FROM CLAN
TO REGIMENT

With best wishes from the author.

FROM CLAN TO REGIMENT

Nicholas Maclean-Bristol

Nicholas Maclean-Bristol
29th May 2007

Pen & Sword
MILITARY

First published in Great Britain in 2007 by
Pen and Sword Aviation
an imprint of
Pen & Sword Books Ltd
47 Church Street
Barnsley
South Yorkshire
S70 2AS

Copyright © Nicholas Maclean-Bristol, 2007

ISBN 978-1844155491

The right of Nicholas Maclean-Bristol to be identified as Author of this Work has been asserted by him in accordance with the Copyright, Designs and Patents Act 1988.

A CIP catalogue record for this book is
available from the British Library.

All rights reserved. No part of this book may be reproduced or transmitted in any form or by any means, electronic or mechanical including photocopying, recording or by any information storage and retrieval system, without permission from the Publisher in writing.

Typeset in 10/12 Garamond by
Concept, Huddersfield, West Yorkshire

Printed and bound in England by
CPI UK

Pen & Sword Books Ltd incorporates the Imprints of Pen & Sword Aviation, Pen & Sword Maritime, Pen & Sword Military, Wharncliffe Local History,
Pen & Sword Select, Pen & Sword Military Classics and Leo Cooper.

For a complete list of Pen & Sword titles please contact
PEN & SWORD BOOKS LIMITED
47 Church Street, Barnsley, South Yorkshire, S70 2AS, England
E-mail: enquiries@pen-and-sword.co.uk
Website: www.pen-and-sword.co.uk

Dedication

This book is dedicated to the memory of the Family of Coll, in particular to tradition bearers without whose diligence much of the history of the family would have been lost. They are:

Allan Maclean of Crossapol-Coll (1760–1832).
Mr Neil Maclean, Minister of Tiree & Coll (1784–1859).
Miss Harriet Maclean, his daughter (1817–1881).
Lachlan Maclean, Glasgow (1798–1848).
John Johnston, Totamore-Coll (1836–1921).
CR Morison, Cuin-Mull (1856–1943)
Hector Macdougall, Glasgow (1889–1954)
John Macfadyen *Iain Hyne* (1880–1974).

Subscribers

Samia Bentayeb, 3 Impasse Jean Baptiste, Lully 57-300, Mandelange, France.
Fedya Bentayeb, 3 Impasse Jean Baptiste, Lully 57-300, Mandelange, France.
Mrs Bessie Bish, PO Box 1298, Swan Hill 3585, Victoria, Australia.
Mrs Berta von Bibra, c/o Mr Chris Faul, Flat 1, 2 Brewhouse Lane, London, SW15 2JH.
Gero Bressel, Winkel 1, Bockenem, D-31167, Germany.
Gisella Bressel, Wanneweg 17, Bockenem, D-31167, Germany.
Wigmar Bressel, 15a, Bremerhaven, D-27570, Germany.
Diarmid Campbell, Kilchoan Farmhouse, Kilmelford, Argyll, PA34 4XD.
Sir Ilay Campbell Bart. Crarae Lodge, Inveraray, Argyll, PA32 8YA.
Court of the Lord Lyon, HM New Register House, Edinburgh, EH1 34T.
David Currie, Ard Mhuirich, Cliasmol, Isle of Harris, HS2 3AR.
Ian de Minvielle-Devaux, 12 Bear Street, Nayland, Suffolk, CO6 4HX.
Truus de Vries-Kruyt, Harinxmaweg 16, The Netherlands, 8E51 AX (3 copies)
Andrina Duffin, 11 Grey Point, Helen's Bay, Bangor, Co. Down, BT19 1LE.
Douglas Fairbairn, Mosswood, Glenmosston Road, Kilmacolm, PA13 4PF.
Gintare France, Kingswood House, 36a Rectory Avenue, High Wycombe, HP13 6HW.
Grahame W Gartside, 3 High Street, Harcourt, Australia, 3453.
Paul Hilton, White House of Aros, Isle of Mull, Argyll, PA72 6JP. (10 copies).
Ben Howkins, Staverton Manor, Staverton, Northamptonshire, NN11 6JD.
Andrew Holman-West, Ibex House, 42–47 Mindries, London, ECJN 1DY.
Keith Howman, Ashmere, Felix Lane, Shepperton, Middlesex, TW17 8NN. (2 copies).
Dr Stephen Janz, Billerbeck 6, 29465 Schnager, Germany, 29465.
Khalid & Rehanna Khan, 169 Lincoln Road North, Acocks Green, Birmingham, B27 6 RT
AJM Kirsop, 18 West Chapelton Avenue, Bearsden, Glasgow, GE1 2DQ.
Angus Macdonald, Auchleeks, Trinafour, Pitlochry, PH18 5UF.
David McDonald, 21 Connaught Way, Bedford, Bedfordshire, MK41 7LB.
The Very Reverend Allan Maclean of Dochgarroch, Hazelbrae House, Glen Urquhart, Inverness.
C Hector MacLean, 71 Lochwinnoch Road, Kilmacolm, Renfrewshire, PA13 4LG.
Charles PB Maclean, Hillend House, Hillend, Edinburgh, EH10 7DX.
Donald F Maclean, 404-4233 Bayview Street, Richmond, British Columbia, Canada, V7E 6T7.
Lieutenant Colonel DA Maclean, Maimhor, 2 Fullerton Drive, Seamill, Ayrshire, KA23 9HT.
Hector Maclean of Dochgarroch, younger, Edinburgh.
James M. McClean Esq, 9275 SW, Cutter Place, Beaverton, OR, USA, 97008-7706.

Subscribers

Dr John MCLean, 7 Drummond Place, Victoria, Australia, 3053.
Sir Lachlan Maclean of Duart and Morvern Bart., C.V.O., D.L., Duart Castle, Isle of Mull.
Captain Marcus Maclean, 10 Princes Gardens, Glasgow G12 9HR.
Marjorie Anne Maclean, 10/6 McLean Street, West Brunswick, Victoria, Australia, 3055.
Mrs Marigold Maclean, Breaneck, 8360 Hamilton Highway, Hamilton, Victoria, Australia, 3300.
Nicolas Maclean of Pennycross, 30 Malwood Road, London SW12 8EN.
Richard Compton Maclean of Torloisk, Newby Hall, Ripon, HG4 5AE (2 copies).
Ronald G. Maclean, Silversand, Vaul, Isle of Tiree, Argyll, PA77 6TP (3 copies).
Sandra L. McLean, 19 Dana Point Road, Chico, CA 95928, USA.
Maclean Library, Tobermory, per the Clan Maclean Heritage Trust.
Alexander Maclean-Bristol, Grishipol House, Isle of Coll, Argyll PA78 6TE.
Miss Amy Maclean-Bristol, Holly Bank, Houston, Renfrewshire, PA5 7HJ.
Miss Phoebe Maclean-Bristol, Holly Bank, Houston, Renfrewshire, PA5 7HJ.
Lachlan Maclean-Bristol & Charlotte Ward, 2 Hawoth Mews, Haworth, West Yorkshire, BD22 8QL.
David MacLean Watt, 23 Dukes Lodge, Holland Park, London W11 3SG.
A Macleod, 23 St Cuthbert's Way, Holystone, Tyne & Wear, NE27 OUZ.
Mrs B. Marriott, 28 Haldon Road, London, 3
Neil Mackinnon, PO Box 20, Evandale, Tasmania, Australia, 7212.
Mrs Jack Mitchell, 21 Tiffany Avenue, Cheltenham, Victoria, Australia, 3192.
Dr Peter Moore, 23 Mount Pleasant Road, London NW10 3EG.
Dr Neil Morison, 19 Carrick Gardens, Ayr KA7 2RT.
Dr Jean Munro, 15a Mansionhouse Road, Edinburgh, EH9 1TZ.
Neil Pattullo, Langlogie, Meigle, Perthshire, PH12 8QS.
RS Robertson, The Village House, Bradfield, Berkshire, RG7 6BH.
Allan Rutter, Arleston House, Cluddley, Telford, Shropshire, TF6 5DR.
Mr & Mrs Kenneth Stewart of Coll, East Bridgelands, Selkirk, Borders, TD7 4 PT.
JK Sommerville, 17 Russell Drive, Bearsden, Glasgow, G61 3BB (2 copies).
Andrew Tod, 2 Atholl Place, Edinburgh, EH3 8HF.
Sir Keith Whitson, Hyndhope, Ettrick, Selkirk, TD7 5HW.
Jean Isabel Whimp, 25 Seavington Road, Elizabeth Park, South Australia, 5113.
Mary-Elizabeth Wilson, 21 Branston Crescent, Petts Wood, Orpington, Kent, BR5 1HA.

Table of Contents

Dedication		v
Subscribers		vi
Table of Contents		viii
Acknowledgements		xi
Abbreviations		xii
Nomenclature		xiv
Maps		xv
Introduction		1
	Part I The making of a Military Tradition	3
Chapter 1	The First Macleans of Coll 1400–1620	5
2	Lachlan Maclean of Coll 1583–1635	18
3	John Garbh Maclean of Coll 1635–1651	27
4	The Battle of Inverkeithing	36
	Part II Campbell versus Maclean	45
5	The first attack on Mull	47
6	Stalemate in Mull	55
7	The disarming of Mull	61
8	Counter-Attack	69
9	The Earl tries again June–August 1679	75
10	The end of the Earl of Argyll?	82
11	The Earl of Argyll's Rebellion	88
12	'The Glorious Revolution'	97
13	Hector Maclean of Coll	108
14	The '45	119
	Part III British Service 1756–1793	131
15	The Seven Years War 1756–1763	133
16	The East Indies and the end of the Campbell-Maclean feud	142
17	The Anatomy of Coll in 1773	150
18	Tenants and their leases	159

Table of Contents

19	The War of American Independence 1775–1783	165
20	A clandestine marriage	174
21	Peace 1783–1793	178
22	The Highland Society of London	187
	Part IV The War with Revolutionary France 1793–1802	193
23	The Raising of the Breadalbane Fencibles	195
24	Alexander's First Military Misdemeanour	207
25	Mutiny at Glasgow	215
26	Captain Hector Maclean, Adjutant	223
27	The end of the 1st Battalion Breadalbane Fencibles	236
28	The Isle of Eigg Company of Volunteers	247
29	The Argyllshire Volunteers	258
30	The War Overseas	265
	Part V Change at home	275
31	The Scottish Society for Propagating Christian Knowledge	277
32	Alexander as an improving laird	286
33	Visitors	297
	Part VI The War with Napoleon 1803–1815	307
34	The Argyllshire & Inverness-shire Volunteers	309
35	A New Generation of Officers & Men	322
36	The West Indies	332
37	The War continues	338
38	The Last Phase of the War	349
39	The War Years at home 1803–1815	356
40	Alexander's Improvements continue	365
41	Gaelic Schools Society & Emigration 1811–1815	375
42	Paris and Plymouth, London and Edinburgh. 1815–1816	385
	Part VII After the War was over	393
43	Things start to go wrong	395
44	The *Beau Monde*	404
45	Australia & India 1820–1828	412
46	Rum to Nova Scotia 1820–1826	419
47	The last years of Alexander Maclean of Coll	429
	Part VIII The Hungry Thirties and Forties	439
48	The first Crisis and the 1841 Census	441
49	Letters from the Tiree Manse	453
50	Juliet Alexa Maclean 1838–1845	463
51	The 'Disruption'	471
52	Famine	480
53	The Clearances	494
54	South Africa, Australia and New Zealand	508
55	'The end of an old song'	520

	Part IX The Victorian Army	531
56	Burmah, China, India and Aden 1840–1860	533
57	South Africa, India and China.1855–1860	545
58	Zulus. 1860–1879	557
59	Africa and Afghanistan 1879–1881	568
60	'The Great Game'	579
61	The North-West-Frontier	593
62	The Second Boer War	608
	Part X A New Regime in Coll	622
63	Reawakening and Radicalism	625
64	Agitation & Fair Rents	636
65	The return of the Macleans of Coll?	648
66	From Regiment to OPMACC	661
	Epilogue	670
	Postscript	672
	Annex A	678
	Tables	680
	Bibliography	693
	Index	707

Acknowledgements

As research for this book has taken nearly fifty years, I have logged up a great many obligations. Firstly I have to thank the Duke of Argyll for allowing me to make use of his archives at Inveraray Castle. He is the third duke to grant me this privilige. It is also a pleasure once again to thank the 12th Duke's former archivist Alastair Campbell of Airds, Unicorn Pursuivant and his assistant Mrs Rae Macgregor for their help in finding my way around the Inveraray archives.

Writing Highland history in Coll would have been impossible without the London Library, whose policy of allowing remote authors to have books out on loan for a very long time, has been invaluable. The Library's staff has also been helpfulness itself. My thanks are also due to the staff of the National Archives of Scotland, the National Library of Scotland, and the National Gallery of Scotland. In London I have also to thank the staff of the British Library, The National Archives at Kew, the National Maritime Museum, Greenwich and the National Army Museum, Chelsea. In France the Archives de Guerre at Vincennes and in the United States of America The Huntington Library have also been of great assistance. Others who have helped are mentioned in notes. Last but not least I wish to thank my publishers Pen & Sword Books with whom it has been a pleasure to work. Without them this book would not have appeared in print.

Nicholas Maclean-Bristol
Isle of Coll
3rd March 2007

Abbreviations

ADC	Aide-de-Camps
APS	*The Acts of the Parliament of Scotland* eds Thomson, T & Innes, C (12 vols, Edinburgh 1814–75)
AT	Argyll Transcripts, made by 10th Duke of Argyll at Inveraray Castle
AV	Argyllshire Volunteers
BCP	Breacachadh Castle Papers
BCT	Breacachadh Castle Transcripts
BF	Breadalbane Fencibles
B&GB D'ton	*Roll of Dumbarton Burgesses and Guild Brethren, 1600–1846*
Beauties of Scotland	Aust, The Hon. Mrs Murray *A Companion and Useful Guide to the Beauties of Scotland and the Hebrides* vol. II (1810)
BL	British Library
CC	NAS Commissary Court
CS	Court of Session Papers
CSD	*Concise Scottish Dictionary*
CSP Scot	*Calendar of State Papers relating to Scotland and Mary Queen of Scots 1547–1603*, edd J Bain & others (Edinburgh 1898–)
CSPD	*Calendar of State Papers Domestic*
DAG	Deputy Adjutant General
DCB	Dictionary of Canadian Biography
DSO	Distinguished Service Order
EUL	Edinburgh University Library
Gens Nostra	*Gens Nostra Ons Geslacht Maandblad Der Nederladse Genealogische Vereniging*
HEIC	Honourable East India Company
HLLRA	Highland Land Law Reform Association
HMCR	*Reports of the Royal Commission on Historical Manuscripts* (London 1870–)
HP	*Highland Papers* Macphail, JRN (ed) Scottish History Society
Huwelijeken Van Militairen	'Huwelijken Van Militairen, behorende tot het eerste regiment van de Schotse Brigade in Nederland, ontleend aan de gereformeerde trouwboeken van 1674 tot 1708' *De Brabatse Leeuw* (Sept. Okt. 1971)
ICP	Inveraray Castle Papers

Abbreviations

IOL	India Office Library
JSAHR	*Journal of the Society of Army Historical Research*
KDG	King's Dragoon Guards
La	Laing MS
NAS	National Archives of Scotland, Edinburgh
NLS	National Library of Scotland, Edinburgh
NMM	National Maritime Museum, Greenwich
NSW	New South Wales
OS	Old Style
OSA	*The Statistical Account of Scotland 1791–1799*
RCAHMS Argyll	*Royal Commission on the Ancient & Historical Monuments of Scotland, Inventory of Argyll* (Edinburgh, 1971–1992)
RD	NAS. Register of Deeds
REME	Royal Electrical & Mechanical Engineers
Report on the Hebrides	McKay, Margaret M *The Rev. Dr. John Walker's Report on the Hebrides of 1764 & 1771* (1980)
RHF	Royal Highland Fusileers
RPCS	*Records of the Privy Council of Scotland*
RSF	Royal Scots Fusiliers
RMS	*The Register of the Great Seal of Scotland*
RT	NAS Register of Testaments
OPMACC	Operation Military Aid to the Civil Community
SC	NAS Sheriff Court
SHR	Scottish Historical Review
SHS	Scottish History Society
SP	State Papers
SRS	Scottish Record Society
SSPCK	Scottish Society for Propagating Christian Knowledge
SW&IHR	Society of West Highland & Island Historical Research
T&AVR	Territorial & Army Volunteer Reserve
TGSI	*Transactions of the Gaelic Society of Inverness*
TNA	The National Archives, Kew, London.
VC	Victoria Cross
VDL	Van Diemen's Land
VSO	Voluntary Service Overseas
WIR	West India Regiment
WHN&Q	*West Highland Notes & Queries*
WS	Writer to the Signet

Nomenclature

The spelling of Gaelic names in a book written in English is fraught with problems. In this book I have adopted the principle that patronymics should be distinguished from surnames. Thus John Macdonald (with a small 'd') is John who belonged to the clan Donald but whose father's name was not necessarily Donald, whilst John MacDonald (with a capital 'D') is John whose father's name was Donald who was not necessarily a member of the clan Donald. The surname Maclean is therefore spelt with a small 'l', the spelling that is preferred by almost all armigerous Macleans with proven descent and all heads of the senior houses of Duart, Coll, Kingerloch and Ardgour. Even Lochbuie uses a small 'l' after Mac, although that family has consistently used the phonetic version 'Maclaine' since the early eighteenth century, by which time several other families who had previously used this spelling had stopped doing so.

In direct quotes from manuscript sources I have printed the spelling as found there. I have also done so when referring to a chief whose style represents his descent from the eponym of the clan.

In an ideal world it would be wise to adopt the Anglo-Gaelic standard version for an individual suggested by GF Black in his work on Scottish surnames, rather than a mixture of English and Gaelic. Thus the seventeenth-century John Maclean of Coll would be styled *Iain Garbh* or Rough John and not a mixture such as John Garbh. It is, however, a fact that this form was often used in the eighteenth-century, even by Gaelic scholars such as Dr Hector Maclean, younger of Gruline. I have followed his example.

I have also followed the method used to-day of describing people belonging to the Isle of Coll as 'Collachs' rather than the correct spelling which is *Colaich*.

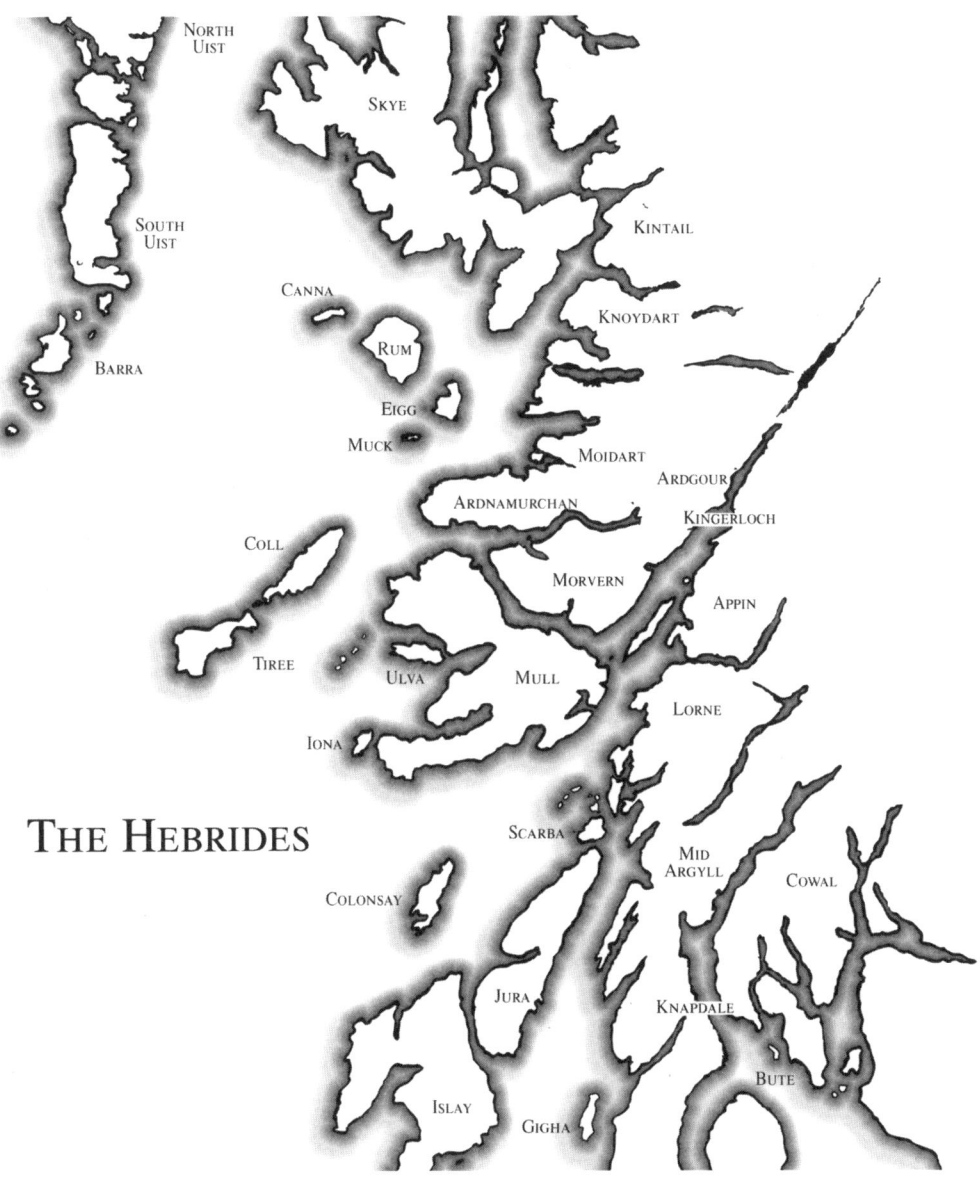

The Maclean of Coll Estate
in Coll, Mull, Morvern, Rum and Muck

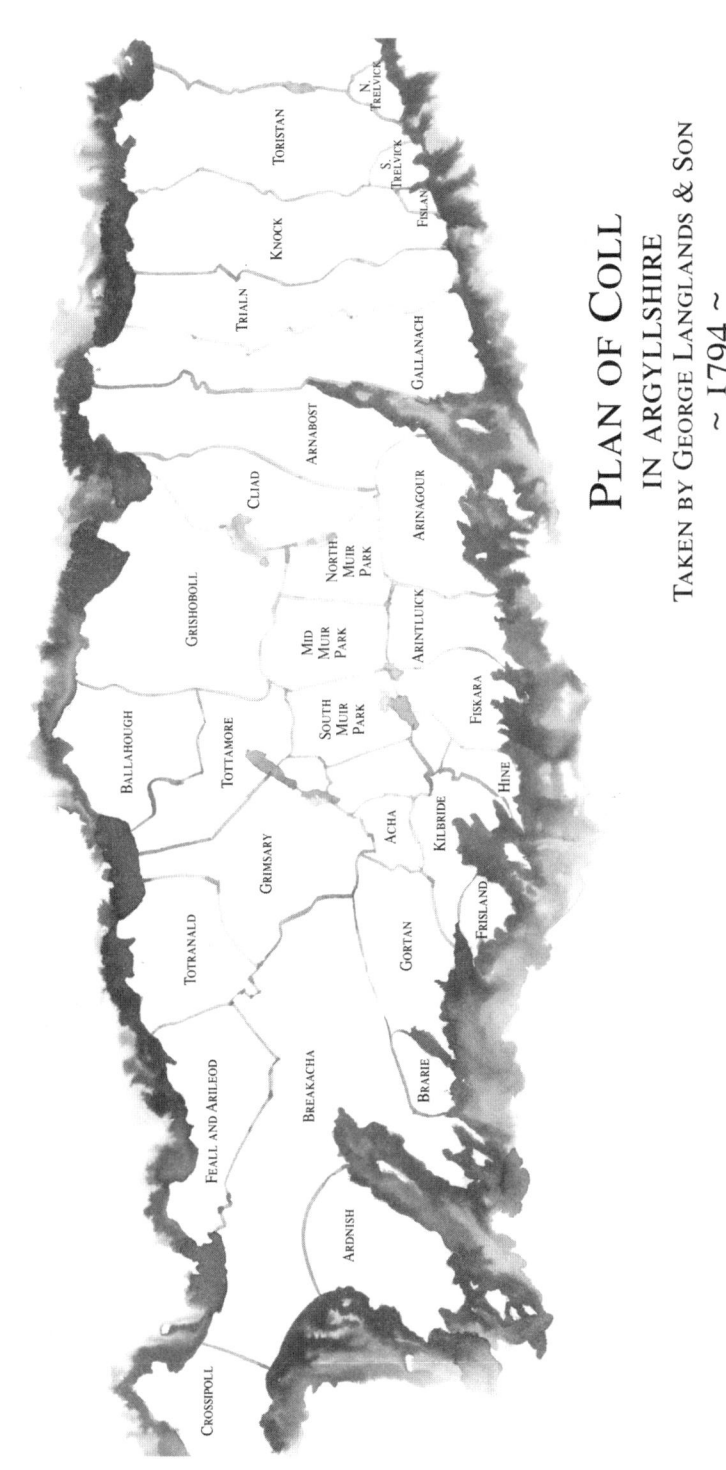

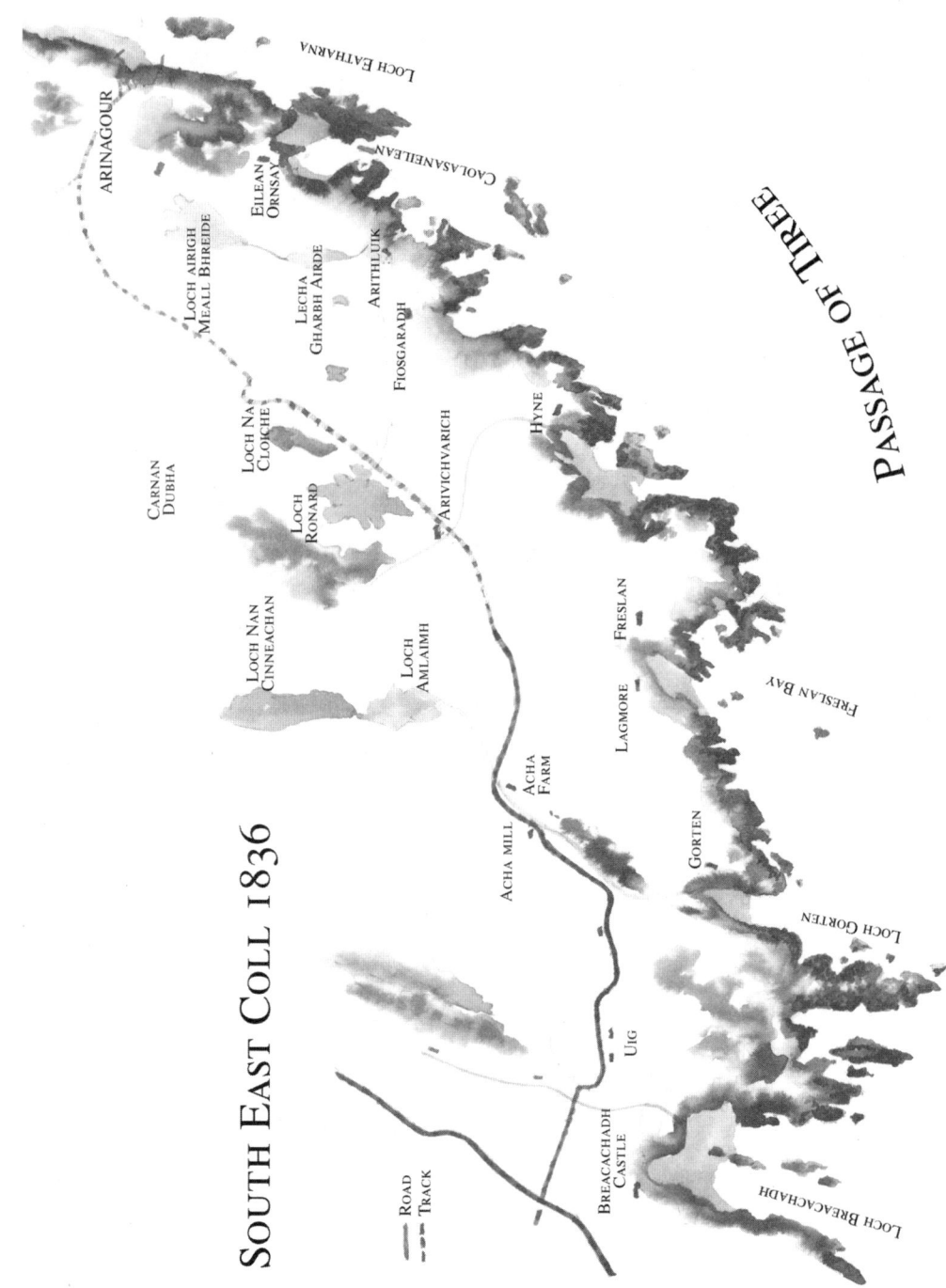

Six Hundred Years in the Hebrides: 1403–2006 Introduction

In 1832 the old man must have looked along the wide sweep of Crossapol Beach in the Isle of Coll with satisfaction. He had almost completed what was to be his most lasting achievement. Soon he could rest with his ancestors in the graveyard between Crossapol House, the simple two-storeyed farmhouse, which he had built some forty years earlier, and the sea.

The task of Allan Maclean of Crossapol (1760–1832) had been to copy out and add to the manuscript 'A Genealogical Account of the Mac Leans' compiled in 1734 by Dr Hector Maclean, younger of Gruline.[1] In doing so he had added to the corpus of genealogical material that still circulated in the Hebrides. What makes Crossapol's account unusual is that his additions include not only the pedigrees of the leading families of the clan, but also those of quite humble people who in the 1830s made up 'the Family of Coll'.[2] It is therefore an invaluable tool by which to identify those men from the Coll estate who flooded into the British Army in the late eighteenth and early nineteenth centuries.

It has recently been said that the 'military ethos of the clan . . . should not be overstressed'.[3] This book argues the opposite. It demonstrates, at least as far as the Macleans of Coll are concerned, that from its origin in the early fifteenth century the clan was organised to support the chief's fighting men. This military structure enabled it to maintain its independence from predatory neighbours. It also made its chief a force to be reckoned with in the conflicts that afflicted the Hebrides from the fifteenth to the seventeenth centuries.

These little wars were mainly local affairs, however, from at least the middle of the sixteenth-century men from Coll had also gone overseas as mercenary soldiers. They went first to Ireland, then to the Netherlands, and after the collapse of Jacobitism, into the British regiments in North America and to the Indian Army.

This movement outwith Scotland involved only small numbers of officers and men. It was not until the Revolutionary and Napoleonic Wars that the Maclean of Coll clan as a whole was mobilised into part time volunteer companies raised to defend the north-west Highlands. They also went into the fencibles. The fencibles were full time regular army units formed to defend Scotland from invasion. Noblemen and lairds raised them from their estates.

The Macleans of Coll served mainly in the Breadalbane Fencibles. It was a regiment raised by the Earl of Breadalbane and his friends, including Alexander Maclean of Coll. The latter provided a strong company and he eventually commanded the 1st Battalion and at one time his kinsmen held most of the key appointments in the battalion.

After the battle of Waterloo men from Coll and Quinish continued to serve in both the British and the Indian armies. Whilst Maclean of Coll owned his estate his tenants still joined the army, but once Coll and Quinish were sold they stopped doing so.

Families descended from the Macleans of Coll who by 1800 had established a tradition of producing commissioned officers have continued to do so to the present day. From the middle of the nineteenth century onwards their loyalty was focused on a particular regiment, rather than on the army itself, and in many ways the regiment became a substitute for the clan, which, once Maclean of Coll had sold his land, had lost its *raison d'être*.

Few of these regimental officers achieved high rank, but they were the backbone of their regiments. Now that all the Scottish infantry regiments have been merged into one Royal Regiment of Scotland it remains to be seen if this tradition will continue.

* * *

In studying one small clan it is possible to examine it in detail, which would not be possible with a larger unit. New patterns emerge. For instance it can be shown that from at least the sixteenth century there were families of professional soldiers within the clan structure. To the best of my knowledge this has not been demonstrated elsewhere. Certainly many Highland families provided officers for the army for several generations, but these were in the main chiefly families with estates to fall back on. The professional military families on the Coll estate were not lairds. They were holders of 'tacks' [leases] of land. They obtained their farms, at least originally, in exchange for service. Some became commissioned officers but many were non-commissioned officers [NCOs] and private soldiers. But whatever their military rank they were conscious of their lineage.

It has been said that the Highlander's capital, and prime resource, was his pedigree.[4] The production of such pedigrees was once the preserve of hereditary genealogists, one of the professional families who served a chief. These families were often descended from the old clerical orders of the medieval Gaidhealtachd, who were one of the casualties of the civil wars of the seventeenth century.

The demise of the professional genealogist did not end the need to preserve a man's pedigree, which could still give a clansman preferential treatment. For instance in the 1840s Lachlan Maclean in Freslan, the lineal descendant of John Maclean of Totronald a seventeenth-century younger son of Maclean of Coll, had his farm rent free 'as a distant connection of the family'.[5]

Allan Maclean of Crossapol was one of the new breed of genealogists who preserved such pedigrees. Without him this book could not have been written and the Isle of Coll would not have inspired the setting up of the Project Trust, an organisation that has continued the British tradition of service overseas. As we shall see, since 1967 it has sent nearly 6,000 eighteen year old volunteers overseas, and dramatically affected the demography and economy of the Isle of Coll.

Notes

1. Dr Hector was a descendant of John Dubh Maclean of Morvern whose offspring were known as *Sliochd Iain Dubh*. They often acted as fosterers to their cousin in Duart to whom they were devoted.
2. It is now in my possession. When it is obvious from the text that it is being quoted no mention is made of it in the notes. It is otherwise referred to as BCP Crossapol MS.
3. Allan I Macinnes *Clanship, Commerce and the House of Stuart, 1603–1788* (1996), 30.
4. Robert A Dodgshon *From Chiefs to Landlords* (1998), 14.
5. Mull Museum. Letter Book. 1846–1850. Captain Donald Campbell at Quinish. 14 May 1847.

Part I

The making of a Military Tradition

Chapter One

The First Macleans of Coll 1400–1620

The first Maclean of Coll probably received his land in about 1400. This was more than 250 years before the British Army was born.[1] However, if one is to understand why Hebrideans, and their cousins on the mainland, had such a reputation as soldiers, it is essential to examine the careers of their warrior forbears. Histories, it used to be believed, are 'the Records of Honour, and everything that is Good and Great ... and, like a Microscope, magnify and illuminate all the Heroick Actions and Exploits of our Ancestors, and create in us an ambitious Emulation to excel them...'.[2] It was this desire that was to inspire Hebrideans to perform extraordinary feats of bravery and make its soldier so prized when attacking.

Lachlan the first Maclean of Coll obtained his land from Donald, Lord of the Isles, who was his maternal uncle. He probably did so at the time of his marriage in 1403, when he had to obtain permission from the Pope to marry his cousin Anna Macleod.[3] At the time Scotland, including the Hebrides, was still recovering from the Black Death of the 1340s.[4] There was a vacuum to be filled and the descendants of Gilleoin na Tuaighe, the progenitor of all Macleans, were ambitious to fill it.

Coll's original holding of land consisted of much of the Isle of Coll, Quinish in north-west Mull and Auchilenan and Drimnin in north-west Morvern. It was an estate that was divided by the sea and the new Chief of Coll required galleys to travel between his possessions and fighting men to preserve them against rivals and raiders.

Galleys and fighting men were the means in the Hebrides in the fifteenth century by which chiefs exercised their power. The great Hebridean galley had changed little from Viking times: it had square sails, but was also propelled by oars; it was shallow of draft, and high in stem and stern. It was a design that gave the galley flexibility: it was able to skim over the waves when the weather was good and seek refuge in shallow inlets when it was bad. Galleys had 18 or more oars and the smaller version, the birlinn, had between 12 and 17. Galleys were an offensive weapon, but they themselves were vulnerable to attack when they were not in the water but drawn up on a beach. This need for protection is the reason why Maclean of Coll built his castle, Breacachadh, where it stands above the beach near the head of *Loch nan Caisteal* in Coll. It has been a symbol of his power for six hundred years.

The first Maclean of Coll[5] did not obtain his land without a fight. The previous owner of the Isle of Coll was a family of Macaulays. They had to be defeated at the battle of Grimsary Hill before they abandoned the island and fled to North Uist. It is not known when the first Laird of Coll died. He may well have been killed in 1411 at the battle of Harlaw. His brother Hector of Duart, who was 'a principal leader under Donald of the Isles', was certainly killed there.[6] Lachlan of Coll may have been as well.

More fighting took place before the Macleans of Coll could be secure in their patrimony. Macneill of Barra, who had married the first chief's widow, tried to defraud his stepson of his inheritance. After a series of exploits, that will have lost little in the telling, the second laird escaped from his stepfather's clutches, invaded Coll with fifty men and slew Macneill at Grishipol, by the shore in the north of the island.

This second laird was John Garbh, 'John Garve More', *Iain Garbh*. Crossapol tells us that

> John Garve More so called from his Gigantic stature and strength, he is also called John Imustich because of his cunningness ... made an easy purchase of the six merk land of Rum from Allan Mac Rury laird of Clanranald who refused to Ratify the same purchase was surprised by Coll at the Island of Eigg and with a Highland Caption was carried to the Island of Coll where he was nine Months till they have settled matters and Joined in a strict friendship which their successors continue to this day.

This is Allan Crossapol's version of the story. Another has it that Clanranald swopped Rum for a particularly prized galley belonging to Coll, but when it was delivered, he found that it leaked, which was why he reneged on his deal.

During the fifteenth century the family of Coll continued to increase their landholding. For a while they held Barra and part of South Uist. They also obtained a grant of Lochiel in Lochaber. It is stated that they held Lochiel for forty years. It was here that they received their first major reverse. Ewen Allansoun defeated them at the battle of Blarnicara, near Corpach, killing the Coll chief *Iain Abrach*,[7] John of Lochaber, and burning all his charters. It was this John who is remembered in the Macleans of Coll's proper name in Gaelic, *Mac Iain Abraich*.[8]

These first chiefs of the Macleans of Coll established the family as an independent power in the Hebrides. What is remembered of their careers is their rôle as warriors. 'Warlords' who fought to gain and retain land. It was this rôle, which their bards recalled in panegyrics that made them the object of reverence. It gave the chief the devotion and deference of their people in a manner that is almost incomprehensible to-day.

* * *

It was the primary duty of a chief to protect his clan and to provide them with land. It was a duty symbolised in his receiving his father's sword[9] when inaugurated as chief.[10] In exchange a clansman was obliged to obey him, to defend his person and property and to make his house open to him.[11] In return the chief was bound to listen to his 'man's advice'. In addition a clansman paid the chief his 'calp'. This was a gift from the clansman's family made to his chief at the time of the clansman's death. This gift was often the tenant's best beast and could be looked on as payment for a lifetime's protection.

The actual protection of clansmen was the duty of the chief's professional fighting men. Who these men were lies at the heart of understanding the make up of a clan. Obviously they did not at first consist of men of the same surname. In the early fifteenth century there were not enough Macleans to go around, and the first Maclean of Coll had to compete with other Maclean chiefs, who were carving out their own empires at the same time.

We have no idea who the first Maclean of Coll's followers were. But in the following generation at least one is remembered. He was a servant of Coll's named 'Giliriamach'. (*An Gille Riabhach*). His leap is still remembered in Coll for during the fight at Grishipol he leapt backwards across the burn and Crossapol tells us 'came up behind Mac Neil and gave him a struck about the houghs by which he fell'.[12]

We can discover something of how Coll built up his following from Crossapol's account. On the back cover of his manuscript Crossapol has an almost illegible 'Account of the different Clanns' in Coll. He states that 'there was one Dugald Lathanach that came to Coll a little after John Garve got the property, he came from [illegible] called himself McLean' and left descendants. He goes on to say:

> The MacKinnons came to Coll when the 3rd Laird of Coll[13] was married to Lord Lovat Daughter, at that time there were two able men about the Laird of MacKinnon's house named Donald Ban & Alister Mor, they were real McKinnons & out of his own family, for refusing Mac Kinnon to go to Slate to apprehend a brother-in-law of their own the Laird of MacKinnon got in a rage against them. Lovat came frequently to see MacKinnon so that the two brothers got well acquainted with him. Lovat on his way to Coll when his daughter [torn] the third Laird of Coll the fore said brothers applyd to him a[nd] wished to go with his daughter to Coll and get a situation as they could not live comfortably where they were [torn] Lovat agreed [illegible], Donald Ban came with him to Coll bringing [illegible] . . .

Iain Abrach's followers at Blarnicara included a family called Maclonich (*MacMhaol Onfhaich*), a 'powerful and fierce family, and were long held in terror by their neighbours'.[14] They were evidently sufficiently 'fierce' to retain their land when the Camerons took over Lochiel, despite the fact that when *Iain Abrach* was killed, they preserved his heir. The Macleans of Coll did not forget their debt to Maclonich and had inscribed in Gaelic above the main door of Breacachadh Castle the words that if a Maclonich should come there at midnight with a man's head in his hand, he should be protected. It also became the tradition that the chief of the Maclonichs was educated by Coll.[15]

The normal method by which Highland chiefs and Lowland lords built up a following was by bonds of manrent. These bonds admitted men who were not of his blood to the same obligations to those that were. They came from an exclusive social group and were considered to be 'gentlemen'. It was rare for anyone below the rank of laird to issue bonds of manrent, and many of those who gave their bond to a chief were men of wealth and position. The point being that it was a chief seeking to attract men to his affinity, rather than the other way round.

The only Coll bond of manrent known to me that has survived is that of 'Jone baine Mcdonelour, and his nephews Neil, Angus, Farchar and Donald sons to Ronald McMeldeny McIllacholm' to Hector of Coll dated 25 February 1568–9. In it they oblige themselves and their posterity to be true and faithful servitors to Hector of Coll their 'kēnking[16] maister and our mane' and his heirs. They also agreed to give him their 'calpes . . . that is to say ane hors for ilk ane of us efter our deces in tokin and sign that he is our maister and chife'.[17]

By the middle of the sixteenth century the family of Coll had produced a number of younger sons to swell the number of the clan. These younger sons might have been expected to have sired cadet branches, however, although Crossapol lists the names of several of them none appear to have left any offspring who were remembered and it was not until John, the fourth laird's time that the 'First Branch of the family of Coll descending from John Garve . . . whose offspring are still extant' is mentioned. Crossapol, who himself descended from this family[18], writes:

The second lawfull son of the third[19] Laird of Coll was Neil More so called from his great stature and strength. He had from his father the Eighteen Merk land in Mull ... He was for a long time haunted by Lachlan Mor and prosecuted by him ... he sent 24 armed men who surprised him in his own house at Benmolach and unjustly killed him at Clachan Dubh near Bellach Roy.[20]

I have told Neil Mor's story elsewhere.[21] The point I want to emphasise here is that by being granted Quinish, Neil Mor was playing a leading role in the defence of the family's territory and was at the fore in the Macleans of Coll's battle for their independence.

* * *

Since the forfeiture of the Lords of the Isles in 1493 the Macleans of Duart had moved in to fill part of the vacuum their master's disappearance had created in the southern Isles. The family of Duart descended from an elder brother of the first Maclean of Coll. Both were the sons of Lachlan Lùbanach Maclean [Lachlan the crafty], who was probably the younger of the two Maclean brothers who first obtained land in the Isles. Certainly the presumed elder brother Hector Reaganach Maclean of Lochbuie originally received a larger estate than his brother. Duart, however, by his ability and the use of his post of chamberlain to the Lord of the Isles, became the most influential Maclean and, when the Lord of the Isles was forfeited, he obtained the Crown lands in Mull and Islay that had been held by the Lord of the Isles himself.

Hector Mor the chief of Duart in the mid-sixteenth century followed his father's example and set about establishing himself as chief of all the Macleans. With the help of his formidable brother *Ailein nan Sop* he first attacked the Macleans of Lochbuie. Their chief was murdered and their power eclipsed. Thereafter the Duart chief was known as *Macgillean*,[22] signifying that he was chief of his name, a claim that was not always accepted by either Lochbuie or Coll.

In the next generation Duart's sons were no less belligerent. In 1561 they invaded Hector of Coll's lands in Morvern. When they were charged before the Privy Council, they claimed that they were justified as Coll, who was known as *An Cléireach Beag*,[23] refused to accompany them on cattle raids or take part in their bloodfeuds. Coll replied that:

> it is of veritie that he aucht him [i.e. Duart] na service, not haldis na landis of him bot of the Quenis Majestie onelie, he being ane fre baroun as any utheris within hir Hienes realme, and sould nocht be subject nor compellit to serve the said Hector of Dowart, nor any utheris bot hir Grace and hir Lieutenants.[24]

This was to be the position of the Macleans of Coll over the next two hundred years. They would often, but not always, follow Duart's lead but they maintained their independence. The quarrel of the 1560s was aggravated, at the time of the Reformation, by the scramble for church land. *An Cléireach Beag*, who was an early convert to the Protestant Cause, obtained grants of the Two Ends of Coll from the church. These grants infuriated the Macleans of Duart.

The worst onslaught by the Macleans of Duart on their kinsmen in Coll took place after Lachlan Mor of Duart succeeded his father in 1574–5. Three years later, when he came of age, Lachlan mounted a successful coup d'état against his cousin Hector Allansoun *Eachann mac Ailean na Sop*, who had control of Duart during Lachlan Mor's minority. Hector Allansoun's daughter was married to Coll's brother Neil Mor, which is probably why Coll was invaded and Hector Allansoun was beheaded at Breacachadh Castle. On this occasion Duart's men withdrew.

They were to come again when *An Cléireach Beag*, the old laird of Coll, died. On the day of his interment Duart's men landed in Coll. The cortege, which was on its way to Coll's burial ground at Kilunaig had only reached Clabbach when news of the invasion reached Neil Mor, who was escorting his brother's remains. Crossapol continues the story:

Neil More and all his men return'd & left his Brothers remains at Clabbach attended only with few men till he would return. He met his Enemies near Totronald [at] Struan na Cean [Stream of the heads] where Neil More and his men fought bravely and put all their enemys almost to the sword. After which Neil More got his brother Interred about nightfall.

Crossapol has another story about *Sruthan nan Ceann*. He says that 'Donald Ban MacKinnon had a son called Donald Mugach who fought bravely at sruthan na ceann with Neil Mor. He was bald headed. Neil Mor said that he was vext that they had no colours to show. Donald Mugach took of his Bonat and said. *Sin agath cular, agus leanaibh e gu oidhche.*' It means: 'There's a battle-standard for you, and follow it till nightfall.'[25]

The Collachs gave a cheer and charged down the brae to slaughter Duart's men. Shortly after this event Neil Mor felt it necessary to retire to Ireland, and the Macleans of Duart occupied Coll. Later, when Neil Mor returned to Mull, he was treacherously murdered, on Lachlan Mor's instructions, at *Dùn na Niall* near Bellachroy in Quinish.

It was probably whilst Hector Allansoun was in charge at Duart, and relations with Coll were good, that Hector of Coll's son *Eachann Ruadh* married Lachlan Mor's sister. She was a considerable catch. Her mother was the legitimate daughter of the Earl of Argyll. *Eachann Ruadh* did not live long after his marriage and died before his father leaving an only child Lachlan, presumably named after his uncle in Duart, who probably brought him up.

In 1593, despite being brought up at Duart, Lachlan of Coll began legal proceedings against his uncle. Three years later they came to a settlement. Duart agreed to hand back his nephew's estate. However, the major bone of contention, the Two Ends of Coll was resolved in an extremely curious manner. One of the Crown's aims at this time was to make one man responsible for his people's behaviour. Dual allegiance, by which a landholder could be the tenant of one landowner and the clansman of another, was one explanation for the disorders in the Isles. Yet the courts now decided that Lachlan Duart should be the landlord of the inhabitants of the Two Ends of Coll, whilst Lachlan Coll was to be their chief. It was the very situation the Crown was trying to eliminate.

The Crown's attempts to bring order to the Isles, and the English government's efforts to bring Ulster to heel, produce a number of documents that give an insight into life in the Isles at the close of the sixteenth century. One such document, compiled in 1596, is the report on the Hebrides made for Sir Robert Cecil by Dionysus Campbell, Dean of Limerick, which was written in connection with the plan to send Hebridean mercenaries to fight in Ireland in the English interest.[26]

In a summary the Dean states that the number of men the Isles are accustomed to raise is:

6,000 men, quhair of the 3rd pairt extending to 2,000 men aucht and sould be cled with attounes and haberchounis, and knapshal bannetts, as thair lawis beir. And in raising or furthbringing of thair men ony time of yeir to quhatsumevir cuntrie or weiris, na labourers of the ground are permittit to steir furth of the cuntrie quhatevir thair maister have ado, except only gentlemen quhilk labouris not, that the labour belonging to the teilling of the ground and wynning of thair corns may not be left undone.[27]

This description of men 'cled with attounes [*Aketon*, a quilted coat worn under armour] and haberchounis [*Haubergeon*, a short shirt of mail armour formed of circular interlocking metal rings] is reminiscent of the effigies of men in armour found in West Highland graveyards, which have been dated to the late middle ages.[28] They underline the conservatism of warfare in the Isles. It was a conservatism that was to last well into the seventeenth century.

Earlier in his report Dionysus Campbell says of Islay that it is

> 18 score merkland and will raise 800 men . . . Ilk merk land in this Ile payis yeirlie three mairtis and ane half, 14 wedderis, 2 geis, 4 dozen pultrie, 5 bollis malt with ane peck to ilk boll, 6 bollis meill, 20 stane of cheis, and twa merk of silver. And ilk merk land sustein daylie and yeirlie ane gentleman in meit and claith, quhilk dois na labour, but is haldin as ane of their maisters household men, and man be sustenit and furneisit in all necessaries be the tennent, and he man be reddie to his maisters service and advis . . .

This assessment would suggest that each merk land produced about 2 men. One presumably being the gentleman 'cled with attounes', whilst the other was probably more lightly armed and was perhaps a servant.[29]

The Dean also states that the Isle of Coll is 30 merkland and could raise 140 men. Therefore, if the Islay formula held good for other islands, each merkland in Coll supported 4.5 fighting men. 46, a third of them, would seem to have been fully accoutred.

Fourteen of Maclean of Coll's holdings in Coll were valued at 20 shillings. Two others, Breacachadh and Feall, were each 3 merkland, whilst Gorten was valued at 6/8d.[30] The east and west ends of Coll were valued at 15 merkland.[31] It would therefore seem that 20 shilling land on Coll was roughly the equivalent to a merkland and that each merk land supported an average of 1.5 fully accoutred fighting men. However, as each merkland on Coll is assessed as producing about the same livestock, grain and cheese as Islay, this statement is surprising.[32] Perhaps the Dean underestimated the percentage of fully accoutred men the Isles could provide. If that is so each merk land on Coll and on Islay supported the same number of men.

* * *

Campbell's description of 'ane of their maisters household men' is the earliest mention I know of the families of professional fighting men within the clan's structure. It is possible to work out who some of these men were. Almost certainly they include those men whose ancestors Crossapol says had come to Coll over the previous two hundred years. There were now several other men descended in the male line from Maclean of Coll. Most of their progenitors were probably illegitimate but in the relaxed sexual mores that preceded the Reformation legitimacy was a debatable issue.

Crossapol states that:

> There is a grand son of the 4th Laird of Coll called Eachan mhic Iain called Niel Bhuidh mac gille challum ic Eachan, who was a brave man, and was the best at the bow and arrow in his time, at the time that his friend Niel Mor was taken prisoner a brother of Niel buidh was also taken by order of Lachlan Mor Laird of Dowart in order to put him to death with the said Niel Mor – Niel Buidh hearing that there was fifty armed men going with Niel Mor and his brother to be put to death at clachan dubh he came upon a precipice above them and cried out with a loud

voice if they would not set his brother at liberty that he had 25 arrows in his bag or *bolg saighed*, and that he was sure of killing one man for every arrow, on hearing this he frightened them so much that his brother was sett free.

Lachlan Mor after that would put a son of Niel Buidh to death, he took him prisoner, when his father heard of his sons imprisonment, he went to Lachlan Mor and told him if he would not sett his son at liberty, that he would apply to the Laird of Coll and the Laird of Loup for assistance and that there would be a good deal of blood shade before his son would be put to death – Lachlan Mor said you'll get your son free if you'll break an Egg upon his head with your bow and arrow, which Niel Buidh did, without touching his son . . .

Crossapol goes on to say 'there was a grand son of Hector Roy the 5th laird Lachlan mac Lachain, a stout man; [both he and] Allan Roy at Feall came out of the family of Coll about that time.' These men left descendants who, as we shall see, survived into Allan Crossapol's lifetime.

Hector of Coll, *An Cléireach Beag*, was married twice. His second wife was a daughter of Macalastair of Loup, in Kintyre. The Laird of Loup was a notable supplier of mercenaries for the wars in Ireland and was of more importance there than at home in Scotland. Coll had two sons by Loup's daughter. Allan the eldest was granted the 27 shilling land of Auchnasaul in Quinish in Mull. John the second received the 20 shilling land of Grishipol in Coll. Both these properties were strategically important for the defence of Coll's territory. Grishipol includes Dùn Dubh. This fort occupies an isolated outcrop of rock. On two sides it has a series of terraces,[33] which fall steeply to the sea. On the south side there is an almost vertical drop. The east side was defended by a series of walls and at the summit there are the remains of two 'sub-circular stone-walled enclosures'. It has 180° observation to the west, from where the threat was from the Macneills.

It is not clear on what terms the brothers received their grants, but as their descendants held them for several generations, and as they are always described as 'of ' rather than 'in' Auchnasaul or Grishipol, it is likely that they were held by wadset.[34] It is also not clear if they received other lands on the Coll estate. It would be surprising if they did not as their cousin Neil Mor's son Allan had, according to Crossapol, 'the six merks lands of Drimnin and Achalinen' in Morvern, which was a more valuable property. It was also Coll's most isolated possession and vulnerable to attack, which suggests that Allan mac Neil Mor was considered to be a reliable fighting man. His half-brother Niall Og certainly was. Crossapol says he was 'a very brave man'. Whilst his 'sweetheart' Mòr Nic Phàidein in her 'Lament for Niall Og' says:

> I am attending the parade ground, with men in order
> Going past: I see none like you among them.
>
> A noble, brave, courageous man, handsome and confident,
> Is the generous one they called Niall Og.[35]

* * *

These cadets of Coll descending from Neil Mor, Allan of Auchnasaul and John of Grishipol were settled on strategic holdings of land that helped defend the clan's territory. The combination of the nearness of their relationship with the chief and the extent of their possessions gave them considerable prestige and they probably lived as mini-lairds each with his own retinue.

These close relatives of the Chief often commanded his men in battle. An analysis of the eighteen occasions between 1580 and 1810 where we have details of who commanded a company of Coll's men shows that the commander was:

The Chief himself	3
Chief's brother	5
Cousin	6
Great uncle	1
Uncle	1
Brother-in-law	1
Friend	1
	18

After the death of the third laird at the battle of Blarnicara, Maclean of Coll seldom led his own men on active service. Instead it seems likely that the Chief, like the colonel of a regiment in the past was responsible for recruiting, clothing and financing it, whilst his lieutenant-colonel fought at their head.

* * *

The control of fighting men, both at this time and later, was a particularly valuable asset to a chief. The wars in Ireland meant that those who could raise men had a commodity, which was in demand. It is not unlikely that Lachlan Mor of Duart was prepared to compromise with his nephew over the Two Ends of Coll because he wanted the use of his men.

Lachlan Mor had done a deal with the English to provide 2000 men in Ulster. They were to be well paid. Each Scot who served with a longbow or halberd was to have 10 shillings a quarter. Every 'shot' with a piece was to have 20 shillings.[36] It is difficult to imagine how and when these men were to be paid. It would seem likely that, rather than being paid individually, the money owing was to be paid to the chief providing them and that he paid each individual soldier, after having deducted a percentage.

In the event Lachlan Mor never took his men to Ulster. Instead he was killed, probably assassinated, at *Tràigh Ghruinneart* in Islay when on 5th August 1598 he went there for a meeting with his nephew and adversary Sir James Macdonald of Knockrinsay.[37] Crossapol says that Allan of Auchnasaul 'commanded a Company of his father's men, under Lachlan Mor, at Gruinart' and that he had previously been 'sent by his father to assist Rory More MacLeod against Mac Donald of Slate ... which was the last contest between these two families'.[38]

* * *

Professional fighting men in the Hebrides were trained from their youth in seamanship and the use of weapons. Allan Macinnes suggests that they received this training in their chief's household.[39] He is probably correct for such training would require central control. They also had a great deal to learn: to handle a broadsword and target, and a bow and arrow.

Mòr Nic Phàidein was perhaps thinking of the training of young men at Breacachadh Castle when she laments:

> And at the approach of evening, when I see no target
> Hit, the playing of the youths has increased my tears.

Perhaps Niall Og had been responsible for their training in archery.

Increasingly the trainees had to learn how to use firearms, and it is worth noting that Lachlan Mor, when writing to Bowes, the English agent, in March 1595–6, says that he will produce 500 'fyermen' for service in Ireland.[40]

Macinnes goes on to say that at the end of their training the ablest students graduated into the *luchd-tighe* or 'household men', who provided the chief with his bodyguard. He also suggests that the *creach*, the cattle raid, was 'in effect, a graduation ceremony from the clan schools'.[41] Certainly Martin Martin says that:

> Every Heir, or young Chieftain of a Tribe, was oblig'd in Honour to give a publick Specimen of his Valour, before he was own'd and declar'd Governor or Leader of his People, who obey'd and follow'd him upon all Occasions.
>
> This Chieftain was usually attended with a Retinue of young Men of Quality, who had not beforehand given any Proof of their Valour, and were ambitious of such an Opportunity to signalise themselves.
>
> It was usual for the Captain to lead them, to make a desperate Incursion upon some Neighbour or other that they were in Feud with; and they were oblig'd to bring by open force the Cattel they found in the Lands they attack'd or to die in the Attempt.[42]

It is argued in this book that membership of this 'retinue of young men of quality' was hereditary in certain families and that they continued to produce soldiers well into the nineteenth century. As we will see, there is evidence to identify some of the families. There is no evidence that younger sons, or landed cousins of the chief, served as permanent members of his bodyguard. It is, however, probable that as young men they received military training with them. It was the normal accomplishment of a Scottish gentleman to know how to use a sword, and as late as the 1670s students at Glasgow University learnt how to handle a pike and musket.[43]

The landed cousins of the chief would have been too busy running their own properties, which were anyhow at a distance from Breacachadh Castle, for them to be much use as a bodyguard. Instead the *luchd-tighe* were settled in farms within striking distance of the chief's residence, such as Ardnish, Uig, Crossapol and Feall.

Membership of the *luchd-tighe* was not limited to cadet branches of the family but became hereditary in other families. Often they were the descendants of men who had lost their own land, and maintained their status as 'gentlemen' by becoming professional soldiers. For example a branch of the old Campbells of Barbreck lost their property when an heiress married back into the Argyll family.[44] At some time by the seventeenth century they joined Maclean of Coll's bodyguard. The Buchanan-Campbells represented them in Coll until the 1950s.

Another family to join Coll's *luchd-tighe* was the MacFadyens. They probably descend from the same family who once owned Lochbuie in Mull.[45] The were certainly in Coll by the late sixteenth century when, as we have seen, one of their daughters was the poetess 'sweetheart' of Neil Oig. There are still MacFadyens in Coll.

* * *

Although their use as mercenaries in Ireland was a means by which Maclean chiefs could threaten, influence, and obtain their gold, its importance to the English should not be exaggerated. In his report to Bowes of April 1596 Dionysus Campbell makes the point that the Macleans 'in any greate nombers, have not come to Ireland, to my knowledge or remembrance and hereinge, theis 30 years ... The ilanders have byn noted better men at home, then in strange countreys'.[46] A statement which is supported by the almost continual warfare in the Isles that took place during Lachlan Mor's 'reign' at Duart.[47]

As we have already seen, the Macleans were not to go to Ireland in 1596 and the death of Lachlan Mor ended the plan to send them there before the end of Tyrone's Rebellion in 1602. The subsequent Plantation of Ulster by Protestant Lowland Scots ended the traffic for the time being.

The end of this trade in mercenaries did not end the need for chiefs in the Isles to maintain professional fighting men. The disturbed state of the Hebrides made the upkeep of at least a nucleus, to train a new generation of soldiers, essential. This was perhaps the rôle of the *luchd-tighe*. The number in the bodyguard probably did not exceed twenty men.[48] However, as in 1596 the Isle of Coll alone could raise 140 men, the number in the *luchd-tighe* was a small percentage of the fighting men that Maclean of Coll had at his disposal. They were needed not only to defend their chief's property but also to carry out the Crown's demands that loyal clans should help put down the rebellions that plagued the Isles at this time.

It is highly likely that Coll's men accompanied Hector Og of Duart to Islay in August 1602, when with 1500 men he ravaged the island to avenge his father's death.[49] Dr Hector Maclean claimed in his manuscript history that the Macleans had a commission of fire and sword for this action. However, no commission appears in the records of the time.[50]

A more official expedition took place in June 1615, when the lairds of Coll, Lochbuie and Mackinnon were ordered to provide men to assist Duart in hunting down Sir James Macdonald of Knockrinsay, who had escaped from prison and was leading a rebellion in the Isles. Two hundred of Duart's and his friend's men were to pursue the rebels both by sea and land 'betuix the row of Ardnamuchine and the marche of Lorne'.[51] They were to be 'prvydit and furnist in manner forsaid' i.e. 'cled with attounes and haberchounis and knapshal bannetts, as thair lawis beir'.

Although the government was quite prepared to use the professional fighting men of the Isles when they needed them, at the same time they were proposing to destroy the very system that supported them. It has long been thought that the instrument the government used were the 1609 Statutes of Iona.

Until recently the Statutes of Iona, which were drawn up in 1608 by Andrew Knox Bishop of the Isles after he captured the leading island chiefs, have been seen as a turning point in the history of the Hebrides. Julian Goodare has, however, convincingly argued[52] that the Statutes of Iona 'did not much matter to the government in 1609–10, or to anyone after that date ...' they were not turning point but an incident in 'the gradual but continuous pressure on chiefs in many related ways between about 1596 and 1617'. He goes on to say that 'The Statutes appeared important to nineteenth-century scholars, who correctly sensed something new about the Highland policy of James VI and searched for a document which appeared to encapsulate this newness. The Statutes were what they found ... [and] leads to a point that ought, perhaps, to have alerted historians to the problem: namely, that the Statutes were *not* implemented'.

What concerns us here is the legislation concerning the military retinue of the chiefs. In 1619 the Council limited the number of 'household men' that a chief might maintain to six [Sleat, Macleod and Clanranald] and three [Coll, Mackinnon and Lochbuie] plus a boy to every two 'gentlemen'. Macinnes suggests that these 'boys' were trainees for the chiefs' bodyguard.

The chiefs were also to:

> purge thair boundis of sornaris and idill men
> sall not beare nor weare hagbuttis nor pistollettis
> thair tennentis sall not weare armour[53]

If these sanctions had been enforced it would have destroyed the military structure in the Isles. There is no evidence that it did. What it does suggest is that at the time there were still many professional soldiers 'gentlemen that labouris not' in the Isles. It also confirms that they were still supported by labourers living in the townships, that they wore armour, and that they were armed with hagbuts and pistols.

It would seem, from what follows, that these 'gentlemen' in the 1620s, as in the 1590s, were allocated a particular township or *baile* by their chief, where they had a house and stock, presumably cattle, in exchange they were on call in emergencies. The labourers who worked the land provided their 'gentleman' with food, peat and other services.

If they were to be effective when required to defend their chief's domain, or to take part in a *creach* these 'gentlemen' would have had to practice their skills. Sword and target, pistol, bow and arrow or hagbut could be used effectively without constant practice. Those who trained them were probably experienced warriors, such as Niall Og. Such men probably were allocated more and better townships than lesser men.

It is possible that something of this military structure in Coll survived into the late seventeenth, or even into the early eighteenth century. Certainly there was still a need for well trained fighting men throughout this period, and the most sensible way for Maclean of Coll to support his soldiers was to let them have a farm at a nominal rent in exchange for service.

Notes

1. Peter Young & JP Lawford *History of the British Army* (1970), 11.
2. An Officer of the Army *Memoirs of the Lord Viscount Dundee* (1711), iv.
3. Francis McGurk (ed) *Papal Letters to Scotland of Benedict XIII of Avignon 1394–1419* (1976), 103. My arguments identifying him as the first Maclean of Coll are in 'The Building of Breacachadh and the Maclean Pedigree' *WHN&Q*, Series 1, XIII (1980), 3–11.
4. Nicholas Maclean-Bristol *Warriors and Priests: The History of the Clan Maclean, 1300–1570* (1995), 19.
5. Crossapol follows Dr Hector Maclean in making John Garbh the first laird. I have argued elsewhere that this is incorrect. See 'The Building of Breacachadh and the Maclean Pedigree'.
6. Donald Gregory *The History of the West Highlands and Isles of Scotland* (1881), 69.
7. He made such an impression on his contemporaries that the Macleans of Coll's patronymic was *Mac Iain Abraich*.
8. Edward Dwelly *The Illustrated Gaelic-English Dictionary* (1977), 1022.
9. Maclean of Coll's two-handed sword is illustrated in CN McIntyre North *The Book of the Club of True Highlanders* (1881), Vol. II, 24. I have to thank Miss Anne Hamilton (Miss Maclean of Coll) for both the gift of the sword and the book illustrating it.
10. Martin Martin states that: 'The formalities observ'd at the Entrance of these Chieftains upon the Government of their Clans, were as follows:
    A Heap of Stones was erected in form of a Pyramid, on the top of which the young Chieftain was plac'd, his Friends [i.e. relations] and Followers standing in a Circle round about him, his Elevation

signifying his Authority over them, and their standing below their Subjection to him. One of his principal Friends deliver'd into his Hands the Sword wore by his Father, and there was a white Rod deliver'd to him likewise at the same time.

Immediately after the Chief Druid (or Orator) stood close to the Pyramid, and pronounc'd a Rhetorical Panegyrick, setting forth the ancient Pedegree, Valour, and Liberality of the Family, as Incentives to the young Chieftain, and fit for his imitation.

11. For example in 1617 the tenants of Caolis in the West End of Coll had to provide: '48 maleas in farine, grano et ordeo, 2 pondera farine et pondus casei pro sustentatione asseationis terre, pro sustentatione unius noctis ½ bollam manseti, ovem 2 annorum, pondus farine et tertiam partem casei, et 3 sol. 4 den. Pro *eik*; [*RMS 1609–1620*, 1628].

12. Samuel Johnson tells us that the *Gille Riabhach*, who he calls 'MacGill' was promised 'certain lands in Mull' if he prevented a sentry, who had seen *Iain Garbh* and his men landing and was running off to Grishipol to warn MacNeill, from delivering his message. 'Upon this promise, Macgill pursued the messenger, and either killed or stopped him; and his posterity, till very lately, held the lands in Mull'. [Samuel Johnson *A Journey to the Western Islands of Scotland* (1817), 189–90]. I have found no evidence to support this statement, however, there were families with the unusual surname *Mcgillireach* in Rum and the Isle of Muck in 1764 [Edin. Uni. Lib. MSS. La. IV 839. Eigg Catechist list, 1764–5]. Ronald Black has an interesting comment on Crossapol's spelling of 'Giliramach'. He says that the -m- in 'Giliramach' makes all the difference in the world. It will be giliriamach, because -mh- and -bh- have the same sound except that the mh is nasal and bh isn't. The error could be argued to suggest that Allan Crossapol had a passive familiarity with the old Gaelic script in which the -h- was generally represented by a dot or omitted altogether. It does not suggest that he was uneducated in Gaelic, because Gaelic orthography is far more phonetic than English: if Allan's pronunciation of riabhach was nasal, it was quite legitimate for him to spell it with an -m- (for -mh-).

13. In fact the fourth.

14. Anonymous *A Breif Genealogical Account of the FAMILY OF McLEAN* (1872), 81.

15. Frederick A Pottle & Charles H Bennett *Boswell's Journal of A Tour to the Hebrides* (1936), 274.

16. Kēnking = *ceann-cinnidh* = Chief, chieftain, head of a clan, chief of a tribe. Edward Dwelly *Gaelic-English Dictionary* (1977), 178.

17. NAS RH6 (Supp) 25 February 1568–9; Niall D Campbell 'An Old Inventory of the Laird of Coll's Writs' *The Celtic Review* (October 1912), 7; Jenny Wormald *Lords and Men in Scotland: Bonds of Manrent 1442–1603* (1985), 328.

18. Crossapol devotes four pages of his genealogy to Neil Mor and his descendants. They are hardly mentioned in any other version of Dr Hector Maclean's manuscript and not mentioned in his original copy at all by the latter.

19. In fact he was the fourth.

20. 'Benmollach' [Crossapol MS, 39] [Penmolloch] was where Maclean of Coll traditionally had his home in Mull. It is where the present Quinish House stands. [Jean & RW Munro *Acts of the Lords of the Isles 1336–1493* (1986), 236.

21. Nicholas Maclean-Bristol *Murder Under Trust: The Crimes and Death of Sir Lachlan Mor Maclean of Duart, 1558–1598.* (1999) 55–60, 208–210, 217, 256, 261, 268, 270.

22. Sir John Mackleane 'Remarks on the Loyal Dissuasive' in Alexander D Murdoch (ed) *The Loyall Dissuasive* (SHS, 1902), 102.

23. He was probably called the 'little clerk' because he was a younger son who was originally intended for the church. He was also a poet. Two of his poems have survived.

24. *RPC*, I, 31–33.

25. P M'F has the same story in 'Bratach Thighearna Chola' *An Teachdaire Gaelach* XIII (1830), 44. I have to thank Ronald Black for a transalation of Donald Mugach's challenge.

26. Will Forbes 'Dionysus Campbell' *WHN&Q* Series 3, No. 6 (November 2003).

27. William F Skene *Celtic Scotland* iii, (1890), 439–440.

28. KA Steer and JWM Bannerman *Late Medieval Monumental Sculpture in the West Highlands* (1977), 23–29.
29. These are the fighting men whom Allan Macinnes [*Clanship, Commerce and the House of Stuart, 1603–1788* (1996), 57] has called *buannachan* from the Norse loan-word *buannacht* which was applied to the maintenance of gallóglaich when billeted upon the people [GA Hayes-McCoy *Scots Mercenary Forces in Ireland* (1937), 17], which is not exactly what we are seeing here.
30. *RMS (1513–1546)*, 712.
31. Both are describes as 'Tirungs' [*RMS (1609–1620*, 1628]. However, the 1558 sasine of the East End says that it was 6 merk land. The West End was presumably valued the same.
32. '5 bollis beir, 8 bollis meil, 20 stane of cheese, 4 stanes of buttir, 4 mairtis, 8 wedderis, twa merkis of silver, twa dozen of pultrie'. *Celtic Scotland* iii (1890), 434.
33. RCAHMS *Argyll*, vol. 3 (1980), 77.
34. A wadset is a mortgage of property, with a conditional right of redemption. It was a popular method for a landowner to provide for his younger sons in the seventeenth century. Earlier generations of younger sons, such as Neil Mor and his son Allan, appear to have received land in liferent.
35. Colm Ó Baoill 'Lament for Niall Og' *WHN&Q* Series 1, Number xxvi (April 1985), 5; Colm Ó Baoill *Duanaire Colach 1537–1757* (1997), 4–6.
36. *Murder under Trust*, 166.
37. *Ibid*, 238–253.
38. This was probably the fight at *Coire na Creiche*, which took place c. 1600. See IF Grant *The Macleods The History of a Clan* (1959), 199. It was not his father, but his nephew Lachlan of Coll, who sent Allan Achnasaul to support Macleod.
39. Allan Macinnes (1996), 57.
40. *CS Ireland*, vi, 382. The cost of equipping their men with firearms was presumably borne by the chiefs. It must have been a significant outlay of cash.
41. Allan I Macinnes (1996), 33.
42. M Martin *A Description of the Western Islands of Scotland* (1716), 101. He says that 'I have not heard an Instance of this Practice for these sixty Years past'. As the first edition of his book was published in 1703, it would appear that the *creach* was one of the many traditions that died out in the Civil Wars.
43. Rosalind K Marshall *The Days of Duchess Anne* (1973), 132.
44. The old Campbells of Barbreck descended from a son of Colin Iongantach Campbell of Lochawe (died 1413). JRN Macphail (ed) *Highland Papers* vol. II (SHS 1916), 93–4; G Harvey Johnston *The Heraldry of the Campbells* (1977), 18.
45. *Highland Papers* vol. II, 86 n. 1.
46. *CSP Scot.*, xii, 198.
47. *Murder under Trust* (1999).
48. See Annex A.
49. *CPS* xiii (1597–1603), 1036.
50. Donald Gregory *The History of the West Highlands and Isles of Scotland* (1881), 285–6.
51. *HP* iii, 250.
52. Julian Goodare 'The Statutes of Iona in Context' *SHR* Volume LXXVII, 1: No. 203: April 1998.
53. *RPCS* xiv Addenda 1545–1625, 583–4.

Chapter Two

Lachlan Maclean of Coll 1583–1635

A chief always had to look in two directions. On the one hand he was responsible for protecting his people. On the other he was the man the government in Edinburgh held responsible for his *oighreachd*.[1] Both responsibilities meant that he needed to have fighting men under his command.

Since King James VI had come of age in 1587 he had made the pacification of the Isles a priority. He had several means at his disposal. For instance within the Gaidhealtachd, as elsewhere in Scotland, it was accepted that the Crown, as part of the royal prerogative, gave title to an estate by the granting of a charter.[2]

As we have seen, Ewen Allansoun burnt Coll's charters after the battle of Blarnicara, and in 1528 Coll received a new title to his estates.[3] Lachlan of Coll was therefore in a better position than many of his peers, when in 1597 the government issued a statute that invalidated all Highland land titles that had not been registered by 15 May 1598.[4] The same year the Fife Adventurers made their first attempt to colonise Lewis.

Slowly but relentlessly the government increased its intervention in the Isles, and made a concerted effort to control the Gaidhealtachd. It was a policy that was boosted, in 1602, by the English victory over the Irish in Ulster. The Union of the Crowns, which followed in 1603, gave James additional means by which to achieve his aims in the Isles. In 1607 further attempts at colonisation on the Irish model were made in Kintyre, and in the spring of 1608 a new expedition to Islay, Mull and Skye was announced.

This expedition, which was led by Lord Ochiltree, eventually set sail in the autumn. His instructions were to reduce the chiefs to obedience and obtain the payments of royal revenues. Ochiltree captured several chiefs and seized Duart Castle, as well as Dunivaig in Islay, which he garrisoned. In December 1608 a government commission to the Isles was established to negotiate a settlement with the captured chiefs and 'all suche other of the Illismen or Heylandis that will come in'.

The commission's aim was not just to extract rents, which the King dismissed as 'the meanest of all motives' but to 'foster general prosperity, economic development and the establishment of Lowland style towns'.[5]

The chiefs were initially reluctant to accept any of the Government's proposals. However, when eventually it dawned on them that the Council meant business, their attitude changed and by the end of February 1609 Hector Maclean of Duart made a series of offers, which appear to represent the position of the other chiefs as well. He agreed to be answerable for all the inhabitants of Mull, with certain named exceptions, and for all the other properties he either possessed or claimed. In order to ensure his obedience, he undertook to enter his sons or brothers as hostages. He also agreed to surrender all his land and take a new infestment of them from the Crown for which he would pay annual duties. He accepted that he would not be able to find a cautioner to guarantee these payments and agreed that if he failed to pay up his land would be forfeit.

In the spring of 1609 Andrew Knox, Bishop of the Isles, who had accompanied Lord Ochiltree to the Isles in 1608, had a meeting with the King in London to discuss the situation in the Isles. By June, perhaps after discussion with the Bishop, James ceased to emphasise his original plan to dispossess the chiefs and colonise the Isles with Lowlanders. Instead he agreed to encourage them to co-operate. He also agreed on another expedition to the Isles. It was this expedition that was to produce the Statutes of Iona.

At a court of justiciary held in Iona on 23 August 1609 the chiefs agreed to establish parish ministers in the Isles and to limit their military retinues. Traditional Hebridean hospitality was to be reduced, Gaelic culture was to be discouraged and the English language promoted.

* * *

Although he met him in the Isles,[6] Lachlan Maclean of Coll was not one of the chiefs seized by Ochiltree. He was, however, one of 'the named exceptions' in Mull for whom Hector of Duart was not responsible.

Coll was present at Iona on 23 August 1609, and was one of the chiefs to be summoned annually to appear before the Council in Edinburgh. In 1615 he appointed an advocate [Mr Thomas Acheson] and writer [Hew Peblis] in Edinburgh at whose dwelling he could be summoned to appear before the Council.[7]

It is possible that the chiefs paid more than lip service to the Council's intentions and on 24 August 1616 in Glasgow Sir Rory Macleod of Dunvegan, Donald MacAllane of Clanranald, Lachlan Mackinnon of Strathordell and Lachlan Maclean of Coll signed a bond of friendship. In it they stress that

> as it hes plesit the Kings Majesty and His Hienes secreit counsale to ordane us to leve in mutuall societie and friendshyp wuth utheris as His Majesteis subiectis aucht to do ... we being maist willingto obey the samen haive agreeit and concludit amovnges our selis and be the tenour heirof bindis and obleiss us ilk ane to utheris, and takand the burdene on us for all our kin, friendis, aleyis, men, tennentis, servandis, and dependaris quhatsumevir ylka or anie of us may command ayer within our awin boundis and landis or outis the samen ... on a penaltie of 5,000 merks scots.[8]

The formidable Roderick Macleod of Dunvegan, *Ruari Mor* led this group of closely related chiefs. They appear to have acted together. Macleod and Coll were even suggested as joint bailies of Duart's estate, when the latter was incarcerated in Edinburgh Castle for failing to pay his dues to the Crown. They also stood caution for each other; agreed to compeir annually before the Council on 10 July; to exhibit close kinsmen, in Coll's case his uncles Allan of Auchnasaul and John of Grishipol. Lachlan also nominated Breacachadh Castle as his dwelling house.

Another party with whom Lachlan was perhaps linked was the Church. His grandfather *An Cléireach Beag* is said to have been pious and, at the time of the Reformation, an early member of the Protestant Party.[9] Lachlan was also well known to Mr Thomas Knox, son of the Bishop of the

Isles, who had negotiated the Statutes of Iona. Thomas Knox, who succeeded his father as Bishop of the Isles, was at this time Minister of Tiree and Coll.[10] It is also worth noting that when Irish Franciscan friars visited the Isles in the 1620s, although Lachlan's allies Lochbuie, Clanranald, and Macleod are mentioned as being either converts or were already Roman Catholics, Coll is not mentioned.[11] In addition his eldest son was well known for his piety and his daughter Janet was to marry Mr Farquhar Fraser, Dean of the Isles. It is this relationship with the Church, which perhaps explains what happened next.

In 1617 Parliament abolished the practice of giving of calps,[12] which as we have seen, was the custom by which a clansman paid his chief for a lifetime's protection. It struck at the very root of the clan 'system'. It was also the means by which the courts had settled the dispute between Coll and Duart over the ownership of the Two Ends of Coll. In theory once the giving of calps became unlawful Coll had no longer any control of a large part of his own island. However, it is by no means certain that such legislation was effective in the Isles and there is evidence that the custom of giving calps prevailed in some parts of the Highlands for a further hundred years or more.[13]

That same summer Lachlan received a new Great Seal charter for his lands.[14] They were erected into a 'Free Barony called the Barony of Coll . . . the Castle of Coll to be the chief Messuage'.[15] A month later Andrew Knox, Bishop of the Isles made him a grant of a feu charter[16] of the 3 merk lands of the Isle of Muck. Muck 'ane little ile of ane mile long and half waid . . . will raise 16 able men'[17] is one of the Small Isles between Coll and Skye. It was said to be very fertile and 'verie gude for fische'[18] It had long belonged to the Bishop of the Isles but for sometime had been possessed by the Macians of Ardnamurchan.

This ancient branch of the Macdonalds had fallen on hard times. They had been savagely persecuted by Lachlan Mor of Duart. Their chief had also fallen out with some of his own clansmen and, after a bloody conflict with them, appealed to Argyll for help. The Earl, whose ancestors had, earlier in the previous century, obtained a claim to Ardnamurchan, was now acknowledged by the Macian chief as his superior. It was a fatal move for his clan. The current earl Archibald, known as *Gill-easbuig Gruamach*, was deep in debt, and when in 1611 John of Ardnamurchan died, leaving an heir who was a minor, Argyll began to enforce his rights.

In 1612 Argyll issued his kinsman Mr Donald Campbell of Barbreck-Lochawe with a commission to occupy Mingary Castle and use it as a base to force the inhabitants of Ardnamurchan and Sunart into submission. At the same time, for some Machiavellian reason, he renewed Donald MacAllane of Clanranald's tack of the lands of Acharacle and Ardtoe, which comprised of much of north-eastern Ardnamurchan. These lands marched with Clanranald's own property in Moidart and were strategically valuable to him. Mr Donald Campbell and Clanranald were now launched on a collision course, which is presumably what the Earl intended.

This was the background to the situation in Ardnamurchan when the Bishop of the Isles made a grant to Coll of the Isle of Muck. Several of the leading Macians had land in Muck. They now became Coll's tenants.[19] Some, perhaps, even moved to the Isle of Coll itself and were the ancestors to the families of Johnstons [Macians] in the island. Others objected to Coll's grant of Muck and, according to Crossapol, kept 'possession of it violently contrary to law' for that and 'other bad practices Coll apprehended fourteen of their men at Ardmor in Mull, sent them to Inveraray, where most of them were put to death'.

The Macians were badly divided. There were family ties between some of them and Coll. Even so it is extraordinary that Lachlan of Coll and his ally Sir Rory took the risk of becoming cautioners for their good behaviour. It was a disastrous decision, at least as far as Coll was concerned.

In the early summer of 1618 *Iain Muideartach* Captain of Clanranald, who had recently succeeded his father, with 'grite pypis blowing afore thame' invaded Ardnamurchan with 200 men. The raiders consisted of both Clanranald's own men and Macians. They drove Mr Donald Campbell from Mingary Castle, ejected his people from Ardnamurchan and Sunart and carried off their booty to Moidart.

On 10th November Mr Donald complained to the Council.[20] As a result he was given letters of horning against the Macians. The leading Campbell lairds, under the command of Sir Dugall Campbell of Auchinbreck, were ordered to apprehend the culprits.[21] Some rebels, however, were still at large when on 17 January 1622 Sir Rory, Lochnell, Lachlan Maclean of Ardnacross,[22] Coll and Dunstafnage were given a commission to seize the Clanranald rebels.[23] A month later they received yet another commission to seize leading Macians.[24] On this occasion the Macians claimed that they had found caution for their good behaviour and had been relaxed from the horn.[25]

Mr Donald continued to harass the Macians and by 1624 the government had a major rebellion on its hands. This rebellion was not limited to the mainland for the Macians captured an English ship and used it for piratical raids up and down the west coast. They soon took other shipping and now became a considerable embarrassment to the King.

Eventually the pirate's ships were captured and the rebellion was doomed when Rory Mor, probably accompanied by Coll and his men, joined Argyll's heir Lord Lorne in marching into Ardnamurchan. Ten rebels were executed, six killed in the fighting and fourteen[26] sent for trial in Edinburgh. The remaining Macians fled. They were now a broken clan. However, as we shall see, several of them lurked in the Isles and were a menace to the Macleans of Coll for many years to come. Crossapol says that some of the Macians hated Lachlan for 'bringing so many of them to justice'.

After the Macians themselves, the major loser by their rebellion was Maclean of Coll. He had stood caution for their good behaviour and that caution was now forfeit. On 4 December 1629 at Inveraray Lord Lorne held a meeting with Lachlan of Coll and his eldest son John. In the minutes of the meeting it was pointed out that Lachlan had become bound

> as one of the cautioners for certain of the Clan Eane for their being answerable to the Laws and for their dutiful obedience and loyal service to the House of Argyll and for thir being obedient tenants to Sir Donald Campbell [as Mr Donald had now become] ... in the said noble lords lands of Ardnamurchan ... whereby Lauchlane as a cautioner became for payment of many great penalties and sums of money which Lord Lorne and Sir Donald might most justly exact of him for all the 'heirschippes and skaith' committed which if done at law 'wald turne to the utter wrack and Ruine of the said Lauchlane' and the said noble lord considering that Lauchlane and his predecessors have been followers and dependers of the House of Argyll, and therefore having a singular regard for his 'weill and standing of his house' has now granted with Sir Donald's consent a sufficient discharge of the haill contracts and penalties in them where Coill and his son bind them to instantly infest and seize Lord Lorne and his heirs male and successors heritably and irredeemably in all and haill the just third part of the 18 Mark land of Queyneis ... all and Haill the Isle of Rowme ... and in the 3 Mk land of Auchillenane, 3 Mk land of Drwnyngne in the Lordship of Morwanne, by sufficient Charters and Infestments ... to be held from the said Lauchlane etc of our sovereign Lord the Kings Majesty and his highnesses successors, and shall deliver up all the old writs of the said Lands or at least authentic doubles of them to Lord Lorne ... [who binds himself] that after he is infest, he will set in perpetual feufarm to the said Lauchlane in liferent and to John Mcleane his eldest lawful son

and heirs male and assignees whatsoever all the above lands. To be held of the said Noble Lord and his heirs etc in feu and heritage for ever for yearly payments of £24 Scots at Whitsunday and Martinmas as feufarm and 'doing and performing' to the said noble lords and his &c all service within the hielandis of this Realme in sic sort as the rest of the said noble lords wassells within the Earldom of Argyll does or shall doe ... And Lord Lorne promises to truly and legally assist maintain and defend the said Lauchlane ...[27]

Lorne had achieved what Lachlan Mor had failed to do. Although Maclean of Coll still held his lands in Coll and two thirds of his property in Mull from the Crown, without the interference of any other party, he had lost the superiority of much of his land and with it his independence. He had also lost out financially. Although Lorne agreed to grant the Mull and Rum lands back in feu to Lachlan the latter had to pay £48 Scots per year for his own property.

Although Lachlan had the good sense not to deliver his original charters up to Lorne he was unwise to do a private deal with the Campbells, rather than take a chance in the courts. Lorne and Sir Donald had hoodwinked him. They were two of the most unscrupulous operators in Scotland.[28] Professor Cowan has argued that the Campbells had an unparalleled reputation for deviousness, treachery and covetousness and that these attributes were largely due to the person and character of Lorne's father *Gill-easbuig Gruamach*, Archibald seventh Earl of Argyll.[29] He goes so far as to say that 'the grasping avariciousness' of the Campbells was part of their genetic inheritance.

Gill-easbuig Gruamach's conversion in 1617 to Roman Catholocism, and his subsequent exile, removed him from the scene but his son Lorne, who was to operate as Earl in all but name from the 1620s, was as ruthless and as grasping as his father. Their henchman Sir Donald Campbell of Ardnamurchan is said by Professor Cowan to be 'a sadly vicious and vindictive character',[30] whilst Sir James Turner, a contemporary professional soldier, describes him as being 'fleshed in blood from his verie infancie'.[31] More recently Alastair Campbell of Airds has defended his ancestor's reputation.[32] However, I suspect Sir Donald's contemporaries in Coll would have preferred Cowan and Turner's verdict.

* * *

Lachlan was Laird of Coll for more than fifty years and his 'reign' witnessed numerous changes in the Hebrides. The most profound was probably increased commercialism. The Crown's new involvement in the Isles and its success in obtaining its rents meant that for the first time the chiefs had a need for cash. In addition their enforced annual attendance on the Council in Edinburgh was expensive and they got into debt. One of the few means they had to raise cash was by the export of cattle.

Cattle had probably been exported from the Isles for many years, and in 1609 Hector Maclean of Duart

and certane utheris chiftanes of the Ylis ... ar maid unable to pay his Majesteis dewyteis of thair landis, be ressoun of a Proclamatioun and Prohibitioun maid within the boundis of Ergyle that no mercheantis or utheris sall buy ony mairtis [cattle fattened for winter consumption], horses or utheris goodis within the boundis of Mule or ony utheris of the West Yllis.[33]

The increased need to export cattle meant that more land was needed for grazing and less was available for crops. Previously the produce of the soil seems to have been consumed locally.

By today's standards the ground was surprisingly productive. Dodgshon calculates that every year Coll produced 240 bolls of meal, 150 bolls of bere 600 stones of cheese and 120 marts.[34] Each merkland on Mull and Coll is said to have paid an annual rent of '5 bollis beir, 8 bollis meill, 20 stanes of chese, 4 stanes of buttir, 4 mairtis, 8 wedderis, two merk of silver, and twa dozen pultrie.'[35]

'Cuddiche, quanhanevir thair master cummis to thame' paid these dues. 'Cuddiche', *cuid-oidche*, was a night's entertainment or lodging[36] given to a landlord when he, or his 'household men' visited a township. One of the objects of government legislation in the early seventeenth century was to abolish this custom. Instead a chief's lands should be set to tenants 'for a certane and cleir dewytie ... [and] ... in all tyme coeming forbeare taking of cowdighis.' Chiefs should 'mak policie and planting ... [and] ... tak maynes about thair housis in thair awne handis, and labour the same with thair awne goodis, to the effect thay may be thairby exercised and eshew idilness'.[37]

These measures were also aimed at curbing the Hebridean habit of hospitality. The amount of food owed by *cuid-oidche* could only be consumed on the spot or when the chief gave one of his legendary entertainments. Several descriptions of these gatherings are preserved in contemporary songs. One of the best known is by Clanranald's bard Neil Mor MacMhuirich and is about a party given by Lachlan of Coll's brother-in-law Sir Rory Mor Macleod

> We were twenty times drunk every day,
> To which we had no more objection than he had;
> Even our food was in abundance ...[38]

Word of these drunken orgies no doubt reached the Court and they were responsible for the regulations limiting the import of wine. Coll was restricted to importing one tun of wine annually.[39] Another statute that did have its effect, or followed a recently established trend, was to make the chiefs send their children to be educated in the Lowlands. Lachlan could not sign his name, at least in Scots in the current secretary hand. John Bannerman has suggested that four chiefs, including Coll, signed the Statutes of Iona in the Gaelic manner as a protest against the implied denigration of their language in the body of the text.[40] The original Statutes no longer exist and this statement is speculation. Bannerman's argument is weakened by the fact that when Lachlan signed his contract with Lord Lorne in 1629 'his hand was led because he could not write' his name. His son John could and does so in a clear confident hand,[41] whilst his younger brother Mr Hector was educated at Glasgow University. He graduated in 1628.[42]

Lachlan's marriage arrangements for his children were, as in the past, to the sons and daughters of other lairds. Certainly the marriage of his eldest son John to Fionnvola, daughter of Sir Dugall Campbell of Auchinbreck in 1620 was original. It was the first time that a Maclean of Coll had married a Campbell and underlines Lachlan's political importance in local society and perhaps his aspirations to play a part in the world beyond the Isles.

Sir Dugall, who had led the Campbells in their assault on the Macians, was considered to be 'the chiefest and greatest under Argyll'.[43] He had married twice. His first wife, Fionnvola's mother, was Lady Mary Erskine sister of Viscount Fentoun.[44] The latter had accompanied King James to London in 1603, where he succeeded Sir Walter Raleigh as captain of the yeomen of the guard. In 1619 he was created Earl of Kellie.[45] John Maclean was therefore marrying into one of the most well connected families in Scotland. This marriage marked the zenith of Lachlan of Coll's alliance with the Campbells.

Mr Hector, Coll's second son, married more conventionally. His wife was the daughter of Allan Maclean of Ardtornish, the scourge of the Macians of Ardnamurchan in the time of Lachlan Mor, who had then married the daughter of their chief and later sided with them against Mr Donald Campbell.[46] Lachlan's daughters also married local lairds. Katherine his eldest daughter in 1627[47] marrying John Mackinnon, son of Lachlan's old ally Sir Lachlan Mackinnon of Strathordell, who was both deaf and dumb.[48] She received a life interest in a number of Mackinnon's lands in Mull. Her attorney, when she received sasine of these lands, was her illegitimate half-brother John of Mingary, who had from his father the important holding of Mingary in Quinish. John had been born in the Lowlands and was known as *Iain Gallda*, 'foreign John'. He was evidently close to his father and in 1629 was a witness to the latter's contract with Lord Lorne at Inveraray.

John, Lachlan's eldest son and Mr Hector were also witnesses of the 1629 contract. Neither Allan of Auchnasaul nor John of Grishipol is mentioned and no other members of the Coll family were witnesses. It would thus appear that we are seeing what appears to be a common feature in the Highlands: that each new generation of younger sons pushed aside and replaced older cadets and the members of unrelated followers, who had held important holdings of land in the past. Certainly this seems to have happened in Sir Rory Mor's family. IF Grant tells us that his

> Four younger sons were provided for by the liferent of large portions of his estate ... by doing so Sir Rory imposed a heavy burden upon his successors and considerably disturbed some of the older families of clansmen. Roderick, the second son, was given Talisker and there is a tradition that a branch of the MacAskills, who had long lived there, was removed to Glendale. Norman, the third son, had the island of Bernera formerly belonging to a family descended from Malcolm, 3rd Chief. William, the fourth son, received Hamer, and Donald got Greshornish.[49]

Crossapol states that Rory Mor 'commited the keeping of his younger childrens portions to witt Sir Rory and Sir Normand' to Maclean of Coll. As the latter's contract of fosterage, in Gaelic dated 8 October 1614 with Eoin mac mic Cainnigh,[50] survives,[51] it is certain that Lachlan was not their foster-father. Whatever the relationship it was, as we shall see, to stand the family of Coll in good stead in the future.

All these Macleod sons established families that were to hold their lands for many generations. It would therefore appear that IF Grant is wrong in saying that they received them in liferent. It is more likely that they held them from their father and his heirs in tack, as the Macleods of Talisker certainly did.[52]

On 4 April 1632, in the presence of John [Lesley] Bishop of the Isles, Lachlan surrendered the six mark lands of the Isle of Muck into the hands of the Bishop, who granted them to his eldest son John.[53] A month later 'John Mak neill vc Gilliechallome,[54] alias McClean servant of Lachlan' appeared before the notary public with charter granted by the bishop and received sasine.[55] The following January Lachlan of Coll, with the advice and consent of his eldest son John, assigned the Isle of Muck to Mr Hector. As a result the Sheriff clerk issued a precept of sasine of the island to Mr Hector's bailie. He was young Neil the son of John Dubh, *nigello oig mak ean dowie*, in Gallanach in the Isle of Muck.[56]

* * *

In the spring of 1632 Lachlan of Coll and Hector Og, younger of Duart, were summoned to Edinburgh to answer the complaints of Sir Lachlan Maclean of Morverne. Duart was heavily in debt and Sir Lachlan, Duart's younger and abler son, agreed to take responsibility for these debts provided that his brother

> resigned the living of Dowart in his favour. Thereupon, having been infest in the said living, he paid the said debts, uplifting the rents of the saids lands etc until last Martinmas that his said father and brother, stirred up by Lachlan McClane of Coill ... [and others] ... disorderly persons in the Isles, gathered together three hundred persons in arms and forbidden weapons and went through the bounds of Dowart, sorning and oppressing the poor people there, compelled them to pay their rents to them, and slew and mutilated their goods and drove the same away...[57]

It is not clear what was behind these events. However, they were soon settled, even before the two Hectors, father and son, of Duart, died. They were succeeded by Sir Lachlan of Morvern.

Crossapol says that Lachlan Maclean of Coll 'lived to a great age'. He was probably born in 1574 and was dead by 8 October 1636.[58] He was thus sixty-one, not a very long life in the Hebrides, where several of his contemporaries lived to be over a hundred. He had, however, been one of the most powerful chiefs of Coll. He is regularly listed before Lochbuie, which is a useful indicator of his position in Hebridean society. His children made advantageous marriages. In the modern parlance he punched above his weight. It was to be a long time before a Maclean of Coll was to be as influential again.

Notes

1. *Oighreachd* = Inheritance, possession, freehold estate, landed proprietor [ED Dwelly *Gaelic-English Dictionary* (1977), 705.
2. *Macinnes* (1996), 5.
3. Thereafter they had a run of charters to the mid-eighteenth century. In the late nineteenth century 49 Maclean of Coll charters, marriage settlements etc were in the possession of the daughters of Hugh, the last Maclean Laird of Coll. It is not known what became of them. Several but by no means all appear in the published *Register of the Great Seal of Scotland* (1912–14). In June 1897 HAC Maclean translated most of them and made extracts from others. Copies of these 'Extracts and Translations' are now among the Coll papers at Breacachadh Castle.
4. *APS*, iv, 138–9, c.33, quoted in Goodare, (1998), 34.
5. Goodare, (1998), 36. The last six paragraphs of this section are based on his article.
6. *RPCS*, VIII (1607–10), 523.
7. Jean Munro 'When Island Chiefs Came To Town' *WHN&Q* No. XIX (December 1982), 11.
8. RC Macleod of Macleod, The Book of Dunvegan (1938), 48–50.
9. *Warriors and Priests*, 139.
10. The two parishes in Tiree and that of Coll were linked in 1618.
11. Cathaldus Giblin (ed) *Irish Franciscan Mission to Scotland 1619–1646* (1964).
12. *APS*, iv, 548, c. 21, quoted in Goodare (1998), 62.
13. Frances J Shaw, *The Northern and Western Islands of Scotland* (1980), 67–8.
14. *RMS* (1609–20), 1653; BCP Charters No. 19.
15. AT Vol. IX, 235.
16. NAS. RH9/4/2.
17. *Celtic Scotland*, iii, 434.
18. RW Munro (ed) *Monro's Western Isles of Scotland and Genealogies of the Clans 1549* (1961), 67.

19. *RPCS* Vol. XIII (1622–25), 605; Professor Cowan in 'Fishers in Drumlie Waters: Campbell Expansion in the time of Gilleasbuig Gruamach' *TGSI* Vol. LIV (1984–86), 295 says that there were 'a substantial number of Macleans in Ardnamurchan who looked to MacLean of Coll'. This is highly improbable. I suspect that Cowan's statement is based on *RPCS* XII (1619–22), 50: that lands in Ardnamurchan were 'possest be the said Clanranald, Clanleane, and utheris'. This is probably a misreading of 'Clanleane' for 'Claniane'.
20. *RPCS* Vol. XI (1616–19), 463.
21. *Ibid*, 643.
22. He was the second son of Lachlan Mor, and was the father of Hector Maclean first of Torloisk.
23. *RPCS* Vol. XII (1619–22), 635–6
24. *Ibid*, 661.
25. *RPCS* Vol. XIII (1622–25), 19.
26. As 14 Macians is the number seized by Coll and sent to be hanged in Inveraray, these two traditions perhaps relate to the same incident.
27. ICP. AT vol. XI (1629–37) includes details of these arrangements.
28. Coll would probably have done better if he had appeared in front of the courts. Other cautioners were burdened with debts for many years to come [eg Edward J Cowan (1986), 278–9] when the object of their caution failed to meet his commitments but they did not lose their property as Coll did.
29. Edward J Cowan, (1986), 268–9.
30. *Ibid*, 294.
31. Sir James Turner, *Memoirs of His Life and Times* (Edinburgh 1829), 48.
32. Alastair Campbell of Airds Unicorn Pursuivant *The Life and Troubled Times of Sir Donald Campbell of Ardnamurchan* (1991)
33. *Collectanea de Rebus Albanicis*, (1847), 153.
34. Robert A Dodgshon, *From Chiefs to Landlords* (1998), 61.
35. *Celtic Scotland*, iii, 428–40.
36. *Dwelly*, 288.
37. *RPCS* Vol. X (1613–16), 775.
38. A Cameron *Reliquiae Celticae*, I, 121.
39. *RPCS* Vol. X (1613–16), 773.
40. John Bannerman 'Literacy in the Highlands', *The Renaissance and Reformation in Scotland* (1983), 231–2.
41. ICP Band L. Coill to the Earl of Argyll 8 October 1636.
42. C Innes (ed) *Munimenta Alme Universitis Glasguensis* Vol. 3, 78.
43. *Calendar of State Papers relating to Scotland 1547–1603* XIII, part 2 (1969), 896.
44. *HP* iv, 59–67.
45. William Anderson *The Scottish Nation* Volume vi (1877), 594.
46. *RPCS* Vol. XII (1619–22), 661.
47. BCP, Coll Charters No. 26.
48. *RPCS*, 2nd Series Vol. IV, 677.
49. IF Grant *The Macleods* (1959), 249.
50. *Ibid*, 374. IF Grant says that Mac Choinich ... was the patonymic of Campbell of Strond in Harris.
51. Donald Mackinnon *A descriptive Catalogue of Gaelic Manuscripts* (1912), 296.
52. NAS. GD248. 29. 2. 88: 15 July 1794 Colonel Macleod of Talisker to Sir James Grant of Grant.
53. BCP Coll, Charters No. 28.
54. He is presumably a son of Neil Buidh.
55. BCP. Coll Charters No. 29.
56. NAS RS/33/230.
57. *RPCS* 2nd Series. Vol. IV, 675
58. AT. Inventory of the 9th Earl of Argyll's Charters 1680, 565.

Chapter Three

John Garbh Maclean of Coll 1635–1651

John Garbh succeeded his father as Maclean of Coll. Crossapol quotes Captain Joseph Witter, the Cromwellian governor of Dunstafnage Castle in 1658,[1] as saying that the second John Garbh Maclean of Coll was 'a wise and pious man and a great lover of music and very hospitable ... [and] that he much resembled King David being a great reader of the Scriptures and a noble player at the harp'. Another version of the same story, handed down in the Maclean of Coll family, has it that

> an English vessel having been wrecked on the island, the captain of which went to the castle of Coll and on seeing a venerable gentleman with a Bible in his hand, and a Harp placed by his side, exclaimed, in the enthusiastic language of that time that he beheld King David restored again to earth.[2]

John Garbh also has the reputation of being an accomplished composer of music for the harp. Two of his compositions survive. One called *Toun Muran* and the other *Caoineadh Rioghail*, 'the royal lament' perhaps composed in memory of the execution of King Charles I.

It has recently been suggested that Mid-Argyll occupies an important place in the history of the harp in Scotland.[3] As we have already seen, John Garbh married the daughter of Sir Dugald Campbell of Auchinbreck, whose property lay in Mid-Argyll, and it is possible that his daughter brought a harper with her to Coll.

It was usual in the Hebrides for an incoming wife to bring her own retainers with her. Fionnvola seems to have done so, as a Mr William Campbell is noted as being in Coll at this time.[4] He is likely to be a relation,[5] and to have been the bailie for her jointure lands. These were considerable as Lachlan of Coll had made over all his lands in Mull, as well as Gallanach, Torestan, Knock and 'Cardnaha' [now Totamore] in Coll, to John Garbh and Fionnvola as part of their marriage settlement.[6]

John Garbh and Fionnvola had eight children. In January 1640 John made a disposition in favour of his seven younger children. His second son John was to receive four thousand merks at the age of 21, which was probably secured by a wadset on the lands of Totronald in Coll. The third son Hugh, who is not mentioned by name in the disposition, was to have 2,000 merks at the same age.

The five daughters were each to receive cattle. Fionnvola, the eldest was to have 240 at the age of 21. The cattle are specified. The first third were to be 'furrow or tydie ky at 20 merks each, the second third 3-year olds at 12 merks each, the third third 2-year olds at 8 merks each'. The second daughter Una, again un-named, was to receive '200 ky' to be divided in three thirds, of type and value as before. The third daughter Margaret was to receive 120 ky, and the fourth Katherine 80 and the fifth Janet [Seònaid] was also to receive 80. All these cattle were to be divided in thirds as above. If any of these children were to die before the age of 21 the 'sums of money and goods destined for that person' were to belong to his eldest son Hector Roy.[7]

John was earmarking 720 cattle for his daughters. When the girls married these animals would probably leave the estate. That John was able to give so many cattle to his daughters is an indication of the number of cattle on the Coll estate, or John Garbh's lack of realism.

In the absence of any estate records for this period it is not possible even to guess how many cattle there were on Coll, but it suggests that on the eve of the Civil Wars the Macleans of Coll had immersed themselves in the cattle trade to the Lowlands.

In the past, as we have seen, the produce of each township had been geared to local needs.[8] For instance, when the chief and his fighting men came to visit, rent in kind was consumed on the spot. This system encouraged the production of arable crops. However, when the chiefs were forced to make extended annual visits to Edinburgh and appear before the Council, they were increasingly in need of cash. The only cash crop they had to export, apart from fish that would not travel, was cattle. As a result more land had to be devoted to pasture. The increased amount of land needed for cattle will have meant that less ground was available to feed the chief's fighting men. As a result, instead of the produce of the soil being used to support a warrior class, it was needed to produce a cash crop, and the chiefs were increasingly drawn into the market economy of the Lowlands.

This change was of immense importance for the future of the Hebrides. Previously a chief might have been thought of as a 'Warlord', whose estate was organised primarily to support fighting men. From now on the need for cash was to be of equal importance. Fighting men were still needed, but so was cash.

Increased contact with the Lowlands, as we have seen, made it a necessity to employ lawyers in Edinburgh. Whilst the export of cattle required not only a drover to take the cattle to market, a nightmare considering the amount of water to be crossed, but also an agent to handle the Chief's interests at the nearest commercial centre. It is therefore worth noting that in 1630 'Rorie, in Creisapoll [Grishipol ?]' in Coll became a Burgess in Glasgow.[9] We will hear more about this branch of the family of Coll, who seem to have been involved in trade from at least this period.

The Coll estate's future prosperity was in some doubt. The estate was burdened with grants of land to younger sons and cattle promised to daughters. In addition Lachlan of Coll had contracted debts that were unpaid and accumulating interest.[10] However, the family's prestige was high and financially it was potentially strong. Otherwise it is unlikely that anyone as ambitious as Hector Maclean of Kellene would have married his eldest daughter to Hector Roy, younger of Coll, John Garbh's eldest son and apparent heir.[11]

Hector Kellene, the eldest son of Lachlan Barrach, 'Lachlan the Superior', Lachlan Mor of Duart's able second son, seems to have inherited his father's ability and his grandfather's ruthless ambition. After a somewhat wild youth, in conjunction with his brother-in-law Hector Maclean of Kinlochaline,[12] Hector Kellene became a Glasgow burgess and must have had commercial interests in the city. He presumably made enough money to purchase a wadset on 'Killene'[13] and appears to have been associated with Lachlan of Coll's party in the 1620s and early 30s. He then moved politically closer to Lord Lorne. In 1636 he witnessed the bond by which John Garbh finally made Drimnin and

Auchlinan over to Sir Donald Campbell.[14] Lorne probably accepted Hector Killene as a follower as his mother was another sister of Sir Dugald Campbell of Auchinbreck.[15]

The contract of marriage between John Maclean of Coll and his son and heir Hector Roy, on one side, and Hector Maclean of Kellene, on behalf of his eldest lawful daughter Marie on the other, was signed on 22 January 1641 at Hough in Tiree. It was a significant occasion. John Garbh settled lands in both Coll and Mull for life on Marie, and the rest of his estate on Hector Roy. Killene provided a tocher 10,000 merks, which 'for the better conservation of the estate and barony of Coill' was to be employed to pay off the debts and burdens on the estate.[16]

The witnesses are also significant. They included Sir Duncan Campbell of Auchinbreck and George Campbell, Sheriff Clerk of Argyll. They were two of the Earl of Argyll's closest confidants.

Lorne, who in 1638 had succeeded his father as Earl of Argyll, was now one of the most influential men in the covenanting party. The Covenanters, who were violently opposed to King Charles I's policies concerning the Church, had taken up arms to oppose the King and had successfully confronted him in the First (1639) and Second (1640) Bishop's Wars.

In 1640 the Committee of Estates granted Argyll a commission of fire and sword to hunt down certain 'intestyne enemes' of the Covenant[17] and in Angus the Earl led a pre-emptive strike against the Royalists, ravaging Airlie Castle and sacking the Ogilvie estates. The Covenanters, however, were not to have everything their own way. In Ulster Ranald MacDonnell, Earl of Antrim had men under arms, and the following November his cousin Alexander Macdonald *Alasdair MacColla* led a raid from Antrim on Islay, which was now owned by Campbells.

The presence of two leading Campbells at Hector Roy's nuptials has to be seen against this background. At such a time of increasing tension, more than family affection for a sister must have induced Auchinbreck to leave the mainland for his nephew's wedding in Tiree. He may have gone there to recruit at the time when he knew that Duart's household men would be there. However, the most likely explanation is that he wished to ensure that Coll would not depart from his alliance with the Campbells. As we shall see, Montrose later thought it worthwhile to write personally to John Garbh to encourage him to send his men to join the royal standard. Auchinbreck too probably thought that Coll's loyalty was worth the discomfort of a winter's journey by sea, especially as word had no doubt reached Argyll that Sir Donald Gorm Macdonald of Sleat was secretly organising an alliance of West Highlanders against the Campbells.[18].

Maclean of Coll is not listed among Donald Gorm's correspondents. Instead he appears to be considered a member of the covenanting party, for when the King appointed Donald Gorm as his commissioner in the Highlands and Islands, his reward was to be a grant of the Isles of Rum, Muck and Canna.[19] The former two islands being part of Maclean of Coll's estate.

* * *

Meanwhile in October 1641 rebellion had broken out in Ireland and refugees were soon fleeing to Scotland across the Irish Sea. After considerable dithering the English Parliament agreed to pay for ten Scottish regiments, which were needed to help suppress the revolt. One of them was to be raised by Argyll. The Lieutenant Colonel was Sir Duncan Campbell of Auchinbreck. The regiment, which was 1,099 strong, was in Ireland by the 1 May 1642. It consisted of ten companies. Many, but by no means all the company commanders, were Campbells.

One company commander, who was not a Campbell, was Hector Maclean of Kinlochaline.[20] His chief Sir Lachlan Maclean of Duart had been imprisoned for debt by Argyll. Whilst he was incarcerated in Carrick Castle on the Clyde, Argyll had probably forced Sir Lachlan to authorise the raising of a company in Argyll's regiment.[21] The muster roles of the soldiers in Maclean's company are mainly in patronymics, and without surnames, it is therefore not possible to say who they were. However, the number of Lachlans, Eachans and Allans suggest that many were Macleans. There are also several Macgilvrays who probably came from Mull. Nobody obviously comes from Coll.[22] Perhaps two MacFadyens in Auchinbreck's company did, but that is pure speculation.

Meanwhile Coll's financial position had not improved. In January 1642 at Inveraray he signed a bond to George Campbell the Sheriff Clerk of Argyll, who as we have seen, had also attended the wedding in Tiree, The bond was for £1,621.11s.4d Scots. Other debts are also listed. They too were assigned to George Campbell.[23] Coll probably now went even deeper into debt. His situation was not improved by political instability as civil war loomed over the British Isles. Increased lawlessness, which must have made the situation even worse, also affected the cattle trade from Coll, especially when John Garbh's illegitimate half-brother John of Mingary was ambushed at sea and murdered by a band of Maciains. It is said that sixteen arrows pierced his body.[24]

John of Mingary had probably played an influential role in the family and it must have seemed to many that the Macleans of Coll were doomed to disappear from the scene. If they had done so at this juncture they would have gone down in history as bankrupt followers of Argyll. However, everything was now altered. Instead of being Argyll's man, Coll changed sides. It was the start of a feud that was to last nearly 150 years.

Perhaps Coll was convinced by the royalist case; perhaps his financial position was so desperate that only political change in Scotland could save him from the clutches of the Campbells. Perhaps John Garbh's situation was exacerbated by the breakdown of his marriage.[25] Whatever the cause, Coll's change of sides had a profound effect on a number of people. The effect on his marriage is vividly illustrated by a poem in Gaelic by his wife Fionnvola Campbell, Lady Coll. In it she curses 'the wicked Seònaid'

> *Turus mo chreiche 'thug mi 'Chola!*
> *Rinn iad mo leab' aig an dorus,*
> *Comaidh ri fearaibh 's ri conaibh*
> *'S thug iad am bràisd as mo bhroilleach,*
> *'S m' usgraichean corrach,*
> *'S thug iad sud do Sheonaid dhona.*

A journey that destroyed me I made to Coll!
They made my bed at the door,
Sharing with men and dogs,
And they took my brooch from my breast,
And my jewels and rounded buttons,
And gave them all to the wicked Seònaid.[26]

David Stevenson has suggested that 'the wicked Seònaid' is Fionnvola's own daughter. Certainly John and Fionnvola had a daughter called Seònaid [Janet] but it is also possible that she is a paramour of John Garbh. Most Macleans of Coll appear to have had illegitimate offspring and it is not unlikely that even the pious John Garbh was not immune to female attractions. However, it is worth noting that in her vitriolic song Fionnvola does not curse her husband.

The incident that sparked off Fionnvola's paroxysm of rage was the battle of Inverlochy. Soon after the Scots regiments landed in Ireland the English Civil War, between the King and Parliament, had broken out. The Covenanters in Scotland sided with Parliament. In order to open a second front for the King, the Marquess of Montrose slipped past the Covenanters and in late August 1644 raised the royal standard in Atholl. *Alasdair MacColla* joined him. The latter had left Antrim in July and sailed to the Sound of Mull. Sir Lachlan Maclean of Duart refused to join him and, having captured and garrisoned Mingary Castle, Alasdair set off in search of Montrose.

The royal army needed to recruit. However, many of its sympathisers among the clans were too much in awe of Argyll and refused to move. Montrose and Alasdair therefore decided to carry out a raid into the Campbell heartland, which was as much a public relations exercise as anything else. Bypassing Campbell outlyers they struck deep into Argyll leaving behind, as they withdrew into Lochaber, a trail of burnt out townships and gutted castles. The effect was devastating. It had proved that the Campbells were not invincible. Waverers, such as Duart, went to pay his respects to the King's Lieutenant and on 30th January 1645 at Kilcumin [now Fort Augustus] he with other clan chiefs signed a band pledging themselves to the

> maintenance of the power and authoritie of our sacred and native soverain, contrarie to this present perverse and infamous factione of desperatt Rebells now ine furie against him.[27]

A Seneachie in his *Account of the Clan Maclean* published in 1838 says that Maclean of Coll was with Sir Lachlan when he joined Montrose in Lochaber. This account is based on Hector Maclean of Gruline's manuscript. However, no version known to me has this information and if John Garbh or Hector Roy was at Kilcumin it is curious that they did not sign the Kilcumin Band.

Meanwhile Argyll was hurrying north in pursuit of the royal army. With him were Sir Duncan Campbell of Auchinbreck and his regiment. They had hurried home from Ireland to avenge the devastation of their homeland. Whether or not the Maclean company was with him is uncertain. Ewen Maclean of Treshnish, a professional soldier who had served for ten years in the French army now, led them. He was certainly on the royalist side at the battle of Inverlochy and it would seem possible that somehow the Macleans had managed to change sides during the battle. This may well be why Argyll's Regiment, hardened by three years fighting in Ireland, broke, ran and was butchered.

Among those taken alive was Auchinbreck. Given the choice of of death by hanging or the sword. His reply became proverbial, *dha dhiu gun aon roghainn*, 'two evil alternatives that give no room for choice'.[28] Alasdair, who loathed him, took the matter into his own hand with a blow from his sword decapitated the Campbell chief. Auchinbreck's sister's despairing song echoes down the centuries

> *Nan robh mis' an Inbhir-Lòchaidh,*
> *'S claidheabh dà-fhaobhair am dhòrnaibh,*
> *'S neart agam gu m' mhiann is eòlas,*
> *Dheanainn fuil ann, dheanainn stròiceadh,*
> *Air na Leathanaichh 's Clann-Dòmhnaill;*
> *Bhiodh na h-Eireannaich gun deò annt,*
> *Is na Duibhnich bheirinn beò as.*[29]

> If I had been at Inverlochy
> With a double-edged sword in my hands
> And strength and skill enough to match my desire,
> I would have shed blood there; I would have torn
> The Macleans and Macdonalds.
> The Irish would lie lifeless there
> And I would have brought the Campbells safely away.[30]

The best piece of evidence that Hector Roy was at Inverlochy is his mother's song where she curses

> Red-haired Eachann of the wicked clan,
> I do not care if you come to harm,
> Or if your line is unfruitful.

Curiously, as has been already noticed, she does not mention her husband, which suggests that David Stevenson is correct in identifying Seònaid as her daughter. Certainly Fionnvola says that

> Seònaid who will never prosper
> May I never see your children gathered together.

If it is her daughter she curses then her curse was effective. Although Seònaid married three times she never had any children. Hector Roy was also to die before his father.

It is probable that Maclean of Coll's loss of a substantial part of his patrimony infuriated his clansmen, particularly men like the descendants of Neil Mor, who had to surrender their property in Morvern. As a Campbell Fionnvola was probably also obnoxious to the clan and according to one account her life was threatened. However, some of the Macleans 'more mercifully inclined than the rest had her securely conveyed out of the house to a boat they had in waiting . . . of course she never returned to Coll nor dared the men who rescued her'.[31] This story bears such a similarity to the early sixteenth-century story of the Campbell wife of Lachlan Cattanach Maclean of Duart who was marooned on the Lady's Rock in the Sound of Mull that it is perhaps apocryphal. Another tradition has it that she became deranged after Inverlochy. She was dead by 1648.[32]

Sir Lachlan Maclean had only thirty men with him at Inverlochy. After the battle he returned to Mull and raised a regiment. He joined Montrose with it after the battle of Alford. Men from Coll were certainly with Sir Lachlan during the Civil Wars. They were under the command of Mr Hector Maclean of the Isle of Muck, who particularly distinguished himself at the battle of Kilsyth. Soon after this victory the Macleans returned home and they were not present at Montrose's disastrous defeat at Philiphaugh.

Montrose himself managed to escape and attempted to reassemble an army. He was evidently joined by two of Coll's sons for on 20th January 1646 he wrote from Strathearn

For my very loving friend the Laird of Coall.

Sir, – I must thank you for all your willingness and good affection to his Majesty's service, and particularly the sending along of your sons, to who I will heave ane particular respect, hopeing also that you will still continue ane goode instrument for the advanceing ther of the King's service, for which, and all your former loyal carriages, be confident you shall fynd the effects of his Mās favour, as they can be witnessed you by your very faithfulle freinde,

MONTROSE.

He wrote again from Petty on 17th April 1646

For the Laird off Coall

Sir, – Having occasion to write to your fields, I cannot be forgetful of your willingness and good affection to his Majesty's service. I acknowledge to you, and thank you heartily for it; assuring, that in what lies in my power, you shall find the good. Meanwhile I shall expect that you will continue your loyal endeavours, in wishing those slack people that are about you to appear more obedient than they do, and loyal in their Prince's service, whereby I assure you, you shall find me ever your faithful friend,

MONTROSE.

James Boswell, who in 1773 examined these letters when he visited Coll,[33] believed that John Garbh's enthusiasm for the royal cause had waned and that Montrose's second letter is not as warm as the first. Who the slack people around Coll are is uncertain but they were probably his neighbours rather than his own 'people' who would not be of concern to the King's Commissioner. Having survived one of the worst winters in living memory Montrose can be excused for appearing a little testy.

Montrose's 1646 campaign proved something of a damp squib. The King was negotiating with the Covenanters and Montrose was ordered to retire to the continent. The Macleans withdrew to the islands. The following year they were to feel the full wrath of Argyll's vengeance. He and General Sir David Lesley with their army moved up through the islands from the south seizing and executing Royalists and any Irish who had not fled with Alasdair to Ulster. In Mull Sir Donald Campbell had to be restrained from demanding that the whole Clan Maclean be put to the sword.

It was probably now that Sir Donald 'with a great party of men' invaded Tiree and Coll. The damage done in Coll was considerable. John Garbh's brother-in-law Mr Farquhar Fraser, the Minister of Tiree and Coll, was to complain that the invaders 'dreave away all the goods therein' that is to say all the cattle on the two islands. In particular they took '70 cowes, 300 sheip and fourscore bolls beir and meall, together with the whole goods and plenishing belonging to the petitioner, quherby and for want of his stipend thrie years after the devastation of the saids islands the petitioner was driven to great straitts and very great miserie for a long tyme'.[34]

The shortage of cattle in the two islands was to last for several years and when in July 1649 at Kilmaluag in Tiree, John Garbh married again, his new brother-in-law Sir Lachlan Maclean of Duart could provide the 180 cattle he promised as his sister's tocher only over a three year period. The handover of the cattle was not to begin until 1650.[35]

The theft of cattle was a constant menace, even in the islands. Landowners, such as Sir Donald Campbell, often encouraged it. This evil old man, who must by now have been in his eighties, was something of a bogeyman to the Macleans of Coll. He is said to have instigated a raid on the Isle of Muck by some of his Macian tenants in Ardnamurchan. They landed by night near Mr Hector Maclean of Muck's house at Gallanach and had begun to drive off his cattle when Mr Hector, who was out for a walk with a servant, disturbed them. He immediately attacked the robbers, but his gun misfired and the thieves shot him dead. They were later apprehended by Lord Seaforth and hanged.[36]

Mr Hector of the Isle of Muck's death robbed the family of Coll of an experienced company commander for their next campaign. It is worth studying this campaign, which culminated in the battle of Inverkeithing, in some detail. Not only did several members of the family of Coll take part in it, but their heroism was to inspire future generations. It also illustrates the Macleans' reputation as fighting men.

Notes

1. FD Dow *Cromwellian Scotland* (1979), 223; Crossapol, probably in a misreading of the manuscript he was copying calls him 'Captain William'; All the other Maclean manuscripts call him Witters. NLS MS 28.3.12 says he was governor of Duart Castle. Sir Walter Scott *Military Memoirs of the Great Civil War* (1822), 253 says that in 1654 he was governor of Blair Castle.
2. John Gunn *An Historical Inquiry Respecting the Performance of the Harp in the Highlands of Scotland, from the Earliest Times until it was Discontinued, About the Year 1734.* (1807), 100.
3. Keith Sanger 'From Taynish to West Meath: A Musical Link'. *WHN&Q* Series 3, No. 4 (August 2002), 15–20.
4. FJ Grant and CB Boog Watson *Register of Apprentices of the City of Edinburgh 1583–1755* (Scottish Record Society, 1906), 290 lists George Campbell, son of the late Mr William Campbell in Coll, as apprentice to James Gairden, litster [dyer], 17 July 1633. I am grateful to Dr Frances J Shaw for this reference.
5. No suitable candidate appears in the 'Genealogy of the Cadets of the Family of Auchenbreck'. JRN Macphail *Highland Papers* iv (1934), 68–90.
6. NAS. RS 1/5. 9 February 1620.
7. NAS. Register of Deeds (hereafter RS). DUR.3, 590–2. I am grateful to Grant G Simpson for help in transcribing this deed.
8. *From Chiefs to Landlords*, 107.
9. GB & GB, I, 6 September 1630. (SRS); C Hector Maclean 72 Lochwinnoch Road, Kilmacolm, Renfrewshire, PA 13 4LG believes that he was the ancestor of the Macleans formerly of Plantation in Glasgow, who were for several generations tenants of the chiefs of the Buchanans, whose estate was on the drove road to Dumbarton.
10. For instance he had borrowed £1,000 Scots in 1630 from Mr Adam Boyd, Archdeacon of Argyll. NAS RD.DAL 58, 131–4.
11. It is not certain where the 'Killene', from which he took his designation, is situated. It is probably 'Killean' in Torosay, Mull, which in 1642 was held by John son of Angus Maclean, minister in Morvern as part of the Knock estate, which his father had a Great Seal charter for in 1620. [*RMS* VIII (1620–33), 27] In February 1642 John resigned the superiority of the Knock estate to Hector Maclean of Kinlochaline [*RMS* IX (1634–51), 1068]. A month later Hector Killene obtained a Great Seal charter of Torloisk, which had been resigned by Sir Lachlan Maclean of Duart [*RMS* IX (1634–51), 1080] and it is under the designation 'Torloisk' that Hector Killene is known to history. It would therefore appear likely that Hector Killene had a wadset of Killean in Torosay, which was discharged when Kinlochaline obtained the Knock estate.
12. *RPCS*, 2nd Series I (1625–7), 28.
13. He was unlikely to have inherited anything from his father. [*RPCS* X (1613–16].
14. ICP Bands. L. Coill to the Earle of Argyll 8 October 1636.
15. *CSP Scotland*, (1547–1603) XIII, Part 2, 896.
16. NAS. RD. DAL 2, 676–84.

17. Edward J Cowan 'The Angus Campbells and the Origin of the Campbell-Ogilvie Feud' *Scottish Studies* Vol. 25, (1981), 25.
18. David Stevenson *Scottish Covenanters and Irish Confederates* (1981), 35.
19. George Hill *The Macdonnells of Antrim* (1875), 254.
20. NLS MS 3018, 52; David Stevenson *Irish Historical Studies* Vol. XXI, No. 81 (March 1978), 83.
21. In the Argyll papers there is a note that tells a different version of this story. It states that: 'Sir Lachlan Maclean was released out of the tolbuith of Edinburgh by the Marquis of Argyll in Anno 1633 who became cautioner and paid the debt for him. Sir Lachlan was not a prisoner as is alledged when ane accompt was fitted and new securitie given in Anno 1642 nor did not joyn with the Marques of Montrose but was a captain against him till after that tym that he fell upon that way as the readiest to pay his debt without money' [ICP. Bundle 470, 136].
22. TNA. SP 28. 120. x/LO8704.
23. NAS. Clanranald Papers: GD 201/1/59.
24. AM Sinclair *Clan Gillean* (Charlottetown, 1899), 372; NAS Synod of Argyll Records. I, 81: 7 October 1643.
25. Despite the number of children John Garbh and Fionnvola produced, a symptom that all was not well with their marriage is the fact that none of their three sons was given a Campbell forename.
26. *TGSI* Vol. XXVI (1904–07), 238–9.
27. Edward J Cowan, *Montrose* (1977), 180.
28. *Ibid*, 185.
29. *TGSI* Vol. XXVI (1904–07), 239.
30. I am grateful to Colm Ó Baoill for a translation of this song.
31. NAS. Stonefield Papers GD 14/151, 12–13. I am grateful to Keith Sanger for this reference.
32. *TGSI* Vol. XXVI (1904–07), 239.
33. *Journey to the Hebrides*, 275–6.
34. *RPCS*, 3rd Series Vol. I, (1661–4), 222–3.
35. BCP Coll Charters, 59–60; *A Tour to the Hebrides*, 276.
36. NLS. MS 3018, 26.

Chapter Four

The Battle of Inverkeithing

The execution of King Charles I by the English Parliament on 30 January 1649 horrified Scotland. It completely altered the political situation. Even Covenanters were appalled, and the majority was prepared to accept Charles II as King, provided that he signed the Covenant. This he eventually did, but not until 23 June 1650, when he was about to arrive in Scotland. In August Charles was forced to sign a humiliating declaration denouncing his parents. Cromwell hurried north to deal with his former allies and on the 3rd September he destroyed Leslie's army at Dunbar in East Lothian.

Even after the Scots defeat at Dunbar they still held Scotland north of the Forth. Charles II had thrown in his lot with the moderate Covenanters led by Argyll, and on the 1 January 1651 he received the crown from Argyll's hands at Scone. Ten days earlier the Scots Parliament appointed Sir Lachlan's heir, Sir Hector, colonel of an infantry regiment to be raised in Argyll and Bute.

Not all those who had followed Sir Lachlan were included in the new regiment. Men, such as Murdoch Maclean of Lochbuie, were under sentence of excommunication for having followed Montrose. Lochbuie's forfeiture after the Covenanters' victory, with its corresponding civil penalties and his excommunication, legally would have prevented him serving in the Scots army. Even in its hour of need the Scots government would not employ such men. Fortunately for the Macleans not all their leaders had been excommunicated. By December 1650 others had made public repentance and been absolved.

Cromwell was sick from February to June 1651 and his illness appears to have halted the land offensive. It did not, however, stop the naval campaign and a series of attacks were made on the royalist fortifications on the north side of the Forth. Then in April the royalist garrison at Inchgarvie was attacked by a flotilla of gunboats. Its artillery was silenced.

The main Scots army at Stirling was in a strong position. It covered the fords across the Forth at Torwood and Cromwell decided to outflank the Royalists by a seaborne assault across the lower Forth. Fife was vulnerable: not only had some of its coastal forts been silenced but Charles had unwisely withdrawn several regiments from it to reinforce the main army at Stirling.

The assault on Fife began with a naval bombardment on the North Queensferry forts. It was followed by an attack, under cover of night, on Rosyth Castle. On Wednesday 16 July, supported by a further naval bombardment, the crossing began. By the morning of the 17 July almost 2,000

Cromwellian troops were ashore, and had taken the Ferry Hills position at North Queensferry. The English began to dig in. They were now at their most vulnerable, but the Royalists, perhaps believing the assault on Fife was a feint to force them to abandon their position at Stirling, did not react quickly enough.

Charles and his advisers knew about the landing by the morning of the 17 July, but it was not until the 19th that his men began to arrive at Dunfermline. By then Cromwell had sent Major-General Lambert with a further two regiments of horse and foot to South Queensferry. By dawn on the 20th they were across the Forth.

Lieutenant-General Holburne was chosen to command the royalist forces sent to destroy the Cromwellian bridgehead. It was not a happy choice. Holburne was a protégé of the Marquess of Argyll. He had served in Mull under Leslie in 1647 and was an anathema to the Macleans. The commander of the Scottish horse, Major-General Brown of Fordell, was a friend of Holburne, and had served in the covenanting army. Among the infantry were Holburne's Foot, consisting of 646 men many of whom were raw recruits; also present were local levies and Buchanan's Foot. The latter's colonel, George Buchanan of Buchanan, was a Covenanter of long standing. Sir Hector's was thus the only regiment which marched into Fife that had fought on the royalist side in the Civil War. There was probably little love lost between it and the rest of Holburne's brigade.

Many of those in Maclean's Regiment were probably men who were too young to have served under Montrose. They will have been keen to prove themselves to their elder brothers. Their leader Sir Hector was also untried in battle, but he had already proved himself decisive in his dealings with cattle raiders. There were also plenty of veterans in Sir Hector's regiment. His lieutenant-colonel was Donald Maclean of Brolas, who had fought at Kilsyth. The major was Allan Macquarrie of Ulva, who had served under Alasdair MacColla. Also among the veterans was Ewen of Treshnish.

Another company commander, who had probably seen plenty of action, was Captain Lachlan Maclean of Hynish in Tiree. As captains were normally lairds he probably held a wadset on Hynish. In addition he almost certainly had previous military experience under Montrose. Perhaps like Ewen of Treshnish he had served in a foreign army. As no other member of the family of Coll is mentioned as being a captain, Lachlan Hynish[1] had probably succeeded the murdered Mr Hector Maclean of the Isle of Muck as the commander of Coll's company in the Maclean Regiment.

Coll's sons John of Totronald and his younger brother Hugh were also present. They had taken part in Montrose's penultimate campaign. Also with them was their young paternal uncle Neil of Drimnacross. These three were perhaps officers in the Coll company, but they could equally have carried a pike and fought as volunteers. This was the usual way at the time to obtain promotion to a commissioned rank.

We know more about the Macleans as a military unit in action from the battle of Inverkeithing than at any other time in its history. For once the whole wider clan was serving together as an officially raised regiment of foot, rather than as rebels.

The Regiment was probably conventionally armed with a combination of pikes and muskets. In addition each man would have had a sword and target. It is also likely to have been organised on normal military lines i.e. each company was led by a captain, who was a chief or local landowner, or one of his younger brothers; a lieutenant who had professional military experience and an ensign who carried the company's colours. A clan regiment, however, differed from normal units in that it was a family affair. Fathers and sons marched together: for instance Coll's cousin Captain Lachlan MacAllan Vic Niel Mor had two of his sons with him; whilst there were five brothers, the sons of Lachlan Odhar of Ardchraoishnish, in the company recruited in the Ross of Mull. It was a regiment whose morale was probably high, that marched into Fife.

* * *

Lambert's men had used their time well. They had survived the most critical time in any amphibious operation and they were now feverishly improving their trenches. They had carefully sited their artillery, some pieces of which had been abandoned by the Scots at the Ferry Hills. By dawn on the 20 July they were ready.

Holburne's brigade appears to have moved into their battle formation straight off the line of march. On the left was the Scottish horse. Next to them was Holburne's own regiment and local men from Fife. On the right was a battle group consisting of Buchanan's foot with more cavalry on the extreme right.

Although the horse on the right wing charged with gallantry and were sufficiently well trained to regroup, those on the left, under the personal command of Brown, were too raw to do so. After some initial success they scattered, leaving Brown, who fell wounded from his horse to be captured. On the right the Buchanans' charge was badly mauled by Lambert's artillery. Even so the fighting must have been intense as the first phase of the battle is said to have lasted for six hours. Then at the crucial moment, Lambert noticed more men in the distance marching to reinforce the Royalists. He ordered the advance. It was an unequal struggle. The Lowland left broke first. They fled accompanied by Holburne himself. The right wing was now isolated.

It appears that the Macleans arrived late, after the battle had begun, which considering the distance they had to travel is not surprising. They had certainly missed the muster at Stirling, and were perhaps the five hundred reinforcements observed by Lambert, whose imminent arrival caused him to attack. It has also been suggested that the Macleans finished their march from Stirling as the first fugitives fled from the field. This would explain the site of the Maclean's stand, which is some distance from the first part of the battle.

Whatever the truth of this scenario, it is clear that it was near Pitreavie Castle that the Macleans made their stand and achieved immortality. Surrounded by Cromwellians they stood their ground, and were slaughtered.

Archaeological evidence and the report that the English suffered minimal casualties suggest that Lambert had quickly moved his artillery forward and opened fire on the Royalists as they fell back. The evidence of both Maclean's bard Eachann Bacach and the Macdonald bard Iain Lom[2] suggest that Cromwell's cavalry played a crucial part in the destruction of the Macleans. Lambert's infantry gave the final coup de grace. As each wave broke on the exhausted Macleans, eight clansman, one after another launched themselves forward to shield Sir Hector from the English pikes and with the cry of *Fear eil airson Eachainn* 'Another for Hector', threw themselves in front of the Duart chief, averting for a while the fate of Sir Hector. One of them was John Garbh's youngest son Hugh.

JP MacLean has a story concerning the Macleans of Coll at Inverkeithing, which is not found in manuscript histories of the Macleans. He says, when he writes of John of Totronald :

> John was severely wounded in the head and body and taken prisoner. Soon after he was imprisoned an English officer came to see the prisoners, and coming to where John was, observed the latter fainting. The officer rendered all the assistance he could, and when he revived him asked him what had been the cause. John replied: 'The shoulder-belt you have on is the cause; for I am certain the owner of it never would have parted with it were he alive'.

The officer answered: 'That is true; for a braver youth was not that day on the field than he to whom this belt belonged'. John replied: 'That was my brother'. The officer seeing Hugh's name was indented in silver and rich ornaments on the belt, he insisted on John's keeping it in memory of his brave brother.[3]

I have no idea of the origin of this story.

News of the result of the battle evidently reached Sir Hector's bard before he learnt of the full casualty list. At first it was thought that the English had captured Sir Hector. Soon, however, the full extent of the disaster reached Eachann Bacach, and he cries out:

> Many a white-handed champion fell into rank around your banner
> and many a handsome youth was mangled under horses' hooves,
> while many a stalwart householder,
> who never brought shame upon his person,
> was drawing his sword, keen as a razor, from the scabbard.[4]

Only forty of Sir Hector's companions returned to the Hebrides. Those wounded, such as Donald of Brolas and John Diùrach, who led the 'forlorn hope', were seriously injured. Others, such as Coll's son John Maclean of Totronald, as we have seen, were also captured. Whole families were wiped out, including that of Captain Lachlan MacAllan Vic Neil Mor and his elder sons, as well as the Ardchraoshnish brothers. The latter were Eachann Bacach's neighbours in the Ross of Mull. He and fourteen of his brothers were at the battle. Eachann was the only one to survive, and he was lame thereafter.

Eachann Bacach appears to have escaped before the final stand where Sir Hector was killed and, when it was believed that the chief had been captured, he declared:

> Although, I left my brothers being slaughtered on the battlefield,
> That is not what I reckon important, but that the noble son of Sir Lachlan
> Is in the hands of English-speakers, and that you have failed to escape them.

Lambert's report on the battle states: 'the reason why the slain exceeded the number of prisoners was because divers were Highlanders and had very ill quarter'. In other words the Cromwellians considered the Macleans little better than vermin. It was an attitude not limited to the English, but was echoed in Lowland Scotland, and underlies much of what is to follow. It also raises doubts over the veracity of JP MacLean's story about John of Totronald.

Inverkeithing was as much a catastrophe for the Macleans as Inverlochy had been for the Campbells. The difference was that the Macleans had stood their ground, whilst the Campbells had turned and run. Perhaps it says something about the extraordinary influence of a chief over his clan. At Inverlochy Argyll had watched the slaughter of his men from his galley and then slipped away to sea. At Inverkeithing the Macleans refused to give in and died around their chief. Perhaps it illustrates a berserk quality in the Macleans that they had inherited with their Gall-Gaidel-Viking genes.

More than 750 Macleans were killed at Inverkeithing. It was a disaster for the Southern Inner Hebrides, but it had earned them immortality. Their sacrifice entitled them to the sympathy of the cavalier party in Scotland, and to the embarrassed gratitude of the royal family.

After their victory at Inverkeithing, Cromwell's troops pushed north to capture Perth. The royal army was outflanked and the Scots generals abandoned Scotland. They made a desperate gamble and invaded England. Cromwell followed. He caught them up at Worcester. The Royalists were soundly beaten and the Macleods butchered as effectively as the Macleans at Inverkeithing. Charles II escaped to the continent. Scotland became an occupied country.

* * *

Two years after Inverkeithing, the Earl of Glencairn left his home at Finlayson on the Clyde, and set off for Loch Awe. The Earl of Atholl, Glengarry, Lochiel and others joined him. The last major phase of the Civil War had begun.

Glencairn's Rising, as it is known to history, was to be a very different campaign to earlier uprisings on behalf of the King. It was also a very different royalist army to that which faced Cromwell at Dunbar in 1650 and in 1651 at Stirling. Geographically and socially it was to be a rising based on the Highlands. Its leaders were nobles and gentlemen, who had an interest in that region and it was their followers and tenants, who made up the army that now opposed Cromwell's major-generals.

The revolt was not only an uprising against a foreign invader, but a re-assertion by the traditional leadership of Scotland of their right to lead the nation. Some might have been moderate Covenanters in the early 1640s, but they had remained loyal to Charles I, and had joined Charles II because of that loyalty, not as the result of the vagaries of Scottish internal politics. The Highland nobility, whether they were clan chiefs, feudal nobles or both, with the exception of the Marquess of Argyll, had never fully assimilated the presbyterian doctrine of church-state relations. They were less concerned than their Lowland counterparts with ensuring that Charles II was a fully covenanted king. They were more interested in seeing that the monarch regained his ancient rights.

Royalist tactics during the summer of 1653 were to avoid direct confrontation with the English: to raid English sympathisers and raise men, money and other supplies from the countryside. Seldom did bodies of Royalists exceed more than a hundred men, and even when several leaders joined forces their combined strength was relatively small. For example in August when Lorne,[5] Glengarry, Glencairn and Donald of Brolas[6] were together they had no more than 1,300 men with them.

Cromwell did not only have a Highland rebellion to deal with, he was at war with the Dutch and feared that they might send supplies to the Royalists via the Hebrides. As a result the Council of State was constantly advising their Commander-in-Chief in Scotland to keep a close watch on the northern approaches, which is why he gave a priority to occupying Lewis and Mull.

In August 1653 Colonel Robert Cobbett sailed for Lewis.[7] Meeting with little resistance he planted a garrison in Stornoway Castle, and on 27 August made for Mull. According to Colonel Robert Lilburne, Cromwell's army commander in Scotland, he did so on the advice of Argyll.[8]

Cobbett's troops reached Mull on 3 September. Eight companies were landed, and 'finding noe opposition, but seeing the people running away,' marched to the castle which they had just left. Cobbett was evidently surprised that the Macleans had abandoned Duart without a fight, as he describes it as 'tenable enough both against great guns and mortar peeces for some time'.

Shortly before Cobbett's invasion, Brolas had returned to Mull to recruit. Glencairn accompanied him. They then went on to Tiree. Not all Macleans supported the Royalists. Some led by Torloisk, as the former Hector of Killene was now, still followed Argyll. 'Yet were both in armes against us', reported Cobbett.

Cobbett was now joined by the Marquess of Argyll himself, who persuaded both Maclean factions to live peaceably, obey parliament and pay the cess, the land tax, to the authorities. They further agreed 'nott to act nor suffer MacCleane the tutor to act anything prejudiciall to affares of the Commonwealth, nor the garrison settled in Dowart, nor to pay any rent to the said McCleane, who still perseveres in rebellion.'

Argyll was to give further assistance to Cobbett, after three of his ships from Ayr, which brought supplies to the Cromwellians, were destroyed off Duart in the equinoctial gales. The survivors made their way overland to Dumbarton.

* * *

It was against this background that George Campbell of Kinnochtrie, the former Sheriff-Clerk of Argyll, who had been buying up Coll's debts for at least ten years, moved in for the kill in his attempt to take over Maclean of Coll's property.[9] Coll's losses were recognised by the Royalists and in 1653 Charles II's secretary had written to John Garbh

> Expressing his Majesties thanks for his affectione to his Majesties service signified be the Earle of Glencairne and assureing him that his Majestie would reward his service and repaire his Losses.[10]

Such sentiments may have warmed Coll's heart but they did not help the immediate situation, and on 3 October 1655 George Campbell obtained a sentence of apprising 'whereby all and haill the barony of Coill and other lands were apprised' from John Maclean of Coll to George Campbell[11] for the sums of £5,124.10s.5d and £256.4s.5d.

A charter of Oliver Lord Protector to Campbell was issued and seizin followed. Officially the family of Coll had lost their inheritance. It was, however, another thing for George Campbell to occupy Coll and the Macleans stayed where they were.

It was probably about this time that Captain Witters visited Coll and, as we have seen, described John Garbh as being like King David. Witters was searching for Coll's son-in-law Brolas, the latter was still in arms against Cromwell and had eluded his pursuers.[12] Witters in a postscript to a letter to General Monck dated 23 May 1657 says that he had 'employed a gentleman, who is nearly related to Donald Maclean [i.e. Brolas] for to bring[13] him in'. It is likely that the 'gentleman' was Torloisk, who in 1648 had successfully held the Macleans' virtually impregnable fortress Carnaburg Castle in the Treshnish Isles for Argyll against Sir Lachlan.[14]

Hector Torloisk was to get his come-uppance in 1660 when the whole island of Great Britain, exhausted by eleven years of republicanism, welcomed back King Charles II. Retribution followed and Torloisk was fined the immense sum of £4,000.[15] His patron the Marquess of Argyll was executed.

* * *

In the heady atmosphere of the Restoration the Macleans of Coll may well have believed that their problems were over. On 11 September 1662 John Maclean of Coll began an action in the Court of Session in Edinburgh against George Campbell and his sons for the return of the charters of the Coll estate, which he had had to surrender and which gave him title to his property. Campbell was no longer Sheriff of Argyll and, as a follower of the late Marquess of Argyll, might have been expected to be vulnerable in an action by a leading royalist. However, although it was heard before Sir Archibald Primrose, who was a fervent royalist, the case appears to have gone against Coll.[16]

Despite King Charles II's promises that he would reimburse the family of Coll for their losses in the Civil Wars nothing appears to have been forthcoming. Crossapol writing of John Maclean of Totronald says that:

> After the revolution he went to London and was introduced to the King by Alexander Roy Laird of MacNaughton [the King] was pleased to intimate that he knew his suffering yet forgot to make him any thing the better, as was too much his custom.

This was not the only setback the family of Coll suffered at this time. Hector Roy, John Garbh's eldest son and heir was dead by 14 October 1661 when the Commissary of the Isles held court at Breacachadh. The Commissary's aim was to assess the 'guids & geir' of those who had recently died in Coll and to appoint executors and cautioners to see that the deceased's movable property passed to the rightful heirs and others who had an interest in his estate.

Although John Garbh was alive he was not appointed one of his grand childrens' executors. Instead this task fell to his much younger brother Neil Maclean of Drimnacross and to John Garbh's own younger son John of Totronald. These two men seem to have had the management of the Clan at this time. John Maclean of Grishipol and his eldest son Lachlan were the cautioners. The former presumably had recovered his standing in the Clan from his position nine years earlier when he is stated to have been among those 'to be sustened upon the publict charge of the presbytery for many reasons suspect and known to us'.[17]

John Garbh was to live until 1673 and by then the prosperity of the family had declined still further. During this time six deeds are recorded in the books of Council and Session, which brought the family into more debt. One of these deeds concerned the marriage settlement of Margaret, Lachlan Maclean younger of Coll's eldest sister, when she married Allan Stewart, brother german to Duncan Stewart younger of Appin. The Stewart brothers agreed to give her 3,200 merks worth of land in liferent, whilst Lachlan, with Sir Allan Maclean of Duart as his cautioner, undertook to provide 100 cows as Margaret's tocher.[18] It was less than half the number of cattle that John Garbh produced for his own eldest daughter in 1640. It says something about Coll's reduced circumstances.

Another indicator of Coll's loss of prestige is that instead of signing his name before all other Macleans, except Duart, in official documents he now appears considerably lower down the list. It is the same story over taxation. In the seventeenth century freeholders had to pay the expenses of their commissioners to parliament. In 1663 the Shire of Argyll was assessed with four pounds for every merk rent they received. Sir Allan Maclean of Duart had to contribute £720, the highest amount in the county. Lochbuie was assessed at £180, Torloisk £60. Coll had only to provide £48.[19]

Lachlan of Coll's own marriage contract with Marion daughter of John Macdonald of Moidart, Captain of Clanranald, cost Coll land in the islands of Coll and Mull[20], whilst Clanranald provided a tocher of 7,500 merks. Marion was a Roman Catholic and appears to have brought a priest with her to Coll which, as we shall see, was to have a profound effect on the family of Coll. She also brought with her a cousin, also named Marion.[21] She was to marry Neil Og of Crossapol, one of Captain Lachlan mac Allan's surviving sons, who was probably too young to have fought at Inverkeithing.[22]

Not all Coll's new debts were the result of marriage settlements. Others were short-term loans. For instance on 21 May at Duart, Lachlan the younger of Coll borrowed £450 Scots from James

Menzies of Culdares, £200 of which had to be repaid by the following July. Coll's leading clansmen[23] acted as cautioners to see that the debt was repaid. This meant that if it were not they were equally liable to be prosecuted. This is exactly what happened and, when Coll did not pay on time, they were all put to the horn.[24]

Coll's debts were to blight the family for more than a generation. According to tradition they could have been reduced if John Garbh were not a teetotaller, a very unusual condition in the Hebrides. Crossapol says that

> He was very temperate as appears from his refusing to visit a friend of his in the Isle of Sky who promised to give him up the evidence of a considerable Debt he had against his familie if he would come but for one night to his house to Make Merry with him, Coll's friends urged him to go but he told them he would not be Drunk once for any consideration which he saw he could not miss to be or disoblige his friend if he went. This piety and temperance he showed through the whole course of his life.

The friend is almost certainly Sir Normand Macleod of Bernerah, who was not only Coll's close cousin but had also been partly brought up by John Garbh's father. After John's death Bernerah enabled Coll's successor to get back his title deeds to the lands and barony of Coll.

George Campbell of Kinnochtrie, the former Sheriff Clerk of Argyll, died at about the same time as John Garbh. However, before he did so, he gave a precept of sasine of the barony of Coll to Sir Normand Macleod.[25] George must have died soon after this event for in Edinburgh on 26 May 1675 it was found that George Campbell had died seized of the lands and barony of Coll and that Colin Campbell was his lawful son and heir. The latter was therefore given seizin.[26] Two months later Colin surrendered the barony of Coll back into the hands of the King's Commissioners who in turn handed them over to Sir Normand Macleod. What money changed hands, other than that Macleod is noted as 'paying the services due and accustomed', is never mentioned.[27]

Notes

1. Crossapol describes his ancestor Lachlan MacAllan VicNeil or both as having Hynish and being a captain.
2. Annie M Mackenzie (ed) *Orain Iain Luim: Songs of John Macdonald Bard of Keppoch* (1964) 40–43.
3. JP MacLean *A History of the Clan MacLean* (Cincinnati, 1889), 296–7.
4. *Eachann Bacach*, 434–442.
5. He was the son and heir of the Marquess of Argyll who had quarelled with his father and taken the opposite side to him in the Civil War.
6. He was now tutor to Sir Allan Maclean of Duart, who was under age. Brolas was the eldest son of Hector Og of Duart's second marriage. He was married to John Garbh of Coll's daughter Florence by whom he had at least two sons Lachlan and Hector Og. He had also had at least one illegitimate child [Nicholas Maclean-Bristol 'A Genealogical Puzzle Solved' *WHN&Q*, 1st Series Vol. XXX (February 1987), 13–17].
7. Walter Scott (ed) *Military Memoirs of the Great Civil War* (1822), 198–9.
8. FD Dow. *Cromwellian Scotland 1651–1660*, (1979), 90–1.
9. NAS Clanranald Papers. GD 201/1/59
10. NAS. GD 174/43.
11. NAS Clanranald Papers. GD 201/1/59.
12. T Birch *Thurloe Sate Papers*, VI(London, 1742), 306; *HMC Leyborne-Popham*, 121. I am indebted to Paul Hopkins for these two references.

13. *HMC Leyborne-Popham*, 121.
14. *Clan Gillean*, 458.
15. APS VII (1661–69), 429.
16. NAS CS 226/5573/1-3 does not give the result of the case. However, as George Campbell's heir was able to transfer the Coll estate to Sir Normand Macleod of Bernerah in 1675 it would appear that Primrose decided in favour of George Campbell.
17. NAS. CH2. 984. 30.
18. NAS. RD. DAL 43, 104.
19. *Northern Notes and Queries, or the Scottish Antiquary*, 23. I have to thank Keith Sanger for this reference.
20. NAS RD MACK 13, 576 dated at Ormcleitt in South Uist 29 June 1665: '16 shilling lands of penniemolloch more, the pennie land of penniemoloch Beg, the pennie land of Cuin, and the half pennie land of Killimoir' in Quinish in Mull. 'the 20 shilling land of Treiland [Triallain], the 15 shilling land of Grimsary and the 20 shilling land of Uige' in Coll.
21. She was the daughter of John of Moydart's sister by 'Alister Mac Ruary Ruarich a son of Clan Glengary' [Crossapol, 40].
22. It was probably as a result of this marriage that Neil Og obtained the farm of Crossapol.
23. NAS. RD. MACK 22, 742. They were Neil Maclean of Drimnacross, Lachlan Maclean in Torestan, Hector Maclean of the Isle of Muck and Hector Maclean of Auchnasaul.
24. ICP Bundle 477. 267. 3 May 1670.
25. NAS. Clanranald Papers. GD 201/1/108, 15 July 1672.
26. BCP. Coll Charters, No. 42.
27. BCP. Coll Charters, No. 41.

Part II

Campbell versus Maclean

Chapter Five

The first attack on Mull

Although he had probably had command of the Clan for sometime, Lachlan is first mentioned as 'Maclean of Coll' in 1673, as opposed to 'younger of Coll'. It was then, with Sir Normand Macleod as his cautioner, that he made a bond in favour of his aunt Kathrine, the daughter of his grandfather's second marriage. In it he agrees to give her 120 cows when she marries.[1]

It was not an auspicious time to take command of the Clan. The struggle between the Earl of Argyll and Maclean of Duart for the control of Mull, which was to overshadow everything that took place in the central Inner Hebrides for almost a century, was about to begin. It is necessary to examine the course of the first phase of the fighting between Campbells and Macleans from 1674 to 1680 in some detail, as it illustrates how both clans were involved in warfare at a time when, if Macinnes were to be believed, commercial rather than military motives were to the fore in the Highlands and Islands.

To understand the origin of these events, it is necessary to look back to the first days of the Restoration. When he was executed in 1661 the Marquesss of Argyll's estate and title were forfeited. However, despite the efforts of the Cavalier Party to secure the final ruin of the House of Campbell, the King was inclined to restore Archibald Campbell, Lord Lorne, to his father's earldom. Lorne had fought for Charles II at the battle of Dunbar, and against Cromwell's generals during the Earl of Glencairn's Rising. In October 1663 he regained most of his father's titles and estates. He also inherited his father's debts. These were massive and the Earl had little choice other than try to obtain the money he himself was owed. Foremost amongst his debtors was Sir Allan Maclean of Duart, whose estate had been adjudged to the Marquess of Argyll.[2]

Sir Allan had succeeded his brother Hector, when the latter was killed at Inverkeithing. In 1661 he reached the age of fourteen and was thus entitled to choose his own curators. He now claimed that during his minority, for want of official curators, 'his estate and fortune had been mismanaged', and neither his tenants nor his debtors would 'pay to him their rents until such times as he be lawfullie authorized with curators fra whom they may receive sufficient discharges'.[3]

Sir Allan was prickly both concerning his own honour and the respect, he believed, was due to him. For example he quarrelled with his cousin Lachlan Maclean of Lochbuie and in 1669 wrote him an extraordinary letter. Lochbuie had apparently insulted him at 'an entertainment' whilst Lochbuie's son had not 'the witt to take leave of me'. As a result he wrote: 'I am going about your destruction. And will perform it tho it cost me halfe of my estate … it will be delayed no longer than till the morrow at night or Sunday morning and the proves you shall sie or Lambess day'.[4]

The new Earl of Argyll was no less sensitive to slights, particularly regarding his legal jurisdictions, and it was only a matter of time until the two men clashed. In February 1665 Argyll wrote to his patron Lauderdale that he had received a letter from Sir Allan:

> shewing me that he had taken a fellow [who] had committed a pitiful murder, and I have sent to put him into Dunstafnage, till I goe to the country, for I resolve not to suffer any Deput to take any lives in my absence ...[5]

Sir Allan was determined that thieves should keep clear of his people. He was less enthusiastic in prosecuting his own tenants when they were accused of theft. On 14 December 1665 Stirling of Keir complained to the Privy Council that 'in August 1664 Duncan McIlenrish 'with his complices, all broken men armed in a hostile manner', came to his lands of Aney and Tunbee in the parish of Callendar ... and drove away twenty-two head of 'goods ky, horses and meires' to the 'far hielands and isles, where it was impossible to recover them'.

Keir asked Sir Allan to get them back, as Duncan lived 'in the Tounbeith in Glengell in the Isle of Morverne'. Sir Allan failed to do so, and both he and Keir were summoned to appear before the Privy Council. Sir Allan claimed that he had made enquiries of his vassals in Tounbech and that they denied that Duncan lived there. Sir Allan was, however, held responsible for Duncan and ordered to pay 2,000 merks compensation to Keir, plus 500 merks expenses.[6]

Sir Allan's people suffered as much as Coll's tenants had by raids from Ardnamurchan, and on 14 October 1671 the former led a massive reprisal against them. Alexander Campbell of Lochnell, who now held Ardnamurchan from Argyll, complained that Sir Allan

> accompanied with all his friends and tennents to the number of 450 men came in a hostile manner and invadut Ardnamurchane having landeit with threttein birlings and boats at Kilchoan for the space of four dayes and four nights during which tyme they not onlie killed with guns and dogs an nowmber of ky, sheep and goats, but also plundreit reft and away took from the tennents of the saide lands meall, butter, cheyse, cornes, burnt and destroyed their peatts and elding to the value of six hundred pounds ...[7]

Lochnell lists the gentlemen who accompanied Sir Allan to Ardnamurchan. It comprises of most of his leading followers and tenants. It also includes some followers of Maclean of Coll such as Neil Maclean of Drimnacross, Hector Maclean of Auchnasaul, Hector Maclean of the Isle of Muck, and Mr Farquhar Fraser's two sons Hector and Mr John.[8]

The Macleans of Duart were not, as has already been stressed, the feudal landlords of all the Macleans: the Macleans of Lochbuie, Coll, Kingerloch, and at times Ardgour and Torloisk, all held their heritable property directly from the Crown. However, the sheer size of the Duart estate, and its chief's policy of setting vast areas of land in tack to his independent kinsmen, gave Duart great influence over them.

Duart was also prepared to appoint Macleans, who were not descended from his own family, to important positions in running the estate. In 1674 Hugh and Lachlan Maclean were joint bailies of Tiree. The former was a member of the Boreray family in North Uist.[9] The latter was the eldest son of John Maclean of Grishipol in Coll. In exchange for his services Lachlan received the 6 merk lands of Ruaig and Vuill in Tiree rent free, but he had to pay £40 for the mill at Hulliboill from which he probably obtained a tidy profit.[10]

The first attack on Mull

Lachlan Grishipol had followed his maternal grandfather Mr Roderick Maclean the Glasgow merchant into trade. In 1669 he was admitted as a burgess of Dumbarton.[11] In the seventeenth century the royal burgh of Dumbarton was a small town situated half a mile from the point where the Leven, a broad un-bridged, fast-flowing river, which is the main outlet for water from Loch Lomond, joins the Clyde. The Clyde itself was then so shallow that ships with cargoes for Glasgow merchants were not able to proceed beyond Dumbarton, a source of considerable irritation and cost to the burgesses of the more enterprising burgh.[12] Dumbarton had a long history of rivalry with Glasgow and the probable reason why Lachlan chose to settle there was that, although other ports on the Clyde traded by sea with the Western Isles, Dumbarton was at the time the only one to have a major cattle market.[13] Lachlan is likely to have looked after the marketing of Coll's cattle, whilst his youngest brother Charles was a drover, who was responsible for bringing them from the islands.[14] In appointing Lachlan as joint-baillie of Tiree Duart's curators may have wanted to obtain his expertise to dispose of their cattle too.

Sir Allan and his curators were also prepared to give large tacks of land to Macleans who were not his clansmen. For instance in 1679 Neil of Drimnacross and John of Totronald were Duart's tacksmen for the Two Ends of Coll. They may well have been in 1671 and that is why Neil of Drimnacross followed Sir Allan on the raid on Ardnamurchan. However, the absence of Coll cadets whose land was solely in the Isle of Coll itself, and the presence of the other Collachs, whose land was vulnerable to raids from Ardnamurchan, suggests that those who followed Duart on this raid did so in order to obtain retribution for the losses they themselves had suffered in the past.

Even before the raid Duart had evidently expected repercussions from Argyll, and on the 8 March 1671 at Fuinary in Morvern Sir Allan drew up a bond. In it Duart promised that if Ardgour defied Argyll on his behalf, and as a result lost his land, Sir Allan would provide him with a merk land for every one he had lost.[15]

He was wise to do so for on 17 February 1672 the Earl of Argyll began an action in the courts in Edinburgh against Sir Allan.[16] However, the law moved slowly and it was not until 25 July 1674, by which time Sir Allan was dead, that the Earl obtained Letters of Ejection against the tenants on the Duart estate.[17]

Argyll evidently did not expect to obtain access without a struggle, for two days later he wrote from Edinburgh to his cousin John Campbell of Glenorchy to say that he had heard that Lachlan Maclean of Brolas, the twenty five year-old tutor to Sir Allan's infant son and heir, intended to refuse to surrender Duart Castle or to hand over the militia's arms stored there.[18]

Brolas's decision to defy Argyll was the beginning of fighting in and around Mull that was to last for six years.

* * *

It is inevitable that we see the campaign through the eyes of Archibald, 9th Earl of Argyll. It is his letters and those of his friends, which have survived. Rebels tend not leave incriminating evidence that could hang them.

Argyll was in many ways a strange man, and a mass of contradictions. He was physically brave. He was also self-righteous and curiously blinkered, unable to appreciate that the spectacle of a traitor's son evading his own gigantic debts, whilst exploiting the machinery of the state to destroy his own debtors, infuriated other men.

The Earl was a devoted husband and a loving father, but he was also aloof and arrogant with his leading clansmen, yet he expected them to sacrifice their interest to his own affairs. His contemporaries blamed much of his behaviour on the fact that he had been 'trepanned'. This had occurred in 1658 after an accident when he was struck by a stone at 'bullets', a game similar to bowls, which he was playing whilst he was a prisoner in Edinburgh Castle.[19] Trepanning involved making a circular opening in the skull with a surgeon's cylindrical saw. Considering the state of surgery in the seventeenth century, it is surprising that he was only subject to 'a trace of instability in manner' and needed to sleep for an hour or more during the day whatever else was happening.

Argyll's most important follower was his brother-in-law John Campbell, younger of Glenorchy.[20] John Campbell, and his descendants will appear again and again in this story. John Campbell was an able, ruthless man. He had married Argyll's sister, the widow of George Sinclair 6th Earl of Caithness, and was closely related, through his father's many siblings, to several Highland chiefs including Lochiel and Lochbuie. He was also, through his paternal grandmother related to the Duke of Hamilton and was part of the family network of the great Lowland magnates. Like them he was highly conscious of his position, precedence, and the need to emphasise his status and his family's history. His father had commissioned elaborate family trees and even had his coat of arms embroidered on his bed curtains.[21] Unlike his Lowland cousins, he still had armed men to impress his contemporaries. As late as 1715 it was believed that he was able to bring 2,000 men to the field within forty-eight hours.[22]

Glenorchy was plagued with debts. He was to complicate matters further for readers of this chapter by becoming Earl of Caithness, as he was the chief creditor of the former earl. The King later decided that this grant of the Caithness title was a mistake and in 1681 Glenorchy was created Earl of Breadalbane, whilst the earldom of Caithness reverted to the Sinclair family.

Glenorchy was not in awe of his chief. He was quite prepared to give him unpopular advice. As a result his relationship with Argyll deteriorated as the fighting with the Macleans progressed. The 'loving cousin' of 1675 is addressed in 1677 by Argyll curtly as 'my lord'.

Argyll's strained relations with his leading supporters, his prickly pride and his vast debts were to affect all his actions. The political manoeuvrings, and squalid squabbles for the King's ear at court, were to have a constant influence on the Earl's affairs. Argyll's patron at court was the able and avaricious John Maitland, second Earl and later first Duke of Lauderdale, the 'L' in King Charles II's CABAL. Lauderdale was the King's Secretary of State. He had the King's ear from the time of the downfall of the Earl of Middleton and the ultra-loyalist cavaliers in 1663. He was to rule Scotland until 1674, when the failure of his policies resulted in the Bothwell Bridge rebellion. Even then, he did not lose his commissioner-ship until 1681.

In 1663 Argyll had warned Lauderdale of the threat from Middleton. Thereafter the Duke protected the Earl. As Argyll was to write to his brother-in-law, the Earl of Moray, another supporter of Lauderdale, in October 1675: 'I am faithful to D[uke] L[auderdale] and what is more I know he trusts me'.[23]

* * *

Argyll's first task, when he received his letters of ejection against the tenants of Maclean of Duart, was to obtain permission from the Council to use royal troops to collect the outstanding public dues in Mull and Ensign Middleton of the Third Foot Guards was sent to demand them. The use of 'red coats', as soldiers who were part of the standing army were nicknamed, underlines the Earl's influence with Lauderdale. Scotland's standing army was tiny. In 1678, when it reached its maximum strength since the Restoration, it only numbered 2,754 men.[24]

The first attack on Mull

The Scots army was designed primarily for use on ceremonial occasions, to garrison the castles of Edinburgh, Stirling and Dumbarton and to keep the peace. Its numbers were quite inadequate for its task, as it was also the only organised body of men the government had at its disposal to undertake tasks, such as those carried out by the modern fire service and to deal with major outbreaks of civil disobedience.

The authorities also had control of the militia. This force consisted of 20,000 foot and 2,000 horse. It was liable to be called out armed and with provisions for forty days service in any one year. The militia plays an important part in this story. From early times every male member of the Scottish community aged from 16 to 60 was liable for military service whenever he was required for the defence of the realm. Until the reign of Charles II the militia had never been effectively organized.[25] It was now essential that it were put on a more regular basis: the threat of foreign invasion, and the circumstances under which Charles had regained his throne made such a force a necessity.

Argyll was to use both the militia and a detachment of the standing army against the Macleans. He also had other military assets. They included two independent companies of Highlanders who had first been raised in 1667 to secure the peace in the Highlands, particularly from cattle thieves. Independent companies of Highlanders were light infantry. They excelled in scouting and were not equipped with the unwieldy sixteen-foot pike that had for some two hundred years been the major weapon of conventional infantry formations, and was still in use. In addition each company was provided with two drums and a set of colours.

These were the forces that were to be launched against the Macleans, when the Council in Edinburgh issued a Commission of Fire and Sword against them.[26] Those written to included the Maclean lairds of Lochbuie, Kinlochaline, Torloisk and Ardgour. Despite the fact that the latter's sons and nephews were with Brolas. A Commission of Fire and Sword was a well-tried method of dealing with Hebridean rebels. It threatened them with disaster if it was launched. At the same time, however, the Council issued an offer of indemnity to the Maclean rebels if they surrendered Duart Castle.

The Macleans, however, refused to surrender Duart and on Monday 14 September the Earl, who was busy preparing to invade Mull, organised a general rendezvous at Oban. He wrote in his diary that he had continued to drill his own men and issue oatmeal and ammunition. However, the day was so foul that the men could not stand to their arms. That night Clanranald came in a twelve-oared birlinn to dine with the Earl and Sir James Macdonald of Sleat, who had already joined him.

On the Tuesday it took from morning to nightfall to divide the boats amongst the different parties and give out orders. Argyll then had to decide whether to leave two companies of foot behind or to abandon his horses. He left the horses.

At last on Wednesday 16 September the armada set sail. Lord Neil Campbell and Campbell of Cawdor took the long route and sailed north up the Sound of Mull for Iona. Argyll and the rest of the invasion force were to meet them there. They travelled by the southern route. The Earl was to write: 'in my passage the wind changed and a part of my companies holding too far to the weather we could only reach Lochbuie'. They were six miles short of their destination and he was only to get there with some difficulty at eight o'clock at night; some of his companies spent the night at sea and did not join the Earl until the next morning. The wind was now so strong that the Earl's party could neither move forward to Iona nor back to Duart. He therefore decided to wait all day to hear how his brother's party had succeeded.

Lord Neil had also been affected by the cross winds and landed on the east coast of Mull and in Morvern, where he drove off the Macleans' cattle. One party captured the infant Sir John Maclean, who was being fostered by Charles Maclean, (formerly at Fuinary in Morvern) who now lived at Ardnacross. The child was stripped of all his clothes and left naked. Lord Neil and his party then proceeded round the north of Mull, raiding and stealing.[27]

The Macleans were in some confusion. Brolas had expected that the Earl's force would besiege Duart and tie itself down. The Macleans had therefore driven off all their cattle and sent their boats to the back of Mull. Now they were surrounded, surprised and many of their cattle were hamstrung, 'which occasioned a great cry by the women and children keeping them'. They ran to their husbands. Once the Macleans realised that they had been out-manoeuvred, they capitulated.[28]

Both Glenorchy and Lochnell, who were with the Earl, had some sympathy for the Macleans. They negotiated a truce at Lochbuie's castle of Moy. By this agreement Brolas was to surrender Duart, lay down his arms and ensure that the gentlemen and tenants living on the estate would renounce their tacks. In exchange those who had defied Ensign Middleton were to be pardoned. Brolas himself was to be confirmed in the wadset that he held from Duart.[29] The infant Sir John Maclean is nowhere mentioned.

On the night of Friday 18 September Argyll sent Glenorchy with five hundred men to receive the surrender of Duart Castle. On the Saturday the Earl himself arrived. He wrote in triumph to his wife. The wind had dropped and it was so calm that he was forced to leave his large boats, which had only sails, behind at Lochbuie 'to come as they could'. He made use of his birlinns, which had oars as well as sails and landed at Duart in the afternoon. He then proceeded to send most of his men home. He would not, he wrote, stay there long himself. His wife was overjoyed.

Brolas's surrender evidently did not include the Collachs, who held land on the Duart estate and had defied Middleton. However, on 23 September they made their peace separately and agreed that they, 'their sub-vassalls, subtenants, servants, cottars and all other persons indwellers upon the lands rowmes and possessions pertaining to or possesst be us ... shall live quietlie and peaceablie as becoming good and loyal subjects'.[30] They were each to forfeit 5,000 merks Scots if they broke their word. Lachlan of Coll, who had now come to meet the Earl and was present, became the cautioner for their good behaviour underlining the fact that Coll was not considered to be under Duart's jurisdiction.

* * *

Argyll had begun his campaign brilliantly. He had also been lucky, launching an armada in the Hebrides at the time of the equinoctial gales is a hazardous undertaking. It had, however, worked. Lord Neil and Cawdor's foray by sea to the back of Mull had caught the Macleans off balance. The invaders had terrorised many of the Mull tenants and forced Brolas to capitulate.

The surrender of Duart Castle was the Earl's reward. Duart is the key to Mull. It lies at the intersection of three major waterways, the Sound of Mull, Loch Linnhe and the Firth of Lorn. It can be used both to observe shipping that travel up the most sheltered sea lane on the western seaboard, and as a base to seize them. Duart is also in line of sight of Dunstaffnage, Argyll's traditional forward base for daunting the Isles, and of other castles such as Dunollie, Achadun and Ardtornish. The rock on which it stands falls almost sheer for some twenty metres on the seaward site, but the landward or southern slope is comparatively gentle and is protected by a ditch.

Glenorchy and Lochnell's treaty with Brolas might have been the end of the affair. However, the Earl now dithered. A note in Argyll's own hand shows that Brolas was quite prepared to abandon his chief and betray his allies, provided that his own property was sacrosanct. Argyll writes:

Brolas is to give me an account of his confederates and of their arrangements with him. He is to discover what engagements are amongst them by word or writs. What good deeds were promised, who hath intromitted with the rents ... who have been his advisors, particularly of late. Who was the writer of his papers betwixt him and Lord Macdonnell and betwixt him and Lochiel. Which papers are to be produced. An account of what boats the Macleans have and what they are. What arms and ammunition they have and how they were procured. To tell, who commands Carnaburg and the castles of Coll and Kinlochaline. Where Macleans papers are?[31]

Whether or not Brolas betrayed his friends is uncertain. The Earl, however, certainly obtained answers to several of his questions. He then quibbled at some of the terms in Glenorchy's agreement. The chance of a peaceful solution was lost and Brolas, who had gone to Edinburgh to meet Argyll, left abruptly to purchase arms and ammunition.

Brolas also began to look for allies. He did not have to look far, for the Earl's actions had thoroughly alarmed his neighbours. In January 1675, at a secret meeting at Kentalen, an agreement in the name of Sir John Maclean's curators was made with Cameron of Lochiel. Lochiel, who was married to Sir John Maclean's aunt, was to receive a pension of 1,420 merks. In exchange he was to come with his clan to assist the Macleans whenever it was necessary.[32]

In order to evade the laws of conspiracy the pension was described as interest on imaginary debts.[33] The pension was secured on Duart's land in Morvern, which had previously been tenanted by Ardgour and his family. Lochiel's tack was to run during Sir John's minority. He was to obtain entry from Whit Sunday 1676. Lochiel and his cousin John Cameron of Glendessary were already tenants of much of Duart's lands in the north-east of Morvern and the Camerons were now in a dangerously powerful position. Brolas probably made similar arrangements with Lord Macdonnell[34] and Keppoch, but the details do not appear to have survived.

It is possible that Brolas had written off Duart's Morvern lands. In April the Earl reported to Glenorchy that there was talk of the Macleans laying Morvern waste and taking their cattle over to Mull. It was the beginning of the end of Maclean of Duart's dominance of Morvern. The other Maclean lairds there were left vulnerable to Cameron ambition.

Amongst those included in the list of Sir John's 'Tutors, Curators Administrators and burden takers' were 'Lachlan Mclain of Coll and Hector Mclain off Iland muck'. It is, however, significant that neither of them signed the bond.[35]

Notes

1. NAS. RD. MACK 58, 877. Aros. 2 October 1673.
2. HP I, 245–8.
3. *Acts of the Parliament of Scotland*, vii (1661–1669), 20.
4. Inveraray Castle Papers [ICP]. Bundle 466.20.1669.
5. *Letters from Archibald Earl of Argyll to John Duke of Lauderdale* (Bannatyne Club, 1829), 28. There is a good explanation of legal jurisdiction at this time in Joy Cameron *Prisons and Punishment in Scotland* (1983)
6. RPCS . 3rd Series. ii, 118–119.
7. ICP. Argyll Transcripts [AT], xv, 104.
8. ICP. AT, 1671.
9. Hugh was also the tacksman of Balliphetrish in Tiree. See TABLE 6.
10. HP 1, 288–95. Rental of Tirie.
11. *B & GB D'ton*, 43.

12. Fergus Roberts & IMM Macphail (ed), *Dumbarton Common Good Accounts 1614–1660* (1972).
13. ARB Haldane *The Drove Roads of Scotland* (1968)
14. ICP 472. 192: 9 May 1679 Bond by Charles, son to John Maclean of Grishipol to the Earl of Argyll concerning 46 cows 'for which he got a pass from the earl to pass through the shire to the lowlands'.
15. NLS. MS. 2134. 'Notes from Ardgour's Papers made at Ardgour, November 1834.'
16. *HP*.i, 251–260.
17. *HP*.i, 261.
18. NAS. GD 112.39.1058. Argyll to Glenorchy. 27 July 1674.
19. John Willcock *A Scots Earl* (1907), 81.
20. His grandfather Sir Colin Campbell of Glenorchy was the 9th Earl's foster-father [John Willcock *A Scots Earl* (1907), 5–8].
21. *Duchess Anne* (1973), 35.
22. HMCR *Portland* x (1931), 299.
23. Moray Mss, Darnaway, Forres. Box 6, 43. 5 October 1675. Argyll to Moray.
24. John Childs *The Army of Charles II* (1976), 197.
25. Nor had the term 'militia' apparently been used in Scotland before the late seventeenth century. Bruce P Lenman argues that it was 'essentially an English concept ... The Scots thought primarily of a general obligation for all fencible men to serve the King's Majesty's interest in arms'. The term 'fencible', which goes back to medieval times, means 'able for defence; fit for and liable to be called upon, for military service'. *Scottish National Dictionary* vol. iv qoted in Bruce P Lenman 'Militia, Fencible Men, and Home Defence, 1660–1797' in Norman Macdougall (ed), *Scotland and War A D 79–1919* (1991), 175.
26. *HP* i, 273; *RPCS*.iv, 272–4;
27. ICP. 467. 57. Ane Accompt of the goods & gear takin be the pairtie commanded be lord Neil Campbell & Hew Campbell of Calder in September 1674.
28. Moray MSS. Box 7.685.
29. David S Macmillan 'The Treaty of Lochbuy' *WHN&Q* Series I, No. XX (March 1983), 3–10; HP I, 275–277.
30. ICP 467. 53. 23 September 1674. Bond by John Maclean of Totronald etc to live peaceably.
31. ICP. 470. 128a.
32. ICP. Bundle 468. 88. 20 [January] 1675. Copy of Bond by Lachlan McLain of Brolas & other curators of Sir John McLain of Duart, minor, to Ewen Cameron of Lochiell for 14,020 merks;
33. I have to thank Paul Hopkins for this suggestion.
34. Aeneas, 1st and last Lord Macdonnell and Aros, 9th of Glengarry. He followed Montrose in the Civil Wars and was forfeited by Cromwell in 1651, unsuccessfully claimed chiefship of Clanranald and after the Restoration was created a peer by King Charles II; *m* Margaret, dau of Sir Donald Macdonald of Sleat, and *d.* 6 December 1680 when his peerage became extinct.
35. ICP Bundle 469, 92. This would appear to be the original bond.

Chapter Six

Stalemate in Mull

In April 1675 Argyll decided to allocate new tenancies in the Isle of Mull. Glenorchy disagreed with him and suggested that the Earl should first settle his differences with Brolas.[1] Argyll, irritated that his plan should be questioned, angrily exclaimed that he 'should go if it were in a fairy [ferry?] boat'. Glenorchy was unabashed. He warned the Earl that he would only alarm the people and that all their work there would be undone.

The Earl was eight days in Mull. He had written to the gentlemen of Clan Maclean to meet him. But only old Torloisk, the Marquess of Argyll's ally, came to meet him. The Macleans claimed that the Earl had broken the terms of their capitulation, worse still Brolas left Mull the day the Earl landed and went to consult with Lord Macdonnell.[2] He now sent a fiery cross throughout Mull. Glenorchy's worst fears had proved to be correct.

On 22 April three or four hundred of Duart's former tenants and friends gathered together at Knockmartin in the west of Mull.[3] They entered into a league and bound themselves together by an oath. The list of those present is instructive. It includes not only Duart's immediate family, but also his former tenants who were the leading men of other Maclean families, such as Lochbuie, Ardgour, Kinlochaline, Torloisk, Inverscadell, the uncles of Macquarrie of Ulva and Major David Ramsay. The latter was Commissary of the Isles and a veteran of the civil wars, who had given evidence against the Marquess of Argyll at his trial.[4] He also had a tack of the farm of Beach on the Ross of Mull,[5] and his son had drafted the secret treaty with Lochiel.

The rebels' first action was to select a raiding party of a hundred men. They then garrisoned the Macleans' traditional stronghold, the virtually impregnable fortress of Carnaburg Mor in the Treshnish Islands. Brolas next appointed captains, lieutenants and other officers. The men were mustered and drilled, colours were displayed. The whole affair sounds highly professional, perhaps helped by the expertise of Major Ramsay. Then, led by Brolas, a raiding party invaded Tiree.[6]

Argyll had stirred up a hornet's nest. It was a situation in which he seemed to revel. On 30 April he had announced that he had sent Captain Middleton to Edinburgh to let the Council know what was going on and to try to get a party of sixty soldiers quartered in Mull.[7] He hoped that he could do the same in Morvern and Tiree. Quartering was a method used by the government to punish Scots who were unwilling to pay their taxes. Regular soldiers were billeted on the delinquent and received free board and lodging until the debt was paid.

One Maclean was notably absent from those assembled at Knockmartin. This was Lachlan Maclean of Coll. There were several reasons why Coll was standing aloof from his kinsmen. One was because his cousin Lachlan Maclean, younger of Grishipol, who had been Duart's bailie in Tiree was kept on by Argyll and re-appointed Bailie of Tiree. It is not certain why the Earl appointed

Lachlan Grishipol to this important post. Probably his time in Dumbarton had made him known to Argyll, who owned Rosneath and was the most important nobleman in the Lennox.[8] Perhaps the Earl was again attempting to divide the Macleans.[9]

Whatever the reasons Lachlan Grishipol was now in an unenviable position. Once Brolas's men landed on Tiree they seized the rents that the bailie had collected. Grishipol fled to Coll's castle from where he wrote to Argyll on 2 May 1675:

My Lord,
I received your lordship's letter of the 18th of April and I was most willing to obey. But I cannot hazard any way without a safe-gaird for all the name of mcleane aim at my Lyfe and sent of purpose to try to apprehend me; but by informatione from the Laird of Coill I escaped, and cam within Coill's Castell where I am and will be till I gett your lordships ordor what to doe. The most of my meanes is taken from me so that I am lyk to Loss Lyfe and meanes except your Lordship prevent it yet I resolve to remaine

My Lord
Your Lordships faithful & reall servant
La. McLaine.[10]

Grishipol also wrote to Lochnell:

Coill May 26th 75.

Honourable Sir,
I could not keip my tym for I was forced to flee for refuge to Coill's Castell and escaped verie narrowly. Brolos's brother[11], and Kenlochaline whoe wer sent of purpous for my lyfe or person so that your lordship is a view profite [?]. I am close here gairding my self and will be so till I got my lords and your[–?] and till Boat and gaird be sent me that may cam me without hazard. Hew McLachlan [Hugh Maclean of Balliphetrish the former bailie] is constitute Bailie be Kenlochalin, and by that [?] it was proclaimed that non should obey our orders from my lord or me as his deput till this debate should be at ane end, and that cowes or other things I poinded for rents or dewteis should return to the owner and so its done, therefore nothing to be expected of that is remaining[.] the oficers hes turned their coats. A great deall of my Kowes & victualls is taken from me & what is remaining I know will not be long at my comand wherfore I trust your lordship will deall with my lord so seriously in my be halfe, as that his lordship will Look for a present Lyvlyhoode to me and myn, and a place of refuge to remaine in saftye, so long as the cuntryes are in truble. So expecting your lordship wi[ll] tak some efectuall course to sie me ther, I am

Sir
Your Lordship asured & humble servant
La McLaine

Sir
If ther wer a vesell in any plaice
About the Sound of Mull. I think
And speidilye I [?]
This leter, and Keip it secret.

The Isle of Coll, however, was not sufficiently remote enough from trouble and Grishipol fled to the Isle of Rum. He wrote to Argyll:

Rowme July 6 1675.

My Noble Lord

This may inform your Lordship that I was forced to Leive Coill, & com to the Hills hier and other places wher I may most contenently shelter my person in saftye, your lordships leters to Coill & me was intercepted Be Ardgour & his children; I met with the Captain of Clanranald heire in this yle; whome I find verie favorable upon your lordship['s] acompt. And now I humblie request your Lordship to writt to him or to any other that can doe it to find out some conveniencie for my safe transportatione to your Lordsh[ip]. And with all to acquent me pairtly of your Lordsh[ip] Dayat with the Captans preast; as for my misery & distress, I omit further to trouble your Lords[hip] with the informatione thereof at present more nor hithertoe I have done, But that I resolve to be a suferer, and am still

My Lord
Your Lordsh[ips] faithful
& most humbl servant
La. McLeane.

It is clear that Maclean of Coll in supporting his cousin had alienated the rest of the Macleans. Not for the first, nor the last time, were they out of step with their kinsmen.

Lachlan Grishipol's discomfiture, however, was soon to be avenged, and from his base at Dunstaffnage the Earl sent letters to his vassals telling them to join him with their birlinns for another expedition to Mull.

* * *

In July the Council issued yet another Commission of Fire and Sword[12] and ordered the heritors of Argyll and the Isles to suppress the rebellion: if necessary Brolas and his accomplices were to be pursued to the death. The Campbells, including Glenorchy, Appin, Lochiel, Clanranald and the Macleods, were expected to support Argyll and regular troops were sent to assist him, although the Earl was again urged to offer the Macleans an indemnity. By September Argyll had assembled 1,500 men at Dunstaffnage. Lochiel, however, unexpectedly wrote that the Camerons refused to serve under him on the terms he had granted. Brolas's secret agreement had paid off.

On 6 August Clanranald wrote to the Earl from Eilan Tiorram concerning Argyll's request that he provided men to support the Earl against the Macleans. It would be difficult, he wrote, to raise his people because:

the harvest tyme is coming one them nowe that [it] shall be very difficult to bring them from it, however, your lordship [m]aye be confident that I shall wait upon you with what I can soe soon as possible.

He goes on to say that

My Lord I thought convenient to show your Lordship that all the name of McLean except the Leard of Colle who is in ane poor condition doth obsolutly resolve to stand stantly against your Lordship at this tyme if your Lordship comes to Mull . . .

Clanranald's explanation as to why his brother-in-law was not with the rest of the Macleans is probably one of the reasons. But it was only part of the story. It should be remembered that 1675 was the year when Campbell of Kinnochtrie transferred the barony of Coll to Sir Normand Macleod of Bernerah. This was the first step in rehabitulation of Maclean of Coll, and it would have been lunacy at this time for the latter to be in opposition to the government in Edinburgh.

* * *

Seaforth now negotiated an agreement for the cessation of hostilities. It resulted in a truce between the Macleans and Argyll. It was to last for two years. During which time the combatants, encouraged by their friends at court, attempted to settle matters between themselves. The Macleans were not without allies on the Council, particularly amongst the old ultra-loyalist cavaliers. Argyll was persuaded to reduce his demands. A draft dispensation in his hand still exists in which he proposes to let Maclean keep the lands of Morvern, 'in order to preserve some memory of the family of Maclean.'[13]

As usual this magnanimous gesture, which might have disarmed some of his critics, was not quite what it seemed, for in October 1676 the Earl wrote to Glenorchy: '... it is certain Lord Macdonnell set Aros and Locheil all Morvern last Wednesday.'[14] In other words the Crown lands of Aros in Mull which had been held by Maclean for more than 150 years were now in Macdonnell's hands whilst Lochiel had a tack of Duart's lands in Morvern. Sir John Maclean's possession of Morvern would now be purely nominal. Lochiel evicted Macleans from the Morvern touns and filled them with Camerons. Lord Macdonnell was less partisan, and evidently was prepared to have Macleans as his sub-tenants in Aros.

All was not quiet in Mull during the truce. In November 1676 Lachlan Maclean of Grishipol, Argyll's titular bailie in Tiree wrote to the Earl:

13th November 1676. Information Lauchlan McClane Baillie of Tirie
Unto the Right honorable and noble
The Erle of Argyll

That where fyftein dayes bypast I sent a man of my owne To
Receive fra my father in law[15] fyfe cowes with thair Stirks, which
He did deliver To Duncan mc dugall brother to downach
Who had a drove of goods [cattle] To convoy to the Lowlands for mercat
And upon the 7th of this instant The Laird of Kengarloch
With Twelve men with him, Came in hostill m[aste]rfull violent maner
And tooke away the saids cowes and stirks belonging to me out of
The said drove, uttering manie boisterous threatnings against
Me, the owner thereof. Whereby it seems the means was not all
their Designe, But evill intendit against my person if present
as they alleadgit, Of which I had onlie intelligence the 11th instant And
so mist oportunitie To wait upon your Lordship at Inveraray
   Heirfore most humblie intreat effectuall course may
   Be taken for recoverie of the loss. And also for prtection
   And securitie of my person and meanes in tyme comeing
            La. McLaine.[16]

* * *

On 25 November 1676 Glenorchy wrote to the Earl from London, where he was looking after Argyll's interest at court and trying to find an heiress for his own son. He had received a letter from the Earl the previous day. In his reply Glenorchy exclaims: 'My lord, most of those things [about which Argyll had written] are so contrary to what you formerly wrote that I am at a standstill to know how to make them agree, and am at a much greater dilemma how to make a fabric of your affairs [which] move according to the flow and ebb of every current'.[17]

The Macleans had left Edinburgh. Until they returned the case against them could not proceed. Until the case was concluded Argyll could not borrow any more money. In addition his Commission of Fire and Sword had lapsed during the truce. Glenorchy wrote that he was not surprised that 'Brolas is advised to stay away as long as he can, but if your garrison do them [i.e. the Macleans] any hurt you will regret it, for when you so confidently pursued for what you did by virtue of your commission what will you be when you have no warrant and they live under protection?'[18]

He goes on to say that he is apprehensive about what will happen if the King hears that the Earl had acted against the Macleans without any warrant. There was still considerable sympathy at court for the Macleans who had, in the past, suffered so much for their loyalty. 'You have the affair at winning or losing [in your hands]', wrote Glenorchy.

The Earl increasingly irritated Glenorchy. The latter wrote: 'You seem not to understand my letter where at I wonder. It is not fit to write too legible but I thought I have you such an account of my commission as was intelligible to those who employed me. I can make a few more attempts until I know your resolution'.[19]

Argyll continued to use Glenorchy as a sounding board for his ideas and to moan about his fate. Writing on 26 December 1676[20] he complained that nobody at court knows the Highlands and despite all the money that the Macleans owed him he got nothing in return, not even the rents of Ardnamurchan. He was still at the expense of paying for garrisons and 'watches', the embryonic police force in the Highlands. In January he writes that he has heard from Inverawe that some of the rebels have 'come about the house of Duart in the night time, if they begin to play it is not my fault'.

Glenorchy replied on 16 January: 'Although the Macleans be so foolish to come about your house at Duart, yet unless they offer some act of hostility I would not wish your lordship to begin, for I can assure you any noise or disturbance in the Highlands will be ill taken here, specially at this time. As you know when wise men and fools contend who bears the blame? Thus I give you true advice'.[21]

Whilst Mull continued to simmer, there was a danger that the South West Lowlands of Scotland would explode. Numbers of people, who were disaffected to the established church, were attending field conventicles. As these openair services grew in size they became increasingly military in character. It was abundantly clear that the ordinary means of obtaining order and obedience to the law was breaking down.[22]

Argyll's enemies could not fail to notice that he was spending more and more time on his private affairs, did not attend the Council regularly and was not concerning himself sufficiently with the public good. In February 1677 Glenorchy wrote from Edinburgh that on his arrival there he had found the Earl's absence from public employment, at a time of crisis, was misrepresented. Argyll had not attended a meeting of the Council since 14 November 1676. Since then there had been much discussion over the peace of the Highlands and in February much thought was given to the problem of conventicles. Argyll hurried from Inveraray and attended the meeting of the Council on 22 February. However much damage had been done to his interest.[23]

Notes

1. NAS. GD 112. 1063. Argyll to Glenorchy. Inverary 10 May 1675.
2. NAS. GD 112. 1061: Argyll to Glenorchy. Dunstafnage 30 April 1675.
3. *RPCS*. 3rd Series iv. 433.
4. NAS. PA 7. 9. 1–83, 243.
5. *HP* I, 282;
6. *RPCS*. 3rd Series iv, 433.
7. NAS. GD112,1061.
8. *Dumbarton Common Good Accounts 1614–1660*, xi.
9. It is worth noticing that on 31 April 1675 at Newport Glasgow Alexander McKorkindale brother germane to the barrone of McKorkindale and Charles McLean in Coll [Lachlan Grishipol's brother] borrowed £24.18d Scots from Alexander Kellie, writer in Edinburgh [NAS. RD. MACK 62, 267]. If, as is likely, this was to finance a drove it would mean that Charles was able to bring cattle from the Isles. To do so he would have to have had permission from the Earl to pass through Argyllshire., which is another reason perhaps why Coll was moving away from his Maclean kinsmen.
10. ICP. Bundle 493. 443.
11. This was Hector Og. He is the ancestor of Major the Hon. Sir Lachlan Maclean of Duart & Morvern Bart, the present chief of the Macleans of Duart.
12. *HP*, I, 308.
13. ICP Bundle 485. 346
14. NAS GD112. 1067. Inverary 30 October 1676 [Badly damaged].
15. Neil Maclean of Drimnacross.
16. ICP Bundle 54. 13 November 1676. Information Lauchlan McClane Baillie of Tirie unto the Right honorable The Erle of Argyll.
17. ICP Bundle 492. 439.
18. Ibid.
19. NLS. MS 975. 21.
20. NAS GD112. 1079.
21. NLS. MS 975. 23.
22. Gordon Donaldson *Scotland: James v–James vii* (1971), 370.
23. NLS. MS 975. 25.

Chapter Seven

The disarming of Mull

In December 1677 the administration led by Lauderdale, with the approval of the King and the Scottish bishops, took the extraordinary step of quartering the Highland Host on the disaffected areas of the western Lowlands of Scotland.[1] On 24 January 1678 the Committee for the West, which was responsible for the host, met at Stirling. Argyll's hereditary enemy the Marquess of Atholl chaired the meeting. The committee included the Earl of Caithness, as Glenorchy had now become. Ominously for Argyll, he was not included.[2]

The Highland Host was principally composed of men from Perthshire, Angus, and from the Lowland Militia. It was withdrawn in May 1678 leaving the conventicling counties embittered and ripe for rebellion. The correspondence between Argyll and Caithness, which I have relied on for much that has gone before, stops abruptly during this period. Caithness had more to do than concern himself with the affairs of his chief.

Argyll was probably in London in June 1678 and tried to make up his quarrel with Caithness. In August the Earl wrote from Glasgow to Caithness that 'I do wish . . . your family well and I desire in what concerns either of us we may be mutually concerned.'[3] In October Lauderdale himself wrote to Caithness from Whitehall. 'It is very acceptable to me [that] all mistakes and jealousies betwixt the Earl of Argyll and your lordship being happily removed'.[4] Despite these outward signs of reconciliation the relationship between the two Campbell Earls remained cool and one of mutual suspicion.

On 10th October 1678 the Council lost its patience with the Macleans and decided that the letters of suspension against Argyll raised by Brolas were frivolous. The same day they renewed their earlier Commission of Fire and Sword against them. Argyll was empowered to call on the assistance of the militia of the shires of Argyll, Bute and Dumbarton, as well as his own tenants. They were to proceed against Brolas and his accomplices. Argyll also had under his command a 'company out of the Earl of Lithgow's regiment that they might put him in peaceable possession of the Isle of Mull'. The latter were one hundred regular soldiers 'out of our Regiment of guards.'[5]

This time the Earl did not make the error of letting Brolas get help from the Camerons. As we have seen Ewen Cameron of Lochiel had married Sir John's aunt and had sworn to assist the Macleans. Lady Lochiel, however, was now dead and Lochiel changed sides. He did so in exchange for the cancellation of a debt of 40,000 merks that he owed to Argyll, which gave rise to the saying *Chaill Eoghan a dhia, ach chaill an t-Iarla chuid aigid.* 'Ewen lost his God but the Earl lost his money'.[6]

A month later the Macleans and Macdonalds revenged themselves on Lochiel for his treachery. The Macdonalds were led by Aeneas, Lord Macdonnell and were presumably armed with the weapons issued to him when he had command of one of the Independent Companies.

Seven to eight hundred Macleans crossed Morvern to the Corran of Ardgour and invaded Mamore, whilst the Macdonalds advanced towards Lochleven. Caithness had hoped that Lochiel's change of sides might help bring the Macdonalds to an agreement, and bring the Macleans to a settlement. He began negotiations with Lord Macdonnell in late November, watched with considerable suspicion by Argyll.

The Macleans and Macdonalds were not to be persuaded and attempted a night attack on Argyll's camp. Argyll and Auchinbreck, the hereditary Colonel of Argyll, were arguing over which of them should be in command of the army. Caithness claimed that only his vigilance saved Argyll's force from being caught asleep.

Rory Macdonald, Lord Macdonnell's cousin, claimed that the confederates had had no intention of fighting but merely 'drew near to the earl of Argyll's camp to hasten the conclusion of the treaty with Caithness'.[7] Argyll, fearing that they were going to fight, withdrew his forces and took refuge in Castle Stalker. This picturesque tower-house of three stories and a garret stands on rocky islet at the mouth of Loch Laich in North Lorn. It has good observation on Loch Linnhe and the Strath of Appin. It was probably built in the second quarter of the sixteenth century. By the third decade of the following century it had passed to Sir Donald Campbell of Ardnamurchan[8] and was inherited from him by Campbell of Airds, who held it in 1678.

Caithness, who joined Argyll at Castle Stalker on 27 November, wrote a letter to the Macleans, which stated that Argyll had agreed to settle with them. In this letter Caithness said that the Earl thought that Castle Stalker was not a suitable place from which to conduct negotiations. It was perhaps too small for the number of men who needed to be present, and Argyll suggested that they should all meet at Duart. He promised to disperse his troops, provided the Macleans did so as well. He also agreed that he would come to Duart with only three or four hundred members of the militia as his bodyguard. Caithness went on to say that Argyll agreed that Lord Macdonnell should act as the mediator between the two sides.[9]

On 27 November Argyll wrote from Castle Stalker to his brother-in-law, the Earl of Moray, to say that Caithness had been negotiating with the Macleans and Macdonalds without his permission.[10] The Earl of Argyll was furious with his presumptuous kinsman and when Caithness left Castle Stalker, and went to Dunstaffnage, Argyll's porter refused him entry. Caithness retired to Balloch where he sulked with toothache.

On 4 December Lochiel reported to Argyll from Inverlochy[11] that the Macdonalds had gone home having spent the previous night in Glen Nevis. He also said that the Macleans were ferrying their people back across the Corran of Ardgour, from there they had dispersed to their homes.

* * *

On 10 December Argyll's armada invaded Mull. The Macleans appear to have been surprised by what appears to have been an extraordinary piece of double-dealing on Argyll's part. Argyll had seized all the boats on the mainland to prevent news of his coming reaching the Macleans. It was winter and Duart's tenants were at their most vulnerable. They could not drive their cattle away to safety of the mountains. Argyll had achieved a remarkable feat in gathering a force of more than 1,500 in winter. Among them were seventy 'redcoats'.[12]

The Macleans were without their Macdonald allies. The great Keppoch bard Iain Lom, in his song to Maclean of Duart, excuses himself for not being present: 'Were it not that the river was swollen in front of us and the flood risen in the fords I would have been at the tryst a day before the others', he exclaims. He accuses the Macleans of giving up too easily: 'A ferret has seized my grandmother's goodly clan in a vice-like grip: feeble is the struggle put up by them although they are a famous family'.[13] It was to be less feeble after Ian Lom composed his song, but the slur has been remembered rather longer than the actual events.

By 18th December Lachlan Grishipol, the Earl's former bailie in Tiree, wrote jubilantly from Duart Castle to John Cunningham of Aikenbar. Provost of Dumbarton

Much Respected

The want of conveniencie was the Rason that I did not writt to you sooner, all the newes heire is that my lord has ferried all his forces to Mull and Morvern. My lord Macdonald was at Mull with a verie few men and went away yesterday home. The Macleans ar upon a traitie thir three dayes but come not to a closs yet, but I know they will agree. I am just now to be shiped to Tirry wher I looke to be repossessed in my owne; Sr I humblie thank you for the Beife you gave to my wyfe, for she writt so to me, And I know my Lord hes wrttin to you concerning her; And I doe earnestly entreat & desyre you to take a caire of my wyfe and children and let them Lacke nothing they stand in neid of[.] This Letter shall obleidge me to pay you thankfullie of all you disbursments in thay behalf at meiting. Hoping you will not faille heir in as my trust is in you. I continow alwayes

Sr
Your most humble servt
La. McLaine[14]

On 21 December 1678 the Earl himself wrote to Cunningham from Duart:

Loveing ffreind

I have all this tyme keeped Lauchlane McLaine with me and I cannot as yet spare him to goe home that he myt provyde for his wyfe and children Therfor I desyre ye will doe me the favor to see she is provyded in any thing they need not exceeding the value of ane hundreth merks scots[15] and this shall obleidge me to see you thankfully repayed I rest

Your Loving ffreind
Argyll.[16]

The disarming of Mull and Morvern followed. It continued throughout January and was effectively carried out and, as far as Mull was concerned, it was efficiently recorded.

On 30 December 1678 Coll's uncles Neil of Drimnacross and John of Toronald brought in the tenants of Quinish with their weapons to Tobermory. They handed in their arms to Argyll's servant Dugald Campbell.[17] The following day Coll's uncles and his cousin Hector Maclean of Auchnasaul made a petition to Argyll in which they acknowledged

The great guiltiness and high crymes committed by us in opposeing the King's Majesties authority & law by unlawful convocation and ryseing in crymes for which we are lyable to the severest punishment of law lykewaye we acknowledge that we have justly incurred the said Earl's displeasure by opposeing ... his possessione of the land and estate of Dowart ... and hereby renounce with kyndness & goodwill any possessions or tacks we have or can pretend to the said estate ... And we bind and obleidge to remove ourselves, wyffes bairns family servants tenants subtenants cottars grassmen goods & geare furth and from any part of the said estate of dowart possessed by us ... And also we in name off & takeing the burden upon us for the said Lauchlan McLain of Coll obleidge us to delyver up the said house and Castle of Coll ...

The petition was witnessed by Argyll's brother Lord Neil Campbell, two other Campbells and 'Lauchlan McLain Baillie of Terie'.[18]

Three days later Hector of Auchnasaull made an individual petition to Argyll. In it he claimed that he was

Very sensible and sory for his opposing his Majesties lawes and concurring in armes with those that wer outlawes and ... did lay hold upon your lordships offer of indemnitie which he acknowledges was a very great favour to him ... [however] your petitioner is lyable to be ruined by those who formerly opressed him and forced him to concurr with them in the illegal actings for besydes what he had formerly suffered from them since your lordship granting him protection they have fallen upon him and killed a great number of his goods which is lyke may bring your petitioner to povertie ...

There follows a list of the cattle stolen from Auchnasaull:

First be Brolos and his substiuts in September 1675 12 cowes
Item be Allan McLaine son to Charles McLaine in Ardnacroish in Apryll or therby in the yeir 76 ane barell of brandie.
Item be Charles McLaine in Ardnacroish his servants and tennents in febry 76 8 cowes.
Item be Lauchlan McLaine of Torloisk acompanied with threscore armed men in May 77 23 piece of horses.
Item be Hector his Cusen germane the said moneth & yeir one mear.
Item efter the Earle of Argyll wes pleased to receive the petitioner in his lordships protection Taken away be Brolos and his Complices now in Carnbulg in the moneth of Janry 79 75 cowes.[19]

Brolas had lost little time in showing that it was wise not to ask the Earl for protection. Safe in his stronghold of Carnaburg he could afford to defy Argyll.

* * *

On 2 January 1679 Donald Campbell reported to his brother, Sir Hugh Campbell of Cawdor, that before he left Argyll the Earl had captured Lochbuies's house and garrisoned it. He also claimed that the Laird of Coll had regained control of his own castle for Argyll and that Macquarrie of Ulva, Charles MacAllan, the bailie of Aros and all his children had surrendered as had all the tenants of Mull and Morvern.[20]

Donald Campbell claimed that Brolas had only forty men with him at Carnaburg and that he could not hold out for long 'as the quarters there are not very good and he has no provisions'. Ardgour, Kinlochaline, Brolas and Torloisk he explained did not come in to the Earl purely because of their 'intromissions with the bygone rents which my lord will not discharge'. Yet it was expected that they would eventually appeal for mercy. Lochiel was being used to bring them in. If they were not willingly he was to bring them in by force. This was far too rosy a picture. Neither Lochbuie's house nor that of Coll had yet fallen.

* * *

Argyll's forces were not to have everything their own way. On 26 December Argyll, who was at Aros, issued instructions for an expedition to Coll and Tiree by fifty of the King's Regiment of Guards and 150 men of the Earl of Caithness's company.[21] The expedition was to be commanded by Campbell of Lochnell. Barbreck's and McIlvernoch of Oib's boats were to transport the fifty redcoats whilst Lochnell's own two boats and the two black boats from Kintyre were to move Caithness' men. Argyll's frigate was to escort the expedition.

Lochnell was instructed that once he had landed on Coll he was to seize the castle and garrison it. He was also to secure all the boats on the island and to use them, and as many of Coll's men as were reliable to help capture Tiree. He was then to make a list of the inhabitants of Coll, those present in the castle and seize their arms. Outstanding public dues owed by Maclean of Coll, which for the period from November 1673 until May 1678 amounted to £345.19s.6d Scots for excise duties,[22] were to be collected as were rents for the Two Ends of Coll, which belonged to Duart.

Argyll notes in his diary that he dispatched his expedition to Coll on 3 January 1679.[23] He was confident of success for the expedition took with it the gentlemen of Coll, Maclean of Coll's uncles[24] who, as we have seen, had already submitted. Argyll planned that fifty of Lochnell and Caithness's men should spend the winter on Coll and Tiree.

January gales are some of the worst each year and it was not a happy expedition that set out. Only fifty of the hundred of Caithness's men who should have been sent were dispatched, as 'they were not expert at sea'. Lochnell wrote to Caithness that he had great difficulty in persuading them to go. Lochnell, however, insisted that they did so as he 'took it to be in your lordship's interest that they should not refuse my lord Argyll's command at the time, as your lordship's cousin Alexander may testify'.[25]

Caithness's cousin, Alexander Campbell of Barcaldine, the second lieutenant in his chief's company, wrote himself on 11 January.[26]

> My lord, I know your lordship marvels that you have not heard from me all this time, but I could not help it for I was commanded by my lord Argyll to go to the Isles of Gometra and Ulva where I have been with your lordship's men this fortnight bypast. Now just when I came back, my lord Argyll commanded fifty of your lordship's company with a sergeant, two corporals and a drummer to go to Tiree and Coll, to receive the house of Breacachadh. Upon which the whole company mutinied and would not go unless I went with them myself. The truth is I know not what to do for I was loath to go ... but because of your lordship's strict command to me in both your last letters ... to obey my lord Argyll's command I held my tongue and prevailed with the soldiers to go there with Duncan Campbell's son.[27]

Barcaldine wrote that he had written to Caithness from Duart to discover if his cousin wished him to obey Argyll's commands, but he had received no answer. He goes on to say that

> it makes me think your lordship did not intend to hinder them, however, if your lordship be not for their staying there after they get the house acquaint me of it and I shall go there myself to bring them out of it, though I be sure they will run away themselves out of it shortly for want of shoes.

Caithness's company had had no pay and Barcaldine had been forced to promise, before the men were prepared to go into the boats, that within a fortnight he would deliver their pay to them and no wonder for it would pity any creature to see them go naked and barefoot as they are, which has made them to use the west country fashion in plundering shoes from everybody that meets them until they have made the Mull men go as barefoot as they do themselves.

Barcaldine asks:

If this be credit for your lordship, your men may be forced to commit such abuse whilst others receive their pay punctually?

He wrote later that week that Caithness's company looked more like beggars than soldiers. This had irritated Argyll, whose 'humour', Barcaldine writes,

bears (as I believe) kindness for no man.[28]

On 19 January there seems to have been a flurry of letter writing at Duart.[29] Argyll wrote to Caithnes:

I have just now received yours and will not delay a return for I am hopeful you will not be alarmed with any meetings of the Macdonalds, for I have had very kind letters from Sir Donald Macdonald and the Captain of Clanranald and have returned them kind answers which they deserved and I look for them both here this week to go with me to Edinburgh.
In the meantime we want no interludes in our scene. Old Lochbuie, old Ardgour and Kinlochaline plays tricks, but you will hear I hope within a week of my way of fighting with these giants. Brolas is also lately be-fooled with Torloisk and he with Lord Macdonald. I spared forty cows pretended belonging to Brolas in hopes of better deportment. Now he has from Carnaburg driven in some cows I had protected which it is like I will pay on his charge.
I told you I had sent a small party of your men and some others to Coll and Tiree upon the assurance of Coll's uncles to deliver me the castle and their arms, but they have failed as all will do here without a present sensible force upon them for visible force is not enough. Your men are all I thank God safe, only we all want shoes except my new recruits from Glenshira and Lochawe that have some spare. I fear your men take them for which I must put guards on them. I am yet hopeful to get Coll and Tiree.[30]

* * *

Maclean of Coll's cousin, Hector Maclean of Auchnasaul was in desperate straits. As we have seen in January 1679 Brolas's men had robbed him of seventyfive cows. Achnasaul's tribulations were not over for as the Laird of Coll's uncles wrote to Culdares from Quinish on 31 January 1679:

Much honoured Sir,
Thes ar shewing your honor that the night before we cam to quinish that ane pirtie off the clan chamrone cam about mid day & tuik away with them from Hector mcLein of Achnasaul the number of ffourtie cowes being all that was left him by the McLeains fformerlie. And as thir goods being fferried upon Johne mcLachlane his botte whoe dwells in Ardnamurchan which your honore knowes is contrar to my Lord Argyll his last order to Locheill & to the Laird off Lochnell therefor your honor may be pleased to wrytt to my lord in all hast & to desyre his

Lordship to congratulate our conditione & to lett him understand howe is this poore corner of coill his contrie is totallie harried excepting som few persons which ar threatned & asalted daylie by the clan chamrons to tack away what they have & their lyffs likways so expecting your honore will tack this to your serious consideratione we rest Much honored Sir

Yours to Serve you
Neill McLean of Drimnacross
John McLeane off totronall[31]

Lord Neil also wrote to Caithness on 19 January.[32] He said that the Clan Ewen [as the Macleans of Ardgour were known] had withdrawn all their cattle and themselves out of Morvern, an event was to mark the end of that family's dominance over that part of Duart's estate. It left the remaining Maclean heritors there to the tender mercies of the Camerons.

Lord Neil wrote that the only members of the Clan Ewen to remain in Morvern were the garrison of the castle of Kinlochaline, which had not yet been taken. Coll, Tiree and perhaps most significantly Carnaburg were still in the possession of the Macleans. Argyll, however, must have considered that he had achieved his immediate aim and needed to cover his back in Edinburgh. He was there by 18 February to attend the Council. In his absence the Macleans reoccupied Mull.

Notes

1. Gordon Donaldson *Scotland James v to James vii* (1971), 370.
2. *RPCS*. 3rd Series v, 304; *Ibid*, 505.
3. NAS. GD112. 1092.
4. Ibid, 1093.
5. *Historical Notices of Scottish Affairs* (1848), 204.
6. James T Clark (ed) *Macfarlane's Genealogical Collection* Vol. i (1900), 138. [This is the published version of part of Dr Hector's Genealogical Account.]
7. ICP. Bundle 470. 134.
8. *RCAHMS* Argyll Vol. 2 Lorn (1975), 188–194.
9. Ibid.
10. Moray MSS Box 6, 51.
11. NLS MS 975, 37.
12. ICP Loose unindexed paper dated 1678. Argyll himself added the number of 'Redcoats'.
13. Annie M Mackenzie *Orain Iain Luim* (1973), 143–144.
14. ICP. Bundle 487, 369.
15. In fact she ran up debts of £69.15s.8d with Provost Cunningham [ICP Bundle 488, 386].
16. ICP. Bundle 487, 370.
17. ICP. Fullerton Transcripts: The Disarming of Mull etc. in the Winter of 1678–1679, 17.
18. ICP. Bundle 467, 54.
19. ICP. Bundle 472, 188.
20. C Innes (ed) *Thanes of Cawdor* (1859), 339–340.
21. ICP. Bundle 472. 179.
22. Ibid. Bundle 486. 352.
23. Ibid. Bundle 470. 143.
24. Ibid Bundle 467.54; NAS GD 112, 1098: Agyll to Caithness Dowart 10 January 1679.
25. NAS GD112, 1099: Lochnell to Caithness Dowart 11 January 1679.

26. Ibid, 1100. Barcaldine to Caithness 11 January 1679.
27. Duncan Campbell the Baillie of Jura's son John received a commission from Argyll on 6 Jan 1679 [NAS. GD 64.2. 24. Campbell of Jura Papers.]
28. NAS. GD112. 1101 'A Campbell to Glenorchy' Douart 19 January 1679.
29. Ibid 1102–6.
30. ICP. Bundle 470. 143.
31. ICP. Bundle 493. 449.
32. NAS GD112. 1102.

Chapter Eight

Counter-Attack

The Council that Argyll attended on 18th February considered the supply of straw and hay for the forces and the iniquities of two indulged ministers. That night the Earl spent the prodigious sum of £2.18/- on 'sack', as sherry was then known. He probably had a hangover the following morning for he then spent 14/- on oysters, bread, sugar and ale. He left Edinburgh for London on 23 February, having changed £50 Scots into English money.[1]

The failure of the Earl's expedition to Coll and Tiree meant that Lachlan Grishipol had not gone to Tiree as he had hoped. On 4 March 1678–9 John Cunningham Provost of Dumbarton repaid £15.8s.8d which 'Lachlane McLaine fear of Grisiboill'[2] had borrowed from Patrick Williamson, younger, Maltman in Dumbarton[3] on 25 October 1678 which was due to be repaid by the 25 December.[4]

Argyll was in London until 28 March to report to the King on his handling of the Macleans and to get permission for another expedition to Mull. Lachlan Maclean of Coll was also in London. He had a meeting with the Earl. On 8 March Coll wrote to his uncles:

Uncles,
I am very sorry that you did presume to raise in armes against my Lord Argyll, as I am informed, haveing no ordour bot your owne. Bot now I doe hereby straitly comand you that tho the Mclaines should ruine all my lands, not to do the lyk againe, as you shall be ansuerable to the King and Kingdom. And as concerneing my house [i.e. Breacachadh Castle] you know it was to yourselves that I gave the charge of it and to no other, bot I do not know what way the divell hes provocked you to suffer my brother or wife to enter into my house for it was well known to you that I was more afrayed that any of the McLaines should enter in it then I was for my Lord Argyll or any of his, and now as I do hereby comands my brother to remove from my house and not to com neere it so long as I shall be from Scotland for if my lord had not carryed a great respect to me my brother had done me mor prejudice than ever he should do me good, and lykwayes over againe comands you to delyver my house to my Lord or his Lordships deputs upon sight hereof as you shall be ansuerable to me and as you wish the security & savety of both your persons and meines and never be found againe contrary to his Lordships comands desyre for be it knowen to you that I am still as I have been formerly his Lordships servant and desyres you lykwayes to be as serviceable to his Lordship as you can. So expecting assuredly you will not faill in doing of this I remaine

Your Loving nephew and
Servant
L McLaine of Coll.[5]

He writes in a postscript:

I have beene plyding with my Lord to send my cousin Lauchlane there to my house and 20 of his Lordship's men 20 of my own, bot whither his Lordship will grant this or not you shall know of it with all dear uncles do not shirk my bussiness for want of litle money for I am forsed to brib[e] som men and if you can at this instant send me bot ten pound and that verie speedily youll prejudge me in mor then foure hundreth pounds Sterling if it shall not be sent for all the money that Charles left me I was forsed to give it away so expecting you will not loose my business or credite I remaine

La. McLaine of Coll

Why Lachlan Coll had to 'brib[e] som men' is not explained. However, the constant complaint of the Macleans of Coll that they had been ruined for supporting the King during the Civil Wars suggests that Lachlan was trying to obtain a pension. On the other hand his subsequent military service in Holland might have needed a helping hand at Court and the ethos of that Court, with its sexual laxity, is likely to have made bribery commonplace.[6]

Lachlan of Coll seems to have been the first leading West Highlander to serve in the Scots Brigade in Dutch Service. Previously it had been the northern clans, most notably the Mackays, who furnished the bulk of Highland Scots mercenaries to the Protestant powers of Europe.[7] In Holland Coll served in a regiment commanded by Colonel Hugh Mackay of Scourie, a skilled soldier who had fought as far afield as Crete. Mackay's lieutenant-colonel was Thomas Buchan. Ironically he and Mackay were to be the commanders of the opposing sides in the Highlands in 1690. In 1684 yet another Mackay succeeded Lachlan.[8]

Lachlan Maclean of Coll had evidently financed his journey to London with money his cousin Charles had raised, presumably as the result of a drove. He had little to keep him at home. As we have seen in 1666 he had married Meve, daughter of John Moidatach Macdonald of Clanranald. She was a Roman Catholic, and it is possible that Lachlan like his brother had converted to Rome.[9] Alternatively he may have refused to do so and this was one of the causes of the breakdown of his marriage. Meve was later to complain to the Council that her husband was not supporting her adequately.[10]

As Lachlan's visit to London was probably an attempt to retrieve his fortunes he had no wish to antagonise Argyll. This may explain the tone of his letter to his uncles, particularly if he expected that the Earl would read it. On the other hand it is possible that Lachlan was genuinely in Argyll's camp and that the letter came into the Earl's possession after he captured Breacachadh.

* * *

Meanwhile in Mull the people were reduced to the brink of famine. Virtually all forms of sustenance had been taken from them and some seven hundred of their cattle killed by Argyll's men. Even worse since Lochbuie surrendered, the Clan Ewen were raiding his people and stolen yet another parcel of cows.[11] On 1 March Brolas, young Ardgour and Torloisk wrote to the Chancellor John Earl of Rothes that Argyll's oppression laid the whole land waste. They feared it would soon not be in their power 'to suppress the violent distemper of our ruinous people . . . upon the author of it'.[12]

On 4 April the Earl returned from London. He attended the Council in Edinburgh and received the King's official congratulations for quieting the disorders in the Highlands. Argyll 'whose prudent deportment in the whole transactions upon that occasion we are very well pleased' was singled out for particular praise. The King now authorised the Council if necessary to make use of the standing forces and militia to take any other steps to reduce the Highlands to obedience.

Preparations for yet another expedition were well under way by 21 April when the Earl's servitor, Dugall Campbell, wrote a memorandum organising provisions for the two regular Highland companies in the King's pay to be used on the expedition; boats and cows were to be procured; the Sheriff of Inverness was to be written to; Cawdor was to get his men in Islay and Lorne to the rendezvous with those of the rest of the sheriffdom; cooking facilities were to be provided for a party of the King's Regiment of Guards; the militia was to be put in a state of readiness; the garrison of Inverlochy was to be provided with 'all necessaries'.[13]

On 25 April Argyll wrote to Caithness, who was at Inveraray, to say that the latter's cousin Barcaldine was with him. Barcaldine had informed the Earl that Caithness's company had dispersed as soon as Argyll had left Mull in January. However, Argyll did not wish to rake up what was past. He told Caithness that he had orders for the militia. They were to be at Achallader, Caithness's castle on the edge of Rannoch Moor, the gloomy bog that was the haunt of thieves and broken men. They were to be there by 20 May.[14]

Argyll goes on to say that the Macleans in Kinlochaline had grown troublesome to Lochbuie and that the Earl was likely to have to go there himself sooner than he intended. Three days later the Earl wrote to Barcaldine to say that he was going to need all the boats he could get hold of and that Barcaldine should send them to Dunstaffnage by the end of May.

There was now a great flurry of activity. Letters were dispatched to and from Argyll's allies. Dugall Campbell's accounts meticulously list the cost of sending boys with messages to Kilberry, Glenorchy and Clanranald. Spies were sent out and paid for. Intelligence was received. The redcoats were given £5.16/- worth of drink to keep them happy.[15]

On 6 May John Cunningham, Provost of Dumbarton, wrote to the Earl that although he had summoned the heritors and other leaders of the shire's militia to meet him that day at Dumbarton, not as many had turned up as he would have wished. Those who had done so were unanimous in saying that they would obey the Earl's commands. They agreed to call out their men the following Wednesday and to rendezvous at the Castle Green of Dumbarton at 10 o'clock. However, all said that it would be very difficult to get all their people to comply with Argyll's orders.[16]

On this occasion the Macleans did not wait for Argyll to attack. Whether or not Brolas and his friends wished, as they claimed, to restrain their people is uncertain. The people, if not their leaders, were bent on revenge. They invaded the mainland.[17] It was an audacious step. Not since Montrose's invasion of Argyll a generation earlier had anyone dared to make a foray into the Campbell heartland.

After Montrose's winter campaign of December 1644 Campbell territory could no longer be considered impregnable. However, the risks in invading Argyll, even in May, were considerable. In addition only six months previously the Macleans had been disarmed. Either they had only handed in useless weapons or Brolas had purchased new swords and muskets. Alternatively the Macleans were poorly provided with weapons and the expedition was even more hazardous. Whatever the facts, it seems that there was anger in Mull that needed to be exorcised.

The youthful leaders of the Macleans were also probably in search of glory, hoping to equal the exploits of their fathers' generation in the Civil Wars. The tenant-touns of Argyll were justified in quaking in their beds at the thought of another *fear thollaidh nan tighean*, 'the destroyer of houses', the nickname given to Alasdair MacColla. Stories of Montrose and his orgy of blood and plunder in 1644 will have lost nothing in the telling.

On 12 May Argyll learned that Brolas was raising the Macleans. His intelligence was that Brolas had forced those living peaceably in Mull to join him.[18] The following day Argyll left for Dunstaffnage.[19] The Earl's frigate was already in the Sound of Mull and it was hoped that it would prevent the Macleans from crossing over into Morvern. In fact Brolas crossed directly to Knoydart, and joined his allies the Macdonalds of Glengarry and Keppoch in Lochaber. Colonel Menzies did manage to capture a small boat near Kinlochaline, which was bringing victuals from Tiree, but it was his only success. Argyll had a major rebellion on his hands.

On 21 May the Macleans linked up with Lord Macdonnell in Keppoch. The following day the confederates were reported to be at Loch Treig. Argyll returned to Inveraray. The rebels now entered the shire of Argyll and on the 23rd were in Glencoe. Argyll thought that they would come by the hills of Glenorchy, so on the 25th he moved his forward base to Kilchurn Castle at the head of Lochawe.[20] He then sent orders to William Campbell, the captain of his frigate, to attempt to seize the rebels's boats.

That day two hundred Cowal men joined the Earl, as did another two hundred men from Argyll proper. Argyll now had a force of 900 men. The rebels probably had more, for Caithness wrote to the Earl of Moray on the 26 May that Lord Macdonnell was reported to be in the Braes of Glenorchy with a force of 2,000 men.[21] Argyll, leaving the Lorne men to guard the castle, moved to meet them. Caithness feared the worst. 'I fear', he wrote, 'that the earl of Argyll has too little time to prepare himself for so surprising a force'. The same day Caithness wrote to Macdonnell offering to act as intermediary between him and the Earl of Argyll. Caithness also wrote to Lord Neil Campbell urging him to put pressure on the Earl to force him to compromise 'but you know', he wrote, 'as you told me, the unfortunate humour of your brother is to be violent'.[22] The rebels were now in the middle of Caithness's territory. There will be 'want instead of tenants and rents', he wrote to Argyll.[23]

On the 30th Argyll himself went to Carrick to collect arms and ammunition that had arrived by sea.[24] He returned early the next morning to Inveraray. The Earl now received intelligence from Inishtrynich, on the south side of Lochawe, that the rebels were quartered close by at Achlian. The Earl paid the fellow who brought the information £4.6s.8d.[25]

Raiding parties from the confederates were now taking cattle from the Earl's tenants in Glenshira. They took 98 cows, 14 two year olds, 25 stirks, 30 calves, 10 horses and 244 sheep from Kilblane alone. Other stock was taken from Campbell of Ardkinglass and Campbell of Strachur's tenants.[26]

On 1 June the Earl distributed the arms and ammunition he had received. Lord Macdonnell was now deep in Ardkinglass's country at the head of Loch Fyne, and the Earl and his men stood to their arms upon an alarm that the rebels were marching towards them. In fact they were to bypass Inveraray on the southern side of Loch Fyne.[27]

Despite the arrival of the ammunition Argyll was outnumbered and he knew it. Reluctantly he agreed to let Caithness negotiate a settlement with the rebels. 'I expect this day to hear of an interview between the two Highland princes E C and L McD', he wrote to the Earl of Moray on 5 June. 'I know L McD and he will make some odd story of it, but so long as I put him out of the shire and dissipate his convocation which by God's blessing I doubt not to do so and make him and other submit themselves I care not what to say'.[28]

Caithness's most effective argument to Lord Macdonnell and the Macleans was that the Primate James Sharp had been murdered, the western Lowlands were up in arms and Claverhouse and the government troops had been defeated at Loudon Hill. The administration was facing its greatest challenge since the Restoration.

The confederates had 'come the length of Inveraray', wrote Rory Macdonald,

> where though they were in a condition to have destroyed all his [Argyll's] country yet being informed of the late insurrection and rebellion in the west against His Majesty they returned immediately home laying aside private quarrels and preferring His Majesty's interest to all they enjoy in the world.[29]

The rebels went so far as to write a petition to the government stating that despite the oppression of the Earl of Argyll that had caused their people to have no means of subsistence left to them, they now wished 'to join with His Majesty's forces ... and to repair to such places as your lordships think fit'.[30] Some of the Council wished to accept the offer. Argyll, however, had proclaimed that both the Macleans and Macdonalds were papists, a statement Rory Macdonald violently denied, but at the height of the Popish Plot [which was supposed to replace the King with his Roman Catholic brother the Duke of York], the administration dared not accept the confederates's offer.

So ended the Maclean-Macdonald counter attack that had started off with such high hopes. Instead it had achieved nothing except once more illustrating the Highlanders' ability to march across rough country in bad weather with remarkable speed. Despite its tactical success the foray failed. It failed because the confederates were torn in two by their loyalty to the Crown and their need to defy Argyll. They had no desire to be rebels. However, whilst the Earl's patron Lauderdale had the King's ear the confederates were doomed. They were never going to win royal favour. Victory between them and Argyll would be decided in Whitehall, not in the Braes of Glenshira.

Notes

1. EUL. Argyll Transcripts 1679. Accounts of Archibald 9th Earl of Argyll.
2. He had evidently now succeeded his father as Maclean of Grishipol.
3. There were a number of Williamsons who were burgesses of Dumbarton in the seventeenth century. This Patrick was treasurer from 1657–58 m [*Dumbarton Common Good Accounts 1614–1660*. 311–2].
4. ICP Bundle 487, 371.
5. ICP Bundle 471, 157.
6. See Eveline Cruckshanks (ed) *The Stuart Courts* (2000) particularly Sonya Wynne 'The Mistresses of Charles II and Restoration Court Politics'; Gerald Aylmer 'Patronage at the Court of Charles II'; Brian Weiser 'Access and Petitioning during the Reign of Charles II'.
7. Ian Grimble *Chief of Mackay* (1965).
8. *Scots Brigade*, I, 505; *Huweliijeken van Miliairen*, 141.
9. In the 1679 list of 'these in the Castle of Breckach in Coll' is headed by 'Donald McLaine, Coll's brother a papist'; he was probably one of those 'deluded by Father O Donnell'.
10. *RPCS* 3rd Series vii, 74.
11. NAS GD112, 1112.
12. ICP Bundle 472. 172.
13. ICP Bundle 472. 171.
14. NAS GD112, 1112.
15. EUL. Argyll Transcripts 1679. Accounts of the 9th Earl of Argyll.
16. NLS MS 975. 45.
17. NAS CH2. 984.1.324.

18. NAS GD112, 1118: Inveraray 12 May 1679. Earl of Argyll to Earl of Caithness.
19. ICP Bundle 472. 180.
20. NAS GD112, 1119: Castle Kylchurn 26 May 1679.
21. Ibid, 1120: Balloch 26 May 1679. Copy Earl of Caithness to Earl of Moray
22. Ibid, 1125: Finlanrig 29 May 1679 Earl of Caithness to Lord Neil Campbell.
23. Ibid, 1129: 31 May 1679 Caithness to Argyll.
24. Moray MSS Box 6, 48 Inveraray 5 June 1679 Argyll to Moray.
25. EUL Argyll Transcripts Accounts of the 9th Earl 1679.
26. ICP Bundle 70: Ane Acompt of the Kowes, horse sheep etc taken away be Aeneas Lord McDonald and his complices in June 1679.
27. ICP 472. 180.
28. Moray MSS Box 6. 48.
29. ICP Bundle 470. 134.
30. Ibid 472. 181.

Chapter Nine

The Earl tries again. June–August 1679

On 5 June 1679 Argyll noted in his diary: 'I had notice McD was on his return'.[1] The Earl went on the offensive. The following day was a Friday and Argyll, having received victuals from the Clyde, prepared to march north. He was unable to start until the following day, by which time the Confederates were past Achallader.

On the way north the Earl met Lochiel. This most plausible of rogues had written to Argyll on 3 June of the misfortunes he had had in

> drawing my men together, though I can confess there can be no excuse when your lordship's interest has so much at stake.[2]

He went on to say that the following day he would be at the Corran of Ardgour and would be ready to march towards the Earl:

> which I think more to your lordship's advantage than to meddle with the rebels cows.

Despite this suggestion it was cattle that were to be Lochiel's chief concern for the next few weeks. Meanwhile things were moving to a climax in the Lowlands. On 7 June the Council wrote to Argyll that the fanatics in the west had formed themselves into a dangerous rebellion whose numbers were daily on the increase. 'We have therefore thought fit', they wrote:

> to desire your lordship may with the greatest expedition your circumstances can allow, to disentangle yourself from your expedition [and] repair to the king's host and to join the forces under the Earl of Linlithgow.

Argyll was to claim that he did not receive this letter until he was in Lochaber.[3] By the time he replied to it he was at Duart, having marched and counter-marched throughout Lord Macdonnell's country before sailing down Loch Linnhe to Mull.[4]

* * *

On 14 June Lochiel had been dispatched from Achallader to Morvern. His orders were to seize any cows there that belonged to the Clan Ewen, plus any others that they owned in Sunart,

Ardnamurchan, Kingerloch and Ardgour. He was also instructed to capture any rebels he found, and that if any of his own people had given shelter to the Macleans, or had concealed their goods, he was to treat them as rebels.[5]

The Cameron chief did not return until after Argyll left the country. Rory Macdonald was to claim that he carried off 800–900 cows from Lord Macdonnell's lands in Morar.[6] Lochiel himself wrote to the Earl on 27 June reporting that the party he had sent to Morar returned to him the previous day. They had taken two days to drive the cattle they had removed through the passes. Not all had returned. A third of the party was missing. 'I believe their own disorder did occasion the most part of the loss', wrote Lochiel.[7]

He also reported that Lord Macdonnell and Keppoch were planning to join together the following week and to fall on Lochiel's country:

> and use us in the same manner they were dealt with themselves, so I think your lordship would do well to prepare for our relief, for if he once ... [indecipherable] ... we have no shelter or strong place to drive our goods in to.

Lochiel had been speaking to Cornet John Davidson about rebuilding the barracks at Inverlochy. Davidson was prepared to make accommodation for 300 soldiers for £200 sterling.

The Cameron chief intended to send some of the cattle his men had 'removed' in a drove to the south. He had arranged with an unidentified Macdonald to take them for him. The latter already had twenty cows for the drove coming from Mull, forty from Tiree and another twenty specifically from Druimgigha, which is also in Mull. Two hundred cows had been taken from Morar: however, some had been 'abused' by Argyll's men. He had

> laid out some cows for your lordship's use, but some of the soldiers got in amongst them and made havoc of all in spite of what I and others could do.

Lochiel spent the next day sorting out the shambles caused by the soldiers' lack of experience in handling the cattle.

* * *

On 26 June the Earl returned to Duart and 'made ready'[8] for the next phase of the campaign. Two days later he wrote to the Earl of Moray to say that the appalling weather had made the rivers unfordable, as a result the Council's letter had failed to reach him; his march had been much slower than he had expected; the River Spey was impassable, and as the whole country had been laid waste, his men were short of provisions. Lochiel had also failed to produce cows for him on time. As usual everybody else, except the Earl, was to blame.[9]

Argyll continues that he had been forced to march to Inverlochy, where he had arranged for boats and oatmeal to be ready for him. He had then proposed to set up his base at the head of Loch Ness from where he could have, he claimed, broken up the rebels' forces. However, when he received the Council's letter he decided that 'it was not proper for me to advance further but return to Inverlochy'. He goes on to say that he had written to Macleod, Clanranald and spoken to Lochiel and Sleat and told them to take their fencible men with forty days provisions to 'make all haste to attend his majesty's forces in the Lowlands'. As soon as it was possible Argyll himself proposed to join them 'with all who will follow me'.

Argyll also wrote a brief letter to the Council on the 27th saying he had done all he could to obey their commands

> which was very much my own inclination, but in the circumstances I was entangled whereof the earl of Moray will give your lordships a particular account it was impossible.[10]

It is evident from his diary that Argyll was being economical with the truth. He had no intention of going to the Lowlands, as he was not going to miss the opportunity of crushing the Macleans once and for all. On the 28th, the same day that he had written to Moray, he set sail. The Earl's first stop was the isle of Carna in Loch Sunart where he seized Ardgour's brothers. That night he slept at Mingary Castle in Ardnamurchan.[11]

The Earl's expedition consisted of his frigate and at least two other boats, including in all probability his galley and one birlinn. There were probably several more. Colonel Menzies was present with his company and the royal troops. The following day the party landed at Croig at Mornish in the north-west of Mull. It is probably now that some of Argyll's party killed Torloisk's brother Hector and two other Macleans. They also murdered James Beaton and Magnus Morison [Ò Muirgheasáin] of Penmore.[12] The latter was the last of an old and illustrious family of poets who for many generations had served both the Macleans of Duart and Macleods of Dunvegan.[13] Later that day the Earl's armada sailed for Loch Eartharna in Coll, spending the night at sea.

The following day they sailed along the coast of Coll. That evening they anchored in *Loch nan Caisteal*, in front of Coll's castle of Breacachadh. The castle is not sited on a naturally defensive position. On the western side the ground is boggy. The sea partially protects it to the south and east. However, this only provides protection at high tide, for when it ebbs a wide expanse of sandy beach is revealed. On the north landward approach is an extensive tract of machair.

The castle consists of a keep of four-storeys and a garret, and a three-storey circular flanking tower. A stone parapet wall joins them. The wall had been raised in the late sixteenth century and provided with musketry loops and other 'gude devices for defence'.[14]

The recent discovery of a cannon ball in the walls of the keep suggests that the castle did not surrender without a struggle. Argyll had, however, brought with him a letter from the Laird of Coll to his brother Donald which, as we have seen, ordered him to give up the castle to his uncles so that they might in their turn hand it over to Argyll's representative.[15] This is presumably what happened, for the Earl notes that the castle capitulated that night.[16]

On 2 July Argyll and Coll's brother Donald signed articles of capitulation. The latter agreed to march out of the Castle of Breacachadh before sunset. He also agreed to deliver up all the arms, ammunition and provisions within the castle. Dugald Campbell, the Earl's servitor, wrote the articles. Lord Neil Campbell, Colonel Menzies and Coll's uncles Neil Maclean of Drimnacross and John Maclean of Totronald witnessed them.[17]

* * *

The following day Donald the captain of Breacachadh Castle handed in two lists of the men he had with him in the castle. Although they are almost identical, one is entitled 'a list of all the men and souldiers that served under Donald McLeane in the House of Breackaich'. The other does not say that they were soldiers. As these papers contain the earliest names of Coll's 'household men' they are valuable to our understanding of the composition of Coll's *luchd-tighe*, and are reproduced at

Annex A. They were written in Scots. The writer was someone with only a rudimentary knowledge of Gaelic, however, they help identify who these men were.

The lists contain the names of more than the 'twenty of my own' men that Coll mentioned in the postscript to his letter to his uncles, but there can be little doubt that these are the men he was referring to. The first man in the list is *Iain Mclachlan vc Allane alias McLeane*. His patronymic makes it certain that he is the son of Captain Lachlan Maclean of Hynish, Tiree who was killed at Inverkeithing. Iain MacAllane's two brothers *Donald McLachlane Vc Allane alias McLeane* and *Neill viz his brother* [Neil Og] are listed as living in *Kealiscollich*[18] [Caolis] and *Kilbryd* [Kilbride].

Allan Crossapol does not mention *Iain Mclachlan vc Allane alias McLeane* in his manuscript, which suggests that he later accompanied his chief to the Netherlands and never returned.[19] He does, however, mention the second of the brothers Donald. Crossapol says that he was:

a remarkably strong man. He was at Holland for some time, at his return there was a challenge between the Laird of Coll and a brave Gentleman of the Locheil family, it seems the Laird of Coll and this man differ'd after dinner and nothing would settle the matter but swords which Coll [had] no experience of, they appointed an hour to meet at the back of the Castle of Breakacha, this Camron came to the ground before the Laird of Coll, but Donald MacLachlan was very much afraid f[or] Coll that he wished if possible to keep back the Challenge, he made up to the foresaid Mr Cameron and asked what he meant by coming there so early, or if it was to fight Coll that it would be more prudent in him to dropt it, Cameron immediately damn'd Donald MacLachlan and began to kick him, Donald Mac Lachlan got hold of him and got on top of him at once and bruised him so much that he was not able to Engage in the challenge any more. The Laird of Coll never allowed Donald Mac Lachlan to leave the Country afterwards[.] He lived at Crossapol for some time and at the Farm of Knock.[20]

It is clear from this list that these three brothers were now permanent members of Coll's *luchd-tighe*. They are just the family one would expect to have done so once they had lost their own land. As we have seen Neil Mor lost Quinish when he was murdered; his son Allan lost Auchillenan and Drimnin when Coll had to hand it over to Sir Donald Campbell; Captain Lachlan's family lost Hynish in Tiree and returned to Coll after their father was killed at the battle of Inverkeithing.[21] 'Iain McLachlan Vc Allane alias McLeane's position in both lists after Coll's brother suggests that he was probably the man in charge of Coll's bodyguard.

This habit of becoming professional soldiers once a family had lost its estate was to be repeated. Other Coll cadets, such as the Macleans of Auchnasaul, Grishipol, Drimnacross and the Isle of Muck, managed to hold on to their properties rather longer than Neil Mor's descendants, and reinforced their hold on them by lending money to their chief. However, when Auchnasaul, Grishipol and the Isle of Muck families eventually lost their inheritance, they too became professional soldiers. It was the only means at their disposal to maintain their status as 'gentlemen' and not descend into the ranks of the peasantry. It was not just in Coll that this pattern developed. As we shall see, it was also to occur in Tiree when the incoming Campbells deprived the Maclean tacksmen of their lands. They, however, had no *luchd-tighe* available for them to join. Instead they joined the British army as private soldiers or the Jacobites or both.

Most of the rest of the garrison of Breacachadh in 1679 are described only by their patronymics. There are, however, two exceptions: *Duncan McDonald Vc Ian* and his brother *Dugall*. They are described as living in *Ardness* [Ardnish] and as being *Mcphaidens* [MacFadyens]. Also in Ardnish are *Iain McNeill Vc Innes* and his brothers *Gwn* [Ewen], *Archibald* and *Donald Baine*. From their living in Ardnish, which according to Coll tradition was the original MacFadyen toun in Coll, and the popularity of the forename Angus [*Innes*] among MacFadyens it is likely that these two sets of brothers are cousins. As we have seen the MacFadyens had probably been members of the Coll *luchd-tighe* since at least the early seventeenth century.

The only other man identifiable by a surname in the list is *Murdo tollick alias Campbell* described as *Murchie Collich* in the second list. He is probably a member of the old Barbreck Campbells, who had possibly served in the bodyguard for several generations. Finally although he is not given a surname but a description: *Finlay the smith* [*Finley McIllmickall smith in Uig* in the second list] it may be possible to identify him as one of the hereditary blacksmiths in Uig surnamed Macdonald who often used the unusual (at least in Coll) forename Finlay.

What I think we are seeing is the late seventeenth-century survival of the chief's *luchd-tighe* or 'household men'. They all live relatively close to the castle and could reach it quickly in an emergency. Lachlan Maclean of Coll certainly had need of a bodyguard in 1679 and was probably to use them as the nucleus for the company of soldiers he was later to raise. They also strengthen my case that service in Coll's bodyguard was a hereditary calling.

It is worth noting that another Collach who probably accompanied Lachlan of Coll to the Netherlands was a Charles Maclean, corporal in Mackay's Regiment in 1685.[22] In that year he married Maria, daughter of Pieter van der Wiel. When their youngest son, Jan, married Anna de Roum he had a drawing painted on wood incorporating the arms of 'Macleane and Roum',[23] which would suggest that Jan was conscious of his ancestry and thought of himself as a gentleman, which of course the *luchd-tighe* were considered to be.

* * *

Argyll spent the night of 2 July at Breacachadh. The following day he left for Tiree, landing at Caolis and began the siege of the fort in Loch Huileboll. The Earl lodged that night at Crossapol in Tiree.[24] The siege lasted five days and the fort only surrendered after cannon had been used on it. The garrison, as in Coll, agreed to march out of the castle by sunset and deliver up their arms, ammunition and provisions to the Earl.

John Maclean in Cornaigmor commanded the garrison in Tiree. He had his tack rent free, presumably as the castle's captain. The garrison also included Brolas's brother Hector Og in Cornaigbeg, Hugh Maclean in Balephetrish, Duart's former bailie in Tiree, Hector Fraser son of the parish minister and seven other Macleans.[25]

On Friday 11 July Colonel Menzies left Tiree with a party to attempt to capture Carnaburg. He returned on the Sunday, having failed to persuade the garrison to surrender. On 11 July Coll's uncles came to Argyll in Tiree and signed an agreement whereby they agreed to keep the Castle of Breacachadh for him, and to have sixteen men there as garrison in the King's service. They also agreed to prevent the boats in Coll falling into the rebels' hands. Another clause in the agreement was that they would give protection to anybody who came to them from the Earl or who was pursued by the rebels. They were to keep in good condition in the castle twenty-four firelocks, six swords and six Lochaber axes, and were to deliver the castle up to the Earl whenever he requested it.[26]

The Earl left Tiree on 15 July, sailed for Carnaburg but landed at Gometra, probably spending the night at Acarsaid Mor on the north-west of the island. The next day he went to visit Iona. In his absence a party sallied out of Carnaburg, killed two of the Earl's men and rescued three prisoners.[27] The Earl was undoubtedly furious. He anchored that night at Fladda, also in the Treshnish Islands and another prisoner, Hugh Maclean of Carna's grandson, escaped.

It was now evident, even to Argyll that he was not going to capture Carnaburg. On the 17th a peace treaty was proposed to the Macleans and the next day was spent in negotiations. On Saturday 19 July the Earl writes in his diary, 'we luffed early but by bringing up my stragglers I fell behind Colonel Menzies.' That night they anchored in the Sound of Mull, opposite Kinlochaline Castle, and Argyll sent to Duart for MacConachie.[28] The following day the Islay men came to the Earl. Later in the day Colonel Menzies joined him at his anchorage in Aros Bay.

On the Monday it blew so hard and continuously that the Earl could do no more than send for more cows. The next day, in contrast, it was calm. The Earl moved to Kinlochaline and the siege there began in earnest.

On 24 July Argyll received a letter from the Chancellor ordering him to report to the Council. Still the Earl lingered. That day he wrote to his brother-in-law, the Earl of Moray, telling him that he had received the Chancellor's letter and that he would do all in his power to obey the Council's demand but 'if I fall a day short' he would let them know. He went on to tell his brother-in-law that Kinlochaline had at last surrendered after very obstinate resistance.[29]

On the 6 August, instead of heading for Edinburgh, Argyll returned to Tobermory in an attempt to finalise arrangements with Brolas. He had hoped that Carnaburg would be surrendered to him on 9 August. However, on the 8th he received a message from Carnaburg's garrison that none of them would come near him on that day because 'it was a dismal day this year'.[30]

The Earl dared not remain any longer in the islands. He handed over negotiations to his brother and then left for Edinburgh. He arrived there on Tuesday 12 August and attended the Council the following day. It was now six weeks since the rebels in the Western Lowlands had been defeated at Bothwell Bridge and the aftermath of the rebellion was discussed. Although several of Argyll's enemies were present at the Council meeting there is no mention in the minutes of disapproval of Argyll's action in failing to bring his men to help put down the rebellion, whilst a process of forfeiture against the Lord Macdonnell, Keppoch and Torloisk was approved by the Council.

Argyll returned to Inveraray on 23 August. The following day he wrote to Moray that he expected that Brolas would now agree to accept the conditions the Macleans had previously refused.[31] In fact a treaty had been signed on 11 August at Tobermory in which the Macleans agreed to release their prisoners, and accept that they were not to travel into the shire of Argyll further than the Isle of Mull without a pass from the Governor of Duart.

The Macleans had also to agree not to molest any of the Earl's tenants. On his part Argyll was to receive Brolas and his new companions into the King's protection until 1 May 1680 and to order all officers and soldiers under his command not to trouble the Macleans. That Brolas obtained such good terms is a testimony to the strength of Carnaburg, and to Argyll's failure to capture it. For while Carnaburg held out the Macleans could withdraw into it when Argyll approached and then sally forth once he withdrew, as he would have to once the weather turned rough. There is a new truculence in the Macleans' behaviour after the Earl's 1679 expedition.

It is, however, impossible not to be impressed by the Earl's tactical handling of the campaign against the Macleans in 1678 and 1679. By invading Mull in mid-winter he had obtained complete surprise and succeeded in disarming most of Mull. The Earl's reaction to the Maclean-Macdonald invasion of the mainland was also impressive. Despite being outnumbered Argyll had deterred the invaders from following Montrose's example and sacking Inveraray. Once the rebels began to withdraw he had kept at their heels until they dispersed. He had then immediately gone on the offensive, launched a naval assault on the Isles and eliminated opposition in the north-west of Mull, Coll, Tiree and Morvern.

Argyll's one tactical failure was in not capturing Carnaburg. It was a crucial failure. Not only did it enable the Macleans to obtain better terms, but gave them a firm base from which to re-occupy Mull once Argyll's men withdrew. It was a lesson that was not lost on the Macleans.

Politically, however, the Earl's strategy was a disaster. By refusing to obey the Council's orders he had confirmed their opinion that Argyll believed he was above the commonweal. It was not a wise strategy, particularly at this time.

Notes

1. ICP Bundle 472. 180.
2. Ibid 471, 165.
3. Moray MSS Box 6, 49: Duart 28 June Argyll to Moray.
4. ICP Bundle 472. 180.
5. Ibid 471. 162.
6. Ibid 470. 134.
7. NLS MS 975. 47.
8. ICP Bundle 472. 180.
9. Moray MSS Box 6. 49.
10. ICP Bundle 471. 167.
11. ICP Bundle 472. 180.
12. Ibid 470, 134.
13. Derick S Thomson (ed) *The Companion to Gaelic Scotland* (1983), 219–20.
14. *RCAHMS* Argyll vol. iii, 177–184; Nicholas Maclean-Bristol *Murder under Trust* (1999), 215–217.
15. ICP Bundle 471. 159.
16. Ibid 470, 180.
17. ICP Fullerton Transcripts 2 July 1679.
18. The second list says 'his wyf in Kealiscollich'.
19. He is likely to be the 'John McLane then in Hayvenesh [Hynish ?] now in Greishoboll' [NAS. CC12. 1. 1. 24(v)].
20. As Lachlan of Coll could not have been described as having no experience in the use of a sword, this event must have taken place after his death.
21. Hynish [Haivenish or Heinishe] was 6merk land. In 1662 it paid £200 money rent the highest in Tiree and in 1663 Lauchlan Mc Lauchlane vc ewine was to pay 'the soume of sextein scoire merks' [EUL. Argyll Rentals. Vol. 2. Mic. M. 676, 28a, 32].
22. It is possible that he is the *Charles McIllespick Vc Rorie* in the 1679 list. Several of those men who came with Coll married Dutch women [*Huweliijeken van Militairen* 152, 154, 155, 157].
23. Private communication to me by the late Dr Johannes Maclean in March 1973. The drawing was then in the possession of Mrs Van der Wal-Havelstadt of Nymegen, *Gens Nostra* (Maart 1973), 61, 62.
24. ICP Bundle 472. 180.
25. Ibid, 194..
26. Ibid, 187.
27. Ibid, 180..
28. This was Campbell of Inverawe's patronymic, almost anglicised out of recognition.
29. Moray MSS Box 6, 53.
30. I have yet to discover what is a 'Dismal Day'.
31. Moray MSS. Box 6, 47.

Chapter Ten

The end of the Earl of Argyll?[1]

In December 1679 the King's brother James, Duke of York arrived in Edinburgh.[2] He came ostensibly as Commissioner to the Scots Parliament. In fact James, who was a Roman Catholic, had been sent into internal exile to take some of the heat out of the anti-popish uproar in London. James's arrival at Holyrood House and his involvement in Scottish politics were in due course to have a profound effect on the future of the Macleans.

James was an able administrator. He was also a weak man, who was influenced by whoever had last spoken to him and his promises were not to be relied on. As the lawyer Fountainhall, a loyalist but a clear-sighted one, noted: James 'was a silly man'.[3]

The Duke's arrival further undermined Argyll's position. As a Roman Catholic James tended to favour his co-religionists, who included Argyll's hereditary enemy the Marquess of Huntly, as well as the Maclean's ally Lord Macdonnell. He was also sympathetic to old loyalists and wished to 'preserve that ancient and loyal clan of the Maclanes'.[4] However, the most serious threat to the Earl's position was James's secret hostility to Argyll's patron John Duke of Lauderdale. It was a hostility based on distaste for Lauderdale's ambiguous political past and his cronies' corruption.

After some initial opposition to a papist presiding over the Council, the Earl of Argyll was successful in exploiting James's obsessive support of hierarchy against disorderly elements in society. He explained to the Duke that both broken men and their patrons hated the Campbells, because they kept the peace in the Highlands. Argyll also flattered James's vanity by suggesting that he should summon the leading Highlanders involved in disputes, and by his superior wisdom resolve them personally.

He also agreed to James's initial plan to end his dispute with the Macleans. This proposal, which would certainly have freed the Earl from his entanglement, was that the Crown should pay off Maclean of Duart's debts. Such an action would reward a loyal clan and maintain the balance of power in the Highlands. For James, like his grandfather King James VI, believed that the Earl of Argyll was 'greater than it were fit for a subject to be'.[5] If he were also to have Maclean's estate the position would be even less acceptable. The only problem was that the Crown had no prospect of finding the money to pay off Duart's debt.

The total revenue of the Scots government was only £60,000 a year and the English Parliament was deliberately starving the Court of funds during the panic over the 'Popish Plot'. Another plan was required. This time James suggested that instead of Maclean's estate, Argyll should receive forfeited property in the south-west of Scotland. This idea was no more acceptable to the Earl. Not only would it involve him in forcibly exacting revenue from a less convenient part of the country, it would also lose him the last vestige of his support among Lowland Presbyterians who still had a lingering affection for the memory of his father.

James returned to London later that month, and in March he wrote:

> his majestie will settle the affaire of the Macklens so as they will have reason to be satisfyed ... tho, may be, all that is desired by them cannot be done; therefore pray advise them that they behave themselves so in the meane tyme not to give advantage against them ...

Unfortunately for the Macleans this warning came too late. In February Brolas, when writing to his cousin Lachlan Maclean, the Earl's bailie in Tiree, stated that James and the Council had summoned him 'and the rest of my friends' to Edinburgh to settle the dispute. He added that he had sent his brother, Hector Og to keep 'the rents upon the tenants hands ... I have given commands to carry themselves civilly to you as to any that belong to my lord of Argyll there'.[6]

Hector Og's idea of treating the Earl's servants civilly was to land in Tiree on 15 February with a hundred fully armed men in a twelve-oared birlinn. He then marched on Heylipol Castle. Alexander Campbell, the governor, who had a garrison of sixty regular soldiers, reported that when they arrived the invaders 'lay two nights near us, soldier like and kept sentries constantly'.[7] They then cut off supplies to the garrison, stopped them communicating with their allies in Coll, prevented them from collecting the public dues or Argyll's rents and obtained free quarter on the Earl's tenants.

The rebels also commandeered twenty bolls of meal ear-marked for the garrison, whose situation now became so desperate that at the end of March the Government was forced to send out a party of twenty-four men led by a sergeant to relieve them. The relief crossed Tiree to Kenovay to treat with Hector Og. Hector told them in plain terms that he had orders from Brolas to keep meal and peats from the garrison, and the relieving party having no orders to engage the rebels, somewhat feebly returned to Heylipol. On the way they confiscated some cows from tenants who owed rent to Argyll. This infuriated the islanders, who gathered from all corners of Tiree. Among them was Hugh Maclean in Balliphetrish. He went up to the castle gate and offered violence to the sentries. Hector Og eventually let the garrison have ten bolls of meal.[8]

When asked by what authority he justified his actions, Hector Og replied that Brolas had a warrant for them from the Council. This was certainly untrue, but it shows how far the balance of power in Edinburgh was believed to be shifting in the Macleans' favour. Another ominous sign for the Earl was that when he brought the first unconfirmed report of Hector Og's action before the Council they were inclined to credit Brolas's and Torloisk's positive denial. Later they even suggested that an outbreak of violence so favourable to Argyll must spring from Campbell manipulation. However, when the truth became clear, official displeasure was reversed, particularly after the Macleans' protector, Lord Macdonnell, was himself discredited by brawling with officials.

On 10 April Lauderdale authorised the Council to investigate affairs in Tiree in order to ensure that Argyll was not prejudiced in his just rights. As the Macleans prevaricated the Council's attitude to them hardened and Argyll felt sufficiently encouraged to suggest that the Macleans should be ordered to surrender Carnaburg.[9]

The enquiry was not completed until July, but it had already exposed the folly of the Macleans' actions. James's one conspicuous ability was as a military, naval and financial administrator. He had quickly noticed that the nation was not getting any return for its expenditure on the two Highland companies. As the captains pocketed most of it, the men were not receiving their pay. They were also seldom mustered except for Argyll's or Caithness's private campaigns. Meanwhile cattle raiding flourished. James saw that the money saved by abolishing the independent companies could be used to finance a scheme that would give the great Highland landowners responsibility for preventing or punishing local raids. Although Argyll was named among those to be given these new powers, he was not happy about the new dispensation and intrigued to save his own company.[10]

Brolas may have been provoked into ordering the attack on Tiree by having soldiers quartered on him. If he had, the result for him was far worse for the crisis brought about by the reprieve of the companies under Colonel Menzie's command, which Argyll sent to relieve Heylipol.[11] They did so, apparently, without further conflict

The reprieve for the independent companies meant that James's scheme was shelved. As it was planned largely to benefit James's favourite, Huntly, it probably prejudiced him further against Argyll.

Argyll also had reason to be pleased with the next official proposal to save the Macleans of Duart, since it was on a far smaller scale than before. In May James proposed to his brother that, if Argyll would fulfil the agreement Lauderdale had obtained from the King to settle lands worth £200 a year on Sir John, the Crown should buy other land from him, worth an equal amount. This would bring Sir John's income to a respectable £500 a year[12] and, to forestall the objection which had wrecked the previous proposal, would let Argyll keep the rents of what land it purchased until the money was actually paid.

Lauderdale's letter to Argyll contained a warning hint that Charles wanted the matter settled quickly. Argyll replied in June expressing his willingness to accept, but quietly reduced the share of the Duart Estate he was to give to Maclean to land worth £200 a year. This change did not at once sink in at Court. Charles expressed his satisfaction and, no doubt with the recent troubles in mind, suggested that the estate given to Sir John should be in Tiree. Argyll probably accepted that Tiree, rather than Morvern, should go to Maclean, as the damage done there that spring greatly reduced its value. King Charles now ordered the Scottish Treasury to enquire into the island's rental value.[13] And Argyll was soon planning to raise Tiree rents to an artificially high level in order to reduce the real value of the estate being given Sir John.

Despite James's irritation with him, Argyll's influence was still considerable. In 1679 Moray had written to the Earl to say he had heard from the Archbishop of St Andrews 'that the Bishoprick of Argyll was again to be vacant. 'And to know yr inclination for filing of it'.[14] In March 1680 he was instrumental in having Mr Hector Maclean Minister of Morvern made Bishop of Argyll.[15] Argyll's choice of a Maclean as bishop is at first surprising. Mr Hector was the Minister of Morvern. He was a pluralist and had also become Minister of Dunoon. Although he had been one of Sir Allan Maclean's advisers, he is suspected of having been behind the impossibly high Tiree rental designed to defraud Sir John Maclean and by 1680 he was firmly in Argyll's pocket. He was not necessarily entirely venal and it is clear that as bishop, he and the Earl planned to revitalise the church in Argyll.

Mr Hector's residence in Dunoon was not far across the water from that of the Bishop of the Isles's seat at Rothesay in Bute. Despite their proximity the two bishops did not pursue a united policy. Bishop Graham of the Isles, for all his later reputation as 'one of the silliest Bishops in the world', began legal proceedings against the Earl for the dilapidation of church property and unpaid teinds amounting to over half the revenue of the Bishopric of the Isles.[16] A similar situation existed in the Bishopric of Argyll, but it is perhaps not surprising that Mr Hector made no such move against his patron.[17] His quiescence contrasts unpleasantly with his sharp practice in his own personal financial affairs. He had purchased a debt due to his wife's uncle from Maclean of Coll. These debts had been outstanding since 1630. The Coll debt was for £1,000 plus the accumulating interest.

In July 1680 Lachlan Maclean of Coll, who was then in Glasgow, was arrested for debt at the Bishop's instance. He was taken before the Lords of Session and Council and it was decided that with his grandfather's estate he had also inherited its debts. Mr Alexander Maclean, to whom his father Bishop Hector had assigned these debts, agreed to liberate Coll, but only in exchange for a new bond which acknowledged both the debt and the interest. Coll's uncle and his cousin Charles Maclean, the drover, son of John Maclean of Grishipol, agreed to stand caution for him. The arrest had come as a surprise for, as Coll wrote to the Earl of Argyll in October 1680, when he next came to Edinburgh he would need letters of protection, 'lest any other deal with me as the Bishop of Argyll did'.[18]

Lachlan of Coll's arrest may have been the final straw that persuaded him to seek his fortunes overseas for he now left Scotland for the Netherlands. He went there initially as a volunteer in the Scots Brigade in Dutch service but, as he took some of his own men with him, he was soon given command of a company. On the 16 December 1681 he took the oath to the States General.[19] He was to serve for three years in the Scots Brigade, and was considered to be 'a man of rare military genius'.[20]

* * *

Lauderdale's ambiguous policies were by now totally discredited. In October 1680 he was finally dismissed as Secretary. His successor and loyal supporter the Earl of Moray, Argyll's former brother-in-law and friend, was a political lightweight. Lauderdale's dismissal was a heavy blow to Argyll, but it was partly balanced by the appointment as Privy Councillor of his son Lord Lorne (admittedly hitherto a playboy) and by the death in December of Lord Macdonnell, the Macleans' most vigorous ally.

Despite Lauderdale's fall Argyll retained a free hand in Mull, whatever the Council decided. For instance when in August, Lochbuie complained to the Council that his son Hector, who had collaborated with the Campbells, and was still illegally holding Moy Castle, the Council outlawed Hector. However, he continued to occupy the castle. When in December Argyll complained that the Macleans had not surrendered Duart Castle the Council brushed aside the latter's argument that it was not part of the Duart estate but a private residence. The Council repeated their order the following February that the Castle be surrendered. Reluctantly the Macleans complied.[21]

In February 1681 James asked Argyll, as a personal favour to himself, to convert to Roman Catholicism. He added a semi-promise that he would make him 'the greatest man in Scotland'.[22] The Duke was apparently prepared to forget the claims of the loyalist Macleans and the Roman Catholic Huntly. This was typical of James's style of favouritism: behind his talk about trusting only loyalists, especially where conversion occurred, he would rejoice more over the one sheep which had strayed and been recovered, than the ninety-nine which had remained in the fold.

Argyll's refusal drove James into the camp of the Earl's enemies at Court. James's anger increased at the 1681 Parliament when Argyll argued in favour of safeguards against Popery. James was furious and gave his tacit consent to the committee's proposal to deprive him of his heritable jurisdictions. James, however, perhaps recalling how his father's callous sacrifice of unpopular ministers had helped bring about the Exclusion Crisis, changed his mind and quashed the committee's plan. Instead, Parliament formally ratified the 1663 charter granting Argyll the Barony of Duart and Tenandry of Aros.[23]

The Macleans hopes seemed extinguished forever. Argyll had already begun to repair Duart and now went ahead with the agreement concerning Sir John Maclean's pension of £500 a year. The terms were, however, revised so that Argyll need only provide lands worth £200 a year, whilst the Crown purchased the other land worth £300. Ignoring the use his enemies might make of this proposal the Earl used the artificially inflated rental of Tiree, as the basis for a settlement.

On 1 October the Scottish Treasury warned the King that it was not advisable to purchase the Crown's £300 year in Tiree. It was better, as a petition in Sir John's name desired, to provide the sum out of the Earl's yearly feu duties. Charles agreed to this plan as an interim measure until both sides could come to a final agreement.[24]

Meanwhile James turned even more forcefully against Argyll and revived the idea of a commission of enquiry into his estates. One reason for this increased resentment was Argyll's efforts in Parliament to tighten the casual provisions in the Test Act against Roman Catholics. This act imposed an oath of non-resistance and acceptance of the royal supremacy in Church and State on all office holders. No conscientious man could take it, without qualification. And Argyll, who was ordered to swear the oath in early November, was too sensitive of his honour to compromise.

The Earl, as several bishops had done, offered to add a codicil to the oath, which he believed James had agreed to accept, hinting at its inconsistency. At first the Duke scornfully appeared to do so, which would have been politically astute, discrediting Argyll forever with the Presbyterians. However, the Duke's advisers persuaded him instead to send the Earl to Edinburgh Castle for a crime, which was speedily inflated into treason. In December Argyll was tried and found guilty. James declared later that the Government's intention had been to restore him to most of his assets, depriving him only of his Highland jurisdictions, the basis of his power, which he had abused against the Macleans.

Argyll, even if he could have accepted, knew that his enemies were baying for his blood and, after James's frequent changes of mind, had no reason to trust him. On 20 December he escaped from Edinburgh Castle, fleeing to England and then Holland. The Government had now to carry through the Earl's forfeiture in earnest.[25] Suddenly, almost by accident, the whole structure of power and landownership, which had prevailed in the West Highlands with one short break for over thirty years, was shattered.[26]

Notes

1. Much of this chapter is based on PA Hopkins and my so far unpublished book 'From the Sound of Mull'.
2. Hopkins *Glencoe*, 68.
3. Sir John Lauder of Fountainhall *Historical Notices*, I , 327.
4. Hopkins *Glencoe*, 69.
5. *Ibid*
6. ICP Bundle 473. 204.
7. BL MS Stowe 199 fol. 18; ICP Bundle 472. 177; Ibid 473. 203.
8. ICP Bundle 489. 395.
9. *RPCS* 3rd Series, vi, 432; NAS GD 112.39. 1153; BL MS Stowe 199 fol. 18; BL Add. MS 23, 246 fol. 26.
10. Hopkins *Glencoe*, 69.
11. *Ibid*, 70.
12. Hopkins *Glencoe*, 70.
13. *CSPD 1679–80*, 487, 544;
14. ICP Bundle 99. Edinburgh 30 September 1679. Moray to Argyll.

15. Mr Hector Maclean was the representative of the Macleans of Knock a family of hereditary ecclesiastics who are the subject of Paul Hopkins & my 'From the Sound of Mull'.
16. *CSPD 1683–4*, 249.
17. *CSPD 1683–4*, 249; Fountainhall *Historical Notices* ii, 717.
18. NAS RD Dal.58, 557; ICP Bundle 473, 205.
19. James Ferguson *Scots Brigade* I (1899), 504.
20. Robert Douglas of Glenbervie *The Baronage of Scotland* (1798), 373.
21. *RPCS* 3rd Series vi, 519–20, 551, 615–16, 618; *Ibid*, vii, 35–6; Hopkins *Glencoe*, 44, 70–1, 84–5.
22. *A Scots Earl*, 249–50.
23. *Ibid*, 250–2; *APS*, viii, 257–9, 446; Hopkins *Glencoe*, 85; Fountainhall *Historical Notices*, I, 312–313, 327.
24. *Ibid* ii, 533; *CSPD 1680–1*, 522–3; *HMCR* 6th Report. Appx., 633., *HP* I, 318–20.
25. *A Scots Earl*, 252–282; Hopkins *Glencoe*, 85.

Chapter Eleven

The Earl of Argyll's Rebellion[1]

At first there were probably doubts about the finality of Argyll's fall. He petitioned the King showing the injustice of his condemnation, but the exposure in 1683 of the Earl's involvement with the English Whigs' plan for a rising connected with the Rye House Plot, which planned to assassinate both the King and his brother, ended that possibility for good.

Meanwhile the Campbells were temporarily without a leader. The most important Lowland Campbell the Earl of Loudoun was in exile in Holland. Glenorchy the most powerful Campbell in the Highlands was close to ruin. His bid to take over the shire of Caithness, by exploiting Sir John Sinclair's debts, had ended in a bloody clan battle. Glenorchy's men butchered a hundred Sinclairs, and the King stripped him of his earldom. In exchange Charles did give him a new earldom that of Breadalbane, but for two years Glenorchy's future was to say the least precarious.[2]

The Macleans did not benefit as completely as they might have expected from Argyll's fall, but they did well enough out of it. In 1682 the Council ordered that the men Argyll had planted in the Maclean strongholds should surrender them.[3] They used every trick to delay doing so. Inverawe even had the audacity to claim that he occupied Duart Castle merely as tenant of the neighbouring farmland.[4] Until he handed over the castle to the Macleans, he was incarcerated in the tollbooth in Edinburgh.

Donald Campbell in 'the Rock of Carnbulg', and John Cameron of Glendessary in Kinlochaline were treated similarly. The latter was also put under caution of 5,000 merks for uttering 'seditious expressions against His Majesty'.[5] Glendessary also tried to deny the repayment of a debt by Ardgour, which he hoped would give him permanent possession of the latter's land.[6] In the past he might have succeeded, but now he failed.

Slowly but surely the Macleans began to regain their prosperity and status. In 1683 several leading members of the clan were appointed commissioners of the militia, cess and excise in Argyll.[7] Nowhere was the Earl's nemesis so complete than in the new organization of the militia. There were companies in Cowal, Mid-Argyll, Mull, Lorne and Kintyre. Brolas was appointed to command the Mull company. The only Campbell to receive a commission was the loyalist Lochnell in mid-Argyll. The other captains were Lamont, the tutor of Appin and Macneill of Gualacholie.[8] In 1684 the Argyllshire militia was called out to provide men to guard the coast when it was expected that, as part of the Rye House Plot, Argyllshire would be invaded.[9]

The main problem in the complete rehabilitation of the Macleans was that Argyll's creditors had first call on his assets, and the Duart estate was one of them. Several creditors were officers of state, who had bought up the Earl's debts in order to obtain preferential treatment. Their rights were paramount. In addition Argyll's children had to be provided for out of their father's estate, and Sir Allan's widow was claiming her jointure of £250, plus eight years of arrears.[10] At the same time this litigious lady was in the midst of a long action in the Court of Session against Katherine Campbell, old Torloisk's widow, who refused to hand back silver plate, gold rings and jewels given to her for safe keeping.[11]

Sir John Maclean of Duart was awarded land in Mull, Morvern and the Two Ends of Coll, receiving a warrant for his charter on 14 June 1684. Other charters, issued on the same day, confirmed leading Macleans in the estates they had previously held from Argyll. They were now to be held of the Crown.[12]

One additional benefit from Argyll's fall was that central government had for the first time an opportunity to establish a judicial system that had some hope of succeeding. It was badly needed. The years of raid and counter-raid by Macleans and Campbells had left a legacy of chaos and demoralisation in Mull and the surrounding area. Too many people, complained Mr John Beaton the erudite Minister of Kilninian and Kilmore, in March 1683 were 'habituated to stealing, robbing from and oppressing others living peacably in those parts'.[13] He himself had suffered. Once it had been the Campbells or Colonel Menzies and his soldiers who drove away his livestock and plundered his house. Now it was his own parishioners who did so in retaliation when he tried to recover his teinds.

* * *

In Holland Lachlan Maclean of Coll, as we have seen, was serving in a regiment of the Scots Brigade commanded by Colonel Hugh Mackay of Scourie. On 24 November 1684 the Hon. Aeneas Mackay, second son of Lord Reay succeeded him.[14] Lachlan presumably returned home to Coll and was there when Argyll invaded Scotland in May 1685. The Earl's choice (in opposition to his Lowland colleagues) of Argyllshire as the setting for his campaign caught the Government off balance. The shire's defences had been neglected. The Earl of Dumbarton was guarding the south-west coast of Scotland, where the hotter Presbyterians seemed about to rise in concert with Argyll and had with him not only the regular army but a contingent of the best men in the militia from the southern Highlands. More men were concentrated on the Forth-Clyde line.

Many of the local forces hastily raised to fight Argyll were lacking in both experience and training.[15] The Government compensated for this deficiency by weight of numbers. Even had the Clan Campbell not been divided, with many gentlemen more or less pro-government, and more neutral or in detention, it could never have matched the Highland contingents now officially called out against it. The Council began 'puringe [pouring] in' men into Argyllshire to oppose the Earl, however, they were largely lacking in discipline. They were also under the incompetent over-cautious leadership of the Earl of Atholl.

Argyll's first landing on his voyage from Holland to Scotland was bungled. It was a ham-fisted attempt to gain support and supplies in Orkney. Instead it merely gave the Government advance warning of his movements. In Argyllshire, having sailed down the Sound of Mull, the Earl landed his son Charles at Dunstaffnage in order to raise Lorne.

On 13 May (five days before Atholl even left Edinburgh), Argyll came close to cutting off Steuart of Ballechin, Atholl's deputy, in Islay with the Government's only local mobile force. He then landed at Campbeltown, set up his standard and advanced, partly by sea, to Tarbert. Later Atholl, with a much larger force, would not dare to advance against Argyll in Cowal for fear the latter should cross Loch Fyne and capture Inveraray.[16]

Had Argyll fully exploited these advantages, or done no more than hold out, he would have given Monmouth, Charles II's illegitimate but Protestant son's crucial English rising a far better chance of success, which should, after all, have been his ultimate aim. The Earl also failed to take the next logical step, to understand that a guerrilla, or partly guerrilla campaign was the best course open to him. Argyll had an inkling of this idea. In Holland he said that 'making the best of a few men in partyes ... would be our first work'. But he failed to live up to his own suggestion. Charles Campbell, having landed in Lorne, started the rising brilliantly. He not only raised perhaps as many as a thousand men, but tied down several times that number by maintaining the initiative, launching raids to keep the enemy on the defensive. He also demoralised Atholl's army with rumours of the treachery of Campbells and Camerons serving on the Government's side. These rumours were not entirely groundless, since one Campbell nearly took Inveraray by a trick.

When Charles moved to join his father, he left a garrison in Carnassary Castle, the house of Sir Duncan Campbell of Auchinbreck. It was an action that paralysed the loyalists in Mid-Argyll. Whilst the gentlemen of the small Kintyre clans, ignoring Ballechin's instructions, retreated into their own, or other people's, local castles, carrying with them men and much needed arms. John Macalister of Loup, for instance, to whom Argyll had written in vain, with others of his name, to join him held Campbell of Skipness's Castle.

Despite Atholl's and Breadalbane's warnings the fire-eater Ballechin was eager to get the rebels to fight. However, the Lowlanders in the Government camp protested and held councils that prevaricated until on 30 May Atholl reached Inveraray with a superior force.[17]

Factional quarrels and suspicion now destroyed the rising's impetus. Argyll crossed into Bute and then to Cowal. The Lowlanders refused to advance on Inveraray, and Argyll, secretly fearing, with increasing foundation, that they might seize the ships and sail away, never dared go far from his base.[18] Mesmerised by an English frigate's damage to Carrick Castle (which provoked Argyll to burn the Bishop of the Isles's palace and other major buildings in Rothesay), the Earl failed to realize that some government warships had only entered the Clyde for provisions. Others had gone north, pointlessly trying to trace his tracks round Mull, giving him a further week's grace.[19]

The Lowlanders, however, were afraid that their ships would be trapped and vetoed the chance of using their ships effectively in Loch Fyne. They then illogically allowed Argyll to persuade them to base their flotilla at Eilean Gheirig (now Eilean Dearg) behind Bute in gloomy Loch Riddon, with the narrow Kyles of Bute as the only outlet. One reason the Earl failed to mention was that it would make it more difficult for them to leave him in the lurch. A few days later four English frigates and two yachts arrived off Bute. Argyll was trapped.[20]

Forced to retreat by land, Argyll left his arms and stores in his castle on Eilean Gheirig, confident that the frigates could never navigate up Loch Riddon, especially under fire from the castle and a new earthen fort he had constructed. That same day they did just that with ease, capturing ships and stores intact.[21]

As he fell back by land towards the Lowlands, Argyll failed to exploit the potential of Cowal's mountainous terrain. His former opponents in the rebel army now urged him to double back into Argyllshire, recruit from the inhabitants aroused by Atholl's plundering, and hasten the disintegration of the Government's forces by retaliatory raids on their neighbours. The Earl ignored this advice. Instead, when it was far too late he advanced into the Lowlands, to the ignominious dispersal of his army beside the Clyde, his capture and execution.[22]

Only in one sphere of irregular warfare did Argyll in early June show any talent. This was in the use of false information to undermine the enemy. His idiosyncratic personality, with its love of 'curiosities' and the bizarre, gave him a natural ability for psychological warfare and he used his gift with skill.

Knowing that Atholl had spies in his camp, he seems deliberately to have fed them with false reports that Lochiel, who had just joined Atholl, was about to change sides. Atholl was ready to believe any such rumours, partly through his old hostility to Lochiel and partly because he was furious that he had criticised his skill as a general.[23]

The suffering of some Camerons since Argyll's fall gave the rumours some plausibility. Glendessary was the most likely suspect. The Macleans now furnished him with a new motive for disaffection. On 2 June, evidently as part of their arrangement of their affairs before they marched off to war, Brolas and Ardgour agreed to turn Glendessary and his tenants out of the holdings they had on the Duart and Ardgour estates.[24]

The Macleans arrived in Atholl's chaotic camp on 7 June. On 11 May the Council, when it mobilised the clans, had instructed Brolas, as Tutor of Duart, to raise three hundred Macleans and join Atholl at Inverlochy. This inappropriate rendezvous, the need to collect provisions and ferry contingents from the remoter islands made them late. Yet the late arrivals were plainly enthusiastic to take part in the coming conflict: Argyll had anchored in Tobermory Bay on his voyage to Lorne, which must have reminded the Macleans of their fate if the Earl's rebellion succeeded.

Atholl estimated that the Macleans' strength was closer to four hundred than the number required by the Government.[25] They also had the flower of the clan to lead them (a fact that we know mainly from the prosecutions later mounted against them for robbery). There were the four Lachlans, Brolas, Torloisk, and his brother John of Tarbert, Lochbuie with his son Hector, and Coll. The latter had his fifteen-year-old son John Garbh with him. The young Laird of Coll at times commanded an independent party of his father's men. Maclean of Ardgour, apparently Ewen, the effective head of the family, was also present with several of his relatives and followers.[26]

Three nights after their arrival a potential disaster occurred. Lochiel (according to Drummond of Balhaldie in his biography of his father-in-law) had aroused Atholl's suspicions by offering to fight Argyll alone with his Camerons and the Macleans.[27] On the 9 June, on a warning that Argyll was planning an attack, Lochiel and his men were sent out on patrol. Lieutenant-Colonel Buchan, however, failed to tell them what standing patrols had been posted. After recognising two of the patrols, the second composed of Macleans, in the nick of time, the Camerons attacked a third, killing several Perthshire gentlemen, before discovering their error. The Macleans, despite their recent disputes with Lochiel, supported him, since gentlemen from one of their outpost had accompanied him and taken part in the attack.

According to Balhaldie throughout the next day the two clans remained together in arms outside the camp, while Atholl's council of war debated whether or not to attack them. Eventually the council decided to treat the incident as an accident. If Argyll had attacked now, the result for the Royalists would probably have been disastrous, but although he quickly heard of the nonsense that had taken place, the Earl did not foresee the disruption in Atholl's camp until the next day. The only advantage the incident brought him was the rumour, spread among his men to keep up their spirits, that the Macleans, as well as the Camerons, were intriguing with him.[28]

After this escapade the Camerons were kept out of the front line, however, Atholl's professional adviser Captain Mackenzie of Suddie, selected the Macleans, with some Atholl men, to act as the vanguard when the army cautiously advanced into Cowal. More than a decade of warfare in the Isles must have made the Macleans into a formidable body of fighting men, a fact recognised by the highly competent Mackenzie.

The Royalist advance guard fought a number of skirmishes as they advanced. Argyll, however, successfully slipped away towards the Lowlands, and Atholl reunited the Macleans with the Camerons. He acted a day too late and they could only pick up a few stragglers. Atholl's army was now rapidly disintegrating. The Highlanders, whose provisions were now exhausted, dispersed and began wholesale plundering. Atholl's only troops, who still had some supplies, and some discipline, were the late-comers the Macleans and, latest of all, the Clanranald Macdonalds.[29]

One last task remained for the Royalists to undertake in Argyllshire. This was to recapture Carnassary Castle. On 23 June, whilst he was in Inveraray, Atholl received reports that the garrison, which Charles Campbell had left there, was causing trouble. They had harassed loyalists, kidnapped some Episcopalian ministers and had acted with such vigour that it was believed that they were two hundred strong. Atholl moved towards Carnassary, but when he arrived he discovered that the garrison was in fact only eighty strong. It was under the command of Captain Colin Campbell of Blairintibbert.

Atholl sent Captain Mackenzie of Suddie forward with a party of Macleans to besiege the castle. Local lairds, such as Donald Macneill of Guallachallie, who had retired into defensive positions when Argyll entered Kintyre, now emerged, plundering vigorously and joined Atholl. Hearing that the garrison of Carnassary resolved to fight to the last man. Atholl, who lacked artillery and siege equipment, sent several captured Campbells, the governor's relatives, to Carnassary with orders to hang them if Blairintibert refused to surrender. The garrison was divided as to what to do next, but the majority insisted on surrender. The commoners were promised their lives, but the commanders and heritors were to surrender unconditionally.

Auchinbreck later complained that the Macleans burned down his house wantonly. However, Atholl's report, a few days later, confirmed by the Suddie's memoirs, shows that on descending to the vaults they discovered powder trails leading to the ammunition store, which had been laid by the more extreme rebels, who intended to blow up the castle and its captors – indeed, according to Atholl, a fanatic actually fired one train, which produced only a small explosion. In a fury the Macleans rushed out and, before Suddie could stop them, seized Auchinbreck's loyalist uncle Alexander Campbell of Srondour, whom Atholl had sent with them to use his persuasion on the garrison. They lynched him. They also wounded a score of the prisoners. As Atholl admitted later, the house was then burned by official order in retaliation for the treachery. It was only sacked after it had been stripped of its contents: 'three scoire horse led [load] of goods & plenishing' were allegedly carried off (although Atholl returned the furniture to Lady Auchinbreck). However, mercy was shown to the prisoners, even the commanders.[30]

The sack of Carnassary was the high point for the Macleans in a massive spree of robbery. Over the past decade, in four major invasions and many smaller raids, the Campbells had repeatedly plundered Mull and Morvern. Now the Macleans had the chance to get their own back on the richer Campbell areas of Argyllshire.

The incomplete *Account of the Depredations* indicates that the Macleans' plunder overwhelmingly consisted of cattle and other livestock. Summary reports of household 'plenishings' they took give less evidence than might be expected from similar accounts of the 1678 Highland Host of the inhabitants of a poorer area seizing upon the agricultural, fishing and other implements for daily labour available in a richer one. There was at least one apparent priority: Brolas and Torloisk evidently organised a massive seizure of horses, both for ploughing and breeding in Mull.[31]

Some accusations against the Macleans, even ones made at the time, were apparently unjust: John Garbh, younger of Coll, who was commanding a party at Inveraray, protested to Atholl on 6 July that he was

> misrepresented to your lordship in my carriage in this country, as those with me should be guilty in spoiling and abusing the country without orders. I can say upon my credit and reputation I neither have nor shall design any advantage ... I doubt not that it will appear that those who misinform of us will find themselves to be at fault.

He had already sent his men home with strict orders not to misbehave. By then much of the robbing in the southern part of the shire was being carried out by the small Kintyre clans, Macalisters and Macdonald of Largie, against their neighbours. The Macalisters were still occupying Skipness Castle as a base for their raids.[32] Although all the Macleans were by now officially on their way home, Brolas and Ardgour planned to use Dunstaffnage Castle as the base for their raiding and to carry off a great bronze cannon there. Ballechin, however, forestalled them by obeying orders to have the castle 'slighted'. In late July some of Lochbuie's followers were still stealing individual cows in Islay and even Colonsay.

Lachlan of Coll is accused of being in the thick of the looting. His sojourn in Holland had not solved his financial problems, nor had he given up hope of a military career. On 15 July 1686 he wrote from Coll to Ann Duchess of Hamilton for her husband's help in obtaining a company in the King's forces;

> Madam,
> My Lord Duik[33] was pleased at Whythall to desyre Hawlks[34] from me and I now hast sent Two Castes of Hawlks to his Grace, I could not omitt to kiss yo[u]r La[dyshi]p hands with my lyn. Having the Hon[ou]r to be related to yo[u]r La[dyshi]p thoe a poore friend and travellor abroad this whylle throughe the Burden that my estat[e] was infested with By what my predccessors did suffer for the Kings interest, and now I humblie Beg yo[u]r La[dyshi]p may be pleased to be a good instrument to [re]mynd my Lord Duik to sie me preferred to the first vacant Companie that falls in his Ma[jes]tes forces. So expecting the Hon[ou]r from yo[u]r Lad[ship] as to send a lyn with the Bearer.[35]

Whether or not he obtained her support is not known and the following year he was drowned in the Water of Lochy.

An unidentified bard composed a panegyric in his honour. The exerpt that follows perhaps gives some of his qualities:

> I shall not speak of your habits, for they are no
> boyish deeds; you were never miserly with precious
> things, and harpers paid you court; you were cour-
> teous to women and friendly to poets and, though
> your hand was hardy in battle, Lord but it was gentle
> with a child.

> You handled a bow well; you were a leader of pipes
> and banners; you were a slayer of deer and a seeker
> of salmon; you were a knight at court, with a well-
> shod, spirited steed, and you were a skipper for the
> cold tempest, frequently plying the English Sea.[36]

Lachlan had done little to reduce his family indebtedness. In fact he had probably increased it. Shortly before his death he had commissioned a distant kinsman Alexander Stewart or Snodgrass,[37] who was a wright by trade, to come to Coll from Greenock as 'undertaker for the building and the finishing of the house of Breakacha'. This was the three storey-house built within the curtain walls of the castle. It made it an infinitely more convenient dwelling place than the old fifteenth-century fortress. It had wide windows looking down the loch towards the sea and at least three fireplaces and cellars.

Allan Crossapol, who was a great-grandson of Alexander Snodgrass, says that 'his father had free houses at Carsdick and a spot of ground which he called Snog Grass, he was married to a daughter of Sir Dugald Campbell Achinbreck, ran through his property by keeping to[o] much rank'. Unfortunately for this statement there is no daughter who fits this description in the Auchinbreck pedigree, However, in a *Genealogy of the Cadets of the Family of Auchinbreck* in the National Library of Scotland it is stated that: 'John Snodgrass Merchant in Paisley[38] married Mary, daughter Colin Campbell of Atichuan'.[39]

Alexander Snodgrass was remembered in Coll by four anonymous lines of poetry, recorded in Dr Hector of Gruline's Collection of poetry made in the 1760s. They speak of him arriving with a couple of bottles in his pocket.[40] He left male descendants who settled at Cornaigbeg in Tiree. They reverted to their original surname of Stewart.[41]

The arrival of the Snodgrass family in the islands underlines the fact that new standards of living, at least among those at the top of society in the islands, needed new skills to make them possible. Lachlan's time in London and the Netherlands had exposed him to new ideas, which he brought back to Coll

Other new blood was brought into the island during the seventeenth century. As we have seen when Coll was building up a body of fighting men in the fifteenth and sixteenth century new families were attracted to the island to become his followers. Another cause of immigration was the custom that when a chief, or one of his immediate family, married outwith the island the incoming wife brought people with her who obtained land in Coll. For instance when the first member of the Auchnasaul family married the daughter of Maciain of Ardnamuchan she brought her Macian (Johnston) foster brother with her to the island. He obtained land at Knock and was known as *Iain dubh na Kille*.

The same happened later in the seventeenth century when Neil of Drimnacross married Flora, a daughter of Macdonald of Morar. She brought her foster brother Murdoch Matheson or Mackenzie with her to Coll. He was so devoted to her son Allan, who became tacksman of Grishipol, that he was always known as Murdoch Allan. Allan reciprocated Murdoch's affection and when his guardian died gave a funeral oration which ended with the words *Och is mi gun Mhurdoch agam*, 'Alas for me I am now without a Murdoch'.[42]

* * *

The turbulent years of Argyll's takeover of the Duart estate, his subsequent fall, rebellion and execution all had their effect on the fortunes on the Macleans of Coll and their cadets. Maclean of

Coll himself survived and eventually prospered. The Macleans of Auchnasaul did not. They were never to recover from the constant raiding of the 1670s and were ruined.

One of the last members of the family was drowned with his chief in the Water of Lochy in 1687. His son became a soldier in the Scots Brigade. He is last heard of when he returned home on leave in 1717 to claim money owed to his grandfather for cattle stolen from him by Charles Maclean of Inverscaddel.[43] He was not successful and presumably died in the Netherlands. Allan Crossapol states that as the family now had 'no freeholding ground there was no men of Consequence of this branch . . . so now are extinct'.

The first family of the Macleans of Grishipol also lost their landholding in Coll. Lachlan Grishipol probably believed it was too dangerous for him to return to the islands after the fighting between Argyll and the Macleans. He remained in Dumbarton. Grishipol's eldest son Roderick, who is never mentioned as 'Maclean of Grishipol', married as his first wife Meve, the widow and estranged wife of Lachlan Maclean of Coll. Part of her jointure lands was Penmolloch in Quinish and she appears to have settled there with her new husband. On her death Rory continued to live there with his second wife. They are said 'by some traditions'[44] to be the parents of Captain Lachlan Maclean in Gallanach in 1776. However, as the latter was born in 1729 and Rory is first mentioned in 1674[45] Rory must have been an old man when his son was born. More probably Captain Lachlan was Rory's grandson rather than his son.

Lachlan Grishipol's second son Mr John Maclean was probably born and brought up in Dumbarton. He was educated at Glasgow University[46] and he too became a soldier, before becoming a minister in Arran. In 1689 he emigrated to Northern Ireland and became chaplain to Viscount Massereene. Two of his three sons became clergymen and the other a surgeon. The eldest was the father of the infamous Lauchlin Macleane, sometime MP for Arundel, manipulator of East India Company stock and the reputed author of the 'Junius' letters. This extraordinary man probably never set foot in the Isle of Coll and, although his father is mentioned in Crossapol's acount, Lauchlin is not.[47]

Notes

1. Much of the first part of this chapter is taken from PA Hopkins and my unpublished 'From the Sound of Mull'
2. Hopkins *Glencoe*, 70–1, 84, 90–1.
3. *RPCS* 3rd Series, vii, 382.
4. *Ibid*, 400.
5. *Ibid*, 420.
6. James NM Maclean 'The Camerons of Glendessary and Dungallon' *The Scottish Genealogist* vol. xviii, No. 4 (December 1971), 77.
7. *Ibid*, 181–2, 229.
8. *Ibid*, 182.
9. *Ibid*, 508–9.
10. *CSPD 1684–5*, 104; *RPCS* 3rd Series vii, 421.
11. NAS Court of Session Papers. 1 Inglis M.1. 7. 1/3.
12. *CSPD 1684–5*, 60.
13. *RPCS* 3rd Series, viii, 93–95.
14. *Scots Brigade*, I , 505.
15. *HMCR Buccleuch & Queensberry*, i, 110–11; Hopkins *Glencoe*, 96–7.
16. Hopkins *Glencoe*, 97–99.

17. *Ibid*, 127; Atholl *Chronicles*, I, 205–6, 219–221; Hopkins *Glencoe*, 99; *Marchmont Papers*, iii, 45.
18. *Ibid*, 42, 49–52; *Wodrow*, iv, 294, 298.
19. Atholl *Chronicles*, I, 212, 219, 221, 226–7.
20. *Ibid*, 232, 236–7; *Marchmont Papers*, iii, 45, 49.
21. *Ibid*, 50–1, 53–4; *Wodrow*, iv, 293–4; *London Gazette* No. 2044; Atholl *Chronicles*, I, 232, 237, 239, 241–2, 252–3.
22. *Ibid*, 240; *Marchmont Papers*, iii, 55–7.
23. Hopkins *Glencoe*, 104.
24. *RPCS* 3rd Series, xi, 45; Atholl *Chronicles*, I, 250.
25. *RPCS* 3rd Series, xi, 45; Atholl *Chronicles*, I, 250.
26. John Crubach Maclean of Ardgour was alive until at least 1690, and is said to have lived to be 95 [NLS MS 3018, 40]. His eldest son Ewen was for many years *de facto* leader of the family. His son Allan (c. 1668–1756) was left to pick up the pieces of the events in 1685–6 [NLS MS 3018, 41].
27. *Memoirs of Locheill*, 212–215.
28. Atholl, *Chronicles*, I, 263–4; Hopkins *Glencoe*, 100–1.
29. Hopkins *Glencoe*, 101–2; Atholl, *Chronicles*, I, 253.
30. *Ibid*, 253–4; *Ibid*, v, Appx., clxx; *RPCS* 3rd Series, xi, 156, 272, 518–19; *Depredations*, 83–4.
31. Hopkins *Glencoe*, 62–3; *Depredations*, 63, 65, 66–70, 79.
32. *Ibid*, 24, 45, 94–7, 103; Atholl, *Chronicles*, I, 249–50.
33. At the Restoration William Earl of Selkirk was created Duke of Hamilton for life as he had married Ann, Duchess of Hamilton in her own right [*The Scottish Nation* vol. V, 434]. Lachlan of Coll was related to the Duchess through his descent from Lachlan Mor Maclean of Duart's wife Margaret Cunningham, daughter of the Earl of Glencairn. The 2nd Marquess of Hamilton had married Ann, the daughter of James Earl of Glencairn [*The Kingdom of Scotland*, 618].
34. Coll probably had a reputation for hawks. In 1549 it is said to have 'ane utter fine Falcons nest in it' [RW Munro (ed) *Monro's Western Isles Of Scotland* (1961), 66].
35. NAS GD 406, 394, which is wrongly dated 1656. I have to thank the late RW Munro for this reference.
36. 'Song to Lachlann, Lord of Coll', *Eachann Bacach*, 49–53.
37. On 11 February 1679 Alex. Snodgrass 'wright in Crawfordsdyke borrowed £137.15s.0d from John Govane merchant in Glasgow [NAS RD3. DUR53. 1]; Inveraray 18 April 1682 Alexander Snodgrass wright in Kilmichael of Glassary takes on Robert, son of James Beatone I Bararay [Boreray?] as his apprentice [NAS SC54. 12. 2]; Glasgow 30 June 1704: Hugh Maclean in Coll & Alex. Snodgrass for present in Crawfordsdyke [NAS SC54. 12. 5.].
38. 11 Oct 1681 Agreement betwixt Archibald Earl of Argyll and John Snodgrass in Bute . . . to win and provide 3000 free stone . . . [AT XVI (1680–9), 80.
39. He was the 2nd son of Duncan Campbell of Ardgaddan, Bailly of Kintyre. *Highland Papers* vol. IV, 77.
40. Photocopy of Doctor Maclean's Collection of Gaelic Poetry, MS 2318, 121 in Aberdeen University Library
41. NAS CH2. 551.1: Parish Registers of Tiree 1766–1819.
42. Archibald Mackenzie to his son Duncan circa 1872. A photocopy of this letter (hereafter Warren 1974) was sent to the late Betty Macdougal in 1974 by Duncan's descendant Thomas Warren, Post Office Box 53, West Vancouver, British Columbia, Canada
43. NAS. Register of Testaments. Cc. 7. 1. 20 November 1717.
44. Crossapol MS, 42.
45. ICP. Bundle 480. 2 September 1674, where he is listed after Lachlan Maclean, Bailie of Tiree.
46. He graduated in 1672 *Mun. Alm. Uni. Glas.* III, 38.
47. He is the subject of a full length biography by the late James NM Maclean *Reward is Secondary* (1963). Although the early part of the book on Lauchlin's forbears is often nonsense, for instance he says that Mr John Maclean was a brother, rather than a son of Lachlan Grishipol, I have no reason to doubt his account of Lauchlin's career.

Chapter Twelve

'The Glorious Revolution'

It was known in Edinburgh as early as September 1688 that William of Orange was preparing to invade England. On the 24 September, on the Earl of Melfort's instructions, the regular army in Scotland, with the exception of garrisons in Edinburgh, Stirling and Dumbarton, marched south to join James's forces in London.[1] Scotland was left without regular troops. It was a disastrous decision.

Trouble was not slow in breaking out. On the 10 October an anti-Roman Catholic mob attacked the Palace of Holyroodhouse. The guards opened fire killing a few young men, including John Garbh Maclean of Coll who was watching the riot.[2] Coll's death following that of his father, Brolas and Torloisk, left the Macleans in the crucial years that followed the Revolution with a leadership that was not only inexperienced but lacked the authority of those groomed to lead from birth.

John Garbh's 'reign' as Laird of Coll was to be the shortest in the history of the family. He was succeeded by his uncle Donald, the 'papist' captain of Breacachadh Castle in 1679, who by 1689 had been 'saved from Rome' by his cousin Mr John Fraser, Minister of Tiree & Coll. Donald kept a low profile in the duel between those who supported William of Orange and the loyalists who sided with King James.

Although men from Coll's estates probably took part in the fighting, no list of them is known to survive, and few of their names have been remembered. One who did take part in this first Jacobite rising was Neil of Drimnacross's son, Hector of Torestan who joined the Jacobite army in Lochaber. Hector is described as one of Sir John Maclean's captains so he will have brought a company of men with him. He was killed in August 1689 in the vicious street fighting in Dunkeld.

Eventually after the fighting had ended Sir John Maclean of Duart surrendered his fortresses to the Williamites. Donald of Coll was one of the few of his friends present at Knocktermartin in Mull when Sir John settled his affairs, and borrowed money, before going into exile.

Once Sir John had surrendered Duart and Carnaburg the isolation of the islands was over. The collectors of the poll tax, which had not been gathered for five years, moved in, travelling 'throw dangerous and impassible seas'.[3] Argyll's representatives moved in as well.

In May 1693 John Cameron of Glendessary, Argyll's bailie, who had returned to his pre-1685 reliance on the Earl of Argyl, held court in Tiree. The latter had been restored by the Revolution to his father's forfeited estates. Glendessary probably brought Alexander Maclachlan with him to Tiree and appointed him bailie of part of that island and of the Two Ends of Coll. The Maclachlans came from Morvern. They were hard tough fighting men and accomplished cattle thieves. They had been staunch allies of the Camerons of Glendessary in their takeover of Morvern.

Glendessary began to uplift the 'meall and duties' outstanding since 1688. The tenants protested. In a letter to the Countess of Argyll they complained that although they accepted that they were by law 'deuly adebted to the Earl of Argyll', however, 'dureing the space of these five years chairgit it was simplie impossible for us to be deutiful payers to the Earl of Argyll, our persons and means lying under the power of Sir John Maclean, who could easily command us a handful in this exentrict and remot yland'.[4]

In addition they continued God had been pleased to bring 'a plague upon our horses by the scab and upon our kowis and sheip as we think be the coldness of winter', so that 'most of us [are] left destitute of our means so that we are not able to labour the half of what we did possess formerlie though in obedience to the earl's factor we have taken as much land as possible for us'.[5]

* * *

It is generally agreed that the weather in Europe worsened from the mid-seventeenth-century and the 1690s were a period of violent storms, which sometimes buried arable land under vast deposits of sand. Such storms were just one of the symptoms of the 'little ice age'. In the 1690s icebergs reached the Faeroes, and the average temperature was 1.5° Centigrade lower compared with the average from 1920–1966.[6] Sunless drenching summer rains, storms, early bitter frosts and deep snow in the autumn damaged crops. Grain failed to ripen. People were still trying to harvest their battered crops in December amidst pouring rain and pelting snowstorms.

There were great regional differences in the famine's severity. The West Lowlands were least affected, North-East Scotland was badly hit and the Highlands worst of all. Mull suffered particularly severely.[7] On 17 May 1695 John Clerk, an estate officer in Netherlorn, wrote to Breadalbane's factor to say that: 'there is a great scarcity of vectuall with us as I have seen this long time but especialie in Mull'.[8]

Most of the islands were affected, including many of those that had previously been 'reputed very fruitful in corn, until the late years of scarcity and bad seasons'.[9] Ireland, in contrast to Scotland, had an abundance of grain. In order to stabilise prices it was against the law to import Irish victual. It was a regulation that was often ignored. Smuggling flourished and, although it was illegal, grain was coming into Argyll from Ireland. For example John Clerk, referred to above, asked permission of Alexander Campbell of Barcaldine to 'tak a start to Ireland for a parsall of meall to supply the contri'.[10]

As the crisis deepened the Government relaxed its ban on imports from Ireland. On 13 December 1695 an act was passed permitting the import of Irish meal. This order was repeated in 1696, but the following year 'there being a prospect of a good harvest', all duties were re-imposed.

Disease followed hunger. In the Uists previously unknown diseases such as 'spotted fever', arrived from Mull. People flocked to the Uists because of its reputation for 'the great produce of barley' there, which 'draws many strangers to this island with the design to procure as much of this grain as they can; which they get of the inhabitants gratis . . . this is a great yet voluntary tax, which has continued for many years; but the late general scarcity has given them an occasion to alter this custom, by making acts against liberality, except to poor Natives and objects of charity'.[11]

It was not only those at the bottom of the social scale who were destitute. Mary Maclean, of the family of Ardgour, described as 'ane poor woman seeking charity for her subsistence' was robbed of her clothes and what money she had on the public highway in Ardnamurchan. She was then murdered.[12] In normal circumstances poor relations were looked after by the extended family. Mary's is the only case of theft and murder at this time from the far west to appear at the Justiciary Court at Inveraray. The complete breakdown of family ties that occurred in other parts of Scotland was not replicated in the Isles. Elsewhere the 'instincts of self-preservation overpowered all other feelings and even natural affection became extinct in crowds of men and women forced to prowl and fight for their food like beasts'.[13]

The famine was not just the result of the appalling weather. Several other factors combined to make it worse. Over-cropping on the fragile machairs of the Hebrides made the land vulnerable to sand blow; the war with France increased taxation, adding to the burden on landowners; many of whom were still in debt as a result of the Civil Wars of the 1640s. Williamite taxation was the proverbial final straw that broke the camel's back.

The scarcity was also unevenly distributed. Ireland, as we have seen, had a glut of corn and acted as a magnet for French privateers, which swarmed around the Irish coast. France had had equally disastrous harvests and a cargo of grain was a valuable prize. As a result Irish corn ships were only allowed to sail in convoys, disrupting normal communications, and depriving remote communities of access to markets.

* * *

The distribution of poor relief was also affected by the religious settlement of 1690, which re-established Presbyterianism. James VII's efforts at religious toleration in 1687 had enabled the 'small remnant of the Presbyterian ministers yet extant'[14] in Argyll to reconvene. They did so at Kilmichael in Glassrie on 29 September 1687. Only seven were present. The ministers assembled defiantly denounced prelacy, but they were now a dying minority.

Once the Revolution was underway it was Episcopacy that was under threat and the Presbyterians began to flex their muscles. On 3 July 1689 Mr Archibald Maclean, the former Episcopalian Archdeacon of Lochgoilhead, appeared before the ministers 'acknowledging of his sin in conformitie with the late episcopie'.[15] His conduct was particularly grievous to the brethren, as he was the son of the old Presbyterian Mr Alexander Maclean, Minister of Kingarth. Mr Archibald was eventually received into the church. He was fortunate. Other Episcopalians were less so and were deprived of their livings. Outed ministers were forbidden to perform baptisms and marriages on pain of imprisonment.[16] As there were insufficient Presbyterian ministers to replace the Episcopalians, the people were deprived of the services of a minister: no minister meant no church service; no church service meant no collection, and as poor relief came from individual kirk sessions there was no money for the poor.

Several outed Episcopalians, such as John Maclean of the Grishipol family, moved to Ireland. Most tried to join the Presbyterian Church. It was now that the triumphant Presbyterian ministers in Argyll showed a vindictiveness that sat ill with their calling at a time when clergy were desperately needed to help relieve suffering. The reputation of the Presbyterian party in Argyll was fatally damaged. As Sir Donald Macdonald of Sleat wrote in 1702, when a massive augmentation of stipends was proposed, it should be prevented, he wrote or the ministers 'wo[ul]d not spare us and our tenants . . . even tho our lands were by sword or famine depopulatt'.[17]

* * *

Mr John Fraser had previously been Dean of the Isles, and Minister of Tiree and Coll and its dependency of Iona. His case is typical of the vindictiveness with which the new order in the church treated the old one. Mr John appeared before the Synod of Argyll on 9 October 1695 'craveing to be received into the communion of the brethren'.[18] The synod, however, 'delayed the consideration of this matter at this season until they be more ripe in the same'. Mr John appeared before them again five days later 'offering to submit to Presbyterian government'. The synod, however, decided that 'not being yet well acquainted with him delays this matter till they be better informed anent his carriage and circumstances'. The following June and the one after that he appeared before them again with the same result.

There can be little doubt that the synod was deliberately enjoying its power and playing cat and mouse with Mr John. Other Episcopalian ministers, such as Mr John Beaton, who were ready to embrace Presbyterianism, were treated similarly. Meanwhile, their parishes were denied their services, or as in the case of Tiree and Coll the minister's duties were carried out illegally and without remuneration.

Mr John Fraser's parishioners were not prepared to accept the situation. On 14 September 1698 the inhabitants and parishioners of the Isles of Tiree and Coll led by Donald Maclean of Coll protested in writing:

> We are verie sensible in what sadd condition we [had] been into if the lord had not inclined the Heart of our pastor to administer the comfort of the word unto us as well since as before the time he has been deprived of his benefice and as we know it is no less grievous to him than the loss of his [indecipherable] to be through malitious groundless misrepresentation suspected of the least stain [on] his behaviour. Soe we think ourselfes bound in conscience to testifie in h[is] behalf for his vindication that the 22 years since he became our minister we have found him laborious in his charge & exemplary in his life ...[19]

Despite their protests Mr John was not reinstated and the parish was to be without an official minister for a further six years.[20] It was not until 1704 that Mr Aulay Macaulay, a strict Presbyterian received a call to Tiree & Coll.[21]

* * *

There is anecdotal evidence that the population of Mull fell dramatically as a result of the famine; where they moved to is uncertain. There were only two Macleans listed in 1695 in the poll tax records in Glasgow, where so many were later to move to.[22] Donald Maclean of Coll in particular was praised for his generosity to refugees:

> You are the centre of attraction for exiles,
> giving them provisions in return for very
> little: Your soul will have its rest in the
> company of angels.[23]

So sang Catriona nighean Eoghainn in her song to 'Donald Maclean, Laird of Coll, when the Campbells were setting the land of Maclean of Duart.'

1698 was the worst year of the famine. The situation was now aggravated by the shortage of seed, and it was believed that God's displeasure was being shown on man and beast. On 10 May 1698 a royal proclamation announced 'that in view of the dearth of cattle and the growing Scarcity' a national fast was to be held.[24]

Although the weather improved in 1699, the shortage of seed was still a cause of great hardship. The worst, however, was over. In 1700 the price of a boll of meal reverted to £4, the price that had been the norm before 1695. It had risen to £8 per boll during the famine years.

* * *

At first Argyll, who had no wish to have another rebellion on his hands left things as they were in Tiree and the Two Ends of Coll. In March 1709, when Sir James Campbell of Ardkinglas received a tack of Tiree and the Two Ends of Coll, things began to change. Sir James continued Alexander Maclachlan as bailie of part of his tack and appointed Colin Campbell, brother to Donald Campbell of Ballinaby in Islay, as bailie of the other part. He also granted him a sub-tack of Ballimartin. Hector Maclean, Balliphetrish's brother-in-law, had previously held this farm.

Dr Hector Maclean, in his genealogical account, describes Hector Ballimartin, the son of John Diùrach, who led the 'forlorn hope' at the battle of Inverkeithing, as 'a very worthy gentleman'.[25] In other words he was rich, and his family had held Ballimartin since at least 1663. Hector himself was probably dead by 1709, but he had sons who were alive.[26] In normal circumstances one of them would have inherited the farm. Instead it went to Colin Campbell.

* * *

In July 1709 the Commissary Court of Argyll, which had not sat for many years in the Inner Isles reassumed it functions in Tiree. By 14 July it had moved to Coll and held court at Gallanach. Its first case was a claim by the Commissary's officer against 'Hector Maclean in Cornaigmore for the sum of 9 merks Scots for 3 stone of meall and against Hector McGilchrist in Balliphetrish [in Tiree] for £3 Scots money resting be him for the teinds at Cornaigbeg'. As the defenders failed to appear the Commissar 'held them as Confessing and decerned them conforme to the lybell'.[27]

The following day the court heard the case of Alexander Maclachlan against Donald Maclean of Coll. Maclachlan argued that Coll owed him rent and other dues

> out of ane pendicle and ane just pairt of Ardneish called gortenagoynen being named to the sd lands and the rents of the sd defenders possession thereof being valued to the soume of ten merks yearly and ilk year of cess year from martinmas 1702 to martinmas 1706 and with tua merks of cess yearly sinsyne and ane firlot of corne yearly sensyne and tua ffulls of meall of setting maill and ane sheep yearly payable be the sd defender out of the proportion posest be him of the [3 merk] landes of Ardneish.[28]

Ardnish was part of the old Duart estate that mixed with Coll's lands. It was a continual cause of friction between the Laird of Coll and whoever was its tacksman, which is why it was usually Coll himself who was the sub-tacksman. Maclachlan appears to have held it himself after 1706 and began to build dry-stone dykes[29] to keep Coll's tenants in Uig's cows from eating his grass.

On 21 July 1709 Hector younger of Coll brought a claim in the Commissary Court against Lachlan Macdonald Bailie of Eigg and his brother John: he accused them of having ferried 13 horses to the Isle of Rum and pastured them there 'without leave or libertie' from the said 'persewer the heretable proprietor of the saides Lands'. Four days later Donald of Coll brought a similar action against the Bailie of Canna. The latter counter claimed against Donald and his sons'. He said that the Macleans had cut off the ears and tails of 15 of his horses and mares. Hector appeared before the Commissariot. He acknowledged that he had ordered that the left ears of the horses should be cut off. The court's decision is not stated.[30]

The dispute with Lachlan Macdonald Bailie of Eigg was transferred to the Sheriff Court at Inveraray. On 8 February 1710 Coll claimed that, as he was the keeper of the King's forest in the Isle of Rum, he was within his rights in seizing the cattle found 'pasturing' at Kinlochscrisort. As such he was 'obleidged to intromet with all goods incroaching upon the fforest under the paine of Tinsell'[31] 'Besydes he hes the power to imprison the person of the delinquents and to confiscate goods found within the fforest as appears by Ja. 5. 4th caput 12 & by Jam. 6 parliat 12: cap. 128'.

The defender answered this charge by claiming:

> it is absolutely denyed that the Lands lyblled are erected as a forrest . . . or that the defender hes any right yrto either as Heretor or keeper the saids land houlding immediately of the Duke of Argyll his Grace hes the only power over the said forest.

Furthermore 'the said Donald McLean of Coll . . . had agreed and transacted with Lauchlane McDonald the pursewer for £20 Scots money for the Graseing of the goods . . . so could not in the first plaice seize or confiscate the goods or any part thereof as pretended keeper of the all [?] forest neither could he poynd or dispose' of them.[32]

The basis of Lachlan Macdonald'd claim that Donald of Coll was not the owner of Rum went back to the 1630s when Lachlan of Coll had been forced to hand over Rum to the Earl of Argyll. Maclean of Coll had, however, continued to receive Coll charters to the Isle of Rum and his position does not appear to have been challenged by the Earl or subsequently by the Duke of Argyll.

* * *

Before 1709, although there were a few Campbells in Tiree, they were, with two exceptions, probably landless cottars and servants. The exceptions were Colin, the bailie and Donald in Gott. Ardkinglas was determined to bring in more and root out the gentlemen of the name Maclean from their tacks in Tiree. On 1 August 1710 he issued instructions to his agents only to award sub-tacks to those of 'no higher degree than themselves'. The days of the Maclean tacksmen in Tiree were numbered.

* * *

Meanwhile Sir John Maclean had wearied of life as an exile at the Jacobite court at St Germains and had after a spell in the Tower of London, returned to Mull. Jacobite intrigue continued to flourish, and after George I succeeded Queen Anne it reached fever pitch. One of the Jacobites' leading agents was Sir John's half-brother Colin Campbell of Glendaruel. Several Campbells were now in the Jacobite camp, and Glendaruel claimed in a report to St Germains that he could count on most of the Campbells in Argyllshire, particularly Auchinbreck and Lochnell.

It was therefore decided that when the Earl of Mar raised the Jacobite standard in the Braes of Mar Glendaruel and young Lochiel should visit Campbell of Lochnell at his house at Mingary in Ardnamurchan. Here Lochiel writes 'I found Sir John McLean and severall of his friends who had occasion to meet there on some private business'.[33]

The 'private business' was the nuptials of Hector Maclean, younger, of Coll and Mary Campbell, sister to Sir Duncan Campbell of Lochnell. Their marriage contract was signed on 14 September 1715.[34] 'I told Sr. John and Lochnell', Lochiel continues,

> finding them merry, that they had reason to be cheerful, for that the King's Standard was to be set up Thursday nixt, Therefore this was the time for all Loyalists to appear for their King and Country.
>
> As all the joy imaginable appeared, not only by Sir John's expressions, but every way about him, to the Contrary Lochnell's and his friends spirits sunk, and begg'd we would keep all as privat as possible for fear of the Garrisson [at Fort William]'s about. I answered Lochnell that it was past all kind of reserve now, since we were immediately to raise in Armes, and that Glendaruale was to be with him that night with a Commission from the Earl of Mar. Sr. John went off next morning to Mull in order to raise his friends.[35]

Hector younger of Coll no doubt interrupted his wedding celebrations to return home and raise his men. It was a half-hearted business. He raised 27 in Coll, 8 in Quinish but none in Muck.[36] The number from Rum is not known. It was a disappointing number. In 1715 there were 49 fencible men in Quinish and 195 on Hector's part of Coll.[37]

One of the reasons behind the poor turnout was probably that there were another eleven well armed men at Sorisdale, who were on the other side. Sorisdale was where Alexander Maclachlan lived with his bodyguard. They are noted as having joined the government militia at Inveraray. However, at the start of the rising when they were at home they were an undoubted threat to the Coll estate. Another reason why Coll produced so few men was probably Hector's lack of enthusiasm for the rising. He did not join it himself, but did not prevent his followers from taking part. Hector sat on the fence and there were no grounds to forfeit him when the rising failed.

Coll produced more than its share of officers who did take part in the '15. Donald of Coll's second son John of Mingary in Quinish, Lachlan younger of Grishipol, Lachlan brother to Hector Maclean of the Isle of Muck and Coll's third son Lachlan Maclean in Achachar in Quinish all took part. They and the other Maclean officers withdrew to Coll after the disastrous Battle of Sheriffmuir, and it was at Breacachadh Castle that they surrendered to the Deputy Lieutenants of Argyll.

* * *

On 26 April 1716, when the Maclean officers surrendered at Breacachadh Castle, a list was made of those males in the island who were of military age.[38] It is worth noting that those listed in the castle itself were eleven officers of the Maclean Regiment who had taken part in the rebellion. They appear to have taken over the castle, either for a last stand, or as an officer's mess.

'Hector Maclean of Coll younger' who, as we have seen, had not been involved in the rising is significantly not in the castle. He heads the list of 31 men in the Breacachadh *baile*,[39] six of whom had taken part in the rebellion. One of those with Hector is 'Murdoch McMurchie harper'. Murdoch had not taken part in the rising. The harper traditionally was 'an accepted member in any household of rank'.[40] He may well, if the Maclean officers, who included Hector's brother John of Mingary, resented the fact that Hector had not taken part in the rising, have been evicted from the castle with his master.

Two of the six men in the Breacachadh *baile* listed in 1716 as having taken part in the rebellion, who are certainly identifiable, came from the same families as those found in the 1679 list of Coll's *luchd-tighe*. They also appear to have lived in the same farms as their forbears: Allan MacNiel Og is said by his grandson to have had Crossapol; Angus MacFadyen who is noted as having 'a sword of Charles roy's in Ardnish' probably lived there too.[41] As in 1679 Ardnish seems to have been a joint-tenant farm with an unusual number of well-armed tenants. The other man listed by his surname in the 1679 and 1716 list in Breacachadh is Malcolm Campbell.

If we accept Allan Crossapol's statement that his grandfather *Allan Mac Neil Oig* had Crossapol at this time, why is he listed at Breacachadh and not in Crossapol?

What I think we are observing in 1716 at Breacachadh, as in 1679, is a situation where the *luchd-tighe* was still functioning. Senior members[42], such as Allan MacNeil Og, had an individual tack to support him, whilst junior members like Angus MacFadyen was a joint-tenant of a farm conveniently close to Breacachadh. If and when the 'household men' were called out to defend their chief they could reach the castle in a relatively short time.

* * *

As he was sick in Perth Sir John had not returned to the islands with his regiment, nor had he taken part in the battle of Sheriffmuir.[43] He died at Buckie during the withdrawal up the east coast of Scotland. His wife had died earlier and in 1709 their only son Hector who was then only five was placed in the care of Donald of Coll.

* * *

Not all the Jacobite army fought at Sheriffmuir. Another body of three thousand men, under the command of Brigadier Mackintosh of Borlum, 'a tough resolute old soldier, formerly a captain in King James the Second's Guards', advanced into Fife and on the night of 12 October about 1,500 of them eluded the Royal Navy and crossed the Forth to Gullane in North Berwick. Amongst them was Lachlan Maclean the eldest son of the dispossessed Hector of Ballimartin in Tiree. He had served in the Scots Guards in Spain and had fought at the Battle of Brihuega, where he was captured. He was now a captain in Mackintosh's regiment.

On the 13 November outside Preston the little Jacobite Army that had marched into England capitulated. The expected Jacobite rising in Lancashire had not taken place and the disillusioned thousand men, who were all that remained of Borlum's force, were surrounded. They had little option but to surrender. The only terms offered were that they became 'Prisoners at Discretion and that they must submit to the King's Mercy'.[44]

Not all surrendered. Six or seven well-armed and mounted Jacobites

> when they saw the rest resolved to surrender endeavour'd to make their Escape; but falling in among Pitt's Regiment, they were all cut to Pieces. They were generally suppos'd to be Persons of Distinction.[45]

Many of those who did surrender were taken to London. On 13 December 1715 King George I was present at the Court of St James. The Council there

> taking into consideration the great number of Prisoners detained in Custody on account of the late Rebellion in Lancashire and how much it imports the Public Peace of the Kingdom that a speedy example be made of some of them, has thought fit to order that the several officers, who are principally intrusted with the custody of the Said prisoners concerned in the late rebellion

shall cause the said prisoners (not being gentlemen and men of estates, or such as shall appear to have distinguished themselves by any extraordinary degree of guilt) to draw lots to the intent, that every Twentieth man, on whom the lot shall fall, shall be appointed for trial in order to due punishment. And if any of the said Prisoners shall refuse to draw, the lots is to be drawn for them in their presence; and the residue on whom the said lot shall not fall, are to be respited from trial, in order to receive H M's mercy on such conditions as he shall Graciously be pleased to think fit.[46]

Among those taken to London and sentenced to death was Captain Lachlan Maclean from Tiree.[47] He was one of 'the undersigned prisoners in the Marshallsea upon account of the Late impious and unnatural rebellion', who

with the greatest humility and contrition throw ourselves att your majesty's Royal feet for mercy. We know we have justly deserved the utmost rigor of the law, and that nothing can parallel the heineusness of our offence but your Majesty's undoubted clemency in alleviating the severity of our punishment. The hopes of this makes us again presume humbly to beg your majesty that instead of the dreadful sentence which by law we may justly expect to be pronounced against us, your majesty may be pleased to transport us where in your royal wisdom you shall think fit . . .[48]

Lachlan escaped death and was 'set at liberty by the King's indemnity'.[49]

* * *

In 1716 Sir James Campbell of Ardkinglas's tack of Tiree and the Two Ends of Coll was renewed. It was done so on the condition that he planted them with tenants of the 'name of Campbell and such as have not taken part in the Rebellion, in the place of the natives, who were for the most part guilty of the same'. Several Campbells settled in Tiree and were at first exposed to raids and reprisals from the Macleans, which reduced some to poverty. Others fled. 'Most, however, remained as a privileged, envied and sometimes hated minority'.[50]

Notes

1. Lord Lindsay (ed) Colin, Earl of Balcarres *Memoirs touching the Revolution in Scotland* (1841), 6–7, 11–12; NAS SP 4. 13, 284–5, 307.
2. NLS MS 3018, 28; *RPCS* 3rd Series xvi, 90.
3. NAS GD170. 22. The Tacksmen of the Poll 1693.
4. ICP. 2 July 1693. Petition of the tenants of Tiree to the Countess of Argyll; AT Vol. xvii, 60a.
5. *Ibid.*
6. Robert E Tyson 'Famine 1695–9'. Lecture at a conference at Aberdeen University in 1989: *Lairds, Landscape and Life 1600–1800.*
7. Ibid.
8. NAS GD170. 654. I am indebted to Dr Frances Shaw for this reference.
9. *Western Isles of Scotland*, 2.
10. NAS GD170. 654. 1.
11. *The Western Isles of Scotland*, 78.
12. John Cameron (ed) *The Justiciary Record of Argyll and the Isles 1664–1705*, i (1949), 174: 19 May 1699.

13. Henry Grey Graham *The Social Life of Scotland in the Eighteenth Century* (1899), 146–148.
14. NAS CH2. 557. iii. The Synod Book of Argyle. 'At Kilmichall in Glassarie'. 29 September 1687.
15. Ibid, 25.
16. *APS* ix, 420–1.
17. NLS MS 1307 fol. 187v.
18. NAS CH2. 557. iii, 141.
19. ICP. 'Petition & Testimony of the Persons in Tiree & Coll, and in favor of the Good Cond[uct] of their Minister-1698. To R. the Moderator & the remanent Reverend Brethren of the Synod of Argyle.'
20. Ibid, iv, 108.
21. NAS CH2. 984. 2; 'the outstanding Harris Minister in first half of the eighteenth century is Rev. Aulay Macaulay, the great grandfather of Lord Macaulay the Whig historian' [*TGSI* vol. XLV, 60].
22. NAS E70. 7. 4, 3–24 & 27–35. I am grateful to Paul Hopkins for a list of 39 Highland-sounding names (Campbell, Buchanan & Colquoun excluded) in Glasgow in 1695, who owed poll tax. There are two Macleans only: J Maclean, maltman, who owed £4.2s; and 'Eliz. Coats Andrew McLeans relict', who owed £1.8s.8d. She is probably the widow of Mr Andrew, the indulged minister.
23. *Na Baird Leathanach*, 57–59. I am grateful to Colm Ó Baoill for a translation of this song.
24. R Steele (ed) *A Bibliography of Royal Proclamations of the Tudor and Stuart Sovereigns 1485–1714* (1910), S.3148.
25. NLS MS 3018. 53.
26. One is possibly 'John McEacharne in Ballimartin' who prosecuted Hugh McEan Roy in Balefuil before the commissary court on 2 July 1709 [NAS CC12. 2. 1]. He is probably the author of 'John Maclean's Journal of the 'Forty-Five' [*WHN&Q* Series 3, No.36 (March 2002), 11–17].
27. NAS CC12. 2. 1.
28. NAS CC12. 2. 1.
29. ICP Tiree Tacks. 40. 127.
30. NAS. CC12. 2. 1.
31. Tinsell = forfeiture of a thing or right by failure to perform some stipulated condition [CSD, 724].
32. NAS. SC54. 10. 2.
33. *TGSI* xxvi, 70.
34. It was witnessed by 'Sir John McLean of that Ilk, John Cameron of Locheill, younger, Donald McLean of Tarbert and Archibald Campbell of Achnatenne.' [Breacachadh Castle Transcripts made by HAC Maclean, 1896].
35. *TGSI* xxvi, 70.
36. *Inner Isles*, 20–22 & 153–171.
37. The total male population of the island listed on 27 April 1716, excluding the officers in the Castle, was 206. As several are said to be 'old' the list is likely to include the whole male population over the age of 15. Those under 15 were perhaps as many as 40 making a total male population of around 250. This would suggest that there were 275 females on Coll, making the total population around 525.
38. *Inner Isles*, 151–3 & 163–5.
39. His father, who had retired and handed over the running of the estate to Hector was living in retirement at Cliad [*Inner Isles*, 157].
40. *Tree of Strings*, 111.
41. He also 'lost his gun in Perth being stolen from him'.
42. As the commisioned officers were in the castle, he is likely to have been a senior NCO. Perhaps like the earlier Neil Og a hundred years before, he was responsible for training the *luchd-tighe*.
43. Iain Ciar MacDougall of MacDougall to his wife. Perth 19 November 1715 where curiously calls Sir John 'Sir Donald'. Quoted in Jean MacDougall *Highland Postbag. The Correspondence of Four MacDougall Chiefs 1715–1865* (1984), 18.
44. *Political State of Great Britain* x July–December 1715, 497.
45. *Ibid*, 498. Report from General Wills.

46. PRO. SP 35. 68.
47. *Political State of Great Britain* xii (July–December 1716), 36.
48. TNA SP35. 77/74: Maclean, Lachlan, Jacobite prisoner.
49. NLS MS 3018, 54.
50. ER Cregeen 'The Changing Role of the House of Argyll in the Scottish Highlands', I M Lewis *History and Social Anthropology* (1968), 160.

Chapter Thirteen

Hector Maclean of Coll 1689–1754

Donald Maclean of Coll died in 1729. In 1773 Boswell found at Coll House what he describes as 'a curious piece on the death of the present laird's father: 'Nature's Elegy upon the death of Donald Maclean of Coll'. There is a leaf missing from the manuscript of Boswell's journal, and all that remains of the 'curious piece' are the lines:

> Nature's minion, Virtue's wonder,
> Art's corrective here lies under.

Dr Johnson read the poem and wondered who wrote it. Boswell supposed it was some country schoolmaster. Johnson thought the epitaph was not so very bad. 'I asked what "art's corrective" meant. "Why", said Mr Johnson, "that he was so exquisite that he set art right when she was wrong"'.[1]

Hector who had already controlled the estate for several years succeeded his father. In 1716, as we have seen, it was Hector who was at Breacachadh when the men of Coll handed in their arms after the '15 Rebellion. Donald of Coll was then living in retirement in Cliad with one male servant.

Allan Crossapol states that Hector was 'one of the bravest Gentlemen of this age for parts and person'. Alexander Maclean Sinclair adds that:

he was a tall, handsome and dignified looking man. He was richly endowed with good sense, and managed his affairs with prudence. He found the estate heavily burdened with debts, but succeeded in paying them all, and also in laying some money by. He built a fine residence near the old castle, and lived in a style becoming his circumstances.[2]

As the eighteenth century progressed landowners benefited both from the higher productivity of their estate, and from the growth of new markets for its produce. Scotland's new investment capital that financed agricultural improvements had also financed new industries based in the towns of the West of Scotland and across the country's Central Belt. The growth of these new urban communities increased the demand for food, drink and raw materials. In this expanding sellers' market, prices continued to rise (the price of oats tripled in a decade), and within a few years even estates, which had been close to bankruptcy became highly profitable.

Increased productivity and expanding markets made agriculture an increasingly attractive investment. Towards the end of the century, rent increases on most estates were spectacular, in some cases over eight hundred per cent. In this new world of commercial farming there were opportunities for lucrative expansion and there was scope for aggressive competition. Some of the less wide awake among the landowners, instead of becoming rich, became the victim of this revolution in agriculture, but the majority prospered and the most active and resourceful became very rich indeed.

* * *

Hector was a staunch Protestant, an elder and a Commissioner to the General Assembly in Edinburgh.[3] He was also the prime mover in getting the Small Isles separated from Skye and made into a separate parish. This action was dependent on the teinds being sufficient to finance an independent parish.

The Small Isles, which at the time consisted of some '700 souls', was predominantly Roman Catholic and there were 'priests still trafficking among them'.[4] The proposed parish consisted of the Isles of Eigg, Canna, Rum and Muck. Eigg and Canna was the heritable property of the Captain of Clanranald, who had been killed at the battle of Sheriffmuir. Three quarters of the population of Eigg were Roman Catholics, as were all the inhabitants of Canna. Rum and Muck belonged to Maclean of Coll. About half the people on Rum were 'papists' and there were several more on Muck.

The islands are described in detail in the petition to establish the new parish. It states that:

> the coasts of these islands are very bad and but one safe landing place in each of them. They lie open to the western sea and Ocean so that by the tempestuous winds and Rolling Seas, which are for ordinary there, many boats are lost away on the Rocks, which lie about these islands.[5]

It was now proposed that the church, manse and glebe of the new parish should be at Kildonan in Eigg and that the minister should preach successively, by turns, in the other islands, where 'meeting places for worship' in each island were to be built. The cost of these developments fell on the heretors according to the value of their teinds[6] and the parties involved appeared before the Commissioners for Plantation of Kirks and Determination of Teinds.

On 22 January 1726 Hector Maclean, then still younger of Coll, wrote to the Lords of Council & Session:

> Sir, Notwithstanding of all the advantages I might plead upon my proof in the valuation of the teinds of my lands of Quinish, Col, Muck and Rumm ... yet, rather than having any hand in stopping that Christian Design of new erection of Parishes, I consent and agree that the teinds of my lands of Quinish be valued at £100 Scots yearly, Coll at £133.6s.8d, Rumm £60 and Muck £60 yearly for Minister and Bishop [teinds][7]

Witnesses were called. They give the earliest insight we have into the detailed running of the estate before everyone on it was affected by the dramatic increase in the population that occurred later in the century.

First to appear was Coll's ground officer[8] Donald Maclean in Uig who stated that: the present rent of the twenty pound land of Coll was £821 Scots silver-rent, plus 24 quarts of butter at 4 merks and

24 stones of cheese at 2 quarts and 31 bolls of victual rent at 6 merks the boll making the total rent worth £945 Scots. This had been the rent from 1722 to 1724. However, in previous years the rent had been less:

        1717: £690 Scots.
        1718: £709 Scots.
        1719: £723.6s.8d Scots.
        1720: £743.6s.8d Scots.
        1721: £623.6s.8d Scots.

The reason why the silver rent fluctuated so much was because 'the lands were much Damnified by the overblowing of the sand'. As a result the tenants were 'considerably impoverished'. He went on to say that 'he had seen the houses on several parts' of the estate removed 'for the space of half a mile and that the possessors were still exposed to the same Inconveniency'. Uig explained that if Coll guaranteed that the tenants lands would not be further 'damnified' by sand-blow they might pay £600 Scots annually, but that if they took 19 year leases and took the risk of further sand-blow themselves they would not be able to pay more than £500, and the laird had recently been obliged to give them a 250 merk reduction in their rent.

Uig further explained that, as their cattle were not housed, they had little or no dung to manure their fields and that if they did not have the liberty to use 'seaware' as fertiliser their rents would have to be cut by 50%. The teinds of the estate in the Isle of Coll were therefore not worth more than 200 merks Scots. This was a vital piece of evidence which was to be forgotten when the kelp boom occurred later in the eighteenth century.

The next witness Donald Macdonald tenant in Totamore stated that the average rent of the estate in Coll was no more than £600 Scots because of 'the frequent Murrane of Cattle'. This infectious disease known in Tiree as the 'bloody flux' had a serious effect on both the payment of rents, which were 'mostly payed by Black Cattle',[9] and the sale of cattle at the great Lowland trysts.

The third witness was Lachlan Macpherson in Cuin, Quinish. He stated that the rent of the £12 land of Quinish was 440 merks Scots silver rent plus the 'casualties' of butter & cheese. 7½ merks of the 12, which had previously been 'waste' was now farmed by Coll himself 'planted with his own stock of cattle'. In 1722 & 1723 the rent of the land not in Coll's hands was 100 merks Scots. He could not remember what the rent was in the four or five years preceding 1722, except that it was less. If Coll's 7½ merk land had been let it would have paid 200 merks. If the whole £12 land had been let to tenants on a 19 year tack it might fetch more than 700 merks Scots. As in Coll the tenants' cattle were not housed and if the tenants did not have the benefit of seaware the rent would be at least 100 merks less. He believed the teinds were worth 155 merks Scots. However, if someone were to take a 19 year lease of the teinds, he could not afford to pay more than 135 merks for them.

Malcolm Johnston in Penmolloch confirmed Macpherson's figures except that he believed tenants would not pay more than 6–700 merks for a 19 year lease. They were not worth more as in the past these lands had been waste and might be again. He also believed that, because of the difficulty in collecting them, the teinds were not worth more than 126 merks for a 19 year tack.

The next witness was Donald Macleod in Kilmory, Rum. Kilmory was the largest settlement in the north of the island. He stated that the rent of Rum was 600 merks silver-rent, 20 quarts of butter and 20 stone of cheese making the total value of the rent for the years 1718–1722, with the exception of 1720, had been 680 merks Scots. The rent for 1720 had been 108 merks less and in 1724 it was as low as 400 merks. If the tenants were offered 19 year leases they could not afford to pay more than 500 merks. 'They could not engage' to pay any more 'without the hazard of being losers'. Further more the tenants of the toun of Kilmory would in future be at least 100 merks 'diminished by reason of the damnages it appeared the saids lands would sustain by the washing of the water and over-blowing of the sand yearly'. He stated that the teinds were worth no more than £40 Scots for a 19 year lease and that a tacksman could not give more 'if he were to have a reasonable profit for his pains in Collecting and drawing the teinds'. John Macquarrie in Harris, the largest township on the island, which is in the south-west of Rum, confirmed Macleod's figures

Patrick Mackay in Kiel in the Isle of Muck stated that the rent of the island, excluding the 3 merk land possessed by Lachlan Maclean of the Isle of Muck, was 246 merks silver-rent, 14 bolls 1 firlot of victual rent, with 18 stone of cheese and 18 quarts of butter. He did not remember what the rent was when half the land now possessed by Maclean of Muck was held by tenants. However, when the other half was set to tenants about five years ago, the rent was 100 merks. For five out of the previous seven years they had paid the same rent, but during the other two years, as a result of the 'Murrane of Cattle' the rent was reduced by 60 merks.

Patrick Mackay went on to say that a tacksman with a 19 year lease might be prepared to pay 500 merks Scots for the whole island. He could not pay more. One reason why was the lack of firewood on the island. It meant that the tenants had to dig their peat in the arable ground, as there was nowhere else to get it. As a result the ground was damaged. As elsewhere the tenants had the use of the seaware of the island. They would need their rents to be reduced by a third if they did not have it. The teinds were valued at £40 Scots. If a tacksman were given a 19 year lease of the teinds, he might be prepared to pay that sum, but certainly no more.

Maclean of Muck had in the past been required to pay 64 merks feu duty each year to the Bishop of the Isles. It was now payable to the Synod of Argyll. He also had to pay a feu of £8 Scots to his feudal superior Maclean of Coll.

* * *

The Synod of Argyll did not accept the valuation provided by Coll's witnesses. They said that they were reluctant to argue with a laird whose support 'they most gratefully acknowledged ... and indeed nothing would have Induced them to have complained ... were it not that ... the Ministers of the paroches that were all ready in Being would be deprived of a Reasonable Subsistance'.[10]

They argued that that the only part of Coll effected by sand-blow 'was but two little villages' which did not make up a tenth of the rental.[11] They also pointed out that the value of the land in Coll's own hands had not been included in the assessment of the teinds as it ought to have been.

In addition there were difficulties in extracting their share of the teinds. They explained that the heretor was a 'Kind of Sovereign'. He would not allow the minister to collect 'his teinds before the Corns were Led, But maintained his people who cutt down the Corns and Carryed them in all the time of Harvest'. Only when 'all was fully Carryed into the Barnyeard' and when the laird 'thought it proper time' was he 'graceously pleased to allow the titular to Come and look at his teinds and if they Could agree upon a Certain quota for his teinds it was well the minister was paid. But if not the minister must take his Corn and Straw at what time the heretor please and must carry them perhaps in the Midle of winter for several miles for he would not be allowed to thresh them out anywhere in the heretors Lands'.[12]

The Synod of Argyll condemned Hector's underestimation of the value of the teinds on his estate. However, as he pointed out the Presbytery of Skye had agreed that without his support it would not have been possible to establish the Parish of the Small Isles, and that he gave it 'Chearfully without hesitation'. It was therefore hardly surprising that he felt aggrieved to be given 'the harshest Character' by the Synod and described as

> ane oppressor and Contemner of all authority . . . he scarce thought there Could be one Instance given of his hindering the Drawing of his teinds. These had, past the memory of man, been led by the Titular and such as had the right therein or by their tacksmen . . . it was observable . . . that it was a variable rent whereof the pursuer was possest. The lands were not set in tack for years nor was that to be done by reason of the great uncertainty of the Cropt and product of the ground in those parts. The cattle where with the ground was stocked were subject to many calamitys and there were but few years in which their Corns Came to full maturity and Perfection and there were considerable parcels of the Land Exposed to the overblowing of the sand and a Considerable rent was got meerly by the Industry of the heretor and his tennants.[13]

The Commissioners appear to have been convinced by Hector's arguments and the teinds were set at the value he had offered at the beginning of the enquiry. The first Minister of the Small Isles was Mr Donald Macqueen.[14] In 1736 he married Marjory, the daughter of Lachlan Maclean of Torestan in Coll,[15] they settled at Sandaneisher in Rum and were the progenitors of a long line of ministers in the Church of Scotland.

* * *

Hector was also responsible for converting Rum from Roman Catholicism. Dr Johnson says that the people of Rum

> Continued papists for some time after the laird became a protestant. Their adherence to their old religion was strengthened by the countenance of the laird's sister, a zealous Romanist, till one Sunday, as they were going to mass under the conduct of their patroness, Maclean met them on the way, gave one of them a blow on the head with a yellow stick . . . Since the use of this method of conversion, the inhabitants of Egg and Canna, who continue papists, call the protestanism of Rum the religion of the Yellow Stick.[16]

Other sources say that the change in religion in Rum was not exactly as related by Johnson. According to Report of the British Fisheries Society Hector Maclean of Coll

> Had a child at nurse in Rume and happening to go and see it of a Sunday, it occurred to him to ask a friend of his, a Clergyman, who chanced to accompany him, to preach. A Roman Catholic man present went out of the room, the Nurse, also a Roman Catholic followed him with the Child, this circumstance enraged Maclean to such a degree that running after the man he beat him most unmercifully with a stick adding 'get back you rascal to the Kirk'. This drubbing frightened the inhabitants so much they none of them ventured more to go to Mass.[17]

Hector of Coll was less successful in his attempt to have Coll separated from Tiree and made into an independent parish. On 1 February 1732 Mr William Morison Minister of the 'United Parishes of Sorabie and Kirkapole' again petitioned the Lords Commissioners for Plantations of Kirks and Valuation of Teinds. In his petition Morison stated that the parish consisted 'of the two Isles of

Tiree and Colle, the nearest of which to the Continent is at a Distance of Sixty Miles'. He claimed that Tiree had 'near 1,500 Catechisable Persons' and that Coll 'has betwixt seven and eight hundred examinable Persons;[18] so that each of the Islands is more than a sufficient Charge for any one Minister'.

He went on to say that 'there lies betwixt the one Island and the other, a dangerous Sea, which at the nearest Passage is four miles in Breadth'. In fact, despite its dangerous nature, the Sound of Gunna, that divides Coll from Tiree, is only 3 miles wide, nor is it likely that the number of examinable people on the island was as many as 7–800. As Boswell, who examined the petition to the Lords for disuniting Coll from Tiree, remarked 'the highest number would be given upon that occasion'.[19] It is therefore likely that in 1729 the total population was 7–800 and that, as we shall see, William Morison, like Mr Hector fifty years later, was being economical with the truth concerning the population of Coll.

William Morison was so keen to have a independent minister settled in Coll that he had executed a deed by which he assigned all his rights to the teinds of the Isle of Coll to any minister appointed by the Presbytery to officiate in Coll plus 300 merks out of his 'two Thirds of the Teinds of Tiree'. Maclean of Coll had also agreed to provide the minister with a glebe in the 'Tack which he has set, comprehending the Ground intended for the Glebe, there is an express Reservation that the Tenant shall be obliged to remove as soon as a Minister shall be there settled'.[20]

The Synod of Argyll claimed that the teinds of the parish 'were so considerable that they can very well afford to defray the Charge of maintaining a second Minister'. The Duke of Argyll, however, stated the opposite, and the petition was dismissed.

* * *

The people on Coll's four properties in the 1720s lived by subsistence farming. They produced a low and uncertain rent. If the weather was bad the full rent could not be paid, and they went into arrears. Natural disasters, such as sand-blow, which had probably begun during the 1690s hurricane, had a dramatic effect on land use. Livestock diseases blighted the export of cattle and it is difficult to see how Hector Maclean of Coll managed to buy out his cousins who had wadsets on parts of the estate, leave 'some money by', build 'a fine residence near the old castle' and live 'in a style becoming his circumstances'.[21] However, as Hector left a considerable number of cattle at the time of his death,[22] the most likely source of the estate's increased income was their export.

The trade in cattle, which had increased considerably since the Union in 1707,[23] was one of a Highland laird's major sources of income. This is perhaps why a family of Kennedys from Lochaber was given land on Coll's estate. They were probably skilled drovers, and cattle thieves. They were almost certainly originally brought to the island by Alexander Maclachlan, bailie of the Two Ends of Coll.[24] He needed them as part of his bodyguard and to help look after his own 'prodigious stock' of cattle.[25]

However useful they may have been to Maclean of Coll, the Kennedys' behaviour was a liability to their neighbours. In 1710 Hector Coll had to stand surety at the Sheriff Court at Inveraray for the good behaviour of Malcolm Kennedy in Gallanach and see that

> Lauchlan mc Harlich vic Lauchlan alias McLean in Trialan in Coll his wife bairns men tennents, cottars and servants shall be harmless and skaithless in their bodys Land, Tacks possessions Goods and Gear and shall be in nowise molested Damnified or Troubled therin by the said Malcolm Kennedy ... under a penalty of 200 merks Scots.[26]

In 1716 Malcolm Kennedy was established in Knock. He is then one of three Kennedys out of five men living there. Both Malcolm and Murdoch Kennedy[27] had been in the rebellion. The third Kennedy, Angus, had not. By 1716 Lauchlan mc Harlich vic Lauchlan was no longer living in the island.[28]

* * *

There are no surviving lists of the inhabitants of Coll during Hector's 'reign' to illustrate in detail how he organised his property. The Kirk Session minutes for Coll only appear to have been kept from 1732–5.[29] The elders by then were all Maclean wadsetters and tacksmen.

Hector maintained the usual following of a Hebridean chief. In 1716, as we have seen, his 'harper' is listed among his men at Breacachadh.[30] As we have also seen Hector's great-grandfather John Garbh has the reputation of being an accomplished composer of harp music. The 1716 list also includes an 'Angus roy McDonald the pyper' living at Arnabost who had taken part in the rising. Whilst the Kirk Session minutes for 1733 mention 'James McLeane Coll's Piper'. Hector was therefore not averse to the music of the pipes. Many lovers of the harp, however, detested the bagpipes. Among them was Lachlan the poet, Hector of Coll's younger brother. He composed a coarse song parodying John Maclean, *Iain Mac Ailein's* the Mull poet's poem *Moladh Na Pìoba* 'in praise of the pipes':

> My lifelong curse, Gilleasbuig, on your pithless body,
> because over all the world of music, you gave first
> place to the pipe. Players of stringed instruments often
> had to listen to your abuse and you repaid them
> badly: yet you were the man to eat bread and puddings
> and meat, you lousy churl!

> Many an earl in Scotland tonight, lying farting in his
> bed having filled his belly with sowens from the pot,
> and developing flatulence, would gladly, for hearing
> her [the pipe] night and morning (they would find it
> distasteful to give her any respect) reward the con-
> fusion of her drones by setting the dogs on it.

> Whatever moron first began to extract a tune from her
> hide I have no doubt that his head had long been
> filled with hallucination and the wildest delirium. No
> brilliant sparkling, fast music comes from her finger-
> holes: she gags and cackles unmelodiously like the
> gaggling geese.

> It is long since I first heard her reputation for
> excessive squawking, dragged out from your ungainly
> arm-pit, the miserable bundle of sticks; she puts
> plenty of fearful thoughts into the hardiest of minds,
> and would serve better as a rattle for clearing the
> horses off the hayfield than inciting armies.

Since downright lies are customary with her, she is a
putrid thing to hold at your breast; she will never play
tunes for you, though you should blow her till your penis
would rise. When you put salt and your breath into the
pig's stomach, this would send out a rancid smell from
the extremities of her body.

He lied who said that she is a sinless spouse, since her
behaviour is not moral and since she has never refused
a romp in her shift in the early hours to anyone at all.
Eight male hooks have their way with her – I disapprove of that, since they would be better equipped to
flay the skins off dogs than to play their minims[?]

We long ago received visible demonstration that her
behaviour was cowardly, for it was at the time for
drawing bravely towards close quarters with an army
that she would take a rest. In disastrous little Sheriffmuir up here (have you heard of it?) she leapt on the
back of a little red-haired boy to flee from the battle.

Pride of place for planting cabbage-seed goes, over all
those my eyes has seen, to Conduiligh who was in Mull
urinating, a mackerel in his hand. Macleod had that
twister MacCruimein – there was a sting in his paw;
Pàdraig and the bleary-eyed Iain Mac Uilleim, two
spongers for drink.[31]

Hector patronised the bard Neil Lamont, who lived at Balevulin in Tiree, and gave him the *bàidse*, the customary reward that a bard received from his patron. Lamont composed a panegyric for his patron when he died in 1755. It includes the words:

> What can I say of one of your quality?
> Pipe and harp would be sounding within your ramparts.
> There would be many kinsfolk and a household of retainers.
>
> This was the house where there used to be great joy
> with servants bustling about noisily in every cellar
> (to ensure) that every man had a glass in his hand.
>
> When Mary of the fine chief's household would come
> requesting that they would retire for the night
> 'My dear' (she would say), 'Do not exhaust any of them'.
>
> Although she would speak them fair, they must sit it out,
> with their host, quaffing the dram,
> and there would be something left over for the dependents.

> It was yourself that saw to it that I was bravely equipped
> from head to toe. After I returned from visiting you
> to my delight I even had a full powdered wig.[32]

* * *

In May 1754 Hector entailed his estate. The entail was established to disinherit the next heir his younger brother Lachlan, who he 'looked on as a prodigall'.[33] Lachlan, as we have seen was a poet.[34] He was also an active Jacobite[35] and a drunk. It is said he was prepared to sell his family or his religion for a drink. He was, surprisingly, a sessioner on the Coll Kirk Session,[36] which suggests that sessioners were chosen for their position in society rather than their moral rectitude. At least he was not an ordained elder.

Those who the entail disinherited says something of the fate of the early cadets of the family. There is no mention in it of the Auchnasaul or the first Grishipol families. As they had left the island their omission is not surprising. However, other families, who were still resident, are also ignored. Most significantly left out is the Totronald family, who after Hector's brothers, would but for the entail have been his nearest heirs.

John of Totronald who, as we have seen, played a leading rôle in affairs in the islands in the second half of the seventeenth century is last heard of in 1694.[37] His son Allan succeeded him in Totronald. Allan, who in the 1730s was an elder in Coll, was educated as a writer [solicitor], but does not appear to have practised outwith Coll. After his death the family rapidly went downhill both economically and socially. In 1776 the eldest surviving son Hector is living in Totamore without servants. He is noted as being able to read.[38] John Johnston, the Coll seanachie, says that he sold Totronald to Maclean of Coll and was a tenant in Totamore living 'in poor circumstances'.[39] He says later that Hector 'became a very poor man, without any land at all, and only a small 'hut' at Grimsary.[40] He did, however, have several sons. It is likely that he was left out of the entail, as in a similar situation in the Lochbuie family he was not 'in the character of a gentleman'.

Those included in the entail were some, but not all, of the descendants of Neil of Drimnacross who were a generation further out than the Totronald family. Drimnacross's heir Captain Hector of Torestan was killed at Dunkeld in 1689. He left an only son Lachlan who had Torestan in Coll as well as Drimnacross in Mull. He was for sometime in the Scots Brigade in Dutch service, where he enlisted as a private soldier and 'being baulked of preferment left the service and came home'. In the 1730s he was an elder of the Kirk Session in Coll, and married a sister of Alexander Macdonald *Alasdair mac Mhaigstir Alasdair*, perhaps the greatest Gaelic poet of the eighteenth century. He was probably dead by 1754 and is not mentioned in the entail. He left only daughters.

Neil of Drimnacross' second son Allan took over the tack of Grishipol. The latter's eldest son Lachlan was an officer in the Maclean Regiment in 1715. He moved to Glasgow, where he became a merchant, dabbling in the trade in tobacco. The second son John succeeded his father in Grishipol. Both the third and fourth sons emigrated to North America settling in Connecticut. The elder Neil, a surgeon, emigrated in 1736. His brother Allan followed him in 1740 and became a merchant in Hartford. He was not successful and claimed that the 'Yankees were too cunning for me'. In the French and Indian Wars he served as a Lieutenant and Commissary.

Allan of Grishipol's three sons who left Coll are mentioned in the entail and were preferred to closer heirs. John who remained in Coll is not.[41] Allan Crossapol mentions all four sons in his manuscript.

Why John of Grishipol and his progeny are ignored is a mystery. Perhaps, with the exception of his brother Hugh, Hector did not think those members of his extended family who were still living in Coll were suitable to inherit the estate.

John of Grishipol was also an elder in Coll in the 1730s. Both his sons eventually left the island and became merchants: John, the eldest, in Virginia, Archibald, the younger son, in Dantzig (now Gdansk in Poland). They were evidently in partnership with their uncle in Glasgow, acting as his agents in the tobacco trade.

These early emigrants kept in touch with Coll and visited the island. 'Virginia John', as he was known, being a fairly regular visitor. These visits were jovial occasions. In 1774 he writes from Glasgow to Murdoch, the future Laird of Lochbuie, to say:

> I am ashamed to have so long neglected to answer your letter, but the gentlemen of this place play so hard in what they call *welcoming me* that I hitherto had time for scarce anything but preparing for the next *drink* – but tomorrow I beat a march for the Highlands where I expect to spend a few regular sober days.[42]

In 1779 there were probably more celebrations as Hugh Maclean, the Glasgow solicitor, writes: 'Allan returned and mett young Coll his brother & Virginia John at Stirling on their way north'.[43] The American Revolution ruined 'Virginia John'.[44] His wife and children there are described in 1781 as being 'in deepest distress for want of succour'.[45]

* * *

Another Allan Maclean perhaps left for America at about this time. His descendants claim that he came from Coll. Allan settled in Philadelphia, which was then a major port of entry for Scottish immigrants. Here he married and practised the trade of skinner and leather-breeches maker. Allan's eldest son, who called himself Allen McLane to distinguish him from Allan Torloisk, was born in August 1746. He describes himself in his will as a 'Friend and soldier of the American Revolution', and it is as a partisan leader that he is remembered. He was the father of Louis McLane the United States Ambassador to the United Kingdom from 1829–31.[46]

Notes

1. *Boswell*, 276–7.
2. *Clan Gillean*, 378.
3. NAS. CH2. 273. 3 March 1731, 14 March 1732 & 18 March 1741.
4. NAS. Decreet of Teinds 1726, 70: 'McLean of Coll against the Minister of Slate'.
5. NAS, Decreet of Teinds 1726, 71.
6. Teinds = portion of laity's estates assessable for clergy stipend. [*CSD*, 1099].
7. NAS. Decreet of Teinds 1726, 78.
8. The man who managed the estate for the laird.
9. NAS. Decreet of Teinds 1726, 96. It is stated that 'the greater part of those were Oxen and young beasts'.
10. NAS. Decreet of Teinds 1726, 98–9.
11. NAS, Decreet of Teinds 1726, 108.
12. NAS. Decreet of Teinds 1726, 103.
13. NAS. Decreet of Teinds 1726, 115.
14. *OSA* vol, XX, 242.

15. *Clan Gillean*, 412.
16. *Johnson*, 196.
17. I have to thank the late JL Campbell of Canna for this reference.
18. It is stated in the Answers for the Synod dated 20 July 1731 that there were 735 examinable people in Coll.
19. *Boswell*, 283.
20. Petition of the Synod of Argyle &c 1 February 1732. BCP. I have to thank the late Miss Hope Macdougall of Macdougall for a copy of this petition.
21. *Clan Gillean*, 378.
22. He left 500 cattle, 180 horses and 500 sheep. He also left 3 ferry boats, implements for making whisky, fishing nets, long lines and other fishing equipment. He was also actively involved in arable farming as he left ploughs, harrows and 'other labouring utensils' plus 130 bolls of bear and 150 bolls of oatmeal [NAS. Register of Testaments. 15 March 1755].
23. ARB Haldane *The Drove Roads of Scotland* (1968), 45.
24. The first member of the family in Coll appears to be 'Ferquhar Kinity alias Macoile eire in Sodistill'. He had two sons John in Toraston and Murdoch [NAS. SC54.12. 6]. John was married to a Christain Cameron, who died in June 1706 leaving an estate worth £142 Scots including 7 cows valued at £93.6s.8d. By 1709 John was living in Gallanach [NAS. CC12. 2. 1]. In 1716 he is possibly the John Kennedy in Caolis [*Inhabitants... 1716, 168*]; 16 July 1709: Murdoch Kennedy in Cornaigbeg against Donald Maclean in Gallanach 'who wrongouslie intrometted with ane sword belonging to the said persewer worth 8 pennies'. [NAS. CC12. 2. 1]
25. NAS. CH1. 2. 49. 266.
26. NAS. SC54. 12. 6. 30 December 1710.
27. In 1733 the Session of Coll 'discharged Murdoch Kennedy of his Intromission with the fines preceeding the date hereof' [NAS. CH2. 70. 1. 15 August 1733.]. Later in 1733, it is stated that he was their collector. If he was a drover, he would be used to handle large sums of money
28. *Inhabitants... 1716*, 155.
29. NAS. CH2. 70. 1.
30. *Inhabitants... 1716*, 163.
31. Colm Ó Baoill *Eachann Bacach* (1979), 55–59.
32. Eric Cregeen and Donald W Mackenzie *Tiree Bards and their Bardachd* (1978), 6.
33. NAS Register of Testaments. 15 March 1755.
34. *Boswell*, 279.
35. NLS MSS. 3733. 61.
36. NAS. CH2. 70.1. Cliad 18 February 1733
37. NAS. SC54.12. 6.
38. NAS. CH2. 70. 1.
39. BCP. John Johnston to HAC Maclean 15 September 1897.
40. BCP. John Johnston to HAC Maclean 19 January 1900.
41. NAS. Register of Tailzies. 24 March 1755.
42. NAS. GD174. 1300.
43. BCP Pennycross folder.
44. Hugh Maclean, Glasgow to Alexander Maclean of Pennycross. 25 February 1779. BCP. Pennycross folder.
45. PRO. AO. 15 February 1781.
46. John A Munroe *Louis McLane: Federalist and Jacksonian* (1973). I have to thank the author for a copy of this book.

Chapter Fourteen

The '45

The improvement in Scotland's economy was interrupted by renewed Jacobite activity. The Government had good intelligence of their intentions. In 1744, when it was expected that a Jacobite uprising would take place, Stonefield wrote to Milton on 16th February from Inveraray:

> if the French fleet puts into the Western Isles or Coast of Scotland I expect to have advice of it soon. I have directed my friends in Ardnamurchan, the northwest part of the continent towards the sea of this shire to send to the Isle of Canna for intelligence because there is in that isle a harbour that lyes central for information.[1]

He wrote again on 3rd March that he had been informed by a friend that Donald Cameron, who had served as 'a soldier in the King's Guards', and now lived in Morvern,

> did about the 8th March go north from Lochiel's to Lord Lovat upon pretence of some ... business, upon his return [he] went to Morvern & Suinard and took lists of the effective men in these countries, that he disclosed himself only to some few Gentlemen, whom he swore to secrecy, and desired them to dispatch the sowing of the seed corns ... From Morvern he ferry'd over to the Isle of Mull with letters to Mr McLean of Torloisk, & McLean of Brolas ... From Mull I am informed that when Torloisk received the first notice of an Invasion, by letters from his son Hector McLean writer in Edinburgh, he sent for his neighbour the Laird of Mackinnon & other gentlemen in his neighbourhood & made merry with them for two days and two nights. That the common people are scouring their arms, and when at their cups which is more frequent than ordinary, do not conceal their joy, and pronounce the vengeance they are to inflict on the name of Campbell in their neighbourhood, once they take up arms ...

He goes on to say that

> the people of the Isles never were so well arm'd as they are at present; that for two years past they were order'd by the Lairds & Chiefs to buy arms and that few men in Mackleods, Sir Alexander Macdonalds & Clanranalds Country but had a Gun Sword & Durk. That they have been plentifully supply'd in guns from Liverpool & Bristoll by smuggling vessels.[2]

The excessive drinking made security lax. On 13th March Stonefield again reported that he had received information of Niel Maclean in Fainmore [in Mornish] in Mull, when in drink that in harvest last, some messages came to the Isle of Mull, from the North ... bearing that there was an invasion intended on Britain by Ireland, to be carry'd to execution in the month of Aprile, and that offers were made to Gentlemen to raise in Mull to favour the designe, that he did not believe any landed gentlemen would engage, but that some young Gentlemen of desperate fortune did agree to it, in the event of a landing from abroad.[3]

* * *

The young Macleans 'of desperate fortune' listed by Stonefield's informant were almost all younger sons: John Kingerloch's brother, Lachlan Coll's brother, Hugh Kilmory [in Scarba]'s brother, and an un-named brother of Killunaig's. John Maclean Tacksman of Icolmkill was the only exception. All were committed to raise companies.[4]

On first glance it would appear that if the spy's information was correct and that the Maclean lairds were playing the old game of backing both sides, ensuring that whoever won they would retain their estates. Such an interpretation is simplistic. Little is known of Kingerloch's brother John at this time, except that in 1743 he owed money to the Loch Etive Trading Company,[5] and that he asked Torloisk's opinion as to whether or not he should become involved in a French invasion. The latter 'disapprov'd & discharged him to be concerned'.[6]

Rather more is known of Coll's brother Lachlan. He took part in the '15, and later attended Glasgow University, although he probably never graduated. His nephew Donald, 'young Coll', told Boswell that he was 'a pretty fellow, and a poet, though very wild'.[7] He is, as we have seen, elsewhere described as a drunk, who 'would sell his religion and his family for a drink'.[8]

Hugh Kilmory's mother was an aunt of Dr Hector Maclean, the genealogist, who had married Hector of Coll's sister. Hugh himself was married to Anne, the daughter of *Maighstir Seathan*, the poet minister and widow of John Maclean in Grishipol, Coll. Hugh Kilmory was tacksman of Kinlochspelve on Lochbuie's estate. He was also a reciter of Gaelic poetry. Dr Hector's daughter Christina Mackenzie writes:

> I remember hearing Hugh Kilmory repeting *Conn Mac an derig* in my father's house in Glasgow in the year 49. I was then Eight years of age, & was much delighted with Conans usage for his forwardness, so much so that I lern'd two or three of the verses from him & still I remember the small variation that is betwext them and the present editions of it.[9]

At first glance it is not clear who Killunaig's brother was. Dr Hector's uncle Charles Maclean of Killunaig had died in 1743. In 1744 his eldest son, Allan was probably serving as a cadet in Marjoribanks' Regiment in Dutch service. The second son, Hector, was tacksman of Torren, which is also in Brolas. Neither is likely to be described as 'Killunaig'. However, Charles's daughter had married Donald, third son of Hector Maclean in Ballimartin in Tiree, and he may well have succeeded his father-in-law in Killunaig. There was certainly a Donald Maclean tacksman of Killunaig in 1748.[10] Both of Donald's elder brothers were known Jacobites and, as we shall see, Donald was probably one too.

The reason why I have gone into such detail on the men accused to Stonefield of being Jacobites is to illustrate that by 1745 Jacobitism was limited to a few closely related families. As we shall see, this is a useful observation, as it helps to work out who the crypto-Jacobites probably were. The draconian penalties for treason probably ensured that only those killed at the battle of Culloden, or like Allan Drimnin were acquitted on a technicality, were listed as Jacobites in later copies of Dr Hector's 'Genealogical Account'.

* * *

The story of the '45 has been told so often that it is only necessary to give details here of what concerned the Macleans of Coll and their immediate relatives and neighbours. Recently the diary of a Captain John Maclean has been discovered and published. Unfortunately the editor wrongly identifies the author.[11] He can be shown to be John Maclean, 2nd son of Hector Maclean in Ballimartin, whose family were the first casualties of the Campbell takeover of Tiree. He was also the grandson of John Diùrach Maclean, who commanded the 'forlorn hope', and was one of the heroes of the battle of Inverkeithing.[12]

Hector Ballimartin's eldest son Lachlan, as we have seen, had served in the Scots Guards in Spain and was taken prisoner at Brihuega. He next appears on record as a captain in the '15; perhaps significantly he did not serve in the Maclean battalion, but in that of Mackintosh of Borlum. Possibly he returned to Britain with Borlum when he was released as a prisoner of war, or more likely after he had changed sides.

John, the author of the '45 diary is less well documented. From the evidence of his diary he writes like a soldier, noting the strategic and tactical organisation of the Jacobite forces, and keeping a cool head in adversity. He evidently had previous military experience. He may well also have served in Spain, and is possibly the unidentified John Maclean, who was the Adjutant of 'Collonel Mackenzie's Regiment', captured at Sheriffmuir and on the 14 November 1715 brought to the Castle of Stirling.[13] He was clearly not in the first flush of youth, and notes on more than one occasion that he was sick. He is probably the un-named brother of Donald Killunaig, mentioned in 1744 by Stonefield. Curiously he is not mentioned in any list of those who took part in the uprising, but then neither is Donald Maclean, who wrote the last few pages of the diary. The probable reason why they have been left out is that, although they were gentleman, John was probably landless and living with his brother Donald, who was tacksman of a relatively small farm and not a laird.[14]

John Maclean was a cultivated man with an interest in what he saw. He inspects old Craigmillar Castle[15] and the Duke of Hamilton's palace, has an eye for an appropriate classical allusion en route to Kendal, comments on meeting 'two violers with their fiddles playing the King Shall Enjoy his Own Again' near Preston, and regrets not seeing 'a Curious Silk Manufactory' at Derby.

Our diarist is also an unquestioning Jacobite. He notes that on

The 14th of August 1745 I went from Broloss in Mull & Crossed the Sound of Mull and arrived the 16th August at Kinlochmudart where I had the honour and Satisfaction to Get a kiss of his royal Highness his hand and after Dinner the Same Day I was ordered by his Highness Back to Mull where I continued untill the 5th Septr being the time I went off from Killunaig in Broloss ...[16]

How many men he took with him to the rising is uncertain. He writes of putting 'myself & Small Company with the Laird of MacLauchlan', and of having on one occasion 'ane Ensign, a Sergeant, and 22 private men' at Musselburgh. Whether or not they all came from Brolas is never made clear.

* * *

Brolas was the estate of Allan Maclean, the only legitimate son of Donald Maclean of Brolas, who as we have seen, had died in 1725. Allan was in an unenviable position. The Duke of Argyll was about to redeem his wadset on Brolas, which would leave Allan and his widowed mother landless. He had also just been refused a commission in Lord Loudoun's Highland Regiment.[17] If ever there was 'a desperate young gentleman' in 1745, it was Allan Brolas. Yet he did not join the rebellion. The probable reason why he did not rebel was that Allan was to marry Una, the daughter of Hector Maclean of Coll, and was already under his influence.[18]

* * *

Hector of Coll was at Talisker in Skye when the Prince landed at Kinlochmoidart. Coll's daughter Mary had recently married John Macleod of Talisker and the local lairds attended the wedding celebrations.[19] On 11 August Sir Alexander Macdonald of Sleat wrote to Lord President Forbes of Culloden to tell him of the reaction of the local chiefs to the Prince's landing. He went on to say:

> Mr MacLean of Coll is here with his daughter, lately married to Talisker; and he assures us of his own Wisdom; and, as he has mostly the direction of that Clan, promises as much as in him lies to prevent their being led astray.[20]

As we have seen Hector of Coll was the guardian of Allan Maclean of Brolas. Allan Brolas appears to have been born circa 1725.[21] He matriculated at Glasgow University in 1737.[22] He was one of several Macleans who joined the Scots Brigade as private soldiers in the early 1740s. He was later to claim that at the outbreak of the '45 'I ca[me] home from Flanders at the desire [of] the Ministry rais'd cloath'd & suc[coured] a company of a hundred un[til] I joined the royal army'. It is likely that it was Forbes of Culloden who was behind 'the desire of the Ministry' that he came home. Hector also sent 60 men, at his own expense to Inveraray for the Militia, but the battalion was complete before they arrived and they were sent home.[23] As they were not officially mustered and received no pay there is no record of who these 60 men were. We therefore have no direct evidence as to whether or not Coll's household men continued as a distinct body in the mid-eighteenth century.

That it is not fanciful to suggest that the *luchd-tighe* might have survived into the mid-eighteenth century is supported by the fact that as late as 1781 it is said that Maclean of Kingerloch 'trusted to the protection of his mountains & his dependents against the authority of the law'. He is described as a 'Highland Chieftain . . . [who] appears more like an Eastern Potentate than an obedient subject' and keeps a bodyguard of 'eight stout fellows determined to defend their chief'.[24]

* * *

Our diarist served throughout the '45 campaign. He took part in the battle of Prestonpans, where the Jacobites defeated the Hanoverian Commander-in-Chief in Scotland. He then marched with his company into England, and went as far as Derby, where Charles Edward was persuaded to return to Scotland. He was sick in Stirling and not present at the last Jacobite success on 16 January 1746 at the battle of Falkirk.

Present at Falkirk, but on the opposite side, was Hugh Maclean, younger of Kingerloch. He had been recruiting in Argyll when the Prince landed, and was one of four 'extra' officers in Loudoun's Regiment, who joined the Duke's cousin Colonel Jack Campbell at Inveraray in September 1745. He was with him at Dumbarton on 27 December. After the battle of Falkirk he was sent to Perthshire with 300 of the Argyll Militia. On 17 March Lord George Murray surprised all the government's militia posts from Kinlochrannoch to Struan. All the officers and men were taken prisoner.[25]

On 16 April two militia officers, who had been captured at Rannoch were interviewed at Inveraray.[26] They claimed they had been starved into joining the rebels, but had eventually escaped. They also claimed that Lieutenant Hugh Maclean had enlisted in the rebel army, worn their badge [i.e. the white cockade] and that he had been dispatched from Fort Augustus accompanied by Allan Maclean, younger of Drimnin to go home to raise his people.

* * *

Meanwhile Captain John Maclean the diarist was sent out to 'bring Meall, White, Corn & forrage and Levie Money' from the Shire of Moray to the Jacobite camp near Forres. Lack of food was becoming an increasing problem for the Jacobite army, and on the 7 April seven officers were ordered to go on raiding parties to seize baggage horses. Captain John was sent with 20 men to the parish of Alves. He succeeded in his mission and returned to Forres with 18 horses on the 9 April.

Also taking part in this detail was the thirteen-year-old Ensign Murdoch Maclean, younger of Kilmory. He had a party of 24 men with him. They had the misfortune to be mistaken for Campbells by a party of Frenchmen in the Prince's army, 'upon which they rushed in upon our men and fell foull of one another. Severall primings burnt and guns snapped upon both sides [.] We had 2 or 3 men wounded but non[e] killed'.[27]

It is suggested by inference in John Maclean's diary that the different bodies of Macleans did not serve together until towards the end of the rising. This suggestion is supported by the claim, that shortly before the battle of Culloden the Macleans were arguing over who should command the clan in the forthcoming contest.[28] The other Maclean contingent was under the command of Charles Maclean of Drimnin.[29]

Both Drimnin and Captain John, and some 100 other Macleans, including Hugh Kingerloch's uncle John, were killed at the battle of Culloden. The diary was, however, carried on by Donald Maclean, who, as we have seen, is probably John's younger brother, the tacksman of Killunaig.[30] He writes:

> It was here that the author of the forgoing part of this Journall was killed and of 200 and upwards of the McLeans there Did not Remain 100 men the particulars of this Battell I cannot tell till further Authority.

He goes on to say:

> In this Battell the greatest Barbaritys was Committed that was heard to be done by Either Christians turks or Pagan, I mean by our Enemies who gave no quarters Kild our men that was wounded in cold blood and continued so doing for three or four Days or any others they could Catch.

The next page in the diary is blank. The new author continues on page 89:

> However I Donald McLean author of this part made my Escape through many Dangers and Difficulties with two more privat men of my Company and being pursued by a troop of Horse I

Came at Last much fatigued by Snow and wind to Strathargag 4 miles from the fild of Battell and began to quarter there...[31]

* * *

Once the Jacobites had been defeated at Culloden retribution began. The West Coast and Islands were vulnerable to the Royal Navy. On the 10 March at 4 am a party was landed in Morvern with orders to burn the houses and destroy the effects of those who had been in the rebellion. They began in Drimnin's toun. By six in the evening they had destroyed the coast of Morvern down to Ardtornish, with the exception of one toun belonging to Macdougals, who declared they had never been out. Captain Robert Duff commanded the appropriately named HMS *Terror*. He covered the infantry from his ship as they made their way along the coast so that the 'service was performed without the loss of a man on our side, although they were often fired at by parties of rebels from behind the hills'.[32]

It was the same story on the other side of the Sound of Mull, where Captain John Hay 'burnt near 400 houses, amongst them were several barns well filled with corn. Stacks of corn, horses, cows, meal and other provisions were destroyed by fire'.[33]

On 19 March Captain Duff reported that he had destroyed boats in Loch Hourn and the coast adjacent. On the 16th he was informed that 'Coll's brother was come over with boats for the Militia, [and] as that Gentleman's conduct has been unsured of late, I sent Capt. Kay out to watch their motions'.[34]

Coll's brother is probably Lachlan, the poet. He had certainly been involved in the uprising and a copy of a receipt survives which shows that on 16 February 1746 at Borrodale in Arisaig he received

> an hundred & Eighty Stand of arms three Casks of Powder three Boxes of Lead, three hundred & sixty flints to arm men for his R[oyal] H[ighness']s Service.[35]

He obtained them from Lieut. Maurice Macmahon of the Ultonia Regiment in Spanish service. Captain Duff later captured him and all his papers were seized.[36]

* * *

Macmahon had been in the Isles for several months. His visit was to have considerable repercussions for many people. On 25 October 1745 someone in the Ross of Mull reported that two days previously

> there passd a large three masted Vessel through the Sound of Icolumkill, piloted from Colonsay, by John McNeill Colonsay's brother & John McIllivoill, and in the Channell John McLean Tacksman of Icolumkill & John Morison went aboard in the Evening – they then droppd anchor off the Lands of Crevick, & Lousd in the night northward having John McLean & John Morison along as also those from Colonsay.
>
> She mounted 16 Guns besides Some Swivells. There appeared 30 or 40 men upon Deck mostly black Complexion, wore their own hair & of Low Stature, also two or three men of Distinction who made a great deall of John McLean & carryed him directly to the Cabin. There appeared also a good many men under Deck, those upon Deck spoke no English Except two of which one spoke Irish ... They seemd to have plenty of Foreign Liquors, gave some to the people & gave out they belong'd to England, & that they wanted to be piloted to Canna or Uist ... it is proper you acquaint the men of war upon Receipt hereof.[37]

John Maclean was reputed to be 'a violent Jacobite'.[38] On 17 July 1746 he was still at large for Airds wrote to Stonefield to say that:

> The party sent to Icolmkill having missed apprehending John McLain Tacksman of the East end of said island, some of his Friends have since applied to me by proposeing his surrendering himself At Inveraray and trust to his innocence as to the crimes laid to his charge, provideing only that his ffamily and effects suffered no dammage in the mean time till his tryal was over...[39]

John surrendered at Inveraray.
On 5 October Stonefield wrote to Milton;

> I send your Lordship the case of John Maclean, a tenant of his Grace in Icolumkill, whose crime is of a singular nature, & of a deep die. Will it not come under aiding and abetting traytors?[40]

The case passed to the Attorney General, who on 20 December wrote to the Duke of Newcastle, Secretary of State in Whitehall to say that:

> I have considered the case of John Maclean... and am of the opinion that there is not sufficient ground appearing... to charge him with High Treason. But as it seems to me very probable that he was Voluntarily engaged in piloting the ship knowing that it came from Spain with arms, money etc for the Pretender's Service (which if true would clearly be treason) I think it will be proper to direct further examination.[41]

John's friends had reason to be concerned for him, and in January 1747 a petition was signed by the ministers, heritors, feuars and tacksmen in Mull and Coll, including two Campbells, stating that he had

> from his infancy been of ane good undoubted Character & lived a good subject free of all disloyall practices known to us hitherto and that from the Commencement of the late wicked and unnatuall rebellion he lived peaceably at home, minding his own private business... untill in October 1745 he with several others innocently boarded a ship which afterwards appeared to be a Spanish Ship & by which he was abruptly carried away with others into the Island of Barra...[42]

One of those who appealed on behalf of John Maclean was his first cousin Lachlan Maclean, merchant in Glasgow, the son of Allan of Grishipol, who had fought as an officer in the Maclean battalion in the '15. Whatever his personal sympathies were in 1745, he was keen to keep in with the government.

On 3 September 1746 Lachlan was on board the *May of Glasgow* with a cargo of 500 bolls of English oat meal belonging to him and to his partners bound for Tobermory and the Clyde. Because of contrary winds he was obliged to put in to Loch nan Uamh in Arisaig. On the 6th in the evening two large French men of war entered the loch. They anchored near to the *May* and sent a boarding party of 20 men to seize her. Lachlan and the rest of his crew were taken prisoner and taken on board the largest ship called the *Happie* (34 guns, 26 or 28 swivels, and around 230 men). The other ship was the *Princess de Conti* (24 guns, as many swivels and 160–180 men).

The French men of war had been dispatched to take off Prince Charles Edward Stuart. It was France's sixth attempt to rescue him.[43] Lachlan was held prisoner for 15 days, during which time several Jacobites came on board the *Happie*, and the French 'were in constant apprehensions of our men of Warr, of which to my great Supprise, as well as to my loss none appeared'.

On 19 September it was agreed that the prisoners should be ransomed. The ransom articles were about to be written when a message from the shore came to Colonel Warren and Captain Bullen, the captains of the two French ships. They immediately 'got up, Dressed very fine, ordered me and my men to go aboard my vessel', and went ashore. When Colonel Warren returned at two in the morning, he ordered Lachlan and his skipper to sign the ransom agreement. He then carried off two hostages and most of their cargo. The Colonel was in great spirits, 'and told us publicklie he had now got the Prince, meaning the young pretender'.

The French ships set sail immediately, and the *May* sailed for Rum, where Lachlan sent his report to Coll's son-in-law, the Hanoverian Captain John Macleod of Talisker. He also sent a copy express to Stonefield.

On 31 December 1746 Lachlan wrote to Lord President Forbes of Culloden, and reminded him of their acquaintance 'by my takeing the farm of Ruag in Tirey in Anno 1740 to give your Lo[rdshi]p the trouble of this missive'. He reminds Culloden of 'John McLean who gott a tack of one half of Icollumkill from your Lo[rdshi]p in the year 1737', and explains his cousin's present circumstances. He says that John was taken to Barra against his will, and had 'to buy a Small boat' there to get him back to Mull. He tells how a warrant for his arrest had been issued by the Sheriff-depute for piloting the Spanish ship to Barra, and not reporting the incident when he got back to Mull; how he had never been to Barra before in his life and was incapable of acting as a pilot, and how he had been sworn to secrecy not to reveal what had occurred.

Lachlan explained that the previous week he had visited Stonefield, who had told him that the chief evidence against John was that he had been seen administering an oath of secrecy to the other Highlanders on board the foreign ship. That could be explained, as he was the only man on board who spoke both English and Gaelic, and therefore had been compelled to do so. He asks Culloden to take up John's case. It is not clear from the papers I have seen what happened to John. However, as none of the versions of Dr Hector's Genealogical Account I have examined mention the case, he was presumably eventually released.[44]

* * *

Coll's brother Lachlan does not appear to have been arrested for his receipt of Macmahon's arms. In his report of the 19 March 1746 Captain Duff of the *Terror* had written to Lord Milton:

> Coll, young Torloisk, and Mackinnon were with me yesterday, and gave great promises for the good behaviour for the people of Mull for the time to come, Coll also undertook for the people of Coll & Tiree, and told me he had wrote to you promising that in 48 hours after his return, he will collect all the boats in his island under his own house to be disabled by any person you please to appoint, reserving two for his own use.[45]

* * *

Hugh Kingerloch rejoined the Argyll Militia after the battle of Culloden, and was subject to an investigation into his conduct after he was captured. In early May Lieutenant-Colonel Jack

Campbell wrote to Lord Loudoun that there was a strong presumption that 'Lieutenant Allan [he means Hugh] Maclean of Captain Mackay's Company had joined the rebels after he had been taken prisoner in Rannoch'.[46]

Colonel Jack, however, wrote again in July that:

> as to Lt McLean we cannot find that there is any truth in the report of his having been employed in the rebel's service. However, as he is but a silly creature, I don't know but he may have uttered caprissions worthy of punishment.[47]

Towards the end of August 1746 the Argyll Militia was disbanded, and Lieutenant Hugh rejoined the Loudoun Highlanders. He found himself in command of Mackay's Company, as the latter was sick in Edinburgh. He was then put under arrest [why he was arrested is not explained]. In December Hugh wrote to Lord Loudoun to answer the accusations against him. He agreed that his conduct might be liable to Lord Loudoun's censure 'as all mortals are subject to frailty so am I', and begged his colonel's pardon. The letter is endorsed 'in arrest'.[48]

Lachlan Maclean of Kingerloch visited Mackay when in February 1747 he rejoined his company at Fort Augustus. Kingerloch and Mackay discussed Hugh's prospects. They agreed that he was unfit for service in the army and that he had large debts.[49] Mackay thought that Hugh's commission should be sold for very little. However, Hugh did not sell up at once. In May he marched with the Regiment from Fort Augustus, and sailed for Holland. There he was at the siege of Bergen-op-Zoom, and it was not until 1748 that he sold his commission.

After the '45 Allan Brolas also served in the Netherlands, where he became a captain in the Earl of Drumlanrig's Regiment in Dutch service. It was a post obtained for him by the Duke of Argyll.[50] The Duke had in 1749 for a payment of £20,000 Scots redeemed the wadset on Brolas, Gribun and Ardmeanach.[51] He granted Allan a nineteen-year lease of his former wadset.

* * *

What were Hector of Coll's politics? Boswell who examined his papers at Breacachadh thought that although the 'laird sent sixty men, he was in his heart of the principles which warmed the breast of his ancestor, Montrose's correspondent'.[52] One fact that supports this view is that his man of business in Edinburgh was Mr John Macleod of Muiravonside, who had a pension of £40 from the family of Coll. He was a longstanding Jacobite agent. His son Alexander, known as 'McCruslick' served as aide-de-camps to Prince Charles during the '45. He escaped to France and his father, who was devoted to him, says in a letter to Hector that he must be supported. He talks of his hopes for *the good cause*[53] and it is clear that, even after the disaster at the battle of Culloden, the Jacobites were still optimistic over the final outcome of their struggle.

Certainly even those who were in arms for the government had sympathy for the Prince. Hector's son-in-law Colonel John Macleod of Talisker expresses what was probably a not an uncommon opinion when in 1794 he wrote to Sir James Grant of Grant appealing for captain's half-pay:

> Which I think myself justly intitled to as I wrought it & risqued my Butt for the family and the throne when I served faithfully & ... was twice within an Ace of catching the *Pretender*. Tho' I thank God I [would] rather be what I am, not opulent, than Rich at the expence which woud have left a slur on myself & clan, tho' we did not escape it at that abominable Era. & then my orders from the D. of Cumberland were, not to trouble him with Prisoners. I would as soon put

an end to my owne life as to that of the young adventurer who did nothing but what any sensible Person would have done who had the same pretensions, and all that I acknowledge to you my very Dear friend, as turning ones coat is no disgrace now a days & now that unlucky family is gone I am as staunch a whigg in Politics as any other & and as stinch to the present administation as any Dutchman.[54]

Hector's eldest daughter Isabel had married Colin Campbell of Balimore. He was killed at the battle of Culloden when commanding a company in Loudoun's regiment.[55] Hector's second daughter Margaret married, as his second wife, Alexander Macdonald of Boisdale, who when he first landed on Eriskay did his best to persuade the Prince to go home. Even so he was taken prisoner on board the *Furnace*.[56] He was confined in London until the summer of 1747.[57] Like many other families in the Hebrides the family of Coll was divided in its loyalties in 1745.

* * *

Hector Maclean of Coll died on 26 October 1754 {OS}. He had retrieved the fortunes of the Macleans of Coll. They had returned to the position they held before the Civil Wars. Hector's prestige amongst his neighbours was such that at his funeral, so Boswell tells us, thirty cows and about fifty sheep were slaughtered and 'there were gentlemen at it from the mainland as well as the neighbouring islands'.[58]

There were significant internal changes on the Coll estate during Hector's 'reign'. Most important was the disappearance of the old wadsetters, who had lent Hector's predecessors money in exchange for land. Their departure is unlikely to have been the result of *force majeur*. It is no more than an impression, but it seems highly probable that it was Hector's deliberate policy to remove the wadsetters on the estate and regain complete control over it. It was not the end of the clan, but it was a different *Clan Mac Iain Abraich* that emerged in the mid-eighteenth century. In many ways it resembled the clan in the sixteenth century rather than in the disastrous bankrupt years of the seventeenth.

* * *

It was not just the wadsetters but also other relatively close cousins of the laird who now lost their land. The second family of Grishipol appear to have had a tack rather than a wadset and their lease came to an end when John of Grishipol died. Hector's brother Hugh, who built the 'White House' followed him as tacksman of Grishipol and was there when he succeeded to the estate. Hugh then set Grishipol in tack to his foster brother Sween MacSween.

In almost every case, once a family lost their land-holding in Coll, they left the island. There was, however, no shortage of candidates with sufficient capital to take their places. There was also no shortage of men on the Coll estate who were prepared to serve as soldiers. However, they were no longer to do so in clan feuds or in Jacobite rebellions. They were, as we shall see, to do so in regiments in the service of the Crown.

Notes

1. NLS MS 16597.
2. Ibid, 3 March 1744.
3. Ibid, 13 March 1744.

4. NLS MS16597. Although John Maclean Tacksman of Iona was his father's eldest legitimate son, his elder illegitimate brother had inherited and lost Treshnish.
5. NAS RH4. 93. 17. 1. 4. Loch Etive Tading Company Papers.
6. Ibid. He is certainly not the John Maclean who was commissioned in the Black Watch in 1739 mentioned by Stewart of Garth in *Sketches of the Highlanders of Scotland* (1822, reprinted 1977), 245. It is an identification that has misled several subsequent authors. [see *WHN&Q* 3rd Ser. No. 3 (2001)].
7. Boswell's *Tour of the Hebrides* (1936), 279.
8. Colm Ó Baoill *Eachann Bacach* (1979), 228.
9. NLS MS 73. 2. 26 f.65 Christina Mackenzie to Mrs Col. MacDonald of Boisdale May 1806.
10. NLS MS 17677 Rental of Broloss Wadset Lands Cropt 1748. He is probably the same 'Donald Maclean Tacksman of Killunaig to attend Presbytery on 13th September 1762 [NAS CH2. 273.1.], and therefore could not be Charles Killunaig's third son Donald, who was serving as an excise officer in Stirling before 2 February 1760 [Alexander Maclean of Pennycross: Genealogy of [torn] family of Torloisk & Kenlochaline. Ane Account of the marriage [torn] Intermarriages of my predecessors Since we descended from Dowart; by my fayr & Moyr. As I cannot make out my fayr's part till I see some friends I shall begin wt my moyr. I note it here from her own mouth this second of feb'y 1760 – She aged 69 years the tenth of July next–]. This paper is among the Pennycross Papers in the possession of the Very Reverend Allan Maclean of Dochgarroch; Donald's identification is strengthened by the fact that he married as his second wife Mary, daughter of John Maclean of Killean, who in 1748 had the tack of Kilimore, Ard & Kilfinchen in Brolas.
11. Iain Gordon Brown & Hugh Cheape (eds) *Witness to Rebellion* (1996).
12. Nicholas Maclean-Bristol.'John Maclean in his Highness's Army', *WHN&Q* Series 3, No. 3 (March 2002), 11–17.
13. T Cooper *The Political State of Great Britain* (1715), 508.
14. In 1748 Killinaig paid a rent of £90 Scots including 'Silver Rents Multure and Presents'. (NLS MS 17677).
15. *Witness to Rebellion*, 23.
16. *Witness To Rebellion*, 21.
17. TNA SP 41.16 folios 70–77. Argyll to Lord Harrington, Secretary for War. 31 May 1745. Argyll recommended the names of officers for the regiment. Donald (sic) Maclean of Brolas was on the original list but was then dropped 'considering there is another of that name who is preferable'. The other was Kingerloch's son Hew. Argyll notes: 'as the clan of that name is generally disaffected, any of them not so, are of great use'. Kingerloch also had a vote in parliamentary elections.
18. In 1733 Hector had bought out Brolas's debts from Colin Mackenzie, son to the Laird of Redcastle for £2,393 Scots as 'a Trust in my person for the behoof of Allan McLean now of Brolas my pupil and that I have in my Tutory Accompts charged him with the sum which I really paid out for obtaining the forsaid Disposition' [NAS RD 12. 27 November 1733].
19. The wedding took place on 28 July 1745 at Talisker. Breacachadh Castle Transcripts No. 46c.
20. Duncan Warrand (ed) *More Culloden Papers* (1929), 17.
21. He says that he was 17 in 1745 [BL, Add. Ms 38211, 34]. As his father died in April or May 1725 [NAS CC 12. 7] this statement cannot be correct.
22. *Alm. Uni. Glas.* 1728–1858.
23. *Boswell's Tour*, 279.
24. NAS CS 237. Mc/5/28. Process Hugh Maclean of Kingerloch against John McKay Messenger at Fort Augustus. 15 January 1781.
25. *Witness To Rebellion*, 34.
26. Huntingdon Museum, Pasadena, California. Loudoun Papers. 12022. I am grateful to Ruairidh Halford Macleod for this and subsequent references from the Loudoun Papers.
27. *Witness To Rebellion*, 35.
28. Frank McLynn (1988), 241. McLynn does not give a reference for this statement.

29. He did 'not acknowledge to have been guilty of rebellion' when he handed in his arms at Breacachadh Castle on 27 April 1716 (*Inner Isles*, 151), and illegally acted as a judge in 1727 (*WHN&Q* 1st Ser. No. xii (May 1980), 19–20.)
30. Donald's granddaughter was married to Allan Maclean of Crossapol in Coll, who in his version of Dr Hector's Genealogical Account describes Donald as 'a very brave man'. It is unlikely that he had a chance to show his bravery save in the '45. BCP, Crossapol MS, 41.
31. *Witness to Rebellion*, 37.
32. NLS MS 3733–3737, 185.
33. Ibid, 192.
34. Ibid, 206.
35. Ibid, 61.
36. JL Campbell & C Eastwick. 'The Macneils of Barra in the Forty-Five', *Innes Review*. I am grateful to the late JL Campbell of Canna, who in 1979 sent me an offprint of this article.
37. NLS MS 3733, 16.
38. NLS MS 16605, 89.
39. NAS GD14, 103.
40. NLS MS 16615, 225.
41. NAS GD14, 118.
42. NLS MS 3733–7, 185.
43. John S Gibson *Ships of the '45* (1967), 119–135; Lachlan's own account is as at NAS GD14, 114.
44. Lachlan's letter to Culloden is at NLS MS 16629.
45. NLS MS 3733–3737, 206.
46. Loudoun Papers 11208.
47. Ibid, 11199.
48. Ibid, 12090.
49. Ibid, 11955.
50. NLS MS 17677, 56. Memorial for Allan McLean of Brolas to the Duke of Argyll Inverary 17 September 1749.
51. Ibid, 53.
52. *Boswell*, 279–80.
53. *Boswell*, 279.
54. NAS GD248. 29. 2. 41.
55. James Ferguson *Argyll in the Forty-Five* (1951), 169.
56. *Ships of the '45*, 13–4, 74.
57. Henry Paton (ed) *The Lyon in Mourning* vol. III (1975), 33.
58. *Boswell*, 266.

Part III

British Service 1756–1793

Chapter Fifteen

The Seven Years War 1756–1763

Two years after Hector Maclean of Coll's death, war began again with France. The Seven Years War (1756–1763) was to have a profound effect on the Hebrides. It brought new ideas and new manners to those who took part. It was also the first occasion in which large numbers of Highlanders in British service fought in North America and opened the eyes of Hebrideans to the possibility of life in the New World.

The Seven Years War was not the first occasion when Highlanders joined the British Army. In 1690 the Earl of Breadalbane had suggested[1] that Highland regiments should be raised for the British service at home or abroad, and Whig chiefs raised four regiments for William III's wars in Europe. These regiments were disbanded at the end of hostilities and the first regular Highland regiment to survive was the 43rd Foot (later the 42nd Foot), better known as the Black Watch (the Royal Highland Regiment). It was formed in 1739 from the Independent Companies originally raised in 1725 by General Wade.

The fame of the Black Watch at the Battle of Fontenoy in 1744, and the exploits of the Highlanders in the '45, convinced British ministers that here was a resource that could be used for the benefit of the nation. William Pitt the elder claimed that he was the first minister to see the potential in the Highlanders. In a famous speech to the House of Commons in 1766 he stated:

> I sought for merit wherever it was to be found... and I found it in the mountains of the north. I called it forth, and drew into your service, a hardy and intrepid race of men! Men, who, when left by your jealousy, became prey to the artifices of your enemies and had gone nigh to have overturned the war before last.[2]

* * *

Although the Jacobite threat had not been eliminated by the battle of Culloden the Government knew from their spies that by early 1755 Prince Charles's offer to the French Court to raise men in the event of war with Britain had been declined.[3] They also knew from their agent 'Pickle', who was none other than Alexander Macdonnell younger of Glengarry, of the threat from the Scots Brigade.[4]

In 1753 Pickle forwarded to Henry Pelham, the Prime Minister, a copy of a report made for Prince Charles by Macdonnell of Lochgarry. In it Lochgarry states that he had agreed with the chiefs that they should provide over 9,000 men for another rising. The Macleans are noted as being able to put 700 men in the field.[5] The Government were also aware that, until he began suffering from the fits of apoplexy that led to his death in Rome in 1750, Sir Hector Maclean of Duart was one of the most active Jacobites in exile. Perhaps one of the reasons why Argyll backed Allan Brolas for a captaincy in the Scots Brigade was to boost him as a rival to Sir Hector. However, once Sir Hector was dead, it was Sir Allan, as Brolas now became, who was the threat. As a result when in 1749 Drumlanrig's Regiment was reduced to one battalion,[6] Sir Allan was out of a job.

In 1755 officers in the Scots Brigade were allowed to transfer to the British service and several Macleans did so. Among them was Allan Maclean, Torloisk's brother. He had distinguished himself in 1748 at the siege of Bergen-op-Zoom and was undoubtedly an able soldier, but the favours he received from the Government were out of all proportion to his importance, and there seems little doubt that this was done to eclipse Sir Allan's prestige.

Sir Allan was to claim that his 'enemy' the Duke of Argyll continuously thwarted his ambitions. Sir Allan probably believed, quite rightly, that as he had the affection of most of the clan he could raise a regiment of Macleans. However, when the time came it was Allan Torloisk, who was given a commission to raise 114th Foot whilst Sir Allan had to make do with a company in the 77th Foot, Montgomery's Highlanders.[7]

Forty men from Coll served in the Seven Years War,[8] rather more than were out in the '15. They probably served under Sir Allan. Certainly there was at least one man from Rum who did. He went with Sir Allan to North America.[9] There were probably others too.

Hector's heir Hugh Maclean of Coll was no soldier and his children were too young to serve in the army and, as son-in-law of the late Hector of Coll, the men from the Island were probably perfectly happy to serve under Sir Allan. He claimed that he recruited his company in two weeks.

Sir Allan took part in various campaigns in North America that won Canada for the British Empire.[10] On 19th June 1759 Major Alexander Campbell wrote from Canada to his father John Campbell of Barcaldine to say:

> Sir Allan Maclean is doing very well, and is much esteemed. If I survive the campaign I shall be more full on the subject. When the Knight gets a little Drink, he swears that he can scarce knows the difference betwixt a Breadalbane Campbell and a M'Lean. I hope if we live to go home to have no discredit in my Tutory of him.[11]

I have not found any muster rolls of Montgomery's Highlanders, nor any lists of Sir Allan's recruits. It is therefore not possible to analyse who were the NCOs and private soldiers from Coll's estate who served in America. The only exception is Charles Maclean in Kilmory in Rum.

Although all of the officers in Sir Allan's company were Macleans, none were from Coll.[12] Two of Hector of Coll's grandsons, sons of Alexander Macdonald of Boisdale, did serve in North America. Both were killed in the war.[13]

* * *

In order to understand the background from which men joined the army from the Coll estate in the second half of the eighteenth century, it is necessary to examine the estate in some detail. There is a great deal of new material available to us.

When Hector of Coll died he left only daughters.[14] His brother Hugh, in accordance with the entail, therefore succeeded to the estate and immediately took over Coll House at Breacachadh. Hugh, as we have seen, had previously lived at Grishipol, presumably working his land with his sub-tenants, workmen and cottars. He also acted as a merchant and discounted bills of exchange.[15] It was Hugh who built the 'White House Grishipol'.[16] However, he never lived there as he inherited the estate before it was completed.[17] He will previously have lived in a small thatched cottage little different to those of his sub-tenants.

In 1748 Hugh had married Janet, sister of John Macleod of Talisker.[18] Their first child was still born, it arrived on 12 March 1749. Over the next nineteen years Hugh and Janet produced thirteen children. One was born each year from 1749 to 1753. There was then a gap until 1755. They then had other children in 1756, 1758, 59, 61, 63, 66 and an after-thought in 1768. Four died as children.[19] It is evident that, unlike English upper-class families [from as early as the last quarter of the seventeenth century], Hugh and Janet were accepting God's will over child birth and not using any form of contraception.[20] The fact that two children were named Hector also suggests that the resigned acceptance of the expendability of children survived, even in the highest echelons of Hebridean society, into the middle of the eighteenth century.[21]

Janet Macleod, Lady Coll, is said to have been 'happy in a pious education and since in the practice of untainted virtue'. However, she was a firm believer in the second sight of which she claimed to have personal experience. She once told her kinsman Macleod of Hamer that

> she heard at different times, in a closet adjoining her bed chamber, a great noise as if the wall was fallen, which so alarmed her that she went in directly into the said chamber and examined every thing about it, which she was surprised to find in the same order she had left them. In a few days a person died in her neighbourhood and the same articles for his sowe [shroud, winding sheet] and coffin were taken out of that closet, after which no more noise was heard therein.

According to Hamer, who wrote under the pseudonym Theophilus Insulanus,[22] 'it is frequently observed that the articles employed for a sowe and coffin are so haunted as to make a noise for some time before they are put in use'. Hamer goes on to say that Lady Coll also informed him that:

> Maclean of Knock, an elderly respectable gentleman living on their estate, as he walked in the fields before sunset saw a neighbour, who had been sick for a long time, coming that way accompanied with another man; and as they drew nearer he asked them some questions, and how far they intended to go? The first answered they were to travel forward to a village he named, and then pursued his journey with a more than ordinary pace. Next day early in the morning, he was invited to his neighbour's interment, which surprised him much as he had [so it] seemed spoken with him the evening before, but he was told by the messenger that came for him the deceased person had been confined to his bed for seven weeks and that he departed this life a little before sun-set, much about the time he saw him in a vision the preceding day.[23]

Hugh's family had considerable influence on him, particularly his brother-in-law Professor Roderick Macleod of King's College, Aberdeen. Roderick was responsible for recruiting 'lads o' pairts' for King's College, and took a fatherly interest in their careers.[24] Roderick was also responsible for Hugh's move in 1765 to Aberdeen[25] to superintend his children's education. He took other young men with him including the heir of the Maclonichs in Lochaber, whose ancestor had preserved Coll's child after his father was killed at the battle of Blarnicara. Young Maclonich wished to join the army. Hugh failed to get him a commission, but found him a place in the train of artillery, where he became a sergeant.[26]

* * *

Hugh was visiting Colonel Macleod of Talisker in Skye when the brothers-in-law had a meeting that was to have some significance for Scottish literature. The meeting was with Mr Ewan Macpherson, then a shoolmaster in Badenoch who was also on a visit to Skye. There he had met an old acquaintance James Macpherson who was in Skye collecting the poems of Ossian. James could not read Gaelic characters. Ewan could and as it was hoped that Ossianic verse would be found in ancient manuscripts in Skye an attempt was made to get him to assist James.

Ewan also had a better grasp of Gaelic orthography than James and was persuaded, against his will, to travel to Dunvegan. When he reached Dunvegan he found Hugh Coll and Talisker there. They insisted that Ewan accompany James Macpherson to the Outer Isles to transcribe the recitation of any people they could find, who could repeat the poems of Ossian. Although Ewan was unwilling to be absent from his charge in Badenoch, the brothers-in-law were adamant and the Macphersons set off for the Long Island.[27]

The outcome of James Macpherson's tour was the publication in 1760 of *Fragments of ancient poetry collected in the Highlands of Scotland*. Few books can have had so great an influence on a particular region of Europe. It immediately caught the public's imagination, and a subscription was raised to enable the 'collector', James Macpherson, to visit the Hebrides. The result of his journey, published in 1762 under the title *Fingal, an ancient epic poem in six books, composed by Ossian the son of Fingal*, caused an uproar. Even patriotic Scots who had welcomed the *Fragments* doubted the existence of an epic as published by Macpherson. We know now that, although he had collected genuine manuscripts, Macpherson's book was a mixture of ancient Gaelic poetry and his own imagination.[28]

* * *

It is uncertain what, if any, influence Hugh Coll had on his other brother-in-law Dr Hector Maclean, who was married to Hugh's only sister. Dr Hector, who had spent many years in Glasgow as a surgeon, returned to Mull in 1767. He was an enthusiastic collector of Gaelic poetry, particularly concerning his own clan. As we have seen, he had also, in 1734, written a brief historical and genealogical account of the Macleans. His contribution to our knowledge of the area is immense.

Dr Hector was acutely conscious of the changes at work in the Hebrides. His collection of poetry and genealogy are attempts to preserve a culture that was rapidly disappearing. He was, however, also an incorrigible snob and it is clear from his genealogical account that he ignores men who he believed, despite the length of their pedigree, had sunk in economic status. For instance the ancient family of Lehir is dismissed with the statement that 'there are a number of commoners in the country yet remaining of the descendants of this family including Hugh Maclean, alias *Mac Eachan vic Ewen vic Ewen vic Ilchalum* . . . and several others too tedious to mention'.

* * *

As we will see Hugh seems to have been content to allow things to continue on his estate much as they had in the past and Dr Walker, the future Professor of Natural History at Edinburgh University paints an idyllic of life on Coll. The hills he writes:

> are interspersed with small Valleys of arable Land, which produce Corn in great Plenty and Perfection. In several parts of the Island also, there are extensive Fields of Excellent Pasturage. The antient Fortress of the Chieftain, and his present House, which is a very good Modern Building, are situate upon the Side of the Bay, by which Vessels have access to the Island, in a much finer Lawn, than many that are modelled by Art. Among several other beautiful Spots of

the same kind, which occur in this Island, there is one upon the north Side, which in the Month of July appeared very remarkable. It is a circular plain, about half a mile over, like so much bowling Green Ground surrounded with Hills. It is a rich sandy Soil, which is entirely filled with red and yellow Clover, a variety of yellow Ranunculus's and a vast Profusion of Bloody Cranesbill and other Flowers, which altogether, form the most beautiful embroidered Carpet that the Earth perhaps is anywhere covered with.

He also notices the amount of sand everywhere, except upon the hills. The sand he says 'driving from the Shore, has become very detrimental. In one place, there is near 500 Acres of excellent Land, laid entirely desolate. The Sand being now several yards deep, where the People yet alive have reaped the best Grain in the Island'.[29]

'The Agriculture of the Inhabitants', he writes:

is in a very simple uncultivated State, from the Disadvantages of their Situation. Their Possessions are very small but equally divided and capable of furnishing them, with all the necessaries of Life, they seem to have any Demand for.

Hugh does not appear to have attempted to change this way of life. As a result he was popular with his tenants. Dr Walker, who visited the island before Hugh moved to Aberdeen comments on this popularity. 'Their chieftain', he writes 'for whom they have the greatest affection, governs them with great equity and mildness, and lives among them in this remote island, like a master of a family consisting of above a thousand people'.[30]

Coll's people on Rum were probably as content as those in Coll. By 1755 they had got used to being Protestants instead of Roman Catholics. Their neighbours in Canna, however, continued to shake their heads over the people of Rum's apostasy. On one occasion in a sermon the priest told the people of Canna that 'if you commit such crimes the Lord will turn his back upon you then what will you do?' Upon hearing this, a poor man got up and said seriously 'if there be amongst us any such wicked person, let them be sent to Rum'.[31]

On 20 March 1765 Neill MacNeill, the catechist for the parish of the Small Isles, reported to the General Assembly of the Church of Scotland. In his report he lists the men, women and children in the parish. He says that out of a population of 302 in the Isle of Rum there were 56 households. All were Protestants.[32] Macleans predominated. In the list of the heads of households 37.5% (21) were Macleans.

Only seven male servants were employed in Rum. Macleans employed six of them. There were also three elders in Rum. All were Macleans. All were recent arrivals on the island.[33] They had replaced the Macleods, Macquarries and Campbells who had previously been the island's leaders.

Dr John Walker, who visited Rum in 1764 and again in 1771, says that some thirty years earlier the island had been almost depopulated by small pox. As a result Maclean of Coll probably encouraged younger sons of cadets of his family to move to there. Their way of life there was somewhat different to living on Coll. Firstly, as already stated, there were then no sub-tenants on Rum, all the heads of households holding their land directly from the laird. Their diet was probably more spartan too. There is little arable land on Rum, just enough to provide the people with sufficient grain to keep them in bread during the winter. In the summer they lived entirely off animal food. As a result they were healthy and long-lived. Walker says that:

The year before I was there, a man had died in the island aged 103, who was 50 years of age before he had ever tasted bread; and during all the remainder of his long life had never eat of it from March to October, nor any other food, during that part of the year, but fish and milk; which is still the case with all the inhabitants of the Island. I was even told, that this old man used frequently to remind the younger people, of the simple and hardy fare of former times, [and] used to upbraid them with their indulgence in the article of bread, and judged it unmanly in them to toil like slaves with their spades, for the production of such an unnecessary piece of luxury.[34]

Rum is a mountainous island of some 15,000 acres. The highest point, Mount Ascheval, is over 2,000 feet. The settlements were all on the coast. The 'capital' was the little port in Loch Scrisort. It had only recently become the island's 'capital' and in 1765 still had only a population of 46. The major centres of population in 1765 were still Harris with 87 inhabitants and Kilmory with 84. However, Kinloch Scrisort has the only sheltered harbour on the island, and even that was exposed to easterly winds. It was the only place from which cattle could be exported. The increased importance of the export in cattle to the estate meant that Rum's potential could no longer be ignored.

Many of Kilmory's population were Macleans, whose ancestor had quarrelled with Maclean of Coll and settled in Skye before coming to Rum, perhaps in the late seventeenth century.[35] One branch of the family in Kilmory in 1765 were *Sliochd Lachlin* who were said to die suddenly if they shot a deer on Mount *Finchra*. Martin Martin was told of several instances of this happening and 'none of the tribe . . . will ever offer to shoot the deer in that mountain'.[36]

* * *

In 1765 there was a population of 138 in the Isle of Muck. 110 were Protestants. The remainder were Roman Catholics. Unfortunately the 'papists' were not divided by household but listed as individuals by the Catechists and it is not possible to identify who they were. Eight were married to unnamed Protestants and there were only two households where the whole family was Roman Catholic.

There were 21 protestant households on Muck. Only 5 were Macleans. One, Hector the laird employed a 'herd' and a female servant. The only other family shown to employ a servant was Duncan Rankin, Hector's piper, who employed two female servants. There was one other male servant, a John Maclean, who was a Roman Catholic. It is not stated who employed him. No other Maclean was a 'papist' and the catechist who made the list says that Hector Maclean of Islemuck and his wife were ardent Protestants who prevented the Roman Catholic priest from visiting the island.[37]

Muck is four miles in circumference, low lying and fertile. It was held of the King by Maclean of Coll for 'sixteen bolls of barley to be paid between the feast of Christmas and the Purification or four merks for each boll'.[38] Coll had set the island in feu to his younger son Mr Hector in the late 1620s or early 1630s.

* * *

One source of income that was not available to Hector Maclean of Coll, but was available to his brother Hugh, was the production of kelp. Kelp, a low-grade alkali, made from the ash of certain seaweeds was used in the manufacture of soap, glass, and many other products. From about the mid-eighteenth century, local supplies from the Hebrides became competitive with those from the Baltic, the Mediterranean, and North America. Kelpers cut the raw material by working along the shore or from boats. They then carried it up the beach in creels, spread it out to dry, and reduced it to ash by burning. At first its value was not appreciated and in 1754 Mr Hector Maclean, the Minister of Coll, sold the rights to the kelp on his farm in Coll to an Irishman for two guineas. The latter made 25 tons of kelp there that year alone.[39]

As no hay was made in Coll the cattle did not have enough to eat in the winter. Walker says that the cattle then eat sea weed 'which they devour greedily, and though at a great distance from the sea, know exactly when to repair to the shore at the time of the ebb'.[40]

There is no comment on what effect the export of kelp had on the fertility of the soil. As we have seen in the argument over the teinds in 1726, the tenants believed that the use of kelp was essential to them. In the long term its loss would have had a disastrous effect on the productivity of the island.

Hugh continued to act as a merchant after he inherited the estate. He lent Lachlan Macquarrie of Ulva money, wadset on part of his property,[41] and in 1764 financed trade with Gothengurg.[42] He was also interested in establishing the linen industry in Coll. Dr Walker says that Hugh was prepared to spend £200 on building a lint mill at Breacachadh, and to provide accommodation for a spinning school at the White House of Grishipol. However this ambitious scheme does not appear to have taken place.

* * *

Although no officers from the Coll estate served in the Seven Years War, several of their neighbours had done so. Before the Seven Years War, gentlemen in the Hebrides kept to the company of their fellow Gaels. The war, however, forced them into the company of those who often ridiculed their homely ways, and those who had been exposed to fashionable southern manners were determined that their friends should not be behind them in adopting a new more sophisticated way of life. For example, Sir Allan's Major in America had, as we have seen, written about him to his father John Campbell of Barcaldine. In the same letter he writes about young Campbell of Ballinaby:

> That as he got no education before he left the country, keeping amongst the people I live with is the only method I can think of to supply the deficiency; he is a very pretty lad but would be lost if I did not take that method; his father may grudge the money but I did it for the best and would expect he would do the same by my son: thirty pounds a year will enable the boy to live in good company, and I am certain 'tis better for him to get much less from his father in the long run and be fit to keep gentlemen's company, than go home as he would do scarce a companion for a ploughman, for when I took him into my charge, he really could hardly read nor write.[43]

Lieutenant Hugh Maclean, tacksman of Langamull on Torloisk's estate, had served in the 114th Regiment of Foot. In 1763, when announcing his imminent return home to his old friend Dr Alexander Maclean, he writes:

> We will endeavour to make you as truly happy in our company and conversation as lies in our power, and make you acquainted with the terms and rules of the art military and other genteel methods of life practised by the army, and especially show you how gentlemen's wives abroad are to be attended and visited according to the newest modes... in short will do everything that may contribute to the care of your person in the genteelest manner.

Gentility became an obsession. It was not only Lieutenant Hugh who was affected. It is ever present in Kingerloch's correspondence. In 1772 he wrote to advise his cousin young Lochbuie, who had recently come of age that 'he ought to consider that he now comes upon the stage of trial and probation and into the world. And it's not the same game that has been acted a century back and will be approved of now – no it's from a prudent cautious genteel behaviour that a gentleman is to gain respect'.[44]

Pitt may have 'sought for merit wherever it was to be found ... [and] ... found it in the mountains of the north'. Those from the North, who served in the army in the Seven Years War, found in gentility something that was change their society as much as they themselves contributed to the conquest of Canada.

Notes

1. Robert Clyde *From Rebel to Hero* (1995), 150.
2. *Hansard's Parliamentary History 1766* (1813), xvi, 98.
3. *Pickle the Spy*, 288.
4. Nicholas Maclean-Bristol 'Jacobite Officers in the Scots Brigade in Dutch Service', *JSAHR*, vol. 82, No. 330 (Summer 2004), 97–108.
5. *Pickle the Spy*, 217–8.
6. Ferguson *Scots Brigade*, ii, 391.
7. Sir Allan did not go to America with the regiment and was not included in the 'General Return ... of the 1st Highland Battalion commanded by the Honourable Archibald Montgomery Lieutenant Colonel Commandant which was made at Charleston in South Carolina' on 18th September 1757. [LO 6695. I have to thank Mary L. Robertson of The Huntington Library, San Marino, California for a photocopy of this document]. Allan recruited three additional companies raised in 1758 [TNA. WO4.56.232–234] which he took to America.
8. *Report on the Hebrides*, 169.
9. He was Charles Maclean of *Sliochd Ruaridh Mhic Ghilleasbuig* [*Clan Gillean*, 401].
10. BL, Add. MS 38211, 34.
11. *TGSI*, xxiv, 35.
12. Niel Maclean 'Military Macleans 1756–9. *WHN&Q* 1st Series, No. III (1976), 5–12.
13. *The Kingdom of Scotland*, 868
14. His two surviving daughters were Una, the wife of Captain Allan Maclean of Brolas and Sibella, wife of the Captain Allan Cameron of Glendessary. They claimed that Hugh had illegally 'intromitted' with £80 of gold and silver & banknotes found in 'the defuncts repositories' after his decease [NAS Commissary Records of the Isles. Reg. of Tests. 15 March 1755].
15. Glasgow City Archives. Inventory of debts owed to Roderick Macleod Merchant in Glasgow 1724–40: his customers in Coll in the 1720s include 'Lady Coll Elder', 'Allan MacLean, alias Mac neill oig in Coll', 'Donald Mac phaden alias Mac Euin Roy in Breakachie'. In the 1730s they include Hector of Coll himself, his brothers Lachlan and Hugh, John Maclean in Grishipol, 'Charles Maclean alias McLachlin vic hearlich, Merchant' and 'Hector McLean alias McEan vic Ewin, Shopman'; Macleod appears to have traded with all the Western Isles as well as with Bristol and Holland; he was buying animal skins in the Highlands [T-MJ 377 (a).
16. RCAHMS *Argyll*, vol. 3 (1980), 231–2.
17. Margaret M McKay *Report on the Hebrides*, 174.
18. B. 20 December 1723; d. 21 July 1780.

19. Maclean of Coll Family Bible. I have to thank Miss Anne Hamilton for the gift of this bible and other heirlooms of the family of Coll.
20. Lawrence Stone *The Family, Sex and Marriage in England 1500–1800* (1977), 415–6.
21. *Ibid*, 70.
22. *Boswell*, 186.
23. Theophilus Insulanus [Donald Macleod of Hamer] *A Treatise on the Second Sight* (1763 [reprinted 1817], 13–4
24. IF Grant *The Macleods* (1959), 590.
25. Signed 17 May 1765; Registered 1 December 1770: Hugh Maclean of Cole Esq sasine of 'all & haill that tennement of land with the closs &ca' belonging to Alex. Burnett 'sometime sub-principal'. *Aberdeen Sasines* Vol. II.
26. *Boswell*, 274.
27. Henry Mackenzie *Report of the Committee of the Highland Society of Scotland on the Poems of Ossian* (1805), 95.
28. The controversy over the authenticity of Ossian's works and Macpherson's influence is voluminous. For a commentary see Malcolm Chapman *The Gaelic Vision in Scottish Culture* (London, 1978).
29. *Report on the Hebrides* (1980), 169–70.
30. *Report on the Hebrides* (1980), 172.
31. British Fisheries Society's Report. I have to thank the late JL Campbell of Canna for this reference.
32. EUL. La. III, 839.
33. They were: John Maclean in Harris, Rum, b. 1724. He was son of Charles, 2nd son Neil Og Maclean in Crossapol, Coll. Later in Kinloch Srisort, Rum; Allan Maclean in Giurdal, Rum, b. 1727. He was son of John, son of Charles, 4th son of John Maclean of Grishipol, Coll; John Maclean in Cove, Rum, b. 1695. He was the grandson of Hugh, 3rd son of Mr Hector Maclean of the Isle of Muck.
34. *Report on the Hebrides*, 196.
35. *Clan Gillean*, 396–402.
36. *Martin Martin*, 273.
37. EUL. La. III. 839.
38. BCP. 1898 Translations of Coll Charters. No. 38a. & 48.
39. Rev. Dr Walker 'Essay on kelp' *Highland Society of Scotland* vol. 1, 4.
40. *Report on the Hebrides*, 173.
41. NAS Register of Sasines. 10. 9. 24 July 1764 & 27 November 1765; GD174. 6. 1762–8: Writs concerning annual rents due by Lachlan McQuarrie of Ulva to Hugh Maclean of Coll from the lands of Ardnacalach, Carnacallich, and others in the isles of Ulva, Staffa and Mull. Macquarrie's portrait painted in 1783 is in the author's possession at Breacachadh Castle.
42. NAS. RD. Mack. 193 & 4. 1. 3. 1764.
43. *Transactions of the Gaelic Society of Inverness* XXIV. Letter from Major Alexander Campbell dated 19 June 1759.
44. NAS. GD 174. 1264. 59.

Chapter Sixteen

The East Indies and the end of the Campbell-Maclean feud

Sir Allan returned to Britain at the end of the Seven Years War. He was placed on the half-pay list. In his absence in America his wife had died. 'That is the end of that family' wrote Alexander Maclean of Pennycross. Although they had a son Lachlan, he had died young and Sir Allan had no immmediate male heir to succeed him. He did, however, have three daughters. They lived with him on the island of Inchkenneth part of his tack of Brolas off the west coast of Mull. Boswell and Johnson, who made their famous visit to the Hebrides in the autumn of 1773, paint an idyllic picture of Sir Allan's life on Inchkenneth. Johnson says:

> Romance does not often exhibit a scene that strikes the imagination more than this little desert. In these depths of western obscurity, occupied not by a gross herdsman, or amphibious fisherman, but by a gentleman and two ladies,[1] of high birth, polished manners, and elegant conversation, who, in a habitation raised not very far above the ground, but furnished with unexpected neatness and convenience, practised all the kindness of hospitality, and refinement of courtesy.[2]

Boswell knew that Sir Allan had served as an officer in Lord Eglinton's Highland Regiment and was 'a great companion of the Earl's'. He therefore expected to find 'a riotous bottle companion and be pressed to drink' but instead he says, somewhat surprisingly, that the 'Knight was as sober after dinner as I could wish'. He goes on to say: 'We dined cheerfully and drank tea, after which Miss Maclean played several tunes on the harpsichord very well. I proposed a reel; so Miss Sibby and Coll and I danced, while Miss Maclean played.'[3]

In 1770 Sir Allan Maclean, when he must have realised that he would have no male heir and that he was the last of his family, began an action in the Court of Session against the Duke of Argyll to reclaim the estate of Duart. He was in no position to do so by himself: his circumstances were such that he could not 'defray the expenses of a litigious lawsuit'. However, certain gentlemen of the name Maclean were prepared to back him. His kinsmen therefore entered into an agreement with Sir Allan Maclean to finance the cost of the suit. They were to be repaid only if Sir Allan's suit was successful.[4]

One of the gentlemen who backed Sir Allan was Hugh Maclean of Coll.[5] He had good reason to do so. Not only had Sir Allan been Hugh's brother Hector of Coll's pupil and son-in-law but, as we have seen the family of Coll had been the leading Macleans in the Isles since Sir John Maclean had gone into exile in 1692. It is therefore worth noting that when 'the gentlemen of the name Maclean' signed the agreement to finance the cost of Sir Allan's case against Argyll, they did so at Breacachadh.[6]

Boswell was to be one of Sir Allan's counsels in his action against the Duke. The Duke perhaps did not know this when in 1773 Boswell called on him at Inveraray Castle. There he found 'the amiable Duke sitting at the head of his table, with Campbell of Airds and several more gentlemen'. He writes: 'I was graciously received' and he and Johnson were invited to dinner the following day. His welcome by the Duchess was less cordial. Boswell says she hated him on account of his zeal in the Douglas Cause[7] and she ignored him totally. Boswell, however, was determined not to be put down and, although he knew it was not the custom at Inveraray to toast anyone's health, he rose and said: 'My lady Duchess, I have the honour to drink your grace's good health'.[8]

Although Sir Allan himself was penniless there was in the clan a new source of income, which was able to help underwrite the cost of litigation. This new source of income came from India.

* * *

The first member of the family of Coll to serve in the Indian Army was Captain Lachlan Maclean, later tacksman of Gallanach in Coll. There is a question mark over both his career and his ancestry. Allan Crossapol states that 'by some traditions' he was the eldest son of Roderick Maclean and Marion, daughter of Donald Maclean of Arihualan.

Roderick was the eldest son of Lachlan Maclean younger of Grishipol, Argyll's bailie in Tiree in the 1670s. Roderick first appears on record in 1674,[9] when he must have been at least 14 and, as Captain Lachlan was probably born after 1729, Roderick must have been an old man when his eldest son was born, which is perhaps why Crossapol doubted his parentage.[10]

The Indian Army, in which Lachlan served, had its beginnings in the need that early British traders had for natives to guard their factories and the warehouses which, until the arrival of ships from Europe, stored their goods. At first they were little more than armed watchmen.

The original Europeans in the sub-continent were supplicants of the Indian princes, who were Viceroys and Governors to the great Mughal Emperor in Delhi. This situation lasted well into the eighteenth century. Everything, however, changed when it became apparent that the Europeans had a military secret, which enabled them to triumph over much larger Indian armies. The secret was discipline.

It was the French who were the first to appreciate that Indians were quite as capable as Europeans to be trained as soldiers in the European manner. And in 1693, with only thirty-six Frenchmen and 3–400 well-drilled native troops, François Martin, defended the French base at Pondicherry for twelve days against nineteen Dutch ships and 1,500 infantry.

The French Indian Army expanded, and in 1746 an engineer officer in the French service, M Paradis with 230 French soldiers and 700 sepoys, but with no artillery, attacked an Indian army of 10,000 across a river and routed it.

The British were slower off the mark. By 1747, although the Madras Army was made up of 3,000 native foot soldiers, it had only 900 muskets. They were also without discipline and had no British officers. The war with France changed the whole situation: peace in Europe did not mean an end to hostilities in India and when in 1748 a peace treaty was signed, fighting continued under the pretext of giving assistance to the Indian princes.

There were now three types of British troops in India. First there were the regular forces of the Crown serving in India to protect British territories from the machinations of the foreigner; then there were the Company's European regiments, paid, recruited and organised by the Company; and finally there was a fast growing army of Indian regiments, recruited locally and officered, so far as the senior ranks were concerned, by British officers commissioned into the Company's service.

At the same time there were three distinct armies in British India, which served the Presidencies of Madras, Bombay and Bengal. The first Indian soldiers recruited for the Madras Presidency were local men, both Hindus and Muslims. Others were adventurers from further north. The Bombay Army employed more northerners, men from Rajputana, Oudh and Behar. This was because the Bombay Army's natural recruits were their neighbours the Mahrathas, who were the enemies of the British. The third army, that of Bengal seldom employed Bengalis; they recruited men from 'up country', which meant from further up the Ganges. They were mostly men from Behar, with others from Oudh and Rohilkand, the Punjab and even as far off as Afganistan.[11]

The princes the British and French supported were the heirs of the aged Nizam of the Deccan, who died in 1748. The succession was disputed. The French supported one candidate, the British another. Meanwhile another disputed succession occurred at Arcot. In both cases the French candidate was appointed.

In Arcot the British backed the son of the previous Nawab as his successor. In 1751 his rival Chanda Sahib besieged him at Trichinopoly. Mohammed Ali, the British candidate, had few troops of his own and a known incompetent commanded the 600 British soldiers, who were the backbone of his army. On the other hand the enemy had 900 French infantry and a considerable number of French sepoys. If Trichinopoly fell nothing could save the British in Southern India.

It was now that the courage, initiative and imagination of two men saved the day. One was Robert Clive, a young civilian who had recently transferred to the military with the rank of brevet captain. He judged that nothing could be achieved at Trinchinopoly, where the opposing sides had reached stalemate. Instead he proposed to strike deep into the Nawab of Arcot's territory. Most Governors of Madras would have dismissed Clive's scheme as folly, but Saunders, who was the current Governor, was a man of vision. He gave Clive 200 of his 350 British soldiers, 300 sepoys and three small field pieces.

On 31 August 1751 Clive and his little army surprised Arcot. He drove out a garrison double his own strength. Then, in a series of sorties, he defeated the enemy gathering against him. Next he set about improving the defences of the town. He was just in time for on 23 September the French began their siege of Arcot. By now Clive's numbers were down to 120 British and 200 Indians. They had to defend a perimeter of more than a mile. Against them were 10,000 of the best troops from Trichinopoly including a contingent of French soldiers.

The siege lasted more than fifty days. It was fought on both sides with great ferocity. Clive made a number of sorties, which were expensive in casualties but were successful in raising the morale of the defenders. By 14 November, however, the enemy made a breach in Clive's defences and the pro-French Nawab's son was ready to launch a major asault. The garrison, which was now down to 80 British soldiers and 120 sepoys, was exhausted but they still managed to beat off this final attack. When reinforcements at last arrived, the French withdrew pursued by a rejuvenated Clive. At Arni he thrashed the enemy in a pitched battle. Clive's inspirational leadership had changed the whole situation in Southern India.

* * *

It was whilst these stirring events were taking place that Lachlan Maclean joined the Madras European battalion. It is not clear exactly when he arrived as at about the time he landed in India his maternal cousin from Tiree did so too. As the latter's name was also Lachlan[12] it is not always clear, although the Coll Lachlan is often described 'Captain Lachlan Maclean, Junior',[13] which man is referred to: until a detailed study is made of all the officers in the Madras army on the lines of Hodson's study of those serving the Bengal Presidency, it will not be possible with certainty to separate the cousins' service in India.

To make matters worse Indian Army historians have turned the two Lachlans into one composite man. They have also been confused with another cousin, the odious Lauchlin Macleane MP. The latter's biographer the late James NM Maclean berates previous authors with confusing the two men.[14] He then goes on to confuse the cousins.

* * *

The two Lachlan Macleans were among the many Scots, who by the middle of the eighteenth century had joined the service of the Honourable East India Company. Service in India was more than just another installment in the centuries-old migration of Scots overseas. It was a major take-over of part of the expanding British Empire. Scotsmen had successfully exploited a niche in the British Army and, by the mid-eighteenth century, one in four British army regimental officers was a Scot. They now turned to India. The martial background of gentlemen from the Highlands, and the fact that a commission in the Company's army was free, made a military career in India attractive. A post in the army also required less use of patronage than the more desirable civil appointments, which probably explains why there were proportionally more Scots, particularly Gaels in the military rather than in the civil service.

The turning point in the involvement of Scots in India, and in Anglo-Scottish relations in general, had taken place in 1725 when, after the Malt Tax riots in Scotland, the Prime Minister Robert Walpole sent the Duke of Argyll's brother the Earl of Islay to Scotland to find out the cause of the disturbances. Islay reported that for some time there had been no effective government in Scotland. Walpole's solution was to sack the incompetent Secretary of State, the Duke of Roxburgh and appoint Islay to manage Scottish affairs.

Islay was to be the dominant figure in Scottish politics, with exception of the period from 1742 to 1746, between the 1720s and his death in 1761. His influence rested on an agreement with Walpole that he would deliver political stability in Scotland, and the votes of most Scottish MPs, in return for the lion's share of patronage and the authority to govern north of the Border.

There were, however, never enough Scottish positions available to bribe the country's tiny electorate. Nor was it easy to surrender to the Scots the existing crown appointments in London, which were claimed by English interests. The rich vein of East India posts instead promised to be an attractive alternative. The Company was in theory an independent corporation, but ministers could always lean on it to provide a source of patronage in return for the periodic renewal of its charter and the promise of commercial favours. East India postings therefore became the foundation of political stability in Scotland and the forging of a stronger union. By 1750 there was already a marked influx of Scots into the Company. By that date they had also taken three out of every eight Writers' posts in Bengal. Jacobite families, who had been 'out' in the '15, received special attention for favour and reward in order to integrate them into the Whig establishment in Church and State.[15]

This early bedrock of Scottish success meant that when in 1757, after Clive's victory at the battle of Plassey demand for Indian posts became insatiable, Scottish interests and networks were firmly established.

* * *

The anonymous scribe of 'A brief Genealogical Account of the family of MacLean'[16] who in about 1763 made his version of Dr Hector Maclean's manuscript says of Lachlan[17] that he 'now commands in the British East India Company's Service as Captain & a Colonell of a Regiment of Seapois or Irregulars in the same Service'. It is therefore probable this is the same Lachlan who in 1762 raised the 8th Battalion of Native Infantry at Burdwan, an incident in the career, which Hodson ascribes to the Coll Lachlan, when he says that he in 1758 'transferred from the Madras European Battalion to the Bengal Establishment'. He goes on to say that in the same year he took part in the expedition to North Circars. He was also present on 8 April 1759 in the storming of Musulipatam and was promoted captain for his gallantry in the assault.[18] The same year, on account of the wounds he had received, he returned home. However, he soon recovered and applied to be re-employed. He received glowing testimonials from Clive and was granted permission to return to India as senior lieutenant on the Bengal establishment. He was to succeed to the next company that became vacant.[19]

Captain Lachlan returned to India in 1761 on the *Chesterfield* and in 1764 took part in the campaign against the Nawab of Bengal & Oudh. He also fought at the battle of Patna. In 1764 the Burdwan Battalion became the 2nd Battalion of Native infantry. Captain Lachlan, however, was removed from command in consequence of complaints of the native officers.

If, as seems probable, this is the career of 'Tiree Lachlan', we know nothing of 'Coll' Lachlan's time in India other than Johnson's remark that he was 'a gentleman who has lived some time in the East Indies, but having dethroned no Nabob, is not too rich to settle in his own country'.[20] He probably served all his time in the Madras Army.

Indian Army officers could accumulate capital in India and it is probably 'Tiree Lachlan' who 'from time to time remitted what money he could spare to Archibald Maclane of London, his friend, but finding his constitution impaired by the fatigue of the service he resolved to spend the remainder of his days in peaceable retirement in his native land'. He therefore sent '£3,500 to Archibald'.[21] He then collected the rest of his effects and dispatched £2,000+ to Maclane & Son and, although he had been offered a majority set sail for London. On his arrival he went to his friend's house but instead of finding him there 'he found the house possessed by the assignees under a commission of bankruptcy'. Archibald was dead[22] and his son Thomas Ashurst had disappeared[23] having forged his father's signature to obtain Captain Lachlan's £2,000.[24]

It is probable that the Coll Captain Lachlan also had dealings with the Cheapside merchants *Maclane & Son* for, at about the same time that Tiree Lachlan returned from India, the Coll Lachlan was advised 'to go to law' with Archibald's brother Duncan 'about my house at

Dallingburn'. Although Duncan states in a letter to the Tiree Lachlan in which he acknowledges that he owes him money implies that his 'namesake Capt. Lau. Maclean of Mull' was also a creditor. However he goes on to say that 'he's a man knows nothing of me nor I of him, nor never had dealing for one shilling'.[25]

Despite their losses both Captain Lachlans were able to purchase properties on the mainland: Tiree Lachlan at Craigbete in Renfrewshire,[26] whilst 'Captain Lachlan, Junior' purchased Craigendmuir of Provan in the barony of Glasgow.[27] The latter also became tacksman of Gallanach on Coll. He was also able to help finance the last act in the feud between the Macleans and the Campbells.

* * *

The two contestants in the battle for the Duart estate were civilised gentlemen. This did not make the contest any less bitter. The stakes were too high, too much blood had been spilt, too many careers blighted and too much land had changed hands for Macleans to forgive Campbells for the loss of their inheritance. On the other hand, as Stonefield had written to the Duke in 1732: 'as the possession of McLean's estate . . . cost your Grace's predecessors no small trouble and expence', it would be a catastrophe for the family if it were lost.

The case did not reach the courts until 13 February 1777. Boswell, who had been drunk the night before[28], opened for Sir Allan. For technical reasons Allan Maclean of Drimnin was the nominal pursuer.[29] Drimnin thrived on 'technical reasons': he had been out in the '45, but on a technicality had not been prosecuted.

Allan Drimnin had a reputation as a hard man. As Lochbuie's agent in Edinburgh wrote to his master in 1767:

> Experience may have taught you that it is not bairn's play to deal with Drimnin, he is the most acute alert antagonist you have, and that he inclines, with all his heart to take a sleeve off your coat.[30]

Drimnin was the prime mover in organising his friends to defray the cost of the case against Argyll. He was less keen to move when it reached its conclusion.

The case was decided on 2 July 1777.[31] Sir Allan made good his claim to the lands of Brolas, which were in a different position to the rest of the Duart estates, but otherwise the action failed.[32] Sir Allan's backers had not got what they wanted, but they were due something. Captain Lachlan had provided £5 in 1772, £7.10s in 1773, £10 in 1775 and £5 in 1776. Sir Allan died in 1783 and although Captain Lachlan applied to his eldest daughter and her husband Charles Maclean of Kinlochaline, his heirs to Brolas, for repayment of the money he had put up to defray the cost of the case he did not receive a penny. He therefore, on 25 September 1787, instructed his solicitor to prosecute Sir Allan's heirs.[33] Ten years later Kinlochaline 'a careless, imprudent and extravagant man'[34] was bankrupt and the Macleans last attempt to regain their inheritance was at an end.

On Sir Allan's death in 1783 the heir to his baronetcy was his third cousin Hector, who lived in Yorkshire and had no involvement in the Highlands. Sir Allan's death therefore marks the end not only of the Campbell–Maclean feud, but also of the Macleans of Duart as traditional chiefs. They could no longer grant land to their kinsmen in exchange for service. The basis of the contract between clansman and chief had disappeared. Had Sir Allan regained the Duart estate it would have been worthwhile for the new Sir Hector and his successors to re-establish their position in the Hebrides. However, without land to be Chief of the Macleans of Duart was an empty title.

Notes

1. Both Johnson and Boswell state that Sir Allan had two daughters. In fact he had three. The third Anna was presumably away from home when the travellers visited Inchkenneth.
2. *A Journey to the Western Islands of Scotland*, 221.
3. *Boswell's Journal of A Tour to the Hebrides* (1936), 316 & 323.
4. NAS. RD1788. Mack 243, 88. Assig. Captain Lachlan McLean to John Campbell, Junior. 18 January 1788.
5. NAS. RD DAL 1. 237, 77.
6. NAS. RD DAL 1. 237, 77.
7. This celebrated case had pitted the Duchess of Douglas, the protector of Archibald Stewart Douglas against the Duke of Hamilton, the heir-male to the vast Douglas inheritance. Hamilton's Duchess was the young and impulsive Elizabeth Gunning, an Irish girl, whose fabulous beauty led mobs to follow her in London. Hamilton died in 1758 and the following year his widow married Colonel Jack Campbell, who in 1770 succeeded as 5th Duke of Argyll.
8. *Boswell's Journal of A Tour to the Hebrides*, 354.
9. ICP. Bundle 480 & 467. 53.
10. As already noticed the most likely explanation is that he was a grandson, rather than a son of Roderick.
11. Philip Mason *A Matter of Honour: an account of the Indian Army its officers and men* (1975), 20–1.
12. His family had previously served in the Scots Brigade in Dutch service [Nicholas Maclean-Bristol 'Jacobite Officers in the Scots Brigade in Dutch Service', *JSAHR* Vol. 82, No. 330, (Summer 2004), 108].
13. Hodson states that Captain Lachlan Maclean was 31 when he returned to India on the *Chesterfield* in 1761. He was therefore born 1729/30. As we shall see I suspect that he muddles up the two Lachlans and as the Coll Lachlan is described as 'Junior' he was probably younger than his cousin.
14. JNM Maclean *Reward is Secondary* (1963), 178.
15. TM Devine *Scotland's Empire 1600–1815* (2003), 268–9.
16. NLS. MS. 28. 3. 12, 12r.
17. 3rd son of Neil [son of Charles *Mac Neil Ban* in Tiree] a pretty Gentleman married to Florence Daughter to Donald Maclean of Arihualan]
18. BL. IOL. Hodson MSS. Vol. 3, 173.
19. BL. IOL. E. 4. 617 [265] Bengal Dispatches 13 March 1761.
20. Samuel Johnson LL.D *A Journey to the Western Islands of Scotland* (1817), 185.
21. Archibald Maclane, of Maclane & Son, merchants, Cheapside, London
22. He died on 13 September 1764 [*Reward is Secondary*, 122].
23. He disappeared in October 1765 [*Reward is Secondary*, 127]
24. NAS. Petition of Rebecca Maclane 21 July 1775.
25. Ibid.
26. NAS. Register of Sasines. Renfrewshire. 1781–1820. 419, 420 & 890.
27. NAS. Register of Sasines Lanark. Barony of Glasgow. 1781–1808. RS 54, 26, 294, 592, 593, 1099, 2532, & 2779; RD 4. 259, 1004.
28. *Boswell In Extremes 1776–1778* (1971), 85.
29. *Highland Papers*. Vol. 1, 243. See also NAS. RD DAL 1. 237, 77. 1770. Bond & Backbond between Sir Allan & Drimnin for £200,000.
30. NAS. GD 174. 1273. 1: 7 November 1767 John Murray to John Maclaine of Lochbuie.

31. *Boswell in Extremes*, 132.
32. *Highland Papers* Vol. 1, 337.
33. NAS. RD 1788. Mack 243, 88. 18 January 1788: Assignation Captain Lachlan McLean to John Campbell Junior.
34. *Clan Gillean*, 440.

Chapter Seventeen

The Anatomy of Coll in 1773

From 1773 onwards there are a number of new sources available about the people on the Coll estate who were to pour into the British Army. Some of this information comes from visitors to the Island. Despite, or perhaps because of its remote location, the Isle of Coll became the destination of travellers who have written about their adventures. Among the first, and certainly the most famous of these visitors were Samuel Johnson, the great lexicographer, and James Boswell, his brilliant if unstable biographer. They visited the Island for ten days in October 1773 and met most of the leading members of the family of Coll. Their accounts complement Allan Crossapol's genealogy and put flesh on his dry skeleton.

The 1770s are, for several reasons, a good time to begin a detailed examination of the family of Coll. Not least is the fact that, through Johnson and Boswell's accounts, the chattering classes of Britain probably first became aware of the island's existence, even to the extent that John O'Keefe, the comic dramatist/librettist set his ballad opera *The Highland Reel*, which was performed at Covent Garden in November 1788, in the isles of Coll and Raasay.[1]

Coll captured the imagination of the British public, partly because of the personality of its young laird, Donald Maclean, 'Young Coll'. Johnson says of him that:

> He is a noble animal. He is as complete an islander as mortality can figure. He is a farmer, a sailor, a hunter, a fisher; he will run you down a dog. If any man has a tail, it is Coll. He is hospitable; and he has an intrepidity of talk, whether he understands the subject or not.[2]

To a public charmed by Ossian and Jean Jacques Rousseau's twin passions, the noble savage and romantic scenery, 'Young Coll' was irresistible.

Boswell explains that 'Young Coll' was not the Laird of Coll, as his father was still alive, but 'the old gentleman gives him full scope'. Donald told him that 'there had been a custom in this family that the laird resigns the estate to his eldest son when he comes of age, reserving to himself only a certain life-rent'.[3]

Young Coll had spent some time in England studying farming, for, as he told them, he was 'resolved to improve his father's lands without hurting the people or losing the ancient Highland fashions'.[4] This resolve was to be the major influence on the policies of subsequent Macleans of Coll.

The travellers met 'Young Coll' at Talisker in the Isle of Skye, where he had 'repaired for lodging' when he was 'weary with following his game' whilst sporting in the mountains.[5] He had originally intended to spend some time on Skye, but instead decided to escort the travellers to Iona and show them the islands of Eigg, Muck, Coll and Tiree. The weather, however, put paid to their plans.

Boswell describes the difficulties of travel to Coll it is a classic reminder of the ever present backdrop to life in the Hebrides. Boswell tells us that:

> When we got in full view of the point of Ardnamurchan, the wind changed, and was full against us getting to the Sound [of Mull]. We were then obliged to tack, and get forward in that tedious manner. As we advanced the storm grew greater, and the sea very rough. Coll then began to talk of making for Eigg or Canna or Coll. Macdonald, our skipper, said he would get us into the Sound. We struggled a good while for this . . .
>
> Our crew consisted of old Macdonald our skipper, a man with one eye, and another sailor. Mr Simson [the owner] himself, Coll, and Hugh Macdonald his servant all helped. Simson said he would willingly go for Coll if young Coll or his servant would undertake to pilot us to a harbour, but as the island is low land, it was dangerous to run upon it in the dark. Coll and his servant seemed a little dubious . . . At last it became so rough, and threatened to be so much worse, that Coll and his servant took more courage, and said they would undertake to hit one of the harbours in Coll; 'Then', said the skipper, 'let us run for it, in God's name', and instantly we turned towards it . . . I had a short relief when I found we were to run for a harbour before the wind. But it was very short, for I soon heard that our sails were very bad, and were in danger of being torn to pieces, in which case we would be driven upon the rocks of Coll . . . Simson and he [Coll] both appeared a little frightened, which made me more so; and the perpetual talking, or rather shouting, which was carried on in Erse [Gaelic], alarmed me . . .
>
> I saw tonight what I never saw before, a prodigious sea with immense billows coming upon a vessel, so as that it seemed hardly possible to escape . . . It was half an hour after eleven before we set ourselves in the course for Coll. As I saw them all busy doing something, I asked Coll with much earnestness what I could do. He with a lucky readiness put into my hand a rope, which was fixed to the top of one of the masts, and bid me hold it fast till he bid me pull. This could not be of the least service; but by employing me, he kept me out of their way of those who were busy working the ship; and at the same time diverted my fear to a certain degree, by making me think I was occupied. There did I stand firm to my post while the wind and rain beat upon me, always expecting a call to pull my rope.
>
> The man with one eye steered. Old Macdonald and Coll and his servant lay upon the forecastle looking sharp out for the harbour. It was necessary to carry much *cloth*, as they termed it, that is to say, much sail, in order to keep the vessel off the shore of Coll. This made terrible plunging in a rough sea. At last they spied the harbour of Lochiern, and Coll cried, 'Thank God, we're safe!'[6]

It was not until daylight that the travellers went ashore and had their first look at the Island. Johnson says that 'Col is not properly rocky; it is rather one continued rock'.[7] Certainly at first sight, at least from the sea, it looks barren and uninhabitable. However, as Allan Crossapol's nephew Mr Neil Maclean says in the *New Statistical Account*: 'Its general appearance is by no means prepossessing, at least in the eye of a stranger'. In fact, although the south-east coast is 'a moorish, barren-looking tract which seems hardly capable of cultivation or improvement, along the north-west coast, the soil is light and sandy. The intermediate space, though interspersed with numerous ledges of rock, contains some fine fields, and many small spots of uncommon fertility'.[8]

* * *

The catechist, who examined the population of Coll in 1776 on its knowledge of the Church of Scotland's Shorter Catechism, lists each inhabitant under individual farms. He found there to be 677 examinable people and 261, who were underage i.e. under seven, making a total of 938. Boswell states that the minister Mr Hector[9] Maclean, whom the travellers met on 5 October, said that 'he had taken up a list of parishioners between seven and seventy by order of the General Assembly, and found nine hundred'. Boswell therefore reckoned that there must be two hundred under seven and about fifty over seventy. As the catechist's list was taken only three years later and makes it quite clear that there were 261 under seven years old, either Boswell misunderstood what he was told or Mr Hector is exaggerating.

Boswell says that Mr Hector's parish consisted of both Coll and Tiree. This was not true. In fact Mr Hector was not the parish minister but was the assistant to the parish minister. The latter lived in Tiree. Coll had been linked with Tiree since 1618. It was a situation, as we have seen, that infuriated successive Macleans of Coll, who tried to get the link broken. It was, however, argued that there were insufficient teinds[10] to establish Coll as a separate parish and, as we have also seen, the Duke of Argyll managed to frustrate all the attempts to divide the islands into two separate parishes.[11]

Mr Hector perhaps exaggerated both his position and the number of his parishioners to impress Johnson. It is a reminder of the danger in trusting too much on a visitor's evidence. It should, however, be remembered that when Dr John Walker visited Coll, shortly before Johnson and Boswell, he also states that the population of the island was about 1,200[12], which increases the likelihood that Mr Hector was lying.

Boswell describes Mr Hector as being 'about seventy-seven, a decent old man in a full suit of black and a black wig'.[13] Johnson says he had the reputation of great learning and had 'the look of venerable dignity excelling what I remember in any other man'.[14] He was said to have a valuable library, but had poor accommodation for it. Johnson describes his house at Cliad as but a single storey hut, which was not inelegantly furnished with windows and a chimney.[15] One room was used for public worship.

Mr Hector died on the 10 April 1775. The Presbytery of Mull, when they were informed, minuted their unanimity 'in regretting the loss to the Presbytery of one who for many years supported the ministerial character with proprietary in our bounds'.[16] Steps were taken to appoint a successor and on 9 November 1775 Presbytery read

> a letter from the ffactor of Tiry Bearing that his Grace the Duke of Argyle is desirous to have Mr Charles Stewart Preacher of the Gospel in Appin settled minister in Coll in the room of Mr Hector Maclean lately deceased . . . and the Clerk is appointed to acknowledge the Chamberlain of Tiry's letter & to converse with the Minister of Tiry about the contents of it & to sollicit his consent that Mr Stewart may succeed the late Minister of Coll.[17]

On 7 April 1776 Mr Archibald McArthur Minister of Kilninian & Kilmore in Mull inducted Mr Charles to Coll. After the Sermon the Session of Coll met. Kirk Session minutes had not been kept regularly during Mr Hector's incumbency. From now on they were written up after each session. They give a useful insight into several aspects of life on Coll in the period from 1776 to 1843.

The duties of the Kirk Session, laid out in *The Form of Process in the Judicatories of the Church of Scotland with relation to Scandals and Censures*, were in 1707 approved by the General Assembly of the Church of Scotland. The scandals to be dealt with were swearing, cursing, profaning of the Lord's Day, drunkenness, and sexual offences.[18] If the culprit was recalcitrant the Kirk Session could appeal to the civil magistrate to carry out their decisions. Before the '45 this was Maclean of Coll, whose lands had been granted by the Crown *in liberam baroniam*. Coll as a baron was therefore a hereditary judge, who had the right of pit and gallows over his people.

Heritable jurisdiction, which was abolished after the '45 Rebellion, was in decline even before the '45 and few baronial courts in the eighteenth century exercised their right to punish in life and limb. In effect the Heritable Jurisdictions Act had effectively reduced Baron Courts to settling minor neighbourhood disputes.[19] In the absence of the Baron Court, the Kirk Session was probably the most influential body of men in the island. The office of Justice of the Peace had, it is true, been introduced by King James VI into Scotland in 1609, but it had never acquired the same prestige as it had in England.[20] Successive Macleans of Coll were JPs but it is unlikely that in 1773 the appointment was of much importance in the eyes of the people of Coll. For example Boswell tells us that on 8 October he saw:

> a good number of people who had come to Coll with complaints of each other's trespasses. Cornaig told them, 'If you do not agree, we have the lawyer here from Edinburgh, who will take you to task ... they said they were never used to take that way. They hoped Coll would settle matters himself.[21]

* * *

The elders of Coll in the 1770s are first listed when on 7 April 1776 the Kirk Session met at Cliad.[22] The list begins with the Laird of Coll. Hugh Maclean of Coll was, as we have seen, living away from the island when Johnson and Boswell visited Coll and they never met him. A caricature of Hugh shortly after this time appears in the anecdotes of the humorist George Colman the younger.

In 1781 Colman had been banished by his father from Oxford to King's College, Aberdeen. He writes:

> During my residence in King's College there was a very worthy old gentleman living in the Old Town, who wore a gold chain round his neck, and whom I always understood to be the provost. This was Mr Maclean, the laird of Col, one of those Scotch western islands called the Hebrides. I met him at dinner, in a mixed party, soon after my arrival in North Britain, when I had everything to learn which appertains to the manners and etiquette of the inhabitants; and observing that marked attention was paid to this ancient chieftain, I was desirous of getting in his good graces. Everybody at table addressed him as 'Col', which appeared to me a familiarity inconsistent with respect; but concluding that they were his old friends, while I was a stranger, I said to him, 'Mr Col, will you do me the honour to drink a glass of wine with me?' He stared me full in the face without speaking, or even deigning to give me a nod of assent. I repeated my proposition, 'Mr Col, do me the honour', &c. &c.; Mr Col maintained his silence, and did not move a muscle. 'Is he deaf', said I, turning to a gentleman on my right hand, 'or what is the matter with him?' 'Gude troth', he whispered, 'ye've e'en

affronted him, by calling him *Mister*'. He then explained to me that a chieftain in the Hebrides, being looked upon as a kind of petty sovereign, is always styled according to the appellation of his dominions . . .[23]

Although domiciled in Aberdeen Hugh Coll spent some time each year in the island. He is recorded as attending the Kirk Session on 27 April 1777. There was then a vacancy in Coll from 16 April 1779 to 18 January 1781 and no meetings of the Kirk Session took place. Hugh is not mentioned as attending in 1781, but he was back again in 1782, 83, 84 and 85. He died in Coll in May the following year.[24]

The most assiduous attenders at the Kirk Session in the 1770s and 80s were Sween McSween, Tacksman of Grishipol and his son Hugh. The McSweens lived at Grishipol 'an excellent slated house of two storeys' close to the sea. Johnson says that he saw more of the ancient life of a Highlander at Grishipol than he had yet found. Mrs McSween, whom he describes as 'a decent old gentle-woman', could speak no English and had never been to the mainland.[25] She was dressed in tartan. She gave the travellers a good dinner and the best goose they had ever eaten.[26]

Johnson thought that life had not progressed in McSween's family; 'for', said he, 'the son is exactly formed upon the father. What the father says, the son says; and what the father looks, the son looks'.[27] Boswell thought young Mrs McSween 'was one of the hardest-favoured women' he had ever seen 'swarthy, and marked with the smallpox, and of very ungainly manners'.[28]

Boswell says that the McSweens had lived in Skye on Macleod's estate 'from a very remote period'. They had left Skye when Macleod put up his rents and got Grishipol from Hugh Coll, who was his foster brother.[29]

The ancient custom of fosterage, whereby a tacksman took the children of the lairds into their family shortly after they were weaned, and kept them until they were ready for their education, cemented relations between classes in the Hebrides. The closeness of the relationship established by fosterage was proverbial.[30]

* * *

Almost as assiduous as McSween in his attendance at Kirk Session meetings was Donald Maclean of Cornaig, a younger brother of Hector Maclean of the Isle of Muck, who Johnson and Boswell had met at Dunvegan in Skye. They described Hector as 'a hearty Highlander', who insisted that his island was not called Muck but the 'Isle of Monk'.[31] Few agreed with him.

The Two Ends of Coll, of which the Isle of Muck brothers were tacksmen, belonged to the Duke of Argyll. Hugh Coll had leased it for £45, but when the Duke put up his rents Coll thought the new arrangement too expensive and would not renew his lease. The brothers, however, were determined not to let a Campbell into Coll. They paid the new rent. It was £105.

Cornaig was a tall stout man with grey hair tied back. Johnson thought him the most distinct man, [i.e. the most original man] he had met in the Isles. He said he did not shut his eyes to what was going on about him, or put his fingers in his ears, which he thought most people they had met in the Hebrides did.

The Session's treasurer was Hugh Maclean, Tacksman of Knock. He does not appear to have met either Johnson or Boswell. Hugh had inherited his tack from his grand mother's second husband, Hector Maclean of Knock, a cousin of Donald Maclean of Cornaig. Hector Knock is the man quoted by Lady Coll, as seeing the vision of his deceased neighbour. Hector died in 1771 leaving an estate valued at £105 Sterling.[32]

Hugh Knock's paternal grandfather, another Hugh, was an illegitimate son of John Maclean of Totronald, and his illegitimacy might have led to a rapid decline in social status. However, his wife was a sister of John Maclean WS the Edinburgh lawyer who died in 1695 and left a sizeable estate.[33] Such inherited wealth enabled the recipient to stock a large farm and made him an attractive tenant.

Landowners needed to attract tenants with capital to their estates. It was easier to build up capital away from the Hebrides than in them. Successful expatriates, however, still wished to settle in their own country. This is probably why Captain Lachlan Maclean, who entertained Johnson and Boswell in 1773, had taken a farm on Coll. As we have already noted, Johnson states that Captain Lachlan was 'a gentleman who has lived some time in the East Indies, but having dethroned no Nabob, is not too rich to settle in his own country'.[34]

Captain Lachlan had only poor temporary accommodation at Arnabost when the travellers descended on him. It was 'just a little larger than the common country house'. However, it was a good haven to Johnson and Boswell after their time at sea. There was a blazing peat-fire, and Mrs Maclean, the daughter of Mr Hector, the minister, got them tea. On their second visit, after they had failed to get away from Coll, their welcome was not so cordial. It is hardly surprising. Mrs Maclean was about to give birth and the house was in some confusion. Although Boswell does not tell us so, Mrs Maclean probably died in childbirth, for by the time the catechist's list was made the captain had built his new house at Gallanach, and was a widower.

The following July the Kirk Session received a letter from Captain Lachlan which perhaps explains why he never became an elder. In it he acknowledges that his servant Ann McKinnon was with child by him and requested that 'both he & she should be exonerated from Church Discipline but [were] quite submissive to any pecuniary Mulct that should be imposed. His Bill to the Kirk Treasure was taken for Ten pounds sterling Payable a month after Date'.[35]

In 1776 Captain Lachlan was living at Gallanach with nine house servants. Only Donald of Cornaig had more. The latter had eleven servants plus 'a chaplain', who was probably the tutor to his children. McSween at Grishipol also had nine servants, whilst Hugh Knock had five. The number of employees is a useful barometer of wealth. With the exception of Captain Lachlan, the wealthiest men in Coll were all elders of the Kirk. Whether this was because of their wealth or because they had other virtues is not clear.

Boswell tells us that there were only three considerable tacksmen on Coll's property on the Island. These were McSween, Captain Lachlan and Mr Maclean of Knock. These 'considerable' tacksmen,[36] with the exception of McSween, were all descended from Coll's own family. However, as we have seen, old McSween was related to Hugh Maclean of Coll by a tie of fosterage, which was even closer than that of blood. Even the minister Mr Hector Maclean, although he was a member of the Treshnish family in Mull, was on his mother's side descended from Macleans of Coll.[37] These tacksmen were also closely connected to each other by marriage.

Johnson thought that the tacksmen in Coll 'live with less dignity and convenience than those on Skye; where they had good houses, and tables not only plentiful, but delicate'. He explains how the tacksmen in Coll ran their farms. He says:

> The tacksman admits some of his inferior neighbours to the cultivation of his grounds, on condition that, performing all the work, and giving a third part of the seed, they shall keep a certain number of cows, sheep, and goats, and reap a third part of the harvest. Thus by the tillage of two acres they pay the rent of one.[38]

Boswell says:

> In Coll it is the practice to have cottars who are obliged to furnish two horses each for work, as also a third of the seed-corn; and for this and their work through the year, they have a third of the crop and three milk cows grazed. This is a good method to make servants have a common interest with their masters.[39]

This cannot be the whole story or the three 'considerable tacksmen' on Coll's estate and Donald of Cornaig on the Duke of Argyll's land would not have needed quite so many servants. The tacksmen must have worked their own part of their tack themselves with their own employees, while the periphery was worked by their 'inferior neighbours' who probably gave their master an agreed number of days work each year. Donald Maclean of Cornaig had 9 sub-tenants in both Cornaig and Caolis in addition to his 5 male and 5 female house servants. Sween McSween had 9 house servants and 8 sub-tenants at Grishipol. In 1776 Captain Lachlan Maclean had 9 house servants at Gallanach. He also had 9 sub-tenants, one of whom employed a male servant. Hugh Maclean of Knock, the third 'considerable tacksman' identified by Boswell, had 5 living-in servants. He also had 6 sub-tenants, one of whom employed a female servant.[40]

* * *

Tacksmen in the Hebrides had a mixed press in the late eighteenth century. James Anderson LL. D the foremost literary improver discusses their status in society, before attacking them. He explains that:

> The class of tacksmen occupy nearly the same rank in the Hebrides, as belongs to that of men of landed property in other parts of Britain. They are called Gentlemen, and appear as such; and obtain a title from the farm they hold, nearly in the same manner as gentlemen in other parts of the country obtain from their estates. Most of these tacksmen are in fact descended from a line of ancestors as ancient and honourable as the proprietors themselves, and therefore reckon them selves equally entitled with them to the appellation of gentlemen. These tacksmen were for the most part, originally younger sons of the proprietor himself, and obtained from their father leases of considerable tracts of ground at a moderate rent, which was bestowed upon them in lieu of a patrimony: The descendants of these have therefore, in general, been accounted as relations of the family of the proprietor, and were treated with a mildness that made them consider their leases rather as a sort of property . . .

He goes on to state the dangers in this state of affairs when the proprietor was an absentee. 'In the absence of the proprietor', he writes:

> these persons aquired a weight and influence in the country, which was very great; so that the proprietor, if he had been so disposed, would have found it a very difficult matter to crush them; and as they found always means to bring the factor to favour their interests, they have been able to continue their sway till the present moment, after most other vestiges of the feudal power have fallen into disrepute.

'These are the men', he continues 'who in general, together with the factors, keep the lower classes of the people in subjection'.[41]

Some contemporary observers believed that the tacksmen were redundant. Others, such as James Campbell of Stonefield found, when he investigated complaints concerning the tacksmen of Morvern, that these complaints were much exaggerated. Whilst Dr Johnson, probably the most astute visitor to the Hebrides at this period, thought that those who wished to get rid of the tacksmen were deluded. He argues that:

> If the tacksmen be banished, who will be left to impart knowledge, or impress civility? The laird must always be at a distance from the greater part of his lands; and if he resides at all upon them, must drag his days in solitude, having no longer either a friend or a companion; he will therefore depart to some more comfortable residence, and leave the tenants to the wisdom and mercy of a factor.[42]

Johnson based his opinions on the islands he had visited: Skye, Raasay, Mull and Coll. He had not visited the Outer Hebrides, where, if the Rev. John Lane Buchanan is to be believed the worst abuses of the tacksmen occurred. Buchanan was a missionary minister who from 1782 to 1791 worked for the Society for Propagating Christian Knowledge in the Outer Isles. His *Travels in the Western Hebrides: From 1782 to 1790* (1793) are violently critical of the smaller lairds and tacksmen's abuse of their 'scallags', i.e. their farm labourers. What he does not make 'sufficiently clear is that the scallags were not directly oppressed by those who their contemporaries regarded as the landlord class – the lairds and tacksmen – but were exploited by the possessor or tenant class by whom they were usually employed, especially in kelping'.[43]

Notes

1. Roger Fiske, *English Theatre Music in the Eighteenth Century*, 2nd edition, (OUP, 1986). I have to thank Dr Paul Hopkins for this reference.
2. *Boswell's Journal of a Tour to the Hebrides* (1936), 323.
3. *Boswell*, 322.
4. *Boswell*, 213.
5. Samuel Johnson *A Journey to the Western Islands of Scotland* (1817), 113.
6. *Boswell*, 247–50.
7. Johnson, 191.
8. *New Statistical Account of Scotland* (1835–45), vol. 19.
9. In the Hebrides a minister was always called *Maighstir* or Mr.
10. *Teind*, the tenth part of the produce of the parish set aside for the support of religion. After the Reformation they were expropriated by the Crown and granted to landowners, who were made responsible to pay the minister's stipend and provide his manse and glebe.
11. The most recent attempt to break the link had occurred in 1732 [The Petition of the Synod of Argyle to the Right Honourable the Lords of Council and Session, Lords Commissioners for Plantations of Kirks and Valuation of Teinds 1 February 1732. & Answers for His Grace John Duke of Argyle and Greenwich, dated 8 February 1732]. I have to thank the late Miss Hope Macdougall of Macdougall for a copy of these documents, given to me when we did get the link between Coll and Tiree broken by the General Assembly of the Church of Scotland.
12. Margaret M McKay (ed) *The Rev. Dr. Walker's Report on the Hebrides of 1764 and 1771* (1980), 169.
13. *Boswell*, 256.
14. Johnson, 186.

15. Neither Boswell nor Johnson mention Cliad as the minister's house. However, their route through Coll suggests that it is. In addition the Kirk Session records describe the 'Bellman' or beadle, who was the principal church employee, as living at Cliad [NAS. CH2. 70. 1]. Finally, during the rebuilding of Cliad House in 2004, it was apparent that the gable end of a single storeyed house had been built into the north wall of the present house. I have to thank Rob Wainwright, the present owner of Cliad, for this information.
16. NAS.CH2. 492. 1.
17. NAS. CH2. 492. 1. 131.
18. JHS Burleigh *A Church History of Scotland* (1960), 268–9.
19. They were never abolished but gradually withered away. David Sellar 'Barony Jurisdiction in the Highlands', *WHN&Q*, 1st Series, No. XVI (September 1981), 22–6.
20. Ann E Whetstone *Scottish County Government in the Eighteenth and Nineteenth Centuries* (1981), 27.
21. *Boswell*, 283–4.
22. NAS CH2. 70. 1. 13.
23. GBB (ed) *Broad Grins* (1898), 479. I have to thank John Yeowell for a copy of this book.
24. *Scots Magazine* Vol. 48 (1786), 259.
25. Johnson, 188.
26. *Boswell*, 260.
27. *Boswell* , 293.
28. *Ibid*, 291.
29. *Boswell*, 259 says that McSween had fostered Hugh Coll, but as they appear to have been of a similar age this is impossible.
30. JL Campbell (ed) *A Collection of Highland Rites and Customs* (1975), 34.
31. *Boswell*, 186–7.
32. NAS. C. 12. 7. 4.
33. NAS. RD 1695. Mack 79, 165. He was the eldest son of Hugh Maclean of Balliphetrish, the former Bailie of Tiree.
34. *Johnson*, 185.
35. NAS. CH2. 70. 1.
36. Any one who had a tack i.e. a written lease was a tacksman, however, the term is often used to describe men who had a considerable landholding. It was these 'considerable tacksmen' who had provided the officers for the Coll Company when the clan went to war.
37. She was the daughter of Neil Maclean of Drimnacross, 3rd son of Lachlan Maclean of Coll (1583–1635).
38. *Johnson*, 198.
39. *Boswell*, 281.
40. NAS. CH 2. 70. 1.
41. James Anderson *An Account of the Present State of the Hebrides* (1785), 164–5.
42. *Johnson*, 134–5.
43. JM Bumstead *The People's Clearance* (1982), 36.

Chapter Eighteen

Tenants and their leases

In 1776 there were two elders on Coll who were not 'considerable tacksmen'. They were Allan Maclean, Cliad and Neil Maclean, Crossapol. They were probably brothers, the sons of Allan Mac Neil Og of Crossapol. Although both they and the 'considerable tacksmen' were tenants and should have been described as 'in' rather than 'of ' the name of their farm, they are almost invariably decribed as 'of ', even by such a stickler for social correctness as James Boswell. He describes Neil's son Donald as 'young Maclean of Crossapoll'.[1] The reason behind this designation is the landholder's position in the family of Coll.

In 1776 both Allan and Neil were employing three servants. Little is known of Allan. He was probably the man who Boswell says 'goes every year to Greenock and brings home a quantity of hardware, ribbons, and other small things; and keeps a little shop at the small village [Cliad], where is the house in which public worship is held as there is no church'.[2] He will have succeeded his father Allan Mac Neil Og of Crossapol as a merchant. The latter it is said 'trades as a merchant betwixt Coll and Glasgow'.[3] Allan Cliad was drowned at Baugh na Coalla at Sorisdale in Coll,[4] leaving three daughters.[5]

Neil Crossapol is better remembered. Boswell, after stating that there were 'but three considerable tacksmen on Coll's property', says that 'the rest is let to small tenants, who pay four, three or even two guineas'. He goes on to say that 'Crossapoll has the highest rented farm of any of them. His rent is £7. Upon this he has always lived creditably for one of his station'. What does this mean?

The Coll seanachie John Johnston (1830–1921) claimed that the Crossapols would not have had 'such a fine farm for £7 per year in 1773 ... unless to support them as near relatives of the Chiefs'. As we will see, as late as the 1840s Lachlan Maclean in Freslan had his farm rent free 'as a distant connection of the family'.[6] There were also parallels in Skye, where the Macleods of Talisker had their farm free of rent for the same reason, until Macleod's financial problems forced Talisker to pay a rent of £100 per year. There is, however, an additional explanation as to why Crossapol's rent was so low.

As we have seen in Chapter 1 the end of the traffic in mercenaries to Ireland did not end the need for chiefs in the Isles to maintain professional fighting men. I have argued that these professional soldiers 'gentlemen that labouris not ' were allocated a particular township or *baile* by their chief. Like so much else in the Hebrides the military profession was probably inherited and the son of a soldier became a soldier, as often as the son of a poet became a poet and the son of a musician became a musician.

I have also argued that both Neil Mor, the ancestor of the Crossapol family, and his sons and grandson were accomplished warriors who led the Coll Company in battle, but after the battle of

Inverkeithing they lost their land as well as commissioned officer status and became full-time members of the chief's bodyguard. In the next generation Allan Mac Neil Og certainly took part in the '15 Rebellion and fought at the battle of Sheriffmuir.[7] The Crossapol family therefore had a firmly based tradition of military service well into the eighteenth century.

There is no evidence that Neil MacAllan of Crossapol in 1776 was a soldier. However, as he was thirty-three in 1745, he was probably one of the 60 men from the Coll estate who attempted to join the militia at Inveraray. From what follows it is probable that he had commissioned officer or at least senior NCO status.

Neil was evidently ambitious for his family and saw the need for his sons to be educated. Boswell says that Neil Crossapol 'is like a judge among his neighbours'.[8] He was probably respected as a member of the family of Coll, and for his descent from NeilMor but it sounds as if it was more than just that and that he was wise. Certainly after the 'considerable tacksmen' left the Island it was his descendants who were to dominate Coll for most of the next century, and they were to regain the status they had lost when the family was almost wiped out at the battle of Inverkeithing.

Boswell describes Neil Crossapol as 'a most industrious man'.[9] He also says that his son Donald, whom he met in Coll on several occasions, was a 'really ingenious lad'. He had 'taken a pretty good view of Staffa'.[10] The tutor of Coll's sons taught other children including Donald,[11] who then went to Aberdeen, where he won a bursary at King's College. Coll then got him another bursary as a student of divinity.[12] Boswell says that 'he goes to Aberdeen from the opposite mainland and returns on foot; and when at home, he teaches his sisters and brothers[13] to read and write. Mr Johnson said there was something noble in a young man's walking two hundred miles and back again, every year, for the sake of learning. He would send him his small Dictionary.[14] He did not know his merit when he was with us, or he would have talked to him. I talked to him. He teaches a few other children besides his father's. He told me he taught them first to read English, and then Erse was easily learnt'.

Boswell says that Donald 'can even read the Irish character too'.[15] Although by 1776 this was an unusual accomplishment, it was not unknown in the Inner Hebrides.[16] For instance Mr Archibald MacArthur, the Minister of Kilninian & Kilmore, who at this time was preparing a Gaelic Dictionary, is said to have corresponded with his collaborators in the medieval Gaelic script.[17] The most probable 'Irish Characters' with which Donald Crossapol was familiar is likely to have been Bishop Bedell's Old Testament published in 1686.[18] It is, however, possible that there were still surviving manuscripts in medieval Gaelic script on Coll. Dr Hector Maclean in his Genealogical Account says, when discussing 'the bare catalogue of names from Gillean upwards to Inighis Teurteamer' that 'there was also another catalogue exactly agreeing with this in an old Genealogical manuscript preserved for a long time in Maclean of Coll's Family, which is now lost'.[19] In addition, as we have seen,[20] Donald's brother Allan probably had some knowledge the old Gaelic orthography.

Before the 1770s the Crossapol family have not left any evidence of any intellectual achievements. Donald's mother, however, was a daughter of Archibald Maclean 'of the family of Lochbuy'. This description is associated with the family of hereditary ecclesiastics the Macleans of Knock in Morvern, who were immersed in Gaelic culture.[21] It is therefore possible that the Crossapol family's interest in genealogy and literature, and Donald's ambition to enter the Church of Scotland, stems from the example of his maternal ancestors.

Neil Crossapol and his son Donald helped young Coll entertain the travellers at Coll House. Boswell notes in his diary for 6 October 1773:

> At night came Crossapoll and his eldest son ... we were jovial tonight. Cornaig sang Erse songs. We had no liquor but whisky punch without souring ... I came to like it well enough. I sat up till after three in the morning with them, and then left them to finish a new bowl.

The following morning he notes: 'Captain Maclean came to breakfast. Crossapol and his son had set out early'.[22]

* * *

In 1776 five other tenants in Coll employed three or more servants. Mrs Janet Maclean in Triallan, the Minister's widow, had five. Allan Maclean in Breacachadh, the gardener 'a very decent-looking man', who probably tended the walled garden at Uig, had three servants as did Neil Rankin, the piper. They served at table when young Coll entertained the travellers. Hugh Macdonald, who was young Coll's own servant, did so as well assisted by Johnson's servant Joseph.[23]

* * *

It is hardly surprising when one examines the population of Coll as a whole that from 1776 to 1793 Macleans dominated the Kirk Session. In 1776 there were 193 households on the island. In almost a third (62) the head of the household was a Maclean. This dominance is even more evident when the number of male servants they employed is examined. In 1776 45 male servants were employed on Coll. 46% (21) were employed by Macleans. Not all Macleans were employers: 10 servants had the surname Maclean. However, only three were working for people who did not have the surname Maclean, which suggests that some were working for their relatives.

We know from Alexander Maclean of Coll's reports on repairs to the roads in Coll sent to the Commissioners of Supply for 1786 that there were then 41 tenants and 112 cottars & servants liable to perform statutory labour on the Island. If we assume that the 29 heads of households who employed one or more male servants were tenants who were the others?

One who was certainly a tenant was Lachlan Maclean in Fiosgaradh. He was Neil Crossapol's younger brother and was an elder in 1793. Lachlan Maclean did not employ a servant. He probably did not need to: Fiosgaradh was a single tenancy of just over 118 acres, including 12 of arable.[24] He had several sons to help him.

Most people in Coll did not live in single tenancies but in joint-tenant touns. Boswell tells us that the island was very populous and that the people

> live mostly in little rural villages, for so I may call a number of houses close to each other ... I saw one place [Feall] near the west end of the island, a village where I counted above thirty houses, and saw they would exceed forty. Fifty-eight families lived in it. Their stacks of corn were not much unlike their thatched houses. The village looked at a little distance like a very full barnyard.[25]

He goes on to say that 'the people in Coll live more comfortably than those in Skye; for each has a little garden – a kale-yard ... and the people here appear better dressed'. Boswell was also impressed by the versatility of the people. He says:

The people are very industrious. Every man can tan. They get oak and birch bark and lime from the mainland. Some have pits, but they commonly use tubs. I saw brogues very well tanned, and every man can make them. They all make candles of the tallow of their beasts, both moulded and dipped; and they all make oil of fish. The little fish called cuddies produce a great deal. They boil their livers to make it. They sell some oil out of the island, and they use it much for light in their houses, in little iron (or unpainted black metal) lamps, most of which they have from England; but of late their own blacksmith makes them. He is a good workman; but he has no employment in shoeing horses, for they all go barefooted here, except some better one's of young Coll's, which were now in Mull. There are two carpenters in Coll; but most of the inhabitants can do something as boat-carpenters. They can all dye. They use heath for yellow; and for red, a moss, which grows on stones. They make broadcloth, and tartan and linen, of their own wool and flax, enough for themselves, as also stockings. Their bonnets come from the mainland. There is a man goes every year with a boat to Greenock and brings home a quantity of hardware, ribbons, and other small things; and keeps a little shop in the small village, where is the house in which public worship is held, as there is no church. It is a wretched hut, pretty long, with four little windows one way and two another, glass in none of 'em; only a bunch of straw is used to stop them in case of rain. There are also two people in the island who occasionally act as pedlars.

Johnson states that 'there are tenants [in Coll] below the rank of tacksmen, that have got smaller tenants under them'.[26] Dr Walker condemned this practice in Mull, observing that the 'most oppressed man in the South of Scotland is the Tenant of a Tenant, and it is not to be supposed that it is less so in the North'.[27] Boswell, however, as we have seen, reckoned that the practice in Coll where cottars 'are obliged to furnish two horses each for work, as also a third of the seed-corn; and for this work through the year, they have a third of the crop and three milk-cows grazed' was a good system as it made 'servants have a common interest with their masters'.[28]

Certainly in Coll the people appeared content. Boswell comments that:

It was very agreeable as we went along to see all the people come from their work and shake hands with the young laird . . . his manners were not those of a chieftain in point of dignity. But if he had not reverence from his people, he had their affection.[29]

Boswell met virtually the entire Coll establishment in 1773. With the exception of the McSweens, all were Macleans descended from the progenitor of the family. There were other families on the estate who played a prominent part in the community especially in Quinish and the Isle of Muck but it was the Macleans who had the best land and who controlled the Kirk Session. Despite these inequalities the people were not unhappy. To quote Samuel Johnson they had 'not yet learned to be weary of their heath and rocks, but attend their agriculture and their dairies, without listening to American seducements'.[30]

* * *

From 1786–1790 there were around 18 tenants and 42 cottars on Coll's estate in Mull. Less is known about them than their peers on Coll's other estates as no catechist's list or rental appears to have survived. The number of individual holdings also changed over the years, as did the number of

Coll's kinsmen living on Quinish. One was Lachlan Maclean in Kilmore. He was a merchant[31] and elder[32] of the Kirk Session of Kilninian & Kilmore, the parish that covered the north of the island.[33]

When the surviving kirk session records begin in 1766 three of the four elders present were tacksmen on Quinish: Hugh Maclean in Achacharra, John Maclean in Mingary, and Allan Maclean in Bellachroy. Only John can be identified with confidence. He was a member of the Boreray family in North Uist. He returned to Uist in 1775 and another Boreray cadet took his place. This was Alexander Maclean, formerly in Gott, Tiree, who also became an elder.

Another well-established family on the Quinish estate was the Morison tacksmen in Auchnasaul. In 1774 Hector Morison was Coll's ground officer for Quinish. He was married to a daughter of Magnus Morison in Penmore on Torloisk's estate.[34] I am not certain if these two families stemmed from the same source. The late Rev. William Matheson did not think that they were.[35] The Penmore family descended from the *Ó Muirgheasains*, one of the principal families of hereditary poet-historians in Gaelic Scotland and Ireland.[36] Magnus Morison was an elder of Kilninian & Kilmore. However, he fell on hard times and became an 'object' [of charity].[37]

There was plenty of movement between Coll and Quinish. For instance in 1799 Hector Morison in Auchnasaul's eldest surviving son married in Coll,[38] and in 1809 his brother Donald married Janet, the daughter of Neil Rankin, Coll's piper.[39]

* * *

The upper echelons of society in the Hebrides were nothing if not sociable. They spent much of their time visiting each other in the Hebrides, entertaining their friends and enjoying a bowl of punch. They also had sociable relations with their 'considerable tacksmen' and with their tenants visiting them and staying in their houses. Sometimes these visits ended in disaster.

On Sunday 25 September 1774 Donald Maclean, 'Young Coll', *Domhnall Òg* and a few companions including 'Young Lochbuie' visited the genealogist Dr Hector Maclean at Erray, near Tobermory. They then decided to pay a visit to Sir Allan Maclean, who as we have seen, lived on the Isle of Inchkenneth on the other side of Mull. As there were no public roads at that period, they followed a path which took them first into Glen Bellart, where they called at Auchnasaul, the house of Hector Morison, Coll's ground officer in Quinish. In conversation with Mr Morison, *Domhnall Òg* said that he was irritated with young Lochbuie's behaviour, as the latter had been shooting game birds all the way from Tobermory.

The party then left Auchnasaul and proceeded up Glen Bellart until they reached the footpath, which led to Lagganulva. They then turned towards the coast. When they arrived at Laggan House,[40] young Maclean of Lochbuie insisted that some of the birds, which he had shot on the way, should be cooked. When they were placed on the dining table, Young Coll got up and threw them on the fire, and refused any more food. The atmosphere must have been explosive.

The party then left, and continued their journey to the ferry. They never reached their destination. Young Coll and young Lochbuie probably came to blows in the boat. It over-turned. Several of those on board were drowned. The only body recovered was that of Donald, and he had a wound on his face. Archibald Lochbuie survived.

Apparently the feud between the two young men had been going on for some time. Both fancied Sir Allan Maclean's eldest daughter, and it was reported that she much preferred young Coll. After *Domhnall Òg's* body was recovered, Sir Allan's daughter came over to the ferry at Ulva and asked for his watch. She extracted a small piece of paper from it. It was presumed that this was a betrothal agreement, which she and *Domhnall Òg* had made.[41]

Notes

1. *Boswell*, 285.
2. *Boswell*, 282.
3. Crossapol MS, 40.
4. Crossapol MS, 44.
5. NAS. CH2. 70. 1, 42.
6. Mull Museum. Letter Book. 1846–1850. Captain Donald Campbell at Quinish. 14 May 1847.
7. *Inner Isles 1716*, 163.
8. *Boswell*, 283.
9. *Boswell*, 269.
10. *Boswell*, 270.
11. He matriculated in 1769. BCP. PJ Anderson, Librarian, University Library, Aberdeen. Private communication to HAC Maclean 24 June 1898.
12. NAS. CH2. 492. 1.
13. One of them will have been Allan Crossapol, the compiler of the Crossapol MS.
14. He was as good as his word and the dictionary was for many years preserved in my family. My grandmother sold it, to avoid family disputes, to Cambridge University, in whose library I understand it is now.
15. *Boswell*, 283.
16. It is suggested in Chapter 1, note 12 that his brother Allan may also have been familiar with the old Gaelic script.
17. I have to thank Ronald Black for this information.
18. *Gaelic Scotland*, 23.
19. NLS. ACC 7609, 2.
20. Chapter 1, note 12.
21. See my 'From the Sound of Mull' (forthcoming).
22. *Boswell*, 283.
23. *Boswell*, 287.
24. NAS. RHP 3368.
25. *Boswell*, 257.
26. *Johnson*, 198.
27. *Walker*, 160.
28. *Boswell*, 282
29. *Boswell*, 258.
30. *Johnson*, 203.
31. He traded 'both in gross & by retail'. In 1790 he became financially embarassed. Most of his creditors were in Glasgow [NAS. CS 234. Sequestrations M1/27. Box 228. 2D & CS 229 Mc/6/54. Box 308]
32. NAS. CH2. 492. 1: He was probably born in Coll. In 1776 he was the 'of age son' of John Maclean in Arinagour, who perhaps kept the 'little poor public house close upon the shore'. [*Boswell*, 252]
33. *Walker*, 152.
34. Neil Morison's memoirs [BCP Card index: Hector Morison]
35. Private communication to the author.
36. Derick S Thomson *Gaelic Scotland* (1983), 219–20.
37. NAS. CH2. 492. 1: 9 September 1777, 25 July 1779 & 13 May 1780.
38. NAS. CH2. 70.1: 22 January 1799 'Charles Morrison from Quinish married to Margaret McInnes in Arnabost in Coll'.
39. Neil Morison's memoirs.
40. It was at the time occupied by Archibald Maclean, Torloisk's brother.
41. Mull Museum Records. D12. 113.

Chapter Nineteen

The War of American Independence 1775–1783

Young Coll's death was universally regretted. Fortunately, however, he had a younger brother, Alexander, to succeed him. Alexander had been studying law in Edinburgh when Donald was drowned. He immediately gave up his studies and took over the running of his father's estate. Boswell reported to Johnson that Alexander, who dined with him on 18 February 1775, was 'a very amiable man, though not marked with such active qualities as his brother'.[1] Be that as it may. He was in his own right an interesting character and, as the man at the pinnacle of the family of Coll for sixty years it was to be his decisions that were ultimately to be responsible for the survival of the clan into the nineteenth century.

* * *

Not everyone in Coll in 1773 had resisted American seducements. Donald of Cornaig's eldest son Lachlan sailed for New England and was in Boston when the American War of Independence began. The inhabitants of the Coll estate were to be far more involved in this new war than they had been in the Seven Years War. As we shall see there were several reasons why the estate was an ideal recruiting ground for the army.

Lachlan Cornaig enlisted as a volunteer and on 14 June 1775 he was commissioned as a lieutenant in the 2nd Battalion of the Royal Highland Emigrants [84th Foot][2] commanded by Major John Small. He then served in Murdoch Maclaine's[3] Grenadier Company.[4] The battalion assembled at Halifax, Nova Scotia. It was mainly recruited from Highland emigrants there, in Prince Edward Island and in Newfoundland. Other men came from Boston. On 19 February 1776 it was reported in Halifax that Lachlan was expected from Boston with a number of recruits.

Later he was stationed at Fort Sackville, near Halifax. He was then in command of 30 men. On 25 August 1778 he was recommended to be adjutant of a 'Grenadier Corps' and later still served in Captain Robert Campbell's Light Company in the campaign in the Southern States. Later he served in Jamaica.[5]

* * *

Many of the men in the 84th had served in Fraser's Highlanders in North America during the Seven Years War (1756–63). Simon Fraser, who raised Fraser's Highlanders, was the son of the infamous

Lord Lovat, who was beheaded after the '45. In 1774 Simon had his father's estates restored to him. He was now in an even stronger position to raise a regiment and in 1775 was authorised to recruit a regiment of two battalions.

Alexander younger of Coll was determined that one of his brothers should obtain a commission in Fraser's new regiment. On 4 December 1775 Boswell, who was in Edinburgh notes that 'Young Coll, who was to go from London next day, sat a little with me'. He gave him a letter of introduction to Johnson,[6] who was pleased with him and took him to dine at the Mitre.[7]

In London Alexander visited the Cecil Street Coffee House. James Maclean, a Kingerloch cadet owned it. During the previous war had served in North America in Montgomerie's Highlanders.[8] He no doubt advised Alexander on how to go about approaching Simon Fraser and on 16 December 1775 Coll wrote from 7 Cecil Street to General Fraser at George's Street, Hanover Square:

> At a time when I know you must be troubled with so many applications, I who am an entire stranger to you, tho' my friends are not, must ask your pardon for intruding upon you with this, in favour of a brother, who is desirous of serving under you in the Regiment you are about to raise.
>
> I would have done myself the honour of waiting of you, but being unacquainted I thought it more eligible to take this methode of acquainting you with my request. – I can with confidence assure you that if you have not already made choise of all your officers you cannot name one, that can with so much ease & expedition raise whatever number of men the commission he gets shall require, for this reason, that my father has not yet by raising his rents or other harsh usages, forced his tenants to leave their country, as too many other proprietors have done. The fact is there are actually at present too many people upon his estate, & more of the antient attachment subsists between him & his tenants than most Highlanders can now boast of, this consequently gives him a command of men – These are the arguments upon which I ground my hopes, tho' to you as a Highlander others might be urged – I hope you will favour one with an answer and forgive the trouble given you by.[9]

It is not known if Simon Fraser replied to this letter. His regiment was oversubscribed and no Maclean of Coll obtained a berth in it.[10] Nor is it certain which brother Alexander was referring to in his letter. It could not have been Hector. He was nineteen in 1775 when he sailed for India to join the Honourable East India Company's service. He obtained a commission as an ensign in the 5th Native Infantry in the Madras presidency and was soon in action on the expedition against the rajahs north of Arcott.[11]

Fraser's Highlanders sailed from Greenock for North America with men of the 1st Battalion of 42nd Foot, the Black Watch. On 23 August 1776 the former Minister of Coll Mr Hector's only son Allan became an ensign in the regiment.[12] He had previously been apprenticed to John Maclean, surgeon in Glasgow. His apprenticeship was for three years and began on 7 July 1770. Although he is described as 'surgeon in Glasgow',[13] he does not appear in the lists of Fellows or Licenciates of the Royal College of Physicians & Surgeons of Glasgow. Presumably he had not paid his dues as he could only practice within the environs of Glasgow with the College's authority.[14]

In October 1777 the British were defeated at Saratoga. This defeat was the turning point of the war. Instead of a civil war between English speaking people, the conflict was now to be waged throughout the world, and there was a need for more infantry regiments. In December Colonel the Honourable William Gordon, brother of the Earl of Aberdeen, was ordered to raise a regiment of Highlanders.[15] It was named the 81st or Aberdeenshire Highland Regiment. Coll's fifth son Roderick Neil was one of the first officers to be commissioned in it. He obtained a lieutenancy on 30 December 1777.[16] He was sixteen.

The reason why he obtained his commission was undoubtedly the result of his family's influence in Aberdeen. On 28 February 1778 the Records of the Merchant and Trade Society note:

> The convener proposed that to testify their respect to the son of their Provost Lieutenant Maclean and the constitutional supremacy of the Mother Country over the Colonies they should, after the example of most of the Corporations in Scotland, offer a Bounty of one guinea over and above all bounties to every recruit that shall enlist within the liberties of the town betwixt this and the first day of May with Lieutenant Roderick Maclean, son of Hugh Maclean Esq. of Coll to which the meeting present, excepting one, did agree and ordered this to be published in the Aberdeen Journal the money to be paid by their boxmaster.[17]

Although the Earl of Aberdeen's lands were in the Lowlands, two-thirds of the men in 81st Foot came from the Highlands. Out of the 82 men in Captain John Ferguson's company, in which Roderick Neil Maclean was a lieutenant, 31 had surnames which suggest that they came from Coll's estate.[18] Supporting Alexander's claim that his father could raise men for the army.

Soon after the regiment was formed it was marched to Stirling, and then shipped to Ireland. They were stationed in Ireland for three years. One officer, Norman Maclean, did not go with them as he was left behind to recruit. He was an ensign. Curiously, although Roderick Neil was the senior officer, he was eighteen months younger than his brother Norman, which suggests that Norman was the brother Alexander had tried to get into Fraser's regiment.

France entered the war against Britain when on 6 February 1778 she signed a formal treaty of friendship and commerce with the 'United States of North America'. There was now a threat of invasion to Britain itself and the Government ordered that fencible regiments should be raised for internal defence. The first to be embodied was the Argyle or Western Fencible Regiment, which was raised by Lord Frederick Campbell, brother of the Duke of Argyll. It was mustered at Glasgow in April 1778. In the absence of the regiment's Colonel, Lord Frederick and the Lieutenant Colonel, Sir James Campbell of Ardkinglas, its effective commanding officer was Major Hugh Montgomery of Coilsfield.[19] Alexander Maclean, younger of Coll, commanded a company. He was twenty-five.

A fencible regiment was for home service only. Otherwise it was little different from any other regular unit and fencible regiments were subject to military discipline. The one important difference concerned the officers. They received pay but they were only temporary officers. They did not hold a permanent commission and were not entitled to half-pay. Many junior officers, however, used a commission in a fencible unit as a stepping-stone to a regular regiment which gave them a permanent commission and when the war was over they were entitled to half-pay.

The Western Fencibles were recruited in both Argyll and Ayrshire. When, on the 9 September 1779, they were mustered at Dundee 41 of the 107 private soldiers who served in Alexander's company between 25 December 1778 and 24 June 1779 have surnames that suggest they came from Coll's estate. Two sergeants, and one corporal did so as well. The list of officers is even more instructive. Apart from Lieutenant William Weir, who presumably came from Ayrshire, they are all Macleans. Although the subsequent careers of one of them named Murdoch is known,[20] nothing is recorded of his antecedents, nor can 'Lieutenant Alexander Maclean' be identified. The others can.

On 25 December 1778 Ensign John Maclean in Alexander's company was promoted into the 2nd Battalion of Royal Scots, the 1st Regiment of Foot, of which the Duke of Argyll was colonel. It was fitting that he should do so as John's father Donald Maclean of Cornaig was, as we have seen, the Duke's tacksman for the Two Ends of Coll. The following day he was replaced as ensign by Allan Maclean, who is probably none other than Allan Crossapol, the compiler of the genealogical account of the Macleans of Coll. In 1780 Allan became the second lieutenant in Coll's company and in May he too transferred to the Royal Scots,[21] serving in the 1st Battalion in England. Dugald Maclean replaced him.[22] He had previously been a sergeant. Promotion from the ranks seems to have been a feature in the fencibles.

There was, confusingly, another Allan Maclean, an ensign in Coll's company in 1780.[23] He evidently had medical training and on 4 July 1780 was transferred to the Colonel's Company as surgeon's mate.[24] This second Allan, who we will meet again, was a member of the Ormsaig branch of the clan. He was known as *doctair ruadh nam blàth shuilean*, the red haired doctor of the warm eyes.

* * *

In 1779 Alexander's company was stationed at Dundee. They were therefore not one of the five companies of the Western Fencibles that mutinied in Edinburgh in October 1779. At the time of the mutiny the Commander-in-Chief in Scotland was Lieutenant-General Sir Adolphus Oughton.[25] Boswell says that he was:

> not only an excellent officer but one of the most universal scholars I ever knew, [he] had learned the Erse language.

Oughton had met Johnson in Edinburgh in August 1773 and as he believed in the authenticity of Ossian's poetry and Johnson did not, Boswell thought that they would have a violent argument.

> But Sir Adolphus, who had a very sweet temper, changed the discourse, grew playful, laughed at Lord Monboddo's notion of men originally having tails, and called him 'a Judge *a posteriori*', which amused Dr Johnson, and thus hostilities were prevented.[26]

Oughton had to use all his tact and charm to diffuse the situation created when the Western Fencible's mutinied. It did so because the men felt insulted by the equipment issued to them.

When it was first mustered the Western Fencibles were given cartridge-pouches that had been discarded by the Glasgow Volunteers. To make matters worse when replacements were issued the new equipment was uncomfortable and impracticable. The men also detested their goatskin sporrans. This resentment was not peculiar to the five companies sent to Edinburgh but was equally felt by the detachment at Dundee. In both places junior officers listened to the men's complaints with some sympathy but, according to John Prebble, did nothing to remedy their grievances.[27]

The result was disastrous. On 8 October 1779 Oughton informed Lord Amherst, who had a seat in the cabinet and was effectively in command of the army, of what was going on in Edinburgh. Oughton wrote from Leith:

> I am sorry to acquaint your Lordship that five companies of the West Fencibles quartered in Edinburgh Castle have mutinied, refusing positively to wear their belts and pouches which

they threw out of their barrack windows. However necessary it was to quell this mutinous disposition and reduce them to obedience it was not advisable to employ force while they remained in possession of the Castle. They were therefore left quiet for a few days, and were this morning ordered to the Links of Leith to exercise. Here they were surrounded by the 10th Regiment of Dragoons. They submitted, grounded their arms, and put on their accoutrements. Lord Frederick Campbell on seeing the Dragoons march into the field seized four of the ringleaders. He was of the opinion that an immediate punishment would produce a better effect than the slow proceedings of a General Court Martial. I consented to this being tried and punishment on the spot was accordingly done.

In the meantime some Highlanders, who were left in the Castle as convalescents, forced the Port Guard, and drew up the bridge declaring they would admit none but their comrades. As the Field Officers did not think their men were to be trusted I ordered them to be marched by companies to the adjacent towns and villages, and have sent an express to Lord Adam Gordon desiring he would immediately send me two or three hundred men to garrison the Castle.

He wrote again at 4 o'clock that afternoon. Colonel Mordaunt with two troops of dismounted dragoons had taken possession of the Castle without any opposition. They then confined all the mutineers they found. Oughton ends his communication with a despairing appeal:

And now my Lord, I must entreat you will send me down an English Regiment for though the Highlanders are brave, and would I believe act very well against a foreign enemy, I have had too much experience of them to put any confidence in them in any domestic broils or tumults: their mutinous and obstinate disposition making them very unsafe when not mixed with other troops. Indeed many strong reasons make it highly advisable to replace the Fencible Regiments in this country with an equivalent number of English troops.[28]

News of the punishment of the mutineers soon reached the detachment in Dundee. The mutineers had first been stripped to the waist, and then bound to a pyramid made from three of the seven-foot halberds carried by sergeants, with a fourth lashed to form a horizontal. The convicted man was next tied at the wrists, which were then drawn upwards above his head and tied to the crossed blades of the halberds. His chest rested on the horizontal halberd and his ankles attached to two of the verticals. The drummers then marched up to the pyramid and on the command 'Go on, drum-major' the flogging began.

Even in an age, which was hardened to brutality, the effect on the convicted man's companions, drawn up in ranks to watch, was devastating. It was believed to be particularly humiliating for Highlanders to have their dignity violated in this manner. If Alexander Maclean Sinclair is to be believed, Alexander Maclean of Coll was not prepared to have his men suffer in this way.

Maclean Sinclair the author of *Clan Gillean* was the grandson of John Maclean *Bàrd Thigearna Collach* Alexander Maclean of Coll's bard, who was later to emigrate to Canada. He collected several stories about his grandfather's patron. He claims that once when Coll was in the Argyll Fencibles:

John Macdonald, of Hogh in Tiree, neglected to perform some duty, which had been entrusted to him, at a bridge. For this act of neglect Major Hugh Montgomery ordered that he should be whipped. Coll was at that time only a captain. As Macdonald was in his company, and as he had been acquainted with him from his youth, he went twice to the major and humbly pleaded with him to forgive Macdonald; but the major was inexorable. When the flogging was to begin Coll drew his sword and cut the cords with which the unfortunate soldier was tied to the whipping-post. Montgomery challenged Maclean to a duel with swords; the challenge was accepted. As there was fear among the soldiers that Maclean might be killed, they sent word to Montgomery that if he should happen to kill Maclean, he would be instantly shot. Coll appeared on the ground; but Montgomery kept away. The duel was never fought.[29]

There is no mention of this incident in the surviving military records. Perhaps Montgomery hushed it up; it is, however, curious that there were no Macdonalds in Hough, Tiree in 1779.[30] There were, however, two John Macdonalds in Coll's company from 25 December 1778 to 24 April 1781, and even if this story is apocryphal it says something about how Alexander was regarded by his men.

* * *

During the war officers from Coll served in campaigns all over the world. In India Hector Coll took part in the siege of the French fortress of Pondicherry, the battle with Hyder Ali and in the reduction of the Dutch fort of Policat.[31] As we have seen Norman had originally spent his time recruiting for the 81st Foot. In May 1780 he was transferred to the 2nd Battalion of the 73rd Foot.[32] They were posted to Gibraltar.

In April 1779 Spain signed an offensive alliance with France against Britain. It was to last until Spain recovered Gibraltar. Since its capture in 1704 the recovery of Gibraltar had been a Spanish obsession and although many British politicians considered trading it for peace with Spain, public opinion in Britain was equally adamant the it should be retained. Gibraltar was under constant siege during the war. The most dangerous attack took place in 1782. On 13 September a Franco-Spanish force of warships and floating batteries, with 40,000 men and 200 guns, anchored 1,000 yards off the Rock of Gibraltar, and with 200 more guns on the Isthmus between the Rock and the Spanish mainland, opened fire.

The British returned fire, concentrating on the floating batteries, with red-hot shot and during the night battery after battery burst into flame. On 14 September the last of them blew up. Gibraltar was safe. The 2nd 73rd Highlanders earned a high reputation during the siege. According to Stewart of Garth 'not a man was punished, or deserted to the enemy'. In May 1783 the battalion returned to England and were marched to Stirling. Here it was reduced.[33] Norman Maclean, who had been promoted captain during the siege, was placed on the English half pay list.[34]

The 2nd Battalion of the 1st Regiment of Foot replaced 2nd 73rd Highlanders in Gibraltar. They had previously been stationed in Cork. Lieutenant John Maclean, Cornaig's younger son was serving with them. He remained there until 1789[35] when he was placed on the half pay list of 87th Foot.

Roderick Neil was also placed on the half pay list. The 81st Foot having spent most of the war in Ireland, where they gained a good reputation. At the end of 1782 they crossed over to England, and, in March 1783, immediately after peace had been signed, they embarked for the East Indies. However, when they enlisted it had been a condition of their engagement that they were discharged once the war was over. The 81st now demanded that the authorities stick to their initial agreement, and the regiment was marched to Scotland where in April 1783 they too were disbanded.[36]

Perhaps as a result of the affair over John Macdonald, Alexander Maclean of Coll was on 24 April 1781 'removed to the Light Infantry' company. Several men were transferred at the same time. None of them had Coll surnames. One sergeant, Allan Maclean who had served in Coll's company was later transferred to the Light Company, as was Francis Maclean, one of the original volunteers who was later commissioned.[37] Sergeant Allan Maclean was, however, reduced to the ranks in April 1782,[38] so he may not have been an asset to Coll. It does, however, seem likely that there was a move to separate Alexander from his clansmen. Maclean of Coll was still in command of the Light Company when the regiment was disbanded at Glasgow on 9 April 1783.

In 1778 Lachlan, younger of Cornaig, married an American lady, Hannah Barbara Cotnam. It is possible that she was the 'very pretty girl' who Captain Alexander Macdonald wrote to Major Small to say 'he had saved Lt. Laughlin McLean from marrying' as although she was very pretty she had 'not a sixpence on Earth'.[39] On 18 January 1779 their eldest son Francis John Small was born in Halifax.[40] He was named after his father's commanding officer John Small and General Francis Maclean who was commanding the troops in Halifax.[41] In 1783 Lachlan was invalided back to Britain.[42] He was home in Coll by 25 November when his daughter Elizabeth Isabella was baptised.[43]

In 1780 Lieutenant Allan, Mr Hector the former Minister of Coll's son, was also invalided home. The 42nd had been in the thick of the fighting since their arrival in America. On one occasion Allan must have been particularly rigorously engaged. This was on 10 May 1777 at the village of Piscattanag [Pisquatua]. Piscattanag was situated astride the lines of communication between 'New York and Brunswick by Amboy'. Stewart of Garth writes:

> The duty here was severe, and the season rigorous. As the houses in the village could not accommodate half the men, officers and soldiers were intermixed in barns and sheds, sleeping always in their body-clothes, as the enemy were constantly sending down nocturnal parties, to fire at the sentinels and picquets. While employed in exciting these nightly alarms, they, however, kept a respectful distance . . . In this manner passed the winter and spring.

Then at 4 o'clock in the afternoon of 10 May 2000 the Americans attacked.

> Advancing with great secrecy . . . their approach was not perceived till they rushed forward on a small level piece of ground in front of the picquets. These they attacked with such promptitude, that the men had hardly time to seize their arms. Notwithstanding this unexpected and sudden attack, they kept the enemy in check till the picquets in reserve came to their assistance. Pushing forward fresh numbers, the enemy became at length mixed with the picquets, who retired, disputing every foot, to afford more time to the regiment to turn out . . . the enemy were driven back . . . leaving upwards of 200 men in killed and wounded. The Highlanders, pursuing with great eagerness, were with difficulty recalled, and were only prevented by the approach of night from pushing on to attack the enemy's camp. The loss of the Highlanders was 3 sergeants and 9 privates killed; and Captain Duncan Macpherson, Lieutenant William Stewart, and 3 sergeants and 30 privates wounded.[44]

Captain Duncan Macpherson was Allan's company commander.[45] There can be little doubt that the latter was involved in the thick of the hand-to-hand fighting.

On 25 June 1777 Allan transferred to the company commanded by Captain Archibald Erskine of Cardross;[46] and on 3 August 1778 he was promoted Lieutenant; then in 1779 at the regiment's camp on New York Island he is reported as being sick. The following year he was invalided home;

however, he soon returned to New York, but is reported dead on 1 January 1781.[47] The edition of the Maclean Genealogical Account, which takes the story up to 1807, says that 'he was lost on his passage from New York to Britain'.[48]

Notes

1. Frederick A Pottle (ed) *Boswell: The Ominous Years 1774–1776*, 67.
2. TNA. WO34. 111. 9738.
3. For Captain Murdoch Maclaine see my 'Murdoch Maclaine, Lieutenant 42nd Foot?' *JSAHR* vol. 77. No. 310, (Summer 1999), 69–70.
4. He appears in that company in a muster at Halifax, Nova Scotia in January 1778 [quoted in John Victor Duncanson *Rawdon and Douglas: Two Loyalist Townships in Nova Scotia* (Mika Publishing Company, Belleville, Ontario, 1989), 400–1]. I have to thank Eugene Quigley for this reference.
5. He was in Charleston on 30 December 1781 [*Rawdon & Douglas*, 400].
6. James Boswell *The Life of Samuel Johnson* (1791), 265.
7. *Boswell's Ominous Years*, 192.
8. James NM Maclean *Reward is Secondary* (1963), 338 says that James was a lieutenant in the regiment, however, the only James commissioned in it was Ardgour's brother. There is also no mention of the Cecil Street James being an officer in his will [PRO. Nelson.Will 36, signed 21 October 1802, proved 3 January 1805].
9. Alexander Maclean, younger of Coll, No. 7 Cecil Street, Strand 16 December 1775. [EUL. La ii, 300]
10. David Stewart *Sketches of the Highlanders* vol. ii, 43–8.
11. *Seanachie* 316.
12. TNA. WO12. 5478. Muster Rolls 1/42 Foot 1759–78 shows that he served in Duncan McPherson's company.
13. NAS. C.12. 7.4 (3). 21 February 1772 when he became cautioner for his mother.
14. John was a son of Mr Archibald Maclean Minister of Kilfinichen & Kilvicewen in Mull. I have to thank Alison Ballantine, Archivist of the Royal College for this information. [BCP. 26 November 1980].
15. *Sketches of the Highlanders* vol. ii, 139.
16. *Army List 1779*, 147.
17. *Records of Old Aberdeen* vol. I, 324.
18. TNA. WO12. 8520; One man with the unusual name Abraham Beatton certainly did. In 1776 he was a servant of Allan Maclean's at Cliad.
19. *Sketches of the Highlanders* vol. ii, 303–4.
20. Murdoch became the Quartermaster and died in 1799 [TNA. WO. 25. 3100].
21. TNA. WO13. 3962. 28182.
22. It is possible that he was the Dugald Maclean, who on 8 June 1778 was in Captain Ferguson's company in 81st Foot at Kinsale [TNA. WO12. 8520].
23. TNA. WO13. 3962. Perth 29 April 1780.
24. Ensign Allan was the son of Dr John Maclean, known as *Iain MacDhòmhnall mhic Thearlaich* the representative of the Macleans of Ross. He was married to Christian, daughter of Captain Allan Maclean, an illegitimate son of Lachlan Maclean of Brolas [*Clan Gillean*, 354].
25. WY Carman 'Lieutenant-General Sir Adolphus Oughton, KB' *JSAHR*, vol. 68, No. 271, (Autumn 1989), 127–9 & Stephen Wood '... By Dint of Labour and Perseverance ...' A journal recording two months in northern Germany kept by Lieutenant-Colonel James Adolphus Oughton, commanding 1st battalion 37th of Foot, 1758, *JSAHR*, Special Publication No. 14 (1997).
26. *Boswell*, 27.
27. John Prebble *Mutiny* (1975), 186–7.
28. TNA. WO1 1003, 589.

29. *Clan Gillean*, 380–1.
30. Eric Cregeen (ed), *Inhabitants of the Argyll Estate, 1779* (1963).
31. *Seanachie*, 316.
32. *Scots Magazine 1780*; *Army List 1781*, 149.
33. *Sketches of the Highlanders* vol, ii, 86.
34. *Army List 1785*, 340.
35. TNA. WO12. 1949.
36. *Sketches of the Highlanders* vol. ii, 140.
37. He is probably the 2nd son of Murdoch Maclean of Kilmory [*WHN&Q* Series 2, No. 1, 11] and the Lieutenant Francis Maclean who on the 22 December 1808 became a lieutenant in 86th Foot [TNA. WO 31. 266].
38. TNA. WO13. 3963. 8809.
39. Captain Alexander Macdonald to Major John Small, Halifax, 19 February 1776 quoted in *Rawdon & Douglas*, 401. At least one of their daughters was exceptionally pretty.
40. BCP. Isle of Muck folder: The Profile of Francis John Small Maclean, Esq. Lieutenant HM Regiment of Foot, died at Dominica in the West Indies on 23 – 1801.
41. Francis Maclean was a de-tribalised Maclean who had served in the Scots Brigade in Dutch service before transferring to the British Army. He raised the 82nd Regiment of Foot.
42. TNA. WO12. 8806. Muster Roll 2/84 Foot.
43. NAS. CH2. 70. 1.
44. *Sketches of the Highlanders* vol. I, 380.
45. TNA. WO12. 5478.
46. Neil McMicking (ed) *Officers of the Black Watch 1725 to 1952* (1952), 36.
47. TNA. WO12. 5479.
48. NLS. MS. 3018, 49.

Chapter Twenty

A clandestine marriage

Meanwhile, whilst his peers were serving in the army, Donald, Neil Maclean of Crossapol's eldest son was continuing his career in the church. On 28 September 1775 he attended a meeting of the Presbytery of Mull. They agreed to 'prescribe him some pieces of training'.[1] Three years later at Fiunary in Morvern 'Mr Donald Maclean, Student from Coll' again attended Presbytery to be admitted to probationary trials. On this occasion the Presbytery

> considering that he was proposed to trials at the Synod two or three years ago and that the Synod had directed the Presbytery to admit him after the Expiration of the Session of College then next ensuring at which they required him to attend, & further that he has produced Certificates of his attendance at the Divinity & his behaviour in other respects is unexceptionable, so far as is known to this Presbytery, do agree in opinion that they may now comply with his Request but think it expedient to pass from the pieces prescribed him bonafide on a former occasion and do now appoint him the following subjects viz . . .[2]

Donald's career was progressing slowly, but it appeared surely, and on 21 October 1779 the Presbytery received a letter from Hugh Maclean of Coll 'in favour of Mr Donald Maclean, Student'. It is not stated what was in the letter, but there can be little doubt that it was to recommend that he should be appointed as Minister of Coll. On 16 April the Presbytery had been informed that 'Mr Charles Stewart Minister of Coll has within these few weeks removed from that Island in order to be settled Minister at Strachur'.[3]

Despite the urgency, the formalities of the church had to be followed and on 18 December 1779, Donald, and his fellow student William Fraser, was examined 'on their knowledge of the Greek Language by explaining each piece of the New Testament from the Original into Latin'. Such erudition was a requirement in the Church of Scotland until the 1970s.[4] It goes some way to explain how at this time city or country ministers of the Church of Scotland met on equal terms with noblemen, judges, advocates, writers to the signet, medical men, and successful business men, and held their own with them, in literary and philosophical discussions at clubs, such as the so-called Select Club founded in Edinburgh in 1754.[5]

The two students were next questioned on their knowledge of divinity and understanding difficult Texts of Scripture. In all of which they gave good specimens of themselves. They then expressed their desire to be licensed, and the Presbytery

> having reviewed the several pieces of Trial gone through by them was satisfied with the result. The Moderator then having taken them under the usual engagement prescribed by the Rules of

the Church of Scotland, and they having declared their readiness to subscribe to the Confession of Faith, the Presbytery did license the said Messrs William Fraser and Donald Maclean to preach the Gospel of Jesus Christ as probationers for the Ministry within the Bounds of this Presbytery.[6]

Then a bombshell struck. On 24 July 1780 Donald was summoned to attend a meeting of Presbytery at Kilmore and was interrogated

> on the common report of his clandestine marriage with Lily Maclean his cousin german in whose father's house he resides, upon which he made an acknowledgement & seemed much affected with his fault, at the same time giving a full and particular account thereof in writing which being read & maturely considered the Presbytery having in view the Interests of Religion in these bounds and also the singular circumstances attending this case did and do hereby discharge him the said Mr Donald Maclean from officiating as preacher of the Gospel till such time as the Presbytery shall see cause to reprove him.

A clandestine marriage was one performed in private without the banns having been read on three consecutive Sundays. It was contrary to both ecclesiastical and civil law, and the Presbytery reacted quickly. On 2 September 1780 they met at Gott in Tiree, a farm held by Donald's father-in-law Mr Alexander Maclean where:

> After reading of the minutes the Presbytry resumed consideration of Mr Donald Maclean's case, and after mature deliberation there upon and upon the advices given by each Brethren of the Synod as were consulted there anent it was agreed not withstanding his application to be reponed to his office that it is too early considering the nature of the Offence. But in order to pave the way for it, as he appears to the Presbytery penitent & not undeserving in other Respects of being encouraged they judge it expedient to have him married this day in their presence, whereupon he & the said Lily Maclean being called & compering Mr Archd. McArthur at the desire of the Presbytery laid before them the folly & blame worthyness of their conduct, rebuked them for the same & exhorted them to make the best amends in their power for the offence they had given and then in presence of the presbytry and of the woman's parents made them join hands and repeat [indecypherable] the usual vows & engagements which parties came under in time of marriage & concluded with declaring them married persons & with prayer.[7]

What is not stated in the Presbytery minutes is that Donald and Lillias's daughter Margaret had been born on 16 July 1780 or that their clandestine marriage had taken place on 25 September 1777.[8] Donald had then been 25[9] and Lillias 28.[10] Why they had to keep their marriage secret is not clear. There can, however, be no doubt that it changed the whole course of their lives.

On 24 July, when Donald had first been interrogated, there was a presentation delivered in favour of a Mr Archibald McColl, who was present. He was asked that if he became minister of the Parish of Tiree

> he was willing to give obligation similar to those granted by the three last incumbents respecting an allowance by them for an assistant minister in Coll, the reasons of which obligations were

fully explained to him; he made answer that he was not prepared for that question & begged the Presbytery would give him time to consider & take advice there upon and particularly to consult his Patron. The Presbytery gave him till their next meeting which is hereby appointed to be holden at Inveraray'.

McColl's patron was of course the Duke of Argyll. He owned Tiree and it is not impossible that it was his agents who had leaked the information about Donald's clandestine marriage. It could, however, hardly be hidden once their daughter was born. The influence of the minister was considerable, and in Tiree hatred of the Campbells lasted well into the 1770s. In 1771 the anonymous author of a report for the Duke remarked that 'the small tenants of Tiree are disaffected to the family [of Argyll] ... and much incited by their chieftains of the Maclean gentry'.[11] This attitude lasted even after Sir Allan had lost his case against the Duke, for as late as 1789 a Maclean bard could sing:

> Our enemies have our places
> And they do not care for us
> Though we are polite to them
> Our hearts are cold.[12]

On 3 August 1780 at Inveraray Mr Archibald McColl ... declared his readiness to give the same allowance for an assistant minister in Coll as had been given by the three last incumbents of Tiree & that he had this day 'the Patron's approbation of this measure'. McColl then signed a voucher addressed to the Moderator of the Presbytery of Mull:

Revd Sir, I as presentee to Tiry agree to the above terms so far as my Interest is concerned & wish how soon Coll may be supplied by any proper man recommended by the Duke of Argyle.

Then the Presbytry, 'after mature deliberation, appointed the Presentee to proceed with all convenient speed to the Island of Tiry & to preach in the different places of worship there & in Coll if practicable'.

It was further agreed to hold a meeting at Tiree on the first convenient day after the 29th 'for the purpose of admitting Mr McColl to be Minister of that Parish' and resolved to petition the Duke of Argyle immediately to recommend some proper person for an assistant minister in the Island of Coll ...'. The Presbytery received the Duke's reply on 21 August 1780. It was that Mr Alexander Fraser, preacher in Craignish, should be assistant Minister of Coll 'upon the same footing with his predecessors in that charge'.[13]

Mr Alexander Fraser was a great-grandson of Mr John Fraser, the late seventeenth-century outed Episcopalian Minister of Tiree & Coll. He was born in 1758 and educated at King's College, Aberdeen. His father was the Duke's tacksman of Gualachaolish in Mull[14] as a result he was less likely to be a thorn in Argyll's flesh than any Maclean incumbent.

On 1 September 1780 the Presbytery met at Hylipol in Tiree and Fraser gave them an extract of his license to preach the Gospel & also testimonials of his character & behaviour as probationer 'which gave satisfaction'. The Presbytery then taking into consideration the situation of the Island of Coll, the difficulty of the communication between that & Tiry, or any other place of residence of an ordained minister and also how impracticable it will be for Mr Fraser to give regular attendance at the meetings of Presbytery and that he cannot be so useful to the people of Coll till he is ordained. For these and similar reasons they resolved to expede his Secondary Trials forthwith & with that view prescribe him for a critical Exercise: John 17 Ch. 12 v. 'Those that thou gavest me I have kept &c'. For a Homily: Heb. 11 Ch. 6v. 'But without faith' &c. For a lecture.[15]

Later that month the Presbytery received a letter from Mr Donald Maclean requesting that they might 'take his case into consideration & repone him in his former office of Preacher'. It was agreed that the letter should be considered at a further meeting. At the same meeting Mr Alexander Fraser, 'assistant minister in Coll having come up & declared his readiness to deliver some of the Pieces of Trial prescribed him'. They were acceptable to the Presbytery and on 1 December 1780 both Mr Alexander and his elder brother William were ordained.[16]

Mr Donald would not have been human if he had not been bitter at how events had turned out. Nor can he have failed to smile when in 1788 it was learnt that Alexander Fraser had been married clandestinely and that the celebrator was none other than the Minister of Tiree, Archibald McColl.[17] However, by then Donald Maclean was settled in a parish of his own. He had eventually been restored to the office of preacher in Mull in September 1781 and was appointed missionary.[18] This meant that he was an itinerant lay preacher with a much lower salary than an ordained minister. He was finally ordained on 5 August 1782.[19]

Notes

1. NAS. CH2. 273. 2.
2. NAS. CH2. 273. 2.
3. NAS. CH2. 273. 2.
4. I have to thank the Rev. the Hon. Robin Buchanan-Smith for this information.
5. JHS Burleigh *A Church History of Scotland* (1960), 301.
6. NAS. CH2. 273. 2.
7. NAS. CH2. 273. 2.
8. James Grant, clerk to the Presbytery of Skye to HAC Maclean 27 June 1898. BCT.
9. Ditto.
10. *Inhabitants of Argyll Estate*, 53.
11. Inveraray Castle Papers *Remarks on the Island of Tiry 1771*, 12.
12. Quoted in A Maclean Sinclair (ed) *Na Baird Leathanach*, [the Maclean Bards], Charlottetown (1900), 4. I have to thank the late Mrs Campbell, of the Roundhouse, Coll for a transalation of this song.
13. NAS. CH2. 273. 2. 21 August 1780.
14. James NM Maclean 'The Frasers of Kiltarlity: cadets of a deposed Mackintosh chief' *The Scottish Genealogist* vol. XVI. (June 1969), No. 2, 33.
15. NAS. CH2. 273. 2. 1 September 1780.
16. NAS. CH2. 273. 2. 1 December 1780.
17. NAS. CH2. 273. 2. 26 March 1788.
18. NAS. CH2. 273. 2. 10 September 1781.
19. NAS. CH2. 273. 2. 5 August 1782.

Chapter Twenty-One

Peace 1783–1793

If Britain had won the American War of Independence, it is unlikely that any Hebrideans who had served in America would have returned home to Scotland. However, despite the fact that Allan Maclean, Torloisk's brother, had obtained settlement rights on extremely favourable terms for the men he was recruiting for the Royal Highland Emigrats: 200 acres instead of the usual 100 per soldier[1] the future of Canada was uncertain and it must have appeared wiser, in the short term at least, to return to Scotland.

Little had changed in the Island whilst those who had been serving in the army had been away. Certainly there had been some deaths. Hugh Maclean of Coll's wife Janet Macleod had died on 21 July 1780,[2] as had her brother-in-law Hector Maclean of the Isle of Muck, but most of the familiar figures were still around. The pattern of life was unchanged. Hugh Coll continued to spend most of his time at Aberdeen, returning to Coll each year and to attend the Kirk Session. The composition of which had not altered since the war began.

The officers and men who had served in the army settled down to domesticity. Alexander younger of Coll had, on 27 March 1780 in Edinburgh,[3] married Miss Catherina Cameron, daughter of Allan Cameron of Glendessary in Morvern. It must have been a love match, for in 1776 Catherina's father's estate had been put up for sale in bankruptcy[4] and she is unlikely to have produced much of a *tocher*. She is said to have been a great beauty. Over the next fourteen years Alexander and Catherine produced eleven children, seven of which grew up to be adults.[5] Two of Alexander's brothers, Roderick Neil and Allan were to marry two of Catherina's sisters. The former, Lieutenant Roderick, who was now on the half-pay list[6] settled in Coll and his daughter Marion was baptised there on 30 October 1790.[7]

Donald of Cornaig's son Lieutenant Lachlan also returned to Coll. He lived initially with his father and stepmother at Cornaig House. It must have been cramped accommodation. On 9 March 1784 Lachlan wrote to Captain Murdoch Maclaine,[8] his former company commander in the 2nd Battalion of 84th Foot to say that 'the house I have on this island is getting too small for us',[9] which is hardly surprising as, in addition to the son born in America, he and his American wife Hannah had six children born in Coll between 1783 and 1791.[10]

In his letter to Captain Murdoch, Lachlan says that the shortage of accommodation in Coll had been the principal reason why, on the death of Sir Allan Maclean in 1783

> I took the Island of Inch, and a farm opposite in Gribun for the space of four years . . . I can get people to take the Tack when I please; and it will serve you and I, until we are ready to go abroad – there is plenty of oisters and Rabbits to be got on the island'.[11]

He was keen to talk about the scheme, which they had obviously discussed in Halifax, to take a grant of land in Canada for he continued. 'Let us settle the plan of operation. I am your man'. He goes on to say:

any interest I have in this Country will not keep me from joineing my old friends – more particulars when we meet; you did not make mention of the Proportion of Land, accruing to each Rank or did you mention your own Return, in so positive a manner as I would wish – this country is damned.

Lachlan's plans to settle in Canada with Captain Murdoch were dashed when the latter instead of remaining, like Lachlan, an impoverished half-pay officer, inherited the Lochbuie estate. Lachlan never returned to America.

Murdoch's cousin Archibald younger of Lochbuie, who had been the cause of the quarrel with Donald 'Young Coll' and the latter's untimely death, had served in the 1st Battalion of the Royal Highland Emigrants in America. He had quarrelled violently with his colonel, Allan Maclean, Torloisk's brother, and been courtmartialled. He had not accepted the courtmartial's verdict and decided to appeal to King George III. On his way back to the United Kingdom he had got into an argument with another officer on the best way to cut up a duck. The argument ended in a brawl in which Archibald was killed.[12]

Murdoch was not the nearest heir to Lochbuie, but his elder brother's children had been passed over when the estate was entailed 'unless they are in the character of gentlemen'.[13] Evidently they were not.

In his letter of 9 March 1784 Lieutenant Lachlan had said: 'I am to have another Farm on this island at May next, but who would be toiling the best part of his life on another man's property (paying an Extravagant Rent) when he can sit on his own lands'.

The farm Lachlan was to have was Grishipol. The McSween's tack was due to run out in 1785, and Lachlan and his family appear to have moved in shortly after the birth of his daughter Flory Ann, who was baptised at Cornaig in June 1785.[14] At Grishipol Lachlan lived like a laird surrounded by his sub-tenants: he had his own piper, a member of the Rankin family.[15] One day whilst he was at Grishipol, Lachlan had a large party to dinner. Rankin was ill and confined to bed. However, his wife Janet was a daughter of Macleod's piper in Skye, and was up to the occasion. Once Janet MacCrimmon had got all the guests into the dining room, she took her husband's pipes and played in the hall, and neither Lachlan nor his guests knew that it was not Rankin who was playing for them.

Lachlan's moan about the rent he was to pay for Grishipol was perhaps the cause of the coolness between him and Alexander Maclean of Coll, which was to bedevil relations between the two families. He was already in financial difficulties, and when on 19 April 1787 he obtained sasine of the Isle of Muck from his father he did so 'under certain reservations and burdens'. In other words there were already loans outstanding on the estate.[16]

Neither Lachlan nor his father lived in the Isle of Muck. A report of 1786 states that:

Muck, which belongs to Donald Maclean, Esq, is nearly two miles in length, by one in width. It is mostly arable, and exports some barley, oats, potatoes, and cattle. The number of people amount to 253, who pay £200 of rent, exclusive of twenty tons of kelp, every year.[17]

In 1787 Lachlan and his father borrowed more money. On this occasion they borrowed from Lady Ann Duff using Muck, including 'the kelp shores', as security.[18]

* * *

Other half-pay officers who returned to Coll at this time were John Cornaig and Allan Crossapol. The impact on rents paid by half-pay officers returning home appears to have been considerable. After the American War of Independence no less than one colonel, a major, eight captains and three lieutenants rented farms on Skye. It is estimated that they brought an assured income of £1,213 into the area from the mid-1780s.[19] Andrew Mackillop argues that:

> Army earnings also helped the financial position of lesser tenantry; indeed they constituted one of the few positive reasons, as opposed to landlord coercion and the threat of eviction, why Gaels enlisted in such numbers.[20]

Mackillop does not believe, as I do, that a laird's people followed their chief out of loyalty and habit.

The Earl of Selkirk, writing at the beginning of the nineteenth century,[21] expresses a point of view that falls halfway between MacKillop's and my opinions. Selkirk claims that the power of a chieftain over his followers ultimately derived from low rents and whilst proprietors continued rents that were well below the real value of the land they kept their authority over the tenantry. Such authority, he suggests, was even greater than in the past 'for, during the feudal times, this authority was tempered by the dependence of the gentry on the affection of their followers for personal safety'. However,

> after the year 1745, the tenantry had no such return to make from the indulgence of their landlord. They felt, at the same time, that he must be under frequent temptations to discontinue that indulgence, and, therefore, were still more anxious than formerly to merit his favour.
>
> The only opportunity they had of rendering him any important obligation was when he undertook to raise men for the army. The zeal with which the followers of any chieftain came forward to enlist was prompted not only by affection and the enthusiasm of clanship, but likewise by obvious views of private interest. The tenant who, on such an occasion, should have refused to comply with the wishes of his landlord could expect no further favour, and would be turned out of his farm. The more considerable the possession he held, the more was it in his interest, as well as his duty to exert himself.
>
> The most respectable of the tenantry would, therefore, be among the first to bring forward their sons; and the landlord might with an authority almost despotic, select from among the youth upon his estate, all who appears most suitable for recruits. The gentry of the Highlands were, in general, too good politicians to make a wanton display of this power; and well enough acquainted with the temper of their people to know that they would come forward with more alacrity, if allowed to indulge the flattering idea that their exertions were the spontaneous effect of attachment to the chief; yet, perhaps, no man of penetration in the country ever doubted the real cause of the facility, with which the Highlands could raise such numbers of men with such magical rapidity.[22]

The reader must judge, from the evidence that follows, which of us is correct. I would suggest that all three points of view were present in the 1780s. Some tenants were sucking up to the chief; some believed it their duty to provide young men to follow him; some sons actually wanted to join the army and return home as heroes. They will not have believed that it was they who would be killed.

* * *

It was important that a laird obtained a tenant, who was not only able to pay the rent, but had the resources to stock and ideally to improve his farm. Coll gained such a tenant when, sometime before 1783,[23] Mr Donald Maclean's father-in-law became tacksman of Mingary on Coll's estate in Mull. Alexander, as we have seen, had previously been the Duke's tacksman of Gott in Tiree. His tack there expired in 1776, but he was still in Tiree in 1779[24], and he probably stayed on until the establishment of the planned village at Scarinish, which incorporated much of his tack, had begun. Alexander Gott was one of the few substantial tenants in Tiree, who actually lived on the island.[25] In addition to his farming enterprise, like many other tacksmen he had a store, and was involved in the distilling of whisky. In 1778 the Bailie of Tiree notes that he spent £1.4s – on whisky from Alexander McLean Gott for recruits joining the Western Fencibles.[26] Alexander also owned a vessel called the 'Lilly', which was wrecked at Port Askaig in Islay in 1771.[27]

James Anderson claims that:

Upon enquiry, I found that most of the principal tacksmen . . . have come into the practice of keeping a kind of store or warehouse of necessaries for the use of his immediate dependents; and that the usual and avowed rate of profit, which they think reflects no discredit upon them to exact, is about fifty per cent and on grain and other articled considerably higher.

He does not consider this unreasonable considering their situation for he says:

Nor are these storekeepers so much to be blamed, as men would in general be disposed to do, on first viewing the matter. The expence they must be at in procuring the articles for sale must be uncommonly great; their sales are languid, credits long, and payments precarious. In these circumstances, very great *apparent* profits must be obtained, before a reasonable profit *per annum* on the stock thus employed can be got . . . it is therefore the circumstances of the country that occasions this misery, rather than the avarice of individuals.[28]

Despite the evident truth of these comments, it did not endear the tacksmen to many of their customers.

Alexander of Gott had moved to Mull by July 1785 when he is first noted as an elder of the parish of Kilninian & Kilmore.[29] In 1787, four years after his first wife's death, he consolidated his position as one of the establishment of Coll's estate by marrying Peggy, the younger daughter of Mr Hector the former Minister of Coll.[30]

Mr Donald Maclean lived at Mingary whilst he was a missionary minister in Mull. One of his duties there was to baptise infants and on 30 September 1782 he baptised John Maclean, tacksman of Lagganulva's son Archibald. Sir Allan Maclean of Duart attended the christening. Also present was an itinerant artist who painted a portrait of Sir Allan in his uniform as an officer of 82nd Foot. He gave the portrait to the parents.[31]

Mr Donald was not to remain in Mull for much longer. On 8 May 1787 he wrote from Mingary to Murdoch Maclean of Lochbuie:

My Dear Sir,
When I had the pleasure of waiting on you at Moy you was pleased, unsollicited, and in a manner truly friendly and benevolent, to observe that your Influence with the Family of Argyle might not be inconsiderable, and that you would, at any time be ready to exert it in order to procure me a Settlement – I think myself in Duty bound to inform you that an Opportunity for Exertion presents itself – The Parish of Ardnamurchan is now Vacant – Argyle presents thereto – May I presume then, My Dr Sir, to request that you sollicit Argyle in my behalf; and that in the manner which you shall think most effectual for procuring me this Parish. Argyle has promised, by a letter to the Late Sir Allan Maclean, & verbally to Coll, to provide for me; it is therefore to be hoped that a suitable Application will have a good effect – Coll was good enough, when the Parish of *Egg*, or the *Small Isles* became Vacant, to write to severals, in order to procure that Birth for me; but the Parish of Ardnamurchan is more eligible for a variety of Reasons, & particularly a situation more desirable for me.[32]

For some reason Mr Donald's application for the parish of Ardnamurchan did not succeed and on 3 October 1787 he was admitted to the Parish of the Small Isles.[33]

Mr Donald did not neglect his family in Mull when he moved to Eigg. On 19 November 1788 he wrote to Lochbuie's factor Mr John Maclaine, Gruline, Mull on behalf of his brother-in-law:

My Dear Sir,
Rory Morison at Tobermory tells me that he has reason to believe that Hugh Maclean, the present Tenant of Tigh-a loin, will be under the necessity of giving up to you the publick house foresaid with its Croft & pertinents at Whitsunday 1789 – Rory at the same time suggests that he judges said house a proper Birth [sic] for himself and family – & expresses a wish to get possession of said House &c as soon as they become open. Tis natural for me to interest myself in the welfare of Rory & his family, & the more so, that he is married to a sister of mine, whose behaviour has always entitled her to my sincere regard. I presume they will give you satisfaction as Tenants, and, I as firmly believe, they may be happy in you as a Master. Permit me then, my Dear Friend, to recommend them to your good offices & let me request that you be pleased to prefer them to the birth foresaid, when Vacant; upon equal terms. I am persuaded you'll find them neither insensible of favour nor ungrateful; and as for me, I shall be ready to acknowledge, whatever favour you'll be pleased to confer upon them, as conferred in a considerable degree upon myself ... I ever remain, My dear Sir, your affct humble servt. Donald Maclean.[34]

* * *

The Small Isles was one of the most arduous parishes to minister to in Scotland. It consisted of the islands of Eigg, where the minister resided, Rum, Muck and Canna. In 1787 Eigg belonged to John Macdonald of Clanranald, who also owned Canna. Rum belonged to Alexander Maclean of Coll and, as we have seen, he feued the Isle of Muck to Donald Maclean of Cornaig.

Clanranald had a valued rent in the parish[35] of £178.16s.6d. Coll and Cornaig's valued rent in the parish was £25.15s.6d each. Mr Donald, as we must now call him was the third Minister of the Small Isles.

Clanranald was not an easy man to deal with. He was at the same time both a Roman Catholic and the principal heritor of the parish. The Presbytery clerk of Skye later wrote 'Clanranald got the Glebe succumbed for the present one, and Mr Maclean appears to have been a master in diplomacy judging from the difficulties he overcame without having recourse to defending himself in the Edinburgh law courts. On 7 April 1789, he interviewed Clanranald in Edinburgh and came home with 'a written plan of accommodation'. On 13 May 1789 the glebe was designed and decree given to have a manse built.[36] Clanranald attempted in July 1793 to create a nuisance by erecting a Mill on the glebe. This attempt was resisted'. The estimated total cost of the Manse was £356.8s.4d. The sum was to be raised in the following proportions:

$$\begin{aligned}
\text{Clan Ranald} &= £276.12\text{s}.11\text{d} \\
\text{Coll} &= £39.17\text{s}.8.5\text{d} \\
\text{Isle na Muc} &= £39.17\text{s}.8.5\text{d} \\
&\,£356.8\text{s}.4\text{d}^{37}
\end{aligned}$$

* * *

In Scotland in the eighteenth century the body responsible for the collection of national taxes and the maintenance of county roads, bridges and ferries were the Commissioners of Supply. The Commissioners were landowners

> enfeost[38] in Superiority or Property, or possessed as Proprietor or Life Renter of lands, valued in the Tax Roll of the County or Stewartry where he acts, to the extent of One Hundred Pounds Scots per annum ...

The Commissioners themselves did not collect the land tax. This task was left to the Collector. But they were collectively responsible to the Scottish Receiver in Edinburgh for any failure on the part of their county to pay the tax, whatever the cause. The Commissioners met annually and received the reports of their local overseers or supervisors.[39]

In May 1785 the meeting of the Commissioners noted that they had received no report from Maclean of Coll either for Coll itself or for Quinish in Mull 'ever since the date of the last Act of Parliament for making and repairing Roads and Bridges in this County'. They instructed their clerk to correspond with Coll and to report his answer to the next General Meeting'.[40]

No reply for 1785 appears in the minutes. However, in 1786 Alexander reported that the number of the inhabitants of the island liable to perform statute labour there amounted to 153. He had therefore paid:

41 tenants 1/6d each	£3.1s.6d
100 cottars & servants at 1/6d each	£7.1s.6d
12 cottars & servants 'neither wrought nor paid'	—

He reckoned that by the labour of 141 tenants, cottars & servants for two days making and repairing roads through Coll at 9d per day he had spent ... £10.11s.6d.

He had also paid for 'road utensils' £3.2s.–
£13.13s.6d

For Quinish he reported that 64 people were liable.

On 12 March 1789: Alexander Maclean of Coll, as 'Surveyor in the Island of Coll and Quinish in the Island of Mull' reported that in 1788:

To the sum charged for 208 Men liable To statute labour in Coll and Quinish At 1/6d	£15.12s.–	
By Balance of last years account due to The Surveyor in the District of Quinish	£2.2s.6d	
By Ditto in the Island of Coll	£2.4s.–	
In Quinish in 1788 he had paid out: 'By 2 days of 60 Men upon the line Of Road from the Harbour of Pollaich Towards the great line at 1/6	£4.10s.–	
By 1 day at 30 Men making and Repairing the road to the church of Kilmore	£1.2s.6d	
By Balance in the surveyor's hands to be accounted for and now in the course of laying out upon the roads and Harbour in the Island of Coll	£5.13s.–	£15.12s.–'

In 1791: Alexander once more sent in a report for the work done in Coll & Quinish in the year 1790 & 1791:

Quinish

1790 By the Charge against 18 Tenants & 42 Cottars 2days work @ 1/6d	£4.10s.–	
By ditto per 1791 both in Quinish	£4.10s.–	£9.–.–
To 2 days work of 60 Tenants & Cottars @ 1/6	£4.10s.–	
Balance due by the Surveyor	£4.10s.–	£9.–.–

Coll

Balance due by Last Report		£5.13s.–
Charge against 43 Tenants & 105 Cottars @ 1/6d per the year 1790		£11.2s.–
Ditto 1791		£11.2s.–
By 4 days work of 12 Men @ 9d	£19.4s.–	
20 men neither worked or paid each of their days	£3–.–	
Balance due by the Surveyor	£5.13s.–	
	£27.17s.–	£27.17s.–

* * *

In addition to the work he was supervising in Coll and Quinish Alexander was also taking an interest in the wider economic development of the area. In 1785 he had become a member of the Highland Society of Scotland.[41] This body (now the Royal Highland and Agricultural Society of Scotland) had been founded the previous year by a group of 'Improvers', who defined their aim as an inquiry into 'the present state of the Highlands and Islands of Scotland, and the condition of their inhabitants' and 'the means of the improvement of the Highlands'. To which they added: 'The Society shall also pay a proper attention to the preservation of the language, poetry, and music of the Highlands'.[42] It was an aim that might have been drafted for the Macleans of Coll, for from all the evidence Alexander, like his elder brother, was 'resolved to improve his father's lands without hurting the people or losing the ancient Highland fashions'.[43]

Notes

1. Andrew Mackillop *'More Fruitful than the Soil'* (2000), 184.
2. Maclean of Coll Family Bible. BCP. Extraordinarily her tombstone is said to state that she was the wife of 'Hector Maclean of Coll' [*Records of Old Aberdeen* II, 313 (63)]. This is a warning for family historians not to believe everything that they read in a graveyard.
3. *Edinburgh Marriages 1751–1800* (Scottish Record Society).
4. Philip Gaskell *Morvern Transformed* (1968), 148.
5. Maclean of Coll family Bible. BCP.
6. *Army List 1784*, 301.
7. NAS. CH2. 70. 1.
8. Details of Murdoch's earlier career and a portrait of him as an officer in the 114th Foot appear in Nicholas Maclean-Bristol 'Murdoch Maclaine, Lieutenant 42nd Foot ?' *Journal of the Society for Army Historical Research* vol. 77, No. 310 (Summer 1999), 69–70; William Y Carman & JA Houlding confirmed my suggestion in *JSAHR* vol. 77, No. 312 (Winter 1999), 301–2.
9. NAS. GD174. 1362.
10. NAS. CH2. 70. 1.
11. NAS. GD174. 1362.
12. Kim R Stacy 'Crime and Punishment in the 84th Regiment of Foot, 1775–84', *JSAHR* vol. 79, No. 318, (Summer 2001), 116–8.
13. NAS. Register of Tailzies XXIII 27, 18 January 1785. I am indebted to the late RW Munro for a note on this entail.
14. NAS. CH2. 70. 1.
15. Neil Rankin Morrison 'Clann Duiligh Piobairean Chloinn Ghill-Eathain' *TGSI*, vol. XXXVII (1934-6), 59–79.
16. NAS. Argyll Sasines, 345; General Register of Sasines 443. 26.
17. John Knox *A Tour of the Highland & Hebrides in 1786*, 75–6.
18. NAS. Argyll Sasines, 344.
19. *'More Fruitful than the Soil'*, 148.
20. *'More Fruitful than the Soil'*, 147–8.
21. The Earl of Selkirk *Observations on the Present State of the Highlands of Scotland* (1806), 64.
22. *Ibid*, 64–6.
23. His wife's tombstone in the cemetery at Dervaig in Mull states that she died in 1783 aged 74.
24. *Inhabitants of Tiree 1779*, 53.
25. ICP. Report on Tiry 1771.
26. ICP. Military Folder – 1803.
27. NAS. CS231 (Currie Mack), Bundle 2/1. Wilson versus McLean.

28. *The Present State of the Hebrides* (1785), 165–7.
29. NAS. CH2. 493. 1: 12 July 1785.
30. NAS. CH2. 70. 1: 26 December 1787.
31. The portrait is now in my possession. On the back it is stated that on 29th July 1855 Mrs Craig said that an artist came to Mull, an extraordinary thing in those days, and after he had taken the Scallasdale family, he went to Laggan (John Maclean's residence) while there Sir Allan came on a visit had his portrait taken, and left it there as a present.
32. NAS. GD174. 1775.
33. Mr Donald was born on 12 May 1752, was married on 25 September 1777 and had at the time of his Admission to the above parish four children:

>Margaret b. 16 July 1780.
>Alexander b. 19 August 1782
>Neil b. 11 July 1784
>Hector b. 3 June 1786.

He later had:
>Julian b. 5 May 1788. [BCP. Letter from James Grant, clerk to the Presbytery of Skye to HAC Maclean dated 27 June 1898.].

34. NAS. GD174. 1419.
35. The valued rent was a valuation of land made in 1667 for the purpose of computing the land-tax and the apportionment for public and parochial expenditure. It replaced the *auld* and *new extents* [*CSD*, 758]. It survived until 1854 [Ann E Whetstone *Scottish County Government* (1981), 74].
36. The manse is a substantial three-storey house, with a good walled garden and view that looks to the south. It now belongs to Keith Schellenberg and is derelict.
37. Letter James Grant, Kilmuir Manse, Uig, Portree to HACM dated 28 June 1898.
38. infeft in = invested with legal possession of Heritable property [*CSD*, 314]
39. *Scottish County Government*, 61–95.
40. Minutes of the Commissioners of Supply for the County of Argyll. 4 May 1785.
41. Transactions of the Highland Society of Scotland, vol. ii, 25 show that he joined the same year as his uncle Roderick Macleod, Principal of the King's College, Aberdeen.
42. Derick S Thomson (ed) *Gaelic Scotland* (1983), 121.
43. *Boswell*, 213.

Chapter Twenty-Two

The Highland Society of London

In 1778, seven years before the Highland Society of Scotland was founded, the Highland Society of London was born. It was the brainchild of twenty-five gentlemen, all natives of the Highlands of Scotland, who met together at the Spring Garden Coffee House in London.[1]

The London society took a lively interest in the establishment of the British Fisheries Society, founded in 1786, whose aim was to raise money to buy land to lease to fishermen and to build storehouses, piers and sheds in order to encourage settlement.[2] Its creation followed a resolution put to the House of Commons by Henry Dundas in 1785[3] 'that a Parliamentary Committee be appointed to enquire into the State of the British Fisheries'.

The seconder of the motion in the House of Commons was George Dempster of Dunnichen MP. He believed in seeing things for himself and accompanied by Sir Adam Ferguson, Bart. MP, and a Mr Guthrie set out to tour the Hebrides in August 1786. They had a somewhat ambitious programme. Dempster was to write:

> We were three in company, Sir Adam Ferguson, Mr Guthrie, and myself; all limited in point of time, but meant to have visited the Long Island, Lewis, and Sky, before our return. In going from Staffa to Coll, we passed Coll's House by mistake; and in making for another harbour there our vessel struck on a sunken rock, about half a mile from the land, and stuck there for two or three minutes; but the day being fine, the sea very calm, and the tide rising, we got the vessel shoved off the rock by the stern after a good deal of thumping on the rock. Very bad weather for two days confined us to Coll, after which we sickened of our expedition, and returned to Strontian in Loch Sunart, and then to Fort William.

The rock in question was marked but not named on their chart. The captain christened it 'Parliament Rock'.[4]

A more useful visit to Coll was made by John Knox, the ex-bookseller and fisheries enthusiast who, after his tour in 1786, gave a lecture to the Highland Society of London. The society published and distributed it. Knox tells us that:

> I crossed the narrow channel to the Island of Coll.
> This island is said to be fourteen miles in length, by two in breadth, though, I believe, its utmost length does not exceed twelve miles. It is greatly inferior to Tirey in fertility, being

composed mostly of rock, some blowing sand, and a very small portion of arable land; yet a number of black cattle are raised here of which, it is said, four hundred are exported annually. The rent of the whole island is only £700 per annum of which Alexander Maclean Esq. has the principal share. The two extremities are the property of the Duke of Argyle ... This island has two indifferent bays, and several small creeks for boats. One of the bays, called Lochachastill, lies on the south side of the island; the other, called Loch Yern, or Irin, lies on the same side, and is more centrical. The entrance of the first is encumbered with rocks; the second is narrow, and the harbour within is dry at low water. Though these bays cannot be rendered of any utility to general navigation, they might to be so far improved as to enable the inhabitants of Coll to prosecute the fisheries.

I too traversed the island from one end to the other, but found very little worthy of notice, excepting the melancholy devastations of the blowing of sand, which has covered some good land, and threatens more. Against this evil there is no remedy; neither does the island admit any considerable improvement: Mr Maclean proposes, therefore, to draw the attention of his tenants to the fisheries, the natural business of these islands, and which would soon place the natives in more comfortable situations.

The only boat upon Coll, in which any person, except those amphibious animals the Highland fishers, would venture himself, belonged to Mr Maclean, and had been taken to Sky by his family, who were on a visit. In this dilemma, a venerable old man offered, with a degree of frankness I little expected, to carry me in his vessel to Bara, or wherever I might think proper to go; not only so, 'but faith' said he 'I can introduce you to any family in the Long Island, for ever body knows William Macdonald, who has been a fisher these five and forty years, and was always respected by the first lairds in the Highlands ... [Knox] found him in Mr Maclean's house, where he enjoyed all the conveniencies of one of the family.

His vessel being a good sailer, and in good condition, I embraced the opportunity, and agreed to embark with him at five in the morning. The night being very boisterous, a less determined passenger would have made that circumstance an excuse for spending another day with Mr Maclean. The morning proved coarse and hazy, attended with rain. Mr Maclean insisted on my drinking tea before I went on board; favoured me with his company to the shore, and sent two of his people to assist in working the vessel out.

Knox's next port of call was the Isle of Rum. He continues:

Rum is a considerable island or rather one continued rock, of nearly thirty miles in circumference. It is the property of Mr Maclean of Coll; contains 300 inhabitants; grazes cattle and sheep; pays £200 rent annually; but has neither kelp, free-stone, nor lime ... Finding ourselves under impending rocks, of prodigious height, we steered to a proper distance, and got safe into the only road upon this bold coast, called Loch Skresort.

Here we landed, at a small village, in a situation not unpleasant. The people were all busy packing herring for their winter provision; and more might have been cured, if they had been provided with salt. Mr Maclean, the proprietor of Coll, informed me that he was determined to give the inhabitants of that island every assistance for promoting the fisheries. I hope he will extend his benevolent endeavours to this bay also, by erecting a small key, and supplying the people with salt and casks, for which they would pay ready money. By means of this aid, they would furnish all the inhabitants of the island in herrings, or white fish, through the whole year.[5]

In February 1787 the Earl of Breadalbane, who was deputy-governor of the British Fisheries Society, wrote a circular letter addressed to proprietors of land in the Highlands and Islands and all persons concerned in the fisheries. Jean Dunlop comments that perhaps the most interesting reply came from Alexander Maclean of Coll, who set out clearly the problem of employing Highlanders in fisheries:[6]

> I must confess to your Lo[rdshi]p that I am one of those who entertain the opinion that the erecting of Wharfs Houses &c. as proposed by the Act of Incorporation will not alone be sufficient encouragement for the extension of Fisheries and forwarding the other views of the Society, my reasons for entertaining this opinion chiefly proceed from the difficulty I apprehend that will be found in inducing the people to inhabit the proposed towns & villages, for it is to be considered that there is not at present in this country any distinct Body of Men who live solely by the Fishing, that, and indeed every other branch of business or trade is carried on by people who are possessed of Lands & who only make the Fishery &c. a mere temporary object or casualty ... If the Inhabitants of those Countries can procure the bare necessaries of life by their Labour they possess their ambition leads them to no farther effort, nor do they in general desire to meliorate their condition by any other exertion of Industry. Their sole attention is in a manner fixed to the produce of the earth, the sole object of pursuit is to get a farm, and a patch of Ground however small is infinitely preferred to any other mode of gaining a livelihood. This is so much the case that the Tradesmen of all descriptions are not to be got without procuring Farms for them or some portion of Land, and no sooner this is procured than they become Farmers solely & they give up their Trade.[7]

Alexander had put his finger on the problem that was to be the undoing of the Society. It also marks the beginning of an acquaintance with the Earl of Breadalbane that was to result in the best documented recruitment of men from the Coll estate into the army.

* * *

During the second half of the 1780s the old establishment in Coll began to die off. As we have seen Hugh Maclean of Coll died in May 1786. He may have given his heir 'full scope' to run the estate, but it was not until after his death that Alexander obtained sasine to it.[8]

Alexander was now in a position to put some of his ideas into practice. His scope was further increased when on 21 October 1788 he obtained a tack from the Duke for £30 beginning at Martinmas 1789 of the lands of Braie, Ardnish, Freisland [Freslan], which mixed with his own land on the south-east coast of the island,[9] and in 1792 the minister of the parish noted that: 'Inclosures are lately begun'.[10]

Alexander followed his father's example in helping to educate young islanders at King's College, Aberdeen. In 1791 he founded the Coll Bursary. It was for £16.10s. per year and was to last for 4 years. The patron was the Chancellor of the University.

* * *

In 1787 Neil Maclean of Crossapol died. He was 75 and was buried in Crossapol graveyard.[11] His second son Allan succeeded him immediately not only to Crossapol but as an elder on the Kirk Session.[12]

On 30 August 1789 the *Scots Magazine* notices the death at Mingary in Mull of Donald Maclean of the Isle of Monk, as Donald Cornaig was now designated.[13] Some years later his eldest son erected a stone over his parent's bodies in Kilunaig Cemetery. Unfortunately he got the date wrong, for the stone states:

Here lye interred the bodies of Donald Maclean Esq, of Isle of Monk who died on the 3[0] Aug 1790 and Flora Maclean his first spouse who died on 1 May 1756. This stone is placed over their remains by their son Major Lachlan Maclean now of the Isle of Monk a mark of respect & duty to the remains of his parents.

A year earlier, on 15 October 1788, Donald had accepted a new lease of the Two Ends of Coll when he wrote to the Duke's Chamberlain Mr James Ferrier:

I am satisfied except as to the clause about the woods. I must build two byres next summer on[e] for my cows and another for my stirks and if agreeable to His Grace I beg the clause prohibiting wood leave as formerly be altered in so far as to allow me what timber may be necessary . . . out of His Grace's wood. However, if this cannot be complied with I must do my best to provide timber elsewhere.[14]

The new tack, which was to last for 19 years from Whitsunday 1789 was for £84, a recognition that the previous rent of £105 was set too high. It was to be terminated in the event of Donald's death if that were to occur before this new tack expired.[15]

Donald's widow was now potentially homeless. However, Alexander appealed to the Duke, who on 24 September 1790 wrote to the Chamberlain of Tiree to say 'You may inform Coll that in consequence of his recommendation I am to allow the late Isle of Monk's widow to remain during my pleasure in the farm of Cornaig.[16]

As we have seen Donald's second son was serving with the 2/1st Foot in Gibraltar and did not return to Britain until 1789, probably arriving home after his father's death. He then married Isobel the daughter of John Maclean Factor of Ardgour. He was living in Cornaig by April 1791 when his son Donald was baptised.[17]

The last member of the family of Coll to die at this time was Captain Lachlan Maclean of Gallanach. He had married for the second time and his wife produced a daughter, baptised Catherine, on 30 July 1790.[18] Lachlan was dead before 14 July 1791 when his will was produced at Inveraray. Two weeks later his eldest son John, the sole executor, proved it in London. Lachlan left £20 per year for life to his wife Isobel Maclean with a third of the furniture, plate &c, and ¼ of the farm of Gallanach 'provided she stay there with my children of my first marriage during her life and duration of tack'. His children Marion, Janet, Ann, fflora, Mary and Lachlan plus any born after his death were to receive £120 Str. His 'natural daughter Mary' was to have £10. His curators to his children were to Isobel 'my' spouse, Alexander Maclean Esq yr of Coll, Donald Maclean Esq of Isle of Muck, and Archibald Maclean Tacksman of Kilmaluag, Tiree. The will had been signed at Glasgow on 8 September 1785.[19]

The death of Donald of the Isle of Muck not only deprived Captain Lachlan of one of the proposed tutors and curators of his children, but it also left a shortage of members of the Kirk Session. To make matters worse on 2 November 1791 the Presbytery was handed in 'and read a presentation by Commission from His Grace The Duke of Argyle appointing Mr Alexander

Fraser Minister of Coll to be Minister of Torosay in Mull'. There was also given in and read Mr Alexander Fraser's letter of acceptance of said presentation dated 22nd day of June Last.[20]

On 14 April 1793 the Kirk Session of Coll met at Clabbach under the chairmanship of Archibald McColl Minister of Tiree & Coll. Also present was Archibald Maclean tacksman of Kilmaluag in Tiree and the Isle of Coll's surviving elders Hugh Maclean of Knock and Allan Maclean of Crossapol. The minutes state that: 'The Session having on this and several former occasions considered' that there were too few elders in the congregation and that 'several Reputable Parishioners (some of whom were formerly Sessioners) were fit to be ordained as such and being accordingly proposed some sabbaths with that view to the Congregation & being all present upon this national fast day, they were accordingly ordained Elders in the face of the Congregation:

> Major Alexander McLean Esqr of Coll
> Captain John McLean at Cornaig
> Alexander McLean Factor to Coll
> Lachlan McLean at Fiosgharadh
> Charles McLean at Arinangoar
> Niel Rankin at Arileoid.

Alexander McLean the factor is the only member of the group whose pedigree is uncertain. If he was a member of the family of Coll, he is likely to be one of the two 'Sanders' Maclean, who have not been identified other than as cadets of the Isle of Muck family.[21]

Lachlan at Fiosgaradh was a younger brother of Neil of Crossapol.[22] He is probably the Lachlan who appeared at Kirk Session meetings in the past without any designation.

Charles at Arinagour had been brought up on Coll, but he was not a member of the family. He was probably a descendant of a refugee from Mull who came to Coll when Argyll took over the Duart estate.[23] In 1776 his father was living without any servants in Ardnish. For a short time Charles kept a shop in Glasgow. He then moved to Coll where he opened a shop at Arinagour.[24] Alexander the Factor and Charles the shopkeeper married sisters. They were the daughters of Neil Crossapol. Crossapol was now the key family who linked the new Coll establishment together.

The last of the new elders, Neil Rankin, was in a different category to the others. As we have seen, he was Coll's piper. A piper was considered to be a gentleman, and the chief's companion rather than his servant.[25] In 1776 Neil Rankin was living at Breacachadh and employed three servants. As we have seen, Boswell notes, when dining at Breacachadh House, that 'we had a bold tune from the piper, a decent comely fellow with a green cloth waistcoat with silver lace; and then he helped to serve at table'. His family had for generations been pipers to the Macleans and until 1757 had run a school for piping at Kilbrennan in Mull. He had previously been an elder of the Kirk Session at Kilninian & Kilmore.[26] Whilst he was living in Mull he had married Catherine Maclean, a relation, perhaps a sister, of Charles Maclean at Arinagour.[27]

These elders and their families were to dominate Coll for the next 60 years. They also, as we shall see, are good examples of how the Hebridean establishment confronted, and was affected by, the challenges, which faced the Hebrides in 1793, 1793 being the year that marked the beginning of hostilities with Revolutionary France which followed the execution of King Louis XVI. It was, as we shall see, the beginning of the last occasion when large numbers of men from the Coll estate went into the army.

Notes

1. Alastair Campbell of Airds, Yr, *Two Hundred Years: The Highland Society of London* (1983), 1.
2. Jean Munro, *The Founding of Tobermory* (1976), 3.
3. In 1784 the Lords of the Treasury commissioned James Anderson LL.D. to tour the Hebrides and explain why the Fisheries had not been exploited by the natives. His report is *An Account of the Present State of the Hebrides* (1785).
4. Quoted in John Knox *A Tour through the Highlands of Scotland and the Hebride Isles in 1786* (1975), 75–6.
5. John Knox, 75–6.
6. Jean Dunlop, *The British Fisheries Society 1786–1893* (1978), 26–8.
7. NLS. MS2619, 30.
8. 10 November 1790: Alexander Maclean of Coll, as heir of his father, seised in parts of the Barony of Coll; the Isle of Muck; on Pr. Ch. 14 February 1787 [NAS. Argyll Sasines, 343].

    2 May 1787: Alexander Maclean of Coll, as heir to Hugh Maclean of Coll, his father, seised 17–9 April – in the third part of Quiynes viz Torresay, Arrigaunichen, Auchenendriesseiche, Weyach, Dirrivey and Arintaunie, Isle of Mull; the Isle of Rowme Ch. Resig. By Archibald Duke of Argyll to the said Hugh Maclean 9 November 1756 & Gen. Reg. Sasines 4 October 1786 [NAS. Argyll Sasines, 342].

    10 November 1790: Alexander Maclean of Coll, as heir of his father, seised in October 1790 – TROTOPOLDO & ARNOPOLDO being parts of the Barony of Coll [NAS. Argyll Sasines, 557].
9. ICP. Tiree Tacks. 40. 125.
10. The Rev. Mr Archibald M'Coll. 'Parish of Tiry', Sir John Sinclair (ed) *The Statistical Account of Scotland 1791–99* (Reprint 1983), 255–280.
11. His simple slate gravestone is broken but readable. It says he died in 1787. However, he is noted as attending the Kirk Session meeting on 11 June 1788. I suspect that the latter is wrong and that it was Allan Crossapol who attended.
12. NAS. CH2. 70. 1.
13. *Scots Magazine* vol. 51 (1789), 465.
14. ICP. Tiry Tacks. 40, 118.
15. ICP. Tiry Tacks. 40, 119.
16. *Argyll Estate Instructions*, 19.
17. NAS. CH2. 70. 1.
18. NAS. CH2. 70. 1.
19. TNA. Will 347. Bevor. Proved 11 July 1791.
20. NAS. CH2. 273.
21. Crossapol MS, 44.
22. Crossapol MS, 42.
23. Nicholas Maclean-Bristol 'A Genealogical Puzzle Solved?' *WHN&Q*, Series One, No. XXX (February 1987), 13–17.
24. *Clan Gillean*, 420.
25. Neil Rankin Morison 'Clann Duiligh: Piobairean Chloinn Ghill-Eathain', *TGSI* vol. XXXVII (1934–6), 5. Translated by Dugald Maclachlan. I have to thank the late Niel Morison for a copy of this translation.
26. NAS. CH2. 493. 11 January 1767.
27. *TGSI* vol. XXXVII (1934–6), 59–79.

Part IV

The War with Revolutionary France 1793–1802

Chapter Twenty-Three

The Raising of the Breadalbane Fencibles

Alexander Maclean of Coll's involvement with the Highland Society of Scotland had brought him into contact with John Campbell, 4th Earl of Breadalbane. In 1782 Breadalbane, who was then only twenty, had succeeded his kinsman the third Earl.[1] Ten years later, when revolutionary France declared war on Britain, he offered to raise a corps of 1,000 men to defend Scotland from invasion.

The offer was accepted. Breadalbane immediately informed John Campbell WS, his agent in Edinburgh, and on 18 February 1793 Campbell wrote to Breadalbane's friends and supporters to tell them the news that Breadalbane 'was to have the nomination of the officers'. He went on to say that the Earl pledged 'himself that they shall not be sent on foreign service', and that: 'His Lordship is to command the Regiment as Colonel and has no doubt that in this emergency he will experience the attachment & zeal of his friends'. He ended 'the footing on which the Corps is to be raised shall be communicated when I again hear from Lord Breadalbane'.[2]

Breadalbane wrote again to John Campbell on 25 February, thanking him for his letter of the 22nd and letting him know that the 'officers appointed in my Corps now stand thus':

Colonel Earl of Breadalbane
Lieut. Col. William Maxwell Morrison
Captains   Alexander Maclean of Coll
         Alexander Macdonald of Boisdale
         John Thomas Erskine [younger of Mar]
         John Campbell of Airds
         5th Not finally resolved
Lieuts   Gavin Drummond a Brother of Kelty's
         John Macdougall of Ardincaple
         Walter Graham Brother of Glenny's
         James Stewart Brother of the Minister of Killin
         Colin Campbell of Ach at Inveraw[3]
         Robert Campbell of Benmore
         Patrick Campbell, son of Balevolin[4]
         Alexander Campbell of Glenfalloch[5]

	Murdoch Maclaine of Kingerloch
	Macdougall of Allinich [Gallanach]
Lieut	[Hector] Maclean, Adjutant
	Allan Stewart Innerhaden
Ensigns	Jura's son & Surgeon's mate
	Robert Campbell, Balevulin's son
	Lochdochart's son
	Campbell son of Lieut Ronald Campbell. Achrioch
	McVean Minister of Kenmore's son
	Achlian's son[6] &c
	Some of the Tacksmen's sons[7]

He goes on to say 'I have not, however, finally settled the arrangements of the subalterns . . . in the meantime the Captains & Field Officers should go on with speed & exertion to the recruiting *service* . . .', which implies that the captains had agreed to serve.

It is a strange list. Both Coll and his brother-in-law Boisdale could be guaranteed to raise men. But why was Airds chosen? As a follower of the Duke of Argyll, he would be expected to join a corps raised by the Duke and not his rival. Curiously, too, none of the Breadalbane's leading cadets are included among the captains and several of the lieutenants and ensigns were not Breadalbane's own tenants but those of Campbell of Inverawe.

A possible answer is to be found in a letter of William Murray of Octertyre to his neighbour Henry Dundas. He writes:

The inclosed is from Mr Campbell of Lochdochart a Breadalbane gentleman who is very much respected and has an Estate of Seven hundred a year. The real state of Breadalbane is that every gentleman in it considers Lord B as a man that neither is or ever will be *good for anything* they therefore, for the sake of their families, wish to connect themselves with some person of influence as Lord B may live many years.[8]

* * *

One of Breadalbane's motives in selecting officers is clear. Later in his letter of 25 February the Earl writes:

I received a letter a few days ago from Mrs Clarke of Comry recommending strongly one Mr Ker as surgeon. She says he is connected with no less than three Perthshire voters. If they would therefore all apply & ask it as a favor perhaps there would be good policy in obliging them.

Breadalbane was an anti-Ministerial Whig and remained one despite his alliance with Henry Dundas, the able and energetic Secretary of State for the Home Department.[9] It was an alliance that was purely tactical. Dundas had an estate in Perthshire and wanted his son, rather than the Duke of Atholl, to represent the county. In order to do so he needed all the support he could get. Breadalbane had the most powerful interest in Perthshire that could be brought against Atholl. It was therefore essential that Dundas had Breadalbane on his side.[10]

Politics also explains why Barcaldine, Breadalbane's most loyal cadet in the 1670s Campbell take-over of Mull, was no longer one of his followers. At the 1774 election the Barcaldine-Glenure family had astonished everyone at the Perthshire election by voting *en masse* for the anti-Breadalbane candidate. They had done so in order to pay off their debts and provide themselves with an alternative income to that of landowners in their own right and tacksmen of farms on the Breadalbane estate. They therefore became professional soldiers. In 1774 the Duke of Argyll was the fountainhead of military patronage in the Highlands and voting for his candidate was a way of canvassing his support. As a result of their action the Barcaldines lost their Breadalbane tacks,[11] which supports Selkirk's suggestion that if a tenant refused to recruit for his landlord he 'could expect no further favour, and would be turned out of his farm'.[12]

Somewhat surprisingly for someone from a Jacobite family Alexander Maclean of Coll was at this time also an anti-Ministerial Whig. However, as he was a friend of Norman Macleod of Macleod, who had recently returned from India and entered politics, he was not the only West Highland laird to follow this course. Macleod had been backed by Dundas as MP for Inverness-shire. He was, however, nothing if not changeable, and was already moving towards radicalism.[13] Alexander attended him when he presided at meetings of Friends of the People.[14]

That such a traditionalist as Alexander was a 'Friend of the People' is at first glance extraordinary. However, much reforming doctrine looked back to supposedly better times and it was an article of faith with many reformers in England, and presumably in Scotland too, that it was not themselves, but the servants and managers of a corrupt executive, who were the innovators. The model followed by the English reformers was 'sometimes traced back very far indeed. One of the most persistent strands in reforming literature was the appeal to Anglo-Saxon purity – that happy state of equality and freedom, which was destroyed by 'the Norman Yoke'.[15] As Gaelic-speaking traditionalists Alexander and Macleod, perhaps looked back to an Ossianic golden era.

The Friends of the People in Scotland were a number of societies founded in Edinburgh and Glasgow in the summer of 1792 with the object of obtaining 'equal representation of the people in Parliament and a frequent opportunity to exercise their right of election'.[16] They intended to do so by legal means and declared that they would defend the constitution and assist magistrates in suppressing riots.

The societies of Friends of the People in Scotland were both popular and democratic. Subscriptions were kept very low and there were no social barriers to membership. As a result the number of branches steadily increased and in November 1792 it was decided to call together a Scottish Convention of delegates from all over the country in order to consider an address to Parliament. It is presumably this convention that Alexander Maclean of Coll attended with Macleod.

Although political awakening in Scotland had started during the American War of Independence, it was not until the French Revolution that the general public began to take an active interest in politics. In 1789 most sections of the community welcomed events in Paris, which many believed would produce similar results to Britain's Revolution of 1689. Few saw it as a threat to the *status quo* and it only gradually dawned on the establishment that the new political order that was emerging in France posed a threat to their own position.

No such fears assailed the bulk of poorer people; to many of them the French Revolution came as a revelation. There was a deep-seated belief in egalitarianism in Scotland and many Scots, with the French example before them, believed that they too could establish political democracy.

Edmund Burke in his *Reflections on the Revolution in France* was the first to draw attention to the dangers inherent in the French revolution. Thomas Paine in his *Rights of Man* challenged this diagnosis. He attacked Burke's reactionary views and set out in a fresh and vigorous style democratic ideals that everyone could understand. He denounced the British constitution as a sham and argued that the ruling oligarchy was never going to reform itself and that the only solution lay in a convention, elected by universal male suffrage, to consider the future government of the country. *The Rights of Man* also had a social vision, which included family allowances, free education for everyone, and old-age pensions.

In May 1792 a royal proclamation against it probably stimulated circulation and by 1793 sales of *The Rights of Man* had reached 200,000. There was even a rough translation in Gaelic. Events in France, from the establishment's point of view, went from bad to worse and when in February 1793 King Louis XVI went to the guillotine and Britain and Austria withdrew their ambassadors from Paris. France immediately declared war. It was against this background that Breadalbane made his offer to raise a corps to defend Scotland in event of an invasion. He might be an anti-Ministerial Whig but he was certainly not a radical.

* * *

In his letter of 25 February Breadalbane goes on to say:

> I hope you will be able to get some clever active Fellows who have already served to act in my corps as Sergeants and Corporals, if some people of this description could be got from Old Regiments it would be fortunate … There is no time now to be lost as I expect the beating orders will be issued tomorrow. The adjutant I have got, formerly a Sergeant Major in 3rd Regiment of Guards, will go to Scotland [at] the end of the week and will be able to give a considerable assistance. My Major young Lude will go of[f] I believe tomorrow with the beating orders. I have just received a message from the Secretary of State with information that there is every probability of my being preferred to command of a 2nd Battalion. Of course I shall now have a double proportion of patronage & the strength of the Regiment from 1,000 to 1,200 men.

On 1 March King George III formally wrote to the Earl to announce:

> We have thought fit to order a Regiment of Fencible men to be forthwith raised under your Command, which is to consist of 8 companies of 3 sergeants 3 corporals 2 drummers & 60 Private Men in each with 2 pipers to the Grenadier company beside a Sergeant Major, 2 Quarter Master Sergeants, together with the usual Commissioned Officers, which men are not to be sent out of Great Britain. These are to authorise you to beat of Drum or otherwise, to raise so many men in any County or part of Our Kingdom of Great Britain …[17]

Breadalbane wrote immediately to tell his friends of the letter from the King and that the men to be recruited must not be under 5 ft 3 in, or less than 15 years of age or over 45. They were all to be examined by a surgeon.

One of these letters survives. In his letter to Gavin Drummond, brother to the Laird of Kelty, Breadalbane writes:

> Relying in your Loyalty and Zeal I hereby invite you to accept of a Lieutenancy in my said Regiment and I flatter myself that besides the above motives your personal regard for me may be some additional stimulus to your accepting.

He went on to say 'it is necessary that certain quotas should be appointed to each Rank, and their seniority in the different ranks will be regulated by their early compleating the quotas allotted them – The proportion for each Captain is 35, for each Lieutenant 8 and each Ensign 6'.[18]

The probability that he was to have a second battalion meant numerous changes in Breadalbane's original order of battle. Many in that list of officers are no longer mentioned, which suggests that their agreement to serve was wishful thinking. There are now fewer West Highlanders and more Perthshire men. Alexander Maclean of Coll is the only one of the original captains still included, and he was now to be a major.

There are among John Campbell WS's papers several notes by Breadalbane on his thoughts on who should obtain commissions, if he was awarded a second battalion. For instance he writes: 'I wonder if Lochiel is still disengaged . . . . . . He might be useful'. Names are suggested to him. He notes the possibility of gaining 'Hugh Maclean, brother to Coll', and Lachlan Maclean of Isle of Muck, 'if he can rase his quota of 35 men'. General Allan Maclean suggests a Maclean who served in the 84th Regiment in America and notes that 'Torloisk must assist him with men'. Airds suggests a couple of names including Murdoch Maclean from the ½ pay list.[19]

* * *

Breadalbane possessed a vast estate. It stretched from Tay Bridge in Perthshire to Easdale in Argyll. The latter being part of the Ardmaddy estate, which the Breadalbane of the day had purchased in the 1690s from Lord Neil Campbell, the 9th Earl of Argyll's brother. It had been sold against the wishes of Argyll and was one of the causes of dissension between the two major branches of the Clan Campbell.

Breadalbane is said to have been able to raise 1,600 men on his own estate.[20] However, he needed more men than that if he was to raise two battalions. The Coll estate was a good potential source of recruits. Why Alexander chose to follow Breadalbane rather than the Duke of Argyll, who was also raising a Fencible regiment, is never mentioned in any of the papers I have examined. There is a possible clue in Major Alexander Campbell's remark that when Sir Allan Maclean had a drink he said he could scarcely tell the difference between a Maclean and a Breadalbane Campbell. Alexander may have felt the same.

On the other hand the Duke of Argyll must by now have known that Alexander's father had been one of the prime-movers in Sir Allan Maclean's attempt to regain the Duart estate. It was hardly the best way for a Maclean of Coll to gain the Duke's patronage. However, by 1790 relations between the Duke and Coll had improved sufficiently for Argyll to offer Coll's brother Norman a place in one of the new Independent companies then being raised. For on 21 October 1790 Alexander, who was staying at Brolas, wrote to the Duke:

My Lord,
I have just been favoured with a letter from Mr Campbell of Sonachan, wherein he informs me that your Grace had been so good as recommend my brother Norman for one of the Independent Companys to be raised. I beg your Grace to accept of my best thanks for this instance of your attention to the interest of my friends. But my brother has been for some years upon full pay, having been disappointed of every opportunity of getting in otherwise, I was obliged to purchase for him into the 68th Regt. which he immediately joined & is now with at Gibraltar.[21]

The evidence of this letter makes it even more surprising that Alexander did not join the Argyll Fencibles. There may, however, have been another reason. As we have seen, Alexander had commanded a company under the Duke of Argyll's brother in the American War of Independence. It is possible that Alexander considered his move to the Light Company, which took him away from his own men, was a slight on his honour. Alexander had a fiery temper and was quick to take offence.[22] Perhaps he had vowed never to serve again under an Argyll Campbell.

Alexander recruited 120 men for the Breadalbane Fencibles.[23] Recruiting began on 6 March, probably in Glasgow and the first 41 men, with the exception of Sergeant John Campbell, Alexander Morrison, Charles Mackay and Finlay Macdonald, had surnames that were not found on the Coll estate.[24] The next 75 men were mostly islanders who began arriving at the rendezvous on 16 March.[25] They were all attested by 13 April. Most came from parishes in which Alexander had estates: Coll [40], Kilninian & Kilmore [11], and the Small Isles [10]. Others came from the Ross of Mull [2] and Tiree [2].[26] Their occupations are also given. There were 2 weavers, 6 tailors and 54 labourers. Details of another 10 men who might have come from anywhere have not been preserved.

Andrew Mackillop comments that Coll's recruits 'belonged to the labouring class ... and suggests that recruitment relied heavily upon cottars and agricultural day labourers'.[27] That this is too simplistic a judgement is clear from what follows.

Most of Alexander's 40 recruits from Coll are aged about 20. Many can therefore confidently be identified in the catechist's list of the island made in 1776.[28] Most were then underage children (i.e. under 7 years old).

It is not so easy to identify recruits from other parts of the estate or those living elsewhere. However, as we shall see, one man who came from Quinish and another from Rum can be identified. One was the son of a tacksman. The other was the son of a tenant. Both are described as labourers.

Sergeant John Maclean, who came from Kilfinichen in south-west Mull, was probably the son of at least a tenant. He is probably the Sergeant John Maclean who served in the previous war in the 81st Foot under Coll's brother Roderick Neil. He is one of the 'clever active Fellows who have already served', that Breadalbane wanted to enlist. He attested on 6 April 1793 when he is said to be 'a labourer, aged 30'. He eventually became Sergeant Major of the 1st Battalion. He was Allan Crossapol's first cousin.

Two other of Allan Crossapol's cousins, Sergeant Allan and Corporal Hugh Maclean, were the sons of Lachlan in Fiosgaradh. Allan had probably served in the Western Fencibles as one of the two Sergeant Allan Macleans in Coll's company. He regained his rank when he joined the Breadalbane Fencibles and is perhaps the Allan Maclean, who became Sergeant-Major of the 2nd Battalion of the Breadalbane Fencibles. Hugh was later promoted sergeant. All these men were descended from Neil Mor of Quinish, whose descendants had latterly formed the backbone of Coll's *luchd-tighe*. Their ancestors had been soldiers for more than two hundred years. Yet historians such as Allan Macinnes believe that military tradition in the Hebrides has been exaggerated!

Another Maclean with a long military tradition behind him was Murdoch, a tailor from Arnabost. According to Allan Crossapol he was a direct descendant of Neil Buidh the sixteenth-century archer.

The sons of both Coll's and Lachlan of Grishipol's pipers were among Coll's recruits. Both are described as 'labourers'. Duncan Rankin's son Corporal Alexander was the older of the two. He probably had previous military service for he immediately became a corporal. Neil Rankin's son Coundullie remained a private soldier. He was 17 when he enlisted and had been training to succeed his father as Coll's piper. One day he was practicing his chanter at Breacachadh Castle when Alexander Maclean, the Bailie entered the room. He saw little future in piping and said: 'Put that from you, when others are with the nobility, you will be with the dogs'.[29] Coundullie took his advice and on 4 April 1793 joined the Breadalbane Fencibles.

Another man who joined on the same day as Coundullie was Donald Morison from Kilmore. He was a son of the tacksman of Auchnasaul in Quinish. Another who joined on 13 April was Will Maclean from Rum. He came from a family with a long military pedigree. His great-grandfather *Iain Gobha*, a cadet of the Auchnasaul family, had served under Lachlan Maclean of Coll in the Scots Brigade in the 1680s. A great-uncle Charles had fought the French and Red Indians in North America in the Seven Years War. An uncle, Neil, had served in 85th Foot in the previous war.[30] Will's family were certainly tenants. However, he could only sign his name with an 'x' when he joined the regiment. Two years later he could at least write his name and, as he later became a sergeant, must have learnt to read in the army.

All the above men were the sons of tacksmen or tenants. They had a stake in the Hebrides. Yet every one of them, save Murdoch the tailor, is described as a 'labourer' when he enlisted. What else could they be called? They probably all worked on their fathers's farms, but they were certainly not day labourers. Many others who joined up with them were in the same situation. For instance the two Macdonald brothers, Donald and Charles, the sons of Neil Macdonald in Totronald were certainly the sons of a tenant. Their brother was perhaps young Coll's servant Hugh Macdonald, who was presumably drowned with his master. Alexander was later to write to his adjutant to get him to let one of Neil Totronald's sons go home to Coll to help their father bring in the harvest.[31] Finlay Macdonald, one of the first men to join, was the son of Malcolm Macdonald in Ballyhough, whose ancestor 'Finlay the Smith' had in 1679 served in Coll's bodyguard at Breacachadh. In 1776 Malcolm was noted as being able to read and was almost certainly a tenant.

Some men who joined the Fencibles from Coll were day labourers, or cottar's sons. Two brothers who enlisted in Coll's company on 6 April 1793 were Donald and John Beaton. They were the sons of Donald Beaton in Gallanach, who in 1776 was probably either a workman or cottar on Captain Lachlan Maclean's tack. They are likely to be related to the two Beaton servants, Abraham and Neil, who served in the 81st Foot in the previous war.

John Beaton left behind him a pregnant girlfriend when he joined the Fencibles.[32] His brother Donald already had an illegitimate daughter Cirsty. He could have been no more than 15 when she was conceived.[33] Two other recruits' illegitimate children are recorded in the session minutes. The dates of their baptisms suggest that the fathers returned home on leave to have sex with the mothers. One girl probably needed little encouragement, as it was 'the third time she was guilty of fornication'.[34] The parents of five other children, who were born to serving soldiers in the Fencibles were married, one probably returned home to marry his pregnant fiancé as his daughter was baptised five months after his wedding.[35]

Five of those in the 1776 list of people in Coll became commissioned officers. Another eight Collachs, who were not in the island in 1776, did so too. Coll thus produced 13 commissioned officers for the war with Revolutionary France. Four of them served in the Breadalbane Fencibles. This is by far the largest number of commissioned officers ever raised on the Coll estate. It underlines the fact that at the start of the war the military potential of the Highlands and Islands was vast.

* * *

In his letter of 8 March 1793 to Gavin Drummond, Breadalbane spells out the financial conditions on which soldiers were to be enlisted. Each enrolled man was due 3 guineas on his arrival at the rendezvous of his company. This statement requires some explanation. Once a recruit had been examined and attested he was to receive half the Bounty Money. When the recruiting officer reached his quota, his men were to be marched to headquarters in Perth Then 'every man who is approved of and enrolled shall have the remainder of the Three Guineas and it ought to be laid out in the purchasing necessaries for him'. If he was not up to requirements he was not to receive the second half of the bounty, but was to be given a weeks pay to make his way home.[36]

The Government paid the 3 guineas bounty to colonels of fencible regiments. The real cost of a recruit on the open market was, however, much higher than that, but whatever a recruit cost the Government paid only that sum. The colonel therefore had to make up the rest of the cost himself. This was expensive. However, if he had a large estate, as Breadalbane did, the colonel could offer tenants land instead of cash for their sons. The recruit then cost the colonel nothing, at least in the short term, and he still got the Government's 3 guineas. Mackillop claims that it therefore made good financial sense for an estate to recruit and he argues that this was another example of commerce not clanship dominating Highland society at this time.[37]

Breadalbane went on to explain to Gavin Drummond that:

As some of the officers may fall short of their respective Complements, and others, it is to be hoped, will have supernumaries, it is but reasonable that the officers who are deficient should pay two guineas per man for every man short of their Quotas, and that the other Class of Officers should receive an extra Bounty of two guineas for each Supernumary. I therefore, in order not only to provide for such deficiencies but to raise a large Body of Men if possible within the time, engage to pay out of my own Pocket an extra Bounty of two Guineas a man for any number of Supernumaries that you or the other gentlemen may raise, provided they are agreable to instructions.[38]

Alexander had a great many supernumeraries. Presumably he pocketed the 2 guineas awarded by Breadalbane. He may as a result have made a profit on his recruiting, but as it is not possible to discover what financial inducements, if any, he gave his men to enlist it is by no means certain that he did.

Almost all of those with non-West Highland names recruited by Alexander went to other companies. His own company was almost exclusively made up of men from his own estate. The only exceptions were the two drummers Bryce and Granger.

* * *

On 20 April 1793 the Earl of Breadalbane approved the 1st Battalion's order of battle.[39] It was somewhat different from his first choice of officers:

First Battalion

Captains
Colonel the Earl of Breadalbane
Lieutenant Colonel Morrison. Major, late 77th
Major McLean. Captain late Western Fencibles
Captains [Lachlan]McLean. Captain late 84th
    Colin Campbell [of Glenfalloch] Lieutenant late 71st[40]
    Alexander Nairne late Ensign Scots Brigade.[41]

The Hon. Francis Gray[42]
William Cunningham late 17th Regt

Lieutenants
Colin Campbell, late Lieutenant 74th
Colin Campbell
Alex. Campbell, late Carolina Rangers
Gavin Drummond, late 42nd
Selkirk Stewart, late Scots Brigade
James Campbell, late 40th[43]
John McDonald, late 76th
John McLean, late 74th
Sinclair, late 42nd

Ensigns
John Campbell
Andrew Mitchell
James Campbell
Wm Campbell
Hector McLean, late Sergeant Major 3rd Guards

Although Campbells outnumbered Macleans, it was the latter who had the key posts. Alexander Maclean of Coll was second-in-command of the battalion. Lachlan of the Isle of Muck was senior captain. The adjutant was an even more crucial appointment. The man chosen had served as Sergeant Major of the Third Regiment of Foot Guards and in the previous war had fought with them on the Continent. His former commanding officer describes him as 'a most meritous old soldier' and it is thanks to his meticulous paperwork that the records of the battalion have survived. Hector was from a cadet family of the Macleans of Boreray in North Uist, which had been settled in Tiree for several generations, and was a nephew of Alexander Maclean, Coll's tacksman in Mingary in Quinish.

On 26 May 1793 Lieutenant-General Leslie inspected the two battalions of Breadalbane Fencibles and found them both complete and the men fit for immediate duty.[44] The following day the battalion was mustered again. There were several changes from the original order of battle of 20 April. One was that the junior ensign was now Francis JS Maclean. He was Lachlan of the Isle of Muck's eldest son. He cannot have been older than fifteen. Officers under the age of sixteen were not allowed to hold commissions.[45]

Breadalbane was concerned over the seniority of certain officers. The draft of a letter to Lord Amherst written in Perth on 30 May survives. In it the Earl writes:

A difficulty has occurred which I shall submit to your decision . . . It happens that in the list of those who have formerly been in his Majesty's service there are two or three Gentlemen who served last war in Royal Provincial Regiments in America, and have half-pay from their former commissions, though I presume they hold no rank in his Majesty's army in Great Britain. I am at some loss how to place these Gentlemen. Were they to take rank in the Regiment in the same situation as in the Provincial Corps in which they served the Gentlemen in the army might complain, on the other hand as the Regiment is only a Fencible Corps, and the officers to have no permanent rank, it might appear harsh not to place all the officers who have served his majesty in whatever circumstances in whatever corps in the rank they formerly possessed and according to the date of their commission.[46]

* * *

The 1st Battalion of the Breadalbane Fencibles marched to Aberdeen where on 1st November 1793 Lachlan Maclean of the Isle of Muck was made an honourary burgess.[47] This was an honour which Aberdeen, to show its patriotism, gave to several army officers at this time, and was useful, particularly to Lachlan as it saved him from paying local taxes.[48] On 18th November Lachlan borrowed a further £500 using the Isle of Muck as security.[49]

On 25th November *The Edinburgh Evening Courant* ran a story that a number of French frigates supposed to be full of troops had appeared off the coast of Aberdeen and spread general alarm. The magistrates gave out orders for the forts defending the city to be manned and the Breadalbane Fencibles were stood to, as it was suspected that the ships were Dunkirk privateers, who were said to have sailed for the North Sea. The editor, however, wisely noted that the story was based on only one report and in the next edition it was it was stated that the story was without foundation. The ships were now thought to be transports taking Seaforth's Highlanders to the south of England.[50]

Notes

1. *The Scottish Nation* vol. 2, 377; the curious story of how he inherited the estate in place of the Glenfalloch family is told in Bernard Burke *Vicissitudes of Families*, vol. II (1869), 39–41.
2. NAS GD50. 18 (1).
3. Diarmid Campbell tells me that the Ach from which he took his designation is to the north-west of Tyndrum. Colin was evidently not living there but in Inverawe.
4. Baleveolin was the name of the old kirk at Ardchattan, which presumably was a tack held by Patrick and Robert Campbell's father. I have to thank Diarmid Campbell for this information.
5. He later served as a major in the 21st Foot. He killed Captain Boyd of the same regiment in a duel in the barracks at Newry and was executed at Armagh [NAS. GD50. 110. 7]; Sir Charles Oman 'A Duel of 1807' *JSAHR* vol. 1 (1921–2), 60–5.
6. The Campbells in Achlian had held their farm for many generations and as kindly tenants were sometimes called 'of Achlian'. They believed that they were MacConnachie Campbells descended from the Campbells of Stronchormaig (who after 1700 called themselves Campbells of Glenfeochan) and were kin to the Campbells of Inverawe. The Achlian family was certainly descended from *Donnachaidh Dubh an Notair*, who was writer in Muckairn, which is now part of Taynuilt. Duncan married Margaret, daughter of Mr Colin Campbell of Achnaba, the mathmatician and correspondent of Sir Isaac Newton. 'Achlian's son' is probably Dugald Campbell, 4th son of Alexander Campbell tacksman of Achlian & Ann, daughter of Archibald Campbell of Inverawe. He was born in 1759 and took over Achlian on his father's death in 1799. I have to thank Diarmid Campbell for this information.
7. This must mean his own tacksmen's sons, as several of those already listed were tacksmen on other estates.
8. William Murray, Octertyre to Henry Dundas 22 September 1800 [NLS Melville Papers Home Defence. 1049, 49].
9. *The Scottish Nation* vol. iv, 97–9.
10. JE Cookson *The British Armed Nation 1793–1815* (1997), 134.

11. Andrew Mackillop *'More Fruitful than the Soil'* (2000), 174.
12. *Observations on the Present State of the Highlands*, 65.
13. Michael Fry *The Dundas Despotism* (1992), 150 & 160.
14. *Memoirs of the Rev. Norman Macleod (senior) DD of St Columba's* (1898), 4.
15. John Ehrman *The Younger Pitt*, vol. 2 (1983), 112.
16. The next part of this section is based on the introduction to Kenneth Logue *Popular Disturbances in Scotland 1780–1815* (1979), 9–13.
17. NAS GD16. 52. 20.
18. NAS GD16. 52. 21.
19. NAS GD50. 18 (9)
20. *Sketches of the Highlanders* vol. ii, 316.
21. ICP. Bundle 691. Letters to 5th Duke on military matters.
22. *Clan Gillean*, 382.
23. NAS GD50.18. Printed paper concerning court martial after mutiny. Only 115 are listed in his recruiting account up to 10 May 1793 [NAS GD16. 52. 24. 20]. Others may have been recruited later.
24. 6 of them were discharged before the end of the month and one deserted [NAS GD16. 52. 24. 20].
25. NAS GD16. 52. 24. 20.
26. NAS. GD112. 52. 15, 116, & 17.
27. *'More Fruitful than the Soil'*, 143.
28. Another 31 have not yet been identified.
29. *TGSI* vol. XXXVII (1934–6), 75.
30. I have to thank Eugene Quigley, Nova Scotia for this information.
31. NAS. GD112. 52. 39. 4.
32. NAS CH2. 70. 1. 17 November 1793: Baptised to 'John Beaton, soldier & Marion Macdonald, Triallain. Flory, a natural child'.
33. NAS CH2. 70. 1. 29 April 1787: Baptised to 'Donald Beaton & Mary McDonald in Gallanach: Cirsty, begotten in fornication'.
34. NAS. CH2. 70. 1. 6 January 1798: Alexander Macdonald, soldier & Janet Mackinnon, Totamore.
35. NAS. CH2. 70.1. 29 April 1795.
36. NAS. GD16. 21.
37. *'More Fruitful than the Soil'*, 116.
38. NAS GD16. 52. 21.
39. NAS. GD112. 52. 24. 1.
40. Colin, of Glenfalloch, b. 30 December 1749, m. 1st 1776 – Drummond (dsps); 2nd the widow of – Constable with issue; 3rd 1793, Jean Ogilvie; d. 29 October 1806 [*Kingdom of Scotland*, 143].
41. Alex Nairn. He later, in 1799, commanded 3rd Bn of the Breadalbane Fencibles [*Military History of Perthshire*, 164]. James Robertson claims in his diary that David Nairne of Drumkilbo, who in 1845 bought Druimfin from Hugh Maclean of Coll, had commanded the Breadalbane's. He must have meant his father. David Nairne is described by James Robertson as 'a plain mannered, unassuming man, as much like a respectable farmer as a polished Gentleman'. His mother is said to be 'a little old Ladylike person in a brown wig ... Ladylike after the old Scotch fashion'. I have to thank James Irvine-Robertson for e-mailing me a copy of James Robertson's journal.
42. The Hon. Francis Gray [later 14th Lord Gray], b. 1 September 1765, m. 17 February 1794, Mary Anne (d. 31 December 1858), dau. of Col. CP Johnston with issue [*Kingdom of Scotland*, 559]; 15th Lord Gray ... was a Maj. In the first battalion of Breadalbane Fencibles ... in August 1807 he was appointed Post-Master General of Scotland. He succeeded to the title the same year, and in 1810 resigned the office of Post-Master General. He was for many years one of the Scottish representative peers. In 1822 the superb edifice of Kinfauns castle, about 3 miles from Perth was built for him, from a design by Smirke ... He d. 20 August 1842, and was succeeded by his son John. [*The Scottish Nation*, vol. v, 374].

43. James, Glenfalloch's younger brother; Capt. Cambrian Rangers, sometime Lieut. 40th Foot; m. after January 1784, Elizabeth Mary Blanchard (d. 1828), widow of Christopher Ludlow, of Chipping Sodbury, Glos., and d. 4 June 1850, with issue. His grandson became 6th Earl of Breadalbane [*Kingdom of Scotland*, 143].
44. NAS. GD112. 52. 24. 25.
45. Tony Hayter (ed) *An Eighteenth-Century Secretary at War the papers of William, Viscount Barrington*, 316–8.
46. NAS. GD112. 52. 1. 24. 25.
47. *Records of Old Aberdeen* vol. II, 3313.
48. Loraine Maclean of Dochgarroch *The Raising of the 79th Highlanders* (1980), 10.
49. NAS. Argyll Sasines, 169; GR527, 221.
50. NLS. *The Edinburgh Evening Courant* 11, 786 (25 November 1793) & 787 (28 November 1793).

Chapter Twenty-Four

Alexander's First Military Misdemeanour

It was during these first months in Aberdeen that events unfold which illuminate Alexander Maclean of Coll's character. In the absence of the Earl of Breadalbane and the Lieutenant Colonel, who was away recruiting, Alexander was in command of the battalion. He now became involved in an affair that also illustrates the rivalry for recruits that soured relations in the Highlands.

The affair, which created a stir at the time, concerned the transfer of 62 men from the Breadalbane Fencibles to the 79th Foot. The Commanding Officer of the 79th had several influential enemies. Its 'Sole Founder' Alan Cameron of Erracht was the representative of a family who believed that they, and not the Camerons of Lochiel, were the rightful chiefs of the clan.[1] Alan, a feisty, quarrelsome, tough old soldier had fought and been wounded in America. In 1779 he married the 14 year-old daughter of a wealthy Jamaican planter. It was his father-in-law's money and Alan's popularity in Lochaber that made the raising of 79th Foot a possibility, and on 7 August 1793 he received a royal commission as 'Major Commandant of our Seventy Ninth Regiment of Foot'.

When he raised his regiment Alan received no bounty money from the Government, and its cost was entirely borne by his father-in-law. He was also bound by his letters of service to obtain his officers from the half-pay list. Among them was his major the Hon. Andrew Cochrane, son of the Earl of Dundonald. Alan had a low opinion of Cochrane and says of him that: 'His head is a Mere Watchwork that requires looking after'. He was, however, engaged to be married to Lady Georgina Hope, whose aunt was married to Henry Dundas, the all important Secretary of State for the Home Department, and in the autumn of 1793 Cochrane spent much time in London with Dundas.

In raising the 79th Regiment of Foot Alan had alienated Lochiel's trustees who were already furious with him for having purchased Erracht and Inveruiskvuillin, the farms of which his family had previously been tacksmen. He had bought them from Lochiel, who was under-age, desperate for money and on bad terms with his trustees. Alan had also crossed the Duke of Gordon, the superior of much of Lochaber, whose mother the Duchess of Gordon, an old friend of the Prime Minister William Pitt,[2] was also recruiting in Lochaber. Even more significantly Alan's ambitions infuriated the Duke's uncle Lord Adam Gordon, who was Commander-in-Chief in Scotland.

Alan, however, had his own allies. Among them was Breadalbane, who agreed to allow 62 volunteers to transfer from the 1st Battalion the Breadalbane Fencibles to the 79th Foot, and on 18th October Cochrane wrote to Alan from Harley Street to say that:

Mr Dundas approves of Lord Breadalbane's letter to the two commanding officers of his battalions relative to their allowing any men who thought proper to enter the recipient's corps: Dundas is of opinion that the volunteers spirit of our country men ought not to be crushed and that as you allow a Bounty to the Regiment of Five Guineas that they can very soon replace those men who chuse [sic] to enter into Established Corps by others, and that the Public Service will be essentially promoted by this reason.

Cochrane goes on to say that 'Breadalbane's letter has so much pleased Mr Dundas that he intends to show it to the King'.[3]

Cochrane had spoken too soon. On 4th November[4] Lord Adam Gordon wrote to Breadalbane from his headquarters at the Abbey in Edinburgh to say that he had received a return from Major Maclean of Coll in Aberdeen. He expresses his astonishment at discovering in it that 62 men had been discharged from the 1st Battalion. He asks 'by whose authority it was done'.[5]

Everyone now ran for cover and proceeded to blame everyone else. On 8 November Dundas had written to Breadalbane expressing the King's 'approbation of recipient's zeal in allowing privates in his fencibles to enlist in a marching regiment'.[6] However, the following day he wrote to the Earl that Major Cochrane has been too quick in writing, for when Dundas looked at Breadalbane's letter it could not be shown to the King, 'for there was an expression in it as if you approved of the plan of allowing your men to enlist partly from an idea that you might in that way get quit of some of your bad men and replace them with good ones. I therefore mentioned in conversation to the King that I had learned that you had very handsomely consented to admit of any of your men entering into a marching regiment meaning to replace them with other recruits. His Majesty very amply expressed His approbation and allowed me to say so to your Lordship.'[7]

The Commander-in-Chief, Lord Amherst followed up Dundas's letter to Breadalbane. He again puts the blame on Major Cochrane for the discharge of the 62 men and says that they should not have been transferred without the King's particular authority and must be returned forthwith. He goes on to say: 'I think it better not to mention the circumstances to the King'.[8]

On 18 November Lord Adam wrote to Erracht to say: 'I am to acquaint you that the Day after you shall receive this – you are to return the 62 men you had received . . . to the Battalion from where they came', as this is an irregular and unmilitary proceeding.[9] In a postscript with a copy of the letter to Breadalbane explaining what he had done he writes that:

> Major Cameron has been given to understand that the Publick must be put to no expense; nor will any charge be admitted in consequence of what has happened; or until things are put just where they were.[10]

At the same time he sent a copy of the letter to Cameron in similar terms. As might be expected Alan exploded with rage. He immediately wrote to Breadalbane complaining that Lord Adam intended publicly to denounce those involved 'with the additional and oppressive view of thwarting me by all possible means in the execution of my present undertaking (founded I am afraid upon lurking something like envy & personal resentment) . . . I should hope your Lordship will be able to counteract so peremptory a mandate as that conveyed in the enclosed letter, by stating & urging forcibly to both Mr Dundas & Mr Pitt, the public & private motives that actuated your Lordship in the moment of allowing me to take these men'. Erracht stresses the need to go to the fountainhead, 'for there can be no doubt that some busy secret engines are at work to vex & disappoint all concerned, by carrying on business with a high hand'.[11]

On the same day he wrote a more restrained letter to Lord Adam suggesting that the 62 ought to be discharged from 79th before they can enlist again in any other regiment. He also writes of his financial losses: 'with respect to the money I have expended upon these men from first to last (not under 14 guineas per man) ... trusting upon the whole to the feelings of a Benign King, in whose service I have made a sacrifice (unprecedented) of about 12,000 Guineas within the last two months.[12]

Lord Adam replied on 21 November pointing out, unhelpfully, that the 62 men were illegally discharged from the fencibles and enlisted in [the] recipient's volunteers, and that this transaction is [therefore] null and void. He adds a 'PS. If you are unavoidably at a distance, they must be ordered to rejoin their Corps at Aberdeen or take the consequences'.[13] Alan took the hint and 55 of the men were marched off that day to Aberdeen under the command of two officers. 7 of the 62 were absent.[14] The remainder, according to Alan, were forced to 'march at the point of my sword, for they would not move otherwise and swore they would never join any other corps – that they were discharged from your Regiment and would never inlist again [even] if cut to pieces'.[15]

The affair now became public knowledge and on Friday 19 November *The Edinburgh Advertiser* announced that:

We have authority to state to the public that the 62 men who had been improperly discharged from 1st Battalion of the 4th Regiment of Fencibles (whereof the Earl of Breadalbane is Colonel) and had inlisted in a corps raising by Major Allan Cameron, having received orders immediately to rejoin their respective companies in the first battalion of Fencibles at Aberdeen.[16]

The other Edinburgh papers also carried the same statement and on 5 December 1793. Henry Dundas wrote to Breadalbane to say. 'Not being very fond of any body defending themselves by paragraphs in the newspapers. I perhaps would have liked as well if you had inserted nothing. At the same time I am very far from being surprised that you was induced to do it when others led the way ... Lord Amherst very much disapproves of the paragraph which induced you to insert one, and has wrote to Lord Adam Gordon to that purpose'.[17]

On 11 December 1793 Lord Adam ordered Breadalbane to repair to headquarters at Aberdeen until the affair of the 62 men is settled. He enclosed the copy of a letter dated 9 December from the 1st Battalion's Lieutenant Colonel, William Maxwell Morrison, who had returned to Aberdeen and written to Lieutenant Colonel Mackay DAG at Scottish Command:

I have to acquaint you for the information of the C-in-C that all the men who were discharged from this and were enlisted into Major Cameron's Corps have joined here except one man left sick at Stirling.

He goes on to say:

I directed the Adjutant this day to order them to take their duty to commence tomorrow, when they all, six excepted, refused to comply alledging that having been discharged from this Regiment, reinlisted with Major Cameron (with which their attestations are now) and having been promised not to be draughted from that Corps they conceive themselves not liable to be turned over to this or any other.

The circumstances are so uncommon and the men so securely determined to resist that I have ventured to defer the matter further till favoured with your advice and further orders how to proceed. I think it is my duty to acquaint you that Major Cameron's conversation to the men gave them the fullest assurance . . . obtained from His Majesty that the men inlisted in his Corps should not be draughted into any other.[18]

The men who refused to 'take their duty' were now incarcerated in the cells. They had, however, obtained the assistance of an Aberdeen merchant, who acted as their spokesman. On 15 December he produced a petition to the commanding officer in the name of the soldiers who considered themselves as having been discharged. First on the list is Donald Beaton. He is none other than the man from Coll who enlisted in Alexander's company on 6 April 1793. At least three other men were from Coll's company. Their petition was that we:

Represent to you Lieut. Collonel Morison of the first battalion of the fourth Scots Regiment of Fencibles and presently Commander in chief of that Regiment in Aberdeen that the said Donald Beaton and all the other Soldiers before named were in the end of October last regularly discharged from the said Regiment of Fencibles by a Field Officer commanding the same and immediately thereafter enlisted as soldies in the Seventy Ninth Regiment of Foot upon express condition published by Major Cameron the raiser of that Regiment that they should only be obliged to serve in the Seventy Ninth Regiment, and should not be obliged to serve in any other Regiment whatsoever. That after the forsaid soldiers were discharged as aforesaid they marched from Aberdeen to Stirling and have continued to serve there ever since under the officers of the said Seventy Ninth Regiment untill of late that the said soldiers were ordered by the said Major Cameron from Stirling the station of their Regiment to Aberdeen. That soon after their arrival there – they were by your orders seized upon – put into close confinement in a prison or guardhouse in Aberdeen, where they are presently detained by your commands – without having to their knowledge committed any trespass whatever – that by these proceedings they the said soldiers humbly conceive that you have been guilty of an infringement upon the laws of your country. A violation of the liberty of your fellow subjects and an undue exercise of military power – and therefore in order to preserve their rights and to obtain redress, I as Procurator for them require you to set them at libertie – and protest that you and all others concerned in their confinement shall be liable to them in the pains of wrongous imprisonment and in every sort of redress which they are entitled to by the laws and in all damages and expences which they either have sustained or may sustain by your illegal or unwarranted conduct towards them – and thereupon I take instruments in the hands of Andrew Davidson Notary Public this fifteenth day of December . . .[19]

On the same day Alan added fuel to the flame by writing to Breadalbane complaining of Lord Adam's behaviour. Breadalbane he suggested had nothing to worry about as 'I can easily perceive that you are well protected from above and that the unhandsome & resentful conduct of Lord Adam Gordon is understood in its proper colours'; he urges Breadalbane to join the regiment at Aberdeen without any delay as the business has come to such a length 'that a very firm & decided line of conduct absolutely necessary to stem his [Lord Adam's] career of malevolent insolence'; he suggests that Breadalbane: 'leave for London to fix the business in a determined manner and stop Lord Adam from giving any further trouble'.

Alan felt that there was a need for discussions with Mr Pitt or Mr Dundas, and with the King if necessary; it was essential to draw their attention to Lord Adam's attempt to bring the men before a court martial and a need to replace them in the fencibles as soon as possible. He goes on to explain that 'the whole business is founded upon old capricious family prejudice towards your Lordship and the Dutches [of Gordon]'s clear chagrin at her son being refused what could not be granted to him – to which add the opposition of a young man (under their wing) to me, carrying the nonsensical tittle tattle of the day from the castle & suburbs to the Abbey,[20] together with the influence of a certain right hand staff man, who suggests military routine with the pragmatic and self-conceited ideas of a Hobbart'.[21]

On 21 December Lord Adam wrote Breadalbane a letter which suggests the Earl was not as well-protected as Alan believed. He writes:

I am sorry to find that I am not to look for your influence towards persuading the 55 men of your first Battalion to return to their duty; and as the consequences most probably must be a General Court Martial, and that your Lordship's conduct and the conduct of other officers may fall to come under their consideration, I think it necessary that your Lordship should remain with your battalion until the Court Martial is over and until their in determination is made public... Your Lordship will please to acknowledge the receipt of this letter and to acquaint me in Course whether my orders sent to Major Maclean of your first battalion to join it, and if such an order is not already sent, an express must be immediately dispatched to him'.[22]

In London it was probably now considered that things were getting out of hand and Amherst wrote to Breadalbane that:

I cannot too strongly express my wishes that the misunderstanding, which has arisen, might be settled to the satisfaction of all parties, and the peace and harmony so very necessary for the good of His Majesty's service.[23]

Dundas, the politician, also wrote to cool the affair. He was thinking of putting the whole problem to the King 'but this depends on the next letter Amherst receives from Lord Adam Gordon'. Certainly there was no need for recipient to influence the men to rejoin his regiment if they are not disposed to do so, 'which will finally end the unpleasant business which has arisen'.

Amherst states that the King 'views with concern that there should be any misunderstanding between the recipient [Lord Adam] and Breadalbane; the King applauded Breadalbane's zeal in promoting the success of the new levies, but could not approve of Major Alexander Maclean's taking upon himself, without proper authority from the King, or consent of the C-in-C of forces in NB, to discharge 62 men of the battalion, at the time under his command at Aberdeen'. He goes on to say that the 55 men in prison are to be released and receive a fresh discharge[24] in the usual form. His Majesty is willing to impute Major's inexperience in his service than to any other cause, and expects it may never again happen'.[25]

Alexander probably did not know at this stage that he was being made the scapegoat for on 18 January 1794 he wrote to Breadalbane to thank him for the 'honourable and spirited vindication in the matter of the 62 men; he leaves the affair to recipient's management'.[26] He evidently expected some form of vindication of his conduct from Dundas. This was not forthcoming and on 28 February he wrote to Breadalbane that he had not yet received a letter from Mr Dundas. He asserts that he is perfectly satisfied with Mr Dundas's conduct during the whole of the affair. However, he would not be satisfied with a letter if it were not official and for publication, at least to the battalion, 'for no private explanation even from the Secretary of State can possibly do away the public censure contained in Lord Amherst's letter'.[27]

On 19 March 1794 he wrote again to Breadalbane that he had never received the promised letter from Mr Dundas. He expresses his anxiety due to the censure in Amherst's letter to Lord Adam Gordon and goes on to say 'It may be possible my conduct deserved that reprimand, but I certainly have reason to complain that a punishment so severe should be inflicted without the opportunity of making any defence. I have therefore wrote to the Commander-in-Chief in Scotland, demanding a Court Martial, which I hope will be granted, unless His Majesty is graciously pleased in some manner to relieve me from my present disagreeable Situation'. If he fails to get either, he resigns his commission.[28]

On 27 March Dundas wrote to Breadalbane returning Alexander's letter. He is evidently relieved that he had not replied to it and refused to become further involved in the affair. He suggests that Breadalbane was mistaken in supposing 'that any approbation which his Majesty expressed to me of your zeal and exertions in his service will operate to any vindication of Major Maclean if anything of blame is imputable to him. I do not know that there is, but what has been related to me by military men is that there was an error in transferring so many recruits from any regiment without the concurrence of the Commander-in-Chief in Scotland. If this was wrong, nothing said to me by the King has any tendency to remove it'.[29]

Nothing seems to have happened until 3 July. The battalion was by then at Queensferry on their march to Glasgow. From there Alexander wrote to Lord Amherst reminding him of the state of their correspondence and informing him that when he reached Glasgow he would write to Lord Breadalbane and resign his commission. On the 11th he did just that. He wrote to the Earl explaining what he had done in a covering letter to his formal letter of resignation. He says that it is with the greatest reluctance he could think of quitting His Majesty's service at this critical period.

> Yet situated as I am it is impossible I can act either with credit to myself or benefit my country; for what can an officer's feelings be or how can he serve after being publicly accused & punished for a crime without ever being heard in his defence and even a trial refused him or how can he pretend to act in, much less command a Regiment in the front of which he was publicly reprimanded for his conduct in that command.[30]

Amherst was at last spurred into action and on 25 July he wrote to Breadalbane to say that he regretted that Major Maclean still demanded a court martial. He would, however, lay all the papers on the case before the Judge Advocate and obtain the King's commands on the matter.[31]

Three days later he wrote to Lord Adam referring to his letter of 3 January concerning the discharging of the 62 men of the 1st Battalion of the 4th Regiment of Fencibles by Major Alexander Maclean. However, that officer's explanation, together with a

> Representation of some circumstances not at the time known, the King has been pleased to say that HM is satisfied the conduct of Major Maclean was not activated by any improper motive, but on the contary that the measures appeared *to him* calculated to forward the public service,

and HM is pleased to permit that this gracious Declaration be communicated through your Lordship to Lord Breadalbane, and to the Major, for alleviating the anxiety under which he labors from an apprehension of having incurred HM's displeasure and for removing any opinion which his brother officers or any other officers may have formed to his disadvantage.[32]

Finally on 31 July 1794 Amherst wrote to Breadalbane to say that the Judge Advocate had laid both Breadalbane's letter and Major Maclean's before the King. The latter not approving that a court martial should take place ordered that a letter should be sent to Major Maclean, which Amherst believed would perfectly satisfy the recipient.[33]

This appears to be the end of the matter. The 55 men who refused to rejoin the Fencibles were discharged on 9 January 1794. Donald Beaton seems to have returned to Coll. He is perhaps the Donald Beaton living at Torestan who on 17 January 1799 married Mary Macdonald in Arnabost. They had several children, baptised on different farms, which suggests that he remained a labourer all his working life. It also suggests that Alexander did not blame him for causing him so much anguish.

Alexander emerges from this affair as being hot headed and quick to take offence. His subsequent treatment of Donald Beaton shows that he was not a vindictive man, even to someone who must have caused him considerable embarrassment. However, he was not prepared to tolerate any reflection on his honour.

Alexander's conduct at this time also illustrates one of the problems for military commanders when they had to deal with territorial officers who were first and foremost independent gentlemen. Fencible officers when they were landed proprietors, as many were, like Members of Parliament who were amateur politicians, gloried in being representatives of their 'countries'. Their roots and allegiances were embedded in local soil and it was difficult, if not impossible, to get them to serve with their battalions when local events demanded their presence. Unlike Members of Parliament who could not be forced to attend at Westminster 'when local business, or a race meetings ... or hunting held prior claim',[34] regimental officers could be courtmartialled for being absent without leave. As we shall see this was a fate that hung over Alexander's head when he decided that it was more important to be in Coll with his wife than to stay with his battalion.

Notes

1. Loraine Maclean of Dochgarroch *The Raising of the 79th Highlanders* (1980). The first paragaphs of this chapter are based on this booklet.
2. *The Younger Pitt* vol. 1, 108.
3. NAS. GD112. 52. 27. 9.
4. According to family tradition Alexander was on leave at this time. His wife was pregnant and Alexander wished to be with her when the birth occurred. He therefore promised Breadalbane that if he gave him leave of absence he would call the child after him. It was a girl who was promptly christened 'Breadalbane'. The name survives in the family in the abbreviated form of 'Alba'.
5. NAS. GD112. 52. 28.1.
6. NAS. GD112. 52. 28. 2.
7. NAS. GD112. 52. 28. 3.
8. NAS. GD112. 52. 28.7–8.
9. NAS. GD112. 52. 28. 7.
10. NAS. GD112. 52. 28. 13.

11. NAS. GD112. 52. 28. 17.
12. NAS. GD112. 52. 28. 16.
13. NAS. GD112. 52. 28. 18.
14. NAS. GD112. 52. 28. 19.
15. NAS. GD112. 52. 28. 24.
16. NLS. *The Edinburgh Advertiser* Friday 15 November to Tuesday 19 November 1793.
17. NAS. GD112. 52. 29.1.
18. NAS. GD112. 52. 29. 9.
19. NAS. GD112. 52. 274. 12.
20. The C-in-C's headquarters was in Holyroodhouse.
21. NAS. GD112. 52. 29. 13.
22. NAS. GD112. 52. 29. 18.
23. NAS. GD112. 52. 29. 18–19.
24. Major Cameron's side of the story is told in a 'Record of His Majesty's 79th Regt, or Cameron Highlanders: By a perusal of his letter of service it will appear that the present Colonel of the 79th Regt was allowed no Bounty Money whatever from Government for his men, and that he was restricted to receive all his officers from the Half Pay list without a step of Rank being allowed any of them; consequently he was obliged to pay Bounty for the few men they incidentally procured for him – and have. It may not be inapplicable as a preliminary remark that, fully aware of his arduous undertaking, Major Cameron naturally had recourse to the local interest of his friends – among them was the Earl of Breadalbane who had previously raised two or three Battalions of Fencible Highlanders from his own Estates for local defence on limited service, with the most friendly disposition, and honourable and patriotic feelings, permitted a certain number of his men to volunteer under the Major's banner – Five Guineas Bounty being paid to each man and five guineas more lodged with the Paymaster to enable His Lordship to replace them from his Estates, which he accomplished in a few days – By these means Major Cameron was enabled to march from 70 to 80 ready disciplined men to Stirling, his intended Head Quarters. Unfortunately, however, the Earl of Breadalbane having omitted the perhaps necessary etiquette of previously formally notifying his intentions, in favour of Major Cameron, to Lord Adam Gordon then Commander of the Forces in Scotland's rank displeasure was the consequence and in the result, after incurring a personal expense of nearly £3,000 for their bounty, clothing, subsistence &c during the time they remained on his parade, Major Cameron to his astonishment received an official mandate couched in harsh terms, desiring him instantly to return the men to the corps from which they had volunteered and threatening to bring Lord Breadalbane, Lieutenant Colonel McLean of Coll, the immediate Commanding Officer, as well as himself to a General Court Martial, and all this not for the good of the service as may readily be perceived, for no sooner had Major Cameron promptly obeyed the order than the whole of the men were discharged at the head of the Regiment and that too at a time when men for general service were urgently required'. MS History of the 79th Regiment by its legitimate Colonel and sole founder [Dochgarroch Papers].
25. NAS. GD112. 52. 30. 7–9.
26. NAS. GD112. 52. 36. 7.
27. NAS. GD112. 52. 31.15.
28. NAS. GD112. 32. 8.
29. NAS. GD112. 52. 32. 11–3.
30. NAS. GD112. 52. 36. 3.
31. NAS. GD112. 52. 36. 14–5.
32. NAS. GD112. 52. 36. 23.
33. NAS. GD112. 52. 36. 24.
34. John Ehrmann *The Younger Pitt: The years of Acclaim* (1969), 31.

Chapter Twenty-Five

Mutiny at Glasgow

On 1 December 1794 John Dunlop, Esq. Provost of Glasgow wrote to Robert Dundas, the Lord Advocate [Henry Dundas' nephew]. It was the letter that made the Government first aware of the next crisis in Alexander Maclean of Coll's military career. 'My Lord', he wrote.

> A very disagreeable affair happened here this forenoon – A Private of the Breadalbane Fencibles having allowed a deserter to escape, he was ordered to be put under arrest and confined in the Guard Room, a Courtmartial was ordered, and this was to have been the day of the trial, but about ten o'clock a considerable number of the Fencibles assembled demanding the release of the prisoner which being refused they loaded in the street, and with fixed Bayonets, charged the Guard which was obliged to acquiesce, and delivered up the prisoner – no person was hurt on either side – There was a considerable number of the Town people present, some of whom it is said, encouraged the mutineers and offered to find them powder and ball ... Major McLean of Coll who commands here has by this post written to the Commander-in-Chief ...[1]

Alexander's previous crisis, 'the affair of the 62 men', has received little comment by historians.[2] The mutiny of the Breadalbane Fencibles on the other hand has attracted much more interest. The most detailed comment is by John Prebble in *Mutiny*.[3] He devotes three chapters to the event.

Prebble's writings have to be treated with caution. He only refers to his sources by listing them at the end of his book and does not tie them in to individual statements. It is therefore difficult to differentiate between fact and speculation. He is also notoriously anti-officer and *Mutiny* is significantly dedicated to 'the Private Soldiers of the 15th Scottish Division – Highland, Lowland, and English Northwest Europe 1944–1945'.

Prebble makes a number of factual errors in his book. For instance he states that Alexander Maclean of Coll 'had been an officer of the Crown for a quarter of a century'. He had not. As we have seen he was very much an amateur soldier, who had served as a captain (not a Lieutenant as Prebble states) in the Western Fencibles from 1778–1783 and in the Breadalbane Fencibles from 1793. He is, however, not unfair on the dilemma facing Alexander when he stood before the armed mutineers in front of the guard-room and told them to their face to return to their quarters.[4]

The details of what actually happened appear in the 'Narrative of progress of a mutiny on Friday 28 December [a mistake for November] among members of the Light Company of 1st Battalion the Breadalbane Fencibles at Glasgow'. It was produced for the Court Martial of the ringleaders, which took place on 28 December 1794.[5]

Prebble states that the trouble began before the mutineers left Aberdeen when Malcolm Macfarlane, a Perthshire man, in the Light Company received a flogging. He says that it had been authorised by Alexander Maclean of Coll. Again this is incorrect.

On 15 November 1794 William Shaw, a soldier in Captain Cunningham's company and Malcolm Macfarlane of Captain Gray's company were courtmartialled in Glasgow for 'riotous & unsoldier-like behaviour in maliciously and unprovokedly beating and abusing Angus Munro a recruit of the Glasgow Regiment in his own house'. Apparently on Wednesday 12 November at 10 o'clock at night the prisoners had demanded that Munro sell them drink. When he refused they beat him up. Both prisoners were found guilty by the court presided over by Captain Drummond. They were then each sentenced to receive 400 lashes on their bare backs by the drummers of the regiment. The sentence was approved by Major Lachlan Maclean of the Isle of Muck, who was acting commanding officer, and not by Alexander Maclean of Coll.[6]

Alexander was quite prepared to authorise a flogging. On 27 November 1794 he approved of 500 lashes being given to another Alexander Maclean and Donald Fraser in Lord Breadalbane's Company. He had grown up since he had cut the cords that bound John Macdonald to the whipping post in the previous war. Alexander was now acting commanding officer and it was his duty to see that the army's punishments were carried out, whether he found it distasteful or not. The Perthshire men in Breadalbane's saw it differently. Perhaps they had heard of the Macdonald incident. Certainly rumours were circulating at the time that Coll favoured the islanders in the battalion.[7] Prebble says that several of them vowed 'that before they would not see or suffer any of them to be punished', in that way again, or 'they would *see the officers' guts about their heels*'.[8]

Their opportunity came when Hugh Robertson, a private soldier in Captain Gray's Company foolishly allowed a deserter to escape from custody. Robertson in turn was imprisoned and a regimental court martial convened. It was about to sit when the Light Company, who had just been dismissed from parade

> assembled in a tumultuous manner before the guard house door and demanded the release of the prisoner, in this they were joined by several individuals of other Companys. – the whole made a push to get into the guard house & had nearly got in when the Sergt of the Guard Nielson, of the Grenadier Company & the two centrys prevented them by placing a Pike & muskets across the door, some of the officers (Lieutenants Maitland & MacLaurin) being present immediately threw themselves also before the Door & pushed them back, others of the officers being in the Officer's Guard room immediately came down upon hearing an alarm as noise below. Captain Colin Campbell & Lieutenant & Adjutant Maclean were first down & assisted in repelling the crowd. The Guard was instantly formed in front of the door & the front rank charged.

At this instant Major Alexander Maclean of Coll, having been informed of the tumult, came to the Guard House accompanied by Captain Nairne. The crowd, 'which was now considerably increased continued close upon the guard & still persisted in requiring the release of the Prisoner'. Alexander, and Colin Campbell of Glenfalloch some of whose men had joined the mutineers, addressed the crowd in Gaelic and used every argument to induce them to return home.[9]

More than once the mutineers seemed to give way and disperse, but as often they made a rush in a body towards the Guard 'with the apparent view of forcing it'. The last time this was done the Mutineers came with so much force that it became necessary to charge them, and they were driven out from below the Piazza in front of the Guard House. No sooner was this done than the mutineers, seeing that the guard were being issued with ammunition and ordered to load, shouted out that they could charge as well as the guard and called on their fellows, who had no arms, to go home and get them. Then the mutineers fixed their bayonets, and yelled out that 'they had or would be supplied' by the people of Glasgow with plenty of ammunition. The civilians in the crowd also offered to bring them stones. They began collecting them in the rear of the mutineers.

The stalemate continued for several hours. Every remonstrance made by the officers fell on deaf ears and things were likely to get completely out of hand and become even more serious. Alexander also had doubts about the reliability of the rest of the battalion. There were no other troops nearer than Hamilton. Something had to be done quickly to remove the impasse. Alexander therefore decided to send the Adjutant to the Lord Provost of Glasgow in order to get him to bring in the Dragoons from Hamilton. They could then be used to assist in capturing the ringleaders. However, before the Adjutant could return, Alexander 'considering the tumult such a measure would occasion in the city & that the result might have been of serious & disagreeable consequence', was persuaded by the majority of the officers to give up the prisoner. It was not, they argued, the right moment to apprehend the mutineers and a more suitable occasion, 'with less danger of disturbing the publick peace' would occur.[10] Reluctantly Alexander agreed to release Robertson who was carried off in triumph by the mutineers.[11] Alexander claimed that Robertson agreed to return the following day to face his courtmartial. It probably surprised no one when he failed to do so.

The authorities in Edinburgh were extremely concerned. They queried the possibility of securing the ringleaders of the mutiny at Glasgow with the proposed assistance of four troops of Dragoons quartered in the neighbourhood & that a very considerable force was necessary. They also believed that if Lord Adam Gordon were to order the Breadalbane Regiment to march out of Glasgow into different places in the neighbourhood, such an order in all probability would not be obeyed. They recommended to the Home Secretary that all the cavalry now in Scotland and such troops of Fencible Cavalry as are capable & fit for duty should be immediately ordered to the different Towns & Villages near Glasgow.[12]

Extraordinarily, however, now that they had made their point the mutineers went back to their duty. 'Every thing has gone on with perfect quietness in the Battalion ever since & the men are in every other respect perfectly submissive to the officers', wrote Alexander on Saturday 6 December to Lord Adam on Saturday. 'As a mark of disgrace I did not allow the Light Company to do any duty for some days, & they seemed to feel it – But lest the rest of the Battalion should complain, of doing duty for them, I again allowed the Common routine to go on, & particularly that they might not take any particular alarm which I apprehend it may be as well for the present to prevent'.[13]

He went on to explain to Lord Adam that:

The whole of this mutinous disposition in the Battalion proceeds from an idea of superiority entertain'd by Lord Breadalbane's own people, and a resolution that seems to be taken by them that no man from that country shall be punished – there being as far as I can discover the only men in the Battalion of this disposition, would appear to make it more necessary that His Lordship should appear in person, and I did write him very pressingly by the first post after the affair and shall again write to him according to your Lordship's request to come down without loss of time as an absolute necessary step & if your Lordship approves I would take the liberty to recommend delaying taking any other measures until he arrives.

Lord Adam had already pressed on Breadalbane the need for his presence in Glasgow. The Earl, however, remained in London and on 6 December, no doubt to Lord Adam's fury, Breadalbane received 'approval to raise a third battalion of fencibles of 1,056 men, allowing him to take 500 supernumaries from the 1st & 2nd battalions plus 500 more if he should find it necessary'.[14]

On 9 December the stalemate continued and Dunlop wrote to the Duke of Portland, who was now Home Secretary, to say that: 'No signs of contrition (I am sorry to say) have been shown by any of the mutineers, although the behaviour of the Regiment seems quite correct, and the routine duty is performed as usual'.[15]

On 12 December the cavalry reached the outskirts of Glasgow. Their presence added to that of Colonel Morrison, the former Lieutenant Colonel of the mutinous Battalion, 'who in a very handsome manner offered and gave his assistance, has had the desired effect of intimidating the Ringleaders & bring back the Regiment to a sense of duty'.[16]

Alexander's policy, and the presence of the cavalry, now bore fruit. The battalion had been subject to a constant battery of arguments by the officers and NCOs as to the effect their behaviour was having on the reputation of their homes, their families, the regiment and their chief. At last they cracked and were persuaded to give in and on 14th December Provost Dunlop was able to write to Portland to say:

> I have to inform your Grace that the Breadalbane mutiny will in all probability be settled very easily – three of the Grenadiers have offered to give themselves up unconditionally and it is reported that this example will be followed by many others at evening parade.[17]

Lord Adam was less happy. In a furious letter to Breadalbane he ordered him to rejoin his regiment at once:

> Your lordship's 1st Battalion, being at present, and ever since their outrageous behaviour on the 1st Instant in a state of absolute mutiny and disobedience to their officers – example must be made – and I expect from your Lordship that you will use what influence you have – and what means you chose – to cause deliver up – in order for tryal by a General Court Martial.

He is, however, able to add that he is glad to learn that four of the mutineers have surrendered. He accepts Breadalbane's reasons for not wishing to have the 1st Battalion ordered to Perth but cannot allow them to remain in Glasgow. They must therefore move to Linlithgow.[18]

The four mutineers who had surrendered were due to be marched on 16 December to Edinburgh with a detachment under the command of Glenfalloch. However, they were not to do so without incident. Captain Leslie, Aide-de-Camps to General Leslie, had just issued his orders to Glenfalloch and seen the prisoners out of town, when he and the Adjutant on their return were assaulted by 'a mob made up of the lowest class of the inhabitants'[19] of Glasgow. They were aided and abetted by Alexander Sutherland, a soldier in Captain Drummond's company. He screamed out that if half a dozen soldiers would join him he would rescue the prisoners and upbraided the rest of the battalion for 'suffering their companions to be [taken] off in that manner'.[20]

Alexander and Provost Dunlop reacted quickly and ordered the guard to disperse the mob. This was promptly carried out and Dunlop was able that evening to write to the Home Secretary, to say 'That mob is however completely quashed for the present and I feel myself much obliged to the Breadalbane Fencibles upon guard, to Colonel Montgomery & to Major Maclean for their assistance upon this occasion'.[21] Whilst on 17 December Major Corbett and the other officers of the Royal Glasgow Volunteers were so relieved that they sent Alexander five guineas to be distributed among the men on guard the previous day under command of Captain Nairne 'for their meritous conduct in support of the Lord Provost & Magistrates'.[22]

Not all the ringleaders had, however, surrendered and in his letter to Portland on 14 December Dunlop wrote:

> I am however very sorry to inform your Grace that one of the principal ringleaders has not been apprehended owing to the Grenadiers, to which company he belonged, having positively refused to give him up ...[23]

Fortunately for everyone the Grenadier Company changed their mind and at 3 pm on the 17 December Dunlop was able to write to Portland to say:

> I have now the pleasure to inform your Grace that the fifth mutineer belonging to the Grenadier Company has a few minutes ago delivered himself up and he will instantly be sent to Edinburgh under proper guard'.[24]

And on 22 December 1794 a relieved Provost could end his part in the affair when he wrote to Henry Dundas to say:

> For some time past, we have had but an unpleasant time of it here; I now think no further disturbance is to be apprehended, either from the Breadalbanes or the townspeople, indeed, the first division of the Regiment, marched from hence today, and the second division goes tomorrow, when the Argyll Fencibles, with two six pounders, are to march in & take the town duty ... That Regiment is I understand a very steady one.[25]

Breadalbane had at last joined the regiment and on Christmas Day Lieutenant Campbell wrote from Bathgate to Alexander in Linlithgow to say that it was Breadalbane's intention to give a treat consisting of 'porter & whisky to be furnished by him [i.e. Breadalbane] to the different divisions'. He also promises 'to procure the use of a Lodge that will accommodate all the Commissioners at once and had spoken to a publican on this topic'.[26] What Lord Adam Gordon will have thought about Breadalbane's idea of reprimanding the battalion does not bear thinking about.

In the same letter Lieutenant Campbell asks Alexander to produce witnesses for the courtmartial of the mutineers. On 20 December 1794 at Edinburgh Alexander Fraser Tytler, Judge Advocate wrote to Breadalbane:

> Its commanded by Lord Adam Gordon to intimate that a General Court Martial is to be held on the following soldiers of 1st Bn of the 4th Fencible Regt commanded by your lordship accused of the crime of mutiny and now present in the Castle of Edinburgh:
>
> John McMartin
> Donald McAllum
> John Scrimgeour

John Malloch
Ludovick McNaughton
Duncan Stewart.

As also:
Alexander Sutherland

of the same Regimentt accused of endeavouring to incite Mutiny and having joined a Mob of Rioters & attacked Major Leslie in the streets of Glasgow.[27]

The courtmartial considered the evidence, which has already been quoted. Evidence was produced that

It appears that a deliberate plan had been formed since the Punishment of Malcom MacFarlane of the Light Company that none of a particular description in the Battalion should be punished as it is thought that it may be proved against Malloch or some others made there of some such impression as that before they would see or suffer any of their number to be punished they would *see the officers guts about their heels* – for some time after the 1st the Mutineers seemed rather by every information that could be got to glory in there exploit.

All the prisoners were found guilty. Breadalbane did his best part to obtain a pardon for the Breadalbane men. He urged Lord Adam to be merciful. He wrote that he believed his regiment needed to be treated differently from others and feared the result of capital punishment would 'leave a wound which will not be easily healed and put an end to any future exertions in Breadalbane.' He was confident that the Regiment was entirely devoted to the service of their King and Country and that 'there is something in the character of these men which require a very different mode of treatment from others'.[28]

No one intervened on behalf of the Caithness man Sutherland. He was shot at Musselburgh. Men of the Breadalbane Fencibles carried out the execution and on 27 January 1795 Lord Adam Gordon wrote to Breadalbane asking him 'to express in Regimental orders writer's satisfaction with the behaviour of detachment of 1st Battalion that day 'upon the melancholy and trying occasion on Musselbugh Sands'.[29] Three days later Lord Adam wrote to Henry Dundas:

By this time you will I hope be informed that the *Mutiny-Business* has ended as near as possible in the way your friend seems to wish & when His Majesty shall be pleased to signify his intention of mercy to the prisoners (still in custody) – a circular order from me to each Corps – will close the unpleasant business ... the Precedent of the year 1742[30] may be adopted by commuting the punishment of death to [?] in a Battalion of Royal American Regiment in the West Indies or in Nova Scotia or Canada and as to those who were ordered corporal punishment – perhaps it were better they should receive *ample mercy* – and be sent to that corps as I never knew a soldier of *any* country improved on flogging.

The example made on the 27th of a *man* Sutherland – a native of Caithness – as I am informed, and I think the *most notorious* of the whole *mutineers*. My original intention was that *two* should have suffered death. But reasons ... induced me to change my opinion and to restrict the punishment of death to one only and as my warrant does not authorise me to *pardon* or *commute* I shall suspend till HM's plans shall be known.[31]

The six other mutineers were offered the alternative to being sent to the 60th Regiment, then a penal battalion in the West Indies,[32] or receive a flogging. Eventually, after the first installment of their flogging, those who had opted not to go to the West Indies changed their minds.

In the publication of the proceedings of the court martial it was suggested on the part of the prisoners 'that a partiality had been shown to the Coll men in the 1st Battalion the Breadalbane Fencibles and this opinion having been rather countenanced by some of the evidence'. It was therefore decided to publish the number of promotions in the battalion. The list showed that since the battalion's inspection at Perth on 10 May 1793 seven men from Coll had been promoted. Thirteen of Lord Breadalbane's men had.[33]

Although Alexander's supposed favour to the men from Coll earned him criticism in some quarters, it does not appear to have done his career any harm. As we have seen, Maxwell Morrison had retired before the battalion moved to Glasgow and in March 1795 Alexander was promoted to succeed him as Lieutenant-Colonel.[34]

Notes

1. TNA. HO102. 316.
2. *The raising of the 79th Highlanders* (1980), 13–4; JE Cookson *The British Armed Nation 1793–1815* (1997), 132 states that 'There was little clan sentiment in what the Highland magnates were doing in 1793–4...' He goes on to say that 'Breadalbane was not above selling 62 of his fencible men into the army'. This I would suggest is a misreading of the evidence.
3. *Secker & Warburg* London (1975).
4. He is, however, unfair in calling Breadalbane 'vain and proud, selfish and self-seeking'. The Earl certainly had his faults, but as David Graham-Campbell makes clear many of his schemes for improving his estate often failed because he was too benevolent to his poor tenants. He is constantly writing in the margin to his chamberlain's proposals, comments such as:
   Where are the poor tenants to be provided for if Anderson gets the whole farm?
   What is proposed by Lochend, here, appears very proper but what will become of all six tenants? Will they be provided for elsewhere?
   '18th Century Chamberlains on a Highland Estate'. Unpublished MS. BCP, quoting NAS. GD112. 10. 2. 5.
5. NAS. GD112. 52. 41–4.
6. NAS. GD112. 52. 213. 5.
7. *A Military History of Perthshire*, 152.
8. *Mutiny*, 323.
9. *A Military History of Perthshire*, 152.
10. NAS. GD112. 52. 41. 33.
11. NAS. GD51. 1. 854. 2.
12. TNA. HO102. 11. 320.
13. TNA. HO102. 11. 334.
14. NAS. GD112. 52. 41. 5–11.
15. TNA. HO102. 11. 344.
16. TNA. HO102. 11. 352. 15 December 1794. Lord Advocate to Home Secretary.
17. TNA. HO102. 11. 350.
18. NAS. GD112. 52. 41. 17–26.
19. TNA. HO102. 11. 356.
20. NAS. GD112. 52. 41. 44.
21. TNA. HO102. 11. 356.

22. NAS. GD112. 52. 41.
23. TNA. HO102. 11. 356.
24. TNA. HO102. 11. 358.
25. NAS. GD51. 1. 857.
26. NAS. GD112. 52. 41. 41.
27. NAS. GD112. 52. 41. 33.
28. NAS. GD112. 52. 42. 19.
29. NAS. GD112. 52. 42. 22–3.
30. He presumably refers to the mutiny of the Black Watch in 1743 [*Sketches of the Highlanders* vol. 1, 259–261].
31. NLS. Melville Papers. 1049. 61.
32. NAS. GD112. 52. 42. 1–5.
33. NAS. GD50. 18. Printed paper.
34. NAS. GD112. 52. 44. 22.

Chapter Twenty-Six

Captain Hector Maclean, Adjutant

The majority of men from the Hebrides who joined the Breadalbane Fencibles were not typical of the rest of the army. The Duke of Wellington notoriously described his men at Waterloo as 'the scum of the earth' and he never modified his opinion considering them as the 'most drunken' and 'worst specimens of humanity'.[1] As we have seen the Collachs were not all angels, but the NCOs in particular came from a very different social background to the increasingly urban underclass that made up the bulk of the army.

The background and career of Hector Maclean the Adjutant of the 1st Battalion of the Breadalbane Fencibles is of interest, as he is a good example of the type of soldier from the islands who became a senior NCO. Hector was a regular soldier[2] who in the previous war had served as a Sergeant-Major in the Scots Guards.[3] As Adjutant he held a key position in the battalion, and was the commanding officer's staff officer. He was therefore responsible not only for the Battalion's drill but also for communicating orders and conducting correspondence. He was also a good listener and had the confidence of the different parties in the battalion.

Hector was descended from the Macleans of Boreray in North Uist who for generations had acted as chamberlains to the Macdonalds of Sleat.[4] It was probably because of their hereditary expertise that Hector's great-grandfather Hugh came to Tiree and was appointed Sir Allan Maclean of Duart's bailie there. He also had a tack of Balliphetrish in Tiree.[5] Hector was probably named after his grandfather who succeeded his own father as tacksman of Balliphetrish. [See Table 12][6] Hector Balliphetrish played a leading part in Maclean resistance to the Campbell takeover of Tiree. His sister was married to Hector Maclean in Ballimartin, one of the first Macleans to lose his tack to a Campbell,[7] which no doubt added to Balliphetrish's anti-Campbell sentiments.

In January 1710 at Inveraray Balliphetrish was found guilty by James Campbell of Stonefield and fined for 'deforcing of messengers'.[8] He took part in the '15 and fought in the Maclean Regiment at Sheriffmuir.[9] In 1738, as a result of the Lord President Forbes's reorganisation of the old Duart estate, Hector lost his tack of Balliphetrish, and was one of the tacksmen ruined by the excessive rent he was forced to pay to get the tack of Gott & Vuill.[10] He was at one time an elder of the kirk, but in 1739 it is said that he had been 'disowned for Elder, by the Session of Tiree some years ago he having fallen in fornication'.[11] He appears to have been married more than once and in 1776 when he was an old man is probably the Hector Maclean living at Knock in Coll[12] with his last wife Catherine Stewart.[13]

The ruin of Hector Balliphetrish meant that his children, with the exception of his son Alexander of Mingary who seems to have recovered some of the family fortunes,[14] had no future in Tiree. Hector, the future Adjutant of the Breadalbane Fencibles had to fend for himself. He was born in 1751, which gives Prebble's description of him in November 1793 as the 'young Maclean' [who] went quickly out of a rear door of the guardroom and over the walls to give Provost Dunlop news of the mutiny,[15] a somewhat different twist to that intended.

He was not the first member of the family to serve in the Scots Guards. His father's first cousin Lachlan Ballimartin had served with them in Spain, probably as a guardsman, before becoming a captain in the Jacobite army in the '15. In June 1774 Hector the future Adjutant was 'entertained' [enlisted?] into Colonel Fawcett's company in the regiment at the Tower of London. He was promoted corporal in 1776[16] and was a Sergeant Major when Breadalbane appointed him as his Adjutant.

Hector, who must have had a good education, was a meticulous preserver of letters. Not just official correspondence but also unofficial letters, including some from his relatives. Their letters too eventually found their way into the Breadalbane archives at Taymouth Castle. Among them is one written in Coll on 30 April 1795 from his cousin Mr Donald Maclean, Minister of the Small Isles who writes to congratulate Hector on his promotion to captain. He goes on to say that he fears that republican principles are gaining ground among members of the lower class. Donald continues 'My cousin Sergeant Major John Maclean writes me he is under the highest obligation to your friendly attention – I hope he will deserve a continuation of it'.[17]

Another family letter is a reply from Hector's brother Alexander who was Sergeant-Major of the 72nd Regiment of Foot [Seaforth's Highlanders] when on 14 August 1795 he wrote to Hector. At the time he was serving in Ceylon in the camp before Trincomallie. He tells his brother of his wife's death in 1793 at Chingleputt and that he had taken part in the siege of Pondichery. He rejoices in hearing family news including 'my uncle Alexander [the Tacksman of Mingary] I am happy to hear is so well'. He had evidently been away from Tiree for many years and sees no hope of returning home soon. He does not expect to see his mother again. Some youthful indiscretion had led him to join the army for he writes 'I hope you will be pleased to represent *mee* and my youthful Folly to my sister-in-law in the most favourable light it will bear'.[18]

These letters illustrate the family network of junior officers and senior non-commissioned officers of the tacksmen class in the early years of the French Revolutionary Wars. They underline one of the strengths of Highland regiments, many of whose senior NCOs were ambitious, able, educated men from families that identified their own interests with those of their officers. For example the Marchioness of Tullibardine says in her *Military History of Perthshire* that in June 1796

> The revolutionary societies appear to have been more than usually busy this year, for it is recorded that on 4 June, the King's birthday, Sergeant-Major John Maclean and Clerk-Sergeant Alexander Knowles, in the name of the non-commisioned officers, drummers, and privates of the 1st Battalion Breadalbane Fencibles, offered a reward of two hundred and fifty guineas for the discovery of any person who should seek to seduce them from their duty.[19]

This she remarks was 'truly an astonishing sum to be voted by some five hundred men, the great majority of whom pocketed less than eighteen pence a week'.[20]

* * *

The Adjutant spent more time with the Battalion than did his commanding officer. In February 1795 Alexander Maclean of Coll was in Edinburgh. On 26th he wrote to Captain Hector to say:

> I expect daily to see my Brother-in-law[21] receive orders to go off for London away, on his way to India, & I wish to see him, besides having business with him to settle. The bearer John Maclean as well as Sergeant Allan Maclean have indispensable business in the country at this time, I wish therefore to let them home, but as they will require to be returned on the recruiting service of Donald Maclean's party to whom indeed a daily [?] order (one of the old ones) might be sent by them – John Mackinnon also requires to my own knowledge to be at home for a little, he might get a furlough for four or at most 5 weeks, as no furloughs are to be granted longer than to the 1st April.
>
> PS. You will be so good as mention this to the [?] office and Major [Lachlan] Maclean [of Muck] at Falkirk . . .[22]

The Adjutant was not able to agree to his Colonel's request and on 12 March the latter replied to Captain Hector in a hurt tone:

> I received yours concerning Allan & John Maclean, I am rather surprised any difficulty should be made as to their absence. You will tell them at any rate to accept of the passes in the meantime; tho there certainly can be no impropriety in sending men on recruiting service to pull up the place of the volunteers. I apprehend the order for the volunteers is a sufficient authority for any commanding officer but Major Maclean may now mention the matter to Lord Breadalbane, who I am convinced will make no difficulty.[23]

In December 1795 Alexander Maclean of Coll was ill, and wrote to Hector to say:

> I intend going to England. It is true I have not been so well as I could wish & Mrs Maclean is by no means well tho much better in some respects than I could have expected; on these accounts I have been talking to her now and then of going to Bath or Bristol to have an opportunity of taking better care of ourselves . . . but many circumstances occur to render this next to impractical tho I am convinced it would be of service . . . As I always wish to keep my promise I will not, without most urgent necessity fail in the one to the Major [Lachlan Maclean of the Isle of Muck] relieving him in two month, so that I will soon have the pleasure of seeing you.[24]

Bath was at this time at its peak as a fashionable spa. The Romans had probably been the first to use its hot mineral waters and the remains of a Roman building connected with the use of the waters was discovered in 1755. Other Roman buildings were found in 1799 and in 1803. The waters were considered to be a cure for a range of diseases from Rheumatism and sterility to skin diseases.[25] The English aristocracy flocked to Bath. Alexander and his wife evidently found the atmosphere highly congenial and it is probably as a result of their time at Bath that they decided to launch their family on English society.

* * *

On 8 April Alexander wrote to Hector, who was now with the battalion in the new barracks at Ayr, to say he had a pleasant journey apart from a heavy fall of snow at Lancaster. They were now at a delightful situation in the village of Clifton. The weather was fine and the country beautiful. They hoped to return in perfect health.[26] This was to be the beginning of regular trips, which took Alexander and his wife away from Scotland.

In May he wrote again to Hector with a doctor's certificate, asking him to get him a prolongation of his leave.[27] He did so again on 1 July writing from Bath. He had originally applied through Breadalbane who, as usual, he complained was dilatory and 'when he did apply for a prolongation of my leave was absolutely refused by my *friend* Lord A[mherst]'; the C-in-C in Scotland had given the writer exactly the time specified in the medical certificate without a day to travel. Alexander was therefore to rejoin the battalion on 20 July and asks where it will be as he will be at Edinburgh on that day; 'both Mrs Maclean & myself', he writes are 'considerably better upon the whole & I am satisfied a few weeks more here would have been of great service. We leave this [place] on Monday for London being obliged to go that way particularly upon account' of his sister-in-law Miss Cameron who was going to India.[28]

In his Colonel's absence Hector was left to make numerous decisions. As the battalion was stationed in Scotland it was possible for some of the battalion to carry out non-military pre-war commitments. Hector was as a result continuously badgered with requests to go home for the harvest or in the case of Sergeant Charles Maclean[29] to extend his leave to collect money owed to him, probably for a drove of cattle.

The Sergeant wrote on 2 January 1796 from Lawers in Breadalbane: 'My dear Captain ... the weather is bad the distance long and the days are very short. As I told you before I came away, I have all my money in small sums among the inhabitants here, & I intend now to collect the whole and to put it all into one place, but the most of them is putting me off from one day to another thinking to get me away as my time is so short now without settling with me'.[30]

The Colonel was not the only officer to be ill, Lieutenant Hugh Mcaskill writing to Captain Hector from the Isle of Eigg on 10 April 1796[31] says he is too ill to rejoin the Regiment. He writes 'I sent Lieutenant Colonel McLean a return of the first Recruits on the enclosed list which I hope he has transmitted to the Regiment. I am at a loss how to send them being giddy Boys, I am afraid it's a risk to send them together'.[32] The list is unfortunately no longer with the letter so we do not know from which island Macaskill had recruited the 'giddy boys'. Previously the only island in the Small Isles to provide any men for the Breadalbane Fencibles was Rum. Lachlan of the Isle of Muck had wanted men from his island to enlist but according to Mr Donald they had refused.[33]

* * *

In May 1795 Holland made terms with France and promised to join her in the war against Great Britain.[34] As a result there was as a threat from Dutch privateers to North-East Scotland. It was not known where they would strike and there was an urgent requirement for a mobile force in the area. However, until there was sufficient fodder for the cavalry's horses, they could not operate effectively and there was a need to garrison the seaside towns of Moray and Buchan.

On 1 May 1796 Major Lachlan Maclean, on his way to the Hebrides, wrote from Glasgow to the Adjutant in Ayr to tell him that the 2nd Battalion of the Regiment had moved to Banff. He warned him that it was likely that there would probably be a general move to the east coast after the review. He adds: 'Please direct for me at Tobermory and let my letters be formed by that direction till I write you to stop'.[35]

Lachlan was probably going to the Isles to try to sort out some of his problems in the Isle of Muck. He was in debt to Allan Maclean Tacksman of Kinloch Scrisort, Coll's factor in Rum and to his brother. Allan now proposed to become tacksman of Gallanach in Muck. Lachlan had, however, been offered a higher rent. He had therefore written to Allan on 4 August 1795 from Musselburgh Camp to say:

Sir, I beg to inform you that I am now offered £140 Str per annum for the farm of Gallanach, which I have declined on your account. I am surprised at a man of your sense and judgment to suppose I would break up my stock in the way you propose, or give my crop on the terms you want. I am certain if we were together for an hour we would settle the whole business easily.

This is what Lachlan was probably intending to do when he travelled to the Isles. He continues:

I am willing to give you the Farm of Gallanach under tack for fifteen years, kelp and all at £120 Str of yearly rents. You are to take my stock, labouring utensils – under comprisement the value of which you are to pay me immediately after the Dumbarton Market. You are to take the whole of my crop under comprisement at the usual time of comprising crops the price to be regulated by what it is generally sold at in the island the whole to be paid at the following Whitsun.

He goes on to say:

The debt I am due you and your brother to be paid off at the rate of £50 a year till the whole is clear. I shall allow the produce of the crop to pay part of the debt, which I hope will reduce it a good deal.

He concludes by saying:

What I have stated is so reasonable that I have no doubt fits meeting your wishes. I shall therefore expect your immediate answer to this which will serve till you get possession, as this letter will be binding on me & the answer binding on you. Any small matters that I may have omitted will be easily put to rights when we meet.[36]

Whatever his arrangement with Allan Kinloch Scrisort was, they did not solve his financial problems. It is not mentioned in Captain Hector's correspondence, but on 12 July 1796 Alexander Maclean of Coll was 'seized in the Isle of Muck with the fishings in security of £800 for a bond of Lachlan Maclean of the Island of Muck dated 30 April 1796'.[37] Why he chose to borrow from Alexander is not mentioned. Perhaps there was no alternative. It is clear from his correspondence with Captain Hector that Lachlan disliked his chief and being indebted to him probably added to his resentment.

This was not Lachlan's only financial worry at this time. On 24 August he wrote from Musselburgh to Captain Hector, who was now in Banff, to say that 'Frank has lost 300 guineas at play in one drunken night to Lord Darlington and Major Lynn'. Francis JS Maclean was now eighteen. A gambling debt was a debt of honour, which had to be paid immediately. It was not to be last scrape that was to cause his father anguish. In 1795 he had transferred to the 11th (North Devon Regiment of Foot) who were stationed at Chatham.[38] They then moved to Colchester. They were to remain there until May 1798.

Lachlan goes on to say that he had had an interview with the Adjutant General concerning leave that he and Glenfalloch wished to take. He adds a postscript: 'Please show this letter to the Lieutenant-Colonel which will save me troubling him at present'.[39] Lachlan had no desire to see Alexander.

* * *

In March 1795 yet another Maclean[40] became an officer in the 1st Battalion of the Breadalbane Fencibles. This was Allan, son of Dr John Maclean in Brolas[41] a member of the Ormsaig family in the Ross of Mull.[42] In the previous war he had served briefly as an ensign in Coll's Company in the Western Fencibles and then as surgeon's mate in Gibraltar during the siege in the 2nd Battalion 1st Foot.[43] He was now to be the Breadalbane's surgeon and Captain-Lieutenant.[44]

As we have seen, Allan was known as *doctair ruadh nam blàth shuilean*, or the red haired doctor of the warm eyes.[45] On 26 September he wrote to Captain Hector to say: 'I was yesterday at Musselburgh to wait on our Major & his family. He was taking his morning ride ... I am to set out tomorrow morning at Eight o'clock with my precious charge for Glasgow ...'

His precious charge was none other then Alexander's wife, who he was to escort to Coll via Quinish, where he wrote: 'I shall drink the health to absent Friends as I have now done after dinner'.[46]

On 2 October Dr Allan writes again to Captain Hector. This time from Oban:

Agreeable to my last letter from Edinburgh I set out thence on Tuesday with Mrs Maclean Coll & family who arrived here in good health and spirits on Friday evening – the weather was very pleasant and we had no extraordinary Adventures on the Road. Indeed Mr Smart of the Tontine Glasgow wish'd to impose on us by demanding 24 guineas for three Chaises[47] which Mr Henry of the Har Inn furnished us for £18 Str of which circumstances you'll please inform Colonel Maclean that he may not employ Smart hereafter. Mr Hugh Coll[48] was here before us with his Brother's barge but a contrary wind has met us to try our Patience. However, we have no cause to complain as yet as we have the whole Inn[49] to ourselves and the young Laird of MacDougald has with some persuasion prevailed on Mrs Maclean to go with some of her flock to Dunolly where I am afraid there is a chance of her remaining for some time. As I am very anxious to see the interview between her & the little wild ones in Coll who call Sandy McLean's wife[50] their mother & do not speak a word of English. I wish to accompany her home & to be able to report her safe arrival, which I hope to be soon. I am afraid that in consequence of HRH the Duke of York's orders for all officers to be with respective Regiments (except MPs) that the Colonel [will] not come to the country so soon as he intended, and I hope that the said order will not overtake me for sometime ... The Gentlemen from Coll inform me that Mingary and all friends in the Country are pretty well ... PS Direct to me at Langamull by Tobermory.

He wrote a postscript the following day:

The wind is Southerly and fair enough with help of Tide for Tobermory so that if it does not run hard we sail at 9 o'clock. Allan Crossapol is our Commodore ...[51]

Allan Crossapol had not rejoined the army in 1793. He had recently married Mary, daughter of John Maclean tacksman of Langamull on Torloisk's estate in Mull. John Langamull was the representative of the Macleans of Lehir, another ancient branch of the Macleans who had lost their property in the early sixteenth century. He was an elder of the kirk, a composer of songs and ardent Jacobite. He married the daughter of Donald Maclean in Killunaig,[52] who is probably the man who escaped from the battle of Culloden with his brother John's diary of the '45.

The 'red haired doctor of the warm eyes' had been correct in assuming that Alexander Maclean of Coll was not going to be allowed to go on leave as soon as he hoped. It was not to be until February 1797 that he set off from Banff for Coll. The weather, so he wrote to Captain Hector, was appalling:

> floods made the way impassable for wheeled vehicles and he had to walk between Fort Augustus and not having much in practice in walking for some years & indeed never so long a one I was extremely fatigued before I got to Fort [William] ... I got with much difficulty & hard walking against the wind next day to Kingerloch's, where the road being impassable & the wind contrary I was forced to remain all Thursday, but on Friday pulled in the same manner to Aross & being informed that Sandy Maclean[53] was in Quinish with my own boat I sent through night an express to prevent his going off which fortunately stopped him & I got home that night, and my family perfectly well & all busily employed in endeavouring to save some wine, several Pipes[54] of which had just been thrown on the shore & suppose from some of the Portugal ffleet, all I have seen being Lisbon. A considerable quantity is come to Ross [i.e. the Ross of Mull]. The vessel must have been lost at no great distance.

He went on to say that Dr Allan's 'wild ones', his two eldest daughters 'that were at home and three months ago could speak not a word of English cannot now speak a word of gallick – Your uncle has been lately complaining he has caught cold and is I am informed far from well. Having come through from Ross straight to the boat. I saw nobody in Mull – Mr Donald[55] is just arrived from Edinburgh. I hope all matters go on well & that you will embrace every good day to practice some drill in case our being early called upon to join other Corps.[56]

Alexander was back in Edinburgh by 3 April when he wrote to the Adjutant in Banff concerning the future of the battalion. He writes: 'I was this morning at the Adjutant-General's office and with the C-in-C. I find the plan is changed since I wrote you last. The five companies now at Banff are to remain there *probably* during the campaign & to be assembled at Banff next week, and I am directed to continue the headquarters there, and the Major to proceed to the Fort upon my arrival. I leave this Wednesday.'[57]

On 13 April 1797 Alexander wrote from Banff to Breadalbane. He had been allowed to remain some days at Edinburgh by the C-in-C:

> Who I found in most unusual good humour ... when I arrived in Edinburgh it was intended that the whole Battalion should be assembled at Fort George but before I left headquarters the plan was changed and I am now to remain here with only a prospect that five companys may be assembled here, for the purpose of a partial review, for a short time the other five being at the Fort and only two here at present ...
>
> Before I left the country above 200 of my people had entered volunteers upon the conditions I had the honor of mentioning to your lordship – but the volunteer plan seems to be for the most part given up although I observe my companys accepted of in places where it is impossible they can ever be of any use ... it seems a militia is now talked of.[58]

As we shall see it was proposed to have companies of Volunteers for home defence in Coll, Quinish and Rum. The Coll estate must now have had nearly three hundred men in arms: 75 in the Breadalbane Fencibled, 200 in the Volunteers and probably another 25 at least in the regular army. It was probably the largest number of soldiers the estate had ever produced.

Colonel Alexander continues in his letter to Breadalbane:

I understand Capt. [Hector] Maclean has wrote to your Lordship applying for your interest to procure him the Adjutancy of some one of the regiments in case the measure of calling out a militia should take place. As your Lordship is already sufficiently acquainted with his ability in that [sphere?] I am confident I need say nothing upon the subject, but I am persuaded there cannot be found one better qualified for such a Situation and would be much the best mode of providing a retreat for him after this war is at an end, as it is the only line he is attached to or qualified for . . .

Major Maclean is to go off in a day or two to command the companies at the Fort but is in the meantime applying for leave of absence upon business, which cannot be granted without the Duke of York's approbation.[59]

* * *

Major Lachlan himself wrote to Breadalbane on 20 April from Fort George. The illness of 'my old and worthy friend' Lieutenant-Colonel Campbell was likely to leave a vacancy and he appealed to the Earl to support him in obtaining promotion, pointing out 'I am the oldest major in your three battalions and the oldest officer in the whole (Colonel Campbell excepted)'. His finances were evidently getting worse and he wished to 'see if I can get my *unhappy business* put in any shape to avoid distraction to my poor family'.[60]

On 16 July 1797 Lachlan wrote a letter to Lachlan Mackinnon Tacksman of Houloun in Eigg, who was his agent in Muck. In it he says he understood that the people of Keill in Muck would pay £110 for that farm. If that was correct he bound himself to give them a letter of tack similar to that of Gallanach 'not forgetting the Harbour and march dyke, and the manufacturing [of] the kelp, if desired'. The tack was to commence from the previous Whitsun 'so that they may have any kelp they make this year for themselves'.

They had agreed to:

Oblige our selves during the currency of our lease to perform the following services vizt. To manufacture into kelp the shores of Ballimeanoch at the rate of 30p per ton to the swimming ware and 40/– per ton the Black ware beginning the same as soon as our labour is finished; to give each of us personally three days labour to the Tacksman of Gallanach and one days labour to the Tacksman of Ballimeanoch yearly during our lease any time the same is required; to cut peats only in such places and in such quantity as you or any other person appointed by Colonel Maclean of Isle of Monk will direct; to keep our march dyke in constant repair & to work three days in the year in repairing the quays and harbours of the island; to give the customary number of hens and spin the usual quantity of yarn annually and lastly to keep a good neighbourhood with each other as well as with the adjoining farm.[61]

Eleven tenants signed the bid [2 Macmillans, 2 Mackinnons, 3 Macleans and 3 Mackays].

Lachlan was not happy at Fort George, which he complains 'is the coldest place he has ever been in'.[62] Fort George is on the coast thirteen miles east of Inverness. It is one of the most imposing fortresses in Europe and is still in use as a barracks. It was built after the '45 to prevent another rising but has never heard a shot fired in anger. However, the war was now entering a new phase and there was an increased threat of French invasion. The Moray Firth was perceived as being a possible place for an enemy landing.

Major Lachlan's problems were not limited to conditions at Fort George. As we have seen his son Frank had left the Breadalbane Fencibles and transferred to the 11th Regiment of Foot.[63] On 8 August 1797 Lachlan wrote to Captain Hector at Regimental Headquarters in Banff to apologise for his delay in not writing earlier. He explains that: 'I was waiting to get some certain intelligence relative to that unfortunate Boy of mine, in whom you have the goodness to be so much interested. I have not heard from him since I came to Fort George till last night. The presentation is entirely given up and he sets out from London in a few days to join his Regiment at Guernsey from where they are to embark for the West Indies, he seems well pleased at the destination. The agents allow him 3/6d per day till his debts are paid, which I believe amounts to £500 Str. Nothing but going abroad would have enabled him to remain in the Regiment . . . You and Mrs Maclean[64] are the only people Frank desires to be remembered to in the Battalion.[65]

* * *

Alexander was at Banff when he heard the news that his brother-in-law Donald Cameron had been killed in India. He writes to Breadalbane to say 'I am very much afraid I have lost my Brother-in-law Major Cameron, which will greatly distress Mrs Maclean being an only brother. I have applied for leave to go to the country'.[66] He set off for Aberdeen to get permission to go home to comfort his wife. Major Lachlan was not pleased and wrote to Captain Hector to say 'I do not understand what [the] Lieutenant Colonel means by not giving me official information of his leaving the Battalion with some instructions'.[67]

On 5 October Alexander wrote from Aberdeen to Captain Hector to say that: 'Sir Hector [Munro, his immediate superior officer] has been so good as allow me to go to Edinburgh I hope when I get there to prevail upon Lord Adam to allow my proceeding to the Highlands'.[68] Lord Adam was not helpful. Alexander had irritated him more than once and the latter wrote to the Adjutant on the 14 September to report that:

> I waited on Lord Adam Gordon & found an answer had been received from the Duke of York by which leave was refused. I have no doubt by the suggestion of his Lordship. I therefore informed him that if I could not otherwise get leave I would be under the necessity of resigning and going off immediately to the country. I have accordingly wrote to Lord Breadalbane and intimated my resignation to Lord AG . . . It will be with regret that I leave the Reg[imen]t as I was in hope I might be able to continue in it to the end, and I at any rate hope to see you all together yet as I will take the first opportunity of visiting your quarters.[69]

His letter to Breadalbane states his intention of resigning and that I 'am today setting off for the country. I will as soon as required send the proper certificate of my resignation which nothing but the necessity of present circumstances would induce me to give in'.[70]

Lord Adam lost no time in accepting Alexander's resignation and on 16 September wrote to Breadalbane: 'My Lord, I have received FM the Duke of York's command to desire that your

Lordship will be pleased to recommend a successor to Lieutenant Colonel Alexander Maclean of the 4th Fencible Regiment'.[71] Alexander's quick temper had once again been his undoing and the tone of his later letters suggests that he had acted on the spur of the moment and half regretted his decision to resign. He had also left Edinburgh in such a hurry that he did not know if his resignation had been accepted. When he cooled down he reflected that as he had left Edinburgh without leave he might be arrested as a deserter.

Alexander lay low in Coll for several weeks and made no attempt to contact the Adjutant or Major Lachlan, who was therefore left without any instructions. On 26 November when he eventually wrote to Captain Hector he is contrite and says:

My dear Sir, you have reason to accuse me of neglect in not answeing your letter sooner but I hope you will excuse me for the reason I mentioned in my letter some time ago to the Doctor. Since I gave in my resignation I had not a scrape of a letter from Lord B. or any other of the *Great* men till very lately, so that I had no idea what I was to do. I did not know whether I might not be tried for *desertion* as I actually left Edinburgh without leave. Lord B being on his way from London. I presume [?] prevented his writing me as well as his receiving my letters. I had a very friendly polite one from his Lordship dated 14th October but being only in general terms, said nothing positive as to what was done about my resignation. I had a few days before the receipt of that letter wrote again to him expressing my anxiety to know what was done & at the same time informing his Lordship that, as the pressure of the cause that had induced me to resign was over, I would, if I could with propriety brought about, have no objection to rejoin, as my resignation proceeded merely from the necessity of a private & tem[p]orary cause & not from any dislike or disregard for the service. I had indeed in my letter to Lord AG upon the subject mentioned my readiness to turn out in defence of the country whenever I should be called upon. This offer I made from a sense of my duty & my real regard to the Batt[alio]n as well as upon acc[oun]t of my own people to show them that it was really no fault of mine I should not again rejoin them. At the same time that it would be allowed with my serious inconvenience & loss to myself. However, I suppose any application that may be made will be too late, and particularly as I have no doubt but the C-in-C in Scotland will [?] oppose any attempt Lord B. might make to withdraw my resignation. I therefore look upon it as now fixed that you will have a new commander . . .

I feel a most sincere regret at parting with the officers and men of the Battn in doing which every possible reason that can be urged to the contrary occurred to myself and perhaps more, yet I feel my situation at the time such as to outweigh to them all & forced me however reluctantly to adopt the step I took. My experience, when I came home, confirmed my opinion and makes me perfectly satisfied with the propriety & necessity of the measure. Any impropriety that my enemies may impute to me upon the subject must rebound on themselves & those who reduced me to the necessity of resigning.

He is honest enough to admit that

altho' I would be pleased rejoin, I was not a little afraid that my offer of returning would have been accepted, as I have begun several operations that it would be extremely inconvenient if not impossible to carry on in my absence.

He continues:

I am much obliged to you for the trouble you have taken about my horses & baggage. I much approve of the sale of the Mare & wish now the Horse was sold. Altho I am really loath to dispose of him but the treatment of Horse in this part of the world is such that I cannot bring him, otherwise would not part with him, nor will I now without he fetches something like his value, had Inverey [?] rented a horse, & I believe Provost Robinson, could you write them & know. I do not know but the Duke of Gordon might take him but forty I will expect *or* keep him.

Alexander's plans for his children to be educated in England had become a fact, for he writes:

I am going off in a day or two for England to see my son settled & I bring my older Girl Jessie with me to leave at some boarding school.

I have not discovered where Jessie was sent to school. His son Hugh was, however, destined for Eton.[72] It was a major change of direction for a West Highlander to send his children south to be educated. His decision was to have vast implications for the future of the clan and can only be the result of Alexander's desire to launch his family into English society.

He concludes his letter to Hector by saying:

I will upon my return see you at Aberdeen. You may rest assured of the continuance of my regards & it would give me real pleasure could I have it in my power to render you service, remember me to all my friends of the Battalion and to the men as a body. Mrs Maclean joins me in my best compliments to Mrs Maclean.[73]

That was the end of Alexander Maclean of Coll's military career. There can be little doubt that he was genuine in his concern that he had let down the men who had followed him into the army, as their ancestors had followed his for almost four hundred years. There can also be little doubt that they did so in that spirit. The whole feel of this correspondence is one of a caring laird and a deferential, loyal soldiery.

Notes

1. Edward M Spiers *The Army and Society 1815–1914* (1980), 77.
2. He was 'entertained [enlisted]' at the Tower of London on 20 June 1774 [TNA. WO 12. 1779].
3. TNA. WO 40. 15. 202.
4. *The Macleans of Boreray*, 3. The account of the Macleans of Baliphetrish is very muddled. Hector who Mackenzie says was the eighth son of Neil Bàn seventh of Boreray does not appear in any contemporary document I have seen. Ewen or Hugh Maclean of Ballipetrish's career is well documented.
5. He first appears there in 1663 when he is described as 'Ewine McLauchlane' [EUL. Argyll Rentals. Vol. 2. MIC. M. 676, 30]. The identity of his father is uncertain. It is possible that he was Lachlan third son of Donald of Boreray whose elder brother was killed at the battle of Inverkeithing in 1651 [*Clan Gillean*, 317]. He is again described as 'hew mclachlan' in 1675 when he was 'constitute Bailie be Kinlochaline'. [ICP. Bundle 492. 433. 2 May 1675].
6. Hector Balliphetrish's maternal grandmother was one of Neil Maclean of Drimnacross's many daughters.

7. He was thus the uncle of Lachlan, John and Donald Maclean the Jacobite brothers who fought in the '15 & '45.
8. John Imrie (ed) *The Justiciary Records of Argyll and the Isles 1642–1742* (1969), 233–6.
9. *Inner Isles 1716*, 119.
10. ICP. Tiree tacks 1748.
11. NAS. CH2. 273. 1: 3 July 1738.
12. Hugh Maclean of Knock who held the farm in 1776 was the grandson of Hector's sister Florence.
13. NAS. CH2. 70. 1. She is probably the daughter of Alexander Snodgrass and widow of Allan MacNeil Og in Crossapol.
14. He was tacksman of Gott & Vuill from 1758 (or possibly 1750 as the figure is indistinct) paying a rent of £17 [ICP. Tiree Rentals. 1758]. He was still there in 1779
15. *Mutiny*, 327.
16. TNA. WO12. 1779.
17. NAS. GD112. 52. 45. 36; Sergeant Major John was the son of Mr Donald's paternal aunt.
18. NAS. GD112. 52. 49. 2.
19. NLS *Caledonian Mercury* 18 August 1796,
20. *A Military History of Perthshire* , 156.
21. Captain Donald Cameron of Mount Cameron, which he had inherited from his aunt Mrs Jean Cameron, daughter to Captain Allan Cameron 5th of Glendessary.
22. NAS. GD112. 52. 43. 33.
23. NAS. GD112. 52. 44. 9.
24. NAS. GD112. 52. 52. 17.
25. Randle Wilbraham Falconer MD *The Baths & Mineral Waters of Bath* (1860), x.
26. NAS. GD112. 52. 57. 3.
27. NAS. GD112. 52. 58. 3.
28. NAS. GD112. 52. 60. 1. She is probably Jean, who was later to marry Allan, Coll's younger brother, who was then serving in the 36th Foot in India.
29. He is probably the Charles, son of Hugh Maclean in Muck [son of John Maclean in Cove, Rum] & Flora, dau. of John, son of Charles 2nd son of Niel Og of Crossapol]. Charles originally joined Lochaber Fencibles. He transferred to Breadalbane's and was eventually commissioned, as an ensign in 8 WIR. He was killed in Dominica in 1801.
30. NAS. GD112. 52. 54. 11.
31. He was presumably the son of the Rev. Malcolm MacAskill, Minister of the Small Isles, whose wife appears to be an illegitimate daughter of Hugh Maclean of Coll [*Na Bard Leathanach* (1898), 258].
32. NAS. GD112. 52. 57. 5.
33. Rev. Donald Maclean 'Parish of the Small Isles' in Sinclair (ed) *The Statistical Account of Scotland* (1983), 230–252.
34. AJ Grant & Harold Temperley *Europe in the Nineteenth and Twentieth Centuries (1789–1939)*, 74–6.
35. NAS. GD112. 52. 58. 1.
36. NAS. GD 201. 5. 206. Missives of leases of the Isle of Muck 1795 & 8.
37. NAS. Argyll Sasines, 953: 12 July 1796; GR 560, 150.
38. He had not joined them by 24 June 1795, but had done so by the end of the year. On 15 December by when the battalion had moved to Colchester he was promoted lieutenant [TNA. WO 12. 2840].
39. NAS. GD112. 52. 61. 18.
40. NAS. GD112. 52. 44. 9.
41. His mother was an illegitimate daughter of Captain Allan Maclean, younger brother of Donald Maclean of Brolas. She was a poetess [*Na Bard Leathanach* (1900), 173].
42. NLS. MS 3018, 23 & 70.
43. TNA. WO12. 1949.

44. NAS. GD112. 52. 44. 9.
45. *Clan Gillean*, 324.
46. NAS. GD112. 52. 62. 15.
47. Pleasure or travelling carriage, esp. light open carriage for one or two persons. *CSD*, 153.
48. Alexander's youngest brother Hugh, who was to serve briefly in the Breadalbane Fencibles.
49. The Oban Inn, which is still a hostelry.
50. Sandy is Alexander Maclean the Bailie. His wife was Mary, second daughter of Neil Maclean of Crossapol. They were then living at Arileod, which is half a mile north of Coll House.
51. NAS. GD112. 52. 63. 5.
52. *Clan Gillean*, 348.
53. Probably Alexander 'the Baillie'.
54. cask for wine, esp. as measure of two hogshead, usu. = 105 gal. *CSD*, 778.
55. Minister of the Small Isles.
56. NAS. GD112. 52. 67. 21.
57. NAS. GD112. 52. 69. 2.
58. NAS. GD112. 52. 69. 6.
59. NAS. GD112. 52. 69. 6.
60. NAS. GD112. 52. 69. 16.
61. NAS. GD 201. 5. 206.
62. NAS. GD112. 52. 69. 21–2.
63. NAS. GD112. 52. 41. 43.
64. Hector had married twice. The name of his first wife is not known but he is described as a widower when on 28 February 1793 at St John the Evangelist, Westminster he married Ann Campbell, spinster of the Parish of Petersham in Surrey.
65. NAS. GD112. 52. 73. 5.
66. NAS. GD112. 52. 74. 4.
67. NAS. GD112. 52. 74. 9.
68. NAS. GD112. 52. 74. 6.
69. NAS. GD112. 52. 74. 22.
70. NAS. GD112. 52. 74. 5.
71. NAS. GD112. 52. 74. 26.
72. HEC Stapylton *The Eton School Lists from 1791 to 1850* (1864), 32a where he is shown under 'Q Lower Division 1799'. He is the first Maclean, the first West Highlander and one of the first Scots to go to Eton.
73. NAS. GD112. 52. 76. 7.

Chapter Twenty-Seven

The end of the 1st Battalion Breadalbane Fencibles

Alexander's resignation caused differing emotions among his fellow officers. Captain the Hon. Francis Gray writing to Captain Hector from Culloden House on 18 September 1797 says: 'I was very much hurt by a letter I had on Friday from Coll, in which he intimates to me his having resigned. He, however, gave me such substantial & cogent reasons for this hasty step that, although I must ever regret his quitting just now, yet certainly he is best judge of his own actions in this particular'.[1]

Major Lachlan was probably delighted. He was increasingly desperate to get promotion and, as we have seen, when in April he heard that his old friend Colonel Campbell was ill he had written to Breadalbane to push his own career. In October Lachlan wrote to Breadalbane again to say: 'I am a good deal surprised that your Lordship has not honoured me with a line since Lieutenant-Colonel Maclean's resignation. It is not idle curiosity that induces me to wish to be in the knowledge of your Lordship's arrangements, but being materially interested, as an officer who has a character to support, and on whose future conduct depends the provision for his Poor Family'. He wishes to know if he 'is to be seconded in a manner that he can undertake the charge of the Battalion'.[2]

Lachlan had also to deal with affairs in the Isle of Muck. On January 1798 he wrote to his agent Lachlan Mackinnon in Howlin, Eigg:

Sir, in consequence of your offer to me of the grass rent of £55 Str yearly for the farm of Ballimeanoch in the Isle of Monk with all its shores and other appendages thereto belonging I agree to the same under the usual restrictions relative to roads, dykes, harbours and cutting of peats – and bind myself to grant you a tack if required for the same number of years as that of Gallanach and Keill – I further bind and oblige myself to deduct £10 Str yearly of the above rent in consideration of your trouble and expence [for] attending on my business.[3]

Lachlan was duely promoted to command the 1st Battalion. His problems, however, were far from over and on 22 February 1798 he wrote to his Adjutant from Musselburgh, where he was on leave with his family to say 'Frank is still in London, and what his fate may be,'[4] I do not know.

He wrote again on the 1 March with more problems. On this occasion they were regimental ones. He had invited the battalion to forfeit four days pay for a military charity. 'I am vexed', he wrote:

> to the heart at the backwardness of the men in coming forward with a moderate subscription. I beg the Major will once more call a meeting of the officers, and produce my last letter to him on the subject as I wish one more trial to be made before the subscription is announced to the publick. I rely on the exertions of the officers commanding companies in prevailing on the men to come forward with four days Pay at once & no more of it. Let it be mentioned that this second trial is at my request as I declined to making the offer of two days pay publick, being so much against their honour and credit and that I trust they have that confidence in me that I would not wish to do anything, but what was proper and respectable to themselves. They ought not to forget the many advantages and comforts granted them lately by their King and Country.[5]

The fact that the battalion had offered a reward of 250 guineas in June 1797 for the discovery of any person who should seek to seduce them from their duty,[6] when Alexander was commanding officer, must have been particularly galling.

'I am distressed' Lachlan wrote on the 8 March to Captain Hector 'we make such a shabby figure ... as to my own affairs they are in a very Embarassed state owing partly to the times, and partly to my inattention to them for these four years back. Frank is still in London, and I dare say will finish his career by a sale [of his commission] and then turn soldier or sailor'.[7]

On 21 March he wrote again to the Adjutant: 'I was asked to announce the subscription to Sir Ralph Abercromby and the Committee. I gave such a explanation to the Adjutant General as I thought necessary to check the officers of any blame .... not a word from Frank.'[8]

Lachlan's world was falling in around him. On 16 April he gave a disposition to the Trustees for his creditors in the 6 merk land of Isle of Muck and fishings. The Trustees received sasine on 3 July.[9]

On the 10 April 1798 writing once more to Captain Hector from Musselburgh, he says: 'You certainly acted as a friend and an attentive officer in corresponding with, and giving me every information necessary for which I feel myself much obliged'.[10] The incident for which he was obliged to his Adjutant was probably the duel that had taken place in the battalion at Aberdeen between Lieutenants George Rae and John McVean, which ended fatally for the latter. Lieutenant Rae was tried for murder by the High Court of Justiciary on the 18 June, and was aquitted.[11]

In his letter to Captain Hector, Lachlan is able to report that his worst fears for his near-do-well son Frank had not come about. Instead of having to sell his commission he had transferred to another regiment. 'Frank has joined and been well received by his Regiment', he writes. 'They are embarked for Ireland with the other regiments'.[12] Despite his letter to his father Frank had not been sent to Ireland nor transferred to another regiment. He was still a lieutenant in 11th Foot and was soon to see active service close to home.

* * *

In order to bring an invading army to England the French were collecting an armada at Ostend. They had recently, at a cost of £5,000,000 Sterling, completed work on a 14 mile long canal from Bruges to Ostend along which they planned to bring men, stores and even gun-boats for a descent on the British Isles. In London it was believed that if the lock gates at Saas, a mile from Ostend, were blown up, not only would the port itself be damaged but the principal internal communication between Holland and West Flanders would be destroyed.

A 'commando' raid was organised, its aim was to destroy the Saas lock. It consisted of the light companies of the 1st, Coldstream and 3rd Foot Guards, the light and grenadier companies of the 23rd and 49th Regiments, the 11th Foot, 100 men of the Royal Atillery, and 9 men of the 17th Light Dragoons, a total of 1,400 men. They were under the command of Major-General Eyre Coote.

On 14 May 1798 the expedition sailed from Margate. It was escorted by a flotilla of frigates and smaller vessels under the command of Captain Home Popham RN. Owing to bad weather it did not arrive at anchor off Ostend until one o'clock on the morning of 19 May. Soon after they had anchored the wind shifted to the west and, as a gale was expected, Popham proposed to go out to sea again. However, intelligence had been received that the transports for the invasion of England were about to move along the new canal from Flushing to Dunkirk and Ostend. It was also reported that the garrisons at Nieuport, Ostend and Bruges were very weak, and Eyre Coote persuaded Popham to land the troops. The men were immediately thrown ashore in a hurry and in any order.

It was not until 4 o'clock when most of the British soldiers were ashore, that the French forward batteries opened fire. The guns of the Royal Navy frigates replied with a broadside and by 5 o'clock the soldiers, with the exception of the 4 companies of 1st Foot Guards, whose transports had strayed from the main body, had all been landed. Eyre Coote pushed forward with six companies under the command of Major-General Harry Burrard and despite some skirmishing with the French, they had soon seized the approaches to the lock.

The main body of the expeditionary force, including 11th Foot took up a position in the dunes to cover the withdrawal, whilst their light company and that of the 23rd Foot under the command of Major Donkin of the 44th Regiment covered the village of Bredin extending to the Blenkenby Road near the sea.[13]

By 11 o'clock the lock gates had successfully been blown up, with the loss of one casualty, and the demolition party withdrew to the beach. What had so far been a copybook exercise in combined operations, now started to go wrong. The on-shore wind increased and the surf was so high that it was impossible to embark the 'commandos'. The covering force began digging in on a ridge amongst the sand dunes and waited for the inevitable French riposte.

It came at first light. The British first saw two strong columns of French troops advancing to their front. They were followed by others marching to the flanks of their defensive position, which was on the ridge of sand dunes overlooking the beach. The action lasted for two hours. Eyre Coote, whilst rallying some broken men, was seriously wounded.

Despite their gallantry the fate of the outnumbered British troops was inevitable. The commanding officers of the 11th Foot and 3rd Foot Guards were both dead. 163 officers and men were killed or wounded and Burrard, who had assumed command, was 'unwilling to sacrifice lives in useless resistance to overwhelming numbers'. He surrendered. 1,100 British soldiers became prisoners of war.[14] Among them was Frank Maclean who had showed 'courage and good conduct in the face of the enemy on a very trying occasion'.[15]

The prisoners of war in 11th Foot[16] were sent to Douai and Fort L'Escape. Morale was low, and a group of sergeants were dissatisfied with the actions of the Sergeant-Major and plotted against him. They were apparently encouraged by Lieutenant Francis Maclean who 'countenanced and supported a cabal or combination of the non-commissioned officers and sergeants against the Sergeant-Major of the Regiment'.[17]

When in July 1799 the prisoners of war were exchanged and returned to England Frank went on sick leave.[18] Complaints about his behaviour whilst he was a prisoner-of-war soon reached the 11th's newly promoted commanding officer Lieutenant-Colonel RS Donkin, who instructed the Adjutant to give him the option of transferring to another regiment or face courtmartial. Frank preferred the second option. Nothing initially happened and he resumed his duties. However, when an enquiry was held into the conduct of the Sergeant-Major 'Lieutenant Maclean's name appeared in so exceptional a light' that the subalterns refused to work with him and his Courtmartial went ahead. It was held at the Royal Hospital Chelsea on 12 December 1799.

Frank was charged with:

1. Improper conduct as an officer during the time he was a Prisoner of War in France in holding communication with the NCOs of the 11th Foot between 1 June 1798 & 1 June 1799 in a manner derogatory to his situation as a Lieutenant in His Majesty's Service.
2. Disrespectful conduct towards and using menacing words and actions to Captain Martin commanding officer of 11th Regiment of Foot on 15 & 16 March 1799.

He was acquitted of the first charge but found guilty of the second and was ordered to be publicly reprimanded 'upon the Parade at the head of the 11th Foot'.[19] He was transferred to Major Hadden's Company and in the pay list for the month ending on 24 January 1800 it is noted that Lieutenant FJS Maclean is 'Dismissed the Service'.[20]

* * *

In June 1798 the 1st Battalion the Breadalbane Highlanders was encamped on the Don Links outside Aberdeen. Towards the end of August Lieutenant-General Sir Ralph Abercromby reviewed them. Two months earlier he had succeeded Lord Adam Gordon as Commander-in-Chief in Scotland. Soon afterwards news came of the French landing in Co. Mayo, and along with the 1st Argyllshire Fencibles (who were also quartered at Aberdeen), the battalion volunteered for service in Ireland. The French landing, however, was so soon crushed that it was unnecessary to bring troops from Scotland, and for the present the 1st Battalion the Breadalbane Fencibles remained in Aberdeen.[21]

On 3 September Lachlan ordered that a Regimental Court Martial should be held at Aberdeen. Charles Maclean, a soldier in the Lieutenant Colonel's own company, who in 1776 had been a servant in Ardnish in Coll had, two days previously, been confined for being drunk at the evening parade. The evidence included that of Sergeant Major John Maclean, who stated 'that the prisoner often makes a practice of getting drunk'. Charles gave no defence, acknowledging 'the crimes laid to his Charge & submits himself to the mercy of the Court'. He was found guilty of a breach of the 2nd section of 24th article of war and was sentenced 'to receive 100 lashes on his bare back by the drummers'. He received 50 lashes[22] before the flogging was halted.

Flogging could not legally take place without the regimental surgeon being present to call a halt, for flogging could and sometimes did end in death. Today there is nothing about military discipline so horrifying as the use of flogging as a military punishment. It also seems extraordinary that such a punishment should have been used so savagely when a great evangelical revival was underway, and when the 'Christian conscience of the nation laboured so earnestly to reduce', and end, the sufferings of black slaves.[23] Whilst at the same time the mutilation of a white soldier received the annual approval of Parliament.

The private soldier's contempt for the pains of moderate corporal punishment[24] explains something of the dilemma facing commanders, and even the great emancipator of slaves William Wilberforce had to admit that 'when he considered what a huge and multifarious body an army was, he should be afraid of adopting suddenly so material a change in what was deemed to be so essential to its discipline' as flogging.[25]

Nothing is easier than to denounce so barbarous a punishment, yet it baffled the wit of the authorities to devise a milder punishment that could control the appalling thugs of whom the rank and file of the British Army was largely composed. For thugs they undoubtedly were and the crimes British soldiers committed were the crimes of thugs and their proclivity for robbery and murder on active service appears with monotonous frequency in Wellington's dispatches from the Peninsula.

There is little doubt that flogging was effective in maintaining discipline in an army where so many soldiers came from the criminal classes. It is also clear from Wellington's observations that his men were usually well behaved while serving with their own units. When they were under the eyes of their own officers and NCOs the chances of getting caught was sufficient incentive to behave. It was when they were overseas in isolated detachments that the most heinous crimes were committed. In other words crimes took place when the men believed that they could get away it. At home serious crimes were rare, but desertion and drunkenness were a constant feature of military life.

As we have seen, Breadalbane urged Lord Adam to be merciful to the Glasgow mutineers and wrote that he believed his regiment needed to be treated differently from others.[26] Were they different? The original cause of the mutiny, the unprovoked beating of Angus Munro when he refused to sell William Shaw and Malcolm Macfarlane, is the type of crime that earned Wellington's men his description as the 'scum of the earth'. Breadalbane may have been living in an unreal world as far as some of his Perthshire men were concerned.

The men from Coll were not innocent of crime but a study of courts-martial in the Breadalbane Fencibles shows that their misdemeanours were minor ones. Certainly men from Coll could and did commit military offenses: Corporal Alexander Rankin was courtmartialled and reduced to the ranks for allowing a deserter to escape at Kilsyth.[27] Private Charles Maclean received a hundred lashes for being drunk on the evening parade,[28] but the overall behaviour of the men from the Coll estate was exemplary. They were serving with their friends and neighbours under the leadership of officers and NCOs they had known since birth. They had every incentive to behave and return home proud of their service and join the ranks of a long line of military forbears. And the stories of their time in the army will have lost little in the telling.

* * *

In October the 1st Battalion of the Breadalbane Fencibles moved to Fort George. The threat of invasion from France was over for the present and by the end of 1798 the British Government, which had joined a new coalition against the French, was once again preparing to take the offensive in Europe. The need for home defence battalions had passed and the Fencible regiments were invited to volunteer for service outside Great Britain. In the middle of March the battalion was abruptly informed that unless three hundred men volunteered to serve unconditionally in Ireland or Europe it would be disbanded. No bounty was offered.

On 20 March it was announced that the Argyllshire Fencible Regiment had volunteered to a man to serve overseas. For a few days the fate of Lachlan's battalion hung in the balance, but by the end of the month it was clear that the necessary number of volunteers would not be forthcoming. Orders were therefore given that the battalion should be disbanded. This took place on 18 April 1799 at Fort George.[29] The battalion's colours and all its records were deposited at Taymouth Castle.

The decision to disband his battalion must, so he thought, have been the final straw for Lachlan. He had a young family, his most recent child had been born on 23 November 1798,[30] and he was now only entitled to the salary as a half-pay captain. The inevitable followed and on 23 July 1799 the Isle of Muck was sold to Ranald George Macdonald of Clanranald. Sasine followed. Clanranald's curators paid off Lachlan's debts. Later Alexander, as superior, confirmed the sale.[31]

Lachlan's traumas were not, however, over. In September 1799, whilst living at Inveresk, he received a letter from Colchester bearing news of his son Frank from the latter's commanding officer. 'Sir', the latter writes 'a very unpleasant task falls upon me by request of your son Lieutenant Maclean, who is about to exchange out of the 11th Regiment ...' Despite Frank's 'good conduct in the face of the enemy on a very trying occasion' he, as we have seen, eventually decided not to transfer but to be tried by General Court Martial.[32] He was found guilty and his sentence was confirmed on 12 December 1799.[33]

* * *

Lieutenant Colonel Lachlan was not the only member of his family at this time to lose their property in the Isles. In the 'Book of Tiree Tacks,' at Inveraray Castle it is noted that after Donald of Cornaig obtained his new tack of the Two Ends of Coll: 'Mr Maclean the Tacksman having died about two years after the commencement of the lease of Cornaig, it fell of course to be possessed by his widow and daughters whose mismanagement of it, with regard to improvements, impoverished the Farm so much during a course of seven years that it will require the labour of many years to bring it to a proper state of improvement'.

Malcolm Campbell, the son of one of Coll's tenants in Torestan in 1776 had, it is said, made a fortune in Liverpool, and on Whitsunday 1798 he obtained the ten unexpired years of Donald Maclean's tack of the Two Ends of Coll.[34]

As a result of this new arrangement the Duke of Argyll wrote to his Bailie in Tiree to say that: 'After paying me the rent which I got from the late Isle of Muck for the farm which he possessed and relieving me of the minister's stipend payable out of it, you are to pay over to the widow and daughters of the Isle of Muck the surplus rent payable by Malcolm Campbell by the new sett, but it must be understood that this is in satisfaction of the claim which these ladies have upon me for £100 by the last lease and they must give up their copy of that lease with a discharge of that claim, otherways I will take the surplus rent'.[35]

Although his mother was the nominal tenant of the Two Ends of Coll, Captain John Maclean had probably tried to help to run the estate when he was home on leave. On 21 January 1798 his son Alexander was baptised at Cornaig.[36] It is the last reference I know of the Macleans of Cornaig in Coll. Thereafter they joined the ranks of Coll exiles in Edinburgh.

* * *

There can be little doubt that when Alexander Maclean of Coll wrote to Captain Hector to say 'as I have begun several operations that it would be extremely inconvenient if not impossible to carry on in my absence',[37] he was talking about his plans to 'improve' the estate. Alexander had been keen to do so for some time. His plans had been delayed by the outbreak of hostilities with France, but before he joined his regiment he had already commissioned George Langlands & Son to survey his part of the Island of Coll.

The survey was carried out in June and July 1794. It shows that the estate consisted of just over 10,926 acres. This was made up of 1,858 acres of arable ground, 1,674 acres of rocky arable, 2,590 acres of Green pasture, 57 acres of meadow, 229 acres of moss, 87 acres of blown sand, and 4,458 acres of Muir.[38]

The Langlands survey very neatly coincides with the report in the *Old Statistical Account* on Tiree and Coll made by the minister Mr Archibald McColl,[39] who states that in January 1793 the population of Coll was 1,041. This means that the population had almost doubled in the 77 years since 1716. Even more worrying, although the population had increased by more than 100 in the 18 years since 1776, the number of households had only gone up by 6, suggesting that there was already serious overcrowding.

The idyllic picture of Coll painted by Dr Walker could hardly be sustained. Even in 1764 Walker said that the people's possessions were very small. They were going to be much smaller when a third of the population, said by McColl to be under 10 in 1793, grew up. Some people in Coll had already seen the writing on the wall. There had been bad harvests in 1790 & 1791 and 36 Collachs left for America in 1792.[40]

Alexander aimed to be true to his family's maxim: 'to improve his father's acres without hurting the people or losing the ancient Highland fashions'. There was now a wealth of advice to help lairds improve their Highland estates. Foremost amongst the literary improvers was James Anderson LL.D. (1739–1808),[41] whose *Essays Relating to Agriculture and Rural Affairs* was first published in 1775. By 1800 it had run to five editions. Copies were passed from one laird to another, and presumably amongst the tacksmen as well. For instance my copy of the first edition is inscribed: 'The gift of A Stuart to Archibald Campbell younger of Jura.1791'. Stuart had purchased the book in 1789.

* * *

Alexander continued to keep in touch with his old battalion. On 18 December 1797 he wrote from Edinburgh to Captain Hector:

> Dear Sir, I received your letter in Course, and am glade to find you are all well. I had a most tedious journey owing to the want of horses & Carriages upon the road. Those at Inveraray were so bad that we only made out two stages a day.
>
> I am much obliged to you for the care you have taken of my horse. Were it not for the abuse he would meet with in the Country I would not part with the horse. I think some of the Gentlemen about Turriff would purchase him for a hunter & I think he ought to fetch 40 Guineas. But I would not let him go under 30, but it might be as well to take that for him as keep him much longer.

He continued to take a particular interest in the Collachs in the battalion.

> As to Coun[42] as he is totally unfitt, because unwilling, to be a servant I suppose he thinks of going to the West today. As I mentioned him to Dr Hector[43] who said he would have no difficulty in procuring a place for him, if qualified to write & keep accounts, which I desired him to attend to when I left Banff. I will in the mean time pay the bounty to a man to exchange for him, as I will get his discharge from the Earl. Were I to ask it, I am persuaded he

would discharge him without an exchange, but I will not ask so improper a thing. Coun may therefore be on the look out for a man to go in his place, in which I hope you will assist him, but I do not think he ought to require his discharge until he is quite prepared to go away & if he has not paid great attention to his writing letters since I left Banff he will not be fitt for going abroad at all.

He goes on to say:

Your uncle is but in a weak state,[44] if he does not soon get better than he was when I saw him, this winter or spring is likely to finish him. I was two nights at his house on my way. I have Jessie[45] with me. I propose leaving [her] at some English school for some time. I leave this today & will return as soon as possible to see you all. I much long to see the men of the Battalion, who I hope have no enmity to me altho' I wished them to do their duty & appear like soldiers and it would give me great pleasure at any time to be of service to any of them if it lay in my power. With best compliments to Mrs M.
  PS. Shuna was sold this day. There were several bidders, which brought the price up to a great height. Major Macdonald of Lindill was the purchaser at £6,210.[46]

On 15 February 1798 Alexander wrote again to Captain Hector, this time from Oban:

I arrived here as I expected on Tuesday night, but have been detained here yesterday & today by contrary winds & extreme bad weather. Showers of sleet & snow from SW-W-NW nor is there much prospect of its being soon favourable but as the weather is so unsettled there may be a chance of a good day when least expected.

He still had unfinished business to complete over the accounts of the battalion, and continues:

I enclose you a letter to the Earl of Breadalbane, which I presume will answer the purpose as it is materially concerning the Roll. I send it you that a copy might be kept and you will then forward it to the Earl & put in a cover.

He was busy with his plans for improvements, probably on this occasion for Quinish for he goes on to say. 'I met my Gardner going for trees & seeds to Edinburgh who informed me the family were all well. I beg my compliments to Mrs Maclean, Captain & Mrs Gray, the Doctor &c'.[47]
He wrote again a week later from Coll:

Dear Sir, I wrote to you from Oban inclosing a letter for the Earl of Breadalbane concerning the Bread money, which I hope you received & forwarded after being perused.
  After a pretty tedious passage from Oban I got home 19 or 20th and found all here well. This will be brought by Charles MacDonald,[48] who lost an opportunity the other day of going off by the Boats or vessels rather sailing through the night. Another lad goes with him, a Brother of Sergeant Hugh Maclean, who his father[49] wishes to get home & he is indeed, as you know, no good acquisition to the Regiment. His father says that by a letter from Hugh to inform him that the Lieutenant-Colonel had said he might be exchanged & therefore now sends this son who may make a good soldier & he is a little drilled in the volunteers that are here. I hope therefore the change may be accomplished.

At Tobermory I found a sloop,[50] which had been storm staid there for above a month with a cargo of Coals for me & by which I came straight here without being in Queenish but I hear your uncle has got most unexpectedly well & is in his usual way. Mrs Maclean joins me …

PS. I will be glad to hear from you when you are at leisure with my Regimental Aberdeen news that may be going. I will be obliged to you to enquire about Sandy Maclean [Sgt Hugh's brother] and give your opinion whether he is likely to brush up so as to be fitt for a servant after the Qrs [?] are over. If you think he will at all do I could wish you would take the trouble of directing him to qualify himself & assist him try what he could do. I have a good opinion of his disposition & could wish to have a namesake & of my own family. Endorsed AM Esq of Coll. Answered 26 March 1798.[51]

That Alexander Maclean of Coll talked of his intended servant Sandy, as 'of my own family', is illuminating. Sandy's father was the small farmer Lachlan in Fiosgaradh in Coll, who was a younger brother of Neil of Crossapol. In their male lines the two families had not been related for more than 200 years, yet Coll still knew the relationship and considered Sandy to be a member 'of his own family'. It says a great deal about relations between officers and men in the 1st Battalion the Breadalbane Fencibles. The Earl probably had a similar relationship as Alexander with his tenants' sons. The Battalion was not a 'clan regiment' in that it was not made up of men from one clan. But it included in its ranks men from two clans, who in the past, had often been on the opposite sides in the feud between the Campbell and the Macleans. It was the last time that they were to be combined into one battalion.

* * *

This letter of February 1798 is the last that I have discovered from Alexander Maclean of Coll to his former Adjutant. These letters show both a degree of genuine paternal concern for his people and his intention of educating his children to take their part in British society. Alexander was not to serve in the army again. From now onwards his energies were to be devoted to reorganising his estate and advancing the interest of his family. His two aims were to prove to be incompatible.

Notes

1. NAS. GD112. 52. 74. 28.
2. NAS. GD112. 52. 75. 8.
3. NAS. GD 201. 5. 206.
4. NAS. GD112. 52. 79. 12.
5. NAS. GD112. 52. 80. 2.
6. *A Military History of Perthshire*, 156.
7. NAS. GD112. 52. 80. 3.
8. NAS. GD112. 52. 80. 5.
9. NAS. Argyll Sasines 1095, GR 588, 193.
10. NAS. GD112. 52. 81. 4.
11. *A Military History of Perthshire*, 156 quoting the *Caledonian Mercury*, June 18th & 21st 1798.
12. NAS. GD112. 52. 81. 4.
13. TNA. WO 1. 177, 421.
14. This account of the raid on the locks is based on The Hon. J W Fortescue *A History of the British Army* (1913) Part I (1789–1801), 587–9.

15. Colchester 3 September 1799. CO 11th Foot to Lieutenant-Colonel Lachlan Maclean, late 1st Bn The Breadalbane Fencibles [TNA. WO 71. 185].
16. '1 Major, 6 captains, 11 lieutenants, 1 adjutant, 1 surgeon, 40 sergeants, 16 drummers & 400 rank & file' [TNA. WO 1. 177, 469].
17. TNA. WO 71. 185: General Court Martial held at Royal Hospital Chelsea on Thursday 12 December 1799.
18. TNA. WO 12. 2242. Monthly Pay list. Captain Rashleigh's Company 11th Regiment of Foot 24 July & 25 July–24 August 1799.
19. TNA. WO 71. 185.
20. TNA. WO 12. 2845.
21. *A Military History of Perthshire*, 156–7.
22. NAS. GD112. 52. 231. 1.
23. Richard Glover *Peninsular Preparation: The Reform of the British Army 1795–1809* (1963), 174.
24. *Ibid*, 178.
25. *Ibid*.
26. NAS. GD112. 52. 42. 19.
27. NAS. GD112. 52. 211. 3.
28. NAS. GD112. 52. 231. 1.
29. *A Military History of Perthshire*, 156–7.
30. *Scots Magazine* vol. 60, (1798), 864.
31. 'Inventory of Title Deeds and papers belonging to Alexander Maclean Esq. of Coll delivered up by Mr Macdonald Buchanan to Alexander Hunter Esq. WS. 1820'. I have to thank C. McLean, 20 Belmont Avenue, Sandbach, Cheshire for a copy of this inventory.
32. TNA. WO 71. 185: GCM held at the Royal Hospital Chelsea on Thursday 12th December 1799.
33. TNA. WO 72. 27.
34. ICP. Tiree Tacks.
35. *Argyll Estate Instructions*, 47–8.
36. NAS. CH2. 70. 1.
37. NAS. GD112. 52. 76. 7.
38. NAS. RHP 3368.
39. Sir John Sinclair (ed) *The Statistical Account of Scotland 1791–1799* vol. xx (reprint 1983), 266. For calculation of the population of Coll in 1716 see Chapter note 36.
40. Not all who left the island at this time went abroad. On 17 April 1792 Hugh Rankin, Neil's second son joined 47th Foot as a private soldier.
41. William Anderson *The Scottish Nation* vol. I (1877), 126–9.
42. Coun Douly (*Con-duiligh MacRaing*) or Quintillian b. 1776; he is listed as underage son of Niel Rankin & Catherine Maclean. in Breacachagh in 1776 [NAS. CH2. 70. 1]; trained to succeed his Father as piper to Maclean of Coll; enlisted in 1st Bn Breadalbane Fencibles, attested 4 April 1793: 17, 5 ft 5.25 ins, Labour, Fair hair, Grey eyes. [NAS. GD112. 52. 539. 17] ; 25 October 1796 [?]: Merchant in Coll [Co6. 1.11. 1]; discharged 24 January 1798; [BCP. Card Index].
43. He was the son of Hugh Maclean Tacksman of Knock in Coll; 1790 MD Marischal College, Aberdeen; Surgeon. 1788–89: *Airly Castle*; 1790–1: *Princess Amelia*; 1792–3: *Middlesex*; 1796: Appointed Assistant Inspector of Hospitals, St Domingo; 25 June 1802: Retired on ½ pay; d. 31 August 1810; Author of *Mortality among troops at San Domingo 1797* [Johnson's roll of RAMC, No. 1504 & E IOL/IMS 1615–1930, 43].
44. Alexander Maclean of Mingary, Mull, formerly of Gott, Tiree. His tack of the latter farm expired at Whitsunday 1776 and was not renewed in order to establish the village of Scarinish [ICP. Remarks on the Island of Tiry 1771]; 'Margaret Maclean wife of Alexander Maclean Tacksman of Mingary d. 1783, aged 74' [Dervaig Graveyard]; 26 December 1787: m. Alex. Maclean, Tacksman of Mingary in Mull and Miss Peggy Maclean at Triallan, [Coll] [NAS. CH2. 70.1].

45. His eldest daughter, born 1 July 1781. In an earlier letter a month earlier [NAS. GD 112. 52. 76. 7] to Capt. Hector he said the same thing, perhaps she had refused to be left at the original school.
46. NAS. GD112. 52. 77. 7.
47. NAS. GD112. 52. 79. 7.
48. The son of Neil Macdonald, tenant in Totronald. He appears to have been at times employed by Alexander as a servant.
49. Lachlan Maclean in Fiosgaradh. Why Alexander was critical of Sgt Hugh is not clear from the Breadalbane papers. He enlisted 16 March 1793 and was immediately made a corporal [NAS. GD16. 52. 24. 20]; He was promoted sergeant by 24 December 1793 [NAS. GD112. 52. 555];
50. Small one-masted fore-and-aft-rigged vessel with mainsail and jib [*CSOD*, 997].
51. NAS.GD112. 52. 79. 8.

Chapter Twenty-Eight

The Isle of Eigg Company of Volunteers

The fencible regiments raised to defend Scotland could never do more than protect the major centres of population and the vulnerability of the remote North-West Highlands and Islands to raids, particularly from French privateers, was a cause of concern to both its inhabitants and to the Government. Once the first fencible regiments had been raised the Government turned their attention to the defence of the rest of Scotland. However, before they could do so they had to set up a structure to co-ordinate recruiting, and in April 1794 a Lieutenancy was established in each Scottish county with orders to raise local volunteers.

In the past Lieutenancies had existed only in times of crisis, such as during the '15 and '45 risings, then noblemen loyal to the government were granted warrants to appoint deputies, recruit officers and call out the militia. These powers lapsed once the emergency was over. It was now proposed to establish permanent Lieutenancies, in the English fashion, with the greatest landlord in each county appointed to be Lord-Lieutenant.[1]

The Lord-Lieutenant appointed for Inverness-shire was Sir James Grant of Grant Bart, MP. He was one of the great Highland magnates who like the Earl of Breadalbane was a political ally of Henry Dundas. Grant had already raised a fencible regiment, and was in the process of forming a regular regiment,[2] when he was appointed Lord-Lieutenant.

On 15 June, after a general meeting of the county of Inverness, Sir James sent in a proposal to form Volunteer companies. Each company was to have two sergeants, corporals and drummers as well as at least 60 Private men. The arms accoutrements, ammunition and clothing were to be furnished by the Government. The Lord-Lieutenant of Inverness-shire was to recommend the officers, who were to have temporary commissions from the King. They were to receive pay, as were the NCOs and private soldiers. The latter were to have one shilling per day for the days they were at exercise. Training days were to take place twice a week.[3]

Grant's next task was to see what support he had in the county and letters were sent the leading men in each district.[4] One of his correspondents was Colonel John Macleod of Talisker[5] who, after commanding a company for the Hanoverians in the '45, had served in the Scots Brigade in Dutch Service. Talisker was overwhelmed to be consulted and on 15 July wrote to Sir James from Gesto in Skye:

Your letter received & answered by last post has not only increased my vanity in being nominated your Lieutenant Depute for a district of this Island, but has likewise awakened in me a principle which has been for many years dormant in me & that is, ambition & which I hope has some foundation that is excisable in my near connection by blood to the Principal, if not all, the landed Proprietors of this & the neighbouring isles of the Hebrides, in whatever County they are Class'd, together with my age & military Rank – which makes me wish to have a principal command under you.

Grant had evidently asked Talisker to let him have a list of the proprietors in his district for he continues:

I imagine you meant either real Proprietors or feuars, & I complied w'it under that idea, but if you want Tacksmen also, you shall have that also, as distinctly as I possibly can in my next & as I stand myself at the top of them by being possessed of a Lucrative one on Macleod's Estates, tho' neither proprietor or Feuar ... [6]

On 15 August 1794 Talisker assembled the leading gentlemen in his district of Skye at Struan in Bracadale. They sent an address to the Lord-Lieutenant, which probably sums up the opinion of the majority of Hebrideans at this time:

We the subscribers Hereby declare our firm and unequivocal attachment to our present happy constitution as established in King, Lords and Commons, and that we abhor and detest all leveling and Republican principles tending to subvert the same and which can only lead to anarchy and confusion, the overthrow of all regular Government and the consequent annihilation of the happiness of all orders of people and therefore we enroll our names hereto under an engagement to obey the call of the Lord-Lieutenant of the County of Inverness or any of his Deputies at all times for all purpose of repelling all foreign enemies, supporting the established Government and suppressing all riots and tumultuos meeetings of any such should happen tending to disturb the peace and tranquility of the Country.[7]

Members of his own family believed that Talisker's enthusiasm had gone to his head, and, on the same day as the address was signed his brother Professor Roderick Macleod of King's College Old Aberdeen wrote to Sir James Grant to say that:

Talisker's letter requires some apology. I need hardly inform you that since a very severe fit of Ague, which he had in Holland above twenty years ago, he has *since that time* [been] subject to high and low spirits. Thank God they do not continue very long & you have seen him in good health & I hope in time [will] recover it again. The distress of Macleod's affairs & the unhappy line he has taken in Politics affected him & depressed his spirits & the knowledge you was so good as to confer on him of making him one of your deputies has now given him the reverse turn & he is continuously writing long letters & moving about which for his age and Clumsiness ... he is very unfit for ... as he is now in the 76th year of his age.[8]

One problem that Talisker foresaw was the Small Isles: Eigg, Rum, Muck and Canna. They were geographically part of Skye. However, when Lord Lorne obtained superiority of part of Maclean of

Coll's property in 1635, Rum and Muck were incorporated into the Sheriffdom of Argyll. Despite Talisker's reputed senility he appreciated that militarily they should be in Inverness-shire and in his reply to Grant's original letter he had written:

> some of the Small Islands adjacent to us [i.e. Skye] are in our County of Inverness as I wish Rum and Isle of Monk likewise were, which are now attached to the County of Argyle ever since the good family of Argyle got possession of the Maclean Esates, as they are yet ... Rum which belongs to my Nephew Mr Maclean of Coll & the Island of Monk would have belonged to another Nephew of mine had my second sister produced a son.[9]

On 13 September 1794 Talisker, in his letter to Sir James Grant, continued on the same theme:

> I humbly think that our neighbouring islands such as Eigg, Rum, Canna & Isle of Monk, all of which except Eigg are in the County of Argyle ... might be added to the district, which Clanranald is your deputy as Canna & Eigg are his property & Rum my nephew the Laird of Coll's property as is the Isle of Monk in some shape.[10]

Talisker thought that Coll's 'good nature & known attachment to Government, he being one of Lord Breadalbane's majors to his Fencible Regiment,' would lead him to accept such a plan as it would not 'detach his property from that County [i.e. Argyll] tho I know even that would not offend him were it added to our County as then he would have a sufficient qualification to enable him to a vote at the Election of Inverness-shire'. It would also make military sense, as Coll 'is located at a distance for the defence of Rum & Isle Monk'.[11]

There were at this time no regular soldiers north of the Great Glen. Those nearest to Skye were stationed at Fort George, Fort Augustus and Fort William. The Royal Navy was also absent from Hebridean waters. If the Islanders did not defend themselves nobody else would. Sir James had therefore written to the Home Secretary to say that the County of Inverness would raise 'as many companies of Volunteer Infantry as are necessary for the internal defence of the County & town.' The Home Secretary, the Duke of Portland replied that the King entirely approved of these measures.[12]

The Government's original plan for local defence in Scotland was to raise a militia. However, they quickly realised that there was little enthusiasm for one and wisely decided to move slowly. It was not until the panic that followed the threat of a French invasion in 1797 that Dundas felt able to push a Scottish militia bill through parliament.[13]

The difference between militia and volunteer units was that the militia was compulsory. Parishes were given a quota of men to provide. Their first task was to produce lists of fit young men of the appropriate age. The quota to be provided would then be selected by ballot. In the event of the balloted man being unwilling to serve he was allowed to find a substitute, or pay a fine of £20. When the average national income was £4 per annum, this was an immense sum, and the Militia was universally unpopular in Scotland. Wholesale rioting followed in the Lowlands in August and September 1797. The men chosen to draw up lists were threatened and in a few cases tenants defied their landlords.[14]

* * *

Among those written to by Sir James Grant in 1794 was Mr Donald Maclean, Minister of the Small Isles. As we have seen, he was now resident in Eigg, which was the one island in his parish that was included in the County of Inverness. Mr Donald therefore convened a meeting of the residents of the island and obtained the signatures of the 101 men prepared to be enrolled as volunteers.[15] No notice appears to have been taken of his letter by the Lieutenancy at this time and it was not until the threat of invasion in 1797 that any attempt was made to take up the people of Eigg's proposal to volunteer. Mr Donald's offer was, however, preceded by one from Macdonald of Morar, who proposed to raise a company from the men of both Morar and Eigg.

The Macdonalds of Morar, who were known as *Clann Mac Dhughail*, descend from a chief of Clanranald who had been deposed and then murdered circa 1520.[16] In 1797 their lands, which had once stretched some fourteen miles from the head of Loch Morar to the sea, were concentrated around Glen Meoble in South Morar. Their chief was Lieutenant John Macdonald, who had been out in the '45 but had returned home before the end of the rising.[17] He had then served in the British Army in Canada in the Seven Years War and in the War of American Independence.[18]

Morar had owned two farms in Eigg, which in 1773 he sold for £1,070 to Clanranald. Morar had also rented two other farms on the island, Galmisdale and Sandevore, which reverted to Clanranald at the same time.[19] In 1797 Colin Macdonald, Morar's kinsman, held the former in tack, and when on 10 February the King accepted Morar's offer to raise an additional company of volunteers 'on the West Internal Coasts',[20] Lieutenant John appointed his kinsman as his lieutenant. He then ordered him to raise 25 men in Eigg. This step provoked a rapid response from Mr Donald who on 28 March wrote to Sir James Grant. He first sets the scene. 'My Lord', he writes:

> This island of Eigg, the property of Mr McDonald of Clanranald is wholly occupied by Eight tacksmen[21] with their workmen, servants and cottars &c. It contains about 400 souls. At the enrollment formerly ordered by your Lordship and which, directed by the Depute Lieutenant of the District, I had the honour to conduct, all the inhabitants to a man, who were able to carry arms gave proof of their Loyalty and attachment to our happy constitution, by cheerfully enrolling their names when required.

He went on in a style no doubt gleaned at Divinity Hall:

> I may warrantably say that the same spirit of loyalty and attachment still prevails; nay, if possible has acquired additional strength in the Breasts of those inhabitants. Permitt me, my Lord, to say that they are worthy of arms, & that they earnestly sollicit your Lordship inter position, and order speedily to procure them arms. Your Lordship knows our detached local situation, our naked & defenceless condition, & that a hundred of armed enemies, would overrun the whole island & carry on Violence and Devastation at will. In addition to the hardships of our situation should we be attacked by an enemy, we have no regular mode of conveyance to communicate our distress to those in power; as we have not been able to obtain the Establishment of a Post Office at Arisaig, tho repeatedly sollicited.

Having set the scene he now goes to the point of the letter. 'We know', he writes

> that, by some unaccountable manoeuvre, Mr McDonald Morar has got letters of service to raise a company of sixty volunteers betwixt Morar & this island of which Twenty five are to be

raised here. This place my Lord, may answer [dis]parate views, but can by no means answer the purpose of Defence, especially at a time when an inveterate and unrelenting Foe were determined to invade our land & deprive us of the invaluable Blessings & privileges secured to us, as subjects of the British Constitution. This island, my Lord, should have a company of volunteers within itself – We can muster about Eighty good men, at least, including the twenty five formerly mentioned, on this island – and we request you with the greatest earnestness that your lordship will procure for us, with all possible speed, arms &c for self-defence; for aiding, as may be in our power, our fellow subjects in the neighbourhood, if molested; and contributing what we can to the protection and security of our countrey, should an actual invasion take place. By this application, we will not interfere with any Gentleman's views & interest. The Public good is our ruling motive.

He has no wish he says to deprive Morar of his command and adds that 'Morar should have a full company on the opposite coast'. He suggests that the 'Lieutenant appointed by him in this island may be continued in that station in the company in view for this'.

He now comes to the crunch. 'If your Lordship think it consistent with my function, I deem it an honour to serve in so good a cause, and your Lordship may command my service'. On the face of it, it was an extraordinary suggestion that a serving minister of the Church of Scotland should offer to serve in an armed body of men was amazing enough. But these were not ordinary times and a few months later, when writing of the preparations being made to repel the threatened French invasion, the Rev. James Macdonald was able to write to KA Böttiger in Weimar: 'You may conceive what a military spirit pervades us, when I assure you that old men past 60 and even 70 have falsified their baptism registers, and called themselves ten years younger in order to be permitted to carry arms; and many of our clergymen are officers of volunteers, and upon actual service every day but Sunday'.[22]

It can hardly be supposed that coming, as he did, from a long line of soldiers Mr Donald was going to miss the opportunity to be one himself. He was quite prepared to step down from the pulpit for the parade ground, despite the criticism such an action would and did provoke. As we shall see what has been called the 'religious avalanche' was about to descend on the Hebrides, and such Erastian behaviour as Mr Donald's was going to attract adverse comment.

On this occasion Mr Donald did not press his appointment. 'Otherwise', he writes 'permit me to recommend to your Lordship Mr Donald McAskill, son of my predecessor in office, a young man of Parts activity & intrepidity, as a proper person to command.' He adds that 'Colin McDonald Tacksman of Galmisdale is the Lieutenant already appointed on this island by Morar – other subalterns may easily got among us, such as Lachlan McKinnon Tacksman of Holoun [Howlin], John McDonald Tacksman of Cliadale – Angus McDonald younger of Laig &c'.

Mr Donald finally comments that 'This letter has been addressed to your Lordship with the particular consent & by appointment of the Tacksmen'. It was later to be said that it was the last time that Mr Donald would consult the tacksmen of Eigg on any subject concerning the military.

Sir James must now have been in something of a dilemma. On 3 April 1794 Henry Dundas had written from Whitehall to his nephew the Lord Advocate to say that the King had received an address from a numerous meeting of the Roman Catholic gentlemen in Scotland, and also their proposal to raise a regiment for HM's service'. HM views with much approbation this proof of loyalty and attachment.'[23]

As recently as 1791 Roman Catholics had been forbidden to hold commissions in the British Army. However, now that the French Revolutionary authorities were increasingly anti-Roman Catholic, British Roman Catholics were no longer prepared to serve in the predominantly Irish regiments in French service.[24] Prince Charles Edward Stuart had died in 1788 and even the most ardent Jacobite now wished to defend Great Britain against France. King George III was keen to encourage Roman Catholics to raise regiments. On the other hand he could not afford to alienate the Protestants, which he would do if he showed too much favour to Roman Catholics.

Morar rapidly heard what was afoot and on 31 March 1797 wrote again to Sir James:

> I have now further to acquaint you that one of my Lieutenants Mr Colin McDonald lives in the Island of Egg distance from the mainland about Eight miles to which a Boat can row or sail in about an hour's time. Twenty five of my men are also there who were meant to be under his command learning to Exercise near their homes except when he & them might be call'd occasionally out to join the main body or when the service might require them to serve under my command elsewhere.

Lieutenant John was being somewhat economical with the truth about the time taken to travel from Eigg to Arisaig. He goes on to say.

> Mr McDonald and these Twenty five men have been engaged with me so far back as 20 December last – I understand now that the other inhabitants of that island begin to make a motion of Raising a company within themselves on the island distinct from mine or any other division on the mainland. Should this offer be approved of, my losing such a proportion of the men I engaged so early and depended on you may naturally conceive be attended with material inconvenience to me. I wish, however, to suggest in the event of my being deprived of these men by the late offer from the island being accepted that you may be pleased to appoint the said Mr Colin McDonald to command the company or such Body of men as shall be enrold on the island – this I think he is entitled to as well on account of his activity in inroling the Twenty five men alluded as for his former services to his King, and Country, for altho' he had not the good fortune of getting a commission he served as a volunteer in one of his Majesty's marching Regiments many years ago, a claim to which no other of the Gentlemen can pretend to and he is well qualified to command as any in Egg – I also beg leave to suggest and recommend Mr Angus McDonald and Donald McAskill both in Egg as proper Persons to be appointed Lieutenants in Colin McDonald's company in the event the plan meets your approbation.[25]

Morar's foreboding that Mr Donald's offer to raise a company in Eigg would be accepted proved to be correct. Sir James agreed to recommend that an independent Eigg company should be raised and on 4 May he asked Mr Donald, Morar and Dalilea for their advice if the company were established of the name of its commanding officer. Mr Donald replied on 18 May 1797. 'My opinion upon this head', he wrote:

> I took the liberty of communicating to your Lordship already – and my reasons being s[?], I find no course now to deviate from what I then suggested Mr MacAskill being a young man of ability, popularity & influence and actuated by no party spirit, I then thought him & still do

think him the properest person to command in this island – I therefore recommend him to your Lordship without the least solicitation of his own, indeed without his knowing that I applied for him.

What he did not mention was that Donald Macaskill's mother was a daughter, presumably an illegitimate one, of Hugh Maclean of Coll.[26] Family loyalty clan rivalry and religion were all tied up in the struggle for pre-emininence in Eigg. Mr Donald continues:

Colin McDonald may be a very good man, but I have reason to be persuaded that he shall not be equally agreeable to the inhabitants in general as Commanding Offficer – Besides my Lord, it may appear odd, that the whole armed force established here and in the neighbourhood, should be *commanded* by officers all of the Romish faith.

This was the telling reason. The penal laws against Roman Catholics may have been lifted in 1793[27] but it was only thirteen years since the Gordon Riots, and there was still a distinct anti-Roman Catholic bias in Scotland, and at Court. William Pitt the younger was later to resign as Prime Minister over George III's refusal, as he saw it, to betray his Coronation Oath and admit Roman Catholics into a Parliament.[28] If there had been no other candidates for commissions than Roman Catholics, Sir James would probably appointed them to command, but as there was a Protestant candidate he could hardly be passed over.

Morar's influence in Eigg was on the wane. Mr Donald goes on to exclaim:

As for Morar's interference with this island we are astonished at it – He has no interest therein: with us he has no manner of business; his Controul is a mere ostentatious [–?–]. Indeed I find his character to be that of a busy meddler – and [–?–] early informed that he would be ready to adopt some measures for frustrating our plan, or directing it, if possible, to selfish authority, he ought to exercise it where it will be admitted. The gentlemen here will not be dupes to his little policy – Colin Macdonald is of his family – That family connection and selfish views must have been the Gr[–?–] of his intermedelling at all in the affairs of this island – Such gentlemen of this island as have conversed with me on this subject declare their feelings hurt at Morar's interference – and I believe it is their case in general. I begin to fear it may hurt the service that Morar has any concern in the Direction of our plan – My opinion therefore is decidely that Mr Donald McAskill should be Commanding Officer here, Colin McDonald first Lieutenant & Angus McDonald younger of Laig 2nd Lieutenant ...

On 4 May the Home Secretary obtained the King's agreement to Sir James's proposal to form an additional company of volunteers in the Island of Eigg. He also got approval for the 25 men living in Eigg who were in Morar Company to be transferred to the Eigg Company. Recruiting could now go ahead and on 12 June 1797 Donald Macaskill was able to report to Sir James Grant that he had engaged 2 sergeants, 2 corporals, 2 drummers and 40 private soldiers. The latter included Mr Donald's eldest son Alexander. He was a boy of fifteen.

Mr Donald's success in getting the nomination of the officers in the Eigg Company was bitterly resented by those tacksmen who had not been included. On 17 July four of them[29] complained to Sir James:

We find it necessary to acquaint your Lordship that Mr McLean Minister of this Parish has been impowered by the several Tacksmen in this Island to correspond in their name with your Lordship in order to procure an order for raising a Volunteer Company for the defence of this Island. How faithfully Mr Maclean wanted that trust the sequel will show – The Correspondence was concealed by Mr Maclean with the utmost Caution excepting your Lordship's answer to his first letter which we all saw, until the Gentlemen recommended by him were appointed officers. These Gentlemen were pointed out by Mr Maclean from interested views, nor was it with the approbation or knowledge of any of the gentlemen of the Island that they were recommended, nor is this the only thing that Mr Maclean has done since his admission to this Parish that has been disagreeable to the inhabitants in general from which you may infer that he has not the smallest influence over any individual in the Island (excepting three cottagers servants of his) and even those if they could procure a footing anywhere else would wish to change their situation – Our reason for troubling your Lordship with this letter is only to convince you of the irr[on]eous line of conduct Mr Maclean has followed unbecoming a Person of his Profession from time to time.

Sir James's reply, if he ever sent one, has not survived. Donald Macaskill, who was now firmly in command of the company took up cudgels with Morar. On 18 July 1797 he wrote to Sir James:

Sir, In consequence of your favor to the reverend Mr Maclean intimating that their was a company of volunteers to be raised in this Island of which I was to be appointed Captain & that the 25 men stationed here, part of Captain McDonald's Morar Company, were to be attached to the Eigg Corps. I acquainted Lieutenant Collin McDonald that this was his majesty's pleasure that he and the 25 men he commanded should join the company to be raised in the island he instantly wrote Captain McDonald Morar who returned a verbal message that he [Lieutenant McDonald] was not to obey my orders but such as he received from him & to continue as he was. Captain McDonald denys having received any notice of this alteration in his corps – in the meantime I called together such of the inhabitants as I thought best qualified to serve his majesty at this time 40 very good men enroll'd their names in one day agreeable to the tenor of your letter.

He continues:

I understand Captain McDonald is making every exertion to retain the 25 men as formerly in his corps which will never answer Equally convenient for the men, Morar being about 12 miles by sea distant from Eigg & being also in a different district – there are 7 of my servants included in the 25 men who as they are once made over to the Eigg company will not nor in any other tho they shall cheerfully follow me whenever I may be ordered. There are a few more of the same disposition on the island [We] will not compleat a company of 60 without the 25.

I have engaged a clever young man (while he remains in the country) a sergeant in the Inverness Fencibles to drill the men & non-commissioned officers – at the same time I shall be at a great loss how to act untill I receive your further orders. Please let me know the compliment of Each company and if it is necessary to return the name height & age of each volunteer.[30]

On the same day he wrote a second letter to the Lord-Lieutenant saying:

I cannot conceive what loss Lieutenant Collin McDonald could suffer from his being detached from the Morar Company as neither officer or men has got any cloathing yet, particularly when I told him from first that I would take the same uniform & accoutrements to accommodate him... There are three more volunteers in Lieutenant McDonald's party that wishes to get into the Eigg Company. I am afraid they will object to their being continued in the Morar Company.

Sir James had in May endeavoured to pacify matters by agreeing that Lieutenant Colin Macdonald should remain with the Morar Company. However, such a decision did not make practical sense, and on the 1 September 797 Captain McDonald of Morar wrote to Sir James to say:

I am happy to have it in my Power to inform you that we have at last prevailed on Lieutenant Colin Macdonald to agree to be attached to the Eigg Company, although with reluctance. I have to acquaint [you] that I have had 15 handsome young men drilled with my company for upwards of three months, over and above my own complement on the mainland, in case Lieutenant Macdonald should be attached to the Eigg Corps as formerly proposed. As these supernumaries have been hitherto at my own expense, I flatter myself that I shall be allowed to appoint another officer in place of Lieutenant Macdonald.

This appears to have been the end of the affair. Lieutenant Colin Macdonald duly appears in *The Army List* from 1798–1800 in the Eigg Volunteer Company, and on 2 October 1797, writing from Whitehall, Portland informs Sir James Grant:

I have the satisfaction to acquaint you that HM has no objection to the detachment of the Morar Company in the Island of Eigg being transferred to the Eigg Company – when I shall receive your recommendation of a gentleman to succeed Lieutenant Colin Macdonald in the Morar Company I will lose no time in taking the necessary steps for HM's Pleasure being received respecting him.[31]

It may have been the end of the argument over the 25 men from Eigg, but it was not the end of the complaints, and on 7 March 1799 Mr John Macdonald, Claidale in Eigg complained to Sir James. 'My Lord, Having taken the liberty to writ your Lordship of date the 24th December last – respecting the Volunteer Company of this Island & by the character your lordship bears as Lord Lieutenant of this county I expected an answer long ago the contents of the above mentioned letter was as viz':

As Doctor MacAskill who commands the Volunteer company of this island is now settled in Fort William and in the event he is not continued to command and that Mr Maclean Minister of this Parish was not kind enough to make mention of my name in the beginning of the Volunteer business I think I have a right to expect that appointment...

Now *My Lord* whether Doctor MacAskill is, or not to be continued I know not, but one thing I know by experience that I am very ill used from the very first outsett of this affair, because in the first place when all the Gentlemen (Tacksmen) in this island in one meeting, consented that Mr Maclean, Minister of this island would correspond with your Lordship to procure a company of volunteers for our defence.

In the second place, I doubt not, but Mr Maclean would be sincere, and that, like every volunteering business, the officers would be chosen by the votes of the volunteers who were to serve in the place, and of course, that Justice would have taken place every honest man had his chance.

In the fourth place I say that Mr Maclean took upon himself, what he had no right, by being too busy in recommending his own favourites to your lordship, and never told me any part of the correspondence he carried on with your lordship till Captain MacAskill came to call for my men; other wise I might have made interest with my own friends.

However, knowing that the Volunteer corps could not be completed without my servants, labourers and cottars & seeing the men daring threats of our enemies, I consent they should accept of Arms & cloaths during my pleasure only which is now ... two years and of course [I have] suffered a deal of inconvenience by it; therefore, cannot up any account without the smallest benefit in return dispense with the service of my servants, labourers & cottars, two days in every week which your lordship may see is a third of a whole year – My whole dependence is my farm. I have no earthly thing to live by, but my ffarm which will require proper attention so that the service of tennants [?] servants, labourers & cottars, two days in the week is very considerable to me as a poor ffermer.

The above *my Lord* are partly [?] my grievance & I would not wish to trouble your Lordship with any more, providing these are heard and a reply sent me in course ...

Whether or not the Lord Lieutenant replied to Cleadle is not known. There can, however, be little doubt who Sir James sided with in the dispute, for on 16 April 1799 the Duke of Portland wrote to him to say that he had laid his letter of 8 April to Henry Dundas before the King recommending Captain Donald Macaskill and the Rev. Donald Maclean to be Deputy Lieutenants of the county of Inverness. He goes on to say: 'I have the satisfaction to acquaint you that HM does not disapprove thereof'.[32]

In 1794 it had been agreed that the Lord-Lieutenant of each county should appoint a certain number of Deputy Lieutenants who were to have charge of a district. They were to be 'Persons of Estate & Character resident in such district'.[33] It is a reflection his personal qualities and on the prestige of the ministry in the Islands that Mr Donald could obtain such an appointment.

Notes

1. *Scottish County Government*, 95.
2. Ronald M Sunter 'Raising the 97th (Inverness-shire) Highland Regiment of Foot', *JSAHR*, vol. 76, No. 306 (Summer 1998), 93–110.
3. NAS. GD248. 28. 4. 40.
4. Some parts of Scotland had begun to form themselves into defensive bodies even before the Lord-Lieutenants received their warrants [JE Cookson *The British Armed Nation* (1997), 138]. This does not appear to have happened in Skye.
5. Norman Macleod of Macleod had written 'to ask Dundas *in justice* to testify that in spite of political differences his ardour, zeal and fidelity may be relied on. His application was fruitless and Sir James's offer to raise a Volunteer Regiment in the Inverness-shire islands was accepted, initially with companies in Skye, Harris, South Uist, Benbecula and Barra [IF Grant *The Macleods* (1959), 530].
6. NAS. GD248. 29. 2. 88; He had originally had his tack rent free but when Macleod of Macleod got into financial difficulties he agreed to pay him 1000 guineas for it 'with which I am tolerably contented' [NAS. GD248. 29. 2. 9]

7. NAS. GD248. 28. 5.
8. NAS. GD248. 29. 2. 20.
9. NAS. GD248. 29. 2. 9.
10. Nas. GD248. 29. 2. 9.
11. NAS. GD248. 42. 43.
12. TNA. HO103. 158.
13. *Scottish County Government*, 97.
14. *Scottish County Government*, 97–8.
15. NAS. GD248. 29. 1. They included James Watt, the schoolmaster, Lachlan Mackinnon Tacksman of Holoun [Howlin], Anthony McDonald the Roman Catholic priest on the island, Hugh Macdonald Tacksman of Sandavore, Colin Macdonald Tacksman of Galmisdale, John Macdonald Tacksman of Claide [Cleadle], Ronald Macdonald Tacksman of Five Pennies, Ronald Macdonald of Laig [the son of the poet Alasdair MacMhaigster Alasdair], Angus Macdonald, younger of Laig & Donald MacAskill Tacksman of Keildonan.
16. *Clan Donald*, 289.
17. Alasdair Roberts 'MacDonalds losing Meoble'. I have to thank the author for a copy of this unpublished paper.
18. NAS. GD248. 656. 6.
19. C Fraser Mackintosh 'The MacDonalds of Morar, styled *Mac Dhugail*' *TGSI*, vol. XV (1889), 63–75.
20. TNA. HO103.2. 118.
21. In 1798 they were: *Rent*.
    1. Kildonan. Dr Donald MacAskill and his mother £65.0s.0d.
    2. Howlin. Lachlan Mackinnon £40.0s.0d.
    3. Sandavore. Hugh Madonald, changekeeper £21.5s.0d.
    4. The Change House. ditto £4.0s.0d.
    5. Howlin. Ranald Macdonald. £25.0s.0d.
    6. Laig. Ranald Macdonald. £41.8s.9d.
    7. Galmisdale. Colin Macdonald. £42.10s.0d.
    8. Gruline. Colin Macdonald as sub-tenant of Lieutenant Fraser's heirs. £11.11s.6d.
    9. Cleadle. John Macdonald. £85.10s.0d.
    10. Sandabeg. Rev. Donald Maclean. £8.0s.0d.
    [Charles Fraser-Macintosh *Antiquarian Notes* (1897), 261–2]
22. A Gillies *A Hebridean in Goethe's Weimar* (1969), 51.
23. TNA. HO103. 122.
24. Ravenhill 'The Hon. RE Clifford (1788–1817) Officer in Dillon's Regiment. *JSAHR*, vol. 69 (Summer 1991), 298.
25. NAS. GD248. 694.
26. 'The Mackaskills of Rudha 'n Dùnain', *Clan Macleod Magazine* (1951), vol. ii, no. 17, 25. She is not mentioned in the Maclean of Coll family Bible.
27. *Dundas Despotism*, 176.
28. *The Younger Pitt* vol. 3, 498–501.
29. They were Lachlan Mackinnon Tacksman of Howlin, John Macdonald Tacksman of Cleadale, Colin Macdonald Tacksman of Galmisdale, Hugh Macdonald Tacksman of Sandavore [NAS. GD248. 192. 3. 38].
30. NAS. GD248. 658. 5.
31. TNA. HO103. 2. 337.
32. TNA. HO103. 3. 50.
33. NLS. Melville Papers. MS 6, 101.

Chapter Twenty-Nine

The Argyllshire Volunteers

The appointment of Lords Lieutenant, on occasions, clashed with previous perceived hereditary rights. For instance the Duke of Argyll on accepting his post wrote to Henry Dundas to point out that: 'It is to be observed that my acceptance of this warrant, does not infer any prejudice to the right I am thought to possess, of being Hereditary Lord Lieutenant of the Shire of Argyll'.[1]

The Duke was one of the first to send in a Sketch Plan for arming & defending the County of Argyll. It was necessary he wrote:

> First to form a company of Volunteers from the inhabitants within the town and Parish of Inveraray to consist of:
>
> One Captain
> 2 Lieutenants
> 2 Sergeants
> 2 Corporals
> 1 Drummer
> 50 Private Men at least to be armed with Firelocks. The officers to be recommended by the Lord-Lieutenant and to have Commissions from him.
>
> To assemble one day in each week to practise.
> To have cloaths from the money raised in the County by Voluntary Subscription that they may be all Uniform.
>
> The Sergeants, Corporals and Drummer to have constant pay from the same fund and to be employed in looking after the arms and accoutrements, and in training such of the volunteers as chuse to assemble for exercise more than once a week as after as designed.

* * *

The Duke of Argyll's original suggestion was for just four companies of volunteers in Argyllshire to be funded and equipped by local subscription. It had not turned out as he had planned. Pay had come from the government, as had the men's uniforms and equipment.[2] There was also a need for far more companies than the four envisaged by the Duke. This was certainly the case after the invasion scare in 1797.

Additional companies plus the original four were formed into a battalion of Argyllshire Volunteers under the command of Humphry Graham the Duke's chamberlain at Inveraray. In April 1797, during the threat of French invasion, when the question of raising volunteers had first arisen, Alexander Maclean of Coll, as we have seen, had been scathing about their positioning and had written to his Colonel the Earl of Breadalbane to say that:

> Before I left the country above 200 of my people had entered volunteers upon the conditions I had the honor of mentioning to your lordship – but the volunteer plan seems to be for the most part given up, although I observe my companys accepted of in places where it is impossible they can ever be of any use.[3]

The first of the three companies raised on the Coll estate was in Coll itself. Allan Maclean of Crossapol was appointed to command it. Both his lieutenant and ensign were his brothers-in-law Coll's bailie Alexander Maclean, and Charles Maclean, who at this time kept a shop in Arinagour. The drill sergeant, who received permanent pay, was Crossapol's cousin Hugh Maclean in Fiosgaradh.[4] As we have seen, he had been a sergeant in the Breadalbane Fencibles before being discharged at his father's request[5] in exchange for his younger brother Alexander.

Alexander had served as a private soldier in Captain Gray's Company. He then transferred to Captain John Cameron's Company on his promotion to corporal.[6] He was still a corporal when the battalion was disbanded.[7] He then returned home to Coll, where he became second sergeant in the Coll Company,[8] replacing Sergeant Allan Maclean, who is probably the eldest of Fiosgaradh's sons. Allan replaced Sergeant Hugh as the sergeant on permanent duty in July 1799.[9] This left a place for the promotion of Corporal Angus MacPhaden to be the third sergeant in the Coll Company.

It is clear from these appointments that in the late eighteenth century the descendants of Coll's bodyguard in 1679 and 1716 still dominated the military establishment on Coll and that the military ethos of the clan lived on. The Coll Company was not the only unit on Maclean of Coll's estate to do so.

The second company to be formed on Coll's estate was the Isle of Rum Company. It was, according to Alexander Maclean of Coll, 'an exceeding good Company'.[10] As we have seen, although the island was geographically in Inverness-shire it was politically in Argyll. Alexander of Coll nominated Captain Donald Maclean to command the Rum Company. He is none other than Mr Donald Maclean the Minister of the Small Isles, who having failed to get command of the Eigg Company, was now not only responsible for their spiritual welfare of the people in Rum, but was also their military commander.

Donald, like his younger brother in Coll, rapidly raised a company of 60 men.[11] He also chose Macleans as his lieutenant and ensign. Both were his cousins. One, Allan Maclean of Kinlochscrisort, was Coll's factor in Rum. The other was Alexander the son of the tacksman of Guirdal, both were descendants of a younger son Neil Og of Crossapol who was in the garrison of Breacachadh Castle in 1679. The drill sergeant was an unidentified Donald Maclean.

Sometime after 16 January 1798 a third company was formed on Coll's estate. This was at Quinish in Mull. The company commander was Allan Maclean, a half-pay ensign in the 73rd Regiment of Foot. He is the 'red haired doctor of the warm eyes', who had served under Alexander Maclean of Coll in both the Western and Breadalbane Fencibles. The lieutenant Lauchlan Maclean is unidentified,[12] whilst the ensign Charles Morison was the son of Hector Morison in Auchnasaul, whose family served Coll as ground officers in Quinish.[13] The drill sergeant, Donald Morison, was his brother.[14]

What is particularly interesting in these lists of junior officers and senior NCOs is how closely they were related. The strict demarcation between officers and other ranks that was to be such a feature of the late Victorian army was far less pronounced at the beginning of the century. It is also perhaps significant that in the pay lists submitted to the War Office, from which these lists have been compiled, the men are listed in alphabetical order by their forenames and not their surnames. This suggests that this is how the company commander, who wrote up the lists, identified them is hardly surprising as the officers will have known their men all their lives.

* * *

One family in Coll, the 'old Barbreck' Campbells in Cornaig and Caolis, are significantly not listed amongst those who served in the Coll Company of volunteers. Their omission gives another insight into Alexander Maclean of Coll's character.

The three Campbell brothers Malcolm, Murdoch and Neil appear in the 1776 catechist's list as the 'over age' sons of Donald Campbell in Toraston.[15] Their father was then employing three servants and had three other families, who are probably cottars, living beside him at Toraston. Donald is therefore probably one of those 'tenants below the rank of tacksmen', described by Johnson as having 'smaller tenants under them'.[16] The similarity of their forenames and their family tradition that they were descended from the 'old Barbreck Campbells' suggests that they also descend from *Murdo tollick alias Campbell* who served as a members of Coll's bodyguard in 1679.[17]

The Campbells in Toraston were ambitious. In August 1786 the eldest brother Malcolm made a bid for the Two Ends of Coll. He offered to pay double the rent paid by the current tacksman Donald Maclean of Cornaig. This bid was turned down, perhaps because the Duke of Argyll did not believe Malcolm could afford to pay it.

Malcolm Campbell is said to have made money in Liverpool and in October 1786 he offered to pay £66 for the west end of the island alone, despite the fact that it was 'most inconvenient in different respects, for the Cattle reared there never will answer for any mercat and the possession itself affords no peats or other fewell but what is brought at a distance of 5 miles to it from Freslan by water carriage, which inconvenience puts it out of the power of any person to afford more rent for it'.

This bid was accepted and it was agreed that the tenant was 'to have peats from the farm of Freslan ... on the condition that if the present tacksman [i.e. Donald Maclean of Cornaig] or some other does not bargain with me for the east end of Coll, this Petitioner if I chuse it must take it also at £84 Str yearly Rent'.[18]

As part of their tack of Caolis and Gunna the Campbell brothers had the privilege of running a passenger ferry between Tiree and Coll. They also had to pay the cess, teinds, minister's stipend, schoolmaster's salary, road money and other public burdens. They had the right to obtain timber from the Duke's woods in Mull and Morvern and cut peat in Freslan. They were also bound to attend the Duke's baron bailie courts in Coll.[19]

As has already been noticed after Donald of Cornaig's death, Alexander Maclean of Coll appealed to the Duke to allow Donald's widow to continue in Cornaig, and the Duke agreed, provided that she remained 'during my pleasure'.[20] The Duke's pleasure ran out in 1798 and the Campbell brothers obtained the remaining ten years of Cornaig's tack. They did so for £120 Sterling.[21]

This move evidently infuriated Alexander Maclean of Coll. As we have seen, Donald of Cornaig and his brother Hector Maclean of the Isle of Muck had resolved to *go the length of their tether* rather than let a Campbell into Coll.[22] It was a decision that had probably helped ruin their family. Now, despite all their efforts, not only had a Campbell obtained land in Coll, outwith the Coll estate but the family had previously been counted among Coll's followers.

Not long after Malcolm Campbell moved to Cornaig, HMS *Caesar*, 84 guns was cruising in the Hebrides when she got into difficulties in a violent storm off Sorisdale. The inhabitants of the East End of Coll thinking that she was a French ship merely watched and did nothing to help, and although the ship's boats attempted to get ashore in the raging surf they failed to do so as no one would point out a safe harbour. Finally the *Caesar* 'still firing minute guns' was blown past Cornaig.

When Malcolm Campbell saw her he said that he did not care if she was a friend or foe. He would try and save her and taking out his own boat with a few of his people he managed to board the Royal Navy vessel and piloted her to Tobermory. Once they were safe the captain gave a great party to his rescuers, which lasted for nearly a week. Malcolm refused any financial reward for his bravery. The captain reported his action to the Admiralty who sent him an inscribed silver urn and a letter saying that 'if at any time he or his descendants should apply for a position under the government it would be granted'.[23]

* * *

Coll must have had a reputation for giving succour to sailors in distress. At about this time Alexander Maclean of Coll was presented with a silver condiment set inscribed: 'To the Laird of Coll For His Humane Treatment to Ships in Distress Upon His Island From the Merchants of Glasgow.[24]

* * *

Although many Macleans joined the lower deck in the Royal Navy in the late eighteenth century there is no evidence that any came from the Coll estate. Few became commissioned officers.[25] One who did was Neil, son of Hector Maclean of Killean, Tacksman of Ardfinaig in Mull. After she left Coll and moved to Edinburgh, the late Donald Maclean of Cornaig's youngest daughter Ann married Neil.

Neil is always described as 'Neal' in naval records. He entered the Navy in 1793 as an Able Seaman on HMS *Argo*, (Captain Burgess).[26] As he was then 20,[27] he was probably not a 'young gentleman' destined from birth for the 'Quarter-deck'. However, he must have had 'a great deal of experience' to have been rated 'able' i.e. Able Seaman by the small committee representing the ship's departmental heads when the *Argo* was commissioned.[28] Unlike Nelson, who was rated as an Able Seaman on the *Seahorse* twenty years earlier, Neil will have slung his hammock with the men on the lower deck and must have had previous service presumably in the Merchant Navy.

Neil spent 17 months as an Able Seaman. When Captain Hall took command of the *Argo* in February 1795 he made Neil a Midshipman and then Master's Mate. He was now on his way to commissioned rank and dined in the Midshipmen's Mess. Its inhabitants were a mixed bag, and varied greatly in age. The most senior members were the Master's Mates, who might be anything from 14 to 40+, according to whether they were of Quarter-deck status, or merely ex-Lower deck men who had risen to be the Master's assistants in the ordinary way. The most numerous of the occupants were the Midshipmen, whose age group could be equally large, and for just the same reasons. But the proportion of 'Lower Deck' Midshipmen would be a good deal smaller than the proportion of 'Lower Deck' Master's Mates.

As the son of a tacksman, whose father and brothers had served as Army officers,[29] Neil would have been considered a 'gentleman' at home. But was he in England when he joined the Royal Navy? He probably lacked the necessary 'Interest' of a patron in the navy to speed up his career. However, his ability and almost certainly his education stood him in good stead and he kept his rank as Master's Mate when in March 1797 he transferred to the *Ville de Paris* (Captain Grey).

In October 1798 he again changed ships and was made Acting Lieutenant on the *Bellerophon* (Captain Darby). He had now served more than the statutory six years needed before he could be commissioned as a Lieutenant and on 6 May 1800 sat and passed his Lieutenant's Examination.[30]

* * *

In 1798 Alexander Maclean of Coll purchased Freslan and the other farms that mixed with his property in the south-east of Coll from the Duke. The following year the Campbell brothers appealed to Argyll. They claimed that:

> Ever since Mr McLean of Coll made a purchase of part of your Grace's detached property in Coll, the petitioners find him, as he has ever been, particularly inimical to their Interest, as to the necessary improvements on the farm of Coalis. This farm was always in use to be supplied with peats and turf from your Grace's Lands lately sold to Coll. But it is now possessed by four tenants who have begun to improve even that part of the hill and moss from which the Farm of Coalis was ever supplied with feuel preserved by your Grace in the Sale and if they are permitted to go on according to their present plan of improvement, which they do merely with the intention of incommoding the Petitioners who are disagreeably circumstanced and against whom the Laird of Coll as well as well as his Tenants harbour ill will and resentment. The moss will in a few years be exhausted and of course no feuel to be got for Coalis, besides the Petitioners are informed and have good reason to believe that when their right of possession over Coalis and Cornaig shall expire that the Laird of Coll and his adherents, merely to gratify their resentment, will make such an offer for these Lands as will put it out of the power of the petitioners to possess them for these and other reasons... the Petitioners... propose... to take a Lease of the said Lands for 27 years from Whitsunday next, including the 8 years that shall then be unexpired...

On 25 October the Duke agreed to let the brothers have a 19 year lease of the two ends of the island from Whitsunday 1800 – provided that they paid a yearly augmentation of £20.[31] The tack specifically included:

> all and whole 28 acres of moss part of the lands of Freslan... as the same shall be selected in one place and distinguished from the rest of the moss in the said lands by the said Malcolm Campbell whom failing by the Chamberlain of Tiry for the time being... for the purpose and free ingress and egress to and from the said moss and all other privileges necessary for cutting drying and leading away peats from the same.

The rent was now £206.[32] It was a considerable sum of money to be found by former tenants. It was also a dangerous investment for men who had crossed the laird to make in Coll.

The brothers' quarrel with Alexander did not abate, and the Duke seems to have become tired of it, for on 6 November 1802 in his instructions to the chamberlain in Tiree he writes: 'Coll and the tacksmen of Cornaig must settle their disputes themselves for I cannot judge of them at this distance'.[33]

Notes

1. TNA. HO102. 11. 1.
2. This is clear from the muster rolls and pay lists in the National Archives for instance see PRO. WO13. 4169. Part 3.
3. NAS. GD112. 52. 69. 6.
4. TNA. WO13. 4169. Part 3.
5. NAS. GD16. 52. 24. 20; GD112. 52. 555.
6. TNA. WO13. 3810. 25 March 1798.
7. TNA. WO13. 3810. 18 July 1799.
8. TNA. WO13. 4171. Part 4.
9. TNA. WO13. 4170. Part 4.
10. NAS. GD248. 661. 1. 1.
11. They were far better recruited than the Argyllshire Militia. The monthly pay lists and muster rolls of the 'First (or Argyll) Regiment of North British Militia' shows that some companies had as few as 17 men. Among them in Major Robert Campbell's Company for the period 28 June–24 September 1797 was a John Maclean. He could possibly be the tacksman of Gallanach balloted in Coll [PRO. WO13. 51; Argyll & Bute District Council. CO6. 1. 11. 1. Minute Book of the General Court of Lieutenancy, 25 October 1796].
12. He is probably Lachlan Kilmore a descendant of Charles (1679 × 80), 4th son of John of Grishipol (1652 × 79). If this is the right man he was a merchant in Quinish, whose affairs 'having gone into confusion', was unable to pay his bills. [NAS. CS229. Mc. 6. 54. Box308].
13. A 'Charles Morrison from Quinish married Margaret McInnes in Arnabost in Coll' on 29 January 1799 [NAS. CH2. 70. 1]
14. In 1809 he was to marry Janet Rankin, daughter of Neil Rankin Coll's former piper. They were the grandparents of the Mull genealogist & antiquarian Coundullie Rankin Morison.
15. Coll Catechist's list [CH2. 70. 1, 47.
16. *Johnson*, 198–9.
17. 'Hebridean Warriors', 148–9.
18. ICP. Tiree Tacks, 111.
19. ICP. Tiree Tacks, 112.
20. *Argyll Estate Instructions*, 19.
21. ICP. Tiree Tacks, 131.
22. *Boswell*, 269.
23. I have to thank Alison McArthur Campbell, 41 Spring Street, Melbourne for a copy of an article 'A Brave Deed at the Island of Coll' in an undated copy of the *Morning Chronicle*, Halifax, Nova Scotia. It describes the urn as being 'surmounted by a silver anchor and chain, and on one side the following inscription:
    From the Right Honorable the Lords Commissioners of the Admiralty to Mr Malcom Campbell, Cornaig of the Island of Coll. As a mark of their Lordships' sense of Mr Campbell's meritorious zeal and exertions in having on the 29th November 1798 (when no other person would venture to quit the shore) gone off to the assistance of His Majesty's Ship *Caesar*, of 84 guns, commanded by Captain Roddam Home, when driven by stormy weather near that Island, and by whose local knowledge she was safely conducted into Tobermory Bay during the storm.
24. It is now in my possession.

25. Between 1751 and the outbreak of the war with Revolutionary France 100 Macleans died outwith Scotland and had their wills proved by the Commissary Court of Canterbury (which had the responsibility for British subjects dying in Foreign Parts). Although 64 were sailors or marines with the Royal Navy or on the ships belonging to the East India Company, not one was a commissioned officer. [BCP. Notes on wills of all Macleans proved by Canterbury Commissary Court previously held at Somerset House transcribed by NMB from 1966–70].
26. TNA. ADM 107. 24, 347 & ADM 107. 66, 13.
27. *Inhabitants of the Argyll Estate, 1779*, 75. Where it states that he was 6.
28. Michael Lewis *A Social History of the Navy 1793–1815* (1960), 85–6.
29. His father was the representative of the Macleans of Killean, who were descended from the ancient family of Ross who had lost so many men at Inverkeithing. He had served as a Lieutenant in the Fencible Men of Argllshire in the Seven Years War; his eldest brother Donald served in America in the 74th Foot. He remained there in 1783 when the regiment was reduced; the next brother Dugald served as a Lieutenant in Alexander Maclean of Coll's Company in the Western Fencibled in the American War of Independence [NLS. MS 7609, 22; *Army List 1785*, 341; TNA. WO 13. 3963]; his immediate elder brother John served as an Ensign in the 6th West India Regiment & 'fell gloriously storming one of the enemies redoubts in St Domingo in March 1798'. [TNA. WO 25. 3100; WO 42. 31, 327].
30. TNA. ADM 107. 24, 347.
31. ICP. Tiree Tacks, 141.
32. ICP. Tiree tacks, 145.
33. *Argyll Estate Instructions*, 65.

Chapter Thirty

The War Overseas

William Pitt the Younger's ideas on how best to fight the war against the French had echoes of his father's preference during the Seven Years War: overseas expeditions and coastal assaults. It was a policy which had the support of the independent country gentlemen who made up the majority in the House of Commons. Other members of the government believed that France was not going to be defeated outwith Europe. They thought that it was going to be necessary either to fight on the Continent of Europe or pay our allies to do so. This fine balance between maritime and continental interests was never easy to maintain, and in the early years of the war it was the blue water school that had the greatest say.

Although most men from the Coll estate served in the Fencibles or Volunteers during the War with Revolutionary France, some took part in overseas campaigns. Several were stationed in the West Indies. Many died there. Britain poured men into 'those pestilential islands' in the expectation that they could destroy France's economy, only to discover, when it was too late, that they had nearly destroyed the British Army.[1]

In October 1795 Alexander Maclean of Coll's younger brother Major Norman Maclean,[2] 68th Regiment, 'a brave and experienced officer', with a handful of men had defended the port of Gouave in Grenada for four months against the Caribs. He then went down with yellow fever. Four days later he was dead and the rebels overran the fort.[3] His younger brother Roderick, then a lieutenant in Colonel Dillon's Regiment of the Irish Brigade, died the same year on his passage from Jamaica to St Domingo.[4]

Lachlan Maclean of the Isle of Muck's near-do-well eldest son Lieutenant Francis who had been dismissed from the 11th Regiment later joined the Ordnance Department. In 1801 he died in Dominica. Charles, the former sergeant in the Breadalbane Fencible, who became an ensign in 8th West India Regiment, was killed there in the same year.[5] However, not all Collachs in the West Indies died there: Neil Rankin 's second son Hugh served as a corporal with the 47th Foot in Bermuda from 1795 until at least 1799.[6] He returned to the United Kingdom in 1803.

* * *

Life in the West Indies comes alive in the pages of the reminiscences of Maria Nugent, whose husband was from 1801–1805 Governor of Jamaica. Mrs Nugent met everyone of importance in the colony, for sooner or later every white man was to be seen at the Governor's mansion in Spanish Town, either calling on business or sitting down to the huge suffocating dinners which were routine during sessions of the Assembly.[7]

When the Nugents arrived in Jamaica, Britain had been at war with France for eight years, and for four years with France's allies or satellites, Spain and the Netherlands. The struggle was economic as well as military, and both sides attached great importance to the commerce of their West Indian colonies. It was even the opinion of Henry Dundas, the British Secretary for War, that the landing of 15,000 French from a superior fleet in Jamaica would be a greater disaster than their landing in the British Isles; as 'the loss of Jamaica would be complete ruin of our credit'.[8]

* * *

Up until the time of the French Revolution, Saint-Dominque had been the richest of all Caribbean colonies, more productive, it was said, than all the British islands put together. But how could a slave colony continue in business under the banner of Liberty and Equality?

In the early stages of the revolution, whilst the National Assembly in Paris debated the rights of free mulattos, there was skirmishing in Saint-Dominique between whites and mulattos and between white royalists and republicans. Some knowledge of what was happening in France inevitably circulated among the slaves. In May 1791 the French Assembly declared political equality between freeborn men of colour and whites. However, soon after the news of this decree reached Saint-Domique, all other hostilities were merged in the much greater upheaval of a slave rebellion.

The nightmare, which haunted every colonial planter, became sickening reality in Saint-Dominique. Plantations went up in flames, towns were looted, murder was avenged with massacre, everywhere there was atrocity, racial fear and hatred. The Jacobin Government in France, after twelve months of havoc, sent out a Commission, backed by military force, to restore order in the colony. But the troops proved ineffective and in order to crush the resistance of royalist-minded colonists, the Commission proclaimed the abolition of slavery and enlisted the support of the revolting slaves. White colonists fled for refuge in the United States, to Cuba, to Jamaica or to Puerto Rico. A deputation even went to England, where they offered the allegiance of the rebellious French colony to the British Crown. They urged its occupation by British troops.

In September 1793 a small British force from Jamaica landed in the south-west of Saint Dominique, where the French planters still retained some control over their slaves. They occupied the principal points on the west coast without much resistance. But this was the limit of their success. Their numbers were drastically reduced by yellow fever and the reinforcements, which they badly needed had to be used elsewhere, partly to deal with trouble in the Eastern Caribbean, where the French recaptured Guadeloupe. They also had to contain a serious rising of the Maroons in Jamaica. The British in Saint-Domingue hung on miserably for five years, but in 1798, worn down by their losses from disease and the skilful opposition of the Negro General Toussaint, they evacuated the island.[9]

Doctor Hector Maclean, Hugh Maclean, tacksman of Knock in Coll's eldest son served with the British troops in St Domingo.[10] He was later to publish a report on the deaths there from disease. In it he states that he was nearly three years at Port-au-Prince where he had the opportunity to observe the progress and treatment of he army in St Domingo. He describes the astonishing mortality among the troops as: 'a mortality almost unequalled in the annals of war, and which has nearly annihilated our army in that quarter, and rendered them incapable of energy or exertion'.[11]

* * *

The chief protagonist of the idea that the French could be defeated in the West Indies, and by small scale raids on the enemy coast, was Henry Dundas who was now the Secretary of State for War. Pitt's cousin, the Foreign Secretary Lord Grenville, opposed him. Grenville, an aloof aristocrat wrapped up in the mutual admiration society of the Grenvilles, was a statesman of European vision, who loathed the revolutionaries and their 'infernal system of atheism and modern philosophy'.[12] He was also 'something of a scholar by temperament, a good linguist and geographer, a planter of exotic trees, and devoted to the interests of his old university and college. He distrusted the products of other environments, such as Dundas with his Edinburgh degree, his barbarous accent, and his slender grasp of syntax'.[13]

Dundas believed that Britain should fight alone, with no allies, no military commitments in Europe, and no subsidies to pay. Isolation was a popular point of view. However, the loss of life in the West Indies and disastrous events, such as the raid on Ostend in May 1798, undermined his position and strengthened that of Grenville. The latter believed that victories at sea might deter invaders and raise morale among the public, but in the long term isolation offered Britain nothing tangible: it would mean strategic paralysis and the permanent threat of invasion; loss of the initiative and the loss of European markets[14] ... the list is endless. To write off the Continent was impossible. France must be driven back behind its pre-revolutionary borders and the revolutionary regime destroyed. Only then would stability be restored to Europe and with stability would come the markets that were essential to Britain's economic success. Such an eventuality could not be achieved without allies. They had to be paid and would also insist that British troops returned to the mainland of Europe.

The member of the family of Coll most effected by the acceptance of Grenville's policy, and the return of British troops to the Continent, was Coll's youngest brother Hugh. He had originally been commissioned into the 42nd and then transferred to the 49th Foot.[15] In 1799 he took part in the disastrous Anglo-Russian expedition to North Holland.

In July 1799 a British army of 12,000 under the command of Sir Ralph Abercromby landed among the sand-hills of North Holland. The aim of the expedition was the restoration of the House of Orange and the conquest of the Netherlands north of the River Waal, including Amsterdam, Rotterdam and Utrecht.[16]

Although the British were reinforced by another 33,000 men, they were mainly partially trained militia under the command of the Duke of York, as well as 12,000 Russians. The army made little progress. The weather was appalling. The troops had to put up with incessant wind and rain. The North Holland plain, always low and marshy was so soaked by continuous rain that it was impossible for the troops to camp on dry ground, even if there had been transport to get tents to them. The men were also so parched with the wind, and by the salt and sand in it, that they suffered agonies of thirst until the next deluge of rain fell on them.

The Duke of York could claim victory of a sort at *Egmont-op-Zee*. There can, however, be little doubt that the French out-fought British in the sand-hills of North Holland. The reason for this fact was that the French had well trained light infantry, whereas the British had none. Major-General John Moore, who commanded the brigade in which both the 49th and 79th Foot were serving, had himself to drive off French skirmishers with the bayonet as he had no skirmishers of his own. It was a lesson that was not lost on him.

It was apparent that there was a danger of the Allied Army disintegrating. Abercromby and his fellow lieutenant-generals told the Duke of York he must retreat. Since landing the army had fought five considerable actions, which had cost them 9–10,000 men. It was also well known that owing to the state of the roads and winter flooding that military operations were impossible by November.

The Duke of York was forced to leave his wounded behind when he withdrew. The French followed up the British withdrawal but they too were badly affected by the weather and their attacks were driven off. They also got word to the British that the French commander favoured an armistice. The Duke's staff eagerly took up the offer and on 18 November a capitulation was signed. It was agreed that the British were to be evacuated by 30 November, and in exchange 8,000 French and Dutch prisoners of war being held in England were to be released. The British negotiator had secured better terms than he had dared expect. However, the French did not know that the British had only sufficient bread for a further three days and that sickness had reduced numbers in the British Army to 24,000 and in the Russian to 9,000 men.

The Allied Army sailed on time. Bad luck, however, continued to dog the expedition and three warships were lost on the Dutch coast, two of them with all hands, whilst a transport ship was also sunk and only 20 of the 250 on board were saved. Eventually the expedition reached England, where the Russians amazed the inhabitants of Yarmouth by drinking the oil from the street lamps. They were eventually quartered in the Channel Islands.

Although Hugh Coll was among the sick, he was offered promotion to the rank of captain in the 60th Foot. His cousin Colonel Lachlan Maclean,[17] who commanded the 60th was keen to take Hugh with him to the West Indies. The former wrote to Colonel Brownrigg at the Horse Guards to say that Hugh had the money available to purchase a captaincy. The Colonel of the 49th was loath to let him go him and wrote that he 'was sorry to lose him from the Regiment as he is a very active and deserving officer'.[18]

* * *

On the other side of the world in India both the British and Indian armies fought France's allies. In August 1787 Alexander Maclean of Coll's brother Allan returned to the active list as a lieutenant in the 36th (or Herefordshire Regiment of Foot) which, when war broke out was serving in India. They took part in the British attack on Pondicherry, as part of a force of 10,000 men. 4,000 of them were Europeans.[19] Pondicherry surrendered on 22 August 1793 after a siege of twelve days.

Also taking part in the siege was the 72nd Regiment of Highland Foot whose Sergeant-Major was Alexander Maclean of the Balliphetrish family.[20] He then served with the expedition, which invaded Ceylon under the command of Colonel James Stuart of the 72nd who, on 30 July 1795 with the flank companies of the 71st and 73rd, sailed from Madras. Two days later the expedition anchored in a bay to the north of Trincomalee. The Dutch commander refused to hand over the fort and a siege began. On the 26th August the garrison numbering 1,300 men surrendered and Trincomalee, with its magnificent natural harbour, passed into the hands of the British for the loss about seventy men.[21] Three years later Coll's brother Hector, who had been promoted lieutenant-colonel in 1798, was appointed to command the native troops in Ceylon.

The 36th Foot sailed for home at about this time. They were certainly back in England by 1 September 1799, when they were stationed at Cirencester. Allan, who had been promoted a captain on 15 April 1796, is noted as being absent with leave from the Commander-in-Chief. In November when the battalion had moved to Winchester he is said to be sick. Although he remained on the strength of the 36th Foot until 1800 he never rejoined the regiment.[22] He probably returned to Scotland when he returned from India, for in May 1800 he married Jean, daughter of the late Allan Cameron of Glendessary,[23] whose two sisters had married his brothers Alexander and Roderick. She is likely to be the Miss Cameron who in 1796 traveled to India, presumably in pursuit of Allan.[24]

* * *

When Tippoo Sahib came to terms with Cornwallis in 1792, he had ceded half his state to the British and surrendered two of his sons as hostages for his good behaviour. He, however, retained Seringapatam. As Napoleon's power grew, Tippoo, who was far better informed about affairs in Europe than most other Indian princes, began to intrigue with the French.

With a French army in Egypt such contacts could not be tolerated and in the spring of 1799 a large army under the command of General Harris advanced on Seringapatam.

On 5 April the siege began. General Baird, at one time himself a prisoner in Seringapatam, was chosen to command the assault with some 5,000 picked men, including some of the 73rd & 74th Highlanders. Under cover of darkness the assault troops made their way silently forward to the trenches closest to the fort and then waited all the next morning sweltering under the sun as artillery fire screamed over their heads.

At 1 pm Baird gave the order to attack and the assault troops rushed across the Cauvery River and up into the breach. A deadly hail of grapeshot and musket balls tore into their ranks but nothing could stop them. In six minutes they had gained the top of the rampart and drove on against a faltering opposition.

On the second breach, where Tippoo Sahib himself led the defence, the attackers ran into stiffer opposition and even fiercer fire. Twice they charged and twice they were thrown back. Fortunately at the breach itself, a captain of 12th Foot led some men onto the inner rampart. They now overlooked Tippoo's men and were able to fire deadly volleys into the ranks of the closely massed defenders. It was soon all over. The defenders, who had previously put up a staunch resistance, panicked and fled into the ditch. The assailants in a blood lust granted no quarter. Some fired down into the mob below, others leapt into the ditch itself to bayonet and club the fugitives to death. The fugitives in turn fought with each other to escape. It was now that Tippoo fell unnoticed under a mound of dead. As a result of the siege of Seringapatam Southern India was to be effectively pacified for the next 150 years.[25]

Fighting a campaign in India held out the prospect of prize money or plunder. Prize money was collected from the spoils of battle and distributed according to a strict scale. The greatest prizes of all could come from a successful siege. Because Indians traditionally hoarded their wealth in towns, a siege held out the promise of spectacular gains. After the fall of Seringapatam Lord Harris is reputed to have returned to England with £150,000. Somewhat less went to the other besiegers: a colonel received prize-money of £297, a subaltern £52 and a British private soldier £3.15s.9d.[26]

Modern scholarship has shown that the 'annual plunder of Bengal' (to use Edmund Burke's phrase) lasted for a relatively short period and involved few people. But systematic pillage on this scale made an enormous impact at home and acted as a powerful incentive to recruitment for the Indian service, and more than counterbalanced the risks and hazards associated with life in Asia.[27]

The destruction of Tipoo Sahib's power-base in Mysore brought the British face to face with the Mahratta Confederacy and there could be little doubt that, sooner or later, there would a violent struggle between these two powers to decide who should rule India. By the late eighteenth century the Confederacy, founded in the seventeenth century, had dissolved in all but name. Five great princes, who were little better than brigands, had carved out independent realms for themselves, each depending on a vast army of undisciplined cavalry for their muscle, and plunder for their wealth. Although they loathed each other, they were still a force to be reckoned with, especially as inevitably the French were advising the Mahratta princes, and they had hired Europeans to train their men and man their artillery.

In 1800 Coll's brother Hector, who was now commanding the 9th Regiment of Madras Native Infantry was attached to the army under the command of Sir Arthur Wellesley. Wellesley's brother the Marquess Wellesley was Governor-General of India. He saw the Mahratta Confederacy as a threat to the peace and security of the rest of India and decided it must be brought under his control. In doing so he was helped by a civil war within the confederacy in which the Peshwa of Poona had been driven from his capital by one of the other Mahratta princes. The Governor-General proposed to restore the Peshwa on condition that he signed a treaty making him a subsidiary of the British. The Peshwa signed and Wellesley ordered his brother to march north from Mysore and place him on his throne.

The first stage of the campaign was for Arthur Wellesley to march from Mysore to Poona, a journey of some 600 miles. This he accomplished. There followed a second period of intense diplomatic activity and military preparation before, in a series of rapid marches, Wellesley endeavoured to bring about an infantry battle. It was essential for his plan that he should be the attacker. The Mahratta aim was to use their vast superiority both in cavalry and artillery to cut Wellesley off from his supplies, surround him, and then when his army was exhausted annihilate him with their infantry. It was not to be.

Wellesley had learned how not to fight a campaign in 1794, whilst serving in Flanders under the Duke of York. His correspondence gives an impression of immense energy, astonishing attention to detail and above all commonsense. It was essential that his army moved quickly and needed to be self-contained. It must not live off the country if he was to win the 'hearts and minds' of the local population and isolate the Maharatta princes from their people. This meant that his men must be well fed and watered. In order to do so he needed to purchase vast numbers of bullocks, if he was to carry his men's food and equipment. No word occurs so regularly in his correspondence as 'bullocks' and their use was to be the key to his success.

Wellesley's march to Poona at the hottest time of the year was a triumph of organisation. He wrote: 'I never saw the troops look better'. And a few weeks later he was able to say that 'I marched the other day twenty-three miles in seven hours and a half and all our marches are made at the rate of three miles an hour'. This was not just how fast the infantry marched, but included the guns and baggage.

At Assaye on 23 September 1803 Wellesley fought the battle he was looking for. Hector was not present. He was serving under the command of Colonel Stevenson who, with a force similar to that of Wellesley, was advancing on parallel lines to the west. They had not joined together as Wellesley believed that a larger army would be delayed in the narrow defiles along their route.

Once he was in sight of the enemy Wellesley decided that if he waited for Stevenson's force to join him, he would present the Mahrattas with just the opportunity they were looking for. He therefore attacked. Wellesley was to claim that Assaye was the bloodiest battle he ever saw. He lost 25% of his force. Casualties were particularly heavy in his Highland regiments.[28] It was an astonishing victory, which changed the fate of India. Until Assaye it was by no means certain that the British would triumph in India. After the battle the British developed a new self-confidence, and an arrogance that was to lead to their undoing at the Indian Mutiny fifty years later.

The remaining Mahrattas, hearing that Stevenson's force was approaching fled, and four of their guns fell into Stevenson's hands. Upon discovering the Mahrattas' movements, Wellesley decided that he himself could not advance north without risking losing Poona. He therefore ordered Stevenson to seize the forts of Asseeghur and Burhanpore on the north bank of the river Taptee. Both of which were seized. Hector Maclean in particular distinguished himself at the capture of Asseeghur.[29]

Stevenson was now ordered to besiege Gawilghur, the chief stronghold of one of the principal Mahratta princes. Before that could take place, a change of plan forced Wellesley to combine his two columns into one and set off after yet another Mahratta army. On 29 November, having driven off small bodies of Mahratta horse, he discovered that the whole enemy army were camped in the plains at the village of Argaum, five miles from where he himself had intended to camp for the night. Although his army had been on the march since 6 am, and it was now 3 pm Wellesley decided on an immediate attack.

The country was covered with fields of grain that was so high that for three miles the marching columns of men could see nothing and were only saved from surprise by their escort of irregular cavalry. The landscape, however, opened up near the village of Sirsoni, where the cultivated land gave way to an open plain, which was cut by watercourses. The enemy was now in full view about a thousand yards to the front. Wellesley had three British battalions (74th 78th and 94th) and twelve Indian battalions including the 9th Regiment of Madras Native Infantry commanded by Hector Maclean.

The Mahrattas knew that the only access to the open ground lay through Sirsoni and they had trained their artillery on the village. As a result, as soon as Wellesley's advance guard, led by a battalion of native infantry, emerged from Sirsoni 50 cannon opened up on them. The barrage threw the bullocks which towed the advance guard's few field-pieces into disorder. The drivers panicked and the bullocks rushed into the ranks of the next body of Indian soldiers causing chaos. Next to the advanced guard were two battalions of native troops who had behaved heroically at Assaye, but even they, seeing their own artillery charging back at them, broke and ran.

Fortunately Wellesley himself was near by. He stepped out in front of the fleeing Indian soldiers, and ordered them to halt. They refused. Wellesley remained calm and told their officers to guide them to the rear of the village and get control of them under cover. This they succeeded in doing and Wellesley, as calmly as before, led the formerly panic-stricken men back to their forming up place. The rest of the army joined them and, having taken up their positions, lay down to avoid the fire of the vastly superior enemy artillery. The British gunners opened fire and Wellesley's infantry drew up in a single line, with Hector's battalion as part of the left wing. The regular cavalry, consisting of five native regiments and the 19th Light Dragoons, were drawn up in a second line to the rear of the right. The irregular horse occupied the same position on the left. The entire force numbered some 11,000 men.

The Mahratta army was formed up in a more primitive fashion. The regular infantry, about 10,000 strong, was drawn up with its cannons in one long line, with a small body of foot to the rear. The cavalry was massed in two huge bands, one in advance and the other to the rear of the right wing. Another body of cavalry was positioned to the rear of the left flank. The Mahratta army probably consisted of 30 to 40,000 men.

Once the British line was in place Wellesley gave the order to advance and the whole army moved forward as though on the parade ground. Wellesley himself leading the cavalry to within 600 yards of the enemy, where he ordered that their 'galloping guns' should open fire. The rest of the cavalry were to charge once the guns produced any effect on the enemy.

Despite the parade ground performance the British left got ahead of the rest of the line and had to halt before the final charge some sixty yards from the enemy. They were badly mauled by grape shot from the Mahratta artillery, whose fire was now masked by a large body of Arabs in the Mahratta army, who with sword and buckler rushed forward, with much shouting, on the British line. Hand to hand fighting followed and the Arabs fell back having suffered some 600 casualties. The dismayed

Mahrattas gave way almost immediately. Two feeble attacks by their cavalry on Wellesley's flanks were easily repulsed and the whole Mahratta army turned and ran, eagerly pursued by Wellesley's cavalry.

Hector again distinguished himself at Argaum and the day after the battle led his men as part of Stevenson's force in pursuit of the enemy. Wellesley followed and the two divisions advanced together to envelop Gawilghur, where the defeated Mahratta infantry from Argaum had taken shelter. The fort of Gawilghur was situated in a natural defensive position high above the sources of the Poorna and Taptee rivers. The citadel was divided into two parts, separated by a deep gorge.

Stevenson, who had already prepared his force for a siege was given the task of capturing the fort. For four days his men struggled with considerable difficulties, dragging their heavy artillery to positions overlooking the fort. By 12th December the cannon were in place and opened fire. Two days later sufficient breaches had been made in the outer fort for the assault to commence and Stevenson's division supported by the Scots Brigade (94th Regiment of Foot) stormed through the gap. At the same time Wellesley launched two columns of the 74th and 78th regiments and a battalion of Sepoys against the southern and north-western gates. They succeeded and the outer fort was seized.

Wellesley's intelligence had been weak and the attacking troops did not realize that they had to cross a gorge before they could reach the inner citadel. A British officer, however, found a track that crossed the gorge and the 94th followed him to the intermediate wall. This obstacle rose steeply from the gorge and could only be climbed with great difficulty, one man at a time, under heavy fire from the citadel. Meanwhile supporting troops came hurrying up just in time to pour musketry fire into the citadel as the 94th clambered over the wall. Yet another wall and gate greeted the attackers and after some considerable effort a place was found where the light company of the 94th could fix their ladders and force their way into the stronghold in sufficient numbers to open the gate for the storming party who put the defenders to the bayonet.

The garrison of Gawilghur was 4,000 strong. It consisted mainly of regular infantry who had fled from Argaum. The slaughter among them was horrendous and in miniature the assault on Gawilghur was as bloody as that on Seringpatam, except that only 14 of Wellesley's force were killed and 112 wounded. Over half the casualties were Europeans.[30]

Hector once again distinguished himself at Gawilghur. The following September he was promoted to the rank of colonel.

* * *

'On New Year's Day 1801 the nineteenth century dawned in gloom', so writes one of the most astute historians of the years of conflict with France. 'In Germany' he continues 'Schiller greeted it with strident verses denouncing the French imperium on land and the British tyranny of the seas, while in London the Tower guns boomed a subdued welcome as the new Union flag was hoisted for the first time, and the people doubtfully wished each other "a happy new century". The hope seemed unlikely to be realised'.[31]

Europe had much to be gloomy about. Napoleon's defeat of the Austrians at Marengo had led to the destruction of the coalition against the French which Lord Grenville, the Foreign Secretary, had so expensively organised. Both Britain and France were exhausted. However, despite Nelson's destruction of the French fleet at Aboukir Bay, Bonaparte held all the cards in the negotiations for peace: he was in an unchallenged position in Egypt; the Baltic was about to be blockaded by the Northern League against Britain's merchant marine; much of Europe was closed to British exports; Portugal was about to be overrun; the Tsar of Russia was considering changing sides and marching on India; Naples was almost prepared to accept a French army of occupation, from which Egypt might easily be supplied. It could hardly have been a worse scenario for the British government.

There was, however, a glimmer of hope. Henry Dundas persuaded his colleagues to send his old friend Sir Ralph Abercromby to the eastern Mediterranean with a British expeditionary force invigorated by hard training and competent leadership. Against all the odds Abercromby landed successfully in Egypt, defeated Napoleon's veterans at Alexandria and retrieved the reputation of the British army.[32] More importantly, had they waited for the news of an unexpected victory, it would have given the British negotiators a stronger hand to negotiate with the French. On 14 March 1802 the Cabinet approved the draft treaty of peace.

The Treaty of Amiens ended hostilities. It also ended the raison d'être for the Argyllshire Volunteers. On 2 July 'Captain Donald Maclean of the late Rum Volunteers' sent a bill to the War Office for £5.5s 'for transporting the arms, accoutrements and ammunition lately in possession of the said volunteers to His Majesty's store at Dumbarton Castle'.[33] The penultimate phase of the Coll estate's rôle as a provider of substantial military units was at an end.

Notes

1. JW Fortescue *A History of the British Army* vol. IV, Part 1 1789–1801 (1915), 385.
2. Alexander was 'obliged to purchase him into the 68th Regiment'. Norman joined them immediately in Gibraltar[ICP. Bundle 691. 21 October 1790 Alexander Maclean of Coll to 5th Duke of Argyll].
3. *Scots Magazine*, vol. 58 (1796), 71; *Gents Magazine*, vol. 66.1 (1796), 167–8; NLS. MS 3018, 30.
4. TNA. WO 25. 3100. 1; NLS. MS 3018, 30. This was presumably the regiment that was raised by the Hon. Henry Dillon. It was the lineal descendant of Dillon's Regiment of the Irish Brigade in French service. It was raised specifically for service in the West Indies [TNA. WO 17. 237 (1)]. It should not be confused with the regiment of émigres raised by Edward Dillon, who had also served in the French Army. This regiment served in the Mediterranean Sea in the British service. [TNA. WO 12. 11698]; AN Ricketts 'Dillon's Regiment in the Peninsula' *The Irish Sword* vol. XII, No. 49, 316; Why a Protestant Scot should have joined an Irish Roman Catholic regiment has defeated my researches. It also confused officers at the Horse Guards when his daughter applied for a pension as he had not served in Dillon's long enough to appear in the Army List. [TNA. WO 25. 3100. I].
5. Letter from Dr Ann Robb, 12 Feddon Hill, Fortrose, Ross-shire IV10 8SP; NAS. GD 112. 52. 54. 1; TNA. WO 42. 31M, 308.
6. TNA. WO 12. 5873. Muster Roll. 47th (Lancashire) Regiment; he stayed in the West Indies until 1803 when he returned to the United Kingdom.
7. *Lady Nugent's Journal*, xi.
8. Quoted in a letter dated 24 August 1796 in *Cambridge History of the British Empire*, vol. 2, 66]
9. *Lady Nugent's Journal*, xviii–xix.
10. The British name for the Spanish half of Hispaniola, which is now the Dominican Republic.
11. Hector McLean *An Enquiry into the nature and causes of the great mortality of the troops at St Domingo*, (London: Cadell & Davies, 1797).
12. Piers Mackesy *The Strategy of Overthrow 1798–1799* (1974), 5.
13. *The Strategy of Overthrow 1798–1799*, 7.
14. *The Strategy of Overthrow 1798–1799*, 4.
15. TNA. WO 31. 67.
16. *History of the British Army* vol. IV, Part 1, 642.

17. He was the second son of Mr Alexander Maclean, Minister of Kilninian & Kilmore and Christian, dau. of Donald Maclean of Torloisk. He was from 1771 to 1775 a merchant in Virginia and lost everything because he would not join the rebels. He then sailed for Britain only with the clothes he stood up in [BL. Add Mss 217333, f. 108], he then joined his uncle Allan Torloisk's 1/84th Foot; in 1787 he transferred to 60th Foot and commanded a battalion in 1799 [*Army Lists* 1799 to 1803]; he was later to serve on the staff in the West Indies as QMG, Lieutenant Governor of Quebec and finally a Lieutenant-General [*Gentleman's Magazine* (1829), 99 ii, 477; he died a bachelor at Leghorn in Italy [TNA. Will 656. Liverpool, proved by Sir James Allan Park].
18. TNA. WO 31. 104. 27 December 1800.
19. *History of the British Army* vol. IV, Part 1, 402.
20. NAS. GD112. 52. 49. 2; he had served in India since at least 1787 [TNA. WO 12. 7925: Muster Roll of Capt. Hugh Campbell's Light Company of HM 72nd Regt of (Highland) Foot 1 December 1787–31 May 1788; he is not mentioned after 13 September 1795 and is perhaps the Alexander Maclean (no mention of sergeant) who was sick in Bengal in June 1797.
21. *History of the British Army* vol. IV, Part 1, 403
22. TNA. WO 17. 146 (1).
23. *Scots Magazine* vol. 62 (1800), 364; Scottish Record Society *Edinburgh Marriages 1751–1800*.
24. NAS. GD 112. 52. 60. 1.
25. *History of the British Army*, 98–9.
26. *A Matter of Honour*, 205–6.
27. *Scotland's Empire 1600–1815*, 258–9.
28. The 74th alone lost 11 officers and 113 men killed and 6 officers and 271 men wounded [*History of the British Army* vol. V, 33].
29. *Seanachie*, 317.
30. *History of the British Army* vol. V, 37–45.
31. Piers Mackesy *War Without Victory: The Downfall of Pitt 1799–1802* (1984), 185.
32. Among those serving in Egypt with the 42nd Foot was Sergeant John Cameron, who was married to Margaret, daughter of Lachlan Maclean in Fiosgaradh. He had wanted her to accompany him to Egypt but her brothers refused to let her go.
33. TNA. WO13. 4174. Part 4.

Part V

Change at home

Chapter Thirty-One

The Scottish Society for Propagating Christian Knowledge

Whilst war with Revolutionary France dominated the thinking of Britain's leaders, changes nearer at home affected the Hebrides. It was to have a profound influence on the future of the Coll estate, Alexander Maclean of Coll's authority and the military ethos of the Hebrides.

There can be little doubt that Alexander's influence was diminished by the arrival of outsiders in the Island. Foremost among them were the schoolteachers of the Scottish Society for Propagating Christian Knowledge [SSPCK], who for a great number of islanders was to transform their attitude to religion.

There is a contemporary witness who left a brief account of Coll's conversion to evangelical Christianity. He was Archibald Matheson or Mackenzie, the name seems to be interchangeable. In his old age he wrote from America to his son Duncan. He says:

> I was born at Grishipol in the Island of Coll March 1798 of honest and industrious parents. I was sent to school when about eight years old, and was considered a promising boy. One day while in school one of the boys was reading Buchanan's hymn on the day of Judgement. Several of us gathered round him. I listened with deep attention and silent awe till he came to the verse *Ach cruàdluchidh Dia &c*, when suddenly a vivid sensation like a flash of lightning shot through me and I very nearly fell.[1]

Such an incident was a not uncommon religious experience at a time when, what has been described as the 'Religious Avalanche', first struck Coll. Archibald goes on to explain that:

> The Bible was not much in circulation in Coll till I was a big boy myself and it was no wonder although gross superstition did greatly prevail among the old Highlanders, but I am not aware of any country where the gospel as soon as it was purely preached among them brought forth its own fruit.

Edward Clarke, who visited the islands in 1797 thought superstition in Mull, and the neighbouring islands, was beyond belief. He quotes for example 'Stones of any singular form, which have been probably originally found upon the beach, have each a peculiar characteristic virtue. They are handed down with veneration from father to son, and esteemed as a remedy for every species of disease incidental to the human or animal view'.[2]

The superficial nature of protestant belief in Coll was of concern to more than late eighteenth-century visitors to the Hebrides. Since the publication in 1703 of Martin Martin's *A Description of the Western Islands of Scotland* the Presbyterian establishment in the Lowlands had been made forcibly aware that the Hebrides were still deeply superstitious and that many pre-Reformation and even pagan practices were still being performed. In 1709 this realisation led to the establishment of the SSPCK. The avowed purpose of the Society was religious and evangelistic,[3] and it was stated that 'The great object of the Society from the beginning has been and still is to send the Scriptures to the Highlanders and teach them to read them'.[4]

Modern Scottish education began in the year 1696, when the Scottish Parliament passed the 'Act for the Settling of Schools'. This act ordained 'that there be a school settled and established and a schoolmaster appointed in every paroch not already provided by the advice of the Heritors and Minister of the Paroch.'[5] In the Highlands it was largely ignored and as late as 1755 there was not a single parochial school in the whole Presbytery of Mull.[6] Whilst in 1790 the people of Tiree, although they all adhered to the parish church, 'still retain some Roman Catholic sayings, prayers and oaths ... such as *Dia is Muire leat*, 'God and Mary be with you', whilst the festivals and saints' days of the ancient Christian Year, were popular events in the Isles well into the nineteenth century. Protestants still cherished the ancient hymns, many which bear obvious traces of their origin in pre-Reformation days. In Argyllshire in particular the sayings and doings of the saints of the Columban Church were preserved as part of popular religious folklore.[7]

The Society's schoolmasters were often designated missionaries, and it was understood that the Society's schools, while they had a lower educational standard than the parish schools, should be more definitely religious. It is true that there was also a strong, and proudly avowed, political motive in the Society's programme: 'these schools have it for their object, to eradicate error and to sow truth, to teach true religion and loyalty, and to strengthen the British Empire by the addition of useful subjects and firm Protestants'.[8]

The schoolmasters were obliged to catechize 'their scholars at least twice a week and pray publickly with them twice a day; poor children would be taught free and also receive further encouragement'; each school would be supervised by the parish minister with 'other prudent and discreet persons.'

In addition to his school duties, each teacher was *ex officio* the catechist of his district. He was bound to visit the people on Saturdays and vacations and also, if the parish church was at any distance, to conduct worship on Sundays. He was forbidden to preach, but allowed to explain the Scriptures. He also read the Scriptures, and other pious books, in his own Gaelic version of the English text.

The selection of the teaching staff was of crucial importance and was made by the central body on local recommendation. The schoolmaster had to be ' a person of piety, loyalty, prudence, gravity, competent knowledge and literature', who would seek to 'correct the beginnings of vices, and particularly lying, swearing, cursing, profaning the Lord's Day, stealing &c'. Each candidate had to submit to a personal interview and examination in Edinburgh. He was examined not only on his knowledge of the educational rudiments, 'but also and most particularly, upon his acquaintance with the Evangelical and his fitness for communicating his knowledge to others'. The teaching of

Latin, as well as Gaelic was forbidden,[9] and until 1767 it remained an offence, punishable with dismissal, for a charity school teacher to help his pupils to read Gaelic.[10]

Certain lords and gentlemen opposed education and 'wished parish schools were suppressed altogether, because their servants were corrupted by being taught to read and write: That they would be more obedient and dutiful, were they more ignorant, and had no education'.[11] This was not the attitude of Maclean of Coll. As we have seen he encouraged education and even had young men from Coll living in his household in Old Aberdeen so that they were able to attend the University.

The first school provided by the SSPCK on Coll's estate was at Quinish. It appears to have been the work of the Minister of Kilninian and Kilmore rather than the Laird of Coll. The minister Mr Archibald MacArthur was a member of the SSPCK and in 1790 he was written to by the Society and asked if he would accept Alexander Stalker, the Society's schoolmaster in Lochcarron, who was to be removed from that station.

The Society's letter stated that 'for the school to be erected at Queenish' in answer to 'Mr McArthur['s] expressed doubt as to some particulars, yet as Stalker appeared on the whole a very fit person for that station, he [the Secretary] had written to Mr McArthur again to propose him to the Heritors and people'. At their meeting 'The Directors approved of what has been done, and in case of the inhabitants of Queenish being satisfied they agree that the school of Lochalsh be suppressed and Alexander Stalker removed to Queenish; but defer making any appointment till Mr McArthur's answer is received'.[12]

Mac Arthur agreed. By 11th November 1790 Alexander Stalker was settled in Quinish and applied for 'travelling charges for himself and his family'. He was allowed forty shillings expenses.[13]

* * *

The Society had strict rules as to what the heritors of the parish were expected to provide for their schoolmasters. These rules are illustrated in a questionaire sent in the 1790s to all their schoolmasters:

Circular Letter to Schoolmasters.

1. Is your house comfortable, properly lighted and kept water tight by the proprietor of the lands, or the tenants in the neighbourhood?
2. Is your school house in good order and provided with sufficient light with glass windows and furnished with tables and forms for the children?
3. Have you a Cows grass in summer? Fodder for her in winter gratis? And is your fewel brought to your house by the people free of expense?
4. Have you a kail yard? And have you any land for grain or potatoes besides and if you have what is the quantity of it? Do you pay rent for it, and to what amount?
5. Are school fees paid by such as are able for their children? What do you receive from each? And what is the average amount of your Quarter Payments in a year?
6. What is the nearest market town to your station? And what price do you generally pay for a Boll of Meal when laid down at your own door?
7. Who is the proprietor of the ground upon which your station is fixed? And what other Heritors are there in the parish?
8. Do you catechise the people in the neighbourhood, and instruct them in the principles of religion?

9. Do you meet with them on Lord's days when they cannot on account of distance or bad weather, attend at the Parish Church, or in the place of stated public worship, and officiate among them by prayer and praise, reading the Scriptures or pious books?
10. Have you books for that purpose? And when was your school supplied with books for the schools?[14]

A similar list of requirements were sent to the heritor and parish minister, there should therefore have been no misunderstanding. That, however, was not always the case and was to be the cause of considerable grief.

* * *

On 1st March 1792 the society received an application 'from Mr Maclean of Coll for a school on his estate'.[15] And on 3rd April 1794 another letter was received from him 'mentioning that the accommodation for that school were now ready'; the Directors therefore appointed John Davidson at Glasgow and his son 'to be removed to that station'.[16]

John Davidson had previously been a SSPCK schoolmaster in Glasgow. He was a controversial character and on 23rd April 1794 Dr Kemp, the SSPCK's Secretary, wrote him a candid letter:

> Sir, I received your letter and am pleased with the temper & spirit that it discovers. The distance to Coll is so great & an opportunity of consequence by sea of so much importance to you & your family that I would wish you to embrace one as soon as it offers. I shall write to Mr McIntosh about a successor to you in your present station.
>
> I find you mentioned Coll's letter by which you will see that he has granted my request in your favour; & you will also see that he mentions the Instruction of young women in the several branches of female Industry of equal importance. If your wife therefore shall succeed in this article it will give me great pleasure & be a strong Recommendation of both her & you to the Laird.
>
> You will observe that the Commission is addressed to you & your Son as [on our Establishment]. Your principal duty will be to superintend the school & to act as a catechiser among the people at large. Your son had an opportunity of seeing the method of teaching here in Mr McDonald's School, which we very much approve of & desire that it may be observed by our teachers. Lady Ross Baillie has interested herself in you & both wrote & spoke to me on your behalf; but she knows your history & character well & is not blind to your defects. Several other people of known piety & respectability have spoken of you to me & the result of the whole is [?] my hopes are mingled with fear. You have ... the blessing of God [to] be extremely useful in that remote Country which hitherto has injoyed but few opportunities – but there are peculiarities in your temper moreover which unless restrained will totally mar your usefulness by rendering you an object of Jealousy & dislike. I cannot in too strong terms recommend to you in duty humility, disinterestness. If you discover any disposition to make yourself contemptuous & angrie to you yourself . . . . . . If you behave to them with any degree of arrogance & affect to give yourself upon an[?] footing with them, if you assume a high tone of authority among the common people or discover any tendency to avarice or greed be assured that you will be very soon despised & complained of nor will it be either in my power or inclination to give you protection. The Directors of the Society will ... be under the necessity of [providing] ... another servant who may more faithfully & prudently fulfill the important office now assigned to you.

I state these things to you plainly because it is my duty in the station I hold to do so & because I am most anxious for your success. I shall hear from you from time to time by Mr McArthur whom I mentioned to you in my last. He is a member of this society & a man of great respectability in that Country in whom we place very great confidence. If you consult him, which it will be your wisdom often to do, he will give you his best advice, & Information concerning many things of which you must be ignorant; the distance is not so great but that you may see him occasionally. The Laird's Boat is frequently come over to that part of Mull where Mr McArthur resides. If you find an opportunity of landing at Coll you will not need to call at Mr McArthur on your way there, but you will but call on him as soon after wards as may be. With respect to Mr McColl the Parish Minister . . . He is a good-natured moderate man. Your duty is to show him all respect & as far as [is] in you . . . inclosed a note to Mr Rob. Scott Moncrieff with which you may call upon him when you are ready . . . & he will give you £5 for the Expence of your Journey and £7.10s being the half year's Salary from the Society from 1st November to full money, which is to be paid with . . . the lateness of your Entry.

I have also ordered a supply of Books to be sent to you by the carrier & the carriage to be paid . . . is done for you. And I can do I have given you my best advice & have only to ad[d] it my prayers that God may take you under his protection & grant you grace to fulfill your duty JK[emp].[17]

The Davidsons were established on Coll by 1 May 1794 and the Secretary reported that he had ordered £5 to be paid for travelling charges.[18] Trouble was not long in coming. The Davidsons had been told to teach at only one school. However, by August the Society discovered that the son, Ebenezer, had opened another school in the east end of the Island. The Directors ordered that they should both be reprimanded and 'if the inhabitants in the east of Coll apply for a school there if so inclined that when such an application is made the Directors may consider of a proper schoolmaster for that station'.[19]

On 11th December 1794 the SSPCK wrote to John Davidson again:

Sir, I should imagine you cannot have forgot (tho you and your son seems to have disregarded), the letter wrote to you by the secretary on the 9th & 23rd of April last pointing out to you most minutely the line of conduct you were both to follow on your arrival in Coll. Of these Letters the Society preserved Copies, & I see from your answer promise implicit obedience; but . . .

Your Commission not only bears that you & your son were appointed joint Teachers of one school; but Dr Kemp most anxiously explained to you how you were both to employ yourselves & no sooner were you landed on the island than you separated. Your son went at his own hand to the to the east end of the island where the Society had never appointed any school of theirs to be erected, & where indeed one was never asked. On this I wrote to you at desire of the Directors on 21st of August last to keep only one school, & in general that you should follow the instructions which had formerly been given. To this letter you gave me no answer. But the Secretary has now received one from your son mentioning that he is still in the east End of the isle, requesting books for this academy of his own Erection (tho books were sent you for the school appointed by the Society,) & requesting also forsooth that Dr Kemp should write a Letter of Thanks to a young Lady[20] there who has shown him some attention.

Now I ask you what can the Society think of such Conduct as this? Were they to act rigidly they would pay no part of your salary. This step they have not yet taken; but the Directors had the matter under their Consideration at last meeting & they desired me to intimate to you their Disappointment of you & your son's conduct & to desire you both to attend literally to attend to the Instructions given you in the Letters above mentioned. Your son will therefore immediately join you & you will continue to teach this one school & in every respect list & show the donations you have received . . . The Society expect & require implicit obedience to orders on the part of all their Servants & you will find it for your interest to comply. I beg an answer to be laid before the Directors & I am &c.

17 December 1794.

PS Since writing the above Dr King has received your Letters of 7th & 22nd November & your son's of 16 & 20th. On considering the whole the Directors continue to the resolution refused in the within Letter writ to your son the officers of the Society will hold no correspondence till he returns to his duty & learns to obey orders.[21]

Davidson had evidently complained of the treatment he was receiving in Coll, and on 20th December 1794 the Society wrote to Major Maclean of Coll, who was serving with his regiment in Glasgow:

Sir, I am desired by the Directors of the Society for Propagating Christian Knowledge to apply to you on the subject of the enclosed Letters wrote to their Secretary by John Davidson their Schoolmaster in Coll. Before he was sent there we were informed both by you and the Minister of the place that all the accommodations were in readiness. The inclosed will satisfy you however that your orders in this respect have not been complied with. The houses it would seem are not yet finished – the poor man has not yet possession of his Croft of Land or Cows Grass. – nor has he obtained any potatoes for his family in terms of the Correspondence between the Secretary & you last Spring. The Society are willing to believe that this ought to be imputed to your necessary absence from the Island. At the same time they must protect their Servants & they therefore desire me to intimate to you that unless the matter is speedily investigated & orders given they must however reluctantly remove their School to another station. This you will at once see the propriety of & I shall therefore expect an answer to be laid before the Directors at their meeting on the first of January a[?]ing to enquire into the truth of the facts stated in the Letters now with you & to grant immediate relief. Be so good to return the Letter with your answers. I have the honour to be &c.[22]

As Alexander was at the height of his problems in the Breadalbane Fencibles he must have been furious with this rebuke. However, he appears to have dealt with the problem, at least for the moment.

There were no further problems with the Davidsons for twelve months. Then 'Ebenezer Davidson assistant schoolmaster in Coll' wrote 'craving leave to go to Glasgow to learn church music – The Directors appointed the clerk to write to him that he cannot expect any such leave of absence from the duties of his office during the winter months when the school ought to be [?] that the Society will at any rate be at no expense on that subject that if he is desirous of acquiring church music he may do so next harvest vacation at one of the neighbouring society schools in Mull without putting himself to much trouble and expense'.[23]

Twelve months later John Davidson was again complaining about his accommodation and other grievances.[24] By now he had made himself so obnoxious to the people of Coll that the Society received a letter from Mr McArthur of Mull on 7th March 1799... suggesting that John Davidson at Coll 'against whom the people there are prejudiced may be removed to Morvern if a school shall be erected there'.[25] Colonel Maclean of Coll wrote 'requesting that John Davidson schoolmaster there may be put upon the superannuated list. That his son Ebenezer & his wife may succeed his father John & his wife, young Mrs Davidson being much better qualified for the instruction of females than old Mrs Davidson'.[26]

John Davidson and his wife moved to Lochgilphead, where he was granted a salary of £7 and told that as he was on the superannuated list he could reside where he liked.[27] However, as he was superannuated his wife could not receive a salary or be appointed to succeed a deceased sewing mistress.[28] She must later have obtained employment for when she died in May 1806 her daughter was appointed sewing mistress in her place.[29] The following year Davidson was the Catechist in Kingussie.[30] He probably died there for on 1st December 1808 his son Ebenezer petitioned for an addition to his salary in consequence of his father's death.[31] Why he should have thought he was entitled to an additional salary is not explained.

Ebenezer Davidson was a far more successful schoolteacher than his father. He was passionately fond of his work and made a considerable impact on the youth of Coll. Archibald Mackenzie writes 'during this period between the my twelfth and seventeenth year [1810–5] I took great delight in reading the Gospels and the historical parts of the old testament. I also got hold of the *Pilgrim's Progress*, which made an impression on my mind'.[32]

Ebenezer Davidson like other part-time catechists went from house to house and was the friend, teacher, and evangelist of the people in his district. However, a people to whom music and poetry was as the breath of life needed something more than sound doctrine, more or less ably expounded. They needed to sing their faith. The spiritual bards who were increasingly composing songs at this time amply supplied that need. The Reverend John Macinnes writes:

The poems and hymns, which these bards created, quickly became the beloved possession of a people who, though innocent of school learning, were passionately fond of verse and were endowed with accurate and tenacious memories. The winter 'ceilidh and the summer migration to the hill shielings were the two social institutions by means of which the ancient ballad literature and the poetry of the secular bards became diffused among the people'. The 'dain spioradail' or 'spiritual songs' gained a wide currency through the same or similar channels.[33]

Davidson also led the singing in church on Sundays and made himself the minister's invaluable assistant in compiling: 'An account of the population Coll' and found that on 20 June 1811 there were:

$$\begin{array}{rl} 623 & \text{Male} \\ \underline{654} & \text{Females} \\ 1277 & \text{Total} \end{array}$$

He notes in the Kirk Session Minutes that

An Obituary has never been kept in this Island & many Baptisms & Marriages have been omitted in the Session Book. It has therefore cost me much labour to make up the above Population account. – Ebenezer Davidson.[34]

* * *

Quinish and Coll were not the only parts of the estate to obtain a SSPCK school. On 6th April 1797 a letter from the Rev. Mr Donald Maclean, Minister of Small Isles, was produced at the meeting of the Society's directors in Edinburgh requesting an ambulatory school for the island of Rum. In it he signified that the tenants have agreed to furnish the teacher with bed board &c in lieu of the usual accommodation. The secretary stated the situation of those islands, their great need of schemes and the impossibility of fixing one to any particular station from the dispersion of the villages, and therefore proposes that a young man, one of its schoolmasters who could best be spared from his present station should be appointed ambulatory teacher in these islands. He was to be appointed provided that he was lodged and boarded at the expense of the inhabitants 'wherever he shall keep school for the time. To such the Directors agreed'.[35]

Roderick Mackenzie was appointed schoolmaster in Rum and on 3 January 1799 he wrote to the Society for his traveling expenses. It was agreed that £3 should be paid to him.[36] On 2 May 1799 they received another letter from Mr Donald 'requesting the erection of a school in the Isle of Muck and an allowance to a schoolmaster when the inhabitants have engaged to provide a school house and to furnish the schoolmaster in Bed board and washing with £6 Str per annum. The Directors remit to the secretary to send a proper teacher in the meantime and agree to allow him a temporary supply of £5 for this year & remit the application for a full erection of the school to the sub committee on the scheme'.[37]

* * *

As has already been suggested the conversion of Coll affected the position of the Laird. Previously he had the undisputed allegiance of his people. Now he had a rival in their affection and as the people learnt to read the bible they began to question his authority. They also began listen to new ideas and to become politically aware. Mr Donald, writing from Coll on 30th April 1795 says 'that he fears that republican principles are gaining ground among members of the lower class'.[38] There is no evidence that Ebenezer Davidson spread such principles but it is difficult to believe that at this time any one else could have done.

Notes

1. BCP. Coll Families. Mackenzie/Matheson folder; Dugald Buchanan 'Latha 'Breitheanais'. A. Sinclair (ed) *Reminiscences of the life and labour of Dugald Buchanan* (1875), 89–110.
2. William Otter (ed) *The Life & Remains of the Rev. Edward Daniel Clarke LLD* (1824), 228.
3. SPCK, Account of the Funds &c, 1796, 28.
4. SPCK, Account of the Funds &c, 1796, 29.
5. John Macinnes *The Evangelical Movement in the Highlands of Scotland 1688 to 1800* (1951), 225.
6. *The Evangelical Movement in the Highlands of Scotland*, 232–3.
7. *The Evangelical Movement in the Highlands of Scotland*, 167.
8. SPCK, Annual Sermon, 1787, Thomas Unwick (Salter's Hall).
9. *The Evangelical Movement in the Highlands of Scotland*, 238–40.
10. *The Evangelical Movement in the Highlands of Scotland*, 245.
11. *OSA*, vol. VIII, 48.
12. NAS. GD 95. 2. 10. SSPCK Minutes of Directors (1783–92), 299.
13. NAS. GD 95. 2. 10. SSPCK Minutes of Directors (1783–92), 357.
14. NAS. GD 95. 2. 10. SSPCK Minutes of Directors (1783–92), 358.
15. NAS. GD 95. 2. 10. SSPCK Minutes of Directors (1783–92), 489.

16. NAS. GD 95. 2. 10. SSPCK Minutes of Directors (1792–1806), 120.
17. NAS. GD 95. 3. 2. SSPCK. Letter Books (1794–1805), 35–6.
18. NAS. GD 95. 2. 11. SSPCK. Letter Books (1792–1806), 124.
19. NAS. GD 95. 3. 2. SSPCK. Letter Books (1794–1805), 50; Minutes of Directors (1792–1806), 161.
20. This was probably one of the late Donald Maclean of the Isle of Muck's daughters. They were still living in Cornaig.
21. NAS. GD 95. 3. 2, 70–1.
22. NAS. GD 95. 3. 2, 70–2
23. NAS. GD 95. 2. 11. SSPCK. Minutes of Directors (1792–1806), 224.
24. NAS. GD 95. 2. 11. SSPCK. Minutes of Directors (1792–1806), 224.
25. NAS. GD 95. 2. 11. SSPCK. Minutes of Directors (1792–1806), 420.
26. NAS. GD 95. 2. 11. SSPCK. Minutes of Directors (1792–1806), 421.
27. NAS. GD 95. 2. 11. SSPCK. Minutes of Directors (1794–1805), 258–61.
28. NAS. GD 95. 3. 2. SSPCK. Letter Books (1794–1805), 277 & 313.
29. NAS. GD 95. 2. 13. SSPCK. Minutes of Directors (1806–13), 27.
30. NAS. GD 95. 2. 13. SSPCK. Minutes of Directors (1806–13), 100.
31. NAS. GD 95. 3. 13. SSPCK. Letter Book (1806–13), 215.
32. BCP. Coll Families. Mackenzie/Matheson file.
33. A Gunn 'Unpublished Literary Remains of Reay Country' *TGSI*, XVI, 267–8; *The Evangelical Movement in the Highlands of Scotland*, 262–5.
34. NAS. CH2. 70. 1, 84.
35. NAS. GD 95. 2. 11. SSPCK. Minutes of the Directors (1792–1806), 413.
36. NAS. GD 95. 2. 11. SSPCK. Minutes of the Directors (1792–1806), 413.
37. NAS. GD 95. 2. 11. SSPCK. Minutes of the Directors (1792–1806), 437.
38. NAS GD 112. 52. 45. 36.

Chapter Thirty-Two

Alexander as an improving laird

Before he went off to war in 1793, Alexander Maclean of Coll had, as we have seen, commissioned George Langlands and Son to survey his estate in the Isle of Coll. Sometime after July 1794 they reported back to him. Alexander now had the first essential tool with which to plan the improvements on his most important estate.

The problem of over-population, which faced every other proprietor in the Hebrides was particularly acute on Coll. Even in 1775 Alexander had complained that 'my father has not yet by raising his rents or other harsh usages, forced his tenants to leave their country, as too many other proprietors have done. The fact is there are actually at present too many people upon his estate'.[1] By the time of the erudite Reverend James Macdonald's visit[2] in 1807 the island was 'over-peopled at least *one-third*'. The cause of the population explosion in the Hebrides is still under discussion.[3] However, it must have increased, at least in part, as a result of improved nutrition, which was caused by the introduction of potatoes, and by inoculation against small pox.[4]

Macdonald explains how the impact of overpopulation effected the policies of Maclean of Coll. He writes that:

> The landlord, like many other Hebridian proprietors, knows not how to dispose of that part of the population, which he cannot accommodate with lands. He cannot bear the thought of turning them at once adrift into the world without having any means of subsistence for themselves and their families; and yet there remains no other alternative in the present situation of the island, except the distressing one of crowding them together upon small portions of land, which even under good management and although rent-free, could scarcely feed such a numerous population. This dilemma is also attended by the additional hardship of retarding or preventing every agricultural improvement. The proprietor cannot possibly effect these, but by means of substantial tenants in possession under leases of considerable quantities of ground: But he would need three times the extent and resources of Coll to bestow suitable farms upon his present tenants, and many thousand pounds to put them into proper condition for stocking them.[5]

Despite this gloomy picture Alexander had his own ideas on how to tackle the problem of an increasing population. Once he had received Langland's survey he began making plans to expand the number of individual holdings on the Island. James Macdonald writes:

Mr Maclean of Coll insisted upon some of his tenants dividing among them the lands, which they formerly held in common, or run-rig, and which they were accustomed for ages to divide annually by lot, for the purposes of cultivation. They obeyed with great reluctance, and each tenant had his own farm to himself. Three or four years experience has convinced them now, that their landlord acted wisely; and the whole of his tenants solicit eagerly the very thing which they lately considered as an act of tyranny or oppression.[6]

Alexander probably made his first experiment in establishing new single tenant holdings, not by breaking up a joint tenant farm, but by dividing into crofts the former tacksman's farm at Grishipol. Lachlan Maclean of the Isle of Muck, Alexander's successor as commanding officer of the 1st Battalion the Breadalbane Fencibles, had probably given up his tack when he went off to war. Instead of finding a new tacksman, Alexander divided the farm into eight individual holdings.[7]

In 1794 Grishipol was the largest farm on Coll, consisting of more than 993 acres. It stretched from the Clabbach to the Cliad burn, and from the sea to the Black Hill in the centre of the island. The new tenants were given linear holdings running parallel to the two boundary burns. Each croft had its own strip of shoreline, arable ground, green pasture, as well as moss and muir beyond the old head-dyke. Some obviously had better land than others and it probably took Alexander's individual attention to get the new tenants to agree to their allocation, which suggests that he did not begin the reorganisation of the estate until after he resigned from the army in September 1797.

Once they had been given their new holdings, the tenants had a massive task ahead of them: the old tenant touns, huddled together like stooks of hay in a barnyard, were broken up and in most cases houses had to be built on the new crofts; this was usually a condition when crofts were allocated; then they had to build stonewalls to separate their own land from their neighbour's farm. Although every man had some skill in building in stone, stonemasons must have been much in demand, which is probably why Duncan Johnston, formerly a servant in Arnabost, who is said to have been a stonemason, was allocated one of the new crofts.

Priority in obtaining one of the new holdings was probably given to the former tacksman's subtenants. Certainly the family of one man who received a croft on Grishipol had been there for more than a century. This was Neil Matheson or Mackenzie, the father of the witness to the coming of the 'Religious Avalanche' in Coll, and the grandson of Ludovic Matheson, *Maoldòmhnich Mac Mhathain*. Ludovic's father Murdoch Allan had come to Grishipol in the seventeenth century. He had done so when Neil Maclean of Drimnacross, a younger son of Maclean of Coll, had married Murdoch Allan's foster sister, a daughter of Macdonald of Morar. Ludovic who was born in 1698 was a man of extraordinary strength. He fought in the '15,[8] and at the age of 100 carried his son across a burn on Grishipol. He lived to be 109.[9] He is listed in 1796 as being among the first class poor in Grishipol,[10] so he probably remained in his own house, in what was then Mibost, when it was made into a croft for his grandson. The latter was still there until at least 1818.[11]

By giving farmers individual holdings Alexander was continuing his father's policy of establishing individual single tenant farms on the former shieling areas in the south-east of the island. The difference now was that most of the new holdings were on farms that had been occupied for hundreds of years rather than on former summer grazings.

The older single tenant farms were at Kilbride and Fiosgaradh. They had been settled before 1776.[12] Samuel Johnson tells us that Donald young Coll had 'attempted what no islander, perhaps, ever thought on. He has begun a road capable of a wheel carriage. He has carried it about a mile, and will continue it by annual elongation from his house to the harbour' at Arinagour.[13]

The corn mill for the west end of Coll was certainly at Acha by 1794[14] and was perhaps there by 1776.[15] The continuation of this road past Acha was to open up a large expanse of land for settlement. However, even before the road was finished, families were established on the coast at places such as Hyne[16] and Arithluic that even in 2005 do not have a road to them. The usual method of moving goods, in any large quantity, to these settlements must have been by sea.

Other new settlements were made on the north-east coast at Fislum, North & South Trelvick, and Leacruadh. The most important development, however, was the expansion of the single tenant farm of Arinagour at the mouth of Lochiron/Loch Ifrinn [now Loch Eatharna] into a village.

In 1813 the SSPCK's school master Ebenezer Davidson wrote:

The above village exhibits a very singular instance of the proprietor's great attention to the welfare of the poor; for here are 25 families ... accommodated with crofts, containing much susceptible of improvement, so as to be equal in value with the best arable land in the island, and seaweed to themselves and all their offspring by long leases. These families were destitute almost, at the time this provision was made for them, and would have been under the necessity of removing to other countries.[17]

* * *

The family at Fiosgaradh, one of the original single tenant crofts, is one of the keys to understanding how the community of Coll functioned in 1800. Fiosgaradh, as we have seen, was a farm of 118 acres, 12 of which were arable, 9 of green pasture and 93 of muir. It was a single tenant holding worked, without servants but with his sons, by a younger brother of the Maclean tacksman of Crossapol. Lachlan Fiosgaradh was a man of influence in the community and an elder of the kirk.

The increased population of the Hebrides meant, even by 1776, that the size of individual families was too great for their place of birth to support them. Increasingly younger sons of tacksmen were forced to leave their farms and move elsewhere. Most had no wish to leave the island, if there was any land available. James Macdonald makes the point that 'the very idea of possessing a spot of land which he can call his own, has an incredibly favourable effect on the Hebridian's mind; and that no people in the world have so great a value for land, or attach so high a notion to the importance of landed property, even in the smallest portions, as the natives of these remote islands'.[18]

Younger sons of tacksmen were prepared to take remote spots of land and Alexander Maclean of Coll's father Hugh had given priority to cadets of his own family in their allocation. He did so both in these new settlements in Coll and, as we will see, in the Isle of Rum. Alexander continued his father's example. That he considered that the Macleans in Fiosgaradh were members of his own family, despite the fact that they had branched off the main stem two hundred years earlier, is clear, as we have seen, from his letter of February 1798 to his former adjutant.[19] In it he describes Fiosgaradh's son Alexander as being 'of my own family'. The paper on which Allan Crossapol wrote his 'Genealogical Account of the Macleans' supports this theory. It is dye stamped 'Bath', and it is likely that Alexander purchased it on one of his visits to the spa, which suggests that Allan Crossapol wrote his *magnum opus* at the instigation of his chief.

The Fiosgaradh family are an important link in the family of Coll as they connect the chief with the majority of the people on the island, acting as the cement that bound together the various bricks that in 1800 made up the population in Coll, and re-establishing the laird's relations with his remoter kinsmen. Marrying into the Fiosgaradh family consolidated one's social position in the Coll establishment.

For example in January 1791 John Mackinnon in Triallan married Fiosgaradh's daughter Catherine. John's predecessors were tenants in Totronald. John himself was working away from home at the time of his marriage. In 1793 he joined the Breadalbane Fencibles. He is then described as a 'labourer'. As he signs for his pay, he was probably literate. On his return from the army he became a tenant in Grimsary and remained there for most of his life. In 1809 he became a sessioner of the Kirk Session. He was to be one until 1839.[20] John's eldest son was to marry a daughter of Charles Macdonald, another tenant in Totronald, whose family had been his parent's next door neighbour when John was a child.[21]

It can be shown [see Table 5] that there were seven marriages between 1790 and 1834 between the Fiosgaradh family and the equally closely related families of Johnston and the Maclean tenants in Arnabost. The former were descendants of a family brought to Coll circa 1600 when Coll's younger son married a Maciain of Ardnamuchan. They originally held the farm of Kiel, near the medieval parish church in Coll at Kilunaig.

By 1776 there were several families of Johnstons in Coll. One was at Uig and another at Arnabost.[22] These Johnstons are said to have been among 'the most respectable in the island'.[23] Despite their respectability one of them had a son born three months after his marriage. He was one of the few Johnstons in 1793 to join the army.[24] Four Johnstons were servants in 1776. One of them, Duncan the stonemason, became a tenant in Grishipol when it was split up into crofts.[25]

The other family, who married into both the Johnstons and Fiosgaradh Maclean families, were the Achamore Macleans known as the *Sliochd Eachainn Mhic Dhòmhnaill*.[26] They probably descend from the illegitimate eldest son of Donald of Brolas, the seventeenth-century tutor to the chief of the Macleans of Duart.[27] If so they probably came to Coll as refugees when the Campbells took over the Duart estate. In 1776 the representative of this family in the centre of Coll, as opposed to their cousins in Ardnish, was Hector Maclean in Cliad. One of his daughters married a Johnston, another married Fiosgaradh's eldest son, Allan, and yet another married his brother Hugh. Both these brothers were sergeants in the Breadalbane Fencibles, whilst Hector's son John married Fiosgaradh's niece Marion, whose father John Cameron was a sergeant in the Black Watch. In 1801 he served under Sir Ralph Abercromby with his regiment in Egypt.

Yet another of Hector's daughters [not shown in Table 5] married John Maclean in Arnabost. He was descended from *Niel Bhuidh mac gille challum ic Eachan*, a grandson of a sixteenth-century Maclean of Coll. He was the famous archer. John's brother Murdoch was a tailor in Arnabost. He served in the Breadalbane Fencibles and signed his initials in the pay list on 24th December 1793[28] when he was promoted corporal in the Second Major's Company. On his return to Coll in June 1803, he became a sergeant in the Argyllshire Volunteers[29] and later, according to Crossapol was a tenant at Toraston,[30] whilst his brother Lachlan became a tenant at Mibost, which was part of the old Grishipol tack.

What is interesting about these families is the broad social spectrum they represent. Sons of tenants become servants, sometimes, but not always to their relations, when they first left home. They then, if they were lucky, married a girl who had a stake in another joint tenant farm, which they took over when their father-in-law was too old to work it. Once these farms started to be broken up into crofts, they had a good chance of obtaining one of these new single tenant holdings. This is what seems to have happened to Alexander Johnston who was in Ballyhough in 1776. He appears to have originally come from Arnabost. By 1776 he was probably a tenant in Ballyhough. He was married to Effie Campbell a member of a well-established family there.[31]

Unlike Grishipol, Ballyhough was never a tacksman's farm but was always held by joint tenants. In 1716 it had a male population of 13. Donald the smith, who had a servant, was probably the leading man there in 1776. He also had a son named Malcolm, who was probably still living at home. As the inhabitants in Ballyhough in 1716 are mostly listed by their patronymics it is not possible to tie them in with certainty to those in the 1776 catechist's list. However, as there was a Malcolm Macdonald in Ballyhough in 1776 who had a son named Finlay, who is later said to be a smith, it is likely that Donald the smith in 1716 was a Macdonald and his son, or more likely his grandson, was the Malcolm Macdonald noticed as being able to read in Ballyhough in the 1776 list. Macdonalds were also present in 7 other households at Ballyhough in the 1776 list, suggesting that they had married into other tenant families there over a considerable period of time.[32]

In 1776 there were three households of Macleans at Ballyhough. Allan Crossapol says that: 'there was a grandson of Hector Roy the 5th laird Lachlan mac Lachain, a stout man of whom descended *Lachlan Mac Neil ic lachain* at Ballyhough, [who] had a son John McLean father to Hector McLean at Grimsary and Lachlan McLean at Kilbride'.

In 1716 there was a Neil bane McLean in Ballyhough, who had taken part in the rebellion and handed in his sword 'being all his arms'. He is likely to be the Neil in *Lachan Mac Neil ic lachain's* patronymic and his son is probably the Lachlan Maclean in Ballyhough in 1776. He was married to a Macdonald and in 1776 had an of age son Neil and underage daughter Ann.

His eldest son John was away from home, perhaps in the army, in 1776. John was back in Ballyhough by 29 December 1782 when his son Hector was baptised. Hector's mother Cirsty Campbell was probably the daughter of the Malcolm Campbell in Ballyhough in 1776. A second son of John and Cirsty named Lachlan was baptised in 1784. Both John and Neil Maclean in Ballyhough had children baptised there until 1795 and 1797 respectively. It is uncertain whether both the brothers obtained crofts there. John certainly did. His son Hector had succeeded him by 1818 as 'Tenant in Balhough'.[33]

Two other sons of men already mentioned as being in Ballyhough in 1716 appear in the 1776 list. They are likely to be living with their fathers and it is therefore probable that in 1716 Ballyhough consisted of 10 households. By 1776 Ballyhough had a total population of 75. It was then made up of 14 households, 9 of whom had children who were under 7 years of age. (There were also two households of women. One consisted of a widow woman and her daughter and the other of a lone woman). Ballyhough was therefore a fairly youthful community in 1776. And although its population had increased since 1716, it was not so great an increase as would be expected and it is probable that the joint tenants strictly controlled the number of people they allowed to live there.

In 1794 Ballyhough consisted of 387 acres. It was made up of 145 acres of arable ground, 67 of rocky arable, 152 of green pasture, 47 acres of moss and 482 of muir. It was then divided into perhaps 6 crofts. It was divided in a way that was uncharacteristic of the rest of the island. It is possible from the walls that survive to see how these new crofts were laid out.[34] Ben Hogh which overshadowed the whole farm was divided into four crofts: *Sròn*, *Am Feadan*, Benmeanach and the Smithy Croft. *Sròn*, Gaelic for a nose was named after the sgurr of Ben Hogh, which dominated the croft. It included fairly large patches of former outfield; it faces south but is very high up for cultivated land on Coll – most of it is above 150 feet and some more than 250 feet and it is exposed to the south-westerly winds; with the help of drainage its lower slopes are workable.

Am Feadan, which is the Gaelic for the whistling of the wind, is fairly descriptive of its site. It had a large section of former arable land, but it must have been marshy ground lying as it does between the ridge of Ben Hogh and the Clabbach burn, and would have had to be drained. On one side it is shadowed by Ben Hogh and on the other by the heather covered slopes of Bernera, which is part of Grishipol's muir. It could not have instilled much hope in its first occupants.

Benmeanach, the middle hill, had no former arable but a large patch of rocky arable and except for the garden near the house and a section near the Clabbach burn was only cultivated by lazy beds. The Beinn Tioraidh croft had more potential. The summit of the ridge on which it stands had been cultivated in the past and was, on its gentler slopes, comparatively sheltered. The Smithy croft had a strip of arable but the rest of its land was extremely poor, either steep rocky ground or boggy.[35]

This distribution of Ballyhough left land for perhaps two more crofts on the former infield, which surrounded the old tenant toun, and the raised beach between Ben Tioraidh and the sea. These two crofts gained the best arable land and the break up of the old arable land was hardly equitable, but was dictated by the landscape.

James Macdonald stresses that:

The example set by enlightened proprietors farming lands judiciously is inconceivably beneficial in remote districts, in which agriculture is not only in its infancy, but where it has a thousand obstacles arising from moral and physical causes to surmount. Nothing short of occular demonstration will convince the common tenant of the advantage to be derived from any inovation in farming.[36]

He particularly commends Alexander for setting an example to his people 'upon a large farm which he keeps in his own hands'. Here he introduced green crops, practicing rotation and the careful breeding of horses and cattle. The large farm, which he farmed himself, probably included the land surrounding the castle. Its acreage was greatly increased in 1798 when Alexander purchased the Duke of Argyll's property on the south-east coast of Coll which mixed with his own land.[37] The 270 acre farm of Ardnish, which begins only a few yards from the castle park, had for centuries been a thorn in the flesh of successive Macleans of Coll.

Alexander had been its tacksman since 1789.[38] Ardnish was now set to the Bailie but it is probably that part was merged with his own home farm and that he built the farm steadings at Breacachadh at this time.[39] At the same time he built the pier at Port na Luinge in Ardnish[40] and Port na Luing House, an inn,[41] whose host Hugh Gray was Alexander's ferry man and land-steward in that part of the island.[42]

The former tenants of Ardnish were removed to other parts of the island. At least one family of MacFadyens was settled at Ballyhough[43], whilst a family of Macleans, who claimed to be members of the Lochbuie family, and were perhaps descended from refugees from Mull, moved to Acha. Malcolm the representative of this family in 1776 had two servants in Ardnish and was probably a tenant. In 1799 his eldest son Allan Maclean was in Acha when he married Anny, a sister of Allan Maclean of Crossapol. She was a widow who had formerly been married to a Sergeant Henry Sutherland, who in 1796 was in Ireland with his regiment when his 'lawful son' Henry was baptised at Breacachadh.[44] In 1810 Allan was to become an elder of the kirk and had a large family of sons and daughters. Allan evidently had a tack of Acha.[45] Unlike many tacksmen he evidently became a successful farmer.

James Macdonald was critical of tacksmen as improvers. He says that:

> However respectable the character of the Hebridian tacksmen, and however proper it is to support that order of men in particular cases ... it cannot be denied that they have been instrumental ... in keeping back the improvement of their country. The very circumstances indeed, which, in one point of view, constituted their respectability, were highly unfavourable to the cultivation of their lands. A tacksman, considering himself and his family as well entitled as any other members of society to the honours and advantages of civilized and polished life, had no idea of enduring the drudgery of a farmer's dull routine. The little that his farm could, by the miserable management of subtenants and servants, supply was either consumed in his family, or laid out in preparing his sons for entering into the army, navy, or some of the learned professions. The profession of a farmer never entered his head. The eldest son might perhaps have the farm, burdened with a provision for the daughters, &c. but it was not meant that he should remain at home to manage it himself, or that he should see one acre of it, until he had first tried to make his fortune in the world.

James Macdonald accepts that tacksmen, the class from which he himself came, '... are exceedingly useful, and often necessary, for maintaining good order and government in the country. Without their aid, the efforts of the clergy and officers of justice would be painful and unavailing; and therefore they ought not to be rashly banished, were they to be viewed in no other light than merely as subsidiary to the police and moral administration of the Isles'. He accepts that in Islay 'most of the improvements ... have been carried on by these tacksmen, under the inspection of the landlord'. Whilst the tenants 'have begun to follow the example of the tacksmen, in draining, enclosing, sowing grass seeds, and adopting a judicious rotation of crops, as well as in reclaiming wild and waste land'.[46]

Did Coll's tacksmen at this time resemble those on Islay or the men critiscised by James Macdonald? There were circa 1800 five relatively large tacksmen on Alexander's estate in Coll. In some respects they fitted into James Macdonald's picture of the generality of tacksmen. Allan Maclean of Crossapol was a half-pay officer in the Royal Scots. One of his sons went off to London to become a wine merchant, another was destined for the church, but the eldest certainly was a serious farmer who appears to have had no other ambitions than to improve his tack and look after the people of Coll's interests in the desperate years ahead.

There is no evidence that Hugh Maclean of Knock ever left Coll, but his sons had no desire to be farmers and both became surgeons in the service of the East India Company. John Maclean of Gallanach, who had succeeded his father Captain Lachlan, late of the East India Company does not appear to have been anything other than a farmer until he was balloted as a militiaman,[47] and it is perhaps significant that when his tack expired it was not renewed. His younger half-brother Lachlan emigrated to Jamaica and became a shipwright.[48]

Gallanach consisted of 700 acres. In 1801 Charles Maclean who had a shop in Arinagour took over as tacksman. Charles was the son of a small tenant farmer in Ardnish. He had a good education, probably thanks to Mr Donald Maclean, who ran a small school at Crossapol during his holidays from King's College Aberdeen.[49] He married Mr Donald's sister and in doing so he joined the Coll establishment becoming both an elder of the Kirk and an ensign in the Volunteers. Charles had one son who, as we will see, trained as a doctor and became a large sheep farmer.

Neil Rankin, Coll's former piper,[50] was by 1798 tacksman of Cliad. His eldest son Hector who was to succeed him at Cliad was, at least at first, a full time farmer. Neil's younger Hugh had left the island in 1791 and joined the army. The youngest son Coun, as we shall see, was extremely ambitious and was to have a career both in and away from the Hebrides.

The last of the large tacksmen was Alexander Maclean, the bailie, who from 1797 was tacksman of Arileod. This was a new tack, created after 1794 from the old joint tenant farm of Feall and what had probably been that part of Breacachadh, which supported the 'changehouse' at Arileod. It was in existence by 1794. This inn, for which the bailie also appears to have been responsible, was situated at the T-junction where the old Totronald-Ballyhough-Grishipol track to the north of the island joined the new road being constructed to the harbour at Arinagour. It was not a very salubrious establishment. The Hon. Mrs Murray of Kensington, writing after a visit to Coll in 1802 says that it is 'not fit for *gentles* (gentlefolk) to put up at'.[51] Alexander Arileod's son remained in Coll as a tenant farmer.

In 1776 Feall had been the most highly populated joint-tenant farm on Coll with a population of 97. As it was gradually cleared to turn it into the bailie's tack the number of baptisms at Feall got less each year. There were none after 1802.

The bailie was responsble for running Coll's baron-bailie court. Since the court's jurisdiction had been severely limited after the '45 Rebellion, its powers were much reduced. It was now limited to arbitrating between neighbours. That baron-courts still functioned after the '45 is clear from the Duke of Argyll's Tiree tack book, which states that the tacksman of the Two Ends of Coll in 1770: 'shall compear and answer at the said Duke's Baron Bailie Courts to be held within the said Island of Coll'. It is also inferred that they existed into the nineteenth century in James Macdonald's eulogy on the Gaelic language when he writes:

> The real uncorrupted Highland or Hebridian language, is noble and energetic. The powers displayed by the natives in conversation, and in the pleadings at the baron bailie courts, are truly astonishing. The eloquence exhibited there would not be believed by any stranger unaquainted with the habits and the language of this people, and certainly is unequalled in the British empire... The powers of language alluded to may, probably, be in a greater measure derived from the manners and habits of the natives, than from any peculiar felicity in their vernacular language; but, whatever may be the cause, the fact is certain: The mountains and vales of the Hebridiaes contain more genuine elegance, more astonishing readiness of expression, a greater command of words and ideas, and these well arranged, luminously arrayed, and powerfully and ingeniously adapted to the speaker's purpose, than we have found among the same classes of people in any other part of Europe.[52]

It is highly probable that the baron-bailie was the man, under Coll's direction, who implemented his reorganisation of the estate. He must have been a convinced improver or he would not have been employed. The other evidence of his dedication to improvement, is that James Macdonald would hardly have said 'that the most valuable parts of the property of Mr Maclean of Coll ... [are] ... exceedingly well managed, and exhibit models of Hebridian industry to all around them,'[53] if the bailie had not been up to his job. He was later made tacksman of Ardnish and Freslan, the land Alexander purchased from the Duke, perhaps as a reward for his hard work. After his retirement he had Freslan rent free.

Alexander Maclean of Coll had no doubt read Doctor Johnson's *A Journey to the Western Islands of Scotland*. He evidently had noted his advice:

> If the tacksmen be banished, who will be left to impart knowledge, or impress civility? The laird must always be at a distance from the greater part of his lands; and if he resides at all upon them, must drag his days in solitude, having no longer either a friend or a companion; he will therefore depart to some more comfortable residence, and leave the tenants to the wisdom and mercy of a factor.[54]

However good or not the tacksmen of Coll were as farmers, they were an essential ingredient in Coll society, if Alexander was to continue to reside there, reorganise his estate and save his people from having to emigrate.

Notes

1. EUL. La ii, 300. 16 December 1775: Alexander Maclean, younger of Coll to Simon Fraser.
2. His report, published in 1811, under the title *A General View of the Agriculture of the Hebrides*, is one of the most valuable studies of the area to be written before the Islands were fundamentally altered later in the nineteenth century. It is different to other surveys because its author is not an outsider looking in, but was brought up in the Hebrides. He was a native Gaelic speaker and a linguist of some repute who had travelled throughout Europe. He was also a shrewd observer of men and manners. [See Alexander Gillies *A Hebridean in Goethe's Weimar* (1969)].
3. Michael Flinn & others *Scottish Population History* (1977), 421–38.
4. Hector Maclean of the Isle of Muck had 80 children up to the age of 18 inoculated by a surgeon in 1772. [*Boswell*, 187].
5. *General View*, 729.
6. *General View*, 132–3.
7. OS. Sheet NM 15 NE (1976).
8. Nicholas Maclean-Bristol (ed) *Inhabitants of the InnerIsles Morvern and Ardnamurchan 1716* (1998), 158.
9. Archibald Mackenzie or Matheson replying to a letter from his son Duncan of 12 July 1872. I have to thank the late Betty Macdougal (Mrs Macrae) for a photocopy of this letter sent to her in 1974 by Duncan's great grandson Thomas Mackenzie Warren, PO Box 53, West Vancouver, British Columbia, Canada
10. NAS. CH2. 70. 1. 29 October 1796
11. NAS. CH2. 70. 2. 4 Fe. 1818.
12. NAS. CH2. 70. 1, 35.
13. *Johnson*, 202.
14. NAS. RHP. 3368: The miller then had a croft of 7 acres, whilst the main holding consisted of 18 acres of arable, 3 acres of rocky arable, 3 acres of green pasture, 10 acres of moss and 74 acres of muir. In addition there was another croft, perhaps what is now known as *Dunanachadh*, south of the road, made up of 4 acres of arable, 8 acres of rocky arable, 1 ruid of green pasture and 4 acres of moss.
15. NAS. CH2. 70. 1, 35 lists 'John Campbell apprentice to Donald Macdonald'. The latter is likely to be a relation of Allan Macdonald *Ailein Muilleir* [*Clan Gillean*, 385], the miller at Cliad in 1776.
16. Hector Maclean & Margaret Maclean were in Hyne by 1794. They evidently succeeded for in the 1830s the father and 3 of his sons were there as tenants [NAS. CH2. 70. 2]. Hector was probably a son of 'Allan Roy at Feall'.
17. Extract from Mr Ebenezer Davidson, dated 19 August 1813. Appendix II. *Third Annual Report of the Society for Gaelic Schools 1813*, [NLS. 1939. 5 (18)].

18. *General View*, 552.
19. NAS. GD112. 52. 79. 8.
20. He was the son of Hugh McKinnon & Ann Campbell in Totronald in 1776 [NAS. CH2. 70. 1, 36]; he married on 13 January 1791 when he was in Triallan and his eldest son Hugh was baptised there on 11 January 1792; on 6 April 1793 he enlisted in the Breadalbane Fencibles: aged 22; 5ft 4 in; Labourer; complexion: fair; Hair: brown; Eyes: grey; Born: Coll [NAS. GD 112. 52. 539]; he signs 'HMcK' when he receives his pay [NAS. GD 112. 52.555].
21. NAS. CH 2. 70. 1, 36. Charles Macdonald was the soldier Alexander Maclean of Coll had written about to his adjutant in September 1794. [NAS. GD 112. 52.39].
22. The elder brother of John Johnston in Arnabost in 1776 was probably Alexander Johnston in Ballyhough who had probably become one of the tenants there by marrying a Campbell tenant.
23. John Johnston (1836–1921) in Totamore Coll to AL Johnston 19 March 1906 [BCP. Johnston folder].
24. 2 November 1791: Neil Johnston m. in Feall Mary Mackinnon; 18 January 1792: son Allan baptised; 6 April 1793 attested 'labourer' aged 26; PM 190; 17 November 1793: son Lachlan baptised [Neil described as 'soldier']; 24 December 1793: signs paybook with x; 24 December 1794 £2.12s.2¼d; 19 July 1801: son Donald baptised;
25. NAS. CH2. 70. 1. 25 December 1796 and subsequent history of family [Nova Scotia Public Archives. Kamloops number. 604-376-8902].
26. *Clan Gillean*, 419.
27. Nicholas Maclean-Bristol 'A Genealogical Problem Solved' *WHN&Q* 1st Series, No. XXX (February 1987), 13–7.
28. NAS. GD 112. 52. 555.
29. TNA. WO 13. 4175 (Part 2).
30. He appears there in the 1841 Census as tenant aged 70 [General Register House. Parish of Tiree & Coll Census. 551. 25].
31. In 1776 there were four other Campbell households in Ballyhough.
32. As suggested in Chapter 9 it is probable that this family were amongst Coll's hereditary luchd-tighe.
33. NAS. CH 2. 70. 2: 3 May 1818 Kirk Session Meeting when Hector 'owned carnal intercourse with' Cathrine McDonald from Kilmore in Mull who had recently been his servant.
34. What follows in the next four paragraphs is based on a lecture by Margaret M. McKay for an 'Awareness course' on the Project Trust's Selection Courses on the Isle of Coll in the 1970s.
35. It is now the Project Trust's croft and the site of its selection course's group task – building a lazy-bed.
36. *General View*, 72–3.
37. NAS. RS10. 15. 2414b–2415b.
38. ICP. Tiree Tacks, 125. Maclean of Coll may have been tacksmen of Ardnish even earlier than 1789, as he appears to have removed MacFadyens from Ardnish to Feall and Ballyhough as early as 1784 [Nicholas Maclean-Bristol 'Ballyhough Farm, Isle of Coll', *WHN&Q* Series 3, No 5 (November 2002), 9].
39. *RCAHMS* Argyll, vol. 3 (1980), 229 & Plate 78b.
40. It was soon after severely damaged in a storm. Information provided by the late Hector MacPhail, Tiree.
41. John Ogg *House in the Hebrides* (2004), 15.
42. He had been employed by Alexander since at least 1801 [NAS. RS10. 15. 2414b]; Holmes Gray 'Hugh Gray, Innkeeper in Coll' *WHN&Q* Series 2 No. 13 (February 1995), 19.
43. John MacFadyen, *Iain Hyne* says in his scrapbook [162–3] that they lived in Beinn Tioraidh.
44. NAS. CH2. 70. 1: 23 June 1796.
45. Extract from Mr Ebenezer Davidson, dated 22 July 1815. Appendix. *5th Annual Report of the Society for Gaelic Schools 1816*, 86.
46. *General View*, 74–7.
47. Argyll & Bute District Council. Minute Book of the General Court of Lieutenancy. CO 6. 1. 11. 1. I have to thank Murdo MacDonald, Archivist for this reference.

48. TNA. Wills. Tebbs 343. Proved 4 June 1831.
49. *Boswell*, 269.
50. Lord Selkirk says that 'the Piper' was a gentleman [*Observations on the Present State of the Highlands of Scotland*, App. B, xii].
51. The Hon. Mrs Murray Aust *A Companion and Useful Guide to the Beauties of Scotland and the Hebrides*. vol. II (1810), 93.
52. *General View*, 563–6.
53. *General View*, 72–3.
54. *Johnson*, 134–5.

Chapter Thirty-Three

Visitors

As we have seen the war with Revolutionary France ended in March 1802. Whilst it was fought wealthy English tourists, barred from visiting the continent, went north to explore the Hebrides. They did so often with letters of introduction to local lairds and ministers, who, perhaps, with so many members of their families away at the war, were deprived of genteel company, and opened their doors to the visitors with amazing hospitality and generosity.[1]

One of these visitors, who did not have a letter of introduction, was Edward Clarke, the future Professor of Mineralogy.[2] In the summer of 1797, when he was tutor to The Hon. Berkeley Paget,[3] Clarke took his charge on a tour of the Hebrides. On a Saturday morning in July they

> entered the harbour of Col, under the Laird's house, landed and proceeded to the top of Ben Fiol [Feall], to take a view of the whole island.

Clarke had evidently found some local people to act as his guides for he remarks when examining the island from the top of Ben Feall that:

> There is very little appearance of cultivation. The island is a ridge of low blue black rocks, chiefly of quartz. While we were on Ben Fiol, they pointed out to me what they called a town, at the foot of the hill; I looked attentively, and saw seveal heaps of straw like ant hills. We descended immediately to examine this curious town. It was built much after that mentioned by Tacitus, which was practised by the ancient Germans, and consisted of about twenty extremely small huts, put together without order or form, not in streets, or straight rows, but standing in all directions, every one places his hut according to his fancy.
>
> The huts of Coll appeared to me the most curious things we had seen. There are several of these *towns* or villages in the island, looking much like the towns in the South Sea Islands, as represented in Cooke's voyages. Any of these islanders will build his house in two days: 'tis only making a circle of stones, and covering the top with straw. It is not exaggeration, when I declare, a stranger might walk over the island, without ever perceiving them.

He goes on to say:

> It is inconceivable how a race of men, so healthy and sturdy as these islanders, can be brought up in such huts as these. I crept into several of them, by a little aperture ... in one side, which serves for a door, and which barely admits a common-sized man stooping, without having

recourse to all fours. I found the inside of all of them without exception interiors filled with smoke, which endeavoured in vain to escape by means of the door, and through several accidental fissures in the roof. It was a sultry morning in July, not withstanding which, in the midst of the suffocating cloud half viewless, a group of nondescript boys, squatting on their haunches, were surrounding a peat fire, without any other apparent object in contemplation than the effect of such an atmosphere upon each others' visages.

On leaving Feall they were making their way back to their ship when they were accosted by Mrs Maclean, wife of the laird of Coll, 'who kindly invited us as strangers to pass the day in her house. Her brother[4] [-in-law], Hugh, hearing of our arrival, had gone in search of us; but as we had taken a different route in our return, we missed him. He soon came in, and apologised for not sending the boat off the last night, but seeing us not to enter the harbour, it was concluded we did not mean to touch at the island'.

Clarke, like most other visitors to the islands, had read Dr Johnson's *Journey to the Western Islands of Scotland*, for he writes:

The proverbial hospitality of this worthy family has been marked sufficiently public by the writing of Johnson and many others. They make it a rule to send an invitation on board any vessel, the moment it enters the harbour, and keep a light burning in the upper part of their house all night as a guide to boats, which may wish to enter. I was happy to be in the company with a brother of the young man so much noticed by Johnson.

Clarke, in conversation with Coll's brother Hugh, asked if there were any cairns on Coll. He was told there was only one in the whole island. It was called *cairn mich Re* (i.e. càrn mhic righ) signifying the cairn or tomb of the King's son. He had for some time wished to excavate one and

expressing a wish to that effect, Mr M. informed me he had often thought of doing it himself, and if pleased we would set out to the spot immediately. Having provided a sufficient number of assistants with spades, a pickaxe &c, we proceeded about 3 miles across the island to a spot mentioned by Mr M. I found here a small cairn by the roadside.

It is situated near the village of Grishipol, in the north of the island. We soon fell to work, and made a rapid progress, endeavouring to perforate the cairn, by opening a channel from east to west. While we were thus employed a venerable figure with hair as white as snow, came slowly up to the cairn, shaking his head and muttering something in Gaelic which I did not understand. Mr M. interpreting for me told me he said 'it was unlucky to disturb the bones of the dead!' As soon as he heard the voice of his Laird, he seized his hand kissing it eagerly poured forth blessings upon every member of the house of Col.

This venerable old man can be none other than of Ludovic Matheson, *Maoldòmhnaich Mac Mhathain*.[5]

Mr M. informed me that his age already exceeded above a hundred years, and he still continued to work, with the perfect use of all his limbs and faculties. He begged for some snuff, and as soon as he obtained it, began to sing a Gaelic song. It was an historical ballad, relating the death of one of the ancestors of the Maclean family, who was drowned, and concluded his account of his exploits, his carriage, and an ode given upon his character and benevolence, foretelling the future honours of the race.[6]

Clarke continues:

I am sorry to add our labours at the cairn were not productive of much information. We discovered nothing; but in casting out the stones, I found several of that description of stones, which are venerated in Mull for their imaginary virtues, also several specimens of beautiful black Mica. Mr M. said, and I believe with truth, that cairns were not erected merely where a person was interred, but often to commemorate the spot on which he died; and also at the place where his body rested, from the place of his death to all the places where his body rested to the place of his interment. The old man informed us, he remembered the time when at any common funeral in Col, if the body was carried by that cairn, every one of the attendants cast a stone upon it. It is an expression of friendship and affection, at this hour among the islanders to say 'I will cast a stone upon your cairn!'

Finding our labour ineffectual, we left our work, and returned to Mr M.'s house. On our road I saw several upright stones, particularly two, called the whispering stones, which they call the giant's grave, and also evident traces of ancient cairns, all of which, though hardly noticed by or known to the natives, bear strong marks of manual labour. On the top of Ben Hough is a large stone, placed on four others,[7] resembling what is called a camlich in Wales.

Upon the seashore at the southern point of the island, is a remarkable vein of the purest lead ore, which runs into the rock. It is extraordinary no person has undertaken to work it. I saw specimens of it at Mr M.'s, and was informed that blocks of the ore amounting to 20 or 30 pounds in weight, had frequently been taken from them by mere curiousity ...

Edward Clarke ends his journal of his time on Coll, which was evidently written for publication, by saying:

I cannot take leave of Col, without expressing a sense of obligation I shall ever feel for the liberal hospitality experienced in the mansion of its Laird. We were utter strangers to the family, and entered their home as wanderers, without any recommendation, and were received not only with a hospitable welcome, but treated with a degree of magnificence during our stay upon the island, which might have done honour to the noblest houses in Great Britain. To heighten our satisfaction, Mr M. himself with the same zeal which his amiable but unfortunate brother showed Dr Johnson and Mr Boswell, offered to accompany us for the remainder of our voyage; and from his general acquaintance with the principal families of all the islands in the Hebrides, we derived a passport to every thing worthy of notice among them.[8]

* * *

They left Coll on the morning of the 23rd and visited Iona and Canna. On 26th July 'we took the long boat, left the harbour' and approached the west coast of Rum landing at a fertile steep-sided glen dominated by the towering ramparts of Bloodstone Hill'. He continues:

A few huts with a small boat or two drawn up upon the beach constitute what the natives term one of their villages ... a farm called Guidill, or Gewdale, and as it is on Mackenzie's chart

Guordil, and immediately several of the islanders came to welcome Mr Maclean, the brother of their Laird ... We accompanied him into a cottage of one of his brother's tenants ... Two of the sons belonging to the old owner of the cottage afterwards conducted us by a narrow path along the north side of the island, over a frightening precipice.

Returning to Guerdil, we found the old man, who received us on landing, waiting with his bonnet in his hand,[9] to request that we would honour his cottage with a short visit.

Mr M. conducted us in where they found 'a clean but homely cloth spread upon a board between two beds, which served us for chairs, upon which was placed a collation of cream, eggs, new milk, cheese, oat cakes and several bottles of fine, old Lisbon wine.'[10]

Eventually after visiting Barra and St Kilda the visitors reached Coll at midnight. Touching the north end of the island, they landed Mr Maclean back home 'and in the morning we found ourselves once again passing down the Sound of Mull'.[11]

* * *

As other visitors followed the pioneers, there was a need for a guidebook to ease their journeys. The Hon. Mrs Murray,[12] of Kensington, who filled this gap in the market, claimed to write

> not for fame, nor for bread ... I write because I think my Guide will be really useful to travelers, who may follow my steps through Scotland, and to the Lakes of Cumberland, Westmoreland, and Lancashire; by informing them of those objects which are worthy of notice, and at the same time acquainting them where, and by what means they can get at them in the safest and most comfortable manner.[13]

She herself was prepared to rough it and in July 1802, en route to Eigg, engaged a boat in Bunessan in the Ross of Mull

> which had conveyed a gentleman and his family with fourteen head of cattle from Barra ... It was a large flat bottomed boat, made on purpose to transport cattle and sheep from one island to another. There was in it one division for beasts, one for passengers, a hole to cook victuals in, and another hole for people to lie down in, which latter dark places I did not approach.

Like Boswell and Johnson before her she did not go where she intended,

> for after being becalmed for a considerable time, the wind arose and blew right a-head of us, and the tide also turned against us. A council was called to determine what was to be done ... It was decided for Coll, and the boat veered to the west. The north end of Coll was at that time nearly opposite to us, which made my heart somewhat light, as I began to be tired of the boat, having been eleven hours in it. The wind blew tolerably brisk, and we were off the land of Coll in the given time; but as it is impossible to land on the north end of the island, there being no harbour for a boat, shelter for man, nor any road leading to any sort of habitation; when we came to the rocky shore, to my grief and astonishment, I found we had to sail south nearly the length of the island, before we could reach Colonel M'Lean Coll's house, a distance of six or seven leagues ...

> We passed point after point but no harbour appeared. The boatmen began to talk loud in Gaelic, and damn in English... the night was fast approaching, and my spirits were far below par, when on a sudden I heard the joyful sound, 'Here it is, here it is!' The wind was high, and we steered into the Loch full sail. The wind was directly for us, but the tide contrary, which made the sea run high, and roar amongst the rocks. The sea was dashing, the sails rattling, the sailors hollowing and shouting... Just at that moment a small fishing boat came down the Loch; I had her hailed to come alongside of us, with an intention for her to pilot us to the anchoring place. There was only one savage-looking man in the boat, and a little girl. The fisherman talked loud in order to direct the sailors, who were swearing, because they could not hear what he said by reason of the noise of sea and wind. The cockle-shell danced backwards and forwards around us, struggling with the waves to get to us, and at last the old man caught hold of a rope thrown to him, by which his boat was drawn close alongside of us; and not withstanding the boat was going full sail, I made no hesitation, but hoisted myself over the side of the large boat, and slipped down into the small one, which was strewed with the refuse of herrings, and half filled with water...[14]

Mrs Murray and her companion reached the shore and 'scrambled over a ridge of slippery rocks

> and gained the grass fields leading to Coll's mansion, where we were received, although I was a stranger, with all imaginable attention and hospitality by Colonel M'Lean and his amiable daughter and family'.[15]

* * *

Another visitor, Necker de Saussure, says that he had the pleasure of knowing Maclean of Coll in Edinburgh. The latter was not at home when de Saussure turned up on the island and he was agreeably surprised when

> Mr Maclean's steward who came out to meet us, hastened to invite us, in the name of his master, to fix our abode at his house as long as we staid at Coll. He offered to accompany us where we chose, and was in every way anxious to make himself agreeable to us.[16]

He goes on to say that at Coll House 'there is a good library, which is a valuable object for a party who often has to while years in a place bereft of all the pleasures of society'.

What Mrs Murray does not tell is that a few months before she landed on Coll, Alexander's wife Catharina had died at Clifton, near Bristol.[17] His wife's death must have been a catastrophic blow to Alexander. They had been a devoted couple and Alexander was not prepared for her to be buried at Kilunaig, the ancient burial ground of the Macleans of Coll, which is seven miles away from Coll House and was beginning to be covered by blowing sand. Instead he built a mausoleum in Ardnish,[18] above the north-east corner of Crossapol beach, within easy walking distance from his house.

Rider Haggard, who visited Coll in 1898, says of the new tomb that:

> a more impressive or desolate resting-place for the bones of a departed family can scarcely be imagined, overlooking as it does the waters of Crossapol Bay, across which the winds moan without ceasing. No church or building is near it, the tomb, a stone enclosure of

about twenty feet square, in the midst of which stands a sarcophagus, being the only trace of man's handiwork upon all the sweep of plain and bents... On the wall of the tomb facing the gateway is a marble slab, which is so rapidly decaying and becoming illegible.

He copied the inscription. It said:

THE LATTER CEMETRY OF THE FAMILY BEING NEARLY OVER WHELMED BY SAND BLOWING, THIS WAS ERECTED, AND THE REMAINS OF HIS REMOVED TO IT BY ALEXANDER MCLEAN OF COLL, UPON THE OCCASION OF THE LAMENTED DEATH OF HIS BELOVED COMPANION, CATHARINA CAMERON, THE BEAUTY OF WHOSE PERSON WAS ONLY SURPASSED BY THE VIRTUES AND AMIABLE DISPOSITION OF HER MIND. OBT. CLIFTON 10 FEB. 1802, AE. 46.[19]

Lightning later destroyed the inscription.

* * *

On 27th July 1802 Mrs Murray set sail from Coll in another cattle boat belonging to the Island. She writes 'the boat was a good one, and the sailors were very civil, attentive men, so that we performed our voyage with pleasure and safety to Eigg... and we landed in a snug little harbour[20]... As soon as we landed on Eigg, we sent up a message to Mr M'Lean to inform him [i.e. Mr Donald Maclean, Minister of Eigg] of our intention of paying him a visit'. Mrs Murray's companion, Mr Dugald Campbell, was a minister in Mull, which is perhaps one of the reasons they 'were received by him and his family with a cordial welcome'. She was to claim that 'his manse is a good one, and pleasantly situated about a mile from the harbour'.[21]

Mrs Murray explains that the majority of the islanders were Roman Catholics and had a priest who lived on the island. A fact that surprised Necker de Saussure when he visited Eigg five years later was that:

Athough the inhabitants of the two kinds of worship live on good terms with each other, I never the less heard in this small island several animated discussions on religious controversy. This is a subject treated with much warmth and spirit without bitterness or intolerance. We heard with surprise a repetition of arguments and a kind of logic, which to all the rest of Europe have for many ages become obsolete.[22]

As we have seen, relations between the two religions were not as cordial as they seemed on the surface. However, the inhabitants generally put on a united front in the face of visitors.

Mrs Murray goes on to sing the praises of Mr Donald. She says:

The worthy Protestant minister's flock in Eigg is but small, but his duty, upon the whole, is exceedingly hard. He is the minister of the small isles, namely Eigg, (where he resides,) Muchd, Rum, and Canna. He attends these isles alternatively, at the risk of his life almost every time he visits the two last named. Fortunately for him he is fond of the sea, and is reckoned the most skilful mariner in the Hebrides.

These circumstances, she believed:

> render him fitter for his allotted duty than most other gentlemen of his profession. He has injured his health by being so much exposed to the hardships of his frequent voyages. His salary too, is very inadequate to his labour and expense, being obliged to keep a large boat, and men to assist him to navigate it.

Mr Donald, like almost every other minister in the Highlands, had a farm in addition to his glebe land. This was the farm called Sandabeg for which, in 1798, he paid a rent of £8.[23] Without a farm no minister could have maintained his family, particularly in the islands, 'as there are no markets, a farm is absolutely necessary to produce cattle, sheep and grain, sufficient for the consumption of every family'.[24]

On the first clear morning after her arrival Mrs Murray mounted Mrs Maclean's pony and set out to climb the Sgurr of Eigg, the dramatic basalt plug that dominates the south-west corner of the island. She was accompanied by her friends, including Ranald Macdonald of Laig, a gentleman of eighty years old, who early that morning had walked across the island to pay his respects to her. Ranald Macdonald was the son of the great Gaelic poet *Alasdair Mac Mhaigstir Alasdair*. In 1776 he had published the first anthology of Gaelic verse ever printed in Scotland,[25] and he was keen to meet a fellow author. Mrs Murray spent one night at his house and was entertained by him with stories of the '45.[26]

On 4 August Mrs Murray set sail for Rum in his boat with Mr Donald. She writes:

> It was one of the clearest days I ever was out in, which procured me the finest treat imaginable of mountain scenery, for nothing can surpass in picturesque form the hills of Culin, and of Strath in Skye, and those in Rum, and the Scur and cliffs in Eigg. We arrived at the head of the harbour in Rum in the afternoon, and left it at six the next morning. The island is so excessively wild and rugged. I was unable to explore any part of it. It is at the head of this bay where Mr. M'Lean preaches in a barn to his Rum flock.[27]

Rum was 'reputed to be the happiest in the Hebrides', wrote de Saussure 'both on account of the low rent which Mr Maclean receives for his farms, and because the isle furnishes a great number of large and small cattle, which supply them all with meat. Their principal occupations are the care of cattle, fishing and getting of sea-weed, which they burn for the purpose of extracting alkali'.[28] Most other commentators say that no kelp was made on Rum.[29]

In 1793 Rum had a population of 443.[30] It had increased dramatically since 1764 when Dr Walker says the population was 288. Then 52 heads of families were paying rent directly to the landlord. By 1793 there were only 43 tenants paying rent. This meant that although the total population had increased the number with a stake in the land had fallen.

In 1793 the total rental of Rum was £209.13s.6d.[31] James Macdonald takes Rum as an example of the problem facing benevolent lairds, such as

> Mr Maclean of Coll [who] might let as a sheep-walk his large island of Rum, containing upwards of twenty-thousand Scotch acres at a profit of several hundred pounds per annum, to two or three farmers, instead of the present three hundred and fifty inhabitants who possess it for a mere trifle, could he find any means of providing for these poor people consistent with

his patriotism and humanity. But although he has been for some years looking out for eligible situations for these persons, who are more and more crowded every year, and consequently must gain by being removed from an island on which they cannot possibly raise a comfortable subsistence, yet he has not hitherto been successful. Few men have had more trouble in this respect, and none has less deserved it.[32]

Neither Mrs Murray nor de Saussure visited Guirdal in the west of Rum. The tacksman Charles Maclean, who had entertained Edward Clarke there in 1797 was dead by 1803. Hector, who now farmed Guirdal with his two brothers Allan and Alexander, was the son of Edward Clarke's host. They were descended from a younger son of Neil Og Maclean of Crossapol (1679). Their grandfather *Iain mac Thearlaich*[33] settled originally in Harris, Rum, and their father Charles moved to Guirdal before 1764 when he married Flora, daughter of John and Mary Maclean in Guirdal.[34]

These sons of Coll tacksmen had probably been sent to Rum after 1735, when the island 'was depopulate' by smallpox.[35] Like their kinsmen in Coll, several of their descendants were elders of the kirk. Some became ministers. Others were officers in the Volunteers. One was persuaded by Alexander Maclean of Coll in 1801 to stock his farm with black-faced sheep. He 'with much reluctance complied with his landlord's injunction, but instead of stocking his farm fully, he only put one half of the number of sheep the farm would feed; notwithstanding, he sold the wool of the half stock of sheep the first year for £50 and the rent of the whole farm was only £60'.[36]

* * *

Mrs Murray and Mr Donald left Rum for Skye on 5th August. It was a clear morning, she writes, 'till we came under the bold cliffs near the mouth of Loch Einort, where Mr. M'Lean's maritime skill was somewhat put to the test, for we experienced several great squalls, which made me shrink from the blast from Culin's towering crags, and seat myself at the bottom of the boat to be out of the way of the gib'.[37]

She continues:

We were a long time tacking and working the boat to its anchorage in Loch Einort, which is surrounded by a shoulder of Culin and other cliffs, and we found that spot as silent and forlorn as an uninhabited island. We landed, and were espied by one solitary man, who came down the mountain to ask if he could assist us. He was useful in aiding our people to carry my baggage to some huts at two miles distance . . .

As we advanced to the huts, the good folks inhabiting them came out to gaze at us . . . It was a very fine day, and we found several very old men and women sitting upon stones and hillocks, near a rattling burn, with their grandchildren playing about them, and the mothers of the young ones sitting and knitting by the old ones, whom they had led out of the huts for the benefit of the fresh air . . . It was a pleasant sight. I entered one of the poorest of the huts, and there found a female, out of her place in society, for she was certainly born in a superior station to that which I found her.

We were informed that from those huts it was no more than three miles to Talisker. Surely, I said, I can walk three miles. No, madam, said Mrs Maclean, (the name of the female in the hut,) you must not think of walking, our Skye miles are not like your English miles; I have two horses not far in the hill; I have sent a boy for them; one you may ride, and the other will carry your baggage.

The horses came, but as I knew my Eigg friend [Mr Donald] could not walk even three miles, I insisted upon his riding, which was soon settled, as the good woman assured us the tall horse would carry double; and for all this civility I could not prevail upon this Skye Mrs M'Lean to accept any recompense. She said she could not bear that a stranger who had honoured her country with a visit, should pay for anything she had in her power to give.[38]

Incidents such as this helped confirm visitors in the belief that the people of the Hebrides really were noble savages. They might live simple impoverished lives but unlike the poor in other parts of the United Kingdom they were not affected by envy of their superiors or dissatisfied with their destiny. In fact many, as we shall see, *were* increasingly dissatisfied.

* * *

Visitors to the Hebrides must have expanded the social horizons of the lairds, ministers and tacksmen who entertained them. They gave their hosts an introduction to a wider world outside the Isles and contacts which helped secure patronage in situations where the lairds had little or no influence. Although they were from very different backgrounds to the missionaries of the SSPCK, these upper class visitors to the Islands also helped to diminish the lairds' monopoly of power and influence.

Notes

1. Donald Macleod, *Memoir of Norman Macleod. D.D.* (1876), 8–9.
2. He was born in 1769.
3. Berkeley Thomas, 6th son of Henry Bayly, 9th Baron Paget and 1st Earl of Uxbridge & Jane, eldest dau. of Very Rev. Arthur Champagne, dean of Clonmacnoise, in Ireland; b. 2 January 1780; m. 22 November 1804, Sophia Askell, dau. of Hon. William Bucknall, & d. 26 October 1842 with issue. [Peter Towend (ed) *Burke's Peerage* (104th Edition, 1967), 75.]
4. This must be a misprint or a misunderstanding. Mrs Maclean's only brother was in India. On 5 September 1797 news of his death was reported to Alexander Maclean of Coll [NAS. GD 112. 52. 74. 9]. The latter could not have been in Coll during Clarke's visit as he was in Banff with his battalion. Clarke's 'brother of the young man so much noticed by Johnson' was probably Hugh about whom Alexander wrote to Breadalbane for a commission in his regiment on 2 September 1797 [NAS. GD 112. 52. 74].
5. See Chapter 11, 94; Chapter 31, 287.
6. This song was perhaps the 'Song to Lachlann, Lord of Coll' by an unidentified Lachlann Maclean [Colm Ó Baoill (ed) *Eachann Bacach and other Maclean poets* (1979), 49–53]. I think he is unlikely to be the same Lachlan Maclean who composed 'Ascaoin *Molaidh na Pioba*' *Eachann Bacach*, 55–9, who is almost certainly Alexander Coll's uncle, the disinherited younger brother of Hector of Coll.
7. It is in fact an erratic, a block of rock brought from a distance by a glacier.
8. William Otter (ed) *The Life & Remains of the Rev. Edward Daniel LLD* (1824), 232–8.
9. The old man is probably the Charles Maclean born in 1737 who married Flora, the daughter of the previous tenant of Guirdal, whose brother Allan he succeeded [EUL. La.III, 839].
10. The latter had been salvaged from a wrecked ship, presumably the same vessel whose cargo Alexander Maclean of Coll found being bottled by his family when he returned home in 1797. NAS. GD 112. 52. 67. 21.
11. *The Life & Remains of the Rev. Edward Daniel Clarke LLD*, 302.

12. She was born Sarah Maese. In 1783 she married Captain the Hon William Murray RN (d. 25 December 1786), second son of 3rd Earl of Dunmore, who had taken part in the '45 and been tried for High Treason. Although he pleaded guilty, he was pardoned. She m. (2) 1 November 1802, George Aust, Under-Secretary of State for Foreign Affairs, and died 5 November 1811 [*The Kingdom of Scotland*, 1073].
13. *The Beauties of Scotland*, vol. 1, vii.
14. *The Beauties of Scotland*, vol. 1, 369–70.
15. *The Beauties of Scotland*, vol. 1, 371.
16. Necker de Saussure, *A Voyage to the Hebrides* (1822), 46.
17. *Scots Magazine*, vol. 64 (1802), 275.
18. *RCAHMS* Argyll, vol. 3 (1980), 158.
19. H Rider Haggard *A Farmer's Year* (1909), 349.
20. *The Beauties of Scotland*, vol. 1, 381–3.
21. *The Beauties of Scotland*, vol. 1, 393.
22. *A Voyage to the Hebrides*, 57.
23. Charles Fraser-Macintosh *Antiquarian Notes* (1897), 262.
24. *The Beauties of Scotland*, vol. 1, 385–6.
25. 'Comh-Chruinneachidh Ovannaigh, Gaidhealach, le Raonuill Macdonhnuill, Ann 'N Eilean Eigg. Vol. 1. Duneidiunn: Clo bhuailt ann le Walter Ruddiman. M, DCC, LXXVI'.
26. *The Beauties of Scotland*, vol. 1, 396–8.
27. *The Beauties of Scotland*, vol. 1, 398.
28. *A Voyage to the Hebrides*, 56.
29. For example *Minutes of Evidence Before Select Committee on Emigration From the United Kingdom: 1827*, 289.
30. *OSA*, 238.
31. *OSA*, 241.
32. *General View*, 104–5.
33. Born 1724; in Harris, Rum in 1764. [EUL. La. III, 839, 10].
34. '*John Mhic Thearlach Guirdal*' (He was the son of Charles, 4th son of John Maclean of Grishipol [of the first Grishipol family] and was dead by 1764). & Mary Maclean, (She was born in 1688. She is described as 'widow' in 1764 when she was living with her dau. Florry & son-in-law Charles in Guirdal). She was the daughter of Allan Maclean of Grishipol (1698 × 1716). See WHN&Q (2004)
35. *Report on the Hebrides*, 196.
36. *The Beauties of Scotland* (1810) vol. II, 398–9.
37. *The Beauties of Scotland*, vol. 1, 404.
38. *The Beauties of Scotland*, vol. 1, 405–8.

Part VI

The War with Napoleon
1803–1815

Chapter Thirty-Four

The Argyllshire & Inverness-shire Volunteers

The Peace of Amiens had been welcomed all over Europe. It was, however, merely an interlude in the struggle with France. War was to break out again in March 1803, and Napoleon determined to invade the British Isles.

As France prepared to invade, Volunteers were once again needed on the Coll estate. The Lord Lieutenant wrote to landowners in Argyll and on 26 May 1803 at Alnwick, on his way to London, Alexander Maclean of Coll replied to the Duke of Argyll's letter to say:

> I have already expressed my ideas as to a Battn in my corner of the country and have no doubt of succeeding even with officers upon the original plan of Government (without pay) – but should your Grace and Lord Lorne recommend a different plan I will be happy to assist in raising there – the same situation as formerly upon my Estate Viz. in Coll, Mull & Rum – I will name the officers most proper to command them – in the meantime it may not be unnecessary to mention that I intend to propose a Brother of mine[1] to command the Coll Company who was captain in the 60th Regt – and Allan McLean an old half-pay officer in the Royals for the Quinish or Mull Company.[2]

Coll was offered and declined the major's post in an Argyllshire Additional Battalion. On 29 September 1803 he wrote to the Marquesss of Lorne to say:

> My Lord, I am this instant honoured with your Lordship's letter of the [indecipherable] [you] are rightly informed that I had some intention of spending the ensuring winter in England, but neither that nor any other consideration would have prevented my using every exertion to forward the service of my country upon the present occasion, no[r?] shall any I can personally render be [?] should the case of necessity occur ... no further wish for being employed than was instigated by my sense of [?] duty ... consideration of rank I assure your Lordship would not in the smallest degree influence me.[3]

Command of the battalion, as in the previous, war went to the Duke's chamberlain Lieutenant-Colonel Graham.[4] Captain Hugh Maclean, who had entertained Edward Clarke in Coll in 1797, took command of the new Coll Company and, although he does not appear to have done any exercise days, received pay for 92 days. Allan Crossapol, who had commanded the company in the previous war, seems to have done all the work. He did so now as a lieutenant.[5]

Alexander's plans for his brother Hugh were dashed when on the 5th October 1803 the latter died in Coll, 'in consequence of fatigue during the Campaign in Holland'.[6] Allan Crossapol, succeeded him as company commander. The other officers were once again his brothers-in-law: the lieutenant was Alexander Maclean, the Bailie and the ensign Charles Maclean.[7] The sergeants were Allan Maclean Fiosgaradh, who was on permanent pay as drill sergeant, his brother Alexander and Murdoch Maclean in Arnabost. The latter is the former soldier in the Breadalbane Fencibles descended from Neil Buidh, the sixteenth-century archer. Both Alexander and Murdoch were only paid for the days they were at exercise.[8] There were also 2 corporals, 2 drummers and 51 private soldiers.

In 1803 the Quinish Company was not re-established as such. However, a Kilmore Company was raised under the command of Allan Maclean 'the red-haired doctor with the warm eyes', with an Archibald Campbell as his lieutenant. It included many of the old Quinish Company including the permanent drill sergeant Donald Morison.[9]

The formation of volunteer companies served to channel the patriotic feelings of the people in the Isles, without their having to serve in line regiments or be balloted for the militia. It also brought in useful additional income.

* * *

Although Mr Donald Maclean Minister of the Small Isles had in April 1799 been appointed a Deputy Lieutenant for the county of Inverness,[10] no one had got round to telling him. And on 1st January 1803 he wrote to Sir James Grant:

> Sir, Having had the honour of being appointed one of your DLs, (for several years, tho' I knew of it not till Summer last), I should with pleasure take an early opportunity of expressing a suitable sense of that honour and of the confidence reposed in me, of which it shall be my study not to appear undeserving.[11]

Mr Donald's reason for writing to Sir James was his concern at the number of people seeking to emigrate. During the war emigration had virtually ceased but with peace it began again.[12] 'Emigration, Sir' he writes:

> is an Object, to which I must beg leave to call your serious attention – In these Isles & along the neighbouring coasts of the mainland, an Emigrant spirit is come to an alarming pitch. It must grieve every lover of his country & its happy constitution, to see these fine fellows, who during the late troubles, *volunteered* for the *National Defence* – who were trained to the use of *arms* and were very capable of doing essential service to their country – now determined to quit their native land for ever – Thus shall we be deprived on future Emergencies, of their valuable Services, towards keeping at a distance the inveterate Enemies of all we hold dear – and towards checking a spirit of licentiousness at home.[13]

As we have already seen in the previous war, Mr Donald had commanded the Rum Company of the Argyllshire Volunteers. He was now given additional duties when on 22nd June 1802 he was made a Justice of the Peace.[14] The lack of JPs in Eigg was one of the grievances of the parish on which he had remarked in the *Old Statistical Account*.[15] Mr Donald was therefore a key player in the area during the war with Napoleon.

Like the Argyllshire Volunteers the Inverness-shire Volunteers had been stood down in May 1802. Their weapons had been handed in at Fort William,[16] and it was necessary to raise them once more. This time it was to be a more difficult task than it had been in 1797.

Instructions to raise a new battalion of Inverness-shire Volunteers went out as soon as the war began. They took time to reach Eigg. On 9 May 1803 Mr Donald wrote to Sir James Grant of Grant, the Lord Lieutenant to say:

> I regret too much time has been lost in its conveyance – on the 5th the proposals were published and the inhabitants invited to enroll on this island – Twenty-three of them only have hitherto got their names enrolled. On 6th [May] 44 enrolled at Islemuck and on 7th [May] 48 enrolled at Rum – Tis probable several others will offer their Services soon. Many of them express their dissatisfaction with the pay offered as too little. Had two days a week been allowed them as formerly, through out the year, it would have met up with a pretty general approbation among them; and many more would readily offer to join

That there was more than just a shortage of pay in the reluctance of men to enroll as volunteers in Eigg is clear from a letter to Sir James from Lachlan Mackinnon in Howlin, Eigg[17] written on 14 June 1803. He writes:

> The want of unanimity among the gentleman of this island will, I am afraid prevent the Company from being raised, as there are no volunteers to be got but their servants and Cottars, besides that some of them have been disgusted with Mr Maclean's conduct when the former company was raised.

Then Mr Donald had been accused of recommending only his favourites for commissions and Howlin was one of those who had complained to the Lord-Lieutenant. Now he was writing again directly to Sir James to claim a commission for his son Hector

> who is desirous of getting a Commission in the Volunteer Company that is to be raised in this island. He has served in the company established here in the last war and is now qualified to act as an officer in such a Corps.

Evidently Mr Donald was not the only person in Eigg who Howlin thought was trying to sabotage his ambitions. For, he writes:

> The Gentlemen who put in for being officers are McDonalds at least two of them, and are of a different persuasion from my son who is a protestant. They perhaps out of partiality for their own names and persuasion indeavour to exclude my son if they have it in their power. But as the whole depends upon your Lordship I flatter myself that you will not forget the only MacAlpine in this Island.

Both the Mackinnons and the Grants claimed descent from King Kenneth MacAlpin, who in 858 had died fighting the Picts.[18] Hector Mackinnon became the ensign in the Eigg Company. However, as Dr Macaskill the previous captain was now living in Fort William, command of the Company went to Laig's son Angus Macdonald, who was a Protestant, whilst the Lieutenancy went to Mr Donald's younger son, Neil.[19]

311

Mr Donald feared that 'From the backwardness shown in Eigg I fear they will scarcely make up a company of 50 privates'. He was more hopeful over 'Islemuck [where] all the inhabitants fit to carry arms have enrolled; yet a complete Company cannot be got there'. But if amalgamated with Rum whose company he had commanded in the previous war, 'I expect a Company of a hundred privates may be collected'.

He had not yet had a chance to visit Canna, where 'if unanimous a small company may be raised'. He goes on to point out that:

> It is proper to observe that the four Islands constituting this Militia District, Eigg alone is in the County of Inverness. Hence it may be proper to ask, is the whole parish, and district to be connected with Inverness County in a volunteer view, as well as in a Militia. In order to a proper arrangement, it is necessary to ascertain this with precision. The inhabitants concerned in Rum and Islemuck will have no objection to their annexation to Inverness-shire in a volunteer view, providing the Lord-Lieutenant and proprietors are unanimous to this point. In this District there is no one officer on half-pay, nor one formerly commissioned in a Regiment of the Line. Dr Macaskill at Fort William had the command of the late Volunteers; and I had the honour of his Majesty's Commission as captain of the late Rum Volunteers, of which I accepted at the desire of Colonel Maclean of Coll the proprietor of Rum, who recommended me for that purpose, believing none on the island maid fit to have the charge – The Volunteers now living in Rum & Isle Muck express their wishes I should have command of them – I have no reluctance to serve my Country in every capacity in which I may with propriety act, and if employed will be ready to accept the command of these men, that their services may not be lost to their Country and shall be well pleased to act under Sir James Grant's command, if matters can be so ordered.

He goes on to say that:

> Should it be my lot to have such command may I presume to recommend for the first Lieutenant my oldest son Alexander aged about 21 years. He has regularly studied Medicine & now practices in these Isles. Such a qualification must be no disadvantage to any Corps with which he may be connected – Besides he has been trained to the use of arms, having been the very first Volunteer who engaged to serve in the late Eigg Company which he did at my request, for Example's sake – Should a second Lieutenant be required, Mr John Maclean, son of a substantial Tacksman in Rum,[20] might be nominated, and Alexander Maclean Guirdale[21] may be a proper person for the Ensigncy in case there be two Lieutenants – I have been this prolix and particular in case it may be necessary for expediting this business.

His chief supported Mr Donald's offer. And on 13th June 1803 Maclean of Coll wrote from London to Sir James Grant to say:

> By a letter received a few days ago from the Duke of Argyll I find that my Island of Rum is placed in respect to Militia & Volunteers in the County of Inverness consequently under your Government.
>
> There was an exceeding good Company there the latter part of the late war, and if you think it advisable I will direct one to be raised there now. I would be happy to serve under your Command myself did not the state of the rest of my property prevent me. In case therefore

that this Company is accepted of, Mr Donald Maclean (the parish minister) who was formerly the Commandant will be the most proper to have the command now & the other officers can afterwards mentioned to you.[22]

* * *

On 11 August 1803 Mr Donald Maclean wrote a long letter from Eigg to Sir James Grant. In it he says:

> In this Parish the People in general have been ready to offer their services as Volunteers – A few Tacksmen of large farms, nurtured in the principles of Bigotry, and activated by selfish views were the only exceptions. Indeed the Eigg people, owing to this cause, were the most backward, and for this cause principally a party at the Islemuck have been admitted into the Eigg Company.
>
> In Rum and Islemuck, the Protestant islands in this Parish, the people expressed a most flattering readiness to enroll as volunteers when proposed to them. This I suggested in part in a former letter, and that a company of 100 Privates might with ease be raised betwixt the two islands, but now I am sorry to find them disappointed.

The request to form a company in Rum and Isle of Muck had evidently been turned down. Mr Donald puts his finger on the fundamental problem:

> This Parish, Sir, has been unfortunately in suspense, if I may so express it, betwixt the counties of Inverness and Argyle. Eigg alone having been heretofore connected with the former. By the former Volunteer scheme the late Rum Co[mpany] was attached to the Argyleshire Volunteers – Hence, in consequence of HM's Proclamation for raising Volunteer Corps, application was made to the Lord-Lieutenant of the County of Argylle for establishing a company in Rum – the application proved abortive; and it was communicated, that the whole of this Parish, by a late arrangement, has been annexed, in respect of volunteers, I suppose, to the County of Inverness.
>
> The application to the Lord-Lieutenant of Inverness-shire, after this arrangement was distinctly ascertained, by the Proprietor of Rum, for a volunteer Co[mpany] on that island, I fear has been too late; so that the People are disappointed, and the county thus deprived in the present critical emergency of the services of a body of men already in a great measure trained to the use of arms, who to do them Justice, are generally able bodied men, and from the best principles attached to King & Country, and it its public established court and religion.

He adds a personal concern when he goes on to say:

> My own feeling too, are not the less hurt at their disappointment, that oblique hints are thrown out, that it must have arisen from inattention in me to the business – After the County volunteer arrangements have been settled I must be sensible of the intricacy in getting them established ...

He was probably well aware of the complaints from the Eigg tacksmen for he adds:

> should it be thought improper to reappoint me their commander, I would take the liberty to recommend my eldest son Alexander for that station, who, I have reason to believe will be

acceptable to the People – has been a volunteer and bred to medicine – Subalterns may be got with ease, according to its strength if established.

At the start of the nineteenth century Nepotism was not thought of as being improper in the Hebrides. Not to look after your own relations was considered far more worthy of condemnation. Mr Donald could not be accused of that sin. In addition to his eldest son, as we have seen, he had his second son appointed as lieutenant in the Eigg Company of Volunteers. He served in it from 1803–6.[23]

* * *

Mr Donald's son Neil was born in Mull on 11th July 1784. In 1797 he matriculated at King's College, Aberdeen.[24] On 17 July 1799 he was recommended by the Synod of Glenelg to receive financial support from their funds to help with his education 'with a view to the Holy Ministry'.[25]

Neil appears at first to have been reluctant to become a minister. Mr Donald writing from Edinburgh in January 1805 in reply to a letter from his eldest son Alexander says:

> Neil attends the Divinity Hall, but cannot get his name enrolled, till an Attestation of his Graduation is procured from Aberdeen. I hope the Sentiments you express relative to his present plan will help to reconcile him to its merit more.[26]

At Divinity Hall in Edinburgh Neil shared lodgings with Norman Macleod (1783–1862) *Caraid nan Gaidheal* (Friend of The Gaels), a sobriquet later bestowed on him in recognition of his work in the Highlands on education and for organising relief during the distress of the 1830s and 40s.[27] He was also to become a doctor of divinity, Minister of St Columba's, Glasgow, and Dean of the Chapel Royal.[28] Norman was 'not only an agreeable and pleasant companion', wrote Neil, 'but capable of assisting and directing my studies'.[29]

Norman Macleod in turn describes Neil as:

> a correct and sober minded young man. He was a great favourite, took the whole management of the bills, and kept landlady and servant in great order. He was a fine performer on the violin, and taught his companion to play a bass accompaniment, and as the performance was often conducted with open windows, a crowd at times collected on the street below.

It was said of him that he was 'apt to stand on the defensive with Lowlanders, and . . . ready to take offence at insults, real or imaginary, and although of short stature, was uncommonly strong and active, and as bold as a gamecock'.

There is a story at about this time told of him that illustrates these qualities:

> One evening, while walking in Prince's Street with some companions, Mr Brewster (afterwards Minister of Paisley, and noted for his Chartist politics), accompanied by some friends, came against Maclean, jostling him violently, calling him a 'Highland Fiddler', and ordering him to 'stand out of the way'. Neil instantly flew at him – there was a cry for 'fair play', and Brewster soon gave in, but not before he had got a black eye, and was compelled to ask Maclean's pardon.
>
> The affair soon became public among the students, and afforded much amusement. The gravity and decorum of the divinity classroom did not, however, prevent the Highlander

from taking further revenge. A few days after the occurrence, Maclean – as was customary – was called upon to deliver his discourse in the Hall. He introduced the history of David and Goliath, and alluding to David's victory exclaimed in a loud voice, looking sternly at Brewster, and shaking his fist at him – 'in this manner, the stripling David leveled the uncircumcised dog with the ground'. The encounter between Maclean and Brewster being well known to all the class, this sally was received with roars of laughter in which Dr Hunter, the grave Professor, was compelled to join.[30]

* * *

The Rum Company was eventually accepted and Mr Donald was able to write on 22nd December 1803: 'The Rum Island Company of Volunteer Infantry is completely enrolled and attested and regularly doing Duty, once a week'. All, however, was not well for 'their arms having not arrived yet – I wrote to Mr C – [?] regarding them soon after you were pleased to communicate they were in conveyance; requesting him to inform *to what* place they were directed, and *when* I might expect delivery of them but neither an *answer* from him, nor *the arms* &c have – [?] to make their appearance'.

He goes on to say: 'The inconvenience arriving from this, it is unnecessary to point out'. This was not the end of his problems for he writes:

> I have not been able to transmit at the regular period, to the Adjutant General's Office & to Major-General the Marquess of Huntly, the monthly return for November last, owing to the weather, but will study to do it, as regularly as my situation will permit. It is to be regretted that there is no established Ferry Boat or packet betwixt this District and the mainland.[31]

Mr Donald's first Quarterly pay list, which covers the period from 24th October to 25th December 1803, was received at the War Office on 22nd March 1804. It shows that the company consisted of himself as captain receiving 9s.5d per day. A total of £4.4s.9d for 9 day's training. His son Alexander received 5s.8d per day as lieutenant and the ensign received 4s.8d. The drill sergeant Donald Maclean was paid a total of £4.13s for 62 days permanent duty at 1s.6d per day. The other two sergeants were paid at the same rate but only for 9 days, whilst the two corporals received 1s.2d per day. One of the two drummers Hector Morison was on permanent pay for 62 days at the rate of 1s per day and received a total of £3.2s. Everyone else received 1s per day. The first 61 men attended every drill available. However, the company's establishment must have been increased for a further 14 men joined after 9th December. In all the company received a total of £48.3s.9d for the period. It must have been a boost to the economy of the island.[32]

In his letter Mr Donald lists the alarm posts in the four islands and the names of the inspector and superintendents. He goes on to say: 'I have been lately in these islands & the necessary instructions, in case of invasion, or an enemy appearing on the coast, have been raised in terms of the Hon. Charles York's[33] letter of 31st October.'[34]

He continues:

> The people of this District seem to have taken an unaccountable prejudice against pioneering – its nature & utility have been pointed out to them, yet their prejudice has not been hitherto overcome.[35] To a man, I believe, they would enroll as *Volunteer Infantry*, if required; but as

Pioneers they show no wish to be imployed – Indeed in any *one* of the Islands Rum, Muck and Eigg, a Company of Pioneers cannot be mustered . . . In Canna *alone*, a company of them might well inroll, as no Volunteer Infantry have been established there. I have *expectations* but no *certainty* that the Canna people will inroll for this purpose. The principal tacksmen is not [at] present at home with them; when he returns I shall again endeavour to see them – if he encourage the Enrollment I'm hopeful it will go.

He has pleasure in telling Sir James that 'the Vote of Thanks & order of the House of Commons have been publicly read to the Volunteer Corps in this district. The most heartfelt satisfaction was expressed on this occasion as well as a determined, resolute not to [–?–] of the very high honour conferred on them'.[36]

* * *

In addition to his duties as parish minister, company commander and Justice of the Peace, Donald had to perform his duties as Deputy Lieutenant. These duties were onerous as they involved implementing the instructions coming from central government concerning the Militia and the Reserve, and could also involve emergency planning for the destruction of buildings and the removal of wagons, cattle &c in case of emergency.[37]

On 20th January 1804 Mr Donald wrote again from Eigg to Sir James Grant:

I had also the honor of receiving your Letter of the 3rd Inst Ordering the levies for the Militia & Reserve due in this District to be immediately completed – I presume Substitutes for our balloted militia men were duely provided by Mr Grant C[lerk to the] G[eneral] C[ourt of] Lieutenancy at Inverness. In this District Here were 5 Reserve men Balloted: viz: 1 in Eigg, 1 in Islemuck, 2 in Rum & 1 in Canna. A Substitute has been got for the Eigg Reserve man, who has joined – I have been lately informed, but not officially, that Substitutes have been provided for the Canna Reserve man; & for one of the Rum Reserve men. If that be the case 2 only are now due viz: one from Rum & one from Islemuck.

That I may remove Reflections against myself, in respect to the management of this business, I must request you'll have the goodness to admit an Explanation. The penalty, in case of Default, imposed by the Reserve Act, is £20 for each man. Inspite of all my endeavours to explain the Reasons & Nature of this penalty in terms of the act, a mistaken idea of it has been taken up & fondly indulged by the persons liable to the Ballot – They could not be dissuaded from a Belief, if the whole penalty was paid, that then not only the person balloted, but all liable to the Ballot, would be free. Proceeding on this idea, the amount of the whole penaltie was collected in the several Islands, but the persons liable to the ballot, previous to the ballot; & this money, according to their view of things, was to be advanced for their general security.

When the Ballot took place, the whole Fines amounting to £100 Sterling collected as above were delivered by the persons drawn or by their agents into the hands of the Preses of the Meeting to be transmitted to the General Clerk of Lieutenancy of Inverness, to be applied towards providing Substitutes. The District meeting were the more ready to concur in this measure, that the General Clerk of Lieutenancy had encouraged them in time of balloting for the Militia, to accept the Fines, if offered, & that he would procure Substitutes at Inverness; & those too (which we thought an object) trained to the use of arms. This plan was accordingly adopted: & as it answered respecting the militia it was expected it might answer also as to the

Reserve – The fines of Course were transmitted; but, it seems Mr Grant has not been able to find Substitutes.

Upon finding the plan misgive, I applied in two letters, at different periods, to Mr Grant for instructions how to act – I have not yet had an answer – & I must Confess that I now find the business attended with some difficulty – The men formerly balloted think themselves free, as the fines paid were apparently on their account at the Ballot will not now pleasantly submit to a new Ballot; & Besides, with few exceptions, they are now under arms as Volunteers. I had the precaution indeed, not to admit into the Rum Company of Volunteers those drawn for that Island.

The Canna man is no volunteer; but the man drawn for Islemuck is a private in the Eigg Company. In consulting Mr Grant above mentioned I hazarded a Suggestion that the money collected in the Deficient Islands might be restored to the Contributors; thinking it the best plan to obviate their pleas of Security arising from that Collection: & Then that there already drawn who could not advance their proper penalties, might be ordered of; or a new Ballot carried on as might be found necessary.

I proposed a question, too whether I might send a party at Government Expense with such men, or not? Or if the Regiment to which they should be attached should send for them – Having received no answer from Mr Grant, I acknowledge I'm at a loss how to proceed, so as to prevent an irritation of the people's feelings; tho I'm perfectly aware that the plea of Exemption above mentioned, is incompetent.

This I have taken the liberty to detail the causes of the Deficiency in this District respecting the Reserve – It arose originally from an expectation that Substitutes could be found at Inverness, a disappointment in which has at length landed us in a difficulty as above represented. My situation unfortunately puts it out of my power to consult with ease & readiness, in this case, I shall receive it with gratitude.

I have often thought the Reserve Act should have been more peremptory in requiring the men balloted to serve in *person* or *by their substitutes*.

He then reverts to being a company commander when he writes:

Our arms &c &c came to hand last week – The Guns need repairs, but they are such as can be executed in the Island. Orders are accordingly issued – The men would be better pleased that the whole were Guns, as being certainly more serviceable. The whole cheerfully agreed to exercise with their arms five days running. I'm sure I have encroached on your time & patience, but hope you'll have the goodness to forgive me.

Only half the number of arms required arrived and it was not till the autumn that Mr Donald was able to send in a bill for the cost of transporting 80 muskets and bayonets, 80 sets of accoutrements, 40 pikes, drum sticks & 1 cask of ball cartridges from Edinburgh Castle to Rum of £5.15s. In addition the cost for carriage and freight of 5 casks of blank and ball cartridges from Fort William to Rum was £3.0s.6d.[38]

Mr Donald had recommended that the strength of his company justified having three subaltern officers and had taken it for granted that this would be approved. He was therefore horrified when he learnt that only two had been appointed. He writes to Sir James that

This led me into a mistake; the three I recommended to your Lordship were Encouraged to do Duty. Mr Hector Maclean[39] has been doing duty as Ensign – A keeness for getting him duly qualified has got the better of prudence. It is – [?] and unpleasant now to be under the necessity of dismissing one of them – Were the Lieutenants of age and Experience Sufficient for the command I could at least be persuaded to resign, rather than disappoint any of them.

His dilemma was solved when his son Alexander was appointed surgeon's mate in the regular army and on 25 April 1804 he was able to write to Sir James:

Sir, I have the honour to inform you that Alexander MacLean Lieutenant in the Rum Island Company of Inverness-shire Volunteer Infantry offers to resign, having a prospect of being immediately more advantageously employed in a medical station in His Majesty's Service – Permit me therefore to request that Mr John Maclean, the present Ensign be promoted to the said Lieutenancy; and Mr Hector Maclean, formerly recommended appointed Ensign.[40]

* * *

Volunteer companies were encouraged to spend time on permanent duty and Mr Donald wrote that the Rum Company 'have all expressed their willingness to go on Permanent Pay and Duty for one month . . . Fort George they prefer as the place best calculated for training them to military duties, if there be room for them there. If not they wish to be in its immediate vicinity . . . They are at present busily employed in sowing there Croft lands, but this work will take no great time to finish'.

However, it was not to be and the company had to be content with doing their permanent duty in Rum, rather than in the bright lights of Fort George. As Mr Donald later wrote:

the inconvenience connected with their local situation, I observe with regret, put it out of the power of the Rum Island Company to go on permanent duty to a distant situation, on the terms proposed. They will, however, examine, with the greatest cheerfulness, the Ten additional Days, without delay, if you be pleased so to order it. Be pleased to recollect that not half of their number have got musquets – the other Pikes – That our sergeants have got no Halberds nor swords – Our Drummer no Hangers but one Drum betwixt them – As to ammunition we never got but one small Cask of Ball Cartridges, which have been dispersed to preserve waiting serious Emergencies. No blank cartridges – have been sent us for improvements in firing. Permit me to request some attention to these circumstances, & that we be put on a level with our neighbours as to the means of useful improvements for service.[41]

* * *

The isle of Canna has a good sheltered port and is strategically sited for shipping passing through the Hebrides. That it could be a useful base for any French privateer operating in Hebridean waters had not escaped Mr Donald's notice and on 11th August 1804 he wrote to Sir James to point out that:

The Island *Canna* makes part of the 17th District of the County of Inverness. It lies in the direct Course of the Ships from the Baltic to the West Coasts of England & Scotland & Ireland. It has a commodious & much frequented Harbour. This, in a peculiar manner, makes it an Object of public attention for should our Enemy appear on this coast, he may have it in his power to do much mischief in that Island. This, with other reasons, makes it desirable to have a company of volunteers on it; and the inhabitants are very urgent in so willing such an appointment on the same footing with those already established in their neighbourhood. They can muster a Company of 52 privates with the proportionate number of commission & non-commission officers on the Island. Donald MacNiel Esq., who resides on the Island, may be recommended for the Lieutenancy & Mr Angus McDonald for the Ensigncy. If you think that Government will accept their offers of service. I would request an early application for the Establishment.[42]

On this occasion Mr Donald's advice does not appear to have been taken. He was, however, soon busy with other things as his company was about to be inspected and on the 16th August 1804, writing from Arisaig Lieutenant-Colonel Macdonell reported to Sir James:

Sir, Inclosed I have the honor send my inspection Report of . . . the Island of Rum Independent Company.

Inspection Return & Report of the Isle of Rum Independent Company of Volunteer Infantry commanded by Captain Donald Maclean at Kean loch Rum 10 August 1804.

	Capt.	Lieut.	Ens.	Sgts	Cpls	Drummers	Privates
Under arms	1	1	1	3	2	2	79
Sick							1
Absent							—
Total Effective	1	1	1	3	2	2	80
Total Est.	1	1	1	3	2	2	80

Officers: Uniformly dressed. Captain Maclean commanded the Isle of Rum Company in last war.
NCOs: Well dressed & expert. Sgts have not received their pikes.
Drummers. Not well instructed. 1 drum wanting to complete.
Men under arms: A fine body of men. Steady & attentive.

Nature & Condition of :
Arms. 40 stand of firearms serviceable. 40 pikes.
Accoutrements. 40 sets serviceable.
Clothing. Complete, good & new.

State of Discipline & General Observations:
This company has been on permanent duty upwards of three weeks, they have made considerable progress in Discipline, and appear fit for any service, they have hitherto not received watch coats, knapsacks, Haversacks or any kind of Camp Equipage. Boats are in readiness, to transport them to the mainland, the nearest point of which (Arisaig) is distant 16 miles – the nearest landing place in the Island of Skye is distant 10 miles.
        Coll Macdonald, Inspecting Field Officer.[43]

In October Donald reverted to his role of Deputy Lieutenant when he wrote to Sir James to say:

Sir, I have the honor of receiving your letter of 22nd Ult with notes of Mr York's three letters therein mentioned annexed.

In this district (17) the arrangements required have been made, as far as its suitability admits. A *sitting Magistrate*, in case of invasion, is appointed. *Superintendents, constablis* and *assistants* are appointed for each of its Islands, Boats are engaged for conveying our Volunteers and carts for conveying their necessary – [?]. There are indeed no provisions stored in any one place for them; but each volunteer is required to have always in readiness provisions for a few days march – Camp billets are not hitherto provided for them, but the speediest measure for getting them would be adopted.

I have the honor . . . &c Donald Maclean DL District 17 Inverness Co.

NB As former communication no pioneers are to be got in this District, tho all, capable of it, are willing to act as Volunteers.[44]

Although, on Mrs Murray of Kensington's evidence, Mr Donald was no longer fit, he still appears to have been able to carry out his numerous duties.

Notes

1. Hugh had served briefly in the 1st Bn The Breadalbane Fencibles & 42nd Foot, he then transferred to the 49th Foot [TNA. WO 31. 67] and finally to the 60th on whose half-pay list he was at the time of his death [TNA. WO 25. 3100, 1].
2. ICP. Folder Military 1800–3, 6.
3. ICP. Folder Military 1800–3, 5.
4. *Argyll Estate Instructions*, 45; TNA. WO13. 4177.
5. TNA. WO13. 4175. Part 2
6. *Scots Magazine* vol. 65 (1803), 639; TNA. WO25. 3100, 1.
7. By 1801 he had become tacksman of Gallanach in succession to Captain Lachlan late of the Honourable East India Company whose son John's tack had presumably expired.
8. TNA. WO13. 4175. Part 2.
9. Ibid.
10. TNA. HO103. 3. 50.
11. NAS. GD248. 656. 3.
12. Selkirk *Observations*, 4.
13. NAS. GD 248. 656. 3.
14. NAS. GD 248. 659. 6.
15. The Rev. Mr Donald M'Lean, *Minister*. 'Parish of Small Isles' *The Statistical Account of Scotland* vol. XX (1983), 251.
16. NAS. GD248. 668. 2
17. Lachlan Mackinnon in Howlin was a member of the Keanouchrach branch of the Mackinnons descended from *Tearlach Sgianach*, the second son of Lachlan Dubh a sixteenth-century Mackinnon chief. His eldest brother Mr Donald Mackinnon, Minister of Strath was born in 1731 and lived to be a hundred. [Mackinnon family tree]. I have to thank Donald Mackinnon of Dalness, Tasmania for a copy of this tree]. Howlin acted briefly as Lachlan Maclean of the Isle of Muck's agent in Muck [NAS. GD201. 5. 206]. I have to thank Catriona White, Frackersaig Farm. Isle of Lismore for this reference.
18. NAS. GD248. 661. 1. 3; Sir Alex. Mackenzie Downie & Alister Downie Mackinnon *Genealogical Account of the Family of Mackinnon*, (1882), 1. I have to thank Donald Mackinnon of Dalness, Tasmania for a photocopy of this book; Majorie O anderson *Kings and Kingship in Early Scotland* (1973), 45.
19. Arrangement for the Eigg Company. [NAS. GD248. 659. 6]; he was to be the lieutenant of the Eigg or 5th Company of the 5th Battalion of Inverness-shire Volunteer Infantry from 1803–7 [TNA. WO 13. 4378].

20. He was probably the son of Allan Maclean, the factor of Rum who had been the lieutenant of the Rum Company in the previous war. As he was born in 1740 he was probably now considered too old to serve. Alternatively he could be the grandson of John Maclean of Sandaneisher (1695 × 1771). John Sandaneisher was in Cove, Rum in 1764 and was married to Marion Macqueen, sister to the first Minister of the Small Isles, who lived at Sandaneisher. He was a cadet of the Isle of Muck family and had probably come to Rum with the other Coll cadets after 1735. John the factor's son is said to have died unmarried. [Nicholas Maclean-Bristol 'Tacksmen in Rum' WHN&Q January 2005. Series 3, No. 7, 19–23].
21. He is presumably the Alexander Maclean who served in the Rum Company in the previous war.
22. NAS. GD248. 661. 1. 1.
23. TNA. WO 13 4378.
24. BCP. Letter of PJ Anderson, Librarian University of Aberdeen to HAC Maclean dated 24 June 1898.
25. NAS. CH2. 568. 3.
26. BCT. Letters to Alexander Maclean 12 January 1805.
27. Derick S. Thomson (ed) *Gaelic Scotland* (1983), 35.
28. Donald Macleod *Memoir of Norman Macleod, D.D.* (1876), 5.
29. BCT. Letters to Alexander Maclean 17 December 1806.
30. John N. Macleod *Memorials of the Rev. Norman Macleod of St Columba's*, (?), 21.
31. NAS. GD248. 656.
32. TNA. WO13. 4383.
33. Charles Yorke was Secretary at War until August 1803 [John Ehrman *The Younger Pitt* vol. 3 (1996), 608 n. 7. He later became Home Secretary [*Ibid*, 819].
34. The alarm post in Rum was to be at Kinloch Scrisort, and in Eigg at Sandaveg,. The inspectors were:

> Eigg. Mr Lachlan Mackinnon, tacksman of Howlin.
> Rum. Mr Allan Maclean, tacksman of Kinloch Scrisort.
> Canna. Mr Donald Macneil, tacksman of Canna.
> Muck. Mr John Mackinnon, tacksman of Gallanach.

The superintendents were:

> Eigg. Mr Hugh Macdonald, tacksman of Sandavore.
> Rum. Mr John Maclean, tacksman of Sandaneisher.
>   Mr Lachlan Maclean at Harris.
> Canna. Mr John Mackinnon, tenant at Keill.
>   Mr Jamieson at Sandy island.
> Muck. Niel McKay & Niel Macmillan, tenants in Keill.

35. He was to write later: 'The men think it an indignity offered them to act as such when their Brethren are in arms – Could they they be enrolled as Volunteers, and a selection afterwards occasionally made; it would suit their humour & spirit better'.
36. NAS. GD248. 667. 10.
37. The Hon. JW Fortecue *The County Lieutenancies and the Army 1803–1814* (1909), 25.
38. TNA. WO13. 4383. 25 June to 24 September 1804.
39. He is presumably the tacksman of Guirdale.
40. NAS. GD258. 659. 5.
41. NAS. GD248. 663. 8. 1.
42. NAS. GD248. 661. 4.
43. NAS. GD248. 661. 4.
44. NAS. GD248. 661. 1. 1.

Chapter Thirty-Five

A New Generation of Officers and Men

The inhabitants of the Isle of Eigg were not alone in their lack of enthusiasm for enlisting in the Volunteers. In Scotland as a whole there was a changed atmosphere to the War. In 1799 the British Government had hoped that when the Fencibles were disbanded the men, who 'from long divorce from any but military employment... would have enlisted in the Line'. It was not to be. The whole nation seemed to be sick of warlike exercises, and recruits were by no means plentiful.[1] James Macdonald agreed with this judgment. He writes:

> A considerable change has, of late years, taken place in the turn of mind common to the youth of this district. They have no longer any predilection for the military life: on the contrary, their abhorrence of it is deep-rooted and inveterate. This is the fact, whatever may be the cause to which we may impute it. The same antipathy exists against the naval service of their country: so that we need not look for any voluntary levies from these isles, as long as the natives remain in their present way of thinking, and the present modes are followed of recruiting our navy and army.[2]

Recruits may have been difficult to find in Scotland as a whole, but they existed on the Coll estate and during the first decade of the nineteenth century many men from the Islands joined the Volunteers. They were, however, only required for home defence. It was less easy to find men for the regular army and navy. Although the number of men the nation had under arms had soared, far too many of them were serving in bodies such as the Volunteers that could not be made to serve overseas. To make matters worse, neither Britain, nor her colonies could be entirely stripped of regular troops. The Government was therefore short of manpower for offensive operations. Though the British endeavoured to employ local auxiliaries and foreign troops, they still did not have sufficient men. This difficulty forced Britain back on methods of war – above all, blockade and colonial aggrandisement – that could only antagonise potential partners on the Continent, and confirm their suspicion that the British were determined to avoid the sort of commitment they required of their allies. These two methods of warfare were also not particularly cost-effective: colonial offensives were notoriously wasteful in terms of lives, whilst blockading Europe's coasts inflicted immense wear and tear on the Royal Navy.

* * *

A New Generation of Officers and Men

Much of the work of the blockade was carried out by frigates, which lay close to the land and were engaged in cutting-out operations in, or all but in, enemy harbours. One such frigate operating in the English Channel was HMS *Leda*. Her log tells of almost continuous operations, watching Boulogne, skirmishing with French gunboats and monitoring sea-borne traffic in the Straits of Dover. On Thursday 21st June 1804, when she was in the Dungeness Roads, it is noted that Lieutenant Maclean joined HMS *Leda*. This was Neil Maclean, who had recently married John of Cornaig's youngest sister Ann.

At the same time as Neil joined the *Leda* she was resupplied with beef and water by HMS *Euryalius*. This method of resupply saved time and enabled the Royal Navy to keep the French under almost constant observation. Two days later in the evening it is noted that HMS *Leda* was 7 or 8 miles off Boulogne. The following morning she joined HMS *Seine* and the rest of the squadron.

HMS *Leda's* logbook is typical of the genre: its tone is semi-literate, official, and its righteous dullness never varies. The wind direction and the weather is always noted first, whilst matters of life and death receive only perfunctory notice. Even so it gives an insight into the every day life of a British frigate in the Channel before the battle of Trafalgar when Napoleon was threatening to invade. For example:

Wednesday 25th July. Variable. WNW. Boulogne ESE 10 miles. PM L[igh]t Air & Variable, 8.15 Anchored in 13 fathoms. Boulogne SSE ½ E 4 miles. AM moderate & clear. 9 weighed & made sail. Fired several shots to bring a Danish Brig too, at noon boarded her, Division in company.

Thursday 26th July. West & Variable. Boulogne East 10 miles. PM. Moderate & cloudy. Sent Lieut. McClean with some men to take charge of the Stad Antonio Christiana Perderson, at 1 she Parted company. Made sail as requisite. AM Lt Breezes ...

Friday 27th July SEBE. WSW Boulogne SEBE 3 leagues. PM Lt Breezes & fine ... 7.10 Anchored in 14 fathoms. Boulonge SE 5or 6 miles. AM Moderate & Cloudy at 6 weighed and made sail. Skirmishing with the flotilla at noon fresh breeze.

Saturday 28th July. SW to WBN. At Anchor in Dungeness Roads. PM Fresh Breezes & cloudy. 2.30 Anchored in 18 fathoms. Dungeness Light House S to W 5 miles. Answer [Signal] No. 214. AM ditto weather. [Crew] employed as requisite. At Noon Fresh Breezes.

Sunday 29th July. W to WSW. Boulogne E to S 9 miles. PM Fresh Breezes and hazy. Joined [by] Lieutenant McClean and two men who went in the brig [&] received fresh Beef. AM moderate & cloudy at 7 weighed and made sail per signal. At 10 exchanged Pendants with the *Sulphur*. At 11 ware & hove to [bring vessel to a standstill, without anchoring]; made [signal] No. 195; at noon ditto weather, mustered ship's company.

Monday 30th July. NNE Calm NBE. At anchor off Boulogne, ditto ESE 405 miles. PM Lt Air. 2.30 anchored with the BB in 30 fathoms. Boulogne ESE 8 milles. Squadron in company at 7 weighed & shifted further into the shore; made No. 63 Gen°; anchored in 22 fathoms; at 10 sent the large & small cutters manned & armed under the command of Lieutenant McClean. AM calm & clear. At 2 observed a very heavy fire of musquetry among the Flotilla, at 3 the small cutter returned with John Simmonds & Nehemiah Taylor dead, 2 marines & 5 seamen wounded. Missing in the large cutter Lieutenant McClean & midshipman. Captain Clerk, 11 seamen & 6 marines having been repulsed in attempting to cut out one of the Grand Flotilla. At noon fine weather

Tuesday 31 July. PM fine weather. Joined company, the Admiral & Squadron; received condemned sores as per orders. AM Lt Air & fine; at 7 weighed & made sail; at ii committed the bodies of the deceased to the Deep with the usual Ceremony. At noon L[igh]t Air.[3]

The anonymous author of the version of Dr Hector Maclean's history of the Macleans who took the story to 1807, adds to the bare bones of HMS *Leda's* log. He says that Neil Maclean, Ardfinaig:

> was Lieutenant on board the Leda Frigate, he undertook to make an attempt to cut out a french ship from – he succeeded in cutting her out, but the tide being against him, and he and some of his people being on board her he was drifted among the french ships and boarded by the enemy, and after making a brave and resolute resistance was overpowered by numbers, yet he fought to the last moment of his existence. He died universally regretted as well by his country, as by his immediate relations. He was only a few weeks married to Ann, second daughter of Donald Maclean of the Isle of Muck.[4]

* * *

Neil Ardfinaig was one of the few Maclean who were veterans of the Revolutionary War, and went on to serve in the Napoleonic War. Most had been killed or had left the service. Some, who were unfit, such as Mr Donald, might be adequate for the Volunteers, but they were hardly suitable for active service. Mr Donald's generation was now too old. Alexander Maclean of Coll, and his brothers, were in the same position. Among the regular soldiers in the family only Alexander's brother Hector, who was now a colonel in the Honourable East India Company's Service, continued on active service.[5] In the extended family it was the same story. Both the Isle of Muck brothers, Lachlan and John, held retired officer's posts: Lachlan was Barrackmaster at Berwick-upon-Tweed; John was a lieutenant in the 6th (Royal North British) Veteran Battalion.[6]

One officer who had served in the Revolutionary Wars and wished to return to the active list was Dr Hector Maclean of the Knock family in Coll. He had, however, for some reason crossed the Duke of York and been placed on the half-pay list. On 17th February 1806 when Mr Donald's son Neil Maclean wrote to his brother Alexander he said:

> I frequently see your friend Dr Hector Maclean who is still at Newhaven. He is applying for full pay, and about the time I came up he had sent a petition and letter to Mr Pitt. He was confident of success and used to tell me that he would triumph over the Duke of York, and the whole of them, and that he would soon write to my father of his victory. He had certainly a good prospect of success, when the death of Mr Pitt, and of course a complete change of Ministry took place. So he'll have his application to make over again.

Dr Hector's misfortunes were perhaps his own fault. Neil goes on to say that: 'I am sorry to say that he is too much given to his bottle of which I have seen several instances, and is neglected by any decent friends he has here. He and his wife are certainly as unhappy a pair as I ever beheld'.[7]

* * *

Lachlan, late of the Isle of Muck's eldest surviving son Hector Alexander followed his uncle by marriage into the navy. However, unlike Neil Ardfinaig he was destined for the quarterdeck from the time of his entry in May 1800. We know that from the fact that he had been born at

A New Generation of Officers and Men

Grishipol in March 1787.[8] He was therefore 13 when he joined HMS *Kent* (Captain Hope) and was rated 'Volunteer Class'.[9] He served only three months as a volunteer before being made a Midshipman on HMS *Zealand* (Captain Minley). He served five years nine months as a Midshipman and was serving on HMS *Majestic* (Captain Hanwell) when he applied to take his promotion exam.

He had now to produce certificates of his service and date of birth as Lieutenants. He could not be commissioned if the had not served for six years in the navy or was under 20 years of age. What follows illustrates the dubious morality of the time and Lieutenant-Colonel Lachlan's determination to get commissions for his sons, even if it meant perjuring himself. This he was quite prepared to do.

Among the papers referring to Hector Alexander's promotion is a certificate dated Coll 12th March 1806 signed 'J Brown, Minister'. It states:

> I do hereby certify that it appears by the Register of Births entered in the Session Books of the Parish of Tyrie and Coll in the County of Argyle, NB that Hector A Maclean, son of Lieutenant Colonel Maclean of the Barracks Department was born in the said parish on the 19th day of March in the year of our Lord 1785.[10]

Unfortunately there was at this time no record of births kept in Coll or Tiree and the Register of Baptisms shows that Hector Alexander was baptised on the 28th March 1787. There was also no 'J Brown' who was ever a minister in Coll or in Tiree. The certificate was nothing less than a forgery.

It seems extraordinary length to go to for Lachlan to gain his son two years seniority at the expense of his 'honour'. However, as Michael Lewis, the former Professor of History at the Royal Naval College, Greenwich points out:

> In all ages 'dishonour' is what men consider dishonourable.
>
> If 'everyone does it'!
>
> If the highest court in the land, the High Court of Parliament, is filled quite openly by every form of bribery: if all – or most – of Civil Service posts are sold, exchanged, inherited or otherwise wangled: if Army and other contractors are scarcely bothering to conceal how they have come by their war profits – if such things are 'done'.

Was Lieutenant-Colonel Lachlan so very dishonest? He was certainly not alone in what he was up to, and no rule was more universally dodged than that of a Lieutenant's minimum age. And, as Michael Lewis goes on to state

> the provision of a birth this was a mere bagatelle. About the turn of the century, Admiral Sir George Elliot tells us, a crown-piece handed to the porter at the Navy Office as one went in to be examined produced a certificate showing one to be any age one liked to mention. This perhaps helps to explain the formula commonly used by Lieutenants' Examining Boards. They seldom wrote 'The candidate is' (mentioning his age). They put 'The candidate appears to be': which covered themselves to some extent and shows how difficult the regulation was to enforce.[11]

Hector Alexander passed his exam.

* * *

There were several new openings in the services for this new generation. The rapprochement between Coll and the Duke of Argyll meant that there was also a new source of patronage available to certain Macleans. In 1801 Argyll, who was Colonel of the Scots Guards, recommended 'Mr McLain, Gentleman to be Ensign in the 3rd Regiment of Foot Guards vice Ensign Lorne Campbell killed'.[12] 'Mr McLain' obtained his commission without purchase.[13] Although the Duke evidently did not know his first name, and the Horse Guards wrongly called him Charles,[14] it is clear from the date of his commission that this man must be Hugh Maclean younger of Coll. On 11 May 1805, under his correct name, he transferred to the 1st Battalion. Four months later, on 26th September, he purchased a Lieutenancy for £1,500[15] and returned to the 2nd Battalion, who continued to perform London duties[16] whilst the 1st Battalion went overseas.

The Coll family spent the winter of 1805–6 in Edinburgh.[17] On 17th February 1806 Mr Donald Maclean Minister of the Small Isles's second son Neil wrote from Edinburgh to his elder brother. Amongst other news he mentions that Hugh Coll had lately come there from London as he had obtained leave of absence. He says that Hugh is 'the same fine frank and friendly fellow you have seen him'. He continues:

> He is now a Lieutenant in the Guards, and by his promotion he avoided going with the Expedition to the Continent, whither I believe his inclination strongly led him.[18]

The expedition that Hugh missed by leaving the 1st Battalion was that led Lord Cathcart. It set sail for the Elbe in November 1805 with the aim of liberating Hanover and threaten Napoleon's flank. In the event Napoleon defeated the Austrians at Austerlitz, forcing the Emperor out of Pitt's final Coalition. The British expeditionary force returned to England.[19]

Hugh took his part in London society. In 1805 he attended the card parties, organised for William Pitt by his sister-in-law the Countess of Chatham, in an attempt to amuse him, but the dying Prime Minister would not be amused. Young Coll often played a card game with him called 'Pope Joan'. According to Hugh, Pitt 'appeared indifferent to every thing around him, like any other invalid, and there was nothing remarkable, or that attracted attention, in his manner or conversation'. In the right company Pitt had in the past, amongst his close friends, been witty and amusing.[20] Hugh was evidently not able to bring out his best in him at the end of his life.

Alexander's efforts to launch his family on English society had duly been rewarded, when on 26th April 1802 in Edinburgh,[21] his eldest daughter Janet (Jessie) married, as his second wife, the Hon. George Hobart, second son of the 3rd Earl of Buckinghamshire. Janet was marrying into one of the leading political families in the English aristocracy: George's elder brother Robert was, from 1801–4, Secretary of State for War[22] in Addington's government; whilst his aunt Amelia was married to Robert Stewart, Viscount Castlereagh, Secretary of State for War in Pitt's last administration.[23]

It is possibly not without significance to his new position in society that on 24th February 1803 Alexander registered his arms in the Public registers of the Lyon Office. Although the family, and other Macleans, had used arms for many generations, Alexander appears to have been the first to register them. He was granted his arms with supporters, recognising that he was a baron, holding his land directly of the Crown, and the representative of a family who before 1592 had been liable to be called to Parliament.[24]

At this time another cadet of the Coll family married into potentionally influential circles: on 22nd August 1805 Flora Ann, daughter of Lieutenant-Colonel Lachlan Maclean formerly of the

A New Generation of Officers and Men

Isle of Muck, married Lieutenant-Colonel James Macleod of Raasay.[25] Raasay's sister had in 1777 married Colonel James Campbell of Lawers, later Earl of Loudoun. Their daughter, also Flora, succeeded her father as Countess of Loudoun in her own right. In 1804 she married Francis Rawdon Hastings, Earl of Moira,[26] then Commander-in-Chief in Scotland. Moira's influence was to be invaluable to his wife's relations.

Lachlan was, as we have seen, at the time of his daughter's marriage, 'a poor barrackmaster' at Berwick-upon-Tweed.[27] Despite his eldest son's somewhat less than illustrious military career Lachlan was determined that his younger sons who were 'a great burden to me with such a large family as I have'[28] should join the armed services. And again as we have already seen, he was even prepared to let them lie about their ages to do so.

Lachlan's third son Donald John was baptised at Grishipol on the 21st January 1789 and was probably born a few days earlier.[29] Yet Lachlan applied for a commission for him on 31st July 1804,[30] when he was only 15, and not the statutory age of 16. Donald John must have said that he was born on the 9th January 1787 for his service records state that he was born then.[31] On 9th August 1804 he became an ensign in the 72nd Regiment of Foot.[32]

The 1st 72nd Foot was part of the Highland Brigade in the expeditionary force, under the command of Sir David Baird, sent to protect the West Indies in 1805 when Villeneuve slipped past the Straits of Gibraltar at the start of the campaign that ended at Trafalgar. Once they had achieved their aim in the West Indies the expeditionary force set sail for Capetown, a Dutch colony. As Holland was now a department of France, it was fair game for the British and after a short engagement the Dutch surrendered.

The commander of the fleet that had taken British troops to Capetown was Sir Home Popham, who had been the prime mover in the raid against the Ostend locks which had ended Francis John Small Maclean's military career. Popham was now to lead an expedition, which was to have an even greater long-term effect on the fortunes of the Macleans of Coll. On his own initiative he persuaded Baird to lend him the 71st Foot, four guns and a handful of dragoons. He collected more men at St Helena and then sailed across the South Atlantic to capture Buenos Ayres. The campaign eventually ended in disaster but not before Sir Home Popham had taken the extraordinary step of sending a circular letter to leading merchants in London inviting them to take advantage of the gigantic market for their goods which his expedition had opened up for them.[33]

Donald John did not join his regiment in the West Indies, but was posted to the 2nd Battalion. However, he failed to turn up and was posted as 'absent without leave'. He later produced a certificate stating that he had been sick and eventually joined the battalion at Dudhope Barracks. He was sent to Inverness to recruit. Later, on 23rd October 1809 he joined the 1st Battalion in Cape Town.[34]

* * *

Lachlan's fourth son George Allan was even younger than Donald John when he joined the army. He was baptised at Grishipol on 11th July 1790 and must have been remarkably big for his age, for on 23rd March 1801 he was already serving in Ireland when he was promoted Lieutenant in the 2nd/46th (South Devonshire) Regiment of Foot. He is then said to have been one of the ensigns who had raised men for an additional two companies.[35]

* * *

Not all those who joined the Volunteers in 1803 stayed with them for the remainder of the war. Some used them as a springboard to gain other more lucrative military employment in the regular army. As we have seen, Mr Donald's son Alexander was one of them. On 25th April 1804 his father wrote to Sir James Grant to say that his son:

> offers to resign, having a prospect of being immediately more advantageously employed in a medical station in His Majesty's Service

Alexander was posted to the Military Hospital at Gosport.

* * *

Mr Donald's father-in-law Alexander Maclean of Mingary in Mull must have died some time after 18th December 1797 when Alexander Maclean of Coll reported to his former adjutant:

> Your uncle is but in a weak state,[36] if he does not soon get better than he was when I saw him this winter or spring is likely to finish him. I was two nights at his house on my way ...[37]

Mingary's widow moved to Glasgow. Their son 'your young uncle Hector', as Mr Donald calls him when writing to his son Alexander, was then 5 years old.

Mr Donald visited the family in Glasgow in January 1805. He writes: 'We stopped three nights at Glasgow at Mrs McLean Mingarry's', Donald adds that 'Hector is lively, contemplates going into Army'.[38] By the following August Hector had achieved his ambition, for when Mr Donald again writes to his son Alexander he says:

> Your Uncle Hector Mingary is now an Ensign in the 14th Foot. He joined his Regiment in August last & is just now imployed on the Recruiting Service at Glasgow & Paisley. This is very favourable to him as he can pass a considerable time with his Mother as a lodger. He wishes if his funds permit to purchase a Lieutenancy; but I fear the funds are short ...[39]

He was, however, to receive promotion 'without purchase'.[40] Eighteen months later he served in England and was ordered to Ireland.[41] He did not, however, go there, for by November 1808 he was with the 11th Foot in Madras.[42]

* * *

It has been worth following the careers of these young officers who were commissioned between 1800 & 1815 in some detail. They are good examples of how the descendants of men who, either as officers or members of the *luchd-tighe* or both had been the backbone of the clan, became regular officers in the army.

One newly commissioned officer from Coll, who had a somewhat different career to the others was Coundullie Rankin the former soldier in the Breadalbane Fencibles. On 8th July 1804 he was commissioned as a Lieutenant and assisted in recruiting in Scotland for the New Brunswick Fencibles.

Coun was back in Coll by September 1804 and living with his father in Cliad, when he married Flora Morison.[43] He was still in Coll on 19th December 1805 when, as we will see, he gave evidence to the Kirk Session. He probably left for Prince Edward Island soon afterwards, where he recruited a further 72 men. In 1806 he was elected to Prince Edward Island's House of Assembly having been endorsed by the Society of Loyal Electors. He became a JP.

The New Brunswick Fencibles subsequently became 104th Foot, making it available for imperial service. Coundulie's career did not continue to run smoothly. On 13th July 1815 he was superseded as a result of a dispute with General Coffin over his accounts, and on 4th April 1816 he exchanged into the 8th Foot and was placed on the half-pay list. In 1814, whilst he was with his original regiment his wife had died, and when he returned to Scotland after the war was over, he married Margaret Maclean, daughter of the tacksman of Kengharair on Torloisks estate in Mull.[44]

Coundullie Rankin's background was perhaps not so very different to the others. He too was a tacksman's son. He had certainly served as a private soldier, but so had Mr Donald's sons, although they were also university graduates. Coundullie certainly was not. The only real exception was William Johnston who was a crofter's son in Arnabost. He was to become a captain in the 2nd Madras Infantry. How he did so is a mystery. He presumably joined as a soldier in the Madras European Regiment and gained promotion through merit.

* * *

One thing all these young men from Coll had in common was that none of them obtained their first commissions by purchase. The system whereby every commissioned rank in the army possessed a pecuniary value originated at the Restoration when 'Tenure by Knight Service' was abolished. However, a colonel who raised men for the King's service still had the expense of recruiting and clothing them. In order to recover some of this expenditure the colonel expected his subordinates to help with this cost. They in turn expected to be repaid by whoever took over from them. As we have seen additional income could come from prize money, which was distributed on a fixed scale according to the rank of each officer. As a result rank possessed a pecuniary value like any other commercial enterprise.[45]

Critics of this system, and there were many, complained that purchase restricted commissions to those who were wealthy rather than those who were competent. In fact a great many commissions were issued 'without purchase' and, as already stated, none the young men studied paid for their first commission. Why was this?

In order to answer this question it is necessary to examine how the system worked. First the candidate for a commission, who had to be sixteen, obtained a nomination either from the Commander-in-Chief at Horse Guards, or, if he wanted to enter the Household Regiments of Horse or Foot Guards, from the colonel of his selected regiment. If approved, his name was placed on the list of those eligible for commissioning and he waited for a vacancy to arise in the regiment of his choice.

In the absence of 'interest', which kept his name to the fore a potential officer could wait for a considerable length of time. For a number of candidates this was a period when they or their parents canvassed supporters to ensure that their names were not overlooked. And it was only by constantly badgering the Commander-in-Chief's Military Secretary that Lachlan, late of the Isle of Muck, managed to keep his numerous sons' names before the Duke of York. Eventually, as we have seen, he succeeded in getting them all commissions without having to pay a penny.

Old officers had a distinct advantage in helping their sons as they had a network of old comrades to contact or names to drop. For instance on 9th August 1804 Lachlan wrote from Berwick-upon-Tweed to the Commander-in-Chief's Military Secretary Colonel Clinton:

Sir, I have great pleaure in hearing you are soon to be appointed to a high situation on the staff; as your duty I understand will remove you at a distance from His Royal Highness the Duke of York I shall esteem it a singular favour if you will have the goodness to forward my wishes respecting the application of my son (Donald Maclean) to a commission as soon as you can bring it about – I took the liberty of mentioning your late worthy father's name in my last letter and I again repeat that if he was living I should not now be a *Poor Barrack Master*.[46]

Lachlan had served under General Sir Henry Clinton in North America during the War of American Independence.

Notes

1. *The County Lieutenancies & the Army*, 6.
2. *General View*, 543–54.
3. NMM. ADM. L. L. 60. Leda Frigate. Lieutenant's Log.
4. NLS. MS 7609, 22.
5. Apart from Hector the last of Coll's brothers to serve in the army was Hugh. He died in Coll in 1802 worn out by his service overseas.
6. *Army List 1810*, 365.
7. BCT. 17 February 1806. Neil to his brother Alexander.
8. NAS. CH2. 70. 1. 28 March 1787.
9. This rating had replaced that of 'Servant', which disappeared officially from the Navy. But since all those previously so called were still there, doing substantially the same work as before, all that the Order of 1st April 1794 did was change names, not facts. Still, the new ruling certainly clarified an obscure position. All ex-servants were now divided into three classes: Classes II & III were real servants but in the words of the Order: Class I. To consist of Young Gentlemen intended for Sea Service . . . to be styled Volunteers and allowed wages at the rate of £6 per annum [*A Social History of the Navy 1793–1815*, 89].
10. TNA. ADM 107. 35.
11. *A Social History of the Navy*, 163 & 4.
12. TNA. WO 31. 110. 2 June 1801.
13. TNA. WO 31. 276. 22 June 1809.
14. *Army List 1804*, 100.
15. He thus became a lieutenant in the regiment and a captain in the army [TNA. WO 12. 1806 Edward M Speirs *The Army and Society 1815–1914* (1980),18] under the system whereby officers in the Brigade of Guards obtained a step in promotion over other infantry officers; his promotion cost him, or his father £1,500 [TNA. WO 31. 191].
16. TNA. WO 17. 87 (1).
17. BCP. Mr Donald to Alexander Maclean. Eigg 30 April 1806.
18. BCP. Neil to Alexander Maclean. Edinburgh 17 February 1806.
19. *A History of the British Army* vol. V (1803–7), 285–97; TNA. WO 1. 631. Frederick, Duke of York to Castlereagh. Horseguards. 1 November 1805.
20. James Robertson's journal. 11 August 1844; in his youth Pitt was aloof and haughty. Even his Cabinet found him uncommunicative. In the right company, however, he could be brilliant and those who had only known him in public were amazed when they caught a rare glimpse of him in private when he could delight in horseplay, nonsense and repartee. [John Ehrmann *William Pitt the Younger* vol. 1 (1969), 587 & 8].
21. *Gentleman's Magazine* (1802), vol. 72, 469.
22. Peter Townend (ed) *Burke's Peerage* (1968), 377.

23. The Castlereagh Stewarts were originally untitled Ulster gentry, who had demonstrated their ability to advance their fortunes by astute marriages. Castlereagh's own father marrying into the influential English families the Hertfords and Camdens. As we will see Jessie's marriage was to be tragically short. However, the connection with her husband's relatives probably did the Macleans of Coll no harm socially.
24. Sir Thomas Innes of Learney *Scots Heraldry* (1956), 130.
25. *Gentleman's Magazine* (1805), vol. 75, 773.
26. *The Macleods* (n.d.) Section 4, 49. In 1816 Moira was made Marquis of Hastings. He was later to be Governor-General of India.
27. TNA. WO31. 164. 9 August 1804. Lt Col Lachlan Maclean to Col. Clinton.
28. TNA. WO 31. 332. 23 September 1811.
29. NAS. CH2. 70. 1. 21 January 1787.
30. TNA. WO 31. 164. 9 August 1804.
31. TNA. WO 25.
32. TNA. WO 31. 164. 9 August 1804.
33. *The History of the British Army* vol. 5, 306–9 & 369.
34. TNA. WO 17. 193. I & 2.
35. TNA. WO 31. 112. 3 July 1801.
36. Alexander Maclean of Mingary, Mull, formerly of Gott, Tiree. His tack of the latter farm expired at Whitsunday 1776 and was not renewed in order to establish the village of Scarinish [ICP. Remarks on the Island of Tiry 1771]; 'Margaret Maclan. wife of Alexander Maclean Tacksman of Mingary d. 1783, aged 74' [Dervaig Graveyard]; 26 December 1787 m. Alex. Maclean, Tacksman of Mingary in Mull and Miss Peggy Maclean at Triallan, Coll. [NAS. CH2. 70.1].
37. NAS. GD 112. 52. 77. 7.
38. BCT. 4 January 1805 Donald Maclean to his son Alexander, Surgeon's mate.
39. BCT. 27 October 1805. Donald to his son Alexander
40. TNA. WO 31. 226. 2 April 1807.
41. BCT. 15 February 1807. Donald to his son Alexander, 99th Regt., Jamaica.
42. BCT. 3 November 1808. Donald to his son Alexander.
43. Dictionary of Canadian Biography, vol. VIII, Rankin, Coun Douly, contributor: Dr Kenneth A MacKinnon, Dept. of English, St Mary's University, Halifax, Nova Scotia, B3H 3C3, Canada.
44. Ditto. It states that he arrived at Fredericton, Prince Edward's Island on 20th September 1805. If this is correct, he must have returned briefly to Coll before the end of the year and sired a son, George, who on 31st December 1806 was baptised in Coll.
45. Gwyn Harries-Jenkins *The Army in Victorian Society* (1977), 62.
46. TNA. WO 31. 164.

Chapter Thirty-Six

The West Indies

On 12th January 1805 Alexander received a letter from his father, whose pleasure at his sons appointment had now abated. Mr Donald wrote:

The probability of your being ordered on foreign service excites an uneasiness, which we cannot suppress. May the Great Over-Ruler of all grant that the W. Indies be not your destination.[1]

Mr Donald had good reason to dread his son being sent to the West Indies. A contemporary described it as 'a dreadful country – it is impossible to imagine the horrors of the W. Indies without witnessing them'.[2] He also had his Chief's family's experience to horrify him at the thought of his own son going to the West Indies. Only recently his chief had lost both his daughter and son-in-law there.

The Hon. George Vere Hobart, Lieutenant-Governor of Grenada, had on 26th April 1802, just six weeks after taking up his post, died in Grenada of yellow fever. His wife, Coll's eldest daughter, Jessie, was pregnant. Her fate horrified the military in Barbados and her cousin Colonel Lachlan Maclean[3] sailed to Grenada to persuade her to come with him to Bridgetown. However, the people of Grenada were looking after her so well that she declined the offer. Maclean reported that 'the island proposed a signal mark of favour for Mrs Hobart on her departure'.[4]

Coundullie Rankin, Alexander's potential servant 'Coun' and the future Lieutenant of the New Brunswick Volunteers, had accompanied the newly wed couple to the West Indies as their major domo. He escorted Jessie on her voyage back home, during which she gave birth to a daughter. During the voyage Jessie caught a cold. It developed into consumption and in 1803 she died in Bristol.[5] She was 22.

* * *

Mr Donald's worst fears were realised, when Alexander was posted to Jamaica as surgeon's mate of 18th Regiment of Foot. Alexander sailed to Jamaica via Barbados. He landed in Jamaica sometime before 26 June 1805. He therefore just overlapped with Mrs Nugent, the wife of the Governor, who on 29th June left Jamaica on the merchant ship the *Augustine Caesar* with a cargo of sugar. On 1st July the *Augustine Caesar* joined HMS *Theseus* and the rest of the convoy assembled and set off for England.[6]

Only once during her time in Jamaica had the island seemed to be in immediate danger of attack. This was early in 1805, when, at one stage of the trans-Atlantic chase, which preceded the battle of

Trafalgar, the French had, for some weeks, a superior force to the British in the Caribbean. Mrs Nugent was still in Jamaica, and she describes the flurry of preparations for defence and the tense period of waiting for the attack, which never came.[7]

Alexander's letter to his father, which left Jamaica on HMS *Theseus*, reached Eigg on 24th October 1805.[8] His father replied immediately:

My Dear S.,

This evening I received your letter of the 26th June last. It relieved us in some degree from anxiety and concern, tho' we cannot be totally free from solicitude and apprehension while you are in that pestilential climate. That Good and Gracious God, who has hitherto preserved you, will continue to preserve you, while your confidence is firm in his protecting providence, & you exert yourself in attending to the means that are in your power. To his fatherly protection we desire to commit you & your concerns ...

I got your letter from Barbados & your first letter from Jamaica. I need not say what degree of happiness from these communications. Your last letter was four months in conveyance. I mean that by the *Theseus*. I wrote you soon after the receipt of your first letter from Stoney Hill Barracks[9] which you could not receive before you wrote last. I hope you have since got it. I wish, my Dr S, you gave me all the particulars, relative to your situation. The Circumstances, which you may think trivial may be thought interesting by us. From the hint you give of a wish to return to Britain we fear your situation is not comfortable. You must not, however, be over impatient. You have heretofore acted with steadiness. Continue to do so, and rely on the superintendence and direction of an all good and all wise God.

To us your Return to Britain, indeed your removal to any situation more salutary would be a high Qualification. The health you have injoyed [sic] to the date of your last affords ground of consolation & we trust you shall not be wanting as to the means of preserving it so far as depends on your self.

You are not to expect news of much importance from me further than that we continue to enjoy a tolerable state of health. Your Mother is not perfectly free from the sore on her Nose. What appears, however, is a mere trifle & makes no progress. Your sisters & brothers [are] well. With publick News I need not trouble you; you'll, no doubt have them from the English papers to which it seems you have access. I am much troubled with weak Eyes so that I can read or write very little. My sight indeed is much impaired within these two last years. Correspondence of Course is not as easy to me as I could wish.

By the last Accounts friends in Coll were well. Coll is building a fine house in Charlotte Square in Edinburgh ...[10]

This was one of a series of letters that Alexander was to receive in the West Indies. They continued for five years, and Alexander was to preserve them against all the hazards from insects and the climate to which they were exposed. They consist mainly of family gossip, and strictures for not writing home regularly. It is a one sided correspondence. Alexander's letters to his father have not survived.

Later in the same letter Donald writes: 'have you ever fallen in with your Cousin Mr Donald Crawford at Kingston. I should imagine he would perhaps try to see & serve you & introduce you to his friends ...'. Donald Crawford was the son of Charles Crawford and Julia Maclean who in 1779 were listed as cottars living at Ballimartin in Tiree.[11] What he was doing there is not clear.

Julia was probably a first cousin of Alexander's mother. If they were really cottars they were certainly educated ones and Donald must have done well in Jamaica, for when he died he is described as Donald Crawford Esq. The trustees of his estate included Alexander Maclean of Coll and Hugh Maclean, younger of Coll.

In an earlier letter Donald mentions a 'Captain John McLean of the Coll family, near relation of Captain Lachlan McLean who lived at Gallanach, whose son was living with Captain John'.[12] 'Captain John' was the son of Neil, an illegitimate son of Roderick Maclean of Penmoloch who had married Lachlan of Coll (1642 × 1688)'s widow. He is said to be 'doing well in Jamaica',[13] and was presumably a merchant.

Captain Lachlan's son by his second marriage, called Lachlan, also did well in Jamaica. He became a shipwright in Kingston and when he died left a considerable estate. In his original will he also named Alexander Maclean of Coll and his son Hugh as his executors.[14]

These exiled Collachs were some of the many Scots in Jamaica. Mrs Nugent says that 'almost all the agents, attornies, merchants and shopkeepers, are of that country, and really do deserve to thrive in this, they are so industrious'. She also says that 'Tradesmen of every description, *if white*, were admitted and invited to the best society'.[15] And on 19th September 1801 she notes that she entertained 'some gentlemen at breakfast chiefly Scotch' and had 'a long discussion on Burn's Poems'.[16]

* * *

Alexander must, however, have complained of his life in Jamaica for his father was determined to get him home. On 30th June 1806 Mrs Murray, who had visited Mr Donald's hospitable manse in 1802, wrote to Alexander, whose regiment were now stationed at Spanish town, Jamaica:

Dear Sir,

A few weeks since I had a letter from your Father wherein he informed me of your situation in Jamaica & that it was not a pleasant one owing to want of friends &c. I immediately wrote to Eigg for particulars which Mr McLean has transmitted to me such as your Education at Aberdeen, your skill, examinations, approbations, certificates &c. Upon those grounds I have applied to some of my friends to give me letters of introduction for you, I enclose two which will I am certain be of service to you whether you continue to be attached to the army, or be advised to practice in private in Jamaica. Should any more letters reach me before the July packet sails I will inclose them also, but should they come too late I will forward them by the August packet. Mr McLean wrote me that he had advised you to leave the West Indies at all events, notwithstanding these letters may still find you in Jamaica.

Mr Aust is acquainted with Mr Keate Surgeon General to the Army, & if you can point out any situation in which he can be of use to you he will be very happy to apply in your favor. Please to direct any letters you may write to George Aust Esq. Chelsea College, London.

Before you left Britain did you know I had changed my name from Murray to Aust. As I shall always remember with pleasure & interest the Days I spent in the Island of Eigg under your Father's hospitable Roof in the year 1802. & if I can at any time be of service to him or any part of his family it will give me infinite pleasure. I am, Dear Sir, your sincere friend & humble servant ...

Mrs Murray had been widowed in 1786. She had now remarried. Her second husband George Aust was Under Secretary of State for the Army and a powerful ally. Alexander was, however, horrified at his father's interference his military career and quickly replied to Mrs Aust's letter. An undated draft of his letter survives:

> I have the Honor of receiving your Letter of the 30th June enclosing letters of Introduction. For the favor, & for the Handsome Manner in which you have expressed your wish to serve me, persuade me to offer my Acknowledgements. In writing my father I allowed some Expressions of Disgust to drop in Mentioning the Fatiguing Round of Medical Duty, & the Dull uniformity of a West Indian Life in my Situation. He has however Concluded my Situation to be much more unpleasant than in reality it is. He likewise apprehends Danger from the Climate, on account of the Considerell Mortality, which has lately occurred here, & of course advised my leaving the country.
>
> I hope from what I wrote him, he may be reconciled to my further stay – which is at the same time a necessary Reason – as the Commander in Chief allows no Medical Officer to resign – For my own part, I should be unwilling to forego all Military prospects – I have been upwards of 2 years an Hospital Mate. (You have dignified me by calling by the appellation of Ast. Surgeon, to which I am by no means entitled). I have served almost the whole of that time in the West Indies – & done the Duty of an Assistant to a Regiment generally in the most unhealthy Situations in the Country – Might I presume then to expect Promotion?
>
> You have Mentioned Mr Aust's acquaintanace with Mr Keate. I should Consider myself under the greatest obligation to Mr Aust – to apply for my Appointment as Assist. Surgeon in any Regiment that has a Prospect of going home soon – for I must own I have no attachment to the 60th or West India Regts which remain abroad permanently – I find I am a Highlander of Scotland who as well as the Swiss sighs for his native Hills, despises the Effeminate luxury of foreign Climes, preferring a frugal fayr, a homely Board & his pristine Simplicity.[17]

George Aust's influence was probably decisive for on 25th November 1806 Alexander was promoted to Assistant Surgeon of the 99th Regiment of Foot in New Providence. He was sent there at a moment's notice 'to do duty with the 99th Regt, the assistant surgeon (the only Medical Officer with the Corps) being dead, and the Corps very sickly'. The Deputy Inspector of Hospitals noted that 'it is hoped that Mr McLean, tho' not the senior by two, and those two being a hundred miles off, could not be sent, will be confirmed in the appointment'.[18]

Mr Keate himself became involved when on 14th March 1807, writing from the War Office, it was noted that:

> Mr Keate ... transmits recommendations from Jamaica with his observations thereon, and states that he has recommended the removal of assistant surgeon Douglas from the 99th Regt to the Royal African Corps in consequence of Hospital Mate Alexander McClean having been sent from Jamaica to New Providence to join the 99th Regiment.[19]

Alexander's commission was dated 19th March 1807 and he had joined his new regiment by the 25th June, when he was noted as being sick.[20] The 99th were scattered among the various islands in the Bahamas. Its regimental hospital, where Alexander presumably was based, was in New Providence. It was from here a bizarre incident occurred in the summer of 1807. Although

Britain was still at war with Spain the Government had decreed that no offensive operations should be taken against any Spanish colonies. The only exception to this rule was to be the port of Baracoa, at the north-east corner of Cuba, which was the base for numerous privateers. The Governor of Jamaica, however, decided that it was not worth risking the lives of British soldiers to eliminate it. Desire for prize money, and the example of Home Popham's seizure of Buenos Aires, on his own initiative, however, led a British naval officer to attempt the same in Cuba.

In the summer of 1807 Captain Tait of the storeship *Chichester* received orders to transport the 99th Foot from the Bahamas to Bermuda. As it was so spread out, it was going to take some time to gather the regiment together for embarkation. Tait therefore persuaded four officers and eighty-seven convalescent men from the hospital join him ostensibly for a cruise to restore their health. He then asked permission of the Governor of Nassau to attack Baracoa. When this request was refused Tait joined force with a privateer and sailed for the prohibited island.

When on 29th July[21] he arrived on the Cuban coast, Tait landed his convalescents and a few marines and ordered them to capture the battery which prevented the *Chichester* from remaining by the shore, and put out to sea again. The unfortunate landing party did their best but under heavy fire from the battery and its infantry, who outnumbered them ten to one the British troops were driven back to the beach. As Tait had left them no boats the detachment was forced to surrender. After a months confinement they were exchanged. However, two officers and eleven men had been killed and twice as many wounded in the assault.[22]

* * *

Alexander Maclean of Coll had no doubt asked Argyll to nominate Hugh to be an ensign in the 3rd Regiment of Foot Guards and the Duke did as he was asked. Alexander could do this for his own son but not for his kinsman. In 1810 when Mr Donald's son Alexander was hoping for further promotion his father wrote to say:

> Your surgeon has been promoted (I see by the Newspapers) and another appointed his successor. This will be a disappointment to you. The interposition of friends is necessary in such a case, but of such you have few or none who have ... influence or even acquaintance with the Medical Board. I applied to Coll for you, but, notwithstanding his wish to serve you, he believed he could do nothing for the above reason ...[23]

Why Mr Donald did not feel able to apply to Mrs Murray Aust again is not explained. It was to be another three years before he became a full surgeon.[24]

Notes

1. The Rev. Donald Maclean, Edinburgh 12 January 1805 to his eldest son Alexander, Surgeon's Mate, Military Hospital Gosport. BCP Eigg Folder.
2. Brigadier-General Marcus Beresford to the Rt. Hon. Lord Hobart. Barbados, 26 November 1802. Beresford himself was to die in Barbados. Buckinghamshire Record Office. D/MH/H. M110.
3. He was Colonel Lachlan Maclean (1754–1829), the second son of Mr Alexander Maclean Minister of Kilninian & Kilmore in Mull, and a grandson of Neil Maclean of Drimnacross. He was thus Mrs Hobart's 3rd cousin several times removed. He had emigrated to America where he was 'for some years a Merchant in Maryland' [JP MacLean *Renaissance of the Clan MacLean* (1913), 131]. In 1775 he joined the Royal Highland

The West Indies

Emigrants, raised by his uncle Allan Maclean, and served as a subaltern until he purchased a company in 1782; in 1784 he was placed on the ½ pay list; in 1786 he returned to full pay by purchase; in March 1794 he obtained Brevet rank of Major; in 1797 & 1798 he was for 11 months a prisoner in France. 10 months of that time was spent in close confinement. In January 1798 he got Brevet rank of Lt Col and in July 1799 'was made an effective Lt Col in the 60th Regt'; in 1802 he returned to the West Indies 'in a very dangerous state of health, which had nearly deprived him of his life and it was a very long time before he recovered'; he was once again placed on the ½ pay list and then in 1811 he was appointed QMG to the Forces serving in the Windward/Leeward Islands [WO 31. 317. 21 Feb 1811]; in 1821 he was made a Lt Gen & Lt Governor of Quebec and died at Leghorn [*Gents Mag* 1829 vol. 99 ii, 477 & TNA. Will 656. Liverpool. Proved 21 November 1829].

4. Buckingham Record Office. D/MH/H. M. 110.
5. NLS. MS 3018, 31.
6. Philip Wright (ed) *Lady Nugent's Journal* (1966), 244.
7. Columbus called the whole island Hispaniola. The British called it St Domingo. The western half was the French colony of Saint-Dominique, now Haiti, whilst the eastern part was a Spanish colony, it is now the Dominican Republic.
8. As he does not mention Nelson's victory and death at the battle of Trafalgar, which took place on 21 October, news of the battle had presumably not reached Eigg.
9. Stony Hill Barracks is on A3 in the hills some 7 miles north of Kingston.
10. 24 October 1805. Eigg Island. The Rev. Donald Maclean to Alexander Maclean. Assistant Surgeon to the Forces, 18th Regiment of Foot, Jamaica. BCT.
11. ER Cregeen (ed) *Inhabitants of Argyll Estate, 1779* (Scottish Record Society, 1963), 62.
12. 5 August 1805. Eigg Island. The Rev. Donald Maclean to his son Alexander, Jamaica. BCP Extracts.
13. NLS. MS 3018, 32; *Seanachie*, 319. I have not discovered if he was a captain in the army or navy.
14. TNA. Will 343. TEBBS. Proved 4 June 1831.
15. *Lady Nugent's Journal*, 29.
16. *Lady Nugent's Journal*, 23.
17. The Rev Donald Maclean Edinburgh 2 February 1805 to his eldest son Alexander, Surgeon's Mate, Gosport Military Hospital. BCP Eigg Folder.
18. TNA. WO 31. 225.
19. TNA. WO 31. 225.
20. TNA. WO 12. 9786.
21. National Maritime Museum. Log of King's storeship HMS *Chichester*.
22. *History of the British Army* vol. 7, 4–5. It is possible that Assistant Surgeon Maclean accompanied the convalescents on the *Chichester* to Barracoa. He is noted as being 'on command' i.e. on detachment at the time of the 3rd undated muster of the 99th Foot between 25th June & 24th Sept. 1807.
23. BCT. 8 July 1810. Donald to his son Alexander.
24. TNA. WO 31. 385.

Chapter Thirty-Seven

The War continues

Although Napoleon failed to invade the British Isles, and had seen the Franco-Spanish fleet destroyed at Trafalgar, there was one method that could be used to defeat his enemy, without first achieving victory at sea. This stratagem was to prevent France and her satellites from trading with Britain. British shipping was banned from entering ports on the Continent.

The Royal Navy's blockade of European ports and seizure of neutral shipping continued. Hector Alexander Maclean played his part in this demanding task, serving as a Lieutenant on HMS *Ganges* and HMS *Flora*. He was then posted as First Lieutenant to HMS *Crescent*. In 1809 she was wrecked off the coast of Jutland and Hector Alexander lost his life attempting to save those who had been wrecked along with him.[1] He left £300, which, as he was a bachelor, went to his father.[2]

There is no doubt that Great Britain suffered severely from Napoleon's 'Continental System': the price of raw materials soared; many industries slumped; unemployment increased; there were many bankruptcies. Matters were made worse by a poor harvest. It seemed likely that Napoleon had only to wait for victory to come. Waiting, however, was not in his nature: he was in any case obsessed by the constant need to secure fresh triumphs and thereby, as he put it, ensure that he continued to be feared.[3] In consequence, no sooner was Britain isolated by Napoleon's deal with Tsar Alexander of Russia at Tilsit, than he was looking around for a new target. The obvious choice was Portugal.

Portugal had frequently allowed British warships to enter her ports. She had not joined the 'Continental System'. She also possessed wealthy colonies and had a large fleet and a tiny army. She was ripe for the picking. Napoleon's break with Spain, the 1808 Spanish uprising, and his subsequent invasion of the Iberian Peninsula gave Britain the opportunity she needed. And the Duke of Portland's government, with many doubts, 'embarked on the Peninsular struggle which enabled us to fight the French on land regardless of what Russia and the other powers might do'.[4]

* * *

It was not just officers from the family of Coll who rallied to the flag in the Napoleonic Wars. During the first decade of the nineteenth century several men from the Island joined 79th Foot.[5] They include Hugh McKay said to be a native of Sutherland[6] and his four sons:

1. William McKay who was born in Coll in 1784. He originally enlisted into the Canadian Fencibles and served with them until 1804. He then joined the 79th.[7]
2. Donald McKay enlisted in 79th Foot on 3rd September 1804 when he was described as a 'labourer in Coll'.[8] His parents were in Cornaig and on 24th June 1787 was baptised there.[9]
3. George McKay enlisted on 15th November 1804 as a drummer in 79th. He was under age. He had been born in Coll and was baptised there on 2 May 1790.[10]

4. Lachlan McKay was born in 1794 and joined the 79th when he was still a boy. He was discharged and returned to Coll to be apprenticed to a blacksmith.[11]

Another William McKay, claimed he was born in Coll in 1774. He enlisted at Thurso in the Reay Fencibles in 1795, Caithness for unlimited service and served a total of 22 years 67 days: On 1 May 1804 he too joined the 79th Foot.[12] Another soldier from Coll who served in the 79th was Dougald Cameron, who is described in the Pay Lists as a 'Labourer of Coll'.[13] Yet another man in 1/79th Foot described as 'labourer of Coll' was John Maclean.[14] He is said to have served in the expedition to Copenhagen.[15] This preventive strike against the Danish navy took place when it was learnt that Napoleon was about to seize it. 79th Foot was part of the expedition.[16] He later served in the Peninsula.

* * *

Many men from Coll fought in the Peninsular War. One family from Coll, who had served as soldiers in Highland regiments for several generations were the Matheson/Mackenzies in Grishipol. Archibald Mackenzie writing to his son Duncan in 1871 says that all of his ancestor Murdoch Allan's second son's descendants became soldiers. Another Archibald Mackenzie, his father's cousin served under Abercromby in Egypt. He took part in all his battles and 'came home nearly blind'. He became a pensioner and kept a little store in Coll.

Archibald also writes of his immediate family's involvement in Spain during the Peninsular Wars. He says:

> My uncle John was upwards of six feet high remarkably handsome, had a pension, went through the retreat under Sir John Moore, and was wounded at Corunna, he took a farm after coming home and lived well, having had no children.

Uncle John was fortunate to survive the appalling retreat to Corunna from 24th December 1808 to 18th January 1809, which followed on Britain's disastrous initial attempt to open a second front in Europe. Sir John Moore had advanced with part of his army from Lisbon into Spain only to find himself outnumbered by Napoleon. Moore possessed 'an important truth, which was never to leave his mind'. It was that he had under his command 'not merely a considerable part of the dispensable force of this country'. It was the British Army. 'Another army it has not to send'.[17] The privations suffered by the retreat were horrendous.

John Mackenzie was not the only member of Archibald's family to take part in the Peninsular War. He continues:

> My uncle Donald ... perished in the Peninsular War. He was one of those brave fellows that volunteered to board the French conway [convoy?] in the Channel, by which a prize of £100 became his, after his death my uncle John [who] was in the same Regiment, the 78th Highlanders, got hold of the money, and my father who was the right heir never saw a penny of it.
>
> My uncle Hector ... went to the army very young had not one word of English, neither could [he] read or write. In the course of a few years he improved so well that he was a colour sergeant, and besides his half-pay was made Barrack Master of Blackness Castle, by which he had 7/6d Sterling ...[18]

Unfortunately for the accuracy of this story, the 78th Foot did not serve in the Peninsula and I have failed to discover in which regiment the Matheson/Mackenzie brothers served. I suspect that they were in the 79th. Not only had men from Coll, who in 1793 served in the Breadalbane Fencibles volunteered to transfer to the 79th, but Archibald's mother had worked in Mull for Lieutenant-Colonel Archibald Maclean of Scour of the 79th. His mother was a sister of Donald Maclean of Cornaig. Scour was one of the original officers of the 79th. He later commanded the 1st Battalion.

Another family said to have served in the Peninsula were the brothers Allan and Alexander Maclean, the sons of Lachlan Maclean in Fiosgaradh. After the disbandment of the 1st Battalion of the Breadalbane Fencibles, Allan became the Drill Sergeant of the Coll Company of Volunteers. He served as such until December 1806.[19] His brother Alexander, who was also a sergeant, left the company sometime before June 1804.[20] According to family tradition Allan served in the Peninsula.[21] It is not certain in which regiment he served. It is, however, unlikely that Allan could have served there for very long, if at all, as he was in Fiosgaradh when his children were baptised there between 18 September 1808 and 29 July 1816 [Three others were baptised there in 1809, 1812, & 1814].[22] It is more probable that it was his brother Alexander who served in the Peninsula. After Alexander left the Volunteers he never again appears in the Coll records. An Alexander Maclean was a sergeant in 2/79th Foot in 1804.[23] He died in Portugal on 19th January 1809.

After the retreat to Corunna the 79th were stationed at Weeley in Essex.[24] They returned to the Peninsula in the autumn of 1809.[25] They were reinforced with men from the Local Militia. This method of reinforcing the regular army had helped bring it back to strength.[26] Several men listed in the muster rolls are named Maclean, but unlike later lists, do not have 'labourer in Coll' written after their name to distinguish them.

These men from Coll are probably good examples of the type of soldier who won the Highland regiments their reputation for bravery and discipline. The fact that so many men in the army came from the criminal classes helps explain why recruits from the Highlands & Islands were so prized. The Earl of Selkirk argued that as long as rents were low:

> the Highland regiment maintained a very superior character. Instead of the refuse of a manufacturing town, these regiments were composed of hardy mountaineers, whose ordinary mode of life was a perfect school for the habits of a soldier. They were composed of the most respectable of the peasantry; men, for whose fidelity and good conduct there was a solid pledge, in the families they left at home, and in the motives that induced them to enter into the service; men, who were previously accustomed, from their infancy, to respect and obey the same superiors who led them into the field; who looked on them as their protectors no less than their commanders; men, in the minds the attachment of clanship still retained a large portion of its antient enthusiasm.
>
> Besides this, each corps being collected from the same neighbourhood, the men were connected by ties of friendship and of blood; and every one saw in his companions those with whom he had to pass the rest of his life, whether in a military capacity or not. Every one was therefore more solicitous to maintain an unblemished character, than he would have been among a medley of strangers, from whom he might soon be parted, to meet no more. The same circumstance tended to give the soldiery a peculiar degree of that *esprit de corps*, which is so powerful an engine in the hands of a judicious commander. The attachment

of the Highland soldier to his regiment was not a casual or transitory nature – it was not a matter of indifference to him, or the result of accident, whether he belonged to one regiment or another – his regiment was derived from his clan, and inseparably connected with it: in the honour of his regiment he saw that of his name; and to it he transferred all those sentiments of glory, which early education had connected with the achievements of his ancestors.[27]

Although no officers from Coll served in the 79th Foot at this time, a distant cousin of Mr Donald did. He was Captain Alexander Maclean later Tacksman of Hosta in North Uist.[28]

* * *

Despite Sir John Moore's disastrous defeat and death there were still 12,000 British troops in Lisbon. In 1805 Wellesley had returned in triumph from India. He was elected to Parliament and briefly was Chief Secretary for Ireland. He was now Lieutenant-General Sir Arthur Wellesley KB. He was originally sent to Portugal in August 1808, where he defeated Marshall Junot at Vimeiro, only to have the fruits of his victory wasted when Sir Harry Burrard superseded him. Burrard was later court-martialled for allowing the French to be repatriated and, after Moore's death, Wellesley was appointed supreme commander in Portugal. His victories were to be the running sore that helped defeat Napoleon

* * *

Hugh Maclean younger of Coll continued to take part in London duties. Escorting prisoners of war from Reading to Norman Cross, and recruiting in London and Newcastle-upon-Tyne. He was stationed at different barracks in London: at Lower Westminster, Portman Street and Knightsbridge.[29] On 13th June 1809 he resigned his commission, when it is noted that he was 'only allowed on retiring from the service to receive the sum of £600 as he did not purchase his ensigncy'.[30]

Meanwhile Wellesley advanced from Lisbon up the Tagus. He now had with him two seasoned battalions from Gibraltar. They joined him on 16th July 1809 at Plasencia. One of them was the 1st 61st Foot,[31] whose senior lieutenant was George Allan Maclean, the youthful son of Lachlan, formerly of the Isle of Muck. In August 1805 he had transferred from the 46th to the 61st Foot,[32] and on 24th March 1808 joined his new battalion at Gibraltar.[33] On the 27th and 28th July 1809 he was to take part in the bloody battle of Talavera, which is described by Fortescue as 'one of the severest ever fought by the British army'.[34]

The 61st was one of the battalions in Sherbrooke's division ordered not to fire until the enemy was within fifty yards of them. They suffered unflinchingly as the French artillery shot them down and then discharged such a crashing volley that it shattered the front line of the advancing French. The French broke and the whole of Sherbrooke's division rashly followed them over the Portiña with the bayonet. The pursuers, however, broke rank and charged in long disorderly lines. They ran straight into the unbroken French second line, which in turn fired volley after volley into the disorganised red coats and chased them back with heavy losses across the Portiña. Wellesley seeing what was happening moved in Mackenzie's division to plug the gap. The Guards and Cameron's brigade[35] rallied and advanced through the ranks of Mackenzie's men and then fought a savage musketry duel with the French.

The crisis was now over on this part of the front, but the battle continued to rage elsewhere. Eventually the French fell back leaving the Allies in possession of the field. Both sides suffered appalling losses. Wellesley's amounted to 800 killed and nearly 4,000 wounded. The 61st lost nearly half its strength.[36] Among the wounded was George Allan Maclean.[37]

George quickly recovered from his wounds and was present with his battalion during the withdrawal back into Portugal and subsequent advance into Spain. He was also present at the investment of Ciudad Rodrigo. Cuidad Rodrigo was one of the key Spanish fortresses. It is situated on the river Agueda and controlled the route from Salamanca into Portugal. It had already changed hands more than once.

The decision to besiege Ciudad Rodrigo was taken and orders were given on the 18th July 1811 to disembark the siege-train on the Douro and transport it by water to Lamego. It was then taken overland to Transcoso. One hundred and sixty boats were required to move the guns and stores as well as over 1,000 country carts besides 400 pairs of bullocks to carry everything over the appalling roads to their destination.

On 1st August 1811 Wellesley moved his headquarters north-west to Castelo Branco and set off with two divisions and one brigade of cavalry for the Agueda. On 11th August the French outposts were driven in and the blockade of Ciudad Rodrigo began.[38] It fell on the 19th January 1812 and the advance into Spain continued.

* * *

Meanwhile in Britain a new cohort of army officers was beginning its military education. It was a very different education from that of their forbears. In the past a young ensign had only received training when he joined his regiment, and was just as likely to learn military vices as virtues.[39] The first serious attempt to raise the standard of young officer's training took place in 1802 with the establishment of the junior branch of the Royal Military College at Great Marlow. Its aim was to educate some (but by no means all) of those who from early life were intended for the military profession; and, secondly as its Royal Warrant stated 'to afford a Provision for the Orphan Sons of those meritorious Officers who have fallen or been disabled in the Service of their Country as well as for the Sons of those Officers in our Military Service who, from pecuniary difficulties, might not otherwise be able to give them an adequate Education'.

One of the early cadets at the college was Donald, eldest son of Lieutenant John Maclean the former Tacksman of Cornaig, who since 1802 had been serving in the 6th (or Royal North British) Veterans Battalion. On 15th June 1809 Donald was commissioned into the 16th Foot.[40] The regiment was serving in the West Indies. Donald, however, failed to join them there. He is consistently noted as being 'absent without leave'. In fact he was serving with the 4 companies of the 16th stationed at Woburn in Bedfordshire and it was the regiment that joined him, rather than the other way round, in July 1812 on their return to the United Kingdom.[41]

Two months after Donald became an ensign in 16th Foot, his brother John Leyburn was commissioned into the 43rd Foot.[42] The 1st 43rd were serving in the Peninsula. Although John was on the strength of the 1st Battalion he was until 1813 to 'do duty' with the 2nd Battalion at Colchester and Bradbourne Lees.[43]

As their father was a serving officer he probably had to pay £40 per year for each of his son's education, board and clothing. This was somewhat less than the sons of noblemen who had to pay £90. Gentlemen cadets came from a wide social spectrum. Some came from quite impoverished homes whilst others came from extremely wealthy backgrounds. In order that they should live at the same level whilst they were at the college, no cadet was allowed to bring more than a guinea with him and pocket money was limited to 2s. 6d. a week. No cadet could be admitted to the college who was under 13 or over 15 years of age. He had to be physically fit and pass an entrance examination in handwriting, grammar and arithmetic. Once at the college he received instruction in 'Mathmatics, Fortifications, and general Principles of Gunnery and Artillery Service'. He was also taught tactics, to draw plans, military geography and history, plus French and German. He also received lectures in 'Natural and Moral Philosophy', and instruction in riding, fencing, athletics, use of the sabre, and swimming.

* * *

Whilst John Cornaig evidently believed in a military education for his sons, his elder brother Lieutenant-Colonel Lachlan relied on contacts and sympathy to get commissions for his children, and the Duke of York's Military Secretaries must have tired of his constant barrage of letters from Berwick-upon-Tweed. For example on 12th December 1810 he wrote to say:

> Sir, after what I took the liberty of formerly requesting you to mention to the Commander-in-Chief respecting my long service, present situation, misfortunes and disappointments through life and reference to character: I will not offer to give you the trouble of going over the same ground again but I have to request you will have the goodness to take an early opportunity of mentioning to the Commander-in-Chief my request, as a singular favour, that he may have the goodness to give a Ensigncy to my third eldest son (Charles Norman) who I certainly intended for a civil employment but *he will* be a soldier and I trust very fit for it. If I am so honoured as to be attended to in this request; I should like him to go to India as I have some friends there, but this must be as it appears best to Sir David Dundas.[44]

There is a note added, presumably by Colonel Torrens, to this memorial: 'When he states the age & eligibility of his son the C-in-C will take the request into consideration.' The Duke of York was concerned over the age of some officers in the army. He had called for a list of captains under the age of twelve and of lieutenant-colonels under eighteen. One of the many improvements to the army carried out by the Duke was to rule that no officer could be promoted to field rank without at least six years service, or to captain with less than two.

The Military Secretary was certainly right to question Charles Norman's age. He had probably been born on 19th April 1796[45] and was now fourteen. Two years under the statutory age.

Lachlan wrote again on the 21st December to say:

> Sir, I had the honour of your letter of the 15th Instant; and agreeable to his Excellencies the Commander-in-Chief's desire I beg leave to inform you that my son is within a few days of sixteen years of age, he is five feet eight inches and stout in proportion; he is active and clever, and has got a good education, and since he has evinced a determination for the army I have had him instructed accordingly so that I hope he will in time do credit to my recommendation...

Despite the lie he had just written, Lachlan had the audacity to continue:

> I have the comfort to think that I have always supported the Character of a gentleman and an officer most scrupulously...[46]

Lachlan must have scrutinised the *London Gazette* with increasing exasperation to see if his request had been accepted for on the 10 May 1811 he wrote:

> Sir, having observed in the last Gazette a *Maclean*, without a first name, appointed to an Ensigncy in the 43rd Regiment, may I hope it is the youth I took the liberty of applying in favour of some time ago – my son's name is Charles Norman – but I have observed things of that [sort] very often happen; and I hope to be honoured with a communication that it is him, although I confess I would prefer an Indian Regiment.

A note added to this letter says: 'I presume it is his son'. In fact it was an unidentified John Maclean who was recommended by 'Viscount Wellington'[47] as Wellesley was now. Curiously he was born in Berwick-upon-Tweed and joined the 43rd in Spain between the 25th August and 24th September 1812. His namesake, Cornaig's son, 'a very attentive & promising young officer', was serving in the 2nd 43rd Foot,[48] and had on 27th March 1811 been promoted 'without purchase'. He then transferred to the 1st Battalion and sailed in the *Harriet* on the 10th February 1813 from Cork for Spain. He arrived there on the 18th March.[49] There were now two John Macleans serving in the battalion.

As there was no answer to his last letter, Lachlan wrote again from Berwick on 23rd September 1811:

> Sir, I am far from wishing to be troublesome to His Royal Highness the Commander-in-Chief but my son Charles Norman Maclean is losing time and is a great burden to me with such a large family as I have – May I therefore have leave Sir, as the friend of all old and distressed officers to remind His Royal Highness, of what I formerly represented that I trust will induce him to honor my son with a commission as soon as possible . . .

On 10th October 1811 Charles Norman was commissioned into the 2nd 60th Foot.[50] He joined the battalion in Barbados.[51]

* * *

The 99th Regiment of Foot was eventually posted to Halifax, Nova Scotia, where it convalesced. The battalion was then sent to Bermuda. It was here that his eldest son received Mr Donald's last letter. It was dated 8th July 1810, Eigg Island. It can only be imagined what Alexander's reaction was, when he read it.

> My Dear A.
>
> Your letter of the 16th May last is come to hand, after a conveyance of about six weeks. The only one received from you in nearly two years. Tis not a sufficient apology that during that period you wrote one other letter; of the miscarriage of which you have been aware. Your long silence was an instance of cruelty, which your Parents did not merit. Of this you appear so sensible that it may be presumed you shall not be guilty of such negligence for the future. In spite of severity of service and press of duty and other unfavourable concomitant circumstances, 'tis impossible but you might have often written to us within that Period. The painful sensations your silence occasioned, 'tis unnecessary to describe. Be careful to prevent such by more frequent correspondence.

The War continues

Besides my letter of the 4th November 1808 I wrote you another, which it appears has not found its way. I think it was directed to Halifax, whither, in your last letter but one, you expected to have been ordered.

Your sufferings have been severe, May God sanctify them to you, and enable you to act with becoming fortitude and patience under them. What appeared like extravagance to us who knew not your misfortune and hardships, is now sufficiently explained away, and we are far from attaching blame to the pecuniary difficulties, which you could neither help nor prevent. I wish you had stated how much you propose to draw on me for, as that would enable me to take some immediate decisive step in your favour, in so far as my circumstances may permit. However, to prevent inconvenient delay I hereby authorise you to draw on Sir William Forbes, J Hunter & Co. Bankers in Edinburgh for £30 Sterling, which I will take care to lodge in due time, with instructions necessary, that your draft may be honoured. Should this prove inadequate, be not shy in communicating, as inclination prompts us to afford you such aid as our circumstances will permit.

Tis extremely hard to be fettered to a profession of hard duty and a dangerous situation the emolument arising from which will not afford a sufficient support. I wish you had not entered upon it. Promotion you may expect, but when it may take place who can say? . . . Your mother is in indifferent health and I cannot boast of mine. Your sisters are well. Hector has been last session in Glasgow College and is now with us. Neil officiates in Coll as Assistant to the Minister of Tyrie and Coll, his salary is £60 per annum. The latest accounts from your Uncle Hector Mingary from India were favourable; and so are those from your cousin Captain Hector Maclean and his wife. Friends in Coll [are] well. All those on this Island in whom you are interested are in usual health. Dr McAskill indeed is distressed with frequent attacks of a severe rheumatism in his right arm. Write me immediately on receipt of this. We have cause of gratitude to the Almighty, who in his goodness has pleased to restore your health. It is Duty and your comfort to study to preserve it. May God bless direct and prosper you. All here offer you their best wishes.

[Note. Bill dated at St Georges Bermuda upon Sir Wm Forbes etc. 5 January 1811].

What Alexander's response was to this letter is not known. He was, however, soon to have another letter from home for on 12th February 1811 his brother Neil wrote unexpectedly from Coll.

My Dear Brother,

I wrote you a few months ago, giving you all the country intelligence which I could collect; and then little thought any circumstances was to occur, which would render it necessary for me to write you so soon again. At that time I was in good spirits, which is more than I can say of myself just now; for I have to communicate an event which I'm sure must afflict you as well as me. To be ever changing and uncertain is the fate of everything below the sun. Losses and misfortunes during the journey of life we must lay our account to, and to leave or to be left by the friends we love, must one day be the fate of us all. By this time you will guess that some calamity has befallen us, and you judge right. Let me then, without further preface, turn your attention to a tale of sorrow. On the 18th November last, our boat was sent in here with information, that my Father had been taken dangerously ill a few days before then with a violent stitch and fever. I set off immediately and understanding that Dr MacAskill was confined by sickness, I called in Mull, and brought our friend Sandy Langamull to attend him.

On my arrival in Eigg, he was in a state of great pain and debility. Everything possible was done to relieve him; but it was beyond the power of medicine. His fever continued unabated, and he had such severe fits and coughing, that he could hardly ever lie down in bed. Why should I hurt your feelings, by giving you an account of what he suffered after this? Suffice it to say, he continued getting weaker and weaker, till at last it pleased God to put an end to his sufferings. He expired early on the morning of the 25th December and had been so much exhausted by six weeks painful illness, that life went out gently and without a struggle. His disease was an inflamation of the lungs (the consequence, I believe, of cold), which brought on the symptoms I have mentioned.

You will easily conceive the distress of your poor Mother and sisters. For my own part, I felt all the unaffected sorrow which a son could feel for the loss of so indulgent and dutiful a father; yet I have endeavoured to bear my loss with all the resignation which became me, and bow with reverence to the Will of God.

Donald was buried in Eigg. Neil was later to commission a tombstone to be erected. It is a simple rectangular stone, with the inscription:

> In rememberance of Rev. Donald Maclean,
> Minister of Small Isles, died 25 December
> 1810 aged 58 years. This Memorial
> was erected by his son Revd
> N Maclean Minister of Tyree Argyllshire.

It stands alongside the grandiose, and decayed, tomb of Donald's predecessor the Rev. Malcolm Macaskill and his son Dr Donald of Kildonan.[52]

Mr Donald had lived a useful life. He was a preacher, a skilled seaman, a farmer and a soldier. He does not appear to have had any ambitions outside the Hebrides. Yet he was quick to encourage his eldest son to attempt to forge a career far from home. He was a scholar who wished to help his eldest son with his 'poetical amusements', although he believed it would be better if he studied politics.

Politically Donald was an arch-conservative, an upholder of the Constitution, and an opponent of radicals. As befitted a descendant of the *luchd-tighe*, he was a staunch supporter of his chief and commanded his men in the Rum Company in the Volunteers.

He successfully guided his family through the transition from the eighteenth to the nineteenth century and all three of his sons followed him to university. They were to form part of the new well-educated non-landed professional establishment.

Notes

1. *Clan Gillean*, 407.
2. TNA. Administrations. 1809. Loveday. 10 February 1809; the log of the *Crescent* stops in 1808. Presumably the journal covering Hector Alexander's time with her was lost when she was wrecked [NMM. ADM. L. C. 221].
3. Charles Esdaile *The Peninsular War* (2002), 5.

The War continues

4. Piers Mackesy *The War in the Mediterranean 1803–1810* (1957), ix.
5. TNA. WO 97. 895. 79th Foot Pensions.
6. This could be a guess. In 1765 there were families of Mackays in both Rum & Muck and it would be more likely that they came from here[EUL. La.III. 839].
7. TNA. WO 97. 895. 79th Foot Pensions.
8. TNA. WO 12. 8393 1/79th Foot.
9. NAS CH2. 70. 1.
10. Ibid; TNA. WO 97. 895.
11. BCP. Wilson letter of 20 August 1871.
12. Ibid; TNA. WO 97. 238.
13. TNA. WO 12. 8383. 1/79th Foot. 25 March to 24 June 1814. He was a prisoner of war.
14. Ditto. He was the son of Lachlan and Catherine Maclean. [Death Certificate 551/2/74] Although the 1871 Census says that he was born in Coll, that of 1851 says that it was in Kilninian in Mull. As no Lachlan & Catherine Maclean have a son baptised in Coll at the right time, he was probably born in Quinish and later moved to Coll.
15. Betty MacDougall *Folklore from Coll* (nd), 35.
16. Loraine Maclean of Dochgarroch *Indomitable Colonel* (1986), 188.
17. Christopher Hibbert *Corunna* (1961), 32.
18. BCP. Matheson/Mackenzie file.
19. TNA. WO 13. 4176. Part 3.
20. TNA. WO 13. 4175.
21. BCP. 8 June 1934. Allan Maclean 5 Glenview Terrace, Greenock to RC Johnston, 158 Crescent Road, Toronto 5, Ontario.
22. NAS. CH 2. 70. 1.
23. TNA. WO 12. 8449: Pay List 25 November–24 December 1804.
24. TNA. WO 12. 8390.
25. *History of the British Army* vol.7, 57n.
26. *History of the British Army* vol. 7, 35.
27. The Earl of Selkirk *Observations on the present state of the Highlands of Scotland* (1806), 66–7.
28. Hector Hugh Mackenzie *The Macleans of Boreray* (1946), 112.
29. TNA. WO 17. 87–91.
30. TNA. WO 31. 276. 22 Jun. 1809.
31. *History of the British Army* vol. 7, 200.
32. TNA. WO 31. 359.
33. TNA. WO 12. 7103.
34. *History of the British Army* vol. 7, 256.
35. Its commander was Alan Cameron, who had raised the 79th and caused Alexander Maclean of Coll so much trouble in 1793.
36. *History of the British Army* vol. 7, 223–256.
37. TNA. WO 12. 7103.
38. *History of the British Army* vol. 8, 252–3.
39. Richard Glover *Peninsular Preparation* (1963), 185.
40. TNA. WO 31. 276.
41. TNA. WO 17. 118.
42. TNA. WO 31. 285. 19 October 1809.
43. TNA. WO 17. 154 (2).
44. TNA. WO 31. 332. 14 May 1810. Sir David had succeeded the Duke of York, who had resigned over the scandal of his mistress having sold commissions and promotions.
45. *Scots Magazine*, vol. 58, 296

46. TNA. WO 31. 332. 10 October 1811.
47. TNA. WO 12. 5574.
48. TNA. WO 31. 319. 27 March 1811.
49. TNA. WO 12. 5574.
50. TNA. WO 31. 276. 10 October 1811.
51. TNA. WO 17. 180. (3).
52. I have to thank Noel Banks, the author of *Six Inner Hebrides* (1977) for letting me have a copy of this inscription.

Chapter Thirty-Eight

The Last Phase of the War

After Tilsit, Napoleon's alliance with the Tsar Alexander I was the cornerstone of his policy against Great Britain. There was, however, no common aim in the alliance. Napoleon merely wanted to use the Tsar for his own purposes. Alexander, not surprisingly, had other intentions. Russia depended on imports from Great Britain, particularly luxuries, which were secretly brought into Russia. She also needed to export her timber, which was less easy to smuggle. Napoleon had also infuriated Alexander by establishing the Grand Duchy of Warsaw from land he had taken from Austria. The Russian Government was always peculiarly sensitive to what happened in Poland. She herself had numerous Polish subjects and the establishment of a Polish state was a dangerous precedent.

The fate of Eastern Europe was to have its effect on one branch of the family of Coll. Archibald, the second son of John Maclean Tacksman of Grishipol, had in 1753 settled in Danzig. He married the daughter of another Scot[1], who was part of an extended family of Scots merchants with extensive trading interests in the Baltic. Archibald, who also became a merchant, maintained his links with Scotland, probably acting as the agent of his uncle Lachlan, the Glasgow merchant, and sending his eldest son to Glasgow University.

Archibald had a thriving business in Poland and East Prussia and acquired an estate at Holm on the river Weichsel. It was badly damaged by Napoleon's troops when in June 1812 the *Grande Armée* crossed the river Niemen to invade Russia. Lachlan, Archibald's second son, knew General Rapp, the military governor of Danzig[2] who introduced him to Napoleon in order to claim compensation for the damage done to his estate,[3] which suggests that Lachlan was working with the French and probably supplying them with stores.

* * *

Not all descendants of the Macleans of Coll fought on the Allied side in the Napoleonic Wars. At least two possible descendants of those who joined the Scots Brigade with Lachlan Maclean of Coll in 1681 served in the French Army.

Sergeant-Major Jean Henri Maclean was born Johannes Henricus at Maastrict in 1783. He joined the Dutch Army in 1799. When the Netherlands changed sides, becoming little more than a French province, he transferred to the 123rd Regiment de Ligny. On 6th September 1813 he was commissioned in the 1st Battalion as a 2nd Lieutenant.

Charles Maclean was seven years younger than Johannes. He was also born in the Netherlands and served in the French Army. From May 1812 to July 1813 he served in the Imperial Guard and took part in the invasion of Russia.[4]

* * *

Before he had decided to invade Russia Napoleon was seriously considering personally returning to Spain where the Anglo-Iberian armies' successes had robbed the French of victory. The invasion of Russia was finally to put paid to any chance of this taking place: it robbed the French Army in the Peninsula of the men it needed to defeat the British and their Spanish and Portuguese allies, and a month after the *Grande Armée* crossed the Niemen into Russia, Wellington defeated Marmont at the Battle of Salamanca.

It is considered that Wellington's victory at Salamanca raised him 'almost to the level of Marlborough, being the most skilful, the most considerable in points of numbers engaged, and the most important in its results that the British had won in modern times'.[5] It was not won without casualties. Those of Hulse's brigade were the worst, and the 61st Foot lost 24 officers and 342 men killed and wounded.[6] As a result of the casualties George Allan was appointed acting-adjutant.[7] Wellington himself recommended him for promotion, 'vice Stubbs killed in action'. The War Office had, however, moved faster than Wellington and had already promoted him Captain in the place of Farell who had died of his wounds.[8]

Wellington's victory at Salamanca attracted a massive concentration of the French armies in the Peninsula. Outnumbered and not helped by drunkenness, when the army discovered the new vintage, Wellington was forced to retreat to Cuidad Rodrigo.

* * *

Meanwhile Lieutenant Donald John Maclean, Lieutenant-Colonel Lachlan's third son at Cape Town was also destined to see active service. In September 1810, the 1st Battalion 72nd Foot embarked in Capetown on the transport HMS *Minerva*. They sailed for Mauritius. This French colony in the Indian Ocean had for some time been a base for French privateers carrying out the *guerre de corse* against British shipping. They had played havoc with British commerce and in 1807 the port of Calcutta alone suffered a loss of £200,000 from their activities over a period of six weeks.

A blockade against Mauritius was mounted and in the spring of 1810 a force of some 35,000 men sailed from Madras for Mauritius. It had always been believed that, as a reef surrounded it, Mauritius was impregnable. However, reconnaissance from the Isle of Rodriguez to the east of Mauritius, which was captured earlier, disproved this belief, and on the 22nd November, an assault was made on Port Louis. The French surrendered on 2nd December 1810.[9]

The 1st Battalion 72nd Foot did not arrive in Mauritius until after 25th November 1810.[10] Donald John claimed in his service record that he took part in the capture of Mauritius.[11] Curiously Fortescue in his *History of the British Army* makes no mention of the 72nd Foot's involvement in its seizure.

Lieutenant-Colonel Lachlan used Donald John's service in the *Isle de France*, as Mauritius was also called, when he wrote to the Duke of York's Military Secretary on 21st September 1811 to obtain a commission for his son Charles Norman. As we have seen Charles Norman was commissioned into the 2nd 60th Foot in the West Indies and was by 25th April 1812 serving with them in Barbados.[12] This was not what Lachlan wanted and on the 27 May 1813 he wrote again to the Military Secretary:

Sir,

I have this day a letter from the officer commanding the 2nd Battalion 73rd Regiment informing me that a Lieutenant Straker was on the eve of being exchanged out of the Regiment and as he knew I wished much to get my son Lieutenant Charles Norman Maclean of the 60th Regiment into the 73rd he assured me, if I had interest at *Headquarters* to effect the exchange, it would be agreeable to the Regiment.

He goes on to say:

I understand that 1st Battalion 73rd Regiment goes to Ceylon, where my old worthy friend General Brownrigg commands, who was so good as promise before he left home he would be of use to that youth, if I could get him out to him – as this is so favourable an opportunity I shall esteem it a great addition to the favours already confirmed if you will have the goodness to promote my views.

On 10th June 1813 Charles Norman was promoted to a Lieutenancy in the 73rd.[13]

* * *

By 1811 Hector Mingary was serving again with the 14th Foot. He then took part in the expedition to what is now Indonesia. 'Our Uncle Hector Mingary was one of the valiant captors of Batavia where he exhibited much prowess', wrote Neil to his brother Alexander in February 1812.[14]

Batavia, now Jakarta, was the capital of Java. It was one of the Dutch colonies in the East Indies and as the Netherlands were now the Batavian Republic and allied to Napoleon, they were fair game for the British. An expeditionary force, under the command of Major-General RR Gillespie, was dispatched there from Madras.

Batavia fell, but the British still had to eliminate enemy strong points elsewhere in Java, including the fortified Cratten of the Sultan of Djokjokarta. Djokjokarta is some 300 miles east of Batavia. Hector Mingary, now in command of the rifle company of 14th Foot, led his men on their march through the steaming heat of Java. On 16th June they began their assault. As they ascended the ramparts the tower blew up killing 23 men and wounding 76. Hector was among those who died of his wounds.[15] His brother officers erected a memorial to him, which was in the old graveyard behind the Pasar of Djokjakarta. It read:

In Memory of Lieut. Hector Maclean, late of His Majesty's 14th Regiment of Foot this column has been erected. It is a votive emblem of esteem to military ardour and early worth by officers who served with him. He commanded the rifle company of his corps in the successful assault of the Craton on 16th June 1812. Towards the close of that conflict he received a wound, which proved mortal in his twentieth year: thus fell a youth. His memory survives in that of his brother officers.[16]

It took time for news of Hector's death to reach Mr Donald's son Neil, who was now the Minister of Eigg, and it was not until 8th September 1815 that he wrote to his brother. Alexander was now part of the Army of occupation in France. In his letter Neil says that: 'Our poor young Uncle Hector Mingarry died of his wounds at Batavia'.[17]

* * *

Also taking part in the battle of Salamanca were the 1st Battalion 79th Foot who had returned to the Peninsula in the autumn of 1809. They were first stationed at Cadiz. It was an unhealthy posting and when the battalion moved to Portugal seven Macleans were left among the sick in Lisbon. One was so ill that he was sent home.[18]

One Private Donald Maclean, who was wounded at Salamanca died of his wounds on 18th October. In the next muster, which covers the period from 25 December 1812 to 24th March 1813, Private Dougald Cameron is decribed as being a Prisoner of War. He is later noted as being a 'Labourer from Coll'.[19] Cameron is an unusual name in Coll. The only family of that name in Coll is that of John Cameron, who is said to have been a Sergeant in the Black Watch,[20] and his wife Margaret Maclean, Fiosgaradh. However, they only have daughters appearing in the Baptismal register.[21] It is, however, possible that Dougald was born during a ministerial vacancy when baptisms were not registered.

* * *

In March 1813 another officer belonging to Coll arrived in the Peninsula. He had sailed on HMS *Harriet*. This was John Leyburn, John Maclean of Cornaig's second son who, since he had left the Royal Military College at Marlow, had served at home with the 2nd 43 Foot. On 16th March 1811 he had been promoted to a Lieutenancy, when the Colonel of his Regiment describes him as 'a very attentive and promising young officer'. He now joined the 1st Battalion as it recovered in Portugal after the retreat from Salamanca.

The 1st 43rd Foot was one of the most experienced battalions in the Peninsula. They were part of the famous Light Division, which had taken part in the siege of Badajoz: 'this (of all others) most dreadful siege'.[22] It must have been a somewhat daunting experience for the unblooded Lieutenant Maclean, who had never heard a shot fired in anger, to join such a veteran battalion, especially as he was senior to several seasoned officers.[23] He had, however, arrived in time to take part in the retraining that took place in Portugal, and when the campaigning season began once more in May 1813 he was present when the 1st 43rd, as part of a rejuvenated army, marched back into Spain and Wellington bade his farewell to Portugal.

Fortescue claims that the British army that marched into Spain in May 1813 was 'in such a state of health and strength as had never before been seen in the Peninsula'.[24] They were going to need to be. The marches they were to perform were both arduous and difficult: the country was barren, rocky and mountainous, the villages few and the roads abominable.[25] It was now that Wellington's organisation, learnt in India, of keeping his army supplied, triumphed. The French were not able to halt or concentrate because they could not feed their troops. 'Wellington's supplies were always hunting for his army; Joseph [Napoleon's brother]'s army was always hunting for its supplies; and thus, whereas to the Allies a halt signified replenishment, to their opponents it spelt starvation'.[26]

All the Collachs in Spain were present in their respective regiments when on the 21st June 1813 at Vittoria the British Army won one of its greatest victories. It was a fitting climax to a great campaign that helped the Allies defeat Napoleon and send hm to exile in Elba.

* * *

When, after Trafalgar, the threat of invasion was over the Volunteers were not stood down. However, the War Office neglected their outlying companies. All seems to have gone well for the Rum Company of the Inverness-shire Volunteers whilst Mr Donald was alive but when he died things went wrong. Although they continued to drill they were not paid. It was not until 1813 that their chief heard what was happening and on the 13th January 1814 wrote a curt letter from Coll to Sir James Grant.

The Last Phase of the War

Dear Sir,

I hope you will pardon my the liberty I now take of representing the situation of a company of volunteers established long, chiefly upon an island of mine which by local situation is placed (with regard to Volunteers, Militia &c) within the county of Inverness-shire consequently under your jurisdiction as Lord Lieutenant of that county – Not having been there for sometime it was but lately I understood the situation of the company & the apparent injustice that has been done to it. Mr Donald Maclean was the captain of this company & during his life everything was conducted regularly. Since then, altho there has been no successor appointed, the affairs of the company appear to have been regularly conducted by the senior officer Mr John Maclean, the annual exercise regularly performed, inspections done, yet the accounts – although regularly transmitted have not been attended to nor the pay [–] at least not paid to either men or officers – I cannot comprehend why this should be the case for as every duty was performed the want of a captain cannot surely effect the rest while they continue to serve. I was at some loss what to recommend to you for the long & indeed expected what I believe has since happened the reduction of their company, besides being at such a distance might be partly owing to my omitting the matter, yet certainly there can be no reason why men that have actually performed their duty should be deficient of their pay – I am persuaded that this matter only requires being properly represented to be rewarded. I think it two years that are due and I trust that you as Lieutenant of the County will have the goodness to make necessary application in the proper Channel to have this mistake (for such it must be) rectified as soon as possible.[27]

* * *

The Allies were in Vienna deciding the future of Europe when the news of Napoleon's return to France fell like a bombshell on to their congress. The Government of Louis XVIII had hardly begun to function but its aims and objectives were clear and the French people did not like what they saw.

Napoleon's return from Elba reads like a romance. He landed at Antibes with a few men, bared his breast to Royalist soldiers who refused to fire on him, crossed half France without difficulty or bloodshed and late on 20th March 1815 was carried up the stairs of the Tuileries by an infatuated cheering crowd. The greatest living soldier in Europe had achieved the bloodless re-conquest of France.[28]

The army deserted Louis virtually *en masse*. The Allies, however, were not prepared to put back the clock and began to assemble their armies in Belgium. The problem facing Wellington was that the army, which had driven the French out of Spain, had been dispersed throughout the world. After Waterloo the Duke is said to have remarked that 'If I had had the same army as in the south of France the battle would have been over in three hours'. Instead he had only 31,000 British officers and men, many of them who had not previously seen active service. He had also under his command 16,000 Hanoverians, nearly 7,000 Brunswickers, 29,000 Dutch-Belgian troops, almost 3,000 from Nassau and 6,000 infantrymen, hussars and light dragoons of the King's German Legion, which had fought so gallantly in the Peninsula.

Napoleon left Paris for the front on the 12th June. His aim was to strike the British and Prussian armies before they could act together. He gained a considerable, but partial, victory over the Prussians at Ligny. However, Blücher, the Prussian commander, was still in a position to promise

Wellington that he would join him at Mont St Jean and it was on the strength of this promise that on 18th June Wellington fought a defensive battle.

In fact Wellington had to fight two separate battles and conduct a withdrawal on the intervening day. The first battle, that of Quatre Bras, was fought on ground that was not of his choosing. It opened badly. Before Wellington could arrive on the scene the Dutch-Belgian troops holding the vital crossroad of Quatre Bras were badly mauled. As the afternoon wore on, his own troops hurried to the sound of firing. As they arrived they were thrown piecemeal into the fray and by their superior firepower held their own against the French columns. Each time the enemy cuirassiers charged the infantry formed squares and drove off the cavalry. Several battalions were, however, caught in line and were so badly damaged that after six hours of carnage Wellington was forced to withdraw to the ridge in front of Mont St Jean.

Torrential rain that night delayed the start of the French advance and they were unable to move forward until the ground was dry enough to allow the artillery to proceed. Even so when the French infantry advanced up the hill they became so covered with mud that their boots were dragged off. Gun carriages sank up to their hubs and when the guns did fire many French shells dropped harmlessly into the morass.

The British position was based on the farms of Hougoumont and La Haye Sainte. Both were on the ridge and consisted of walled gardens, hedges and orchards. As we have seen most of the men from Coll were serving in the 79th Foot. It was part of Kemp's Brigade in Picton's division, which was held on the ridge to the east of La Hay Sainte. Picton drew up his two brigades consisting of less than 3,000 men side by side in a line two rows deep. 150 yards in front of them behind a hedge on the crest of the ridge was the Dutch-Belgian Brigade.

On the afternoon of the 18th June 80 guns of the French artillery bombarded the ridge. French columns 18,000 strong then advanced up the long slope and attacked. At the approach of the French the Dutch-Belgian Brigade, which had received numerous casualties in the bombardment, fired one volley then turned and fled. Kemp's men moved forward and occupied the hedge vacated by the Belgians. The over-confident French columns halted and began to deploy into line only thirty yards in front of the British line. Picton seized the critical moment and shouted at Kemp's Brigade, 'a volley, and then charge!'

The volley had a devastating effect and with a fierce hurrah, the British fell on the enemy with the bayonet. Picton was shot dead as he ran forward, but Kemp's Brigade pushed on with cold steel. The French fell into disorder. The next moment they were flying in confusion down the slope pursued by the 79th, their comrades in Kemp's Brigade and the Allied cavalry. Many Highlanders grasped the horses' stirrups and dashed forward beside the cavalrymen.

Throughout the day the 79th were in the thick of the fighting. Few regiments had such heavy casualties. They had begun the battle with a full complement of officers and men. When the day was won it was left to a lieutenant to bring what was left out of action. 32 officers, over half the 40 sergeants, and 424 of the 684 other ranks were casualties.[29] One of the dead was a son of Allan Fiosgaradh.[30]

Notes

1. He was John Simpson the Town-Major of Memel.
2. Danzig had since 1805 had a French garrison [Adam Zamoyski *1812: Napoleon's Fatal March on Moscow* (2004), 79].

3. John, Archibald's eldest son died in 1799 at Königsberg [Kaliningrad] on a business trip to what was then East Prussia [BCP. Letter dated Berlin 6 August 1972 from Angus William Maclean].
4. Archives de Guerre, Chateau de Vincennes, Paris. Arch. Admin. Officiers 1791–1847: Letter from Johannes Macleane 'S-Gravenhage, Holland & copy of reply from Vincennes dated 6 March 1968.
5. *History of the British Army* vol. 8, 502.
6. *Ibid*, 506.
7. TNA. WO 17. 181 (3).
8. TNA. WO 31. 359 30 October & 19 November 1812.
9. *History of the British Army* vol. VII, 602–5.
10. TNA. WO 17. 193.
11. TNA. WO 25.
12. TNA. WO 17. 180 (3).
13. TNA. WO 31. 374.
14. BCT. 5 February 1812. Rev. Neil Maclean to his brother Alexander.
15. Major H Davidson *The History & Services of the 78th Highlanders 1793–1881* (1901), 88.
16. Dr J MacLean 'Queries', *Scottish Genealogist*, vol. 16, No. 4 (December 1969), 93.
17. BCT. 8 September 1815. The Rev. Neil Maclean to his brother Alexander, Surgeon 64th Regiment of Foot, British Army, France.
18. TNA. WO 12. 8390 & 8391.
19. From now on several men are identified as 'Labourers from Coll or Mull' presumably to distinguish them from other men with the same forenames.
20. BCP. Coll Families Box file. 'Memoirs of Jane Macinnes. 9 April 1888'.
21. Marion 19 November 1787 & Jane 28 September 1789. [NAS. CH 2. 70. 1].
22. BCP. Strachan Folder: Camp before Badajoz 8 April 1812. Lieutenant JWH Streaphan to his wife Mary.
23. Including his namesake John Maclean, who had served for 6 months with the Portuguese army [TNA. WO 17 154 (2)]; arrived with the 1st Battalion in August 1812 and had taken part in the retreat from Salamanca; he had been promoted Lieutenant on the instructions of Wellington.[TNA. WO 25. 788].
24. *History of the British Army* vol. 9, 131.
25. *History of the British Army* vol. 9, 154.
26. *History of the British Army* vol. 9, 192.
27. NAS. GD 248. 671. 4.
28. AJ Grant and Harold Temperley *Europe in the Nineteenth and Twentieth Centuries* (1948), 162–75.
29. Peter Young & JP Lawford *History of the British Army* (1970), 122–5; W Richards 'The Camerons at Waterloo' in *Scotland for Ever*, (nd), 109; David Stewart *Sketches of the Highlanders* vol. 2, 213–4.
30. BCP. 8 June 1834. Allan Maclean, 5 Glenview Terrace, Greenock to RC Johnston, 158 Crescent Road, Toronto 5, Ontario, Canada.

Chapter Thirty-Nine

The War Years at home 1803–1815

The old Duke of Argyll died at Inveraray on 25 May 1806. The Marquess of Lorne, who was an intimate of the Prince Regent, succeeded him. Lorne is reputed to have sired 400 illegitimate children.[1] The new Duke immediately began to sell off some of the vast Argyll estate. Included in this disposal were the Two Ends of Coll. These were promised to Maclean of Coll. The Campbell brothers were, however, desperate to save their investment. They are said to have turned up at Inveraray with gold in their saddlebags. Cash was something the Duke could not resist.

'The two ends of Coll have been sold by Argyle', Mr Donald Maclean wrote to his son Alexander on 15 February 1807: 'Our worthy friend[2] Coll was promised preference by the Duke ... but was disappointed. Malcolm and Murdoch Campbell have bought them for £8,000'.[3]

That the Campbell brothers dared bid against Maclean of Coll shows how times had changed. Some tenants, particularly those who had lived outwith Coll and made money, were no longer prepared to accept that the will of the Laird was to be obeyed without question.

The Campbell brothers are an interesting family. Despite the antagonism of the Laird and his allies, they were to become landowners in their own right, Justices of the Peace and were to marry into the leading family of the Coll establishment. Yet they were linked horizontally to a number of quite humble people, who made up the bulk of the population. Their rise illustrates the opportunities that were available at the beginning of the new century to men who had initiative, ambition and luck.

The Campbell brothers' mother was the daughter of an unidentified Neil Maclean. Her sisters were married to tenants in Coll. One of them married a John Mackinnon, who in 1776 was one of Donald of Cornaig's sub-tenants in Caolis. He is described as 'a respectable farmer in Coll'. Another sister, Catherine, was married to Murdoch, the son of *Maoldòmhnich Mac Mhathain* in Grishipol. In 1798 their grandson Archibald was born at Grishipol. He is the Archibald Mackenzie, who has already been mentioned on several occasions. In 1872 he wrote two long letters to his son Duncan Mackenzie giving him stories about his ancestors. These letters not only illustrate the lives of tenants in Coll at the beginning of the nineteenth century. They complement Allan of Crossapol's 'Genealogical Account of the Macleans'.[4]

Archibald says that his father Neil:

had when a boy the King's evil in his right arm, he went to a great doctor by the name of McKinnon in Mull, with him he continued for three years, and came home quite well only a little stiffness in his arm which continued all his life ...

He continues:

My mother was dairymaid to Colonel McLean of Ross [Lieutenant-Colonel Archibald Maclean of Scour 79th Foot[5]] in Mull, and was married there. Her husband died shortly after the marriage. She left Mull and was engaged as chief dairymaid with the Laird of Coll, where she and my father were married. In this profitable employment they continued for some years, and then took a farm ...[6]

He goes on to describe the sort of houses tenants lived in at this time when he writes:

The top of the walls of the houses in the Highlands were like those of the Jews very wide. My father was building a new house at the time, and made the top of the wall quite narrow. My mother who was in the habit of drying some cheese on the wall, fell down on a stone pavement, and received such internal injury as brought her to her grave in a few months.

Archibald says that when his mother died 'My poor father was almost distracted for he loved her most tenderly'. He says also that his father's female cousins who lived with him 'threw themselves in his way'. They were 'neither servants nor mistresses' but did everything to ruin his house and did most things improperly'. There was another girl in the house, which my mother brought up ... In the course of three years he got married to this girl,[7] imagining she would be good to us, to me, and my sister, and indeed she was to me. They had a family consisting of two sons and three daughters.[8]

His stepmother was 'a decent humble girl then about fourteen years old'. He married her when she was seventeen.[9] These were humble people. They were not at the bottom of the economic pile in Coll, but they were not far off it.

* * *

Another example of the potential within Hebridean society is illustrated by the careers of Murdoch Maclaine of Lochbuie and his extended family. In June 1804, when he lay dying at Moy House, two sons and seven daughters were present. Also there to say farewell to the old chief 'who was sinking fast, but hanging on to life with true Scottish tenacity' were the lairds of Ulva, Coll and Airds who in turn held the old man's hand and engaged him with 'rational conversation'.[10]

It was a fitting end to an ancient chieftain, yet Murdoch had not always been a chief. He was a younger son of the 4th son of Hector Maclaine 12th of Lochbuie. As such he had few prospects and had in his youth 'served for seven years regular apprenticeship to a linen manufacturer in Edinburgh'.[11]

If it had not been for a series of deaths and the fact that his elder brother's sons were passed over in the entail of the Lochbuie estate if 'they were not in the character of gentlemen', which they evidently were not, Murdoch would never have inherited the estate. However, thanks to hard work and his success as a linen merchant in Edinburgh, he was able to finance the raising of 25 men in the Seven Years War for the 114th Foot. This action gained him a commission as a lieutenant and the character of a gentleman.

Before Murdoch had risen to prominence his sisters had both married. One had married Hugh Maclean, a tenant in Barchindroman in Mull. He died in February 1760 when he was 'working at cutting of the woods – your poor sister I pity she is big with child & has four children & nothing to support them'.[12] Another sister Margaret married Lachlan Macquarrie a joint-tenant at Oscamull on the Sound of Ulva.[13] Their daughter Elizabeth was married to Farquhar Maclean, a joiner[14] who shared his farm with his in-laws. They were hardly an affluent family, yet one of Elizabeth's brother's was to become a major-general, Governor of New South Wales and a considerable landowner in Mull, and another was to be an officer in the 42nd Foot and also a landowner in Mull.

The point I am trying to make is that even in chiefly families at the turn of the nineteenth century economic failure led to social ruin. Whilst economic success, such as that of the Campbell and Macquarie brothers, led to social advancement, however humble their extended family might be. Whilst some of those of the tenant class were ascending the social ladder those at the top were also seeking new opportunities.

* * *

Alexander Maclean of Coll was also ambitious for his family. As we have seen he wanted his family to play an appropriate part in the wider society of the United Kingdom: in 1795 he became a member of the fashionable New Club which met at Bayle's new tavern in Shakespeare Square in Edinburgh's New Town;[15] he visited the waters at Bath; in 1796 he also purchased a house in the New Town. It was located on the north side of George Street, between Castle Street and Charlotte Square.[16]

Whatever the charms individual Macleans had for the aristocracy, there can be little doubt that part of this attraction was that Highlanders were now 'all the rage'. The event that led to the transformation of the Highlander from barbarous rebel in the public's imagination into 'noble savage' was the publication in 1760 of *Fragments of ancient poetry collected in the Highlands of Scotland*.

Ossian's poems can be considered as having paved the way, and wetted the public's appetite, for the works of the Edinburgh advocate Sir Walter Scott whose first poems began to appear in 1796. His first literary success *The Lay of the Last Minstrel* appeared in 1802 and was an immediate best seller. Marmion followed in 1805.[17] Scotland was now highly fashionable in English society, particularly with rich romantic females.

Although he was a Borderer and had little, if any, Gaelic, Scott had from an early age been fascinated by the Highlands, its history and its traditions. As a schoolboy he had paid the first of many brief visits to the Highland where he was captivated by the scenery. However, it was not until 1793 that he spent any length of time there. He did so with his friends who had estates in the area, exploring Lomondside and Loch Katrine.

One of Scott's greatest friends, with whom he explored Loch Lomond, Arrochar and Loch Sloy, was Hector Macdonald Buchanan WS who had married the heiress of Robert Buchanan of Drumikill and Ross Priory in Dunbartonshire. Hector was the youngest son of the first marriage of Colin Macdonald of Boisdale and had taken the additional surname of Buchanan when he married the heiress. Hector's eldest brother Alexander had married Marion, Alexander Maclean of Coll's only sister. It is therefore certain that Scott and Alexander Coll knew each other, especially as at about the time Coll purchased his house in the New Town of Edinburgh, Scott moved in to North Castle Street.[18] They were thus relatively close neighbours and moved in the same circles.[19]

Scott had an astonishingly retentive memory for the traditional tales he heard. And in his publications he put all he had gleaned from the Highlands to good use. As a result he did more than any other individual to stimulate curiosity in Scotland's heritage and draw tourists in thousands to the Highlands, particularly to the Trossachs. One view of Scott is that he 'spread a romantic patina' over the reality of the Highlands, producing a 'synthetic myth'.[20] Whatever the truth of this assertion, it is clear that Scott's journeys and contacts in Highland Scotland directly inspired a significant part of his work. Without Scott ignorance of Gaelic speaking Scotland would have remained even greater than it was.[21]

* * *

In 1807 a young shoemaker from Tiree made his way to Glasgow to buy leather. He carried with him a 'letter of guarantee' from Alexander Maclean of Coll. It was an auspicious journey. Not only did the young shoemaker find himself a wife in Glasgow, but he was so grateful to Alexander that he composed a panegyric in Gaelic in his honour. It was the beginning of one of the last patron-poet relationships in the Gaidhealtachd.

John Maclean *Iain Mac Ailein mhic Iain mhic Thearlaich mhic Lachain mhic Eoghain mhic Lachainn Fhin* was born on 8th January 1787 at Cnoc Mhic Dhùghaill in Caolis, Tiree.[22] His maternal great-grandfather Neil Lamont had been Maclean of Coll's bard in the mid-eighteenth century[23] whilst his paternal ancestors were descended from the Macleans of Hynish in Tiree, who were in turn cadets of the family of Ardgour. Several members of the family were poets. Most are forgotten but John is remembered in Canada as the *Am Bàrd Mac-Gilleain*, or the Bard Maclean and in Scotland as *Bàrd Thighearna Chola*, or the Laird of Coll's poet.

John's first surviving song is *Òran do Thighearn Chola* or A Song for the Laird of Coll: even in English it gives something of the ideas behind their relationship. It begins:

> It is strange for me to be idle
> And not to start on a poem
> That is running about my brain,
> About the noble, precious Colonel,
> The man who gave me the token of respect
> That I shall not forget,
> I came to him twice
> To resolve my difficulty.
>
> I received this without denial
> It wouldn't be worth it to say,
> That he'd forsaken his clanspeople,
> Who would plead with him trustingly,
> When he enquired of me conversationally.
> And I gave him the proof,
> Of my reason for pursuing him,
> Before he took a step on my behalf.
>
> It didn't surprise me that he did that
> If he were to remember the rest,
> The nobles from whom he is descended.

> Were manly, brave, and clannish,
> Their natural qualities are contained in him,
> Courageous without (a hint) of fear,
> It was their hardiness itself in the time of need,
> Which made them (so) useful to their guard.
>
> There is many a virtue to report,
> That was possessed by the ancestry from whom
> The pure fine MacLean had sprung,
> From the clan that was royal,
> From the forest that was without decay,
> That would not surrender without good reason,
> In the face of a battalion, without any fear,
> While facing destruction on a battlefield.[24]

John's reference to the battle of Inverkeithing was perhaps too apt. The Macleans of Coll had not, so far, been slaughtered in the Napoleonic Wars. But they had lost several members of the clan. None more so than Coll's own immediate family. As we have seen his younger brothers Norman, Roderick and Hugh had all died as result of illness on active military service. His next younger brother Hector was a bachelor in India. Allan, his youngest surviving brother was, as a result of his time in India, living in retirement, perhaps as an invalid in Portobello, Edinburgh's sea-side suburb. Alexander's only surviving son Hugh was serving in the 3rd Foot Guards in London. If he were sent on active service, would he return unscathed? Would the family that had survived Inverkeithing survive this much longer campaign against Napoleon?

John Mac Ailein's songs give an insight into what the people thought was happening in the family of Coll in the first two decades of the nineteenth century. Whether the gossip and rumour were correct or not is not important. He gives us a picture of the possibilities that the surviving documentary evidence lacks. For instance in his first surviving song to the Laird of Coll he says of young Coll:

> If he would ask my advice.
> And his affairs would be as I wish,
> We would be joyful,
> When we would hear that Miss Clephane,
> Is to be married to him.

Marianne, the only child and heiress of Lachlan Maclean of Torloisk had, to the disappointment of the clan, married Major-General William Clephane of Carslogie in Fife. Clephane died in Grenada in 1803 leaving three daughters and Sir Walter Scott, who was a great friend of the family, was appointed their guardian.[25] Scott thought highly of Mrs Maclean Clephane and her accomplished daughters, who regularly dined with him on Sundays when they were in Edinburgh. He was impressed by their knowledge of the poetry and music of the Gaidhealtachd.

The sisters collected harp music and their manuscripts are an important source of our knowledge of its surviving detritus. It was this enthusiasm for the harp that led Scott and other members of the Highland Society of Scotland to commission a Perthshire man Alexander Campbell, who was an Edinburgh organist, to tour the Highlands to collect harp tunes and save the music of the Gaidhealtachd from extinction. He collected 189 tunes, some of which were, with the help of Walter Scott, published in *Albyn's Anthology* in 1815.[26]

It was probably Scott who directed Campbell to Mull where he not only met the Maclean Clephane sisters, but also Mrs Christina Mackenzie who lived in Dervaig.

Christina Mackenzie was the daughter of Dr Hector Maclean, the genealogist, and Catherine Maclean, who was Alexander Maclean of Coll's aunt. Christina had so impressed Dr Johnson when he visited Mull that he said of her:

> She is the most accomplished lady I have found in the Highlands; she knows French, music and drawing, sews neatly, makes shell-work and can milk cows. In short she could do anything.

She was also the only person Johnson met in the Hebrides who could translate Gaelic into English.[27] Christina, who now lived at Quinish, had inherited her father's collection of Gaelic poetry, which Campbell inspected. He continues:

> The voice of Harps may yet be heard in the Highlands and Western Islands. As a proof it is well known that the accomplished ladies of Torloisk are admirably skilled in the harp. I myself while in Mull was delighted with the tasteful execution of the improved harp of Mrs MacLean at Cuinish [Quinish]. This instrument as an accompaniment to the voice is well adapted to support and give affect in what is called musical expression to say nothing of its being of all others the best calculated to exhibit in performance the symmetry and grace of the female form to bewitching advantage . . .[28]

Alexander Maclean of Coll probably considered that Margaret Maclean Clephane was an ideal wife for his son Hugh.[29]

Hugh continued his career in the Scots Guards until June 1809 when he resigned.[30] I have not found any contemporary document that states why he suddenly left the army. It was hardly a tactful time to resign. The following month the flank companies of 2nd Battalion of the 3rd Foot Guards embarked for Spain.[31] The 1st Battalion, who they presumably reinforced, then took part at the battle of Talavera. Three captains, one ensign, one adjutant, four sergeants and 45 guardsmen were killed. The lieutenant colonel, the major, one captain and three ensigns, eleven sergeants, one drummer and 249 other ranks were wounded.[32]

The only explanation as to why Hugh should have resigned at this time is that his father insisted that he come home and find himself a wife. The situation was getting desperate. None of Alexander's brothers had produced a male heir or looked like doing so. The next heir by entail of the Coll estate after Hugh was Lachlan Maclean, formerly of the Isle of Muck, who was probably an anathema to Alexander. All Alexander had tried to achieve was in the balance. Hugh had to marry and produce a son.

Hugh was launched on Edinburgh society. In 1809 he became a member of the New Club, which was at the height of its popularity among Scottish noblemen and country gentlemen. In 1809 it acquired new premises at 3 St Andrew's Square.[33]

* * *

The revival of interest in Highland culture brought some curious oddities to the fore. None was odder than Alasdair Ranaldson Macdonell of Glengarry (1773–1828). Lord Adam Gordon described him as: 'a young chieftain composed of vanity and folly'.[34] Glengarry, who was a clan chief, a major landowner, a Deputy Lieutenant of Inverness-shire, and a Colonel of Fencibles, had a quick temper. This temper, and his arrogance, resulted in a duel with a fellow officer. It was caused by a quarrel over a girl who refused to partner him at the last dance at a ball at Fort George. His opponent died of his wounds and Glengarry was tried for murder. He was acquitted.

Glengarry's most curious behaviour occurred on his Grand Tour. In Florence when he gave a dinner party to some noblemen, during the dinner

> he laid hold of the Marchese (who sat at the post of honour on his right) with both hands, stretching out his vigorous arms at full length. 'In this way', exclaimed our chief, seizing the unfortunate man by the collar, 'one takes the cow by the horns, while another lays hold of the tail, pulling the beast to the ground'. Conceive the astonishment and dismay of the poor Florentine, thus grappled by a powerful man armed to the teeth' with pistol, sword and dagger, and bellowing in a barbarous and to him unintelligible language . . .

The guests left in some alarm. Later on the Tour Glengarry noticed a swelling in his left testicle. He decided to treat himself and to this end had 'tied a cord tight round the scrotum' and sort assistance in procuring 'a second cord for the same useful purpose'. Glengarry's reasoning behind this unusual treatment was:

> He told us [was] that a witch had insinuated herself into his scrotum. That after she had tormented him for some time he determined to destroy her. That for this purpose he had fastened some whipcord round his scrotum and had by that means secured the enchantress bodily and prevented her escape. That her head was still at liberty – that she had bit the vessel which convey the seed to the left testicle, that he had been under the necessity of fastening a second cord with which he dextrously got hold of her neck and strangled her, which was fortunately accomplished before Dr Decarro cut the cord.

There was another side to Glengarry who could be charming. Sir Walter Scott summed him up in his Journal when in 1826 he wrote:

> This gentleman is a kind of Quixote in our age, having retained, in their full extent, the feelings of clanship and chieftainship, elsewhere so long abandoned. He seems to have lived a century too late . . . Warm-hearted, generous, friendly, he is beloved by those who know him, and his efforts are unceasing to show kindness to those of his clan who are disposed fully to admit his pretensions.

Those who did not suffered the full force of his enmity.

Glengarry was obsessed with traditional Highland society. In June 1815, at Inverlochy near Fort William, he held the inaugural meeting of the True Highlanders a

> pure Highland Society, in support of the true Dress, Language, Music and Characteristics of our illustrious and ancient race in the Highlands and Islands of Scotland, with their genuine descendants where ever they may be.

Several Highland chiefs were at this meeting including possibly Alexander Maclean of Coll[35], accompanied by his bard. When the gentlemen went in to dinner the bard John Maclean was left outside. Glengarry then arrived and when he saw John took him by the arm and led him into the dining-hall, treating him as if he was a gentleman. When the assembled company was seated at the dining table, Glengarry offered the poet a dram. John drained the glass and declaimed the song *Deoch slàinte Mhic-ic-Alastair Tighearna Ghlinne-garadh*. In it he declared that Glengarry and not Coll was the King of the Gael and his Gaels were beyond comparison *Rìgh nan Gàidheal uil' e agus nach robh coimes dha fhèin is d' a chuid Ghàidheal*.

Coll was furious at the insult and turned to John 'his anger clear in his face', and said *Iain, Iain, cioda rinn thu orm a-nis; carson nach deanadh tu rann mar siud dhòmhsa*? 'John, John, what have you done to me now; why wouldn't you compose a verse like that for me?' The poet, himself reportedly greatly angered at having been left outside by his patron, replied *Cha laigheadh e ort* 'Because it would not befit you.'[36]

* * *

In March 1814, a year before Margaret Maclean Clephane married Lord Compton, Hugh married Miss Janet Baird Dennistoun, second daughter of James Dennistoun of Colgrain.[37] Neil Maclean who visited the newly weds in Mull writing to his brother Alexander says that she was 'rich and I believe of good prospects'.[38]

The Dennistouns of Colgrain in Dumbartonshire were an old Lowland family who claimed Norman descent. James Dennistoun, who succeeded his father in 1796, was for nearly thirty years convenor of the county of Dumbarton. He was also vice-lieutenant of the county and colonel of the Dumbartonshire militia.[39]

Notes

1. Alastair Campbell of Airds, Unicorn Pursuivant *A History of Clan Campbell* vol. 3, 292–3.
2. He is using the word in the Scots manner i.e. to mean 'relative, or kinsman' [Mairi Robinson (ed) *The Concise Scots Dictionary* (1987), 215].
3. BCT. Letter Donald Maclean to his son Alexander, 99th Foot, Jamaica dated Eigg 15 February 1807.
4. See my 'Hebridean Warrior' (forthcoming), 3.
5. His mother was a sister of Donald Maclean of Cornaig [NLS. MS 3018, 45].
6. A croft on Grishipol, probably Mibost.
7. She was Flora Beaton, who was probably the 'natural child' of John Beaton, soldier, who was baptised on 17 November 1793.
8. BCP. Matheson File. Archibald Mackenzie to his son Mr Duncan McKenzie c. 1872.
9. BCP. Matheson File. Archibald Mackenzie replying to his son's letter of 12 July 1872.
10. MH Ellis *Lachlan Macquarrie* (1958), 121.
11. NAS. GD174. 2059. 1.
12. 26 February 1760. Gillean Maclaine to Mr Murdoch Maclaine, Linen Manufacturer in Skinner's Close, Edinburgh GD 174. 1244. 29. 8. 1].
13. John Ritchie *Lachlan Macquarie* (1988), 12.
14. Nicholas Maclean-Bristol 'The Maclaines of Kilmory', *WHN&Q* Series 2, No. 1 (March, 1988), 9–12.
15. It had been founded in 1787, three weeks after the idea had been conceived at a Caledonian Hunt Ball organised by the Earl of Glencairn to mark the opening of the New Assembly Rooms in George Street in the city's New Town. [Morrice McCrae (ed) *The New Club* (2004), 1 & 26].

16. It was a tenement on the north side of George Street, between Castle Street and Charlotte Square [NAS. Edinburgh Sasines (1781–1820), 6627.
17. His first publication of ballads in the German style began in 1796 [JG Lockhart *The Life of Sir Walter Scott, Bart* (1879), 90]. Scott's first literary success was his *Minstrels of the Scottish Border* which appeared in 1802. In the same year he began the first canto of the *Lay of the Last Minstrel*. It was published in 1805 and in the following 25 years sold 44,000 copies [*Poetical Works of Sir Walter Scott, Bart* (1882), 4].
18. *The Life of Sir Walter Scott, Bart*, 103.
19. LA Necker de Saussure in his *A Voyage to the Hebrides* (1822), 46 who visited Coll in 1806–7 says that he knew Mr Maclean of Coll in Edinburgh.
20. Hugh Trevor-Roper *The Listener*, 3 March 1977 quoted in Derick S Thomson (ed) *Gaelic Scotland* (1983), 263.
21. *Gaelic Scotland*, 263.
22. *Clan Gillean*, 337–41.
23. Rev. Hector Cameron *The Tiree Bards* (1932), 1
24. Robert Dunbar 'The Poetry Of John Maclean, 'Bàrd Thighearna Chola', 'Am Bàrd MacGill-Eain'. As yet unpublished PhD thesis University of Glasgow (2005). I have to thank Rob Dunbar for allowing me to use this work.
25. *Life of Sir Walter Scott*, 394–395.
26. Keith Sanger & Alison Kinnaird *Tree of Strings* (1992), 160–1.
27. Samuel Johnson *A Journey to the western Islands of Scotland* (1817), 212.
28. *Tree of Springs* 162.
29. This may be the reputed engagement referred to in Mr Neil Maclean's letter to his brother dated 29 October 1810, Coll [BCP. Coll Transcripts].
30. TNA. WO 31. 276. 22 June 1809.
31. TNA. WO 17. 91.
32. TNA. WO 1. 238. 310.
33. *The New Club*, 64.
34. Brian D Osborne *The Last of the Chiefs* (2001), 76. The rest of quotations in this section, except where stated are from this book.
35. He does not, however, appear in the list of those attending in the *Inverness Journal* 15 June 1815 and it is possible that the gathering was on the occasion of the opening of the Jacobite monument at Glenfinnan or at a Falkirk Tryst.
36. A Maclean Sinclair *Clarsach na Coille* (1928), 283. This edition edited by the Coll seanachie Hector Macdougall tells this story from oral tradition in Coll and Tiree. I have to thank Rob Dunbar for drawing this reference to my attention.
37. *Scots Magazine* vol. 76, (1814), 318.
38. BCP. Neil Maclean to his brother Alexander. Eigg 8 September 1815.
39. *The Scottish Nation*, vol. IV, 30–31.

Chapter Forty

Alexander's Improvements continue

The Napoleonic Wars meant high prices for both cattle and kelp from the Coll estate. Alexander Maclean of Coll was therefore able to continue his improvements. After he had broken up the old joint-tenancies and established new tacks Coll continued to 'improve' his estate. Whether or not these arrangements were for the long term good of his immediate family and his tenants remains to be seen.

Sometime between the 16th July 1809 and 24th July 1810[1] Alexander Maclean, the Bailie, gave up his tack of Arileod and moved to Freslan. As 'an old servant of Coll's' he had it rent free.[2] Freslan, it will be recalled, was one of the farms that Alexander Maclean of Coll had purchased from the Duke of Argyll in 1798.[3] It had been let to four sub-tenants and was immediately the cause of friction between them and the Campbell tacksmen of Caolis who had the right to draw peats from the Freslan moss. As we have seen the Campbell brothers complained to the Duke.[4]

It is possible from the Register of Baptisms in Coll[5] and the lists of recruits for the Breadalbane Fencibles to[6] work out who some of the sub-tenants were.[7]

Two patterns emerge from this analysis. Firstly that Maclean of Coll gave tenancies in Freslan to those who followed him into the Fencibles. Perhaps this was a condition of their enlisting.[8] Secondly that as he cleared Feall some tenants there were resettled on the new settlements in the Freslan-Gorten-Lagmore area.[9] In 1776 there was only one family living at Freslan, and none in the other two farms. By 1798 the work to improve the land had begun. It is only necessary to look at the land today to appreciate just how much work muct have gone into draining the land, making lazy-beds and building their houses and byres.

As we have seen, sometime in the twelve months between July 1809 and July 1810 Alexander Maclean, the Bailie, left Arileod and moved to Freslan, which he had rent free.[10] He seems to have given up being Coll's factor at much the same time for his brother-in-law Charles Maclean of Gallanach is first noted as being factor on 8 May 1812. Alexander had a tack of the lands purchased from the Duke including Ardnish and Freslan. It is not certain what was now the position of the tenants who were already there. Hector MacPhaden and Hugh Mackinnon appear to have moved out but Roderick Macdonald stayed on in Lagmore and Murdoch Maclean in Gorten/Freslan may have done so too.

Alexander the Bailie was to go downhill after he moved to Freslan. By 1805 at least he had developed a taste for the bottle. Perhaps his wife was dead. She had been entrusted, when their parents were away, with the care of Coll's children. As we have seen Dr Allan Maclean wrote:'the little wild ones' call 'Sandy McLean's wife[11] their mother & do not speak a word of English'.[12]

Rumours about his conduct were rife and on 29th July 1815, in the presence of the Minister and the Session Clerk, he acknowledged 'his guilt with Mary Macdonald his maid, which he says happened about the end of March last'.[13] Mary acknowledged 'having guilt with Alexander' who paid her fine. He was suspended as an elder of the Kirk.

* * *

Whatever the long term viability of his improvements on the south-east coast of the Island, there can be little argument over the benefit of planting trees. On 15th February 1798 Alexander had written that in Mull, 'I met my Gardner going for trees & seeds to Edinburgh'.[14] These trees were probably for the Quinish estate. The Highland Society of Scotland encouraged planting. They gave grants to proprietors of estates on the north and west coasts of Scotland,

> who should plant the greatest extent of ground after being properly enclosed; half of the plants to be larix or hardwood. This last condition was annexed from the consideration of that predilection which long established custom had introduced in favour of *Scots firs* exclusively, though it seems certain that many other species of trees are preferable, not less on account of their certainty of growth, than their value when grown.
>
> These premiums excited the attention which the Society hoped, in districts where such encouragement was most necessary; such were awarded to ... Mr Maclean of Coll [and other proprietors] each of whom had made plantations on an extensive scale on their respective estates ...[15]

The introduction of sheep into Coll was a more controversial subject. James Macdonald says that 'Hebridean farmers never thought of rearing sheep with any other view than merely supplying their own families with wool and mutton; and accordingly maintained only a very few of the common breed of the country along with their stock of black cattle'. He goes on to say:

There are now three different breeds to be met with in almost all the larger islands, viz.

1. The native aboriginal breed, common to the whole Hebrides forty years ago, and still more numerous than the other two breeds taken together;
2. the *Linton*, or black-faced sheep of the south of Scotland;
3. the well known fine-woolled *Cheviot* breed.

He believed that the blackface should be restricted to the higher ground of the isles, where they have abundance of range, and where the finer Cheviot breed cannot so well succeed. They ought to be pastured on the higher and more stormy islands, such as Rum.[16]

Alexander had experimented with the new breeds of sheep in the farm he managed himself. Macdonald says that

> Finding that sheep proved pernicious in tearing up the roots of the *arundo arenaria* and other plants which served to check the devastating progress of blowing sand, he has greatly diminished their numbers upon his estate; and he has also, by means of roads, and the aid of carts, which soon followed the making of roads, greatly reduced the number of horses kept by the tenants.[17]

1. View from Crossapol House, Isle of Coll looking towards Mull. Allan Maclean of Crossapol, his father and eldest son are all buried here, as are the Campbells of Carnaig and Caolis and many other Collachs.

2. Lachlan MacQuarrie last of Ulva (c. 1715-1818) in the uniform of the 74th (Argyle) Regiment of Foot. He was a neighbour of Hugh Maclean of Coll from whom he borrowed money. In July 1777 his estate, which he claimed had been in his family for 900 years, was sold for £9080. Coll had wanted to buy it but thought the price too high. Later in December 1777 MacQuarrie joined the 74th Foot as a Lieutenant and took part in the campaign in America against the rebellious colonists. On his return home he lived a lonely existence on Little Colonsay as a pensioner of Murdoch Maclaine of Lochbuie.

3. Sir Allan Maclean of Brolas, Baronet of Morvaren (1725-1783) in the uniform of the 82nd Regiment of Foot. He was the ward and son-in-law of Hector Maclean of Coll. It is said that shortly before Sir Allan's death he visited Laggan-Ulva. An artist was also present who had come to Mull 'an extraordinary event in those days, and after he had taken the Scallasdale family, he went on to Laggan (John Maclean's residence). While there Sir Allan had his portrait taken, and left it as a present'.

4. Donald 'Young Coll' with his fiancée Miss Maclean of Brolas by an unidentified artist. After Donald's death she married Charles Maclean of Kinlochaline. The late Major AMGS Forbes, King's Own Scottish Borderers, owned the original.

5. Portrait of Captain Allan Maclean, 36th Regiment of Foot (1763-1829), by an unidentified artist. Painted in 1822 at the time of King George IV's visit to Edinburgh, it was given to his niece Mrs Macleod of Talisker when she visited Edinburgh from Australia in 1857. It is said to have survived two bush fires in Australia.

6. Janet Macleod (1781-1803), eldest daughter of Alexander Maclean of Coll (1753-1835); married 26th April 1802 to Hon. George Vere Hobart, 2nd son of 3rd Earl of Buckinghamshire.

7. The Hon. George Vere Hobart (1761-1802), Lieutenant Governor of Grenada.

8. Lady Vere Hobart (1803-1888), only child of Hon. George Hobart & Janet Macleod Maclean (1781-1803). On 31 July 1832 she married Captain Donald Cameron of Lochiel and on 9 September she was granted precedence as an earl's daughter.

9. Sibbella (1784-1830), 2nd daughter of Alexander Maclean of Coll (1753-1835).

10. Catherine (1787-1862), 3rd daughter of Alexander Maclean of Coll (1753-1835), wife of Major Donald Macleod of Talisker. Miniature by Alexander Galloway of 6 James's Square, Edinburgh 1807.

11. Ensign John Norman Hector (1829-1882), 7th Madras Light Cavalry, 2nd son of Hugh Maclean of Coll (1782-1861). Painted in 1846 before he joined his regiment in India. The artist had not completed painting the legs when John had to leave for India and another man acted as model for them.

12. Major-General John Norman Hector (1829-1882). The last Maclean of Coll. Portrait by an unknown artist.

13. Captain Henry Donald Neil Maclean DSO, the King's Own Scottish Borderers, after receiving his DSO from the King on 24 October 1902. He was the last of the direct male line of the First Branch of the Family of Coll.

14. The author in the uniform of a Lieutenant in the King's Own Scottish Borderers. Painted by Peregrine Heathcote from a photograph taken in Glasgow in 1959 when he was Aide-de-Camps to Major-General JFM Macdonald CB, DSO, OBE, General Officer Commanding Lowland District & 52 (Lowland) Infantry Division (TA).

15. Breacachadh Castle and Breacachadh House from a watercolour by Poole (1841).

16. The author and his wife in the 1970s during the restoration of Breacachadh Castle, Isle of Coll.

17. Breacachadh Castle in 2006.

Macdonald believed that little thought in the Hebrides had been given to the breeding horses. He writes:

> very little has hitherto been done . . . [in] bringing this breed to perfection, or preventing it from degenerating. In general, the tenants pay no manner of attention to their stallions or breeding mares, but leave them almost entirely to chance. In summer and early autumn, one-half of their horses and mares range freely and unconfined amidst the mountains, whence they are not brought to the different farms and hamlets for work until the harvest is ended, the crop to be carried home, and the peats or fuel to be secured. They are then hunted after, like so many wild beasts, and each tenant or proprietor endeavours to procure his own, which he has not perhaps seen for many weeks before. They are driven into inclosed fields or pen-folds, frequently into bogs and morasses, before they can be laid hold of, and sometimes injured severely in the process. Their manes are then cut, the hair laid up for rope-work and other purposes, and the young horses are gradually broken in for the labours and cruel hardships of winter. Very few are housed, or in any other way protected from inclemency of the weather and the rigours of a scanty and unsheltered pasture, than merely by a winter in-closure fenced with a miserable turf-dyke or wall, along the sides of which they stand shivering with cold and half famished with hunger, the live-long winter nights. Any horse brought from other districts of Britain, to undergo this treatment all at once, fall off rapidly and soon perish.[18]

It is hardly surprising that when he resigned from the Breadalbane Fencibles, Alexander had written to his adjutant Captain Hector to say: 'I am much obliged to you for the care you have taken of my horses. Were it not for the abuse he would meet with in the Country I would not part with [them]'.[19]

There can also be little doubt that many of Alexander's initiatives were good for everyone on the estate. For example before 1801 he had established a ferry between Coll and Quinish. In October 1801 the Chamberlain of Tiree suggested to the Duke that he should copy Coll's example and encourage the ferry that had been inaugurated between Tiree and Mull

> for letters and the accomodation of passengers, for which it is hoped your Grace will be pleased to get some encouragement from the Post Office as she goes regularly every Thursday if the weather permits, and to give a situation to the packet-man. It is hoped your Grace will be pleased to order him a croft at Scarinish upon more easy terms than others are to have them; otherwise the people of the island will be induced to go by Coll to Mull, as Mr McLean of Coll gives very considerable encouragement to his packet-boat, and his fare is very low. Your Grace's factor is informed that Mr McLean gives the grazing of four cows and their followers, and a large croft free of rent to encourage his packet in Coll.[20]

Despite the encouragement he gave to the ferry operating out of Arinagour, it seems to have lapsed. At a meeting of the Commissioners of Supply on the 10th April 1810 a petition was heard from Alexander Maclean of Coll requesting the establishment of a ferry between Pol-laich in Mull and Loch Eartharna in Coll. The meeting agreed that it should run once a week

> and that the Fare for Passengers and cattle should be as under viz one shilling for each Passenger; and one shilling and sixpence for each Cow or Horse; on the regular Packet

Days. Twelve shillings for the whole Boat, on other days than the regular sailing days and Ten shillings and sixpence for a small row Boat with Four men in Calm Weather.[21]

The Chamberlain of Tiree complained about the movement of cattle between Tiree and Coll. He wrote to the Duke that he had:

frequently had occasion to observe the bad effects of the small boats kept for the purpose of the ferry betwixt Tyree and Coll, in which neither cows nor horses can be ferryed without throwing them down and tying them on their passage, a practise that often produces serious effects, and at times the death of these animals. The ferryman on the Coll side will not alter the custom that was there when he got the tack, as it would subject him to the expence of keeping a proper large boat, but on the Tyree side there is no such restriction and relief should certainly be derived from this evil, which the factor begs to represent to your Grace.[22] The Duke, however, did not believe that there could be sufficient intercourse in transporting cattle from Tyree to Coll to defray the expence of providing and keeping a large boat, and I cannot therefore at present interfere in the manner that is pointed out by the chamberlain.[23]

The advantage of an estate in the Hebrides being owned by a resident Laird, rather than an absentee Duke, however able and knowledgeable, is underlined by the value of cattle produced in Tiree as compared to Coll. As early as 1794 the Duke had commented to his Chamberlain that:

The price of both cows and stots is from one third to one fourth below what such cattle bred in Mull or Coll usually sell for, which together with the difficulty in disposing of them discourages the tenants from paying much attention to the rearing of cattle . . .[24]

The cattle in the Isles are the ancestors of today's Highland Cattle. James Macdonald thought that

The breed of cattle in the Hebrides was perhaps originally the same in all the isles; but it now varies so considerably, that it would be difficult to fix on any part of the whole region, where the *real ancient* Hebridian breed can be found. Some persons imagine it to be the Skye, others the Mull, and others the Lewis or Long Island species.

He goes on to say:

Of this description of live-stock there are about 110,000 head in the Hebrides; and of these *one fifth* are annually exported to the British continent, and fetch at a moderate average £5 each, or £110,000, which is somewhere more than the present rental of the isles. The use of the four fifths, which are kept, yields nearly one third of their subsistence stock to the inhabitants in meat, milk, manure, and money circulated among themselves by home purchases . . .

He further explains that the breed of cattle found in the Isles are 'of the Kyloe breed'. The term 'kyloe' being a corruption of the Gaelic word meaning *Highland* pronounced as 'if spelled Kaêl by the common people'.

Alexander's Improvements continue

He says that a *Kyloe* bull

> should be of a middle size, capable of being fattened to fifty stone avoirdupois. His colour should be black (that being reckoned the hardiest and most durable species), or dark brown, or reddish brown, without any white or yellow spots . . .

Strangers, he says 'cry out against the folly of the people in keeping cattle of a small breed; when by changing it for the Irish, or Lowland Scotch, they might greatly enlarge the carcases of their stock'. However, he states:

> The great question in Hebridian grazing and rearing, is, what breed will best answer the land and climate, and what size can be most easily and securely raised at the *smallest expence*? Heavy cattle cannot seek their food in bogs and marshes, leap over ravines, rivers, and ditches, or scramble through rocks, and in the faces of cliffs and precipices, like the present breed, which is almost as nimble as a Chamois goat.

He continues:

> A moderate size is accordingly preferred by all skilful graziers, *i.e.* bullocks or stots, which, fattened at the age of five, weigh 30–36 stone avoirdupois, and heifers, which weigh, at the same age, 24–30 stone. This rule, no doubt, admits of considerable latitude of application; and while the weight or size now specified answers extremely well for the common average of the best breeds used by gentlemen farmers in Islay, Mull, Coll, Tyree, and Skye.[25]

John Knox writing in 1786 said that 400 black cattle were exported annually from Coll.[26] James Macdonald, however, writing some twenty years later claims 'that nearly 220 head of black cattle are annually exported and perhaps 80 or 90 slaughtered in the island. This in proportion to the other Hebrides, give a total of 1400 or 1500 for the whole of Coll, and is perhaps very near the truth'.[27] There is no evidence to say that Alexander had reduced the number of cattle on Coll, so it seems that Knox's figure is an overestimate.[28]

Mrs Murray says: Colonel M'Lean sold his cattle in 1802 upon the island at the high price of £14 a head, without being at any expence for transporting them.[29] This will have been at the sale in Coll on 3rd October 1802 about which the Chamberlain of Tiree wrote to the Duke:

> There was a market held [in Tiree] on 3rd May, which brought but few purchasers. On the 3rd October the second market was held, when a good many fat cows appeared, but as there was an unforseen coincidence of the market of Coll on the same day instead of the 6th, few dealers appeared in the island. Upon a communication with Coll upon this interference, he has explained it was accidental, and that in future it would be prevented.[30]

If Alexander was able to sell his cattle at nearly three times what Macdonald says was the average price, he must have had some very good cattle indeed. And even if the island was producing less, but probably better cattle, than it had been in 1786 he was still making a tidy income from Coll in cattle alone.

* * *

The Laird was of course not the only man in Coll to own cattle. All the tacksmen and tenants would have had them too. Archibald Mackenzie/Matheson writing of the first decade of the nineteenth century says that his father, after he returned from working in Mull he

> got the superintendence of the Laird of Coll's large stock, a very profitable situation I assure you ... My mother was dairymaid ... in Mull ... she left Mull and was engaged as chief dairy-maid with the Laird of Coll – where she and my father were married. In this profitable employment they continued for some years and then took a farm, he then was reckoned to have the best stock of cattle in the Island, twelve splendid milch cows, with a proper number of young ones, they made a vast quantity of butter and cheese.

High cattle prices must have given Alexander Maclean of Coll confidence in the future: his improvements had transformed the estate on Coll; praise had been heaped on him by commentators such as James Macdonald whose *General View of the Agriculture of the Hebrides* was published in 1811; he must have felt that he could do nothing wrong and set out to rectify some of the mistakes his extended family had made in the past.

* * *

As we have seen Lachlan Maclean of the Isle of Muck had in 1798 been forced to sell his island to Macdonald of Clanranald. Lachlan had held the island on a feu from Alexander Maclean of Coll and despite the sale Alexander remained the feudal superior. It evidently infuriated both him and his clansmen that part of his patrimony had been lost, particularly as there was a considerable income to be gained by the sale of its kelp. He therefore decided to buy back the island. Clanranald was in financial difficulties and had been forced to hand over his property to trustees. They might be prepared to sell.

John Maclean *Bàrd Thighearna Chola* probably expresses the feelings of the people on the estate when they learnt that Alexander had gone off to Edinburgh to purchase the island. Despite their disagreement, Alexander seems to have forgiven his bard for in 'a Song to the Laird of Coll, when he purhchased the Isle of Muck' the poet says:

> News arrived from Edinburgh
> The story gave me satisfaction
> That Alastair had gone on a journey
> Today I heard it with certainty
> When he went amongst the nobility
> He won victory over those who were gathered
> He took home the title to the place
> Though the rest had long striven against him.

> Each laird wanted to have it,
> And were bidding up its price,
> It was not an easy business for them,
> Since he set his mind on the matter,
> He'd be despised through his life for it,
> Since it had been owned by his ancestors,
> If he had let the place get away from him,
> Even if its price went up a thousand.

Alexander's Improvements continue

> He did a deed that was tidy,
> When he went to engage in the matter,
> Many of the moneyed-classes were gathered
> He made an offer that released them,
> Though it had been lost quite foolishly,
> He had been trying to get it for ages,
> Many a person had an eye on it,
> If it had gone to them cheaply.
>
> No use to them in its direction,
> It wouldn't be wise, it would be foolish
> To enter into such silliness,
> He has a feu rent of the land,
> And a pledge to get it,
> If he were to sell it in a while,
> It would always double its price.[31]

It would take more than high cattle prices to buy back Muck. Fortunately he had his family to rally round him.

On 10th October 1815 Coll's brother Major-General Hector Maclean was created a Knight Commander of the Bath. Sir Hector, as we must now call him, was a rich man. The following month he lent his brother £5,000. It was secured on the 6merk land of the Isle of Muck.[32] Alexander and his son Hugh had purchased it together. They had paid £ 9,175.[33] It was to be paid in three installments over three years.

There was jubilation on the Coll estate when the news reached them:

> Every person who heard the account,
> Gave praise to him for what he'd done,
> That Rum, and Coll, and Quinish are
> Now secured under his title,
> And the Isle of Muck, the low-lying land,
> That they had [been] lost as part of the estate.
>
> His tenants are all rejoicing,
> About the way in which he is proceeding:
> A message had arrived for them,
> About the missing thing that they wanted,
> All his lands all together,
> Fires of joy on every hilltop,
> With them drinking to his good health,
> Of strong spirits of (great) purity.[34]

As we have seen, according to his bard Alexander had purchased the Isle of Muck against stiff opposition. He was, however, determined to regain the island.[35] John Maclean says that it was 'foolishly given' away through negligence. But that now:

> Though it was lost to them for a while,
> Since it has returned to where it shouild be,
> It will now never again be sold.

It is clear from this song that the Isle of Muck was purchased before Hugh married his wife so it was not her money that paid for it. Alexander appears to have borrowed £1,000 from his uncle Roderick Macleod at this time, secured on Ardnish.[36] This loan, Sir Hector's £5,000 and other borrowings[37] probably helped pay for Muck.

It has been suggested that Alexander purchased Muck as a speculative investment. The Napoleonic Wars had cut off the rival sources supplying kelp. Its value soared as the demand for soda ash, used in the manufacturing of soap and glass, which could be made by the burning of seaweed, increased. In 1810 the average price per ton reached £20. In 1808 alone Clanranald had made £42,000 from kelping.[38] This suggestion may of course be true, but it appears from John Maclean's verses that clan sentiment also played a large part in the purchase.

It was probably the same emotion that in 1817 led Hugh to purchase Tenga in Mull for £2,999 from the trustees of George Duke of Argyll. It had never been part of the Coll estate. Tenga[39] is tongue of land between the Aros and Ledmore rivers. The property, however, seems to have extended north-west over the watershed up Glen Bellart for it includes Pennymore & Aird and the Penmore Mill[40] in Mornish, which march with Coll's lands in Quinish. They had until 1737 been the home of the Ò Muirgheasains, the hereditary bards to the Macleans of Duart and were surrounded by Torloisk'e estate.[41]

It is possible that Hugh purchased Tenga and Penmore partly with the tocher he received when on 22nd March 1814 in Edinburgh[42] he married Janet Baird, daughter of James Dennistoun of Colgrain, in Dunbartonshire.

More purchases of land were to follow. In June 1817 Alexander and Hugh purchased the 24 merk 5 shilling land of Aros from the Duke of Argyll. This was a massive undertaking. It included 'Arrois, Kantalin, Kilmalen and Arle' which were let to James Maxwell, 'Ardnacross and Drumfin' let to Captain John Campbell, Calve Island which was let to the British Fisheries Society, 'Lettermore, Letterbeg and Strone' let to John McNiven and 'Ledmore and Ledbeg' let to various tenants.[43]

On 29th September 1818 Hugh and his father had borrowed £2,000 from Neil Snodgrass of Cunninghamhead. It was secured on Tenga.[44] It likely that it was this loan as well as Janet's tocher that helped them to buy his new property in Mull.

Notes

1. These are the dates when the Kirk Session of Coll met [NAS. CH 2. 70. 1].
2. Mull Museum. Captain Donald Campbell's letter book. 14 May 1847.
3. NAS. RS 10. 15. 2414 B to 2415 B.
4. ICP. Tiree Tacks, 131. 25 October 1799.
5. NAS. CH 2. 70. 1.
6. NAS. GD 112. 52. 539. 5.
7. Hector MacPhaden is the only Hector to appear in 1776 in the Catechist's list. He was the youngest 'of age' son of John MacPhaden in Grimsary, who is later described as a tailor. Hector himself is also described as a tailor when on 9th April 1793 he enlisted in Coll's Company in the Fencibles. He is back in Coll by the 29th June 1798 when his daughter was baptised in Ardnish. Other baptisms follow in 1800 when he is again

said to be a tailor [no place of abode is mentioned]; in 1801 he is in Gorten, in 1804 and 5 in Freslan, and in 1806 and 1808 in Lagmore. As Low Gorten is next door to Lagmore, which was part of Freslan, he was probably living in the same place throughout this period. In 1811 he moves back to Grimsary. He was still there in 1815.

Roderick Macdonald was baptised on 23rd March 1777. He was the son of Allan Macdonald in Ardnish, who in 1776 was employing a servant there. He is the only Roderick Macdonald in Coll to be baptised at this time. On 22nd March 1793 he enlisted in Coll's Company in the Fencibles. On 24th October he signs for his pay with the initials 'R McD', so he could probably read and write. He was back in Coll by 25th December 1798 when he was a corporal in the Argyll Volunteers in Coll. He was a sergeant by 25th December 1808. On 19th May 1801 he is described as being in Lagmore when he married Ann Maclean in Grimsary. They had their children baptised there from 1802–1818.

Hugh Mackinnon. In 1776 he was the 'under age' son of Hector Mackinnon in Feall, who had probably served in 81st Foot from 1778–1783. On 30th December 1794 Hugh married Margaret Maclean also in Feall. On 28th July 1799 his son Donald was baptised in Freslan and he was there until at least 1803 when another son was baptised. The next son was baptised in 1810 in Triallan. Hugh served in the Coll Company of the Argyll Volunteers from 1799 to 1808.

Murdoch Maclean was in 1776 the 'of age' son of Neil Maclean in Feall. Murdoch was still in Feall in 1787 when he maried Catherine Mackinnon who also belonged there. They had five children baptised in Feall. By 1803 they had moved to Freslan where they had a son baptised. They had two more children in Gorten. As in Hector MacPhaden's case they were probably living at the same place all the time. Murdoch's wife died, and on 23 February 1809 he married Catherine Maclean in Totronald formerly in Feall. They had three children baptised in Gorten, the last in 1811.

Lachlan Maclean and Mary Mackinnon had one son baptised in Freslan in 1800. They had been married in Feall in 1789 and had several children baptised there. Lachlan is probably one of two men of that name who served in the Argyllshire Volunteers between 1798 and 1803. In 1807 five Lachlan Macleans were serving in Allan Crossapol's Company.

Malcolm Maclean and his wife Cirsty Lamont had a son baptised in Freslan in 1803. They had previously lived at Arnabost where, in 1783 their first child was baptised. They then moved to Grimsary where they had another eight children, so they may have been at the end of their reproductive lives by the time they moved to Freslan. Malcolm does not appear to have served in either the Fencibles or the Volunteers.

8. Betty MacDougall quotes John MacFadyen, Hyne as saying that a Neil MacDonald, who lived in a remote croft known as *Am Buaile Bheag*, 'the Little Fold' had inherited this plot of land from his father John, who had it freehold from Maclean of Coll in recognition of his army service 'on the battlefield'. Neil refused to give it up when in 1856 John Lorne Stewart purchased the estate. When he tried to remove Neil the latter met the factor's men at the border of his ground brandishing his father's sword and shouted out in defiance: 'Take one step over that march and your head will be on one side, your body on the other and God alone knows where your soul will be'! [*Folklore from* Coll, 23]. All that remains of his house now is a pile of stones. *Buaile Bheag* is near *Bagh Feisldlum*. Ordnance Survey. 1:50,000 First Series. Coll and Tiree. Sheet 46.
9. Others such as Malcolm Campbell in Feall, who had served from 1778–83 in the 81st Foot with Coll's brother Roderick, did so too.
10. Mull Museum. Captain Donald Campbell's letter book. 14 May 1847.
11. Sandy is Alexander Maclean the Bailie. His wife was Mary, second daughter of Neil Maclean of Crossapol. They were then living at Arileod, which is half a mile north of Coll House.
12. NAS. GD 112. 52. 63. 5.
13. NAS. CH 2. 70. 2: 29 July 1815.
14. NAS. GD112. 52. 79. 7.
15. Highland Society of Scotland Prize Essays &c (1816), vii–viii. I have to thank Sir William McKay for this information.
16. *General View*, 446–58.

17. *Ibid*, 727.
18. *Ibid*, 468–84.
19. NAS. GD 112. 52. 77. 7.
20. *Argyll Estate Instructions*, 62.
21. Argyll & Bute District Archives.
22. *Ibid*, 94–5.
23. *Ibid*, 97.
24. *Ibid*, 33.
25. *General View*, 422–7.
26. John Knox *A Tour through the Highlands of Scotland and the Hebride Isles in 1786 (1975)*, 74.
27. *General View*, 727–8.
28. In 2005 there are around 300 cows on Coll, including folds of Highlanders at Grishipol and Lonban (of Grimsary). There are, however, a great many more sheep in Coll today than there were in 1800.
29. The Hon. Mrs Murray Aust *A Companion to the Beauties of Scotland* (1810), 372–3.
30. *Argyll Estate Instructions*, 72.
31. I have to thank Rob Dunbar for a copy of his translation of this poem.
32. NAS. Argyll Sasines (1781–1830), 2751.
33. NAS. Argyll Sasines (1781–1830), 2305.
34. Rob Dunbar (ed) 'A Song to the Laird of Coll when he purchased the Isle of Muck'.
35. NAS. Argyll Sasines (1781–1830), 1095, GR 588, 193.
36. NAS. Sasines Argyll (1781–1830), 2392.
37. On 22 September 1813 Sir Gilbert Stirling of Teirlogue lent Alexander £1,500. It was secured on the Isle of Muck and on Ardnish & its pendicles [NAS. Argyll Sasines (1781–1830), 2391]; Sir Gilbert was the son of Sir James Stirling, Bart, Lord-Provost of Edinburgh who had made a fortune in the West Indies. When he returned home he became a partner in the banking house of Mansfield, Ramsay & Co. Sir Gilbert who succeeded his father in 1805 was then a lieutenant in the Coldstream Guards. [*The Scottish Nation* vol. IX, 523]. Hugh may have known him in London.
38. Noel Banks *Six Inner Hebrides* (1977), 78.
39. Ordnance Survey Landranger Series. Sheet 47: Tobermory & North Mull (513458).
40. *Ibid*, (407525).
41. NLS MS 17677, 100: Hector Maclean of Torloisk, Mull 1749 to the Duke of Argyll.
42. *Scots Magazine* vol. 76 (1814), 318.
43. NAS. General Register of Sasines. C2. 165.
44. NAS. Argyll Sasines (1781–1830), 2955. Neil Snodgrass is presumably a relation of Alexander Snodgrass the 'undertaker' for the new house within the curtain wall of Breacachadh Castle.

Chapter Forty-One

Gaelic Schools Society & Emigration. 1811–1815

On 8 May 1811 the SSPCK received a letter from the Rev. Neil Maclean. He had, as we have seen, left Coll and succeeded his father as Minister of Small Isles, and explains 'that on account of the illness & death of his predecessor the Society's school on the island of Rum had not been examined for two years'. The Directors sustained the excuses.[1]

The initial antipathy towards Gaelic on the part of the SSPCK had defeated its aim. However, not all the Society's teachers refused to teach in Gaelic and in 1812 the Rev. Daniel Dewar, who had just toured most of the Hebrides, as well as Arisaig and Morar, on behalf of the Gaelic Schools Society stated in his report:

> I had almost forgot to mention the case of a most deserving Schoolmaster in the island of Col. He belongs to the SPCK. He teaches his scholars to read Gaelic, on the Lancastrian plan, with more success than any other Teacher I have seen in the Highlands. The poor man, whose very soul is in the business, is greatly at a loss for Gaelic Bibles. If you could give him a donation in Gaelic spelling-books and Bibles, you would materially promote the object of your Institution.[2]

Most Highlanders who attended the SSPCK schools did not have the benefit of an Ebenezer Davidson. Many learned to read in English, but it was often mechanical reading without much understanding and the vast majority of the Highland population remained un-anglicised and unlettered. The men, who in 1811 set up the *Edinburgh Society for the Support of Gaelic Schools*, deplored this illiteracy. And at its inaugural meeting it was agreed that:

> The sole object of the society shall be to teach the inhabitants of the Highlands and Islands to read the Holy Scriptures in their native language.

The modest resources of the Society, collected by subscriptions from individuals and organisations, were spent as soon as they were received. They were mainly used to provide equally modest salaries for their diligent schoolmasters. In addition their funds were used to distribute Gaelic Bibles, Testaments and Scripture extracts, which were the sole teaching aids used in their schools. No funds were available for housing and it was left to the inhabitants of the Highlands and Islands to provide suitable accommodation for the schoolmaster, and the word 'suitable' had many interpretations.

The school usually consisted of a small thatched house, sparsely furnished with little heating or lighting. The dedicated men who laboured in these unsatisfactory conditions were of varying degrees of ability and education. They must have been devoted to their duties for little financial inducement was offered to them. The normal salary in 1811 was £12 per annum. However, the favourable reception given to their efforts usually proved sufficient compensation for their lack of material rewards and physical comfort.[3]

Shortly after the Gaelic Schools Society received Dewar's report they had a long letter from the Rev. Neil Maclean in Eigg dated 7 September 1812. In it he wrote:

I am just favoured with your letter of 21 August. Having no regular conveyance, our communication with the mainland and nearest Post Office is at times rather precarious. Should my answer not reach you as soon as you might have expected, you may assign what I now mention as the cause. I am sincerely happy that this Parish has engaged the attention of your Society; and most cheerfully shall I contribute anything in my power towards the promotion of the pious and benevolent object they have in view.

That you may more readily perceive the inconveniences and difficulties arising from its local situation, with which the conveying of instruction is attended to this quarter, and the expediency of obviating them as far as may be done permit me to call your attention to the following short statement.

The Parish of Small Isles, containing a population of upwards of fifteen hundred, comprehends four islands, viz Eigg, Islemuck, Rum, and Canna, separated by boisterous seas, the navigation of which is difficult and dangerous. In winter and spring it is often totally impractical to cross from one to the other. During a tract of severe weather in these months, I have been unable for five, six, or even seven weeks, to go to the remotest of these islands, and even then at the risk of my life.

In this island (Eigg) where the Parish Church is situated, there has been a Parochial School established for a considerable time; no Gaelic, however, is taught, the schoolmaster being a young man from Aberdeenshire. According to the best enumeration, its population amounts to 442 one half of which at least are Roman Catholics.

Rum is a large mountainous island, containing, I think, about twenty-one thousand acres. Over this surface is dispersed a population of 445. There is a Society Schoolmaster appointed among them; but owing to the extent, the extreme ruggedness, and detached nature of the country, much general benefit cannot be expected to result from his labours.

There was a Society School likewise established in *Islemuck* not long since, but for particular reasons the Teacher was removed, a few years ago, and the School discontinued.[4]

Canna I certainly consider as most destitute of means of instruction. It is the remotest of the Small Isles, being I suppose, 24 or 25 miles by sea from hence; and I do not know that there was ever any such thing as a Public School of any description erected there. As to book knowledge they must of course be in a deplorable state. Here a difficulty of another kind occurs: all the inhabitants (392), with the exception of seven or eight families, profess the Roman Catholic religion. Among a people whose minds are in general strongly biased by religious prejudices, and who are remarkably tenuous of their own opinions, I have considerable doubts whether the introduction of any person of a different persuasion as a Teacher would be encouraged or countenanced, even if he should profess to teach nothing but the reading of the Scriptures 'without note or comment'. It might, however, be thought worth a trial. In the other islands

I have mentioned, a considerable number may be found capable of reading English and Gaelic, though with the bulk of the people the case is otherwise.

If it were consistent with the plan of your Teachers to remove occasionally from one farm to another, I am of opinion that in Rum most good might be done; but having the School stationary, I presume, for the reasons formerly mentioned, that not above 40 or 50 could conveniently be assembled in one place. The remaining islands particularly Islemuck and Canna, which are the smallest, I take it the greatest part of the population might be collected. When the Teacher intended for this station comes forward, I shall probably see him here, and shall be happy to grant him every facility in my power. In the meantime I shall endeavour to impress the minds of the people with a sense of the advantage they may derive from this instruction. I remain &c.

NB. The Parish of Small Isles was vacant when the inquiry was set on foot respecting the state of the Highlands. I have been rather particular, as no report had been sent from this Parish.[5]

Ebenezer Davidson in Coll took an interest in education throughout the island, and not just in his own SSPCK school. On 19th August 1813 he wrote to the Gaelic Schools Society to say:

I had the singular satisfaction to receive your very interesting communication in March last... [The island is] 15 miles long and about 3½ broad... contains a population of 1277 souls. In order to obtain an authentic account of the state of the people on this island, I employed persons, on whose fidelity I could depend, in the different farms throughout the Island, and requested of them to give faithful answers to the queries proposed, which they very readily and cheerfully did. I shall now state the answers in the order required. I find the number of persons, within the bounds of this island who read English alone to be 94, of these 49 understand what they read; 216 read English and Gaelic; and the number of those who cannot read either English nor Gaelic, amounts to 556. There is no school here save the one under my charge, which has been established here 19 years ago, and which is stationed in the centre of the island.[6] The number who have been taught at this school to read English and Gaelic, and who are now residing in other countries, would appear paradoxial, perhaps to strangers.

The situation of the people in the east end of this island, and a few families in the west end, in regard to instruction, is truly claimant; being situated at too great a distance from the school, they are consequently destitute. It is a lamentable case to relate that there are more than 70 children here totally devoid of the means of instruction. A boy from my school was employed by these people for some time in teaching their children; and the scholars under his charge made good progress in reading English and Gaelic; but owing to the great difficulty of procuring books and, as the people could not permit many of their children to attend school during the summer and harvest seasons, he resigned his charge about two years ago. Those, however, who could not afford to pay for their children, were deprived of the benefit, and as the school was not in a centrical situation many of the people were prevented from sending their children thither. The school under my charge was established here in May 1794. Till then they never had a stationary school in this island for any considerable space of time... I have been conversing on this subject say that they would frankly give all that they have in their possession, on condition that they might be enabled to read the Sacred Scriptures. A teacher might be usefully employed in various places here. I shall have to mention two of the most needful.

He goes on to outline the places where schools could most necessarily be situated:

Arinagour, a small village at the mouth of the harbour called Loch Ifrinn, containing 25 families and 152 souls; but including 5 other families in the vicinity, the number of souls is 176. There are 77 who are unable to read either English or Gaelic. One of the inhabitants told me a few days ago that he himself would build a house accommodating the school &c. The above village exhibits a very singular instance of the proprietor's (Col. Maclean, Esq of Coll) great attention to the welfare of the poor; for here are 25 families . . . accommodated with crofts, containing much susceptible of improvement, so as to be equal in value with the best arable land in the island, and secured to themselves and all their offspring by long leases. These families were destitute almost, at the time this provision was made for them, and would have been under the necessity of removing to other countries . . . Exclusive of the 77 . . . there are 12 persons in this place who read English, but do not understand what they read. This village is four miles from the school.

The next place is *Torraston*. This farm is more than 3 miles east of Arinagour; and here the people from the following farms may assemble for instruction – namely Trealn, Knock, Fislum, Traleveg, Lechruadh and Cornaig. These places contain 42 families and 291 souls. The number, who are unable to read either English or Gaelic in this quarter, amounts to 162. Having laboured in this station for 19 years, I am acquainted with the circumstances of the people young and old, in regard to instruction, and aware of the many grievous obstacles to instruction which occur here, which I believe are generally to be met with in every Highland district.

PS. – I spoke to the proprietor, who seems pleased at the prospect of a teacher being sent here.[7]

The Directors of the SSPCK took notice of Davidson's reputation and on 21st March 1814 wrote to him to say:

Sir, I have the pleasure of informing you that the SSPCK have been pleased to make an addition to your salary of £2 and to that of Mrs Davidson. They are well informed of the diligence zeal and success with which you discharge the duties of your office and they trust that this spontaneous mark of their approbation will encourage you to persevere in your exertions for promoting the great object of the Society, particularly the improvement of the youth under your care.

I received only a few days ago your letter of 8 ffeb with which I am much pleased as it expresses a laudable concern for the benefit of your scholars, without any claim for yourself. As the arrangement on the scheme which I have notified above was made before your letter was reached me, you will perceive that the Directors never will overlook a teacher who discovers more attention to the interest of his scholars than to himself, I regret that on account of the Librarians indisposition and some of his [?] losses the Society's library has not for some time past been so accessible as usual. But I hope it will not be long so; and as you state that six years have elapsed since you received a complete supply of books I shall with much pleasure as soon as I have it in my power order a new supply, attending as much as possible to the wishes expressed in your letter . . .[8]

* * *

On 8th November 1812 the Rev. John Maclean from Grandtully in Perthshire was ordained as assistant minister in Coll in succession to Neil Maclean.[9] In 1814 he examined the newly established Gaelic Schools in Coll and in the Society's following annual report it was stated:

Torraston. At the examination of the school there during last summer, out of 68 persons on the list 46 were present with whose proficiency the Rev. Mr Maclean and the other visitor, were highly pleased 'it afforded me' says the minister 'much pleasure to find among the men and women, of from sixteen to thirty years of age. Many of these, who did not know the letters in December last, and now able to read the Psalm-book with tolerable ease. Upon the whole it is gratifying that of 66 persons attending this school eight read the Bible, 22 the Psalm-book, and 36 spell and read the First Book'. It is expected in consequence of the representations received from Coll, since the date of the above letter, that the Teacher at this station will in the course of the present Winter open a school at *Arinagower* in the same island. About 90 persons resident there are stated to be unable to read either English or Gaelic, and they have most earnestly petitioned the Society for the benefit of your Teacher as soon as he is removed from Torraston.

On 15th August 1814 the Rev. John Maclean had written to the Gaelic Society to say that:

The Session of Coll, joined by the people, are anxious that their sincere thanks should be conveyed to the Society for the Support of Gaelic Schools for sending a Gaelic Teacher to us, who was introduced to this island by a letter to me, as assistant Minister, from the Rev. Archibald McColl late Minister of Tiree & Coll to your Society for their attention to the Spiritual interest of the people committed to my pastoral care, I consider myself much indebted.

Some weeks ago, accompanied by a few of the Elders, and Mr Davidson, Schoolmaster, I visited your school in the district of Torraston. There were 40 present that day from the list produced by the Teacher, I understand that the number usually attending the School was 64. On examining the Scholars, I was highly gratified to find some among them who could read none at the commencement of the Session, now able to read parts of the Psalm book and New Testament, and with the progress of the whole I had every reason to be satisfied. Finding that some of the Scholars were necessarily absent on the above occasion, I again, accompanied by Mr Davidson, visited the School on the following Sunday, after Divine Service. There were 46 present.

He continued that he trusted the Society would 'permit the Teacher Alexander Mackenzie, to come to them as soon as the Session expired at Torraston, which, I understand happens on 15 September. The population of Arinagour exceeds 160 souls. Of these about 90 are unable to read either English or Gaelic. Indulging their laudable request, will, in my opinion promote the views of your Institute'.[10]

The following annual report noted:

Arinagour School opened 10 months ago. In April last the number of persons attending was 74; but from the avocation of the season, it was reduced, in the month of July to 30. As, however, the Teacher was in the practice of going from house to house, among those who have not been able to attend with the view of preventing them from forgetting what they had learned, the disadvantage consequent upon non-attendance, were in a great reason counterbalanced. At the close of the summer session the number of scholars had very considerably increased; and, when the School was examined, 54 individuals were present, who acquitted themselves to the entire satisfaction of their examiners.

The situation was less happy in

Torraston... In this place one your schools was formally established; but, in consequence of the prevalence of measles, the Teacher was compelled to quit it, and settled at Arinagower, long before the intended term of his services had expired. An intelligent correspondent of your committee[11], in a letter lately received, says:

I now beg leave with all earnestness to draw your attention to the district of Torraston. The poor people here are extremely urgent in requesting me to present their case to you. They all seem grateful for the favours already conferred upon them. Owing to various impediments, a considerable number of persons in this district have been deprived of the benefit of instruction during the time the Teacher officiated among them. As he had but few books (in consequence of the delay in their passage to the island) for a considerable space of time after the school was opened, the number of such as shared and benefited of his teaching was limited. After the books arrived, an epidemic disease, the measles, prevented many from attending. Their humble wishes are that your Society may have the kindness to favour them with a Teacher for a few months. An account of the population of this district was made up a few days ago, and the following statement, which may be depended on, will serve to show the necessitous condition of this district.

The total number of inhabitants amounts to 258. Several families, included in a former account, are omitted as they can attend the school at Arinagower; which was 291. Of the 258, 179 are unable to read either English or Gaelic; and to this number may be added 8 persons who read but imperfectly

In consideration of the circumstances mentioned in the letter just quoted, your committee have thought it indispensible to send a Teacher again to Torraston where the need of his services is pressing and the prospect of his success favourable.

This request was granted and the following year's report shows that:

Coll. The number of Scholars attending your school is 68.

	No. of Males	No. of Females	Age	Total
35. John Johnston. Torraston	41	27	4–25	68[12]
36. Alex. M'kenzie Arinagour	45	33		78[13]

The teacher at Arinagour wrote on 22nd July 1815:

I arrived here on 13th June; and according to orders opened the School on the 15th. The number of scholars is 30. We are prevented from having a regular night school; for the people take such a length of time at their daily employment, that I despair of having any till the end of August. Manufacturing of kelp, and peats for firing are their main objects of pursuit at present. 16 of my scholars are away off the island, some of these who are heads of families are expected soon back; this will of course increase our numbers; but to preserve in their memories what they have attained, I go from house to house and thus employ every convenient opportunity for their improvement. Monday last being the day of rewards, all the children were present who usually attend here and many more who have it not in their power to make their appearance but very seldom. We meet on Sabbath morning at 7, continue til 9; and at half-past 5 in the evening and continue while we have daylight.

Ebenezer Davidson wrote from Coll on 19th October 1815 to say:

Alexander M'kenzie, Teacher of your school in the district of Arinagower, intimated to me that, agreeably to the regulations of the Society, your school in the said district ought to be examined on, or previous to, the 15th Ult. And the minister of this island being then absent and the time of his arrival uncertain, he requested me to examine the school, starting at the same time, that the [?] appointed for examining the school was nearly expired, it is with much pleasure I beg leave to acquaint you that I did on the 10th Ultimo examine your school in the said district, having along with me at the same time two respectable tacksmen, both resident in this island, viz: Messrs Allan M'Lean, Crossapol, and Allan M'Lean, Acha. The scene presented to my view on entering the school house was truly gratifying, where I observed married men and women with their infants in their arms, diligently reading their books. This scene appeared more interesting to me recollecting that some years ago it then appeared to me a thing impossible, that I should ever enjoy the pleasure I have felt. A serious view of the effect of your bounty, under divine blessing, must impress the hardest heart, unless it is totally void of any concern for the eternal happiness of precious and immortal souls. A prospect of this nature ought to incite every heart in fervent praises to God.[14]

* * *

In 1815 one of Ebenezer Davidson's pupils Archibald Mackenzie, who was now seventeen, set off for Rum to act as tutor to the Macleans who were tacksmen at Guirdal beneath the towering ramparts of Bloodstone Hill. He later wrote:

In my 17th year I was engaged by three brothers of the name McLean of Guirdhill in the Island of Rum to teach their children. I eagerly accepted this offer, but no sooner went there than my heart was nearly broken regretting that I went there, the love of home, of my father and his little family (for he had married again) filled me so much that I used to travel three miles to a place from which I could see the Island of Coll, as for religion or the means of grace, I heard no sermon during the two years I spent there. My religious impression wore off, except when I thought of the prayer meetings kept by Mr Davidson. My companions were profane and I soon learned their habits.[15]

* * *

As we have seen Ebenezer Davidson had observed that 'the number who have been taught at this school to read English and Gaelic, and who are now residing in other countries, would appear paradoxical, perhaps to strangers'. Whilst at Arinagour School the teacher noted that '16 of my scholars are away off the island, some of these who are heads of families are expected soon back'.

It is therefore clear that one of the side effects of teaching people in the island to read and write gave them skills that enabled them to find work outwith the island. It was the beginning of an un-quantifiable trend. Unlike overseas emigration those leaving Coll to work elsewhere in Scotland returned home, but it must have given them a taste for a new life and when things got tough on Coll they left.

In his letter to his son Archibald Mackenzie implies that the happy state of affairs when his father 'was reckoned to have the best stock of cattle in the island' did not last.[16] It is likely that one reason why was that the fertility of the soil was declining. In the 1720s when the tiends of the Coll estate were being assessed it was stated by the tenants that 'if they did not have the liberty to use 'seaware' as fertilizer, their rents would have to be cut by 50%'.[17] Edward Clarke, however, noted in 1797 that

> the neglect of tillage, which is universally experienced since this discovery [kelp] was made is already sensibly felt; and promises to overvalue the ground which is derived from it. The lands lie neglected, and without manure, and if naked rocks are to succeed corn fields and the barbary desert to [?] of husbandry to gather sea-ware, the profits arising from kelp to individuals, will ill repay the larger [occasion ?] in the community at large for want of these necessaries they are accustomed to derive from their lands'.[18]

It is probable that by 1810, or thereabouts, the fertility of the island had deteriorated and was no longer able to produce the rich grazing needed to feed large numbers of cattle. Either the number of cattle had to be cut or the tenants had to accept that the quality would get worse. In both cases their incomes would suffer.

Members of Archibald's family had already emigrated. He says that before he was born his aunt Ann had gone to North Carolina. As Archibald was born in 1798, it is likely that she was one of the 36 who left Coll for America in 1792.[19] Emigrants then did so after two dismal seasons when the crops failed, and the price for kelp and cattle was low. He goes on to say in his letter to his son that Ann and her husband Archibald Mackinnon 'had a splendid farm' in North Carolina 'on which they kept 30 cows'. They also had 'a great many slaves, to whom they learned the Gaelic'.[20]

The example of successful emigration was dangled before the people. There was now also an active recruiter of emigrants on the island. This was Charles Maclean, the former shopkeeper in Arinagour, who had made money out of kelp. In 1801 he had taken a lease of Gallanch and he was perhaps behind the proposed emigration from Coll in 1803.[21] This emigration was prevented from taking place by the Emigation Act of June 1803.[22] By 1810 Charles had probably replaced Alexander Maclean the Bailie as Coll's factor and was now in an ideal position to persuade people to emigrate.

The prime mover behind the emigration movement in Scotland at this time was the Earl of Selkirk. On 6 May 1812 he wrote to his friend Alexander Macdonald of Dalilea about Charles. Charles Maclean he writes.[23]

> has collected a few families as settlers on the terms which we talked over: they appear to be well selected having scarcely any children below 8 years old, & a number of lads & lasses, fully or

nearly grown; & withal the parents not superannuates. He has got as many families (& more) than we can take this year so that there is no object (even if we had time) to look for more; but I think it not impossible that when the goodness of the Country & Climate is known from an eye witness, some people may be anxious to get a promise of being taken out next year on these terms, & many thereby induced to send some of their young men on wages at present.

Two months later, on 9th July, Selkirk wrote again from London to Dalilea to say that 'Charles Maclean brought a few families, engaged on the terms which we concocted together, & who were the means of bringing with them 15 or 20 fine young men. This, I think will have a very good *nest egg*. A year later on 6th June 1813 Selkirk wrote once more to Dalilea.

I believe I mentioned to you that I gave great encouragement to Mr Maclean, not so much with a view to his personal services, as for the sake of having one settler of the rank of a gentleman. He is to have a township of land, free passage for himself his family & two servants (a man & a woman), & he is to have a years provisions free after his arrival at the settlements.

Charles Maclean mentioned to me some other families who would be willing, as he thinks, to go on similar encouragement, particularly Mr John Maclean, Tiroran in the vicinity of Loch Lewin in Mull, parish Kilfinichen. Charles Maclean believes him to have property to the value of £6 or 800: he has a numerous family, many young children: & one of his sons is in the service of the North West Company. Charles Maclean also mentioned a relation of his own in Tiree: Neil McDonald, in Kenovay, he does not represent him as a man of education – he is a small tenant holding a tenement of 8 or 10 cows stock but a man of personal influence in that island, where [with] his assistance a good supply could be got of able young boatmen for the Company's service.

He also mentions a Mr McKillop, at North Sanox in Arran, a farmer of some property who is inclined to go ... Mr Maclean writes that he thinks, his brother-in-law Dr Alex Maclean at Langamull in Mull would be inclined to go out but this is only a guess: & I have no information as to this young Doctor, Character & qualification ... *Bloody Papist* as you are, you can perhaps distinguish merit, even in a presbyterian Minister (no difficulty in finding one 'as that market is very well stocked') ... will you allow me to refer Charles Maclean to you with respect to his entering into engagements with any people either as settlers or Servants. He is very zealous, but his zeal is apt to get the better of him; & I cannot trust to his discretion unless he can report his proceedings to some person, who is within reach of more frequent & immediate communication than I have at this distance. He is very active, & anxious to do his best, & judges well in many points; but he cannot be made to understand the necessity of a precise observance of his instructions, & he some time misinterprets them in a way that surprises me. He cannot go very far wrong if he has an authority within reach to refer to, but when weeks must pass before he can have an answer to a letter, a great mischief may intervene ...

How many people from Coll's estate were among those recruited at this time for Selkirk is uncertain. Perhaps, as the Laird was at home, none were.

Charles was to become something of a bogeyman in Coll folklore. John Johnston, writing in 1898 states that Charles attempted to clear Coll when Alexander Maclean of Coll was in the 'Militia' 'but the Coll people were too much for him, and appointed a deputation of their number to search out where the Laird was, and represented the matter to him, whereupon the attempt was departed from ...'. It is possibly this attempted emigration was the one cancelled by the passing of the Emigration Act and no major emigration from the Coll estate is recorded after 1792 and before Waterloo. It was to be a different thing once the war was over.

Notes

1. NAS. GD 95. 3. 13. SSPCK. Letter Book (1806–13), 378.
2. *Annual Report of the Society for Gaelic Schools* (1812), 23 [NLS. 1939. 5 (18)].
3. Murdo Macleod, 'Gaelic in Highland Education', *TGSI*, vol. XLIII (1960–3), 312–3.
4. It was noted earlier that Muck had a population of about 190. A teacher was due to be sent to them by the Gaelic Schools Society in December. *Annual Report of the Society for Gaelic Schools*, 11, viii.
5. *Annual Report of the Society for Gaelic Schools*, 19–20 [NLS. 1939. 5 (18)].
6. Langland's plan shows it to have been in Grimsary (now Lonban) NAS. RHP.3368.
7. *Annual Report of the Society for Gaelic Schools*, Appendix II. Island of Coll. [NLS. 1939. 5 (18)].
8. NAS. GD 95. 3. 3. SSPCK. Letter Book (1806–14), 391.
9. NAS. CH 2. 70. 1. Mr John Maclean's ancestors are said to have come from Ardgour Circa 1500 [James Robertson's letter book 1843].
10. *Fourth Annual Report of the Society for Gaelic Schools* (1815).
11. Probably Ebenezer Davidson.
12. 'Reads chiefly the New Testament and Psalms'.
13. 'Many good readers'. *Sixth Annual Report of the Society for Gaelic Schools* (1817).
14. *Fifth Annual Report of the Society for Gaelic Schools* (1816).
15. BCP. Coll Families. Mackenzie/Matheson file.
16. BCP. Coll Families. Mackenzie/Matheson file.
17. NAS. Decreet of Teinds 1726, 96.
18. *Edward Clarke*, 259.
19. *OSA* vol. XX, 278.
20. BCP. Mackenzie/Matheson file. Archibald Mackenzie to his son Duncan, c. 1872.
21. *Argyll Estate Instructions*, 66.
22. The Passenger Vessels Act (43 Geo. III, 56), which was passed in June 1803. Its aim was to prevent the serious privations that had been endured by passengers in emigrant ships. The Act laid down regulations for the provision of adequate space for passengers (one passenger to two tons of burden as a minimum), higher standards of hygiene, and sufficient supplies of food, water and medical stores. Vessels carrying more than fifty persons were to have a qualified surgeon on board. *Argyll Estate Instructions*, 73, n.1.
23. Charles, son of Lachlan, was born in 1760. He received a good education, and was a clear-headed and shrewd man. He kept a shop in Glasgow for a short time. He removed from Glasgow to Arinagour in Coll, where he also kept a shop. He entered into the kelp business and made a small fortune by it. He rented the farm of Gallanach, and was at the same time appointed factor of Coll. [*Clan Gillean*, 420].

Chapter Forty-Two

Paris and Plymouth, London and Edinburgh. 1815–1816

In the Spring of 1815 reinforcements for the British Army in the Netherlands were scattered around the world. Most arrived too late to take part in the battle of Waterloo. For example the 1st Battalion 43rd Foot, in which Lieutenant John Leyburn Maclean was serving, were in New Orleans when they were ordered to France.

On the 25 May 1815 HMS *Ceylon* sailed from Halifax, Nova Scotia. She carried with her the 64th Regiment of Foot. Among the officers on board was Mr Donald Maclean's eldest son Alexander, who had transferred from the 99th Regiment of Foot in Bermuda and was now a 'full surgeon'.[1] On 29th June the *Ceylon* docked at Ostend and the regiment set off on their march to catch up with Wellington's army who were advancing on Paris.

Wellington had crossed the border into France on 21st June. Even hardened Peninsular veterans, who were hardly strangers to forced marches, were startled by the severity of the pursuit. But for those who were not part of the advance guard the army's progress was a triumph: regimental bands played, *feu de joies* were fired and on the 3rd July Paris capitulated. On the 13th Napoleon, having failed to obtain a guaranteed safe passage to America, threw himself on the mercy of the Prince Regent.

> Your Royal Highness . . . I have ended my political career and come, like Themistocles, to seat myself at the hearth of the British people. I put myself under the protection of her laws and address this entreaty to Your Highness as the most powerful, the most steadfast and the most generous of my foes.[2]

On 15th July, having inspected the weeping French sailors who were to row him to HMS *Bellerophon*, he sailed for Plymouth. He was exiled to St Helena. Meanwhile the British Army camped in the Bois de Boulogne, which was transformed into a white-tented town. It was probably here that the 64th joined Wellington's Army.

Surgeon Maclean must have met several acquaintances in Paris, probably including his cousin Captain Alexander Maclean of the 79th Foot who had been wounded at Waterloo.[3] It is also possible that he was detached from his regiment to assist the medical officers in Brussels who were working frantically round the clock. Hundreds of the wounded had waited their turn for hospital treatment. They had been deposited on lines of straw along the Brussels streets and washed by public-spirited ladies. As the carts rumbled by, fastidious shopkeepers sniffed eau-de-Cologne or camphor. Many of the French had lain on the battlefield for several days. When they arrived in Brussels several were wearing carters' smocks to cover their nakedness, for contrary to Wellington's orders they had been robbed of their rich uniforms.[4]

Whether or not Alexander was detached to help the surgeons in Brussels to deal with the carnage is not known. He was certainly in Paris by September 1815 when he wrote to his brother Neil. Unfortunately neither this letter nor the diary he is known to have kept has survived.

* * *

Paris was all of a bustle as Europe's leaders and tourists assembled. The leaders of the victorious alliance arrived to decide the fate of France. The tourists came to gawk. Amongst the delegates at the Peace Conference was Tsar Alexander I of Russia, and at the grand review of the Allied Armies that took place on 26th September he announced the formation of the Holy Alliance. This was a near Messianic crusade for a Christian brother-hood of rulers and nations, which he hoped would extend Russia's influence by sweeping under its wings all Christian nations.

The Tsar had more on his mind than politics. In the neighbourhood of the Tuileries there was a small fair, where apples, toys and cakes were sold. One day when the Tsar was strolling through the fair he noticed a very pretty girl, who stared at him from one of the stalls. He asked her why she looked at him so intently.

'I am looking at you, Sir' she replied 'because you are the very counterpart of the Emperor of Russia; but you cannot be that great personage or you would not lower yourself by talking to a poor apple-girl'.

The Tsar retorted 'whether I am the Emperor or not rest assured, my dear, that were I to stay much longer in your company I should lose my heart'; however, he continued, presenting her with a louis d'or 'can you tell me the address of the Emperor of Russia, for I am anxious to find it out?'

The girl handed over her stall to one of her friends and volunteered to show him the way. On their arrival at the hôtel, he invited her in. 'No Sir', she replied 'I have shown you where the Emperor lives, which I think is all you require; so good morning, to you, Sir'.

'No, no, that is not all, my little angel; you must now tell me where you live'.

'Well, Sir I am to be found at my stall'.

The result of this encounter was that the apple-girl found her way to St Petersburg, where she lived under the Tsar's protection and afterwards married a Russian nobleman.[5]

In London the Emperor was to try the same tactics, but with less success, on the daughter of Lachlan Maclean of the Isle of Muck.

* * *

The 64th were not to remain part of the army of occupation in France for long. In January 1816, the main body of the Regiment was landed at Dover and set off on their 287 mile march for Plymouth.[6] The Regiment was to spend the next eighteen months there. Most of their time was spent recruiting and making up their losses after their long sojourn in the West Indies.

It was not a happy time for the Regiment. As happens at the end of hostilities Ministers were determined to save money. Cutbacks followed. Officers were placed on the half-pay list. Among them was Lieutenant Campsie of the 64th Foot. On 15th February 1817 he wrote from Dublin to Surgeon Alexander:

My dear McLean,

I take the opportunity of Chambers going to Plymouth to write you a few lines. I little thought that on leaving, I was not to see you for a considerable period, but see the unfortunate state of the subs of the Regiment – almost all reduced, and I among the number!

I have every hope of getting on Full Diet as soon as affairs become settled, at present the state of them will not warrant my using interest to get in, as it is imagined that a further reduction of two companies will yet take place.

With regard of my debt to you I really am ashamed to tell you that at the present I cannot discharge it. I am somewhat involved which I hoped to have wiped off by my remaining on Full pay and an extension of leave while I remained with my friends here, but trust to my honor the moment shall not escape me when I am the least able to remit you with my most grateful thanks.

Alexander had, as in the past been too generous with his pay. He was not, at least in the short term, going to see it again. As he had lost some of his baggage on the journey from France, he was financially embarrassed. He in turn wrote to his brother Neil for help.

On 15 May. Neil replied to his brother's letter. He brought him up to date with his own affairs and with local news:

My Dear Brother,

Your letter of the 17th April we had the pleasure of receiving some days ago. Your last communication to me came to hand in September 1815, and was answered in a few days. I then gave you all the information regarding ourselves and our friends which could occur to me, or which I believed you would reckon most interesting; but as I had no acknowledgement to that letter, and indeed never had a word from you *since*, till within a few days, I am to this moment ignorant whether it ever reached you; neither did I know how to address you again.

In my last letter, among other things, I think I informed you of our intended removal to this quarter [Tiree],[7] which we effected in the month of December following. Having now been settled here nearly a year and a half, I am the better able to form some correct idea of the place and its inhabitants. Hitherto we cannot much boast of the comforts or pleasures of our new situation. Since our arrival, we have had to encounter many inconveniences and vexations frequently incident to new settlers. The dwelling house had been left by the possessors in a most ruinous and uncomfortable state, and tho' it had been repeatedly promised me, it should be put into a habitable situation before we entered it, we had to pass the first winter under it in this style. It has been since repaired, but it can never be made very comfortable or commodious, as it is both small and ill planned. Our other accommodations of the same kind are in proportion.

With regard to the Natives (my worthy parishioners) I am sorry to say I cannot speak in very favourable terms. The great body of them appear to me to be an irregular untractable set, with little moral or religious principles among them, whom nothing but the dread of punishment can keep in order, and who as they have no Heritor or even Factor resident among them cannot readily be reclaimed. I am almost constantly pestered with checking those irregularities, which fall under my own particular cognizance. Tho' this I am afraid will be found to be the general character, it is but justice to add that there are many exceptions.

It was, Neil believed, a very different society to the life they had led in Eigg. There they had been amongst gentlemen farmers. Their opposite numbers in Tiree had been driven out of the island on the Duke's instructions almost a century earlier.

Neil was not the only observer to be critical of the Tiree people. Dugald Sinclair, the Baptist preacher, who visited Tiree in June 1814 was scathing about both the people and Neil's predecessor. On the 21st he writes that he met:

An old man, who according to his own account had not heard a sermon for *six* years past till yesterday: others there are, I have been told who for *fourteen* years have not heard a sermon! They are at a little distance from the Kirk, and are said to be too indolent to come to it. Education is at a low stage here, and no women of the common class that we have seen can read. At worship a man or two have a Bible, and a few of the men can read.

He goes on to say that

I read Roman iii, 9–21. On reading verse 10 'There is none righteous, no, not me'. One of my female audience abruptly said '*Air Moire, tha ceud*', literally 'By Mary, there are a hundred'. I began to reason with this poor creature, assuring her that what I had read was the Divine record. To call which in question was a great sin.

Echoes of Roman Catholicism lingered in Tiree. Sinclair also complains that 'we found to our grief, that some young persons [were] employed a great part of the Lord's Day in singing idle or profane songs'.[8]

Neil goes on to say that:

Even of the better sort, the habits are so different from what we have been accustomed to, that there are few or none with whom we would wish to put ourselves on an intimate footing, or associate much. Except the prospect of a greater income alone, I can conceive no inducement to settle for life in this remote sequestered corner; and even that, tho' in general good, is by no means a certain or fixed thing. In every other respect it is in my opinion far inferior to our former situation. Time may reconcile us to the change, but I cannot help regretting as yet that I ever thought of it.

The winter we came here, we had no crop of our own, so that besides the expenses attending our removal, and our common outlays, we had for that year to purchase all the necessaries of life. Our last crops completely failed, and our prospects during this year are not better. All this would have been more tolerable, had I not by a train of unlucky circumstances attending my release from my former charge (too tedious to mention) been kept out of *rank and pay* till Michaelmas last. I have now done about a year and a half's duty in this parish, and have not as yet handled a farthing of its *Temporalia*.

This you will own is a hard case. The Presbytery of Mull, in consequence of some blunders and informalities above alluded to, thought proper to delay my admission to this parish till after the term I have mentioned, and regular admission is necessary in order to establish a legal claim to the emolument. From these circumstances you will easily perceive I do not at present overflow with money, and that I am more in the way of requiring than giving assistance. I am grieved it should not be in my power to relieve your wants when they appear so urgent; and more so, that you should be under the necessity of applying for pecuniary aid. I might confess it vexes as well as surprises me: surely it is not likely that the loss of a little baggage should occasion such serious inconvenience.

It may probably be in my power some time after this to assist you, if your necessities continue: at present I find it impossible, however much inclined. Indeed I shall be well satisfied if I can muster money and credit sufficient to keep our family for this year in the necessaries and common conveniences of life. This is a time of general distress over the country; both proprietor and tenant feel its pressure, and many of both classes in this quarter are failing fast.

Neil could not have moved to Tiree at a worse moment. In April 1815 the vast Tambora volcanoe on the Indonesian island of Sumbawa exploded in what is thought to be the biggest volcanic eruption in documented times. Billions of tiny particles were thrown into the heavens accompanying billowing clouds of sulphur rich gas. In subsequent weeks, the tiny specks of rock fell to ground, producing a layer of dust for hundreds of miles around the epicentre. The invisible sulphurous gases, however, remained in the atmosphere and travelled around the globe. The gas when combined with water droplets produced sulphuric acid, which when suspended in the atmosphere, blocked out some of the incoming solar heat. The result was devastating. In parts of the northern hemisphere temperatures were held down throughout the summer of 1816. Crops failed, people starved and it went down in history books as 'the year without a summer'.[9]

* * *

Despite Alexander's financial difficulties all was not doom and gloom for him in Plymouth. He had met a girl. She was Anna Maria Williams. Like Alexander she came from a military family, however, unlike his, hers were in the navy: her eldest brother John Poulton was a lieutenant on the *Euryalius* at the battle of Trafalgar. He was still serving on her in 1809 when he was killed off Toulon in an attempt to cut out a French merchant ship;[10] another brother Thomas joined the navy in 1805 as a cadet. He served on the *Pygmy*, 16 guns and was engaged in cutting out two French vessels from St Malo. In the war of 1812 he lost an arm on the *Opussum*, 14 guns whilst in the West Indies chasing an American Man of War; the youngest brother Poulton was also a lieutenant. He was to be wounded at the battle of Algiers whilst serving under Lord Exmouth;[11] the eldest daughter Mary was married to Lieutenant Henry Strachan of 73rd Foot, who she accompanied to the Peninsula. He was killed on the withdrawal from Quatre Bras.[12]

Alexander and Anna Maria became engaged. And on 14th October 1817 Alexander's cousin Captain Hector Maclean, who had once been Maclean of Coll's adjutant in the Breadalbane Fencibles, wrote from Dublin Royal Hospital.

My dear Cousin,

Your welcome letter of the 4th Instant dated Plymouth Citadel, I received on the 11th, and I assure you it made all our little society very happy to hear from a friend whose long silence we were unable to account, but my dear Sir, you have now accounted for it in the most satisfactory and agreeable manner seeing that you have been *courting* and that courtship has been crowned by a happy union, upon which occasion Mrs Maclean and me unite in most sincere and affectionate congratulations and best wishes to you and the most worthy lady who is to become the partner of your life and that you may be long spared the support and comfort of one another, and that you may increase the united clan of Williams and MacLean.[13]

Alexander was the first member of his family to marry outside the Gaidhealtachd. For at least the last five generations his ancestors had married their cousins. Like his kinsman Hugh Maclean of Coll he was marrying into a new gene pool.

On 20th January 1818 Neil wrote from Tiree to congratulate his brother on his marriage.[14] Neil himself had married in 1814.[15] Whilst his brother was marrying outwith the islands Neil was marrying into the Hebridean establishment. His wife's father was Major Alexander Macdonald of Vallay, in North Uist. Her mother was a sister of the three Macdonald brothers: Alexander Macdonald of Boisdale, Scott's friend Hector Macdonald Buchanan of Drumkill and Ross Priory, and Sir Ranald Macdonald of Staffa.[16]

* * *

As we have already seen Flora Ann, daughter of Lieutenant-Colonel Lachlan Maclean formerly of the Isle of Muck, had married Lieutenant-Colonel James Macleod of Raasay,[17] whose niece had succeeded her father as Countess of Loudoun in her own right. By 1811 her husband Francis Rawdon Hastings, Earl of Moira,[18] was Constable of the Tower of London.[19] As it was the Constable's, and not the Commander-in-Chief's, privilege[20] to appoint the Major and Deputy-Governor of the Tower of London, it is certain that it was through his influence that Lachlan obtained his post. It had a salary of £172.17s.6d per annum.[21]

Lachlan was not to hold his new job for long. On 13th November 1815 he had been to a meeting at Carlton House with the Prince Regent's secretary. On his return to the Tower, the Sheriff of London's officers arrested him for common debt. He was taken to the 'Lock up House'.[22] The Tower of London is a Royal Palace and it was claimed that the Sheriff's officer's action was illegal as it was carried out within the boundaries of the Tower, without the authority of the Prince Regent. The protest does not appear to have done Lachlan much good and he died six months later.[23]

Lachlan's daughter Mary Gavine MacLean is said to have been an example of Scotland's most perfect type of beauty. Her kinswomen described her as possessing:

> a lovely complexion, and beautifully shaped neck and arms. My miniature of her, which belonged to her daughter, does justice to her lovely colouring, her brown hair, large brown eyes, and also her very sweet expression of face. A lock of her hair, still preserved, is of rather a reddish brown.

She was also modest and of an amiable disposition. She once said that 'she supposed she must be pretty, for everyone told her so, but that she was unable to see it herself'. She was the 'reigning beauty' of 1816 and 1817 at a time when people literally crowded around the holder of that title. The following extract from a newspaper illustrates some of the problems associated with the post of 'reigning beauty':

> Now and then, in my time, some paragon of beauty, independent of rank, or attractive dress, was occasionally to be seen. I remember a friend telling me Miss Maclean was so beautiful that

whenever she appeared in Edinburgh, where she resided, a crowd collected. On one occasion when he accompanied her to a shop in Prince's street, a policeman had to be sent for to clear the way; and when that evening she entered the theatre the audience stood up in homage to her charm.

On one occasion, in Prince's street, a naval officer had his arm broken in the press of escorting her from a shop and that when she entered the Edinburgh Theatre the audience stood up whilst the band played 'The Bonniest Lass in all the Town'. It is also said that an old gentleman told one of her nieces how he used to escape from school and run down a side street to see Miss MacLean pass. Whilst an aged Highland lady used to narrate how the beautiful Miss MacLean had to be veiled when going to the opera in London, because the people stared at her.[24]

Mary Gavine's career as 'reigning beauty' coincided with the Tsar of Russia's visit to London. As with the Paris apple-girl he tried to persuade her to accompany him back to St Petersburg, but she firmly refused, 'for she was just as good as she was beautiful'. She also had a quick wit. On one occasion in London she was passing two dandies who admired her complexion, but could not believe it to be natural. One said 'Painted, by Gad'. Mary Gavine overheard him and witheringly replied 'No, painted by God'.[25]

Both the Duke of Grafton and the Marquis of Huntly were enamoured of her. However, she preferred Captain Colin Clerk of the Rifle Brigade who she married and accompanied to India.[26]

* * *

Surgeon Alexander Maclean and his wife were not destined for a lengthy marriage. In March 1818 the 64th embarked at Plymouth for Gibraltar. Alexander sailed with them. He was already sick, worn out by service in the West Indies. He died at sea. His posthumous son Alexander was born two months later and baptised on 5th June 1818.[27]

Notes

1. He was promoted on 1 November 1813 [TNA. WO 31. 385] and joined the 64th Regiment of Foot on 31 March 1814 [TNA. WO 12. 7325: 25 March–21 September 1814].
2. Quoted in Elizabeth Longford *Wellington Pillar of State* (1972), 17. I have to thank my sister Mrs Peter Gray for a copy of this book.
3. Alexander 4th of Hosta, North Uist, who subsequently got a tack of Baleloch. He was a Captain in the 79th Cameron Highlanders, saw much service in the Peninsular War, and was wounded at Waterloo. He took up residence at Baleloch on retiring from the army, and acquired a tack of the farm of Griminish, which he relinquished in 1829 on that farm being added to Vallay, and relet to the Rev. Finlay MacRae, Parish Minister. Captain Alexander Maclean of Hosta married Alice, dau. of the Rev. James Macqueen, Parish Minister of North Uist, by his wife Susan, dau. of William Macdonald, of Vallay, with issue:
   1. Donald Ewen, fifth and last of Hosta.
   2. Alexander.
   3. John.
   4. Allan.
   5. Margaret.
   6. Jamima.

   Margaret and Jamima were both married. After Captain MacLean's death, which took place in 1843 at Baleloch, his widow with all her family emigrated to America in 1846 ... [*The Macleans of Boreray*, 112].

Alexander's parents were John MacLean, 3rd of Hosta and Margaret, dau. of the Rev. Donald Macqueen, minister of North Uist (who died on 28 March 1770), by his wife, Marjory (who died 13 February 1801), dau. of Lachlan Maclean of Torestan, Coll (*Fasti Ecclesiae Scoticane*, vol. 7, 191) [Hector Hugh Mackenzie *The Macleans of Boreray*, 111. I have to thank the late Mrs Campbell, The Roundhouse, Coll for a copy of this book].

4. *Wellington Pillar of State*, 4.
5. Rees Howell Gronow *The Reminiscences and Recollections of Captain Gronow* (1889) vol. 2, 251.
6. TNA. WO 12. 7326: 25 December 1815–24 March 1816.
7. He had in 1814, through Alexander Maclean of Coll's influence, been appointed Minister of Tiree and Coll [BCP. Coll Transcripts 10 September 1815].
8. Glasgow University Library Special Collections [Bf67 – m 23] *Journal of Itinerating Exertions in some of the more destitute parts of Scotland* (1816), 13.
9. Jeremy Plester 'Weather Eye' *The Times* 17 March 2004.
10. Robert Holden Mackenzie *The Trafalgar Roll* (1913), 273–4.
11. BCP. Maclean Family Folder: Copy of Services of Lieut. Thomas Williams RN and family.
12. BCP. Maclean Family Folder: Letters of Lieut. JWH Strachan (formerly Streaphan) to his wife 1812–5.
13. BCP. Maclean Family Folder. Letters to Alexander Maclean, Surgeon 64th Foot.
14. BCP. Coll Transcripts.
15. *Fasti Ecclesiae Scoticae* vol., 121.
16. He later changed his name to Seton-Steuart when he, through marriage, succeeded to the Touch estate in Stirlingshire [*The Kingdom in Scotland*, 867].
17. *Gentleman's Magazine* (1805), vol. 75, 773.
18. *The Macleods* (n.d.) Section 4, 49. In 1816 Moira was made Marquis of Hastings. He was later to be Governor-General of India.
19. *Army List 1811*.
20. TNA. WO 94. 61. 2.
21. *Army List 1813*.
22. TNA. WO 94. 61. 3.
23. *Gentleman's Magazine* (1816) vol. 86. 1, 571.
24. JP MacLean *A MacLean Souvenir* (Ohio, 1918).
25. I have to thank Alastair Campbell of Airds for this family anecdote.
26. Captain Clarke was the younger son of Andrew Clark of Comrie (Fife). His elder brother Robert married Isabella Wellwood of Garvock. They were the parents of the Rev. William Clarke-Preston, who inherited Ardchattan from a cousin. I have to thank Alastair Campbell of Airds for this information.
27. TNA. WO 25. 3100.1.4.

Part VII

After the War was over

Chapter Forty-Three

Things start to go wrong

Archibald Mackenzie/Matheson tells us that after his mother's death his family started to go to rack and ruin. His father saw disaster ahead. Perhaps others on the Island felt the same. As has already been noticed, in August 1813 Ebenezer Davidson commented that:

> The number who have been taught at this school to read English and Gaelic, and who are now residing in other countries, would appear paradoxial, perhaps to strangers.

Ebenezer's comment implies that once they were able to speak English, or better still read and write it, the people could see the possibility of achieving a better life away from Coll and were already leaving the Island for the mainland. That people were seeking work, at least temporarily away from home, is confirmed by Archibald Mackenzie's own sojourn in Rum. It is also implicit in the schoolmaster at Arinagour's statement that: 'sixteen of my scholars are away off the island, some of these who are heads of families are expected soon back'. The Kirk Session minutes also mention Collachs shearing in Mid-Lothian, and girls in service in Glasgow.

Something was going wrong. In his pioneering work *The Highland Economy 1750–1850* Malcolm Gray writes:

> 1815 is a date almost as significant in economic as it is in political history, and for the Highlands, it serves fairly well to define the end of an era, when confident planning gave way to nervous attempts to hold together the existing agrarian system.

He makes the point that the date, 'like most in economic history, cannot be made too precise'. It did, however, mark 'a tumble in cattle prices into a trough from which it did not climb till late in the century'.[1]

* * *

The difference in the number of the poor in Coll in 1815 and 1817 is surprisingly[2] small. However, on 22nd June 1817 it was noted in the Kirk Session minutes that:

> The Session having taken into consideration the state of the poor's funds resolved that the poor on account of the general dearth shall be served this year with meal &c are happy to understand that Coll has commissioned a supply for that purpose.

In 1817 there was no meal to be purchased in the Island and 33 stone was imported by the Laird and distributed to the poor at an increased value i.e. the first class poor now received 10/– worth each.[3] In 1815 they had received 7/–.[4]

Despite the 'general dearth' young men and women still were able to enjoy themselves. Sometimes, however, a party could end up in the participants appearing before the Kirk Session. On 12th January 1819 a number of young people met at Mibost for a dance 'and, after drinking some whisky in Malcolm Campbell's house[5], went all to his barn to resume dancing'. The only exceptions were Roderick Johnston the shoemaker, son of Duncan Johnston, tenant in Grishipol and Peggy, daughter of John Maclean, tenant in Arnabost, 'who continued in the drinking apartment by themselves'.

Rory Johnston was later rumoured to have committed fornication with Peggy and complained to the Kirk Session of the people making the allegations. The Session ordered those who had been at the 'Ball' to appear before them and on 18th March 1819 they began to examine witnesses:

Archibald McDonald at Mibost stated that he was in Malcolm Campbell's house between 11 & 12 o'clock, as he supposed, & his sister having come from the Barn for the light, he went to the closet, where Rory Johnston & Peggy McLean were sitting on a bed, took the light & gave it to his sister at the door, but waited himself to listen a little to them & slept on a bed. On awakening he went to the barn, & a little after Peggy McLean came in to the barn & by & by Rory Johnston.

Lachlan Johnston at Grishipol stated that he came in to Malcolm Campbell's House about one o'clock in the morning, as he supposes, & went to the door of the apartment where Rory Johnston & Peggy McLean were. He tried to open the door but did not find a sneck [= latch *CSD*, 638] or string wherewith to open it. He went to the kitchen floor & whistled once or twice, & went to the barn where they soon followed.

Archibald McKenzie at Grishipol went to Malcolm Campbell's in quest of Rory Johnston & enquired, 'Are you there Roderick?' On which Rory answered 'Is it you, Archy? He replied 'It is' and added 'You have better join the rest of the company that no person may be speaking of your being here'. As to the time they remained in the Closet together he is not very sure only that he danced at least one reel during the time.

Neil McDonald at Mibost stated that Robert Norris, strolling tin smith, said to him the morning after the Ball that there was not a greater whore in Glasgow than Peggy McLean & that Rory Johnston had actually criminal connection with her the preceding night.

Lachlan McKinnon at Grishipol declared that the said Robert Norris a few days after the Ball told him that, while searching in the dark for his little boy, he entered the Closet & came to the bedside where he found Rory Johnston & Peggy McLean in the very act of committing fornication.

Neil Campbell at Mibost stated that the said Robert Norris, about a week after the Ball told him that he caught Rory Johnston & Peggy McLean together in Neil's bed on the night of the Ball in his father's house.

After hearing the evidence the Session decided: 'To give time to examine more minutely into this matter the Meeting adjourned *sine die*'. They met again on 19th April under the chairmanship of the Rev. Neil Maclean, the Parish Minister. Also present were the Rev. John Maclean, assistant minister and Coll's son-in-law Major Donald Macleod of Talisker, Allan Maclean of Crossapol and Allan Maclean of Arileod, who had formerly been in Acha. Why it was not necessary to have such a heavyweight session is not explained. The minute states:

> The session resumed consideration of the case of Roderick Johnston at Grishipol reported to be guilty of Criminal connection with Margaret Maclean, daughter of John Maclean Tenant at Arnabost.
>
> Archibald McDonald & Neil Campbell at Mibost, and Archdibald McKenzie & Lachlan McKinnon at Grishipol being interrogated adhered to the declaration formerly made by them before the Kirk Session on the 18th of March last. But Lachlan McKinnon & Neil Campbell peremptorily refused to make oath to them although strongly & repeatedly admonished so to do.
>
> The Kirk Session considering that there was no proof or even strong presumption of guilt against Roderick Johnston, except certain allegations said to have been uttered by Robert Norris, a strolling tin smith for some time resident in this parish, but which he positively denied by his letter of 6th March last signed in presence of two witnesses and laid before this meeting, were unanimously of opinion that the said Roderick Johnston's oath should be taken in vindication of his own and the above mentioned Margaret Maclean's character. After being suitably exhorted and having the solemn nature of an oath duely explained to him the oath was accordingly administered.
>
> The Session are further of opinion that the above calumnious report originated with either Lachlan McKinnon & Neil Campbell the above witnesses, or with Robert Norris the above mentioned strolling tin smith, And recommended to the Minister of Coll to order public intimation of this decision to be given on the following Sabbath before the Congregation is dismissed.[6]

I have dealt with this case at some length because it gives something of the atmosphere of life on Coll. It also sheds a different light on the early life of Archibald Mackenzie/Matheson in Coll, compared with the picture he gives of himself some fifty years later. It was also the last time that many of those at the Ball at Mibost, were to appear in the Coll records. Later that year they were to emigrate. As in the past bad harvests led to people leaving the Island and the 1816–17 season had been a very bad one.

Attitudes to emigration had changed. On 26th March 1819. Macdonald of Dalilea wrote to Lord Selkirk to say:

> The Highland proprietors are now becoming sensible of the truth of your Lordship's valuable & enlightened remarks on the state of the population of that part of the country, they find that the consequences of throwing obstacles in the way of immigration are now come to an alarming height & that their Estates are consumed by the useless pernicious & increasing population; they are now as eager to get rid of the people as they were formerly to retain them; but it is now too late, the people have consumed the means they formerly possess'd & are become so poor that they cannot transport themselves to any other place.[7]

Archibald Mackenzie/Matheson had not been among the unemployed. He says that Major Macleod of Talisker wanted a valet. He calls it a 'body servant' and says:

I was engaged with him and, as far as a good living and easy work would do, I had a good time of it with him. I continued for four months till he sold his property and prepared to go to England, my father disapproved of my going with him and I returned home once more. I was then advised to go to Glasgow and endeavour to procure a situation as clerk and in the event of being disappointed to try to get to be a Gaelic schoolteacher. I travelled on foot to Glasgow, and had strong letters of recommendation but was unsuccessful. I then went to Edinburgh, was examined, and was to get a school in the Island of Uist, a place I did not like.

He returned home. Colonel Simon Fraser[8] recruited him as an emigrant. Fraser had property in Pictou, Nova Scotia as well as being tacksman of Kingharair on Torloisk's estate in Mull. He was also the owner of the ship *Economy* of Aberdeen.

Another emigrant proposing to sail on the *Economy* was John Maclean, the Laird of Coll's bard. His agreement with Colonel Fraser has survived:

Tobermory, July 29, 1819.

It is agreed between John MacLean Bard to MacLean, of Coll, and S. Fraser of Pictou as follows: John MacLean will with his wife and three children be accommodated with a passage to North America, which amounts to Twenty-seven pounds, Six shillings, and in addition S. Fraser will endorse the said John MacLean's bill for Thirty-three pounds, Six shillings due to Mr. Robert Menzies, Printer, Edinburgh; for all which the said John MacLean will now pay Twenty-three pounds, Twelve shillings in cash an assign over to the said S. Fraser three hundred and eighty Gaelic song books in security of the balance.

S. Fraser.
John Maclean.

The songbooks referred to in the agreement were the bard's 1818 *Collection*. Despite whatever financial assistance he had received from Alexander Maclean of Coll, John still owed the printer a sizeable sum of money. He had only sold twenty copies of his book. Simon Fraser must have had sufficient faith in it to accept the remaining 380 copies in security for the fare and attach a value of £37 to them.[9]

Apparently Coll was not at home when the poet decided to emigrate. Mrs Macleod of Talisker, who was then in Coll with her family, however, wrote to tell her father about John Maclean's decision. Alexander wrote to the poet as soon as he received his daughter's news, but his letter urging him to stay in Scotland arrived too late. Maclean Sinclair claims that even if the bard had received the letter he would not have been persuaded to stay on account of his stubborn character.

He was not a man that could easily be coaxed or advised; he was very stiff in his own opinions. When he had resolved to do a thing, it was almost useless to try to persuade him not to do it.[10]

Archibald Mackenzie goes on to say: 'I got letters of recommendation to the Reverend Mr Fraser of McLennan's Mountain and to a Mr McNiven, a merchant in Pictou'.

The Rev. Donald Allan Fraser was the son-in-law of Allan Maclean of Crossapol.[11] The latter was probably responsible for the Archie's letters of introduction. Donald Allan had himself emigrated to

Halifax, Nova Scotia in 1817. Archibald ends his letter by saying: 'I parted with my dear father on the 27th of July and set sail from Tobermory on the 4th August 1819'.[12]

Another family to sail on the *Economy* was the Johnstons led by Duncan Johnston, the former stonemason and tenant in Grishipol. He took his family with him including his son Rory of Mibost Ball fame and his brother Lachlan, who had given evidence to the Kirk Session. Duncan's brother Donald who had been living in Arinagour and his family were also on board. His son Hector had with him, to the fury of Alexander Maclean of Coll, Coll's piper's set of bagpipes.[13]

Duncan was bitter at leaving Coll. He was about 59 at the and said on leaving that he was sorry his house was made of stone 'it was his great lament that there had no way to burn it when they left for Nova Scotia'.[14]

Archibald writes that:

> I was not long on board the vessel before I perceived that we had two parties on board. The Colonsay people [had] heard the Gospel powerfully preached among them by evangelical missionaries sometime before and many of them were converted to God ... arguments and religious disputes commenced ... I remember one incident which I think is worth relating. One of the most violent opposers was a man by the name of Kennedy from Coll. He took hold of the windward shrouds, where I and another person took shelter during a very heavy storm, a dreadful blast came and the vessel seemed very nearly capsized. Kennedy went down upon his knees and implored mercy. This being made known to the other passengers the fellow held his tongue afterwards.

Donald Johnston's daughter Mary had a beautiful singing voice and she was often invited on deck during the voyage to entertain the passengers.[15] After what must have seen a very long time, especially to Lachlan Johnston's wife, who gave birth to a son during the voyage, the family arrived in America.

On their arrival in Nova Scotia the emigrants went their separate ways. The Johnstons spent the winter in an abandoned logger's shack. The children were kept busy gathering moss to stuff in the holes and cracks to keep out the cold winds. Inside the shack was an old stove used both for cooking and heat, beside its oven door hung a switch. Outside was a small clearing with a rope strung from tree to tree around the edge. Any child who so much as touched the rope soon learned the use of the switch, for outside the limiting rope was nothing but miles of woods and anyone who strayed stood little chance of ever being found.

* * *

It is probable that there was another emigration from the Coll estate in 1820. One of those who left was Hugh Campbell from the Isle of Muck.[16] This emigration was organised by Coundullie Rankin. His father Neil Rankin had died in 1819. Although Neil's eldest son Hector had been running the farm for some time, Neil's death may have been the event that led to Hector and his family to emigrate to Canada. However, he had other problems that may have led to his departure. Hector had two illegitimate children by different women before 1815, when he married his second wife Susanna Macdonald. On the 19th April 1819 he was summoned to appear before the Kirk Session, when he was described as 'Hector Rankin tacksman of Cliad' so his father was probably dead. He was accused 'of adulterous intercourse with Mary McDonald wife of Donald Bethune workman at Cliad'.

It is stated in the minutes that before Christmas he had gone to Arinagour to buy some cloth for his boys. When he returned home, his wife being absent in Tiree, he went to Donald Beaton's house 'to obtain some necessary apparatus to dye' the cloth. At the door he met Beaton's wife. She said that she did not have the necessary apparatus. As he did not believe her and was drunk he 'put his hands on her shoulders and thrust her in before him to the house'. In the meantime Hector MacFadyen, the son of another workman in Cliad, came into the house to get a knife in order to skin turnips. He claimed he saw Hector Rankin lying on the bed, 'having hold of part of her cloaths'. Mary told him to keep quiet and when MacFadyen left she followed him and began to spin.

Hector MacFadyen's father said that when he met Mary McDonald the following day, she told him that if his son had not come in 'she would have been in danger of improper treatment at his [i.e. Rankin's] hands'. The Kirk Session decided 'there appears to them no proof' of the charge and Hector Rankin was discharged. His lease, however, was not renewed.

Coundullie's brother-in-law Roderick Morison from Drimnacross in Quinish probably sailed with him to Prince Edward Island. In September 1821 he opened a school at a place called Flate River, twenty miles from where the Rankins were living. Coundullie was now High Sheriff of Charlottetown in Prince Edward Island. He was then living on a 109 acre farm on Lord Selkirk's estate near Belfast.[17]

Educated able tacksman like Coundullie and Roderick Morison were people the Hebrides could not afford to lose. Not all of those who left Coll went to the colonies. Some as we shall see went to Glasgow.[18]

* * *

Angus Johnston a tenant in Ballyhough succeeded Hector Rankins as tacksman of Cliad. It is an interesting comment on the success of Alexander's reorganisation of land holding on Coll that a former joint-tenant was financially in a position to take on a tack of a substantial farm and stock it.[19] Some of the profit from Cliad may have come from kelp making, which survived the Napoleonic Wars[20]

Additional labour was required on the main kelping shore in the south-east coast of Coll and more new settlers moved into the Hyne-Kilbride-Freslan-Acha-Gorten area [See Map: South East Coll 1836]. Among them was Lachlan, the grandson of Allan Maclean of Totronald, who moved to Freslan. He had once been tacksman of Arinagour. He moved to Arnabost and then in 1817 he settled in Freslan., which he shared with 'Bailie Freslan'. They will have brought workmen with them and had the farm free of rent.[21]

In 1820 another Lachlan Maclean and his wife Christian Macniven moved from Ballyhough to Kilbride and settled close to the shore to the south-west of Hyne.[22] Lachlan came from a well-established family at Ballyhough. They are said by Allan Crossapol to be descended from 'a grandson of the 5th Laird of Coll Hector Roy'.[23] The rewards to be gained by moving to Kilbride must have been considerable for such a tenant to flit to the barren south-east coast.

In addition to the manufacture of kelp, whisky was being made in the area. Since 1707 revenue officers had made a vigorous, if largely unsuccessful campaign to impose excise duties in the Highlands and Islands. Widespread illicit distilling took place until in 1823 a Royal Commission resulted in an Act, which set more reasonable rates of taxation. Alexander Maclean of Coll attempted to stamp out illicit distilling. Lord Teignmouth says that in 1827 near Bellachroy in Mull there was a hamlet 'on the desolate brow of a steep ridge' known as *Siberia*, to which Coll exiled people found 'guilty of smuggling and other crimes deserving exile'.[24]

* * *

Things start to go wrong

The new settlements in the Gorten-Freslan-Hyne area does not appear to have had the same social controls as older established crofting communities on the north coast, and there was something of a wild west atmosphere about the place. On 22nd July 1822 the Kirk Session interrogated Flora Macinnes, a servant of the Cooper's at Acha. They demanded to know if she was 'with child'. She said she was and named the Bailie's son Norman as the father. He appeared before them a week later and denied the charge, and implicated other young men in the area.[25] He also said that 'Rory son of Niel Mclean at Gorstan [Gorten] was desired by the Cooper … to avoid his house on account of Flora McInnes'. The session therefore summoned 'these lads to attend on Sunday first'.

Flora appeared before the Session again on 5th August at Clabbach and owned guilt with Hugh Maclean, son of Hector Maclean at Hyne. She could not say when 'only that it was after they began distilling whisky'. She denied ever 'having Crim. Con with any' of the others. They, however, all admitted that they had had intercourse with her. Flora gave birth on the 4th November and appeared before the Session on the 16th of December. All the parties involved maintained their former positions and the Session decided that from 'the pertinacity of the Parties, that the matter could not be finally decided without the oath of some of them' and that it should be taken the first time that the Minister of the Parish came to the Island. Flora then said that 'she hoped that Norman's oath would not be taken but in the presence of the Cooper'.[26]

It was not to be until 6th February 1822 that Mr Neil visited the Island and acted as Moderator. All the parties assembled at Clabbach, including the Cooper. The latter claimed that on a Sunday in summer 1820 he caught Rory Maclean & Flora in the very act of committing fornication. Once that irrelevance was out of the way Mr Neil administered the oath to Flora. She stuck to her original story and the child was fathered on Norman Maclean. He, however, said that he would never acknowledge that the child was his, and 'strongly suspected that it was the Cooper who was the father of the child'. Mr Neil, who was Norman's first cousin, did not agree and ordered that the child should be baptised forthwith.[27] He also ordered that the fornicators should do penance and pay their fines.

This was not the end of the story. The Cooper's wife now enters the affray and handed in a petition to the Kirk Session who agreed that it should be handed in to the Laird. The content of the petition was not minuted, but it presumably asked that Flora should be banished from the Island for on 23rd August 1823 when the Beadle went to Acha to cite Flora McInnes to appear before the Congregation he was told that she had left the Island.

Flora was not the only girl in Coll to be complained of as a danger to the morals of the Island. On 28th March 1825 Peggy McMillan, who was 'generally believed to be of a disorderly & irregular character', appeared before the Kirk Session who agreed 'that immediate application should be made to the Proprietor for removing her out of this Island'.

More complaints of the Cooper's behaviour followed. On 22nd June 1826 noted that John McNeil weaver, late at Acha, now at Totamore compeared with his wife complaining that Alexander Maclean tenant at Acha [the Cooper] had on several occasions used 'improper language & liberties with Mrs McNeil to induce her to commit adultery'. The Cooper again appeared before the Session & gave in his defences. However, at the same time and Place yet another complaint was heard when 'Neil Campbell, workman at Acha' compeared before the Session with his wife 'saying that owing to conversations between Alexander Maclean tenant of Acha and the said Mrs Campbell the Complainer will not be satisfied till one of the parties frees the other on oath'.

On 10th February 1829 the case of Alexander Maclean, tenant at Acha and 'Margaret McLeod wife of John McNeil weaver lately residing in this Island' was heard. 'Both parties having compeared the said Alexander McLean did voluntarily offer to make oath that he never had any criminal intercource with the said Margaret McLeod'. The case was dismissed. More complaints from settlers in the Freslan-Hyne area followed. On 10th February 1830 Lachlan Maclean tenant at Kilbride complained that Hugh Maclean son of his neighbour Hector Maclean tenant at Hyne had 'been scandalizing his daughter Mary with Donald son of Donald Maclean tenant at Kilbride – the said Donald Maclean appeared and Deponed that he never had any criminal intercourse with the said Mary Maclean'. There was more to this case than appears in the Kirk Session Minutes for on 4th December 1833 Hugh and Mary were married. It was one of several marriages between the families of new settlers to the area.

These cases that appeared before the Kirk Session illustrate the fact that despite of the 'Religious Avalanche', which is said to have struck Coll in the late eighteenth century, the behaviour of young men and women on the Island was not much different from what it had been in the past or the future. It also shows that the Kirk Session was inclined to give those accused of sexual misdemeanours the benefit of the doubt and the Coll establishment were neither puritans nor hypocrites. They were also even-handed when dealing with their own relations as with their servants.

Notes

1. Malcolm Gray *The Highland Economy 1750–1850* (1956), 155.
2. In August 1815 there had been 8 first class poor at 7/– each in Coll making a total of £2.16s, 6 second class poor at 5/– a total of £1.10s and 7 third class at 4/– £1.8s. They were all paid in cash as were Widow McDonald at Arinagour 10/6, Duncan Rankin at Cliad 7/–, the 2 Kennedy boys at Clabbach at 4/– each i.e. 8/– and Effy McDonald one of the first class poor who got an additional allowance of 5/–. These sums were paid by Sunday collections: £6.16s.6d, fines collected by the ground officer: £2.3s.5d, additional fines 'from persons found guilty of cutting Bent grass: £1'. When marriage money &c was collected the Session had a total of £14.8s.6½d to distribute, leaving a balance of £7.4s.½d in their hands and it was noted that Coll's annual donation of £2.10s 'shall remain in in his hands till it be necessary to demand payment [NAS. CH 2. 70. 2: 9 August 1815].
3. NAS. CH 2. 70. 2: 1 August 1817.
4. Ibid. 9 August 1815.
5. In 1776 Malcolm Campbell is listed as the unmarried son of Neil Campbell in Feall. From 1778–1783 he served with Lieutenant Roderick Maclean in 81st Foot. In 1785 he married Ann Maclean in Ballyhough. Their son Neil was baptised in Feall on 24 February 1790. They remained in Feall until 1797. On 5 January 1800 they had a son Donald baptised in Grishipol.
6. NAS. CH 2. 70. 2.
7. EUL. La.II. 202. 44.
8. Son of Captain John Fraser 82nd Foot, and a grandson of Captain Andrew Fraser master mariner trading between Leith and the Baltic and Tacksman of Gualachaolish, Torosay, Mull; [he was married to Anna Isabella Maclean, dau. of Baron David Maclean of Gasevadholm, Sweden, youngest son of Sir John Maclean alias Macklier, 1st Baronet of Dowart and 1st Adlad Macklier]. He was 4th son of Mr John Fraser (1647–1702) Minister of Tiree and Coll]; born c. 1769; served in Peninsular Wars as a major. Later Colonel of 80th Foot; he was a collector of Gaelic poetry; m. Margaret, dau of John Maclean of Langamull [James NM Maclean 'The Frasers of Kiltarlity: Cadets of a Deposed Mackintosh Chief' *The Scottish Genealogist* vol. XVI, No. 2 (June 1969), 29–30].
9. I have to thank Rob Dunbar for this information.
10. *Clarsach na Coille*, xvi.
11. On 3 October 1814 in is noted in Coll's marriage register that 'The Rev. Mr Donald Fraser Minister of the Gospel in the Island of Mull and Miss Catherine McLean Crossopoll were married at Crossopoll at

8 o'clock Post Meridium'. It was also noted that 'The day on which the above Mr Fraser was married ... was the market day in this island' [NAS. CH 2. 70. 2: Marriages & Baptisms in Coll 1814]. Donald Fraser was the son of Mr Alexander Fraser, Minister of Coll 1780–91 [*The Scottish Genealogist*, vol. XVI, No. 1 (March 1969), 33–4].

12. BCP. Mackenzie/Matheson folder.
13. Alexander Maclean Sinclair in an article in the *Oban Times* (14 July 1900) writes: 'Hector was educated by that noble specimen of the Highland chieftain *Alasdair Ruadh, Tighearna Chola*. He could read and write both English and Gaelic. He spent about four years learning pipe music with Duncan MacMaster, Coll's piper, and about four years more with Mackay at Dunvegan, the successor of Donald Roy MacCrimmon. He became one of the best pipers in Scotland. He succeeded MacMaster as piper to the Laird of Coll. He came to this country [i.e. Canada] with his father and took the best bagpipes in Coll with him'. He became a Baptist minister and died in September 1845.
14. I have to thank Thelma I Johnston, RR # 2 Scotsburn, Pictou Co. Nova Scotia, BOK 1RO for this information dated in a letter of 5 January 1976 to Donald F Maclean.
15. [NS Public Archives (Kamloops no. 604–376–8902).
16. *History of Inverness County*, 512.
17. Public Archives of PEI. Accession 2716. 14 July 2003; DCB vol. VIII, Rankin, Coun Douly.
18. *Clan Gillean*, 385.
19. Angus Johnston's father Alexander had probably become a tenant on Ballyhough by marrying Effie Campbell a member of a well-established family on Ballyhough. He is probably the grandson of a William Maclean in Arnabost in 1776. This Johnston family was closely related to the Macleans in Arnabost, who were descended from Neil Buidh, the sixteenth-century archer. They also constantly married into the Fiosgaradh Maclean family and are a good example of how some non-Maclean tenants in Coll at the beginning of the nineteenth century could be upwardly mobile whilst other members of the same family got left behind: Angus's eldest son John succeeded his father as tacksman of Cliad [NAS. CH2. 70. 2. 27. November 1832–1842]; Donald was a shoemaker in Cliad; Lachlan was initially a tenant on Cliad. He then became the estate's ground officer and a member of the Parochial Board in Coll; Hugh became a tenant on Cliad [NAS. CH2. 70. 2: 8. 6. 1832–19 December 1843]. He had by 1851 lost his tenancy and become a cottar [1851 Census]. In 1855 he was back in Arnabost when he was appointed Inspector of Poor in Coll.
20. William PL Thomson *Kelp-Making in Orkney* (1983), 91–2. I have to thank Brigadier Sidney Robertson, Kirkwall, Orkney for a copy of this book.
21. Mull Museum. Captain Donald Campbell at Quinish's Letterbook 1846–50. 14 May 1847.
22. The settlement, which now consists of three well-built ruined cottages is now known as 'the Bachelors'. The name Kilbride has moved more than once to its present location to the north on the road between Acha and Arinagour. I have to thank the present proprietors of Hyne, Ken and Barbara Jones for taking me round their land and discussing it with me.
23. Crossapol MS, 43a. 'Hector Roy' was in reality the 6th Laird.
24. *The Coasts & Islands of Scotland*
25. He named:

    Hugh son of Hector Maclean at Hyne.
    Hector son of Donald Maclean also at Hyne.
    Allan Maclean at Gorten.
    Donald Cameron, tailor at Mannal, Tiree.
    Rory son of Niel Maclean at Gorten.

26. NAS. CH2. 70. 2.
27. Baptisms. 12 March 1822. Norman Maclean, Freslan & Flora McInnes, Acha: Alexander, Bastard.

Chapter Forty-Four

The *Beau Monde*

The beau monde, to which Alexander's family now belonged, spent much of the year on the move. As we have seen this peripatetic way of life had always been a habit in the upper echelons of Hebridean society. But now, instead of only visiting their neighbours, they travelled further afield.

The English tended to spend the summer in the country and winters in the nearest attractive town. In Scotland the lairds and their families moved to Edinburgh. Others migrated to the South – to Bath, or Clifton and similarly clement resorts to escape the harsh isolation of winters in the country.[1]

In 1814 Alexander's family were in Bath whilst he remained at home superintending the alterations to Coll House.[2] Bath was not what it had been. By the end of the eighteenth century it was already on the decline. 'One set of critics dismissed it as old-fashioned and too staid: another took the opposite stance, and thought that the society had become indiscriminate and vulgar'. Nevertheless, it had its adherents amongst traditionalists such as the Macleans of Coll and to quote Venetia Murray

> the *haut ton* of the Regency, mainly descendants of the great families who had patronised Bath in the days of Beau Nash. After all, the main attraction of the city had remained for two thousand years – the medicinal properties of the local spring.
>
> Generations of invalids had claimed miraculous 'cures' both from drinking and bathing in the warm, sulphurous waters. By the beginning of the nineteenth century, however, there was a new emphasis on hygiene, and it was realized that the baths were run on such insanitary principles that they were likely to cause more problems than they solved ... This principle of communal immersion meant that people with infected wounds and running sores shared the same water as those with contagious diseases ... For the dedicated minority who continued to patronize Bath, however, there were plenty of alternative attractions. Life began early, with the first customers arriving in the Pump Room at eight or nine in the morning to drink their daily dose. The orchestra would already be in position and played background music throughout the day. Dancing began at noon every day except Sunday and there were formal balls twice a week, starting at six in the evening.[3]

It was perhaps this new attitude to hygiene that caused the Macleans of Coll to desert Bath and begin to visit York. York was at this time the capital of the North of England, acting as a magnet for local landowners who did not aspire to a house in London, in much the same way as Edinburgh appealed to Highland lairds, whose opposite numbers in the North of England would rent a house in York for the winter months. They could then attend assemblies and balls, the races and musical festivals, and enjoy the cosmopolitan atmosphere in a medieval city dominated by its magnificent cathedral.

Alexander is first noted as being in York on 11th December 1819 when he signed a bond there. He was travelling in some style. His daughters accompanied him and at least two servants, one being his piper Duncan McMaster.[4] The following year his fourth surviving daughter, Marion Christina, married George Lloyd Esq. of Clifton, near York.[5] The Macleans evidently paid an extensive visit to York at the time of the wedding and took a house in Coney Street, where they entertained their friends. On 15th February 1820 they had a supper party at which they played cards and danced a quadrille to the accompaniment of a piano.[6] One of the guests was Anne Lister, a small landowner and an inveterate snob. She was also a predatory[7] lesbian who kept a secret diary, written in code, which tells, in some detail, of her conquests and her failures. She was to be involved with two members of the Maclean of Coll family.

Marion Christina died on 15th June 1821.[8] The Macleans, however, continued to visit York and on the 24 October 1821 Anne Lister records that she 'went . . . to the Macleans' to play chess with Miss Breadalbin Maclean. Played 1 game – won it in an hour'.[9]

* * *

As his father reached his seventieth year, Hugh Maclean, younger of Coll, took an increasing part in running the estate. Hugh, who is described by his daughter as looking old in his youth, as his hair was silvery-grey at 30, and young in his old age, was popular in Argyll, chiefly on account of his amiable character, and for the interest he took in the welfare of his tenants. She goes on to say:

> He used to be much out of doors. I can see him now going about making improvements in the grounds with his head gardener, and a great dog. He wore generally 'Shepherds plaid' clothes . . . He used to delight in making new walks, and would cut down trees himself to let views of the sea be seen. I can see him also in the library, his 'den' as it was called sometimes, where he used to write and receive people on business.[10]

Hugh took his civic responsibilities seriously. He was a director of the company that owned the steamboat the *Highlander* which took tourists from Tobermory to Staffa, and in August 1822 chaired a meeting to look into complaints concerning its captain.[11]

He was also a member of the Argyllshire Game Association which was concerned with the decrease of muir fowl on their estates. In July 1822 it resolved that in future 'they shall not commence shooting of grouse and black game upon their properties nor grant premission [sic] to any other person to do so previously to the 22nd day of August'.[12]

Hugh and his wife Janet were to have four daughters. They were born in quick succession, the youngest, Isabella Sibella, was born on 14 May 1819.[13] Six months later Janet was dead.[14]

* * *

In August 1822 King George IV made a state visit to Scotland. It was the first time a reigning monarch had visited Scotland since 1650, when Charles II was crowned at Scone. The visit was a triumph. Sir Walter Scott was responsible for the organisation of the ceremonies and, as might be expected, it was a theatrical display of Gaelic splendour. Glengarry did his best to push himself to the fore and infuriated a great many people by his behaviour. Stewart of Garth later complained to Sir Walter that 'had it not been for Glengarry the King's visit would have passed without an angry word',[15] being only marred by the suicide on 12th August in London of the Foreign Secretay the Marquis of Londonderry as Castlereagh had become the previous year.

On Saturday 17th August the King held a levée at Holyrood. The great and the good of Scotland were well represented and listed in the newspapers. Although the Duke of Montrose presented Hugh's brother-in-law Major Dennistoun of Colgrain to the King, there is no mention of any of the Coll family being present.[16] The only Maclean to attend either the levée or the subsequent drawing room the following Tuesday was Maclean of Ardgour.[17] There was in fact a dearth of West Highlanders taking part in the whole proceedings.[18] Why this should be the case is nowhere mentioned. Perhaps, as far as Maclean of Coll was concerned he had withdrawn from such events after the humiliation he had received when dining with Glengarry. He may also have considered the whole affair somewhat bogus.

* * *

Hugh was still without a male heir and it was imperative that he married again. On 1st August 1825 he did so in London. Hugh had met his second wife at his brother-in-law's house in Edinburgh. She was Jane, the eldest daughter of William Robertson Esq. of Edinburgh. She came from a very different background to either Hugh or his first wife. William Robertson, who was at one time an assistant secretary of the Bank of Scotland in Edinburgh, had by 1792 become a merchant on his own account in Glasgow. He was one of the merchants to respond to Sir Home Popham's invitation to 'leading merchants in London inviting them to take advantage of the gigantic market for their goods which his expedition had opened up for them' in South America.[19]

In December 1806 Robertson, accompanied by his eldest son John Parish, who was then only 14, set of for South America. By the time they arrived Buenos Aires had been recaptured by the Spanish and they landed instead at Monte Video. They did so on the very day that Monte Video was occupied by the British troops. John was to claim that he acted as a 'powder monkey' distributing cartridges during the subsequent siege.

John was sent home when the Spanish recaptured Monte Video but returned to South America in 1808 to work as a clerk in Rio de Janeiro. He then went to Buenos Aires where he was to remain for two years before moving to Paraguay. He reached Asunción in 1812 and began to trade from there with Buenos Aires. In 1814 his brother and lifelong business-partner William Parish Robertson joined him. Paraguay was then remote, undeveloped and dangerous. John was to claim that he was the first 'Englishman' to visit this anarchic country in the lawless years of the revolution. The only rival to that accolade was Don Pedro Campbell an immensely strong Irish deserter from the British Army. He was hired by the Robertsons to bring discipline to the estancias of Corrientes. He proceeded to do just that, thanks to his dexterity with his knife with which he reduced the mutinous gauchos of the pampas to obedience

The brothers Robertson attracted the attention of Paraguay's notorious and eccentric dictator Dr José Francia, who made good use of them in his increasingly confrontational relationship with Buenos Aires. Later Francia sent John to London to encourage the British Government to establish closer links with Paraguay. He failed, and on his return to Asunción lost Francia's patronage. In 1815 the brothers were expelled from Paraguay. They were, however, nothing if not persistent and they established themselves just over the border in Corrientes and Goya on the Parana River. They now made a fortune trading in hides which, as a result of the war, were in a short supply in Europe.[20]

In 1816 the brothers moved back to Buenos Aires from where they continued to control their business in Corrientes, Goya, Santa Fé and Paraguay. They then went into partnership with another Scot Thomas Fair who had financed their earlier operations. John was now able to return to Britain and armed with letters of introduction from his wealthy grandfather John Parish, a retired Scots Hamburg merchant living in Bath, set up a merchant house in Liverpool. It had correspondents in London, Glasgow and Paisley. John then went on to develop trade between European and Asian ports and the east coast of South America.

John Robertson sailed for South America again in 1820 and extended his interests to Chile and Peru. He and his brother were now major figures in the merchant community in South America, and when John next returned to the United Kingdom he not only had assets of £100,000, but was the accredited representative of the governments of Buenos Aires and Peru. The brothers were also involved with the *Banco de Descuentos y Banco de Bueno Aires* and in 1824 acted as intermediaries in arranging the 1824 bond issue by Barings for the government in Buenos Aires. They were to be involved in other issues made between 1822 and 1825 for the Peruvian Government.

Hugh met Jane again in London, where she lived with her brother in a large house in Baker Street, Portman Square, which was then extremely fashionable. They were evidently very rich. Jane must have seemed the answer to Hugh's problems. The economy of the Highlands was getting worse day by day, as were Hugh's debts. Even at a time when one of the classic characteristics of the aristocracy was a sublime indifference to economic reality and debt was a way of life, Hugh must have realised that an injection of capital into the Coll estate was essential.

John Robertson was also extremely persuasive. One of his pet schemes was to settle Scottish emigrants in Argentina. The brothers had purchased 16,000 acres of good land 'six leagues' from Buenos Aires. 250 emigrants were recruited in South West Scotland. In May 1825 they assembled them in Edinburgh and set sail on the *Symmetry*. On the 11th August the colonists arrived at Buenos Aires.[21] Perhaps Hugh saw the Robertson brothers' settlement as the answer to his own overcrowding problems?

Whether or not Jane was already displaying the unpleasant characteristics, which, as we will see, appear in her daughter's journal is not clear. What was certain was that his peers were going to mock Hugh for marrying beneath him. Some wag wrote:

> The Laird of Coll he's proud and he's great
> His ancestors they are quite out of date.
> He married a Lowlander girl for her siller,
> And when that one died he married anither.
> The Lowlanders they were beneath his own rank
> Did e'er a Heeland Laird play such a prank.[22]

To the Robertsons the Macleans must also have been attractive. As with other *nouveau riche* their aim was probably: to 'better themselves', to move up the social scale, to send their sons to public school, marry their daughters into the peerage and in every way possible emulate the ruling classes. As Venetia Murray has written:

Historically wealth in England derived from land, but with the advent of the Industrial Revolution the emphasis began to change. Scions of the great estates during the seventeenth and eighteenth centuries had some justification for their reckless extravagance: they were brought up to believe that they would inherit the earth, in a literal sense, and that land was a commodity which could not fail. They had been rich for generations and there seemed no reason why they should ever cease to be so.[23]

It was not quite the same in the Hebrides. The Macleans of Coll had been impoverished by the Civil Wars, but that was a long time ago, and they had managed to escape from that financial disaster. Since the mid-eighteenth century they had been wealthy. If there was an injection of capital into the estate they could live well and carry out their responsibilities to their tenants.

As part of their marriage contract it was agreed that Jane should obtain an annuity of £700, and Hugh receive a tocher of £5,000. Jane's annuity was secured by a sasine on the Coll estate. Alexander agreed to give sasine at Quinish on 21st July and Hugh and Jane signed in London on their wedding day. It is probably significant that their wedding was not in Edinburgh but at Marylebone Church in London and that their signatures were witnessed by two of John Robertson's servants. The inference being that John was looking after his sister's interest and was preparing to put up more money than is mentioned in the Register of Sasines.[24]

That he was expecting far more than £5,000 from the Robertsons is clear from their daughter Juliet Alexa's Journal. Jane was said to have money of her own 'but somehow she had not got it when she was married ... It was always only 'coming', never there to spend'. Hugh, however, was completely taken in. Instead of living in Coll or Quinish he was probably persuaded by Jane, who was extravagant, that they must build a new house. In 1825 Hugh commissioned the fashionable architect William Burn to build him a large dwelling-house in simple Tudor style[25] at Drumfin near the head of St Mary's Loch by Tobermory in Mull. As Jane's money had not yet arrived he had to borrow.

Shortly after Hugh's wedding the South American loan bubble burst. The loans the Robertson brothers had negotiated in theory had made them huge profits but they were on ruinous terms, as far as the governments were concerned and the Buenos Aires issue acquired a notoriety that was remembered for many years in South America. In 1826 the government of Buenos Aires defaulted on their agreement. The Robertsons were ruined.[26]

* * *

Alexander's brother Sir Hector retired from the Madras Army as a Lieutenant-General and settled in London, living at 3 Northwick Terrace in St John's Wood. In 1823 he decided to settle some money on his nieces. He therefore paid Alexander and Hugh a capital sum of £6,000. It was to be used to give Alexander's four surviving daughters an income of £200 a year. Payment was to begin six months after Alexander's death.[27] Until then their father was to have the use of the capital.[28]

It is perhaps worth noticing that Alexander's orphaned granddaughter Vere Hobart is not a beneficiary of Sir Hector's generosity. Perhaps it was considered that her father's family should provide for her.[29]

Both her parent's families shared the responsibility for Vere's upbringing. On her father's side her great-aunt Louisa Stuart looked after her. She was the widow of Lieutenant-General Sir Charles Stuart, the third son of George III's first Prime Minister, and was the mother of Charles Stuart,[30] who from 1815–1830 was the British Ambassador in Paris. In 1828 he was created Baron Stuart de Rothesay. Vere's other guardian was her devoted aunt Sibbella.

Sibbella appears to have been seduced by Anne Lister shortly after they met in 1820. By 1828 she was a sick woman and was being treated by a Mr Long in Harley Street. He also had designs on Sibbella and Anne, who had at first encouraged her to see Long, became intensely jealous of their relationship.

Sibbella moved from the house of one relation to another. She often stayed in Edinburgh with her sister Maria, who was married to Alexander Hunter WS, or in Mull with her brother at 'Coll House', as Drumfin was then called. In July 1828 the two friends toured the islands together. Anne Lister stayed with her at Coll House and in March 1829 she writes that she 'thought Miss McL' looked no better than 'when I parted with her last in Mull'. She was certainly not fatter.[31] In London Sibbella rented 13 Nottingham Terrace, near York Gate, Regent's Park. Anne stayed with her there, meticulously noting her expenditure.[32] On one occasion whilst she was staying there the two women went to Whitehall to see Lady Stuart. She was, however, ill and confined to her room, only Miss Hobart was at home. This appears to have been Anne's first meeting with Vere, who was now 26. She describes her as:

> a very nice lady-like girl, her manner remarkably pleasing. Sat ¼ hour with her. She shook hands with me on meeting and I did with her at coming away, leaving on the table at which we had been sitting, my card for Mrs Foster.[33] Could not quite determine in my own mind whether I had done this well or not. Perhaps it was not the thing, but Miss McL had said something to Vere about leaving our cards, tho' she did not leave hers. I wish I could see a little of fashionable life. I should feel to understand things better.[34]

Anne's self conscious lack of social assurance is a regular feature in her journal. She confesses to Sibbella that she had been 'over head and ears in love' with her when they first met 'but how could I presume to think a person like her would care for me'.[35] The positions were now reversed: it was Sibbella who was in love with Anne. Sibbella said 'she was as good as a married woman . . . not an old maid'. Others had noticed their affection for each other and more than once Sibbella is accused of being Anne's mistress.

Vere Hobart was concerned about Sibbella's finances and discussed them with Anne. Long had offered not to charge her for his services. Sibella had rejected the suggestion. She writes:

> My Highland pride will not allow me to give up giving fees to my doctor tho' he has sometimes proposed it, tho' in a very delicate way.[36]

As her father was still alive, Sir Hector's annuity had not started to arrive and Sibbella was living on £50 a year, plus the interest she received on some capital of £500, from which she had withdrawn £150 and needed to withdraw a further £50. Sibbella explained that on her father's death she would have another £250 a year, but he might live for several years. What should she do in the meantime? Anne thought of asking Vere to give her friend an allowance but felt at this it that it would be inappropriate.[37]

The two friends planned to go together to Paris. Sibbella's youngest sister Breadalbane, begged her not to go on account of her health. Anne, however, was determined to go and confides to her diary that Sibbella 'has quite as much as told me I might have her as much as I liked in Paris'.

The Stuart de Rothesay's now invited Vere to stay with them at the embassy in Paris. They wanted her to travel on the 15th April with the Miss Berrys. Mary and Agnes Berry had a famous literary salon in North Audley Street. Although they were neither rich nor particularly aristocratic, they were amongst the most entertaining women of their generation and were for more than fifty years the most popular hostesses in London. The great appeal of the Berry's salon was that it was informal and apolitical. In the words of Venetia Murray their guest list:

> ranged from Horace Walpole (who was one of their greatest fans and lent them Strawberry Hill, his beautiful house at Twickenham, for years), via Fox and the brilliant Whig society of the late eighteenth century, to the Duke of Wellington . . .
>
> They liked mixing people, the débutante and the dandy, the young and the old, artists and patrons, choosing their guests for their conversational worth alone.

Mary Berry reckoned that £2,000 a year was the absolute minimum you needed in London to entertain 'agreeably all those friends who should prefer a neat plain dinner or supper, and *our agreeable society* to a French cook and dull company',[38] which has something to say about Sibbella's worry about living on £50 a year.

Sibbella was now too ill to travel and Anne jumped at the chance to stay with the Stuart de Rothesays. She told Sibbella she would go to Paris with Vere, who wrote a note to Sibbella to say she had accepted Anne's 'obliging offer' and had decided to go to Paris with her rather than with the Misses Berry. Anne was now revelling in her friendship with Vere and her aristocratic relations. Invitation to dinner from Lady Stuart, visits to the opera and calls to and from the Misses Berry followed. It was, however, not just snobery that was exciting Anne. She was becoming increasingly excited by Vere and was worried that she might not be able to control herself.

By the 16th November 1830 Sibbella was failing fast. Vere writes that she

> slept soundly for a couple of hours, a thing she had not done for many days or nights. She then roused & asked Jessy for some gruel, but when she tried to taste it her head fell back on Jessy's shoulder, and then there was a struggle for about ten minutes & it was all over – She had insisted on Albane's leaving her at 11 o'clock, but she was with her to the last moment, as well as Sir Hector. The funeral is to be on Tuesday & at Marylebone, soon after which Albane will return to Scotland.[39]

Sibbella died of consumption. Vere was overwhelmed with grief. The following year she went to live with Anne Lister in Hastings. Anne longed for a romantic relationship with her, but Vere was more interested in marriage and accepted a proposal from Captain Donald Cameron of Lochiel. On 31st July 1832 they were married. Anne had to pretend to Lady Stuart that she was delighted.

Notes

1. Venetia Murray *High Society: A Social History of the Regency Period, 1788–1830* (1998), 113.
2. *Highland Postbag*, 170.
3. *High Society*, 125.
4. NAS. RD 5. 512. 613; On 3 March 1805 he & Mary Taylor 'in Breacha' were married [NAS. CH2. 70. 1].
5. *Burke's Landed Gentry* (1952), 1540 & NAS. RD 5. 788, 119: Their marriage contract is dated 5 December 1820. In it Alexander agreed to pay £1,000 as her marriage portion, 'which sum should be the absolute property of the said George'.
6. Helena Whitbread (ed) *I Know My Own Heart* (1988), 116.

7. Jill Liddington *Nature's Domain: Anne Lister and the Landscape of Desire* (2003), 35.
8. BCP. Maclean of Coll Family Bible.
9. *I Know My Own Heart*, 170.
10. BCP. 'The Journal of Juliet Alexa Maclean'. I have to thank the late Alba Windham for a copy of this journal.
11. *Caledonian Mercury* Saturday 24th August 1822.
12. *Caledonian Mercury* Thursday 25 July 1822.
13. BCP. Maclean of Coll Family Bible.
14. *Edinburgh Magazine* vol. 6 (1820), 94: 11 November 1819 died at Ruchill, Mrs Maclean, wife of Hugh Maclean Esq. younger of Coll.
15. John Prebble *The King's Jaunt* (1988), 266.
16. Coll's son-in-law George Lloyd is said to have been present, but was not at the levée. However, he wore Highland dress. The outfit he wore is now in my possession.
17. He had married Lady Margaret Hope, daughter of the 2nd Earl of Hopetoun. Her sister was married to Henry Dundas.
18. *Caledonian Mercury* Monday 19th August & Thursday 22nd August 1822.
19. *The History of the British Army* vol. 5, 306–9 & 369.
20. Before the discovery of rubber hides had a number of uses which rubber was to replace.
21. John Dodds *Records of the Scottish Settlers in the River Plate and their churches*, (1897), 11 & 18.
22. 'The Journal of Juliet Alexa Maclean'.
23. *High Society*, 62.
24. NAS. RS 3. 1381, 85r–106r.
25. RCAHMS *Argyll* vol. 3, 38.
26. HS Ferris *Britain and Argentina in the Nineteenth Century* (1960); *Dictionary of National Biography* (1896), Robertson, John Parish (1792–1843); *Oxford Dictionary of National Biography* (2004) vol. 47, 251–2.
27. NAS. RD 5. 430. 78. 152.
28. Roy Jenkins estimates that the approximate value in 1995 would be ×50 i.e. £300,000 [Roy Jenkins *Gladstone* (1995).
29. In 1816 Vere's half-brother George had succeeded his uncle as 5th Earl of Buckighamshire as Vere is frequently called Lady Vere Hobart she had presumably been granted precedence as if her father had been an earl.
30. He had had a remarkable Diplomatic career: in 1805 he was Lord Gower's 'Secretary of Embassy' in St Petersburg, where he was 'a firm supporter of the English system of embroiling the continent in a war, to make a diversion for itself, but without any views for the benefit of the allied powers' [Piers Mackesy *The War in the Mediterranean 1803–1810* (1957), 61]; after Spain changed sides he was British ambassador to the Spanish Government, and was quite prepared to use his initiative. On one occasion removing himself from Spain to Vienna 'to act as the unaccredited and unauthorised representative of his country' when he felt that the Austrians were neglecting the Adriatic [*Ibid*, 320].; he was married to a daughter of the Earl of Hardwicke and in 1828 was created Baron Stuart de Rothesay..
31. Helena Whitbread (ed) *Anne Lister's Journal 21 March to 18 April 1829* (1998), 278. I have to thank Nicholas Rowland for a photocopy of the journal.
32. I have to thank Nicholas Rowland for this information.
33. She was Vere's half-sister and the wife of the Rt Hon Sir Augustus John Foster, Bart. The British Ambassador in Turin.
34. *Anne Lister's Journal*, 285.
35. *Ibid*, 292.
36. Sibbella Maclean to Anne Lister January 1829.
37. *Ibid*, 296.
38. *High Society*, 78.
39. Vere Hobart to Anne Lister. I have to thank Nicholas Rowland for this information.

Chapter Forty-Five

Australia & India 1820–1828

It was not only tenants who wished to emigrate. Alexander Maclean of Coll's daughter Catherina had married Lieutenant Donald Macleod of Talisker.[1] In 1816 Donald was in financial difficulties. He sold his tack of Talisker and moved to Durham. Shortly afterwards he came to live in Coll, where his fourth son was baptised.[2]

On 14th February 1820 Alexander was staying at Ibbotson's Hotel, Vere Street, in London. Ibbotson's was one of London's fashionable hotels. The charges were, however, more economical than at similar establishments and it was chiefly patronised by clergymen and young men from the universities.[3] From Ibbotson's he wrote to the Earl of Bathurst, the Colonial Secretary, concerning Donald Macleod 'who' he writes has had 'the misfortune to fall into rather distressed circumstances from causes unnecessary to trouble your Lordship with'.

He explains that Talisker 'was for many years a Lieutenant in the 72nd Regiment serving in the East Indies, and is now on upon the half-pay'. He goes on to say he had also served as a major in the Volunteers and Militia in the Isle of Skye. He now wished to emigrate to one of the British Settlements with his family and, as he is 'married to a Daughter of mine, I am ready to advance any sum of money that may be necessary for defraying the expenses of passage and establishing him'. He continues 'As far as information has hitherto been procured, New South Wales would appear to be the most eligible situation for such a family.

'It would be extremely obliging if your Lordship would have the goodness to direct a grant of land to be given to him, and also permission forthwith to proceed there with his family'. Bathurst replied that he had much pleasure in agreeing to Coll's request and would write a letter of recommendation to General Macquarie, 'which will ensure to Mr Macleod on his arrival in the colony a grant of land proportionate to his means of cultivation'.[4]

Talisker was later to claim: 'I was, I believe the very first of the class of respectable settlers that ever came to this colony from Scotland'.[5] He was certainly the first to go there directly, sailing from Leith on the *Skelton* on 19th June 1820 and arriving in Van Diemen's Land in November. He thus arrived there eighteen months before Major-General Lachlan Macquarie, his wife's third cousin twice removed,[6] sailed from Sydney for home.

Lachlan Macquarie had spent almost twelve years as Governor of New South Wales. When he arrived it was a prison-colony of 10,452 souls. There were a further 1,321 in the dependency of Van Diemen's Land and 177 on Norfolk Island.[7] When he left there were 13,401 people living in

Sydney alone, 5,506 in the district of Windsor, and 4,778 around Parramatta. In addition there were 5,542 in the southern parts of Van Diemen's Land and 1,643 in its northern settlements.[8]

Macquarie had done much more than preside over an increased population. He had transformed the colony. When he arrived he came with orders to send home the New South Wales Corps, which had mutinied two years earlier and whose morale was at rock bottom.

In 1788 the first convict ships arrived at Botany Bay. Most of those who sailed in them were in chains. They were the sweepings of the gutter, thieves and prostitutes, social outcasts who their fellow-countrymen did not wish to see again. The convicts had been sent to the antipodes as a punishment, and Ministers in London wanted the fear of transportation to deter potential criminals and reduce numbers in British prisons. The legislation, warrants and letters patent that established the colony were designed solely for a penal settlement.

There were no free settlers amongst the first ships to arrive at Botany Bay. They came later and by 1807 some 166 free settlers and 500 ex-convicts, who had been granted plots of land, had sown 13,146 acres and owned cattle and sheep. The rural economy of New South Wales was also being privatised: free settlers received huge grants of land and became expert graziers. They saw convicts as cheap labour and believed that New South Wales was to be a convict colony in the same way as a West Indies island was a slave colony.

Macquarie saw it differently. In 1817 he 'freely admitted that he viewed the colony as an asylum, a place of sanctuary or refuge in which he offered hope to the downtrodden by trying to raise them from subjection'. His guiding principle, one that was approved by both his head and his heart was to treat men according to their merits and to restore prisoners to the position in society they had forfeited by their crimes.

While some free settlers admired the governor for his dedication to the well-being of every inhabitant in the colony and found it natural to rub shoulders with emancipists, ex-convicts who had completed their sentences, 'a coterie of exclusives vilified the governor's policy and made a point of affronting former felons'. The greater their opposition, the more angrily Macquarie reacted, declaring that the emancipists were 'the best class in the colony' and angrily exclaimed 'that there were but two types of individuals in New South Wales – those who had been transported and those who should have been'. On numerous 'public occasions he deliberately paid more attention to emancipists than the free, much to the latter's chagrin'.[9]

Before 1810 no emancipist or native-born Australian talked of the colony as his own. After 1819 such revolutionary 'chatter swelled audibly'. It began at grassroots level, was aided and abetted by the governor and soon developed into a belief that the colony belonged to the convicts and their descendants, and to them alone.[10] Not surprisingly Macquarie's critics complained to Lord Bathurst, who appointed a commission of enquiry to look into the administration of New South Wales and report as to how the colony might be restored to its original purpose.[11]

It was to this rapidly developing colony that Donald Macleod and his family wished to emigrate. He was not alone in doing so. Public interest in Australia developed more slowly in Scotland than in England, and it was not until Governor Macquarie had been in the colony for some time that a favourable impression of Australia and its prospects began to reach Scotland. It did so in letters written by friends and relatives who were already there, either on Macquarie's staff or in the 73rd Foot which had formerly been a Highland Regiment.[12]

There were other factors besides Macquarie's governorship that helped bring about a change of attitude to Australia. The opening up of South America to British trade was one. Another was the need for other commercial outlets and colonies. In Scotland in particular the Peace of 1815 had brought a serious check to manufacture and commerce. Markets were needed to replace the demands of war and were difficult to find. Scots began to look further a field for land and markets, and the fact that Macquarie had successfully repaired the damage done by his predecessors, made Australia appear to be a practicable proposition for both settlement and trade.[13]

The Highland element among the Scottish settlers varied considerably from year to year. In the first three years of the emigration surge, from 1820 to 1822, about a dozen applications were received each year from Highland landowners, tacksmen, and half-pay officers. Many doubtless suffered from the economic gloom that was spreading over the Highlands, although they often did not wish to admit that they were economic migrants, and claimed that the reason they wished to emigrate was the lack of military employment and the falling in of tacksmen's leases.

One of the reasons why the Highland element was so prominent in the very earliest stage of emigration was undoubtedly Governor Macquarie's reputation and the number of his friends and relations among Hebridean landowners and tacksmen. For instance Alexander Macdonald[14], son of Major Alexander Macdonald, tacksman of Vallay, in North Uist[15], stated in his application for a grant of land in 1820 that he was 'known to His Excellency, Governor Macquarie, and prefers going to NSW to any other colony'.[16] He also explained in his letter to the Colonial Secretary that 'the termination of a beneficial lease held by your petitioner's father and his ancestors for many generations compels him to remove'.[17]

Donald Campbell, another tacksman, of Craig by Dalmally in Argyll, who applied in 1823 stated that his reason for wishing to emigrate was because 'of the high rents and the low price of cattle in this country'.[18] Most Highland tacksmen, who applied were not poor, judged by the standards of the time, and their salaries, half-pay, or savings as military officers in the East India Company supplemented their capital.

There were few among the Highland tacksmen, or half-pay officers, who would admit that they were in financial difficulties: Donald McDonald of Balure, Appin, a half-pay lieutenant, however, complained that he was unable to support his family 'in a manner befitting his rank'.[19] More typical were those with pretensions to some capital and plans to take out a small retinue of servants: Alexander McNab of Degnish near Oban, claimed to have between one and two thousand pounds available in cash;[20] and even Donald McLeod of Talisker, while pleading 'distressed circumstances', stated that he could take out several Highlanders.[21]

He was to take twenty-two people with him. All travelled cabin class[22] and cost him, or more likely Alexander, £800. They did not come from his old estate but were provided by his father-in-law. Heading the list was an unidentified 'Mr Allan Maclean'. He does not appear to have been one of Coll's tacksmen. It is possible that he is the former Drill Sergeant in the Coll Company of Volunteers.[23]

Another Maclean was Flora, the daughter of Allan Maclean, formally in Acha who by 1820 was tacksman of Arileod. Another of Coll's tenants was Roderick Macdonald, in Lagmore, who had been a corporal in the Argyllshire Volunteers. He took with him his wife and ten children. He was perhaps going out as Talisker's ground officer and there is little doubt that Donald Macleod saw himself living in Van Dieman's Land as a laird in much the same manner as he had on Skye.

Not all those on the *Skelton* came from Coll's estate. Donald Macdonald was from Eigg. He was the second son of Angus Macdonald Tacksman of Laig, who had commanded the Eigg Company of Volunteers in the Napoleonic Wars.

Donald Campbell and his cousin Colin were also among the cabin passengers. Donald was the son of Murdoch Campbell, one of the proprietors of the Two Ends of Coll. Whilst Colin was the son of Murdoch's brother Neil, tacksman of Sunipol in Mull, who had married Allan Maclean of Crossapol's youngest sister Ann. Also travelling on the *Skelton* were Dr and Mrs Cameron and their five children. In 1798 Dr Cameron had served as surgeon's mate on the East Indiaman *Good Hope* and in 1808 had taken part in the expedition to Argentina.[24]

The *Skelton* sailed from Leith Roads on the 19th June 1820. She had a crew of 17 and 57 passengers. A further 21 passengers joined at Portsmouth. On the 18th July off Cape Ortugal Mrs Macleod was 'delivered of a fine boy'. She recovered so quickly that she jokingly said she would recommend ladies to give birth on board ship.

On 21st August, when the ship crossed the Equator ceremonies of homage to Neptune were performed and the God of the sea put his usual questions to the passengers. The day was fine and spent in conviviality. In the evenings the ladies and gentlemen danced reels, which was considered to be good exercise.[25] The voyage, however, was not without friction and when the *Skelton* stopped at Table Bay in the Cape of Good Hope. There was some disagreement between the Macleod and Cameron children, which caused their fathers to quarrel violently and only the intervention of Captain Dixon, the owner and master of the *Skelton*, stopped them from fighting a duel.

Dixon came of a well-known family of seafarers and ship owners in the flourishing seaport of Whitby, and early in 1820 he was seeking employment for his vessel. He states: 'The difficulty of procuring employment for ships at that time naturally suggested to the owners of vessels the idea of fitting them out as transports for the conveyance of such persons as were desirous to emigrate to the new settlements. The terms were made as reasonable as possible ... seventy guineas for a cabin passage, and forty guineas for steerage'. The voyage proved highly successful, and on his return, Dixon, much impressed by what he had seen, and no doubt anxious to publicize the potential of the colony with a view to encouraging the flow of emigrants who might take passage with him, wrote a *Narrative of a Voyage to New South Wales and Van Diemen's Land in the year 1820*. Dixon was a keen observer. He was particularly impressed by the system of land grants he saw in Van Diemen's Land, which he considered was by far the more attractive of the settlements.

On his arrival in Van Diemen's Land Donald Macleod received a grant of 2000 acres in the north of the island ten miles from Launceston. He christened it Talisker. Two years later he was dissatisfied with his grant and wrote to Lord Bathurst to say that apart from the 2000 acres, the labour of seven convicts 'victualed from the stores' and provisions for his family for six months, he had 'received no encouragement whatever'.[26] Bathurst evidently wished to encourage him and he was granted a further 2100 acres. His holding was increased still further when his brother Colonel Alexander Macleod of the East India Company's cavalry was allocated 3000 acres. He died soon afterwards and Donald inherited his land.

* * *

Alexander Maclean of Coll also supported another potential emigrant's application when he signed the petition of Allan Mackinnon, Struan, Bracadale, Skye. Allan was the son of John Mackinnon, a member of the Keanouchcrach branch of the Mackinnon family. His mother, Mary, was the daughter of Allan Maclean, tacksman of Kinloch-Scrisort in Rum.[27] His uncle was the historian Mr Donald Mackinnon of Strath who died in 1831 at the age of 100. His other uncle was Mr Donald Maclean's old adversary in Eigg, Lachlan Mackinnon of Houloun.

On 1st March 1822 Allan Mackinnon arrived in Van Diemen's Land, having sailed out on *Castle Forbes*. He brought with him capital of £500 and received a grant of 200 acres in the Breadalbane district and the promise of 300 more. Initially he had problems over his grant, which was not settled until 1826. In the meantime he accepted the post of keeper of the Launceston Gaol. This experience gave him an insight into the lives of the convicts and was to be useful when he employed them when he got his land.

At Talisker Donald Macleod had his problems. He had difficulties in keeping his employees[28] and he was denounced in the press for his treatment of the convicts allocated to him.[29] This was only the beginning of his troubles and in 1825 he was fined for selling spirits without a licence.[30] Help, however, was on its way for in May 1825 Hugh Maclean, younger of Coll, applied for a grant of land for his nephews Magnus and Alexander Macleod, who were on the on the point of returning to Australia on the *Triton*.[31] They are described as young men who 'have been for some years engaged in the study of practical agriculture and are possessed of the required capital of £500 each. I therefore trust that your Lordship will be pleased to order the usual grant of land on their arrival in Van Diemen's Land'.[32]

Sailing with the Macleod brothers on the *Triton* in 1825 was an Angus Mackinnon. He became Donald Macleod's overseer at Talisker from 1826–28.[33] Also on board was Colin and Neil[34] Campbell's brother Alexander. Colin met the *Triton* in Hobart. He had taken a grant of 700 acres at White Hills, near Launceston and the brothers, having sent Alexander's luggage on by cart, preceeded to walk the hundred miles to Colin's farm.

Later Colin purchased more land on the Tamar River, which Alexander managed for his brother, growing wheat and potatoes and keeping 50% of the profit. After a year or two Alexander moved on and managed the emancipist Simeon Lord of Sydney's Bona Vista Station, which employed 14 convicts. In 1829 he left Lord's service and rented White Hills from his brother, who had returned to Scotland for a visit.[35] Whilst Alexander was at Bona Vista, Aborigines speared one of his shepherds. Alexander played a major part in hunting down the murderer.[36]

Not all those from Coll had sufficient capital to obtain a grant of land. Hugh Maclean son of Allan Arileod sailed from Leith in the *City of Edinburgh* and arrived at Hobart on 13th April 1825. He later explained that the reason why he had not 'brought my capital with me, was my having been young & unexperienced in the world and my friends wont intrust me with the whole, untill such time as I might have some knowledge of the Colony'. As he was unable to farm he took a post for two years in Launceston with Simeon Lord's firm. By January 1828, thanks to a remittance of £500 from his relatives in Scotland and his investment in stock, he had accumulated capital of £725 (£300 in cash, 200 head of cattle at £4 each and 300 sheep at 15/–). He therefore applied for a grant of land and the Lieutenant-Governor ordered 640 acres be provided on the condition that he resided on them. Donald Macleod vouched for him.[37] Despite his promise to reside permanently on his grant, in 1828 Hugh is noted as having 'just set out on a sealing voyage'.[38]

The Campbell cousins also flourished. Neil's letter of the 23rd December 1828 to his mother at Sunipol in Mull has survived. He writes that he had 'entered into partnership with Mr Beveridge in the purchase of a saw mill here at which I now reside'. He says that it is in the wildest part of Van Diemen's Land and that he was to spend Christmas with Allan Mackinnon from Rum. There was evidently a family quarrel underway between his father and Neil's cousins, presumably over the estate of his uncles Malcolm and Murdoch Campbell, who had died in 1821 and 1818.[39] He hoped that they could reach a settlement without resource to a third party.

Neil also mentions the Macleods. 'Major Macleod's family are well', he writes 'in their usual way carrying their heads as high as they can fly'.[40] Donald Macleod had not got over the fact that he had been a laird. His attitude to his neighbours evidently irritated them. Once they had reached Australia his father-in-law's tenants were no longer prepared to doff their caps to anyone.

Not all the emigrants on the *Skelton* stayed in Australia for very long. In 1822 Mr Allan Maclean is listed as the licensee of the 'Black Swan' hotel in Goulburn Street, Hobart. In 1824 he announced that he was leaving the colony 'for a short time' and on 16th January a notice appeared in the *Hobart Town Gazette* requesting that any claims against him should be presented at the 'Black Swan'. Allan had been allocated a grant of land. In June 1827 the Surveyor General received a letter from a Peter Lette, who stated that it was now six years since Allan had received his grant but that he had not carried out any improvements on it or had not even felled a single tree. As it was now three years since Maclean had left the colony, he requested that the land should be transferred to him.[41] Allan does not appear to have returned to Tasmania.

* * *

Sometime in the 1820s John Maclean of Cornaig's youngest son Alexander Campbell sailed to India. Unlike his other brothers, instead of becoming a soldier, he became a merchant in Bombay.[42] On 16th August 1825 he married Mary Elizabeth, the only child of Henry Travers of Fairfield in Devon. If he was not already successful Alexander's marriage was the making of his career. Henry Travers had been a member of the Bengal Civil Service and had numerous useful connections and when their first son was born at Moorshedabad in Bengal on 14th November 1826 he was named after his maternal grandfather.

Notes

1. *Scots Magazine* 1806 vol. 68, 397. He was the eldest son of Colonel Magnus Macleod 5th of Talisker who had succeeded his elder brother Colonel John in 1798. Major Donald had served as a lieutenant [20 August 1794] in the 72nd Regiment of Foot in the East Indies and later as a major [24 September 1808] in the 3rd Battalion of the Inverness-shire Militia; [Donald Mackinnon and Alick Morrison *The Macleods – The Genealogy of a Clan* section 2 (nd), 11.
2. NAS. CH 2. 70. 2: 7 January 1819 where it is stated that he was born on 30 November 1818.
3. *Captain Gronow*, vol. 1, 54.
4. TNA. CO 201. 102. 186.
5. TNA. CO 201. 147. 18.
6. Macquarie was, through his mother, the great-grandson of Catherine, dau. of John Garbh Maclean of Coll (1617 × 1675).
7. John Ritchie *Lachlan Macquarie* (1988), 108.
8. *Ibid*, 144.
9. *Ibid*, 160.
10. *Ibid*, 160.
11. *Ibid*, 153.
12. *Sketches of the Highlanders of Scotland* vol. 2, 164.
13. David S Macmillan *Scotland and Australia 1788–1850* (1967), 26–7.
14. He was an only son who had served latterly as a major in the local Volunteers & Militia [TNA. CO 201. 102. 277].
15. He had served 'during the whole of the first American War as Capt. Lieutenant of the late 76th Foot or Macdonald Highlanders to 1783'. He was 'Major of Volunteers during the French War'. [TNA. CO 201. 102. 277].
16. *Ibid*, 82–3.
17. A. McDonald's petition, 20 November 1820. TNA.CO 201. 102.
18. D Campbell's application, 17 December 1823, TNA. CO 201. 148.

19. D McDonald's application, 28 July 1820, TNA.CO 201. 102.
20. A McNab's application, 14 July 1820, TNA. CO 201. 102.
21. D McLeod's application, 14 February 1820, TNA.CO 201. 102.
22. They can therefore be identified. At this time there is virtually no information about those who travelled steerage.
23. He last appears in the Coll records on 29th July 1816 when his son Lauchlan is baptised. [NAS. CH2. 70.1].
24. He was the 2nd son of John Cameron, merchant of Greyfriars, Edinburgh [KR von Stieglitz *A History of Evandale* (1967), 33–5.
25. James Dixon *Narrative of A Voyage to New South Wales & Van Diemen's Land in the Ship Skelton during the Year 1820* (1822), 14–16.
26. TNA. CO 201. 147, 18.
27. *The Macleods* Section 3, 141.
28. Letter from Neil Campbell, Launceston to his mother in Sunipol, Mull. 23 December 1828. The original of this letter is in La Trobe Library, Melbourne. I have to thank Roddy Balfour, Torran Gorm, Cantray, Croy, Inverness for extracts from this letter
29. Tasmanian State Archives. Colonial Secretary's Correspondence: Van Diemen's Land (1824–1836). CSO 1. 106. 3926.
30. Tasmania State Archives [TSA]. Wayne Index of Immigrants. I have to thank Roddy Balfour, for this reference and for drawing my attention to others both in the National Archives in Kew and in Tasmania.
31. TNA. CO 201. 170. 295.
32. TNA. CO 201. 170. 290.
33. I have to thank Donald Mackinnon of Dalness, PO Box 20, Evandale 7212, Tasmania for information in the previous three paragraphs.
34. He had petitioned to join his brother, with support from Hugh Maclean, younger of Coll, in 1823 [TNA. CO 201. 113, 175].
35. He had returned home with the intention of persuading his father to bring the rest of his family to Australia. [LSD 1. 92, 518–533]. Neil Sunipol was not, however, persuaded. He died in 1851 still Tacksman of Sunipol and is buried beside his brothers in Crossapol graveyard.
36. 'Sixty-Five Years in Australia' *The Argus* (Tuesday 27 May 1890). I have to thank Brian Campbell for this reference, which was dictated, shortly before his death, by his ancestor Alexander Campbell.
37. TSA. CSO 1. 240. 5795.
38. 23 December 1828: Neil Campbell to his mother at Sunipol, Isle of Mull.
39. Crossapol Graveyard, Coll. All three brothers are buried close together beneath ornate gravestones as though defying the Macleans around them.
40. 23 December 1828: Neil Campbell to his mother.
41. Archives Office of Tasmania. CSO1/134/file 3224. I have to thank Robyn Eastly, Senior Archivist Reference Services for a copy of this letter and other material relaying to emigration to Tasmania from Coll.
42. BL/L/MIL/12/73, 187.

Chapter Forty-Six

Rum to Nova Scotia 1820–1826

Juliet Alexa[1] claims that her father Hugh Maclean younger of Coll was: 'too kind a landlord for his own interests'. As the 1820s progressed he had much to concern him. Emigration to Canada continued. In the summer of 1822 six MacMillan brothers and their sister left the Isle of Muck. They sailed from Tobermory on the *Commerce,* of Greenock and landed at Plaster Cove, now Port Hastings, Cape Breton.[2]

Not all movement was away from the Isles. 'Lachlan Maclean Esq', the shipwright son of Captain Lachlan of the East India Company who had done well in Jamaica, returned to Coll for a visit. He brought with him his black servant Macfarlan. And on the 20 May 1820 Neil Campbell in Mibost complained to the Kirk Session that Christian Bethune, also in Mibost, had defamed his wife Marion Kennedy's character by saying that when she was a servant with her brother at Totronald she 'had been guilty of fornication with McFarlan'.[3]

Lachlan Maclean the shipwright was only home on a visit and returned to Jamaica.[4] Major-General Lachlan Macquarie, the former Governor of New South Wales, who returned to Mull in August 1822, came home with the intention of living on his estate. However, he returned to find the local economy in ruins and the people starving. They were 'unemployed, restless and emigrating *en masse*'.

His own financial situation, as the result of his spending spree on land in 1804, was in tatters. Instead of the handsome credit he imagined he had accumulated since 1809, he learned to his horror that his bankers held a mere £166 in his account. His tenants could not pay their rents, and because the market for land had collapsed, he was unable to sell his Loch na Keal estate for anything approaching the price he had paid for it.[5]

The whole basis of the economy in the Hebrides was under threat. On the 14th November *The Scotsman* noted:

It gives us pleasure that Alexander Maclean of Coll, Esq., besides endearing himself to his tenants by residing amongst them, last week reduced their rents 25 per cent. His tenants are seldom ever changed, but remain in their ground as long as they are well doing.[6]

If the tenants were unable to pay their rent, it would not be long before the landowner was facing a financial crisis, and on the 5th October 1823 Hugh Maclean, writing from Coll to the Earl of

Bathurst outlined the dire position that the Isles were in. He also had a solution. It is worth quoting this letter in full as it gives an insight into the situation when there was still time to do something about it:

My Lord,

with the view of obtaining a settlement in Canada for a part of our suffering population permit me to lay before you a sketch of our condition in the Hebrides. The excess of our population seems to be unknown beyond our own bounds & may well appear incredible to those who compare the extent of our surface with our numbers. But it is an undeniable fact that every estate of £1,000 per annum has at least 500 supernumarie parties to support. An example will but show this. I take my father's estate, not an extreme case & in which much has been successfully done for the improvement & comfort of the people. On an estate of £3,000 per annum, we have a rapidly increasing population of 2700 no fishery or manufacture except 100 tons of kelp which would give full employment for 3 months to about 70 individuals: cattle and sheep our only saleable produce: in the best seasons not raising grain sufficient for our own consumption.

In such a dreadful season as the present it is needless to state to your Lordship the misery that must exist. In the very best at least half the people are in a state, which would be considered actual starvation in any other part of Britain. It must be evident that the entire income of such a property could not afford adequate relief in a season in which by no possibility half the rent could be collected. The poor people have no resource but the humanity of their Landlords & have suffered much without complaint. In permanent relief they look to emigration alone and they have not the means of transporting themselves now they have been rapidly increasing & impoverishing since the War & the relaxation in the instruction on emigration formally imposed by the Government. We are willing to give every assistance in our power for the transport say of 100 families as an experiment if government will take charge of them on landing at Quebec placing them on their allotment of land free of every expense & a years rations (in cash at stated periods, to save expence & the constant complaints).

It is understood that the Government of Canada is anxious for the settlement of the new districts on the Ottawa river near Montreal where these poor people might be fixed at a small expence. Relief has been given to the Irish, we are as needful, surely as deserving altho less clamourous.

I trust that your Lordship will be able to give a favourable answer. Our state is fast approximating to that of Ireland a few such partial reliefs may perhaps prevent the necessity of any general measure for our assistance, which cannot otherwise be much longer delayed. If my proposal may not meet with the success your humanity might wish it, might I presume to inquire from your Lordship how far we may expect his Majesty's Government to grant us assistance in the attempts to provide for our superfluous population and make the Hebrides a source of wealth instead of a burden on the Kingdom?[7]

* * *

It is against this background that Hugh's marriage with Jane Robertson must be seen. News that he had married a rich women coming at a time when morale on the estate must have reached a nadir, seems, if the number of surviving songs in Gaelic praising Drumfin are anything to go by, to have been greeted with enthusiasm by his people. It was no doubt particularly satisfactory that Drumfin was being built on land that had once belonged to the Macleans of Duart but had been lost to Argyll.

This potential source of income probably gave Alexander and Hugh the means to tackle the estate's major problem. This was the Isle of Rum. Alexander had done his best for the island. He had taken John Knox's advice and built a pier at the head of Loch Scrisort, solely for the use of the islanders. James Macdonald says that the loch was not much frequented by outsiders 'as mariners are always afraid of the squalls, which rush from the lofty mountains and rough shores of Rum. And accordingly keep a respectful distance from every part of its coast'. However, during a storm when Macdonald had to take shelter in Loch Scrisort, he found to his surprise a good anchorage and 'a pier or quay at the head of the loch'.[8]

Alexander had also rented land at Arisaig to hold cattle from Rum so that they could recover from their journey by sea before they joined a drove for the long trek to the Lowland markets.[9] He had also probably introduced new tacksmen to the island. Letters from Van Diemen's Land talk of 'Allan Mackinnon from Rum'. I suspect that this is the Allan Mackinnon (1796–1877), Struan, Skye whose petition to emigrate was supported by Alexander.[10] As we have seen, Allan sailed on 1st March 1822 on the *Castle Forbes* and obtained a grant of 500 acres in the White Hills area of Tasmania.[11] His father John Mackinnon may well have taken a farm in Rum in addition to his land at Struan in Skye, especially as he was married to the daughter of the factor of Rum.

* * *

As has already been noticed the number of people on the island had increased dramatically and the collapse in the price of their black cattle meant that the people of Rum were unable to pay their rent. It has been suggested that even when they had the means they were unwilling to do so,[12] which suggests that the landlord tenant relationship was beginning to break down. By 1825 they owed £2,000 in arrears and the vile weather in the early 1820s was going to make the situation even more desperate. Everyone agreed that something had to be done. But what?

In the first decade of the century, as we have seen, Necker de Saussure had written that:

The islanders of Rum are reputed the happiest in the Hebrides; both on account of the low rent which Mr Maclean receives for his farms, and because the isle furnishes a great number of large and small cattle, which supply them all with meat. Their principal occupations are the care of cattle, fishing and getting of seaweed, which they burn for the purpose of extracting alkali.[13]

James Macdonald, however, painted a less rosy picture. He commented that:

This island is the most mountainous and rugged of all the Hebrides, Jura itself not excepted, and ought to be entirely converted into a sheep walk or a deer park . . . In point of agriculture, it is one of the most backward of all the Hebrides, nor is this in the least degree surprising. The surface of the island is so rugged, its climate is so boistrous and rainy, and there is such a scarcity of manure, that it would be a very difficult matter to prosecute agriculture with any advantage even supposing it peopled by a colony from East Lothian or Berwick.

East Lothian and Berwick were considered to have the most advanced agriculture in Scotland. Macdonald spells out the problem of the climate in Rum with a personal anecdote.

Conversing with a young man at the head of Loch-scrisort in 1807, during a *down-pour* of rain which had persevered in deluging the island for a week, the reporter asked, 'Does it perpetually rain in such torrents in Rum?' He answered, *Cha bhi, ach sneachda na-uathriogh*, i.e. No Sir, not always torrents of *rain*, but sometimes of *snow*.

Macdonald went on to say that:

although in general unfit for agriculture, and especially for white crops, there are some hundred acres of good low-lying land in the sheltered valleys, where green crops and grasses might be cultivated with success. Were the island, therefore stocked with a hardy breed of sheep, it would pay four times its present rent; and 300 individuals, who are now a dead weight upon Mr Maclean of Coll the proprietor, and cannot maintain their families in any tolerable degree of comfort, would elsewhere seek for labour and subsistence. The proprietor attempted to introduce sheep instead of the black cattle and horses; to which the natives had been accustomed, and they answered exceedingly well, but the prejudices of the inhabitants soon overcame their reason; and, as the landlord was not on the spot, or in a condition to superintend and enforce the system of sheep-farming, they soon returned to their former live stock and their ancient habits.

He shakes his head in despair when he writes:

In an agricultural light, therefore, Rum is a blot on the map of the Hebrides, and its population, however, simple and virtuous, are in their present state a dead stock to the community and to themselves. Although Mr Maclean should not exact a shilling of rent from an island that might, if under sheep stock, pay him £1,200 or £1,300 per annum, the natives would be poor and miserable; so there is no resource but to turn them off in some way or other.

He argues that Alexander's benevolence was misplaced and complains that:

The proprietor's humanity prevents him from depopulating this island, although his good sense must convince him that his benevolence is, in the long run, cruelty to the poor creatures whom he feeds at his expence, and a loss to the community, who are deprived of the population in question as effectually, in every point of national resource, (useless militia service only excepted,) as if they lived in Borneo or Sumatra.

By the 1820s Alexander was probably convinced that James Macdonald was right. Tourists might still be charmed with what they saw on Rum and revel at a glimpse into a world that they had lost. For example in 1824 John MacCulloch was storm-bound at Guirdal where he ... was 'devoured by kindness'. He and his crew fell in with the nearest Maclean who could converse in English and were provided with such fare as the house afforded:

There was an old fiddle hanging up in the corner, very crazy in the pegs and in the intestines, but still practicable ... A ball here requires no great preparations ... The lassies had no shoes and marvelous little petticoat; but to compensate for these deficiencies they had an abundance of activity and good will ... The ceilidh became prolonged 'in tender pity to the prettiest girl of the party, who had been sudden and quick in falling in love with a handsome lad belonging to my crew, and was weeping bitterly at the thoughts of parting'.[14]

Others were less complimentary about the inhabitants of Rum. Lord Teignmouth writing in 1827 and quoting Coll's son-in-law Alexander Hunter states:

The people of this island were an indolent race of *gentlemen*, some of whom had held commissions in the Fencible Regiments; fishing for their amusement, living on good mutton, lying in bed in rainy, and on the grass in fine weather, and paying little or no rent. At the time of their emigration, they owed Coll, their landlord, upwards of £2,000, which he could have recovered by sale of their stock, which amounted to double that sum. But he not only declined this mode of indemnifying himself but contributed £600 towards the emigration of the poorer class. The island has since yielded a rental of £800.[15]

In fact I can identify nobody in Rum who had held a commission in the Fencibles, but as we have seen, they had served as both officers and men in the Volunteers.

* * *

In 1820 people from Rum emigrated to Nova Scotia with those from Coll. As already noticed, this emigration had not been organised by Maclean of Coll. If he was to solve the problem of Rum he was going to have to organise the move himself. He chose his son-in-law Alexander Hunter WS, the Edinburgh solicitor to do it for him.

It has been suggested that it was not Alexander, who was responsible for the Rum clearance but his 'hard-hearted son Hugh,'[16] who 'may have been of a more mercenary disposition'.[17] However, Alexander did not retire until 1828 and it is highly unlikely that he was not involved in the unpleasant but inevitable decision to clear Rum.

Plans were made to find a single tenant for the whole island. It was advertised and the people given notice to quit. Dr Lachlan, Charles Maclean of Gallanach's son, says that he happened to be in Edinburgh when he heard that a 'Club were [about] to offer for it, who would show no sympathy for the people'. He therefore made

an offer which was accepted. This was in 1825, and the following year, 1826, I took possession. I bought, or rather took at valuation, all the livestock and everything they had to dispose of.[18]

Archibald Mackenzie/Matheson says of his father that

such was the opinion of the Laird of Coll of his Judgement and independence that when the people of the Island of Rum were coming to America the valuation of the whole stock of the Island was left by the proprietor and the tenantry to his bare word and that of another farmer in Coll, one Angus Johnston and the proprietor a stern man and the inhabitants of six large villages were both satisfied.[19]

Dr Lachlan goes on to say that

> About 130 0f the inhabitants being poor, they did not take the benefit of this generous offer. These remained on the island for two years, and were all employed by me and fairly paid. Hearing reasonable accounts from their friends, they at last followed – their passage being paid, to which I contributed £150.
>
> On 12th July 1828 the last of the old inhabitants of Rum sailed on the *Saint Lawrence* for Ship Harbour, Cape Breton.[20]

* * *

Maclean of Coll was the subject of much criticism for clearing Rum and the following year his agent and son-in-law Alexander Hunter was called to give evidence before the Select Committee on Emigration from the United Kingdom. The questions put to him and his answers give the flavour of the case.

Lord Binning chaired the Committee.[21] Hunter was examined:

> Question 2907: You were employed in superintending an emigration? Answer: From the island of Rum; the estate of Maclean of Coll.
> 2908. At what period did that emigration take place? Last year; in the month of July last year.
> 2909. Of how many persons did it consist? The last emigration, about 300.
> 2910. Were they embarked in one ship? There were two ships.[22]
> 2911. State to the Committee the terms upon which those persons were freighted out together, with all the particulars relative to the expense of their nourishment, and so on? The expense came to £5.14s per head of each adult person, upon the average.
> 2912. What was the expense of those who were not adults? Two children from seven to fourteen years of age are reckoned as an adult, and three under seven.
> 2913. What was the duration of their passage? About 37 days.
> 2914. Will you have the goodness to state to the Committee the particulars of their allowance of provisions; does the £5.14s include all the expenses? Every expense.
> 2915. Passage and all? Every thing.

Alexander Hunter went on to explain that there was an Act of Parliament, with regard to the allowances; but in this case, upon application to Government, they dispensed with the allowance, and oatmeal instead of beef was substituted, only a very small proportion of beef. The weekly allowance to an adult was, eleven pounds of oatmeal, three and a half pounds of bread or biscuit, one and a half pound of beef, half a pound of melasses, half a pound of pease or barley (either), a quarter of a pound of butter, and the allowance of water, of course that cost nothing, but it is 35 pints.

2917. What portion of that quantity of provision did they consume during their voyage? The allowances were laid down for 12 weeks, that is according to Act of Parliament; but they were told when they went on board, that whatever was over, they were to get for themselves, and of course they were very sparing, and they had provisions when they arrived, equal to serve them for two or three months. They were on board 37 days. But I must explain, that a number of them had salt mutton of their own, and potatoes, exclusive of the ship's allowances.

2918. Of what class of persons were these emigrants generally? What we call Crofters, in the islands, and some of them were farmers; some of these people had money, a good deal of money.

2919. What is a Crofter? A man who pays rent from 30s to £5.

2920. A man who has a small bit of land? Exactly so, a small bit of land.

2921. Where were they taken to? To Cape Breton.

2922. But not located there? Not located certainly, but merely landed there.

2923. The expense that you have named, is merely the expense of their landing? Merely the expense of their landing.

2924. Are these individuals satisfied in their situation at Cape Breton; have you any evidence of that kind, of any satisfaction that there is? I have only one letter from those who went last out; I have one letter declaring themselves perfectly satisfied; but I have some letters from those who went out some years ago, which perhaps may throw some light on the satisfaction they felt.

2925. Have you any particulars relative to the other emigrants you also superintended? I did not superintend the first.

2926. It appears then, that these people were amply supplied with provisions, and that part of that expense might have been spared? Certainly.

2927. Can you form any judgment at all how much might have been spared, as for example, do you think that they might have been shipped and landed at Cape Breton for 30s. less per head, or how much in your judgment? Why they might; there is a risk, however, because instead of 37 days, they might have been 47 or 57 days in passage; by the average of the passages, certainly one half might have been saved.

2928. How was this £5.14s paid; was it paid by the people themselves? No, by the proprietor, who gave a sum of money to assist them.

2929. Are you not of opinion, that the highland proprietor has consulted his own interest by this arrangement? He certainly has.

2930. Because in seasons of scarcity, I presume they feel themselves bound by custom to support the population? By humanity.

2931. And somewhat also by usage? Why, a man cannot allow his population to starve.

2932. Was it in consequence of the introduction of sheep farming, the improvement in farming in that district, that it became desirable for these people to emigrate? In the island of Rum, it is all sheep-farming; it never was anything else, nor is it adapted for raising crops.

2933. Then that emigration did not take place in consequence of any act of the landlord in the improvement of his estate: Certainly not.

2934. But it enabled him to do it? In an island for sheep alone you could hardly suppose it possible that they could raise as much grain as would feed so large a population, therefore the proprietors got little or no rent, the tenants were obliged to lay out the price of their sheep in supporting themselves.

2935. Then I suppose they drew their rent from kelp? There is no kelp on that island.

2936. What has been the effect on these persons; what is the present population of the island, compared to its former situation? Instead of a population of 350[23] people, there is a population now of 50, and one person has taken the whole island as one farm, and of course he is enabled to pay a higher rent, as he has not to maintain so many people.

2937. Could you give the Committee any idea of what would have been the state of the island, if that population had not emigrated? Certainly.

2938. Will you be good enough to do so? The population would have gone on increasing, and of course as the population increased, the rents would diminish.

2939. Can you furnish the Committee at all, with any data of the number of individuals it would be expedient, if it were possible (and I will suppose for a moment it is possible) to send from the western isles of Scotland, from the western coast of Scotland? I think they could spare one-third of the population very easily.

2940. Do you mean in the islands? In the western highlands and islands.

2941. Was the whole of that expense borne by the landlord, or only part? The landlord paid the whole of that expense.

2942. Of £5.14s per head? Yes.

2943. Have you stated how many went? I think about 300.

2944. Have there been many people settled in the island since? No person can settle there without the leave of the proprietor.

2945. Of this number (300) that went, how many were children? I believe I have an account of that at home, if I had it here I could tell you exactly.

2946. Can you state the whole amount of the expense in, in a round sum? About £2,000 I think, somewhere thereabouts.

2947. For removing this number? Yes; the way it was done was this: these people owed a great deal of arrears of rent, and Maclean, of Coll, agreed to give them their arrears of rent, and to advance a certain sum of money in order to assist them out, and give them a little money in their pockets when they arrived there.

2948. What was the usual extent of the possessions of the persons that were removed? Why, they possessed land, perhaps from £4 to £100; some paid £4 and about £100 I think the highest was.

2949. There could not be many paid £100? Not many, one or two.

2950. Be so good as to state the extent of the general class of the property farmed by the smaller class of farmers? It is impossible to say; the land there is rented at £800 a year, and it contains 30,000 English acres; it is impossible to say what extent any one person possessed.

2951. Did you go with these emigrants? I did not.

2952. Were they willing to go? Some of them were, others were not very willing; they did not like leaving the land of their ancestors.

2953. You stated there had been a letter from them? I have one letter only; there have been several.

2954. What account does he give? A very good one.

2955. When did this emigration take place from Rum? In the month of July last. There was an emigration partially, but not at the landlord's expense, four or five years ago, from Coll and Rum.

2956. How is the contract made with the ship owner, for the removal? At so much per head; and he is bound to give them certain provisions, according to the scale that I have stated.

2957. Was the contract made by a person well acquainted with shipping? Why, we know the average rate per ton of the ship, and how many passengers she would carry, and in that way we came pretty nearly to know whether it was a fair contract.

2958. What became of them when they got to Cape Breton? They landed there, where they met with a great number of friends, who had gone from the neighbouring islands a few years ago.

2959. Did they get land? They got land; a number of them had a little money with them; the friends of those who had no money assisted them, and they became labourers to their friends; and those who had money got grants of land.

* * *

As no rentals survive for Rum it is not certain who the 'one or two' tenants who paid £100 were. It is probable that one was the Tacksman of Kinlochscrisort. Allan Maclean the former factor was presumably dead by 1826 and his eldest son appears to have died young. The second son, Donald, had since 1818 been Minister of the Small Isles. The third son James was factor of the Isle of Muck in 1826, so this family did not emigrate to Nova Scotia. One other tacksman family was that of Sandaneishir. The tacksman there in 1803's grandson later lived at Dunoon, so it is possible they too did not emigrate either.

One tacksman family that did emigrate were the Maclean brothers in Guirdal. All with one exception sailed for Cape Breton. The exception was Hector's daughter Mary, who was betrothed to her cousin James who, as we have seen, became factor of Muck.[24]

Another Maclean family on board the ships sailing for Canada was that of Neil in Kilmory, who had served in the 85th Foot in the American War of Independence. He had then returned to Rum and remained there until July 1826. He and his son Hector entered into an agreement with two Morisons for a lot of land on the west side of Lake Ainslie in Nova Scotia. After they had paid they found that the Morisons did not own the land for which Hector had paid his life savings.[25]

Notes

1. 'The Journal of Juliet Alexa Maclean', 1. I have to thank the late Miss Alba Windham for a copy of her ancestor's journal.
2. *History of Inverness County*, 511–12. They were the children of Lachlan Macmillan and Catherine Campbell. Her brother Edward who had served in the Breadalbane Fencibles was drowned in 1813. His wife Margaret (Peggy) Maclean claimed 'near relationship to the Laird of Coll'. [BCP. Canadian Emigration File 1820 1840: Letter from Jean Matheson Fries]; NAS GD 16. 52. 24. 20.
3. NAS. CH 2. 70. 2: 28 May 1820.
4. He died there. His will was proved in 1831 [TNA. Will 343. TEBBS. 4 June 1831]. When he made his original will in 1814 he had appointed Alexander Maclean of Coll and his son Hugh as executors of his estate in Great Britain and guardians of his reputed children by two 'women of colour'. Also mentioned in his will are his two negro slaves named 'Coll and Hugh'.
5. *Lachlan Macquarie* (1988), 198.
6. *The Scotsman*. 14 November 1972: '150 Years Ago'. I have to thank Maj. AJC Hewat, late the King's Own Scottish Borderers for this reference.
7. TNA. CO 384. 9. 353. A reply was drafted and approved by Lord Bathurst. It does not appear to have survived. [Ibid, 352].
8. *General View*, 743.
9. I have to thank Catriona White for this information.
10. TNA. CO 201. 102, 309.
11. Information from his descendant Donald Mackinnon of Dalness, Tasmania.
12. *Celtic Monthly* (1901).
13. LA Necker de Saussure *A Voyage to the Hebrides* (1822), 56.
14. John MacCulloch *The Western Islands of Scotland* (1824), quoted by Magnus Magnusson *Rum: Natures Island* (1997), 16–17.
15. Lord Teignmouth *Sketches of the Coasts and Islands of Scotland* vol. 1 (1836), 94–5.
16. Magnus Magnusson *Rum*: Nature's Island 1997), 20.
17. John A Love *Rum*: A Landscape Without Figures (2001), 124.
18. Dr Lachlan's article of 1872 was published in the *Celtic Monthly* (1901).
19. BCP Mackenzie/Matheson Folder.

20. John L MacDougall *The History of Inverness County*.
21. Thomas Hamilton, only son of 8th Earl of Haddington (d. 17 March 1828), b. Edin. 1 June 1780, was educated at the University of Edinburgh. He graduated at Oxford. In July 1802 he was elected MP for St Germains; in 1807 for Cockermouth; and for Callington, at the general election the same year. He was afterwards member for Rochester, and a commissioner for the affairs of India. In 1814 he was sworn a privy councillor. In July 1827, during his father's lifetime, he was created a peer of the United Kingdom as Baron Melrose of Tyningham, and in 1828 suc. his father. In December 1834, he was appointed lord-lieutenant of Ireland, but continued in that post only to the following April. He was first lord of the admiralty from September 1841 to January 1846, when he was constituted lord-privy-seal, but retired from that office in the following July. In 1843 he received £43,000, as remuneration for the office of hereditary keeper of Holyrood Park, that office being abolished. He m. Lady Maria Parker, dau of 4th earl of Macclesfield, without issue. He d. 21 December 1858. [*The Scottish Nation*, vol. V, 396].
22. They were the *Harmony & Highland Laddie*. I have to thank Eugene J Quigley for this information.
23. As there were 443 people in Rum in 1806.
24. Relations between the tacksman families in Coll and Rum are discussed in my 'Tacksmen in Rum' *WHN&Q* (Jan. 2005). Series 3, No. 7, 19–23.
25. I have to thank Eugene J Quigley for this information.

Chapter Forty-Seven

The last years of Alexander Maclean of Coll

Alexander Maclean Sinclair says that in 1828 Alexander Maclean of Coll handed over his estates to his son Hugh and went to live at Quinish in Mull.[1] Alexander certainly appears to have spent an increasing amount of time at Quinish in the 1820s.[2] Lord Teignmouth notes in 1827 that on his return from Staffa 'a boat pushed out from the Bay of Quinish, in Mull, and soon introduced us to the hospitality of a neighbouring mansion'.[3] This mansion is probably Quinish House, which was built on land that was previously called Penmolloch.

After his marriage Hugh probably first lived at Quinish in the house either he or his father had built at Penmolloch[4] and, when he moved into Drumfin, Alexander probably at first took over his house there. By 1822 Alexander had handed over the running of his home farm to Donald Campbell, when the latter is first noted as being in 'Brekack'.[5]

Donald Campbell was formally the tacksman of Killundine in Morvern.[6] In 1821 he purchased his former tack from the Duke and immediately passed it on to Dr John Maclean of Ardow in Mull.[7] During the war Campbell had served as a 2nd Lieutenant in the Royal Marines and was on HMS *Agamemnon* at the battle of Trafalgar.[8]

On 24th October 1822 he was married in Coll to Miss Jane Gregorson. She was the sister of John Gregorson of Ardtornish, in Morvern, who was Sheriff-Substitute in Tobermory. Donald is described as a 'mild, intelligent and pleasant man', 'a good fellow', 'safe' where money was concerned and was 'allowed to be an active and judicious Highland agriculturist',[9] 'winning prizes for butter and pigs'. However good a farmer he was, Collachs must have been turning in their graves to see a Campbell taking over the best farm in Coll. Donald Campbell played an active part in the community: in January 1823 he became an elder of the Kirk; in 1826 he was made a Justice of the Peace.[10] He was to succeed Charles Maclean of Gallanach as factor of Coll.

* * *

Charles Gallanach was, at least financially, the most successful of Neil Maclean of Crossapol (1712–1787)'s sons or sons-in-law. In 1821 he had purchased a small property in Mull.[11] At his death he left an estate valued at £1109.14s.11d.

Neil Crossapol's children formed a caring and supportive unit, who took a keen interest in each other's careers. For instance in December 1809 when Mr Donald wrote to his son Alexander in Halifax, Nova Scotia he says:

Your Uncle in Coll some time ago had a dangerous cut. His two youngest children are promising boys. You aunts at Gallanach, Achadh and Sunipole and families are well.[12]

They were now the nucleus of the family on Coll. Mr Donald's other sisters were probably dead. Mary Arileod certainly was. Since her death her husband Alexander had been dismissed as an elder and had to marry his maid.[13] His family then began to slide down the social scale. He had, however, been given a share of the farm of Freslan 'gratis' as 'an old servant of Coll's'.[14]

In 1810 Mr Neil had written from Coll to his brother to tell him, amongst other family news, that: 'Our Cousin Lachlan Gallanach has been studying medicine in Edinburgh'.[15] Lachlan 'never got a degree'. Instead he turned his attention to sheep farming. He began by managing Lord Glenelg's estate in Lochalsh and afterwards rented Talisker in Skye before leasing Rum. On his father's death he gave up Gallanach 'as Rum (about 27,000 acres) was quite large enough for his capital'.[16] Lachlan married Isabella, daughter of Captain Donald Mackenzie of Hartfield, the brother and heir to Mackenzie of Applecross. Their mother was Anne, yet another sister of James Macleod of Raasay. Lachlan's son Major-General Charles Smith Maclean was to claim that Alexander Maclean of Coll treated his father like a son.[17]

When Lachlan Gallanach was a medical student Alexander Maclean of Coll did his best to further his career. Apparently George Hobart's elder brother[18] visited the islands and, presumably, stayed in Coll. He had in his gift a post in India, which Alexander persuaded him to offer to Lachlan. The latter, however, didn't want to leave home and turned it down. John Macneill, son of Macneill of Colonsay, was also a medical student. He heard about the post and, although he was very young and married, he hurried to Windsor to persuade Hobart to give it to him.[19] It was the start of a highly distinguished career as a diplomat, which culminated in him becoming Sir John MacNeil GCB, FRSE, PC.[20] Lachlan's career, as we shall see, was rather less successful.

* * *

The Crossapol extended family is a good example of how the tacksman class responded to the challenges of the 1820s & 1830s. The senior member of the family in Coll, Allan the tacksman of Crossapol, had almost completed his 'Genealogical Account of the Macleans' at the time of his death in April 1832. He was writing about the descendants of John Maclean of Totronald and had reached his great-grandson 'Lachlan McLean at Freslan' when he ends in mid sentence.[21] Perhaps he died as he was writing.

After Coll's son and surviving brothers Lachlan Freslan was his nearest male Maclean relation, however, as we have seen, when the estate was entailed in 1754 his father had been disinherited. The fact that Lachlan was a sessioner may have had something to do with his remaining prestige in the community of Coll. In the Island he was always known as *Lachin Mac Eachin Mhic Fir Throtraoil* i.e. 'Lachlan the son of Hector the son of Totronald',[22] and when he moved to Freslan he received his croft rent free as 'a distant connection of the Family'.[23] Allan Crossapol also mentions six other descendants of the Macleans of Coll in his manuscript who were resident in Coll shortly before he died.[24]

He was buried in the Crossapol Graveyard, between the two-storeyed farmhouse he had built in the 1790s and the sea. His youngest son Donald, who was studying for the ministry, had in March 1831 predeceased his father. He was aged 22. His elder brother John had left Coll and set up as a wine merchant in London. In 1831 he married Anne, daughter of Alexander Maclean, tacksman of Kinnegharair on Torloisk's estate in Mull.

Allan's eldest son Neil[25] succeeded his father as tacksman of Crossapol. He did not become an elder of the Kirk. In March 1839 his illegitimate son Neil was baptised at Crossapol. The child's mother was Isabella Macarthur in Totamore, another farm of which Neil was the tacksman. At the time of the 1841 Census[26] there was a family of cottars in Totamore named Macarthur, and Isabella was presumably a member of this family. Neither she nor the child was living in Coll at this time.

What is significant for this book is that none of the new generation of the Crossapol family, who remained in Coll went into the army. This was probably a reaction to the end of the war and to the cut back in the number of regiments. There were however, as we will see, other reasons.

* * *

The senior representative of old Neil of Crossapol's family in the Isles was Mr Neil Maclean, the Minister of Tiree and Coll. Like his uncle in Coll he took a keen interest in his family history and in 1829 began to write articles for *An Teachdaire Gaelach*.[27] This was one of the publications that Dr Norman Maclead, Neil's former flatmate whilst they were both at Divinity Hall in Edinburgh, had founded. Macleod's aim for the publications, which he also edited, was to provide the reader with 'every kind of useful information' which had hitherto been locked up', as far as monoglot Gaelic speakers were concerned 'in English books'.[28]

An Teachdaire Gaelach, to which Macleod himself contributed[29], consisted of articles on history, geography, current affairs, poetry and religious subjects. Neil, writing under the pseudonym P. M'F also managed to include stories from Coll tradition such as *Bratach Thighearna Chola*, which tells of his ancestor Neil Mor's victory over the Macleans of Duart at *Sruthan nan ceann* and John Garbh's victory at Grishipol in *Leum a Ghille riabhaich*.[30] There were other contributors from Coll, including 'Eoghan Og' and 'Mactalla' who in the final issue, published in 1831, wrote an elegy on the death of Sibbella Maclean of Coll.[31]

'Mactalla' was the pseudonym of Lachlan Maclean, better known as *Lachainn na Gàidhlig*, who was born in Arnabost in 1798.[32] In about 1821 he went to Glasgow and became a hosier. He was the author of several articles in *An Teachdaire Gaelach* and in *Cuairtear nan Gleann*. In 1837 he published *Adhamh agus Eubh*, 'Adam and Eve' and in 1840 the 'History of the Keltic Language'. Both these publications argued that Gaelic was the language of Paradise.[33]

Neil's most valuable literary legacy is probably his contribution on his parish for the *New Statistical Account of Scotland* (1845). His article which was drawn up in 1840 and revised in 1843 gives an account of the topography and natural history, civil history, population, industry, parochial economy, and miscellaneous observations about his parish. It is an invaluable insight into life in Tiree and Coll, rather than the general picture of life in the Hebrides, in the last decade before famine destroyed all that Alexander Maclean of Coll had tried to achieve. Once again Mr Neil does not miss the opportunity to laud the achievements of his ancestors John Garbh and Neil Mor.

Neil also carried on a lengthy correspondence with his elder brother's widow in Plymouth. She was living on a small pension and finding it hard to make ends meet. Neil's own lot was not always a happy one. In November 1831 he writes:

> Towards the end of Spring, several of our young people were in succession attacked by the Scarlet fever, but recovered tho' after a severe indisposition. The other children were sent from home for some time for fear of infection. About the middle of July, our second oldest

Daughter, who had escaped the former malady, was taken ill, and after a severe illness of nearly three weeks, died on the 5th August, aged between twelve and thirteen years. Her head seemed chiefly affected, and Medical friends who attended her, said her complaint was caused by an effusion on the brain. This was a severe trial to us, especially as it was the first break in our young family. Ann Maria Flora was a lovely and dutiful child, of the most amiable and engaging disposition, nor had we any of better promise or talent . . .[34]

He writes again two years later and comments on his new accommodation:

This last season we got a new dwelling house, or manse, as the house intended for the Clergyman's accommodation is termed in Scotland, our former residence being very small and incommodious.[35]

The campaign for a new manse in Tiree had begun in May 1831, when Mr Neil laid before the Presbytery a petition, which stated that:

That, although it is provided by law that the Parochial Clergy of the Church of Scotland should have certain accommodation, yet true it is that your petitioner has hitherto wanted such accommodation. May it therefore please the Reverend Presbytery to appoint a day for visiting the Parish of Tyree and to take such steps as may appear to them expedient for obtaining this proper legal accommodation . . .[36]

A Presbytery delegation visited Tiree and 'finding the Minister of Tyree wholly unprovided with a Manse and Office Houses direct Mr Gilchrist [the architect who was present] to submit to them for Consideration at next meeting Plans and Specifications of a Manse of a size and description usually built in these parts and the neighbouring bounds. Further they direct Mr Gilchrist to lay before them plans and Specifications of Office Houses containing . . . a Barn 27 feet long' walled garden, 'Byre for five Cows, Potatoes, Coal, Cart, and Milk Houses as also a poultry & Pig House &c of the usual size and description'.

These outhouses were as essential to the minister, as to any other farmer, for in addition to preaching, visiting the dying, catechising his parishioners and his other duties, ministers had their 'glebes'. This farmland was a payment in addition to their stipend and was needed to provide their sustenance. Servants probably did most of the farm work on the glebe, with the minister taking key decisions.

Work on the manse &c commenced under the control, and cost, of the heretors of the parish.[37] By 22nd June 1833 it was reported that, apart from a few adjustments to be made by the contractor Mr Fletcher, 'the building should be taken of[f] his hands'.[38]

Mr Neil also took an interest in his deceased brother Alexander's son's education. On 3rd July 1834 he writes to his sister-in-law in Plymouth:

I am well pleased with Alexander's letter, and the spirit he shows to be independent. I am aware the expenses of his education must bear pretty hard on your limited income; but trust he may live to requite it all by his future good conduct, and his gratitude for the exertions you are making in his behalf. It would certainly be very desirable if a situation could be soon procured for him. I fear I can be of little or no service in promoting his present views:

I shall, however, keep the matter in mind; and if I can find that any friend or acquaintance of mine is possessed of any influence in that profession to which his views point, I shall be extremely happy to use my endeavour to run it to his advantage.[39]

* * *

Although old Neil of Crossapol's male descendants were content to remain in the Isles, his daughters were not. Allan Maclean, tacksman of Arileod had married old Neil of Crossapol's penultimate daughter.[40] They had a large family of four sons & seven daughters. As we have seen, the eldest daughter Flora sailed to Van Diemen's Land on the *Skelton* with the Macleods in 1820, and the eldest son Hugh had done the same in 1825 on the *City of Edinburgh*. Instead of becoming a farmer Hugh became involved in sealing. In 1828 he was shipping seal and wallaby skins to the United Kingdom. In 1831 he returned to Scotland and persuaded his father to bring the rest of the family to Australia.

In the meantime Hugh's brother Neil had also gone to sea and obtained a master's certificate. The two brothers now purchased the *John Dunscombe*. She was a schooner of 88 tons, built in Prince Edward Island in 1819, which had crossed the Atlantic and was based at Greenock. It was used to bring wine and fruit to Glasgow from Continental ports. In *Lloyd's Register of Shipping* for 1829 she is described as having a draft of 8 feet and to be a remarkably fast sailor.

The Arileod family embarked on the 16th September 1832 and sailed from Glasgow for Van Diemen's Land on a voyage that is perhaps unique in the history of emigration to Australia, in that virtually all the crew and the passengers were from the same family. They called at St Helena, where she took on water, and then at Tristan Da Cunha. On the 15th December the *John Dunscombe* sailed into Table Bay. She had with her a cargo of coal, which was in short supply in Cape Town and she took on wine, which sold well when, on 10th February 1833, the *John Dunscombe* reached Hobart. She then sailed for Sydney arriving there on the 6th March.[41]

In 1831 Donald Macleod had put up *Talisker* for rent. The Macleods' stay in Tasmanian Talisker had not been a happy one. Edward Markham, Surveyor of Van Diemen's Land on 18th July 1833 wrote in his journal:

> rode out to Major Macleod's house at Perth(sic), a most miserable affair considering how well off they might well have been but for all consumming pride of birth she being daughter to a Highland laird old Coll of Coll and Mull. The daughters are delicate but fine grown girls and can play scotch jigs and reels c but none of them have married, as they do not take about here. Under the floor of the room they live in, the native cats had borrowed and bred and the smell and effluvia arising is terrible it is like living over a wild beast show: we had a badly dressed dinner, chump ends and bits [?] the horns &c, rode with the Major who is next to imbecilic now (as Mrs Macleod wears the Breeches) rode to Talisker the name of his farm now let to a clansman of the Macleans, the old Major is in difficulties and all is at sixes and sevens. The grounds [are] slovenly and the back parts out of order and filthy. There are 5 girls and 3 or 4 sons. Magnus or Magnose, as he has a large nose is a fine young fellow. I did not see the others as they were away in the bush ...[42]

As his sons could not get good land in Tasmania they moved to the mainland and became successful Squatters. Major Macleod and his family followed them, having let Talisker to Allan

Arileod.[43] He is described as 'Mr Mc'Lean, of Talisker' when his daughter 'Miss McLean' was married at the Scotch Church on Tuesday 28th November 1834. She was married to a 'George Hamilton Esq'.[44]

* * *

Other Coll tacksman families, who had emigrated were having mixed successes. In 1832 Coundullie Rankin was appointed Inspector of Militia in Prince Edward's Island. The Militia there consisted of fourteen battalions. He had been promoted to be a major and had command of a battalion of 700 Highlanders. Every single one was 'a genuine Highlander by father & mother'. His two eldest daughters were married in Cape Breton, but his eldest son George had moved to Demarara, where he was doing well. His brother Hector Rankin was not. Coundullie says: 'Poor Hector is but muddling. He has a large family & but little to support them'.[45]

In 1832 Coundullie was living on a 'fine farm' in the country some 75 miles from Charlottetown. He was active in local politics, and in 1834 was an unsuccessful land reform candidate in elections to the House of Assembly. In April 1836 he presided at a meeting in Belfast that passed a resolution excluding land agents from the Assembly. Probably as a result in 1839 Lord Selkirk's attorneys had him removed from his Point Prim farm. He was still active in the affairs of Highland emigrants and in 1846 & 1851: was President of the Highland Society of Prince Edward Island.[46]

* * *

Whilst the tacksmen of Coll were adjusting to the new conditions in the Isles, the nation's leaders were arguing over Parliamentary Reform. In 1830 the rulers of Britain were still landowning aristocrats. For example the Duke of Newcastle controlled nine constituencies and on occasions had evicted a tenant for voting the wrong way. He was astonished at his action being criticised and exclaimed: 'Have I not the right to do what I like with my own?'.[47]

Out of 513 English and Welsh members 415 represented cities and boroughs, but those boroughs were almost all in the hands of major landowners. The electorate had not changed with the demography of Britain, and was often absurd. The members of parliament for Rye and Dunwich represented six and fourteen electors respectively, whilst Manchester and Birmingham were not represented at all. The greatest absurdities were the 'pocket boroughs'. Most infamous of all was Old Sarum, where one elector was qualified to vote by the ownership of a ploughed field.[48] Scotland was little better. In 1790 Argyllshire had 43 voting freeholders and 49 in 1811.[49]

Demand for reform came to a head in 1830. Unemployment was rife, Luddite destruction of machines and poaching was getting out of control, whilst the ousting of King Charles X and the Ultras in France and his replacement by his cousin *Philippe Œgalité* heightened the tension in the United Kingdom. In the last election of the old unreformed Parliament the reformers: Whigs, Radicals, Irish and Scots swept all before them and the Tories were routed.

The result of the subsequent Reform Bill enfranchised those tenants-at-will paying £50 in rent.[50] In the Parish of Tiree & Coll there had previously been two electors – Alexander and Hugh Maclean of Coll. They were now joined[51] by Mr Neil Maclean the minister in Tiree and his cousin Neil 'tacksman of Crossapole' in Coll. Tiree had only one other new voter: 'Duncan Campbell tacksman or tenant of the Farm of Reef &c'. The other new voters on the Coll estate were 'Donald Campbell Esq tenant of the Farm of Breachachacoll', who was now living at Breacachadh; 'John Campbell Esq', who was tenant of his late father-in-law's farm of Gallanach and John Maclean, the assistant minister's namesake and brother-in-law who had moved from Grishipol to Arileod on the departure to Australia of the *John Dunscombe* family.[52]

There were five new voters on the Caolis & Cornaig estates.[53] John Campbell evidently found it more profitable to move to his wife's old home at Gallanach and let Cornaig to Archibald McInnes. He was already in financial difficulties and with his cousin Alexander Campbell of Caolis had in 1832 signed a bond for £400 secured on the Cornaig estate. Their creditor was Dr Donald MacArthur Minister of Kilninian & Kilmore in Mull, who in 1810 had succeeded his father Mr Archibald MacArthur.[54]

* * *

Juliet Alexa, Hugh Maclean younger of Coll's eldest child by his second marriage was born on 21st July 1826. Her 'Journal' written up before her father's death in 1861 gives a detailed insight into the family of Coll in the 1830s and 40s. She says that her father took a great interest in politics both 'general and local. He went with Sir Robert Peel and has always been a moderate conservative, though he was a supporter of the great Reform Bill.'[55]

At the end of his life Alexander Maclean of Coll evidently came to live at Drumfin. He came there at a time when the religious revival was at its height. Juliet Alexa describes 'a strange enthusiastic and fanatically religious child' from the nearby village where the people were frightfully superstitious and 'lived in huts with a fire in the middle of the floor, the smoke going up through the chimneyless thatch. None wore shoes or stockings and the boys no trousers. They were generally miserably poor'. This child was supposed to have 'no ends of "signs of Grace"' and was held up as a pattern to us . . .

> She used to tell me of wonderful fights she used to have with the Devil, every now and then, hand to hand active fights. And I used to feel perfectly certain that she only dreamt it all, though I was not so uncivil to say so. One day she rushed in to Grandpa's room, where I was sitting reading to him, and looking quite scared and much excited she told him that she had 'just met the Devil in the drawing-room and he was there now', Grand-father said, highly amused, 'What is he like?' 'Oh Sir', she said, 'He's got great horns and a long tail, and –'. Here grandpapa began to laugh. Mary terrified said, 'O Sir, Sir don't laugh'.[56]

James Robertson, who in March 1842 became Sheriff-Substitute of North Argyll, also kept a diary when he came to live in Tobermory.[57] He says that Mrs Maclean of Coll told him that Alexander Maclean of Coll was beloved by his people and at the end, when he could no longer talk:

> people on the estate used to come to Drumfin and wait until he was wheeled out in his easy chair to the lawn on fine summer evenings and form a circle round him, some of them standing at a little distance, and some leaning on the back of his chair. In this position they would stand for an hour looking at him without speaking a word and quietly take their departure. They appeared to be gratified and pleased by simply looking upon him, and the kind old Gentleman seemed to reciprocate their feeling and enjoy their presence. Mrs Maclean's phrase was: 'they evidently understood each other'.[58]

Alexander Maclean of Coll died on 10th April 1835. News of his death appeared in the newspapers as far away as Australia. One dated 12th September 1835 published an account by an anonymous correspondent, which announced:

DIED – On the 10th of April last, at Coll House in the Island of Mull, Alexander M'Lean, Esq, Laird of Coll, in the 84th year of his age – the venerable Parent of the Lady of Major M'Leod. The respect, in which the deceased was held by his numerous tenantry and friends, was truly indicated upon the melancholy occasion of his Funeral. The steamboat that conveyed the respected remains from the scene of his death to the vault in the family Chapel of Coll, was crowded with anxious multitudes eager to evince by their attendance the last sad offices that can be paid to decayed mortality. Every countenance bore the impression of deep – unfeigned sorrow, which, although tending the more firmly to impress on the minds of the surviving relatives – the extent of their irreparable loss – convinced them, that the deceased's worth was imprinted indelibly upon their hearts. The deceased went with honor to the grave. He lived in the hearts of all who had the pleasure of his acquaintance, and was justly esteemed the 'Father of his People'. He was the best of husbands – the most affectionate of fathers – an indulgent master – a liberal landlord – and as he lived a sincere Christian, so he died in the firm hope of his enjoying hereafter the rich rewards of a well spent life. The Deceased Laird is succeeded by his only surviving son, Hugh.[59]

Alexander had led a remarkable life. He had guided the family of Coll's destinies for half a century during one of the greatest periods of change in Hebridean history. Fortunately for him he was not to live to see the collapse of his 'improvements.' His policy to integrate his family into the English aristocracy was to have equally disastrous results.

Notes

1. *Clan Gillean*, 383.
2. He signed a number of legal papers there: Eg NAS. RD 5. 430. 78. 152 when on 15 March 1823 he signed Sir Hector's annuities to his nieces.
3. Lord Teignmouth *Sketches of the coasts and islands of Scotland* (1836), vol. 1, 44.
4. George Langlands & Son, Land Surveyors *Map of Argyllshire* (1801) shows Penmolloch where Quinish House now stands [*Acts of the Lords of the Isles 1336–1493* (1986), 236]. I have not yet discovered when Quinish House was built.
5. NAS. CH2. 70. 1. Marriages 24 October 1822.
6. His father was Hugh Campbell, tacksman of Killundine (1775 × 1796), who was 'the lawful son of … Alexander, brother german to Donald Campbell of Airds' [*Clan Campbell* vol. III, 40, 137 & 170]; in 1754 Alexander leased Killundine for a rent of £19, increased to £38 in 1773; in 1792 the Morvern estate was reorganised and Hugh had Laggan added to his tack at an increased rent of £98.8s.1d which in 1802 was raised to £160 [*Morvern Transformed*, 152–3].
7. John Maclaine of Ardow's wife Christian Campbell [NAS. Sasines of Argyll 1781–1830. 908] was probably the sister of Donald Campbell [*Morvern Transformed*, 46 &153].
8. Quinish 19 June 1848. DC to HG Ward Esq. MP, Secretary to the Admiralty, London [Mull Museum Donald Campbell's Letter Book.]
9. *New Statistical Account*, Tiree & Coll, 212–3.
10. NAS. CH2. 70. 1. 10 January 1826.
11. This was the Ardow estate which he purchased from Dr John Maclean of Ardow when the latter purchased Killundine [NAS. Sasines Argyll 1781–1830. 788 & 908]. John Maclean had been assistant surgeon of the 84th Regt. of Foot; in February 1821 he purchased the lands of Arivolchyne, Ardrioch & Duchorine from Eoin Maclachlan of Killiemore, residing at Laudle in Morvern; in June 1821 he purchased a feu disposition of Ardow from the trustees of the Duke of Argyll [ibid 11 & 55].

12. BCT. Donald Maclean, Eigg Island, 30 December 1809 to Alexander his son in Halifax. Charles's daughters were: Catherine (bapt. at Arinagour 5 June 1791) m. 6 June 1815 at Gallanach Hector Mackinnon, tacksman of Derrichuaig (d. 2 May 1837) with issue [BCP. Extract from the Journal of Mrs Margaret Maclean (née Mackinnon)]. Sibella (bapt. at Arinagour 17 January 1798) m at Gallanach in Coll 28 September 1828 Mr John Campbell of Cornaig (bapt. at Cornaig 11 July 1803). Isabella m. 5 February 1822 The Rev. Donald Maclean, Minister of Small Isles (ordained 1818) with issue.
13. He was to live until at least 1831 when his son Alexander was baptised [NAS. CH2. 70. 2. 12 May 1831].
14. Mull Museum Archives. Captain Donald Campbell's out letter book 14 May 1847].
15. BCT. Neil Maclean to Alexander (his brother) in Bermuda. Island of Coll, 29 October 1810.
16. BCT. Major-General CS Maclean CB, CIE, Shanklin, Isle of Wight, 25 November 1896 to Mrs Francis. This statement is confirmed by *Gradum Medicinae Doctoris in Academia . . . quae Edinburgh* (1846).
17. Major-General CS Maclean, Dean House, Ryde, Isle of Wight, 23 January 189 to CR Morison.
18. The Hon. Robert Hobart, Sec. of State for War & the Colonies 1801–4, Chancellor for the Duchy of Lancaster in 1805 & 1812, PMG 1806–7; d. 4 February 1816 [Burke's Peerage (1967), 377].
19. James Robertson's Journal. Friday 3 May 1844. I have to thank James Irvine Robertson for a copy of this journal.
20. In 1851 he conducted a special inquiry into the condition of the Western Highlands & Islands [*The Scottish Nation* vol. VII, 56–7].
21. Lachlan is in 1776 the 'of age' second son of Hector Maclean in Totamore. In 1801 he is described as 'of Arinagour' when at Grishipol he marries 'Ann Maclean from Lochaber'. They remain in Arinagour until 1809 when the family move to Arnabost. They remain there until after 1815 when they may have moved to Freslan. In 1816 Lachlan becomes a sessioner of the Coll Kirk Session and is still on it in 1835.NAS CH2. 70. 1 & 2]. He is not listed as a tenant in Freslan in 1836 as he was not paying rent. [NAS. RD 5. 604. 194. 9 January 1836] he is still in Freslan for the 1841 Census.
22. BCT. Coll Families Box File. Johnston Folder. John Johnston to HAC Maclean 29 April 1898.
23. Mull Museum Archives. Captain Donald Campbell's out letter book 14 May 1847; he had moved to Freslan by 1834 [NAS. CH2. 70. 2. 28 September 1834].
24. They are:
    1. The descendants of 'a grandson of the 4th Laird of Coll Eachan Mac Iain called *Neil Buidh Mac Gillechallum ic Eachain*':
        a. John Maclean in Arnabost m. in Arnabost 1 February 1792 Flory Maclean with issue.
        b. Murdoch Maclean tenant in Toraston. He was a tailor. In April 1793 he enlisted in Coll's company in the Breadalbane Fencibles; he was able to sign his name; in 1807 he became a sergeant in the Coll company of the Argyllshire Volunteers; m. Margaret McPhail with issue.
        c. Lachlan Maclean tenant in Mibost m. in Arnabost on 17 May 1809 Barbara Maclean with issue. He was presumably dead before 1841 when his widow and children were living at No. 4 Cliad.
    2. The descendants of 'Hector Roy 5th Laird [called] Lachlan mac Lachain s stout man of whom descended Lachlan Mac Neil ic Lachain at Ballyhough [who] had a son John Maclean father to:
        a. Hector Maclean at Grimsary m. 4 February 1834 at Grimsary Mary Maclean. He was dead by 6 January 1840 when his widow m. Roderick Macphaden. Both were absent at the time of the 1841 Census but her children were living at Kilbride with Christie Maclean a cottar aged 80, who is perhaps their maternal grandmother.
        b. Lachlan Maclean at Kilbride m. before 1809 in Ballyhough to Christian Macniven; in Ballyhough until 1818 and then to Kilbride where he is listed with 'others' as paying rent of £53 on 9 January 1836. He was dead by 1841 Census when his son Neil aged 20 is listed as 'farmer'.
    3. The grandson of descendants of Allan Roy at Feall 'who 'came out of the family of Coll about that time' i.e. late sixteenth century:
        a. John Maclean, miller at Cliad m. 2 August 1827 Janet Macdonald at Cornaig with issue; 1828 in Toraston; 1830 1834 miller at Cliad.

25. The 1841 Census says that he was then 35. He was therefore born in 1805–6. No Neil appears in the Baptismal Register. A son named Hugh was baptised on 15 November 1805. Either Neil was born earlier or his name was wrongly entered as 'Hugh' in the register.
26. NAS. Parish of Tyree & Coll *Census 1841* (551/21).
27. John N Macleod *Memorials of the Rev. Norman Macleod (Senior) DD of St Columbas* (Edinburgh, 1898).
28. *Gaelic Scotland*, 35.
29. *Memorials of the Rev. Norman Macleod (Senior DD) of St Columbas*, 85.
30. *An Teachdaire Gaelach* XIV. Aireamh. 1830, 44 & 67.
31. *An Teachdaire Gaelach* XXIII. Aireamh. 1831, 263.
32. He was the son of John Maclean in Arnabost [see note 20. 1a.]
33. A Maclean Sinclair *Na Bàird Leathanach*, The Maclean Bards (Charlottetown, 1900), 83.
34. BCT. Mr Neil Maclean, Island of Tiree, 10 November 1831 to Mrs Maclean, 21 Devonshire Place, Plymouth.
35. BCT. Mr Neil Maclean, Island of Tiree, 16 December 1833 to Mrs Maclean, 21 Devonshire Place, Plymouth.
36. NAS. CH2. 273. 4. Aros 3 May 1831.
37. Hugh Maclean younger of Coll & The Duke's Chamberlain Colonel D Campbell.
38. NAS. CH2. 273. 4. Tobermory 7 May 1833.
39. BCP. Neil Maclean, Island of Tyrie, 3 July 1834 to Mrs Maclean, 21 Devonshire Place, Plymouth.
40. Una or Hannah. She was a widow on 4 April 1799 when she married Allan Maclean who was then in Acha. He was a sessioner of the Coll Kirk Session from 18 July 1813 to 13 July 1831.
41. *The Independent*. Saturday 9th March 1833.
42. Mitchell Library Sidney.
43. Bruce D Macleod, a descendant of Major Donald says that the family 'did not fail' in Tasmania, but left because 'his sons could not get good land so they moved to the mainland as Squatters'. *WHN&Q*, No. IX (January 1979), 22–26.
44. *The Independent* Launceston VD Land Saturday 1 November 1834; her elder sister was married to Donald Campbell, Caolis.
45. CD Rankin to his brother-in-law Donald Morison 25 February 1832. Public Archives of PEI. Accession 2716. Item No. 2. 14 July 2005.
46. DCB, vol. VIII, Rankin, Coundully.
47. *Wellington – Pillar of State*, 263.
48. Charlotte M Waters *An Economic History of England* (1949), 432–5.
49. *Political State of Scotland at Michaelmas* (1812), 14–17.
50. *Wikipedia Free Encyclopedia*. Reform Act 1832.
51. NAS. GD 174. 1973.
52. One of the reasons for his move was subsidence at the 'White House', which had caused the east gable wall to crack.
53. Caolis: Charles Campbell, John Kennedy, Donald Macdonald & Neil Mackinnon; Cornaig: Archibald McInnes.
54. BCP. Cornaig papers. Letter of 20 May 2003 from Hilary Peel, Creag a'Croman, Salen, Aros, Isle of Mull who I have to thank for this information.
55. BCP. 'The Journal of Juliet Alexa Maclean (married Ashe Smijth-Windham 1859)', Part 1, 1. I have to thank the late Mève Windham for a copy of this journal.
56. Ibid, 7.
57. Joseph Buist Loudon (ed) *The Diary of James Robertson, Sheriff Substitute of Tobermory 1842–1846* (2001).
58. James Robertson's Journal 5 August 1844.
59. *The Chronicle* 12 September 1835.

Part VIII

The Hungry Thirties and Forties

Chapter Forty-Eight

The first Crisis and the 1841 Census

Alexander Maclean of Coll's death in April 1835 was marked by cold wet weather. The following month was also wet and crops were sown in the worst possible conditions. The summer, however, turned out dry and warm, and where the land was well drained the harvest was no worse than usual. On wetland, which made up three-quarter of land under tillage in the Western Highlands and Islands, the crop was much below normal.

The potato crop was also affected by disease, whilst the wet late harvest prevented corn from ripening and made the storage of those potatoes that could be saved problematical. As a result the people of the Hebrides met the spring of 1836 with greatly diminished supplies.

The weather continued to be vile. In February 1836 snowfall was unusually deep. It continued to fall, alternating with rain and sleet, until the end of April preventing the people working on wetland from getting their crops into the ground before the dry weather arrived in the middle of May. Because there had been low prices for their cattle the previous autumn, farmers had hung on to their livestock, which now quickly eat up what few potatoes were left, leaving even fewer to be sown. Many of the seed potatoes were also diseased.

The short spell of dry weather in May was succeeded by non-stop rain throughout the rest of the summer and autumn, only to be followed by severe frosts in October. The result was disaster. Not only had the crops failed to ripen but the wet weather made it impossible to bring in the peats. The people of the Hebrides had to face a winter without adequate food or heat. Unless supplies were brought from the mainland the people were going to starve.[1] In the event disaster was averted. It was achieved by the combined effort of government, landlords and Lowland charitable agencies.[2] Much of the latter's efforts were inspired by Mr Neil's friend the Rev Dr Norman Macleod, Minister of St Columba's in Glasgow, whose efforts earned him the sobriquet *Caraid nan Gaidheal*, 'Friend of the Gael'.[3]

* * *

The fall in cattle prices, which had followed the end of the War, was in 1826 briefly reversed. This reversal may well have encouraged Dr Lachlan to take his lease of the Isle of Rum. The transformation of Rum into a profitable stock farm was going to demand investment and it was recognised that although a good deal of land could be brought into good pasture, land at Kinloch and Kilmory ... 'a considerable expense must necessarily be incurred in improving the said land, building office houses at Kinloch, shepherds' houses and fanks in different parts of the island, and also a tup park, and in making drains and stone dyke inclosures'. It was therefore agreed that at the end of the tack Dr Lachlan should be paid up to £1,500 for his improvements, provided that the Laird approved them in writing before they began. At the end of the tack the landlord was obliged to take the whole stock of sheep, black cattle and horses that were on the island.[4]

Dr Lachlan agreed to pay an annual rent of £600 for the first two years of his tack and £800 thereafter.[5] He failed to do so. The rise in cattle prices in 1826 proved to be an aberration and they continued their slide, as did the value of sheep. As a result one of Hugh's first actions after the death of his father was to sue Dr Lachlan in the Court of Session. Eventually the dispute was settled out of court. Hugh agreed to reduce the rent of Rum from Whitsunday 1826 to 1834 to £400 per annum. From Whitsunday 1834 to the end of the current lease the rent was to return to £800. It was also agreed that Hugh's process of sequestration was withdrawn; Dr Lachlan's claim that Hugh had failed to deliver sheep as promised was also withdrawn; both sides were to pay their own costs and Dr Lachlan had 'that very day' to pay £1,000 for the outstanding Rum rents. He did so at the Falkirk Tryst on 11th October 1836.[6]

The dispute may have been settled, but the cost of the lawsuit is said to have been the cause of Dr Lachlan's bankruptcy. In 1839 he left Rum penniless 'much worse off than the comfortable people he turned out of Rum 13 years previously'. He went to Australia.[7]

Dr Lachlan blamed Hugh for his failure. His son was to write of Hugh that:

I cannot say that I feel any sympathy with the latter, whose behaviour was disgraceful. I hold his father's memory on the other hand in the greatest veneration for Alexander was an honourable man and a true friend to my grandfather. In fact he treated him like a son.[8]

* * *

Despite worries about its future, kelpmaking was profitable until 1830. It survived the early tariff reforms without too much difficulty, and in 1825 prices were still as high as £10 to £15 per ton. The following year, in Orkney at least, what was probably the largest amount of kelp ever was made there.[9] However, in 1830 the reduction of the remaining duties saw a collapse in the price of kelp which was both as sudden as it was terminal. The industry never recovered.

The Gorten-Acha-Freslan-Kilbride-Hyne area had by 1836 a population of not less than 210 people. It comprised of 36 households and was dominated by Macleans. Most could claim to be relatives of the chief. Macleans owned 23 houses and Mackinnons 7. There were 6 with other surnames. The dominance of Macleans is even more pronounced when the number of tenants is counted. Out of a total of 18 tenants, 14 were Macleans & 4 were Mackinnons. In addition there was a miller at Acha named Smeaton, who was from Monzie in Perthshire. In 1836 he had replaced a Maclean as miller. There was also a teacher at Arivichvarich, a pendicle of Kilbride. He was also a Maclean.

It was an intensely Gaelic-speaking community, which included several people who made songs. One was the Cooper. Some of his songs have survived.[10] Alexander Maclean Sinclair says that the Cooper was 'a cheerful companion'. He was also an expert seaman, perhaps a smuggler,[11] and, as we have seen he liked girls.

Another composer of satirical songs was Lachlan Freslan's daughter Uney. She admitted that she had composed part of a song about John Maclean, also in Freslan.[12] He responded by spreading a story that she 'lay several nights with John Mackinnon in Gorten'. He did so because of the 'provocation he had received on account of her song'.

The first Crisis and the 1841 Census

In 1836 Lachlan Maclean 'and others' in Kilbride were paying a rent of £53. Lachlan was dead by the time of the 1841 Census. The 1841 Census was the first decennial census in Scotland. It lists each member of a household by age, occupation and where he or she was born. It and its successors are invaluable aids for studying the population of the Coll estate.

Lachlan Maclean in Kilbride's younger son Neil succeeded him. Neil, 20, is described as a 'farmer', and in 1841 had his mother and younger siblings living with him. Their farm was made up of one house and 4 out buildings. In 1841 Lachlan's eldest son John, 30, was also a 'farmer' in Kilbride. He had a dwelling house and 3 unoccupied out buildings. He had married outwith the area, to the daughter of a Maclean tenant in Totronald.

This was not the last involvement of this family in Kilbride. Lachlan's elder brother Hector was a tenant in Grimsary. In 1834 he had married, probably for the second time, to a Mary Maclean from Kilbride. Whilst still at Grimsary they had rapidly produced three children, the last was baptised in 1837. Hector must have died soon afterwards for in 1840 his widow married a Roderick MacPhaden. Mary and her new husband left the Island before the 1841 Census, leaving her three children with Christie Maclean, an 80 year-old cottar in Kilbride. They lived in one building with no out houses.

There were in all seven tenants in Kilbride listed in the 1841 Census. All were Macleans. Kilbride on this occasion includes Hyne, where Hector Maclean, the original 1794 settler, is still mentioned as being the tenant in 1836.[13] He had one occupied house and 2 out buildings. Hector's son Donald also married away from the area. His wife Mary was the daughter of John Mackinnon in Grimsary, a member of the Kirk Session. They settled at Hyne, at first as cottars, and then in 1835 as tenants. Donald's wife is described as a widow in May 1838, when their son also named Donald was baptised. In 1841 she was a cottar in Lagmore, where her father had moved after he left Grimsary. Hector Maclean's son Hugh is also described in 1834 as a crofter in Lagmore, when his first child was baptised. By 1840 he is a tenant in Kilbride.[14]

The largest farm in Kilbride consisted of one occupied house and 6 unoccupied buildings. The tenant living there in 1841 was a 75 year-old widower called Donald Maclean. He originally came from Feall and is perhaps another son of Allan Roy. At the time of the Census Donald was living there with his three unmarried sons and two female servants. Their house, which still stands, is roofless. It is a particularly well-constructed house with two small windows facing the sea. It is, by Coll standards, a substantial house.[15] Old Donald had previously lived, for at least a couple of years at Acha, perhaps as a sub-tenant, before in 1800 coming to Kilbride. On 23 May 1839 his youngest son John married Mary, the daughter of John Maclean the current tenant of Acha. John was dead, perhaps drowned, before 1841. His widow and her two children moved back to Acha, where she later is described as a house servant to her widowed mother.[16]

There were frequent movements between the tenants in the area. For example John[17] & Flory Maclean came originally from Grimsary to Kilbride in 1800. By 1834 John was tenant of Acha Farm, having succeeded *An Cubair Colach* when the latter moved to Lagmore. John and Flory had 3 sons and 2 daughters, who all married their neighbours' children. Cut off as they were from much of the rest of the Island, the children of tenants in the Gorten-Hyne area often married each other's children. Sometimes they first lived as cottars on their father or father-in-law's croft before succeeding him or moving to a better situation in the area. It was probably an inward-looking yet vibrant community who enjoyed the boom years and tightened their belts when the crops failed and the kelp price collapsed.

* * *

In 1837 the Government sent Robert Grahame, Professor of Botany at Glasgow University, to investigate the distress that had occurred in the Highlands and Islands. He reported that the islands Tiree and Coll 'are portions of the country which have most materially suffered, not so much from the influence of one or two bad seasons, as from the loss of the kelp trade, and from the excess of the population which that manufacture had gradually engendered'.[18]

Mr Neil Maclean goes into further detail in his report in the *New Statistical Account*. He says that the manufacture of kelp 'may now be spoken of as one of those things which have been'. None had been made since 1837. At the height of the kelp boom Coll had produced 150 tons a year and employed 140 adults. The cost of production varied from £2 to £3.10s, the cost depended on 'the ruggedness of the shore'. 80 tons were made in 1837. Since then the manufacture had entirely ceased.[19]

He blamed the present crisis on the increase in population, which

> had been accelerated... by the system of crofting, or dividing the land into minute portions – a system adopted at first with the humane intention of accommodating as many poor families as possible, but which afforded only a very temporary relief, and I fear has been the means of increasing the evil. It is no uncommon practice with such tenants to subdivide their lots of land among their families, when they grow up; and thus a croft originally designed for the maintenance of one family, and perhaps scarcely sufficient for that purpose, is frequently portioned among two or three, and the whole are reduced to poverty.

Mr Neil is probably speaking of Tiree, where overcrowding was endemic, but he could equally well have described the situation in the Gorten-Hyne area of Coll. Mr Neil goes on to say that: 'Emigration seems to be the great resource; and the proprietors must either assist them to accomplish this measure or apply to the Legislature to hold out encouragement and aid.'[20]

Not all those who left the Island at this time went abroad: John Maclean the former miller at Cliad went to Glasgow.[21]

*   *   *

On the other side of the world there were changes that were to affect the future of a great many people from the Coll estate. By the late 1820s vacant property in Van Diemen's Land was in short supply. Tasmania at this time, in spite of its perfect climate, fertility and beauty, was a detestable place to live in because of the convict settlement. In the remoter districts in the early thirties, a door was never opened after dark without the householder having a shotgun in hand. The only assistance obtainable was from indentured convicts, and an atmosphere of crime and violence pervaded the countryside.

There was also trouble from the Aborigines. As we have seen, in 1829 Colin Campbell returned to Mull for an extended break. In his absence his brother Alexander, known as 'Captain Campbell', rented his brother's farm at Whitehills. While he was there he 'took part in an expedition against the blacks, who had given much trouble to the settlers and one of his shepherds was speared by them'. In his memoirs, dictated to his daughter and published with his obituary, it is stated that:

> At Norfolk Plains Captain Campbell was placed in charge of 15 ticket-of-leave men and prisoners and they started to for the Western Tier, camping at night near the head of the Great Lake, under pouring rain. Another night was spent at the homestead of Mrs Patterson, mother of John Hunter Patterson, now in Riverina. Eventually the party arrived at Pittwater,

and a line of sentries being placed 80 yards apart. Captain Campbell was then ordered, under Captain Moriarty, to scour inside the lines as far as East Bay. No blacks were seen there, but several other detachments met at Prosser's Plain, and great difficulty was experienced in obtaining provisions. Captain Campbell went with Batman to the headquarters at Pittwater... While there he was introduced to Governor Arthur, who spoke very kindly to him and promised that if he were to recommend any of the men under him for indulgence, he would see that they received the benefit of it. Four or five of the men afterwards obtained their tickets-of-leave, and one became a wealthy man in Melbourne.[22]

Entrepreneurs in Launceston were now looking across the Bass Strait for new opportunities. Europeans had not yet occupied New Holland, as the southern coastline of New South Wales was then known. The only exceptions were seasonal visits by whalers and sealers. The Government in Sydney was opposed to allowing Europeans to settle in New Holland. However, in late 1834 an illegal settlement was made at Portland Bay. Its aim was to exploit the extensive grazings to the west of Western Port and the Colonial Government in Sydney reluctantly accepted the inevitable and set up the necessary administration to run the new colony.

The Macleods of Talisker were among the first settlers in Van Diemen's Land to decide that the game was not worth the candle and move across the Bass Strait to Victoria. They settled in the Port Philip area. Their tenant Allan Maclean, formerly of Arileod in Coll followed them. He became a squatter in his own right at Strathallan.

News of the opportunities in Victoria must have reached Coll, for when Dr Charles Boyter[23] visited the Island in 1837 he found several potential emigrants. In the past, when people from the Hebrides had emigrated, they had chosen to go to Nova Scotia and Prince Edward Island. The situation there had, however, changed. In 1837 the Colonial Office decided to extend the bounty available to emigrants to Australia to include agricultural labourers and married couples, whilst political disturbances in Canada, and a financial panic in the United States, discouraged emigration to North America.[24]

* * *

On 27th September 1837 seventy-two people from Coll, plus a further eleven from the Small Isles, sailed on the *Brilliant* from Tobermory for Australia. They sailed via the Cape of Good Hope and on the 20th January 1838 docked at Port Jackson.[25] The emigrants from Coll represented a cross-section of people on the Island. Of the twelve heads of household all, save two, were in their thirties: six were farm servants; four were tradesmen; and two were tenants.

The farm workers had a varied standard of education: two could read and write; two could neither read nor write; two could read a little but could not write; all had good characters, certified by the Minister and in one case by Hugh Maclean of Coll himself.

Lachlan Mackay, the blacksmith, his wife Anne Stewart and his four sons could speak a little English. His two elder daughters, who had both been housemaids, one in Glasgow and the other in Coll, could both speak English. The youngest daughter who had also been a housemaid in Coll could 'hardly speak English'. Their good character was vouched for by Hugh Maclean of Coll. Lachlan Mackay said he was 45. When he was a boy, he had served for a short time in 79th Foot, but had been invalided out of the army.

Allan Maclean, the failed miller at Acha, is described as a 'boat builder and carpenter'. He had evidently learnt his trade from his father John Maclean, who had also been a boat builder in Coll.

He could read and write English. His eldest daughter, 20, who had been in service in Glasgow could also speak English. The next daughter, 18, who had not been in service, could only speak a little English, whilst the third daughter, aged 8, could not speak any at all. The three sons, 12–16, were all attending the school.

Another tradesman was Hugh Mackinnon. He was a 'joiner and house carpenter' in Grimsary. He had probably learnt his trade in Glasgow, as his wife was from there. Her father is described as 'a rope maker of Glasgow'. Both could read and write. Also from Grimsary was Hector Mackinnon. He was a ploughman and his wife a dairymaid. He too could read and write. These two Mackinnons were probably brothers and the sons of John Mackinnon the member of Coll Kirk Session. Mr Archibald Nicol, the Assistant-Minister in Coll gave both 'very good' character references. Also sailing on the *Brilliant* was a dairymaid named Julia Mackinnon, 27. She is stated to be the daughter of John Mackinnon, and is probably the sister of Hugh and Hector Mackinnon, although she does not appear in the Baptisimal Register.

The two tenants[26] who left the Island at this time were married to sisters. Both came from well-established families in Coll. The wives had both been off the Island in service in the Glasgow area. They had married away from Gorten where they were born. The only other family from the Gorten-Hyne area, who chose to emigrate at this time, was that of Donald, the son of Donald Maclean, the former cooper in Bute. Donald Junior's wife, Effy Maclean was the daughter of John Maclean the tenant at Acha. Mr Neil gave both good character references. He stated that they were members of the Church of Scotland. Both could read, presumably in Gaelic, but could not write. At the time he emigrated Donald was as a cottar on his father-in-law's farm. He is listed as a 'farm servant' on the passenger list when the *Brilliant* landed at Port Jackson.

* * *

One family who appear to have gone to Australia at their own expense was that of Alexander Maclean, *An Cubair Colach*. The bard himself died in 1836 and the family left Coll before the 1841 Census. In about 1842 the family, including the Cooper's sons John, Allan and Robertson sailed for Australia.[27]

These emigrants from Coll were, like the earlier tacksmen, just the people the Island could not afford to lose. This was a general complaint throughout the Highlands, and those organising the emigration came into conflict with the relief committees, who objected to the 'cream of the Highland population being shipped abroad, leaving only poverty-stricken, aged, and destitute people in the area'.[28] This was as exageration, as far as Coll was concerned, but there is little doubt it was those with initiative who left on the *Brilliant*.

Several other families left Coll at this time. Some of them settled in Glasgow. Among them was John Maclean the former miller in Cliad.[29] The Macleans of Fiosgaradh may have gone there too or to Greenock. They had certainly left the Island by 1838 when a new tenant moved into Fiosgaradh.[30]

* * *

On 25th November 1837 Hugh Maclean of Coll complained to Lord Glenelg, Secretary of State for the Colonies[31], that his people who had gone to Australia that year had at the most only three weeks notice between their being chosen, and the day they sailed. This lack of organisation put both the emigrants and himself to a great deal of expense. 'Respectable Emigrants connected with land' he wrote require at least 'six months notice' to dispose of their stock and say their good byes.

In another letter of the same date to Sir George Grey[32] Hugh explained that:

I am a Highland Proprietor, who having lost one third of his income by the annihilation of kelp manufacture, have consequently a large surplus population, which must either ruin me, starve or emigrate. These poor people naturally look to me for help. I am utterly unable to afford – and I feel most keenly the responsibility of recommending their going into almost certain destruction of convict contact and example. They are themselves aware of the great danger and importune me for location apart.

Instead of allowing them to mix with the convicts he proposed, without expense to government, to settle a great number of our poor countrymen in a location apart in Australia. By it the cruelty of sending them into the certain contamination of a convict population will in a great measure be avoided, and themselves set down at once in comparative comfort in a manner congenial to their feelings under pastoral Superintendence of their own choice, all points so justly dear to every Highlander.

Hugh argued in his letter to Lord Glenelg that as his people had been 'rendered destitute chiefly by the acts of Government for the greater benefit of trade'. He believed that the least the Government could do was to allow them the value of the bounty that the Government had already provided. He went on to say:

I do not wish to interfere with Emigration or [?] Colonial Bounty further than as obtaining an equal share of what is offered to all enables me to affect a great good without expence to the British Government.

He continues: 'Considering the Cause & its probable effects . . . I do not think it unreasonable to expect that your Lordship will obtain for me the requisite land in lieu of Colonial Bounty to Emigrants.

3000 is the number embraced in my calculations, to be carried out 300 each year for 10 years. 67 families of 4.5 averaging 3 adults: £18 present cost to government.

$67 \times 3 - 200$ adults at £18 = 3,600 each year = in 10 years	£36,000
Interest in 10 years at 4%	6,400
Cost of bare transport of 3,000 in 10 years	£42,400

12 months rations at 1/– per day = £18.5s – exceeding cost of passage. On these data my proposition to government, is that in 5 years £42,000, (£8,400 per annum) be advanced by them for transport (as at present to Australia), 12 months rations for 1,500 persons. On my engagement to repay the whole expense at above rates and carry out 1500 more persons within the succeeding 5 years.

Colonial government to sell to me 100 acres for each family carried out and 20,000 for private stock, giving the price as Bounty to Emigration land to be accessible to sea in the unsettled district (say) about Port Philip.

In execution of this plan it would be my desire and interest to accelerate to [?] utmost the rate of Emigration it need be limited only by the ability of the Colony to furnish rations, it is not too much to expect that after 3 years it may be continued at 600 per annum.

'The increased value of land occupied' he wrote 'and the rapid increase of stock would be ample security against any possible loss'. He concludes: 'Should this offer or any modification of it be likely to meet your Lordship's approbation I am ready to go to London. Not a moment may be lost without danger of losing a whole year. Emigrant Ships must proceed direct to the point of debarkation on the proposed Colony ... Another cause of haste is that the Highland Destitution Committee have a large surplus applicable to emigration and desire to wait the result of this application for their guidance in distribution'.[33]

Hugh's plan did not fit in with Government policy for the disposal of wasteland in Australia and Grey's comments on Hugh's plan are damning. He writes:

> Reduced to plain terms, Mr Maclean's proposal is that Government should give him a very large tract of land and should advance him £42,400 in the conveyance of labourers to it, upon condition of his engaging to repay the amount, if this scheme answer as well as he feels sure it would ... It also seems pretty evident that unless Government be prepared to give away an extensive district and lend 40–50 thousand pounds for its improvement to, any respectable proprietor who may apply for this purpose ... is to be extended to all who are willing to enter in the speculation, it must be a well stocked Treasury that is to stand the drain. In short the proposal seems obviously one that will not bear a moment's investigation, and the only difficulty is that the objections are so many. And each so sufficient, that it is hard to know which to put forward without doing injustice to the others of equal importance. Whatever be the reasons, however, that may be assigned, they would, I believe be connected with the administration of the Public lands, and as that is a branch of the service kept under the immediate direction of the Secretary of State, Lord Glenelg would probably think it wise that the answer to Mr Maclean would proceed from the Colonial Department and not from me.[34]

Glenelg agreed and an opportunity to solve the problems of the people on the Coll estate and Hugh's own financial crisis was lost.

* * *

Glenelg would not help Hugh, but he was prepared to help his own relations.[35] As we have seen his cousin Jane Eliza Grant had married Captain John Leyburn of the 43rd Foot, John Maclean of Cornaig's son. And when John Leyburn exchanged into the 50th Foot and went on to the half-pay list, he went to live at Lochletter in Glenurquhart. Lochletter was part of Jane Eliza's brother, Patrick Grant of Redcastle's estate.

By 1837 Patrick Grant of Redcastle was in financial difficulties. Glenelg came to his rescue and offered him an influential position in Australia. However, Grant chose this moment to make an attack on the government. Even Glenelg's family affection could not fail to notice this attack and Grant had to be content with becoming a police magistrate at West Maitland in the wilds a hundred miles north of Sydney.[36]

The post of Principal Superintendent of Convicts intended for Redcastle was still vacant. Glenelg decided to keep it in the family and it was offered to John Leyburn. He accepted and set sail with his family on the *Earl Durham*. He took up his new job on 31st August 1837. He also purchased land on the south coast of NSW near Broulee. He named his new property *Glen Duart*.[37]

* * *

The first Crisis and the 1841 Census

In 1836 Alexander Maclean Campbell,[38] 'Captain Campbell', also crossed the Bass Strait. He had been recruited to manage the Portland Bay whaling station, and in 1837, when a new whaling station was set up at further along the coast at Port Fairy, he became its manager.

When the Arileod Macleans settled at Strathallan, Donald, the youngest son, took up land for himself in 1836 on the Darebin Creek. The eldest son, Malcolm, remained with his father. The sailor brothers Hugh and Neil continued to work the *John Dunscombe* and traded throughout the Southern Hemisphere. On at least one occasion they sailed to Valparaiso, on another to Java. In 1835, whilst looking for a cargo in New Zealand they had the misfortune to run aground in the little harbour of Opotki, in the Bay of Plenty. Maoris surrounded the schooner in their canoes and seized the *John Dunscombe* and its contents. The crew, with the exception of the cabin boy, was kept as prisoners for nine months. The cabin boy, who escaped made his way overland through hostile Maoris territory to Auckland.

News of Hugh and Neil's mishap reached Scotland and on 24th February 1835 the Rev. A Maclaine, Minister of Ardnamurchan wrote to the Earl of Aberdeen, who was now Secretary of State for the Colonies. In his letter he included an extract from a letter from his brother J Maclaine of the merchantile house *Maclaine Wilson & Co*, Batavia:

> A few days ago a respectable looking young man called at my office and introduced himself as a Mull man. His name is Morrison. He appears to have had a good education and is now settled at Hobart Town VD Land and I believe in good circumstances.

He goes on to say that 'Hugh Maclean and his brother Neill who, after visiting Java, had gone on to New Zealand, where they had been captured by Maoris'. Hugh and Neill Maclean he explains are natives of the Isle of Coll. 'Morrison is a native of Mull and an acquaintance and friend of the unfortunate captives'.

Maclaine continues that in Hugh Maclean's character

> there was a remarkable combination of steady prudence, great enterprise [and] kind and honourable feeling. After having established himself comfortably in VDL he returned to his native island and purchased a vessel, manned her chiefly with his own brothers, bold and hardy isles men and conveyed his parents and whole family to his residence in the colony. He then betook himself to the traffic with the Dutch settlements and the other islands in those seas in the course of which he fell into the hands of the savages of New Zealand. The fate of this young man and his brother emits deep feeling in this part of the Highlands, where they are known and respected – his aged parents and family in VDL have lost their chief support.[39]

In the meantime the New Zealand authorities had sent a Royal Navy vessel to Opitiki to rescue the captives,

> but the Maoris became aware ... that such an order had been given, and hastily got the schooner afloat. With the help of the sailors they ... patched the remaining sails, gave them sufficient provisions for the voyage, and the *John Dunscome* had the luck to make Aukland harbour safely. The brothers had won the confidence and affection of the Maori chief so completely that on their leaving he entrusted two orphan nieces to their care to be educated

in the European fashion. The McLeans discharged the duties thrust upon them faithfully, but the indignation of [their mother] Anne was great ... when she found herself acting as nurse maid to these 'niggers'.

Hugh's luck now ran out. A few years after his adventure in New Zealand he had purchased a ship called *Britannia*. As he could not insure her in Melbourne he sailed in her for Sydney, and was presumably wrecked during a fog on his way north. It was believed that he managed to get ashore on the inhospitable Gippsland coast 'among other proofs the initials HML were found cut on a tree; but that was all, the degraded aborigines alone knew the rest'.[40]

Notes

1. Edinburgh 6 May 1837. Mr Robert Graham to Mr Fox Maule. *First Report of the Select Committee on Emigration, Scotland* (1846), Appendix, No. 1.
2. TM Devine *The Great Highland Famine* (1988), 27.
3. *Gaelic Scotland*, 35.
4. NAS. RD5. 526. 733.
5. NAS. RD5. 526. 733.
6. NAS. RD5. 570. 728. The detailed papers for this case are no longer in West Register House.
7. John A Love *Rum* (2001), 128 where he quotes a letter from James Maclean, plumber Greenock to the Rev. Alexander Maclean Sinclair dated 31 March 1897.
8. BCP. Brolas File. Letter Major-General CS Maclean to CR Morison. I have to thank Dr Niel Morison for allowing me to make a photo copy of this undated letter.
9. *Kelp-making in Orkney* (1983), 94–5.
10. *Na Bàird Leathanach* vol. II, 8–16.
11. The little port *Acasaid falachaidh* 'the secret Harbour' in Farsachd, where he is said to have hidden when the excise men were after him is still known in Coll.
12. He is probably the Bailie's eldest son by his second marriage who was baptised at Freslan on 12 February 1819.
13. In 1841 his wife was dead and he is the 75 year old farmer there employing one male servant. He was probably a son of Allan Roy at Feall.
14. He also had 1 dwelling house and 2 out buildings.
15. By 1851 old Donald Maclean was dead and his three sons were running the farm. They are likely to be the 'Bachelors' of Coll tradition.
16. NAS. 1851 Census.
17. He had probably been born in Arnabost and was the son of Donald Ban and Mary Mackinnon. Donald is remembered in his great-great-grandson's sloinneadh *Aonghas MacNeil ich Neil ich Ian ich Donal Ban*. Angus was born in 1892 and in 1928 became Professor of Religious Education at the Theological School of St Lawrence University in Canada. He was the author of several books including *God and the Devil at Seal Cove* (1976).
18. *First Report of the Select Committee on Emigration, Scotland* (1841), 87.
19. *New Statistical Account of Scotland*, vol., 216.
20. *New Statistical Account of Scotland*, vol., 222.
21. *WHN&Q* series 2, No. 12 (May 1994), 20 & no.13 (February 1995), 21–2. He is among the descendants of the Macleans of Coll mentioned by Allan Crossapol. Greenock was another lowland centre to receive migrants from Coll and at the time of the 1851 Census there were 12 people there [8 males and 4 females] who said that they came from Col. 159 came from Mull. [RD Lobban 'The Migration of Highlanders

into Lowland Scotland (c. 1750–1890) with particular reference to Greenock' (Edinburgh University Unpublished PhD Thesis 1969), Vol. 2, 450]. One family who left were the Macleans in Fiosgaradh. As we have seen they had been a prominent family in Coll. They probably went to Greenock. In 1836 Allan Maclean the former sergeant in the Bradalbane Fencibles is still listed as the tenant in Fiosgaradh. He was either dead or had given up his tenancy by 1841 when another unrelated Maclean was tenant. Allan's family had probably left the island. His nephew Lachlan, Sergeant Hugh's eldest son was probably a joint tenant of Fiosgaradh with Allan. He evidently failed and by 1834 was a cottar in Freslan. In 1851 his family was receiving support from the Highland Destitution Committee. [NAS. CH2. 70.2]. He sailed to Australia in 1852 on the *Flora Macdonald* and landed at Portland, Victoria [I have to thank Beverley Koschitzke, PO Box 336, Warracknabeal, Victoria 3393 in a letter dated 7 November 2006 for this information about her ancestor].

22. Extract from *The Argus*. Tuesday 27 May 1890. I have to thank Captain Campbell's descendant Brian Barbreck Campbell for a photocopy of this article.
23. In 1835 he was appointed Colonial Emigration Agent in Scotland by the New South Wales authorities [David S Macmillan *Scotland and Australia 1788–1850* (1967), 272].
24. *Scotland and Australia 1788–1850*, 266.
25. Archives Office of New South Wales: Report of a ship arrived in Port Jackson 20 January 1838. Copy made by Margery Christine Foster in January 1976. I have to thank the late Betty Macdougall for a photocopy of this paper.
26. They were John Maclean, tenant at Ballyhough and John MacPhaden at Clabach. Their wives were Catherine & Mary Mackinnon the daughters of John Mackinnon tenant in Gorten. They had both been in service in the Glasgow area.
27. A. Maclean Sinclair *Na Bàird Leathanach* (Charlottetown, 1900), 8; Crossapol Graveyard.
28. *Scotland and Australia 1788–1850*, 278.
29. *WHN&Q* series 2. No. 12 (May 1994), 20 & No. 13 (February 1995), 21–2. His ancestor 'Allan Roy at Feall came out of the family of Coll' in the mid-sixteenth century.
30. NAS. CH2. 70. 2. Coll Baptisms 16 February 1838; Allan Maclean the former sergeant in the Coll Company of the Argyll Volunteers is probably the Allan Maclean who is listed as being responsible for the rent of 'Fisgara' in 1836 [NAS. RD 5. 194]; Sergeant Hugh, who was last mentioned as being in Fiosgaradh in 1819 [NAS. CH2. 70. 2. Coll Baptisms 14 August 1819]. His eldest son Lachlan probably succeeded him as the tenant. He is noted as being in Fiosgaradh from 1828–32 [NAS. CH2. 70. 2. Coll Marriages 10 September 1828]; [NAS. CH2. 70. 2. Coll Baptisms]; His wife was employed as a handloom weaver. Lachlan, the youngest of Allan & Hugh's brothers, was a crofter in Fiosgaradh from 1814 to 1835 [NAS. CH2. 70. 2. Coll Baptisms]. In March 1839 Lachlan's daughter Mary gave birth to an illegitimate daughter named Catherine Gillows [NAS. CH2. 70. 2. Coll Baptisms]. Catherine's father John Gillows was a servant in Strathaven, so it is likely that Mary had been a servant there too. Lachlan and his family had left Coll by the time of the 1841 Census.
31. Lord Glenelg, a title in the peerage of the United Kingdom, conferred in 1835 on the Right Hon. Charles Grant, eldest of 3 sons of Charles Grant, for many years MP for Inverness-shire. Born in 1783 and educated at Cambridge, his lordship was in 1807, called to the bar at Lincoln's Inn. Elected, in that year, MP for the Fortrose burghs, he continued to represent them till 1818, when he was chosen for Inverness-shire, for which county he sat till raised to the peerage in 1835. From December 1813 to March 1819 he was a lord of the treasury, and from August 1819 to December 1821, chief secretary for Ireland. In 1823, he became vice-president of the board of trade, and in September 1827 president of that board, and treasurer of the Navy, but ceased to hold these offices in June 1828. In December 1830 he was made president of the board of control, and continued so till November 1834. From April 1835 to January 1839 he held the office of secretary of state for the colonies. [*The Scottish Nation*, vol. V, 314]. His sister Maria was married to Patrick Grant of Redcastle, whose sister married Captain John Leyburn Maclean late 43 Foot. Dr Lachlan Maclean of Rum began his career as a sheep farmer by managing Lord Glenelg's estate.

32. The Rt. Hon. Sir George, 2nd Bart., PC., GCB., b. 11 May 1799, who was called to the Bar in 1826, became JAG and filled various high ministerial offices. He was Chancellor of the Duchy of Lancaster in 1841; Secretary of State for the Home Department from 1846–52 and again from 1855–58; Secretary of State for the Colonies from 1854–1855; again Chancellor of the Duchy of Lancaster in April 1859 and Secretary of State for the Home Dept. 1861–66. He represented Devonport 1832–47; Northumberland 1847–52 and Morpeth 1853–74; m. 14 August 1827, Anna Sophia (d. 8 July 1893), eldest dau. of Rt. Rev. Hon. Henry Ryder, DD., Bishop of Lichfield and Coventry, and had issue [Peter Townend *Burke's Peerage, Baronetage and Knightage* (1967), 1108].
33. TNA. CO 384. 44. 180.
34. TNA. CO 384. 44. 182.
35. Elizabeth Grant of Rothiemurchus *Memoirs of a Highland Lady* (1967), 283.
36. *Grants of Shewglie*, 27.
37. Glenelg was perhaps also responsible for finding a post for John Leyburn's brother Donald Maclean. He became a stipendiary magistrate in Bermuda. [BCP. Isle of Muck Folder; JNM Maclean. Draft Pedigree Maclean of Muck dated 4 May 1969. Most of the unreferenced information above concerning the descendants of Donald Maclean, 5th of Muck comes from this document].
38. He was the son of Neil, the youngest of the three Campbell brothers who had purchased Caolis & Cornaig in 1798 from the Duke of Argyll. His mother was Ann Maclean, the youngest daughter of Neil Maclean of Crossapol.
39. Mitchell Library, Sidney. Dispatches to the Governor of New South Wales. January–December 1835, 869–870.
40. Anon. *Coll* (Wellington, 1911), 13–14. I have to thank Sarah Fitzgerald for a photocopy of her ancestor's story.

Chapter Forty-Nine

Letters from the Tiree Manse

The weather in 1836 was a universal topic of comment. 'We have had a very bad summer here indeed', wrote young Alexander Maclean in Tiree to his mother in Plymouth. Alexander, Surgeon Alexander's posthumous son, was now eighteen. He was on his first visit to his uncle Mr Neil at the Manse in Tiree. They had given him a warm welcome. He writes to say that:

My Dear Aunt and Uncle... since my arrival have treated me as one of their own. My Aunt is the most kind hearted affectionate creature imaginable. Her health is not of the best but does not prevent her from attending to domestic duties. She desires me to present her kind love to you. My Uncle is naturally reserved, but notwithstanding, when you know him, you find him an honest hearty, hospitable old Highlander. My Cousin Harriet is without exception the prettiest girl I have seen since I left Plymouth, accomplished and good-natured beyond anything. Lylyas the next is about 13 years old, and of great assistance to her Mama, in fact I may say she is the house keeper. Isabella the youngest is a very pretty girl about 12 years old, has musical genius. She plays the piano very prettily, and composes walses by far preferable to some I have seen in print, in fact they are very superior children, and one cannot be with them a week without loving them. Donald is near one and twenty, he is studying the medical line and attends the university during the winter months. Sandy has just attained his 16th year, and is as to size quite a prodigy, he is about my height, but as stout again not one of my things will go near him and has whiskers nearly equal to Uncle Poulton.

He goes on to say that there had been several visitors from all over the Island to the Manse, who were old acquaintances of his father and wished to see *Allister Mackindoter*, which he says 'means in English the doctor's son'. He says that:

One old man of 85 years old paid me a visit a few days hence and after taking my hand in both of his, turning me round and round to have a full view of me, said that he should live ten years longer for the sight of me. Nor do they all this for the sake of gain, for I could not give them a greater affront than to offer them money, but from real affection to the sons of those who have been kind to them.[1]

It was perhaps Mr Neil, although the note is not in his handwriting, who on this visit gave his nephew a list of his ancestors: 'Alexander Maclean, son of Alexander, son of Donald eldest son of Neil, son of Allan, son of Neil, son of Lachlan, son of Neil son of Neil Mor son of Maclean of Coll – The Chief'.[2] This pedigree is different to that in Allan Crossapol's manuscript, as it inserts another Neil between Neil Mor and Allan. Other sources suggest the second Neil was the brother, rather than the father of Allan. Two other pedigrees illustrating Alexander's father's maternal descent from Maclean of Coll were, in the 1890s, to confuse Alexander's second son the genealogist HAC Maclean.

The family at the Manse paid an annual visit to Lochalsh, where Mr Neil's younger brother Hector, the Minister lived with his two unmarried sisters. Alexander writes that their luggage had been packed for four days but until the weather improved they were unable to set off. He anticipated 'much sport when I arrive at Lochalsh'.

Whilst he was in Tiree, Alexander visited Staffa, which he says is 'well worth seeing and more than realized my expectations'. He eagerly read letters from Plymouth, which afforded him 'much pleasure', but he complains 'through the negligence of the young lady who superintends the post office at Tobermory, intervals of 3 and 6 weeks occur without receiving letter bags, although opportunities may and do take place nearly every day. She is I understand about to be married . . . she deserves she should be well whipped'.

In his letter to his Aunt Strachan he ends by saying:

> My Aunt has just informed me that a boat leaves the Island early tomorrow morning, also that the letter must be on board tonight, and as I am now writing by candle light I must conclude as it is my intention to write Mama a few lines.[3]

* * *

The letters in this chapter give a brief insight into the life of Mr Neil Maclean's family in the first years of the 1840s. It was a time when a huge question mark hung over the future of the Hebrides. Although the letters are generally cheerful and outward looking they see the future of the family in India or Australia. They tell little about what is going on in Tiree. As Mr Neil's sister Margaret wrote to her sister-in-law Anna Maria Maclean in Plymouth: 'You know so little about this part of the world, that you would feel no interest in anything in the way of news from it, and indeed there is little to be said in that way, particularly at this season, and a person living in a town can hardly form an idea of the dull life we lead, in this quarter, during the winter months.[4]

The letters also tell of the trials and tribulations at this time for a professional family with little money and few influential friends. Commissions in the army and in the East India Company's Service required both money and or influence. It is, however, curious that nowhere in these letters is any mention made of appealing for help to Hugh Maclean of Coll. Perhaps the proof has been lost, but other evidence suggests that there was later a coolness between Hugh and Mr Neil. Certainly the warmth that Mr Donald's letters showed for his chief and even Mr Neil's early letters to his brother describing Hugh as 'the same fine frank and friendly fellow which you have seen'[5] are not repeated.

* * *

Young Alexander, or 'Alick' as his cousins call him, had an uphill struggle to get into the Army. On 6th October 1834, when Alexander was sixteen, his mother had written to Major-General the Right

Honorable Lord Fitzroy Somerset enclosing a Memorial to Lord Hill the Commander-in-Chief in which, after repeating her earlier petition of 1819 to the Duke of York, she says that she has:

> With her small means given the best education in her power to ... her orphaned son ... and watched assiduously over his Morals as well as his education in order to fit him for the Honorable profession of the Army, hoping one day to see him provided for therein through the bounty of His Majesty in compassion to the peculiar circumstances of his birth and the hardships of the Memorialist's case.

After repeating 'that her connections are of the most respectable characters both Naval, Military and Civil', she goes on to state 'that she is unable to purchase a commission for her son and humbly hopes that what she has represented will induce your Lordship to recommend him as a fit and worthy subject to the bounty of his Majesty for a commission without purchase where ever a vacancy may occur in any regiment at home or abroad'.

The Commander-in-Chief replied on the 14th October expressing his regret that 'on account of the list' he was unable to help.[6] The 'list' was of those officers on the half-pay list who wished to be employed. In addition places had to be found for those cadets being educated at the Royal Military College. The Commander-in-Chief therefore was unable to help the sons of deceased officers.

Four years later the 'list' had been reduced and in May 1838 Alexander himself wrote to Lord Fitzroy Somerset requesting an interview so that he might be granted a commission without purchase. He repeats his mother's reasoning and states that 'although unable to purchase, I have received a classical education, and have sufficient means, in addition to the pay of a Subaltern, to support the rank and respectability of an officer and a gentleman'. On this occasion the War Office accepted that the circumstances which Alexander had brought to the attention of the Commander-in-Chief were deserving of support. They were therefore pleased to add his name to the list of candidates for a commission without purchase.

The battle was not over yet. On 20th September Anna Maria wrote to thank Lord Fitzroy for the kind reception that her son's petition had received. However, as she pointed out, it was four years since she had first applied, and she trusted that he would use his influence to get her son a commission as quickly as possible.

Nothing had happened by February 1839 and Alexander wrote again:

> My Lord,
>
> I am encouraged by your Lordship's official letter to me of the 14th May, and your esteemed letter to my widowed mother, to trespass on your patience, while I respectfully solicit the favor of your Lordship's advice as to the propriety of approaching the Commanding-in-Chief Lord Hill by letter, to repeat to his Lordship the increasing anxiety I feel for the attainment of the favorable assistances it has been my good fortune to receive from his Lordship of being brought into the service. Beseeching your Lordship not to attribute my present application to an intrusive impatience, but to the true motive, an anxious desire, I daily feel, as I advance in years, to relieve my Mother from partly supporting me, an expense heavily on her limited means (her pension only). I feel assured I shall receive your Lordship's attention, it being the characteristic of your Lordship to bestow indulgent consideration, on every case brought before the War Office, in which the interest of the widow and orphan are concerned.

On 24th October 1839 Alexander at last received his commission, without purchase, and became an ensign in the 94th Regiment of Foot. The War Office had originally intended him for the 2nd West India Regiment, a graveyard for Highland officers. However, somehow or other he had obtained a commission in a much more suitable regiment.

* * *

The 94th Regiment of Foot had first been raised in 1794 from officers who had previously served in the Scots Brigade in Dutch service.[7] It was a highly appropriate regiment for Alexander, as a Coll Maclean descended from the chief's household men, in which to serve. The regiment had distinguished itself in India at the battles of Seringapatam and Argaum, and in the Peninsula. It had been disbanded after Waterloo but had been reformed in 1823, once it was appreciated that there was to be a need for more battalions to defend the British Empire.

The army in the period after Waterloo was different to the one that had fought Revolutionary France and Napoleon. Then it had needed as many regiments that it could raise and it was not too particular where its officers came from. The post war army had been taken over by the English ruling class. As Edward Speirs has written:

An officer had either to be born and bred a gentleman, or be prepared to act and behave like a 'natural' gentleman within the confines of regimental society. Embodied in the norms of gentlemanly behaviour were requirements of dress and deportment, an emphasis on honour and integrity, and a conformity with the manners and etiquette of polite society. Upholding these standards of behaviour was deemed necessary for maintaining the harmony and concord of the officers' mess.[8]

Alexander's mother had made sure that his education fitted him for this role and what he lacked in cash he made up with persistence. One of his brother officers was later to write: 'I retain a very vivid recollection of your telling me how you obtained your first commission, it is a history which must ever redound to your credit'.[9]

On 1 May 1840 the *Diamond* slipped away from Gravesend with Ensign Alexander Maclean, 94th Foot, on board. Four months later he arrived in Madras.[10]

* * *

Whilst Alexander was still at sea his pretty cousin Harriet wrote to Alexander's mother:

My dear Aunt,

I have for some days contemplated writing you, which affords me greater pleasure than I could have expected in addressing one I have never seen, and whom I regret being a total stranger to us. It is also a wish of Mama's that I should enquire for you all, more especially yourself, as I fear you must be in very low and depressed spirits since your dear son sailed, though he has been away from you for some time, you could hear frequently from him. We had accounts of dear Alick's departure first in a few hurried lines from himself, written the day before they first proposed embarking. We had next a much more minute account from our cousin John Maclean,[11] with whom Alick is a most particular favourite and he had just returned from seeing him off. We were delighted to hear he left him in good spirits, and that his departure was altogether a happy one. John went as far as the Dover/Deal, and came ashore with the pilot regretting much he could go no further, as the ship was not to call at any port. The *Diamond* is such a fast sailor that I trust they may have a quick passage, as we cannot expect to hear of them till they reach India. So I hope dear Mrs Maclean you will avoid distressing yourself over much, as dear Alick leaves his friends under the most favourable auspices and (if he lives) have no doubt but his excellent steady conduct and extremely gentlemanly bearing will promote him to fame and fortune which should reconcile his friends to the loss of his agreeable society.

Harriet goes on to say that her brother Donald (the doctor) 'is still with us, practices much, more I may say for the benefit of the poor than his own profit. Likely he too, poor fellow may be in India some day. Several of our friends are using interest to get him into the EIC Service, but it may take some time to obtain an appointment ... Our establishment is very thin at present and likely to be so for sometime. Papa went to Edinburgh about a fortnight since, took the dear girls with him to be left at school where I am sure they will be happy and comfortable as I always liked Miss Wilson. We expect Papa at the end of the week and send the boat to meet him tomorrow to Mull'.

Harriet wrote to Mrs Strachan again in October 1840. She was staying 'with our good friends the Camerons'[12] at Calgary Castle, the small castellated Gothic mansion which their Eigg friend Captain Allan McAskill had built in 1823, after he had purchased the Mornish estate from the Duke.[13] The family in Tiree had evidently been carefully scanning the gazette for news from India, particularly of Alick. 'We long much to hear of him now and think it possible there may be letters this month, if he wrote immediately on his arrival which I think he would not fail to do'.

Reading between the lines of her letters, it is hard not to feel that Harriet was taking a more than cousinly interest in Alick's progress. She says that she 'wrote a long letter, which I hope would overtake the overland mails for August, and gave him a full account of his Scotch friends and anything also that I thought could interest or amuse. I forget whether I formerly mentioned that our Cousin John McLean sent us a full-length profile of him, in bronze and in undress uniform, which is certainly like, tho' not flattering to the original'.

She says that her brother Donald 'has not yet heard anything satisfactory about his India appointment, so I fear it is not forthcoming, if not, he must like many, buy his fortune in some distant land as there is but a poor field for medical men in this country, particularly in the Highlands if they only do well by their profession. Indeed I fear that our two only brothers may both go abroad'.

In February 1841 Harriet writes to apologise for holding on to Alick's letter for so long. She had kept it so that her brother Donald might see it, but he had been called away professionally and was away longer than he intended. She had since received a letter from Alick herself, written on 20th October. He had been held up in Madras and was impatient to join his regiment. In November he embarked for Bombay and eventually joined the 94th at Cannanore.[14]

Donald's Indian ambitions had not prospered. 'He must, I think, give up all hope of the Company's Service most unfortunately being now above the age required', wrote Harriet, 'otherwise a General Sir John Rose near Inverness could in all probability procure it through time. This old Gentleman has considerable interest, and is a great friend of our Uncle Mr McLean in that quarter, this is very vexing, but he must seriously think of some other good appointment. We are now for different reasons anxious he should obtain one. An old Grand Uncle Colonel Macdonald[15] thinks he could get him into his old Corps the Artillery, but Don is quite undecided whether he will accept the kind offer, if not perhaps the same interest may be turned to Alick's advantage somehow ...'[16]

Donald himself wrote from Tiree on 11th March 1841. He said he had despaired

or at least nearly so, of the prospect I had of getting a medical appointment in the Hon. Co's Service, there is such a vast difficulty in procuring them as the India Directors turn their patronage generally to good pecuniary advantage. I have, however, a chance of getting into the *Artillery*, and am at present anxiously expecting an answer to a letter my Uncle Col. Macdonald wrote Sir John Will, the Director General of Ordnance Hospitals relative to my appointment.[17]

Alick's letters from India were eagerly awaited in the Manse. 'We long dearly for dear Alick's next', Harriet wrote to her aunt on 14th April, 'they must be very amusing and written in high spirits from the specimen you give. Donald had been out that night and carried in letters home about three in the morning, when he came to my room with them, and read yours aloud, and tho' more asleep than awake, had a most hearty fit of laughter, when the Cousin's meeting was described. [Alick had met his cousin Harry Strachan 39th Foot who was about to leave India]. It must have been a rich scene altogether ... Indeed I rejoice you are all to be made so happy and trust your long expectation of seeing your dear Nephew may soon be realized, you will soon think every ring at the door is to announce him'.

Harriet's sisters in Edinburgh, Lillias and Isobella, were enjoying school and 'have been kept so busy between studies and amusement that they have been on the whole but lazy correspondents. Miss Milne has lately been very generous to her young Ladies. Lilly gives me an account of a splendid ball, she had given, entirely at her own expense, and upward of a hundred and fifty came and danced all night to the music of four professional people, and what was better, the young Ladies might ask any friends they wished. Our girls had near fifty of their own wishing, all enjoyed the thing extremely well, and allowed they had not seen a more delightful, the whole season'.[18]

Donald continued as a doctor in Tiree but his younger brother, also Alick, seeing no prospects for him at home decided to emigrate to Australia. In an undated letter at about this time Harriet writes: 'Poor Alick sails for Australia in about 3 weeks from London in the *Lord Sausmarez*'. Its captain Neil Maclean, of *John Dunscombe* fame, was their cousin from Van Diemen's Land. When the latter arrived in London he found he could spare a little time and had travelled to Tiree to pay his Highland cousins a visit. Harriet's brother Alick was, however, away in Lochalsh saying goodbye to his uncle and aunts. He 'returned leaving them in low spirits, not having heard of his intention, till he went to take leave of them'.

Tiree Alick had been obliged to make up his mind to go to Australia in a hurry, 'but we ought to be thankful', Harriet writes, 'that he leaves us under promising circumstances, and that his first outset in the world is with so excellent and steady a young man as Neil Maclean, who is very well acquainted with the Country and so interested that he will be at the trouble of giving all the information which his experience can make useful'. Alick was to settle near Port Phillip, which she writes 'is highly spoken of.'

Harriet had heard that the 94th were ordered to China. 'Alick will see some service sooner than he expected, and I trust get some prize money', she writes to her aunt, adding 'I daresay you will not rejoice on first hearing it, the loss on our side is generally trifling, and we are persuaded it is a good thing for Alick'.

Harry Strachan was now back in Plymouth and sent news of his cousin. Harriet continues. 'We rejoice to hear such accounts of dear Alick, and of his being so happy and comfortable with his Regiment. His being selected for the Light Company speaks volumes'.[19]

There was then a pause in the correspondence and it was not until September 1841 that Harriet writes again to her aunt:

After a lapse of some time, I . . . enquire for you again. We have had so many interuptions before and since our beloved Alick's departure that I hardly remember how our correspondence stands. But should the difference be with me, I am sure you will forgive me. Knowing so well how the time and mind can be occupied in similar circumstances as we have lately experienced and of so painful a nature a parting with our dear young brother for such a very great distance and such an existence as it appears ere we can see him. Nor can we expect to hear from him till May, as the *Lord Sausmaurez* had no intention of calling anywhere. She is thought to be a capital sailer, so that I trust they may have a speedy, prosperous passage.

She goes on to say that:

We all felt in such bad spirits for some time. Indeed the blank he makes in our small circle, appears as great as ever. But we must manage to feel reconciled to all changes ordered no doubt for our ultimate benefit, though we do not see it at the time. And what of your dear Alick? It is no lack of affection to be so long of speaking of him, for in this house he is often spoken and thought of with the fondest interest. We have heard nothing of him for a long time, except through our friend John Maclean, that he was very well and happy in July last, which we are delighted to hear, but should like to see it confirmed by his own account.

Had the cousin's affection for each other began to fade? There is just the hint of irritation and disapproval in Harriet's letter. However, she cannot be cross for long and she remarks that her cousin John Maclean, the London wine merchant, 'was very well pleased to find the 94th was prevented getting to China, after being under orders for a march. It might be a disappointment to some, but Alick may get something to do in India, and I trust he may want no opportunity of bringing himself forward to get promotion as soon as possible. It seems Sir Archibald Maclaine[20] and he are the only Macleans who have ever been in the 94th, the former was much thought of as an Officer, and wished Alick to keep up the credit of the Clan, as the black fellows had behaved so well since he punished them. It is my pleasure that Alick should be on so happy a footing with his brother officers. I could hardly fancy it otherwise, at home as well as abroad it cost dear Alick no exertion to get the esteemed approbation of all who knew him for his good disposition and gentlemanly conduct, and he really does very great credit to those who brought him up. It can be no flattery to say so'.

She goes on to say:

I must tell you we have got three likenesses of our dear Alick which are thought very good, one in plain dress clothes, and one in Highland Costume, very striking, some defects about the hands, and features of it, and also some touches in the miniature. I am glad to say we managed to put all right to Papa's satisfaction and all of us. They are so like that we can hardly look at them very long without being affected, indeed we have often found poor Papa weeping alone.

Harriet recounts a remarkable incident on the *Lord Sausmaurez*'s voyage. Off the Scilly Isles someone on board had thrown a bottle over the side with a message in it for ' S McLean'. A copy was sent to the Manse. Harriet says that the ship had very few passengers on board and that 'Alick took a nice new bagpipe, and his old violin' with him. Her brother Donald was now talking of emigrating to Port Phillip. She comments that 'the Climate has certainly many advantages, which would be some consideration of account of one so dear to him as himself', which sounds as though at this time there was little love lost between brother and sister. Donald had just become engaged. 'I don't think I have told you', Harriet writes, 'that I expect to have a sister-in-law . . . how soon not being yet fixed, though others can plan so well, it is really astonishing how such things transpire and often without any foundation'.

Harriet is sounding waspish. She writes: 'I rather think Alick has not written to Lochalsh since going to India, which may somewhat offend, so that I shall take the liberty of giving him a gentle hint, first time to write'. She complains about the weather. 'We have had dreadful weather for some time but promises to improve. We hear that a little country boat has been lost with a number of men, the poor creatures. It is thought they were quite near home at the time, and the hope of their friends has been a little raised by a report that a gentleman in Mull spied with his glass a tent erected on one of the small uninhabited Isles, where sheep are kept. Which I hope may be true'.

She had at last heard from 'Cousin Alick'. Harriet writes: 'He is quite well and seems happy, but I can plainly see he is not over fond of India. Though he does not complain, he has all the leanings towards home and old friends natural to his kind heart. They are amusing themselves just now with theatricals. Alick seems to take an active part. I am glad to hear he has no taste for Tiger hunting, being a dangerous and unwholesome amusement, penetrating those jungles. Mama felt some apprehension and sent him messages . . .[21]

Harriet is evidently embarrassed by the tone of her last letter and on 1st November writes:

Only a few days since I sent off a long letter and I fear tiresome epistle to you. Since then I have had a letter from Aunt Margaret in which she mentions having received a nice kind letter from you, enclosing some of your dear Alick's and which in compliance with your request she forwarded to us. Opportunities are less frequent now, and in case of no conveyance for weeks (which must appear very *outlandish* to *most* but Highlanders.). I enclose your letters after being perused by us all over and over with much gratification.

She goes on to say that: 'I fear many of his friends in this part of the world (particularly the Lady part) must sympathise much with Alick in his regrets at not being sent to China, but I am glad to see that much better judges are of a different opinion in the event that he might still go there. We have a Lt. Campbell staying near us just now, who has been a good deal in India, the account he gives of the heat, and the annoyance from those horrid insects is really dreadful.[22]

Six months later Harriet is writing a letter that has not survived, when her brother Donald gives her a letter to add to hers:

As my sister is writing to Plymouth, I shall just pop this note into the same envelope with her epistle, but my modesty will not allow me to call it an answer to the kind letter you wrote me about a year ago. I write with a greater degree of pleasure on the present occasion to inform you of a *certain event* which is to happen about the middle of June and which is to terminate my career among those singularly uninteresting *Bipeds* called *vulgarly* Bachelors, and altho' my earthly pilgrimage has not been of very long duration, I have generally come under the denomination of that class of Worthies. The young lady whose *fate* is to be linked to mine is a Miss Cameron, living not far from ourselves, and who likely may be known to you by name from the circumstances of our Cousin Alick's being acquainted with the family when in the Highlands ...

Alick's maternal first cousin and great friend Harry Strachan of the 39th Regiment of Foot was now at Plymouth. Donald writes that:

If Mr Strachan your nephew, who I heard had some intention of visiting the Highlands, will think a Highland Wedding an inducement to come, we shall be delighted to see him, and will give him a *Highland Welcome*. Only please tell him that there is a very important condition to be made namely that he must take *bitters* (an old Highland custom) every morning before breakfast, also two or three *salt herrings* with a share of all the other substantialities of a *Scotch Breakfast*; which I fear may be rather revolting to the *stomach* of an *old Indian*.

News of events in Afghanistan had reached Tiree and Donald continues 'You will naturally feel very anxious at present about dear Alexr as the 94th have been ordered to Cabool [Kabul], but I hope the worst there is over, the former mismanagement will teach them in future how to act more vigorously, and with better effect against those rascally savages. Alick like every soldier must run his chance of the fortunes of war and I hope a little active campaigning will have no worse effect than to give him speedy promotion.[23]

This is the last letter from Tiree to Plymouth for almost ten years. It is inconceivable that others were not sent, but they have not survived and we are left with a brief vignette of a civilised little household on the brink of disaster.

Notes

1. BCT. Alexander Maclean, Tyrie Manse, 1836 to his mother.
2. BCP. Folder Colonel Alexander Maclean 94th Foot. Genealogical Information.
3. BCT. Alexander Maclean, Tyrie Manse, 1836 to his aunt Strachan.
4. BCT. Manse of Lochalsh, 6 March 1841. Margaret MacLean to Mrs MacLean, 21 Devonshire Place, Plymouth.
5. BCT. Edinbugh 17 February 1806. Neil Maclean to his brother Alexander.
6. TNA. WO 31. 793. 1174.
7. The 94th (The Scots Brigade) regarded themselves has the oldest Regiment in the British Army. It was raised in 1572 for service in the United Provinces and served in the pay of the State's General until 1782 when the Dutch government sided with the American colonies and demanded that the officers renounce their allegiance to King George III. Sixty-one refused, left Dutch service and were placed on the British half pay list. In 1793 and 1794 they were brought back on to full pay and four battalions were raised with the name the Scotch Brigade. These four battalions were reduced to one battalion, which in 1797 was sent to India, where it distinguished itself at Seringapatam and Argaum. In 1802 the battalion was renamed the 94th (Scotch Brigade). In 1807 the 94th returned to the United Kingdom and adopted the kilt. However, by 1809 there were insufficient Highland recruits coming forward to man all the Highland regiments and it was argued that non-Highlanders, because of their dislike of Highland dress, were reluctant to join Highland regiments. It was therefore decided that 'His Majesty's 72nd, 73rd, 74th, 75th, 91st, and 94th Regiments

should discontinue to wear in future the dress by which His Majesty's Regiments of Highlanders are distinguished; and that the above Corps should no longer be considered as on that establishment' [Adjutant General's Memorandum 7th April 1809]. In 1818 the 94th was disbanded in Dublin. It was reformed in 1823. [Diana M Henderson *Highland Soldier* (1989), 13–14.]
8. Edward M Speirs *The Army and Society 1815–1914* (1980), 1.
9. BCT. W Davenport Davenport, Bramall Hall, Nr Stockport, Cheshire. 26 July 1852.
10. BCP. Alexander Maclean's Commonplace Book 1840–52.
11. John Maclean was Allan Crossapol's second son, a wine merchant in London.
12. Alexander Cameron of Calgary 'a landed proprietor with financial problems'. James Robertson's Letter Book, 430307, 431226, 440110, 440817, 440826, 450625, 450808, 450820.
13. RCAHMS *Argyll* vol. 3, 229–30.
14. Cannanore on the Malabar Coast in south-west India was in 1507 one of the first forts built by the Portuguese in the Indies.
15. Lieutenant-Colonel Robert Macdonald, 1st of Inchkenneth and Gribune, Isle of Mull, CB, JP, DL, late RHA [*The Kingdom of Scotland*, 868].
16. BCT. Tyrie Manse, 2 February 1841. Harriet Maclean to Mrs Maclean, 21 Devonshire Place, Plymouth.
17. BCT. Tyrie Manse, 11 March 1841. Donald Maclean to Mrs Maclean, 21 Devonshire Place, Plymouth.
18. BCT. Tyrie Manse, 14 April 1841. Harriet Maclean to Mrs Maclean, 21 Devonshire Place, Plymouth. Isabella was to marry Alexander Wentworth Cameron whose great-grandfather Allan Callart had been wounded at Culloden. He was banished and his estate forfeited [*Clan Cameron*, 195–196; *Jacobite Estates of the '45*, 8, 23, 237, 244].
19. BCT. Tyrie Manse, undated. Harriet Maclean to Mrs Maclean, 21 Devonshire Place, Devon.
20. Lieutenant-General Sir Archibald Maclaine, second son of Gillean Maclaine of Scallasdale; b. 13 January 1777; in 1810 he was a captain in the 94th and greatly distinguished himself by his gallant defence of Fort Matagorda for 55 days against 8,000 men under Marshal Soult. His services on this occasion earned him a knighthood and accelerated promotion into the 87th Foot; he died a Lieutenant-General in March 1861 [*Clan Gillean*, 275].
21. BCT. Tyrie Manse. 25 September 1841. Harriet Maclean to Mrs Maclean, 21 Devonshire Place, Plymouth.
22. BCT. Tyrie Manse. 1 November 1841. Harriet Maclean to Mrs Maclean, 21 Devonshire Place. Plymouth.
23. BCT. Tyrie, Argyllshire, NB. 10 May 1842. Donald Maclean to Mrs Maclean.

Chapter Fifty

Juliet Alexa Maclean 1838–1845

There is a vivid picture of life at Drumfin in the Journal of Juliet Alexa Maclean. She was Hugh's eldest child of his second marriage. As we have seen, Juliet Alexa was born on 26th July 1826. She was born, much to her later irritation in Edinburgh, as she would have preferred to be born in the Highlands.

She was an observant child, quite old enough in the late 1830s to notice the under-currents in Maclean of Coll's household. There were two distinct parties at Drumfin: Hugh's party and that of his wife. Juliet Alexa was devoted to her father, although she did not see much of him. Her siblings felt the same. Hugh always had 'a kindly word or a joke when he happened to see us, and would now and then arrange amusements for us. I can remember fireworks and a magic lantern and a swing, of which he was the manager. When he went to London he would bring us back presents of books &c'.

Juliet Alexa's opinion of her mother, Jane Robertson, was somewhat different. Her clearest memory of her mother was 'in her own room, alone, reading the Bible, or with her sister talking gloomily or in rhapsodies on religious subjects'. Mrs Maclean's sister, 'My Aunt of Unpleasant Memory', was then unmarried and lived at Drumfin'. She was believed to be of vast importance in the household and was 'considered before Papa himself. Mama was much devoted to her, believed in her to the utmost extreme and gave her entire confidence. They used to pride themselves on what was called a "romantic attachment" to each other. This Aunt entirely ruled Mama, who heard and saw everything through her, and would stay late in her room at night talking, which I – sleeping in an adjoining dressing room – heard much against my will. And which I afterwards thought I should have been happier had I not heard'.

Juliet Alexa's chief complaint concerning her mother was that she would reproach her for being:

> 'a Maclean, a regular Maclean'. I had 'no imagination or enthusiasm'. I was commonplace and uninteresting a regular Maclean. All true enough, though I neither cared nor much understood what she meant. But I did not like to be told by way of reproach that I was 'a Maclean'. Why, what else should I be? Why, of course I was. And glad of it too. Was not Papa a 'Maclean'? And besides, there was an enormous quantity of family pride in our family. And it was thought a very grand thing to be of so old a Highland family. And it seems to me Lowlanders were rather

despised. I well remember the mixed feeling at the time, how it seemed actually wrong that Mama should talk so, and yet, that being one of 'the Elect' it was impossible that she could be wrong.

Jane Robertson's brothers, John and William Robertson, were both religious. They used to visit Drumfin. John, the elder, joined the 'Irvingites'.[1] Juliet Alexa says that

> He was like all the rest of his family supposed (by themselves) to be very 'clever', very 'superior'. He was now quite fantastically religious. He would talk much of the 'Millenium' when Jesus Christ might be expected to arrive from heaven on a cloud to judge us all, and send most of us to the devil.

The children at Drumfin were afraid of this uncle, who used to catch them and make them learn hymns. He would himself sing psalms and hymns for hours. Religion completely dominated the Drumfin children's lives. When their lessons were over and before tea, they used to

> play at church. We turned a chair topsy-turvy over another for a pulpit and installed my brother John Norman there in. Alick used to be the clerk and 'give out psalms' and the rest with the nurses were the congregation. We used to sing a psalm, then our parson would read us a chapter in the Bible and once he attempted to preach, but finding he had nothing to say began to cry.[2]

Hugh's attitude to the Robertson's religious enthusiasms was mixed. He describes himself as 'an old Evangelical'[3] and seems to have been rather more balanced, though no less intense, than his wife in his attitude to religion. She was obsessed and considered his daughters from his first marriage as being:

> very worldly-minded and so were their aunts and cousins the Dundases, Baillies and Campbells. I remember when they were to make their first communion. They had many secret communings with Mama on the subject. In the end Margaret after hysterics, refused to attend, fearing she was not in a fit state to communicate and might therefore 'eat and drink damnation to her soul'.

Hugh's 'worldly guests' did not have an easy time at Drumfin. On one occasion Lord Stuart de Rothesay, the former British Ambassador in Paris, committed the unforgivable 'sin' of falling asleep at 'Prayers'. As a result Jane spent all the next day, a Sunday, in her private rooms with some 'Christian Friends', while the 'worldly minded' members of the family were left 'to entertain Papa's guests'.[4]

Unsurprisingly Juliet Alexa did not enjoy her childhood at Drumfin. She says that 'The time I liked best was once when we all went in a large boat to Coll and stayed for a week or so and had splendid hot weather and holidays, and were out on the beautiful sands'. She was thought to be delicate. So when her Aunt Breadalbane, always referred to as Aunt Albane, visited Drumfin she took her back with her to London. Old Sir Hector had invited Juliet Alexa to stay at his house for twelve months.

On their arrival in London they found 'the good old uncle waiting dinner for us. I quite well remember him. He was always most kind to me and took more notice of me than I had expected. My Aunt was as kind as ever. I, of course, in those days, never dreamed of making comparisons, but it is easy to see how much fitted [she was] by nature to understand and manage me as a child than my Mother. She did not demand of me what I could not be, i.e. demonstrative, enthusiastic, imaginative, and she made a kind of companion of me, so that altogether I did not feel that there was a great distance between her, as between Mama, and myself, although Aunt Albane was one of the Elect of Course'.[5]

Aunt Albane told me much family history, and I heard many things new and startling. She talked much and often about my sisters. Margaret[6] and all the Hamiltons [who] were then in Jersey. The other three sisters were always in Scotland still with their aunts,[7] who were friends of Aunt Albane's. From the way I had always heard them spoken of, Shakespeare, Byron, Voltaire, all Roman Catholics, the entire French nation and my sisters' relations, the Dundases, Baillies &c, had all been classed together in my mind as specimens of the world, 'worldly', 'unregenerate' lost souls, unmistakenly in hell ... and most unlikely associates for our pious Aunt Albane. I now learned that they merely 'hadn't such extreme views on religion' as Mama or indeed as she herself had.[8]

Religion coloured every aspect of life at Northwick Terrace but it was not oppressive as it was at Drumfin and Juliet Alexa, for the first time, started to enjoy going to church, and occasionally, of her own free will, accompanied her aunt to church on Wednesdays. The family at Northwick Terrace were Episcopalians and there was usually a popular preacher whose sermons were practical and short, unlike a 'Scotch church' where the clergyman would 'pour forth a volley of variations on the old, old story of our wickedness, and in long, long prayers which were in reality no prayers at all but a wonderful kind of "complimentary address" to the Deity with insulting remarks on human nature in general'.

She was also taken on expeditions to the Tower of London, Westminster Abbey, the Zoological Garden, Madame Tussaud's, Richmond and Hampton Court. Sometimes they went to the Serpentine to watch the skating and to see the carriages going with family friends to the Palace. She first saw the Queen out riding with Lord Melbourne and even met her, which 'was quite an event'. Sometimes Sir Hector would take her himself. He wanted to take Juliet Alexa to the theatre, but Aunt Albane objected.[9]

* * *

Meanwhile at Drumfin Hugh's financial position had gone from bad to worse and on 24th September 1838 he accepted the inevitable and placed his estate into the hands of trustees. His brother-in-law Alexander Hunter WS led them. Hugh's debts now exceeded £65,000.[10]

Placing an estate under trust meant that the owner no longer controlled his own property. The trustees were empowered, without advice or consent from the estate's owner or from his creditors, to uplift the rents, take, and convert into cash his whole moveable estate and dispose of all his unentailed land. The factor of the Coll estates took his orders and reported to the trustees. Although, as we shall see he kept Hugh in the picture on what was going on. The factor's job was not made any easier by the fact that Hugh often ignored his new position and continued to act as though he controlled the estate.

A tenant, a Mrs Douglas, was initially found for Drumfin and the Macleans moved out. It was a bitter blow. Hugh's own purchases in the north-east of Mull were particularly dear to him. The trustees allowed him £400 a year to live on.

Aunt Albane broke the news to Juliet Alexa that the family was to leave Drumfin. She explained how the Macleans of Coll had once been rich, but were now poor. Juliet Alexa writes: 'Papa came to see us at Northwick Terrace and we all went to Drumfin to get ready' for a final visit before Mrs Douglas could move in. At Edinburgh en route to Mull they stayed 'at Lady Baillie's, where I saw my three sisters. They were very kind and Catherine made me promise to write to them, and gave me presents'. It was settled that they should stay with Aunt Albane till some place in Germany had been decided on for them 'to take up our abode as a family'.

What concerned Juliet Alexa most during her short stay at Drumfin was the fate of her half-sisters. Her mother's sister now talked even more openly than ever against them. She likened them to 'Regans and Gonerils' and said that they had left their father's house like the prodigal son, and wasted their substenance in riotous living.[11]

The family dispersed. Aunt Albane took the elder sisters to Wales and the rest of the family went to live by the Rhine. It was believed that Germany was an inexpensive place to live and that if they were able to live on £400 a year for seven years all might be put right again. Aunt Albane, however, 'feared we might remain away much longer than that and the poor kind Aunt seemed grieved at the possibility, and cried and hoped we might not forget her. I loved her very much, I told her, and I was sure I should never forget her'.

The Macleans were to live at several different places in Germany.[12] One was Ehrenbreitstein. Where Juliet Alexa writes:

We had Sunday lessons as of old with Mama, and we were kept in the house all day. We lived opposite a house where there was music and dancing every Sunday, so we lived for the day in the back rooms with no prospect but the rock of Ehrenbreitstein about a yard from the balcony on which the windows opened. (We could touch the rock) ... Papa read newspapers of a Sunday though Mama hid them (and John Norman used to think it a joke to take them out and put them in his way).

They later lived at Coblenz and Juliet Alexa once more enjoyed early morning walks with her father. They went to the parade to see the soldiers and hear the bands. Juliet Alexa learnt to play many marches by ear. She writes: 'Papa liked these marches and for years I used to play them to him every night while he marched up and down the room'.

The family was not to spend long in Germany and Juliet Alexa returned to Northwick Terrace. Her two eldest brothers were now at Highgate Grammar School on the edge of Hampstead Heath. It was a good grammar school, which had been founded in 1565, but it hardly had the same social cachet of Eton. Sometimes her brothers visited them at Northwick Terrace. Sometimes they were all taken to dinner by their Uncle Robertson at the house of one of his City friends. Juliet Alexa dreaded these dinners, but she was obliged to go to them as she was under his charge as well as that of her Aunt Albane, 'which he took care to let me know'.

In August 1843 they all left London for Devonshire to stay at Budleigh Salterton, 'a pretty little watering place where Papa, for £100, had taken a house for a year'.

* * *

Hugh Maclean of Coll's wife and children were not the only members of the extended family of Coll to seek temporary exile away from the islands, although their absence was somewhat different to that of their distant relations. There had always been movement between the different parts of the Coll estate. However, as the nineteenth century progressed an increasing number of islanders were seeking seasonal employment away from home and by the early 1840s the income earned by seasonal migrants throughout the Highlands and Islands was a key factor in the economy and enabled tenants to pay their rents after the collapse of the manufacture of kelp. At the time of the 1841 Census there were 'about 50 persons' away from Coll 'temporarily absent in search of employment'.[13]

An example of a family in the 1840s, who depended on seasonal employment in the Lowlands, were the *Sliochd Ailean Mhic Ghilleasbuig*. They descend from a branch of the Macleans of Auchnasaul in Mull, who in the early seventeenth century had settled at Kilmory in Rum. One late eighteenth-century member of the family, also named Allan, had moved to Coll where he had charge of the Laird's galley. He lived at Totronald.[14] Totronald was one of the best farms in multiple posession on Coll. In 1776 it had a population of 82 divided into 18 households. It was later laid out in linear crofts. In 1836 the tenants paid a rent of £92 per year.[15] Captain Donald Campbell was to write that it 'will support itself. It was the only farm on Coll that 'will completely do so'.[16] It was in this happy position because it had controlled its population.[17] 1841 Totronald's population consisted 51 people, considerably less than there had been in 1776. They were living in 11 households. 8 were tenants.[18] One tenant was a tradesmen and 2 were Cottars.[19]

Totronald was a close knit community. Most of the tenants there in 1841 were descended from families who were there in 1776, and there were several marriages between the sons and daughters of tenants. They also had a close relationship with Maclean of Coll. As we have seen one tenant ran his galley and Alexander of Coll had specifically requested that another tenant's son Charles Macdonald, who was later his servant, should be given leave from the Breadalbane Fencibles to help his father with the harvest.

One of the tenants in 1841 was Neil Maclean who was a recent arrival in Coll. He was, however, the great-nephew of the man in charge of the former laird's galley and had cousins already living on the farm.[20] He had lived for some time in the Isle of Muck, where his cousin Rory Mor was Ground Officer. He then moved to Coll and settled at Totronald. Neil was married to a Flora, daughter of Lachlan Macdonald a farmer at Kilchoan in Ardnamurchan. They had three sons. They are the authors of a unique series of letters from a crofting family, which survive. Their mother Flora Macdonald's brother James was evidently a *lad o pairts*, who was a writer in Inveraray. When he died James's widow hid his correspondence in a hole in the wall of their house in Inveraray.[21]

Neil Maclean's eldest son Lachlan writes his first surviving letter to his uncle on 16th March 1843. He says: 'I suppose that it is very difficult to get work this year, but if you have any acquaintance on one of the steamboat captains if you please to look for a place for me'. He goes on to say 'I was at the herring fishing last year at Fraserburgh... I left home in June for Glasgow, the worst place for work that I never saw. Then I went away with one of the fishing boats from Portnundas to the east and ingaged there with one of the fishers for a shilling the cran without meat or lodging... we fish 200 crans... it was dear enough to me many nights to draw up the nets, thirty three feet of boat against sea and storm twenty miles from land... I hope that you will write to me where is Donald my uncle in Edinburgh that he will get some work for me till I go to Leith to the fishing... excuse me for it is my own hand... your affectionate nephew, the bad writer, Lachlan MacLean'.

Lachlan's uncle James evidently replied to his nephew, for the latter wrote again on the 18th April to thank him for it and to say that he was sorry to hear that his uncle Donald was ill and that his wife was dead. The family was to come home to Ardnamurchan. Uncle James had advised his sister to take one of Uncle Donald's daughters. Lachlan writes to say 'we are very willing to take one of the eldest daughters and I hope you will send them home as soon as possible. The school is not a quarter of a mile from us'[22] and she may go to it as soon as she will come'. He goes on to apologise for his 'bad English, bad spelling and bad writing' and to beg for help in finding a job ' Dear Uncle, I know that the hands on the steamers are hard wrought indeed but I would be glad to get in one of them in such a bad world as this. I would get imployment at the herring fishing but it will not last but two mounths the lo[n]gest and it will th[r]ogh me out of nine mounths work'.

Lachlan was not alone in getting work away from Coll. By the early 1840s the income earned by seasonal migrants from the Highlands and Islands was a key part of the economy. At the time of the 1841 Census there were 495 temporary workers absent from Tiree & Coll. This was 12% of the inhabitants of the parish.[23]

The herring fishing was now concentrated around the coastal towns of North-East Scotland. They could not find enough local men in July and August to man all the boats at the peak season of the fishing. By the 1840s it had become a firmly established custom for crews to be strengthened each year by men from the Western Isles.

Lachlan wrote again to his uncle from Fraserburgh in June 1843. He had failed to get work on the steamers and although he was in good health complained of 'very sore feet with travelling through the Country without work'. He was 'out of employment yet but got some promice to get in the next week a kind of work that is going on at the harbour'. He said he had gone 'up to Portnundas and I met with my last sgibber [skipper] and he took me away to this place telling me I would get plinty of work till the herring fishing would begin'.

James, Neil and Flora's youngest son, and the most prolific letter writer of the three brothers, wrote to his uncle on 5th December 1844. He was then 15 and was keen to learn book keeping. He writes: 'I wish to find out what kind of school will I learn than to be going on farther in great countings'. His elder brother 'Donald is readey of the Book Keeping he finished it a week ago and he think you will look out some place for him'. He also hopes his uncle can find a place for 'a lad here in the neighbouring, who were very kindly to us when we came here'. This was Malcolm MacDonald the son of Alexander Maclean of Coll's protegé Charles MacDonald.[24] Malcolm had served his time as a blacksmith but 'he hath no place yet and he thinks if any place be fit in Ardnamurchan this year will do for him'.

Donald himself wrote from Totronald on the 23rd January 1845:

I embrace the opportunity of writing you these few lines to let you know the way that I can write and spell but it is impossible to me to this in order that it may please you when my brother must hold on to the Selling Book yet for he is very often in the school. I do not know what I shall do when I am not at the School but every winter you mentioned in James's letter what kind of work I was for if I would get in a shop or in a Warehouse. I suppose it will be a fine work to me . . .

I intend now to give you a short description of my unprofitable journey round the east side of Scotland last summer. We landed about Ardnamurchan and we travelled to Inverness myself and Lachlan and another some people. We took the steamer to Inverness at ten o'clock at night and we did not reach Fraserburgh till 4 next evening. The weather was so bad that we were not at sea but about half of the time and we did not gain nothing but we should be thankfull that our lives were spared – Lachlan was driven away to Peterhead with a strong gell [gale] from the Nor West in company with another 100 boats, distance 20 miles and we got our passage with a boat belonging to Queensferry and we travelled to Linlithgow and we took the steam coach to Glasgow.

In November there was a rumour going the rounds in Coll that Uncle James was dead and James Maclean wrote on the 11th to discover if it was true. 'For I am most anxious to here with perfect certainty about you'. He goes on to say 'whosoever will read this scroll will send me an answer whether he is alive or not for there is a long time since I do not hear from him for I will be very anxious to hear from day to day about you till I will receive an answer'. He evidently thinks his uncle will read the letter for he continues to give him family news: 'Donald went to the East Country Herring Fishing this year too and I suppose that he did not gained anything on his journey better than last year and I heard he is now sailing between Glasgow and Liverpool by one of the Packets'.

Uncle James was not dead and sent his nephew some newspapers, which gave him great pleasure and he wrote to ask for more as they 'give me an interesting stories'. Donald was back at home 'always working with horses drawing weeds from the shore'. His parents were not willing to let him go to sea and there was 'no Schoolmaster in Coll that can teach him Navigation . . . [and] Donald would loose himself in this desolate place'. He was writing in January 1846.

The eldest son Lachlan had by now married his cousin and since November had been building his own house. James writes 'I think it will be a while before it will be finished in this dreary winter'. In the meantime he was living with his parents. 'He hath a nice son was born on the 24th July who is called Niel'. He goes on to say that 'the cow that you gave to my mother is on our hands yet and she is very lean fleshed this year and also looking very old in her appearance and digestion are faileth away so that I am afraid of [for ?] her. She had a good calf this year and I think it will be the best of our cattle the one that she had coming from Mingary'.

James was still hoping to get away from Coll. On 21st February 1846 he writes: 'Dear Uncle, I do wish that you will send me an answer soon and let me know if you are to bring me out of this desolate place this year'. Uncle James did not reply and his nephew wrote again from Totronald on 1st April:

I was expecting your letter would come every day since I wrote you on 27th February and am sadly disappointed towards every vain hopes I wrote you. I am sure it did not please you at all and there was no wonder it was the second day of my illness and a few days after I sent for the Physician he told them that I had the fever and they left the house all except the old folk. Lachlan went to his father-in-law's House and Donald and Grace were out in a little house till Lachlan got his own house finished but they may come home now for we cleaned everything two times for I smoked the house yesterday with Sulphur and a thing called *Eudhar Beinne*.

Dear Uncle, I hope you will do something for me this summer to get me out of Coll. If I will remain another two or three years it will break my heart with work for I shall never forget last harvest before I reaped the one third of our crop and after that that took it to lie in the bundles and lift it on to the horses side to bring it to the barn yard insomuch that my arms are sore yet after it.

Notes

1. Edward Irving (1792–1834) was a tragic figure. He came from a humble background in Annan, Dumfriesshire and struggled through an arts course at Edinburgh University. A scorner of patronage and ecclesiastical intrigue, he found no one to present him to a parish in Scotland. Eventually he accepted a call to a small Scots congregation in London, where his new 'natural style' of preaching at once attracted attention. In 1828 he visited Scotland and preached to gigantic congregations in Annan, Edinburgh and Kirkcaldy. However, there were doubts about his doctrine, and, when he returned to Scotland in 1829, he found he was banned from Edinburgh pulpits. He was then accused of allowing people claiming 'the gift of tongues' to take part in services in his London church. He was expelled from the Presbytery of London, tried on a charge of heresy and deposed.
2. BCP. Juliet Alexa's Journal, 17.
3. *Minutes of Evidence taken before Select Committee on Sites for Churches (Scotland)*, 3.
4. Juliet Alexa's Journal, 1–6.
5. Juliet Alexa's Journal, 24.
6. Margaret was married to James Hamilton of Barns & Cochna in Dumbartonshire [Maclean of Coll Family Bible].
7. The sisters of their mother were Elizabeth Dreghorn Dennistoun, wife of Duncan Campbell of Barcaldine; Dame Mary Lyon Dennistoun, wife of Sir William Baillie Bart of Polkemmet; They were the coheirs of their mother Margaret, dau. of Robert Dreghorn of Blochairn [NAS. RD5. 426. 159. 3].
8. Juliet Alexa's Journal, 28.
9. Juliet Alexa's Journal, 26.
10. NAS. RD5. 604. 194.
11. Juliet Alexa's Journal, 31.
12. Juliet Alexa says she was 12 when the family went to Germany. They must therefore have gone soon after the Trust Deed was signed in September 1838 [Journal, 37].
13. NAS. Census 1841 (551). Enumeration. Abstract of the Answer & Returns 1843.
14. *Clan Gillean*, 39. In 1776 he was living with his nephew Donald Maclean in Totronald 3.
15. NAS. RD5. 194. 24 September 1838.
16. Mull Museum Archives D 12. 113. 20 March 1847.
17. Several families had left Totronald during the 1830s. They included Hugh Mackinnon, a tenant who in 1838 moved to Gorten; Hector Maclean, a cottar who in 1834 moved to Torrindeich a pendicle of Arileod; Donald Kennedy, a cottar who in 1837 probably left the island; and Charles MacPhaden, a shoemaker who may have done so too.
18. 4 Macleans, 2 MacPhadens & 1 Mackinnon.
19. 2 Macleans, 2 MacPhadens & 1 Macdonald.
20. He was aged 60 in 1841.
21. Arthur Littlewood, then warden of Auchindrain Farm Museum, found them hidden in the wall of the old Sheriff's House in Inveraray. They are thought to have been placed there by Uncle James's widow. I have to thank him for copies of the correspondence from Coll.
22. At this time there was a school at Arileod.
23. *The Great Highland Famine*, 147.
24. He had died in 1835 and is buried in Crossapol graveyard.

Chapter Fifty-One

The 'Disruption'

Juliet Alexa notes in her journal that one year her father went briefly and alone to the Highlands. Although she never gives a date, it is possible to work out that the year in question must have been 1843. It is an ominous year in Scottish history for it is the year in which 470[1] ministers seceded from the Church of Scotland. In doing so they split the church, and divided communities as bitterly as in the 1690s. The north and west Highlands and Islands were particularly affected and the Free Church in that part of Scotland became the church of the people.

The 'Disruption' had begun in a controversy over the right of the patron of the parish of Auchterarder to have his candidate imposed, against its wishes, on the congregation. The presbytery backed the congregation. However, when the patron and his nominee sued members of the presbytery for damages the Court of Session gave in favour of the pursuer. An appeal to the House of Lords was turned down and the 470 ministers signed the 'Act of Separation and Deed of Demission' and constituted themselves as the first General Assembly of the Church of Scotland Free. Thomas Chalmers, one of the most distinguished ministers in the Church of Scotland, became its moderator.

Not all those involved in the controversy were against patronage *per se*, and even Chalmers believed that good use could be made of it to secure an effective ministry, and realized the danger of unbridled popular liberty of choice, for he was no democrat.[2] The point at issue was 'the encroachments of the civil courts on the spiritual powers of the Church' for, if 'the State refused remedy, conscience demanded the abandonment of the civil advantages of establishment'.[3]

The 'Disruption' may have been triggered off by the Auchterarder incident and increasing dissatisfaction with the legal position of the Church of Scotland. But behind

> this lay a more fundamental if unexamined question. It had been the historic Calvinist standpoint that the Christian Church ... could so impress itself upon the surrounding community that the standards of the Gospel became the rule of life for society at large. Was this assumption consistent with the New Testament and practicable, or even realistic, in a nineteenth-century industrial situation?[4]

The Evangelical wing of the Church of Scotland, which 'laid emphasis on the great Christian doctrines of sin, grace and redemption', and whose aim was to awaken in their hearers a deeper personal religious experience',[5] gradually gained influence in Scotland, as the nineteenth century progressed, although it was not until 1834 that they replaced the Moderates as the majority at the General Assembly. To this new majority, and its numerous sympathizers throughout the country, it appeared that the Church was shaking off its century-old lethargy.[6] But the leaders of the Evangelicals had been misled by the enthusiasm that greeted their oratory. As late as April 1843 they still believed that they would have their majority at the next General Assembly when the crucial vote for a policy of a Disruption, not within the Church, but between Church and State was to take place. However, the country at large was not ready for such a breach. In Scotland parish ministers had civil as well as religious functions and the courts of the National Church were part of the legal structure of the land. And, as the lists of commissioners being sent to the Assembly showed, there had been a change of outlook. The Evangelicals had lost their majority. Too late to turn back they decided on a change of tactics. If they could not persuade the Assembly to side with them they would leave the Church.

It was a dramatic decision. It was also an expensive gesture for the seceders relinquished all the emoluments and privileges they had enjoyed within the Establishment. It was a considerable financial and social sacrifice for the sake of principle.

* * *

One of the ministers to sign the 'Deed of Separation' was Archibald Nicol, the assistant minister in Coll and on the 15th August he was ordered to compear before the Presbytery of Mull.[7] Instead of doing so he wrote a letter admitting that he had seceded and the Presbytery minuted the fact 'that Mr Nicol is no longer a Minister of this Church'.[8] Mr Neil Maclean, who was absent from Presbytery, was ordered to report in order that the Presbytery could 'take the earliest and most efficient means towards having the vacancy of Coll supplied'.[9] It was to be 15 years before a new Church of Scotland assistant minister was appointed to Coll.

Despite his dismissal Mr Nicol continued to act as though nothing had happened. He continued to hold services at Clabbach, to chair Kirk Session meetings with his old elders, minute its actions in the same session book and distribute funds to the poor. On 2 May 1844 a Free Church delegation visited Coll and preceded to ordain new elders selected from a list nominated by the people.

One member of the delegation was the Reverend Peter Maclean Minister of the Free Church in Tobermory, who had arrived in Mull in August 1843. He came originally from Stornoway and had spent some time in Cape Breton. James Robertson, the Sheriff Substitute of Tobermory, who knew him well, describes him as a 'ranting parson' whose 'noise and vehemence enchants the Saints of Tobermory'. His intemperate language was to sour relations between Hugh Maclean of Coll and the Free Church.

It might have been expected, from the Maclean of Coll family's evangelical fervour, that Hugh would have sided with the Free Church. However, he objected to the violent language used by several Free Church ministers, particularly Dr Candlish, who was quoted as saying that it was the duty of all Free Kirkers to use all means in their power to pull down the Established Church.[10]

It was perhaps the controversy over the Church that persuaded the trustees of the Coll Estate to agree to Hugh returning to live at Drumfin before the Aros estate was sold. On 11th July 1844 he arrived at Tobermory on the *Toward Castle*. James Robertson, the Sheriff Substitute of Tobermory, now met the Coll family for the first time. He thought that they appeared to be 'very amiable and good people' and hoped to see more of them by and by, and anticipated 'much pleasure in their society'.[11] He was impressed with Mrs Maclean, who he believed was far cleverer than her husband, but from a very different class, 'that is to say she is not quite so much a lady as he is a gentleman'.

James Robertson soon became a close confidant of Hugh, seeing him almost every day, and accompanying him to church. On one occasion they heard Mr David Ross the new Church of Scotland Minister preach. Robertson thought his sermon 'beautiful, affecting, well composed and well delivered'. Another man present 'thought he strained his voice and spoke too loud. Coll and Mrs Maclean thought the same, and further appeared disgusted with poor Ross's Scotch accent, ungainly manner and the length of his sermon'. Robertson wrote 'I must not let the poor fellow know what the Colls think of him for he is a modest man, and as I believe easily discouraged and disheartened'.[12]

Juliet Alexa was the only one of Hugh and Jane Maclean's children not to be at Drumfin that summer. James Robertson met the rest of the family. He describes young Coll as 'a handsome well grown youth of sixteen or seventeen, near six feet tall, quiet and modest. He is dark, round faced and black-eyed. John is a very smart gentleman-looking little lad of 14 or 15, also dark, easy in his manner, talkative, longish faced and pleasing looking'.[13]

Hugh kept the news that Coll House had been sold from his family and they only discovered what had happened when the purchaser, David Nairne, was coming up to the door of the house. Hugh then hurriedly mentioned to his wife what had occurred. Robertson felt for Hugh as 'he was strongly attached to the place and the loss of it is a severe blow to him'. He goes on to say that the Colls 'are such very amiable people that it is impossible to make their acquaintance without feeling a warm interest in all that concerns them'.[14]

David Nairne is described by James Robertson as 'a plain mannered unassuming man, as much like a respectable farmer as polished Gentleman'.[15] He says his mother is a little old Ladylike person in a brown wig and very deaf; the daughter is a second though not improved edition of the mother'.[16]

The purchase of Drumfin was not to proceed amicably. Hugh was determined to exclude Drumdarroch 'a very beautiful locality' where he intended to build a cottage and threatened to cancel the sale unless Drumdarroch was excluded. Nairne considered that such an exclusion would destroy his privacy, and refused to agree. Hugh believed that there were other reasons: that Nairne wished to keep a woman there.[17] He was, however, in no position to cancel the sale and his dream of a cottage faded.

The handover was a drawn out affair and was not completed until May 1845. In the meantime the aftermath of the 'Disruption' continued to be felt. The curious state of affairs in Coll, whereby Mr Nicol continued to act as though nothing had changed lasted at least until the end of 1844. On 30th December, one of the last entries in the Kirk Session minutes notes that he paid £2.2s.6d 'to such of the poor as received nothing or but little of the clothes sent for distribution by Mrs Maclean of Coll'.[18]

* * *

In January 1845 an increasingly acrimonious correspondence began between Hugh Maclean of Coll and the Free Church Minister of Tobermory. The Rev. Peter Maclean had attacked David Ross the Church of Scotland's minister. On 2nd January Hugh wrote to the Free Church minister:

Rev. Sir,

Previous to my return to this country, I wrote to you my reasons for not joining the Free Church, my predilections having been in favour of the old Evangelical party. It was my wish on my arrival, to have made your acquaintance; but too-well authenticated reports of the language, demeanour, and actions of many members of the Free Church (yourself, I regret to say, included), have hitherto deterred me, desiring to judge for myself. I consider it a desirable preliminary, most just towards you, and satisfactory to me, to ascertain from yourself the truth of the allegations . . .

1st Whether you believe that ministers of the Established Church (as such, independent of individual demerit) are ministers of Satan, going themselves, and leading their people straight to Hell?

2nd Did, or do you from the pulpit hold them up to condemnation, collectively or individually, especially Mr Ross. And debar your congregation from any intercourse with them, as so doing raised a barrier between them and Heaven?

3rd Do you believe groaning and loud lamentations in church (not at home) indispensable, essential, or any mark of grace?

4th Do you hold vociferation, violent gesticulation, repetition, &c, to be similar marks of the same in a minister?

5th Do you hold out to your people, that having once signed to support the Free Church, it would be perjury . . . to rejoin the Establishment?

6th It being notorious that your congregation do hold these absurdities, do you combat them?

Hugh went on to say that 'I shall most truly rejoice in your disclaiming all these things, my earnest desire being, if the re-integration of our church be impossible, to make both divisions as efficacious as possible in disseminating real Christianity . . .'

Peter Maclean replied the same day, saying that 'I have little leisure at any time to engage in a lengthened correspondence. It is therefore far from my intention at present to enter on a minute vindication of my own opinions, or those of my people, far less to disprove the numberless calumnies and falsehoods circulated by our enemies, with a desire to injure our cause; at the same time, I am far from wishing to evade the subject of your letter. You having no personal acquaintance with me proves that all your information is collected from others; and as I agree with you entirely in thinking that no Christian minister should hold opinions he fears to confess, I beg to see my accuser face to face . . .'.

Hugh wrote on the 7th January once again asking for direct answers to his questions. Peter Maclean replied on the 8th:

Sir,

I was too much engaged when your messenger came last night to answer your note. I beg leave to refer you to the plan suggested in my letter of the 2nd instant, as the only one I intend to adopt . . .

Hugh replied, writing from Drumfin on the 9th 'Rev. Sir, Although you are certainly not legally responsible to me, I may presume on your belief that every Christian minister is enjoined to be ready to give to my inquiries such answers as I requested. You quoted Gamaliel's advice for my guidance. Is it not you, who glory in acting diametrically contrary to it, who must need to be reminded of it?'.

The 'Disruption'

Peter Maclean returned to the attack. On 11th January he wrote: Sir, although you persist in demanding answers to queries, which I consider absurd and trifling, I must decline to give them. In following this course, I have the example of the Blessed Saviour, who declined to answer questions which were asked with the intention of ensnaring him ... As you refused my method of settling this question, I beg to decline any further correspondence on the subject'.

Hugh agreed, and[19] he too went on to the attack. He had checked all his letters to Peter Maclean with James Robertson. The latter notes in his diary that on 28th January Hugh showed him the draft of a letter he had written to Archibald Nicol in Coll. This letter has not survived. Presumably it told him to stop using the church and manse at Clabbach. If so Nicol did as he was told and moved to Ballyhough. Here the tenant, Charles Campbell, one of the elders ordained by the Rev. Peter Maclean, built him a simple thatched cottage. It is situated on the march with Totronald and the field where he preached to the people in the open air is still known as the 'Minister's Field'.

Disagreements with David Nairne continued and there was an argument with him over the furniture to be left at Drumfin. All was settled by 1 May when Mrs Maclean of Coll and her children left Tobermory on the steamer. 'A melancholy day', James Robertson notes in his diary.

Hugh, however, had unfinished business to complete. On 7th Robertson 'walked with Coll to Drumfin, and went through the house with him. Poor fellow', he writes, 'I felt deeply for him. He came up after dinner to show me a kind friendly letter from Nairne'. Hugh had by now moved out. On 8 May the Sheriff went up to the house. In his diary he says: 'I felt destroyed and disgusted at seeing the house laid open to the unhallowed intrusion of a mob. There was a great gathering but I left immediately. The following day Hugh left for Quinish. His factor Captain Donald Campbell sailed the same day for Rum. He took with him an agent of the Marquis of Salisbury who was interested in buying the Island.[20]

On 16 May Hugh accompanied by Mr Ross sailed for Coll. Hugh had evidently got over his poor opinion of Ross and had chosen him to persuade the people of Coll to leave the Free Church. He had a daunting task ahead of him. Since the days of Ebenezer Davidson the population had become increasingly devout. It was a piety accentuated by suffering.

When Charles Maclean of Gallanach died his son-in-law John Campbell of Cornaig had succeeded him at Gallanach and not his son Dr Lachlan, who had his hands full with Rum.[21] John Campbell now cleared the people from Gallanach and settled them at Bousd on his Cornaig estate. In 1830 they were visited by one of the interim inspectors of the Gaelic Schools. 'There he found 25 families, most of whom had been cleared out of the interior of the island. Eleven of these families he found living in tents on the seashore in conditions of great squalor. He noted how even in this state they read their Bibles as taught by the Society, prayed & sang psalms. "Happy people!" he exclaimed, "for although you are deeply sunk in poverty, you are rich in faith and good works: the Spirit of God and your Bibles, have taught you that it is your duty, in whatever situation of life you may be placed, to be therewith content".'[22]

If this was the attitude of the majority of the people of Coll they were ripe for recruiting by the Free Church. What happened next is recounted by the. Dr Macintosh Mackay[23], Minister of Dunoon, who had joined the Free Church and was to be the Free Church's convenor for famine relief. The author of *Annals of the Disruption* writes:

Though nearly the whole population of the island had joined the Free Church, the chief believed that if proper arguments were addressed to them, and if personal influence were brought to bear, they would return to the Establishment. He engaged a minister he had confidence in to accompany him to Coll; sent word fixing a particular Sabbath, and invited his clansmen and dependants ... to come and meet him.

Duly at the appointed time the chief was on the spot with his champion. The people whom he had called were seen gathering along the roads, but instead of meeting him at the Established Church, they kept streaming past, on their way to the Free Church service in the open air. It was in vain that the chief addressed them, placing himself on the road along which they had to go, reasoning and remonstrating with groups and with individuals, urging them to come and at least give his friend a hearing. Their reply was a respectful but firm refusal. 'Ask us anything but this', they said, 'and we are ready to comply; we will serve you – we will follow you as our fathers have followed your fathers in days of old – we will stand by you to the last – but our consciences are our own, and our religious conviction we cannot surrender'.

Dr Mackay went on to say that despite this incident 'there is still a very strong feeling of attachment to Mr Maclean and his family', and they were 'universally beloved by the people'.[24] This statement argues against those like James Hunter, who in *The Making of the Crofting Community* claims that:

In the Highlands the Disruption was not just an ecclesiastical dispute. It was a class conflict. Its battle line was the line of class demarcation, the line between the small tenantry on the one hand and sheep farmers, factors and proprietors on the other. In that fact is to be found the explanation of what is otherwise inexplicable: the intensity of proprietorial opposition to the Free Church.[25]

As we have seen Hugh Maclean of Coll's dislike of the Free Church was based on the intemperate language used by the Rev. Peter Maclean, and not on class warfare. That class played little or no part in the community of Coll in the 1840s is clear: the Laird was the cousin of the tacksman, the tacksman was the cousin of the tenant, the tenant could be the father or brother of a cottar. Most of the people in Coll probably still regarded themselves as being part of Maclean of Coll's family.

James Robertson, when talking of Highland impostors quotes the case of 'the girl Maclean a Boat carpenter's daughter from Coll, who gave herself out as Coll's cousin'.[26] She would not have been Hugh's first cousin, but she will have known her relationship to him and he probably knew his relationship to her, which is why Allan Crossapol's Genealogical Account is so valuable, as it proves these relationships. For instance Murdoch Maclean at Arnabost, the elder 'nominated by the people' in 1844, was a descendant of Neil Buidh the sixteenth-century archer. Murdoch's father appears in Allan Crossapol's manuscript as 'John M'Lean at Arnabost'. Each stage of his ancestry is then given back to the 5th Laird.

During the first winter after the Free Church seceded congregations had to put up with the weather and their services were conducted in the open air. The second winter, however, was more severe and it was felt that things could not go on as they were, and the Assembly of 1845 appointed a committee to take charge of the problem. Graham Speirs Sheriff of Mid-Lothian was appointed convener.[27]

In 1845 the people of Coll applied for a site for a Free Church. Alexander Hunter replied that there could be no objection, provided 'the doctrine proclaimed by Dr Candlish that it was the duty of all Free Kirkers to use all the means in their power to pull down the Established Church, was not only not held but denounced by the applicants'. The committee, who had approached him said they were 'strongly against such doctrine as being unchristian, and stated that a minute to that effect' would be sent to him.

The Free Church leaders in Coll were in a weak position. Their leases were due to expire at Whitsun 1846. And in March Alexander Hunter obtained Summons of Removing from the Sheriff Court in Tobermory against the Rev. Archibald Nicol, John Mackinnon, shoemaker & church warden in Clabbach, Charles Campbell in Ballyhough and Widow Catherine Maclean in Triallan.[28] As three of the four were not in fact removed,[29] it would appear that this was merely a threat, but it cannot have helped relations between the Free Kirkers and the estate.

Hunter heard nothing from the Coll people about a site until June 1846 when he was again approached. He repeated that as soon as he received the minute he was sure that Coll, who was now in England, would grant them their request.

Speirs wrote to Hunter on 2nd July 1846 thanking him for forwarding his letter to the Laird of Coll and stating that Dr Candlish was not the Free Church, and claiming not to know what doctrine was imputed to him. He also stressed that he believed that the granting of sites to the Free Church would 'allay any bitterness on its part against the Establishment'.

His letter crossed with another from Hunter who said he had heard from Coll, 'who says he has never had any objections to give a site in Coll to the Free Church, at a reasonable distance from the parish church' and that it was his earnest wish that the people should abjure the unchristian doctrine about which he had written. Such doctrine he said 'had not reached the ears of the inhabitants of the island when the deputation waited on me', but as they were well known in Edinburgh, Hunter believed that they should be 'denounced by the simple people of the island before giving them a place of worship'. He says that if he were a Free Churchman, 'I would have been delighted to have the opportunity of denouncing such doctrines'.

Speirs wrote back on 9th July:

My dear Hunter,

I am very glad to understand that Coll has agreed to give the sites required on his property, which leaves me nothing to do but beg you will convey him my thanks for his attention to the subject.

He then goes on to quote from a passage in a pastoral address issued by the Free Assembly in 1845 and appointed to be read in all churches:

With reference to the footing on which our friends of the Establishment and ourselves ought to stand towards one another, whether collectively or individually, there may be room for the exercise of sound discretion, and the most conscientious may differ as to the kind and degree of intercourse to be kept up, according to the strength of their convictions, and the circumstances in which they may be placed. We are not disposed to lay down any instructions on the subject beyond the simple apostolic rules 'Let every man be fully persuaded in his own mind', and, 'Let all things be done in charity'. We exhort you to avoid all bitterness and evil speaking, and that wrath of men which worketh not the righteousness of God'. I cannot conceive anything more calculated to promote a spirit of peace than this address ...

The Free Church minister and elders had, however, not yet made the declaration that Coll required and Hunter wrote once more to Speirs to say that once he had received it Coll would at once give a site at a suitable distance from the parish church.[30]

Captain Donald Campbell, the trustee's factor on the Coll estate was equally critical of the Free Church and when Hugh wrote to him asking that he forward a letter to Archibald Nicol he replied: 'I am surprised you waste argument with him. It is quite useless'. In his letter Hugh complains that Nicol has not answered an earlier letter enclosing a copy of Sheriff Speirs denial on part of the Free Church of 'the unchristian tenets of Mr P Maclean'. Nor had he answered several other letters. He continues:

> I have ... been unable to get from you either denial or confession of holding these obnoxious doctrines, nothing but 'I have never preached them'. I judge that distrusting your own judgement (which I am sure in this case you had better have followed) you are afraid either of Mr Peter Maclean or of your people. But now that your Church are desirous of throwing off this merited opprobrium, you may discard it also and practise and preach the contrary to undo the mischief done to your own church if from no higher motive. You or your people have not only compelled 60 poor children to abandon the only school of industry they could ever hope for, yet you assume the appelation of the *free* Church! And have destroyed the schoolmistresses' garden. Both these outrages must be repaired *publicly and indubitably* before I can believe your denial. You wish to leave Coll I see, and you know that in doing so you necessarily leave the poor people to any illiterate fanatic.[31]

Many Highland proprietors were severely criticised for their action during the 'Disruption' in refusing the Free Church sites for churches.[32] And on 9th March 1847 the House of Commons appointed a committee of inquiry before which Chalmers and others gave evidence, with such effect that the offending proprietors gave in and legislation was not required.[33]

One curious fact that comes out in Coll's actions during the 'Disruption' is why he relied on Mr Ross of Tobermory to try and win the Collachs back to the established Church and not on Mr Neil Maclean, the parish minister. Mr Neil was certainly not a Free Kirker and the people of Tiree remained in the Established Church, but it seems that there had been a break down in relations between the two Macleans. There is an entry in James Robertson's Diary on the 11th March 1845, which says: 'The Minister of Tyree and [Hugh] Coll called; not together, indeed they do not seem to have any great affection for each other'.[34] Hugh had already fallen out with Dr Lachlan, who was advising the Free Church minister in Tobermory and had joined them. He was accused by Captain Donald Campbell of doing all he could to 'annoy me or Coll'.[35]

Notes

1. Andrew L Drummond & James Bulloch *The Church in Victorian Scotland 1843–1874* (1975), 8.
2. JHS Burleigh *A Church History of Scotland*, (1960), 336.
3. *A Church History*, 350.
4. *The Church in Victorian Scotland*, 1.
5. *A Church History*, 328.
6. *A Church History*, 340.
7. NAS. CH2. 273. 4.

The 'Disruption'

8. NAS. CH2. 273. 4, 75.
9. NAS. CH2. 273. 4, 76.
10. *Select Committee on Sites for Churches (Scotland)*, 195.
11. James Robertson's Diary, 11 July 1844.
12. James Robertson's Diary, 21 July 1844.
13. James Robertson's Diary, 9 August 1844.
14. James Robertson's Diary, 6 September 1844.
15. James Robertson's Diary, 6 September 1844: He claimed to be 'the heir male of the family of Strathaird, afterwards Lord Nairne, and the last substitute in the Entail of Drumkilbo, which he is now selling to buy lands in Mull'. He was a relation of Alexander Nairne, Alexander Maclean of Coll's brother officer in the Breadalbane Fencibles.
16. James Robertson's Diary, 8 September 1844.
17. James Robertson's Diary, 12 & 19 September and 25 October 1844.
18. NAS. CH2. 70. 2. 30 December 1844.
19. *Select Committee on Sites for Churches (Scotland)*, 3–6.
20. James Robertson's Diary, 9 May. 1845.
21. His son Major-General CS Maclean says Rum 'was quite large enough for his capital' [BCT. Brolas folder. Letter to Mrs Francis 25 November 1896].
22. *20th Annual Report of the Society for Gaelic Schools* (1831), 35.
23. He appears to have taken interest in Coll and James Robertson notes in his diary on 16 February 1844 that 'the Cocker' or dissenting Minister Mackay has left Coll'.
24. Thomas Brown *Annals of the Disruption* (1893), 422–3.
25. James Hunter *The Making of the Crofting Community* (1976),104.
26. James Robertson's Diary, 23 December 1843.
27. *Annals of the Disruption*, 410.
28. NAS. SC59. 2. 4.
29. All except Widow Catherine Maclean were still in the same farms in 1851 as they were in 1841.
30. *Select Committee on Sites for Churches (Scotland)*, Appendix to the Third Report, 195–6.
31. Mull Museum Archives. Capt. Donald Campbell's Out Letter Book. 7 Sept. 1846.
32. *The Church in Victorian Scotland*, 12.
33. *A Church History*, 355–6.
34. *James Robertson's Diary*, 140.
35. Mull Museum. Captain Donald Campbell's Out Letter Book 12 March 1847.

Chapter Fifty-Two

Famine

On 24th June 1846 Captain Donald Campbell, factor of the Coll estate, wrote to Alexander Hunter, the trustee to whom he reported to say: 'We have a very fine Summer but rather dry, yesterday & today, however, we had a fine rain'. Three weeks later the situation had entirely changed. He writes 'I regret to tell you the Potato Disease is spreading widely among us'. The Great Highland Famine, which followed the failure of the potato crop, was to have a devastating effect on the Western Highlands and Islands. It was to destroy the Macleans of Coll.

The most recent commentator TM Devine[1] justifies the term 'Highland Famine' on three counts:

> First, for almost a decade between 1846 and 1855 the potato, the main subsistence crop of the population of the Western Highlands and Islands, failed in whole or in part and threatened a large number of the region's inhabitants with both malnutrition, severe destitution and the killer diseases associated with these conditions.
>
> Second, massive external assistance was required to reduce the real danger posed to the lives of many thousands of people.
>
> Third, the subsistence crisis had a fundamental impact on such crucial social indicators as birth, marriage and migration.

The Coll estate in particular was affected. It is possible to study the effect of Devine's three counts on it at first hand: in addition to the statutory returns and reports, there is one surviving volume of the Factor's out letter book for the years 1846–1850;[2] a rental for the part of the estate in the Isle of Coll for 1854; a collection of letters written between 1843 and 1847 from the sons of a crofter living in Totronald to their uncle in Inveraray;[3] the minutes of the Parochial Board of Coll from 1847–1856[4] and the Journal of Coll's daughter Juliet Alexa. It is therefore possible to examine the crisis from a number of different angles.

Hugh Maclean of Coll, who was now living at 24 Queens Terrace, Bayswater, London, was first informed of the catastrophe in a letter from Donald Campbell of the 3rd August who writes:

> I regret to tell you the Potato Disease has spread fearfully all around us particularly in Coll where the Ground Officer writes and some tenants do not expect to dig one according to all appearances. There will be a famine in the Country such as has not been heard of unless timeously guarded against. How can it be other ways if the food the people depended upon for 10 months of the 12 is destroyed?

Famine

He goes on to say:

The Disease this year has appeared quite in a new shape. Potatoes were never more promising until the rains commenced the beginning of July. They soon thereafter began to wither first showing black spots on the leaves which spread by degrees to the Stem and Roots – I am told my own at Breachacha & Gallanach are as bad as can be but here [i.e. in Quinish] some of them as yet look healthy but how they prove is quite uncertain. The other crops look well and will be early . . . I intend going . . . to Coll to examine myself into the state of the Potato Crop.

On the 10th August, when he returned to Quinish from Coll, the factor reported to Hunter that:

the Ground Officer gave me of the miserable state of the island and he did not represent the state worse than I found it. The Potato Crop is utterly destroyed and there are scores of Families that have not a meal of meal in their houses. There are poor Cottars for whom something must be done immediately to relieve them or they will starve. I have directed the Ground Officer to send me a list with the number in each family which I expect tomorrow and how soon I receive it will send it to you . . . I confess I am much disheartened at this Calamity which falls so dreadfully heavy on the Small Tenants and Cottars and the more so as I congratulated you and myself on their prosperous state at Whitsun. It is now that the evil of these small possessions will be felt, not that great part of Coll is adapted for large ones. What to recommend . . . I hardly know.

He continues:

If it was possible to send these Cottars and some of the poorest Tenants to America it would be some relief and it would perhaps be as cheap as supporting them in Coll for one year if the Potato Crop is doomed as it appears to be. Next year it will be worse. Write me I beg you fully what appears to you best to be done. I will write to Coll this day making him aware of the state of matters. Oatmeal and all cheap food must expect to rise considerably but I will apprehend it will have a Contrary effect on Butcher meat. But you will have better access to be informed as to this than I have. I must also affect the Value of Highland Properties where the population is Dense . . .

PS. I strongly recommend that £1 be given to every Cottar who takes himself and his family away entirely from the island immediately . . . harvest work is now come on and such as are able and willing will get work, Railways and other work. I would order that houses of such be raised to the ground whenever they leave so as to prevent any from returning.

It is possible that this letter persuaded Coll to take the disastrous step that was to ruin the family. Hugh had seen the effect of the 1837 crisis on his people and knew that he was going to need a new source of funds if the Coll estate was to ride out the failure of the potato crop. Julia Alexa writes:

In this year in an evil hour my Uncle Robertson persuaded Papa, and Papa Aunt Albane, to advise a transfer of some money of Sir Hector's (they being trustees) from Coutt's bank into certain 'Peruvian Bonds' for the sake of higher interest. £8,000 was thus transferred, and this was eventually to increase to £30,000. My Uncle Robertson and the Peruvian Minister were to

481

go shares with Sir Hector in the profits. Then everyone would benefit and the money was to be as safe as at Coutts (of course!) The transfer was made in due form, correctly and in order, and people from Coutt's with various documents, people from the India House, lawyers, doctors and all were assembled in the drawing room of No.3 Northwick Terrace. Certificates, signatures, in all due form were given, received and signed. All was right as possible.[5]

Despite the failure of Jane Robertson's money to arrive twenty years earlier, Hugh, the Panglossian eternal optimist, was completely taken in by his brother-in-law's persuasive tongue. He wrote to Captain Campbell with the good news and explained that that he was going to be financially independent of his rents. In the meantime he wished to pay for Indian meal for his people. On 17th August 1846 Donald Campbell replied:

My dear Sir, I am favoured with yours of the 11th. I rejoice exceedingly at what you say regarding your own prospects. Nothing that regards [concerns ?] your welfare can be indifferent to me. I have made enquiry regarding Indian meal and from all I have been able to learn I doubt if it is superior to Oatmeal. It is certainly cheaper but if ground for any time it gets sour and it is not so palatable to the people as the other and I would recommend that only part of the sum you mention should be at first laid out in the purchase of it. I do all I can to induce Cottars in Coll who have no land to take themselves and families out of the country.

As we have seen, Donald Campbell was considered 'a safe man' where money was concerned.[6] He advised Hugh to be cautious and when wrote on 7th September 1846 said: 'I am exceedingly rejoiced that your own prospects are so bright, but do not be too sanguine till you actually handle the cash. These South American Governments are so changeable'. He then goes on to say 'I shall not lose a day in applying the money you mention after it arrives purchasing Oat & Indian Corn Meal. It will be much required'.

The situation in Coll was indeed dire. James Maclean, the tenant's son in Totronald, had written to his uncle as early as the 7th July to say: 'Our crop is looking well except the potato. It is most lamentable to look at it for it is of no use altogether except a very little'. The situation was even worse in November when he wrote:

Our potatoes are all perished here long ago. It would not supply us with two days the produce of 15 barrels that we sowed in spring, but we have a good de[a]l of corn as much as will supply us with Meal during the year, but not half so fruitful as it was last years for the rains passed over it in July and also in August. Even then our barley will not weigh 40 lbs per bushel instead of 50 lbs it weighed the last three years.

Hugh might wish to help his people, but until he produced the cash Donald Campbell would do nothing. On 14th September he wrote to Hugh to say that he doubted if Hunter would advance the £100 Hugh proposed to spend on Indian corn. He continues: 'Your poor people will now for the present have to depend on what you can spare yourself'. This was to be Hugh's problem throughout the Famine. His heart might be in the right place, but unless his gamble on the Peruvian bonds succeeded, he was not in a position to give much help to anyone. He was, however, tireless in his efforts to persuade the government to do something. His neighbours did not always appreciate his efforts. On 21st September William Clark, who now owned the Isle of Ulva, wrote to Captain Campbell at Quinish.

> We are all much obliged to Coll for the trouble and attention he has taken in London and at the Treasury regarding the potato calamity, but I fear the goodness of his heart and with the view of obtaining more ready Government assistance, he may have represented us richer and able to come forward than we really are. Which would just make the Government a greater [?] leave us to our own resources. Coll in his letter to me [of] the 11th Inst. (After leaving the Treasury where he met Sir E Coffin on the eve of his departure for here) proposes that we, the distressed [proprietors], should assess our selves of £1,000 & lay up in the store Indian Corn at Tobermory. He has other proposals as to carrying on & completing the Mull roads – as to the roads I perfectly agree with Coll provided Government help us as they did in Ireland – Coll also proposes making the poor rate assessment much higher – now like him I consider the Mull proprietors at Martinmas fair and Whitsun next can look for no rents from their tenants. I mean those under £20 . . . I will just ask where and how are we to get money to carry through these three plans – we should never lose sight of telling Government . . . that we the Mull people both proprietors and tenants *are really poor* and in as much want and poverty as any of the Irish . . . the poorer we show ourselves to be, and the less our ability to come forward so much the more are the Government bound to aid and assist us and so they will if it be properly represented.[7]

Hugh's proposal to lay up a store of Indian corn at Tobermory was similar to the plan put forward by the Marquess of Lorne, soon to become 8th Duke of Argyll, who wanted such a store to deal with the immediate problem.[8] Such a suggestion was commonsense and was not contraversial. Hugh's proposal to increase the poor rate assessment was.

The Poor Law Amendment Act of 1845 had made it clear that the able-bodied poor in Scotland would not be supported by the state. The proprietors on whose estates they lived must, as in the past, provide for them, although there was no legal liability that they should do so it was the accepted practice that the proprietors would. That they would continue to do so was the core of the government's thinking.[9] 'The new poor law will be a grievous one. We have yet felt all its weight and I must make you aware there will be a woeful falling off in the payment of your rents from the smaller tenants. Do not expect to get a shilling', Donald Campbell wrote in September 1846.[10]

At the beginning of the month the local leadership in Mull, Coll and Tiree met to consider what measures should be taken to relieve the situation. Alexander Maclean, younger of Coll and Captain Donald Campbell represented the Coll estate. Mr Neil Maclean Minister of Tiree and Coll were amongst the ministers who attended. Young Coll pointed out that most of his crofters and cottars were dependent on the potato for their sustenance and had not the means to buy meal. The wealthier tenants had also lost heavily and were in no position to help their poorer neighbours.

At the meeting the proprietors agreed to continue to support the destitute until the government announced their plans to deal with the emergency. They also decided to appoint a standing committee to oversee measures to relieve the current situation. Coll was to be represented by Donald Campbell the factor, Neil Maclean of Crossapol, John Campbell of Cornaig and Alexander Campbell of Caolis.

The government also moved with surprising speed: Charles Trevelyan, Assistant Secretary to the Treasury, who had been the Whitehall end of those administering famine relief in Ireland, was to direct similar operations in Scotland; Sir Edward Pine Coffin, who had just spent the first months of 1846 in the west of Ireland, was appointed Commissary-General and sent to Scotland to report on the situation there. He visited most of the west coast islands but, as a result of the weather, failed to reach Coll. He did, however, see Captain Campbell in Mull and in Oban met Hugh, who was on his way to Mull with meal to be distributed amongst his people.

Although the government was adamant that the proprietors were responsible for their people, they accepted that it would place a substantial financial burden on them. And as early as August 1846 they brought in an 'Act to authorise the Advance of Public Money to promote the Improvement of Land in Great Britain and Ireland',[11] which was part of Sir Robert Peel's policy of compensating British agriculture for the loss of the protection it had had before the repeal of the Corn Laws. The new act gave landowners and tenants grants to drain and fence land. They were to be repaid over 22 years and were charged at 6½% per annum. The act enabled landowners not only to improve their land, but also saved them money as their crofters, when they were paid wages could buy meal and pay their rents. At the same time the government sent depot ships to the islands from which proprietors could obtain supplies at cost.

Hugh Maclean of Coll was the first landowner in Scotland to apply for a grant under the Drainage Act. He was allocated £1,000.[12] It would not, however, be paid immediately and in October 1846 he wrote to Charles Trevelyan:

From the statement I have made of my own case you must see that I can do no more. I have full expectation that if these loans are obtained and work forthwith set a-going, my own people will require no further public assistance. But I fear that if all the usual formalities be insisted on, and no assurance of such loans being speedily granted reach us, the extreme of destitution must overtake us and the absolute starvation of many ensue.[13]

The government's speed in sending its inspectors could not, however, be faulted. By the end of October an inspector had visited Coll and reported on the suitability of land for drainage. Work started and Hugh could write to Trevelyan that:

I find my tenants so eager in the matter of drainage, that I propose doubling the amount of my first application . . . a great part of the drainage must be in small portions, from desire to bring work to the doors of lesser tenants.[14]

In December he applied for another grant for £3,570. Donald Campbell was less enthusiastic about drainage. On 25th September he had reluctantly written to Hunter to say:

if Coll persists in borrowing money on the Drainage Act. I am willing to try one of the Parks at Breachacha.[15]

Hunter was probably no more enthusiastic than Campbell. Drainage grants could ease cash flow and enable to the people to pay for food, their rents and even arrears, but they had to be repaid. Creditors on the estate would also not be enthusiastic, as money owed to the government would take precedence over their loans, some of which had been bought up by Hunter and his partners.

Hugh now proposed to move to Mull to superintend famine relief. The problem was he had nowhere to live. However, his loyal factor came to the rescue and on 21st September wrote to say:

> I regret at hearing you say you have no house in Mull while I reside here you may make it as much yours as mine & it is much my desire that you turn me out by building me a farm house at Mingary.[16]

Money to help the people in Coll and Quinish continued to come in from various sources. In September David Ross in Tobermory sent £20. The major source, however, was from Hugh's sister Breadalbane and their uncle Sir Hector Maclean. They sent £30 in September and a further £50 three months later. Coll's own finances also seem once again to have given cause for hope and in October when Donald Campbell wrote to Hunter he said

> You will see the farm of Caolis is also on the market. If they are sold reasonably will Coll make an attempt to purchase? Caolis is worth £150 rent.[17]

Progress in carrying out his plans for drainage at Breacachadh was slowed down by the refusal of Glasgow manufacturers to make tile drains that were suitable for the sandy soil. Then in the autumn work had to stop because of the appalling weather.

The situation in Coll was getting increasingly desperate. On 27th October Donald Campbell wrote to Hugh:

> I hope the Government meal will soon arrive. They are beginning to cry loudly from Coll, where the destitution will be felt first.[18]

As soon as he was back in Mull, Hugh wrote to Trevelyan to say that:

> The distress begins to be severely felt in this quarter. All my people are fully employed, yet they cannot obtain the needful supply, there being nothing for sale at Tobermory; and I have distributed all the Indian meal I could procure in Glasgow on my way home.[19]

The government, however, was also experiencing difficulties in procuring grain of acceptable quality for its supply ship. In addition to the famine in Ireland the blight had affected other European countries contributing to the shortage. As a result the store ship the *Belvidere* did not reach Tobermory until December. When it did arrive its cargo was immediately sent on to Coll. Neil Maclean of Crossapol then distributed it.

Hugh was now sharing Quinish House with his factor. Hugh's proximity seems to have dampened Campbell's optimism for in December he writes:

> The Laird is still confined to the house by his sore foot. I fear his expectations are too sanguine as to his Peruvian speculations. Some of his plans here are at best rash and I have endeavoured to persuade him from them altho' his great aim in them is to give to people employment. But should his expectations in which he is sanguine fail where are the funds to come from?[20]

Mr Neil Maclean's old flat mate the Rev. Dr Norman Macleod was now Convener of the Central Board of Management for Highland Relief. On 23rd December 1846 Campbell wrote to him to report on the situation on the Coll estate. He writes:

My dear Doctor,

I have just received your circular of the 19th. I rejoice to hear of your charitable inclination towards the poor Highlanders. Relief cannot be sent too soon. The cases of destitution that come daily to my knowledge are most distressing and altho' Coll has been here for some time back on purpose that he may know the state of his people and do all he can to relieve them, yet he finds it impossible to do [all] their destitute cases requires. He has ground work and drainage works &c for the greater part of the able bodied but there is a class and a large one of poor people, male and female who are not able to work and yet have no legal claim to be put on the poor roll who are very destitute. There is at least 100 families on his estate of poor cottars that have no land that are in a state of destitution that I cannot describe. They are indeed at this moment principally supported by his charity and that of other members of his family.[21]

Shortly before Christmas when Coll left for London. Campbell writes that:

He was more full than ever of his plans & improvements here. I trust he may be able to accomplish them. He is a man of the most amiable and benevolent aspirations I ever knew, but I wish he would sometimes consider more before rashly entering into some of his plans.[22]

The situation in the Islands was getting worse and the people were rapidly reaching the limit of their sparse resources. Some were reduced to a diet consisting almost entirely of shellfish, and to one meal a day. Others were reported to be 'sending their children to bed early to reduce the pangs of hunger'.[23] Sheep stealing was reported to be on the increase,[24] and was taking place in Quinish. The factor wrote:

sheep stealing is going on to a great extent. I yesterday on some suspicion I entertained sent McGregor with a warrant & assistants to search a house in Dervaig where a young man of the name of Maclean & a sister lived with an old woman their grandmother Callich Eustin as she is called & they found no less than 3 carcases of sheep that had been killed the night before & were identified as belonging to Ardow & the young man and his sister are likely bound to see Botany Bay.[25]

In January Campbell had been loud in his praises of Hugh's efforts on behalf of his people. For instance he had written to Clark of Ulva to say:

Coll left me 10 days ago for London. He is so sanguine of his plans that he would leap over all forms of obstacles to accomplish his object. Still it is all from Benevolence, & his wish to do good'.[26]

In his letters to Hunter, however, he was becoming critical of the Laird. Towards the end of the month he wrote:

The report that the proprietor of Coll has furnished meal & bere for his people arose probably from my purchasing a good deal of meal for the store for the tenants with their own money...[27]

He was equally scathing about some of his plans to improve the land in Quinish he was intending to take from Campbell for his own use. In another letter to Hunter he writes:

I think I wrote to you that Coll has given instructions to drain & trench some fields within the grounds he intends (on coming to live here) to reserve to himself, they are such as I would on no account undertake to improve for myself, not being a paying concern.[28]

He was also getting irritated with Coll for writing to him to hurry up with his plans for drainage and was quite prepared to let him know it. On 12th February he wrote:

You tell me to go on with work, but the main spring is wanting *cash*. I have advanced all I could for the Drains already.[29]

It is clear from his correspondence that the strain on Donald Campbell was beginning to tell. At the beginning of the famine he comes through as a concerned if realistic man. However, as the winter dragged on a new hardness is apparent in his dealings with people on the Coll estate, including his own employees. For instance on 15th February he writes to Martin McCaill his ploughman at Gallanach to say:

I have sent word to Peter McPherson to give you some meal, but you must be aware you are running in my debt. I take this opportunity of giving you warning that I will not require your services after Whitsun first. I give you this early notice that you may look for another place yourself. There never were better wages for good workers in the Low Country than now and your son Donald might earn 5/– a day. You may not expect any place from me.[30]

Alexander Hunter had been contemplating the long-term future of the Coll estate. His solutions all involved getting rid of a great part of the population. Campbell agreed. But how was it to be done? He writes:

I differ with you in thinking that Coll is adapted for dairy[ing] with a very few exceptions. The whole south side from Freslan eastward is a sheet of black heath with the exception of a few patches of reclaimed moss. The north side with the exception of Breachacha, Cliad, Mibost & Gallanach so interspersed with rock that you will not get two acres of arable adjoining and every rough acre of it in want of draining. But it would puzzle Smith of Deanston to set about it. I have got the survey of Coll, which I will send you. That of Quinish is mislaid somewhere at Drumfine where the Laird could not find it. When I have maturely considered the matter I will give you my ideas. At present my idea is that sheep would pay. A considerable range might be joined on the south side from the march of Breachacha all the way to Arinagour...[31]

It was not until 20th March that the factor put his detailed thoughts on paper concerning the present state and possible future of the different farms on the estate. In a letter to Hunter about the attitude of the population he says: 'you are in a mistake they will never move of their own accord – they will rather die of starvation. I mean the Cottars. Once we are quit of the greater part of the people I have no doubt a better arrangement could be made – I have been giving it the best consideration in my power. The following is the best I can propose':

Totronald will support itself, the only farm on Coll that will completely do so.
Grimsary would do so by doubling the crofts.
Crossipol along with Totamore would take the three small crofts of Ballyhough.
Ballyhough the other two crofts of this farm being double ones will support themselves.
Acha the miller at Acha would take Acha & all Gorten to the march of Freslan for which he has plenty subject.
Freslan and all the south side I would be inclined to put in one to put in tenement [piece of land held by an owner] as there is a good deal of heather & hill ground attached it all way to Arynagour.
Grisipol The state of this farm can only be improved by doubling the crofts.
Mibost Should support itself.
Cliad This also should support itself but it is in Lachlan Johnston [the ground officer] and His late brother's families' possession but they want subject and have fallen much in arrears.
Arnabost This farm will only do by having the crofts doubled – the tenants [are] all poor.
Toraston This might do in one possession or as well join Gallanach – but I am not inclined to take more land. The tenants are poor.
Trelvaig very small possession that should be joined to Toraston.
Arinagour A nest of paupers that will pay no rent.
Penmore & Dervaig will rank with the worst farms in Coll owing to excess of population – But what is to be done – if we dispute normal obligations to support the people. Sir E Coffin will tell as he did Mr Clark of Ulva that it is a question if necessary he will refer to Parliament whether proprietors were not legally as well as morally responsible . . .[32]

Despite everyone's efforts the people of Coll had had a desperate winter. There had been 'Great mortality among the old people this year', Campbell wrote to Hugh adding that: 'Lachlan McPhaden, Lonban & Duncan Mckinnon, Grimsary died lately. They were two of your oldest tenants'.[33] As usual Hugh's sister Breadalbane and Sir Hector had been of enormous help. Miss Maclean had hopes of getting some potatoes from Spain. 'I pray to God she may succeed' wrote the factor.[34] The same day he wrote to Miss Maclean of Coll. 'If you can be the means of sending a cargo of potatoes to Tobermory to be sold to the *Tenants* at a moderate price you can bestow no benefit on the half so great'. She also promised to send £100 cash from Sir Hector. Campbell acknowledged the donation immediately saying 'Good Sir Hector's benevolence knows no bounds. I will not apply the £100 you are to send until I advise you how this must be spend'.[35]

The donation was timely, as the factor had just written to Coll to say that 'your tenants in Coll & Mull will require at least 300 bolls of oats & 100 of beir'.[36] The situation in Coll was even worse than Campbell believed. A delegation from the Island arrived at Quinish to inform him 'that unless seed oats are got for the island a great part of the ground will be unsown as many have been obliged to consume their seed Corn for food. Can any thing be done? Even 100 Bolls of oats & 50 Bere would be much'.[37] On the same day he alerted Coll to the new crisis:

488

The account I have today from Coll of scarcity of seed oats is alarming. I wrote to Glasgow last week regarding them. But as ready cash is required I fear my funds will not allow me to go far. Be so good as to write in course of Post what you can do.[38]

Sir Hector's donation was diverted to the purchase of seed instead of foodstuff. He wrote to tell Hunter what he had done:

I have sent for 50 Bolls seed oats for which I am to pay by cash sent me from Sir Hector through Miss Maclean – but this will not suffice & I fear a great part of the ground will be unsown. It will be impossible to get them to dibble it.[39]

In addition to the support from the Coll family help came from the Free Church. A large number of its followers lived in areas worst affected by the potato blight. It also had a large following among congregations in the cities, who could be expected to come to the aid of their co-religionists, and by the end of December 1846 Free Church congregations in the Lowlands had, after five Sunday collections, raised over £10,400.[40] They also had practical ways they could help and on 9th January 1847 Donald Campbell reported to Hugh that:

Dr Mackay, Dunoon & some other Free Chuch men were lately in Coll & took away about 40 from the island to work at Railways.

Investment in railways reached its peak in the 1840s.[41] Constructing them was labour intensive and labourers could earn 15–16 shillings a week. This was good money when most tenants in Coll were paying £7.10s.0d per year for their crofts.

It is impossible to say just how many men from Coll were to work on the railways in the 1840s, but one man who certainly did was Lachlan Maclean, Neil in Totronald's son. On 2nd April his brother James wrote to their uncle to say:

Lachlan my brother had left Coll on the 4th March for the Low Country and a letter came from him last weekend he began to work at the railroad on the 15th at a place called Larbert near Falkirk where he met with his cousin John MacDonald and James McNiven from Oban, wages from 15/– to 16/– a week. I hope he will get some place for himself this year for a great number of farmers were warned in Coll last week.[42]

'Warning farmers' meant giving them notice that they were to be evicted. In order to do so Campbell had to get a 'Removing notice' from the Sheriff Court in Tobermory. He had consulted Hunter on what to do when on the 13th March he wrote:

Now that the time of warnings is come, what is to be done regarding the estate this year – I am perfectly at a loss to give my advice regarding it. No doubt some would require to be removed, but removing any this year will create a great outcry and sensation . . .[43]

Both Campbell and Hunter were well aware of the danger of a bad publicity. The potato famine had caught the attention of the national press and both the *Scotsman* and the *Times* had sent investigative reporters to the Hebrides. Their search for a good story having been made considerably easier now that a regular steamship service was available.[44]

Despite the need for caution Hunter obtained Removing Summonses against twelve tenants in Coll and two in Quinish. The summons stated that 'the pursuer has oft and divers times desired and required the said defenders to flit and remove themselves their wives bairns families servants sub-tenants cottars . . .' from 'the expiry of their title and right of possession'.[45]

It is clear that summonses of removal were often used as a threat to compel the payment of arrears of rent. For instance Roderick Morison at Bellachroy was still in his tack when Campbell wrote to him in May to say: 'it is necessary that you come here to know the exact conditions on which you are to occupy part of the land of Bellachroy and Kilbeg.' One was that he was 'allowed to keep or sell no spirits in the shop or house. This Coll makes an express condition' of his remaining.[46] As Roderick kept the Bellachroy Hotel, he was hardly going to make any profit or pay his rent in future. That Campbell was not entirely heartless is clear from his treatment of Allan MacPhaden in Totronald who had been given notice to quit. As he explains to Hunter:

> An old man Allan McPhaden in Totronald who for some years had only half a croft is fallen so far in arrears it is no use keeping him there. I have joined his half croft to the other giving him his house & a cow grass deducting of the rent for [?] access the sum of £2. He is 87 and has paid rent to Coll for 60 & I could not bear to cast him wholly adrift.[47]

Seven of those warned in Coll do not appear in the 1851 Census. They had presumably left the Island. On 28 June 1847 the factor wrote to tell Coll that

> he had returned from Coll on Saturday night. The rent collection has not been good but not worse than I expected. I return to Coll in a few day's time to take the Crop of the Emigrants at Valuation, at least of such as cannot otherwise be disposed of. There are about 120 going in all.[48]

Only 40 are accounted for among the families of those warned to leave, so another 80 must have left of their own accord. On the 9th July Campbell writes to Hugh to say

> The Emigrants are away from Coll to the number of about 100 – This relieves us but little as it is not the most destitute that are gone.[49]

The emigrants made their way to Liverpool from where they were to sail to Canada. They were in a pitiable state and someone wrote to Miss Maclean to complain. She in turn asked the factor for an explanation. As he explained to Hunter:

> It seems that some one has been writing Miss Maclean an account of the Destitute state of the emigrants on their reaching Glasgow, which have been grossly exaggerated. This getting of their land was the Voluntary act of them all & I believe every one of the tenants with the exception of Campbell whose wife wrote you had the means of transporting themselves & families. I cannot speak with such certainty as to those who were not tenants but I believe they had also had the means.[50]

Hugh himself wrote a furious letter to his factor who told Hunter that:

Coll writes me also in great consternation about my charging such of the Tenants as emigrated for the seed corn they received – even of a reduced rate, with the exception of Campbell at Arinagour. I considered all that I charged able to pay the trifle charged which in the whole amounted but to £2.16/–. I wish Coll would enquire a little into matters before he writes so hastily.[51]

However destitute the emigrants were when they reached Liverpool, their plight was nothing to what happened to them next. One of the tenants Murdoch Johnston was later to write from Canada to his brother William in India:

My very beloved William,

It is with pen of grief and ink of tears that I fabricate a letter of sympathetic feelings and renew my melancholy wounds which are marked so deep in my heart that it will not be heeled or made up this side of Jordan ... I left Coll in the year 1847. You know that the Lord blessed me with children. He gave me seven boys and two girls so that I could stay no longer in Coll with my poor family when The Lord cut the staff of bread from our mouths ... I left Liverpool on the 7th July 1847 with a number of Irish men who had fever among them. There was also the pox, even the smallpox ... After ten days at sea, the disease broke out with mortal power to all of us. My wife, myself and all the children were seized with the smallpox and after four days my most lovely Alexander was interred in the watery grave of the Atlantic Ocean ... We came after a voyage of seven weeks and five days to a place called Quarantine Island ... Hospitals and doctors were there to inspect the immigrants and when we landed we were taken away, the men to one hospital, the women and the children to another. I was kept in the hospital with the black fever for two months. When I recovered a little I searched for the children and my dear wife. I found my wife and one of the children in one of the hospitals. They did not know what had become of the other children but they expected that they had all died. I was told to search in Quebec and in Montreal for them as maybe they were some of them alive and been sent away with the well people in the steamboats. I was sent away from Quarantine Island and left my dear wife behind with the fever as they would not allow me to await her, which proved to be the last sight of my dear espoused wife.

Eventually Murdoch found some of his children his children in Montreal. He made his way to Mara, near Lake Simcoe, where several people from Coll had settled. Neil Mackinnon, who had been on the Laird of Coll's wherry had taken care of two of the children.[52] Murdoch was to live to become a prominent citizen in Mara and be one of the two Collachs responsible for the building of a Presbyterian church there.[53]

Notes

1. TM Devine *The Great Highland Famine* (1988), v.
2. Mull Museum Archives D12/113.
3. When the uncle James McDonald, Sheriff-Substitute of Inveraray died his widow hid his correspondence in a wall in their house. Copies of the letters from Coll are in BCT. 1840s folder.

4. Argyll & Bute Archives. Minute Book of Coll Parochial Board. CO 6. 7. 5. 1.
5. Juliet Alexa's Journal, 103.
6. *The Diary of James Robertson*, 3.
7. Mull Museum Archives D12/113.
8. Parliamentary Papers, LIII *Correspondence from July 1846 to February 1847 relating to the Measures adopted for the Relief of the Distress in Scotland* (1847), 17.
9. *The Great Highland Famine*, 83.
10. Donald Campbell to Hugh Maclean of Coll 19 September 1846. Mull Museum Archives D12/113.
11. 9 & 10 Vic. Cap. C1 (1846). *The Great Highland Famine*, 100.
12. Parliamentary Papers (1847), XXXIV. Application for advance of Public Money under provision of Act 9 & 10 Vic. Cap. C1, 101.
13. Parliamentary Papers. Correspondence relating to the measures adopted for the Relief of Distress in Ireland and Scotland (1847), LIII, 95.
14. *Ibid*, 169.
15. 26 September 1846. Donald Campbell to Alexander Hunter WS. Mull Museum Archives D12/113.
16. 21 September 1846. Donald Campbell to Hugh Maclean of Coll. Mull Museum Archives D12/113.
17. 2 October 1846. Donald Campbell to Alexander Hunter. Mull Museum Archives D12/113.
18. Parliamentary Papers. Correspondence relating to the measures adopted for the relief of Distress in Ireland and Scotland (1847), LIII, 169.
19. *Ibid*, 168.
20. 19 December 1846. Donald Campbell to Alexander Hunter. Mull Museum Archives D12/113.
21. 23 December 1846. Donald Campbell to the Rev. Dr. Norman Macleod. Mull Museum Archives D12/113.
22. 29 December 1846. Donald Campbell to Alexander Hunter. Mull Museum Archives D12/113.
23. *The Great Highland Famine*, 43.
24. *The Great Highland Famine*, 43.
25. 24 February 1847. Donald Campbell to Hugh Maclean of Coll. Mull Museum Archives D12/113
26. 4 January 1847. Donald Campbell to Clark of Ulva. Mull Museum Archives D12/113.
27. 26 January 1847. Donald Campbell to Alexander Hunter WS. Mull Museum Archives D12/113.
28. 1 February 1847. Donald Campbell to Alexander Hunter WS. Mull Museum Archives D12/113.
29. 12 February 1847. Donald Campbell to Hugh Maclean of Coll. Mull Museum Archives D12/113.
30. 15 February 1847. Donald Campbell to Martin McCaill, Ploughman, Gallanach, Coll. Mull Museum Archives D12/113.
31. 22 February 1847. Donald Campbell to Alexander Hunter WS. Mull Museum Archives D12/113.
32. 20 March 1847. Donald Campbell to Alexander Hunter WS. Mull Museum Archives D12/113.
33. 22 January 1847. Donald Campbell to Hugh Maclean of Coll. Mull Museum Archives D12/113.
34. 5 February 1847. Donald Campbell to Hugh Maclean of Coll. Mull Museum Archives D12/113.
35. 24 February 1847. Donald Campbell to Miss Maclean of Coll. Mull Museum Archives D12/113.
36. 24 February 1847. Donald Campbell to Hugh Maclean of Coll. Mull Museum Archives D12/113.
37. 13 March 1847. Donald Campbell to Alexander Hunter WS. Mull Museum Archives D12/113.
38. 13 March 1847. Donald Campbell to Hugh Maclean of Coll. Mull Museum Archives D12/113.
39. 20 March 1847. Donald Campbell to Alexander Hunter WS. Mull Museum Archives D12/113.
40. *The Great Highland Famine*, 117.
41. In 1846 and 1847 there were no fewer than twenty-seven separate companies operating in Scotland and 'three hundred miles of track were under development utilising the labour of 3000 horses and 29,000 men'. [*The Great Highland Famine*, 160].
42. 2 April 1847. James Maclean to his uncle James Macdonald. [BCT. Totronald Folder].
43. 13 March 1847. Donald Campbell to Alexander Hunter WS. Mull Museum Archives D12/113.
44. *The Great Highland Famine*, 175–6.

45. They were in Coll: Widow Ann MacDonald, Ballyhough; John Kennedy, Grimsary; John McInnes, Donald McPhaden, Malcolm Campbell, Trelvaig; John Maclean, joiner Arileod; Allan McPhaden, Totronald; Angus McInnes, Lachlan McInnes & Murdoch Johnston, Arnabost; Widow Mary Johnston, Cliad; Charles MacDonald, Grishipol, and in Quinish: Roderick Morison, Bellachroy & Kilbeg; & Neil Maclean, Kilmore [NAS. SC 59. 2.4] Several of these documents are very fragile and have probably suffered from damp.
46. 17 May 1847. Donald Campbell to Mr R Morison, Bellachroy. Mull Museum Archives D12/113.
47. 7 April 1847. Donald Campbell to Alexander Hunter WS. Mull Museum Archives D12/113.
48. 28 June 1847. Donald Campbell to Hugh Maclean of Coll. Mull Museum Archives D12/113.
49. 9 July 1847. Donald Campbell to Hugh Maclean of Coll. Mull Museum Archives D12/113.
50. 27 July 1847. Donald Campbell to Alexander Hunter WS. Mull Museum Archives D12/113.
51. 23 August 1847. Donald Campbell to Hugh Maclean of Coll. Mull Museum Archives D12/113.
52. BCT. Johnston Folder from file made up by The Rev. CH Johnson, Kamloops, British Columbia 13 January 1973. (Kamloops number. 604-376-8902) Nova Scotia Public Archives.
53. 31 May 1989. Mr Dave Sargeant RR # 1 Hawkestone, Ontario, Canada LOL 1TO to Betty Macdougall.

Chapter Fifty-Three

The Clearances

In Coll folklore Captain Donald Campbell is something of a bogeyman. He is accused of having cleared Feall and Torestan.[1] As Feall was cleared in the first decade of the nineteenth century,[2] long before he came to Coll, this is hardly fair. Torestan is another matter.

We know more about Torestan at this time than any other farm on Coll. This is, in part, because of the evidence John Johnston, Coll's sanitary inspector, gave to the Royal Commission (Highlands & Islands 1892), the so-called *Deer Forest Commission*. In addition to the printed edition Johnston made a hand written draft of his evidence, which has survived. In it he lists the rent for 1848–9 paid by each tenant in Torestan.[3] This information does not appear in the printed report, which merely states that the total rent paid by the Torestan tenants was £60. This is considerably lower than the rent of £76 the Torestan tenants paid in 1836, a reduction of almost 21% over the famine years.

In 1848–9 the man who paid the lowest rent was Donald Beaton. He was then aged 45 and had been born and brought up on Torestan. His father Abraham Beaton, in 1776 a servant of Allan Maclean in Cliad, had perhaps become a tenant at Torestan as a reward for serving with Coll's son Roderick in the 81st Regiment of Foot during the American War of Independence.[4]

The man paying the highest rent in 1848–9 (£8.10s.0d) was Murdoch Maclean, aged 80. He was a descendant of Neil Buidh and had been a soldier in Coll's company in the Breadalbane Fencibles. He later became a sergeant in the Argyll Volunteers. Another tenant, who was in Torestan in 1841 aged 80, but who was dead by 1848–9, was Hugh Maclean who had been in Torestan since 1793 and came originally from Caolis. He was married to Catherine,[5] the daughter of Coll's piper Neil Rankin, who later became tacksman of Cliad.

These three tenants were all men who were likely to be given a priority when tenancies were allocated. Torestan, which had included Trelevaig, was previously a tacksman's farm, one of several given to a younger son of the Coll family.[6] In 1794 it consisted of 70 acres of arable ground, 307 acres of green pasture and 468 acres of muir. It was good grazing. In addition its attraction at the beginning of the nineteenth century was probably its coastline and potential for cutting kelp. Torestan's profitability disappeared with the collapse of its manufacture. And when Donald Campbell wrote his report in March 1847, he says of Torestan that the 'tenants are poor'. He also says that it 'might do in one possession or as well join Gallanach – but I am not inclined to take more land'.[7] In a postscript to the same letter he writes:

> The ground officer of Coll has come in as I am writing. 5 of the best tenants have given up the lands – they are in different farms and it is difficult to replace them – I will clear Torestan if I can, but not unless I find room for the tenants – the two best in that farm are offering to have it.[8]

The best of the crofters pay £8 to £9 rent in about 8 head of cattle, a couple of horses or ponies & they generally own about 4 Bolls of oats, a Boll of bere & used to plant about 10 bags of potatoes.

North and South Trelvaig were two of the new settlements on the south coast surveyed in 1794. They were both very smallholdings and were geographically part of Torestan. North Trelvaig consisted of 8 acres of arable, 16 of green pasture and 34 of muir. South Trelvaig had only 6 acres of arable, 27 of green pasture and 22 of muir.[9] On the coast to the south and adjacent to South Trelvaig was the little farm of Fioslum, which consisted of an acre of arable and 17 acres of muir. It had, however, a good anchorage where a jetty had been built, presumably in order to load seaweed gathered on the surrounding coastline.

In his letter of the 20th March Donald Campbell describes Trelvaig as a 'very small possession that should be joined to Torestan'. Two days later he had removing summons issued to three of the crofters in Trelvaig.[10] As none of them appear in Coll at the time of the 1851 census, they presumably left the Island. One other family in Trelvaig fared better. They had left Trelvaig by 1851 but instead of leaving the Island were settled as crofters in Kilbride.[11]

In 1841 three of the Torestan tenants were 70 or more years old. Two of them are not heard of again and were probably dead.[12] On 22nd January 1847. As we have seen Campbell had written to Coll to say there was: 'Great mortality among the old people this year'.[13] Murdoch Maclean, who was 70 in 1841, was still a tenant in Torestan in 1848–9. He is not listed in the 1851 census and was presumably dead. His son Hector does not appear in the 1851 census and, after his father's death, had presumably left the Island. Murdoch's other son John was also a tenant in 1841. In 1848–9 he was paying a rent of £7.10s.0d. In 1851 he was a tenant in Grishipol.

Campbell was in no hurry to clear Torestan, and was concerned that too many tenants on Coll were intending to emigrate. As we have already noticed on 30th March he had written to Hugh to say that 'Some of the Coll tenants are going to Emigrate in whom to replace them puzzles me exceedingly as they go from different farms'.[14] And again on the 10th April he wrote to the ground officer 'if James Maclean is determined to leave Torestan who do you propose in his place?'. As James was not there in 1841 or 1848–9, he must have been in it for a very short time.

Campbell goes on to say that: 'the Torestan people must take Trelvaig. I have written permission to take John McInnes & his brother's crop at valuation'. He was also clearing Fioslum, which had no rôle now that there was no kelp to export. The only male there in 1841 was a lone cottar named Charles Macdonald, and the factor instructed the ground officer to 'try to make room for' him.[15]

Three new tenants, who were not in Torestan in 1841, appear in the 1848–9 list. All three were paying £7.10s.0d rent. One, Neil Mackinnon is perhaps the former cottar in Trelvaig in 1841. Another Lachlan Macdonald was living with his father, a tenant in Arivarich, in 1841. He is probably the man of whom Donald Campbell wrote in 1849 to the ground officer: 'I will give Lachlan MacDonald accommodation no longer. There is no need in his asking favours'.[16] If this was the same man, he again prevailed over the factor, for in 1851 he is listed as a farmer in Arnabost. The third new tenant is a Malcolm Kennedy.[17]

As far as the tenants in Torestan are concerned Donald Campbell kept his word. Donald Beaton, Euphemia Macdonald, and John Maclean all obtained crofts on Grishipol. Hector Maclean, Hugh Maclean and Catherine Rankin's son, obtained the double croft at Elan Ornsay. Only John Mackinnon who was a tenant in 1848–9 lost out economically. In 1851 he became a cottar in

Arnabost.[18] The last of the tenants, Neil Mackinnon, was not in Coll in 1851 and had probably left the Island for good.

Donald Campbell looked after the former tenants when, despite all his protestations to the contrary, he merged Torestan with his farm of Gallanach. What happened to the cottars did not concern him.[19] It is quite clear from reading Donald Campbell's letters between 1846–1850 that although he felt responsible for those who had paid rent to the Coll estate, he had no responsibility for those who had not.

By the time of the 1851 census there were no tenants living on Torestan, or on Trelvaig or Fioslum. The people there had all been cleared. However, apart from those who had emigrated, apparently voluntarily, the tenants in Torestan had all been found other berths on the Coll estate. The clearing of Torestan is not the *cause célebre* that Coll folklore would have it to be, at least as far as the tenants were concerned.

* * *

From the start of the famine Donald Campbell had been convinced that the number of landless cottars on the Coll estate must drastically be reduced. On 12th March he reminded Alexander Hunter:

> You are aware that in the beginning of last winter I offered £1 to every Cottar in Coll that removed to the Low Country with his family. A very few availed themselves of my offer but I directed the ground officer immediately to pull down the houses of those who did which was done. Among them he pulled down the house of Donald Maclean which he found unoccupied on the moor of Arnabost. He and his family having removed from the island, this man did not apply for or get the £1 having previously gone south on an intimation I sent him [by] the ground officer that he had better do so as he would certainly be removed at the first term. The man has wrought in the Low Country till now but has called here today claiming great damages for pulling down his house. His wife I understand has been serving as a nurse in Doctor Maclean of Rum's family and I have no doubt the man is urged by the doctor to see whether he can annoy me or Coll in this matter, and he will, if he can, make a case of it – the man paid no rent, had no lease, cow or horse. He built his house there by sufferance from me two or three years ago and was liable to be removed whenever I thought fit – the potato failure rendered it desirable to reduce the population as much as possible consequently finding this house unoccupied as it had been for some time it was pulled down.[20]

This is just the sort of story that was remembered on Coll and blackened the factor's reputation.

Whilst Donald Campbell's reputation plummeted that of the leading Maclean still living in Coll soared. As we have seen Neil Maclean of Crossapol had been appointed a member of the 'standing committee to oversee measures to relieve the current situation in Coll'. In particular he was responsible for the distribution of oats and barley sent to the Island.[21]

In 1847 Neil was a 41 year-old bachelor living at Crossapol House. At the time of the 1841 census he had a household of 9. They included his aunt Margaret, who was presumably the widow of Charles Gallanach, a housekeeper, two female servants and a boy. There were also living in the house three other people who were probably relatives. Neil worked the farm with three male servants who lived in a separate building. Crossapol was a good farm. It comprised of 278 acres, made up of 50 acres of arable, 23 acres of rocky arable and 204 of green pasture. In addition Neil

Crossapol rented Totamore, which consisted of 335 acres (114 arable, 96 rocky arable, 27 green pasture, 42 moss, 54 blown sand and 31 muir). In 1841 the population of Totamore was 25 people living in 5 houses. 4 of the heads of families were cottars, the other a John MacPhaden has no description after his name.

Neil was keen to expand his holding at Totamore for in April 1847, when the factor was trying to get the small tenants into more viable holdings, the latter writes:

> I think I can get the three small crofts of Ballyhough joined to Crossapol's farm of Totamore & make room for the tenants there on land of others who emigrate or leave ...... There are two of the vacant crofts not yet let because I could not get a tenant to my mind ... I will try and put the small crofters of Ballyhough in their rooms & join their crofts to Totamore, which Crossapol will be glad to get.[22]

Neil Crossapol was one of those on the Island who had obtained the vote as a result of the 1832 Reform Bill. He was thereafter addressed as 'Neil Maclean Esq. Crossapol'. He had, however, been educated on the Island and Donald Campbell perhaps considered that he was something of a country bumpkin. And when a Parochial Board was established on Coll to look after paupers supported by the Scottish Poor Law the factor wrote to Neil to say:

> I find circumstances prevent my going to Coll till after the Mull market. Consequently I cannot attend the meeting of the Parochial Board on Monday 16th August but if you have the Minister of Tiree you will be all right. If not I must I suppose adjourn the meeting till after the Mull market about the 24th. I send you the new act for your guidance you will have to study it that we may be more regular[23]

It was a somewhat patronising letter, implying that all would be well provided his cousin Mr Neil Maclean, the minister was there to hold Crossapol's hand.

Neil Crossapol's irritation comes through in the minutes of the meeting, which was held at Arileod on the 16th August. After the list of those present, which included 'Neil McLean Esq. Crossapol, Mr John Maclean Arileod, assisted by the Rev. Neil Maclean Minister of Tyree and Coll', the minute states:

> The Chairman having failed to attend Mr Maclean Crossapol was elected Chairman.[24]

Neil was to continue to be chairman for the next seven years, even when the factor was present and was to receive glowing plaudits for his work during the famine.[25]

Donald Campbell had cause to regret not attending that first meeting of the Parochial Board. In June 1843, when he had given evidence before the Poor Law Inquiry for Scotland, he said that 'the tenants in Coll and in Mull are particularly kind to the poor in their neighbourhood. There is no person in danger of being in destitution in this country'. He had, however, 'not a doubt but it would destroy the disposition which at present exists amongst the farmers to assist their poor neighbours, if a legal assessment were laid on for the maintenance of the poor'.[26]

At the beginning of the famine Campbell had written to Coll to say that: 'the new poor law will be a grievous one. We have yet felt all its weight'.[27] He had also said in his letter to Crossapol 'I think we must assess for 8d in the £1 – the same we do here. I spoke to Mr Nisbet as Trustee on the Caolis and Cornaig estates who will go along with whatever is decided upon'.[28]

The Parochial Board did not agree with the factor. At their first meeting, it was minuted that:

> taking into consideration that the funds hitherto provided for relief of the Poor of this Island by voluntary contribution has been totally inadequate to that purpose, resolved that the sum of one hundred and fifty pounds Sterling is required for their support during the ensuing year and that this amount must be raised by legal assessment.
>
> They have further agreed to adopt the third mode of assessment pointed out by the act, and to impose an equal percentage of 4% on the annual value of lands & heritages in the island as well as on the estimated income of the inhabitants derived from means & substance.[29]

Later at their meeting on 14th February 1848 the Parochial Board agreed to exempt crofters paying rent of £5 & under from being assessed. However, they directed 'the Collector to intimate to Mr Campbell Breachacha Factor for Coll that the Parochial Board have assessed him in the full amount of his salary as Factor as well as his income as Inspector of Drains, estimated at £100 Stg per annum'.

At the same meeting the Parochial Board unanimously elected three new members for the following year:

Rev. Archibald Nicol.
Alexander Campbell of Caolis JP
Mr Alexander Stewart, Teacher.[30]

They replaced John Maclean, Arileod and Lachlan Johnston, the Ground Officer. The new Board members were hardly likely to be congenial to the factor. Two were certainly Free Church[31] and the third, Alexander Campbell, probably was too.[32]

Perhaps in addition to the rivalry between the two churches, there was a lingering anti-Campbell attitude still prevailing in Coll. Not only was the factor's advice ignored, and his poor law assessment made a high one but he was not consulted, as he probably had been previously over anything concerning the estate. On the 14th January 1848 he wrote somewhat wistfully to the Laird

> I believe the Local Committee of Coll had part of a house at Arinagour for a store for their meal for which they paid the *owner of the House* something, but what the sum was I do not know. I was never consulted. It was I suppose done with Dr Boyter's sanction.

However, he cannot resist implying that the Committee's decision was wrong:

> The Session House has been for some time the store house here and as the Rats have completely destroyed the floor to get at the Meal. Dr Boyter has agreed (for the Destitution Board) to put a new floor in it and to fill up between the sleepers with stone & lime.[33]

* * *

The Poor-Law Amendment Act of 1845 exacerbated the problem of Tiree and Coll being one parish. Initially both parts of the parish agreed on the same method of assessment, however, in September 1848 the Parochial Board of Tiree decided to change their method and wrote to Coll to 'to know the sentiments of the Coll Board'. The latter were, however, unanimous that the original system suited their part of the parish and Neil Crossapol and Alexander Campbell were authorised to attend the Tiree Board's meeting on 21st September at Kirkapol with full power to act for the Coll Board.[34] The two boards could not agree on the same method of assessment. Coll's representatives arguing that if the second method were adopted: 'the assessment would fall on a few tacksmen, the land being generally subdivided into small crofts under thirty pounds rent, & with exception of a Free Church Minister few people of income exceeding thirty pounds reside on the island'.[35]

The Board of Supervision refused to accept the Coll Board's request that they should continue to use the original method of assessment. They agreed that the cost of supporting the poor in the island over the next twelve months would be £177. In addition the Barony Parish Glasgow claimed that they were owed £18.7 Stg for the support they gave to three Collachs who now lived there. The Board accepted responsibility for one of them but not the other two.

* * *

Paupers supported by the parish were not the only people in the Highland famine area requiring help. In addition to those legally entitled to support, there were a great many other people, particularly the able-bodied poor, who were in desperate need. However, the political philosophy of the time was that state interference should be at a minimum. This doctrine was dealt a body blow by the Irish Potato Famine, which affected several million people and killed between 1 and 1.2 million. In the West Highlands and Islands the number of people seriously at risk was never more than 150,000 and although mortality rates did start to rise the crisis was successfully contained.

The Scottish famine also occurred a year after that of Ireland and the government had learnt a great deal from its Irish experience. As we have seen the government did intervene in 1846 and 1847 but by August 1847 when it ended its operations, it was more than happy to leave the administration of famine relief to the Central Board of Management for Highland Relief. This body had been set up to co-ordinate the activities of the benevolent societies in the Lowlands, whose extraordinary growth since Waterloo was a symptom of the nation's new wealth, and of the powerful influence of the church which stressed that it was a Christian's duty to help his less fortunate neighbours. Response to the crisis in the Highlands was unusually generous, even by the standards of Victorian philanthropy, and by the end of 1847 the Central Board had £209,376 at its disposal for famine relief in Scotland.[36]

The Central Board's money enabled it to assist those who were outside the scope of the Poor Law. Its policy was, however, strictly in line with the dominant philosophy of the Victorian middle class, who loathed the 'demoralising effects of gratuitous relief'.[37] Help would only be given in exchange for work. As a result all over the West Highlands and Islands gangs of men, women and children were found repairing and building walls and constructing roads and piers. Inevitably this work was done in co-operation with the landowner, who was required to pay a proportion of the cost. The estate was involved in deciding what work should take place for on 13th March 1848 Campbell writes to Hunter:

> I saw Crossapol lately and all the suggestions you made as to Coll roads I gave him instructions regarding – I told him to employ Caldwell & get from him the drainage tools that would be of use for the roads.[38]

Equally inevitably this 'cooperative system' was attacked for diverting charitable money into the pockets of landowners.[39]

The number of people in the islands who were suitable to act as the Central Board's representatives was limited. They were inevitably the same men who ran the Parochial Board. Men with experience of the islands were also limited and Dr Boyter, who had been employed to recruit emigrants for Australia in 1836, was employed to report on how the Central Board's money should be spent. In March 1847 he visited Coll, having already spent some time on Tiree. He writes:

On Saturday the 25th I rode a considerable distance over the eastern portion of Tyree, and crossed by the ferry to Coll in a very heavy gale of wind with rain, which continued that day and the following; and having appointed the *Torch* to call for me at the eastern extremity of Coll, and to bring a supply of meal ... During this journey I had an opportunity of seeing various parties employed in road making and repairing, but such is the sandy formation of the country, and the want of material for that purpose, that I see no great chance of doing much good at that work.

He goes on to say that:

Mr Maclean [of Coll] intends laying before the Board the estimates and plan of a pier, which, as an accommodation for fishers, would be most serviceable and when I mention that there are 100 families who have neither land nor means of living, I conceive that employment at this pier would be the most serviceable way of employing their time. I therefore most earnestly recommend Mr Maclean of Coll's claim for some pecuniary assistance in the erection of this pier.[40]

When on the 13th April he reached Tobermory he wrote a specific memorandum on Coll. It was published as Appendix No. III to his report:

Island of Coll.
This island, with the exception of the farms of Caoles (Alexander Campbell Esq, proprietor) and Cornaig (John Campbell, Esq, proprietor) belongs to Mr Maclean of Coll; it is 14 miles long and 3 broad. Population 1200.

Mr Neil Maclean of Crossapol has held the appointment of sub-inspector, and a more intelligent, impartial man could not have been found in the island. The work done under his superintendence has been:

1st a line of of road thirteen feet in breadth [running], from the march of Arinagour to Cliad – distance about 2 miles. The principal advantages of this road are that the numerous population on the farms in the immediate vicinity will thereby be enabled to lead their peats in summer and their manure in winter. It is also useful as forming a connecting link with the public road to the east end of the island.

2nd a piece of road one mile and a half long, and 15 feet broad running from the farm of Ballyhough to Grishipol in the centre of the island. This piece of road will be of use to the whole inhabitants of the island, particularly in so far as it enables them to get with horses and carts to the ferry of Arinagour, to the district mill, to the church, and indeed to any part of the island where roads are made.

3rd Two miles and a half of road 14 feet broad from Totronald to Breachacha forming the connecting link of a now complete communication to the west end of the island.

4th A road about 1 mile in length through the village of Arinagour to a piece of ground used by the villagers for raising crops. In consequence of this road and the facility thereby afforded for taking out manure, the poor people have this year been able to cultivate 5 or 6 acres of land, which they could not otherwise have done.

The Committee did not provide employment for the females, but Miss Maclean of Coll had been carrying on extensive operations and established a frock manufacturing at Arinagour. However, the report states: 'I regret to learn, however, that not with standing her great exertions, this employment has been attended with so much loss that she will be obliged to discontinue'. It goes on to say:

It will be remembered that two boats, and four of the east country fishermen, were employed at this island for the last two months of their engagement with the Committee. The success which they met with was very encouraging, the value of the fish caught during that short period being £73.5s.6d, and I understand that these men are so elated with their success, and so confident of continued good fortune in prosecuting the fishing off this island, that they intend returning to settle there. Since their departure, the natives who have been fishing with the Committee's materials have not been so fortunate, principally in consequence of the rough and boisterous weather, and the imperfect state of the tackle, &c. The fish caught and sent to market was sold for £7 but the value of the meal given as wages to the men while fishing was only £2.12s.6d, so that the Committee have incurred no loss in the matter. The fishers, however, expect that they will be paid one-half the proceeds of the fish, as an encouragement to future exertions, and I would recommend the Committee to allow them this.

The proprietors on this island being all under trust, little or no remunerative employment has been provided, or is in prospect. Mr Maclean of Coll applied for and obtained a loan of £1,900 under the Drainage Act; but hitherto very little of it has been expended, as only twenty men were employed for three weeks in the beginning of the year; and I am informed that very little may be expected next year.

The garden plants and seeds, which were sent here were carefully planted and cultivated by the poor cottars and crofters. They have come up well, have been of the greatest service to the poor, and are now the only food left to the cottars.

The other crops (with the exception of the potatoes) are about an average, and have been well got in. The cottars and crofters' crop of potatoes is already consumed, and the tenants' crop is diseased to the extent of two-thirds.

Of the state and condition of the people, the Committee will have some idea when they are informed that, out of a population of 1200, 535 have been fed by the Relief meal, and 70 by the Parochial Board; 125 families are cottars, who have no lands, consequently no crop; 12 families are cottars, who hold small plots from crofters; 84 families are crofters, paying from £2 to £5 of rent; and 6 families are tenants or tacksmen. The whole of those cottars who hold no land are very destitute. The 12 families of cottars holding from crofters, and about 18 families of the crofters, will be in a similar state from February next.

The Parochial Board is assessed at the rate of 6% on rental, and 4% on means and substance; and allow the 70 paupers on the roll an average subsistence of 8 lbs.

On 21st November Neil Crossapol wrote a letter that was published with Dr Boyyter's Appendix. He writes:

I have for the last two days been going through the island to satisfy myself as to the real state of the people at present, and I beg to state for those of your Committee that many families who have no holding are this moment entirely destitute and cannot get a days employment. These poor people are at present living on the charity of the few in the place who have anything like a sufficiency for themselves; and even those who, I am aware will not have any of their own by the beginning of May, are at present aiding their more unfortunate neighbours which shows a very grand feeling on their part.

Whilst in an extract from his letter of 29th December Lachlan Johnston the ground officer wrote:

I have never heard such cries for food in Coll before and had it not been for the drainage works at Gallanach, great numbers of families would have been very ill off. These drains are now nearly finished, and I am afraid some of these people will starve.[41]

* * *

Coll's family continued to take steps to improve the situation in their old home. In April Campbell wrote to Miss Maclean of Coll to say that

Mr William Maclean returned from Coll a couple of days ago where he went to teach them the mode of drilling their crops. He is an uncommon nice lad. He amuses himself with his gun & fishing rod. I am only fearful of his over fatiguing himself.[42]

Mr William was Coll's younger son. His elder brother Alexander, known in the family as Alick, had gone to the Highlands every autumn since the family returned from Germany 'to encourage keeping up acquaintance with the people and a feeling for the place'.[43] He made a very good impression on everyone. 'I am rejoiced to hear he pays such attention to agriculture', wrote Donald Campbell.[44]

There was much concern in the family over what was to become of Alick. These worries are stressed by Juliet Alexa in her journal when she writes that Alick:

did not care for the cadetship promised Papa by Lord Ripon then in the Government. I heard this voted a very good thing as it would be undesirable for him to go out of the country for his own interests and yet at the same time the estate was so much in debt, that if some law should first pass which should enable the entail to be broken that all the debts might be paid. If this were not done and Alick inherited the estate he would be so very poor as never to be able to afford to live on it.

She herself had strong views on inherited estates:

Inherited estates, I thought were fearful things in those days for most Highland proprietors, unless very well off indeed, so as to be independent of the rents of tenants. If those poor creatures were too poor to pay rents the landlords who depended on this must be ruined. It seemed to me a disagreeable thing to be obliged to depend on the rents of those very poor people, and that in attendant better days it would be fortunate if poor Alick had something to do to keep him independent of them on arriving at possession.[45]

Other members of the family continued to take an interest in the Island and to visit it. At one time Hugh himself toyed with the idea of going to live at Breacachadh. In 1847 his sister Maria, Mrs Hunter, proposed to spend the summer in Coll for in June 1847 Campbell wrote to Hunter to say:

> On my arrival at home on Saturday I learnt that Mrs Hunter had some intention of going to Coll for a few months of the summer with her family for the benefit of bathing & that she was prevented by hearing that Coll himself had some thoughts of going there. This need not now prevent Mrs Hunter as I had a letter from him by last post that he is to take a cottage at Epsom & relinquishes all thoughts of coming to Coll – will you have the goodness to say to Mrs Hunter from Mrs Campbell & myself that if she will put up with what accommodation the Castle affords we would be delighted that she would occupy it for what time suits her and it would cost her nothing but milk.[46]

It was, however, Sir Hector and his niece Breadalbane who did most for the people on the estate. As we have seen they were continually sending money to buy meal for the people or financing new initiatives to help them to earn money. Sir Hector was now a very old man living out his dotage in amiable forgetfulness. Juliet Alexa says that 'From having so long seemed only worried and unhappy he was now always quite pleased, placidly happy and contented with everything ... He always seemed to know and be pleased to see Papa. He did not care to say much, but several times a day he used to remark apropos money matters: 'Formerly I used to occupy myself a great deal about them', but laughing cheerfully 'somehow I cannot trouble myself about those things now'!

Unlike Sir Hector, Breadalbane was extremely worried about money matters. Juliet Alexa says that Aunt Albane would get into a great state about them. She would say to her:

> You (meaning the family) must be spending too much, and where did the money come from? Where indeed? And how on earth could I ever know? Was it not ridiculous and out of the question to confront Mama and ask her? And from dear Papa it was still more impossible. It was decidedly neither my business nor my 'duty' to try and find out. (Margaret used to write as if it were!) Where did the money come from? To my Aunt I used to 'suppose' it might come from my uncle Robertson perhaps. He might be paying back more than the originally proposed £200 a year. And had she [Aunt Albane] not said that the £8,000 could not be touched? This I said to her, but to myself, my suspicious fears said 'I wish all may be right about that £8,000'.[47]

Juliet Alexa seems to be implying that her parents had been misusing the money that Sir Hector had invested in Peruvian bonds. However, it is more likely that Hugh had borrowed again on the belief that he was Sir Hector's heir. On the 18th March 1847. Donald Campbell had written to say: 'I am rejoiced to learn that your prospects are so good & hope you soon will touch the cash'.[48] Perhaps he had news that his brother-in-law's schemes were reaching fruition. Whatever the source of his income there was always a hope, whilst Sir Hector was alive, that all would turn out for the best for Hugh Maclean of Coll.

Hugh was one of the few people in London in 1847 who was optimistic about the future. It was a bad time in the city. A number of companies failed, including Sherwell & Co, who according to

Juliet Alexa, were somehow connected with the Peruvian Bonds and the missing £8,000. She had no faith in her Uncle Robertson and was terrified that her father as well as Uncle Robertson would be held responsible for the money.

* * *

There were, however, still some lighter moments. On 27th November 1848 the young Laird of Coll reached his majority an event that was probably celebrated throughout the estate, although printed evidence only survives for what occurred in Mull:

Rejoicing

On Coll's Estates of Quinish & Peinmore, Mull to celebrate the anniversary birthday of Alexander son & heir of Hugh McLean Esq, of Coll.

As early as 11 AM of the 27th November the festival commenced. Crowds were seen with their flag staffs and banners waving in the air assembling at a conspicuous eminence in Quinish on which were placed cannons, which towards the evening were kept successively firing and whose tremendous echo reverberated from the surrounding hills and throughout the romantic vale of Glenbelart.

Bonfires illuminated both sides of the Glen. A similar demonstration was given at the same time at Peinmore. In the evening the whole tenantry of both Estates enjoyed themselves at a comfortable repast whence spirits, wines &c were served in abundance.

The usual toasts being given, the health of the young heir of Coll, whose ancestors for upward of four hundred years have been the benevolent and generous Proprietors of the soil, was drunk with demonstrations of great joy and hilarity. The healths of the other members of the family and others were given in succession.

The toast of the Duke of Argyle, Lord McDonald, Lochbuy & Captain Campbell the Factor on the property being given. The party separated with harmony and good feeling much delighted with their meeting.[49]

The list of those subscribing is headed by Captain Campbell who donated £1, as did Donald Maclean tacksman of Kengharair on Torloisk's estate. Dr MacArthur the minister followed (10/–), as did Henry Nisbet the banker in Tobermory and other leading men in the North of Mull. The list of tenants subscribing is led by Niel Morison, Cuin (5/–) and Lachlan Morison, Bellachroy (6/6d) followed by 67 other Quinish tenants, who gave at least 1/– each, whilst the tenants of Peinmore gave £1.13s.6d. It is a remarkable display of affection for the family, especially at the height of the potato famine.

The participants got their money's worth. 11½ gallons of Tobermory whisky, 1 gallon of Rum, 1 dozen bottles of London Porter, ale and wine were drunk. A cask of gunpowder was also used. In all, including 3/6d for broken windows at the schoolhouse, the cost came to £16.1s.7½d.

It was the last time the tenants on the Coll estate had any cause for celebration, for on 11th December 1848 Sir Hector died at his home in Northwick Terrace. He was ninety-two. Sir Hector had always intended to make Hugh his heir. He was his only nephew with the name Maclean and was head of the family. It was, however, known that Sir Hector had destroyed an old will and was to make another. If no will was found Sir Hector's money would be divided among all his relatives and as Aunt Albane pointed out Hugh had already had his share and the missing £8,000 would have to be repaid.[50] The family was penniless. At this crucial moment Uncle Robertson was in Mexico[51] and no one knew what he had done with the £8,000. Hugh and Alexander Hunter searched frantically in the city for any papers left behind by Robertson to shed some light on what he had planned. Nothing could be found.

It so happened that at this time Juliet Alexa had an extremely rich admirer who wanted to marry her. Her sisters said she must do so for the sake the family. Mr — was to come 'on the day after tomorrow' to ask Hugh for his daughter's hand, and she knew that, despite the fact she did not want to marry Mr — the answer must be 'Yes'. Then after a dreadful night when Hugh did not come home at all, papers were discovered showing that Uncle Robertson had, after all, left money and made arrangements for some to be paid monthly until his return. Juliet Alexa writes:

And thus the marriage was no longer a necessity, and entirely a wrong thing. And Papa wrote for me to Mr — to ask him not to come that day. And that ... on further acquaintance I found that we really should not suit each other and the answer must be 'No'. I also wrote to him myself. He was very polite about it but still rather seemed to think 'she was daft to refuse the Laird of Cockpen'.[52]

Sir Hector's will was never found. He left some £20,000. Breadalbane Maclean was the sole executor.[53] On the 30th December Donald Campbell wrote to Hugh to say:

I was apprehensive you would suffer by your uncle's death — It is most unlucky that Mr Robertson should also be absent at this time when his presence in London is much required.[54]

On the same day he also wrote to Alexander Hunter:

Sir Hector's death will I fear be severely felt by him [Hugh] as well as others ... The Rent Collection is about over. So far, as I expect the tenants to come in for the present, there is of course a deficiency but not more than I expected — on the contrary several have made a wonderful exertion to pay up but they have encroached on their stock to do so. This will cause a further deficiency another time. The greatest defaulters are the tenants of Torestan, Arinagour, Penmore & Dervaig as you might expect ... I am in hopes of getting some of the crofters about Acha cleared at Whitsun and that Smeaton the miller will take them. The occupants there can pay their own passage ... Thorburn [the tenant of the Isle of Muck] makes a further difficulty about signing his lease.[55]

In his letter of the 30th to Hugh, Donald Campbell said that the 'young Laird' who had presumably been in Mull for his 21st birthday celebrations was intending to go south on the steamer 'the week after next'. He also says that Alexander had showed him a 'pamphlet upon Natal'. It would therefore appear that even before Sir Hector's death 'young Coll' was considering emigrating to South Africa.

Notes

1. Hector Macdougall & Hector Cameron *Handbook to the islands of Coll & Tiree* (Glasgow ND. C 1930), 51.
2. See Chapter 40.

3. Torestan is the only farm in Coll whose rental is known to survive for the year 1848–9.
4. TNA. WO12. 8520.
5. She is 'my poor sister Catherine' who Coundullie Rankin mentions in his letter to Donald Morison of 25 February 1832. Public Archives of PEI. Accession 2716. Item No. 2. 14 July 2005.
6. In the seventeenth century it was one of the farms belonging to Neil Maclean of Drimnacross and was inherited by his son Hector, who in 1689 was killed at the battle of Dunkeld. It then went to his son Lachlan, who served in the Scots Brigade in Dutch service but returned home in disgust when he did not obtain promotion. As Lachlan had only daughters Torestan reverted to the estate when he died. In 1776 Donald Campbell, whose sons later purchased the Two Ends of Coll from the Duke of Argyll, held it.
7. 20 March 1847. Donald Campbell to Alexander Hunter WS. Mull Museum Archives D12/113.
8. In 1848–9 the rental of Toraston was:

Mrs McEachren	£7.10s
Donald Beaton	£6.10s
John McKinnon	£7.10
Lachlan McDonald	£7.10s
Murdoch McLean	£8.10s
John McLean	£7.10s
Neil McKinnon	£7.10s
Malcolm Kennedy	£7.10s

[BCP. *Report of the Royal Commission (Highlands & Islands, 1892)*, John Johnston's Draft Evidence]. Murdoch McLean was almost certainly one of these two tenants. It is not possible to say who was the other.

9. NAS. RHP. 3368.
10. They were John McInnis, Donald MacPhaden and Malcolm Campbell [NAS. SC 59. 2.4]. Only John McInnis was in Trelvaig at the time of the 1841 census.
11. In 1841 there were two households of Kennedys in Trelvaig. John was a crofter whilst his father Murdoch and brother Donald (who lived with his father) were presumably cottars.
12. They were: Hugh Mackinnon, 72. Hugh Maclean, 80. Murdoch Kennedy in Trelvaig, 70 who did not live to move to Kilbride.
13. 22 January 1847. Donald Campbell to Hugh Maclean of Coll. Mull Museum Archives D12/113.
14. 30 March 1847. Donald Campbell to Hugh Maclean of Coll. Mull Museum Archives D12/113.
15. 10 April 1847. Donald Campbell to Lachlan Johnston. Mull Museum Archives D12/113.
16. 12 June 1849. Donald Campbell to Lachlan Johnston. Mull Museum Archives D12/113.
17. There is only one Malcolm Kennedy in Coll at this time. He was a crofter in Grimsary in 1841 and 1851. Perhaps he was in Torestan in between these dates.
18. He later was in Knocleathan where his son John died of fever in 1855.
19. It is also, unless new evidence appears, impossible to work out what happened to them. Too many of them have the same names.
20. 12 March 1847. Donald Campbell to Alexander Hunter WS. Mull Museum Archives D12/113.
21. 26 March 1847. Donald Campbell to Alexander Hunter WS. Mull Museum Archives D12/113.
22. 7 April 1847. Donald Campbell to Alexander Hunter WS. Mull Museum Archives D12/113.
23. 13 August 1847. Donald Campbell to Neil Maclean, Esq, Crossapol.
24. Argyll & Bute District Archives. Minute Book of Coll Parochial Board. CO 6. 7. 5. 1. He chaired every meeting of the board until his death on 1 January 1855, having been elected chairman annually.
25. *Highland Destitution Reports. Glasgow Section.* 9th Report. 2 August 1848, 17. Appx. No. 3.
26. Parliamentary Papers. *Report from the Commissioners appointed for inquiring into the Administration and Practical Operation of the Poor Laws in Scotland* (1844), XXVII–XXXVI. Minutes of Evidence, 123.
27. 19 September 1846. Donald Campbell to Hugh Maclean of Coll. Mull Museum Archives D12/113.

28. 13 August 1847. Donald Campbell to Neil Maclean, Esq, Crossapol.
29. Minute Book of Coll Parochial Board. Minute No. 1. 16 August 1847.
30. Coll Parochial Board. Minute No. 5. 14 February 1848.
31. This seems to have been a Free Church coup. The Church of Scotland retaliated by taking back the Parish records. Until March 1847 baptisms had continued to be registered in the old Parish Books. This practice now stopped and the Parish Minister the Rev. Neil Maclean came over to Coll to baptise the few people on the island, mainly employees of the estate, who remained in the Established Church [NAS. CH2. 70. 2, 13 March 1847–27 August 1854].
32. His cousin John Campbell of Cornaig certainly was [NAS. GD 112. 52. 625].
33. 14 January 1848. Donald Campbell to Hugh Maclean of Coll. Mull Museum Archives D12/113.
34. Coll Parochial Board. Minute No. 8. 18 September 1848.
35. Coll Parochial Board. Minute No. 9. 25 September 1848.
36. *The Great Highland Famine*, 111–115.
37. *Ibid*, 119.
38. 14 March 1848. Donald Campbell to Alexander Hunter WS. Mull Museum Archives D12/113.
39. *The Great Highland Famine*, 134.
40. 9th Report of the *Highland Destitution Reports Glasgow Section 1848–50* (2 August 1848), 14.
41. *Ibid*, 17.
42. 24 April 1847. Donald Campbell to Miss Maclean of Coll. Mull Museum Archives D12/113.
43. Juliet Alexa's Journal.
44. 22 February 1847. Donald Campbell to Alexander Hunter WS. Mull Museum Archives D12/113.
45. Juliet Alexa's Journal, 86.
46. 14 June 1847. Donald Campbell to Alexander Hunter WS. Mull Museum Archives D12/113.
47. Juliet Alexa's Journal, 149–50.
48. 18 March 1847. Donald Campbell to Hugh Maclean of Coll. Mull Museum Archives D12/113.
49. Mull Museum Archives D12/113.
50. Juliet Alexa's Journal, 162.
51. The European revolutions of 1848 had left governments with a distinct shortage of silver. Mexico was now a major source and for several years Rothschild mercury from Spain had been sold to the Mexican silver mines [*The House of Rothschild*, 467]. It is possible that it was because of silver that Robertson was in Mexico. New discoveries of silver had also recently been found in his old stamping ground of Chile and Peru and it would be surprising if he were not involved [*Ibid*, 470].
52. Juliet Alexa's Journal, 163.
53. TNA. PROB 6. Admin 1848. Sir Hector Maclean, Knight.
54. 30 December 1848. Donald Campbell to Hugh Maclean of Coll. Mull Museum Archives D12/113.
55. 30 December 1848. Donald Campbell to Alexander Hunter WS. Mull Museum Archives D12/113.

Chapter Fifty-Four

South Africa, Australia and New Zealand

It was perhaps the financial crisis in Australia of the 1840s that led Hugh Maclean of Coll to decide to send his sons Alexander and William to South Africa. Apart from officers in the army during the Napoleonic Wars, and colonists on their way to Australia, few Collachs if any probably had experience of the colony.

The first Europeans to settle in South Africa were the Dutch, who in 1652 founded the Cape Colony. Thirty years later French Huguenot refugees, who left France after the revocation of the Edict of Nantes, joined them. The British first arrived in 1795 when they seized the colony during the French Revolutionary War. In 1800 it was returned to the Dutch. Six years later it again capitulated to the British.

British settlement was slow to start. The Dutch East India Company had in 1780 declared the Great Fish River to be the eastern boundary of the Cape Colony and it was not until 1812 that Colonel John Graham drove an estimated 8,000 Xhosa over the Fish River and fortified the boundary with a line of blockhouses. At about the same time the Zulu king Chaka the 'South African Attila' was advancing south burning villages and driving all before him. In 1820 there was a major movement of emigrants from the British Isles to the Cape Colony and in 1823 Dr Farewell and other Englishmen set out to explore Natal. They made a treaty with Chaka, which gave them Port Natal plus about 50 miles of coastline to a depth 100 miles inland. Farewell persuaded 20 Englishmen to found a colony with him in Natal. Africans driven south by Chaka sought protection from these first colonists and joined them in their precarious little settlement.

Missionaries and traders penetrated far inland and along the eastern coast. In 1835 the settlers made a second treaty with Dingaan, Chaka's brother and successor. This treaty ceded them the southern half of Natal, and when in 1837 the voortrekkers left the Cape to escape British domination the British settlers warned them that they had every intention of keeping Port Natal for the British Crown.

In 1838 Dingaan promised land to the Boers who had moved into north Natal, but instead of keeping his word he murdered their leader Piet Retief and attempted to wipe out the voortrekkers. The Boers avenged Retief's murder by defeating the Zulus at Blood River. In 1840 Dingaan's 'place' was destroyed.

Flushed with victory the Boers set up Dingaan's brother Panda as their own Zulu king and proclaimed Natal to be the independent republic of Natalia. They advanced towards the coast and besieged the small British garrison of 27th Foot in their camp at Port Natal. A settler, however, escaped and made a dramatic ten days ride to warn the British authorities at Grahamstown and the Cape government sent 100 men of the 27th and a detachment of the 25th Foot by sea to raise the siege.

The following year Natal was annexed by Britain and the majority of the disgruntled voortrekkers took their wagons back over the Drakensburg.[1] Under Panda's rule, although the different Zulu factions fought among themselves, and the kraals of those who irritated him were 'eaten up', the frontier was relatively quiet. The British held to a policy of non-intervention in native affairs, but most people believed that sooner or later they would be drawn into a war with the Zulus and that Zululand would be annexed.[2]

* * *

It was to the unstable frontier between Natal and Zululand that Hugh Maclean of Coll proposed to send his two sons. How much he knew about the actual situation there is not known. No doubt the tense atmosphere on the border was glossed over in the prospectus for prospective settlers.

Plans were underway for Alick and William to sail for South Africa and on 26th January 1849 Alick wrote to the Ground Officer in Quinish:

Neil,

I got your letter a few days ago asking me about the lads who were anxious to go out with me to Natal & I now write to tell you that at all events I should like to take out two men & the two I would fix upon are if possible John Maclean & Beaton from Penmore who from all I have heard & know about them are well behaved industrious fellows & to be depended upon – they however will be obliged to find their own way to London, which I have no doubt they are perfectly able to do as a trifling sum will carry them there – their passage to Natal of course will be found them & as their wages when there must be agreed upon afterwards but they cannot expect them to be very high at first – The ship we are to leave in sails from London on 15th of February which gives them plenty time to prepare for going out. In the event of their leaving me they will be bound to repay me the amount of their passage money viz £10 – I have just ascertained that the fare from Glasgow to London per Railway is 34/– (shillings). I shall write again soon & I have no doubt I shall be able to take out more than two men – Remember me most kindly to all the Quinish people & am yours ever Alexr Maclean.[3]

Hugh once more attempted to obtain support to settle his people overseas. His original plan, which he put to the government, was to relieve 'my starving redundant population'. He proposed to send out useful settlers to Natal. But as he received no encouragement 'it falls to the ground except so far as my two sons . . .'are concerned. Hugh had been warned that 'There is very little good land at government disposal in Natal and I am strongly advised not to preclude the purchase of more eligible land, by lodging the purchase money here, at least until my sons see & judge for themselves'.

He went on to say:

My object in now writing is to request you obtaining from Earl Grey assurance that money paid for government land in Natal should be allowed the same privilege in nomination of settlers to be carried out as is accorded to money lodged at home for that purpose and also the necessary extension of the time with what they must take out. I may hope that every reasonable facility will be allowed to so desirable an object. [4]

The Colonial Office appear to have lost Hugh's original letter and when the recipient Elliot received his letter of 30th January he wrote an office memorandum which stated that:

Mr Maclean's former letter does not appear to have been received in the Department. I suppose the writer wishes that his sons should not remain at Natal if they cannot find suitable land & he is unwilling therefore that any purchase money should be paid down in this country: but should his sons find land in that colony which suits them he asks that the purchase money may be expended in the introduction of settlers on the same terms as if the money had been previously deposited here.

The particulars of the case are as follows. Mr Maclean the Laird of Coll in the Hebrides is anxious to remove some of his people to Natal but his means have become very limited and he is resolved to begin by sending his own sons to judge for themselves of the capabilities of the place. This is just such an enterprise as Lord Grey would, I think, feel desirous to encourage. Mr Maclean does not like to bind himself to buy Crown land until his sons reach the spot. What he asks is, that if when he makes a purchase, he may be allowed the privilege of nominating Emigrants for a free passage as if he had deposited the Purchase Money here. I apprehend that this may be conceded, telling him of course that the Emigrants must be according to the Regulations and explaining what the Regulations are. A Deposit could then be written to the Governor accordingly and the Land Board should be informed.[5]

Alick was in a hurry to get the young men from Mull, who had agreed to go to Natal and on 2nd February wrote again to the Ground Officer:

Neil,

In case you may be waiting for another letter from me before sending off the men I wrote you of before, I write to say that there is no time to be lost as the ship we sail in leaves London on the 15th of this month but if they could be here by the 11th they would be in time enough. I don't know exactly the days of the steamers but if they don't suit let them come by Achnacraig. They will only take one day between Glasgow & London by going by the Caledonian Railway. I shall be very much disappointed if they do not arrive in time so please do your best to make them start immediately if you cannot get the two men I wanted try & get other two but I should like very much if you could get John Maclean to go – The more I hear about Natal the more I like the thought of going there – it is the finest Country in the world – By next packet I hope a number more will come out to me – men who can plough well would be the best hands. Tell the men when they arrive in London to make their way to No. 29 Queens Terrace, Bayswater. We are all very well here, which I hope is the case with you in Mull. Whenever you get my letter give me an answer by return of post & Believe me as ever attached to you all, yours Alexr Maclean.

Tell them to bring as little luggage as possible. AM.[6]

Things were now moving apace and on 6th February 1849 Elliot sent a memo to the Colonial Land and Emigration Committee:

Gentlemen, I am directed by Earl Grey to enclose for your information and guidance, copies of a correspondence with Mr Maclean, Proprietor of the Isle of Coll in the Hebrides, by which you will perceive that he is about to send his two sons to Natal, and that if they should make a purchase of Crown lands, Lord Grey has consented that he should have the same privileges of naming eligible Emigrants in respect of that Purchase as if he had deposited the same amount of money in this country.[7]

On the same day he wrote to Hugh to say:

Sir,

(1) I am directed by Earl Grey to acknowledge your letter of the 30th Ultimo stating that you are about to send your sons to Natal, but that until they reach the place and can exercise their judgement on the spot, you are unwilling to confirm their choice by making that deposit of money for the purchase of crown lands which would entitle you to name an equivalent number of eligible Emigrants for a free passage. Under these circumstance you request that if, after your sons' arrival, they should buy Crown lands, you may be allowed the same privilege of nominating Emigrants for a free passage which you would have had if their payment had been made previously in this country.

(2) I am desired to acquaint you in answer that Lord Grey is desirous to afford every reasonable encouragement to Gentlemen who send out their sons under the circumstances you describe and that he will be happy to authorise the Commissioners of Emigrants to allow you the privilege you request in virtue of any actual payment for Crown land made by your sons to the Government of Natal, and officially repaid to this country.

(3) The Governor will be instructed to report the fact upon being applied to by your sons for the purpose and to requisite directions will be given to the commissioners of Emigration.

(4) You will of course understand that any Emigrants who you may name must be strictly conformable to Commissioner's Regulations for the time being, and be applied by the Colonies at present eligible are:
Agricultural labourers.
Mechanics.
Skilled labourers & small farmers, accustomed to some labour, and intending to work for their subsistence.

On 8th February Elliot wrote to Sir Harry Smith, the Governor of the Cape Colony, to let him know what had been agreed with Hugh and sent him copies of the correspondence.[8]

* * *

The Ground Officer appears to have had problems in getting the young men Young Coll had hoped to get to accompany him, and on 10th March Coll himself wrote to him:

Sir,

I send to you, as I see Alexander has written to you today, two forms of application for Emigrants to Natal given to me by the government office to be filled up, & sent addressed as directed, or to me. Any agency [?] to go must wait directions from London as to the ship in which they are to proceed – *after being approved of*. Mr Hunter has written to Capt. Campbell the proposed terms for a man & wife. For a single man: free passage to London & thence to Natal. The *outfit* here is just £4. For either man or woman to engage for three years. Wages £10 per ann[um] & living. If leaving the service before end of three years, after arrival, to repay all expenses of passage. Alexander is most anxious that *Johnny* Maclean should go, and Jane Fergusson & her husband. But he has I suppose written to you fully. Mr Hunter will pay the expenses & forward them to London to me.

The time cannot, you see be fixed as yet: but I can get it made at any time most suitable; vessels go every month. All may be sure that the Climate, and every thing else is of the very most favorable, or I would not send two of my sons there. Hundreds are going: the first are sure to be best off. Plenty of good people are to be had here but we desire the benefit of our own people first. Alexander says they expect to reach Natal in six weeks from Plymouth.

After a few years labour there any active fellow can become a landowner on his own account. I am anxious of ascertaining whether it would do to send out many of our young couples to cultivate the land. Subsistence is very easily got – three crops, certainly two, in every year. As soon as certainty comes I shall propose it to my people – purchase land & have them sent out free to a Country as Superior to England as England's best land & climate is to Mull. Let me hear as soon as anything is doing. Roderick Morison has a *Natal* book for anyone's information about it.[9]

Alick and William seem to have had to delay their departure and to have sailed without the Penmore young men, for on 30 May Donald Campbell wrote: 'I could not at present get two young men to go to Natal as Coll wishes. Those that were proposing to go have drawn back'.[10]

He went on trying and on 26th November Captain Campbell wrote to Coll

My dear Sir – I was favored with your letter of the 12th. I assure you that it is not for want of will on my part that the emigrants are not yet from this to Natal – Mr Hunter also I think offers very few – the following are the conditions he authorises me to give for the passage outward £5 allowed to cloathe them and bring them to Leith where they will be shipped to London. For the above they are to serve 3 years and they will housed and fed – at the end of 2 years 20 acres of land will be allotted to them and a couple of cows given them and during the third year half of their time will be allowed for working their own land – if a man and wife go the wife also to work for her meat & passage – of all that have yet offered not one has stood firm – some wife, father or mother has interfered to prevent it.[11]

The factor therefore had to try again and on 26th December 1849 wrote to Alexander Hunter to say that 'three men from Coll express a desire now to go to Natal'.[12] It was, however, not until 30th January 1850 that he was able to write to Hunter:

Two men at last have come forward from Coll who seem desiring to go to Natal. I think they may answer. I enclose your form of application for each of them (they are brothers). I understand there is a ship to sail from the Clyde between the middle and end of February by which Coll wishes them to be shipped... There is another man John McPhaden most anxious to go if you are inclined to send.[13]

In the end only the two men from Coll were sent to Natal.[14] Despite destitution people on the estate were reluctant to go to South Africa.

* * *

Alick and William settled at Umhlali north-east of Port Natal near the coast not far from the Tugela River which was the boundary between Natal and Zululand. The brothers traded into Zululand exchanging blankets and beads for cattle, which could be sold at a considerable profit. A blanket bought in Port Natal for 10 shillings was sold for a 'beast', which could be sold in Natal for £4.[15]

It was, however, a dangerous business. When the Macleans first arrived Panda killed anyone who displeased him or whose cattle he coveted. Whole kraals were massacred and Alick said that 'he was once near a kraal which was entirely "eaten up" and the people exterminated. He was near enough to hear everything that was going on'.[16]

* * *

In Australia the Macleans had to face different but equally terrifying experiences. Allan Arileod's youngest daughter Anne had, at the age of 21, married Mathew Holmes, a merchant in Geelong; they lived at Glencairn in the Barrabool hills, beside the Barwon River.

On the 6th February 1851 the whole of the south-eastern coast was ablaze from the borders of South Australia to Gippsland. Borne on the wings of a hurricane, the fire swept over the land. It was ten o'clock in the morning when Hugh Campbell [son of Donald Campbell, Caolis & Flora Maclean, who was living with his aunt at Glencairn], a lad of sixteen, hurried in to tell his young aunt that the fire had crossed the Barwon and was coming down their land. There was no question of saving any property. It was their lives, and their lives only that mattered. The first thought of Ann Holmes was to drag blankets from the house and plunge them in the river. At first the five children were placed in the stone dairy beside the river, but when their mother noticed the concentration of heat in the large trees on the river banks she hastily removed them and, with Hugh Campbell's help, got them through the fire on to burnt ground, and there till the afternoon they fought with heat, raging wind, and flying fire of all sorts. The blankets were redipped in the river as chance offered and were their only protection. Many families in the neighbourhood perished completely, but when the groom who had driven Mathew Holmes to his office in the morning returned about 4 pm in desperate haste when he saw the line the fire had taken, he found a miserable group of eight beings black beyond recognition, huddled in grimy blankets on a log which was burning inside, but cooler than the baked ground.... [the groom] summoned Mathew Holmes, and they brought an express to convey the miserable family to Katherine [Anne's unmarried sister] McLean's cottage, where they were cared for and nursed through the after effects of their terrible experience.

The baby, however, was past saving. The family removed to Geelong where the firm of Holmes, White & Co. prospered.[17]

* * *

In 1851 gold was discovered in a waterhole near Bathurst in New South Wales. It marked the beginning of the Australian gold rushes and the gold frenzy that gripped the whole nation. The discovery not only had a huge effect on the Australian economy. It had a profound effect on the national psyche: the camraderie and 'mateship' that developed amongst 'diggers' in the gold fields and their open disdain for authority is still an integral factor in how Australians see themselves and how others see them.

The prospect of moving in a short space of time from poverty to untold riches gripped the nation and

> A complete mental madness appears to have seized almost every member of the community. There has been a universal rush to the diggings.[18]

This exodus from agriculture was of great concern to the authorities who attempted to control the flight from the land. And the Victorian government did their best to prevent their people from following the example of New South Wales. However, six months after the discovery of gold there it was found in Victoria itself at Ballarat and Bendigo Creek.

The Victoria discoveries dwarfed those of New South Wales and during the 1850s Victoria produced more than a third of the world's gold output. Immigrants poured into the State and in just two years its population grew from 77,000 to 540,000. Immigrants came from all over the world. Most were British but the largest foreign contingent was made up of 40,000 Chinese under contract to other Chinese or foreign businessmen. In exchange for their passage money they worked until their debt was repaid. Most returned to China. These Chinese were hard conscietious workers but they were often unpopular as they were seen as rivals by the racist white diggers.

Between 1851 and 1854 tension in the goldfields increased. There were clashes between diggers and the authorities. In December 1854 a riot led to the police from Melbourne storming *Eureka Stockade* on the outskirts of Ballarat and the death of 22 diggers.

Life in the goldfields was rough and tough: places of squalor, greed, crime, self-interest and racism. Diggers were perceived to be beyond the reach of British civility. They were 'transient creatures, lacking geographical attachments and social responsibilities'. Mining towns proved themselves to be incapable of supporting the churches, schools and charities. They, however, had an irresistible attraction to settlers who knew that every 22½ ounces of gold dust they found would buy them an 80 acre freehold property of virgin soil.

Many people from Coll must have tried their luck in the goldfields. The fate of many of them is unknown. For instance Donald or Daniel Maclean, Dr Lachlan's eldest son ended up in the gold diggings and was not heard of again.[19] The fate of Mr Neil, the Minister of Tiree & Coll's son Alexander is even less certain. He is last heard of in 1851 and I have been unable to discover what happened to him. John and Allan Maclean the 'Cooper of Coll' of Coll's sons were more successful.

> John found the otter skins, which he brought with him useful in washing for gold . . . they did well as gold buyers; and also sold stores to the diggers. One day, when John was gold digging he was warned by a Chinaman, named Fan So, of a plot to murder him and steal his gold.

The warning saved his life. In 1852 the family decided to sell their farm and move to New Zealand. They brought with them their capital, which consisted of 500 ewes, cattle and horses.[20] As they probably left Coll with very little they must have done extremely well in the goldfields.

* * *

By the middle of the nineteenth century it was possible to return from the colonies for an extended holiday in Scotland. Several of those who could afford to do so visited the Hebrides. The steamer had cut travelling time significantly, and emigration was no longer a life sentence

Among those who returned to Mull was Dr Lachlan Maclean. On 9th July 1844 Sheriff Robertson notes that 'Dr Lachlan Maclean called, and told a number of stories about the aborigines of Australia, South Sea Islands, America &c.[21] He had returned from Australia in 1842, after only three years, leaving behind his eldest son there, 'much against the boy's will'.[22]

Also back in Mull was Colin Campbell, Sunipol. Sheriff Robertson, who was a snob, saw him in Tobermory in February 1843. He points out that he was no relation of the previous Campbells in Sunipol, who were Airds' cadets.[23] Robertson describes Colin's family as 'ordinary peasants'.[24] He was, however, not too superior take tea with his wife and her sister,[25] and when he saw Colin the following year he describes him 'as a good manly fellow'. Poor Colin's 'eyes were red and his usual spirits dashed'. He was to go off that day in the steamer from Tobermory on a journey that would take him back to Australia.[26]

In the 1970s The *Sidney Morning Herald* had an extraordinary article about Colin. It was written by one Paul Derriman, who says that his story is a composite of three separate accounts of the 'Sunipol hauntings', which he was given in Mull. He says that:

The central character in the affair was a local man called Colin Campbell. Legend has it that he emigrated to an unidentified part of Australia in the early 1800s, became a bushranger, and was identified by a ferryman called Cameron, whom he forced at gunpoint to give him a free ride. He then fled home to Scotland, settling again at Sunipol. Campbell was popularly known by a Gaelic name meaning Big Colin. Even today he is remembered in Mull, fairly or unfairly, as a strong and violent man. The hauntings at Sunipol began soon after Campbell's return. Stones from the beach 200 metres away came flying through the windows. Lights were seen about the house at night. Voices spoke to people out of the darkness. But the most intriguing manifestation of all was the appearance of the ghost of a black man, reckoned to be an Aboriginal murdered by Campbell in Australia. All this supernatural activity caused understandable alarm in the area. The minister of the local kirk warned people to avoid Sunipol at night. The farm was deserted by most of its employees, including a kitchen maid who claimed to have been accosted by a ghost when she went outside at night to the water pump. Campbell, no doubt suspecting a natural cause for the disturbances, posted an armed guard outside after dark. Curiously, Campbell's ultimate fate seems to have been forgotten. No one could tell me when he died or where he is buried. The hauntings at Sunipol, however, are said to have continued until early in this century, and the ghost of Campbell himself is said to have taken part in them . . .

Philip Derriman goes on to say:

This then is the bizarre tale of Colin Campbell, according to the folklore of Mull. Unfortunately, the story of his stay in Australia, as recorded in Australian libraries, is not nearly so complete. Research for the *Herald* by the Mitchell Library in Sydney, and in the State Library of Tasmania, failed to find any record of a bushranger called Colin Campbell. Possibly, Campbell spread the bushranging story as a boast after his return to Mull. Both libraries, however, did discover that a well-known Australian whaling captain, named Alexander Campbell listed in the Australian Dictionary of Biography, as having been born at Sunipol, Mull, in 1805, had an elder brother in Australia, called Colin. The State Library of Tasmania further discovered that this Colin Campbell, whom we can safely assume to be Big Colin, had emigrated in 1820, had secured a grant of land for farming near Launceston, Tasmania, and had, in a document dated 1829, declared his intention to return temporarily to his 'native place' to bring back his father and other members of his family. Thereafter, so far as Australian records are concerned, Colin Campbell drops out of sight. Certainly there seems to be no record of any lawbreaking to justify his subsequent notoriety. But a clue may lie in the career of his brother Alexander, who was closely associated with Colin in Tasmania at least until 1829 and probably until 1831. Alexander is said to have taken an active part in Governor Arthur's 'war' against the Tasmanian Aborigines in 1830. Perhaps Colin did too – and was pursued by the ghost of one of them to the other side of the world.[27]

What on earth is one to make of this story? It is not clear when Colin returned to Australia after his departure in 1829. It is, however, unlikely that he returned there only in 1843. His father never went to Australia but remained at Sunipol until his death in 1851.[28]

As we shall see the tradition about him in Coll is of a very different Colin Campbell. According to his gravestone in Crossapol graveyard:

Colin Campbell of Cornaig and Caolis Island of Coll and of Auchnacloich in Lorn who died at Cornaig 18 Jany 1867 in the 71st year of his age. He became a successful settler in Australia and thereafter came back and purchased these three properties in his native country and died much respected and deeply regretted by all who knew him. His sorrowing widow and children place here this monument to the memory of a kind and affectionate husband and father.[29]

Whether or not Colin took part in Governor Arthur's War against the Tasmanian Aborigines is not known, but there were plenty of opportunities to kill Aborigines when he is known to have been in Van Diemen's Land. In 1826 the Tasmanian Aborigines began guerilla warfare against the settlers, who they accused of stealing their land and raping their women. In revenge they speared both white men and women. The settlers responded by hunting them down, shooting them, setting steel traps and poisoning them. By 1835 there were only 300 left. These survivors were transported to Flinders Island, where most died of disease. Only 46 remained when the camp was closed in 1847.[30]

The charge that Colin was a bushranger probably says more about the imagination of people in Mull, who had to find a reason for his financial success in Australia, rather than any propaganda put about by Colin. If there is any truth in this story the events recorded at Sunipol probably took place before he returned to Australia in 1843 and may explain why he did not settle in Sunipol after he had made his fortune.

* * *

Colin's brother Alexander 'Captain Campbell', who as we have seen moved across the Bass Strait to Victoria, considered that it would be more interesting to go sperm-whaling than run a whaling station. Accordingly he went to Sydney and joined the *Sir William Wallace*, a vessel of 272 tons, which was setting out on a long voyage. A whale was caught near the New Hebrides, where the sailors landed, and saw a burning mountain, and the ship went as far north as the coast of Japan, visiting Stewart's Island, Guam, Howe's group and the Landrones. The voyage lasted over two years, and was not a success. In 1835 Captain Campbell again went whaling with Captain Mills as mate, in the schooner *Mars*. Near Mauranga Bay, New Zealand they met Captain Hugh Maclean, who as we have seen had just narrowly escaped destruction at the hands of the Maoris. Bad weather plagued this voyage and no sperm whales were found so the *Mars* went to Cloudy Bay and caught a number of black whales. The second mate and a boat's crew were lost overboard in a gale.

At this time too many vessels were engaged in whaling and in 1842 Messrs Griffiths and Connolly failed. As Captain Campbell had been their partner he lost all his savings. Griffiths failed for £70,000 and Connolly for £90,000. All that was left to Captain Campbell was a claim to a whaling station, including the site at Warrnambool, which he sold to Messrs Foster & Strong for £80. He then began life afresh as captain of various vessels trading between the ports of Sydney, Launceston, Port Fairy and Melbourne. However, Captain Griffiths soon re-established the whaling station, and Captain Campbell joined him.

In 1844 he built a cottage in Port Fairy, and continued to own it till his death. While living there he married. Whaling at this time was very successful, Captain Campbell taking 11 himself. During the next three years he continued whaling during the season and trading along the coast and to Tasmania during the rest of the year.

By 1847 whaling ceased to be profitable. Captain Campbell therefore joined the civil service as harbour master in Melbourne, just before the outbreak of gold fever in 1851. He retired in 1869, aged 64. In 1877 he took a trip to Scotland with his wife and daughters. He died on 25 May 1890 aged 85.[31]

* * *

Whaling was not the only industry in Australia in crisis in the 1840s.[32] Among the casualties was John Leyburn Maclean, whose *Glen Duart* estate was sequestered in 1846.[33] Although John Leyburn was to return to the United Kingdom and die a Military Knight of Windsor,[34] the children of his first marriage were to remain in Australia and become distinguished public servants. The eldest son Mordaunt was to continue the earlier Maclean of Coll tradition of marrying a cousin, when in August 1844 he married Marion Christina Lloyd, the daughter of Donald Macleod of Talisker[35] and Catharina Maclean of Coll.

In 1842 the second son Alexander Grant was appointed to the Surveyor-General's Department, becoming chief draftsman in 1856. In 1861 he became Surveyor-General.[36] When he was sixteen in 1845 the third son Harold became a clerk in the Colonial Secretary's Office. He was eventually to be Sheriff of New South Wales.[37]

* * *

In 1852 the Cooper's sons purchased Ashfield, a 10,000 acre property near Christchurch in New Zealand, and in 1855 they acquired another 30,000 acre block near Ashburton, which they christened Lagmore, after their old home in Coll. They were, however, ambitious for more and when in 1858 John Maclean heard of a great tract of land, which no white man had ever seen, he set off with a horse and a pack-horse laden with supplies for the Waitaki River. Here he met up with a Maori chief named Huruhuru who guided him to the land he was looking for. It was a vast area of almost 400,000 acres, which hardly surprisingly the Waste Land Board was reluctant to grant to any one settler. John Maclean, however, got round the problem by dividing it up among his brothers and sisters. They called it Morven Hills Station. By 1871 the brothers were running 110,000 sheep on their property.[38]

Notes

1. Lynne Bryer & Keith S Hunt *The 1820 Settlers* (Cape Town, 1984); Rosemary Dixon-Smith *The Conch 1828–1869* (2000).
2. Juliet Alexa's Diary, 307.
3. Mull Museum. Campbell of Quinish 01-003. item 3.
4. TNA. CO 179. 9. 399, 908. 30 January 1849. Hugh Maclean, 29 Queen's Terrace, Bayswater to FF Elliot Esq.
5. TNA. CO 179. 9. 401.
6. Mull Museum. Campbell of Quinish 01-003. item 3.
7. TNA. CO 179. 9. 403.
8. TNA. CO 179. 9. 405.
9. Mull Museum. Campbell of Quinish 01-005. item 5.
10. 30 May 1849. Donald Campbell to Alexander Hunter WS. Mull Museum Archives D12/113.
11. 26 November 1849. Donald Campbell to Hugh Maclean of Coll. Marine Terrace, St Helier, Jersey. Mull Museum Archives D12/113.
12. 26 December 1849. Donald Campbell to Alexander Hunter WS. Mull Museum Archives D12/113.
13. 30 January 1850. Donald Campbell to Alexander Hunter WS. Mull Museum Archives D12/113.
14. 23 March 1850. Donald Campbell to R Bevins Esq. 8 Princes Square, Glasgow. Mull Museum Archives D12/113.
15. Juliet Alexa's diary, 307.
16. Ditto.
17. Anon. *Coll* (Wellington, 1911), 17–19.
18. *Bathurst Free Press* quoted in James Cowie *The Australian Gold Rush* [http//www.sbs.com.au/gold/story.html].
19. *Rum*, 139–140.
20. Helen Maclean Buckley *From Little Towns in a Far Land We Came* (1950), 31.
21. *The Diary of James Robertson*, 9 July 1844.
22. *Rum*, 139–40.
23. They had employed the poet Thomas Campbell as a tutor to their children.
24. *The Diary of James Robertson*. Note. 5 February 1843.
25. *Ibid*, 25 July 1843. She was a Maclean from Balaphetrish in Tiree.
26. *Ibid*, 11 May 1844.
27. *Clan Campbell Newsletter 1980*. I have to thank Alastair Campbell of Airds for a copy of this article.
28. He is buried in Crossapol Graveyard beside his brothers Murdoch and Malcolm.
29. Crossapol Graveyard, Coll. He died at Cornaig on 18 January 1867 aged 71.
30. Benjamin Madley 'Patterns of frontier genocide 1803–1910: the Aboriginal Tasmanians, the Yuki of California and the Herrero of Namibia' *Journal of Genocide Research* (2004), 6 (2), June, 167–192; Runoko Rushidi *Black War. The Destuction of the Tasmanian Aborigines* (1998).
31. *The Argus*, 27 May 1890.
32. *Scotland and Australia 1788–1850*, 318.

33. Mitchell Library, Sidney. Extracts of G Gipps's despatches. I have to thank Anne Maclean, 1017 Mclean Street, West Brunswick, Victoria 3055, Australia for this and other information below concerning her ancestor Captain John Leyburn Maclean.
34. Edmund H Fellowes *Military Knights of Windsor 1352–1944*.
35. LM Mowle *Pioneer Families of Australia*, (1978), 251.
36. *Australian Dictionary of Biography* Vol. 5. (1851–1890), K-Q, 182.
37. *Ibid*, 183–4.
38. Geoffrey P Duff *Sheep May Safely Graze* (Christchurch, 1998), 23–4. I have to thank Angus Kennedy, Tighan Lochan, Isle of Coll for a loan of this book.

Chapter Fifty-Five

'The end of an old song'

Whilst *An Cubair Colach*'s sons were making their fortune in New Zealand, Hugh Maclean of Coll's was running out.

I have not been able to discover the fate of 'Uncle Robertson's' Peruvian bonds, but it would seem pretty clear that his speculation failed, and Sir Hector's heirs lost their money and with it any hope of saving the estate. The fate of the family of Coll was sealed. No 'white knight' was going to come to their rescue and it was only a matter of time before everything was sold. What prevented it from happening now was that the estate was entailed.

As we have already seen, in May 1754 Hector Maclean of Coll entailed his estate.[1] An entail was then the fashionable device to exclude unsuitable heirs from succeeding to landed property. As it also prohibited the owner from selling an estate, which was only his for life, he was unable to use it as security on which to borrow money. This prevented profligate heirs from ruining their families, but it also stopped conscientious landowners from borrowing money to improve their estates.

Numerous methods were used to get around entails. For example land that was purchased after the entail was made was not subject to its conditions. Thus Maclean of Coll was able to borrow money on the land in Mull and Coll that he had bought from the Duke of Argyll but not on his original barony.

In the 1840s entails were denounced as one of the causes of Highland destitution. Robert Somers writing in 1848 states:

> The law of entail places the heirs in possession in a most humbling and powerless position, while it retains the privilege of administering the property in hands which have long withered in the grave, it gives its revenues to money-lenders, whose shadowy forms are equally wrapped up from public responsibility and public view ... The true owners of property must be dragged forth from that insubstantial framework behind which they conceal themselves ... The heirs in possession must be free agents. They must have power to improve, to borrow, to sell part or the whole of their estates, to bear the burdens of their station, or, if not able, make room for those who are. To this end, it is essential that the law of entail be entirely abolished.[2]

Although Hugh Maclean of Coll had sold the land he and his father had purchased, the proceeds from their sale had not extinguished his debts.[3] Nor had the sale of Rum, which had not been included in the entail. All he now had to sell was the core estate in Coll and Mull and until entails were abolished they were unsellable. As Donald Campbell wrote on 26th November 1849: 'the state of Coll's affairs . . . are lamentable and concern me exceedingly'.[4] In the meantime the running of the estate continued as before, although steps were probably being taken to prepare it for sale, if and when the entail was abolished.

Even as early February 1847 Campbell and Hunter were discussing the long term future of Coll. Hunter thought that the island was suitable for dairying. The factor disagreed. He wrote:

> I differ with you in thinking that Coll is adapted for dairy[ing] with a very few exceptions. The whole south side from Freslan eastward is a sheet of black heath with the exception of a few patches of reclaimed moss. The north side with the exception of Breachacha, Cliad, Mibost & Gallanach so interspersed with rock that you will not get two acres of arable adjoining and every rough acre of it in want of draining[5]

Campbell's problems increased. On 5 May 1849 he wrote to Hugh to say:

> The arranging [of] matters for Coll I found much more difficult than for Mull. One of the Torestan Crofts has remained in our possession for the last year because I could not get no tenant for it and now there are only three out of all of them that has taken any land. These I provide for in other vacant crofts so that it is clear, as I mentioned to you in my letter from Edinburgh. Nor do I know where to get a tenant for it which was my inducement to make Mr Hunter the offer of joining it to Gallanach – it has you know no accommodation for a respectable tenant and its bounds are too narrow to keep sheep in its own marches.[6]

One tenant who did wish to renew his tack was Mr John Maclean Arileod. He wrote to the factor on 15 May 1849:

> Sir, I hereby offer to take a lease of the farm of Arileod & Feall including Pendicle of Torndach for the term of 15 years from Whitsunday 1850 – at the yearly rent of £50 Str giving me a break in the lease in my favour at the end of 7 years from the commencement – you know for some years past, particularly for the last three since the potatoes failed, I have been losing considerably by the farm & that I used to pay a great part of my rent by my crop. Under all the circumstances and the prospect of the fall in price of both corn & cattle I have no doubt you will think I have offered you a fair rent for the farm and that you will state the same to the trustees. There is one year of my lease to run but I throw myself on the liberality of the trustees that they will not see old tenants removed in Coll. I may get a new lease my office houses require considerable repairs. They are old thatched houses in bad condition & I need them properly repaired along with the main house.[7]

The following day Campbell sent Arileod's offer to Hunter with the comment:

> I enclose an offer made by Mr Maclean, Arileod for a new lease. The representations he makes of the state of his circumstance is but too true, they have been going back for some years. He is honest & very industrious and if he quits, as he is half inclined, I would have difficulty in finding a tenant for the farm. Under the circumstances I recommend that his offer is accepted, making a break in the lease mutually & declining any outlays in the office houses except assisting him with timber from the thinning of the woods here. They are certainly in a

bad state but with the assistance proposed he may repair them. Yesterday was our market day but there were few cattle and fewer buyers. The few sold brought low prices 20% under last year.[8]

As we have seen, Campbell had been criticised for his treatment of the Torestan crofters and wrote indignantly:

The situation regarding the removals in Coll is entirely incorrect. Every tenant and cottar removed from Torastan has got some other possession, except one man who is a notorious thief and his brother is allowed to give him a house where he will not have such opportunities for dishonesty – one of the tenants removed from Arnabost is going to America, being enabled to do so by the indulgence you have empowered me to grant to old tenants as to their arrears.

Two will be removed from Arinagour but they are unmarried men without any burden but still have fallen in arrears. Lachlan Maclean loses his croft at Dervaig because he has fallen considerably in arrears & has no stock to pay rent.[9]

On the same day he instructed the Ground Officer to put these adjustments into practice in a letter which underlines the complicated arrangements the factor was having to make to ensure that as little land as possible was lying 'waste':

I am not sure whether Charles Macdonald will go to Knocklean to serve me. If not I understand Dugal McNiven will be glad to go. I have only further to say that the crofters of Arinagour [?] the tenants have been obliged to remove are first to be served. I mean particularly Charles McDonald, Dugal McNiven & Donald Beaton. One of the two farms will probably be provided at Kocklean. But I see Donald Beaton can have but one croft this year. If it can be avoided I do not wish the other Beatons that have been warned at Arinagour to be removed. The Campbells removed from Arnabost I have no plans for – they do not deserve it. See that John McKinnon Cannada removes at the term day. I spoke to his brother that I had no obligation to or shall give him a home.[10]

On 30 May he wrote to him again:

You will take one of the loads of Indian meal, that is [to say] two Bolls & divide [them] among the poor cottars of Torestan, those that go, as well as those that stay, giving the largest share to the most needful. Lachlan McInnes & Neil Maclean are the only ones to stay. See that John Cannada removes at once.[11]

Hunter had turned down Arileod's offer. Campbell responded:

As to the Arileod lease it may wait for another year, but unless our prospects materially mend you will have to come down to the offer made. What is the use of keeping up a rental that cannot be realised?[12]

On 12th June he wrote again to Johnston:

I have written to Mr Nesbit for the necessary warrants to eject Alexander Maclean & the McInnes lads. These people will only irritate me to sequester their crop. As to the Torestan cottars they must remove immediately, except the two that I allow to remain. I will otherwise hand ejections against them also – I did not intend to give any meal except to those who are submisssive – I will give Lachlan McDonald accommodation no longer. There is no need in his asking favours. Mr Caldwell will shortly be out again to finish his drainage. He is instructed to give preference to such of the Torestan cottars as have removed, but if any pressure to remain they will get neither work or meal from me. What would be the use of them remaining where they would not be allowed to make a particle of crop ... I will call a market in Coll immediately on my return when I will collect the rents which you will inform the tenants must be paid at any rate.

NB. Exert yourself to get the Torestan Cottars away. I would be sorry for their own sakes to be obliged to resort to severe measures.[13]

* * *

The increased impatience, apparent in Captain Campbell's correspondence, reflect the contemporary attitude to the Highlands and Highlanders. It was generally believed in influential circles that 'poverty was a reflection of personal failure and economic success an achievement which merited moral approval'. This view underlines the thinking of Sir John MacNeill[14] and Charles Trevelyan,[15] the two men who were to have the greatest influence on famine relief in the Highlands and Islands.

Both men shared similar attitudes. MacNeill argued that there was 'nothing so injurious to the people and to the country as the gratuitous distribution of food'. Such misplaced charity only encouraged 'the cancer of pauperism, the habit of the poor depending on the help of others rather than their own efforts'. Instead, MacNeill stressed 'that rather than inflict such "demoralisation", charitable funds should be used to "promote habits of industry and self-dependence by increasing the productive powers of the soil"'. Both men also believed that Highlanders were lazy and needed to be taught a moral lesson. Only then would they change their ways and bring an end to their endemic destitution.

Although official government involvement ended in 1847, when the store ships in Mull and Skye were withdrawn, Trevelyan remained highly influential, leaving the direct administration of relief to the Edinburgh and Glasgow committees of the Central Board of Management for Highland Relief. Men who had much the same views as Trevelyan, and could be trusted to carry out his policies, took over the responsibilities of existing Relief Committees. The Government was thus left free to concentrate on monitoring landlord's policies, and bringing pressure to bear on the inactive. It also, in conjunction with the Central Board, could bring employment to the area, with financial help made possible by the Drainage Act.

The man who had responsibility for the Central Board's operations on the Coll estate was Charles Baird, Secretary of the Glasgow Section. He had been active in relief work in 1836–7 and was joint author of a pamphlet published in 1838, entitled *Remarks on the Evils at Present Affecting the Highlands and Islands of Scotland*. In it he praised the Highlander's many virtues, their valour, religious loyalties and their kindness to kin and the poor. He, however, also says that they were feckless, guilty of having too many children, too fond of 'ardent spirits' and were notoriously idle. Although he evidently visited Coll Baird's picture of the Island is superficial, taking no notice of Alexander Maclean of Coll's earlier valiant efforts to bring the island into the nineteenth century.

* * *

In 1849 the weather improved and in October the factor was able to write: 'we have at last splendid weather for securing the crops. A couple more days will finish all'. The improved situation enabled the Central Board's operations to come to an end in 1850. The managers knew that this was to happen twelve months earlier and on 2nd October 1849 Donald Campbell wrote to Hunter to say:

> Mr Baird the Secretary of the Highland Relief Board, Glasgow called on me Saturday. I had a long conversation with him regarding the state of the people on the Coll estate – Their funds will last another year and not longer – He asked what permanent work would most benefit the island of Coll. I replied the quay at Arinagour, which would cost £1,000. He then asked me if they built the quay would we support our own poor in the island. That was a question I said to put to you and not me . . .[16]

The building of a pier at Arinagour would have a significant effect on the island. On 10th October Donald Campbell wrote to Hunter to say:

> the meal distribution in Coll last year (I mean the one now ended) was not quite 400 bolls, half Indian and half oats – in the event of the quay going on it would furnish work for the greatest part of the recipients from the Destitution Committee as they live round Arinagour – and we have between £4 and £50 in road money which I have no doubt the trustees will allow to be laid out in roads on the island so I do not think the support of the poor people will cost you much for the next year in the event of the pier going on.

He goes on to say: 'What they will do afterwards if not thinned by emigration is more to be dreaded'.[17]

* * *

One of the problems of receiving Government finance lay in the small print: loans incurred administrative charges. On the 19th October Campbell wrote to Hunter:

> The last post brought the enclosed for Coll which being from the Inclosure Commissioners I opened and now forward to you – I find £99.19s.5d is retained for expenses. There will I hope be no difficulty in charging this to the estate being a charge by Government & sanctioned by Act of Parliament – you will bear in mind that the whole interest of 6½% is paid by myself and the other tenants so far as the drainage . . . I have just received a letter from the Laird complaining that Drainage and other improvements are not carried out on the estate with spirit – never enquiring how the means are to be supplied for doing so.[18]

Hugh was in Jersey staying with one of his daughters when he received a letter from his factor:

> in regard to the improvements on the estate Mr Spooner's last inspection amounts to above £400 – to this is added the expenses reclaimed by the Commissioners amounting to £99. I do not think the estate should bear this expense – as it is enough for the tenants to pay 6½% on the actual expenses of draining – but I do not expect Mr Hunter will allow it as he complains so

much of the burden of the estate with regard to the Arinagour quay. I have some hopes of it – it has been surveyed by the engineer of the Fishing Board ... [the cost will be] £1,400. If the Fishing Board give help the Destitution Committee will assist.[19]

The good harvest meant that the tenants should have been in a position to pay their rents. However, he writes:

The only satisfactory rent payers at this term has been the Coll tenants (always accepting Arinagour) and they are deserving of any assistance that can be given them ... In regard to the mosses that Coll has had drained and trenched here [i.e. at Quinish], I have come under no obligation for them nor will I. Until manured and cultivated they are dead and useless to the estate – and if I manure and crop them it is all that can be expected from me particularly as they will not bear horses & all must be done by spade work – it was much against my wishes that Coll meddled with them but he would have them done – it is perhaps fortunate that no more has been done as Coll's views excluded much [?] – I must allow these mosses so near the house was a great eye sore & their improvement will give the place quite a different look.[20]

The failure to spend money on maintenance was having its effect. On 18th December 1849. Campbell wrote to Hunter to report that:

The public houses at Bellachroy & Arinagour are getting into such disrepair that they must immediately [be] looked to. The school-house at Dervaig also requires some repairs.[21]

Donald Campbell's out-letter book, which has given an invaluable insight into the running of the Coll estate during the Potato Famine, stops abruptly in April 1850. Others that he kept do not appear to have survived. The last entries continue to reflect the problems that affected the factor and the people he was responsible for in the aftermath of the famine. For instance in January 1850, a rumour was circulating in Coll that if a man was moved from one farm to another he lost the right to support from the Central Board.

On 24th January he attempted to kill this nonsense by writing to Charles Baird to say that:

An absurd idea has gone abroad in Coll that if a man is removed from one farm to another he is thereby disqualified from receiving any allowance of meal from your Board. I will be obliged by your writing Mr Maclean Crossapol setting this to right. I do not for a moment suppose that you mean to interfere with landlords or their factors in removing tenants & cottars from one farm to another as they see cause.

He went on to say:

Will you excuse me from giving a hint that any person keeping unnecessary dogs should be excepted from any right to get much. An order from your Board to this effect would be of immense benefit, as these dogs fed on your meal are not always kept for the best purpose.[22]

In February the saga of the clearance of Torestan finally came to an end. In a letter to the Ground Officer he writes:

I am glad you have at last removed John Morison from Torestan. See that every house has been pulled down how soon it is empty.[23]

In March he has a final blast against the iniquities of the inhabitants of the two new villages that fifty years earlier Alexander Maclean of Coll had been praised for establishing:

The small crofters of Arinagour & Dervaig are a great evil but you know they are not of my creating – The purpose of granting leases to such now is the getting the Destitution meal which will encourage them to work their crofts better & the ground officer shall have instructions to see they do it – the attempt to double crofts at Arinagour will not do because no one there is able to stock or pay rents for a second one – the ground is now not drained & on such ground will have little effect – it has been hitherto a kind of Botany Bay – where all that had gone back in their circumstances had r[efuge] – what rent they paid now by the earnings of their sons & daughters when in service. Until the potatoes failed they had an abundance of them for food.[24]

He did, however, take pride in the modern housing he had encouraged. On 25th March he writes:

building houses of turf with divot roofs I consider in these days retrograde. But at any rate we do not require houses – those already inhabited at Dervaig & Arinagour and all over the Coll estate were very superior to any that can be built of turf. Had the price of potatoes kept at what it was four years ago & the root itself not failed every house in Dervaig would by this time be slated.[25]

He is not without sympathy for those in arrears. On 2nd April he wrote:

I have been obliged to send summonses of removal to several of the crofters of Dervaig & Penmore for having fallen in arrears of rent, also the same in Coll. What to do with the poor people I know not – if I turned them off they will only be thrown on the pauper list. One poor man came here a couple of days ago – and on my telling him it did not rest with me to keep him on he went away weeping bitterly – you may suppose how I felt for him. Whatever am I to do with him or such? Had you not better allow them to creep on as they are for this year & pay what they can? – I before mentioned to you that the tenants of this estate generally make a wonderful exertion to pay their rents last year'.

Hugh Maclean of Coll was once again proposing to come and live in Quinish. Campbell's lack of enthusiasm is apparent in the penultimate letter in his letter book. On the 3rd April 1850 he writes:

I am favoured with your letter of the 27th March. I will be no bar whatever to your coming to Penmolloch as you propose. The land you take being valued by arbiters and the loss I sustain thereby being deducted from the rent. But I object to any taking a sum of money and building myself accommodation. Let them be specified and calculated for – The extended farm you allude to was never contemplated by Mr Hunter or me when I took the lease. Still when required I will not be adverse to coming to equitable terms regarding it at a future time.

Finally on 15th April 1850 he writes to Hunter to say: 'I am sorry to say that two of the best tenants in Coll have thrown up their lands intending for America. They are wise while they have anything'.[26] It is not an inappropriate end to Donald Campbell's surviving correspondence.

* * *

Although the Central Board ceased to operate in 1850, both Trevelyan and McNeill continued to take a close interest in the Highlands and Islands. Sir John McNeill was commissioned to write a report for the Board of Supervision in Scotland, which he chaired. He visited Mull and on the 18th February 1851 was present at a meeting of the Parochial Board of Kilninian and Kilmore held at the Mull Hotel in Tobermory. He put the following questions to the meeting:

1. Are there at this date in the parish ... persons suffering from want, who are not, by the existing law entitled to demand relief and who cannot find employment whereby they might earn the means of subsistence; and if so what may be their number?
2. Is there good reason to believe that there will be such persons, as the season advances? And if so, what is the greatest number of such persons that will probably be suffering from want at any one time before next harvest, notwithstanding every exertion they can possibly make to procure the means of subsistence?
3. What measures have been taken, or are proposed, to be taken, by the parochial board with a view to such emergency?

The Board answered:

1. The board is not aware that there is ... any person ... in circumstances so destitute as to endanger health.
2. The board are of the opinion, that throughout the ensuing season, destitution will press harder than at any previous period, on those who are not by law entitled to demand relief. The board, however, should hope, from the cheapness of provisions, and from the facility of obtaining employment in the south that none will suffer in his health from want of food.
3. No new measure has been adopted ... The inspectors having had and exercised discretionary power of relieving cases of extreme distress amongst those not legally entitled to demand it and that discretionary power will be continued.[27]

Among the landowners and factors present at the meeting was Captain Donald Campbell. He stated that he had been Coll's factor in the parish for twelve years, although he had been acquainted with the property, presumably when he was factor of the Isle of Coll for a further twelve years. He said that up until Martinmas 1846, the tenants had been 'in comfortable circumstances' and had generally paid their rents regularly. However, 'since the failure of the potatoes, they have been unable to sell any part of their crop; but on the contrary, have been obliged to import food', They were also falling into arrears with their rents.

He claimed that he had persuaded Coll to reduce his rents of all the tenants paying less than £50 by 10% since Whitsunday 1849. Even so none of those paying a reduced rent was able to pay it in full. Those paying over £15 were able to pay a larger proportion of their rent than those paying less than £15. He was of the opinion that there was no danger of anyone under his charge dying, but that there would 'necessarily be much privation and distress'. He went on to say that he was authorised to grant nine-year leases at the present rents and had gathered all the people on the Mull estate together to explain the offer to them. A few accepted, some declined and the rest were unenthusiastic.[28] He believed the reason was that 'tenants on the Coll estate were never removed but for strong reasons'.[29]

In 1851 there were 664 people on Coll's property in Mull. 51 were tenants paying a rent of £10 or less and another 19 were paying over £10. There were also 38 cottars who were paying nothing to the proprietor. The rent due was £779 per year but in the four years to Whitsunday the proprietor only received £1,280, an average of £320 a year, whilst the arrears due were £836. At the same time the expenditure on wages and gratuities to the people on the Mull estate during those years was £789, and the taxes and public dues amounted to £484.[30]

MacNeill does not appear to have visited Coll. He, however, reports that there were 130 families of cottars on the Island who had no land from the three proprietors. Three of the cottars and 25 families of crofters were paying less than £5 rent. Only one was not receiving relief from the destitution fund. Another 51 crofters were paying from £8 to £15 a year in rent. The total population of the Island was 1109[31], a fall of more than 400 since 1841.

Coll had one advantage in that it was not far from Tobermory, where there was 'every facility for proceeding to seek employment elsewhere; and about 100 of the inhabitants of Coll have recently had recourse to that mode of obtaining their subsistence, having been supplied by individuals residing on the island with the means of going to the south'. The sum of £70 had also been employed by the Roads Trustees for the construction and repair of roads in Coll, which has furnished a considerable amount of employment. Seed had also been provided to enable those who had none to plant their corn and potatoes.

MacNeill sums up by saying that:

There is good reason to hope that this season will pass away, not without painful suffering, but without loss of any life in consequence of the cessation of eleemosynary aid. But if henceforward the population is to depend on the local resources, some fearful calamity will probably occur before many years, unless a portion of the inhabitants of those parishes remove to where they can find the means of subsistence in greater abundance, and with greater certainty, than they can find them where they now are.[32]

* * *

MacNeill's report finally discredited charitable relief as a solution to Highland destitution and made a powerful case for assisted emigration. It led to the Emigration Advances Act, which provided loans at low rates of interest to proprietors who wished to assist the 'surplus' population of their estates to emigrate, and led to the founding of the Highland and Island Emigration Society. Between 1851 and 1856 it supported the movement of almost 5,000 people to Australia.

The first to leave from the Coll estate were ten families mainly from Arinagour and Dervaig, who sailed from Liverpool for Moreton Bay on 28th August 1852 in the *Marmion*. They were followed the following year by six families in the *New Zealand*, in June1854 by a further thirteen families in the *Edward Johnston* and by a further family from Gallanach in Coll in the *Hornet* in July. In all before the estate was sold 95 people left for Australia, under the auspices of the Highland and Island Emigration Society.

In 1854 an Act of Parliament broke the entail and the following year the Coll estate was sold. The breaking of the entail involved the consent of the next three heirs. All were abroad and had to return to the United Kingdom to sign away their inheritance.[33]

Before they left Alexander, younger of Coll and his brother William visited the islands to say goodbye. Harriet Maclean says that the visited her family at the Manse in Tiree and remained a week. 'She says: 'they felt much the loss of all the old estates'.[34]

It was not the only tragedy now to strike the Crossapol family. On 16th December 1851 the Rev. Neil Maclean had written to his sister-in-law in Plymouth to say:

My Dear Sister,

After a long interval of silence, I wish it were in my power to communicate anything, which might be gratifying to you: but alas! This is not at present the case, for you are already aware of the severe and unexpected domestic calamity with which we have been lately visited. It has pleased God to call away our dear Donald, after one day's illness ... In the midst of our affliction, however, it is a source of some gratification to know the great attachment and affection felt for him by all classes of persons here, and the feeling of deep sorrow and regret which was manifested on hearing of his untimely death. When the tidings spread, [torn] there was scarcely a dry eye in the whole Parish. Even the people [at] the Light house Establishment here, whose families he was in the habit of frequently visiting professionally, tho' in some measure strangers, were observed to shed tears in abundance over his grave.[35]

It was not to be long before Neil was to join his eldest son in the little family graveyard at Kirkapoll. He was to die on 26th August 1858. He was 75. Four years earlier, on 10th January 1855 his cousin Neil Maclean tacksman of Crossapol had died in Coll. He is buried in Crossapol Cemetery.

Notes

1. NAS Register of Testaments. 15 March 1755.
2. Robert Somers *Letters from the Highlands on the Famine of 1846* (1977), 178–9.
3. As a result of the arrangement with the Earl of Argyll in the 1630s the Isle of Rum was not included in the entail [NAS. Register of Tailzies. Vol. 2, 286–294].
4. 26 November 1849. Donald Campbell to Alexander Hunter. Mull Museum Archives D12/113.
5. 22 February 1847. Donald Campbell to Alexander Hunter. Mull Museum Archives D12/113.
6. 5 May 1849. Donald Campbell to Alexander Hunter. Mull Museum Archives D12/113.
7. 15 May 1849. Donald Campbell to Alexander Hunter. Mull Museum Archives D12/113.
8. 16 May 1849. Donald Campbell to Alexander Hunter. Mull Museum Archives D12/113.
9. 24 May 1849. Donald Campbell to Alexander Hunter. Mull Museum Archives D12/113.
10. 24 May 1849. Donald Campbell to Lachlan Johnston, Ground Officer, Coll. Mull Museum Archives D12/113.
11. 30 May 1849. Donald Campbell to Lachlan Johnston, Ground Officer, Coll. Mull Museum Archives D12/113.
12. 30 May 1849. Donald Campbell to Alexander Hunter. Mull Museum Archives D12/113.
13. 12 June 1849. Donald Campbell to Lachlan Johnston, Ground Officer, Coll. Mull Museum Archives D12/113.
14. He was the man who had jumped at Hobart's offer of a place in the East India Company's Medical Service, when Dr Lachlan Maclean turned it down. He served in both India and Persia and later became a diplomat and special envoy to the Shah of Persia. In 1845 he was appointed the first chairman of the Board of Supervision of the Scottish Poor Law.

15. He had also served the East India Company. In 1840 he was appointed Assistant Secretary to the Treasury, a post 'that might be better described as Permanent Head of the Treasury with a very considerable influence over policy as well as administration' [*The Great Highland Famine*, 124].
16. 2 October 1849. Donald Campbell to Alexander Hunter. Mull Museum Archives D12/113.
17. 10 October 1849. Donald Campbell to Alexander Hunter. Mull Museum Archives D12/113.
18. 19 October 1849. Donald Campbell to Alexander Hunter. Mull Museum Archives D12/113.
19. 26 November 1849. Donald Campbell to Hugh Maclean of Coll. Mull Museum Archives D12/113.
20. 12 December 1849. Donald Campbell to Alexander Hunter. Mull Museum Archives D12/113.
21. 18 December 1849. Donald Campbell to Alexander Hunter. Mull Museum Archives D12/113.
22. 24 January 1850. Donald Campbell to CH Baird HRB, Glasgow. Mull Museum Archives D12/113.
23. 12 February 1850. Donald Campbell to Lachlan Johnston, Ground Officer, Coll. Mull Museum Archives D12/113.
24. 11 March 1850. Donald Campbell to Alexander Hunter. Mull Museum Archives D12/113.
25. 25 March 1850. Donald Campbell to Alexander Hunter. Mull Museum Archives D12/113.
26. 15 April 1850. Donald Campbell to Alexander Hunter. Mull Museum Archives D12/113.
27. PP. *Report to the Board of Supervision by Sir John MacNeill on the West Highlands & Islands* (1851) 9–10.
28. *Ibid*, 21.
29. *Ibid*, xviii.
30. *Ibid*.
31. *Ibid*, xxv.
32. *Ibid*, xlvii.
33. NAS. RD5. 960. 198.
34. BCP. Extract from Harriet Maclean's letter [probably written by Alexander Maclean 94th Regiment] dated 21 November 1885.
35. There is a story in Tiree that Donald committed suicide and that his ghost haunts the Manse. It is said that he had a problem with drink. One evening he went to visit a woman in childbirth. He was drunk and knocked over a candle. The woman and her child were burnt to death and in a fit of remorse Donald killed himself. Thereafter there were noises in the attic of the Manse that sounded like someone dragging furniture around.

    In the 1960s the Church of Scotland sold the Manse to Robert Beck the Tiree vet. It is now owned by Ian and Eileen Tainsh who have turned it into an extremely comfortable guest-house. When they were renovating it and it had no electricity they heard the noises and Beck told them the legend of Dr Donald. However, when Ian Tainsh and his son stripped off the plaster board in the attic they found that loose pieces of mortar moved in the wind between the stonewall and the lath that held up the plaster board. Since they replaced it the noises have stopped.

    'Donald Maclean, surgeon' is buried in the small walled family plot at the west end of the roofless medieval parish church at Kirkapoll. His 'affectionate father' erected it. Neil's daughter Mary Flora, his wife and the Rev. Neil himself are buried in separate graves beside him. As this is consecrated ground Donald could not have been buried there if he committed suicide. It would therefore appear that the Tiree story is incorrect.

Part IX

The Victorian Army

Chapter Fifty-Six

Burmah, China, India and Aden 1840–1860

The French Revolutionary and Napoleonic Wars, unlike earlier conflicts, had divorced the extended family of Coll from its base in the Hebrides. After earlier wars officers had returned to their tacks in Coll and Mull. Now, either because their fathers had given up their tacks and emigrated, or because the time they had spent in the tropics had made them reluctant to return to the cold and wet the officers did not return home. There were other less obvious reasons as to why the officer class in the Hebrides did not return home at the end of their military service.

As Edward Spiers points out: In the 1840s in London 'balls, theatres and country visits relieved the not over arduous duties even of a subaltern'.

Although

the social scene was less hectic and less expensive in the more remote stations of Ireland and Scotland. Officers still amused themselves, however. In the afternoons they rode, hunted, shot, fished, attended race meetings, or possibly, in summer, played cricket. In the evenings the unmarried officers dined in the mess.[1]

This way of life could not be replicated in the Hebrides. Officers therefore tended to retire to Cheltenham and Bath, where they could continue to follow these interests.

* * *.

When Ensign Alexander Maclean of the 94th Regiment of Foot arrived in India in September 1840 he was not the only Maclean of Coll serving there. Nine other members of the family served there as officers between 1840 and 1860.

The last of the previous generation of Coll officers in India, died in 1839. He was Alexander Lockhart Maclean, Lachlan, last of the Isle of Muck's youngest son. He had seen active service with the 67th Native Infantry in the Arakan during the First Burmese War (1824–6). This nearly disastrous campaign was only undertaken when an arrogant over-confident Burmese king launched an unprovoked invasion of the south-east frontier of Bengal.[2]

The British were totally ignorant of the problems of warfare in a tropical country of swamp and jungle like Burmah. This ignorance resulted in massive casualties through disease, including cholera and malaria. No one at the time realised that mosquitoes caused malaria. At one time 25 officers in one of the British battalions were on the sick list and the campaign richly deserved its title as the worst managed of all the nineteenth-century colonial wars.[3]

Alexander Lockhart was to spend at least two tours of duty in the Arakan. During his second, in 1837, his wife died there. She was 23. Alexander himself died two years later having recently given up command of the Recruit battalion of his regiment at Meerut.[4]

Lachlan Alexander Maclean, Alexander Lockhart's nephew,[5] joined the 67th Native Infantry in June 1837.[6] It was the beginning of a trend amongst the Macleans of Coll to join family regiments. Previously there seems to be little family loyalty to a regiment and officers moved from one to another.

Lachlan Alexander was not to add to glory to the reputation of the Macleans of Coll in the Indian Army. Within 18 months of arriving in India he was in prison for debt. He compounded the offence by beating up a Mr Bryant, 'in his own shop at Benares', after the latter refused to give him any further credit.

The Commander-in-Chief, with surprising mildness, stated that if Ensign Maclean 'should have misconstrued, or so foolishly rejected the admonition which he received by His Excellency and also from his Commanding Officer... in beating Mr Bryant [and] if [he]... hopes to rise in the service he must change'. He also pointed out that Lachlan Alexander had two court martials pending and warned him that the 'early and disreputable termination which will infallibly attend such a career as this; trusting at the same time to that officer's respect for the army, and for his Family, for a return to the honorable conduct always suggested by the feelings of an officer and a gentleman'.

Lachlan Alexander seems to have got off lightly. In 1841 he was given leave to go up river 'for the benefit of his health' and in July 1842 he was promoted Lieutenant.[7] In September 1842 at Benares he married. He died at Delhi on 23 December 1846 and was buried at the Rajpura Cemetery. His short career perhaps illustrates some of the characteristics in a new generation of British officers, whose behaviour was one of the factors that led to the Indian Mutiny a decade later.

It is, however, worth noting that the shopkeeper 'Mr Bryant', who Lachlan Alexander had beaten up and 'affects to despise' was presumably white and tells us nothing of his attitude to the native population. Although someone who despised a European he believed to be his inferior is hardly likely to have had a high opinion of the natives at a time when 'the fashion in Calcutta and to a lesser extent in the larger stations up-country' was to look down on everything 'black'.[8]

The attitude of many British officers to their Indian soldiers had changed as the frontier of British India moved further to the north-west. South of that frontier there was now no enemy we were not confident of beating. And with increased confidence came an unattractive arrogance.

* * *

The next member of the family of Coll to arrive in India was a very different character to his cousin Lachlan Alexander. Lachlan Hector Gilbert Maclean was yet another grandson of Lachlan Maclean late of the Isle of Muck, being the son of Captain Donald Maclean 2nd (Queen's) Regiment of Foot, who had died at sea on his way home from India in 1834. The same year LHG Maclean was commissioned into the 49th Foot. The following year he was posted to the East Indies.

On 30 May 1840 the 49th were part of the expeditionary force assembled in Singapore that set sail for China. Although the Opium War of 1841 that followed was about much more than opium, there is little doubt that the British and others made a great deal of money out of the drug. It went some way to redress the previous balance of payments deficit in China's favour in its trade with Europe.[9]

The primary cause of the conflict was the failure of two cultures to understand each other and the refusal of Chinese Emperor to accept that Europeans were anything other than impertinent barbarians. Like the King of Burmah he underestimated the power of British arms and believed that because Chinese silk and porcelian were superior to that of Europe it followed that a Chinese army was superior to that of Britain

The aim of the expedition, as detailed by Lord Palmerston, the Whig Foreign Secretary was: to punish the Chinese for seizing British goods, mainly Indian opium, and to open Chinese ports to international trade. Palmerston's orders to Admiral Elliot were that he should: blockade Canton, occupy the island of Chusan, deliver a letter addressed to the Minister of the Emperor of China and then sail north to the mouth of the Pei-ho to sign a treaty with a duly accredited representative of the Imperial Chinese Government. It was easier to give such orders than to carry them out.

As in Burmah disease was a greater threat to the army than was the enemy. The combined attack of dysentery, diarrhea, malaria, exhaustion and intense heat resulted in an appalling death toll. By the end of 1840 out of the 3,000 men in Chusan 450 were dead.[10]

A battalion of Madras Native Infantry reinforced the British in Chusan and Elliot[11] was able to assemble some 1,400 men for an assault on the forts of Chuenpi and Taikoktow. This operation was carried out without casualties from enemy fire, although 38 British soldiers were injured when, after it was captured, an explosion of ammunition occurred at Chuenpi.

This first clash between British and Chinese troops underlined the difference in their capabilities. Although some of the British were only armed with old smooth bore flintlocks, they were infinitely superior to the ancient matchlocks used by the Chinese. An agreement between the two commanders followed by which the Chinese ceded Hong Kong to Britain and agreed to pay 6,000,000 dollars to the British Government. China was to be opened to international trade.

The Chinese Emperor furiously denounced the agreement and sacked his Commissioner. The treaty was equally unpopular with the Viceroy of India Lord Auckland, who believed the indemnity was far too small and that Elliot's evacuation of Chusan was a mistake.

1841 saw spasmodic military operations in and around Canton: forts were captured, batteries silenced and a flotilla of 40 junks destroyed. The following year the arrival of British reinforcements resulted in the rout of a Chinese counter-attack and a leisurely advance through south-east China that carried the war up to the walls of the great city of Nanking. It was here that the Chinese reluctantly accepted defeat.[12]

Lieutenant Lachlan Hector Gilbert Maclean, who had a reputation of being 'an attentive steady officer', was present in every action (Segoan excepted) during the campaign in China. He then returned home with his regiment in August 1843 and was in command of a company until October 1845 when he joined the 'recruiting service'.

In August 1847 he wrote to his colonel requesting promotion. In his letter he pointed out that he had served in the army for thirteen years, and had for some time been the Senior Lieutenant and the only subaltern in the regiment who had served in both India and China. He was keen to continue serving in the 49th, but, if there was not a vacancy in the regiment he wished to be posted to any regiment on foreign service, or to an unattached company. He also drew attention to the fact [which was not true] that he was the 'sole survivor of numerous members of my family who have had the honor [sic] of serving in both the army and navy'. The crux of his dilemma appears when he writes that 'I have always been with my regiment and would naturally wish to remain in it if I saw any chance of promotion except by Purchase which is unfortunately not in my power'.[13]

The same desire to serve overseas, especially in the Indian Army, where an officer could live on his pay, is apparent in other letters to the Commander-in-Chief. For example when in December 1845 the Rev. Samuel Emory Day appealed to the Duke of Wellington for a commission for his son William Deane Hoare Guinness Day, an undergraduate at Wadham College, Oxford, he makes that self same point. William obtained an ensigncy in the 94th Regiment of Foot. It cost his father £450.[14]

* * *

In 1841, as we have seen, news reached London that the 94th, who were then at Cannanore, were to be sent to join the expedition in China. Although the 94th appear to have been ordered to march, the order was cancelled and the battalion remained at Cannanore. They were soon to be stood to for another campaign, this time in Afghanistan.

In 1838 the first Afghan War had commenced when the British, fearing that a Russian backed Persian siege of Herat was the prelude to a Russian takeover of Afghanistan, seized Kabul. A puppet was placed on the Afghan throne. However, it soon became clear that his rule depended on British bayonets and it was necessary to occupy Afghanistan. An Afghan revolt followed and in January 1842 it was decided to withdraw the army back into India. It was a disastrous decision. In the high, snow covered Afghan passes tribesmen ambushed and destroyed the withdrawing army. Dr Brydon escaped to bring news to Jellalabad. An army of 16,000, including camp followers, had been slaughtered. It was one of the greatest disasters in British military history. It also underlined the point that a British army was not indestructible and was yet another step that led to the Indian Mutiny.

That summer another British army set out to avenge this humiliating defeat. It was this army that the 94th were rumoured to be joining. 'You will naturally feel very anxious at present about dear Alex as the 94th have been ordered to Cabool [Kabul] wrote Dr Donald MacLean from Tiree on 10 May 1842:

> but I hope the worst there is over, the former mismanagement will teach them in future to act more vigorously, and with better effect against these rascally savages. Alick like every soldier must run his chance of the fortunes of war and I hope a little active campaigning will have no worse effect than to give him speedy promotion.

Once again, however, Alick was to be disappointed and the 94th remained at Cannanore. No doubt his belligerent cousins in Tiree, who kept a vigilant eye on what was happening in an empire, where so many of their relatives and friends were serving, were equally disappointed.

On 23rd March 1843, Alick, who on 20th January 1842 had purchased a Lieutenancy in the 94th,[15] at last left Cannanore and marched for Trichinopoly[16] with the Right line and Headquarters of his regiment to join the Left wing who had been there since December 1841. They remained united until January 1845 when the Left wing proceeded to Burmah whilst the Right wing set sail for Aden.

In 1839 Commander Haines of the Indian Navy had been sent to purchase the Aden peninsular from Sultan Mahsin of Lahej. The latter feared that the Egyptians would take Aden and pay him nothing.

In 1839 Aden was a derelict village of 600 inhabitants. Haines turned it into a thriving market place and a key port of call on the route to India. The British wanted Aden as a coaling station.[17] Despite the fact that they had no territorial ambitions in the interior of South Arabia the British were unable to ignore the neighbouring tribes. And the 94th were sent to Aden to reinforce the small garrison there when news reached India that an Arab attack was anticipated.[18]

On the morning of the 27th February 1845 'after an agreeable passage of one month, we described in the distance from the poop of the good ship *Scotia* the dim outline of the Arab Coast enveloped in mist. Great indeed was our curiosity and excitement; telescopes were in great demand'. So writes 'An Officer in the Queen's Army' in *Historical & Statistical Sketches of Aden in Arabia Felix during a two year's residence in that Colony* (1848). Although the author is anonymous, he was almost certainly Lieutenant Alexander Maclean, who had been appointed Adjutant of the 94th on 10th September 1844.[19]

The 94th's first task in Aden was to improve the colony's defences. Henry Viscount Hardinge had examined them, when he visited Aden in 1844 en route to India to take up his post as Viceroy.[20] They were based on the old Turkish Wall around Crater. The Arab attack, led by a religious fanatic named Syed Ishmael did not materialise until August 1846. On the 12th intelligence was received that the enemy were approaching Aden and

> at about sunset the whole of the Queen's troops were formed into a column by sound of bugle in double time, and shortly afterwards moved with great steadiness, and in the best of spirits to their various posts on the heights ... An attack from the enemy that night was considered certain, but they did not appear until several days afterwards, and the troops were a good deal exposed to the sun.

It was not until 1 am on the 16th that an enemy reconnaissance party came close to the walls and the garrison opened fire.

> In a moment, the signal being given, a destructive fire and shrapnel was opened upon the Arabs who alarmed and discomforted fled in great confusion, leaving some of their wounded, a number of creases, matchlocks &c &c., behind them in their flight ... For several days after the petty demonstrations of Syed Ishmael nothing could be seen of the enemy – their efforts were considered paralysed, and it was thought that being in all probability disheartened by failure, and weakened by dissensions among themselves, as well as deprived of the necessary means of carrying on the siege, the cause of Syed Ishmael had been forsaken ... On the morning, however, of the[1]9th August, at about 8 o'clock they were descried advancing to the number of 1,200 towards the Turkish Wall – Some might be perceived mounted on their war-camels, others on horseback, galloping at full speed, and not a few on foot, moving to almost certain destruction; without order or regularity, and evidently without any pre-arranged plan of attack. As might be expected, this unorganised rabble were soon dispersed by the fire of the British guns, to which some shots from the gun-boats in the bay under Lieutenant Hamilton, materially contributed.

Syed Ishmael thus baffled in his futile demonstration upon Aden, endeavoured to stop British supplies from Arabia, in which for a time he was successful, for during a period of three weeks none could be obtained.

As in Burmah and China the 94th suffered more from disease than from enemy fire. In the period from 1st April 1845 to 31st March 1846, 947 men were admitted to hospital, of which 26 died. As the 94th were only 536 strong, many must have been admitted to hospital more than once. Then in the six months from 1st April 1846 cholera reached Aden and another 14 men were lost. The impact of these deaths had a profound effect on the 94th Foot, which is vividly expressed in a barrack room ballad dedicated to Lieutenant Maclean:

> In this land both of sunshine and sorrow,
> where we make friends today, but to lose them tomorrow
> And the comrade with whom I have revelled at night
> May render his soul to its Maker ere light.

The author, Mathew Arkins who is evidently an educated soldier writes:

Sir,

I hope, I am not trespassing on the limits, which the humility of my station prescribes, in submitting for your approval, or censure the enclosed regimental songs, if there is any error ... I must take leave to remind you, that a barrack room is a very uncertain source from which to obtain correct information. In conclusion, I have only to say it may appear rather presumptuous in me, thus to address you, but I throw myself on the kindliness of your character, to acquit me of any unworthy motive ...

His songs give a picture of garrison life that, rather than driving off Arab attacks probably took up the greater part of the 94th's time in Aden:

> Oh – saw ye, the parade today
> Oh saw ye the parade,
> The ninety-fourth in proud array,
> marched past a bold brigade;
> of men who seemed, as if they deemed,
> dull life not worth their care;
> but in fray or field – would never yield,
> whilst doing what brave man dare ...

He also shows that, as in every remote garrison, entertainments were organised to amuse the troops. In India Alexander Maclean had organised amateur theatricals. Perhaps he did so in Aden. Certainly the officers took part in horse racing whilst the men enthusiastically bet on their favourites. Arkins wries:

> We've had races in Aden – such never were seen
> in Arabia before though in India there might
> have been horses as fresh aye or jockeys as light
> for Lieutenant A[shto]n to weigh down ten stone
> had to girt at least six pounds of shot to his zone
> 'twas a pity, faith, after the trouble he took
> our soldiers his claims to reward should o'er look
> when he won the first race though it scarcely was civil

> they wished him and his high-trotting mare at the devil
> but the truth must be told, he rode 'gainst their pet
> it was vexing to think Captain I . . . should be beat . . .

He continues:

> the races kept up, till the sun had come down
> to the mouldering rocks like a Seraph's bright crown
> And the ladies remained while the red light yet rolled
> All over the skies like a mantle of Gold.
> Happy matrons and mothers, coquettes of eighteen
> were pleasing and pleased with gay Mr M[aclea]n
> 'homo ad unquem est' rely on his word
> for his honor's unsullied and bright as his sword.

The comment about ladies in Aden is surprising. In his *Sketches of Aden* its author complains that: 'One very great drawback in Aden is the almost total want of ladies' society . . . and as the number of spinsters are sadly disproportionate to that of bachelors, it is rarely, very rarely that people are united there in the holy bond of matrimony'. Certainly the want of a wife was on Alexander Maclean's mind. In his commonplace book he writes:

A man may admire accomplishments and be dazzled by genius, but he seldom loves a woman for these things. He loves her for what is essentially distinct from, though not positively incompatible with them – her woman's nature, the woman's heart.

It was to be some time before he found his ideal. In the meantime the author of *Sketches of Aden* complains that:

I am inclined to think that few, very few of the British possessions are so wholly destitute of those mundane enjoyments that can render life so little agreeable, as Aden. There happiness is but a by-word, the warmest feelings become stagnant, and 'the souls' of men 'dry as summer's dust, burn in the Socket'. Fortunate is he whose habits of reflection and self-denial are such as enable him to withstand the grosser pleasures of existence, and whose mind disregarding such paltry and transitory joys, can still receive light from the inexhaustible and never failing lamps of knowledge. But the young and thoughtless spirit, full of hope and generous sentiments in seeking pleasure there will assuredly grapple with a phantom. The climate too, is often an enemy of study, and in what manner to 'beguile the lazy time' becomes a matter of serious reflection. In such a place the most trifling incident, or the most trivial circumstance, absorbs the attention. Indeed it has often been to me a matter of surprise how people possessing no resources of their own, can manage to get through the day, for indeed in the paucity of recreations, Aden has not its equal.

Pedestrianism and acquatic excursions, though often indulged in, weary by repetition, and angling soon becomes a toil instead of a pleasure. I have blistered my feet over the stony roads of Aden, and destroyed all my shoes. I have sailed in her bays and been scorched by burning sun. At home, I have sought entertainment in books, but in vain. I have dosed over Zimmerman, and tried to love solitude. I have yawned over Shakespeare, and crimsoned the most heart-stirring passages of that exquisite poet with the vile blood of the moschettos [mosquitoes]. Again with respect to the pleasures of the table, *tiffins* and cold beer, as in India are held in high estimation, yet a new person newly arrived from England and accustomed to good living would view with astonishment a European dinner in Aden – the emaciated forms of sundry superannuated cocks, the tough beefsteaks more suited for the stomach of an ostrich than a human being, the unsightly joints of beef and goats' flesh, and tarts deprived of their just proportions of gooseberries and cherries, would be little calculated to satisfy the cravings of hunger or allay ill humour . . .

The 94th left Aden on 3rd December 1846 and returned to Madras. They were to spend a year there before they returned to Cannanore.

It was whilst he was still Adjutant in Cannanore that the subject of his promotion came up for discussion. Several of his rivals for a company were back in England to put their case to the Military Secretary. On 25th April 1849 Alexander's old friend Laurence Desbrough wrote to say:

I met Peatt at Chatham . . . I met him again at Lord Fitzroy's last Tuesday when he told me that he was about to return his name for purchase. On the same day I met Sykes and Donhill – the latter was in town for the purpose of waiting upon the Military Secretary anent returning his name for purchase, and the upshot of his interview was that should Meik send in his papers he will be gazetted to the Company . . . I must tell you the way he (Donhill) has raised the needful. His mother has the life interest in some certain monies that come to George and his brother and sister upon her death – some lawyer has managed to raise the necessary funds upon his prospects. He proposes exchanging into a West Indian Regiment upon his promotion – the very best thing he can do. Sykes was in town for the purpose of thanking Lord Fitzroy for his promotion. The mail . . . will convey the welcome intelligence of Nicholl's retirement on full pay whereby Mercer was promoted and my dear old friend Mac has obtained a step. I only wish it had been you instead of Mercer that had got the Company. However all in good time – and now Mercer, if he meant anything, can assist you with the money. What I do hope you will be able to make up – in a short time, but to do so you must economise in real earnest – you must not give a *single tiffen party* – no not even to a *single individual*. If you pursue this system you will be astonished at the amount of savings which one year will produce – indeed I am sure that this year's forbearance will enable you to put by the whole purchase money . . .

Desbrough stresses that if Alexander 'Should be so fortunate as to succeed in returning your name for purchase, I think you ought to ask the Colonel as to the person who he may propose as your successor [as Adjutant]. Without flattery he will find it very difficult to fill your place. Indeed I know not one of the subs who is fit to do so'.

Alexander was a conscientious officer, who took considerable pains to write to the parents of both officers and soldiers who died whilst serving with the Regiment. For example the parent of Private Grimes from Dublin wrote to say:

I cannot feel at ease till I have in the Most Humble and grateful manner returned our thanks to you – for the feeling and Christian like manner in which you condescended to give us the details of our dear Son's death – the source through which you sent it – and *all* the trouble you have taken on his account. Rich and poor have their troubles – therefore I pray the Lord may bestow in treble portion of that Balm of comfort and consolation in any and all trouble on you kind Sir – which you condescended to administer to us your inferiors in our Affliction. I thank God that our dear departed son gained the notice and esteem of so kind and feeling a Superior – and I hope poor little David may prove himself worthy of your notice kind Sir to which you so kindly intimated in your letter . . . [PS] Dear Sir pardon all the errors of this scroll owing to my limited education. James' mother.[21]

Desbrough goes on to point out that the Chancellor of the Exchequer had announced that regiments were to serve in India for 15 years and Alexander had not been there a full eleven. He goes on to say:

The only draw back is the necessity of postponing your visit to your mother until you have realised the amount required, but I am sure she is too reasonable to wish you to come home before you have compassed this most desirable end . . .

Despite his friend's advice Alexander embarked for England on 9th January 1852. He landed at Plymouth from a Cowes Pilot Boat on 28th April 1852. He had been away for almost twelve years.

Whether or not it was to see his mother that he came home, or to secure promotion is not clear from his papers, but whatever the cause on 23rd July he was promoted to command a company of the 94th. It was highly popular in the Regiment. But it came too late for Alexander's career. In 1854 the 94th were ordered to return to England. The men were given the option of staying in India and transferring to another unit. 343 volunteered to do so, and it was a much reduced battalion of 4 officers and 277 men who sailed from India on 21st March 1854.

Whilst the 94th was at sea the Crimean War had broken out and by the time the Regiment reached England recruiting was well underway for those units who were being sent to Russia. As a result the 94th had difficulty in obtaining new men. To make matters worse 400 men of the 94th were drafted to the 18th Foot who were being sent to the War.[22]

What was left of the regiment stayed at home. In July 1854 Alexander became Adjutant of a Provisional Depot battalion at Omagh in Ireland. He therefore missed the chance of active service in the Crimea and the opportunity of obtaining accelerated promotion.

On his return from India Alexander visited the Reverend Samuel Day, Vicar of St Philips & Jacobs in Bristol. He was the father of Lieutenant William Day of the 94th Foot, who had died in India. There he met his friend's only sister Olivia. In 1857 he married her.

The Days were an old established Bristol family. Olivia's mother was the only daughter of the Reverend William Hoare, Vicar General of Limerick, who had married yet another Olivia, the daughter of Arthur Guinness of Beaumont, County Dublin and the aunt of Sir Benjamin Lee Guinness 1st Baronet.[23] Alexander had married into an extremely wealthy influential family. Perhaps it made up for his missing accelerated promotion.

* * *

No officers from the family of Coll appear to have taken part in the Crimean War. However, seven men from Coll's estate of Quinish joined the army at this time and four of them took part in the battle of Alma. They had been inspired to join the Army by old soldiers who had served at Waterloo 'and when we saw them dressed in the kilt ... our heart went into it'. They wished to join one of the old Highland regiments and went off to Edinburgh to enlist. All joined the 79th.[24]

Although these soldiers were keen to join a Highland Regiment no officer of the family of Coll appears to have done so. They joined the Indian Army or served in English Line Regiments. None went into a Highland Regiment. Perhaps this was because there was no senior Maclean of Coll serving in a Highland Regiment to promote their career. Instead in the 1840s and 1850s they joined the Madras Army, where even after his death old Sir Hector still had some influence.

The first to join was John Norman Hector,[25] son of Captain Donald Maclean late 16th Foot, who had died in 1835.[26] He was recommended by his mother's cousin Lord Glenelg and in 1839 was commissioned into the 32nd Madras Native Infantry. Hugh Coll's son John Norman, who as we have already seen, was sponsored by his father's friend Lord Ripon,[27] followed him in 1845. He was commissioned into the Madras Cavalry and was in turn, in 1852, joined by his youngest brother Evan who had been nominated by 'the late Sir Hector'.[28]

Another source of patronage was the Bombay merchant Henry Travers, whose daughter had married John of Cornaig's youngest son Alexander Campbell. In 1844 their son Henry Travers was commissioned into the Bombay infantry.[29] The Isle of Muck family tended to go into the Bengal army. In 1839 Lachlan HG Maclean 49th Foot's younger brother Wellwood George Mowbray became a cadet in the Bengal Infantry.

Finally Charles Smith Maclean, Dr Lachlan's son, on the recommendation of C Webb Smith, also applied for a cadetship in the Bengal Infantry.[30] India House wanted him to join the Madras Army. Perhaps because of the influence of the Coll family in Madras and his father's quarrel with Hugh Maclean of Coll, he had no wish to do so. Eventually he got his way.

CS Maclean had been educated at Madras College in St Andrews and had the most glowing reference from John Smith, who had directed his studies. He writes:

> I have known few young gentlemen of so good character or disposition, and fewer still of superior talents. He has shown great aptitude for all kinds of learning and his restless curiosity has urged him to gather up from books more useful and amusing information than serves to content most men who fancy themselves well-educated. For his years he is an excellent scholar, especially in those subjects, which HEIC's Board of Directors has seen fit to prescribe. He is an intelligent talker, a pleasant companion, a true friend. Generous in the extreme, resolute almost to a fault, regardless of self, a hater of whatever is mean and grovelling; to me he seems very likely to realize much that is noble and honourable in the character of a soldier.[31]

CS Maclean arrived at Fort William in India on 6th March 1854. He was posted to the 44th Native Infantry. Five months later he was transferred, at his own request, to the 3rd European Regiment. On 28th June 1855 he passed the colloquial examination in Hindustani.[32]

* * *

Whilst the military members of the family of Coll were following their careers in India, their cousin Alexander Campbell Maclean had moved to Hong Kong. He arrived in 1849. He had probably already had dealings with Jardine, Matheson and Co for he soon became a partner. Alexander's wife had died in 1840 and he brought his eighteen year-old daughter Adelaide with him to Hong Kong. In the early 1840s it had been the convention that partners should be unmarried. There had been no provision for married quarters and the partners had messed together. However, the company's move to Hong Kong made a more normal social existence possible and the arrival of Miss Maclean was greeted with enthusiasm. Alexander Matheson writing on 23rd October 1848 from London to Donald Matheson in Hong Kong says:

> I am quite sure you will find Miss Maclean a most agreeable acquisition to your society. I saw her only once and was much pleased with her manner as well as greatly struck with her resemblance to her mother... If you only knew the trouble and botheration in getting suitably married in this country, you would think twice before neglecting the present opportunity. I do not address this to *one* but to *all* of you...' [33]

She did not stay unattached for long and in Hong Kong in 1850 the social highlight 'was the merry wedding at East Point [of Miss Maclean], some fifty at breakfast which was wound up with by a dance'.[34] However, she neither married a Jardine nor a Matheson but a Captain Edward Fisher, Royal Artillery.

Notes

1. *The Army and Society 1815–1914*, 23.
2. JJ Snodgrass *Narrative of The Burmese War* (1827), 1. Major Snodgrass was Military Secretary to the Commander of the expedition. He was the heir of Neil Snodgrass of Cunninghamhead who had lent money to Alexander Maclean of Coll to buy land in Aros [NAS Argyll Sasines (1781–1830), 379. 6 October 1823].
3. George Bruce *The Burmah Wars 1824–1886* (1973), 26.
4. VCP Hodson *List of the Officers of the Bengal Army 1758–1830* (1946).
5. He was the son of Charles Norman Fitzgerald Maclean, who had left the 73rd Foot in Ceylon in mysterious circumstances. He had been born in St Helena.
6. BL. L/MIL/11/31/63, 351.
7. BL. L/MIL/10/31/55.
8. *A Matter of Honour*, 176.
9. It is estimated that by 1817 China had received £150,000,000 worth of bullion from European traders for her exports.
10. Edgar Holt *The Opium Wars in China* (1964), 111.
11. Captain Charles Elliot RN was the cousin of Admiral Elliot who had returned to the United Kingdom.
12. *The Opium Wars in China*, 122–131.
13. TNA. WO31. 938.
14. TNA. WO31. 938.
15. He seems to have purchased his promotion through his savings and a loan from his commanding officer Lieutenant-Colonel HR Milner [BCT undated letter HR Milner to Alexander Maclean 'Referring to the purchase of my Lieutenancy'].
16. The 'Rock at Trichinopoly', the site of Clive's crucial victory against the French, is illustrated by Francis Swain Ward (1736–92) in 1772–1773. See BL Images on line.
17. Gordon Waterfield *Sultans of Aden* (1968), 1–4.
18. HFN Jourdain & Edward Fraser *The Connaught Rangers* (1926), 313.
19. BCP Alexander MacLean's framed commission is in the Hall at Breacachadh Castle.
20. BL. L/MIL/5/437/432.
21. BCT. 25 April 1849. J&M Grimes, Phoenix Park, Dublin to Lieut and Adjutant McClean, HM 94th Regt.
22. *The Connaught Rangers*, 320.

23. Peter Townend (ed) *Burke's Peerage* (1967), 1343.
24. Report of the Royal Commission (Highlands & Islands, 1892), 2274–6.
25. BL. L/MIL/9/190, 329.
26. TNA. WO 42. 31M, 313.
27. BL. L/MIL/9/211, 460–3.
28. BL. L/MIL/9/226, 864.
29. BL. L/MIL/9/206, 374–383.
30. I have not discovered who he was. It is curious that Dr Lachlan did not get Lord Glenelg, whose factor he had been, to sponsor his son. Perhaps he had fallen out with him too.
31. BL. L/MIL/9/230, 580–592.
32. BL. L/MIL/10/59, 636; /63, 636; /61, 636.
33. Maggie Keswick (ed) *The Thistle and the Jade* (1982), 30. I have to thank Sir David Landale for a copy of this book.
34. *Ibid*, 200.

Chapter Fifty-Seven

South Africa, India and China. 1855–1860

After the sale of the estate the family of Coll was scattered. Even the delicate Juliet Alexa went overseas. On 24th September 1857, with her companion Emily, she left Number 14 Upper Westbourne Terrace, Hyde Park for Natal in order to escape 'two home winters'. She writes:

> It had long been a wish of mine dating from the days of childhood and the reading of Robinson Crusoe to know what it would be like to live far away from civilization, and later on I longed to live where there should be neither calling nor returning calls, neither church nor clergymen... At last I hoped to enjoy real solitude and to live entirely beyond the pale of any 'society' for the space of a year.[1]

Her father saw them off on the 25th on board the ship *Devondale* barque, 450 tons, bound for Cape of Good Hope. She writes:

> Papa came on board and remained till we began to sail. Saw him taken in tow in his boat by a large steamer. We anchored for the night eight miles below Gravesend. Every one but myself was ill.

The 27th was very rough but the 28th was a beautiful day. By now she was comfortably established in her cabin and she had 'determined on the hours I shall keep during the voyage as to reading, exercise &c'. She meant to spend as much time as possible on deck and sat there watching the cliffs. Despite her frail health Juliet Alexa was tough. She notes that everyone on board was 'ill and miserable', except herself and the sailors. She thought that Hastings and St Leonards were the last places in England that would be visible by daylight and on the 29th she was on deck at 2 only 'to see Brighton, a long line of light'. But when day broke Beachy Head was still in sight.

It was very stormy on the night of the 29th and boards were put up to prevent the passengers from falling out of bed: she spent the rest of the day in bed like the rest, as it was no use trying to stand. On 1st October she notes that there were:

> No more white cliffs – no more was old England to be seen. We are fairly out of the Channel and the sensation is curious... We zigzagged out of the Channel. First you ask 'What coast is this?' You are told 'England'. The next time you ask it is seen to be 'France'.

On the night of the 4th a gale began.

Just at the end of the Bay of Biscay. I had wanted to see one, and the mate and Mr C at my request hauled me along to a place in the bulwarks where they could hold on tight and also take care of me. The waves seemed really 'mountains high'. I could not have believed it unless I had seen them, they kept coming up against us like great black walls, and it seemed as if each wave must come down right on top of us, and smash the masts, but instead of this on getting pretty near they always seemed to go *under* the ship.

Pretty little 'Mother Carey's Chickens' out flying about all the time quite close to us. I got tied on with a rope to prevent me slipping down. The noise of the wind was great and it was pretty dark, the waves seemed to get even larger. The sensation I experienced was that it was very frightful but I was not frightened, as the sailors did not seem to be. No one spoke a word.

So the voyage continued and on 7th December Table Mountain was in sight 50 miles away. The journey, however, was not yet over, even after landing. And on the 28th she notes: we left Cape Town by mail steamer *Waldenstein* for Natal.

At the time there was no easy way to land at Port Natal and the *Waldenstein* had to lie off the coast whilst the passengers and freight were taken ashore through the surf in open boats. In her diary for 9th January 1858 she notes:

In the morning boats began to put off to and fro from shore and I saw Zulu Kafirs for the first time. Though nearly literally in undress, or not dressed at all, one somehow does not fancy this. They look like living dark bronze statues. They seemed very cheerful and lively.

Dear Alick came early on board to fetch me, having only this morning heard of the steamer's arrival, so now I had the pleasure of seeing him again. He looks very well but is nearly copper-coloured and does not weigh as much as when he is home. He was in good spirits and told me his carriage and fourteen, a covered wagon with oxen, was waiting to take me, and my luggage to Durban, and he would 'ride on horseback after me' . . .

We started then for Alick's place, ninety miles from Durban, through deep sand into thick bush of which there is two miles between the Point and Durban. It is very pretty indeed the trees are shiny like evergreens mostly. Alick's wagon driver had been one of Dingaan's warriors. His natural and usual costume is a fringe of buffalo hair and tails round his waist, a string of large beads with an ostrich feather stuck into his wooly hair which is done up into a ring or crown as a sign that he is married . . .

Durban is utterly unlike any place I ever saw before. It is not like a town at all . . . Imagine rows of long thatched one storied and verandahed houses in occasional gardens with banana and other trees in front dispersed at intervals pretty far apart along a sandy shore between the sea and the bush. Three wide streets with smaller ones across and this is Durban . . . In Durban every man's house is of necessity founded on sand . . . It is even a foot deep where one crosses the streets . . . and where on a darkish night it is a common thing for the 'oldest inhabitant' to lose his way. St Pauls (in the sand) is like a real home church, like St Saviour's Westbourne Grove and many others, but not so large and having no windows as yet.

Juliet Alexa explains that there were many rivers along the coast of Natal and that each district was called after the nearest river. In Alick's case his land was on the Umhlali River. He owned a sugar estate, Oaklands, which was let to a Mr Reynolds, and lived at Glenalbyn. Sugar had proved to be a success and many people were now growing it and were making rum. Alick's was called 'Umhlali Water'.[2]

She goes on to say that there have been 'wars and rumours of wars' in the Zulu country. And just on the banks of the Tugela, the boundary river a few miles from the Umhlali, there was a frightful battle in the Zulu country between two of the king's sons, and in case 'of our savage neighbours coming across to fight on our side of the Tugela', a fort called 'Fort Scott' had been built and garrisoned 'with three officers and 40 soldiers'.

Her arrival at Glenalbyn was full of surprises:

[We] arrived at a signpost in the middle of a kind of field. At first it seemed to me to lead nowhere and the words on it 'To Glenalbyn' seemed too mysterious, but Alick interpreting showed me a ploughed furrow. This we followed and it stopped at a gate where Alick's land begins, and we went through a field of sugar cane. And I must say that no field I ever saw is to be compared to a cane field as to beauty ... we crossed the river, the Umhlali, as wide there, perhaps wider, than the Serpentine at the little bridge ... During the rains it was impassable but now alright again. The river is beautifully clear and very good to drink. It is sandy like the sea to look at. We went on through the middle of a ploughed field again straight up to the house which is not yet finished, but quite enough so to be comfortable in ... The house is a very nice one, built of brick and will be thatched. When finished it will have in the body of the house five rooms. Dining room, drawing room, two bedrooms and a kitchen. And two more verandah rooms with doors out into the same but none into the house. One of these I live in and I like it so much.

We sat out in the verandah until late listening to the wonderful noises and 'Voices of the night', the most curious and pleasing, and to the distant roaring of the sea about three miles off.

In the evening Alick brought Mr Koch here, [he] had sent off the *Herald*, a small vessel, to try and open a trade with native chiefs ... and Willy sent to act for him, as he knows how to get on with savages here and the language where he has gone is not unlike Zulu. Mr Koch sent up the *Herald* to open a trade in ivory with a native chief who lives on the King George's River, which flows into Delagoa Bay, being assured that it was lawful and right to do so. But the Portuguese Government it seems dispute this and have always opposed themselves to anything of the kind, claiming both the river and the trade. Willy cannot lose anything, and as he has been much in Zulu country may stand the climate better than the others who have not ... Mr Koch is frightfully angry about it and says he will send up another ship 'armed'. Take the place and blow it up.

By the 19th January people were beginning to be alarmed at not hearing any news of the *Herald*. There was to be a meeting in Durban to incite the Governor of the Cape, Sir George Grey, to do something, as 'it seems that many hear give up the whole party for lost'.

In February news at last arrived:

a Portugese sailor, who had come overland from Delagoa Bay through the Zulu country to Tugela, told the boatman there that the *Herald* was there alright, in the Bay. Captain Macdonnell, one of the officers at the camp, heard this from the boatman and at once came and told us. Since then a Mr Paton has arrived from the Zulu country and brought news, since then confirmed, that the *Herald* had been there, seized by the Portugese authorities and the crew sent up as prisoners to Quilmane, Willy included.

Juliet Alexa writes: 'so now it is most probable we must remain a long while without any news from them. Alick is going to-morrow to Durban to see Mr Koch about it'.
Meanwhile there was nothing to do but wait. She describes the daily routine at Glenalbyn:

At sunrise ... the Oaklands mill bell rings for the Kafirs to begin the daily work. Alick gets up also and sets his to work, and works himself also with his white man Lachlan Mackinnon, who could speak nothing but Gaelic a year ago. Flora, his wife, bakes our bread for us. We send our flour to her when she bakes her own. And she irons Alick's shirts. But there is not much ironing done here ... Alick is never happy unless he has some work in hand, something to do, and he works away like a common man at home, in shirt and trousers only. Except on a Sunday, which, as on board ship, is celebrated by wearing white shirts, a light coat added on going out. Alick bathes in the river, and I have had a bath in my room (half a huge cask) and at nine we have breakfast. Then he goes out again to his cane ...

She describes her life in letters home her brothers and their friends all have nicknames. Willy was known to his contemporaries as 'Moses' and William in her letters to her father. She explains:

1st May. 'Alister'[Alick], 'Dingaan' [Frank Woodcock] and Mr Lewis Reynolds are away hunting in the Zulu country ... We have still no news of poor Willy from his prison. But the war steamer, sent from Simon's Bay by Sir George Grey, passed here some three weeks ago ... Alick has not got that grant of land Willy wanted ... After a grant is got, you require capital to set it up, and then it seems you are not likely to make money, but only to keep yourself alive. And be thankful you are out of debt ... Things do not appear at all to an eye-witness out here as they sound or are read of at home[3] ... I fear to write too cheerfully in case you think Alick and I say different things and I fear to write too despondingly about his affairs in case he may not like it. But he is not as well off as he is believed to be at home. The Mr Reynolds rent Oaklands from Alick at £300 a year for nine years ... But Alick has still a mortgage to pay off on the original price of Oaklands. £600, and some must be paid on the 1st January next, 1859. And there is the interest to pay for the £2,000 borrowed money. And everyone borrows from him!! And Mr Koch is in difficulties and he is Alick's agent ...

On 10th June news reached Glenalbyn that HMS *Lyra* had returned from Mozambique 'with Poor Moses and two remaining prisoners. The other two, poor Captain Duncan and a sailor, died of fever'. Then on 12th June while riding down the cane field 'Willy came suddenly down upon us, looking so fearfully ill that I did not know him at first. He was riding very slowly he was so weak and he says it is a wonder he is alive. And so it is after all his adventures'. He had lost three stone in weight since he left for Delagoa Bay.
She writes home later about the political situation:

You will see by the papers what excitement there has been of late here on account of the dissolution of the Natal 'parliament' (legislative council) and the consequent elections. Most people hereabouts were very anxious that Alick should stand for this county, Mr Tom Reynolds, who believes greatly in Alick got 38 votes for him at once ... but of course Alick would not hear of it, and has been canvassing for Mr Harry Milner instead ...

Willy had now recovered. Juliet Alexa writes that he:

is going to the Zulu country for Mr Koch with whom he seems to have made a very good arrangement. He is to have under him all Mr Koch's wagons and Kaffirs and to go shares in the profits of the trading which, as he has nothing to lose will be clear for him. And he is far better off than Alick now. I should like to visit him should he set up a house in the Zulu country as he talks of doing. The worst is that horses will not live there.

Alick's finances continued to deteriorate.

This is a strange place as to money matters. It seems all the poor fellows who have money and are safe and honourable payers have to suffer from the sins of all the rogues who will not pay what they owe. Alick has really no alternative but to let Glenalbyn for the present. At the end of the month he is going with his wagon into the Zulu country for two months and wishes me to accept a kind invitation I have had from Mrs Colenso [the wife of the Bishop] to go again to Bishopstowe for as long as he is away ...

The Colenso family became close friends of Juliet Alexa. Although she had not, as she had wished, escaped from the religious environment in London, Juliet Alexa probably found the intellectually stimulating liberal atmosphere in the Colenso family more to her taste than conventional Christianity at home.

In her letters she answers questions put to her about the problems settlers faced in running their estates. She writes:

You ask about ploughing. Kaffirs are supposed not to be able to plough straight, and therefore sugar planters require a white ploughman. Poor Lachlan [gets] £5 a month, a house, garden and milk, Alick has had to pay £40 of his debts and seems to be always losing money by some means or other.

Once he had let Glenalbyn Alick had to apply for a job. To his surprise he was chosen as manager of the new Umzinto sugar company. Juliet Alexa was disgusted. In her letter home on the 8 May 1859 written from Bishopstowe, Pieter Maritzburg to say:

I did not write home by the last mail. I knew Alister would write and give my news as well as his own. You would be glad to hear of his improved prospects. I, of course think it a great bore and very hard that he should have to accept any place at all. But he said he was glad when it offered, affairs looked so bad. I have had two letters from him, and he seems to think the 'berth will fit him' ... I don't know if he means to remain more than a year at the Umzinto. It is a river a long way off below Durban not far from 'No Man's Land'.

On 21 May 1859 she notes that Mr Windham, Resident Magistrate, Umvoti, arrived to stay. She had said earlier that 'the Resident Magistrate is the great man of each place here, the only one in authority in small places, and is also often it seems the only "gentleman" in his county'.

In July Juliet Alexa travelled to Umzinto to be with Alick. She writes:

Every day now I go for a ride with Alick. The country hereabouts is very pretty. He has eighty odd Kafirs here at work, and plenty to do looking after them all.

Africans were not an easy labour force to manage. One of the initial problems the sugar industry had to face was to induce the indigenous natives to work on the plantations, and in 1858 a few Chinese and Malay labourers were imported from Java on behalf of the Umzinto Sugar Co.[4]

Juliet Alexa's life now began to take an unexpected turn. On the 21st July she noted that 'Ashe Smith-Windham arrived on a visit to us'. On 28th the foundation of the sugarhouse was laid. And on 19th August she notes laconically: 'Marriage day. We were married at the Bishop's private chapel by the Bishop'. After the reception the newly wed couple set off on the six-hour's drive to Hoghton, the home of Mr Eastwood, who she describes as one of the only gentleman in Umvoti. And on the following day, after another three hours ride, they arrived at Greytown.

* * *

Not all the movement of Maclean of Coll ladies was in one direction. After her experience in the bush fire Anne Holmes was taken ill and ordered back to England with her family. They sailed for home on the *Australian*. The children caught measles but on 18th June 1854 eventually reached London. The years from 1856 to 1864 were spent in Edinburgh. Mathew Holmes divided his time between his business in Geelong and his family in Scotland. In 1859, having made enough money, he was on the point of retiring when he decided to visit New Zealand. He was much taken with the new colony and with his brother-in-law Donald McLean decided to settle there. He was soon followed by several of his wife's nephews and nieces.[5]

* * *

In 1857 Catharina Maclean, Mrs Macleod of Talisker visited Scotland. She stayed in Portobello with her aunt Jean, the widow of Captain Allan Maclean late 36th Regiment of Foot. Aunt Jean gave her niece the life-size portrait of her husband in full Highland dress,[6] which is now at Breacachadh. It is the front cover of this book. She was also given, probably by her brother, part of the dinner service that Vere Hobart had given to their grandfather Alexander Maclean of Coll for bringing her up. Sadly when the packing cases were unpacked in Melbourne the dinner service was found to have been smashed to pieces on the journey.[7]

* * *

Whilst the ladies of the Coll family were travelling to and from Scotland, the British were facing their greatest challenge in India. The Crimean War had drained British regiments from India and it was scarcely over when the Bengal Army mutinied at Meerut. The event, which triggered off the Indian Mutiny was the issue of the new Enfield rifle. Its cartridge had to be rammed down the barrel. To make the ramming easier each cartridge was greased. Owing to almost incredible insensitivity the grease used was made of a mixture of pig and cow grease. Since the cartridge had to be bitten, any sepoy using it tasted pig if he were a Muslim, or cow if he were a Hindu. Both animals were forbidden to sepoys by their religion.

As we have seen the underlying cause of the Mutiny was a mixture of other factors, but it was the use of these cartridges that caused Mangal Pandy, a sepoy of the 34th Native Infantry, to run amok and shoot his adjutant dead. When he did so the Quarter-Guard stood idly by. General Hearsey, who commanded the Calcutta garrison, rode fearlessly at the assassin who ran off and shot himself. The Indian guard commander and his men were court martialled and the 34th were disbanded. Then in the intense heat of the Indian summer in an almost unbelievable combination of harsh discipline and weakness by the British commanders in Meerut the mutineers were sentenced to ten years hard labour in irons. To the sepoys this was a far greater punishment than death. That evening all the Indian regiments in Meerut mutinied. They shot their British officers, released their comrades and the common criminals in the jail and ran amok.

The revolt now spread to Delhi, where no British troops were stationed and where Bahadur Shah the aged heir of the Moghuls still lived. He was proclaimed Emperor. After an epic defence of the arsenal, which the British blew up with themselves in it, rather than let it fall into the hands of the mutineers, Delhi was taken.

The recapture of Delhi was essential if the British were to have any hope of crushing the revolt. A Field force was assembled and marched on Delhi. They managed to defeat a much larger army of mutineers but were too few in number to assault the walled city and were anyhow without a siege-train. They therefore settled down on the Ridge outside Delhi and were in turn besieged by the mutineers.

Having failed to crush the revolt before it got out of hand, the British were now to see the Bengal Army, to which more than half the Indian Army belonged, mutiny. They did so from Calcutta to Peshawar. Throughout Oudh there were several small isolated British detachments and bodies of native troops who remained loyal. Atrocities became legendary. At Cawnpore the little European garrison put up a magnificent defence. For eighteen days they held off all attacks. Then the mutineers, now under the command of Nana Sahib, the adopted son of the last of the Peshwas, offered the garrison safe conduct to Allabad, under flag of truce. As the end was otherwise inevitable the offer was accepted. On 27th June the garrison with the women and children embarked. Once they had started off down the river the boatmen deserted them and the mutineers opened fire from the riverbank. The boats ran aground. Five men escaped. The remainder were shot down or captured and executed. The women and children were seized, held in captivity for two weeks and then literally butchered. The sepoys refused to perform this ultimate act of treachery; Nana Sahib hired Cawnpore's butchers to perform the task.

At Lucknow Henry Lawrence fortified the residency. Bands of mutineers were now in the surrounding area and on the 29th June Lawrence unwisely allowed himself to be persuaded to attack a large body of them near Chinhat. A badly planned and worse executed attack almost resulted in a disaster. Many of the British were killed, including Wellwood G M Maclean of the 71st Native Infantry.

The British withdrew into Lucknow and so began one of the most famous sieges in British military history as some 900 Europeans and 700 loyal sepoys resisted a besieging army that was never less than 6,000 and often more than 10,000 strong. Meanwhile John Lawrence, who had by August pacified the Punjab, sent his men and the siege train to join the British Army on the Ridge outside Delhi. Among these reinforcements was CS Maclean who had since January been serving with 1st Sikh Irregular Cavalry (Probyn's Horse). In September 1857 he transferred to the Guides Infantry.

Six hundred of the Guides took part in the storming of Delhi. 350 of them were killed and the British officers had to be replaced four times. One officer was wounded on six occasions and yet survived.[8] CS Maclean and three other officers were wounded twice.[9] The gallantry shown by the attackers, particularly the sappers, became a legend and on 20th September resistance ceased. And 'Hodson, the beau sabreur of the Ridge', found the last of the Moghuls hiding in a tomb. He brought him back a captive.

Although the war was to continue for another twelve months the crisis was over. Reinforcements began to pour into India. Among them were men from Dervaig, who after the Crimea had volunteered to transfer from the 79th to the 92nd (Gordon Highlanders). On 16th November Sir Colin Campbell, with a Field force that included the 92nd Foot, fought his way through to Lucknow and brought off the surviving women and children. It was not, however, until the spring of 1858 that he managed to conquer Oudh.

In central India during the spring and early summer of 1858 Sir Hugh Rose, with an army from Bombay and Madras, conducted a brilliant campaign against the mutineers. Rose, who had learnt his trade in Prussia where his father was a diplomat, had trained his Field force so differently to the troops in other sectors that his men seemed almost like an army from the future: 'unlike the brightly dressed, slow-moving and deliberately deployed soldiers in the other British forces, Rose's men, of whom only half were European, were dressed in khaki and so heavily supported by larger and better-equipped supply trains that they could move faster, further and more effectively than any other force'.[10]

Rose with a total of 6,000 men captured Jhansi, which had, under its former Rani, a garrison at least twice the size of his army. He also defeated Nana Sahib's henchman Tantia Topi and drove off his army of 22,000, which had been sent to relieve Jhansi. Rose then marched through the desert, took Kalpi and defeated a vast new army that Tantia Topi and the Rani had assembled at Gwalior.

Two Macleans were part of Rose's Field force: John Norman Hector Maclean served as Adjutant of the 32nd Native Infantry at the battle of Batwa and the storming of Jhansi. He was mentioned in dispatches;[11] Coll's son John Norman was Adjutant of the 7th Light Cavalry and helped intercept the rebels under Tantia Topi. He also served with the column of observation on the Wurdah River 'for suppression of disturbances in the Nizam of Hyderabad dominions'.[12]

In November 1858 the East India Company was dissolved and India came directly under the Crown. Many reforms were undertaken and the Indian Army rose like a phoenix from the ashes of the Mutiny. Historians have since argued about its origins. Peter Lawford probably is correct when he writes: 'The great sepoy mutiny was not a satanic conspiracy, as some Victorian historians suggested nor a nationalist uprising as have others. It was the tragedy of a joint stock company that had overgrown its strength'.[13]

* * *

The army in India was not to rest on its laurels. China had failed to honour the Treaty of Nanking, which ended the First Opium War by which the ports of Canton and Shanghai were opened to European trade. In 1856 a second conflict took place, which was ended by the 1858 Treaty of Tientsin when Britain and France brought pressure on the Chinese to allow a Resident Minister from each country to be based in China. The following year a British fleet of nineteen ships commanded by Admiral Hope escorted the two Resident Ministers when they set out to take up their posts. Hope went ahead of the main fleet and anchored off Taku at the mouth of the Pei-ho River, which leads to Peking. However, when he sent an envoy ashore to make arrangements for the arrival of the two Ministers, he was met by an armed mob who refused to allow them to land.

After several days of arguments the Admiral decided to seize the Taku forts that controlled the entrance to the Pei-ho River. He opened fire from his gunboats and landed a force of 1,100 marines to storm the forts. The Chinese, however, responded with accurate artillery fire. Four gunboats were disabled and the Marines were pinned down. Admiral Hope was seriously wounded and the Marines eventually withdrew having suffered 430 casualties. The mission was a complete failure.

This affront to Anglo-French prestige could not be allowed to go unpunished and the British and French Governments decided on a joint expeditionary force to enforce the Treaty of Tientsin. 10,000 British from India and 7,500 French from France were detailed for the task. They were under the command of Sir Hope Grant, an intensely religious, dour Scot who had distinguished himself during the Mutiny and was loved by the men.

Among the British troops were Probyn's and Fane's Horse. These two irregular Indian cavalry regiments operated on the *silladar* system, whereby each trooper owned his own horse. However, whilst they were to serve in China the Government undertook to provide them with their mounts. They were brigaded with the King's Dragoon Guards. All the cavalry were to give invaluable service in the campaign that followed.[14]

In March 1858 CS Maclean had gone on sick leave to Europe. He returned in November 1859. Whilst he was on leave he was promoted to a captaincy in Probyn's Horse.[15] In August 1860 he took a drop in rank and transferred to Fane's Horse,[16] the newly raised irregular cavalry unit commanded by Captain Walter Fane.[17] Fane's Horse wore light blue tunics and red turbans. In August 1860 it consisted of 14 officers and 330 other ranks.[18] The men were Sikhs, Pathans and Punjabi Moslems.

By the middle of June 1860 the expeditionary force started to arrive at Talienwan, on the Manchurian peninsular (near the present site of Port Arthur). It is an excellent anchorage and gave plenty of room for the army to spread itself out. The Cavalry Camp where all the Artillery, the King's Dragoon Guards, Probyn's Horse and Fane's were based was alive with activity. Thomas Bowlby, *The Times*'s correspondent with the expedition writes:

The horses are in excellent health; there are but 40 sick out of 1775. The Indian Cavalry Regiments laid on a display of tent pegging. Probyn led and Fane was second. Both went near but neither succeeded, their horses being out of practice. Next came a Sikh at a tremendous pace, shouting at the top of his voice, with his body extended, and spear close to the ground. He carried away the peg amid great cheering. It was afterwards carried off four or five times in succession...[19]

The army embarked again and on 1st August started to land in the Gulf of Pechilli opposite the small town of Pehtang, some twenty miles from the mouth of the Pei-ho River. It was not an ideal site for an assault landing. The shore was made up of flat slippery mud through which everyone had to wade for at least three-quarters of a mile before reaching harder ground.

At 4 am on the morning of the 3rd a strong allied reconnaissance, under the command of a French general, advanced along a causeway through the mud towards the Pei-ho and the Taku forts. The allies advanced for three miles, when they came to a bridge guarded by a Tartar vedette, which galloped off to join a larger body of Chinese cavalry. As the French crossed the bridge the Chinese opened fire. After some skirmishing the advance guard withdrew to a more secure position until the main body landed. The Chinese failed to follow up the withdrawal but reports of a great Chinese victory reached Peking.

Meanwhile the disembarkation continued and by 6th August the 2nd Division and the Cavalry Brigade were both ashore. On 9th August Grant sent out a second reconnaissance party, consisting of two troops of the King's Dragoon Guards two squadrons of Probyn's Horse, and a hundred infantry, to report on the country to the north of the causeway. Major Probyn, who commanded the party, was given strict instructions not to engage the enemy, and although several bodies of Tartar horsemen were seen hovering quite close by, they were ignored.

Probyn made a long detour to within a mile of the Chinese position on the Pei-ho. He discovered that the route was practicable to all arms. Grant now had the information he needed to advance in earnest. Reconnaissance was only one of the roles for which the cavalry were well suited. They were also invaluable at protecting the flanks when the advance got under way.

As soon as it began, a mass of Tartar cavalry trotted forward to threaten the left wing of the 67th Regiment (Hampshires), who were armed with the new Enfield rifle. The 67th managed, with accurate fire, to halt the Chinese but the Tartars merely withdrew out of range until

> with a loud yell Probyn's and Fane's Horse, supported by two squadrons of the KDGs, charged and scattered the enemy, cutting down numbers of them. This was too much for the Tartars, who turned and fled, pursued for five miles by the Indian sowars and British troopers...[20]

The cavalry was also required to do escort duty. During the advance one troop of Fane's Horse under Lieutenant MacGregor were required to stay behind with Stirling's battery, supporting the 2nd Division, who were making slow progress through the mud. A body of about a hundred Tartar cavalry spotted them and, hoping to capture the guns, charged 'uttering wild and unearthly cries'. Stirling managed to unlimber his guns and get off two rounds before MacGregor led his 25 sowars in a spirited counter-attack against four times his own number:

> One of the leading Sikhs ran his spear right through the body of a Mongol horseman, the head entering his chest and going out at his back. The spear broke in the middle, the Mongol fell to the ground spitted, and never moved a limb. Lieutenant MacGregor singled out his man, and was in the act of spearing him, when another Tartar fired his matchlock within ten yards pointblank. The slugs hit the Lieutenant in five places, three lodging in his chest, two in the forehead. For a moment fire blinded him and burnt his face, but the work was done. The Tartars dispersed in every direction...[21]

Skirmishers of the Royal Scots led the advance of the 1st Division along the Causeway. A large body of at least 2,000 Tartar cavalry immediately charged them. Instead of receiving them in line, the 1st Brigade formed regimental squares, which greatly impressed the Tartars who bravely came up to the guns and rocket battery which were firing straight into them.

Once again the escorting cavalry fell on the Tartars, who beat a hurried retreat, hotly pursued by the cavalry. Unlike regular cavalry the two Indian regiments did not rally at the end of the charge but for over an hour continued to pursue individual parties of Tartars. At one stage some 3 or 400 Tartars surrounded Lieutenant Anderson of Fane's Horse, with five of Probyn's and two of Fane's men.

Anderson killed seven of the enemy with the help of Sowar Wayeer Khan of Fane's Horse, who rode beside him and when Anderson was disabled by a sword cut on his arm, rushed back to assist him and killed a further four Tartars.

Brigadier Pattle of the KDG, who commanded the Cavalry Brigade, now sent an aide-de-camp to recall the Indian cavalry. However, Major Probyn had seen Anderson's plight and told the aide-de-camp that he would rescue his men first. He galloped off to Anderson's assistance. The Chinese fled, but not before Probyn had killed several of them with his own sword.

Pattle, who had no previous experience of irregular cavalry, complained to Grant that Probyn had ignored his orders. Grant reprimanded Probyn. But also reminded Pattle that Probyn and Fane commanded irregular cavalry, who did not behave in the same way as regulars. He advised him to let them have their heads in future. The independence shown by Probyn, Fane and no doubt CS Maclean, was typical of a certain type of British officer. They could be infuriating subordinates, but when given their head could be magnificent.

After heavy fighting the Allies captured the Taku forts and advanced up the Pei-ho. Eventually they seized the Emperor's Summer Palace. It was destroyed in revenge for the Chinese treatment of the British and Indians taken prisoner when negotiating with the Chinese under flag of truce. One of those who died in captivity was Lieutenant Anderson. He had commanded the detachment escorting the negotiators. His body was left lying in the cage with the other prisoners for three days before it was removed. Another to die in captivity was Thomas Bowlby *The Times's* war correspondent.

Notes

1. Juliet Alexa's adventures enroute to and in Natal are taken from her Diary, 244–302.
2. At this time the demand for Natal sugar provided the largest source of exports for the Natal. The failure of commercial cotton and other tropical crops among the early settlers had led to the cultivation of cane in the late 1840s and 1850s. Between 1854 there were 318 acres under cultivation in the counties of Alexandria, Durban and Victoria. By 1866 it had risen to 12,781 acres [Bill Guest & John M Sellars *Enterprise & Exploitation in a Victorian Colony* (Pietermaritzburg, 1895), 183.
3. The Utopian picture of Natal painted in emigration propaganda succeeded in persuading a few thousand British subjects to make a fresh start in the newly acquired Colony. However, by 1852 it was evident that Natal could not compete with North America and Australia in attracting a sufficient number of settlers to sustain and expand its economy. Reports from settlers themselves of the harsh reality did nothing to improve the situation. Many also who had come out were short of capital. They also had little experience of living in a rural environment. [*Ibid*, 8].
4. *Ibid*, 10.
5. *Coll* (Wellington, 1911).
6. BCP. Australia File. 25 October 1962. MKR Cole, Beckenham, Kent to NMB enclosing a letter from her grandfather Roderick Maclean Macleod, eldest son of Hector Allan Macleod.
7. Information from Anne Hamilton.
8. G J Younghusband *The Story of the Guides* (1908), 75.
9. He was recommended for, but not granted, the Victoria Cross and when a second recommendation was made it was again refused 'on account of lapse of time' [BL/IOR/L/MIL/7/5675].
10. *Palmerston*, 435.
11. BL. L/MIL/11/80, 91.
12. BL. L/MIL/11/85, 121; /73, 29.

13. James P Lawford 'The Indian Mutiny 1857–58' *History of the British Army*, 171. Much of that part of this chapter that deals with the Mutiny is based on this account.
14. Michael Mann *China, 1860* (1989), 8.
15. BL. L/MIL/10/67, 636.
16. TNA. WO 17. 1723.
17. It was raised on 1st January 1860 [TF Mills *Land Forces of Britain, Empire & Commonwealth. 19th Lancers. Fane's Horse.* (World Wide Web).
18. *China, 1860*, 40 & 164.
19. *China, 1860*, 40.
20. *China, 1860*, 60.
21. *China, 1860*, 60.

Chapter Fifty-Eight

Zulus. 1860–1879

Greytown was to be Juliet Alexa's home for the next eight years. She says of it:

You would not know Greytown for a town at all. There are at present about 54 inhabitants, counting as 1 the small babies, black and white, and 16 houses of which only two [are] stone, and none brick. There is a post office in the town and [we] have letters on Sundays and Wednesdays and have to answer them on Saturdays and Tuesdays! There are two large rivers between this and Durban, the Umgeni and Umvoti, and in the rainy season they are often unfordable.

She goes on to say that:

The courthouse, Ashe's office, is in the Laager, which is one of the features of Greytown. It is a square stone walled enclosure with loopholes for shooting from all round.

The Laager was meant to accommodate all the Umvoti people in case of a Zulu attack. It was only about five minutes walk from her own house, which had been built by a Boer and was in the usual Boer style: stone with a wooden plank ceiling and beams. The roof was thatched. All the rooms opened 'one into another'. It had a storeroom, dining room, drawing room, bedroom and the verandah room', which was 'the stranger's bedroom'. The kitchen and her Scots maid Flora's room were in a detached building. The whole property consisted of 2 acres. It had cost Ashe £150. He had also built a stable for £100.

Ashe was the second son of Joseph Smijth-Windham DL, JP, of Wawne Hall, Yorkshire. He was born on 18th March 1830 and educated at Eton and Trinity College, Cambridge. In 1857 he was appointed Resident Magistrate at Greytown.

In a letter home Juliet Alexa describes her husband as being:

by nature somewhat of an agriculturist, but as a magistrate he must not undertake regular farming. He does a little in that way, having sheep and horses, and of course a few cows. He has land in the colony besides that on which we live. He is fond of planting and pruning trees and growing flowers and vegetables and gained the prize for English vegetables at our agricultural show. We had lettuce, beetroot, round potatoes, carrots, vegetable marrows, pumpkins, broad beans and French beans and cucumbers. He is a very good shot and of a Saturday afternoon, when he is free after twelve, he goes out shooting and always brings home something. He is an artist, but unfortunately he has very little time in which to draw... He plays on the cornopean, and we play duets.... Ashe's duties make him half a fixture and half a vagabond. He goes daily to the office at ten, and is there till three nominally, but often is detained till five... Occasionally he has to go away for a 'breach court', at some far away place where he has, of course, to ride. And two or three times a year he has to go off for a fortnight at a time collecting, to collect taxes from the natives.[1]

Juliet Alexa's concerns about her brothers continued. On 13th June 1860 she wrote:

It is a great bore that Alick and I now are in such remote parts of the colony and so far removed from each other that when you enclose a letter for me to him, or vice versa, nearly a month is gone and another mail due before the letters arrive which came by the last mail.

Her worries about Willy were more serious:

Ever since he returned here he has had nothing but bad fortune. First the loss of his expensive imported horse, and his Mozambiqui adventures and misfortunes then the lung sickness getting into the Zulu country and spoiling the trade there, and now it is the delay of the compensation money alone which prevents him being able to settle down. I wish the Portugese would make haste.

She writes later, at the time of Prince Alfred's visit to Natal:

'Moses' has now been some weeks here, waiting, waiting, poor fellow. He cannot get the land formerly applied for by him to the Government it seems, because he did not pay the necessary fees when the time came. But when that time came he was a prisoner at Mozambique! I wish the Government could have taken this into consideration. However, we have done our best for him, and they can't. I suppose if they gave him the land now no end of rogues would take advantage of the precedent. All the Government people here are perpetually abused for almost everything they do, by all the colonists it seems to me. They are never contented. There is some talk at present of creating more 'Government border agents' like Mr Almsley. Such a post would suit 'Moses', but he has no chance from the Government here, as he is quite like other colonists in the above respect!

Since she married Ashe she had, not surprisingly, taken the Government's side in their disputes with the colonists, both Boer and British. It was said that the only thing that united the two races was 'a reckless disregard for justice and prudence in handling the natives'.[2] She also took a keen interest in the history of Natal and wrote a potted version of the history of the Zulus.

Although she dismissed any idea that she was in awe of the tribes the other side of the Tugela River she was certainly aware of their presence. The Tugela River was only 30 miles from Greytown. Reports from Zululand appear constantly in her letters home. Soon after her arrival at her new home she writes:

The only public event which has made any 'noise' here of late years was that battle at the Tugela which happened scarcely a year before I came out. Its history was thus. Panda [the Zulu king], though not 60, is getting old and is gouty, and cares now only for peace. He orders the death of merely individuals who displease him or those whose cattle he may covet, instead of ordering whole Kraals to be massacred wholesale ... He is not as savage as Chaka [who Bishop Colenso described as the 'South African Attila'] and Dingaan, nowadays at least. His two sons Ketchwyo and Umbulazi each had a party on his side and hostile to the other. To prevent a quarrel between them he divided part of the country between them, for each to remain in, separately and in peace. Ketchwyo, who is supposed to be rather savage and quarrelsome was dissatisfied with this arrangement, and it is said, rather wanted to fight about something, quarrelled with his more peaceful brother saying the division was not fair and collected an impi (a body of fighting men) and brought them close up to Umbulazi, who with his people was very near the Tugela, the boundary river between the Zulu country and Natal. Umbulazi sent across to Mr Walmsley, the Border Magistrate, to ask what he should do, and Mr Walmsley sent at once for Mr Shepstone in this emergency, for per what the Zulu messenger said he feared they meant to fight this side of the river. In the end Mr Dunn and Mr Walmsley's police went across to Umbulazi and fought on his side on the Zulu bank of the river. Ketchwyo gained the day, his impi being far more numerous. Umbulazi was killed and every man of the police, and thousands of people, men, women and children were driven into the river with assegais or drowned in attempting to cross. Still, many escaped across to Natal, among others Umbulazi's mother and her younger son, Umkungo, now at school at the Bishop's Station ... All who cross from the Zulu country here are called refugees and have to go before a magistrate who sends them out to work for white men at fair wages ... There was another disturbance in the Zulu country since I came here to Greytown, between Ketchwyo and another brother, O'Ham, and there was more fighting and more refugees crossed.

Both her brothers had dealings with the Zulu king and her knowledge is presumably based on their views, and on Holden's *Colony of Natal* and *Cloete's Lectures*, which she recommends that her correspondents at home should read. She continues:

Although Panda is alive Ketchwyo is now supposed to have most power. 'Moses' has seen him twice lately and he has promised to give him a grant of land. He is supposed to be a rather good fellow now that he has all his own way! They say he has a splendid impi and is a very great man among his own people, after savage fashion. It is supposed that when Panda dies there will be another disturbance as another son of his, O'Ham has got up a party in opposition to Ketchwyo.

She dismisses the value of 'Fort Scott' with its garrison of forty men:

it is said that if many such little camps were stationed all along the border they would be useless as protection against the thousands of Zulus who are ready to come down on us at Ketchwyo's order. It seems should he choose to eat us up he easily may, but we never think about him here, or feel at all afraid, somehow. Though, of course, it is easy to see that if they chose to eat us up, we should have no chance against those thousands.

In 1411, before the battle of Harlaw, the inhabitants of isolated settlements in the Mearns must have had a similar attitude to Donald of the Isles' hordes that Juliet Alexa had to Ketchwyo's.

* * *

News from home brought Juliet Alexa fresh worries. On 18th February 1861 she notes 'I had a letter from dearest Papa which made me think he must be very seriously ill and feel most anxious that he should get home as he so evidently wished it himself. And now I thought was the time to go on a visit but it could not be done'. On 3rd April she wrote to her father to say:

> We have at last had a visit from Alister. At last, dear old fellow, he says a change of country always does him good. I do wish we saw him more frequently, but it requires five days ride up here from Umzinto, and he cannot of course as manager be spared for any time. He looks very well, and his income is as yet quite secure, but we can't help longing for him to be once more on his own account and on a place of his own. He promises to come here whenever he can . . . Willy is reported to be still in the Bay and to be coming here soon. I long now more than ever before for the mails and trust that this one now due may say you are at home again as you wished to be, as I fear the cold Scotland weather has been too much for you. I wish you had left before Christmas.

In her letter to her father of the 13th February Juliet Alexa had written:

> There is another report that Ketchwyo has had his brother O'Ham murdered, and the fighting in the Zulu Country goes on and refugees are daily expected. Another border magistrate has been appointed. Some of the Boers in this county are alarmed but they always are, and *we* are not yet thinking of 'trekking'! I can't even imagine a Zulu invasion. They never yet have crossed the border since this, Natal, was a British colony. And old Panda knows well enough it is his interest to be friends with us. It is only his son Ketchwyo who is dangerous and he is not yet king.

On the 25th April she wrote again:

> There are various rumours and reports from the Zulu Country, Mr Shepstone was here a few days ago on his way to see Panda and try to induce him to name his successor with a view to prevent his sons continuing to quarrel among themselves, and to see Ketchwyo to try and incite him to keep the peace. There are various speculations as to whether this is a wise move or not. Of course whatever the Government does is sure to be voted wrong, but much is not published in the papers as yet about this. They merely mean to wait and see whether Mr Shepstone's mission is successful first. He has never been in the Zulu Country before. He has been 'Secretary for Native Affairs' to every Governor that has been, and so it is said the natives believe him to rank highest, as they see others depart . . .

Theophilus Shepstone, who Juliet Alexa mentioned in her letter, was a close personal friend of Bishop Colenso and the two men were to fight to protect the African reserves in Natal from land-hungry settlers.[3]

In May Juliet Alexa writes:

> You need not be alarmed about the Natal Zulus. Ashe is obliged to have, however, a policeman watching in the location near this [place] to give warning of what may be reported of doings on the other side of the Tugela. Nobody believes there is any danger of our Colonial natives

joining Ketchwyo. They are far more afraid of him than we are. He would kill them all if he could, it is said, as runaways. He is at present going on as usual burning Kraals and killing the people, and now it seems would prevent any refugees crossing here for protection. Whoever would go he kills ... Soon after the show Mr Shepstone and one of his sons were here on their return from the Zulu Country. He had gone to try and persuade Panda to declare his successor, and, as you know, he has named Ketchwyo.

It was now believed that Ketchwyo would invade Natal. Panic spread like wild fire but Juliet Alexa stayed calm. On the 19th July she wrote to Alister:

I daresay you will like to hear about all the fuss as we are here at 'headquarters' (the seat of war!) and doubtless the papers have not got hold of the true story yet. Last Friday some Kafirs from the Nordsberg road party came away from their work to the courthouse here in a great fright, saying that a Zulu impi had crossed the Tugela and that they must go to their Kraals. The N'kos [the Zulu name for a great chief, by which she means Ashe] thought they were only lazy as he had had no reports, and when he had a letter from Mr Paterson, angry at their desertion, did not quite know what to do. Only none of us dreamed of believing the story, and on Saturday the men were told it was all nonsense and went back to their work.

On Sunday morning Mr Wheeler (from Player and Wheeler's Maritzburg) who have a second store here, arrived in a dreadful state of mind to fetch his children away from this 'dangerous place', ... saying that the Government proclamation was out in Maritzburg that the Governor had had a message from Panda to say Ketchwyo had crossed somewhere near s'mahashis, a few miles from here, that special messengers were on their way here, and that troops were to be immediately sent up to the Laager. And on Monday the messengers arrived with printed notices to be sent round to the Field Cornets to collect an armed force, and a private letter from Mr Shepstone to say the Governor himself would arrive in a day or two here, and that the Cape Corps and the 85th were already on their way. We could really hardly believe it all. As for being frightened, that you may be sure we were not. Only it was evident there was a panic in the city. Johnny had gone out for mealies to the thorns that morning, but came back in a hurry, the report having spread, and he had seen many Boers riding hard and one had advised him to trek back as hard as he could. Then arrived Mr Peters with pistols in his belt, and full of news about the panic they were in the city. They thought Ketchwyo had sent an impi across to kill Umkungo at the Bishop's Station, and so he had been sent off to the camp for protection! The Governor was to be here about sundown, and he had seen the Cape Corps at the Umvoti! ... Then came the Chief Justice in command of the armed Boers, then Carbineers under Mr W Proudfoot, and Karkloof ditto under Mr W Barter. It was a good thing we had plenty of beef for tiffins and dinner. On Wednesday arrived many wagons full of frightened families of Boers to take refuge in the Laager, and German Missionaries with wives and families from Hermansburg, fifteen of whom we put up in Flora's room. Then came Colonel Grey and Mr Taylor and the rest of the 85th all in red coats and swords &c. In the course of the day Mr Allen and more Carbineers, and then, just in time for dinner, the Governor, Major Erskine and Mr Shepstone and his three sons.

Some Boers had rushed into Maritzburg on the first rumours and told how the Zulus had already burned farms and killed D Pretorious near Greytown (who had that very day been here all right!). And all the ladies were quite alarmed at the Governor and other gentlemen deserting them all and going to such a dangerous place as Greytown, where they made sure of course that we must all have been in a great state of danger and alarm, and were astonished to find that we should never have believed a word of any even probable Zulus crossing, but [for?] the Governor's proclamation. And we still only found all this only rather good fun, by way of a change.

Everybody made himself very pleasant and no one more so than His Excellency himself. It seems there is no doubt Ketchwyo is up to something at present, as he is close to the boundary and he has with him mounted Basutos. But what he meant, if ever did mean anything more than a hunting party, it is not likely we shall ever know. The last report is that he has gone from this down towards the coast on his own side of the Tugela. Troops are to be sent to Mr Walmsley's in consequence, and more stationed somewhere near Hermanburg.

The government now moved to calm the panic and Juliet Alexa enclosed a letter from Colonel Erskine the Colonial Secretary:

The following is the latest information from the 'seat of war', which was published by the Mayor yesterday afternoon:

Grey Town, half past 6 pm
17th July 1861.

Sir, I am desired by the Lieutenant Governor to inform you that on our arrival here we found all quiet, and that all the rumours which were this morning in circulation at Pietermaritzburg are groundless.

Mr Duval Pretorious has been in Grey Town today, Ketchwyo is said to have gone further down his own side of the Tugela. His Excellency would thank you to make this intelligence known to the public.

On 28th July she wrote to her brother once more to report that:

Patrols have been sent out in all directions from Greytown since I last wrote, and the last news is that Ketchwyo is peacefully at his Kraal, and had sent a message across to know what we meant by all our preparations and did we mean to 'eat him up?'.

On the 29th August in her letter home she wrote:

We have no news here since last mail. Ketchwyo has gone back to his Kraal and remains quiet, but our camps and defences are to go on, as he is not to be trusted. We are to have a camp between this and the Tugela, and another lower down by Mr Walmsley's.

Ashe has been publicly thanked by the Governor in the papers for his services in the late affairs... There is now no chance till next dry season of any Zulu invasion thanks to the Tugela. If the Zulus had really come it would of course have been dreadful. Their mode of proceeding is this. They come on quietly in thousands together in single file marching all night and hiding till about an hour before sunrise, and then fall on the people and burn their places and steal their cattle. The Dutch were always thus taken by surprise in former times...

So ended the 'affair'. There was, however, worse news from home for on 3rd August 1861 Hugh Maclean of Coll died at Woodville, the home of his eldest daughter Margaret.[4]

Hugh's last years cannot have been very happy. He was probably desperate for money. In January 1835 he had taken his first wife's sisters to court over money due to his daughters since 1815 from his marriage settlement. On this occasion he had won the case. However, in May 1857 it was referred to the House of Lords. They reversed the earlier judgment.[5]

Hugh's second appearance in court in 1857 was no more successful. Although the estate in Coll had been sold in May 1856 by public roup, arguments over who should receive the rents and pay the public dues on the estate since Martinmas 1855 continued after the purchaser obtained entry. On the 18th November 1857 Alexander Hunter (as Maclean's Trustee) took the purchaser John Lorne Stewart to court. The case was tried in the Court of Session, which found against the plaintiff.[6]

Both Juliet Alexa and her brother Alister went home at last in March 1862. When she returned to Natal she seems to have stopped writing her diary, except for an occasional entry and she makes no mention of the problems of her friend Bishop Colenso, which must have affected her. He had scandalized his fellow Christians in the 1860s by his assertion that the Bible, especially Genesis, was not to be taken literally. He had been inspired by talking to some of his Zulu parishioners to look at the Bible more closely. In doing so he tried to build a bridge between Darwin's new discoveries and traditional Christianity. In 1863 he was tried for heresy, was deposed and excommunicated by the Archbishop of Cape Town. Colenso appealed to the Privy Council who upheld his tenure as Bishop of Natal.

* * *

Alister also returned to Natal, but probably only after extended leave during which time he seems to have visited South America and British Columbia. On his return he visited the Diamond Fields near Kimberley. In 1867 an African shepherd had picked up a strange glittering piece of rock from the veld. Diamonds were discovered, first in the river diggings in West Griqualand, close to the river Vaal, then at Colesberg kopje twenty miles away. In five years the revenue of Cape Colony rose five times. The colony seemed set to exchange rags for riches. Tens of thousands of diggers scrambled for the blue mud of Kimberley, especially white Englishmen (like young Cecil Rhodes) and black Africans from all over South Africa.

1867 was a traumatic year for Juliet Alexa. On 3rd June her brother Willy died. He may have tried to make his fortune outwith South Africa as *Clan Gillean* says he died in India.[7] 1867 was also the year when Ashe gave up being the Resident Magistrate in Greytown.

Another result of the discovery of diamonds was that African wages soared. It was already difficult to get African labourers to work on the settlers' farms and plantations. The mines at Kimberley acted as a magnet for thousands of blacks. Not all of them spent their wages on beer. Some used their earnings to better themselves. After a few months in the mines they returned home to their kraals dressed like white men, and with breech-loading rifles.

* * *

King Panda died in October 1872. He was buried with several of his servants, as it was an ancient Zulu tradition that servants, wives and girls of the *isigodlo* (the royal enclosure) were killed when a king died so that they could serve him in the spirit world. The same month Ketchwyo was inaugurated as king. The ceremony was carried out before Shepstone, who had said he wished to be present, arrived at kwaNodwengu. Shepstone was furious. He had announced that his presence at the coronation was essential as it underlined British recognition. Ketchwyo was perfectly aware of what was happening and wished to stress his independence. He, however, assured Shepstone that he would not allow his men to move outside the borders of Zululand.

In 1873 Langalialele the chief of some seven thousand Hlubi tribesmen, who had fled from Zululand and settled and prospered in Natal, was ordered to register his people's firearms. He was ordered to appear before Shepstone at Pietermaritzberg. Langaliele panicked. He knew that another chief had concealed his weapons, come unarmed to a peaceful meeting with Theophilus Shepstone's brother John and had, with thirty of his tribesmen, been killed. He was too afraid to meet Shepstone. Instead a force of British regulars, Natal volunteers and 5,000 African levies went after him. The tribe fled into the Drakensberg.

The Government forces blundered around in the mists of the Drakensberg passes. Three colonists and two Africans were shot in a skirmish with some Hlubi stragglers. Most of the volunteers initially fled only to return and avenge their humiliation by smoking women and children out of the caves where they were hiding. They then burnt kraals and carried off cattle and grain. Thousands of women and children were marched off to Pietermaritzberg and handed over to the settlers as forced labour. Basutos, who had sided with the settlers, rounded up Langalibale and his men. He was tried for high treason and imprisoned in Robben Island. The colonists then occupied the Hlubi reserve.

There was outrage in London when in 1875 Bishop Colenso brought documentary proof of the atrocities in the Hlubi reserve to the notice of Lord Carnarvon, the Colonial Secretary. The Governor of Natal was sacked and Langaliele and his people were released. To his dismay, when he was collecting evidence of these atrocities, Colenso found that his friend Theophilus Shepstone, who he regarded as a champion of African rights, was a liar who had condoned the atrocities and been hand in glove with the settlers.[8]

* * *

On 11th July 1875 Alister Maclean, who had inherited his father's empty title of Maclean of Coll, died of dysentery at Umgeni, near Durban. His illness was so brief and his end so sudden that only his closest friends were aware that he was ill and the general public were shocked to learn of his death and burial. The *Natal Colonist* in his obituary says:

> The deceased gentleman was one of our oldest colonists, and the predecessor of Mr T Reynolds in the proprietorship of Oaklands, Umhlali. He was the eldest member of a very old Highland family, a considerable traveller, having visited South America and British Columbia. He was also one of the earliest visitors to the Diamond Fields, but he invariably returned to Natal after these more or less protracted absences. One of the gentlest yet bravest of men, Mr Maclean was thoroughly esteemed by all who knew him. He was not only a considerable traveller, but was an enthusiastic hunter and sportsman, and his commanding and powerful frame gave no token of so early an end. He was not married, and his only near relative in Natal is Mrs AF Windham, who was near him when he died; The funeral took place on Monday morning in the burial ground of the Church of England, and was attended by many of the friends of the deceased, whose loss will be most sincerely deplored by them. Archdeacon Lloyd read the offices of the church.

Zulus. 1860–1879

The British press picked up the obituary and an anonymous correspondent wrote:

A paragraph in the *Natal Colonist* gives intelligence of the death of Alex. Maclean, Esq, of Coll, on 11th July [1875], at the early age of 47. . . . the subject of this short memoir emigrated to Port Natal in 1849. On two or three occasions he revisited England, and thirteen months ago spent a short time in his native district of the Highlands. Though so long absent and so young when he left, he yet retained the most lively recollections of his old acquaintances and associates, who can never forget the pleasure it seemed to afford him to meet them again, nor the eager grasp of his hand and the sparkle of his eye, lighted up by sincere affection, when they chanced to meet. To those who knew Mr Maclean from boyhood as some of us did, when the slim gentle youth headed our many deer-hunting parties on his father's estates, accompanied by his younger brother – now also no more – and our boating expeditions in quest of wild fowl, &c – to such, certainly, his outward appearance was much changed – a tropical climate had ripened that youth into manhood of the most prepossessing appearance. That splendid figure, manly form, straight as a pine, a man among a thousand struck us with admiration, and still more so when we found the same gentle, mild, unassuming, affectionate disposition that distinguished his youth.

* * *

When the Boers had shaken off the dust of Cape Colony and trekked north they had founded the impoverished independent republics of Transvaal and the Orange Free State.[9] The Transvaal in particular was in a dire financial state. Few taxes were being collected and a disastrous foreign loan to build a proposed railway from Pretoria to Delgoa Bay in Mozambique had emptied the Treasury. This had not, however, stopped the Boers' aggressive dreams of expansion and in 1875 they had poured into Zululand in an attempt to annexe the land south of the Phonge River. Shortly afterwards they invaded the Bapedi land to the north-east of the Transvaal.

Since 1861 Chief Sekukuni had ruled the Bapedi who had purchased firearms from traders in Delagoa Bay. He considered his land to be independent of the Transvaal and drove out the miners who were prospecting for gold on his side of the Steelpoort River. He also carried off Boer cattle and repulsed a retaliatory raid by President Burgers of the Transvaal.[10] For the first time in history the Boers had been defeated in a war against the natives.[11]

It was feared in London that the Transvaal would destabilise British South Africa. It was therefore decided to take over the Transvaal as the first step in creating a federation of Cape Colony and Natal with the two Boer republics. Carnarvon the Colonial Secretary decided to appoint Sir Bartle Frere, an Indian Mutiny hero, as Governor of the Cape and the future High Commissioner of the Federation. At the same time Theophilus Shepstone was recalled to London and given instructions to take over the Transvaal.

On 12th April 1877 Shepstone did just that in an astonishing bloodless coup d'etat. Carnarvon had acted without consulting the Cabinet and Lord Salisbury was furious. He had had earlier dealings with Frere, who he considered 'quarrelsome and *mutinous*'.[12] He was quite the wrong man at this moment to send to South Africa. Shepstone was also the wrong man to be made Governor of the Transvaal. He had no experience in dealing with the Boers and did his best to reconcile them to his rule by doing a U-turn and siding with them against Ketchwyo.

For several years there had been a dispute between the Zulus and the Transvaal Boers over a strip of land on the north-west border of Zululand. Shepstone had always wanted to secure it for Natal and Panda had offered it to the British, in order to defend his people from the Boers. In October 1877 Shepstone went to Blood River, the border between Transvaal and Zululand, and told Ketchwyo that he must handover the disputed territory to the Boers. Ketchwyo's reply was unequivocal. He had called Shepstone his 'father' and now he had deserted him. He was both a cheat and a fraud.

Shepstone was incandescent with rage. He wrote a furious letter to London, which Frere read. Ketchwyo, he wrote must go. Unless his anachronistic regime was removed there could be no progress in South Africa:

> Cetewayo [sic] is the secret hope of every ... independent chief ... who feels the desire that his colour shall prevail ... The sooner the root of the evil ... which I consider to be the Zulu power and military organisation, is dealt with, the easier out task will be.[13]

Frere was convinced by the soundness of Shepstone's advice. Ketchwyo, however, was not just an ignorant savage, but an astute diplomat who had once said:

> I love the English. I am not Mpande [Panda]'s son. I am the child of Queen Victoria. But I am also a king in my own counrty and must be treated as such. Somsteu [Shepstone] must speak gently to me. I shall not hear dictation ... I shall perish first.[14]

Ketchwyo now appealed to Bishop Colenso and the Governor of Natal for advice and the latter ordered that a Commission of Enquiry should look into the whole matter. To everyone's astonishment it found in favour of the Zulus. Frere was mortified. He had already decided that Ketchwyo must be removed. He kept the Commission's finding from the public, a half-secret from London, and began a public relations campaign against Ketchwyo. He then sent an ultimatum to the Zulu king. He must accept a British Resident in Zululand, and abolish his military system. If he failed to accept these terms in thirty days, Britain would invade. There was no way Ketchwyo could accept such a demand.

The ultimatum expired on 11th Janury 1879. The next day the British Commander-in-Chief Lieutenant-General Lord Chelmsford launched a three-pronged attack on Zululand.

On 23rd January 1879 the Zulu impi of 20,000 warriors slipped past Chelmsford's column and fell on his rear echelon at Islandlwana. 858 British soldiers, including 52 officers, and 471 black troops were slaughtered.[15]

The disaster at Islandlwana was the most costly defeat Britain had suffered at the hands of a native army in Africa. Lord Chelmsford asked for three more regiments to be sent to reinforce him. The Cabinet decided to send five. One was the 94th Regiment of Foot.

Notes

1. Juliet Alexa's diary, 313.
2. *The Scramble for Africa*, 47.
3. *The Scramble for Africa*, 49.
4. *Clan Gillean*, 383.
5. NAS. CS 235. M 70/15.
6. *Cases decided in the Court of Session*. No. 16. 18 November 1857.
7. *Clan Gillean*, 383.

8. *The Scramble for Africa*, 46–49.
9. In his *Saturday Review* article in 1860 Lord Salisbury, who in his youth had visited South Africa, suggested that the Boers had only trekked out of British jurisdiction because 'They could stand the loss of their nationality but not the loss of their slaves'. The Transvaal Republic, which they had set up as their last retreat was somewhere where they could 'maltreat the natives to the utmost of their heart's content'. Andrew Roberts *Salisbury: Victorian Titan* (2000), 716.
10. *The Scramble for Africa*, 42; The South Africa Military History Society. *Military History Journal*, Vol. 2 No. 5. HW Kinsey 'The Sekukuni Wars'.
11. KW Smith: 'The campaigns against the Bapedi of Sekukhune, 1877–1879', *Archives Year Book for SA History*, 1967, II.
12. *Salisbury*, 225.
13. Sir T Shepstone to Lord Carnarvon, 11 December 1877 [TNA 30/6/23 quoted in *The Scramble for Africa*, 52].
14. *The Scramble for Africa*, 56.
15. *The Scramble for Africa*, 57–71.

Chapter Fifty-Nine

Africa and Afghanistan 1879–1881

On the evening of the 11th February 1879 the English newspapers were full of the disaster at Isandlwana, 'and it was felt that England would make a great effort to retrieve that reverse; but that it should come home to us as individuals was not so clear', wrote Captain WE Montague of the 94th Regiment, who were quartered in Aldershot.

The following day he continues was intended as a 'Brigade day' and after an early breakfast Montague went up from his married quarter to the barracks in order to take part. But instead of finding the companies on parade ready to be inspected, he found the men standing about in groups, not saying much but just standing around 'as if they had heard something, and expected to hear more'. The suspense did not to last for long. On the orderly-room table were orders that that the regiment was to prepare for immediate embarkation to South Africa. Montague went straight home.

> My wife met me in the entrance to our hut; it was unusual for me to return so early. Besides that, there must have been something in my face, which had not been there before.
> 'We're ordered off to the Cape at once Nelly!' I said. It was no time for begging one's words.
> Nelly gave a slight shiver, and I saw her hand press on the handle of the half-open door she was holding, a trifle heavier than it had done before I spoke. That was only for a second – little more. Then she gave a faint smile, and laid both hands on my shoulders, saying, as she kissed me, 'I am so glad, Ned, because I know that you are glad'. And after that she burst out crying.[1]

The manner in which the officers and their wives greeted the news of the regiment's mobilization says a great deal about attitude to war in Britain at the zenith of the British Empire. At least as far as the army was concerned. To go and fight the Queen's enemies was an adventure. The wives may have wept, but they were proud of their husbands and would themselves do their duty.

Hurried preparations followed. For the officers journeys to London followed, with visits to tailors, boot makers and the Army and Navy Stores. Tradesmen descended on Aldershot with samples of their wares and received many orders. When Montague's garments were delivered he suggested, as a joke, that he supposed he could pay when he returned. Only to receive the reply that, 'when gentlemen are going out as you are, sir, it is always a case of ready money'. Whilst his boot maker 'a well-to-do gentleman in the West End', shook his head and said of Isandlwana: 'Sad business, sir – very sad; nothing like it in England since I can remember. We lost three customers by it, sir!'

* * *

One newly joined officers of the 94th was Second-Lieutenant Alexander William Day Maclean. He was the son of Colonel Alexander Maclean, late of the 94th, who was now the senior member of the Crossapol family. Young Alexander, or Willie as he was called at home, was one of the first members of the family of Coll to join his father's regiment. He had been educated at Clifton College and the Royal Military College, Sandhurst. On 30th January 1878 he was commissioned into the 94th.[2] He was one of the few members of his extended family to join the army at this time.

The descendants of the family, who had swarmed into the armed services from 1800 to 1840 failed to do so in the 1870s. None of Hugh Maclean of Coll's sons produced a male heir who survived infancy.[3] Only two of Lachlan of the Isle of Muck's grandsons had male issue: Francis John Small's grandsons emigrated to Australia; and neither of John Francis Gray's sons entered the army.

Although John of Cornaig's descendants served in the Volunteers in Australia, none became professional soldiers, preferring to become surveyors and lawyers. Even the sons of the most successful soldier amongst Cornaig's grandsons, Major-General John Norman Hector Maclean of the Madras Army, did not follow their father into the army. Alexander Campbell's only soldier son, who had joined the Bombay army's[4] own son emigrated to New Zealand. His brothers became merchants. At least one, Hector Coll, joining Jardine, Matheson and Co. in Hong Kong.[5]

As we shall see one other Coll family who was to continue send its sons into the army were the Gallanach Macleans. They too, like their Crossapol cousins, were descended from, if only in the female line, Coll's *luchd-tighe*.

* * *

In 1878 the 94th was a very different regiment to the 94th of the 1840s. Firstly it was no longer Scottish. In 1873 its depot had been moved to Armagh and most of its men were now Irish.[6]

Although the 94th were under strength and had to receive some 300 volunteers from other units, not everyone in the regiment could go to South Africa. Montague writes that 'we, the lucky ones ... were easily to be distinguished from the unlucky ones left behind, who walked slowly and carried no parcels. Poor fellows, how we pitied them!'

The soldiers too were carried away in jingoistic euphoria. Long lines of people, all shouting and cheering, greeted the regiments as they arrived at Southampton to embark on the *China*. The men were stowed below 'like so many sardines in a box; the officers snatched a minute now and again to consume bottles of champagne with their friends in the saloon'. The Commander-in-Chief, the old Duke of Cambridge paid them a flying visit

And at last we cast off from the quay, and steamed slowly past the dock head.

The crowds, there as elsewhere unmindful of the bitter wind, cheered and waved their handkerchiefs, while the band on board played *Auld lang syne* and *The girl I left behind me*, till the men could blow no longer ... The steam-tender alongside blew her whistle ... and a few minutes after the order 'Full speed ahead'. England was once more a thing of the past.

* * *

It was not until 2nd April that the steam ship *China* anchored off Durban. When it did it was announced that the ship's owners Messrs Burns and M'Ivor in a patriotic gesture wished to present the officers of the 94th 'with the wine which they had drunk in no half-hearted way throughout the voyage'.

The 94th now had to experience the difficulties of getting ashore over the bar between deep water of the Indian Ocean and the Durban beach:

> As soon as the ... ladders were slung over the side, the men began swinging down them, passing their rifles first, and following themselves into the arms of a couple of sailors placed to catch them in the much-heaving tug.
>
> 'Catch a hoult of me legs, Barney darlint!' and appeals to 'Holy Mother', or half the saints in the calendar, were frequent. And elicited shouts of laughter from those already down. It seemed as if the stream of struggling red-coated bodies would never cease. In vain the captain held up his hands and shouted that the boat was full – still down they came, tumbling and sprawling, till there was really no more squeezing room; and then it was only one company and the moety of another that were out of the ship, and there were ten in all. The crew gave three cheers, and we pushed off, tossing and rolling quite as deep in the big swells ...
>
> We passed some small vessels hard and fast on the bar, the water sucking in and out of the hatchways with a dismal sound. 'Swish' came a spray, like a whip, right across our faces, and those who had waterproofs put them on; the men, crouching under the low bulwarks, grinned, and let off more jokes. Then came a huge roller, sending our boat down into the depths of the green water, and we were introduced to the Durban bar. Another and another followed, broad, greasy swells, and with many lurches and splashing of salt spray, we got through into the quiet water inside.

After their long journey the reception they received did not live up to expectations. Only a few children came out to cheer. The colonists, who in Durban were largely of British stock, turned out only to stare. Their view of the war was that England had got them into the mess and it was up to her to get them out of it.

Troops poured in. Not only from England but from Ceylon, Mauritius and St Helena. Durban cheered up. The 'scare' was over and merchants made money faster than they could have dreamed possible. The clubs made 'all military men members, to the discomfort of their own, who were elbowed out of ... their own particular places, by eager, hungry new-comers'.

Whilst they waited to go to the front the battle of Kambula was fought and Etshowe relieved, and order after order reached the regiment. One of the first was to 'dye our white helmets the colour of the ground', to make targets less obvious to Zulu snipers. Officers were also advised to remove badges of rank and make themselves indistinguishable from the men. The Zulus were believed to know the number of officers in each unit. They also were said to have detailed ten men to each British officer and were prepared to sacrifice their own lives to see that no officer survived. One order produced much annoyance at the time. It was that the campaign was to be teetotal. No alcohol was to be taken on the expedition. Thus saving the expense of extra waggons and to ensure that 'the men were at all times ready to fight with their wits about them'.

* * *

At long last the regiment set off by train for Pietermaritzberg. The men travelled in cattle-trucks whilst the officers went in the second-class carriages of Natal State Railways. The track rose steeply at first through the bush, then past open park-like spaces dotted with clumps of trees. Up mountain passes and by impassable gorges filled with a tangle of semi-tropical vegetation. Flat-topped mimosa bushes with long thorns were everywhere. Occasionally blue gums came in sight, which were a sign of habitation as farmers planted them in a circle round their houses for shelter and firewood. Higher up the bush gave way to more grassland. At the top of the range the train halted and the men disembarked.

The train was left behind and the column marched on. Native kraals came in sight with cattle grazing all around. The inhabitants 'fine looking men grinning good naturedly, and saluting, greeted the soldiers and shouted: 'Oolay Johnnie! Go cut dam Zulu throat'. The men were delighted and gave a cheer in return. 'Kloofs', the Dutch word for a ravine, were passed on either side. A flat-topped mountain came insight, its upper slopes scarred with a wall of naked rock.

The white helmets issued at Aldershot had disappeared; 'the spikes, so martial looking there, had gone, with every vestige of pipe clay washed out of the belts: but the men stepped along cheerily, whistling or singing popular airs, till the dust got in their throats, and there was a rush at the first halting-place to fill their water-bottles'. But the streams, tempting at a distance, proved to be dried up.

Maritzburg at last was reached at the end of a broad valley on the banks of a 'tolerably good river, its pools prettily shaded with willows, and fringed with a setting of wild-flowers'. In order to honour the capital of the colony, instead of going directly to their camping place the column marched down the main street. 'Crowds of well-dressed townspeople turned out to see us, and in their honour our half-dozen drummer-boys moistened their lips sufficiently to play a bugle-march at the head of the column. But no answering cheer met our poor efforts at military pomp, no friendly hand put out even a bucket of water to wet the soldiers' lips. Dry and dusty they marched to the campground above Fort Napier, and threw themselves on the ground quite tired out'.

The road between Pietermaritzburg and Greytown was considered to be unsafe for traffic and the 94th were sent to protect it. They marched north across the Umgeni River, which flowed through a valley of the greenest grass, sometimes 5 foot high. Unlike other rivers they had seen in Natal, the Umgeni was full of water, which in places cascaded through pillars of basalt on whose summits bushes grew where weaverbirds had hung their nests. The roar of the water could be heard long before it was seen. Near Greytown they came across a herd of hartebeests in an otherwise boring plain, cut by the Umvoti River, which in places was sufficiently deep for oxen to stand knee-deep.

Montague says that Greytown contained only a few houses surrounded by blue gums. It had probably changed little in the ten years since Juliet Alexa had lived there. He says that the inhabitants were mostly Dutch. People of the neighbouring district, who sought sanctuary in the town, dramatically increased its population. He describes the laager as being an enclosure surrounded by a wall 10 feet high. Inside was a house containing the munitions of war; round the wall ran a banquette for the men to stand upon ... Admittance was by a door strongly barred. Outside ran a ditch. Beyond this was the camp of some infantry, also strongly fortified.[7]

The 94th were now split into two unequal parts. C Company, commanded by Captain Froom and E Company (Captain Pöe) were detached from the rest of the regiment to relieve two companies of the 4th Foot to form the Greytown garrison.[8] On the 16th April the rest of the regiment continued its march through the thorn country until on the 24th they reached Dundee, where the Second Division under Major-General Newdigate, was assembling for the advance into Zululand.

Willie Maclean was one of the officer's left behind at Greytown. He therefore missed the battle of Ulundi, which destroyed Ketchwyo's impis and where the British avenged Isandlwana. The 94th, the largest unit to take part in the battle particularly distinguished themselves.[9]

Once Ketchwyo was captured it was decided to resume operations against Sekukuni. The detached companies at Greytown rejoined the regiment and marched north with them to the mountains east of Pretoria. The troops to be employed against Sekukuni, the 'Transvaal Field Force' were under the command of Sir Garnet Wolseley, who had arrived from England and succeeded Lord Chelmsford as Commander-in-Chief in South Africa.

Middelburg was selected as Wolseley's operational base and the 94th pushed forward to build three small forts to protect his lines of communication. One of them was 'Fort Burghers', which was held by D Company (Captain GRS Bowlby) and some native irregulars. On 12th November it was attacked by some 5,000 of Sekukuni's warrriors who were beaten off.

On 24th November the 94th began their advance towards Sekukuni's Town and on 25th completed a 20 mile forced march that brought them to within striking distance of their objective. The enemy's main position consisted of a fortified mountain with a spur, which ran at right angles to it. In the angle between the two positions was a kloof that led up to the top of the mountain. Sekukuni's town and the chief's kraal were at the lower end of the kloof.

An isolated mass of piled up boulders 100 feet high, honeycombed with caves was directly in front Sekukuni's Town. It was known as the 'Fighting Kopje'. Its defences had been improved by the construction of a number of loopholed sangars. It was well supplied with water and was the key to the whole position.

Lieutenant-Colonel Murray of the 94th was given command of six companies of his own regiment and eight companies of 2nd/21st Foot the Royal Scots Fusiliers. His task was to take the Fighting Kopje and Sekukuni's Town. The attack on the spur was the responsibility of Major PR Anstruther of the 94th, who had under his command one company of the 94th and some native troops. The attack on the left of the position was the task of the mounted infantry companies of 94th, 2nd/21st and two local units. Once the caves were cleared the Right and Left attacks were to swing inwards and assault the town from the rear. At the same time the remaining two companies of the 94th plus 6,000 Swazis warriors, who were deadly enemies of the Pedi, were to scale the north face of the mountain, seize the summit and join in the attack on the town from the rear.

The attack began at 10 am Each section carried out its orders and by noon the caves in the mountain had been cleared of the enemy. The Fighting Kopje was now surrounded and an artillery bombardment began which preceded the general assault. The attackers rushed forward and seized the summit of the kopje, but Sekukuni's men were so well concealed in the caves below, that it was impossible to get to grips with them. Attempts to dynamite the kopje's caves failed to dislodge the defendants. Many of them had worked in the diamond fields and were used to handling explosives. They cut the fuses before the dynamite could explode and it was to be another twelve hours before Sekukuni's gallant garrison surrendered.

Meanwhile Sekukuni himself had disappeared. B Company 94th was sent after him with a detachment of native levies. On 2nd December they overtook him and brought him back a prisoner to Headquarters.

Two private soldiers of the 94th rescued Lieutenant Dewar of the KDG, who was wounded when he was attached to the 94th's mounted company. As he was being carried down the hill by six of the native levies, 40 of Sekukuni's men attacked them. The levies dropped their charge and fled. The two men of the 94th dashed to rescue the wounded officer. One carried him on his back, whilst the other kept the enemy at bay. Both men were awarded the Victoria Cross.[10]

Willie Maclean also distinguished himself on the attack on Sekukuni's Kraal and was awarded the medal and clasp.[11] He was now posted to the Depot and therefore missed the final tragedy of the South African campaign.

* * *

Shepstone's takeover of the Transvaal might have been achieved without bloodshed, but it had not reconciled the Boers to British rule. One of the few advantages that the Boers perhaps accepted was that the threat to their security from Ketchwyo and Sekukuni no longer existed. In retrospect to destroy the two most powerful native regimes was a disastrous decision. Both could have been contained and were an ever present threat to the Afrikaners who were Britain's real enemy. The British, however, underestimated and despised the Boers who they believed would never dare risk rebellion. They were wrong.

They also did not expect that the Boers would throw away the rulebook and fail to behave like English gentlemen.

* * *

On 5th December 1880 two companies of the 94th left Sekukuniland for Pretoria. Lieutenant-Colonel PR Anstruther who had recently taken over command of the battalion[12] led them. He had with him eight other officers and 248 men plus 34 baggage wagons and the military band.

By 20th December the unwieldy column had covered 130 miles, but in two day's time should reach Pretoria. At 1 pm Anstruther and Egerton, the transport officer, who had gone ahead to select a camp for the night at Bronkhorst Spruit, noticed that the band had stopped playing. 150 armed and mounted Boers had appeared in the thorn trees to the left of the track. One of them rode forward carrying a white flag with a note for Anstruther. It stated that at Heidelberg four days earlier the Transvaal Republic had been proclaimed. Anstruther and his men must stay where they were or the Boers would not be answerable for the consequences.

Anstruther replied that he had been ordered to go to Pretoria and to Pretoria he would go. He turned round and galloped back to the column shouting at his men to stand to. As he did so the Boers opened fire. Bandsmen dropped their instruments and rushed to get their rifles from the waggons. They were shot down. The men returned fire, but the Boers had disappeared in the smoke, to snipe from behind the rocks. Others fanned out to encircle the column, 'picking off the leading oxen with each wagon and killing the African drivers'.

Anstruther, who had been shot in the legs five times, had little alternative but to order the bugler to sound the cease-fire. Five officers, including Anstruther were dead or dying. A third of the men were dead and another third seriously wounded. A white flag was raised and the Boers galloped down from the rocks. They grabbed the soldier's rifles, pulled off their helmets and forced them 'to squat like Africans'. The Boer leader shook Anstruther by the hand and said he was sorry that he was hurt. He dealt humanely with the other wounded and marched the unwounded to Heidelberg.

* * *

The newly installed telegraph brought the news of the disaster rapidly to Europe. On Christmas Eve 1880 WS Wilson who had served in the 94th was at the New Club in Edinburgh, when he heard the news. He wrote the following day to his old friend Colonel Alexander Maclean, who had now retired and was living in Bristol.[13] Wilson had evidently met Colonel Murray, who was just back from South Africa, for he writes:

> Only want of time prevented my writing yesterday to tell you how much gratified I was hearing Murray's account of your son. He tells me that he very much resembles what you were in times gone by, and that is as much as I should care to hear of a son of mine: for I can remember when I joined looking upon you as the beau ideal of a soldier: the time is so long gone by that one may say so without hesitation . . . I am greatly shocked at the news; and am thankful that your son is safe at the Depot. What a time of anxiety it must be to poor Mrs Anstruther till we get details. Now wishing you and yours many a happy Christmas and New Year . . .[14]

* * *

After the massacre of the two companies of the 94th at Bronkhorst Spruit the Boers in the Orange Free State rushed to join their cousins in the Transvaal. They invaded Natal. Major-General Sir George Colley, who had succeeded his patron Wolseley as the new High Commissioner in South Africa, commanded the British troops in Natal who advanced against the Boers, only to be repulsed on 28th January at Laing's Nek and on 7th February at Ingogo. London ordered Colley to offer the Boers an armistice and an invitation to peace negotiations. He was appalled.

Colley's orders were vague enough to be misinterpreted. Instead of giving the Boers sufficient time to reply, he gave them twenty-four hours. When they failed to meet this impossible deadline he attacked. He had noticed that Majuba Hill, which overlooked the Boer position, was unoccupied. If he could seize it he could force them to fall back into the Transvaal and the British defeats would be avenged.

Colley led a remarkable night advance up the hill, which in places could only be climbed on hands and knees and the British reached the summit without having to fire a shot. At dawn they could look down on the Boer trenches. It was a remarkable achievement. The success went to their head. The British were also exhausted. One battalion had only been in South Africa for two weeks and was not yet acclimatized. Instead of strengthening their position, they lay about in the sun and failed to dig in, build sangars or post sentries.

Although the Boers had been surprised, once they saw what had happened they were quick to realise the seriousness of the situation. They divided their men into two parties and covered each other with fire, as they clambered up the hill and occupied a small kopje which overlooked the British position. The British were either slaughtered or ran for their lives. One man who did not run was Sir George Colley. He was last seen walking towards the Boers with his revolver in his hand. A moment later he was shot through the head.

Paul Kruger, the Transvaal President had in fact accepted an armistice before the battle. Majuba Hill need never have been fought. Gladstone's government was forced to make a humiliating peace. The Transvaal was once again a republic. It was almost independent, except in foreign relations and the dream of some in Cape Town and London for a British South Africa was put on hold.

* * *

Whilst Ketchwyo and Sekukuni were being defeated in South Africa, half way round the world on the North-West Frontier of India, the British were engaged in a more justifiable struggle.

The British Empire's first line of defence, and the foundation of her strength and prestige was the Royal Navy. So long as we maintained our naval supremacy nine-tenths of the Empire was secure from attack. The missing tenth was India. India's long land frontier extending from Tibet in the east to Afghanistan and Persia in the west was, of course, far removed from the sphere where naval superiority could be exerted. But for hundreds of miles along this frontier the highest mountain barrier in the world insulated India geographically from Central Asia. Only in the north-west was she really vulnerable.

Throughout its history India had hypnotised invaders from the west. They had entered India through its North-West Frontier. Most recently Napoleon, and his one time ally Tsar Alexander I of Russia, had planned a joint offensive through the passes to seize India's fabled wealth from the British. Their plans had come to nothing, however, Alexander was not the first Russian to look covetously at the Sub-Continent and even Peter the Great was supposed to have said in his will:

> We must progress as much as possible in the direction of Constantinople and India. He who can once get possession of these places is the real ruler of the world...

Most historians believe that the story of Peter the Great's will is apocryphal but its sentiments certainly expressed the aims of many Russians and one of the problems facing the British was the difficulty in interpreting Russian motives. Some observers believed that she was after a port on the Gulf. Some held that she aimed at incorporating the four northern provinces of Persia and that the Shah's kingdom might be used as a convenient route for the eventual conquest of India.

Others believed that no Russian statesman dreamed of the *conquest* of India. But they certainly contemplated the invasion of India. Their real objective was not Calcutta but Constantinople. An invasion of India would keep England employed in Asia and allow Russia a free hand in Turkey.

Even so, the danger was not acute as long as Persia, Afghanistan and the great deserts beyond them separated the Russian and British Empires. That safeguard was lost in 1880 when Russia finally succeeded in pushing her frontiers southwards to the borders of Persia. The British in India were now faced an entirely new problem: meeting an invasion from the front, while at the same time having sufficient troops in place to defeat a possible rebellion to the rear.

Many soldiers considered that the north-west frontier that the British had inherited from the Sikh's was indefensible. Lord Roberts who was Commander-in-Chief in India from 1885 to 1892 expressed it best when in 1898 in a speech in the House of Lords he said:

> When the responsibility for the defence of the North-West Frontier devolved upon me... I never contemplated any defence being possible along the Frontier, as marked on our maps by a thin red line... which did well enough so long as we had only to guard against tribal depredations. A Frontier more than 1,000 miles in length, with a belt of huge mountains in its front, inhabited by thousands of warlike men, over whom neither we nor any other Power had control, and with a wide, impassable river in its rear, seemed to me then, as it does now, an impossible Frontier, and one upon which no scheme for the defence of India could be safely based.[15]

Imperialists in London and Delhi, who believed in a Forward Policy, thought that the frontier should be pushed as far as the 'natural boundary', the Hindu Kush. Such a strategy meant controlling much of Afghanistan and in 1876 Benjamin Disraeli sent Lord Lytton, the new viceroy to India, to reinstate the Forward Policy reversed after the disastrous First Afghan War.

Lytton's first step was to establish a British mission in Kabul. The Amir, Sher Ali, however, refused, arguing that if he did Russia would want one too. Matters came to a head in 1878 when Russia assembled an army of 30,000 in Turkestan and sent an uninvited diplomatic mission to Kabul to try to persuade the Afghans to join the Russians in invading India.[16]

Britain protested at the Russian presence in Kabul. They demanded that the Amir accept a mission from Britain too, and when Sher Ali failed to reply sent an envoy with small force into Afghanistan. It was stopped by Afghan troops at the Khyber Pass and on 21st November 1878 the British retaliated and invaded Afghanistan.

Sher Ali turned in desperation to the Russians but their bluff had been called. They refused to give him any assistance and to the dismay of the hawks in St Petersburg the invasion of India was called off. The Amir, therefore, appointed his son Yakub Khan as regent and went to Russia to beg the Tsar to change his mind. Instead of helping him the Tsar told the Amir to return home. He did so and died in February 1879.

British forces now occupied Kabul and Kandahar, and in May 1879 Yakub Khan signed a treaty by which he was left in control of much of Afghanistan but was obliged to accept a British representative in Kabul and hand foreign affairs over to him.

The British representative Sir Louis Cavagnari arrived in Kabul in July 1879. Two months later an Afghan mob lynched him. Unlike 1841 when an incompetent old man had led the British army, Frederick Roberts VC, thought by many to be the most able British soldier since Wellington, was in command. He marched on Kabul and hanged those he deemed responsible for the murder of Cavagnari and his men.

Despite Robert's victory by March 1880, even the most enthusiastic supporters of a Forward Policy agreed that it was not practical politics to occupy Afghanistan. This decision was made before the General Election in Britain, at which Afghanistan was a major issue, threw out the Tories and returned Gladstone to power. At the same time Abdur Rahman, a claimant to the Afghan throne, who had spent twelve years in exile in Samarkand under the protection of the Russians, entered Afghanistan from the north. Tribesmen flocked to his standard.

Although the Russians backed Abdur Rahman, he was not a Russian stooge and the British reasoned, correctly, that he was firstly an Afghan nationalist. He had also seen the Russians let down too many of his predecessors. The British decided to back him. A Muslim agent would represent Britain in Kabul and the army would withdraw. In return Abdur Rahman agreed not to have relations with any other foreign power. However, he only controlled the area around Kabul and the rest of the country was in turmoil. There were other claimants to the throne and before Roberts could return to India news reached him that another rival for the throne, Ayub Khan was marching on Kandahar.

Kandahar had only a small British garrison and 2,500 British and Indian troops, under command of Brigadier-General George Burrows, were sent from India to intercept Ayub Khan. As he approached Kandahar, more tribesmen joined him and by the time he reached the city his army was 20,000 strong. He was also well armed and had modern artillery. British intelligence was poor and Burrows grossly underestimated Ayub Khan's strength. By the time he realised his error it was too late. Outmanoevred, outnumbered and outgunned at the battle of Maiwand the British suffered one of their worst defeats in Asia and almost 1,000 of Burrow's men were dead.

The shattered remnants of Burrow's army withdrew into Kandahar and the horrified garrison prepared for a siege. As his first troops were leaving the city, news of the disaster reached Roberts in Kabul. He set off with his 10,000 men on an epic 300 mile forced march from Kabul to Kandahar.

'The entire force, including infantry, cavalry, light infantry, field hospitals, ammunition and even mutton on the hoof, reached the beleagued city in twenty days'.[17] It was one of the fastest forced marches in military history.

On hearing of Roberts' approach, Ayub Khan took fright and tried to parley. But Roberts was in no mood to do so. As soon as he reached Kandahar he reconnoitred the Afghan position. The following morning Roberts struck. At first the Afghans, who had more artillery than their opponents, put up a fierce fight, pouring a devastating fire on the advancing British and Indian troops. But by mid-day the Afghan artillery had been silenced and by last light it was all over. The British had lost 35 dead, whilst the Afghans left 600 dead on the field and carried off as many with them.

Among the British dead was Allan Macdonald, the last of the little band of Hugh Maclean of Coll's men from Dervaig, who had joined the army in the 1850s. They had fought in the Crimea and in the Indian Mutiny. Macdonald was the last of them and died serving in the 92nd Regiment of Foot (the Gordon Highlanders).[18]

Another of Coll's former tenants' sons who took part in the campaign was the ubiquitous Charles Smith Maclean. He served throughout the Afghan campaign and commanded 1st Punjab Cavalry. He was mentioned in dispatches for his gallant conduct at Saif-un-din, and for his valuable work during the campaign[19] he received the medal and clasp. In 1881, by now a colonel,[20] he was serving in Waziristan, a mountainous territory on the Afghan border inhabited by a turbulent tribe of Pathans. Once again he was mentioned in dispatches and awarded the CB.[21]

Notes

1. Captain WE Montague *Campaigning in South Africa: Reminiscences of an Officer in 1879* (1880) 1–3.
2. *Ibid.*.
3. His eldest daughter Emily Agnes, however, married Lieutenant-Colonel Henry Charles Hamilton of the 2nd Lancers Hyderabad Contingent in the Indian Army [Burke's *Peerage & Baronetage* (1923), 1119, under Hamilton of Silverton Hill; Reginald George Burton *A History of the Hyderabad Contingent* (Calcutta, 1905), 290–292. I have to thank Anne Hamilton for a copy of this book].
4. Capt. Henry Travers of the Bombay Army.
5. He died on 24 March 1894 and is buried in the European cemetery in Happy Valley. His tomb reads 'Sacred to the Memory of Hector Coll McLean/ … aged 57 years/Erected by Ho Tung'. [British Association of Cemeteries in South Asia *Chowkidar*]. I have to thank Phillida Purvis for an extract from this publication.
6. *The Connaught Rangers*, 371.
7. *Campaigning in South Africa* 37–71.
8. *The Connaught Rangers*, 337.
9. *Ibid*, 347.
10. *Ibid*, 350–353.
11. *The Celtic Monthly* Vol. VI (1898), 156.
12. He was appointed in August 1880 [*London Gazette*, 6 August 1880].
13. On his return from India he served as Adjutant to the Depot Battalions at Preston, Parkhurst and Chatham. In 1859 he was appointed Staff Officer of Pensioners at Omagh County Tyrone. He was subsequently transferred to Northampton and finally to Bristol District where he served till his retirement as Colonel on 1st July 1878 [BCP. HAC Maclean's undated notes on the Macleans of Crossapol].
14. BCT. The New Club, Edinburgh, Christmas Day 1880. WS Wilson to Col. Alexander Maclean.

15. *PD*, Fourth Series, Lords, 7 March 1898, liv, 752–3. Quoted in Rose Louise Greaves *Persia and the Defence of India 1884–1892* (1959), 197.
16. Peter Hopkirk *The Great Game* (1990), 380.
17. *Ibid*, 400.
18. *Report of the Royal Commission (Highland & Islands)*, 1892, 2276.
19. BL. L/MIL/7/5675.
20. On 19 June 1879 he was recommended by Major-General PS Lumsden, Adjutant General in India for brevet promotion to Lieutenant Colonel [BL/L/MIL/7/5675, 21].
21. BL. L/MIL/9/300/79.

Chapter Sixty

'The Great Game'

Britain may have decided to abandon its Forward Policy, but Russia had no intention of doing so. Within weeks of the last British troops leaving Afghanistan, the Russians were once more on the move. Their next objective was to overthrow the Turcoman tribes who controlled the Karakum Desert. The Turcoman tribesmen were notorious for robbing any caravan that dared to trade across its desolate wastes, carrying off their captives into slavery. Their territory was bounded in the west by the Caspian Sea, in the north by the Khiva khanate (under Russian rule since 1873), the great River Oxus in the east and the northern provinces of Persia to the south.

The Russian's first task, once they advanced into the Karakum, was to capture the great Turcoman stronghold of Geok-Tepe, which lay on the southern edge of the desert, half way between the Caspian Sea and Merv. Geok-Tepe eventually fell on 24th January 1881, but only after sappers had burrowed under the massive walls of the fortress and blown a gap in it nearly 50 yards wide. Ferocious hand-to-hand fighting had been followed by the headlong flight across the desert of the defenders. The Russian cavalry had pursued 40,000 terrified civilians across the steppes, and 8,000 are said to have been slaughtered.[1]

The capture of Geok-Tepe did not, in itself, cause undue alarm in London. There was a feeling that the Turcomans, who had been the cause of so much human misery, had got no more than they deserved. What did disturb the British was the thought of what the Russians would do next. Would they press on eastwards and occupy Merv? If they did they would be in a position to march into Afghanistan and occupy Herat.

The names Herat and Merv were to reverberate around the corridors of power in London and St Petersburg. Herat was an ancient city, which had, in the days of Tamerlane and his son, been a metropolis of Muslim culture and the glory of Asia. Now it was poor and ruinous, important only for its strategic position. For the British its position had an ominous significance. It was on one of the traditional conqueror's routes, along which a hostile army could enter India through the Khyber and the Bolan Passes.[2]

Merv, the Turcoman capital, was another ancient city built around a famous oasis. It is said to have been founded by Cyrus the Great (559–580) and in ancient times had been known as 'the Queen of the World'.[3] In February 1221 its days of glory ended, when a Mongol army commanded by Tolui, son of Genghis Khan sacked the city and slaughtered most of its inhabitants.[4] Opinions in London and Calcutta about Merv were mixed: Northbrook called Merv 'a few mud hovels in the desert', whereas in 1877 Lytton described it as 'undoubtedly the most important spot in Central Asia'.[5]

After the fall of Geok-Tepe, St Petersburg, which was aware of British fears, was not ready to move again. The Russians were concerned, however, lest London should decide on a pre-emptive strike itself and seize Herat and perhaps even Merv. Such a strategy was certainly being proposed, as the cheap option, by the hawks in Simla and in the War Office. They argued that if Herat fell to the Russians, India's armed forces would need to expand dramatically. While if Kandahar too was taken, the increased number of troops needed to defend India would be even greater.

The hawks' advice fell on deaf ears. Gladstone's Government had abandoned the Tory's Forward Policy and, with trouble in the Sudan, had no desire to stir up further trouble in Central Asia. Kandahar was evacuated and in February 1884 the Russians annexed Merv.

The chiefs of staff's worst fears were coming true. Of particular concern was the Transcaspian Railway, with its capacity for transporting troops and artillery, which Russian engineers were extending eastward at an alarming rate. Work on the line had begun in 1880 on the orders of General Skobelev, when he was preparing for his advance on Geok-Tepe.[6]

The Government of India was equally aware of the threat. In April 1885 Lord Kimberley, Gladstone's viceroy had written:

In two or three years at longest the Russian railway will be extended to Merv ... I fully anticipate that ere long Khorassan will fall into the hands of Russia. A march on Herat will then be comparitively easy.[7]

Khorassan, the Parthia of the Romans, had for a long time been a bone of contention between Turcomanistan and Persia. It was currently the north-east province of Persia and was a valuable area to the British from which to observe what was going on in Central Asia. As a result, as early as December 1882, officers of the Indian army were sent to Khorassan to organise an intelligence service and, if possible, inject an element of stability into the border regions.[8]

In order to eliminate any cause of conflict Gladstone's Government agreed to dispatch a commission to discover what they called a 'scientific frontier' with Russia. After much official correspondence and arguments, it was agreed that the Joint Afghan Boundary Commission would rendezvous at Sarakhs on the 13th October 1884.

Although the British commissioner General Sir Peter Lumsden[9] arrived on time, there was no sign of the Russians, and it was soon apparent that whatever St Petersburg had agreed, the Russian military were determined to extend the boundary to as close to Herat as possible.

The immediate bone of contention was Pendjeh, a remote oasis halfway between Merv and Herat. The British considered it to belonged to Afghanistan, as did the Afghans. The Russians said that it belonged to them, as part of the territory they had taken over with Merv. As Pendjeh lay astride the approach to Herat, London had no intention of letting it fall to the Russians.

Still the Russians did not come to the rendezvous and Lumsden had to sit out the winter in Sarakhs. It was now clear to Lumsden that the Russians had no intention of negotiating until they had taken Pendjeh, and they could not do so until the snows melted. In India two army corps were mobilised, ready to march into Afghanistan to defend Herat. Meanwhile the Afghans sent troops to Pendjeh. The Russians, who had moved closer and closer to the oasis, angrily ordered them to depart. The Afghan commander refused. The Russian commander then attempted to persuade Lumsden to order the Afghans to depart. He too refused.

The Russians now changed tack and goaded the Afghans into opening fire on them. They were now less than a mile from Pendjeh and when at last fighting broke out the Afghan cavalry fled. The infantry, however, stood its ground and two of their companies were slaughtered. Finally the remainder of the Afghan infantry fled too, leaving 800 of their men dead.

When news of the Russian seizure of Pendjeh reached London it caused panic on the Stock Exchange. Everyone believed that war was inevitable. To the Government's surprise, however, instead of demanding that the British fulfilled their treaty obligations and shed Russian blood, the Amir, who had no desire to see his country once more a battlefield, shrugged his shoulders.

The Russians withdrew just out of Pendjeh and the Boundary Commission began its work in earnest. It was eventually agreed that the Russians would retain Pendjeh in exchange for the Zulficar Pass, which the Amir and his British advisers were anxious to control.[10] The pass, which runs from east to west, connects Khorassan with north and western Afghanistan. As it was the old Turcoman plundering road and was the traditional 'way out of Persia', it concerned Persia more immediately than it did Herat and India.

* * *

In addition to his other problems Gladstone now lost the vote on his Budget and resigned. The Tories, led by the Marquess of Salisbury with a minority government, replaced him. Internationally, Salisbury could hardly have inherited a worse situation. The Sudan had been lost to the Mahdi; Russian generals were plotting to seize Herat and their troops were reported to be around the Zulficar Pass. Afghanistan's status as a buffer state was in jeopardy.[11]

The Zulficar Pass, at least to the 'Forward' school of Indian strategists, was the place through which the Russians, who were now closer to Herat than were the British at Quetta, could bypass the Hindu Kush and march into India. General Sir Frederick Roberts, by then Commander-in-Chief in Madras, had written to Salisbury on the day the Gladstone Government lost his Budget vote, warning that the Russians were 'at the gate of Herat' and saying that Britain needed to recapture Kandahar, as soon as possible, to counter the threat if Herat should fall.

A paper Roberts had written, urging the British garrison in India to be increased from 65,000 to 80,000 men, stressed, what in another age would be called the 'domino' theory: if Russia's influence were to be felt in Kabul, it would gradually extend through Chitral, Yasin, Gilgit and Kashmir to India itself.

Roberts was not a lone voice crying in the wilderness. Major-General Sir Charles MacGregor, who was the Indian Army's Quartermaster-General, also called for increased urgency to be given to the construction of strategic roads and railways to and within the frontier regions. He pointed out that the Russians were working flat out to advance their own railway systems towards Afghanistan. MacGregor was uniquely qualified to comment. Not only did his duties make him head of the newly formed Intelligence Department at Simla, but he had travelled extensively in Afghanistan and north-eastern Persia. He had written about his travels and had recently published an extremely influential book on the defence of India.[12] It had been sent to politicians in London, presumably including Lord Salisbury.

Salisbury's strategic philosophy for the North-West Frontier was based on containment. This meant preserving the integrity of Afghanistan. In order to do so it was essential that a British officer should be stationed near Herat. In the past the Amir had refused to allow this to happen. The crisis at Pendjeh made him change his mind.

The officer chosen was Brigadier-General CS Maclean CB, like MacGregor he was well qualified for his task. As we have seen, he had served in numerous campaigns in India and was a competent linguist.[13] He was appointed on 21st March 1885. His instructions from HM Durand, Secretary to the Government of India were concise. They were:

> To watch from the Perso-Herat border the course of events in the Afghan frontier districts, and the movements of the Russians beyond, and to collect such information on these subjects as might seem useful to your Government...

He was to cultivate friendly relations with both the Afghans and the Persians, and to act at all times in compliance with 'any advice or directions you might receive from the British Minister at Teheran'.[14]

Brigadier-General Maclean arrived at Herat whilst the Pendjeh crisis was at its height. As we have seen it was immediately followed by another war scare, when it was rumoured, inaccurately, that the Russians were about to seize the Zulficar Pass. Then in August the 'doves overcame the hawks in St Petersburg'. Salibury's determination that the Russians should not be allowed to upset the *status quo* in Central Asia had probably been the decisive factor in persuading the Tzar to accept the current situation.[15] In the summer of 1887, a protocol was signed, which agreed the boundary between Afghanistan and Russia.[16]

Durand goes on to say in his instructions to Maclean that despite the Amir's change of mind about having a British officer on the Perso-Afghan border, Brigadier-General Maclean was not to settle differences between the Afghans and Russians. Durand wrote:

> You are aware that His Highness the Amir refused to permit the location of British officers on the border for the purpose of settling such differences, and that His Highness declined to allow his officers to consult you. Nevertheless the Governor of Herat has lately asked for your advice with regard to certain important questions concerning the border. In this apparent change of attitude the Government of India, while reluctant to accept responsibility which might, unless carefully guarded and exercised, lead to complications, would not object to your giving friendly and unoffical advice in emergent cases.[17]

Although he was not allowed to intervene in the negotiations between the Afghans and the Russians, Maclean was not short of work and had plenty to do collecting intelligence. For example in December 1886 he reported that Alikhanov, the aristocratic Caucasian Muslim in the Russian army, who had largely been responsible for the seizure of Merv[18] had been removed as Governor. He also said that 2,000 Russian troops had gone from Pendjeh to Chargai; that Afghan nomads had purchased Russian arms; that there were rumours of a religious war; and that the Mullahs were objecting to the extension of the railway to Bokhara.[19]

The value of Maclean's work encouraged the Government of India's Foreign Department on 5th August 1887 to apply to Lord Cross, the Secretary of State for India, in a secret letter for an increase in his staff. They wrote that:

> The duties upon which Brigadier-General MacLean is employed are in our opinion of the highest importance. He is the main channel of information with regard to the movements of the Russians in Central Asia, and he has been directed to watch the course of events in the northern provinces of Afghanistan. It is also desirable that he should gain influence in Eastern Persia itself, and establish friendly relations with the local Governors and officials on the Khorassan frontier.

They went on to point out that the 'arrangements originally contemplated by Her Majesty's Government for watching the Russo-Afghan frontier included the appointment of several British officers, and the establishment of a Central Asia news-agency on a much larger scale than the present. The attitude of His Highness the Amir and his refusal to allow English officers to reside on the Afghan border, or to interfere in frontier affairs, have resulted in the abandonment of this scheme, and the large expense which it would have entailed has thereby been saved'.[20] Maclean had his establishment increased by a doctor and a chief clerk.

Maclean seems to have satisfied his masters in Simla for on 6th October 1887 HM Durand, Secretary to the Government of India wrote to say:

> Your organisation of an intelligence agency has had a considerable measure of success; and what you have done in this direction has the approbation of the Government of India. The system needs however further extension and improvement, and with this view the additional establishment asked for in your telegrams . . . has been sanctioned. With this establishment, and the enhanced sumptuary allowances at your disposal, His Excellency in Council trusts that you will be in a better position than before to gain full and accurate information as to the state of affairs in and around Khorassan, and to promote friendly relations with the local Governors and officials, and with the border tribes.

* * *

Another of Maclean's tasks was to keep an eye on Afghan refugees in Meshed.

When Gladstone had ordered the British to abandon Kandahar they had offered the city to the Amir. He, however, was slow to occupy it. And his cousin and rival Ayub Khan, the man who had defeated Burrows at the battle of Maiwand, seized Kandahar. He was not to hold it for long as Abdur Rahman, stung by its capture, marched on the city. Ayub Khan fled to Herat, and when his cousin followed, took sanctuary at Meshed.

Meshed is the most important Muslim holy city in Persia. It is the site of the tomb of the eighth imam, Ali al-Rida and Shia theologians rank it as the seventh most holy place in the whole of Islam. At Meshed Ayub Khan was safe from pursuit. However, despite the fact that 'his attempt to disturb Afghanistan has signally failed', he was too dangerous to be allowed to remain there; the Government of India wanted him away from the border and not to have an opportunity to go over to the Russians. On 22nd September 1887 the Legation in Tehran was instructed that: 'If possible Maclean should secure and surrender Ayub Khan to the Persians' He was to offer Ayub considerable sums of money to get him to co-operate.[21]

Arthur Nicolson, the Chargé d'Affaires at the Legation in Teheran now received a barrage of telegrams from the Foreign Secretary of the Government of India. Most were passed on to Maclean. On 1st November he was told:

> It must be remembered that Ayub has broken faith with us and that his attempt to disturb Afghanistan has signally failed . . . it will be well to let him understand that we appreciate these facts & also perhaps that his adherents are showing some readiness to make terms for themselves.

The solution Simla believed was that he should go into exile in India.

> He can then be informed that if he comes to India he will receive same allowance as Gakoob Khan[22] to support himself and family & dependants. He will be honourably treated & allowed

to live in Rawal Pindie. His travelling expenses will be paid & his journey through Persia will be facilitated, as far as possible in manner desired. Reasonable allowances will be granted to such of his adherents as elect to come to India.

His rights over his own household will be respected so long as the laws of India are not broken. With regard to his claims in Afghanistan it is evidently impossible for me to make any promises. Ameer would naturally resent such a course but Maclean may if necessary give him privately such general assurance as will satisfy him that Government of India bears him no ill will.[23]

As Ayub Khan had, at the battle of Maiwand, inflicted on the British one of their worst defeats in Asia the terms he was being offered were remarkable. However, when he was in India, he would be a useful piece in the game of chess being played on the North-West Frontier, as he could be used if Abdur Rahman the present Amir needed to be brought into line.

Maclean's negotiations with Ayub were fraught with difficulties and he did not always interpret Simla's instructions as they wished.

For example on the 22nd November 1887 they complained to the Legation in Tehran:

Regarding Ayub I did not intend to accept his fourth condition but as promise has been given it must be kept. Maclean's proposals to him are approved. If he rejects them Maclean may accept any reasonable alternative subject to my approval.

They wrote again on 1st December 1887: *'Afghan refugees*. We cannnot accept responsibility for debts, but will pay arrears on the understanding money is applied to payment.' And on 11th December: 'Both Secretary of State and I are agreed that Ayub's demands are exorbitant, but Lord Cross is willing to sanction the proposed arrangement provided the total annual expenditure for all purposes . . . can be limited to 4 lacs'.

On 16th December a telegram from Benares to Teheran underlined the problem of negotiating at a distance:

Your telegram 13th. Maclean sent assurance to Ayub. I am very much dissatisfied with this document. Why has Maclean kept it back till now? It ought to have been communicated at once both to your self and to the Government of India. Although Maclean states that in accord with my instructions he told Ayub that he could give no promise of any sort or kind in regard to Ameership it appears he has given an understanding 'that all Ayub's rights in Afghanistan should not be forgotten'. Inspite of the awkward wording the natural inference to be deducd from the foregoing sentence & the use of the word 'rights' is that some pledge has been given that Ayub's claim to succeeding the present Ameer will be favourably considered which is an expectation I was unwilling to hold out as it would be most unwise to commit ourselves prematurely on such a point. If on the other hand as Ayub complains the phrase is meaningless, it ought not to have been introduced at all. In dealing with Orientals it is both unfair & dangerous not to be explicit. It is just possible when Ayub found he could obtain no promise about the Ameership he may have desired to secure his [?] proprietary & other rights as an Afghan Sirdar on the occasion of any possible settlement of Afghanistan's affairs & that it was in this view that he accepted & interpreted the expression 'rights'. If this conjecture is correct, the phrase would be less objectionable. But this seems unlikely. In any event Ayub must be told & we must have some proof that he has been told that while his present surrender need not & will not compromise or prejudice any political chance he can consider himself to possess. The British Government continues to decline to give him advance pledges or promises whatsoever in regard to the Ameership.

Later the same day a more conciliatory telegram followed. Someone in Simla wrote:

I can quite understand that a good deal of inconvenience might now arise from asking Ayub to subscribe a fresh agreement. I am afraid however that the undertaking already executed by Maclean hardly secures the objects desired both by the Government of India & the Secretary of State. It does I think give us full power to regulate the movements of Ayub & his Sirdars. Term 4, upon which Maclean relies for enabling us to control the distribution of his allowances to Ayub's followers will hardly effect that purpose. The wording 'are' held to imply right of Ayub to distribute & redistribute the allowance pretty much at his own caprice . . . I suppose however that the matter must now be left to stand on its original basis.

Maclean must have objected to the criticism and on 24th December his superiors, who were now in Calcutta telegraphed:

Please forward to Maclean following telegram as from me: begins your telegram to Mr Nicolson[24] of 21. I am quite satisfied that in the Matter referred to you acted to the best of your judgement & I fully appreciate embarrassing nature of the emergency which you had to deal.

The matter was now resolved to the Government of India's satisfaction for on 26th December 1887. Nicolson received a telegram, which must have pleased him:

I congratulate you heartily on the success of your negotiations. Please also convey to Maclean. The only point I am at all anxious about is that we should be in a position to (show) should Ayub Khan hereafter try to place wrong interpretations upon secret agreement that he was clearly & distinctly told that the India Government's position & implicitly declined to give him any promise or assurance in regard to Ameership.

On the 2nd January 1888 Nicolson was able to report to Lord Salisbury that 'General Maclean has reported to me by telegraph that Sirdar Ayoub Khan has agreed to the Government of India's conditions' and was about to leave for India.[25] Salisbury replied that he proposed 'with the concurrence of Viscount Cross, to instruct Mr Nicolson to inform General Maclean that HM's Government highly appreciates the valuable services which he has rendered in this matter, and the skill with which he has conducted the negotiations'.[26]

* * *

Although Maclean was forbidden to become involved in any Afghan dialogue with the Russians, such a ban did not extend to Perso-Afghan relations and both countries' rulers found his services increasingly useful. The boundary between the two states was a cause of potential conflict. For instance both rulers claimed the district Hashtadan, near Herat. The Afghans said it belonged to them by 'ancient pasturage rights'[27] and in 1885 the Amir claimed to have a 'deed of grant of Hashtadan', but who had made it was not known.[28] The Persians complained that soldiers from Herat persecuted their people and the disagreement had reached a stage where it could have come to war. Neither the Shah, nor the Amir, wanted this to happen and it was agreed that the British should appoint an arbiter to recommend where the border should run. It says much for his reputation with both sides that Maclean was chosen.[29]

Complaints, however, continued. On 17th December 1887 it was reported that the Governor of Herat had to write to Maclean to say:

> There is no truth, as alleged by Persian officials, that some of the Herat people were cultivating and digging a canal at Hashtadan. On the other hand the Persians have brought their flocks to Hashtadan and dug wells there. He complains that Persian sowars had ridden to Tirkisht and had entered the Ghurian district and filled up the wells of the Karez: if such things occur again it will certainly lead to a quarrel.[30]

Maclean went to investigate and reported that:

> he had visited Hashtadan and found about 100 flocks of sheep grazing the lands belonging to Hashtadan all these belonged to Persians with the exception of 15 which belonged to Afghans. The Kazez called Tirkisht, about two forsakhs from Hashtadan towards Herat, has been used by Herati herdsmen for the irrigation of their land and for its cultivation during the last 2 years, and they claim it is their own property. Several Persian officials rode to Tirkisht and ordered the Herati herdsmen to clear out. They however refused and replied that they would only do so if compelled by force.[31]

* * *

Until Russia advanced into Turcomanistan, Persia had been a low priority for the Foreign Office, and after the minister was withdrawn in 1885 the legation had been run, as we have seen, by the chargé d'affaires, Arthur Nicolson. He had performed his duties assiduously, but he was a junior diplomat and lacked the necessary prestige to influence the court in Teheran. He was well aware of his limitations and recommended that a man of standing should be appointed as minister.

The man chosen, Sir Henry Drummond Wolff, MP (1830–1908),[32] was certainly a heavy weight diplomat and politician, who had enormous experience of the intricacies of an oriental court. He was also an ally of Salisbury's rival Randolph Churchill and the Prime Minister had good reasons to want Wolff out of the country.

In Salisbury's brief to Wolff he pointed out that it had been HM's Governments object to prevent the Russians from occupying Merv. However, the failure of that policy and 'the settlement of the north-western frontier of Afghanistan' had greatly changed the situation. If Russia were now to acquire territory in Khorassan, Salisbury wrote, the security of Herat would be at risk. In addition, as the Intelligence Department at the War Office had pointed out, the construction of Russian railways in Khorassan could be a disaster for the defence of India:

> Khorassan is not only the base from which serious operations against India will be undertaken, if ever they should be attempted, but its possession is essential to Russia even for operations in western Afghanistan. This is clearly set down in important Russian secret official publications.

> Even if we admit that sooner or later Khorassan must become a Russian province, and that Herat and Northern Afghanistan must fall to Russia, it is desirable to postpone the evil day as long as possible. Nothing would so hasten its arrival as the construction of such railways as here contemplated, and nothing would so greatly add to Russia's power for still further advance.

He went on to stress that:

> the matter is one which should be closely and carefully watched. It has not been lost sight of by the War Office... of the importance of settling the frontier between Persia and Afghanistan... It was agreed last summer by the two parties that the question should be investigated and decided by Brigadier-General Maclean, an officer of the Government of India, who is stationed on the Perso-Afghan border for purposes of observation, and for the settlement of any matters which may arise between the Persian and Afghan officials. It does not appear that the inquiry has yet taken place. Should the dispute be settled fairly to the satisfaction of both parties, which, perhaps, is too sanguine an expectation, an opportunity might be afforded to propose a definition of the whole frontier. But the question is one of much delicacy...[33]

* * *

Drummond Wolff's appointment, and the opening up of the Karun River at the head of the Persian Gulf to international trade, raised the temperature in the war of words between Great Britain and Russia. St Petersburg had for some time been demanding that she be allowed to establish a consulate in the holy city of Meshed. The Shah had in the past always refused but now, as a sop to the Russians, he gave in. However, he proposed the Britain should have one too in order that the 'Russian flag would not fly alone',[34] and 1st February 1889 Maclean was appointed Her Majesty's Consul General for the Province of Khorassan and Seistan. He was instructed to reside in Meshed.[35]

The Seistan basin, on the Perso-Afghan border, commanded the western entrance to the Helmand valley, one of the routes into India. It had from time to time been ruled by Persia, but in the nineteenth century the Shah's authority was only vaguely felt in the area and much of it was either quasi-independent or under Afghan rule. Seistan's potential was not limited to its command of one of the gates to India, but it had never really recovered from Tamerlane's devastation and in the nineteenth century it barely supported 100,000 people.[36]

On 4th March 1889 General Maclean arrived at Meshed from Teheran. ERC Thomson, the Vice Consul, described his arrival:

> His Public Entry, as Her Britannic Majesty's Consul-General, took place on the 11th March 1889. At 9 A.M... the Union Jack was hoisted, for the first time, in the garden of the Consulate-General, a suitable flagstaff not having been procured sooner.
> At 1.30 P.M. General MacLean in plain clothes and accompanied only by a couple of servants, rode, by the Ark Gate, to the suburbs, where a tent and a marquee had been erected by the authorities. Shortly afterwards Nawab Hassan Ali Khan, accompanied by about fifty British subjects, (or rather persons claiming British protection), all mounted, passed by the Eed Gate to the same spot.
> On arrival at the tents, General MacLean entered the smaller one, and dressed himself in full uniform. The Persian Officials and the British-subjects meantime assembled in the marquee.

The following is the list of the Istkbals sent to receive the Consul-general:

On the part of the Prince Governor.

Sartif Muhammad Jaffar Khan, (in full uniform)
One Mastaufi
Two Munshis[37]
One Yuzbashi, & ten Ghulams
One Major of Artillery & four mounted orderlies
One Major of Infantry & four orderlies
One Led horse, with gold trappings
One Naib of the stables
One Jilandar
One riding horse with English saddle & gold trappings
Ferashes.

On the part of the Foreign Agent

Mirza Hussein Khan, Sarhang, Naib Karguzar (Deputy Foreign Agent)
One Munshi
One Ferash Bashi & ten Ferashes
One Led horse
One Jilander
At the gate One Naib and Ferashes

On the part of the Beglar Begi (Mayor)

Muhhammad Sadik Beg, Kālā Begi
One Darogha
Two Ked Khudas
One Led horse

General MacLean was received in the marquee by the Sartip and the leading officials above mentioned. It had evidently been arranged that, if possible, the Consul-General should advance alone to where the Istikbal was seated, at the other end of the marquee. The trick, however, failed for General MacLean remained at the entrance, enquiring for the people who had been sent to receive him. At the same time the Nawab, in a loud tone, enquired of the Sartip what he was doing. Thus humbled, he hastily advanced and led the Consul-General to the centre of a semi-circle of chairs. He, and the Persians, seated themselves on the right, and the British officers, on the left of the Consul-General. After sherbet had been handed round, General MacLean proposed to start, and the procession entered the town, something in the following order:

Ferashes
Ghulams
A Led horse

'The Great Game'

A Duffadar of the corps of guides and two sowars in uniform, with arms and accoutrements
Ferashes
The Consul-General on a horse with gold trappings
The Sartip
The British officers
The Deputy Karguzar and other members of the Istikbal
British subjects

Along the whole route crowds of people lined the roads and housetops, and gazed, in silent wonderment, at the novel spectacle. Very few of them, apparently, realized that this procession had thrown open the gates of their holy-city to the wide world, and that henceforth they were to be civilized in spite of themselves. It is understood that the religious classes protested against both the appointments of the Consul-General and the hoisting of the flags within the holy city. But apparently they have realized now that neither can be prevented, and are silently acquiescing. Some of them understood that the English are the only check on the Power now hovering on their frontiers.

The Jews were especially conspicuous on the housetops. Since the general massacre of their sect, in Meshed, fifty years ago, they have been compelled to profess the Muhammadan faith, while secretly performing the rites of their own.

On reaching the Consulate-General the Istikbal partook of tea, sweetmeats, and pipes and then departed. Next day the Karguzar (Foreign Office Agent) paid an official visit to General MacLean, and on the 14th March the latter visited the Prince Governor.

On 21st March, in his own hand, the General added a *note*:

Mr Thomson went out to see the procession, and wrote the above account, which I now send as it may prove useful for future reference.[38]

Maclean was in his element, probably revelling in his importance and enjoying every moment, particularly when he got one over on the Russians. On 30th March in a private letter to Wolff he wrote:

My dear Sir Henry Wolff,

Since I last wrote, the Russian Consul-General has arrived. His reception by the Persians was similar in almost every respect to mine. He has not yet hoisted his flag, but I believe he will do so today. The house he has secured does not please him, but he cannot get a better. There are only two houses in Meshed that would suit him, but both are occupied ... The Consul-General's escort consists of only 4 Cossacks and 4 Turkomans. At first 50 Cossacks were told off to accompany him, but he contented himself with the smaller number on the grounds that if 4 are not sufficient neither would 50 be. It follows that if he at any time thinks himself in danger he will summon help from Ashkabad.

My flag attracted no notice at first, apparently but within the last few days the religious school and some fanatical mullahs have been talking about pulling it down, and also that of the Russians when it is put up. The chief Muftahid whose advice they asked has dissuaded them from making the attempt. This man is a well wisher of ours, and in secret communication with us and I think his influence together with that of the other muftahids and of the Prince Governor will prevent any attack taking place.

I sent the Nawab to the Muftahid to say that I had heard reports of the students intention . . . anything of the sort would in all probability lead to an immediate Russian occupation of Meshed. He agreed and said he had & would use his influence to keep things quiet. He approves of the British flag, and looks upon it as hoisted for the good of Persia . . .

Maclean continued to report Russian troop movements and rumours from the bazaar. He says that 'the Meshed people are convinced that the Russians have designs on Afghanistan and I am constantly asked what we are going to do'. Maclean saw it as his rôle to kill such speculation and writes that: 'I always tell my Persian friends that our Government knows everything and will do what is proper if occasion arises'.

* * *

In 1889 the Shah planned to make a trip to Europe, his third and last. Maclean was also due to go home on leave. As the ownership of Hashtadan had not been resolved by the time of the Shah's visit to the United Kingdom, the General was summoned to Brighton to brief the Shah. In his report written on 1st August 1889 at his home in St Andrews Maclean writes:

On Sunday afternoon (28th July) the Shah sent for me.

On being shown into the room His Majesty caused all other persons to go out, and carefully examined the map [of Hashtadan, which Maclean had brought with him]. He said that he desired me to speak to him, not as the Shah, but as if he were an ordinary individual. He asked me to mark distinctly in red the direction of the line of frontier, as suggested by the proposals for a compromise. This I did. He then asked me to point out the provinces of Herat, Kháf, Bakharz, and Jám. When this was done he suddenly asked me to whom Hashtadun belonged. I replied that that this was the very point under dispute. He then pressed me to give him my own opinion on the subject, which he said he would keep quite secret. I said that as far as I could judge Persia had lost Hastadan when Ahmad Shah conquered Eastern Khorassan, and there is nothing to show that she has regained it since.

On the other hand, although the Afghans do not appear to have occupied the valley for about 50 or 60 years, they have always opposed its attempted occupation by Persia. I pointed out that for at least a generation it had been a rendezvous of Turcoman raiders, which His Majesty admitted.

He then asked on what principles the basis for a compromise rested. I replied that it rested on a division of the old water canals (kanats), of which the northern and southern (sic? central) groups would fall to Persia, the southern to Afghanistan. The Persians would then be able, if so inclined, to apply their share of the water, after cleaning out the kanats, to the irrigation of old cultivated lands falling to them, while the Afghans would have the water for the irrigation of the Kafir Kala and Darband lands, below the Darband defile. The professed wishes of both parties would then be met. He then said that the map I had did not show the relative position of Hashtadan with regard to the neighbouring Afghan and Persian districts with sufficient clearness, and that I must provide myself with another map which I should show him at Teheran, ten days after his return there. He said that I must not go to Mashad before coming to Teheran... He said that he looked upon the Afghans as nothing, and were it not for the feelings of friendship he entertained towards the English Government, he would give them nothing...[39]

Maclean's return from leave coincided with the visit of the precocious Conservative Member of Parliament George Nathaniel Curzon. In the autumn of 1889, as the correspondent of *The Times*, Curzon went to Persia. He was highly critical of Maclean's accommodation in Meshed. In one of his letters to *The Times* he writes:

> It is to be regretted that so far the British Government has not been able to house its representative in a suitably becoming fashion... the building which now bears the insignia of the British Consulate and flies the British flag, is one that affords the scantiest possible evidence of the rank and importance of its inmate. It is little short of discreditable that the British Consul General should be compelled to reside in such attenuated and miserable surroundings... General Maclean, the capable representative of Great Britain in Khorassan contemplated at first the purchase of a well-wooded and well-watered garden nearly thirty acres in extent, outside the walls of the city... The staff of the Consulate-General, when fully organised, will consist of the Consul-General, his assistant, and a Vice-Consul. A private guard is provided by two sergeants and three privates of the Indian Corps of Guides, whose picturesque uniforms and smart appearance create a favourable impression, while a native guard of one sergeant and six men is furnished by the Persian Government. Attached to the British Consulate is also a body of 22 Turkoman *sowars*, mainly Sarcks of Penjdeh... who are now employed upon a private postal service between Meshed and Herat, where their post enters into correspondence with that of the Amir of Afghanistan... Both the Russian and British Governments have several hundred subjects residing in and passing through Meshed for trading purposes...[40]

It is probable that Curzon is echoing Maclean's complaints about his accommodation in Meshed. If so he was not to have to endure it for much longer for in 1891 he left Persia and retired from the army. He had been a local Major-General in Meshed, but he now reverted to his substantitive rank of Lieutenant-Colonel, although he continued, as was usual, to call himself Major-General CS Maclean.

Notes

1. *The Great Game*, 406.
2. *Persia and the Defence of India*, 74; *The Great Game*, 42.
3. *The Great Game*, 403.
4. http://www.thebritishmuseum.ac.uk/ane/anereexmerv.html
5. *Salisbury*, 293.
6. *The Great Game*, 438.
7. *Persia and the Defence of India*, 31.
8. 18 December 1882 Foreign Office memorandum [FO 65/1153].
9. He was said in 1879 to know more about Afghanistan than 'any officer available in India... from his personal experience in Afghanistan and from a close study of our connection and dealing with the country from 1840 to the present time' [BL/L/MIL/7/5675, 21].

10. *The Great Game*, 418–433.
11. *Salisbury*, 340.
12. *The Defence of India* (Simla, 1884).
13. BL. L/MIL/61/636.
14. TNA. FO 248/450.
15. *Salisbury*, 342.
16. *The Great Game*, 432.
17. TNA. FO 248/450. October 1887.
18. *The Great Game*, 411.
19. TNA. FO 248/450. January 1887.
20. TNA. FO 65/1377. No. 123 of 1887.
21. TNA. FO 248/477. Tel. No. 185 sent to Maclean 27 Sep, 1887.
22. Yakub Khan, the Regent appointed by Sher Ali, who was Amir when Cavagnari was murdered. That Ayub Khan was to have the same treatment in India as Yakub Khan is highly significant.
23. TNA. FO 248. Simla. 1 November 1887.
24. Arthur Nicolson, later Lord Carnock, in charge of the Legation in 1886 and 1887 [*Persia and the Defence of India*, 87].
25. TNA. FO 248. 7. Teheran 2 January 1888. Nicolson to Salisbury.
26. TNA. FO 248. 68. FO 10 January 1888.
27. TNA. FO. 60/491. 29 February 1888. Marquess of Salisbury to Sir Henry Drummond Wolff. No. 14, Very Confidential. From TNA. FO 60/491 quoted in *The Defence of India*, 256–268.
28. TNA. FO 248. 450. 18 January 1885. Tel. From Viceroy.
29. TNA. FO 248. 450. 25 February 1887. Tel. From Viceroy.
30. TNA. FO 248. 450. 167. Military News. 17th December 1887. Governor of Herat to General Maclean.
31. TNA. FO 248. 450. 167. 18th December 1887. Mirza Ali Jan to General Maclean.
32. Oxford Dictionary of National Biography (2004), Vol. 59, 974.
33. 29 February 1888. The Marquess of Salisbury to Sir Henry Drummond Wolff.
34. *Persia and the Defence of India*, 171.
35. TNA. FO 60/505, 202.
36. *Persia and the Defence of India*, 17 & 18.
37. Secretary or language-teacher in India [Urdu].
38. TNA. FO 60/500.
39. BL/IOR/L/P&S/18/C61.
40. George N Curzon *Persia and the Persian Question* (1966), 171–3.

Chapter Sixty-One

The Northwest-Frontier

Whilst Major-General CS Maclean was serving in Persia his eldest son Hector Lachlan Stewart Maclean, who had been born in a tent at Sheikh Budin on the North-West Frontier of India,[1] was at the Royal Military College Sandhurst. On 24th April 1889 he was commissioned into the Northumberland Fusiliers. He joined them at Rawal Pindi but was not to serve with them for long. On 17th February 1891 he became a probationer for the Indian Staff Corps and was attached to the Guides, the regiment his father had served in during the Indian Mutiny at the siege of Delhi.

The Guides were then taking part in the Hazara Campaign of 1891. Once that expedition was over Hector Lachlan accompanied them to their headquarters at Mardán where he obtained a permanent commission as a Wing Officer. He was thus following the current fashion of serving in his father's old regiment. In August 1892 he became a Squadron Officer in the Guides Cavalry. In 1895 he served with them on the Chitral Relief Expedition.[2]

* * *

In the 1890s the Russian threat to India had not lessened but had shifted from Persia to the High Pamirs. Both the Russians and the British sent in officers to examine the remote and virtually unknown passes through the mountains, which separated Afghanistan, China, Russian Central Asia and British India. However, the Russians did so in strength and expelled the British officers.[3]

By August 1891 the Russians were claiming territory right down to the Indian watershed. Their claim included the independent state of Chitral, which received subsidies from and was under the protection of the Government of India. However, the death of its aged ruler now plunged Chitral, which was sandwiched between Afghanistan and Kashmir, into anarchy. Successive rulers were rapidly deposed and the final straw came when it was learnt that the Chitrali Amir's southern neighbour Umra Khan of Swat was preparing to advance into Chitral and annexe his turbulent northern neighbour's territory.

If Russia had now decided to march into Chitral little could have prevented her from doing so. To forestall such a situation a small British force in Gilgit rushed north and occupied the royal palace, which the expedition's commander saw as the best place to withstand a siege. His thinking may have been correct, but in doing so he united Umra Khan and the Chitralis against him. The siege began in earnest.

Meanwhile two British expeditionary forces were hurrying north to relieve Chitral. Colonel James Kelly in Gilgit commanded one, which was 1300 strong. Major-General Sir Robert Low from Peshawar led the other. It was made up of 15,000 men. On the 3rd April 1895 the main force stormed the 3,500 foot Malakand Pass leading into Swat. It was held by 12,000 of Umra

Khan's Pathan warriors. But they were no match for Low's men and were forced to flee. Two days later a squadron of Guides Cavalry destroyed 2,000 of the enemy and on 13th April their infantry battalion eliminated an even stronger body of Pathans killing 600 of them.

The Swatis prepared to defend Munda but when they too realised just how formidable the army coming against them was, they abandoned their capital. The 10,000 foot high snow-filled Lowarai Pass was now all that remained between Low and his objective. Low's army was, however, still struggling over the pass, when the much smaller body from Gilgit reached Chitral, only to discover that the besiegers had abandoned the siege.

The British Government annexed Chitral and the frontier between the Russian and British Empires, after a century of intrigue, was at long last settled. The Russians had, however, got most of what they wanted and were in a strong position to invade India if ever war broke out between the two empires.[4]

* * *

Meanwhile, whilst Hector LS Maclean was with the main expedition sent to relieve Chitral, his somewhat older third-cousin, 'Willie' Alexander WD Maclean, was stationed at Castlebar in County Mayo. As we have seen, in 1873 the Depot of the 94th Foot had moved to Armagh and the regiment had become Irish. The 1881 army reforms reinforced this decision: the Infantry were now to be organized into 'Territorial Regiments of Four Battalions' of which the 1st and 2nd were to be Regulars and the 3rd and 4th Militia. All were to bear a Territorial Designation in common, corresponding with the localities with which they were connected.[5] The 94th became 2nd Battalion of the Connaught Rangers.

In 1887 Willie was serving with the 2nd Battalion and at the Aldershot Army Athletics Meeting was in the winning officers' tug of war team. In July 1889 he married Rose Eaden Abinger, daughter of Admiral William Fenwick. She accompanied him to Malta and on 4th February 1891 was present at a ball at which the officers of the Malta garrison entertained HRH the Duke of Cambridge. The centre-piece in HRH's supper room at the ball was made up of relics of the 94th campaigns in South Africa, including the ragged remains of the colours saved by Lieutenant Egerton, when the Regiments's headquarters was massacred by the Boers.[6]

The symbolic importance of the colours to a regiment cannot be over-emphasised. They were the regiment's rallying point in battle; they represented those members of the regiment who had died in past battles. On them were emblazoned the regiment's battle honours. For the 94th they included Seringpatam, Badajoz. Vittoria and Orthez.

Willie spent much of his service in Ireland and in 1892 he became Adjutant of 3rd Connaught Rangers. It was an amalgamation of the 3rd South Mayo and 6th North Mayo Militia. He and his wife set up house together in J Block in the Barracks at Castlebar. Their life comes alive in the scrapbook they kept from 1894.[7] For example on 2nd June 1894 the *Mayo Examiner* had a piece on the training of recruits which, as the senior regular officer in the 3rd Battalion, was one Willie's responsibilities:

> General the Hon. WHA Feilding, the Inspector-General of Recruiting for the Army, inspected the recruits 3rd Battalion Connaught Rangers at the barracks on 31st May last. The men were drawn up in column of companies, under Major Maclean, each man a pace and a-half apart, thus giving the General every facility to thoroughly examine each man. The men presented the same clean and smart appearance as they usually do, and the Inspector-General was pleased to

express himself as thoroughly satisfied with all that he saw, and specially remarked out the fine physique of the recruits; and it is only fair to add here the men are a credit to all concerned, especially so on account of their good behaviour, there being an entire absence of crime amongst them.

The piece ended with the announcement that: 'An entertainment will be held in the Long Room Military Barracks, on Friday next, the 8th inst., consisting of singing, readings &c.'

Another of the Major's responsibilities was not only to entertain the troops but to take part in the affairs of the local community. Both he and his wife entered into the spirit of amateur dramatics with enthusiasm. Their efforts received glowing reports in the local press. For example on 15th January 1895 the *Chronicle* announced:

On the evenings of Tuesday and Wednesday next a very attractive entertainment will come off at the Courthouse, Castlebar, in aid of the Soldiers and Sailor Families Association. The entertainment will commence with a Christy Minstrel performance by Major MacLean's Minstrels, followed by an original sketch in dumb show 'A Lesson in Photography'. The second part will consist of a screaming farce, entitled Incompatibility of Temper. Judging by the well-known abilities of the performers, whose names appear in the programme, and the success which invariably attends Major MacLean's efforts, we may predict most enjoyable evenings for those who can attend.

Athough they were to spend five years in the far west of Ireland, the Connaught Ranger Macleans were not completely cut off entirely from British metropolitan society. For instance Willie attended a Levee in London, when on 21st February 1893 he presented his younger brother HDN Maclean, who had recently been commissioned into the King's Own Scottish Borderers, to the Prince of Wales. The Adjutant-General later presented Willie after he was promoted to the Queen at Buckingham Palace on 9th March 1895. On this occasion the Marchioness of Tweedale presented Rose Maclean to the Queen. *The Court Journal* gave a detailed description of her dress:

Gown of rich duchess satin in a pale shade of salmon pink, petticoat draped with handsome flounce of old point de Venise lace; corsage covered with lace and clusters of orchids and lilac; train of exquisite white brocade with raised designs lined with pink satin, with lace falling from each shoulder and fastened with same flowers on the train. Ornaments, pearls and diamonds.

These occasions helped to integrate an officer in the army into the British upper classes.

The brothers AWD and HDN Maclean's financial situation seems to have been very different from that of their father when he was a junior officer. Life in the army in the 1890s was expensive and officers had to have a private income, except in India. For instance when Lieutenant HDN Maclean[8] was Rawalpindi in June 1896 he wrote to his mother over his overdraft at his bank to say:

I wish I knew how I stand a[t] Cox's. You had better put a hundred there for me or better still get him to let you know direct for I am overdrawn & tell him you will put a hundred there if necessary.

He also asks her to 'let me have a book with all my investments put down & when paid in &c I should feel more secure against Cox's carelessness'. It is highly unlikely that his father had any investments when he joined the 94th and it was presumably money that HDN Maclean (or Neil as he was known in the family) had inherited from his maternal grandfather that enabled him to play polo, go pig-sticking and take part in the other activities that passed an officer's time when his battalion was on garrison duties in India.

* * *

Neil's choice of regiment: the King's Own Scottish Borderers rather than the Connaught Rangers suggests that he rejected the Irish connection and wished to renew his family's Scottish origins. The Earl of Leven had in 1689 raised the regiment that was to become the KOSB to defend Edinburgh against 'Bonnie Dundee' and the Jacobites. Dundee's army, as we have seen, included a company of Macleans of Coll's men and the Regiment and Neil's ancestors were on opposite sides of the political divide that split Scotland into two opposing camps in the late seventeenth and early eighteenth centuries. The Regiment returned to Scotland to oppose the Jacobites in both the '15 and '45.

Leven's Regiment remained on the permanent establishment of the British Army. Although it was for many years considered to be the Edinburgh Regiment, it was never officially named as such in the Army List. Instead it was known by the names of its colonels and took its place as the 25th Regiment of Foot to be raised since the Restoration.

Soon after it was raised, in memory of its origin, the Regiment was granted the privilege of marching through the streets of Edinburgh with colours flying and drums beating without having to ask the permission of the Provost.

The Regiment took its share in the wars of the eighteenth century and earned particular fame in 1759 as one of the British infantry who defeated the French cavalry at the battle of Minden. In 1782 in order to stimulate recruiting the War Office announced a scheme whereby the names of English counties were conferred on infantry regiments. Scottish regiments were not affected. However, by chance at the time a recruiting party of the 25th was in Edinburgh and was prevented by the magistrates from exercising its old privilege of beating for recruits without their permission.

The Colonel of the Regiment in 1782 was Lord Lennox, the Duke of Richmond's younger brother whose family seat was at Goodwood in Sussex. Lennox was so furious at the insult to his regiment that he asked George III to make Sussex the designation of the Regiment. The King agreed and during Lennox's lifetime the 25th was the *25th (Sussex) Regiment of Foot*. Lennox died in 1805, and the same year, at the command of King George III, the Regiment became the 25th King's Own Borderers. In 1832 William IV permitted it to bear on its colours the arms and motto of the City of Edinburgh.

Until the Cardwell reforms in 1873 all regiments of the line were itinerant. Regiments had no regimental home and no regimental recruiting area and when the regiment was overseas there was no system for providing replacements on a geographical basis. The 25th Foot's only point of contact with Scotland was the memory of its origin in Edinburgh. It was a tradition that the 25th held to with tenacity.

Whilst a regiment was overseas, depot companies were left at home usually in Scotland or Ireland. It was in 1829 when the Regiment was in the West Indies that Major Courtenay Chambers, the officer commanding the depot companies, used his initiative to recover the 25th Foot's ancient privileges.

He appealed to the Lord Provost of Edinburgh who replied:

Sir, I this day read your note to me of 11th current to the Magistrates and Council; and I was authorized to inform you, that so far as they can restore the privileges of the 25th Regiment, they are most happy to do so; and therefore your men may beat up for recruits through all streets any day of the year, Sunday of course excepted. The Magistrates and Council hope also that your Regiment may soon be restored to its primitive name and honours; and if they can in any way aid you to obtain them, it will afford them much pleasure.

It is clear from this letter that the name they wished restored was that of *The Edinburgh Regiment*. It was not to be. In 1873 when Cardwell began his reforms his aim was to weld together the regular army and the reserve. The system of two-battalion regiments was introduced: one battalion was to serve at home and the other overseas. Single battalion regiments such as the 94th were paired with the 88th to become the Connaught Rangers and lost its Scottish identity. The 25th were more fortunate as since 1855 they already had a second battalion. However, each regiment was to have a permanent depot in its regimental district where it was to be brigaded with reserve battalions. In his wisdom the Secretary of State decreed that the 25th Regiment of Foot's depot should be at York and the Yorkshire militia should become its reserve battalions. It was further proposed that the Regiment should be named *The York Regiment (King's Own Borderers)*.

A furious campaign in Scotland followed and the War Office was persuaded to move the depot to Berwick-upon-Tweed, which became Headquarters of the 25th Regimental District. Eventually the 25th Regiment was linked to the Scottish Borderers Militia, which incorporated the Border counties of Dumfriesshire, Selkirk and Roxburgh, with Berwickshire and Kirkudbright and later Wigtownshire. The original 'Borderers' of the title granted by George III had probably been that between the Highlands and Lowlands rather than between England and Scotland. This fact was tactfully forgotten and although Edinburgh Castle remained the major theme of the Regiment's cap badge Edinburgh became the domain of the Royal Scots.

It was not to be until 1887 that the Regiment finally became the King's Own Scottish Borderers.

* * *

Although the Russian threat to India had diminished, everything was not quiet on the North-West frontier. In 1897 the Frontier tribesmen were everywhere in arms and it was necessary to mount four major and two minor punitive expeditions against the Pathans. In the Swat Valley the clans were roused by a fanatical preacher known to the British as the 'Mad Fakir'[9], whose followers on 26th July began their revolt with an attack on the British detachment on the road to Chitral at the summit of the Malakand Pass. They also attacked the little fort of Chakdara, described by Winston Churchill as being 'peeked up on a rock like a miniature Gibraltar'. It defended the long swinging bridge across the Swat River.[10]

Immediately after the attack the Corps of Guides received orders to reinforce the Malakand Pass. Both the Guides infantry and cavalry did so by a forced march. In the action that followed Lieutenant Hector LS Maclean was badly wounded, having been shot through the cheek. The bullet came out behind his ear but miraculously did not damage the bone. He continued fighting until he fainted through loss of blood. The tribesman who shot him did so at point blank range 'as his face was blackened with the powder of the discharge'.

Maclean was taken to hospital, however the wound was not considered sufficiently serious to detain him. His regiment was now in the Swat Valley and it was anticipated that they would soon again be in action. And although his wound had not yet healed, Hector hurried forward to join them.

On 17th August at Landakai the Guides were once more in action. In a letter dated 22nd August 1897 from the Guides' Cavalry Camp, Mingárra, Swat Valley Lieutenant-Colonel RB Adams, Commanding Officer of the Queen's Own Corps of Guides wrote to Mrs CS Maclean:

The enemy held a long spur, round the end of which the road we had to go passed along a narrow, stony causeway between the spur and the river. As soon as the enemy were cleared off the hill the cavalry started to go round by this road. Some dismounted men, with whom your son went, led the way to clear away obstacles in the shape of stone walls placed by the enemy to block the road. I also accompanied them. Your son led the way and was full of spirits, and eager to get on in pursuit of the enemy, whom we could see running away over the plain in the valley beyond. As the road was cleared the mounted men followed in single file; and the first party to reach the open ground beyond formed up and galloped in pursuit. Your son's horse was being led some way behind and he was, therefore, somewhat delayed by having to find it. Our course to reach the enemy lay for a certain distance along a nullah[11] up past a village and over an open plain of soft, ploughed up ground. In crossing this the leading squadron became very much scattered, most of the men falling behind, as their horses were unable to keep up with those of the officers.

Most of the enemy had reached another spur before the Guides could catch them, and they opened 'a very hot fire on all of us as we approached'. Colonel Adams continues:

What we should have done and what I intended to do, was collect the scattered men behind the nearest available cover, and with the dismounted men, to open fire. Unfortunately, at this moment Lieutenant Greaves, who was out with us as a press correspondent, was runaway with by his pony, and carried up to the foot of the spur amongst the enemy, one of whom shot him, and on his falling from his horse, others proceeded to hack at him with their swords. Several of us who were nearest at once rushed to his rescue. Immediately as this happened your son arrived – with Lieut. Norman 11th Bengal Lancers, who was attached to us – at the corner of the village, where I had thought of dismounting the men. He at once said to Norman 'we must get some men together' and collecting about a dozen or so, who arrived at the same time, he brought them into the nearest point of cover left to them, under the orders of Norman, to open fire on the enemy. He himself came out into the open in front at once, where we were struggling to get poor Greave's body on to a horse, in order to carry it away. As he approached us he dismounted, and said 'Here, put him on my horse', and he himself assisted largely in lifting the body and placing it across the saddle.

We had all started to return with the body to the nearest cover, and had carried it about fifteen yards, when your son exclaimed that he had been hit in the thigh. He was unable to mount his horse, and so two of our men, who had come out after him, and were alongside him at the moment each seized his arm, and brought him along in that way for about twenty or thirty yards to the corner of the wooded graveyard, where he had placed the dismounted men, and which was the nearest point of cover. He then sunk unconscious and had to be lifted up and carried in front of three men on their saddles, back to where Dr McNab was... Dr McNab could do nothing to save him; and without recovering consciousness, he very shortly afterwards expired. But for his action in placing those dismounted men in the graveyard, whence their fire checked the enemy, the small party round Lieutenant Greaves' body would most certainly have been rushed; and but for his coming out so readily to our assistance, we should have had great difficulty in lifting and carrying away Lieutenant Greaves and Norman would have been so much longer delayed under the hot fire the enemy were pouring down upon us from the hill close by, when every additional minute increased the risk of further loss.

Adams received the Victoria Cross for his gallantry in attempting to save Greaves. Lord Fincastle, Sir Bindon Blood's Aide-de-Camps, who also took part in the rescue attempt, did so as well. In a letter he wrote to Mrs CS Maclean Fincastle says that:

We managed to get hold of Greaves but I think would certainly have been rushed if your son had not come out with three sowars to our assistance. We owe our lives to his coolness, as he first dismounted his squadron in a [?] of trees some fifty yards away who by their fire gave us something to retreat to, beside keeping the tribesmen from rushing us... Most of our horses were shot – all except one were wounded or killed and the fire was so hot, so your son would certainly have got a Victoria Cross. He certainly deserved one for saving the whole situation and I hope he will get one as a tribute to his memory.[12]

Hector Maclean's body was carried to the Guides' headquaters at Mardán, where 'most, if not all of the gallant dead of the Guides repose'. He was buried with full military honours.

In 1897 the Victoria Cross could not be awarded posthumously. It was to be almost ten years before the regulations were changed and Hector Maclean was awarded the ultimate British award for gallantry in battle.[13]

* * *

At Rawalpindi in September 1897 the 2nd Battalion The King's Own Scottish Borderers was mobilized as part of the Tirah Field Force. It consisted of a division of two brigades under the command of Lieutenant-General Sir William Lockhart. This was the largest of the expeditions in 1897 against the Pathans. Its aim was to exact reparations on the Afridi and Orakzai tribes for their seizure of forts in the Khyber Pass and other border posts. As no British troops had ever before entered Afridis or Orakzai territory, it was to be a major undertaking.

Of all the Pathan tribes living on the North-West Frontier the Afridis were the most numerous, powerful and possibly the most warlike. They numbered at least 25,000 men and spent their winters in the Bara Valley and around the Khyber Pass. In the summer they moved with their flocks and herds to Tirah. This is the name given to the high open valleys from which rise the two streams, which combine to form the Bara River and those that become the Khonki and Kurmena rivers. It is an area of 6 or 700 square miles. The Afridi were notorious raiders and were said 'to know little and care still less for the tenets and doctrines of the faith' they professed. Captain Shadwell the *Pioneer* and London *Daily News*'s special correspondent with Lockhart's expedition goes on to say that: 'Only when religion forms an excuse for plunder and breach of faith, as it did in 1897, that an Afridi considers himself in some way bound to the Koran'.

It had always been the Afridi's boast that Tirah, which includes valleys and plateau's some 6,000 feet high, had not only never been invaded by a hostile foe, 'but was of so difficult and inaccessible a nature as to practically preclude any operations being undertaken against its inhabitants'.

The Orakzai's country, which lay to the south-west of that of the Afridis was only slightly less remote. They too could muster some 25,000 men, and were believed to pay more attention to religion than did the Afridis. In the past several small expeditions by the British against various sections of the Orakzais had, from time to time, been successfully mounted, but Tirah proper had never been penetrated.[14]

For the British to invade Tirah required them to have a considerable administrative tail.[15] This was not a problem for the Frontier tribesmen, who like the Highlanders of Scotland of old, could live for days on the grain they carried with them. Consequently it was not necessary for the Afridi or Orakzai to protect their lines of communication. They were also 'so nimble of foot' and so 'conversant with every goat track in their mountains that they can retreat in any direction'. This mobility enabled them quite unexpectedly to attack from any direction, and to disperse as quickly as they came. For this reason the rear of a European force was as much exposed to attack at its front or flanks.[16]

Again, like the Highlanders of Scotland, who they resembled in many ways, the Pathans were formidable fighting men. They were never without weapons: 'when grazing their cattle, when driving beasts of burden, when tilling the soil they are still armed'. Like the Highlanders the Frontier tribesmen were perpetually at war with each other. 'Every tribe or section of a tribe has its internecine wars, every family its hereditary blood feuds ...'. How similar his new foes were to his own ancestors is not apparent from Neil Maclean's surviving correspondence. It would, however, be surprising if he did not appreciate the irony of the situation.

* * *

2 KOSB were to be part of 4 Brigade in 2 Division. They left Rawalpindi in two trains on 6th October 1897 and the following morning reached Khosagarh, the railhead on the Indus River. They then marched to Kohat and arrived there on the morning of the 9th October. They were then joined there by their commanding officer Lieutenant-Colonel Dixon CB, who resumed command of the battalion, having just returned from leave in the United Kingdom.[17]

The Tirah Field Force continued its march up country for a further 45 miles. Its objective was now Shinawari, which was still in British India and was to be the base camp for the expedition. The plan was to march north into tribal territory. 4 Brigade was to move through the Chagru Kotal[18], a 5,500 foot high pass to the north-east of Shinawari, whilst 3 Brigade was to attack the enemy's flank and rear west of the Shinawari-Chagru Kotal road. This last movement required the brigade to carry out a long circuitous march over exceedingly steep and difficult country.[19]

Brigadier-General Westmacott left Shinawari Camp with 4 Brigade at 5 am on 18th October. He headed north for the Dargai heights. This feature was another 1,000 feet higher than the Chagru Kotal. It dominated the pass and had to be seized. Captain LJ Shadwell, who was with 4 Brigade writes:

> The village of Dargai lies on the northern side of a small plateau. The eastern edge of this tableland breaks off, at first in an almost abrupt cliff, but some distance lower down the ground, though very steep, shelves away less precipitously. This slope is thrown out from the bottom of the cliff in the form of a narrow and razor-like spur, with the path or track

lying along its northern side, well within view or range of the cliff-head. But by climbing along the southern side of this spur troops can move from Chagru Kotal ... unseen by the enemy. Connecting the crest of the spur, however, and the foot of the cliff there is a narrow neck or saddle an hundred yards long ... whose sides were far too precipitous to allow any movement along them. Though devoid of all cover and completely exposed to the heights above this ridge had to be crossed so as to reach the path ascending to the summit.[20]

Westmacott ordered his Brigade to make a frontal attack on the heights with the 1st Battalion 3rd Gurkhas leading, 2 KOSB supporting them, and with the Northampton Regiment in reserve. Shadwell who was watching the attack writes lyrically that:

The spectacle of the 3rd Ghoorkhas rushing across the dangerous zone on the ridges and of the KOSB, who had started 800 yards behind them when the attack began, straining every nerve to catch up or even pass them was a stirring sight, and the advance up the cliff side led by Lieutenant Beynon DSO [of the Gurkhas] with a revolver in one hand and a climbing-stick in the other. Was a thing ever to be remembered.

The Gurkhas fixed bayonets and charged, whilst the KOSB gave them covering fire and then scrambled up after them. The enemy did not stop to wait for Lieutenant Beynon's arrival, but abandoned the position. They had seen 3 Brigade's scouts in the distance moving to cut them off and when 4 Brigade reached the summit they were virtually unopposed. Four companies of 2 KOSB under Major Mayne occupied the heights but there was no water for a considerable distance and neither battalion was equipped to hold Dargai. They were therefore ordered to withdraw.

Westmacott has been severely criticised for not holding Dargai. Not only was the withdrawal continuously under fire from the tribesmen who rushed back to the high ground when they saw what was happening. But it was necessary to do the whole thing over again two days later.

On the 20th the tribesmen did not make the same mistake that they had made on the 18th and the 2nd/2nd Gurkhas and Gordon Highlanders had 200 casualties retaking the heights. It was on this occasion that Piper Findlater of the Gordons won the Victoria Cross by playing his pipes and cheering on the assailants, although he had been shot through both legs. The Gordon's epic charge captured the imagination of the British public and overshadowed events on the 18th. However, as Captain Shadwell pointed out:

it must be remembered that when the 1st/3rd Ghoorkhas advanced over the ridge to the attack the enemy, for all our troops knew, might be in overwhelming strength, and prepared to stand to the last; and the bravery of 1/3 Ghoorkhas and that of the KOSB who followed them with such eagerness, should not, because their losses were fortunately small, be too much overshadowed by the magnificent courage showed by 2/2 Goorkhas and the Gordon Highlanders and other regiments two days later.[21]

Both Afridi and Orakzai tribesmen are thought to have joined together to defend Dargai and prevent the British from entering their territory. Some 12,000 of them were believed to be in the area. After the seizure of the heights the Orakzai avoided pitched battles and thereafter only harassed the Field Force from a distance.[22]

The advance continued through the Sampagha Pass and into the Mastura River Valley. Shadwell says that:

> We had all heard a good deal of the fertility of Tirah; but I think I may say that, despite this, everyone was astonished at the appearance it presented. Well watered, highly cultivated, comparatively speaking flat and open, with massively-built homesteads surrounded by fruit trees, and with large stacks of fodder in the courtyards or on the mud roofs, and with numerous trees dotting the steep sides of the valley – it seemed like a Garden of Eden in comparison with the barren, inhospitable country which is generally so characteristic of the North-West Frontier.[23]

2 KOSB led the reconnaissance in force out of the Mastura through the Arhanga Pass and into the Maidan Valley. The KOSB were therefore the first battalion into Tirah. This was the summer home of the Afridis and the most fertile and important portion of country in all Afridi Tirah. Shadwell states that it 'had never before been visited, and, as far as I know seen by a single European'.[24] Once they were into the valley the KOSB set up Camp Maidan on a hill at a height of 6,300 feet. No food or blankets reached the camp that night. It was now November and bitterly cold.

Camp Maidan was to be the Task Force's base for the next two weeks. From here they carried out a reconnaissance of the road to Bagh and raided and burnt the villages of the Zakka Khel Afridis. When they retired the tribesmen attacked and one Borderer was wounded. A few days later the Task Force returned to complete the burning of the Zakka Khel villages and the Northampton Regiment suffered heavy casualties.

On 12th November 2 KOSB formed part of a force covering a foraging party north of Camp Maidan and had three men wounded taking a high difficult hill. H Company led the attack supported by G Company, two men of H Company, having their bayonets broken by enemy bullets. Three others had bullets through their clothes or accoutrements.

On the 18th the force began to move camp to Bagh. Half 2 KOSB covered the left flank of the advance and the other half formed the Brigade's advance guard. They were continuously sniped at and one Borderer was killed. On 21st the battalion provided picquets for the move of 3 Brigade from Camp Maidan to Bagh and in the evening as G Company were going out to reinforce the day picquets they were suddenly fired on. One man was killed and two were dangerously wounded.

On the morning of the 22nd November 4 Brigade, less the Northampton Regiment, provided the bulk of an adventurous, but highly successful, reconnaissance in strength down the Sholaba defile to Dwatoi (or two rivers, where the Rajgul and Sholaba streams met to form the Bara River).[25] About two miles out from Camp Bagh the stream entered a extremely narrow gorge and, although the Gurkhas picqueted both sides of it, several tribesmen, who could not be discovered continued to snipe at the column and four KOSB were wounded.

Dwatoi was reached at 4 pm and B and H Companies had to mount two distant picquets in the dark. Once again no blankets or food reached the camp that night, and all ranks, who had been thoroughly soaked by having spent much of the day knee deep in icy water, spent a miserable night.

The rear-guard, which was provided by 36th Sikhs, did not arrive at the camp until 5 pm on the following day. In the meantime the tribesmen had assembled in some force on a hill to the north-east of the camp from which a picquet had been withdrawn and four weak companies of 2 KOSB under Captain Haig were sent to drive them out. This they succeeded in doing, but only after hand-to-hand fighting with the officers using their revolvers.[26]

The following morning at 6 am the force commenced its return to Bagh. The picquets were withdrawn without difficulty, but the rear-guard of 36th Sikhs and C and F Companies of 2 KOSB were closely followed by tribesmen who attacked them at the entrance to the Sholaba defile.

Once they returned to Bagh the Task Force had a few days rest, interrupted by the occasional foraging parties. Then on 4th December the surplus baggage, including the tents were sent back to Shinawari with some of the wounded and an escort of 40 men under the Quartermaster.

The weather was now threatening to close in, and 4 Brigade was ordered to return to Dwatoi. On the 7th they began their move with three companies, who had been picqueting providing the right flank guard. On emerging from the defile into the Bara Valley the KOSB, who now formed the advance guard, were fired on from the hill above Dwatoi, which Captain Haig's men had previously assaulted.

On this occasion Captain Macfarlane led the assault with F Company. The hill was taken to the sound of the pipes, and with the loss of one man wounded. But once the piquet was in position F Company came under constant fire from an enemy position some 300 yards away. During the night the tribesmen, having crept up through the thick scrub, tried to rush the picquet. On three occasions they came sufficiently close to throw stones into the Borderer's sangars.

An officer in F Company wrote:

When it got dark the Afridis began to fire at us, but we didn't reply. Suddenly one of the sentries called out, 'Stand to! They're on us!' We all sprang to our posts and opened fire independently on a mob of men who were charging down with loud shouts. Some of them were within twenty yards. Our fire checked them and they drew off. We could hear groans, and the noise made by bodies being dragged and carried away. One dead man was left within ten yards of our wall.

They now established themselves under cover all round us within very short ranges, fired frequently, shouted abuse in Hindustani, and threw stones, by which several of us were hit. We took no notice, by Captain Macfarlane's orders, but waited to give them the bayonet should they come on.[27]

Two KOSBs were killed in Macfarlane's spirited action.

On 9th December a force of 1000 men, including C and E Companies 2 KOSB, reconnoitred the Rajgul Valley, whilst G Company provided the escort for the mountain battery, which covered the withdrawal. This was the last offensive action of the campaign. General Lockhart's aim to show the tribesmen that there was no safe haven for them anywhere in the whole of Tirah had largely been achieved; 1897 was coming to an end and the Task Force was not equipped for a winter campaign in the mountains. It was therefore decided to withdraw down the Bara Valley and towards Peshawar and re-establish the Task Force's base in the Peshawar Valley.

At its upper end the Bara Valley was wide and the going was easy, for there were many dry rice beds; and though the stream flowed sometimes on one side of the valley and sometimes on the other, occasionally breaking up into several channels, there was nothing to prevent the transport moving on a wide front, fording the stream at various places.[28]

The tribesmen interpreted the withdrawal as a retreat and the Task Force was persistently harassed by tribesmen, mainly those of the Zakka Khel, whose territory included the Bara Valley, and from the morning of the 10th, when the withdrawal began to the evening of the 14th some part of the Task Force was under fire.

On the 10th December the Division left Dwatoi, with 4 Brigade in the lead. That day they reached Sandana. Although they did not encounter too much opposition the column was fired on from both flanks and the Brigade suffered 10 casualties, and one mule belonging to the Maxim Gun Detachment of 2 KOSB was hit.

On 11th December the march was resumed, 2 KOSB forming 4 Brigade's rear-guard. It was heavy going as the transport strayed into wet fields near the riverbed and became bogged. It was also bitterly cold. 2 KOSB's war diary records that some:

Kahars and drabies[29] left their baggage and went to warm themselves at fires they had lighted, and the men of the Battalion had to carry several wounded Sikhs and Gurkhas, who had been deserted by their dhooly-bearers, nearly the whole march.

Captain Shadwell says that:

now began the chief disaster of the march, for animals got bogged in all directions and slipped up in watercourses and could not get out. The drivers in many cases left them and went into houses to get firewood; dhooly bearers put down their dhoolies and did likewise; others broached or found a cask of rum already broached, and got so hopelessly drunk that three of them who came into the camp died from the effects during the night.[30]

Despite these dramatic events, by 5 pm 4 Brigade's rear guard had arrived at Sher-Khel and set up camp. 3 Brigade's advance guard was close on its heels, but it was apparent by 9.30 pm that its rear guard, whose baggage had become entangled in the wet fields, was not going to reach camp that night. It was also reported that the tribesmen had attacked 3 Brigade's rear guard. 2 KOSB was therefore stood to. Eventually only H Company was sent out to assist 3 Brigade. However, it saw no sign of the enemy but about a mile from Sher-Khel it found many camp followers and ponies, which were driven into camp.

As the mist cleared away the following morning and the sun shone out, all the hills round were seen to be covered with snow, down to within a few hundred feet above the level of the camp. Shadwell comments that 'we had not left Maidan a day too soon'[31] or they would have been trapped.

On 12th December 2 KOSB formed part of a force sent back to help 3 Brigade's rear guard into camp. It had spent the night in a village about 2½ miles from camp, and had had a hard days fighting and suffered some 40 casualties. Once they had completed their task the two brigades swapped places and 4 Brigade took over as the Division's rear guard.

The following day saw the heaviest and most continuous fighting of the whole campaign. The tribesmen emboldened by their successes of the previous day had had their appetite whetted by the hope of still more plunder and showed a complete disregard of danger. Even before the baggage had left camp, and while the KOSB and 1st/3rd Gurkhas were loading up, the enemy opened a heavy fire, killing ten of the animals.

By 11 am all the baggage was clear of the camp and the picquets began to withdraw. The tribesmen now increased their fire, and two of the KOSB's picquets were wounded. So accurate was their shooting that, as one of the KOSB came in from picquet and fell wounded, two more bullets struck him as he lay on the ground. One of the jocks was also nearly captured. He had been wounded in a village without being noticed by his colleagues. However, he managed to run in to camp just before the tribesmen entered the village.

From the very start of the withdrawal from Sher-Khel the rear guard was so heavily pressed that some of the KOSB and 1st/3rd Gurkhas ran out of ammunition. About 3½ miles from the camp the path left the river and ran through thick scrub intersected with nullahs.[32] It then continued over a low pass, the Lakarai Kotal. At the point where the road left the riverbed the baggage became blocked and delayed the withdrawal for thirty minutes. The tribesmen kept up their attacks and it was now that 2 KOSB had the worst of their casualties.[33] The tribesmen made a rush across the stream to try to take the baggage, instead they unexpectedly came under cross fire from the KOSB, a machine gun on the one bank and from 1st/3rd Gurkhas on the other. Shadwell says that: 'Many a tribesman threw up his arms in the water and floated down the stream a corpse'.[34]

Once the rear guard started to move on again through the scrub the enemy took advantage of every bush to creep up unseen. As dusk drew on Brigadier-General Westmacott's force was so reduced by casualties, and still more so by the fighting men having to carry their wounded comrades that only 200 Northamptonshire Regiment, 110 KOSB and about 150 each of the RSF, 36th Sikhs and 1st/3rd Gurkhass, and a wing of the 1st Battalion 2nd Gurkhas were left as rear guard.

As it was now getting dark Westmacott decided that if the rear guard went on for another two miles to join the rest of the division they would have even heavier losses. He decided to halt and spend the night on a ridge to the west of the pass. The exhausted troops had just occupied this position, and were beginning to sit down and rest when as Shadwell writes:

> the enemy made a most determined rush. The men were in their places in a moment & a withering fire was poured into the yelling tribesmen, and the troops had again shown that they were invincible. The foe seemed to melt away before this fire, but our troops suffered too; and when the smoke had cleared, it was seen that Lieutenant West, the gallant adjutant of 1st Battalion 3rd Ghoorkhas . . . had fallen dead with a bullet through his head . . . The troops who had thus held the enemy at bay, and had repulsed this last desperate rush with such stern determination, have good cause to be proud of their deeds; for never had the enemy fought with such determination, and never were they more favoured by the ground. Not a mule or a follower was cut off; and though our losses were one officer killed and three wounded, and above 24 men killed and 80 wounded, the enemy had learnt a lesson. When he again followed up and harassed the retreat next day, it was in a very different manner from the day before when caution had been thrown to the winds.[35]

The rest of the night passed quietly.

Relief was in sight. A column had been sent out from Peshawar to meet the Task Force and had set up a firm base at Swaikot. The rear-guard therefore set off from their ridge at the double. They were fired on from the adjoining heights but not with the same intensity as the previous day and at about 5 pm they reached the safety of the camp at Swaikot. The rear guard had been 30 hours without water.

The following day the Chief of Staff of the Tirah Expeditionary Force sent an order to the General Officer Commanding 2nd Division:

> General Sir William Lockhart will be obliged if you will convey to the GOC 4th Brigade his appreciation of the excellent work done by himself, his staff and the troops under his command on the 13th and 14th December, when a very difficult operation was most successfully carried out: Sir William regrets the hardships to which the troops covering the withdrawal from the Bara Valley were exposed, but these were unavoidable.

The Task Force remained across the river from Swaikot until 17th December when 4 Brigade moved higher up the hill to Camp Mamanai. On 29th January 2 KOSB took part in a raid to drive off the Afridi's cattle from the Kajaori plain. This action finally brought the Afridi to heel. By the beginning of April they had paid the fines levied on them.

The campaign was over and on 7th April 1898 the KOSB returned to India. The Task Force had achieved its aim. It had not done so without significant casualties. Captain Shadwell states that its Casualties to 14th December were:

	Killed	Wounded
British officers	17	41
Native officers	5	12
British R & F	80	292
Native R & F	137	345
	239	690

The Kings Own Scottish Borderers under Colonel Dixon are said to have been 'one of the finest regiments in the Force'.[36] They were to add 'Tirah' to their battle honours.

Second-Lieutenant HDN Maclean had been with 2 KOSB throughout the campaign, although I have been unable to discover in which company he served. On 26 May 1898 he wrote to his mother from Cawnpore to say:

We are all very pleased at what our Colonel got. I suppose of course you saw it in the paper viz. ADC to the Queen. It is certainly a great compliment to the Regiment as well as the Colonel, Sladen also secured a DSO and I hope the Major and Haig secures something also.[37]

Tirah had been Neil's first taste of active service. It was not to be his last.

Notes

1. *Celtic Monthly* Vol. IX (1901), 181.
2. BL. *Graves in India*, 225.
3. *The Great Game*, 465–470.
4. *Ibid*, 483–501.
5. General Order 41 dated 11th April 1881 quoted in HFN Jourdain & Edward Fraser *The Connaught Rangers* 2nd Bn, formerly 94th Foot (1926), 371.
6. BCP. Castlebar Scrapbook. Lieutenant Egerton tore the colours from their poles and carried them on foot for 42 miles to Pretoria, despite having been seriously wounded.
7. BCP. Castlebar Scrap book.
8. He was promoted Lieutenant on 22 May 1895: Sir O'More Creagh VC, GCB *The Victoria Cross & Distingushed Service Order*.
9. Major CAP Hobday RA *Sketches on Service during the Indian Frontier Campaigns of 1897* (1898).
10. Winston S Churchill *My Early Life* (1930), 143.
11. Stream, watercourse, ravine [*CSD*].
12. *Celtic Monthly* IX (1901), 170. Major-General CS Maclean to the Editor.
13. TNA. WO 98/7. List of Recipients of the Victoria Cross 1856–1914. Maclean, HLS. Lieutenant Indian Staff Corps 9.11.97/15.10.05. Tirah Campaign, India 17.8.97.

14. *Lockhart's Advance through Tirah* (1898), 1–49.
15. The baggage of the Division was carried on the back of mules. When it left Shinwari it is described as 'going slowly out of camp all day [and] it soon became evident that the Rear-Guard would not move that night – Accordingly 1/3 Gurkhas and 4 Companies 2/KOSB were sent forward to picquet the road on which the baggage was blocked during the night' [KOSB Regimental HQ. 2 KOSB Digest of Services: KOSB D1. 1].
16. *Ibid*, 103.
17. Regimental Headquarters the King's Own Scottish Borderers. 'Second Battalion's Digest of Service'. I have to thank the Regimental Secretary Lieutenant-Colonel Colin Hogg OBE, DL for his help when I was examining the Regiment's records. Except where stated the story of 2 KOSB in Tirah is taken from this document.
18. Kotal = pass.
19. *Lockhart's Advance*, 116.
20. *Lockhart's Advance*, 117.
21. *Lockhart's Advance*, 122.
22. Robert Woolcombe *All the Blue Bonnets* (198), 76.
23. *Lockhart's Advance*, 165.
24. *Lockhart's Advance*, 171.
25. *Ibid*, 230.
26. *Ibid*, 235.
27. Colonel HD Hutchinson *The Campaign in Tirah 1897–98 (1898)*.
28. *Lockhart's Advance*, 262.
29. Native doolie bearers and transport drivers.
30. *Lockhart's Advance*, 262.
31. *Ibid*, 277.
32. Anglo-Indian: stream, watercourse, ravine.
33. 2 men killed and 1 colour sergeant, 1 sergeant and 11 men wounded.
34. *Lockhart's Advance*, 282.
35. *Ibid*, 284.
36. *The Campaign in Tirah 1897–98*.
37. BCP. Indian folder.

Chapter Sixty-Two

The Second Boer War

In 1899 Lieutenant Neil Maclean was posted from 2 KOSB in India to 1 KOSB in Dublin. He was not there for long, for on 18th December the battalion was mobilized for war in South Africa.[1]

During the nineteen years that had passed since the First Boer War there had been many changes in South Africa. In 1886 gold had been discovered in the Witswatersrand and the European population of the Transvaal had shot upwards. Most of the Uitlanders, as these new arrivals were called, were British. The Boers did not love them, mainly because they were British, but also because of their hedonistic life-style, which was somewhat different to that of the Calvinist Afrikaaners. They, however, had to be tolerated: the Transvaal was chronically short of cash and the Uitlanders paid most of the taxes. Even so Johannesburg, with a population of some 50,000 Uitlanders, was not allowed an un-elected municipal council, whilst English was banned in official communications and, most infuriating of all, it was almost impossible for non-Boers to obtain full citizenship.

In 1896 Paul Kruger the Transvaal President proposed to visit London to re-negotiate Gladstone's humiliating 1884 London Convention.[2] He was not encouraged to do so and was told, in no uncertain terms that under no circumstances would Article IV of the 1884 Convention, which prevented the Transvaal from making treaties with outside powers without British consent, be rescinded. Furthermore the Cabinet made it clear that if he came the Uitlanders's franchise would be under discussion. Pretoria was proposing that the franchise should be limited to people who had lived in the Transvaal for fourteen years. As most Uitlanders had settled there since gold had been discovered in 1886, this was a piece of blatant gerrymandering.[3]

The Boer treatment of the Uitlanders was only one factor in the increasing tension between Great Britain and the Transvaal. Of even greater significance was Kruger's purchase of arms from Germany, which were smuggled in through Portuguese-owned Delagoa Bay. By April 1897 Chamberlain was warning Salisbury that the Transvaal had 'a stock of artillery, rifles and ammunition of all sorts to furnish a European army'.[4]

Transvaal was on its way to be the dominant power in South Africa. It was the only possible market for the agricultural produce and manufactured goods of the Cape Colony and Natal, whilst its potential wealth, population and aggressive leadership made it the focus for Boer discontent throughout the region.

The British Government was not, however, prepared to allow South Africa to fall to the Boers, and in January 1897 Alfred Milner was appointed High Commissioner for South Africa. Milner a 'fanatical imperialist of unbending will'[5] made it clear that his aim was to engineer a clash with the Transvaal. That he was not alone in having imperialist ambitions is clear from the top-secret memorandum Jan Smuts made to the Transvaal Executive. In it he wrote:

South Africa stands on the eve of a frightful blood-bath out of which our volk shall come ... either as ... hewers of wood and drawers of water for a hated race, or as victors, founders of a United South Africa, of one of the great empires (*rijken*) of the world ... an Afrikaans republic in South Africa stretching from Table Bay to the Zambezi.[6]

As 1899 progressed South Africa moved inexorably towards war. Negotiations continued, but at the same time British reinforcements were sent to the Natal border. Then on the evening of the 9th October Milner received an ultimatum from FW Reitz, the State Secretary of the Transvaal, threatening war at 5 pm on Wednesday 11th October unless various demands were met. It was one of the most extraordinary actions in the nineteenth century. In it Pretoria demanded 'that the troops on the borders of this Republic shall be instantly withdrawn', 'that all reinforcements of troops which have arrived in South Africa since 1st June 1899, shall be removed' and even 'that Her Majesty's troops which are now on the high seas shall not be landed at any port in South Africa'. The Boers with a population of 430,000 were challenging the British Empire at the height of its powers.

For them to have any hope of success the Boers needed to strike first, before any further reinforcements arrived. If they could do so they believed they would receive foreign assistance from an increasingly anti-British Europe and that Salisbury's government would fall. They also expected that after some initial defeats Britain would come to terms, as Gladstone had done in 1881. In doing so 'they failed to appreciate that in Salisbury they had to deal with a very different type of politician', to Gladstone.[7]

When the Boers invaded Natal there were only 12,000 British troops in South Africa and the first weeks of the war followed an almost inevitable pattern. As Andrew Roberts has written:

The Boer War followed the classic pattern of most modern British wars, including the Napoleonic, Crimean, Indian Mutiny, Zulu, Afghan, First and Second World Wars – of humiliating initial defeats followed by national arousal and exertion before ultimate victory.[8]

Certainly the Second Boer War could not have begun more disastrously for Britain. 'Black Week' which began on the 10th of December with the ambush of General Sir William Gatacre at Stormberg, where 700 men surrendered, was followed the next day by Lieutenant-General Lord Methuen's 1st Division being repulsed by Piet Cronje at Magersfontein. Methuen failed to relieve Kimberley and lost 210 killed, 675 wounded and 63 missing, against negligible Boer losses. On 15th December Louis Botha routed Sir Redvers Buller VC at the Battle of Colenso.

Salisbury had, however, learnt the lesson of the Zulu War, and acted ruthlessly. He replaced Buller with Lord Roberts, the hero of Kandahar, leaving Buller in charge of the army in Natal. Salisbury also insisted that Lord Kitchener, who in September 1898 had defeated the Mahdi's army at Omdurman, should join Roberts as his Chief of Staff.

* * *

In the aftermath of 'Black Week' one of the reinforcements sent out to Cape Town was 1KOSB. On the 4th January 1900 it embarked on the *Braemar Castle*. Its total strength was 27 officers and 1082 other ranks, including 470 reservists.[9] A surprising number of both officers and men had recently served with the 2nd Battalion on the North-West Frontier.

The Battalion disembarked at Cape Town on 26th January 1900. They left almost immediately by train on a six hundred mile journey to the Orange River, arriving there on 29th. They left again 5 days later and marched to Enslon where they joined the 14th Brigade (Major-General Chermiside), which was part of the 7th Division (Lieutenant-General Charles Tucker).

Private William Fessey, an old soldier in the Maxim gun detachment, takes up the story:

10th February. Reveille at 4 am, breakfast 5 am, then on trek again to a place called Ramdam, where we halted for the night. **11th February.** As usual, early breakfast – what we had to call it – cold coffee and hard biscuit. We then went to a place called De Kiels Drift on the Riet River, and I must say that it was an awful hot day, and we was in full marching order, same as we dressed in England, and in addition to that 220 rounds of ammunition, and the troops began to fall out one after the other – no wonder. My Corps, most of us [had] seen foreign service in India and Egypt and it told on us I can assure you [in] this place. There were dozens fell out through the heat and drought. It was only a small march, 19 miles and when we got to the river it was good to see the troops charging for water. (57 officers and men had to be sent to the rear in ox-wagons prostrate with heat and exhaustion). **13th February** ... so we went on the march 5.30 pm to a place further up river – a place called Wagon's Drift, arriving there at 2 am **14th February.**[10]

The following day the King's Own Scottish Borderers were to see their first taste of action in South Africa.

* * *

On 23rd December Roberts had left Southampton in the *Dunottar Castle*. Kitchener joined him off Gibraltar. They arrived at Cape Town on 10th January 1900. During the voyage they had endlessly paced the deck discussing Roberts' plan to defeat the Boers. It was not the plan proposed by the War Office, who had recommended an advance on Bloemfontein with three columns: one each from Cape Town, Port Elizabeth and East London. Instead Roberts and Kitchener decided to advance up the western flank of the enemy republics, along the railway, which ran from Cape Town through De Aar junction to Kimberley, Mafeking and eventually to Bulawayo.[11]

South of Kimberley, which was under siege, the Boers were astride the railway line at Maggersfontein. Facing them, south of the Modder River, was Lord Methuen's 1st Division. Roberts' plan entailed concentrating behind Methuen's Division then doubling back to Enslin followed by a rapid march east to the Riet River and then back north to the Modder, outflanking the Boers and lifting the siege of Kimberley.

As Roberts explained at the enquiry after the war was over, the advantages of this plan were:

1. It was on that line only we had possession of a railway bridge over the Orange River.
2. It was by that line only that Kimberley could be relieved in time.
3. It was by that line only I could deal with the Boer forces in detail, and defeat Cronje before he could be reinforced.[12]

In its essence Roberts' tactical dispositions were extremely simple. While the 1st Division under Methuen contained Cronje at Magersfontein and the 7th Division (Tucker's) secured the important township of Jacobsal to the south-east, French's cavalry, the 6th Division (Kelly-Kenny's) and the 9th (Colville's) were to make a wide left-handed loop round Jacobsal and reappear unexpectedly 14 miles east of the Boer position and seize the drifts on the Modder. From there French would press on to Kimberley itself, thus cutting Cronje's communications, while the infantry waited to pounce should he try to retreat east along the river.

By the evening of 10th February a formidable advance guard was established at Ramdan 20 miles south of Maggersfontein. From here they had only to march 10 miles due east to cross the Riet, a tributary of the Modder running SE-NE, then a more formidable march 30 miles north to the Modder itself – a considerable distances for un-acclimatized infantry to cover in a country without water.

It was noon on the 11th before Cronje heard that there was a British concentration at Ramdam; however, he did not believe that the British would leave the railway line, and assumed that their move was a demonstration, such as he had been carefully accustomed to, on his flank.

* * *

On 6th February, just under four weeks from the day of their arrival in South Africa, Roberts and Kitchener left Cape Town in deepest secrecy. Two days later they arrived at the camp on the Modder River, where 37,000 men, 12,000 horses and 22,000 transport animals awaited them. Two days later, to deceive Cronje, the bulk of the army south of the Modder River dashed back to Enslin, then east to Ramdam and east again across the Riet River, then north to the Rondeval and Klip Drifts on the Modder. They were in position by 14th, whilst Roberts and his staff, together with the 9th Division reached Wegdrai, half-way between Klip Drift on the Modder and Waterval Drift on the Riet.

Meanwhile between the 12th and 13th of February the 7th Division reached De Kiel's Drift on the Riet River. They then received their orders to take Jacobsal and on the 14th started their march. Finally on the 15th French with his cavalry entered Kimberley. The first object of Roberts' strategy had been achieved.

Not everything was going according to plan. Because of bad scouting by all units, Roberts had much less intelligence about the enemy than he should have had. Cronje was believed to be still at Maggersfontein, whilst De Wet and his commando were thought to have withdrawn to the east. As it was not known exactly where De Wet was, the wagons of the supply column, which had not yet crossed the muddy drifts of the Riet, were told to fall back on Ramdam. This order was not obeyed, and shortly after the news of French's success reached Roberts, De Wet attacked the supply column on the east bank of Waterval Drift. Fortunately the Boers had failed to cut the field cable to Wegdrai and as soon as Roberts received the news that his supplies were being attacked he ordered three companies of the 7th Mounted Infantry, the 18th Field Battery and 1KOSB to help the convoy.[13]

Private Fessey writes:

> Orders were then given that our Corps was to go a distance of 10 miles along the river to a ford over the river called Waterfall [Waterval] Drift to relieve a convoy belong to Lord Roberts' troops, escorted by a company of Gordon Highlanders, which was being shelled in all directions by the enemy.
>
> **15th February.** This was the commencement for the KOSB to be under fire. We fought for 8 long hours and then it came over dark and we had to take up a position along the river bed

until 3 am, then a message came from Lord Roberts that we were to retire and leave the convoy, which consisted of about 150 wagons conveying food and provision for troops, so we had no meat for 3 days, only coffee and biscuit.

General Maurice says that the reinforcements came up in time to 'repulse an attempt of the burghers to work down the river bed, but the accurate fire of the Boer guns [2 Field Guns & 2 pom-poms] and rifles' made it quite impossible for them to move the convoy and carry out Lord Roberts' orders. He goes on to say that 62 Brigade reached the scene of action at sunset, but at midnight Tucker, who was in command of the operation, sent a signal to the Commander-in-Chief to say that he could not be certain of extricating the convoy, unless he was reinforced by at least two more battalions and another battery. Roberts was in a dilemma. If he abandoned the convoy his troops would be short of food. However, although the loss of the convoy with its supplies would be serious, its abandonment would be a lesser evil than the dislocation of his plans. Every man was needed for the fight with Cronje.[14] The convoy was therefore abandoned.

Meanwhile Cronje, his communications in his rear severed by French, his left threatened by Kelly-Kenny and faced by a heavy frontal bombardment from Methuen, was in a critical situation. At dusk on the 15th, he decided to withdraw by the only road left open to him – east along the Modder towards Bloemfontein between French's rear and the van of the 6th Division. This move should have been discovered within a few hours of its commencement either by Methuen or Kelly-Kenny's scouts; but it was not till about 6 am on the 16th that one of the outposts at Klip Drift observed 'a vast cloud of dust rising behind the broken line of kopjes to his right front'. Cronje had passed right through the jaws of the trap prepared for him; but the very effort, laden as he was with baggage train and camp followers, proved his undoing. Kitchener at once sent the news back to Roberts, who had meanwhile advanced with his HQ to Jacobsal, and then swung the 6th Division into harassing the Boer's retreat. The speed with which he moved was to play a vital part in Cronje's downfall.[15]

Cronje knew that if he crossed a ford on the Modder and moved south he would almost certainly meet up with De Wet, as well as the reinforcements, which were being rushed up from Bloemfontein. He was also confident that the British could never intercept him. He therefore decided to cross the Modder at Vendutie Drift east of Paardeberg, but after a day's hard fighting he felt obliged to rest his men and horse for some hours. This halt gave time for the British infantry to occupy all the drifts on the Modder except the one at which Cronje was heading. At 10.30 am on the 17th Cronje arrived at the drift that would mean safety for him and his men. His first wagons had just reached the water's edge when shells began falling among them. French's guns had arrived in the nick of time.[16]

With every bolthole stopped Cronje's destruction was inevitable. However, he was not going to admit it. 'He therefore bared his teeth like the old wolf at bay, and proceeded to dig himself into a naturally strong defensive position'[17] and prepared to fight it out. 'Cronje's laager' as it is called, was on the north bank of the Modder at Vendutie Drift not far from Paardeberg. High hills, which slope gently down to the river, surround it. Whilst at Vendutie Drift the Modder is no more than a shallow stream about 50 yards wide, which winds its way through steep-banks that rise to an average height of 30 feet. The banks, and the ground immediately adjoining them, were covered with mimosa, thorn and other scrub, which gave excellent cover on an otherwise bare and shelterless plain. Innumerable ravines, which run into the river on both sides, make admirable trenches for a defensive position.

Throughout the remainder of 17 February, and throughout the night, the Boers improved these trenches and where necessary dug fresh ones. They worked feverishly to construct an elaborate system of defence, which gave all-round field of fire over the surrounding veldt. They also built dug-outs in the steep river-banks which provided complete protection for women and children, whilst the overhanging banks of the river provided the Boers with a two mile covered way from one end of the laager to the other.[18]

Kitchener who, as Roberts was sick, was in command, resolved to attack at dawn on the 18th February. He did so with two of Roberts' infantry divisions and a brigade of mounted infantry. The whole force investing Cronje's laager totalled some 15,000 men.[19] Kitchener knew that speed was essential if he was to take the laager before Cronje could break out. He examined the intended battlefield and could look down on the Modder River from a dominant kopje south of Vendutie Drift, soon to be known as Kitchener's Kopje, and announced to the few officers who accompanied him on his dawn reconnaissance: 'Gentlemen! It is now six-thirty. By ten-thirty we shall be in possession of that laager'.

Kitchener gave his divisional and brigade-commanders precise orders. His tactical plan possessed the merit of simplicity: Kelly-Kenny was ordered to launch a frontal attack from the south at 10 am, and to engage the enemy's attention while simultaneously attacks were launched upon the laager by Colville from the east, along the north and south banks, and by Hannay's mounted infantry from the west along the north bank. Kitchener also tried to get French to attack from the north with his cavalry; but French explained by heliograph soon after dawn that his men were too exhausted. Kitchener accepted his explanation, and French undertook to prevent the enemy from escaping northwards. He also undertook to deal with any Boer commandos that might attempt to intervene from the north.

The guns opened fire and soon Kitchener could see Cronje's carts and tents in flames. The divisions then advanced across the open veldt. Then everything started to go wrong. As the British lines advanced, man after man dropped, hit by accurate fire from smokeless rifles. Kitchener saw the converging divisions, one after another, falter then stop. Then Stephenson (18 Brigade) and Hannay (Mounted Infantry Brigade), on the northern flank, suddenly turned their men away from the laager: Boer snipers, approaching the battlefield undetected from Bloemfontein, were attacking from the rear and causing havoc. Philip Magnus says that:

> The battlefield presented an extraordinary spectacle of the Boer laager, like a bull's eye, encircled by a British army, which was ringed, in its turn, by a number of Boer commandos of unknown strength.[20]

Kitchener, believing that these casualties should be accepted and that nothing should impede the main advance, sent furious messages to his subordinates. But the impetus was lost.

At about half-past one he rode down from Kitchener's Kopje to regroup his divisions and inch them forward. An hour later a staff officer withdrew the experienced troops on the kopje and sent them to reinforce the crippled advance below. He replaced them with men of Kitchener's Horse, who were untried in battle. They were thus given the task of holding the most important feature of the field, a fact which Kelly-Kenny had recognised as the key to victory, even if Kitchener had not.

All that dreadful Sunday afternoon under the blazing sun the casualties on both sides mounted. The British suffered more dead and wounded in that one battle of Paardeberg than in any single action of the South African war.

While the battle continued below, still undecided, with gallant charges, which pushed back the Boers but could not reach the laager, a disaster occurred on Kichener's Kopje. At about four o'clock. De Wet, who had abandoned the siege of Kimberley when French broke through, had ridden hard with three hundred men and several guns to aid Cronje. Undetected, he had crossed the Modder River higher up and galloped behind the British lines and up to the kopje, surprising the inexperienced young troops, who put up a poor fight and then surrendered. De Wet seized the whole southwest ridge and trained his guns. The first shells fell on the hospital tents.[21]

When night fell and the battle died down. Cronje had still not escaped and Kitchener was determined to renew the attack at dawn, despite the fact that he had failed to dislodge De Wet from Kitchener's Kojpe. British reinforcements were, however, on their way.

On the 17th 7 Division had arrived at Jacobsdal. Witnesses in 1 KOSB, who were present, give different timings for what followed.

1 KOSB's war diary notes that:

on the following day the now famous march to Paardeburg began, continuous marching from 9 pm till 7.30. The following day, Klip Drift was reached, all the troops were utterly exhausted and to make matters worse the baggage with rations was far behind and emergency rations had, therefore, to be used, but the great object had been attained. General Cronje was cut off from Bloemfontein & had been surrounded in the bed of the Modder River

Private Fessey wrote in his diary:

We moved off again the same night to the Modder River, where we heard of General Cronje being hemmed in on a riverbed. We marched all night long till 6 am then we had our breakfast and rested for two hours after marching 19 miles . . . We started again the same evening, got to where General Cronje was in the riverbed, marched another 16 miles up the side of the river, making a total of 35 miles in about 27 hours – we had reached Paardeberg.

General Maurice says that: Chermiside's Brigade (14th), which included 1KOSB, had marched on half rations for more than 30 miles in less than 24 hours, which he comments was 'a fine performance considering the great heat, lack of water and the thick clouds of dust which choked and parched the throats of the men'.[22]

Fessey continues:

We arrived there 6 pm on Monday evening (**19th February**) ordered to lie down as we were without food or drink for the next day because the baggage did not come with us. We had a bit of fresh mutton for dinner that was all right, we then started away on a night march to get closer to the enemy position, but as luck had it we got too close. We marched about 4 miles and then the Boers started to fire at our baggage guard but it was too dark. We could not see where we were going so our General said we was far enough, we had better lie down till day break with our rifles loaded ready for we knew that we were close to the enemy, and I can tell you this much, I was nearly starved to death with the cold.

20th February. So when day-break came we got up and took our blanket back to the wagon when all at once the enemy opened such a tremendous heavy fire on us about 700 or 800 yards off us and the Boers were on both sides of us. Cronje was on our left in the riverbed and the old famous De Wet on small kopjes [Kitchener's Kopje] on our right. He was trying to reinforce Cronje, but he failed.

When we found out that we were so near the river bed Major Mayne gave orders to the right half battalion to retire further out of range of fire, so we commenced to move. We got a smart reception, they opened fire on both sides of us at the same time, we could not tell where they was [sic] coming from. They fairly rattled into us so we thought the best thing to do was to lie down for a bit. We got on to our stomachs and blazed away at one another for three and a half hours, and how we got through that terrible fire so near the Boers at pitch dark I don't know. Before if they had liked they could have swept us off the earth, for we marched and marched in the dark until we was on top of the trenches, although I must give my Corps praise, took everything cool and calm and not many of them was hit. It was a mystery to the world, God only knows, I don't. The bullets landing all around me and the whole of us, came like hail stones . . . We had several of my Corps hit but I do not know who they are at the present moment, but shall know at roll call.

Late on the afternoon of 20th February Roberts, who was now fit, resumed command and cancelled Kitchener's orders for another attack. Roberts' inspection of the ground and the evident exhaustion of his troops convinced him that the laager could not be taken without considerable loss of life 'which did not appear . . . to be warranted by the military exigencies of the situation'.[23] Instead he proposed to tighten the cordon, bombard the laager, and mount a minor offensive to drive De Wet from Kitchener's Kopje.

On the 20th I KOSB's war diary states that:

the Battalion moved up to a position on the east of Cronje's laager, and came under a very heavy fire – retreating towards Kitchener's Kopje, then held by the enemy. We again came under heavy fire, but continued the march eastward to cover the rear of the Force investing Cronje and resisting General De Wet's attempts at relief.

Chermiside's march to the east was part of Roberts' plan to eliminate De Wet. They started to move before dawn on 21st but his men were hardly in motion when they came under fire from three separate enemy positions. Chermiside therefore moved his men south, in order to get out of range of the laager. He then pushed on to Vandenbeg Drift, which he reached having suffered 38 casualties.[24]

On his arrival at Vandenberg Drift Chermiside sent the Lincolns supported by a ½ battalion of 1KOSB to reconnoiter Kitchener's Kopje. Roberts intended that French's cavalry should attack it from the south and drive De Wet into the arms of the infantry. De Wet, seeing that he was being encircled rapidly withdrew. As the retreating Boers drew near some of them dismounted and fired on French's troops. General Maurice states that: 'the arrival of the Lincoln's & KOSB had contributed much to the success' of the operation.[25]

Fessey puts it more graphically if with less clarity. He writes:

We got under good cover then we saw the party that was on our right flank on a kopje, we opened fire again at 1700 yards but it took no effect, it was amongst big boulders but now our artillery starts shelling them. My word they soon felt them. I could see them retiring in full haste but we kept sending them a few pills into them for an hour or two – which made them shut up for a while. Then my Corps advanced to a farm close by where they had been on the kopjes. We started at the kopjes and chased De Wet for his life as well as giving his troops a severe doing, the best cutting up that he ever had as yet the Borderers did.

De Wet may have suffered a reverse but he had not given up his attempt to relieve Cronje. He had withdrawn down river and was re-organising his burghers at Poplar Green. He had evidently got a message through to Cronje and the two Boer commanders planned a joint attack of 3,000 on Hills A&B which were now held by 1 KOSB.[26]

The author of *With the Flag to Pretoria* writes:

The Boer Relief Force made its last desperate effort to reach Cronje. De Wet and Botha and some 2,000 men tried to break the British line but Roberts was ready for them. Every kopje they attempted to seize was held by the British. First of all they rode towards a kopje not seemingly held, but as they neared it the Scots Borderers who were under cover on it opened a vigorous fire. For possession of a fourth kopje the Boers raced the Scottish Borderers but the Borderers won the position. The Scottish Borderers advanced to Osfontein.[27]

Osfontein Farm is at the foot of Kitchener's Kopje. The KOSB were to be there for eight days, standing to each morning at 4 am. It was at stand to one morning that a sentry saw some men in front of them on the veldt. He reported to his officer, who examined them through his glasses and confirmed that they were Boers. Fessey goes on to say:

He ordered the Maxim to get ready at once which we was all ready to move at a moment's notice. We went out and saw them coming rather thick, so we came into action at 1,730 yards, but it was a bad position for us. Their Pom Pom was playing at us for a while, so we shifted to a place where we could see them.

We let them come within 300 yards of us and then we started and rattled them, Maxim and volleys, all we were worth. We emptied belt after belt and could see them fall and I am sure they suffered heavily. We could see their horses fall by the score and running about riderless. They got a surprise – they made a rush for a kopje where one of our Company [sic] was and the Boers were driven back, with very heavy losses three times that morning. We was lucky, on our side we had only 5 men wounded, and one Officer. We were relieved off outpost at 10 am so we remained in camp.

Eventually on the 27th February, the anniversary of Colley's defeat at Majuba Hill, Cronje surrendered.

Roberts now had his best chance of finishing the war. If French's cavalry, Horse Artillery and mounted infantry had moved faster they could have intercepted the enemy's line of retreat and captured their guns, wagons, and a considerable number of prisoners. As the presidents of the Orange Free State and the Transvaal were with the Boer army their capture could have led to an end of hostilities. It was not to be.[28]

On 13th March, four weeks after the start of Roberts' campaign, he entered Bloemfontein the capital of the Orange Free State. There was now a pause whilst the transport caught up with the army. During the halt at Bloemfontein the country around was harassed by small patrols of the enemy in and around Dewetsdorp[29] and by others working from Karee a point about 20 miles north of Bloemfontein.

Karee Siding is on the railway line north, where the Boers occupied a formidable line of hills. On the 28th of March a force, of which 1 KOSB was a part, was sent up the line to dislodge the enemy. The action that followed was the most costly of the campaign, as far as the Battalion was concerned.[30]

On 28th March Chermiside received his orders. Fessey writes:

Paraded at 6.30 am and we sat down in the sun till 10 am, we then got orders to advance. We got in sight of the enemy about 12 mid-day and the Boers opened a terrific fire on us as soon as we got into the open veldt. Karee Siding Hills is a horseshoe shape and the Boers had occupied this when we had orders to advance. A deadly fire was put into us, but we took the position that day.

We were fighting till dark all day long without water or food. It was the severest fight the Borderers have had to the present. We had 5 men killed with one of the enemy shells. We only had nine-pounders with us on this occasion, for we thought there was only a small party of them which we could shift easy, but we found the difference, I am sure . . . We had 86 killed in action that day. I shall not forget it in a hurry. My Regiment suffered the most that day, but as long as we drove them out of it and beat them it was all right, but poor chaps we left 86 at Karee Siding.

Conan Doyle, who was a medical officer with the army, has much the same story:

Tucker's Division, consisting of Chermside's brigade (Lincoln's, Norfolks, Hampshires and Scottish Borderers) and Wavell's brigade . . . assembled at Glen prior to advancing towards Karee. At Karee Tucker advanced his infantry, the eight regiments going forward in echelon of battalions imagined from the silence of the enemy that the position had been abandoned. They were undeceived by a cruel fire, which beat upon two companies of the Scottish Borderers from a range of two hundred yards. They were driven back, but reformed in a donga. About half-past two a Boer gun burst shrapnel over the Lincolnshires and Scottish Borderers with some effect, for a single shell killed five of the latter regiment . . . the casualties, and of the honour, falling to the Scottish Borderers and the East Lancashires.

1KOSB's war diary says that:

The loss of the infantry amounted to 160 killed and wounded and of this number 83 were Scottish Borderers. One officer (Captain Going) was killed outright and another (Lieut. Young) died of wounds the following day. So ended a terrible days fighting and although the success was dearly bought, yet it was strategically important – for the ridge captured was the last before the north was reached, & from 29th March to 2nd May it was the most advanced post.[31]

Lieutenant Neil Maclean, who had taken part in all the earlier battles in the campaign, wrote after the battle to his brother Hector in his only letter from the war that has survived:

My dear old Boy, Just a line from here to go by the mail i.e. Storebank., 2/4/00. I have written card to Mother telling her of the fight: It was [?] hard fighting as you can see from our casualties considering it was a success as when we have lost heavily it has usually been the other thing. I am afraid that there will be a lot more still to come for though after all it is business it is not nice losing so many good fellows. How many more of us were not knocked over goodness knows. One of their shells made a terrible mess of five of our men simply leaving nothing recognisable.[32]

On 3 May Lord Roberts' main force assembled at Karee and commenced its great march to Pretoria – 220 miles away. The Battalion's war diary records that:

1 KOSB took part in the actions at the Vet River on May 5th and 6th and Zand River on the 10th. On May 12th it was part of the force that occupied Kroonstad where a halt was made for eight days . . . . . . On May 22nd the army moved 15 miles to Honingspruit; on the 23rd it took part in a march of over 20 miles over fine rolling prairie, which brought us to Rhenoster River, which was crossed without opposition. On the 26th the vanguard crossed the Vaal River at Vilgoen's Drift. On the 28th the troops marched 20 miles and crossed Klip River and on 31st of May the army entered Johannesburg. Two days were spent there and then a move was made on Pretoria, 30 miles distant.

On June 4th we came within sight of the southern forts of Pretoria. The enemy were in force on the ridges commanding the narrow nek which led to the Boer capital. Henry's Mounted Infantry supported by J Battery and the guns of General Tucker's division began the fight. The answer from both cannon and rifle was very hot for a time but by half-past two the enemy fire slackened, and soon after the ridge was taken.

All that night we lay on the hills, hungry and cold, with the twinkling electric lights of the town below us.

On the following morning the 14th Brigade, following the Guards marched into Pretoria.[33] Five days later Lieutenant Neil Maclean was promoted captain.[34] He took over command of F Company.[35]

* * *

The capture of Pretoria made Britain's ultimate victory inevitable. Roberts hoped that capture of the capital of the Transvaal would mean the immediate end of hostilities. It was not to be. After the fall of Pretoria, the burghers' morale could hardly have been lower. Deneys Reitz, son of the Transvaal State Secretary who in October 1899 had signed the ultimatum to Britain, tells of dissolution and desertion in the Boer commandos.[36] And even such a lion-hearted adversary as De Wet recorded how his spirits sank and it became almost impossible to prevent his men from returning to their farms.[37]

Despite the initial despair, Boer morale recovered and instead of making peace they determined to continue the war by the use of guerilla tactics, which they believed were 'better suited to the genius of the Boer people than regular field operations'.[38]

Despite their vast experience in colonial wars, or perhaps because of their very diversity, the British had not formulated any coherent doctrine on how to deal with guerillas. It was not until 1896[39] that any anti-guerilla manual was produced, and Lord Kitchener, who at the end of 1900 succeeded Lord Roberts as Commander-in-Chief, was compelled to devise a sophisticated anti-guerilla strategy from scratch. He did so with his customary efficiency, thoroughness and tenacity. First, highly mobile mounted British columns were sent to sweep the veldt, harrying the Boer commandos, whose ability to manoeuvre was further restricted by the use of barbed wire and the erection of lines of forts and blockhouses. Farms and livestock belonging to recalcitrant Boers, who were still on commando, were systematically destroyed, and Boer women and children were confined in what were called 'concentration camps' – a phrase that was later to acquire sinister overtones.[40]

By the end of September 1900 the whole railway network in South Africa, with the exception of the section north from Pretoria to Petersburg, was in British hands.[41] This was a considerable advantage to the British, as it gave them the ability to switch troops rapidly from one part of the country to another. It, however, had the disadvantage in that it was also a tempting target for Boer commandos to sabotage. And bridges and other vulnerable points had to be guarded.

* * *

Christian de Wet had been brushed aside in the grand march through the Free State, but he now began to disturb the British lines of communication, blowing up bridges, tearing up the railway, destroying telegraphs lines and capturing small posts.

1 KOSB played their part in guarding the railway. The war diary says that:

Major AE Haig, of the Scottish Borderers commanded at railhead Krommellenberg with a force of 1,000 details when Vredefort Road Station was attacked and captured by De Wet with 1400 men and six guns. The garrison consisted of 18 men, mostly of the AS Corps, but included 3 of the Borderers. Major Haig drove off the enemy who then moved to Roodewal, where the Derby Militia were encountered and completely overpowered. Major Haig's men were then merged into a force commanded by Colonel Spens. Co-operating with Lord Methuen's Division this force met and defeated De Wet driving him from his strong position on Rhenoster Kopjes and occupying it.

It goes on to state that: 'On the 13th July Colonel Godfray with a mixed force moved out from Pretoria to the relief of two companies of the Lincolns and one squadron of the Scots Greys, who were attacked by De La Rey at Nitrals Nek. Colonel Godfray's force arrived too late, however, as the small force had been overpowered after a hard fight'.

The war diary continues:

The Battalion was then drafted into General Ian Hamilton's new force. This force joined in the combined movement eastwards and went as far as Balmoral, where a storm of unprecedented violence was encountered, resulting in the loss by exposure of over 300 animals. Beyond sniping and some shelling of our convoy at De Wagon Drift, very little resistance was met with.

About this time De Wet was attempting to break into the Transvaal and join hands with De La Rey who was harassing the garrison of Rustenburg, and

Colonel Hore was held up at Brakpan on the Elands River. Hamilton's Force was therefore recalled and dispatched westwards . . .

So the advance continued and the war diary states that:

Passing through Witwatersberg at Nekpoort, Hamilton's force marched on through Kaalfontein to Vlakfontein and Olifants Nek where slight resistance was met with and overcome. Marching through difficult bush country brought us to Warn Bathe from where we trekked back to Pretoria... Early in May 1901 the Battalion moved to Krugersdorp and thence to Naauwport West to join the mobile Column commanded by Brigadier-General HG Dixon CB himself an old Scottish Borderer [He had commanded the 2nd Battalion on the Tirah Expedition]. Much work was done in clearing farms in the difficult country north & west of Naauwport.

On 29th May the column was fiercely attacked by General Kemp near Vlakfontein and had 175 casualties, mostly belonging to the Derbyshire Regiment, Scottish Horse and Yeomanry. For a time in this fight our [?] were in the hands of the enemy but were retaken again before evening & On this occasion according to the sworn testimony of numerous witnesses the Boers killed several of our wounded. This killing of the wounded was denied in the House of Commons but was afterwards confirmed by Lord Kitchener, who sent the depositions of the witnesses to the Boer Generals without any result.

HDN Maclean took part in the action at Vlakfontein and was mentioned in dispatches.[42]

Colonel RG Kekewich of Kimberley fame then took command of the Column and from June to September hunted the kloofs and dongas of the Magaliesbrg with singular success. The most notable incident of this period was the capture by Major Mayne with a few men of the 2nd Volunteers Service Coy of Commandant Wolmarians & 30 armed Boers in a kloof at Damhoek.

In September 1901 the Battalion relieved the West Yorks on the Mob[...] River Blockhouse Line. Several unsuccessful attempts were made by the enemy to break through this line.

It was probably during these incidents that Captain Neil Maclean earned his DSO. How he did so does not appear in the records and all he told his family was that it was 'for driving a train'. His award was noted in the *London Gazette* on the 27th September 1901 'in recognition of services during operations in South Africa'. He was also mentioned in despatches and on 24th October 1902 was decorated by the King.

By then the war was over. Kitchener's severe methods had eventually been successful; but they increased the odium under which Britain already lay in world opinion. By the beginning of 1902 both sides were tired of war. In May of that year peace was signed at Vereeniging under which the Boers were promised eventual self-government.[43]

Notes

1. RHQ KOSB. Historical Records. KOSB Q14, 94.
2. *Salisbury*, 291–2.
3. *Salisbury*, 655–6.
4. *Salisbury*, 657.
5. *Salisbury*, 657.
6. *Salisbury*, 733.
7. *Salisbury*, 739.
8. *Salisbury*, 740.
9. RHQ KOSB. Historical Records: KOSB Q1. 4, 94.
10. Heather Wilson (ed) *The Diary of Private William Fessey DCM* (1998), 16.
11. Philip Magnus *Kitchener* (1958), 160.

12. *Lord Roberts*, 280.
13. Major-General Sir J Frederick Maurice KCB *History of the War in South Africa 1899–1902* Vol. II (1907), 76.
14. *Ibid*, 77; *Lord Roberts*, 289.
15. *Lord Roberts*, 282–9.
16. *Lord Roberts I*, 291: French had started at 3 am and despite the exhaustion of many of his men and horses had covered the 30 miles from north of Kimberley in record time.
17. *Kitchener* (1958), 163.
18. *Ibid*, 164.
19. John Pollock *Kitchener* (1998), 177.
20. *Kitchener* (1958), 166.
21. *Kitchener* (1998), 179.
22. *Maurice* (1907), 147.
23. Roberts' Despatch No. 3 dated 28 February 1900 quoted in *Roberts*, 292.
24. *Maurice*, 157–9.
25. *Ibid*, 160.
26. *Maurice*, 168.
27. *With the Flag to Pretoria*, 21.
28. *Lord Roberts*, 298–9.
29. Winston S Churchill *My Early Life*, 351–7.
30. Historical Records: KOSB Q1. 4, 99.
31. Ibid.
32. BCT. Family Military Box file. Letter Card 2 April 1900. Lieutenant Neil Maclean KOSB to HAC Maclean.
33. Historical Records: KOSB Q1. 4, 100–1.
34. *The Victoria Cross and Distinguished Service Order*.
35. BCP. Captain Neil Maclean DSO's Christmas card 1901.
36. Deneys Reitz *Commando* (1930).
37. *Lord Roberts*, 327.
38. *Commando*, 126.
39. CE Callwell *Small Wars*.
40. Robert Corbett *Guerilla* Warfare, 18; History *of the British Army*, 193.
41. *Lord Roberts*, 342.
42. *Hart's Annual Army List for 1906* (1906), 268 b.
43. *History of the British Army*, 193.

Part X

A New Regime in Coll

Chapter Sixty-Three

Reawakening and Radicalism

The sale of Maclean of Coll's estate coincided with the Gael's loss of confidence in himself. Famine and emigration had done their work and destroyed the Highlanders' belief in his way of life. Robert Somers, who visited the Hebrides during the Famine, and published his findings in the radical North British Daily Mail, was an industrious investigator. He visited people in their own homes and noted their conditions. He even followed them to Glasgow, where he saw hundreds of Highland families sleeping on the Green, as they had no accommodation in the city. Somers described the circumstances, which he believed gave rise to the people's disillusionment with life in the Highlands and their desire to escape from the misery of the last few years. This attitude developed into an indifference to the 'way of life' and its associated Gaelic culture.[1]

This indifference was not limited to those who had been cleared from the land. The editor of the *Celtic Monthly* ', writing in 1917, complains that:

50 years ago most of the representatives of the houses that once led the clans were indifferent to those things that are especially associated with the Highlanders. If one reads, for example, the *Life of Elizabeth, last Duchess of Gordon*, a woman of noble character and great piety, one would scarcely believe that she was the widow of a great Highland Chief. The same is true to take another instance, of the biography of John, 8th Duke of Argyll who, as well as being MacCailein Mor, was a distinguished statesman and scientist. When the present writer read it, he was struck by the fact that there was not, as far as his memory serves him, a single reference to the language and history or music and traditions of the Highlanders. The one exception was a statement by the Duke that he was proud that Sir Colin Campbell, the hero of Lucknow, was a member of his clan.[2]

It is against this background that the Gael forgot his past. In the old days it had been a source of family pride for parents, probably usually the mother, to pass on to their children their *sloinneadh*, their pedigree, and traditional tales of their ancestors' exploits. By the end of the century this habit had almost completely disappeared. It certainly had in Coll, a fact that was to cause considerable confusion when a new generation, to whom the famine was only a folk memory, once again began to take an interest in their past. This change in attitude appears to have begun in the 1870s. It was encouraged by the re-publication in 1881 of Donald Gregory's *History of the Highlands and Isles of Scotland*, which had originally been published in 1836.

Among those who purchased a second edition of Gregory's classic was Colonel Alexander Maclean,[3] late of the 94th Regiment of Foot, who had spent the last years of his service, from 1865–1878, as a staff officer at Bristol District. After his retirement he started to take an interest in his Highland ancestry. His cousin Harriet was still alive, living with her niece Isabel Cameron in Scarborough, and he seems to have written to her to ask for information about the family. As his mother was English and had been married to his father for such a short time, his own knowledge of his ancestry was probably limited to the stories he had been told in Tiree and the list of his ancestors that he received from his uncle when he visited the Island in 1836. In 1885 Harriet wrote to say:

> One thing is quite certain that we hail in a direct line from Niel Mhor that Gigantic Hero from father to son down to the present date – poor Niel Mhor met with treachery & was slain near Tobermory by his Br-in-law – his wife was angry with Niel Mhor for imagining her brother would injure him, but so it turned out.[4]

* * *

This renewed interest by Macleans in their ancestry intensified when in December 1883 Sir Fitzroy Donald Maclean of Duart, Bart succeeded his father.

As we have seen Coll's son-in-law Sir Allan Maclean, the sixth baronet had died in 1783. He died without leaving a surviving legitimate son, and had no immediate male relations to succeed him. Once again the *Sliochd Iain Dubh* came to the aid of their chief. Alexander Maclean, the doctor and cattle-dealer, had in 1765 purchased the Pennycross estate in Brolas. He was one of the many, but by no means the senior descendant, of John Dubh of Morvern. What was more to the point was that he was a noted genealogist. It is clear from Pennycross's surviving correspondence that after Sir Allan died, there was some doubt as who was his heir.

Torloisk's brother General Allan Maclean was married to the daughter of a Brolas cadet, the Glasgow merchant Donald or Daniel Maclean, sometime Collector of Customs at Montego Bay. As two of her brothers had served under him in the Highland Emigrants, General Allan seems to have considered himself their guardian and to have written to Pennycross to find out if they were in line to succeed to the Maclean baronetcy.

Pennycross replied.[5] After outlining the descent of the Collector's family from *Donel McEachan Oig*, first of Brolas, he writes:

> Eachan oig brother to Lachlan [2nd of Brolas] married McNeil of Barra's daughter. [He] left issue John, father to the above Collector, your father-in-Law... You [can] easily now see from the above tree that seeing the issue of old branch of the first Daniel McEachan Oig is extinct in the person of Sir Allan, the issue of the 2nd brother *Eachan oig mcDonel vic Eachan oig* must of course be the heir of blood & line to title or estate if there was on[e], your brother [-in-law] is unfalably [sic] the heir to both. If Hector, brother to your father-in-law, is dead no living person will dispute that, he is to take up the title as the seventh Baronet.

General Allan's elder brother-in-law became the seventh baronet. He died without issue and was succeeded by his younger brother Sir Fitzroy Jeffreys Grafton Maclean, a highly successful soldier, who died a full general in 1847. The latter's eldest son Charles Fitzroy succeeded Sir Fitzroy. He was educated at Eton, commissioned into the Third Regiment of Foot Guards and later commanded the 81st Foot. Neither Sir Fitzroy nor Sir Charles lived in or owned land in Scotland and the latter's son and heir first came to Mull in 1850 when he was a boy of fifteen.

Sir Charles was a keen yachtsman and it was on a sailing trip around Mull that his son young Fitzroy Donald first saw Duart Castle. He writes:

> We then proceeded to Oban and from there sailed across to Mull and lay at Duart Bay in order to allow us to land and see Duart Castle ... My father would not land, but allowed us to do so in order for us to make our first visit to the ancient stronghold of our family. We went all over the ruins little dreaming it would ever be in my possession.[6]

* * *

Not everyone in Scotland had lost interest in Gaelic culture. However, as was pointed out in a Gaelic periodical in 1875,[7] the re-awakening of interest in matters Celtic was a southern, middle-class affair. It was primarily concerned with linguists and culture, but this new Gaelic movement also acquired something of the status of a political pressure group and conducted a campaign that led to the creation of a Chair of Celtic at Edinburgh University. Its influence, however, did not extended to the Highland peasantry.

The man who was largely to transform the situation, was John Murdoch (1818–1903). Born at Ardclach in Nairn, he was brought up in Islay, where he 'acquired a deep and enduring interest in Gaelic culture and an equally enduring hatred of Highland landlordism'.[8]

In a long career, as an Inland Revenue officer in Dublin, Murdoch was influenced by a number of radical political writers, particularly Fintan Lalor, whose analysis of the Irish land problem 'gave pride of place to the peasantry as the main agent of agrarian change'. And when, in 1873, Murdoch retired to Inverness he founded a weekly newspaper, *The Highlander*.[9]

The 1860s and 1870s witnessed increasing agricultural prosperity in the Hebrides and once the 1861 clearances were over the crofters, even those in Coll, were on a more secure footing than they had been for twenty years. Crofters' incomes were also rising and discontent was hidden well below the surface. It was, however, still there and social peace in the crofting counties was essentially precarious. Any deterioration in crofting incomes was bound to precipitate a new crisis.[10]

The winter of 1879–80 once again brought near-famine conditions to a large part of Ireland. And as James Hunter has written:

> the distress that followed encouraged the remarkable rise of the Irish Land League, an agricultural tenants' movement founded in 1879 ... its strength lay, not so much in its considerable parliamentary representation, as in its mass following in rural Ireland where rent strikes and other forms of direct action organised by the League quickly threatened to undermine, and even destroy, the enormous power of the Irish landlord class. Having failed to crush the League by the deployment of all the coercive apparatus at its disposal, Gladstone's administration [resolved] to reform the Irish agrarian system – the outcome being the Irish Land Act of 1881

Irish unrest and its legislative consequences did not go unnoticed in the Highlands,[11] especially as the Highland harvest of 1881 was uniformly poor; and though the following summer began with the promise of an unusually large crop, it ended with crofters' potatoes being destroyed by blight more completely than at any time since the 1850s.[12] All the ingredients were in place for the discontent, which simmered beneath the surface, to explode.

The 1882 failure of the potato crop in the Hebrides was the event which started the trouble. It was followed by the refusal of crofters in Skye to pay their rents. The crofters of the Braes, in particular, demanded more land and proceeded to follow the Irish example. Summonses to remove the ringleaders were issued but, instead of accepting them, the summonses were burnt. Attempts to arrest prominent crofters failed and the authorities had a major outbreak of civil disobedience on their hands.

The battle of the Braes received massive publicity for the crofters' grievances. And in its aftermath John Murdoch's campaign for a political union between the crofters and the adherents of the Gaelic revivalist movement at last began to bear fruit.

Other incidents followed and in February 1883 the government announced the setting up of a royal commission to look into the conditions of the Crofters and Cottars in the Highlands & Islands of Scotland. It began taking evidence on 8 May under the chairmanship of Lord Napier.

The crofters' allies in parliament suspected that the Napier Commission was merely a delaying device. They therefore set up the Highland Land Law Reform Association as an alternative method by which to achieve their aims. The HLLRA was loosely modelled on the Irish Land League. It demanded 'fair rents, durability of tenure and compensation for improvements'. However, much to the surprise of its critics, the Commission had the unexpected effect of allowing crofters to speak their minds without fear of retribution from their landlords' representatives.[13]

* * *

The surviving crofters in Coll were not immune from the new radicalism. Not only had they, like the Skye crofters, been removed from their traditional holdings of land, they had seen them given to incomers. Little has been written about the 'troubles' in the 1880s in Coll, however, a remarkable collection of letters survive which make it quite clear that Coll was in the forefront of the crofting agitation.[14] They were written to George Sutherland, the Highland Ladies Association's schoolmaster at Bousd. In 1935 his daughter gave them to a 'Mr MacDougall'[15]

The incoming laird, who had purchased the estate in 1856, was John Lorn Stewart. His family were cadets of the Stewarts of Ardshiel and his grandfather had been killed fighting for the Jacobites at the battle of Culloden. However, despite his impeccable Highland antecedents, Stewart came to Coll with a dubious reputation.

He had succeeded his father as the Duke of Argyll's Chamberlain in Kintyre. He was a talented farmer, and was largely responsible for the introduction of improved breeds of cattle into Kintyre, and establishing the dairying industry there. Despite this undoubted benefit to the economy of Kintyre, the tenants on the Duke's estate had little love for him. This was the fate of most factors. But in addition, he seems to have earned the dislike of his peers in Campbeltown. One of them, Captain Charles MacKay, wrote a scurrilous poem about him that was circulated throughout the town:

BUBLY JOCK

Bubly Jock, Your Mother's a Witch/And A' Your Weans are Warlocks.

Robbie Burns' lines on another factor had evidently inspired MacKay's verses. For the former's lines:

Poor tenant bodies, scant o'cash/How they maun thole a factor's snash/He'll stamp and threaten, curse and swear/He'll apprehend them, poind their gear/While they maun stand, wi' aspect humble/And hear it all, and fear and tremble.

Are echoed in MacKay's poem, which includes the words:

A hundred cottar-bodies poor/Ye caused to turn outside the door;/And for to make their ruin sure/Ye tax'd the peats,/Quist, dried and drawn frae moss and moor/Wi' toilsome sweats.[16]

To give Stewart his due, when he had taken over Coll it was in a dire state. As we have seen the first clearances had taken place when Hugh Maclean of Coll still owned the Island,[17] but the people do not appear to have blamed the old laird. Any criticism was levelled at his trustee Alexander Hunter or the factor Captain Campbell. In addition the largest and most disastrous emigration from Coll were to take place after Stewart purchased the estate.[18] But, whoever he was, the new laird was never going to replace the old one in the affections of his people. However, Stewart hardly helped the situation. Even if the legend of him collecting his rents with a pistol on the table is exaggerated, and his snatching a crofter's bonnet off his head as a deposit until he paid the penny he still owed is apocryphal, they say something about how he was regarded.

Stewart kept most of the farms he initially cleared in his own hand and ran them with salaried managers. He stocked them, as he had in Kintyre, with cows from Ayrshire.[19] For the Island it was a complete social and economic revolution: commercial dairying requires a different life-style to crofting. The old Collachs preferred looking after their Highland cattle.[20]

New houses and steadings had also to be built, both for the new managers and incoming tenants. They must have cost a great deal of money, which had to be recovered with higher rents, which were not going to be paid by local people. By 1861 four of the seven large farms (i.e. those over 100 acres) not in hand were let to incomers from Ayrshire (2), Perthshire (1) and Islay (1).[21] Only Arileod, Cliad and Mibost remained in the possession of Collachs. Some of the old families were eventually to take to cheese making, but most of the Collachs did so only as servants to the incoming managers and dairy farmers.

* * *

Stewart had his favourites among the old inhabitants of the Island. For instance John Hyne says that his grandfather *Aonghus Mac Ailein Mhic Aonghus* was born in Ballyhough and probably lived in one of the Project Trust's two small thatched cottages at Beinn Tioraidh.

One of his brothers Hector later had a croft at Grishipol and had a family of boys and girls. The eldest son was named John. John Hyne says that his Aunt Mary used to tell him of the 'jolly evenings they had at Uncle Hector's house, John was a fiddler and he usually stood in the bed to give the young folks more floor space and have more elbow room to use his bow'.

As a young man Angus had gone to Greenock to learn to be a boot maker. When he returned to Coll he married Catherine the widow of James Johnston in Arnabost and settled down on the croft. They had a family at Ballyhough and then moved to Arnabost.

John Hyne says that when Stewart came to Coll he laid down such severe conditions on the small holders that no one was prepared to accept them. Stewart, however, was impressed with Angus and asked him where he learned his English and said:

You are not going away Angus. I'll see that you will be comfortably settled on my estate.

The family therefore moved to Acha 'where they were in comfortable circumstances'.
One of the original dairy farmers brought by Stewart to Coll was a man named Cowan who built the new farmhouse and steadings at Ballyhough. When he moved to Crossapol, Angus asked Stewart if he would let him have Ballyhough. Stewart agreed. Angus sold his Highland cattle bought in Ayrshires and began to make cheese. The family prospered and his descendants are still on Coll.[22]

* * *

It is clear from a comparison of the 1861 and 1871 censuses that most of Stewart's first phase in clearing the Island was restricted to land that had been rented by Captain Donald Campbell. However, between 1861 and 1871 he went on to clear Arithluic, Ballard, Cliad, Freslan, Grishipol and Totronald.

The statements made to George Sutherland illustrate the method he used to clear Totronald. It was made by John Maclean in Sorisdale, one of the tenants who was removed:

John L. Stewart bought Coll in 1856. The first Whitsunday after coming into possession Stewart gave notice that each tenant in Totronald would be required to make 80 'rods' of drains before next Whitsunday under penalty of £1 additional rent yearly. Five years after this he sent word to us to come to him in order that he might settle with us about the land.

We went to Breacachadh, where he was & he said to us. I have sent for you to settle with you about the land. I am going to raise your rents. Perhaps you will not take it when the additional rent is put on, but if you will, I would prefer you to any others. There were six crofts in Totronald then paying about £78 between them.

The terms on which we were to be allowed to retain our crofts were as follows. The rent was to be raised to £150 and was to continue for three years at this figure. At the end of this period it was to be raised to £200 [and] to continue at that figure for another three years. Then at the expiry of this second period it was to be raised to £250 and to continue at that till the expiry of the 19 years lease.

The rent was to be paid by the township even should one or two or more fail, and a new man was not to be brought in on any condition whatever. Go home, said he, and meet together and consider these terms, and then send one of your number to me to let me know whether you are willing to take the land on these conditions or not.

The result was, of course, that we came to the conclusion that we could not take it on such terms.[23]

John Gilchrist from Islay replaced the Totronald crofters.

* * *

The clearing of Grishipol caused particular ill will. In 1861 there were eight tenants on Grishipol, each had between 30 and 40 acres. In addition one croft had previously been broken up for a Free

Church manse, church and presumably a glebe. After the minister Alexander Fraser was transferred to Lairg, his successor was persuaded to give Grishipol up and move to Arinagour, where a new church and manse were built. The old church and manse became a dairy farm run by the estate and the crofters' hill ground became a sheep farm.[24]

Stewart treated the old tacksman class as harshly as he did the crofters. Norman Maclean, the son of Coll's old factor was evicted from Freslan,[25] as was Catherine Campbell from Cliad. Incomers replaced both of them.[26]

Some of the incoming tenants did not remain in Coll for long. For instance John Craig from Ayrshire, who became tenant of Crossapol in 1856 had left the Island by 1871. It is said that Stewart's rents were too high for incomers as for the natives.

For a long time the people suppressed their resentment. However, on the 18th October 1884 a letter under the heading 'The *Scotsman* on Stewart of Coll' appeared in the *Oban Times*, the newspaper that had taken over *The Highlander's* role in supporting the crofters. It was signed with the pseudonym '*Fear Cuairt*' [a sojourner, visitor, tourist]. As it probably expresses the sentiments of many of the crofters in Coll, and was continually quoted by them, it is worth quoting in full:

> 1856 was a black year in their Callander [sic], for at once the work of Clearing off the population Commenced with no sparing hand, at Whitsunday 1857, the very first term it could be done, a great number of the tenantry had to take themselves off the best way they could, and to see old men and women of 80 weeping bitterly and lamenting their fate, was a sight those that saw it will never forget. The most of them Emigrated to Tasmania, as there was a door open in that direction then. But we are informed 15 of them perished on the way and met a watery grave, fever having broke out in the vessel; often the case at that time in Emigration Vessels – will their Blood be on the head of any one!
>
> The proprietor of the East End of the Island – Cornaig, the late Colin Campbell Esq., when he saw the work of desolation carried on with such unfeeling, took pity, as he said on the old people, that is old men and women who would not likely survive a long sea passage ... Mr Campbell to his lasting praise be it remembered gave his Estate of Cornaig entirely to those families who were not willing, or able, to go away in order to keep them in their native place, when he could have got a much higher rent by letting it as one tack.[27]

In 1861 Cornaig had a population of 50, plus a number of fishermen from Aberdeenshire. By 1871 it had risen to 143 plus fishermen. However, only two of the families present in 1861 were still there ten years later,[28] and it would appear that John Campbell cleared Cornaig before he sold it to his cousin Colin and that the latter, instead of inheriting a population of cottars and paupers, filled his property with former tenants from the Coll estate. They will have brought their stock with them.[29]

What is remarkable about the 1861 settlement of Cornaig is that when the people moved there they did not organise their new land into individual holdings, but reverted to the old pre-crofting practise of runrig[30] that had been abandoned for almost a century. It was a damning condemnation of the policies of Alexander Maclean of Coll, which for a short time had brought the Island such prosperity.

The new crofters in Cornaig, the East Enders, were the only people in Coll not beholden to the new laird and they were prepared to complain about him. In December 1884 they sent a letter to the *Oban Times* testifying to the accuracy of *Fear Cuairt*'s letter 'in all its details regarding what the Coll people suffered at the hands of the proprietor of the Coll estate, especially the late proprietor'.

John Lorn Campbell had died in 1878.[31] His son Colonel John Lorn Campbell succeeded him. After 1886 he does not appear to have spent as much time on his estate as had his father. His initial enthusiasm as a farmer may also have waned.[32] Certainly after 1885 he stopped entering stock under his own name at the Coll Agricultural Show, which since 1878 had been an annual event on the Island. And in the preface to the *Coll Almanac for 1888*, it is noted that: 'the smaller dairies have made a bold bid for pre-eminence; and it is worthy of remark that success has been attained in proportion as makers have followed with minute care the instructions for the manufacture of Coll Cheddar'. Several tenant farmers were prize-winners. Some were even Collachs, but the best stock still came from farms held by the estate, although entered by the manager rather than in Stewart's own name.

The East End do not appear to have taken much interest in the Show until 1888 when several young men won prizes at the Highland games, and in 1889 Kenneth Mackinnon's Cornaigmore football team beat the one led by the Minister's son.[33]

* * *

There is another, rosier, picture of Coll at this time. It is by Rider Haggard, who published an account of his 1898 visit to Coll.[34] Rider Haggard is best remembered for his romances *King Solomon's Mines, She* &c. However, he also wrote political history and sociology, on agriculture and on travel. In 1877, when he was a twenty year-old clerk, he had accompanied Sir Theophilus Shepstone to Pretoria. They were there for the annexation of the Transvaal, and when the Secretary to the Mission was so overcome by emotion that he was unable to continue to read the proclamation, Haggard had to take-over.[35]

Rider Haggard travelled to Coll in September 1898 to visit his friend Colonel Lorn Stewart. He explains that:

> From Oban to Coll the traveller goes by steamboat, a journey of six or seven hours, past the rugged heights of Appin, for so long the home of the Stewart clan; past the rock where a particularly truculent Duart, desiring to be rid of his wife, hit upon the expedient, admirable in its simplicity, of taking her out for a day's sea-fishing and, just as the tide began to rise, finding that he had business on shore. Unfortunately for him the lady had good lungs and was rescued.

The steamer that took him to Coll was the *Fingal*. He says of her that

> even at the best of times she does not seem to care to undertake the adventure of mooring by the little stone pier, preferring to anchor a hundred yards or more away. Presently a broad-bottomed boat comes out, into which we are bundled with our luggage, some other passengers returning from the gathering at Oban, several black-faced rams, and a sheepdog.

> Half an hour later they were driving towards the Castle. He reckoned that little had changed since Boswell's visit, 'except that a good road now runs across it, with telegraph poles at the side ... Another mile and the Castle is in view – a three storied and naked-looking building coated with grey cement and backed by the massive ruin of the old home of the McLeans, who owned this island for many generations. Round about the Castle are lands more or less enclosed and improved, upon which wander some of the Laird's herd of beautiful Ayrshire cows – a noble herd it is numbering 250 or more. Here also oats stand in stooks, and beyond them appear a field of magnificent swedes'.

After dinner they discussed farming in Coll. He had no doubt about its potential. It could grow very fair crops of oats, was well suited to cattle and sheep, and where the land was improved, produced good hay and magnificent swedes and turnips. He goes on to say that:

> Thirty, or even twenty years ago, when it was more highly farmed than it is now, it used to be a prosperous place. To-day, however, the blight of agricultural depression lies as heavy upon it as it does upon the Eastern Counties. Thus the cheese that it produces can barely hold their own in the Scotch market against the imported Dutch and American article, and as it does not pay to ship young cattle to the mainland, the throats of most of the pedigree calves are cut so soon as they are born.

He then makes the surprising statement that 'another obstacle to the success of farming in Coll is the deficiency of labour.' As we shall see, there was a lack of employment at the time of the Deer Commission in 1892, when the population was 536[36], it would therefore appear that since then the population had dropped dramatically.[37]

Rider Haggard's aim in coming to Coll was probably to enjoy the shooting. He considered that the Island was a paradise

> to a certain kind of sportsman . . . He must be a person who doe not mind hard work and who is a lover of Nature and its voices. To such a one there are few places like this island, for here wild things abound, and though the bags may not be heavy, they will certainly be varied. In the bogs there are snipe, among the bents lie partridge, and yonder on the moor land grouse may be found; both the partridge and the grouse having been introduced since Boswell's day, when *he* went out shooting in Coll, was content with starlings, which he ate. Then there are hares in great numbers, wild duck if you can get near them, golden and green plover, the last so plentiful that they are not shot, and in winter woodcocks and wild geese.

He goes on to say that:

> Ravens may be seen also, and not far from them a pair of peregrines hanging about the face of the Green Mountain, although, because of their destructiveness, neither of these birds are allowed to increase. Out of the caves, too, flash rock-pigeons with a noise of rattling wings, and from time to time a curlew, surprised in a hollow of the sandpits, twists away like a great snipe filling the air with his ringing, melancholy notes; while yonder on the sea-shore the gulls wheel and clamour.

He did not go shooting by himself. He explained that:

> At a quarter to ten o'clock or thereabouts a tall bearded figure with a genial and weather-beaten face may be seen striding across the golf-green towards the Castle, accompanied by a pointer dog or dogs. This is the keeper, Lees, of whom I will say – that his walking powers are demoniacal. Not that he seems to go fast, but his length of stride is tremendous, and – and it is my sole complaint – he never stops. From ten o'clock in the morning till seven at night, with the shortest possible interval for refreshment, that stride will continue through

snipe-bogs, over sand-bents, across heather and peat-hags, with the fearful regularity of a machine, till even the inexaustable pointer begins to look tired and droops its tail.

He also examined Maclean's tomb and took a copy of the inscription.[38] He remarks:

This is the first time that ever I remember seeing the personal appearance of the deceased alluded to upon a monument.

He went on to wonder

how in those days, when there was neither railways nor steamboats, her husband contrived to convey the body of the beautiful Catharina Cameron from Clifton to Coll. I am told, however – for a piece of gossip of the sort lasts for a long time here – that while the tomb was building, and the bones of the old McLeans were being moved into it, her body lay for a year in a packing-case in some shed at the harbour without any one suspecting what the fatal box contained.

On Sunday 25th September he and his host walked to Clabbach to attend the service at the Parish Church, which he says:

is joined to the manse, and is a very plain building, white washed and shed-like in appearance. At the end of it, clad in a black silk gown, sat the minister, the Rev. D Macechern, in a high pulpit, and beneath him were gathered a congregation of about twenty people. The service consisted of hymns, extempore prayers, two lessons, and a long, but on the whole very good and well-reasoned sermon. The Psalms were sung from a metrical paraphrase.

Finally he mentions that when his host was 'laying out a golf green my' he discovered 'four skeletons buried beneath the turf. On investigation it was found that the ancient name of the site was Cnoc-na-Crochadh, or Hangman's Hill'. These were probably the murderers of Neil Mor.[39]

Notes

1. Robert Somers *Letters from the Highlands on the Famine of 1846* (1977) [First published in 1848].
2. *Celtic Monthly* Vol. XXV (1917), 1.
3. His copy inscribed 'A Maclean' is in my library at Breacachadh Castle.
4. BCP. Genealogical information collected by Colonel Alexander Maclean: extract from Harriet Maclean's letter of 21st November 1887.
5. Pennycross Papers in possession of the Rev. Allan Maclean of Dochgarroch, who I have to thank for an extended loan of them.
6. Short History of the life of Col. Sir FD Maclean, Bart as told by himself to EE Greenhill, 7.
7. *An Gaidheal*. Vol. IV, (1875), 250.
8. James Hunter, *The Making of the Crofting Community* (1978), 129; *Gaelic Scotland*, 206.
9. James Hunter, 'Politics of Highland Land Reform, 1873–1895', *SHR*. Vol. LIII, No. 155: (April 1974), 47.
10. *Crofting Community*, 128.
11. *Ibid*, 132.
12. *Ibid*, 131.
13. *Crofting Community*, 143–4.

Reawakening and Radicalism

14. BCP. Johnston Box File.
15. He is presumably the Gaelic enthusiast and Glasgow policeman Hector MacDougall. His daughter, the late Betty MacDougall, Shore Street, Isle of Coll who gave them to me shortly before her death.
16. AIB Stewart, 'Bubly Jock', *The Kintyre Magazine*. No. 27, (Summer 1990), 3–4.
17. NAS. Highland Emigration Society Papers. HD 4[3D]2 & HD 4/5.
18. On 25 July 1857 the *Persian* sailed from Liverpool with 81 passengers from Coll. Seven died on the voyage [HD 4/5, 952–963.
19. F Fraser Darling (ed) *West Highland Survey* (1956), 385.
20. *Report of Her Majesty's Commission of Inquiry in to the Conditions of the Crofters and Cottars in the Highland & Islands of Scotland 1884*, Vol. 3, 33858.
21. Arinagour [McDonald, Perthshire], Ballyhough [Cowan, Ayrshire], Crossapol [Craig, Ayrshire] & Fiosgaradh [Gilchrist, Islay].
22. BCP. John MacFadyen's scrapbook, 51–55.
23. BCP Johnston Box File.
24. Stewart is said to have brought in professional shepherds at this time and blackface sheep.
25. He settled in Cornaig.
26. John Galbraith, an Ayrshire miner, who after 1861 took over Cliad, is said to have helped the Pattersons flit to Arnabost in 1856. He was also offered a farm but said he was not well enough off to stock it then. However, he was determined to get a farm and with the help of his relations cut so much coal that he was able to stock Cliad. The family were to be tenants there for the next hundred years.
27. *Oban Times* 18 October 1884.
28. One was Sibella Campbell, the previous proprietor's widow [she was the daughter of Charles Maclean of Gallanach] and Donald McKinnon a shepherd.
29. It also appears from the dates of the first death in Cornaig of an incomer from the Coll estate [19 January 1862] that the move took place late in 1861.
30. *Coll Almanac for 1888*.
31. Stewart, of Coll mausoleum, Arinagour Isle of Coll.
32. He won numerous prizes at the Coll Agricultural Society Show in 1886, but had no entries in 1887 [*Coll Almanac 1887*].
33. *Coll Almanac for 1890*.
34. *A Farmer's Year*, 340–358.
35. *The Scramble for Africa*, 40.
36. *Royal Commission (Highlands & Islands, 1892)*, 874.
37. I do not have the total for 1901. By 1911, it was down to 389. This is 50% of the number in 1861 [*West Highland Survey*, 382].
38. See Chapter 33.
39. *Clan Gillean*, 387.

Chapter Sixty-Four

Agitation & Fair Rents

George Sutherland, who for three years was the Highland Ladies Association's schoolmaster at Bousd, was instrumental in collecting the complaints of the East End crofters, and it was Sutherland, under the pseudonym *Fear Cuairt*, who had written the article in the *Oban Times*. It infuriated Stewart, who took legal measures to find out who was the culprit. According to John Johnston, Stewart made great efforts to discover the author's identity, and believed that it was Johnston.

Most of the letters from the Island to Sutherland between 1883 and 1889 were from John Johnston, who was one of the leaders of anti-Stewart agitation. He was the most remarkable man the Island produced in the nineteenth century.

John Johnston belonged to the Arnabost branch of the Coll Johnstons, and was born there in 1836. In the 1861 Census he is listed as a shoemaker, living at Arnabost with his father, John Johnston, senior. The latter was a grocer.

When Arnabost was cleared, to make room for John Patterson, a farmer from Ayrshire, the Johnston family moved to Cornaig. Young Johnston was not to remain there long. In 1865 he emigrated to Canada. After some time there he moved on to the United States and returned to Coll in 1870.[1] By the time of the 1871 Census he was back in Cornaig, where he is described as a 'house carpenter'. In 1880 the whole family moved to the old smithy croft on Ballyhough, which was now known as Totamore.[2] By 1884 he was the Parochial Board's inspector and Collector of Rates.[3] At the same time he was secretly organising the agitation in the Island against the laird and promoting the HLLRA.

Johnston did not always get his own way. On 23rd December 1884 he wrote to Sutherland: 'The meeting of the East Enders collapsed owing to none of the west end people meeting them at Arinagour'. He complained that those tenants on the Coll estate were completely cowed. It was hardly surprising, and at least he had the grace to admit: 'Of course most of them, if not all, are in arrears'. Without security of tenure the remaining crofters on the Coll estate were highly vulnerable, as was Johnston himself. In May 1885 he said to Sutherland that the laird and his allies believed that 'if they can get us removed from Coll they shall have no further trouble'.

On 20th March 1885 John Johnston wrote to George Sutherland to say:

> I understand that Mr McKenzie, the Secretary of one of the Societies in Edinburgh, has sent some papers to the East End people to be signed by them and returned back – which they did everyone of them signing – likely the Petition for the Bill of Suspension of Evictions to be presented soon to Parliament, and that was a matter every one in the Highlands ought to

support. It was not signed by any on Stewart's Estate – nor were they asked – I believe they would not put pen to paper for such matters, as they are such complete slaves. I am a little doubtful of some of them when the Election comes but they may prove servile – but they shall be well watched, and if they do – then the Irish remedy will have to be partly applied for such cases.

The Irish remedy could mean only one thing. By the spring of 1884 a new wave of unrest was underway and crofters in some islands were using terrorist tactics of one kind or another. The overnight destruction of fences and dykes became commonplace. In South Uist telegraph wires were cut and a boat belonging to a farm manager destroyed.

Crofters in Skye and South Uist were instructed by their HLLRA branches to do no work for sheep farmers. And it was made abundantly clear that anyone who dared to occupy the holding of an evicted tenant would be made to feel the displeasure of his fellow crofters. This was no idle threat: in Kilmuir in Skye, for example, a boat belonging to a crofter who refused to take part in the agitation was destroyed, his windows smashed and his byre burned down; the corn stacks belonging to two North Uist crofters who refused to join the HLLRA were similarly sabotaged and their cattle mutilated.[4]

The situation in Coll never seems to have gone as far as this, perhaps because the people were not united. Coll was split in several directions. By the 1880s the Free Church was no longer identified as being automatically anti-landlord. In fact the Free and Established Churches had swapped positions. It was the ministers of the latter body, many of whom had practically no congregation, who had least to lose by joining the HLLRA.[5] This was certainly true in Coll, where Neil McDougall, the parish minister from 1877 to 1895, only preached to incomers.

Johnston, although nominally a member of the Free Church, was highly critical of Roderick Ross the Free Church minister, whom he considered as 'a flunky to Stewart'. Ross had been instrumental in moving the Grishipol church and manse to the village. Johnston tells Sutherland that 'My father... opposed Ross's settlement here and all his doings since he came at least in the matter of removing the Church to Arinagour in order to please McCorkindale and the laird'. Duncan McCorkindale was the estate clerk, the manager of the shop, a member of the Parochial Board and a power in the land.

Ross, who had been writing letters to the *Oban Times* attacking the agitation in Coll, was not popular with his predecessor Alexander Fraser, who in April 1885 returned to the Island for a holiday. Fraser was alarmed at the changes that had occurred since he left the Island and wrote to George Sutherland to tell him so. He writes:

I understand that a correspondence is going on at present between himself [Ross] & some parties who conceal their names but are supposed to be Rev. N. Mcdougall, Weir & young Johnston and it is supposed that you are in the secret too & lend a helping hand... If it be true that you are the medium thro which these so called agitators in Coll receive their information I will only say *that I am sorry* and *would not expect it of you*. I am not opposed to agitation, under certain circumstances, for certainly from the first of days my heart is *with the oppressed* all I would take exception to in this case is your association (if it be true) with *such a low set* for the trio: McDougall, Weir and Johnston *Can't be* such *characters as you can respect*. I would wish you better company. I'll not say more at this stage as I know but little as yet. Old Johnston never came to church.

Sutherland replied indignantly:

I could not understand what Mr Ross meant in that foolish, weak letter of his which appeared recently in the *Oban Times* when he spoke of a certain trio as being at the root of the agitation in Coll... that the Rev. McDougall and Johnston & Weir have been at the root of this agitation and that I have been the medium through which they work is a *pure falsehood* and I take it as an insult to myself that anyone should think that I am so characterless and brainless as to be made a tool of by anyone... the agitation began with the people of the East End and with them alone, and I gave expression to their views in that letter of mine to which you refer. I did so because my whole heart went out in sympathy towards these poor people and then I am a thorough going radical in politics and I believe in Land Nationalisation. As for the Stewarts of Coll their conduct cannot be sufficiently reprobated, and the present Mr Stewart is a chip of his father... as to my informants I may say that I have been collecting information on the subject, at least three years... of course the East End people have been my principal informants... You know & Mr Ross and everybody else on Coll knows, that I am as ardent a Free Churchman as any one can be, and it grieves my heart that Ross is playing into the hands of the Moderates as he is doing.

Johnston in his turn attacked Fraser. On the 5 May he wrote to Sutherland to say that:

Fraser himself has taken a house from the laird in Coll & is coming to reside here – that is partly how he was so keen to serve the 'laird'... The East End people has slept on the matter of meetings, Ross has succeeded in muffling them in the meantime, poor ignorant creatures, they will follow their *priest* like the Catholics without enquiring for themselves, and he will get a *fat* treatment and presents from the laird for his being their leader and for his services to keep them down.

A week later, however, he was happy to inform Sutherland that:

The East End people through my guidance (secretly) has constituted themselves into a Branch of the HLLRA in form, and have appointed a Chairman Duncan Campbell, Secretary Allan McKinnon, Treasurer Alexander McLean.

Johnston took a keen interest in politics outside his Island and on 20th April 1885 wrote to George Sutherland to ask for his opinion:

What think you of our aristocracy starting this *War* with Russia, if it goes on we may rest assured it was purposely got up to divert attention from home affairs and to take the chance of any opportunity that might arise in the attendant confusion, to extend their present privileges – we are aware this was a former dodge and was successful too – but we have some hope as we know that a great difference exists between the intelligence of the People of the present day, from those of the beginning of the Century.

An election was due. It was the first under the new franchise brought in by the Representation of the People Act 1884, which gave the vote to rural householders. And in August 1885

DH Macfarlane, the sitting Liberal MP for Argyllshire, held a meeting at Arinagour. In November he was returned again. But six months later in the June 1886 election, to Johnston's dismay, Gladstone's Liberals were defeated. It was a defeat of massive proportions, the equivalent to the Tories' defeats in 1906, 1945 and 1997. In Argyll Macfarlane, with 3045 votes, lost to the Conservative John W Malcolm, younger of Poltalloch, who polled 3658 votes.

The most significant measure passed by Gladstone's short-lived third administration was the Crofters' Act of 1886, which followed the Napier commission's deliberations. Coll was invited to send a delegation to Tiree, but no one turned up and Alexander Buchanan, who had married Colin Campbell's daughter, was the only person questioned about the Island. He gave only the most non-committal replies. For example when asked about Stewart: 'Did he not improve a great number of people off the face of Coll?' He answered 'I am not aware of that'.[6]

The Crofter's Act of 1886 guaranteed security of tenure to crofters and gave them the right, on relinquishing a holding, to claim compensation from the landlord for improvements made to it by themselves or by their family's predecessors. The Act also enabled a tenant to bequeath his croft to a member of his family and, in the most important of its provisions, set up a land court, the Crofters' Commission, which was empowered to fix fair rents for crofters' holdings, subject these rents to a septennial revision, cancel all or part of any accumulated arrears, and generally administer the Act and any subsequent crofting legislation.[7]

Johnston was keen to get the East End crofters to apply to the Commissioners for a review of their rents and they 'one and all expressed themselves anxious to do so'. However, Ross, the Free Church Minister, was now taking an interest in such matters. As a result, Johnston wrote to Sutherland on 18th February 1887:

Whether he is really in earnest remains to be seen, at all events he has succeeded in ruling the East people to sleep on their oars, and you don't see anything now in the shape of either meetings or resolutions by the East End people.

He goes on to say that:

I am now almost persuaded that unless some one who have [sic] really the good of the people more at heart than the smiles of a Landlord take the matter up at once, the chance will escape, you will perhaps then exclaim why I don't do so myself. The reason is that I was not consulted by them in any thing or asked to do anything for them since Mr Ross got so much into their confidence they discarded my advice altogether and will not come near me for any help in these matters, the consequence is that they are well hushed up now – at all events – perhaps if you forward these forms with an urgent appeal for them to proceed they may do it – But they seem to me extraordinary lax and careless about the matter. Some one have [sic] undoubtedly been tampering with them.

In fact the Crofters' Commission did play a flying visit to Cornaig in 1887, 'where the peculiar run-rig system in its most ancient form, taxed their rent making – or unmaking – abilities to the uttermost'.[8]

As a result of the visit of the Crofters' Commission the East End crofters received a 30% rent reduction and the write-off of half their rent arrears. The surviving five crofters on Stewart's estate also had their rents reduced. The rent of Johnston's croft, Totamore, was reduced from £12 to £7.[9]

In 1888 George Sutherland became a Free Church minister and Johnston's correspondence with him tails off. In his last letter to have survived, which is dated 8th October 1888, he writes:

> I know very well though our own Island is Liberal and Radical to the Backbone, and has a large majority of Land Leaguers too. Still a Radical Minister would stand no chance of being elected through the influence of a few Elders who are Landlord flunkeys.

Ross had married and to Johnston's surprise was 'now as much a Land Leaguer as any here. He, in fact behaved after all, far better than I expected he would'.

* * *

Ross' conversion coincided with the arrival in Coll of Alexander Darroch. The new factor is something of a bogeyman in Coll's oral history. He was in position by 1887, and by 1891 was living at the newly built lodge just outside Arinagour. He had evidently been hired to raise the profitability of the estate and Stewart from now on appears to have taken a back seat. In his evidence to the 1892 Deer Commission, Ross implies that Stewart 'from want of practical knowledge of his business' placed the running of the estate in the hands of the new factor.

Coll's prosperity depended mainly on the dairying industry,[10] but it also once had a useful income from the sale of Blackface sheep, and the 1861 Census lists 12 full time shepherds on the Coll estate. By 1891 this number had been cut by half.

Coll had specialised in hirsels[11] of wedders on the black hill, at the centre of the Island and on the north and southeast coasts. Wedders were reared both for their wool and mutton: there were prizes at the Coll Show in 1886 for wedder lambs, and for two and three year olds.

In 1880 the price of wool had fallen dramatically. Between 1880 and 1885 the number of sheep in the counties of Ross, Inverness, Argyll and Sutherland, which between 1875 and 1880 had fallen by about 1.4%, fell by a further 5.2%. The wool trade continued to be undermined by foreign competition. Imports increased from having been worth £500 million in 1887 to more than £671 million in 1894. One Highland proprietor even claimed that the value of wool had fallen by half since 1883, and wedder farmers, caught between rigid costs, falling returns and by now relying completely on their wool revenue for profit, did not share in the brief recovery at the end of the decade.

Breeders of wedders were also affected by fashion, and in the 1880s Southern consumers developed a taste for lamb rather than mutton. They also preferred cheaper frozen mutton from Australia, which, after 1880, began to replace more expensive meat from the domestic flocks as the main source of mutton in the London market. The situation deteriorated still further in 1885 when, in order to overcome the problem of distribution, which, until then had sheltered British producers, importers began to build cold storage facilities for New Zealand lamb. And Highland hill farms were gradually forced to become a reservoir of store lambs, for lowland dealers to fatten and make a profit.

Darroch's solution to meet the coming crisis was to cut back on sheep numbers and reduce the amount of the estate's arable ground under tillage. He could do so as much less ground was now required to grow root crops for the sheep during the winter months. He was also able to cut back on labour. Unfortunately for the twelve men made redundant there was no other employment for them on Coll, and they were the sole providers for some 50–60 people.

Most of the day-labourers on the Coll estate were cottars living in Arinagour. They claimed that before Stewart's arrival their fathers had had crofts there, which enabled them to keep a couple of cows and cultivate enough 'potato ground' to feed their families. Now they had only their houses, for which they had to pay rent, and no means of subsistence.

Darroch was unsympathetic. Ross claimed that he said that they should leave the Island as 'the cities have more need for them than the country, apparently'. The Free Church minister was in a dilemma. He was later to tell the Commissioners that:

> Formerly, on personal grounds, I had anything but cause to complain of the proprietor: to me, personally, he was most kind, nor had I, until this vindictive spirit began to manifest itself, the slightest occasion to find fault with the proprietor on personal grounds. I was asked to identify myself, because of these troubles with the people, and I felt bound to do it.

Ross organized a petition to the laird, asking that two acres of land should be given to each cottar for 'potato ground'. Darroch was authorised to give them some land, but the conditions attached were so draconian that the men could not profitably undertake to fulfill them.

Ross continued to try to persuade the factor to relent and wrote to him on 21st April 1890. Darroch replied on the 23rd only to say he had left it too late:

> As the villagers' application for potato land has been allowed to lie over so late in the season, it is impossible now to have the arrangements completed in time for planting this summer; and, besides, the land which they may get is taken up for the grazing of your own and the villagers' cows.

* * *

In 1886 Crofters had obtained security of tenure but nothing had been done for the cottars on Highland estates. 1892, however, witnessed a change of government and the Liberals were returned to power with considerable support from the crofting counties.

Yet another royal commission was set up to report on the amount of land in the crofting counties, which although now under sheep or deer, could be more profitably used for those without any land.

On 15 May 1894 the Royal Commission (Highlands & Islands, 1892) proceeded to take evidence in Coll.[12] The first witness was the Rev. Roderick Ross, Free Church Minister, 49. He was asked:

Do you appear here on behalf of the people? – I do.

Have you a written statement? – Yes, I have.

Kindly read it – My acquaintanceship with Coll dates from 1882, exactly twelve years ago. Amongst the first things that reached my ears as a stranger settled down in the island was the somewhat disheartening story that Coll was a poor place – that the people in general were poor, and some were very poor. On the surface, that did not appear: the cottar class was kept in employment, but I had been told that rents were high, and that farmers and crofters were in arrears. The former were chiefly on the Coll Esate, and the latter, with four or five exceptions, on the Cornaig Estate, where there are too many and the crofts are too small. The Cornaig crofters are a thrifty, hard-working people and, since the fixing of Fair rents by the Crofters Commission, are as prosperous as low prices for cattle and the size of their holdings would lead to expect. The great cry with them, and the great need with them, is enlarged holdings.

At the census of 1841 . . . the population of Coll had stood at the high figure of 1442 people; in 1851 it was 1109, and in 1881 it was 643, whilst in 1891 it was only 522.

'If', Ross remarked

> fifty-three years ago, nearly three times the present population, and 43 years ago, more than double the present population could live on Coll, how unfounded and utterly unreasonable and shameless is the cry kept constantly ringing in our ears, that the population of Coll is still too large to enable them to live in comfort, and that they should move away to the large cities. This is the policy that, by fair means and foul, has been carried on for years, and been brought to bear oppressively on the cottar class.
>
> The truth is, that the policy is one of extirpation of the Highland race from their native soil, and it would ill serve the purpose to improve the condition of those allowed for a time to remain. On the contrary, as the little band grows smaller and smaller, like the remnant of a once noble army surrounded by savages, their condition becomes every day more critical and less bearable.
>
> It is not for me to say who is responsible for all the evils that I know exist. At the same time that I was told that Coll was poor, I was told that the laird would make a good proprietor if he had good advisers. Indeed the laird was usually painted white by those of his own estate, and his advisers as black as black could be

Ross went on to say to the Commissioners that after Darroch refused to give land to the Arinagour cottars:

> I was deprived of the grazing of my own cow about 8 days after this, for my pro-cottar propensities, and my intimation that I was to apply to the Crofters Commission . . . in less than 24 hours' notice I was deprived of the grazing of my cow, . . . My cow is now fed in the byre.

He was also asked: 'Have the doors of your house been barricaded with barbed wire by the estate? – Well I would rather not go into the matter. There is an action pending in reference to that'. Donald Macinnes, a mason in Uig had fewer qualms of complaining about Ross's treatment. In his evidence on the iniquities of the behaviour of the Coll estate he says:

> I cannot conclude my statement without stating a case in proof of my assertion. For some years past the respected Free Church minister of Coll has incurred the loyal displeasure of the powers that be for advocating the cause of the poor people, with the result that he is boycotted beyond human endurance. The latest move against him was the erection of a six-row barbed wire fence to the front door of the manse, while the same was done to the kitchen door. A more scandalous action was never before committed in Scotland. Not only was it put up one time, but three times in succession, and pulled down on every occasion. In addition to this the well from which the manse was supplied with water was filled in with all sorts of rubbish . . .

That people on the Coll estate were no longer afraid to denounce the laird and his minions shows how far things had deteriorated. As might be expected John Johnston also gave evidence[13] and a long list of complaints. As a result he was replaced as the Parochial Boards Inspector and

Collector of Rates. Charles Macfadyen in Arinagour also paid a penalty for voting against Colonel Stewart at the County Council election. He was dismissed after 19 years service to the estate. He was not the last to feel Darroch's wrath. Robert Sturgeon, the postmaster, fell out with the estate and was turned out of his shop. The people in the village, however, were no longer prepared to put up with such arbitrary behaviour. They therefore built him a house on stilts below the high-tide mark, which belonged to the Queen and not to the estate. Stewart eventually relented and Sturgeon's grandson still lives on the Island.

* * *

The Commission also took evidence from Maclean of Coll's other old estate in Mull. The inhabitants of Dervaig were as bitter as those in Arinagour. Lachlan Kennedy, a crofter aged 33, claimed:

> Our grievances may be said to have commenced when the late Mr Forsyth bought the Quinish estate in 1857. Before collecting the second half-year's rent we received intimation that our rents were to be raised. In the course of a few years it was raised a second time, so that now we pay fully £1 more for our crofts than we did when he got possession of the estate, besides being deprived of other privileges, which we then possessed. There were at that time twenty-seven crofters in Dervaig possessing in common the hills of Monabeg and Torr, which enabled us to keep fifty-six cows, one bull, and twenty-eight horses.

When asked if the had been happy under the laird of Coll? – He replied that 'Every person was', and when asked: 'Was it a bad day for Dervaig when the laird of Coll sold it?' said 'Yes, all the world knows that'.

John Campbell, a crofter's son from Dervaig and soldier, aged 51, who now lived in Greenock, was even more explicit on the consequences of the departure of Maclean of Coll. He was asked: 'Are there any men in the army from Dervaig but yourself?' As we have already seen, he explained that:

> In the time of the Crimean war there were seven of us out of that locality in Her Majesty's service, and four of us went up to Alma, and I am the most insignificant of the whole. We went through the whole Crimean war. Three of us again went through the whole of the Indian Mutiny. In Afghanistan we were represented by one of our number, and he was killed in the last battle. That is the last belonging to our place, who was in Her Majesty's service.

He went on to say that his comrade, who was killed at Kandahar was originally in the 79th and then the 92nd. Campbell himself was first in the 79th, and then transferred to the 92nd in India. He said with pride that they had 'no less than fourteen war medals, a star, and twenty-one clasps in our village'.

Fraser-Macintosh went on to query the fact that 'notwithstanding all these services you have been ill used in the matter of your possessions?' Campbell replied: 'We complain bitterly that we cannot get these houses for which our forefathers paid for'.

Sheriff Nicolson then asked: 'Did you use to have a good many men in the army from the island of Mull? Campbell answered: 'I cannot speak for the whole island, but I remember four Waterloo men in my own parish'.

There were rumours that men had been bribed with the promise of land if they joined the army and Nicolson asked: 'Have you ever heard that there was any particular benefit given in former times to men who enlisted? Campbell said: 'Never in our place that I heard of' and when asked 'Is there any difficulty in recruiting men for the army?' replied 'No; but there are no men in our parish – nothing but sheep and game'. The questioning continued in the same vein:

35969. Does the recruiting sergeant ever come to Mull? – I never saw one. We generally found our way into the army. We went because others came home, and we saw them dressed in the kilt, and when we saw that our heart went into it. I went to Edinburgh to enlist, and others followed me.

35970. Have you any idea how many men from Mull are in the army just now? – I cannot say, but I don't think there is more than one belonging to our parish. I am not aware of any at all; but in my time there were seven of us out of that wee spot – one in the navy and six in the army.

35971. Do you know any gentlemen, officers in the army, from the island of Mull? Not belonging to Mull properly.

35972. Was the army ever popular in the island of Mull? – I could not say, but there was this feeling, that they would like to be in one of the Highland regiments. The old Waterloo men came home and told stories, and the young men would be delighted to be connected with the army.

35973. Is it less popular than it used to be? – I think so.

35974. Why? – Because of the way the people are crushed down now. All their life is crushed out of them.

35975. Is not that the more reason why they should better their position by going into the army? – Formerly, when people had more to come and go upon, young men lived more with their parents, and now no one can keep a child, they cannot keep themselves, and it was an easy matter in those times. In those times men came home in the wintertime and went away in the spring, and now they cannot do that. In the crofts of Dervaig there are about two acres of arable land, and the biggest croft in that island has been turned over for the last eighty years, and that has impoverished it. The people have neither plough nor horse nor anything. The old people have to carry peats nearly three miles. The old men complain of the peat carrying, but they must do it.[14]

It was a damning indictment. The gloomy prediction made by Mr Donald Maclean during the Napoleonic Wars, that if the people were allowed to emigrate the reservoir in the Highlands and Islands for the armed services would dry up, had been proved true. Men who had followed their traditional leaders to war would not volunteer to follow incomers.

* * *

The situation in Coll was similar to that in Dervaig. Whilst the Macleans owned the Island former servicemen returned home once their military service was over. At the time of the 1841 Census there were three army pensioners in Coll. Two were members of the Mackenzie/Matheson family.[15] The third was William MacKay, late of the 79th Foot. A William Matheson, 85, and a John Maclean, 75, who had served in the 93rd Regiment of Foot, had joined them by the time of the 1851 Census.[16]

These pensioners were probably all veterans of the Napoleonic Wars. William MacKay certainly was. He was one of the four MacKay brothers in Cornaig, who joined the 79th. Their father Hugh, who was also an army pensioner, had probably also served in the regiment.[17]

* * *

William's career is well documented. He enlisted into the Canadian Fencibles and served with them until 1804. He then joined the 79th. He too took part in the Corunna debacle and saw action at Busaco, Fuentes de Honor, Salamanca, the Pyrenees, Nivelle, Toulouse and finally at the battle of Waterloo.[18]

When the Army was retreating to Corunna William became separated from his comrades and was in danger of being captured. However, he noticed that those men who fell alive into the hands of the enemy had their clothes and other possessions stripped from them. When he saw that capture was certain, he took off all his clothes, hid them and pretended to be dead. His pursuers therefore passed him by. When they had gone he recovered his clothes and eventually rejoined the Army.[19]

Another story is told of William MacKay. John MacFadyen, the gardener in Coll in the 1940s, recalls in his collection of Coll place names and tales that in the 1780s there was a woman living at Cornaig known as:

Mor Abrach, as she was familiarly called lived with her brother Donald in an isolated cottage on the moor, attending to their cattle and plot of cultivated lands, by many she was reckoned to have supernatural gifts, and could foresee coming events &c. On one occasion she visited the MacKay family and was offered a seat by the fireside, William a curly haired laddie of seven or eight years came along to welcome her and stood by her knee, she was passing her fingers through his golden hair, she said its a pity that some day these locks will be entangled in the seaweed on the beach.

William grew to be a strong man, entered the army and fought in most of the Continental wars of his time, had many adventures, and narrow escapes, after being discharged from the army he came home with his wife and family and settled down in the little thatched cottage by the roadside on Ballard farm, where he intended to spend the rest of his life quietly, and prove that Mor Abrach's prophecy concerning him was all nonsense, he would never again cross the oceans or leave the Island.

For sometime everything seems to be going according to plan. He was fond of fishing off the rocks when the weather was favourable. His favourite place was Grianaig, Arileod. One afternoon he went off and didn't return when expected, a party went to look for him, but darkness fell and the search had to be given up till the following day, when his corpse and his fishing rod were found entangled in the seaweed where the high tide had left him on the beach. Mor Abrach's prophecy seems to have been fulfilled to the letter.[20]

In the register of deaths for 13th December 1860 it is stated that William MacKay, 77, died from 'drowning. Fell off a rock while fishing'.

* * *

By the time of the 1861 Census another pensioner, Donald McInnes, 55, had returned to Coll. He settled in Grimsary. He was not the only pensioner to do so and the pair of houses he and John Maclean lived in were as a result known as the 'Barracks'.

John Maclean, who lived to be 94 was remembered in Coll for his 'gigantic proportions and good nature' and 'was often chosen to officiate as "caller out" at funerals, which he conducted with impressive skill'.[21] He was known as 'Pensioner Mor', and although he later served in the 93rd Regiment probably originally served in the 79th. He was with his regiment at Copenhagen and throughout the Peninsular War. He attributed his safe return to a charm he had learnt in his youth:

The charm Mary put on her son/and Bridget put on her banners/and Michel put on his shield/and the son of God before the throne of clouds/a charm art thou against arrow/a charm against sword/a charm against the red tracked bullet/an island art thou in the sea/a rock art thou on land/and greater be the fear these have/of the body round which these charms goes/in presence of Colum Cille/with his mantle round thee.

Other charms, which were remembered in Coll well into the late nineteenth century, were used to protect cattle against diseases and drowning at sea.[22]

Both these pensioners died in 1874. No new pensioners in the nineteenth century returned to the Island after them. McInnes was one of the few Collachs who had joined the army since the Napoleonic Wars. The Potato Famine, Emigration and the Clearances had cost the army one of its most valuable recruiting areas.

Notes

1. *Oban Times*, 14 May 1921.
2. It had at one time been included in the Totamore sheep farm held by Neil Maclean of Crossapol.
3. *The Coll Almanac* (1886), 1.
4. *Crofting Community*, 149.
5. *Crofting Community*, 155.
6. *Report of Her Majesty's Commission of Inquiry in to the Conditions of the Crofters and Cottars in the Highland & Islands of Scotland 1884*, Vol. 3, 33854.
7. *Crofting Community*, 161.
8. *Coll Almanac for 1888*.
9. BCP. Johnston Box-file. Rent of farms on the Estate of Coll as per Valuation Roll of the County, year 1898–99 in Johnston's handwriting.
10. *Coll Almanac for 1888*.
11. *Hirsel*= a flock of sheep looked after by one shepherd. In 1891 there were shepherds living at Grishipol [John Cameron]; Kilbride [Donald Kennedy]; Totamore-Grimsary [William Gilchrist]; Breacacha [Neil Kennedy]; Arnabost [Neil McLean]; Gallanach [John Hadow].
12. *Royal Commission (Highlands & Islands, 1892)*, 870–881.
13. He gave a great deal of evidence on the structure of the population of Coll both before and after Stewart's arrival in the Island, which has already been used.
14. *Royal Commission (Highlands & Islands, 1892)*, 2251–2253.
15. One was Archibald Mackenzie, 70, who was living at No. 5 Cliad with his wife and one male servant. He was probably the son of Donald Mathieson in Grishipol in 1776. He was still in Cliad in 1851, but had probably died before the register of deaths began in 1855. The other was John Mackenzie, son of John Mathieson & Margaret McKay. He married Betty Sutherland and was living in Arinagour in 1841 & 1851. He died 22 February 1857, aged 90. She died three years later.
16. William Matheson, who born at Dornoch in Sutherland was dead before 1855.

17. BCP. Letter. Wilson 18 September 1971.
18. TNA. WO 97. 895. 79th Foot Pensions.
19. Betty MacDougall, *Folklore from Coll* (nd), 36.
20. BCP. John MacFadyen's collection, 83–4.
21. *Folklore from Coll*, 35.
22. Ditto, 79–80.

Chapter Sixty-Five

The return of the Macleans of Coll?

John Johnston was married to a Maclean. Both his mother and grandmother were also Macleans. It was a fact of which he was extremely proud. His views were similar to John Murdoch's in that he was both violently anti-landlord and was interested in Gaelic culture: he was an enthusiastic piper and expert at *ceòl-mór*, the classical music of the bag-pipe and claimed that one of his reasons for going to Canada was to recover the pipes belonging to Maclean of Coll's piper, which had been taken, to the fury of Alexander, to Canada in the 1820s. Unlike Murdoch, he was loyal to his own chief and was an uncritical supporter of the Macleans of Coll. In his final letter to Sutherland he had written:

> I have to inform you that one of the Branches of the old family of Coll came to the Island some three weeks ago with the direct object of buying the estate from Stewart and taking it back to the McLeans again. He is a young man – hails from New Zealand, and seems to be connected with a Bank there, has plenty of means and would give Stewart a fair price tomorrow if he would sell, but after speaking to him on the subject he declined coming to any arrangement for the present – so the man left Coll, but he has written me about the matter asking me to be on the alert, should any indication come that Stewart wants to sell out and let him know at once.
>
> It would be a great day for the poor people if this were to happen as this man would give them all the land available at once, whereas Stewart is getting worse and worse every day.

The visitor from New Zealand was George Alexander Maclean Buckley. He was a grandson of Alexander Maclean, *An Cùbair Colach*. As we have seen the Cooper's widow and children had emigrated to Australia, where they made a fortune in the Gold Fields. They had then moved to New Zealand and become extremely successful sheep farmers.[1]

It is perhaps significant that the last Maclean of Coll was dead before George Maclean Buckley came to Coll. Major-General John Norman Maclean of Coll had died on the 29th August 1882, leaving only daughters, his son having died as an infant. John Norman had no immediate male heir and was the last of the direct line of the Macleans of Coll.

Although George Maclean Buckley's paternal Maclean ancestors were Lochbuie cadets. His Coll blood came through the Crossapols, and it is remarkable that he wished to purchase the Coll estate.

The return of the Macleans of Coll?

If the entail had not been broken the estate would have gone to the senior descendant of Donald Maclean of the Isle of Muck. But the entail had been broken in 1854 and the nearest male heirs were not the family of Muck but the descendants of John Maclean of Totronald, who had been disinherited when the entail was made in 1754. There was therefore doubt as to who was the rightful heir to the name and arms of Maclean of Coll.

* * *

Interest in Maclean genealogy increased in 1889 with the publication of JP Maclean's *History of the Clan Maclean*. Its author was a dentist in Ohio and much of the new interest in the history of the Macleans was in North America. In 1893 the Clan Maclean in America invited Sir Fitzroy to visit the Chicago Exhibition. He landed at New York in full Highland dress. 'Needless to say' he writes in his memoirs 'I was an object of interest to the New Yorkers who saw me'.[2] He was greeted in New York by Archibald Maclean of Pennycross, who was one of the leading lights of the Clan Maclean Association, which had been instituted in Glasgow in 1892.

1892 was the year in which Colonel Alexander Maclean, late of the 94th Regiment of Foot, died. He does not appear to have passed on to his children much of what he knew about his ancestry. What he did tell them was that they were descended from the Macleans of Coll, and that, 'in certain circumstances', they would succeed to the chieftainship. Quite why he thought this was so is nowhere made clear in his surviving papers. Perhaps it was the wishful thinking of an old man.

Allan of Crossapol's manuscript history of the clan had disappeared and Alexander never saw it, but the evidence he had received from his uncle the Reverend Neil Maclean and his cousin Harriet should have shown him that the Crossapol family was the senior Coll cadet, *not* the most recent. That no one was able to tell his children the truth is an illustration of just how much had been forgotten since the diaspora of the Macleans began.

It was only after Alexander's death that his children became interested in their Maclean heritage and it is uncertain, when they were living in Bristol, how conscious the family was of its Highland roots. Certainly the eldest son Willie appears as a child in an early photograph draped in tartan, but the Maclean's life in Clifton, as shown by the family photograph album, was more affected by their mother's relations, than their father's. The former were becoming increasingly important. One cousin WH Wills, of the tobacco dynasty, was MP for East Bristol and was to become Lord Winterstoke. He was the godfather of Neil, the youngest of the Clifton Maclean brothers.[3] Other cousins were the Guinnesses, who at this time collected two peerages. The ennoblement of these new men exasperated the old nobility. Lord Salisbury is said to have complained to the Duke of Devonshire, when yet another rich Wills' cousin, who was also a MP, was recommended for a baronetcy: 'Please let your baronet or baronets be as presentable as possible … No more tobacconists I entreat you'.[4]

As far as wealth was concerned the Macleans could not possibly compete with their cousins, but the possibility that Willie was the rightful Maclean of Coll was attractive, especially to his wife Rose, and the Maclean brothers, who were all in Castlebar over the summer of 1895, probably then began their quest to get Willie recognised as Maclean of Coll.

The following summer most of the Clifton Macleans were once again in Castlebar when, on 22nd August 1896, an article appeared in the *The Oban Times*.[5] It was entitled 'The Macleans of Coll' and included the paragraph:

The Macleans, I am sorry to say, have lost Coll, but there must be someone somewhere who has the right to style himself chieftain of the Macleans of Coll. It may be an empty title, so far as the representation of land or money is concerned, but from an historic point of view it is an honourable title, just as honourable as some of those in Burke's Peerage. But, be that as it may, I should like to know the name and address of the man who is really entitled to use it.

Possibly as a result of this article Willie and his brother Hector decided to attend the 1896 gathering of the Clan Maclean Association. It was to be held in Glasgow. Daniel Maclean, the Association's secretary replied to Willie's application for a ticket:

My dear Clansman,

We are very glad that your brother & yourself are coming to the Clan Gathering on the 16th Inst.

You will get a hearty Highland welcome. Enclosed is the card of the Hotel all the McLs go to. Mrs Robertson being a Maclean & an enthusiastic one. I would advise you to be here on the Thursday leaving Dublin or Belfast on Wednesday night so as to get a letter to me to go into the matter of the Chieftainship of Coll.

Reports of the Gathering were somewhat premature when they described Willie as 'Major AWD Maclean, of Coll', listing him after Sir Fitzroy and Lady Maclean.[6] There is, however, little doubt that members of the Association were keen to have him recognised as such. A descendant of a branch of the family that had emigrated to Dantzig was claiming to be the Coll chieftain and his German nationality probably made him an unpopular choice.

All the natives of Coll living in Glasgow were said to be in Willie's favour, and their spokesman Alexander McLean Johnston, another leading light in the Association wrote to Hector to say:

I have also written to America and Australia and by the account I give of your brother am certain the Coll friends in these places will be anxious to have him as the Chieftain of the Macleans of their beloved Island.[7]

Before this could happen Willie, or rather Hector, who with Rose was now the prime mover in the quest, had to prove his case to the Lord Lyon King of Arms. It was not going to be easy. Several people claimed, correctly, that the Crossapols were descended from Neil Mor. However, with the exception of his son Neil Oig, they did not know the names of any of his descendants. This lack of generations convinced Rose that the family must only have descended from Neil Mor in the female line and that their male ancestry was from a much more recent source. A vast correspondence, which survives,[8] argues all the possibilities. It shows that the family's descent from Neil Maclean the tacksman of Crossapol in 1773, was accepted by the Lord Lyon but more research was needed to fill in the earlier gaps.

Rose was adamant the Crossapol's could not be descended from Neil Mor as both the Isle of Muck family and the Germans, would certainly have a stronger claim, and how could her dear father-in-law have made such a claim to be the Coll chieftain unless he was certain of its truth. She was convinced that the family must be descended from the most recent cadet, the Macleans of Totronald. Shortly after the Gathering she received evidence that supported her belief.

At the Gathering the brothers met Flora, the daughter of Norman Maclean sometime in Freslan. She was therefore a cousin, 'tho I fear the connection is not aristocratic', wrote Rose on 30th September 1896.[9] Flora lived at Cornaig in Coll, but she was staying in Glagow with Alexander McLean Johnston when in October 1896 she wrote: 'I think we can prove that you are off the Totronald family, if so your Brother is the rightful chieftain of the Macleans of Coll'.[10] The pace now began to quicken.

Hector had been advised to write to John Johnston in Coll and the latter replied to his letter on the 2nd November 1896:

Sir,

I duly received your letter of 25th ult with thanks. It is a great pity the inquiry contained in it was not made some four or so years ago, as Mrs Campbell from the Crosspoll family – (a sister of the Allan you refer to being her mother) she knew all about them, as she was very intelligent, and of a long age (96) before she died. My own father also who died in July last, aged 90, was a very good authority on the pedigree of all the families of note belonging to the Island. These both were alive then, and would between them put the matter on its proper footing. However we must do all we can towards it.

I cannot make out the exact relationship between the Totronald and Crosspoll families as the time is so long since they parted, but of course all the McLean families of note in Coll sprang from the same root ...

There were of the Totronald family: John, (from John Garbh 7th of Coll) – Hector, Allan, Hector (who sold it to Coll of the day) and Lachlan, who was the last of the direct male line, having lost his two sons by drowning when children. This was the Grandfather of the Miss Flora McLean you saw in Glasgow ...[11]

Hector had evidently offered to pay him for his services for Johnston wrote again on the 18th November:

I trust you will not feel yourself under any obligation to me for any little help I can render in tracing out your relationship with Coll. I shall be most happy to serve any that come within a fraction of consanguinity to that illustrious family of whom the old Coll people were so proud, and held in such affection – that even today the little remnant of them left on the Island would be ready to follow any of the family through thick and thin, to the shedding of their blood, so much of the old 'fire' is left after all the 'Terrible' vicissitudes these poor people came through ...

He continues:

Since I wrote last I have been making all possible inquiries about the Crosspoll family and I found another piece of information from a woman of about 88 years who is in Coll. She says that the Crosspoll family comes 'direct' from the Coll family and not from the Totronalds ... she says also that 'Hector' was the name of the Neil's father whom I found in the church records under date 2nd December 1776, and that 'Hector' was son of Ewen or 'Hugh' 3rd son of John Garbh 7th of Coll. This puts us on solid ground.

Who this old woman was and where she got her story from is never explained. It was quite wrong and suggests that Johnston was making it up. A new Maclean of Coll could be a valuable ally in his war with Stewart, whose reputation he constantly blackens in his correspondence with Hector.

Both Rose and Hector jumped at the story that the Crossapols were descended from John Garbh's son Hugh, who was killed at the battle of Inverkeithing. The problem was that there was no proof that Hugh was ever married. Johnston, however, was determined to get Willie recognised as Maclean of Coll. He even went as far as to get a number of Collachs at a public meting to attest that this pedigree was correct. The surviving daughters of Hugh Maclean of Coll, who were old ladies living in England, did the same, but the vital documentary evidence was still not forthcoming and there was at least one new claimant in the field.

He was none other than Willie's second cousin Major General CS Maclean, the former British Resident in Seistan, who had retired to Shanklin in the Isle of Wight. The general claimed that he was descended from the eldest son of the Donald Maclean of Coll, who died in 1729 and that this son had been disinherited. Johnston dismisses the claim and says that the general and his wife had visited Coll some 4 or 5 years previously but that at the time no mention was made of him claiming the chieftainship.

> He did, however, try to find out how his relationship with the Colls stood, I understand, and consulted some of the old people on the subject, whatever the result was I cannot say, but I can assure you that nothing was reported through the Island at the time about the matter, and that the Coll people never acknowledged him . . . as Chief . . .
>
> If General MacLean took the interest which the Coll people showed in him to mean they considered him as Chief, he was greatly mistaken though he is a very fine man and a real gentleman.[12]

As he was the son of Dr Lachlan Maclean, the man held responsible for clearing Rum, General Maclean was not popular with many of the old Coll people. One who had denounced Dr Lachlan was James Maclean, the letter-writing crofter's son in Totronald in the 1840s, who was now a plumber in Greenock. He wrote to Maclean Sinclair in Nova Scotia about the clearance of Rum. In his letter he says 'Dr L's mother was a sister of Allan of Crosspoll, that was all the connection to the family of Coll'.[13]

General Maclean really seems to have believed that he was the rightful Maclean of Coll and that his ancestor had been cheated out of his birthright. He refused to attend Maclean Gatherings. In a letter to Hector Maclean in June 1900 he says: 'I have made a rule of never taking part in any of the clan gatherings except in my proper position as the lineal representative of John Garve, in virtue of my descent from Hector, the eldest son of Donald of Coll and Macleod of Harris's daughter'.[14] It was a claim that the Association considered 'preposterous'.

Unfortunately for his theory a cousin of General MacLean, who had emigrated to Australia had a different origin for their family. She does not mention any paternal relationship to Maclean of Coll, but rather to the Macleans of Duart. The General's family were certainly known as the *Sliochd Eachainn Mhic Dhomhnaill* 'the seed of Hector son of Donald'. What I believe happened is that the family muddled up two different families and that they were in fact descended from the first Donald of Brolas. He did have two sons called Hector: Hector Mor and Hector Oig, the latter being the ancestor of the present Chief of Duart. The elder Hector was perhaps illegitimate and his family were among the refugees given sanctuary in Coll after the Campbells took over the Duart estate.[15]

This wishful thinking of prominent Highlanders, and the desire to make their ancestors more distinguished than they were, is one of their curious habits throughout the ages.[16] It was particularly prevalent in the Victorian era when people with quite humble origins had become extremely wealthy and wished to have an illustrious pedigree to go with their new wealth. There was no lack of unscrupulous genealogists then or now, who, for a sum, were perfectly prepared to do what their patrons wished.

* * *

On 9th March 1897 Willie Maclean resigned his appointment as Adjutant of 3rd Battalion the Connaught Rangers.[17] He had spent four and a half years in Castlebar and his departure was marked by the presentation of an illuminated address acknowledging his popularity with all classes in County Mayo and their thanks for his courtesy and public spiritedness during his time amongst them.[18] He was posted to the 1st Battalion, who were then in Sheffield and on 15th April sailed on the P&O steamer for India.

In his absence Hector continued to seek for evidence for his brother to be recognised as Maclean of Coll, and on 25th November 1898 Francis J Grant, the Lyon Clerk wrote to him to say:

> The Lord Lyon has again gone over the whole facts and I am glad to say feels himself justified in granting your brother a matriculation of the Arms as representing the family of Coll. The extract is therefore being written out and I hope will be ready in about a fortnight. I shall then communicate with you regarding the fees payable.[19]

The following day a letter appeared in the *Oban Times* from Charles James Maclean, of the Isle of Muck family who claimed that they were the Coll heirs. Hector wrote to the Clan Maclean Association pointing out that, although the Mucks had been heirs of entail, that entail had been broken in 1854. He went on to announce to the Association that he had just received the Lyon Clerk's letter. They informed the press. All hell now broke out: Frank Hunter, the grandson of Alexander Hunter the Coll Trustee wrote to Lyon to say that Hugh of Inverkeithing had never been married; James Maclean, the Greenock plumber wrote to the *Oban Times* to say that the Muck's were the rightful heirs, and on 15th December Francis Grant wrote to Hector to inform him that:

> The announcement made in the newspapers which was quite premature, has had the result of producing several rival claimants to the chieftainship of Coll who have protested against the issue of the Extract. The Lyon has requested particulars of their claim and until these have been furnished and disposed of I will be unable to have the Extract completed.
>
> I presume you have seen the correspondence, which has been going on in the *Oban Times*.

Hector protested, but to no avail and on 21st December Lyon himself wrote to him to say:

> You are of course aware that your case at the best is rather a thin one; still in the absence of any opposition and on the footing that your brother's claims were acknowledged by the clan in general I should have felt justified, as I stated, in matriculating the Arms of Coll to him, but this matriculation could only have proceeded on the narrative that some of the steps in the descent rested upon generally received family tradition. When, however, there is distinct and categorical contradiction, and one family tradition is put against another the matter assumes a

different aspect and I must take some time to consider or if possible get further light. I am not in the least taking up a position hostile to your brother's claim: I only say it must be dealt with from a different point of view.

I do not think the question of the entail need enter into consideration.

Although Hector continued to search for further evidence, this was really the end of the affair. It was to be several years before Allan of Crossapol's manuscript which seems to have been in the possession of a member of the Fiosgaradh family, came to light.[20]

* * *

Although the confrontation between Hector and General Maclean was fought out in the columns of the *Celtic Monthly*, they continued to have civilised social relations. In 1900, after remarking that Alexander Maclean Sinclair's *Clan Gillean*, which had been published the previous year, had treated both families' descent 'rather unkindly'. The General goes on to say:

I hope you and yours are all well and that your brother in South Africa is sound & hale where so many have been cut down. My son Donald is, or rather was at Wepener when he last wrote fretting at not being at the front. Colin is in *Prince George* & Alastair is going up for his exam for Sandhurst in a few days.[21]

The General's son Donald had been educated at Clifton College. In 1895 he was commissioned into the Royal Scots. He was also to win the DSO in South Africa and to be mentioned in dispatches. He died in 1909.[22] He was the father of Vice-Admiral Sir Hector Charles Donald Maclean, KBE, CB, DSC,[23] who continued to claim to be the rightful Maclean of Coll.

* * *

Whilst Harry Maclean, as Neil was now called, was serving in South Africa, his eldest brother Willie was in India. Since leaving Castlebar he had served in the North-West Frontier Province. He was for some time Commandant of Kailana Camp. He died on 20 May 1901 at the Station Hospital in Nasirabad. In notifying his death in orders the Commanding Officer stated that: 'Major Maclean had endeared himself to all. In his death the battalion has suffered the loss of a most highly talented and efficient officer'.[24]

In 1909 Harry Maclean took over command of the KOSB's Depot at Berwick-on-Tweed. He was still there when in August 1914 the First World War began. He was ordered to raise a Service battalion in Kitchener's New Army. It was named the 6th Service Battalion the King's Own Scottish Borderers, and was part of the 9th (Scottish) Division. It had the distinction to be one of the 'First Hundred Thousand'.

* * *

After two World Wars, it is almost impossible today to imagine the enthusiasm of those young men who flocked into the army in August 1914. Harry Maclean moved his headquarters to Bordon in Hampshire, where the new battalion was to assemble. By the end of September they were almost overwhelmed by the number of men from the Borders wishing to join up. 'CW' the anonymous author of the story of the 6th Battalion writes that:

at one period my Company totalled over 600! I think the strength of the Battalion was more than 2000, and it was with great difficulty that we fed and paid them in Barracks with accommodation for only one Battalion.[25]

As a result it was necessary to raise two more battalions of Borderers and when their COs and officers arrived and other Barracks in the district were available, the men were drafted off to the 7th and 8th Battalions respectively. They were to become part of the 15th Scottish Division.

6 KOSB worked from dawn to midnight, with only one week's holiday at Christmas. CW writes:

but it was work that showed good result in a very short time. By means of preliminary route marches, handling arms, and recruit drill, Company, Battalion, Brigade, and Divisional training, not forgetting musketry... we eventually developed into one of the finest Battalions ever raised.

6 KOSB was a family affair. Its men were from the towns and countryside of the Borders, and were as clannish as Highlanders. On occasions this clannishness could be overdone. CW, who had to bring three hundred recruits from Berwick-on-Tweed to Bordon, writes that 'for instance, twenty men, evidently all belonging to the same football club, insisted on being together in one carriage, while the next was empty'.

The battalion were at Bordon until March 1915. It then moved into huts at Bramshott for Divisional training. Almost all the original officers had by then left to fill the many vacancies in the 2nd Battalion, which had gone to France in August 1914 with the British Expeditionary Force. They were all either killed or wounded before 6 KOSB left England. Not one, as had been hoped, came back after convalescence. The result was that all the battalion's officers, with the exception of the CO, Second-in-Command, Adjutant, one or two Company Commanders, and Quartermaster, had when they joined been cadets, with only volunteer or OTC training. They had no doubt, like the rest of the army's new officers, soon been imbued with the traditional paternalism of the pre-war regular officer.[26]

On 13 May 6 KOSB left England for France. They arrived at Boulogne an hour or so late. Led by Harry Maclean and his Adjutant the battalion marched off the boat, and formed up on the quays. CW writes that 'Though it was after midnight, and we had only just arrived, we immediately ran up against the realities of war, as the hospital ships lined alongside the wharfs were busily taking in the wounded'. They set off for St Omer and then to the village of Tatinghem, where they had the first taste of French billets.

Time passed and 'after a while we began to wonder when we should be going into the trenches, as we were getting very tired of the inactivity. Route marches were insisted upon every morning, with physical exercise and bayonet fighting, to keep the men fit, and in the afternoons we used to play soccer.

'We had quite enough of this, and great was our joy when Company Commanders, with the CO and Adjutant, went off to look at the trenches outside Armentières. The rest of the Battalion followed next day, and the men were billeted at a convent'.

On their march they met their fellow Borders. The author of the 7/8th Battalion writes:

On the last day of August we had the pleasure of meeting the 6th Battalion KOS Borderers. They were marching through Fouquereuil on their way to Verquin, where they were to be billeted for the night. Work was stopped, and the 6th Battalion halted for a few minutes to allow the men to talk to one another. The 6th looked very fit.[27]

Eventually they went into the trenches. CW says that:

The main communication trench was a work of art, with wooden fascines and revetments all the way along. It seemed to be of an interminable length, and all we could see were the stars just beginning to peep out, and the gaunt shell-shattered willow trees ... The Hun lines were about 400 yards away, and I was told they were held by Saxons who were very quiet.

He continues:

The state of our trenches is difficult to describe. They had recently been captured from the Germans, and were ornamented by decomposing legs, hands, and other parts of the body sticking out of the parapet, parados, and even from the bottom of the trench, where the corpses had evidently been hastily buried. It was very hot weather at the time and one could never get accustomed to the stench of the dead.

After a few days it began to rain in torrents, and the trenches were soon half full of mud, which reached to the waist in parts.

The battalion's trenches were in a dreary part of industrial Artois. It was poor, chalky ground, overgrown with long grass. The remains of rows of mean miner's cottages surrounded pit-heads and mounds of slag. There was only about one to five hundred yards of No Man's Land between the brown parapets of the British lines and the wall of dull grey sand-bags that formed those of the Germans.

It was known to everyone on either side that Haig was preparing a major offensive. As the days passed, the bombardment grew more intense, and CW writes that

our excitement grew to fever pitch. On Friday morning, 24th September, we marched by platoons and took up our battle positions prior to the attack, which was to be some time the following morning, Saturday 25th September 1915. A and B Companies held the front trenches, C and D in the immediate rear.

Orders were that we, D Company, were to assemble in A Company's trenches immediately they went over the parapet, and then to follow them directly we received word from the second in command.

By the evening the whole Battalion was in position. Everybody was watching the wind as it had been decided that the attack would be preceded by the use of gas, which had been developed to counter the enormous advantage machine-guns gave to a defender.

The German lines were on the crest of a low line of downs. On the first crest rose 'a great German fortification some 500 yards in diameter, which was built around the path from Vermelles to Loos, and dominating with its machine-guns and its sunken quick-firing turrets of steel armour the bare, grassy hollows through which our men had to advance. There were three lines of barbed wire to get through, machine-gun positions sheltering behind slag heaps to storm, and rows of colliers' cottages'.

A gas attack requires not only a current of air flowing in a regular movement from the advancing force to the defending force, but the current must be 'of a nice quality, neither too strong, or it will disperse the gas before the effect is obtained, nor too gentle, or it may not carry the cloud of heavy fumes quickly and far enough'.[28]

CW writes:

> It had been decided in the event of the wind being unfavourable to launch the attack without the assistance of gas. However, fortune seemed to be on our side, as a steady breeze was blowing towards the Hun line. After a final inspection to see every man was ready with bayonet fixed &c. I waited for the fatal hour. Sharp at 6, immense volumes of smoke were seen emerging from our front line, and rolling very, very slowly towards the Huns. These were the smoke bombs thrown out with the gas, and our engineers were doing their work well. We were all wearing gas helmets on our heads so that they could be pulled over the face immediately if the gas turned in our direction.
>
> At this time it seemed as if hell was let loose. Every available gun from the 18-pounder to the heavy siege was firing rapid, and the Huns, too, pored shell after shell into us as they knew an attack was imminent ... Everything looked as if things were going splendidly for us, as the gas seemed to have reached the Hun line, and was still rolling forward. Our spirits were sky high then, and the men were dancing with anxiety to get forward.

As soon as CW saw the silhouettes of A Company going over the top he took his men up the communication trench. It took only a few minutes to get into position and D Company were ready in A Company's trench as the last of its men disappeared into the smoke.

Morale was sky high and the excitement was at fever pitch as D Company waited for the order to follow on. Then everything changed.

> ghastly forms re-appeared from the smoke and came tumbling into the trench. Some were quite green, coughing and spitting, and shouting 'For Christ's sake, kill me', others were covered in blood shot in dozens of places, and some so mangled that as they fell quivering in their death spasm, you could hardly recognise them as human beings.
>
> This was our A Company, which went forward with such confidence, and there we were waiting for orders before we could go to their assistance. My Company Commander came up to me, and as we had no word to advance, we decided to go forward at once, as I guessed our second in command had been killed. With a shout we were over – there was no delaying – everybody went over as one. We half walked, half ran – but the men were dropping round me like ninepins – the barrage was so terrific. I can remember distinctly the expression on the faces of those near me, and it was whilst pointing out our direction with my stick, when we were half way across, that I felt a terrific shock in my right leg, and toppled over, forgetting everything for the moment. I had been shot clean through the right leg, but I regained sufficient consciousness to see our poor devils falling all around me, and some disappearing in the smoke. Blood must have been spouting from me like a fountain, but my servant, to whom I owe my life, was quickly at my side, and ripping the field dressing from my coat, bound up my leg. We both lay there for some considerable time until I felt I had sufficient strength to crawl on my stomach back to our lines.

During this slow and painful progress he got hit in the back, but he said it was only a splinter, and did not hurt him, and he still stayed with me. After a while he left me for a minute and crawled to a dead KOSB to get me his water bottle as I had left mine behind with my haversack and I was parched with thirst. He returned shortly with the news that he had seen our Company Commander lying dead near the parapet, shot through the head.

It took us roughly two to three hours to get back to our front trench, and it was a marvel we were not killed as we crawled over the parapet.

Outside, on No Man's Land, it was a pretty bad sight, but what met our eyes when we got into the trench, no pen could describe.

On the firing step where I lay was our Pipe Major sitting bolt upright, shot through both legs. He had been playing his pipes from the top of the trench until he was hit and toppled back. I got my servant to give him some morphia, which I had with me, and I think that relieved him temporarily. I heard later he died in hospital. He was the finest and grandest old man in the Regiment, and we were justly proud of him.

At the bottom of the trench and piled in dugouts lay the dead and wounded. There was still the nauseating smell of our gas, which clung about the trench, and every engineer seemed to be suffering from it. Walking hither and thither were men who had lost their units and did not know where to go. Confusion and chaos seemed to reign everywhere. Men were running about shouting for stretcher-bearers, and others were crying out that the Huns were counter-attacking.

I attempted with the assistance of my servant to crawl down the trenches until we came across a stretcher-bearer. During this slow and tortuous journey I heard on all sides of the terrible tragedy that had over-taken the poor old KOSBs. 'A' Company had lost every officer; the whole Company had been held up on the wire, which had not been cut effectually. The same had happened to all the other Companies.

When he reached Battalion Headquarters CW met his Colonel and Adjutant. Both were going off. Harry Maclean had been hit in the head as he went up the communication trench to lead his battalion into No-Man's land.[29] His Adjutant assumed command until he was wounded in the foot. The Battalion had been cut to pieces, and every officer had been killed or wounded except the second machine-gun and transport officer who did not have to go over the top. The British gas affected most of the wounded. It was still to disable them when their other wounds had healed.

Few of 6 KOSB had reached their objective. Too many things had gone wrong. The wind at daybreak on Saturday morning had been too gentle and too aslant of the enemy's main positions. It had therefore drifted back on the battalion. Despite the artillery barrage the shells had failed to cut the German wire. Also at the crucial moment CW writes:

Our gunners had ceased fire. I learnt afterwards they had no more ammunition, but the Huns were throwing every single projectile they had into us. Bullets were spluttering and licking up the earth all round, and shells were bursting near and over our heads every second.

CW's picture of the battle bears little relation to the account in the weekly illustrated newspaper *The Great War* of the battle of Loos. In the caption under a picture of the British Storming A German Trench Near Loos. *The Great War* states that:

between September 25th and 27th 1915, the Allies made a combined advance in Artois, in the course of which there was some exceptionally heavy fighting, resulting in tremendous loss to the enemy and the capture of the important village of Loos. After a terrific preliminary bombardment by our artillery, the infantry rushed the trenches, racing their officers, one of whom was heard to call out: 'Faster, boys! Give them hell!' There was some rapid bayonet work, which brought the Germans to their knees screaming for mercy, and an immense number were taken prisoners.

News of the reality of the battle of Loos, which saw around 60,000 British casualties,[30] was kept from the British public and it must have been extremely galling for those who took part to see no mention of the 9th Division in the newspapers. And no account of their achievements, 'other than a very jejeune account which was published many months afterwards, has reached the public, and their friends only know of their glory and of the heavy fighting in which they were engaged, from private letters, or from announcements of the casualties'.[31]

CW writes in his Finale:

in spite of our terrible casualties and unfulfilled hopes, there is the consolation of knowing that we played our part and did credit to the undying history of our Regiment. Other Battalions in that Division were more lucky and did great things but for all that, if fortune had been on our side, I am sure we should have done well, and what we did will have helped in no small way to bring victory and freedom to our great Empire.

Winston Churchill was more generous. In a speech in the House of Commons on the 31 May 1916 he said:

I will tell the House the story of the 9th Scottish Division. This Division was the premier Division of Scotland, the first of the New Army to be raised by Scotland at the beginning of the War. In the battle of Loos, this Division, with the other Scottish Division, the 15th, played a very notable part. Out of the 9500 infantry who advanced to the attack, 6000 men were killed and wounded in the battle. Some of the Battalions lost three-fourths of their strength, but nearly all succeeded in achieving the task which was set them of gaining the positions, some of the most important positions, and they were only lost when they were subsequently handed at a later stage to other troops.

The author the *History of the KOSB in the Great War* gives the statistical details: 358 were killed or missing, 272 were wounded or gassed. Two thirds of the NCOs and men were casualties. 11 officers were killed and 8 were wounded. He adds that 'it was all over in minutes. The wonderful product of months of zeal, energy and patriotism were "knocked out" without opportunity of doing more than set an example to posterity by their bravery'.[32] It was the battle of Inverkeithing all over again.

Notes

1. Helen Maclean Buckley *From Little Towns in a Far Land we came* (1950), 31–49. The only one of the Cooper's children to marry was his daughter Alexandrina. George Buckley was her son. He failed to buy Coll and instead bought the Isle of Shuna, where he built the present castle.
2. 'Life of Sir FD Maclean, Bart', 269.

3. BCP *The House that Jack built* inscribed to 'Harry Maclean from his affect. Godfather WHW, January 7 1878'. Henry Donald Neil Maclean was known as both 'Harry' and 'Neil' at different stages of his career. WH Wills was Sheriff of Bristol from 1877–8; MP for Coventry 1880–5, and for East Bristol 1895–1900; High Sheriff of Somerset 1905–6; created a baronet 12 August 1893, and raised to the peerage as Baron Winterstoke, of Blagdon, co. Somerset 1 February 1906. He *died* 29 January 1911, when both his barony and baronetcy became extinct. [*Burke's Peerage & Baronetage*, (1928), 2424].
4. *Lord Salisbury*, 662.
5. BCP. AWD Maclean's scrapbook. The letter was written by the Rev. Alexander Maclean Sinclair, the grandson of John Maclean the Laird of Coll's bard. He was later to publish *Clan Gillean* (Charlottetown, 1899).
6. Ditto. *The Glasgow Herald*, Saturday 17 October 1896. Clan Maclean Reunion.
7. BCP. Johnston Box file. 1 December 1896. Alexander McLean Johnston, 13 Franklin Terrace Overnewton, Glasgow, to HAC Maclean.
8. BCT. Pink Folder. Copies of 'Letters to Hector Arthur Coalson Maclean concerning the claim of the Macleans of Crossapol to succeed as Barons of Coll. 1896–1916.'
9. BCT. Pink Folder. 30 September [1896]. Rose Maclean to Hector Maclean.
10. BCT. Pink Folder. 10 October 1896. Flora Maclean to Hector Maclean.
11. BCT. Johnston Box File. 2 November 1896. Johnston to Hector Maclean.
12. Ibid.
13. *Rum*, 128.
14. BCP. 14 June 1900. Shanklin. CS MacLean to Hector Maclean.
15. Nicholas Maclean-Bristol 'A Genealogical Puzzle Solved?' *WHN&Q* No. XXX, (February 1987), 13–17.
16. David Sellar 'Highland Family Origins – Pedigree Making and Pedigree Faking', Loraine Maclean of Dochgarroch (ed) *The Middle Ages in the Highlands* (1981), 103–116.
17. *London Gazette* 9 March 1897.
18. BCP. AWD Maclean's scrap book.
19. BCT. 25 November 1898. Lyon Clerk to Hector A Maclean Esq. 50 Bessborough Street, London.
20. In 1921, after Hector's death, his brother Neil, who was staying at the Constitutional Club in London, received a letter from the Association saying an Allan Maclean in Greenock had written to ask them to advertise for the *Leabhar Dearg* of the Macleans of Coll which had been in the custody of Neil Maclean of the Fiosgaradh family and lent by him to John Maclean, wine merchant, London. It is likely that this was the Crossapol manuscript but there is no other evidence as to where it was from the time it was written until it turned up in HDN Maclean's papers. Most of his possessions were left with his sister Mrs Francis-Hawkins, who was my grandmother.
21. BCP. Brolas Box File. 14 June 1900. Shanklin. Major General CS Maclean to HAC Maclean.
22. *Who Was Who 1897–1916*, 458.
23. *Burke's Peerage &c* (1970).
24. *The Connaught Rangers*, 384.
25. CW *From Bordon to Loos* (1917), 6.
26. GD Sheffield *Leadership in the Trenches* (2000).
27. J Goss *A Border Battalion the History of the 7/8th (Service) Battalion King's Own Scottish Borderers*. (1920), 27.
28. HW Wilson (ed) *The Great War* vol. V (week ending 11 December 1915), 116.
29. Stair Gillon *The KOSB in the Great War* (nd), 326.
30. Niall Ferguson *The Pity of War*, (1999), 307. I have to thank the author for a copy of his book.
31. Winston Churchill MP. House of Commons 31 May 1916.
32. Stair Gillon *The History of the KOSB in the Great War* (nd), 327.

Chapter Sixty-Six

From Regiment to OPMACC

Lieutenant-Colonel HDN Maclean spent the eighteen months after the battle of Loos recovering from his wounds. By August 1917 he was sufficiently recovered to resume command of his battalion. He joined 6 KOSB on 9th August 1917.

The offensive known as 'Third Battle of Ypres' had started 10 days earlier. It was doomed before it had even begun. The scene of the last phase of the battle, where Harry Maclean was to lead his battalion into the attack for the last time was the low, flat country near the northern end of the Passchendaele Ridge and was pitted with shell-holes holding water. It was reclaimed marshland, which was too wet for cultivation. Heavy shellfire would and did destroy the intricate drainage system and turned it into a swamp.

27 Brigade, of which 6 KOSB was a part, was moving forward to the start line when at about midnight on the 11th October the weather broke completely and the march of the Brigade, under torrents of rain along the slippery duckboards was one prolonged ordeal. How heavily laden infantry were expected to cross this morass and take their objectives beggars belief.

As the brigade moved forward to the forming up place [FUP] a company of 6 KOSB was caught in the open by the hostile barrage and suffered considerable casualties. Sir John Campbell of Ardnamurchan,[1] the descendant of Maclean of Coll's old ally Campbell of Airds, who was commanding 11 Royal Scots transferred a company to 6 KOSB who, thus reinforced, went on forward to the FUP. They were heavily shelled and gassed by the enemy's artillery. Many of the taping parties were killed or wounded, and all had to wear their respirators for several hours. At 5.35 am the British barrage began and the battalions moved forward. The leading men, without the marking tapes, lost direction almost at once.

To say that the battle of Passchendaele was a disaster is something of an understatement.[2] The historian of the 9th (Scottish) Division, of which 27 Brigade was a part, writes:

> Rain and mud constituted the chief explanation for the failure of the Division in this battle, which should not have been fought; no man could progress at more than a snails pace, and shear exhaustion was a factor more potent than the enemy in bringing the advance to a standstill.[3]

Among the losses 6 KOSB suffered on 12th October were 15 killed, 154 wounded and 27 missing (probably drowned). The illustrated periodical *The Great War* has a harrowing description of the suffering of the army in the mud of Passchendaele:

Many British soldiers found themselves up to their armpits in mud. When comrades tried to pull them out the result was that the would-be helpers were pulled in. In one case two battalions took three-quarters of an hour to get over two lines of undefended trenches. Entire platoons were overwhelmed in bogs like quicksands, into which they slipped when trying to climb out.[4]

The physical strain proved too much for Harry Maclean's constitution. It was a young man's war and the 'gallant Colonel was evacuated sick on the 19th [October 1917]'.[5]

By 1920 he had improved sufficiently to take command of 2 KOSB, but his recovery was premature. On 4th February 1922 he was invalided out of the army.[6]

Harry took a keen interest in the War. He owned all the books written about the KOSB and purchased several of Bruce Bairnsfather's original cartoons to add to the drawings by R Caton Woodville of the Second Boer War. He died in France in 1927. He was 55. With his death the direct male line of the *Sliochd Neil Mor*, as recorded by Allan Maclean of Crossapol, came to an end. There were, however, numerous descendants of the family through the female line. I am one of them.

* * *

Some explanation is required to explain why I have spent almost fifty years of my life collecting information for this book. As a child I was constantly told that I looked like a Maclean and behaved like one. I am not sure that this was meant to be a compliment and I wanted to be a Bristol like my father. However, slowly but surely my imagination was captured by stories of the Macleans of Coll: of how my great uncle was really the rightful chief; but that he had somehow been cheated out of his inheritance; the Castle should have belonged to us.

My new enthusiasm was wetted by my great grandfather's copy of Donald Gregory's *History of the Western Highlands and Isles of Scotland* and Maclean Sinclair's *Clan Gillean*, which I read avidly whenever I visited my Aunt Elspeth in London. She was the custodian of most of our Maclean family artefacts, which she had inherited when her uncle Harry and her mother died.

The other major influence on me was the Second World War. I was eight in 1943, when the battle of El Alamein was fought. It is impossible for those who were not children at that time to understand the excitement of that victory. We listened every day to the six o'clock news and marked the Eighth Army's advance across North Africa and into Europe with pins on wall maps. We also fought battles with our toy soldiers. There was no doubt in my mind that I would be a soldier and follow my uncle Alec and great uncle Harry into the KOSB.

After Wellington I joined up as a recruit at Berwick-on-Tweed. After Sandhurst I was commissioned into 1 KOSB. In 1955 they were stationed at Ballykinlar in Northern Ireland. We were then ordered to Malaya and took part in the campaign there against the Communist Terrorists. I was then appointed as ADC to the GOC 52 (Lowland) Infantry Division & Lowland District in Glasgow.

It was in Glasgow that my interest in the Macleans really flowered. In particular I obtained an extended loan from my cousin Mona Pattullo of her father's papers concerning his claim to be Maclean of Coll. At about the same time I acquired Allan Maclean of Crossapol's manuscript.

As my boss General JFM Macdonald CB, DSO, OBE was commanding a Territorial Division much of our work took place at weekends. There was not much to do in the office, either for me, or the General's PA Miss Russell. Miss Russell, who soon became Mrs Barrie's forbears had lived on the estate of Mackenzie of Gairloch, and she was immensely loyal to them and was interested in the Highlands in general. It therefore did not take much persuasion to get her to type out my great uncle Hector's papers.

Whilst I was living in Glasgow I explored the Highlands and visited Coll for the first time. It had not changed a great deal since Rider Haggard's visit in 1898. The steamer still anchored off Arinagour and a ferryboat carried passengers and parcels to the shore. I stayed at the Coll Hotel. Guy and Jean Jardine were my generous hosts. The hotel appeared in the *Good Food Guide* and lived up to its reputation.

Thanks to *Hughie Broadhill*, who amongst his many other jobs, drove the Island's one taxi, I was shown much of the Island. I was also taken to meet many of the old people still living on the Island, and added their stories to those I had gleaned from my great uncle's papers.

The weather was good and the Island was magical. I decided that this was where I wanted to spend my life. Hughie also took me to see the Castle. It stood gaunt, roofless and empty. No one had lived in it since 1750; apart from my family no one had ever lived there; it had never been blown up or burnt down; it had just decayed quietly like an old warrior once his active life was over. But was Breacachadh's use over? Could it be restored?

I knew of old Sir Fitzroy Maclean's restoration of Duart and MacNeill of Barra's at Kishmul. I decided that I would take on the third restoration of a mediaeval Hebridean castle. Kenneth Stewart, who had inherited the Coll estate, and who I met on my first visit to the Island, was prepared to sell Breacachadh Castle to me and shortly after I stopped being ADC it became mine.

When I returned to 1 KOSB they were stationed in Berlin. Then after some time at Redford Barracks in Edinburgh I was off on the advance party to Aden. It too did not appear to have changed all that much since my great grandfather had been there in 1846.

Since I bought Breacachadh, I had been trying to work out what I would do with it. Certainly I wanted it to be the home for my wife and children if and when I got married, but I also saw it as the centre of an international organisation. I knew from my study of Maclean history that many Collachs, who had gone overseas, had been remarkably successful. They had first left as mercenary soldiers, then as colonists, and finally as soldiers in the British Army. Was there something in Coll's environment that could inspire a new generation in Britain to serve overseas, and return to enrich their own communities?

It was when I was walking down the High Street in Maala in Aden that I had a chance meeting that changed my life, and that of a great many other people. A motorcade drove past me, and when I looked to see who the visiting dignitary was, to my surprise I recognised someone who had been in my form at Wellington. It was Prince Alexander Desta, the grandson of Haile Selassie, the Emperor of Ethiopia.

He was staying with the Governor of Aden. I gave him a telephone call. We had a drink and he invited me to visit him in Ethiopia. I was due some leave and I spent ten days exploring Ethiopia with Desta. He had his finger in an enormous number of pies and was passionate about the future of his country.

One of the people he took me to meet was Professor Rowse, who ran the Technical Agency. He had on his office wall maps of Ethiopia that were littered with symbols. He said that every circle was a potential Kariba Dam. He claimed that if they were built Ethiopia could not only feed itself, but the whole of North East Africa. It was stirring stuff. It made me think.

Before I returned to Aden, Desta told me that he might be his grandfather's successor. Would I be interested in leaving the army and help him develop Ethiopia. He said that there was room in

Ethiopia for anyone, whatever the colour of his skin, who fell in love with the country. It was an amazing offer. I had recently spent two and a half years in Malaya, where 50% of the population appeared to want to throw out the British. All over the developing world everyone was crying for 'decolonisation'. Yet here was an articulate black politician who actually wanted the British to stay. It was then that I saw my 'blinding light on the road to Damascus'. I said that my future was in the Hebrides, but that I would send him able young Englishmen. It would be up to him to capture their imagination. They could then help him to achieve his dream.

* * *

We left Aden in February 1964. 1 KOSB had been there for two years. I was on the rear party. We were then stationed at Shorncliffe in Kent. In my spare time I started to explore the possibility of recruiting young men to serve in Ethiopia. I had a lot to learn. For instance I did not even know of the existence of Voluntary Service Overseas, which since 1958 had been sending eighteen year old volunteers to Nigeria and Sarawak.

My researches had, however, to be put on hold when, inspired by Nasser, an uprising began in the Radfan, on the border between the Aden Protectorate and the Yemen. In an attempt to put down the rising a battalion of the Parachute Regiment was to be dropped into the Radfan. In order to mark out the DZ [the dropping zone], a party of SAS was sent ahead into the Radfan. They were seen by a shepherd and were attacked. Two of the party were killed. The remainder fought their way out, but they had to leave the bodies of their dead comrades behind. Their heads were cut off and put on poles across the border.

A punitive expedition was launched against the tribesmen in the Radfan, as 1 KOSB was spearhead battalion, it was immediately sent back to Aden. The next four months were amongst the most exhilerating in my army career as we put down the rebellion in much the same manner as 2 KOSB had in Tirah.

When we returned to England, I was sent on a staff attachment to 19 Infantry Brigade Headquarters in Colchester. In a matter weeks we were sent to Borneo. Indonesia was threatening to invade Sarawak and reinforcements were needed. 19 Brigade Headquarters was stationed to Sibu in the Third Division of Sarawak.

In the short time since we had returned for the first time from Aden and our return to the Radfan I had met my future wife and become engaged. At a cocktail party in Colchester Brigadier David Fraser had said to my wife to be that of course she must come out to Borneo. Once we got there he changed his mind. We had, however, sent out our wedding invitations, and the Brigadier allowed me to hitch a lift home on a RAF plane and get married. We spent the first half of our honeymoon in Coll and the second half in Singapore. I then went back to the war and Lavinia got a job working for Special Branch in Kuching, which was not part of Brigadier Fraser's bailliewick.

In the meantime 1 KOSB had been sent to Hong Kong, and when 19 Brigade Headquarters returned to the UK, the Battalion was posted to the Third Division of Sarawak. As 1 KOSB were short of captains, instead of going home with 19 Brigade, I went up river to become second-in-command of B Company at Nanga Gaat.

Whilst I was with 19 Brigade I was able to visit Kuching every six weeks or so, but when I rejoined 1 KOSB this was not going to be possible. I therefore smuggled Lavinia to Sibu and took her up river. She went to live for a short while in a longhouse on the Rejang River, where she lived with a community of Ibans. Most had never seen a white woman before.

Then to my relief I was posted to the Ministry of Defence and became a very junior staff officer in the Directorate of Army Training. My job was to help organise army exercises in Africa and the Mediterranean.

* * *

When President Kennedy founded the Peace Corps, people in Britain said that we should have one too. It was pointed out that VSO had been doing the same sort of thing for some time, but instead of the experts the Peace Corps was sending to developing countries, VSO was sending out eighteen year olds.

It was decided that VSO should follow the Peace Corps' example. Alec Dickson, the founder of VSO, was replaced. The eighteen year olds were rapidly phased out. There was now no organisation to enable eighteen year olds, who had a year to spare before going to University, to serve overseas. A number of people felt strongly that this was a mistake and that a new initiative should be launched. Among them were friends of mine, including George Edinger,[7] and Alec and Mora Dickson.[8] In our spare time we recruited three young men, who we sent to the Abba Hanna Jimma home for street boys in Addis Ababa. Prince Alexander Desta had been responsible for its foundation. The boys sailed for Ethiopia in December 1967.

Despite numerous dramas, the experiment was sufficiently successful for us to replace the first three with a further five. They were sent to work with the Ministry of Mines. It was, however, decided that in order to select suitable volunteers it was necessary to have more than just a half an hour interview. Instead we would run a selection course on the lines of the Army's Regular Commissions Board. As an experiment, when the Ministry of Mines boys returned to the UK, we brought them up to Coll. Here we made them do orienteering and other practical tasks. Work on the Castle had begun and they were able to camp with us in Breacachadh. We found that living and working with them enabled us to know them really well. Since then every volunteer we have sent overseas has first come to Coll.

Shortly before I was posted to the Ministry of Defence the concept of Military Aid to the Civil Community [OPMACC] was born. A number of people, notably Gerry Reynolds MP, the Parliamentary Under-Secretary of State for the Army, Major-General DB Lang CB, DSO, MC, Director of Army Training, and the journalist Hugh Hanning, had developed the idea of the peaceful use of military forces and formalising the help the Services already gave to the civil community.

The Government of the day had taken the decision to withdraw west of Suez and there were going to be a considerable increase in the number of servicemen in the UK. How could they best be used in 'areas where the training requirements and skills of a military unit' could 'be harnessed to do a particular task which the community as a whole would like undertaken'.[9] Many of the ideas concerned assistance in a natural disaster or other emergencies. Others were routine tasks such as the improvement of amenities in the countryside, assistance to youth organizations &c. There was, however, Category C, which visualised the full time attachment of volunteer officers and NCOs to social service organizations. I was asked if I would consider becoming the Army's first volunteer. I jumped at the chance, and when my two-year tour at the Ministry of Defence came to an end I became the Army's first director of the Project Trust.

My wife and I had purchased a small terraced house in Waterloo, which became the Trust's headquarters. It was in walking distance of both Whitehall and the City, which was invaluable as one of my first tasks was to raise the funds to make the whole idea possible. It also involved waiting for potential donors to reply to my requests. Once again, as in Glasgow, I had time on my hands. Much of it was therefore spent working on Highland history at the London Library and copying out extracts from the Register of the Privy Council of Scotland &c. [I didn't know about photocopiers then, but the exercise had the advantage of making me remember facts I might otherwise have forgotten].

One of the people I approached to sponsor Project financially was Field-Marshal Sir Gerald Templer, who had been largely responsible for the defeat of the Communist Terrorists in Malaya. He had a somewhat brusque reputation and it was with some trepidation that I went to visit him. 'No' he said when I outlined my case. He would not give me any money. However, 'it was time that Jackie Ward, became involved in something like that'. He would speak to him about it.

Colonel EJS Ward, MVO, MC had commanded the Life Guards and the Household Cavalry Regiment. He was a rich man and was to turn up each day at our office in Whittlesey Street in his chauffeur-driven Rolls-Royce, much to the twitching of lace curtains. He would then write begging letters to his friends. They were highly supportive and Project raised enough money to send the next batch of volunteers overseas. It also provided sufficient funds for me to fly to South America and find projects in Chile, Peru and Mexico in addition to those in Ethiopia.

I later flew to Australia and found further openings. In Tasmania I had a letter of introduction to Donald Mackinnon of Dalness, near Launceston. He was descended from Allan Mackinnon, the son of Coll's tenant in Rum and Jessie, the daughter of Allan Maclean in Arileod, who had sailed to Australia with her family on the *John Dunscombe*. We therefore called our first Tasmanian project Project Dunscombe II.

We now had twenty-five volunteers overseas, and my two years with Project was coming to an end. Several people said I should not leave Project. Instead I should leave the Army and turn Project into a major force in the voluntary sector. However, it was hardly fair on the Army if, after two years on full pay doing something I really wanted to do, I handed in my commission. It was also only another couple of years until I qualified for a pension. I was going to need every penny I could get if I was to restore Breacachadh and support my family. I therefore handed over Project to Major Peter Lewis in the 15/19th Hussars, whilst I became deputy-chairman of Project.

* * *

My next job was as 2nd Training Major of the 51st Highland Volunteers. 51 Highland was a T&AVR battalion based in Perth. It consisted of the volunteer companies of the five Highland Regiments and had drill halls from Lerwick in the Shetlands to Campbelltown in Argyll, with the London and Liverpool Scottish thrown in for good measure. David Saunders of the Gordon Highlanders, the other Training Major and I divided the work between us, and when he left the battalion was split in two. I looked after 1/51 Highland whilst David's successor had the second battalion.

I became responsible for training the Black Watch and Argyll & Sutherland Highlander Companies. My major task was to run weekend exercises. I did so all over the Highlands on land belonging to friends of mine. Before the battalion was split in two, I ran one for the Queen's Own Highlanders Companies on Coll. The 'enemy' were flown in from Stornoway and the invading force landed from a landing craft on the beach in front of the Castle. Led by Corporal Sharp, playing the pipes, the men poured ashore up to their waists in water, as live ammunition was fired across their front.

As the jocks were weekend soldiers, most of whom had not done National Service, they were perhaps not ready for such an ambitious exercise. However, I wanted to show them what they could do, capture their imagination and give them something to talk about. I certainly succeeded in the latter. I am told that my exercises are still talked about some thirty-five years later.

Meanwhile the Castle was slowly coming alive. Mainly thanks to William Flett, the Coll builder, who took on the work when I could not get an outside contractor to do the job.[10] I continued to run selection courses for Project during my annual leave and the candidates helped clear rubble and do a bit of pointing at the Castle. As they were only there for five days they never became very expert, but it gave rise to the rumour that they restored the Castle, which was something of an exaggeration.

Peter Lewis did a year with Project. He then handed over to Major Stewart Maclennan REME, who in turn was succeeded by another officer, who was not very satisfactory. The number of volunteers fell. By now the Troubles in Northern Ireland were underway and the Ministry of Defence said they could not provide a major or a captain to take over as Director of Project. Would we be prepared to accept a lieutenant-colonel? I of course said yes. I was therefore in the unusual position, as a serving army major, of having a serving lieutenant-colonel reporting to me. It says a great deal for Ken Todd of the Royal Highland Fusiliers, who had previously been Defence Attache in Vienna that he was prepared to take on the job. He made a considerable improvement in Project's administration and in the briefing and training courses.

It now really was time to leave the Army. Project had to stand on its own feet. A serving soldier did not replace Ken Todd and I once again became the director. I had, however, not quite finished with the army. My family's move to Coll was made to coincide with another exercise on the Island. My wife and two children, one aged three and the other six months old, went ahead to set up house in the semi-restored castle. I was to follow with the exercise's advance party. However, Caledonian MacBrayne's steamer *Loch Seaforth* broke down and could not sail. Luckily there was a Royal Navy minesweeper moored in Oban. I asked the Captain if he could give us a lift. 'Certainly' he replied and we set sail. The wind now started to get up and by the time we reached Coll it was very rough. There was no way the minesweeper could land. I was therefore put ashore in a rubber dingy, told my wife what was going on, took off some of the NCOs already on Coll and returned to the mainland to transfer the exercise to the army's training area at Garelochead. My wife, not surprisingly, was somewhat upset. 'Don't worry Mummy', said our three year-old. 'Let's go to Kilunaig [the Island's Cemetery] and see our ancestors.

When I eventually retired my time with the Army was still not quite over. The Company Commander of D (Argyll & Sutherland) Company had also retired and there was no-one ready to take over from him. I was asked to do so. I thus stopped being a regular soldier one day, and joined the Territorial & Army Volunteer Reserve the next. My company included sub-units in Argyll and Dumbartonshire. We had detachments in several places, including the Isle of Coll, where there were six men, which caused the tabloids some excitement. I was, unbeknownst to me, following in the footsteps of my great-great-great-grandfather and his brother who had commanded companies of the Argyllshire Volunteers in the war with Revolutionary France.

Two years later the post of director of the Project Trust became a full time job and I retired from the Army for the last time. Since those early days Project has become a major organisation. It is the senior of the 125 or so which send young people overseas, and the market leader amongst Gap Year organisations. We have sent almost 6,000 young men and women overseas. All have come to Coll for selection, and latterly for briefing, training, and de-briefing at the end of their year. We now have a full time staff in Coll of ten plus two part-time, and a further two full members of staff in our 'branch office', for school's liaison, in London. In addition we have eleven households on Coll that act as hosts for the candidates on selection. Originally I insisted that one member of each family of hosts had to be Gaelic speaking. Sadly they no longer exist.

Candidates coming to Coll do more than a selection course. The traditional way that the people grew crops here was by constructing mounds and furrows. Mounds to give a sufficient depth of soil and furrows to take away rainfall. The landscape of the Island is covered with 'lazybeds', as the strips are called, although there was nothing lazy about the people who made them, as candidates soon find out. Each group on selection has to build one. They discover what hard work it is to be a subsistence farmer. We find out who is capable of hard work.

Coll is also used as a model to make volunteers think. They study a developing community, where development failed. At the end of their week each candidate has to give a presentation on some aspect of the Island's history, geography, culture &c. This presentation acts as a model for the community report they have to write when they are overseas.

Needless to say Project has made an impact on the Island's demography and its economy. In the early days all volunteers lived at the Castle. They had lectures there and were taught how to dance reels by Hughie Broadhill's wife Chrissie. Project, however, grew too large for the Castle. We therefore purchased Ballyhough farmhouse and transformed it into a purpose built Selection and Training Centre.

The Castle later obtained a collection of artefacts that belonged to the family of Coll. I also gathered together a library about the Hebrides and a collection of manuscripts, and compiled a card index of the inhabitants of the Island from 1750 to 1900. All have been used for this book. They will also be used to make the past come alive to a new generation of Project Trust volunteers.

* * *

We now send up to 250 volunteers overseas each year. This is the maximum number we believe we can look after properly overseas. They have served in 50 different countries. Ethiopia, sadly, is no longer one of them. When their revolution took place Haille Selassie and his grandson were both murdered. Alexander Desta's dream was never realised, but volunteers have, since leaving university, played their part in many different parts of the developing world, for instance 10% of all volunteers are now in medicine. Many would not have been had we not sent them overseas and captured their imagination.

I retired as director of Project when I reached my 60th birthday. My wife succeeded me. I am still President of Project and in 2002 was instrumental in setting up projects in Niger and Mauritania. However, since my retirement I have concentrated my energies on my fold of Highland cattle, my flock of blackface sheep, and on Hebridean history. In 1972, with another group of friends, I founded the Society of West Highland & Island Historical Research [SWHIHR]. It publishes *West Highland Notes & Queries*. Much of the research for this book first appeared in its pages.

SWHIHR also published my *Hebridean Decade: Mull, Coll and Tiree 1761–1771* (1982). Whilst John Tuckwell published my *Warriors & Priests: The History of the Clan Maclean 1300–1570* (1995) & *Murder Under Trust: The Crimes and Death of Sir Lachlan Maclean of Duart 1558–1598* (1999). The Scottish Record Society published *Inhabitants of the Inner Isles & cá1998)*. Other books on Hebridean History will, hopefully, follow.

Notes

1. Sir John Bruce Campbell of Ardnamurchan, 2nd Bart. He served with the West Australian forces in the South African War. He was to win the DSO in 1917. [*Burke's Peerage and Baronetage* (1923), 489].
2. Lidddell Hart *A History of the World War 1914–1918* (1930), 423.
3. John Ewing *The History of the 9th (Scottish) Division 1914–1919* (1927), 242.
4. *The Great War* Part 179. (Week ending 19th January 1918), 439.
5. *The KOSB in the Great War*, 357.
6. BCP. Illustrated Certificate signed by King George V stating that 'Lieutenant-Colonel HDN Maclean DSO. The King's Own Scottish Borderers served with honour and was disabled in the Great War. Invalided from the Service 4th February 1922'.
7. He was the author of *The Twain Shall Meet* (1960). I had met him in Singapore during the Malayan Emergency. [Nicholas Maclean-Bristol (ed) *Project Trust Directory 1967–1998* (1999), ix.
8. See Mora Dickson *A World Elsewhere: Voluntary Service Overseas* (1964).
9. Denis Healey, Secretary of State for Defence. *Military Aid To The Civil Community* (Ministry of Defence, 1968), i.
10. Our architect was initially Ian G Lindsay, who had restored Iona Abbey. When he died Richard Avery succeeded him. Richard was also Project's architect when we built the Hebridean Centre in Coll with a team of local builders. They were led by John Fraser who has worked for Project for more than twenty five years.

Epilogue

If National Service had continued after the 1960s, it is doubtful if organisations sending young volunteers overseas would ever have been born. Most young men could not have afforded a year overseas in addition to undertaking their National Military Service, and they would not have seen the need to undertake such service once they had experienced military service abroad.

Even if it cannot be argued that volunteering replaced National Military Service the Army certainly had a considerable influence on many of the organisations who now send volunteers overseas: several have been run by ex-soldiers; without Military Aid to the Civil Community the Project Trust would never have got off the ground.

Military skills have numerous applications in civilian life, but these skills will not be learnt if young men and women do not join the armed services. As WF Deedes has recently written in the *Daily Telegraph*: 'for the first time in a century – or longer – we have almost no one left among our rulers or in Parliament who has experienced war service'.[1] Not only does this mean that those who make the decisions over peace or war have no experience of a soldier's life, but also that most of the traditional leaders of this country may never have had the opportunity to know someone from a different social background to their own. Those who did National Service certainly did. You get to know people very well in an ambush in the jungle. It is a pity that the new leader of the Tory Party David Cameron never served in the army. I understand he claims to descend from a cousin of Alan Cameron of Erracht, the founder of the 79th Queen's Own Cameron Highlanders.

* * *

When on 23rd June 2006 the King's Own Scottish Borderers march down Prince's Street in Edinburgh for the last time, there will be five members of my family present. Both my brothers served in the KOSB. One served in Malaya and Berlin, and one in Aden, the Radfan and Borneo. My eldest son served in the battalion in Northern Ireland,[2] as did my niece's husband, who is still a serving office in the Regiment. We have been King's Own Scottish Borderers for four generations. Before that we served in the 94th and I suspect that Great-uncle Harry did not join the 94th because it became an Irish, rather than a Scottish Regiment. Certainly the disappearance of the old Scottish regiments will not encourage young men and women from Scotland to join the Army. It remains to be seen whether or not they will join the new Scottish regiments once their own family regiment has been disbanded.

* * *

Epilogue

The regiment had many of the virtues of the Clan: loyalty, paternalism and deference. Could the Clan have survived into an age when deference is a dirty word? It is hardly likely. But the regiment did. It died when for a variety of reasons the Ministry of Defence reduced the size of the Infantry and forced the remaining individual infantry regiments to reorganise in Large Regiments, thus all Scottish Infantry Regiments are now formed into five battalions as part of The Royal Regiment of Scotland with every member wearing a kilt with a common tartan and a common capbadge; the only distinguishing item being a different coloured hackle for each battalion. Individual regimental links with families and regional areas will inevitably suffer.[3]

* * *

Once wartime restrictions of the Napoleonic Wars were over, cheaper barilla was always going to destroy the kelp industry. But could the death of a clan have happened gradually, without the trauma of clearance, if the potato crop not been affected by blight?

There are innumerable 'what ifs' in the story of the Macleans of Coll. Would the estate have been able to keep its population longer, if Alexander Maclean of Coll, who in the fifty years he had control of it and was largely responsible for its future, had not divided the joint-tenant farms into crofts? I doubt it, but if the tenants themselves had continued to regulate the number allowed to live on their joint-tenant holdings, as they appear to have done in the past, there would probably have been less bitterness. But on the other hand successful crofters would not have amassed sufficient capital to better themselves, and afford to emigrate.

The establishment of crofts was the fashionable answer both to improving the lot of the people and increase the income of the Laird. And Alexander was certainly affected by fashion. His moves to Edinburgh, Clifton and York for the winter undoubtedly altered his horizons. If he had not sent Hugh to Eton and the Scots Guards, would his son still have got ideas above his income? He might not even have married Jane Robertson, who brought so much disaster with her tocher.

> Did ever a Highland Laird
> Play such a prank?

Perhaps both Clan and individual Scottish regiments had outlived their usefulness. Perhaps they are rightly relegated to romantic memories. But perhaps the Coll estate has a lesson for the future of other peripheral communities.

Notes

1. *The Daily Telegraph* Friday 2 June 2006, 23.
2. His younger brother joined 1st Battalion Argyll & Sutherland Highlanders. He too served in Northern Ireland.
3. I have to thank Brigadier AD Myrtle, CB, CBE late KOSB for improvements on the original draft of this paragraph.

Postscript

I was correcting the page proofs for this book when I had a message from Alan Borthwick at the National Archives of Scotland to say that the Maclean of Coll charters and other papers had turned up at a house clearance sale in Port Elizabeth, South Africa. Bob Horlock who had purchased them offered to let the National Archives have them on loan for a short time in exchange for translating the Latin charters. The National Archives were unable to help and put me in touch with Bob.

It was quite extraordinary. I had been searching for the charters since 1958. I knew about them as my great-uncle HAC Maclean had transcribed the charters in 1897. They were then in Torquay in the possession of Hugh Maclean of Coll's youngest daughter Mrs Hamilton-Dundas. What had happened to them since had defeated all my researches.

To cut a long story short I purchased them from Bob and they are now back at Breacachadh Castle in Coll where they probably were from 1528 until the castle was abandoned in 1750 when the family moved up the hill to the 'New Castle' where Boswell and Johnson examined them in 1773.

The archive consists of 54 vellum charters and precepts of sasine from 1528 to 1756. In addition there are another 84 documents including the two letters of 1646 from the Marquess of Montrose to Maclean of Coll printed in Chapter 3. Boswell had copied them. Most of the other letters he saw are in the archives. The only exception is the letter from Coll's lawyer the Jacobite agent John Macleod of Muiravonside. Perhaps it will turn up in the future.

There are many other documents that were not noticed by James Boswell. Several concern the lawsuit between John Maclean of Coll and Ewen Allansoun in 1536. Coll then attempted unsuccessfully to get the lands of Locheil restored to him. The family, however, never gave up hope and tried to get them returned after the '45. They were then among the forfeited estates held by the Governmement and could perhaps have been given to a loyal supporter of the regime. This is the inference of an undated memorial of Hugh Maclean of Coll written some time after the Seven Years War (1756–1763). It also adds to our knowledge of the Macleans of Coll's rôle as recruiters for the British Army. It is woth quoting in full:

'Memorial for Hugh Macklane of Coll Esqr to His most Gracious Majesty, & the Great Officers of State – Humbly Sheweth, – That in the year 1528, James the fifth granted to John Macklane of Coll a charter of Twenty Pounds worth of Old Extent of the Lands of Locheill, Lands of Druma & Achlinan, now called the lands of Stron & Errich, & Inish Skire Valine, & Muir Shirlich, &c with the pertinents, lying in the Lordship of Lochaber, & County of Inverness; As a copy of said Charter, dated at Edinburgh, the 1st of December 1528, and of the Sixteenth Year of his said Majesty's Reign, bears. – That a Precept of sasine is granted, along with the said Charter; & where upon the said John

Postscript

Macklane was infest in these Lands, conform to a Copy of his Instrument of Sasine, bearing Date, the 27th of April 1536 – In consequence of which, the said John Macklane was in peaceable Possession of these Lands. But, soon thereafter, the said John Macklane was slain; & the foresaid Lands were taken Possession of by Ewin Allanstown ; & the same being called in Question; and an action brought before the Lords of Council & Session, & after a Commission, & Proof of the Fact, there is a Decreet, finding the said Twenty Pounds worth of Land to belong to the Memorialist's Predecessors; as appears by a Copy thereof, of Date the 5th June 1538. – That the Memorialist's Family, notwithstanding of all these Writes & Evidents, have never recovered Possession of the foresaid Lands. – That the Memorialist, within these three years past, has lost (by it's being blown over with sand) almost one half of his arable land in the Island of Coll; which can be attested, & certified as a Fact, by the Ministers of the Neighbouring Islands; & all the Gentlemen in the neighbourhood; and that, by the most moderate Computation, the Memorialist, within these thirty years, has as much arable Land, covered with sand, & rendered useless, as would yield him, at least, £22 Sterl per Annum; and, that misfortune is still encreasing, & the sand covering more of his Ground: Notwithstanding of which, he pays the same Cess, & publick Burdens, as if no such Misfortune had happened; and, as if the whole Island had been in the same good state as formerly. And, it is to be feared that, in Time, the whole Island will be rendered useless, by the blowing of the Sand, & it's covering the same; To that Depth, as to render it unfit for Culture, & without Vegetation of any sort. – That, in the Year 1744, McDonald of Barrastyle[1] [Barrisdale], & Doctor Cameron[2], & their Accomplices, sent a considerable Number of their Dependers, to the Memorialists Island of Rum; and, at one Time, carried off from him 40 Cows; And at another Time, 20 Cows, & Horses. – That he went in Quest of them, accompanied by a small number of his Tennants, at the Risque of his, & their Lives; &, upon Discovery of them, he raised a suit for Recovery of them; & was at a very considerable Expence. – But, the Commotions, that arose in the Country, in the Year 1745, put a stop to his Recovering his Cattle, & Horses; or the Value thereof. – That, in the Year 1745, Major General John Campbell, afterwards Duke of Argyle, sent ane Order to the Memorialists Brother, Hector Macklane, then of Coll; to raise, in his Islands, One hundred Men, & send them to Inverera, under proper Officers; in order to Join his Grace, the Duke of Argyle; & be assisting in quelling the unnatural Rebellion. – The Memorialist did undertake to raise this Number of Men, upon the different Parts of his now Estate; And tho' in the Dead of Winter, & at the Risque of his Life, & those, who attended him, passed from Island to another, & succeeded in the raising of these Men; And, when Raised, he gave them a considerable sum in Cash; to bear their Expence to Inverera: With thirty Bullocks, & sufficient Quantity of Oatmeal, for Provisions. – These men joined his Majesty's Forces, & went to Culloden; & few of them ever returned. – And neither the Memorialist, or his Brother, ever received, or were ever reimbursed of a single shilling of that great Expence; which they laid out, & were at, in Raising, Collecting, & Sending these Men, for the Support of Government; and, which they did, out of their true Zeal for the present Constitution. – Some Years thereafter, when the War broke out in America; altho' the Memorialist had no Relation to serve, by raising Men for them; Yet, for his Love to his King, & Country; He raised, & sent above 200 Men, for General Fraser, Lord Eglinton, Sir Allan, & Major Allan Macklane. – These are Facts, that can be well attested; & the most unexceptionable Evidence given. Therefore the Memorialist hopes, That some Consideration will be had to this simple Narrative thereof; And, That Government will take the same under Review; & grant such Relief to the Memorialist, & his Family, as will make some Recompence to him, for the Loss of the foresaid Lands; the Carrying off of his cattle, & Horses; the Expence he was at, in Raising the foresaid Men, for the Service of

Government, in the 1745; And, for the great Zeal He, & his Family has always had, & shown for his King, & Country; And, to his most Gracious Majesty, & his Privy Council, shall seem proper'.

I have not discovered what became of this memorial nor if any muster roll of the Argyll Militia survives for the '45. Hugh Coll's statement that men from his estate fought at the battle of Culloden is contradicted by James Boswell who says that 'They were sent home as the Argyllshire battalion was made up before they arrived' at Inveraray.[3] Sir James Ferguson, however, implies that one of the Maclean militia companies was sent to reinforce the Government troops at Dalmally. They could then have gone on to take part in the battle at Culloden and among the Argyll Militia who tore down the stonewalls which restricted the movement of the Government cavalry. They then fired four vollies at the Jacobite second line, with considerable effect, before drawing their broadswords and falling on the Camerons. When they broke they pursued them. They were the only infantry to do so, but probably only for a short distance and did not take part in the butchery that followed.

Twenty men of the Argyll Militia were killed at Culloden.[4]

An explanation for Boswell's story is that he was a sentimental Jacobite. The whole tenor of his account on Coll is that the family were Royalists and covert Jacobites. Perhaps young Coll did not wish to disolution him and tell him that men from the Coll estate had actually fought for the Government at Culloden. Alternatively Hugh was lying. I think that is unlikely as there were too many people about in Government who must have known the truth even though the evidence now no longer exists.

* * *

The second document that adds to our knowledge of the family's military career is a letter dated the 18th June 1782 at Calcutta from Hector, Hugh Coll's third son to his father. As we have seen in 1775 when he was nineteen Hector had sailed to India to join the Honourable East India Company's service. He obtained a commission as an ensign in the 5th Native Infantry in the Madras presidency and 'was soon in action on the expedition against the rajahs north of Arcott'.[5]

By 1780 he was in action against a more formidable adversary. This was Hyder Ali the Muslim adventurer who had made himself ruler of the Hindu state of Mysore. In 1766 the Madras Presidency had joined the Nizam of Hyderabad in a war against Hyder Ali. The Nizam dropped out of the conflict leaving the East India Company to fight it out alone with the able and astute ruler of Mysore. They were fortunate to escape from the fighting without too much loss of face. Their subsquent behaviour, in refusing to keep to their treaty obligations with Hyder Ali, however, turned him into an uncompromising enemy. In June 1780 he marched out of Bangalore and invaded the Carnatic [now Karnatka]. He burnt villages, and drove off cattle from around Madras and Vellore. Black columns of smoke dominated the landscape and the people fled before the supine Government of Madras reacted. They had little excuse. The 1st Battalion of the 71st Highland Regiment of Foot had recently arrived in Madras and the garrison was stronger than was usual.[6]

The flank companies of the 71st Foot were part of the force that eventually, under Colonel Baillie, marched out of Madras to engage Hyder Ali. On 10th September they were defeated and butchered. Some were captured and imprisoned in disgraceful conditions at Seringpatam. Hector was probably not with Baillie. In his letter to his father he says that he was captured in January 1781. He was therefore probably detached at Amboor when it surrendered on 13th January 1781.[7] For some reason Hector was not sent to Seringpatam but sent to Madras, where as he was considered to be 'a prisoner of War and therefore not permitted to take the field, finding myself rather disagreeably situated at Madras I resolved on taking a trip to Bengall in hopes that I might persuade Mr Macpherson to do something for my brother and myself'.

Hector's younger brother Allan had recently joined him in India. Allan accompanied John Macpherson to India, presumably in the hope of getting a post in the civil administration. Macpherson who was the son of Mr John Macpherson a minister in Skye, and as his mother was a daughter of Donald Macleod of Bernera, he was cousin of the family of Coll. Whatever hopes they had from Macpherson were soon to be dashed.

Macpherson who was born in 1745 had first come to India as purser in an East India Company ship commanded by his uncle Captain Alexander Macleod. In Madras he was introduced to the Mohammed Ali, Nabob of the Carnatic who had borrowed vast sums of money, at enormous interest, from the merchants in Madras and his affairs were in chaos. Hard pressed by his creditors he entrusted Macpherson with a secret mission to London to obtain help from the Government. Macpherson arrived back in London in November 1768 where he so impressed the Government that he became the Member of Parliament for Cricklade. In January 1781 he was apointed to a seat on Supreme Council in Calcutta.

Hector is scatheing about Macpherson who 'would do nothing for my Brother Allan tho' he brought him out along with him, but left him with me at Madras and as I could do nothing better for him was obliged to apply to Lord Macleod to take him into his Regiment. He got an Ensigncy in a few days, and is still with the Regimentt'.

Hector writes that the power Macpherson

has (of serving his friends essentially is immence) but I am affraid it will be to no purpose – the truth is that his highland friends can be of no service to him in promoting his views in life, friendship I take entirely to be out of the question with him, and I am persuaded he will only serve those how [who] by themselves or friends can be usefull in promoting his own interest, he now not only is a great man, but also in every respect considers himself as such, and pretends to be much affraid of the common talk that highlanders are partial to one another (should be imputed to him), if this observation is just I am almost certain that he will be an exception to it.[8]

Hector continues:

Hyder Ally is now in possession of almost every Fort in the Carnatic and the whole country so effectually destroyed that the Army under Sir Eyre Coote cannot move but a little distance from Madras on account of provisions with which they must be constantly supply'd from there. – Madras has but few resources at present either of of Men, money, or provisions but what it receives from Bengall.

Relief was, however, to come when in December Hyder Ali died. His son Tipoo Sahib succeeded him and Allan presumably took part in the operations against him and the French that followed. He first appears in the *Army List* in 1784 when he apears as a Lieutenant in 1st Battalion 73rd Foot. His Lieutenancy is dated 15th May 1783.

*   *   *

The final extract from the Maclean of Coll papers does not concern the army. It is a letter from Sibbella Maclean to her brother Hugh who was in London to see his Macleod nephews back to

Australia and staying at Ibbotson's Hotel. He was also courting a new wife. Since his first wife's death in 1819 Sibbella appears to have looked after Hugh's four daughters. On 6th May 1825 she writes to him from her father's house at 51 Castle Street, Edinburgh. It gives an insight into the family that complements the earlier evidence. She writes:

My dearest Hugh

This morning I received your letter, and did not xpect more decided news so soon – but most anxiously trust that, so ardently desired by us all may not be long withheld, but do not be too precipitate you must have a little patience, such a woman is not to be got without a little trouble, by all I hear she is just the person to make your happiness[.] I only wish she knew you better, & I do think her hesitation would end, you know it is a serious concern for any woman to accept a man with four children, & the more [?] she is, the more she will reflect on this, had she seen your children, she would think less on the difficulty they are every one of them, such kind open hearted, affectionate creatures, they would soon love her as a mother, the two governesses they have had, had the charge of Many children before them, and both declared they never saw such well disposed children, both were like to break their hearts at parting – they are boistrous poor darlings but that is from the absurd indulgence of their last governess – and it must take patience to conquer it, & I have no doubt Mrs Maser when she arrives will very quickly polish them, at present I fear the evil is increasing as their cousins are here, and the house full of trunks, boxes & work women, you [?] can scarcely conceive the bustle we are in the hurry is so great. – As I am as busy as my frail carcase will allow me.

The children were off to stay with their relations at Duddingston. Sibbella was to send the two carriages to collect them on Sunday evening as

they get their lessons of dancing in the week, I cannot get more as masters are so much occupied – Elizabeth is the worst performer she tries to set them all laughing instead of doing the steps – I have all along made them having a mama some time a thing of course as a circumstance that would greatly add to their happiness, so that if you succeed, which God grant you the children, will receive their Mama, with the greatest affection, and you may be sure, (if this most desireable event comes to pass,) I shall never interfere with any new arrangement & ways with the children, and will always be most happy to assist my new sister (if I am blessed with one) in any way she wishes.

Sibbella was fraught. She continues

an answer has just come from the governess, who will be here in a day or two, I shall look for sets of books, but I do not know what you formerly sent her, I shall send Shakespeare as I do not think she has a copy and what else I can find her [?] be acceptable from you, there is such a bustle I scarcely know what I am writing I would have written sooner but know not where to direct to you and could not beer to send a letter to Mr Robertson's where I grieve to think your hopes are still so uncertain – May God bless you, dearest Hugh – and grant you your wishes, and believe me ever most affectionately S MacLean

Postscript

Jane Robertson accepted Hugh's proposal and they were married that August with disastrous results for the family, especially for Hugh's four daughters by his previous marriage. Jane was, as we have seen in Juliet Alexa's journal, always to be critical of them and after their mother's death these happy boistrous girls cannot have had a very enjoyable childhood.

Sibbella paints a sad picture of her father in his dotage. She writes to Hugh:

My father's health is very good, but his head sadly confused – Miserably anxious for news of you. It is a great pity Alex [Hunter] spoke on the subject [of money ?] to him but did it with the best intention, thinking to make his mind easy – but his memory is unhappily so bad, he adds as well as forgets – he longs to get home, but I rather think he will not go, till I return with the children. If you wish to see Mrs Maser, she is to be heard of at Mrs Paine's, 36 Fetter Lane, Fleet Street, but is visiting about in various places, I wish she were arrived. You would receive a sad letter from Catherine [their sister in Australia] but it was written under disappointed feelings, Alex Hunter wrote rather a severe letter on their children being sent home which she had just received we have since received a letter written a week before in high spirits, a most flourishing account of the great increase of their stock, [?] and seemingly quite happy, and says how much more so she would be had she all the children at home with a governess.

Although the remainder of the Maclean of Coll papers do not contradict the main thrust of this book, they provide numerous opportunities for articles which will illustrate the challenges that faced a major Hebridean family from 1400 to the present day.

Notes

1 Barisdale was a notorious thug who betrayed both sides in the '45. He was captured by the Prince's companions and taken to France in irons. The French did not release him until 1749. On his arrival in Scotland he was lodged in Edinburgh Castle where he died [*Bonnie Prince Charlie*, 280].
2 Dr Cameron, a brother of Lochiel was the last man to be executed in Scotland for taking part in the '45 [*Charles Edward Stuart*, 413–414.
3 *Boswell's Journal*, 279.
4 *Argyll in the '45*, 172; *A History of Clan Campbell* vol. 3, 142–143.
5 *Seanachie* 316.
6 *History of the Army* vol.3, 432; Lord Macleod, the former Jacobite son of the Earl of Cromartie, in 1777 raised the 71st Foot as it was known in India. It was, however, numbered 73rd Foot in the *Army List*. To confuse matters further in 1786 it was officially renumbered as 71st Foot. In 1808 it was renamed 71st (Glasgow Highland) Regiment of Foot and eventually merged with 74th Foot to become the Highland Light Infantry. In 1960 it was amalgamated with the Royal Scots Fusileers. It is now 2nd Battalion Royal Regiment of Scotland.
7 *History of the Army*, 447.
8 BCP. Coll Charter Chest.

Annex A

Third of July 1679. A list of all the men and soldiers that served under Donald McLeane in the House off Breackaich as follows:

Iain McLachlan Vc Allane alias McLeane
Iwire McDonald
Donald McAngus bane
Rory More
Donald McLachlane Vc Allane alias McLeane
Hew roye
Donald McDonald Vc Lachlane
Hector McDonald Vc Lachlane
Malcome McIane roye
Donald McNeill Vc Eane Vc angus
Rory McDonald Vc murdoe and his sone
Donald Mcfi – ista
Finlay the smith
Murdo tollick allias Campbell
Iain McEwen Vc Lachlane
Niall vize [i.e Og] alias McLeane
Dougall McDonald Vc Eane and his brother
Duncan McDonald Vc Eane VcAngus
Iain McNeill Vc Eane Vc Angus and his brother
Donald McNeill Vc Eane VcAngus
Donald bane
Donald Mceane
Rory McCane Vc donald Vc finly
Murdo McNeill Vc Eane

'I Donald McLaine doe heirby declaire that the above writtine lyst faithfully given up be me as witness given under my hand alt Colle. 3 July 1679. 'Donald McLean'.
1679 List of these in the Castle of Breckach in Coll.

Donald McLaine, Coll's brother – Captaine a papist
Iain McLauchlane Vc Allan – alias McLaine

Annex A

Donald his brother – his wyf in Kealiscollich
Neill viz his brother in Kilbryd
Donald McIllphadrick in Nealis – he hath two brether in that town
Iain McNeill Vc Ian Vc Innes in Ardness – married
Gwn, Archibald and son his brether
Donald Baine McNeill there
Duncan McDonald Vc Ian there his wyfe ther
Dugall his brother there – his wyfe these two are Mcphaidens
Finley McIllmickall smith in Uig
Rorie McDonald Vc wurchie there – his wyfe ther
Donald McGreeht ther hes beine maried
Charles McIllespick Vc Rorie in Arnabost maried
Hector viz his good sonn
Rorie moir – a papist
Donald McNeill Vc Illchallum
Donald McInnes Baine
Iwer tayleor
Murchie Collich
Hector Mcdonald McLauchlane
Malcome McIan Roy

Tables

Tables 1–12 are intended to help the readers to identify individuals mentioned in the text. They should be used in conjunction with the index. In addition to the name of the individual, he can be identified by the dates when he is mentioned in contemporary documents, i.e. Hector -Ruadh (1558 × 1564/5). If the dates of his birth and death are known they are shown, i.e. Alexander (1753–1825). Where '×' is shown, no contemporary evidence of birth or death is known. The dates are when he appears in contemporary records. Where no dates are shown, the individual's existence is known from one of the Genealogical Accounts of the Macleans.

Except where shown all individuals are surnamed Maclean.

The spelling of Maclean as a surname is used throughout the book, except when spelt otherwise where an original document is quoted. The term of Mac followed by a capital, i.e. Mac Donald indicates that the individual mentioned had a father whose forename was Donald. It does not indicate his surname.

In most documents, females are left out for simplicity. They can be identified in the text.

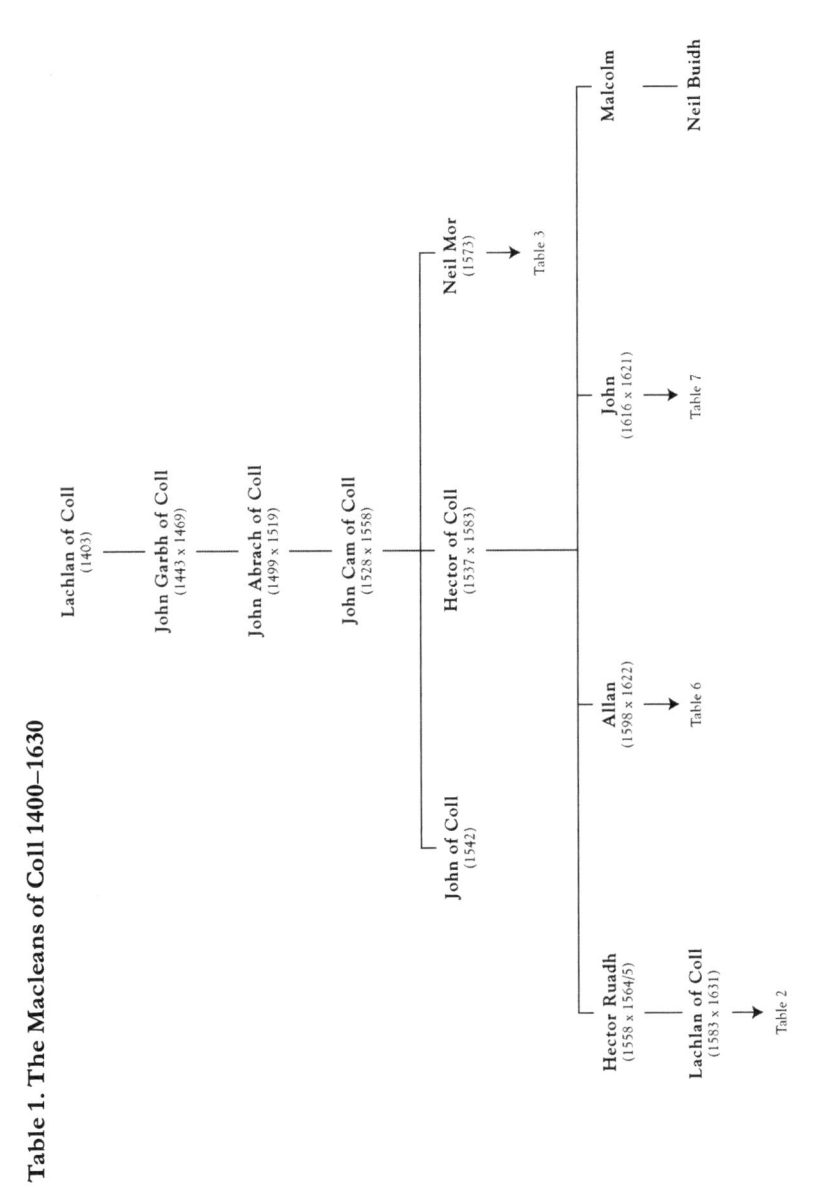

Table 1. The Macleans of Coll 1400–1630

```
Lachlan of Coll
    (1403)
     |
John Garbh of Coll
  (1443 x 1469)
     |
John Abrach of Coll
  (1499 x 1519)
     |
John Cam of Coll
  (1528 x 1558)
     |
     ├─────────────────────┬──────────────────────┐
John of Coll                              Hector of Coll         Neil Mor
  (1542)                                   (1537 x 1583)          (1573)
     |                                         |                    → Table 3
     ├──────────────┐                          ├──────────┬──────────┐
Hector Ruadh    Lachlan of Coll             Allan       John      Malcolm
(1558 x 1564/5) (1583 x 1631)          (1598 x 1622) (1616 x 1621)    |
                   → Table 2              → Table 6    → Table 7   Neil Buidh
```

NMB 10.08.06

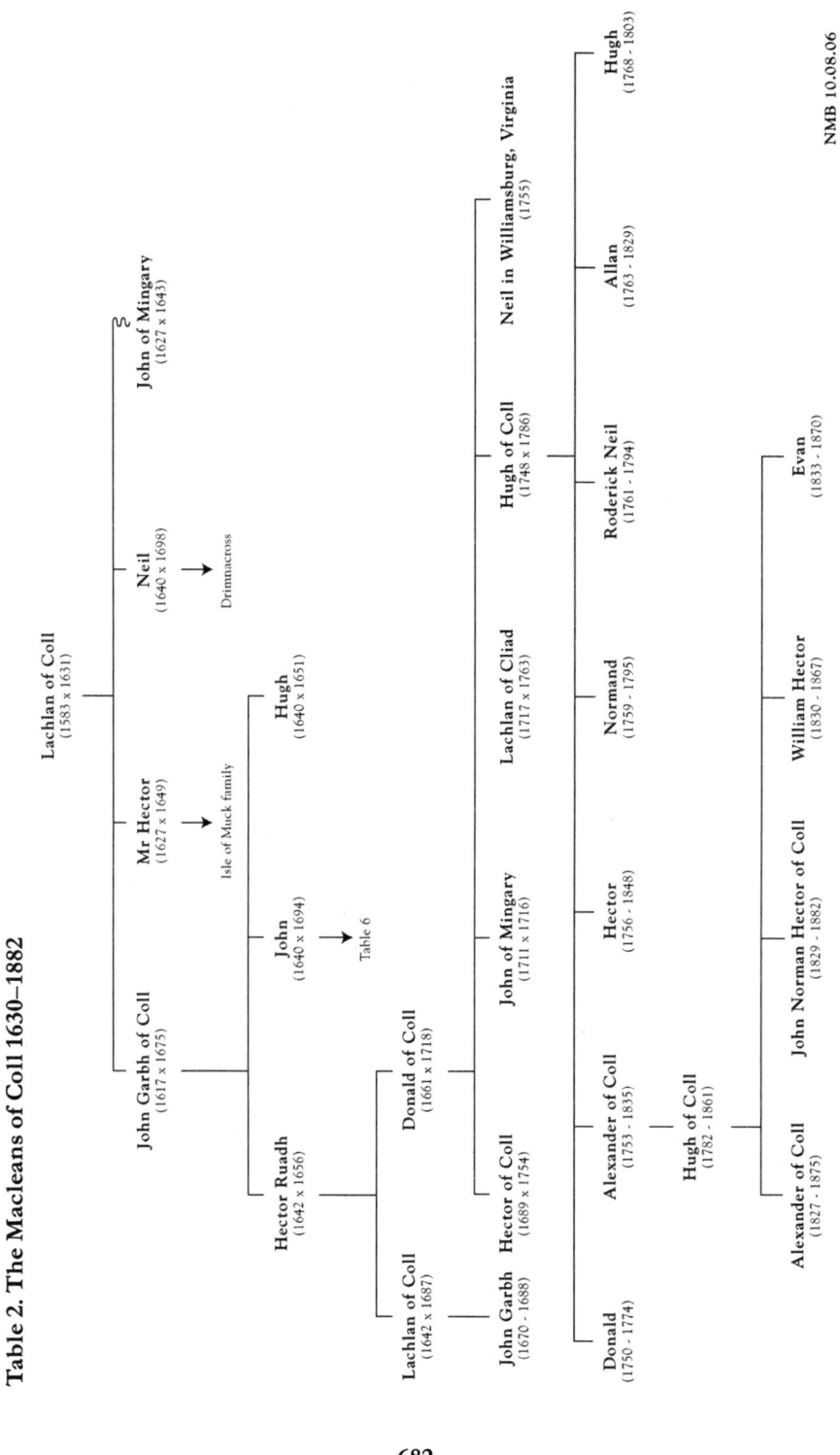

Table 2. The Macleans of Coll 1630–1882

Lachlan of Coll (1583 x 1631)
- John Garbh of Coll (1617 x 1675)
- Mr Hector (1627 x 1649) → Isle of Muck family
- Neil (1640 x 1698) → Drimnacross
- John of Mingary (1627 x 1643)

Mr Hector's children:
- John (1640 x 1694) → Table 6
- Hugh (1640 x 1651)

John Garbh of Coll's descendants:
- Hector Ruadh (1642 x 1656)
- Donald of Coll (1661 x 1718)
- John of Mingary (1711 x 1716)
- Lachlan of Cliad (1717 x 1763)
- Hugh of Coll (1748 x 1786)
- Neil in Williamsburg, Virginia (1755)

- Lachlan of Coll (1642 x 1687)
- John Garbh (1670 - 1688)
- Hector of Coll (1689 x 1754)
- Donald (1750 - 1774)
- Alexander of Coll (1753 - 1835)
- Hector (1756 - 1848)
- Normand (1759 - 1795)
- Roderick Neil (1761 - 1794)
- Allan (1763 - 1829)
- Hugh (1768 - 1803)

- Hugh of Coll (1782 - 1861)
- Alexander of Coll (1827 - 1875)
- John Norman Hector of Coll (1829 - 1882)
- William Hector (1830 - 1867)
- Evan (1833 - 1870)

NMB 10.08.06

Table 3. The First Branch of the Family of Coll

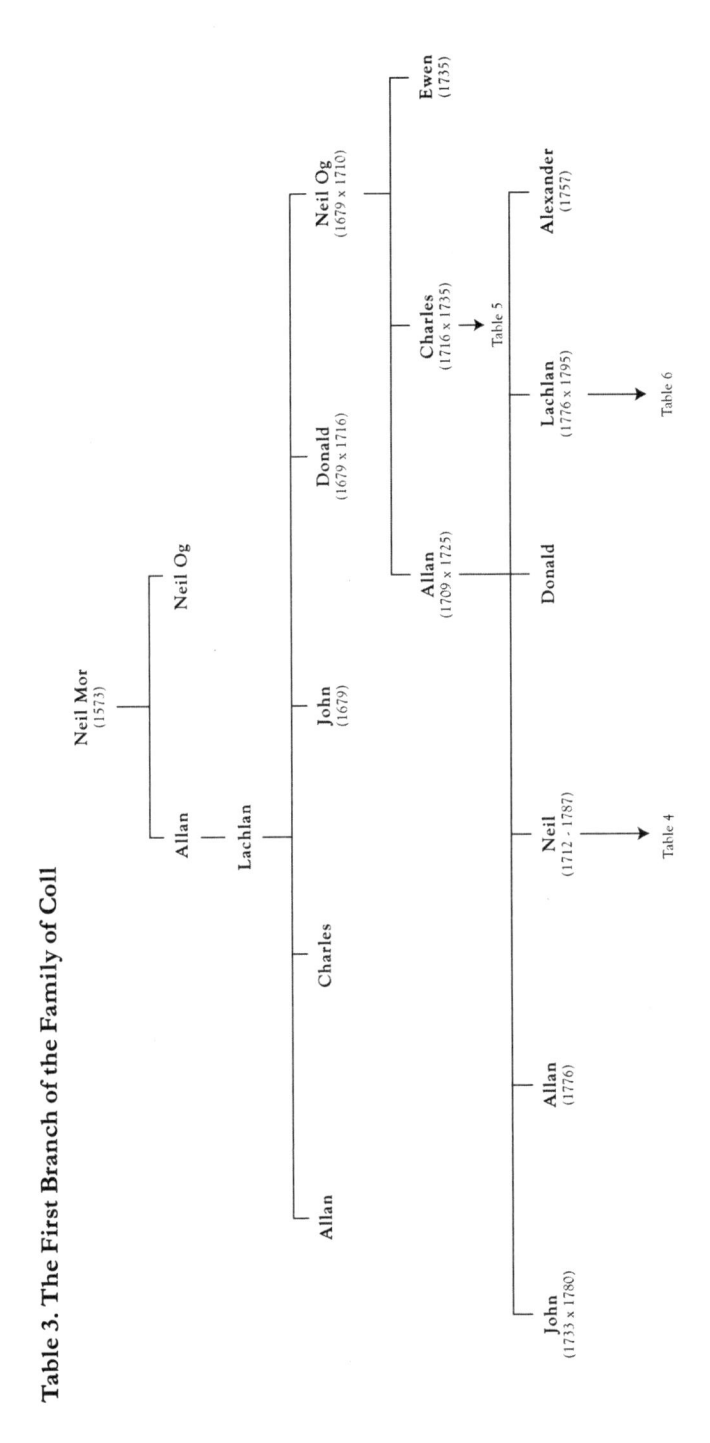

Neil Mor (1573)
├── Allan
├── Lachlan
│   └── (children): Allan, Charles, John (1679), Neil Og
│   └── John (1679)
│   ├── Donald (1679 x 1716)
│   │   └── Allan (1709 x 1725)
│   │   ├── Neil (1712 - 1787) → Table 4
│   │   └── Donald
│   │   ├── Allan (1776)
│   │   │   └── John (1733 x 1780)
│   │   └── Lachlan (1776 x 1795) → Table 6
│   │   └── Alexander (1757)
│   └── Neil Og (1679 x 1710)
│   ├── Charles (1716 x 1735) → Table 5
│   └── Ewen (1735)
└── Neil Og

NMB 10.08.06

683

Table 4. Later Macleans of Crossapol

Neil Maclean in Crossapol (1712 x 1787) — Ann = Donald Maclean Sgt. Maj. John 1BF (1758 x 1798)

Children of Neil Maclean:
- Lachlan
- Allan, in Crossapol, Capt. Coll Volunteers (1760 - 1832)
- Neil (1766 - 1787)
- Marion = Roderick Morison in Tobermory (1774 x 1789)
- Ann = Neil Campbell in Sunipol, Mull (1766 x 1854)

Children of Lachlan:
- Mr Donald, Capt. Rum Volunteers (1752 - 1810)
- Mr Neil, Min. of Tiree & Coll (1784 - 1859)
- Mr Hector, Min. of Lochalsh (1786 - 1869)

Children of Mr Donald:
- Alexander, Surgeon 64F (1782 - 1818)

Son of Alexander:
- Lieut. Col. Alexander 94F (1818 - 1892)

Son of Mr Neil:
- Dr Donald (1815 - 1851)

Children of Lieut. Col. Alexander:
- Maj. Alexander 94F (1858 - 1901)
- Hector (1861 - 1918)
- Lieut. Col. Henry Donald Neil KOSB (1872 - 1926)

Child of Mr Hector:
- Alexander (1836 - 1851)

Children of Allan:
- Neil in Crossapol (1806 - 1855) [son: Neil (1839 x 1855)]
- John, Wine Merchant, London (1808 - 1886)
- Donald (1812 - 1834)
- Mary = Alexander Maclean, Bailie of Coll, Lieut. Coll Volunteers (1791 x 1831)
- Margaret = Charles Maclean, Bailie of Coll, Ensign Coll Volunteers (1776 x 1829)
- Janet = Capt. Allan Macdonald of Darracha
- Una = 1 Sgt. Henry Sutherland (1796); 2 Allan Maclean in Acha (1776 x 1833)

Child of Mary:
- Norman in Freslan (1797 x 1871)

Child of Margaret:
- Dr Lachlan of Rum (1789 - 1881)

Son of Dr Lachlan:
- Maj. Gen. Charles Maclean (1856 - 1921)

Child of Janet:
- Malcolm (1790)

Children of Una:
- Hugh, Capt. John Dunscombe (1801 - 1839)
- Capt. Neil (1809 x 1899)

Children of Ann:
- Colin of Caolis & Cornaig (1796 - 1867)
- Capt. Alexander of Port Fairy (1805 x 1890)
- Neil (1828)

NMB 10.08.06

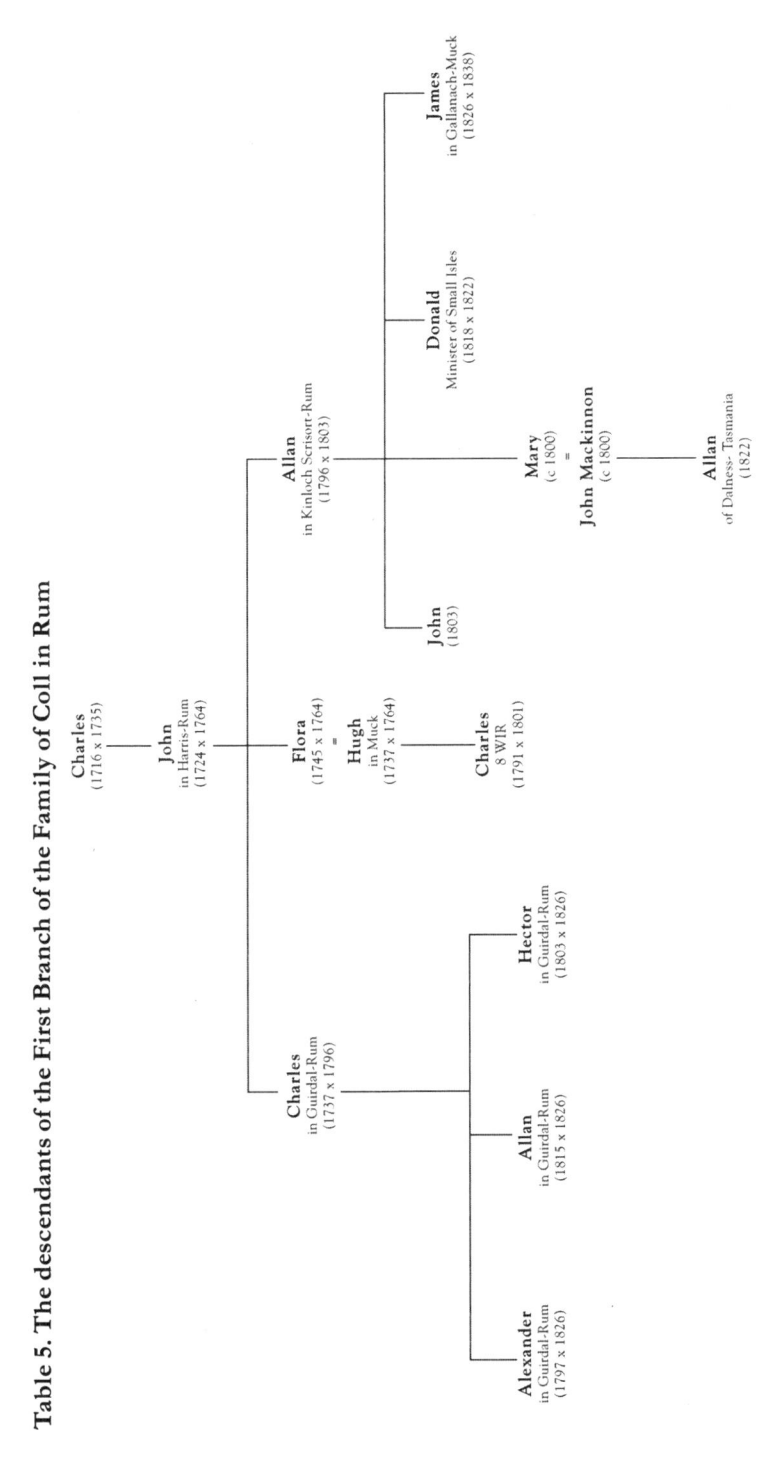

Table 5. The descendants of the First Branch of the Family of Coll in Rum

```
Charles
(1716 x 1735)

John
in Harris-Rum
(1724 x 1764)
│
├─────────────────────────────────┐
│                                 │
Charles                           Flora
in Guirdal-Rum                    (1745 x 1764)
(1737 x 1796)                     =
│                                 Hugh
│                                 in Muck
│                                 (1737 x 1764)
│                                 │
│                                 ├──────────────────┐
│                                 │                  │
│                                 Charles            Allan
│                                 8 WIR              in Kinloch Scrisort-Rum
│                                 (1791 x 1801)      (1796 x 1803)
│                                                    │
│                                                    ├────────┬─────────────────┬──────────────────┐
│                                                    John     Mary              Donald             James
│                                                    (1803)   (c 1800)          Minister of        in Gallanach-Muck
│                                                             =                 Small Isles        (1826 x 1838)
│                                                             John Mackinnon    (1818 x 1822)
│                                                             (c 1800)
│                                                             │
│                                                             Allan
│                                                             of Dalness-Tasmania
│                                                             (1822)
│
├──────────────┬──────────────┐
Alexander      Allan          Hector
in Guirdal-Rum in Guirdal-Rum in Guirdal-Rum
(1797 x 1826)  (1815 x 1826)  (1803 x 1826)
```

NMB 12.08.06

Table 6. Some relationships between Coll tenants producing NCOs

```
                                    Lachlan Maclean
                                     in Fiosgaradh
                                      (1776 x 1795)
                                           │
                    Hector Maclean          │
                        Cliad               │
                       (1776)               │
                          │                 │
       Lachlan           │                 │
       Arnabost          │                 │
        (1776)           │                 │
           │             │                 │
   ┌───────┴────┬────────┼─────────┬───────┴──────────┐
   │            │        │         │                  │
 Flora  =  John      Murdoch   Ann = Sgt. Allan 1BF   Margaret       Sgt. Alexander
        (1776 x 1836)  Sgt Av        in Fiosgaradh      =            (1776 - 1798)
                     (1776 x 1841)   (1776 x 1826)   Sgt. John Cameron
                                                         42F
                         │                  │
                    22.12.1834              │
                    Duncan = Catherine      │
                    (1802 - 1890)           │
                                            │
John Johnston = Isobel                      │
  in Arnabost                               │
    (1776)                                  │
       │                    8.3.1803        │      3.1.1810
       │         Jean  =  Sgt. Hugh 1BF     John    2
       │                  in Fiosgaradh    in Leacruadh  =  Marion
       │                  (1776 x 1819)    (1776 x 1860)
       │                                        │
 Capt. William                                  │
 2nd Madras Inf.                           Catherine = John Mackinnon
 (1799 - 1861)                                              1BF
       │                                                (1776 x 1841)
   Margaret
   (1800 x 1819)
       │
   Lachlan
   (1798 - 1848)
       │
  22.11.1831
  John  =  Janet
 (1805 - 1896) (1802 - 1885)
       │
   Murdoch
  (1793 - 1867)
       │
    John
  in Totamore
  (1836 - 1921)
```

NMB 12.08.06

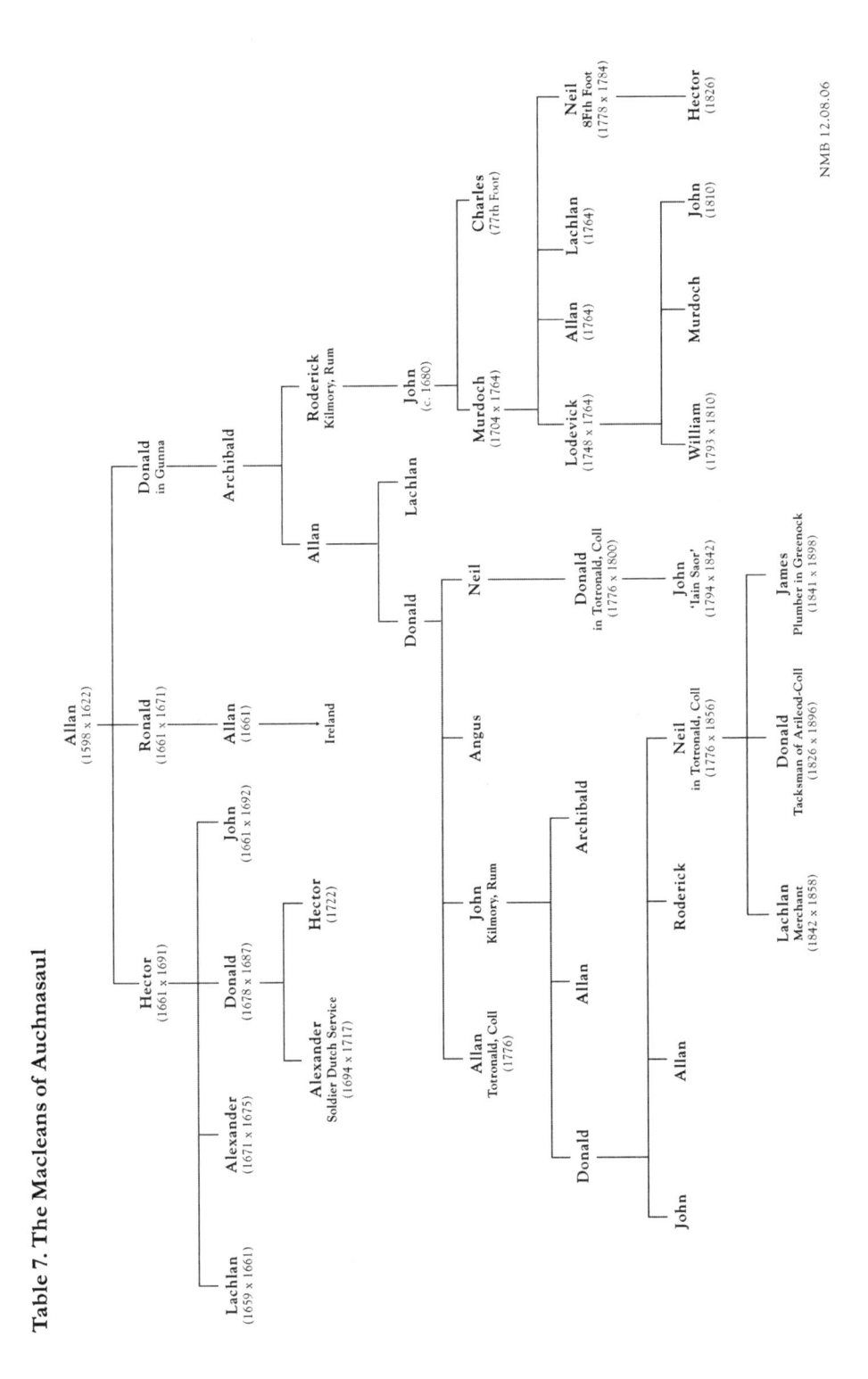

Table 7. The Macleans of Auchnasaul

- Allan (1598 x 1622)
  - Lachlan (1659 x 1661)
  - Alexander (1671 x 1675)
  - Hector (1661 x 1691)
    - John (1661 x 1692)
    - Donald (1678 x 1687)
      - Alexander, Soldier Dutch Service (1694 x 1717)
      - Hector (1722)
  - Ronald (1661 x 1671)
    - Allan (1661) → Ireland
  - Donald in Gunna
    - Archibald
      - Allan
        - Donald
          - Angus
            - John Kilmory, Rum
              - Allan Totronald, Coll (1776)
                - Donald
                  - John
                  - Lachlan Merchant (1842 x 1858)
                  - Donald Tacksman of Arileod-Coll (1826 x 1896)
                    - James Plumber in Greenock (1841 x 1898)
                - Allan
                - Roderick
                - Neil in Totronald, Coll (1776 x 1856)
              - Archibald
            - Neil
              - Donald in Totronald, Coll (1776 x 1800)
                - John 'Iain Saor' (1794 x 1842)
          - Lachlan
      - Roderick Kilmory, Rum
        - John (c. 1680)
          - Murdoch (1704 x 1764)
            - Lodevick (1748 x 1764)
              - William (1793 x 1810)
            - Allan (1764)
              - Murdoch
                - John (1810)
            - Lachlan (1764)
          - Charles (77th Foot)
          - Neil 8Fth Foot (1778 x 1784)
            - Hector (1826)

NMB 12.08.06

Table 8. First Macleans of Grishipol

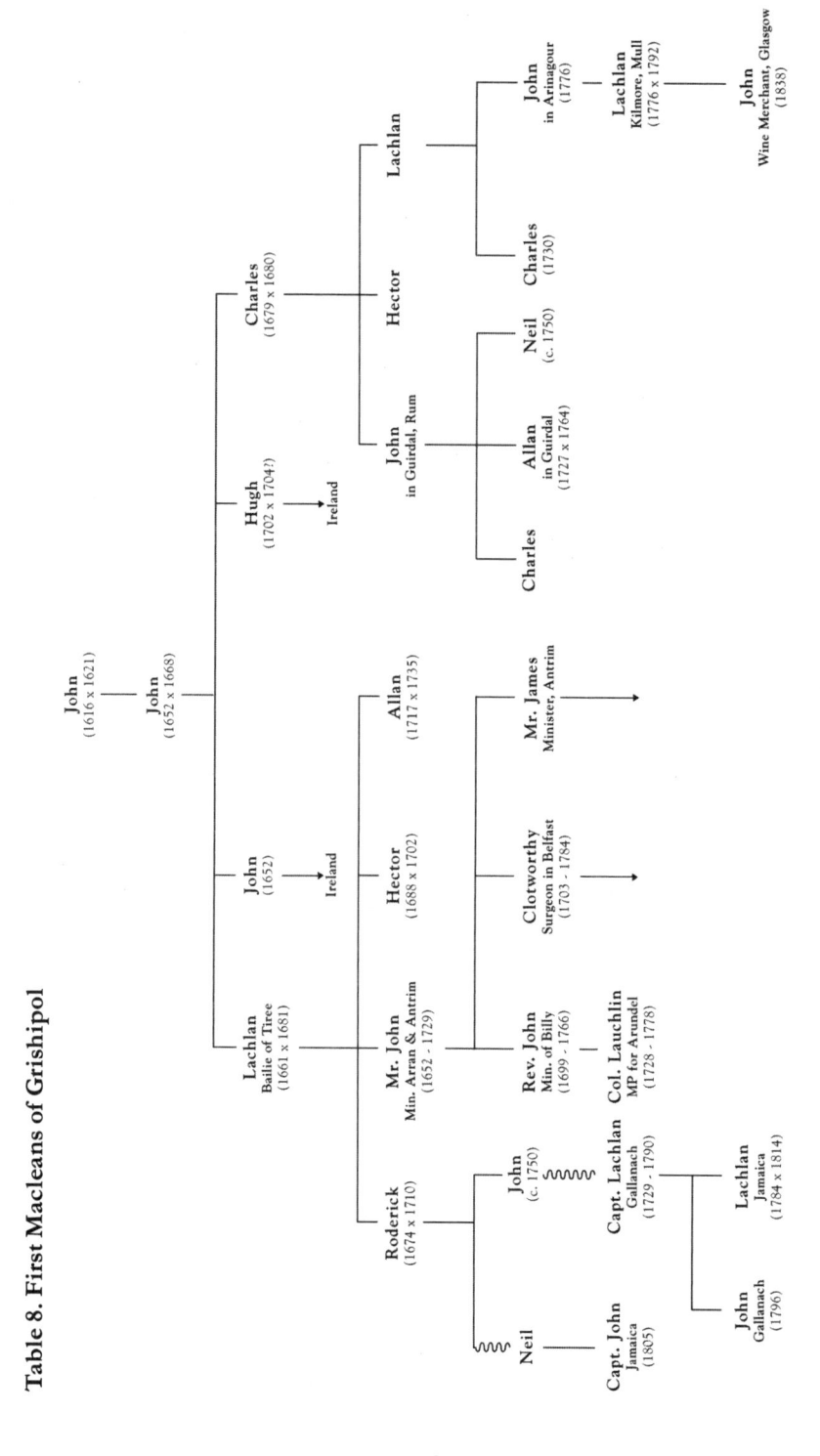

```
John
(1616 x 1621)
│
John
(1652 x 1668)
├─────────────────────┬──────────────┬─────────────────────────────┐
Lachlan              John          Hugh                         Charles
Bailie of Tiree      (1652)        (1702 x 1704?)               (1679 x 1680)
(1661 x 1681)        → Ireland     → Ireland                    │
│                                                               ├──────────────┐
│                                                              Hector         Lachlan
│                                                               │              │
│                                                    ┌──────────┼──────┐      ├──────────┐
│                                                   Charles   John    Charles John        
│                                                            in Guirdal, Rum (1730)  in Arinagour
│                                                             │                      (1776)
│                                                    ┌────────┼────────┐             │
│                                                   Allan    Neil                   Lachlan
│                                                   in Guirdal (c. 1750)            Kilmore, Mull
│                                                   (1727 x 1764)                   (1776 x 1792)
│                                                                                    │
│                                                                                   John
│                                                                                   Wine Merchant, Glasgow
│                                                                                   (1838)
│
├──────────────────────────────┐
Mr. John                      Hector
Min. Arran & Antrim           (1688 x 1702)
(1652 - 1729)                 │
│                             ├──────────────┐
│                            Allan          Clotworthy
│                            (1717 x 1735)  Surgeon in Belfast
│                            │              (1703 - 1784)
│                           Mr. James       → 
│                           Minister, Antrim
│                           →
│
├──────────────┬──────────────┐
Rev. John     Col. Lauchlin   
Min. of Billy MP for Arundel  
(1699 - 1766) (1728 - 1778)   

Roderick
(1674 x 1710)
├──────────────┬──────────────┐
Neil          John           Capt. Lachlan
~~~           (c. 1750)      Gallanach
│             ~~~            (1729 - 1790)
Capt. John                   │
Jamaica                      ├──────────────┐
(1805)                       Lachlan        John
                             Jamaica        Gallanach
                             (1784 x 1814)  (1796)
```

NMB 12.08.06

Table 9. The Macleans of the Isle of Muck

Mr Hector (1628 x 1649)

- Hector (1666 x 1684)
  - Capt. Lachlan (1715 x 1716)
    - Hector (1719)
  - Donald of Cormaig (1730 x 1789)
    - Hector (1764 x 1780)
  - Capt. John (1778 - 1809)
    - Maj. Lachlan (1771 x 1816)
  - Donald 16F (1791 x 1882) = John Leyburn 43F (1794 - 1873)
    - Francis John Small 11F (1793 x 1800)
    - Hector Alexander RN (1787 - 1809)
    - Donald John 72F (1789 x 1830)
    - John Francis Gray EICS (1799 - 1827)
    - Alexander Lockhart 67th Bengal NI (1804 - 1840)
    - Alexander Campbell (1798 - 1863)
  - George Allan 61F (1790 - 1820)
  - Charles Norman 73F (1796 - 1822)

- Lachlan (1671)
  - John (c. 1715)
    - Lachlan
  - Lachlan (c. 1715)
    - Alexander

- Hugh (1651)
  - [John]
    - Hector in Knock (1733 x 1771)
      - John (c. 1770)
        - Hector (c. 1750)
    - Donald (c. 1750)
      - Alexander (c. 1770)
    - John in Cove, Rum (1695 x 1771)
      - Hugh in Muck (1737 x 1764)
        - John Sandeneisher, Rum (1803)
        - Hugh (1778 x 1824)
          - Charles Ensign 8 WIR (1797 x 1801)

NMB 12.08.06

Table 10. The Macleans of Drimnacross & Torestan

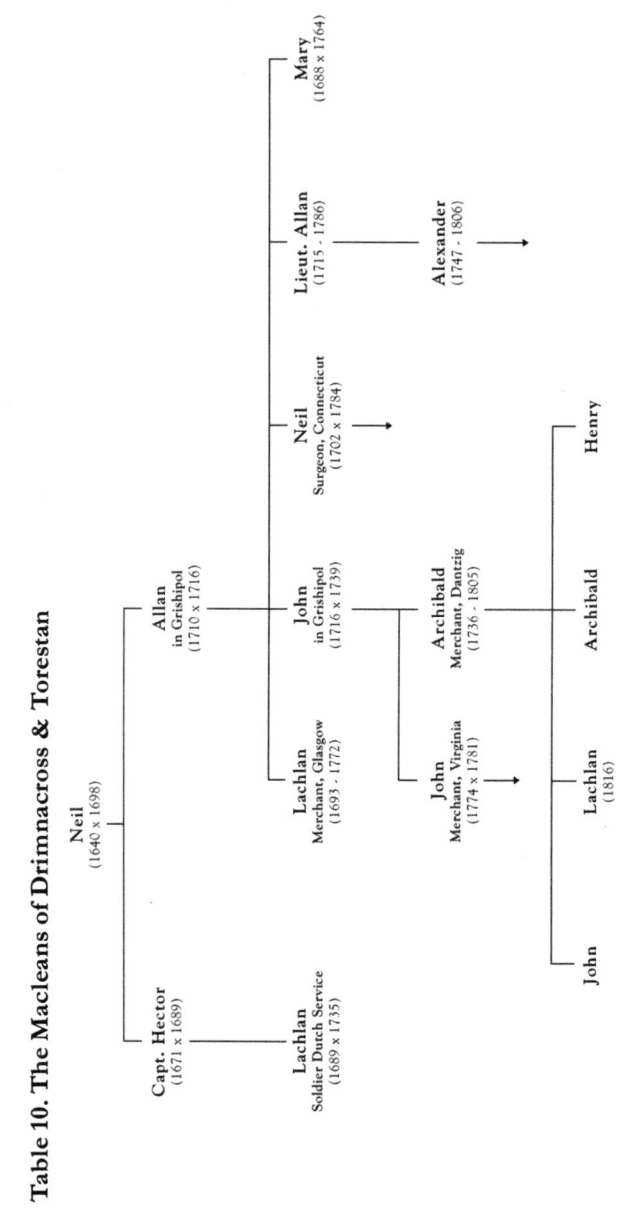

- **Neil** (1640 x 1698)
  - **Capt. Hector** (1671 x 1689)
    - **Lachlan**, Soldier Dutch Service (1689 x 1735)
  - **Allan** in Grishipol (1710 x 1716)
    - **Lachlan**, Merchant, Glasgow (1693 - 1772)
    - **John** in Grishipol (1716 x 1739)
      - **John**, Merchant, Virginia (1774 x 1781)
      - **Archibald**, Merchant, Dantzig (1736 - 1805)
        - **John**
        - **Lachlan** (1816)
        - **Archibald**
        - **Henry**
    - **Neil**, Surgeon, Connecticut (1702 x 1784) →
    - **Lieut. Allan** (1715 - 1786)
      - **Alexander** (1747 - 1806) →
    - **Mary** (1688 x 1764)

NMB 12.08.06

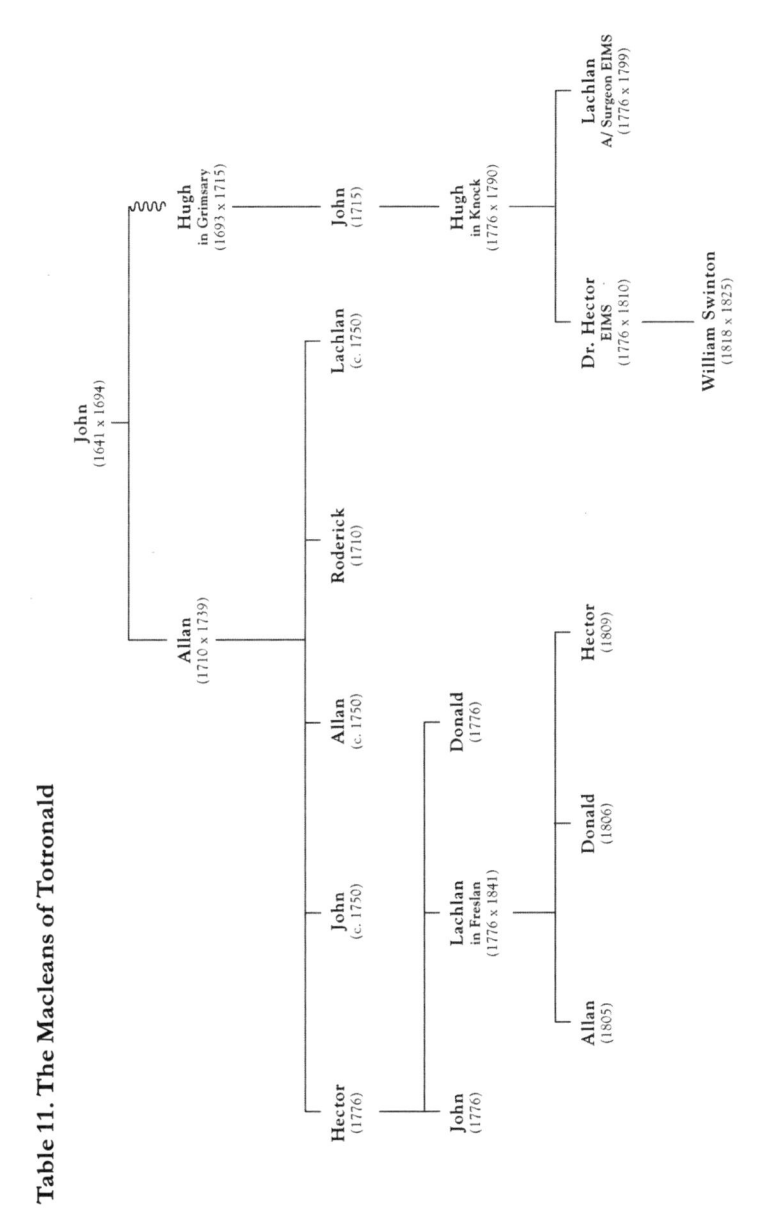

Table 11. The Macleans of Totronald

- John (1641 x 1694)
  - Allan (1710 x 1739)
    - Hector (1776)
    - John (c. 1750)
      - John (1776)
      - Lachlan in Freslan (1776 x 1841)
        - Allan (1805)
        - Donald (1806)
        - Hector (1809)
    - Allan (c. 1750)
      - Donald (1776)
    - Roderick (1710)
    - Lachlan (c. 1750)
  - Hugh in Grimsary (1693 x 1715)
    - John (1715)
      - Hugh in Knock (1776 x 1790)
        - Dr. Hector EIMS (1776 x 1810)
          - William Swinton (1818 x 1825)
        - Lachlan A/ Surgeon EIMS (1776 x 1799)

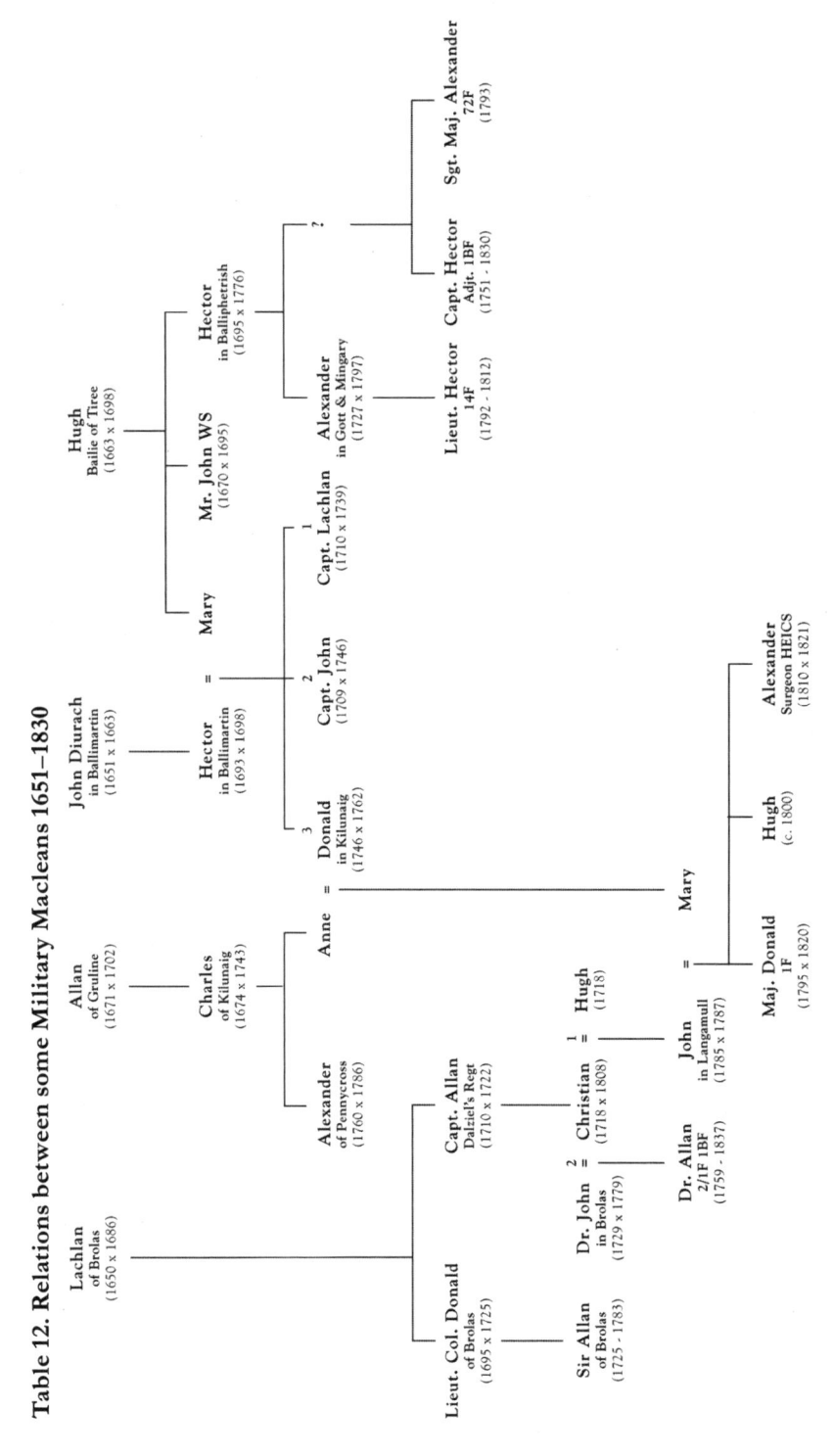

Table 12. Relations between some Military Macleans 1651–1830

```
                                                                          Hugh
                                                                     Bailie of Tiree
                                                                      (1663 x 1698)
                                                                            |
                              ┌─────────────────────────────────────────────┼──────────────┐
                              |                                             |              |
                      John Diurach                                    Mr. John WS       Hector
                      in Ballimartin            Mary          =       (1670 x 1695)   in Balliphetrish
                      (1651 x 1663)                                                    (1695 x 1776)
                              |                                                              |
                              |                                                         ┌────┴────┐ ?
                       Hector                                                           |         |
                     in Ballimartin                                                Alexander
                     (1693 x 1698)                                              in Gott & Mingary
                              |                                                  (1727 x 1797)
                    ┌─────────┼─────────┐                                              |
                  1 |       2 |       3 |                                         ┌────┴────────────┐
           Capt. Lachlan  Capt. John   Donald                              Lieut. Hector      Capt. Hector     Sgt. Maj. Alexander
           (1710 x 1739)  (1709 x 1746)  in Kilunaig                           14F              Adjt. 1BF              72F
                                         (1746 x 1762)                     (1792 - 1812)      (1751 - 1830)           (1793)

           Allan
         of Gruline
        (1671 x 1702)
              |
          Charles
         of Kilunaig
        (1674 x 1743)
              |
      ┌───────┴───────┐
      |               |
  Alexander         Anne   =   ────────────────────────────    Mary
  of Pennycross
  (1760 x 1786)

  Lachlan
  of Brolas
 (1650 x 1686)
      |
 ┌────┴─────────────┬───────────────┬─────────────┐
 |                  |               |             |
Lieut. Col. Donald  Capt. Allan                        
 of Brolas         Dalziel's Regt
 (1695 x 1725)      (1710 x 1722)
      |
 ┌────┴──────┬─────────────────┐
 |           |                 |
Sir Allan   Dr. John      Dr. Allan             1
 of Brolas  in Brolas   =  2/1F 1BF   Christian  =  Hugh
(1725 - 1783) (1729 x 1779) (1759 - 1837) (1718 x 1808)  (1718)
                                             |
                                          2  |
                                          John
                                       in Langamull
                                       (1785 x 1787)
                                             |
                                             =   Mary
                                    Maj. Donald
                                        1F
                                   (1795 x 1820)
                                             |
                              ┌──────────────┼──────────────┐
                              |              |              |
                          Alexander         Hugh            
                       Surgeon HEICS       (c. 1800)
                        (1810 x 1821)
```

NMB 13.08.06

Bibliography

UNPUBLISHED PRIMARY SOURCES.

Archives de Guerre, Chateau de Vincennes, Paris. Arch. Admin. Officiers 1791–1847.
Archives Office of New South Wales. Report of a ship arrived in Port Jackson 20 January 1838.
Argyll & Bute District Council Archives. CO6. 1. 11. 1. Minute Book of the General Court of Lieutenancy.
    Minute Book of Coll Parochial Board. CO 6. 7.
BCP. Crossapol Manuscript.
    The Journal of Juliet Alexa Maclean (1859).
BCT. Coll Charters.
BL IOL Hodson MSS.
    E. 4. 617 Bengal Dispatches.
    L. MIL.12.73, 187.
    MS ADD 38211.
    MS Stowe 199.
Buckinghamshire Record Office. D/MH/H. M110.
Dochgarroch Papers, Record of His Majesty's 79th Regt, or Cameron Highlanders.
Dunbar Rob. 'The Poetry of John Maclean 'Bàrd Thigearna Chola' (unpublished PhD Thesis. University of Glasgow (2005)).
EUL. MSS. AT 1679. Accounts of Archibald 9th Earl of Argyll.
    AT Argyll Rentals. Vol 2. Mic. M. 676, 28a, 32.
    Laing.II, 300].
        III.
        IV 839. Eigg Catechist list, 1764–5.
General Register House. Parish of Tiree & Coll Census. 551. 25.
Glasgow City Archives. T-MJ 377 (a).
Glasgow University Library Special Collections.
King's Own Scottish Borderers Regimental Headquarters, Berwick on Tweed 2 KOSB Digest of Services: KOSB D1. 1 (1897).
    Historical Records. KOSB Q14, 94.
La Trobe Library, Melbourne, Australia.
Mitchell Library, Sidney, Australia. Dispatches to the Governor of New South Wales. January December 1835.
    Extracts of G Gipps's despatches.

Moray Manuscripts, Darnaway, Forres. Box 6, 43.
Mull Museum. Letter Book. 1846–1850. Captain Donald Campbell at Quinish.
NAS. CC12. 2.
       CH2. 70.
       CH2. 273.
       CH2. 492.
       CH2. 493.
       CH2. 551.
       CH2. 557.
       CH2 984.
       CS 1 Inglis M.1. 7.
       CS 226.5573.
       CS 229 Mc/6/54. Box 308.
       CS 234. Sequestrations M1/27. Box 228.
       CS 237.
       Decreet of Teinds 1726.
       Highland Emigration Society Papers. HD 4.
       GD 14. Stonefield Papers.
       GD 16.
       GD 50.
       GD 51.
       GD 95. SSPCK Minutes of Directors & Letter books (1783–1813).
       GD 112. Breadalbane Papers.
       GD 170. 22. The Tacksmen of the Poll 1693.
       GD 174. Maclaine of Lochbuie Papers.
       GD 201. Clanranald Papers.
       GD248. Grant Papers.
       RD DAL 1.
       RD. DAL 2.
       RD. DAL 43.
       RD.DAL 58.
       RD.DUR 53.
       RD MACK 13.
       RD. MACK 22.
       RD. MACK 58.
       RD. MACK 62.
       Register of Sasines.
       Register of Tailzies.
       RHP.3368. Plan of the Island of Coll in Argyllshire.
       RT. CC. 7. 1.
       RS/33/230.
       SC 54. 12.
       SC 59. 2.4.
       SP 4. 13.
       Synod of Argyll Records.

Bibliography

NLS   Melville Papers Home Defence. 1049, 49].
        MS 28. 3. 12.
        MS73.
        MS 975.
        MS 2134.
        MS 2619.
        MS 3018.
        MS 3733-3737.
        MS 16597.
        MS 16605.
        MS 16615.
        MS 16629.
        MS 17677.
        Caledonian Mercury.
        Edinburgh Magazine.
        The Edinburgh Advertiser.
        The Edinburgh Evening Courant.
NMM. Lieutenant's Log *HMS Leda.*
        Log of storeship *HMS Chichester.*
        Log of *HMS Crescent.*
Nova Scotia Public Archives. Kamloops number. 604-376-8902.
Prince Edward Island Public Archives, Accession 2716.
Tasmanian State Archives. Colonial Secretary's Correspondence: Van Diemen's Land (1824–1836).
TNA. CO179. 9.
           201. 102.
        FO 65.1153.
        HO102.
        HO103.
        SP 28. 120.
        WO1 1003.
        WO 12. 11698.
            1779 Muster Rolls of 3rd Regiment of Foot Guards.
            2242 Monthly Pay List. 11th Foot.
            5478 Muster Rolls 1/42nd Foot.
            5479 Muster Rolls 1/42nd Foot.
            5574 Muster Rolls 43rd Foot.
            5873 Muster Rolls 47th Foot.
            7103 Muster Rolls 61st Foot.
            7325 Muster Rolls 64th Foot.
            7326 Muster Rolls 64th Foot.
            7925 Muster Rolls 72nd Foot.
            8002 Muster Rolls 73rd Foot.
            8390 Muster Rolls 1/79th Foot.
            8393 Muster Rolls 1/79th Foot.
            8449 Pay List 2/79th 1804.

8520. Muster Rolls 81st Foot.

8806. Muster Rolls 2/84 Foot.

WO 13 51 Muster Rolls First (or Argyll) Regiment of North British Militia.

3810. Muster Rolls 1st Battalion Breadalbane Fencibles.

3962. 28182. Muster Rolls Western Fencible Regiment.

3963. 8809. Muster Rolls Western Fencible Regiment.

4169. Part 3. Muster Rolls Argyllshire Volunteers.

4170. Part 4. Muster Rolls Argyllshire Volunteers.

4171. Part 4. Muster Rolls Argyllshire Volunteers.

4175. Part 2. Muster Rolls Argyllshire Volunteers.

4378. Muster Rolls of Inverness-shire Volunteers.

4383. Muster Rolls of Inverness-shire Volunteers.

WO 17.

WO 25.

WO 31.

WO 34.

WO 40.

WO 42.

WO 71.

WO 97. 895. 79th Foot Pensions.

WO 98/7. List of Recipients of the Victoria Cross 1856–1914.

The Huntington Library.

LO 6695.

SECONDARY SOURCES

Books

Aberdeen Sasines.

Alphabetical List of the Officers of the Indian Army at the Madras Presidency 1760–1834 (1837).

An Officer in the Queen's Army [Alexander Maclean ?] *Historical& Statistical Sketches of Aden in Arabia Felix during a two years residence in the Colony* (1848).

An Gaidheal, 5 vols (1871–1877).

An Teachdaire Gaelach (1829–1831).

Anderson, James *An Account of the Present State of the Hebrides* (1785).

Anderson, William *The Scottish Nation* (1877).

Anonymous *A Breif Genealogical Account of the FFAMILY OF McLEAN* (1872).

Anonymous *Coll* (Wellington, 1911).

An Officer of the Army *Memoirs of the Lord Viscount Dundee* (1711).

Army List 1779.

Atholl, J Duke of, *Chronicles of the Atholl and Tullibardine Families*, 5 vols (Edinburgh 1908).

Aust, The Hon. Mrs Murray *A Companion and Useful Guide to the Beauties of Scotland and the Hebrides* (1810).

Australian Dictionary of Biography Vol. 5. (1851–1890).

Banks, Noel *Six Inner Hebrides* (1977).

Bibliography

Beauclerk Dewar, Peter (ed) *The Kingdom of Scotland* (2001).
Birch, T *Thurloe State Papers*, VI (London, 1742).
British Fisheries Society's Report.
Brown, Iain Gordon & Cheape, Hugh *Witness to Rebellion* (1996).
Brown, Thomas *Annals of the Disruption* (1893).
Bruce, George *The Burmah Wars 1824–1886* (1973).
Brumwell, Stephen *Redcoat: The British Soldier ans War in the Americas, 1755–1763.* (2002).
Bryer, Lynne & Hunt, Keith S *The 1820 Settlers* (Cape Town, 1984).
Buckley, Helen Maclean *From Little Towns in a Far Land We Came* (1950).
Bumstead, JM *The People's Clearance* (1982).
Burke, Bernard *Vicissitudes of Families*, vol. II (1869).
Burleigh, JHS *A Church History of Scotland* (1960).
Burton, Reginald George *A History of the Hyderabad Contingent* (Calcutta, 1905).
Calendar of State Papers Domestic 1680–1.
Callwell, CE *Small Wars*.
Cambridge History of the British Empire, vol. 2.
Cameron, A *Reliquiae Celticae* (1894).
Cameron, John (ed) *The Justiciary Record of Argyll and the Isles 1664–1705* (1949).
Cameron, Joy *Prisons and Punishment in Scotland* (1983).
Campbell, Alastair of Airds, Yr *Two Hundred Years: The Highland Society of London* (1983).
Campbell, Alastair of Airds, *The Life & Troubled Times of Sir Donald Campbell of Ardnamurchan.* (SWH&IHR 1991).
Campbell, Alastair of Airds, *A History of Clan Campbell* 3 vols (2000–2004).
Campbell, JL (ed) *A Collection of Highland Rites and Customs* (1975).
Campbell, JL (ed) *Highland Songs of the Forty-Five* (1933).
Celtic Monthly (1901).
Chambers, James *Palmerston: 'The People's Darling'* (2004).
Chapman, Malcolm *The Gaelic Vision in Scottish Culture* (London, 1978).
Childs, John *The Army of Charles II* (1976).
Churchill, Winston S *My Early Life* (1930).
Churchill, Winston S House of Commons 31st May 1916.
Clan Campbell Newsletter (1980).
Clark, James T (ed) *Macfarlane's Genealogical Collection* i (1900).
Clyde, Robert *From Rebel to Hero* (1995).
Coll Almanac.
Collectanea de Rebus Albanicis, (1847).
Cookson, JE *The British Armed Nation 1793–1815* (1997).
Cooper, T *Political State of Great Britain* (1715).
Corbett, Robert *Guerilla Warfare* (1986).
Cowan, Edward J *Montrose* (1977).
Cregeen, Eric (ed), *Inhabitants of the Argyll Estate, 1779* (SRS 1963).
Cregeen, Eric *Argyll Estate Instructions 1771–1805* (SHS 1964).
Cruickshanks, Eveline (ed) *The Stuart Courts* (2000).
Curzon, George N *Persia and the Persian Question* (1966).
Davidson, H *The History & Services of the 78th Highlanders 1793–1881* (1901).

Devine, TM *The Great Highland Famine* (1988).
Devine, TM *Scotland's Empire 1600–1815* (2003).
Dickson, Mora *A World Elsewhere: Voluntary Service Overseas* (1964).
Dictionary of Canadian Biography.
Dictionary of National Biography (1896).
Dixon, James *Narrative of A Voyage to New South Wales & Van Diemen's Land in the Ship Skelton during the Year 1820* (1822).
Dixon-Smith, Rosemary *The Conch 1828–1869* (2000).
Dodgshon, Robert A *From Chiefs to Landlords* (1998).
Dodds, John *Records of the Scottish Settlers in the River Plate*, 1897).
Donaldson, Gordon *Scotland: James v-James vii* (1971).
Douglas of Glenbervie, Robert *The Baronage of Scotland* (1798).
Dow, FD *Cromwellian Scotland* (1979).
Downie, Sir Alex. Mackenzie & Downie Alister Mackinnon *Genealogical Account of the Family of Mackinnon* (1882).
Drummond, Andrew L & Bulloch, James *The Church in Victorian Scotland 1843–1874* (1975).
Drummond of Balhaldies, John *Memoirs of Locheill* (Maitland Club, 1842).
Duff, Geoffrey P *Sheep May Safely Graze* (Christchurch, 1998).
Duncanson, John Victor *Rawdon and Douglas: Two Loyalist Townships in Nova Scotia* (Mika Publishing Company, Belleville, Ontario, 1989).
Dunlop, Jean *The British Fisheries Society 1786–1893* (1978).
Dwelly, Edward *The Illustrate Gaelic-English Dictionary* (1977).
Edinger, George *The Twain Shall Meet* (1960).
Ehrman, John *The Younger Pitt* 3 vols (1969–1996).
Ellis, MH *Lachlan Macquarrie* (1958).
Esdaile, Charles *The Peninsular War* (2002).
Ewing, John *The History of the 9th (Scottish) Division 1914–1919* (1927).
Falconer, Randle Wilbraham MD *The Baths & Mineral Waters of Bath* (1860).
Fasti Ecclesiae Scoticae.
Fellowes, Edmund H *Military Knights of Windsor 1352–1944*.
Ferguson, James *Scots Brigade* (1899).
Ferguson, James *Argyll in the Forty-Five* (1951).
Ferguson, Niall *The House of Rothschild* (1998).
Ferguson, Niall *The Pity of War* (1999).
Ferris, HS *Britain and Argentina in the Nineteenth Century* (1960).
First Report of the Select Committee on Emigration, Scotland (1846).
Fiske, Roger *English Theatre Music in the Eighteenth Century*, 2nd edition (1986).
Flinn, Michael & others *Scottish Population History* (1977).
Fortescue, The Hon JW *A History of the British Army* (1913).
Fortescue, The Hon JW *The County Lieutenancies and the Army 1803–1814* (1909).
Fraser Darling, F (ed) *West Highland Survey* (1956).
Fraser Mackintosh, C *Antiquarian Notes* (1897).
Fry, Michael *The Dundas Despotism* (1992).
Furgol, Edward M *A Regimental History of the Covenanting Armies 1639–1651* (1990).
Gaelic Schools 3rd Annual Report of the Society for Gaelic Schools 1813.

Bibliography

Gaelic Schools 5th Annual Report of the Society for 1816.
Gaskell, Philip *Morvern Transformed* (1968).
GBB (ed) *Broad Grins* (1898).
Gentleman's Magazine.
Giblin, Cathaldus (ed) *Irish Franciscan Mission to Scotland 1619–1646* (1964).
Gibson, John S *Ships of the '45* (1967).
Gillies, A *A Hebridean in Goethe's Weimar* (1969).
Gillon, Stair *The KOSB in the Great War* (nd).
Glover, Richard *Peninsular Preparation: The Reform of the British Army 1795–1809* (1963).
Goss, J *A Border Battalion the History of the 7/8th (Service) Battalion King's Own Scottish Borderers* (1920).
Graham, Henry Grey, *The Social Life of Scotland in the Eighteenth Century* (1899).
Grant, AJ & Temperley, Harold *Europe in the Nineteenth and Twentieth Centuries 1789–1939* (1948).
Grant, IF *The Macleods The History of a Clan* (1959)
Grant, FJ & Boog Watson, CB *Register of Apprentices of the City of Edinburgh 1583–1755* (Scottish Record Society, 1906).
Grant of Rothiemurchus, Elizabeth *Memoirs of a Highland Lady* (1967).
Grants of Shewglie.
Gray, Malcolm *The Highland Economy 1750–1850* (1956).
Gregory, Donald *The History of the West Highlands and Isles of Scotland* (1881).
Greaves, Rose Louise *Persia and the Defence of India 1884–1892* (1959).
Grimble, Ian *Chief of Mackay* (1965).
Gronow, Rees Howell *The Reminiscences and Recollections of Captain Gronow* (1889).
Guest, Bill & Sellars, John M *Enterprise & Exploitation in a Victorian Colony* (Pietermaritzburg, 1895).
Gunn, John *An Historical Inquiry Respecting the Performance of the Harp in the Highlands of Scotland, from the Earliest Times until it was Discontinued, About the Year 1734* (1807).
Haldane, ARB *The Drove Roads of Scotland* (1968).
Hansard's Parliamentary History 1766 (1813).
Hart, Liddell *A History of the World War 1914–1918* (1930).
Harries-Jenkins, Gwyn *The Army in Victorian Society* (1977).
Hart's Annual Army List for 1906 (1906).
Harvey Johnston, G *The Heraldry of the Campbells* (1977).
Hayes-McCoy, GA *Scots Mercenary Forces in Ireland* (1937).
Hayter, Tony (ed) *An Eighteenth-Century Secretary at War the papers of William, Viscount Barrington.*
Healey, Denis Secretary of State for Defence. *Military Aid To The Civil Community* (Ministry of Defence, 1968).
Hibbert, Christopher *Corunna* (1961).
Highland Society of Scotland Prize Essays &c (1816).
Hill, George *The Macdonnells of Antrim* (1875).
Historical Notices of Scottish Affairs (1848).
Hobday, CAP *Sketches on Service during the Indian Frontier Campaigns of 1897* (1898).
Hodson, VCP *List of the Officers of the Bengal Army 1758–1830* (1946).
Holt, Edgar *The Opium Wars in China* (1964).
Hopkirk, Peter *The Great Game* (1990).
Hopkins, Paul *Glencoe and the end of the Highland War* (1986).

HMCR Buccleuch & Queensberry.
HMCR Leyborne-Popham.
HMCR Portland x (1931).
Hunter, James *The Making of the Crofting Community* (1976).
Hutchinson, HD *The Campaign in Tirah 1897–98* (1898).
Imrie, John (ed) *The Justiciary Records of Argyll and the Isles 1642–1742* (1969).
Innes, Cosmo (ed) *Munimenta Alme Universitis Glasguensis Thanes of Cawdor* (1859).
Innes, of Learney, Sir Thomas *Scots Heraldry* (1956).
Irvine Robertson, James *The First Highlander* (1998).
James, David *Lord Roberts* (1954).
Jenkins, Roy *Gladstone* (1995).
Johnson, Samuel *A Journey to the Western Islands of Scotland* (1817).
Jourdain, HFN & Fraser, Edward *The Connaught Rangers* (1926).
Journal of Itinerating Exertions in some of the more destitute parts of Scotland (1816).
Keswick, Maggie (ed) *The Thistle and the Jade* (1982).
Kincaid, A (ed) *An Account of the Depradations committed upon the Clan Campbell and their followers during the years 1685 & 1686* (Edinburgh, 1816).
Knox, John *A Tour through the Highlands of Scotland and the Hebride Isles in 1786* (1975).
Lang, Andrew *Pickle the Spy* (1897).
Lauder of Fountainhall, Sir John *Historical Notices of Scottish Affairs* (Bannatyne Club, 1848).
Letters from Archibald Earl of Argyll to John Duke of Lauderdale (Bannatyne Club, 1829).
Lewis, Michael *A Social History of the Navy 1793–1815* (1960).
Liddington, Jill *Nature's Domain: Anne Lister and the Landscape of Desire* (2003).
Lindsay, Lord (ed) Colin, Earl of Balcarres *Memoirs touching the Revolution in Scotland* (1841).
Lockhart, JG *The Life of Sir Walter Scott, Bart* (1879).
London Gazette.
Longford, Elizabeth *Wellington Pillar of State* (1972).
Logue, Kenneth *Popular Disturbances in Scotland 1780–1815* (1979).
Loudon, Joseph Buist (ed) *The Diary of James robertson Sheriff Sudstitute of Tobermory 1842–1846* (2001).
Love, John A *Rum: A Landscape Without Figures* (2001).
MacCulloch, John *The Western Islands of Scotland* (1824).
Macdonald, James *A General View of the Agriculture of the Hebrides* (1811).
MacDougall, Hector & Cameron, Hector *Handbook to the islands of Coll & Tiree* (Glasgow nd).
MacDougall, Jean *Highland Postbag. The Correspondence of Four MacDougall Chiefs 1715–1865* (1984).
MacDougall, Betty *Folklore from Coll* (nd).
MacDougall, JL *History of Inverness County* (New York, 1917).
Macinnes, Allan *Clanship, Commerce and the House of Stuart, 1603–1788* (1996).
Macinnes, John *The Evangelical Movement in the Highlands of Scotland 1688 to 1800* (1951).
Mackenzie, Annie M (ed) *Orain Iain Luim: Songs of John Macdonald Bard of Keppoch* (1964).
Mackenzie, Hector Hugh *The Macleans of Boreray* (1946).
Mackenzie, Henry *Report of the Committee of the Highland Society of Scotland on the Poems of Ossian* (1805).
Mackenzie, Robert Holden *The Trafalgar Roll* (1913).
Mackesy, Piers *The War in the Mediterranean 1803–1810* (1957).
Mackesy, Piers *The Strategy of Overthrow 1798–1799* (1974).
Mackesy, Piers *War Without Victory: The Downfall of Pitt 1799–1802* (1984).

Bibliography

Mackillop, Andrew *'More Fruitful than the Soil'* (2000).
Mackinnon, Donald *A descriptive Catalogue of Gaelic Manuscripts* (1912).
Maclean, Fitzroy *Bonnie Prince Charlie* (1988).
Maclean, James NM *Reward is Secondary* (1963).
Maclean, James NM *The Macleans of Sweden* (1971).
MacLean, JP *A History of the Clan MacLean* (Cincinnati, 1889).
MacLean, JP *A MacLean Souvenir* (Ohio, 1918).
MacLean, Lachlan *An Historical Account of Iona* (1833).
MacLean, JP *The History of the Celtic Language* (1840).
MacLean, Loraine of Dochgarroch *The Raising of the 79th Highlanders* (SWH&IHR, 1980).
MacLean, Loraine of Dochgarroch (ed) *The Middle Ages in the Highlands* (1981).
MacLean, Loraine of Dochgarroch *Indomitable Colonel* (1986).
Maclean-Bristol, Nicholas *Warriors and Priests* (1995).
Maclean-Bristol, Nicholas *Inhabitants of the Inner Isles Morvern & Ardnamurchan 1716* (SRS 1998).
Maclean-Bristol, Nicholas *Murder Under* (1999).
Maclean-Bristol, Nicholas (ed) *Project Trust Directory1967–1998* (1999).
Maclean Sinclair, A *Clan Gillean* (Charlottetown, 1899).
Maclean-Sinclair, A *Na Baird Leathanach* (1898 & 1900).
Maclean-Sinclair, A *Clarsach na Coille* (1928).
Macleod of Macleod, RC *The Book of Dunvegan* (1938).
Macleod, Donald *Memoir of Norman Macleod. D.D.* (1876).
Macleod, John N *Memorials of the Rev. Norman Macleod of St Columba's* (nd).
Macmillan, David S *Scotland and Australia 1788–1850* (1967).
Macphail, JRN (ed) *Highland Papers* vol. II (SHS 1916).
Magnus, Philip *Kitchener* (1958).
Magnusson, Magnus *Rum: Nature's Island* (1997).
Marshall, Rosalind K *The Days of Duchess Anne* (1973).
Martin, Martin *A Description of the Western Islands of Scotland* (1716).
Mason, Philip *A Matter of Honour: an account of the Indian Army its officers and men* (1975).
Maurice, Major-General Sir J Frederick KCB *History of the War in South Africa 1899–1902* Vol. II (1907).
McCrae, Morrice (ed) *The New Club* (2004).
McGurk, Francis (ed) *Papal Letters to Scotland of Benedict XIII of Avignon 1394–1419* (1976).
McIntyre North, CN *The Book of the Club of True Highlanders* (1881).
McKay, Margaret M *The Rev. Dr. John Walker's Report on the Hebrides of 1764 & 1771* (1980).
McLean, Hector *An Enquiry into the nature and causes of the great mortality of the troops at St. Domingo*, (London: Cadell & Davies, 1797).
McLynn, Frank *Charles Edward Stuart* (1988).
McMicking, Neil (ed) *Officers of the Black Watch 1725 to 1952* (1952).
Memoirs of the Rev. Norman Macleod (senior) DD of St Columba's (1898).
Moncreiffe of that Ilk, Sir Iain *The Highland Clans* (1982).
Mowle, LM *Pioneer Families of Australia*, (1978).
Munro, Jean & RW *Acts of the Lords of the Isles 1336–1493* (1986).
Munro, Jean *The Founding of Tobermory* (SWH&IHR 1976).
Munro, RW (ed) *Monro's Western Isles of Scotland and Genealogies of the Clans 1549* (1961).

Munro, RW & Macquarrie, Alan *Clan MacQuarrie* (1996).
Munroe, John A *Louis McLane: Federalist and Jacksonian* (1973).
Murray, Venetia *High Society: A Social History of the Regency Period, 1788–1830* (1998).
Necker de Saussure, LA *A Voyage to the Hebrides* (1822).
New Statistical Account of Scotland (1835–45).
Northern Notes and Queries, or the Scottish Antiquary.
Oban Times, 14 May 1921.
Ó Baoill, Colm *Eachann Bacach & other Maclean Poets* (Scottish Gaelic Texts, 1979).
Ó Baoill, Colm *Duanaire Colach 1537–1757* (1997).
Osborne, Brian D *The Last of the Chiefs* (2001).
Otter, William (ed) *The Life & Remains of the Rev. Edward Daniel Clarke LLD* (1824).
Oxford Dictionary of National Biography (2004).
Parliamentary Papers, *Minutes of Evidence Before Select Committee on Emigration from the United Kingdom* (1827).
Parliamentary Papers, *Report from the Commissioners appointed for inquiring into the Administration and Practical Operation of the Poor Laws in Scotland* (1844).
Parliamentary Papers, *Minutes of Evidence taken before Select Committee on Sites for Churches* (Scotland).
Parliamentary Papers, LIII *Correspondence from July 1846 to February 1847 relating to the Measures adopted for the Relief of the Distress in Scotland* (1847).
Parliamentary Papers, XXXIV. *Application for advance of Public Money under provision of Act 9 & 10 Vic. Cap. C1, 101* (1847).
Parliamentary Papers, *Highland Destitution Reports. Glasgow Section.* 9th Report (2 Aug. 1848).
Parliamentary Papers, *Report to the Board of Supervision by Sir John MacNeill on the West Highlands & Islands* (1851).
Parliamentary Papers, *Report of Her Majesty's Commission of Inquiry in to the Conditions of the Crofters and Cottars in the Highland & Islands of Scotland* (1884).
Parliamentary Papers, *Report of the Royal Commission* (Highlands & Islands 1892).
Paton, Henry (ed) *The Lyon in Mourning* vol. III (1975).
Political State of Scotland at Michaelmas (1812).
Pollock, John *Kitchener* (1998).
Pottle, Frederick A & Bennett, Charles H *Boswell's Journal of A Tour to the Hebrides* (1936).
Pottle, Frederick A & Weiss, Charles McC *Boswell In Extremes 1776–1778* (1971).
Pottle, Frederick A & Charles Ryskamp *Boswell: The Ominous Years 1774–1776* (1963).
Prebble, John *Mutiny* (1975).
Prebble, John *The King's Jaunt* (1988).
RCAHMS *Argyll,* vol. 3 (1980).
Records of Old Aberdeen.
Denys Reitz *Commando* (1930).
Rider Haggard, H *A Farmer's Year* (1909).
Ritchie, John *Lachlan Macquarie* (1988).
Roberts, Fergus & Macphail, IMM (edd), *Dumbarton Common Good Accounts 1614–1660* (1972).
Robinson, Mairi (ed) *The Concise Scots Dictionary* (1987).
Rose, GH *Marchmont Papers: A Selection from the Papers of the Earls of Marchmont*, 3 vols (London 1831).
Rushidi, Runoko *Black War. The Destuction of the Tasmanian Aborigines* (1998).

Bibliography

Sanger, Keith & Kinnaird, Alison *Tree of Strings* (1992).
Scots Magazine Vol 48 (1786).
Scott, Sir Walter *Minstrelsy of the Scottish Border* 1802).
Scott, Sir Walter *Lay of the Last Minstrel* (1810).
Scott, Sir Walter *Military Memoirs of the Great Civil War* (1822).
Scott, Sir Walter *Poetical Works* (1882).
Seanachie *The Clan Maclean* (1838).
Selkirk, The Earl of *Observations on the Present State of the Highlands* (1806).
Shadwell, LJ *Lockhart's Advance through Tirah* (1898).
Shaw, Frances J *The Northern and Western Islands of Scotland* (1980).
Sinclair, Sir John *The Statistical Account of Scotland 1791–1799I* vol XX (1983).
Skene, William F *Celtic Scotland* iii, (1890).
Somers, Robert *Letters from the Highlands on the Famine of 1846* (1977).
Smith, Annette M *Jacobite Estates of the Forty-Five* (1982).
Snodgrass, JJ *Narrative of The Burmese War* (1827).
Speirs, Edward M *The Army and Society 1815–1914* (1980).
Stapylton, HEC *The Eton School Lists from 1791 to 1850* (1864).
Steele, R (ed) *A Bibliography of Royal Proclamations of the Tudor and Stuart Sovereigns 1485–1714* (1910).
Steer, KA and Bannerman, JWM *Late Medieval Monumental Sculpture in the West Highlands* (1977).
Stevenson, David *Scottish Covenanters and Irish Confederates* (1981).
Stevenson, David *Irish Historical Studies* Vol. XXI, No. 81 (March 1978).
Stewart of Ardvorlich, John *The Camerons* (nd)
Stewart of Garth, David *Sketches of the Highlanders of Scotland* (1822).
Stone, Lawrence *The Family, Sex and Marriage in England 1500–1800* (1977).
Teignmouth, Lord *The Coasts & Islands of Scotland* 2 vols (1836).
The Argus (Tuesday 27 May 1890).
The Chronicle (12 September 1835).
The Daily Telegraph Friday (2 June 2006).
The Glasgow Herald, Saturday (17 October 1896).
The Independent, Launceston, VDL (Saturday 9 March 1833).
The Independent, Launceston, VDL (Saturday 1 November 1834).
Theophilus Insulanus [Donald Macleod of Hamer] *A Treatise on the Second Sight* (1763 [reprinted 1817).
Thomson, Derick S (ed) *The Companion to Gaelic Scotland* (1983).
Thomson, T & Innes C (eds) *The Acts of the Parliament of Scotland* (12 vols, Edinburgh 1814–75).
Thomson William PL *Kelp-Making in Orkney* (1983).
Towend, Peter (ed) *Burke's Peerage* (104th Edition, 1967).
Tullibardine, The Marchioness of *A Military History of Perthshire* (1908).
Turner, Sir James *Memoirs of His Life and Times* (Edinburgh 1829).
Warrand, Duncan (ed) *More Culloden Papers* (1929).
Waterfield, Gordon *Sultans of Aden* (1968).
Waters, Charlotte M *An Economic History of England* (1949).
Whetstone, Ann E *Scottish County Government in the Eighteenth and Nineteenth Centuries* (1981).
Whitbread, Helena (ed) *I Know My Own Heart* (1988).
Whitbread, Helena (ed) *Anne Lister's Journal 21 March to 18 April 1829* (1998).

Who Was Who 1897–1916.
Wikipedia Free Encyclopedia.
Willcock, John *A Scots Earl* (1907).
Wilson, Heather (ed) *The Diary of Private William Fessey DCM* (1998).
Wilson, HW (ed) *The Great War* vol. V (week ending 11 December 1915).
Woolcombe, Robert *All the Blue Bonnets* (1980).
Wormald, Jenny Lords and Men in Scotland: Bonds of Manrent 1442–1603 (1985).
Wright, Philip (ed) *Lady Nugent's Journal* (1966).
Young, Peter & Lawford, JP *History of the British Army* (1970).
Younghusband, GJ *The Story of the Guides* (1908).
Zamoyski, Adam *1812: Napoleon's Fatal March on Moscow* (2004).

Articles

Bannerman, John 'Literacy in the Highlands', Ian B Cowan & Duncan Shaw *The Renaissance and Reformation in Scotland* (1983).
Campbell, JL & Eastwick, C 'The Macneils of Barra in the Forty-Five', *Innes Review*.
Campbell, Niall A 'An Old Inventory of the Laird of Coll's Writs' *The Celtic Review* (October 1912).
Carman, WY 'Lieutenant-General Sir Adolphus Oughton, KB' *JSAHR*, vol. 68, No. 271, (Autumn 1989).
Cowan, Edward J 'The Angus Campbells and the Origin of the Campbell-Ogilvie Feud' *Scottish Studies* Vol. 25, (1981).
Cowan, Edward J 'Fishers in Drumlie Waters: Campbell Expansion in the time of Gilleasbuig Gruamach' *TGSI* Vol. LIV (1984–86).
Cregeen, Eric R 'The Changing Role of the House of Argyll in the Scottish Highlands', I M Lewis (ed) *History and Social Anthropology* (1968).
CW *From Bordon to Loos* (1917).
Forbes, Will 'Dionysus Campbell' *WHN&Q* Series 3, No. 6 (November 2003).
Fraser Mackintosh, C 'The MacDonalds of Morar, styled *Mac Dhugail*' *TGSI*, vol. XV (1889).
Gaelic Schools 5th Annual Report of the Society for 1816.
Goodare, Julian 'The Statutes of Iona in Context' *SHR* Volume LXXVII, 1: No. 203: April 1998.
Graham-Campbell, David '18th Century Chamberlains on a Highland Estate'. Unpublished MS.
Gray, Holmes 'Hugh Gray, Innkeeper in Coll' *WHN&Q* Series 2 No. 13 (February 1995).
Gunn, A 'Unpublished Literary Remains of Reay Country' *TGSI*, XVI.
Hunter, James 'Politics of Highland Land Reform, 1873–1895', *SHR*. Vol. LIII, No. 155: (April 1974).
Kinsey, HW 'The Sekukuni Wars' The South Africa Military History Society. *Military History Journal*, Vol. 2, No. 5.
Lawford, James P 'The Indian Mutiny 1857–58' *History of the British Army* (1970).
Lenman, Bruce P 'Militia, Fencible Men, and Home Defence, 1660–1797' in Norman Macdougall (ed), *Scotland and War AD 79–1919* (1991).
Maclean, James NM 'The Camerons of Glendessary and Dungallon' *The Scottish Genealogist* vol XVII, No. 4 (December 1971).
Maclean, James NM 'The Frasers of Kiltarlity: cadets of a deposed Mackintosh chief' *The Scottish Genealogist* vol. XVI, No. 2 (June 1969).

MacLean, J 'Queries', *Scottish Genealogist*, vol. 16, No. 4 (December 1969).
Maclean-Bristol, Nicholas 'Military Macleans 1756–9.' *WHN&Q* 1st Series, No. III (1976).
Maclean-Bristol, Nicholas 'The Building of Breacachadh and the Maclean Pedigree' *WHN&Q*, 1st Series, XIII (1980).
Maclean-Bristol, Nicholas 'A Genealogical Puzzle Solved' *WHN&Q*, 1st Series Vol. XXX (February 1987).
Maclean-Bristol, Nicholas 'The Maclaines of Kilmory', *WHN&Q* Series 2, No. 1 (March, 1988).
Maclean-Bristol, Nicholas 'Murdoch Maclaine, Lieutenant 42nd Foot ?' *JSAHR* vol. 77, No. 310, (Summer 1999).
Maclean-Bristol, Nicholas 'John Maclean in his Highness's Army', *WHN&Q* Series 3, No. 3 (March 2002).
Maclean-Bristol, Nicholas 'Ballyhough Farm, Isle of Coll', *WHN&Q* Series 3, No. 5 (November 2002).
Maclean-Bristol, Nicholas 'Jacobite Officers in the Scots Brigade in Dutch Service', *JSAHR*, vol. 82, No. 330 (Summer 2004).
Maclean-Bristol, Nicholas 'Tacksmen in Rum' *WHN&Q* Series 3, No. 7 (2005).
MacLean, Ir J 'Huwelijken Van Militairen, behorende tot het eerste regiment van de Schotse Brigade in Nederland, onleend aan de gereformeerde trouwboeken van 1674 tot 1708' *De Brabatse Leeuw* (Sept. Okt. 1971).
MacLean, Ir J 'Genealogie Macleane' *Gens Nostra Ons Geslacht Maandblad Der Nederladse Genealogische Vereniging* (Maart 1973).
Mackinnon, Donald 'The Mackaskills of Rudha 'n Dùnain', *Clan Macleod Magazine* (1951), vol II, No. 17.
Macleod, Murdo 'Gaelic in Highland Education', *TGSI*, vol. XLIII (1960–3).
Madley, Benjamin 'Patterns of frontier gencide 1803–1910: the Aboriginal Tasmanians, the Yuki of California and the Herrero of Namibia' *Journal of Genocide Research* (2004).
Mann, Michael *China, 1860* (1989).
Mills, TF *Land Forces of Britain, Empire & Commonwealth. 19th Lancers. Fane's Horse.* (World Wide Web).
Montagu, WE *Campaigning in South Africa: Reminiscences of an Officer in 1879* (1880).
Morison, Neil Rankin 'Clann Duiligh: Piobairean Chloinn Ghill-Eathain', *TGSI* vol. XXXVII (1934–6).
Ó Baoill, Colm 'Lament for Niall Og' *WHN&Q* Series 1, Number xxvi (April 1985).
Ogg, John *House in the Hebrides* (2004).
Oman, Sir Charles 'A Duel of 1807' *JSAHR* vol. 1 (1921–2).
Pakenham, Thomas *The Scramble for Africa* (1992).
Plester, Jeremy 'Weather Eye' *The Times* 17 Mar. 2004.
Mackleane, Sir John 'Remarks on the Loyal Dissuasive' in Alexander D Murdoch (ed) *The Loyall Dissuasive* (SHS, 1902).
Macmillan, David S 'The Treaty of Lochbuy' *WHN&Q* Series I, No. XX (March 1983).
Munro, Jean 'When Island Chiefs Came To Town' *WHN&Q* No. XIX (December 1982).
Ravenhill, William 'The Hon. RE Clifford (1788–1817) Officer in Dillon's Regiment. *JSAHR*, vol. 69 (Summer 1991).
Ricketts, AN 'Dillon's Regiment in the Peninsula' *The Irish Sword* vol. XII, No. 49.
Roberts, Alasdair 'MacDonalds losing Meoble' (forthcoming).

Roberts, Andrew *Salisbury: Victorian Titan* (2000).

Sanger, Keith 'From Taynish to West Meath: A Musical Link'. *WHN&Q* Series 3, No. 4, (August 2002).

Sellar, David 'Barony Jurisdiction in the Highlands', *WHN&Q*, 1st Series, No. XVI (September 1981).

Sheffield, GD *Leadership in the Trenches* (2000).

Smith, KW 'The campaigns against the Bapedi of Sekukhune, 1877–1879', *Archives Year Book for SA History* (1967).

Stewart, AIB 'Bubly Jock', *The Kintyre Magazine*. No. 27, (Summer 1990).

Sunter, Ronald M 'Raising the 97th (Inverness-shire) Highland Regiment of Foot', *JSAHR*, vol. 76, No. 306 (Summer 1998).

Walker, Rev. Dr 'Essay on kelp' *Highland Society of Scotland* vol. 1.

Wood, Stephen 'By Dint of Labour and Perseverance' A journal recording two months in northern Germany kept by Lieutenant-Colonel James Adolphus Oughton, commanding 1st battalion 37th of Foot, 1758, *JSAHR*, Special Publication No. 14 (1997).

Index

The first part of this index is primarily designed for use, in conjunction with Tables 1–12, to identify individuals on the Coll estate. It also helps define their territorial status. Landowners, whether feudal superiors holding their land directly from the crown, feuars holding of a feudal superior or wadsetters, who held their land in security for a loan, are described as 'of' their holding of land. They plus commissioned officers, ministers, merchants and doctors & their children are listed in the first section. Tacksmen who had a tack or lease are usually described as 'in' a holding. They appear in the second section. Some tacksmen such as the Macleods of Talisker and later Macleans of Crossapol, who held their tacks for many generations were almost invariably described as 'of', although technicaly they were only entitled to be 'in'. Tenants at will are listed with a comma after their name before the name of the toun or town, which they worked with a number of other tenants are listed in the third section. 'At' merely denotes where someone lived. Those whose land holding is not known are listed in the final section.

Part 1 Men and women whose paternal ancestors were members of the Family of Coll.

Landowners, commissioned officers, ministers &c

Maclean
    in Arileod-Coll, 449, 550.
    in Arnabost-Coll, Table 6, 403.
    of Auchnasaul family, Table 7.116, 467.
    of Coll family, Tables 1–2, 405, 408, 452, 466, 476, 503, 520, 533, 541, 542, 545, 550, 569, 648, 649, 650, 651, 664, 672, 677.
    of Crossapol family *Sliochd Neil Mor*, Tables 3–5, 390, 649, 651, 652.
    of Drimnacross family, Table 10.
    in Fiosgaradh family, Table 6, 403, 446, 451, 654, 662.
    in Gallanach family, Table 4, 569.
    at Germany, 650.
    of Grishipol 1st family, Table 8, 116.
    of Grishipol 2nd family, Table 10, 128.
    in Guirdal-Rum family, Table 5, 381, 422, 427.
    of Isle of Muck family, Table 9, 650, 651.
    in Lagmore-Coll and New Zealand family, 515, 517, 518.
    of Torestan family, Table 10.
    of Totronald family, Table 11, 650, 651.
Adelaide, daughter of Alexander Campbell, Jardine Matheson & Co, Hong Kong (1840), 542, 543.
Alexander of Auchnasaul-Mull (1671 × 1675), Table 7.
Alexander of Coll (1752–1835), Table 2, 1, 161, 165–167, 169, 170, 179, 181, 183–185, 187–192, 195, 197, 199, 200–203, 207, 208, 211–217, 219, 221, 225–232, 236, 237, 241–245, 249, 259–263, 265, 268, 270, 273, 277, 280–284, 286, 288, 291–295, 298–303, 305, 309, 312, 324, 326, 333, 334, 336, 347, 352, 353, 356–361, 363–368, 370, 371, 372, 378, 383, 385, 389, 392, 398–406, 408, 409, 412, 414, 415, 419–424, 426, 428, 429–431, 433–436, 441–454, 467, 468, 500, 520, 526, 543, 550, 631, 635, 648, 673, 677.
Alexander, soldier in Dutch service (1694 × 1717), Table 7, 78, 95.
Alexander of Coll [Alick or Alister] (1827–1875), Table 2, 464, 473, 483, 502, 504, 505, 508, 509–513, 528, 529, 531, 545, 545–549, 551, 552, 558–565.
Alexander, Surgeon 64th Foot (1782–1818), Table 4, 186, 253, 312, 314, 315, 318, 321, 324, 326, 328, 330, 331, 332, 334–337, 344, 345, 346, 351, 355, 356, 363, 364, 385–387, 389, 390–392, 429, 432, 437, 453, 456.
Alexander Campbell of Haremere Hall, Sussex, merchant in China (1798–1863), Table 9, 241, 417, 542, 569.
Alexander Macdonald Lockhart, Captain 67th Bengal Native Infantry (1804–1839), Table 9, 533, 536.
Alexander [Alick], Lieutenant-Colonel 94th Foot (1818–1892), Table 4, 391, 432, 453–461, 530, 533, 536–541, 569, 575, 577, 596, 626, 634, 649, 652, 664, 665.
Alexander [Alick/Sandy] son of Mr Neil Minister of Tiree & Coll (1820 × 1851) Table 4, 453, 458, 459, 460, 514.
Alexander [Willie], Major 94th Foot (1858–1901), Table 4, 569, 572, 573, 576, 594, 595, 649, 650, 652, 653, 654, 662, 664.
Alexander in Guirdal-Rum, Ensign AV (1797 × 1826), Table 5, 259, 304, 312, 321, 429.
Alexander Grant, Surveyor General NSW (1861), 517, 571.
Allan of Auchnasaul-Mull (1598 × 1622), Table 1 and 6, 11, 12, 24, 94, 289.
Allan of Auchlinnen & Drimnin-Morvern (c.1600), Table 3, 11, 17, 78, 159, 454.
Allan (1651), Table 3, 39.
Allan (1717 × 1735), Table 8.
Allan (c.1750), Table 11.
Allan, Captain 36th Foot (1763–1829), Table 2, 178, 234, 268, 360, 550, 675.

Allan in Crossapol-Coll, Captain AV (1760–1832), Table 4, 1, 2, 6, 7, 10, 16, 21, 25, 34, 43, 78, 94, 98, 108, 116, 143, 151, 160, 164, 168, 180, 189, 191, 200, 228, 259, 288, 290, 292, 310, 356, 373, 381, 386, 396, 398, 400, 415, 430, 431, 454, 462, 476, 649, 652, 654, 656, 662.

Allan in Kinloch Scrisort-Rum & in Gallanach-Muck. Lieutenant Rum Company AV (1796 × 1803), Table 5, 226, 227, 230, 259, 312, 321, 415, 427.

Allan, Lieutenant & Merchant at Connecticut (1715–1786), Table 10, 116.

Allan of Totronald-Coll, writer in Coll (1710–1739), Table 11, 116, 400, 651.

Ann, daughter of Donald in Cornaig-Coll (1798), 261, 323, 324.

Ann, daughter of Neil in Crossapol-Coll (1776 × 1828), 291, 415, 452.

Ann Maria Flora, daughter of Mr Neil. Minister of Tiree & Coll (1819–1831), 432.

Archibald, Merchant at Dantzig (1736–1805), Table 10, 117, 349, 652.

Archibald in Dantzig (c.1780), Table 10.

Breadalbane [Albane], daughter of Alexander of Coll (1793–1887), 213, 405, 409, 410, 464, 465, 466, 481, 485, 488, 489, 490, 501, 502, 503, 504, 505, 509.

Catherine, daughter of John Garbh (1650), 417.

Catharina, daughter of Alexander of Coll (1787–1869), 398, 412, 415, 433, 436, 517, 550, 677.

Catherine, daughter of Donald of Coll (1773), 361.

Catherine, daughter of Allan of Crossapol (1814), 402.

Catherine Cameron, daughter of Hugh of Coll (1816–1898), 465, 468, 654.

Catherine, daughter of Captain Lachlan in Gallanach (1790).

Charles (1651), Table 3, 39.

Charles, drover (1679 × 1680), Table 8, 49, 54, 60, 70, 85, 263, 306.

Charles, Sergeant 1st BF later Ensign 8 WIR (1795 × 1801), Table 5, 226, 234, 265.

Charles Norman Fitzgerald, Lieutenant 73rd Foot (1796–1822), Table 9, 343, 344, 350, 351, 543.

Charles James (1898), 651.

Clotworthy, Surgeon at Belfast (1703–1784), Table 8.

Donald of Auchnasaul-Mull (1678 × 1687), Table 6, 95.

Donald of Coll (1661 × 1729), Table 2, 69, 73, 77, 78, 97, 100, 104, 596, 654, 678.

Donald of Isle of Muck formerly in Cornaig-Coll (1730–1789), Table 9, 153, 154, 155, 156, 161, 165, 168, 178, 179, 180, 190, 241, 260, 261, 285, 363, 649, 652.

Donald, 'Young Coll' (1750–1774), Table 2, 142, 150, 151, 153, 162, 163, 165, 287, 324, 340, 674.

Donald MA, DL, Minister of the Small Isles & Captain Rum Independent Company of Volunteers (1752–1810), Table 4, 159, 160, 161, 164, 174, 175, 176, 177, 181, 182, 183, 186, 224, 226, 229, 234, 235, 250, 251, 252, 253, 254, 255, 256, 257, 259, 273, 284, 292, 302, 303, 304, 305, 310, 311, 312, 313, 314, 315, 316, 317, 318, 319, 320, 324, 326, 328, 330, 331, 332, 336, 337, 340, 344, 345, 346, 351, 352, 353, 356, 363, 373, 375, 385, 417, 429, 430, 437, 454, 644.

Donald MA, Minister of the Small Isles (1818 × 1822) Table 5, 437.

Donald, theological student (1809–1831), 430, 439.

Donald MD, Tiree (1815–1851), Table 4, 453, 457, 458, 460, 462, 463, 464, 529, 530, 536.

Donald John, Captain 72nd Foot (1789 × 1830), Table 9, 327, 350.

Donald, Lieutenant 16th Foot (1791–1834), Table 9, 190, 330, 342, 452, 534, 542.

Elizabeth Dreghorn, daughter of Hugh of Coll (1817–1914), 467, 468, 654, 676.

Emily Agnes, daughter of Major-General JNH Maclean of Coll (1855–1943), 579, 650.

Evan, Lieutenant Madras Infantry (1833–1870), Table 2, 542.

Fionnvola, Daughter of John Garbh (1640), 27.

Flora Ann, daughter of Lachlan of the Isle of Muck (1785 × 1805), 179, 326, 390.

Francis John Small, Lieutenant 11th Foot (1779–1801), Table 9, 171, 203, 227, 231, 234, 236, 237, 238, 239, 241, 245, 265, 569.

George Allan, Captain 61st Foot (1790–1820), Table 9, 327, 341, 342, 350.

Harold, Sheriff of NSW (1845), 517, 571.

Harriet, daughter of Mr Neil Minister of Tiree & Coll (1817–1881), 453, 456, 457, 458, 459, 460, 464, 529, 530, 626, 636, 649.

Hector of Auchnasaul-Mull (1661 × 1691), Table 6, 48, 63, 64, 66.

Hector of Coll, *An Cléireach Beag* (1537 × 1583), Table 1, 7, 19, 437, 478.

Hector of Coll (1689 × 1754), Table 2, 101, 103, 108, 109, 112, 113, 114, 116, 122, 126, 127, 128, 129, 133, 134, 138, 140, 153, 305, 520, 673.

Hector Ruadh, younger of Coll (1558 × 1564/5), Table 1, 9, 290, 400, 405, 437, 476.

Hector Ruadh, younger of Coll (1642 × 1656), Table 2, 28, 31, 32, 42.

Hector of Isle of Muck, MA (1627 × 1649), Tables 2 & 9, 23, 24, 32, 33, 34, 37.

Hector of Isle of Muck (1666 × 1684), Table 9, 48, 53.

Hector of Isle of Muck (1719), Table 9.

Hector of Isle of Muck (1764 × 1780), Table 9, 138, 154, 178, 260, 294.

Hector of Torestan-Coll, Captain Jacobite Army (1671 × 1689), Table 10, 97, 116, 506.

Hector of Totronald later at Totamore (1776), Table 11, 116, 651.

Hector, Lieutenant-General Sir (1756–1848), Table 2, 166, 170, 268, 270, 271, 324, 360, 371, 372, 408, 409, 410, 436, 464, 465, 481, 482, 484, 485, 488, 489, 503, 504, 505, 507, 520, 542, 674, 675.

Hector Alexander, Lieutenant RN (1787–1809), Table 9, 324, 325, 338, 346.

Hector MD, EIMS (1776 × 1810), Table 11, 242, 245, 266, 273, 292, 324.

Hector in Guirdal-Rum Ensign Rum Company Inverness-shire Volunteers (1803 × 1826), Table 5, 304, 318, 429.

Hector MA, Minister of Lochalsh (1786–1869), Table 4, 186, 345, 454, 457, 458.

Hector Arthur Coalson (1861–1918), Table 4, 25, 385, 386, 439, 454, 617, 649, 650, 651, 652, 653, 654, 662, 663, 672.

Hector Coll (1837–1894), 569, 577.

'Hector', according to John Johnston he was the son of John of Totronald, 651.

'Hector', according to John Johnston son of Hugh of Inverkeithing, 651.

Hector in Guirdal-Rum Ensign Rum Company Inverness-shire Volunteers (1803 × 1826), Table 5, 304, 318, 321, 382, 424, 425, 427.

Henry in Dantzig (c.1780), Table 10.

Henry Travers (1826), 542, 571, 579.

Henry Donald Neil DSO [Neil or Harry], Lieutenant-Colonel King's Own Scottish Borderers (1872–1926), Table 4, 595, 596, 602, 606, 608, 617, 618, 620, 623, 649, 654, 655, 660–662, 671.

Index

Hugh [Ewen] of 'Inverkeithing' (1640 × 1651), Table 2, 27, 37, 38, 651, 652, 653.
Hugh (1651), Table 9.
Hugh (1702 × 1704), Table 8.
Hugh of Coll (1748 × 1786), Table 2, 117, 128, 134, 135–140, 141, 143, 153, 154, 155, 156, 158, 166, 167, 174, 183, 189, 192, 199, 234, 243, 278, 288, 672, 673, 674.
Hugh of Coll, Lieutenant-Colonel 3rd Foot Guards (1782–1861), Table 2, 25, 205, 233, 235, 326, 330, 334, 336, 341, 360, 361, 363, 372, 390, 405, 406, 407, 408, 411, 416, 419, 420, 421, 423, 427, 429, 434, 435, 438, 442, 445, 446, 447, 448, 454, 463, 464, 465, 466, 467, 472, 475, 476, 477, 478, 479, 480, 481, 482, 483, 484, 485, 486, 488, 489, 490, 491, 493, 494, 495, 496, 498, 499, 500, 501, 503, 504, 505, 506, 507, 508, 509, 510, 511, 512, 513, 514, 520, 521, 523, 524, 526, 528, 529, 532, 542, 545, 560, 563, 569, 577, 625, 629, 643, 652, 675, 677.
Hugh, Captain 49th Foot (1768–1803), Table 2, 199, 267, 268, 298, 299, 300, 305, 309, 310, 320, 330, 360.
Isabel, daughter of Hector of Coll (1689–1754), 128.
Isabella Sibbella, daughter of Hugh of Coll (1819–1901), 40, 467, 468, 654.
Isabella, daughter of Mr Neil Minister of Tiree & Coll (1836), 453, 458, 460.
James MA, Minister, Antrim (c.1750), Table 8.
Jane Breadalbane, daughter of Hugh of Coll (1836–1928), wife of George Hamilton-Dundas, 654, 672.
Janet (Seònaid), daughter of John Garbh (1640), 28, 30, 31, 32.
Janet Macleod, daughter of Alexander of Coll (1781–1803), 229, 233, 243, 246, 326, 330, 332, 336.
Johannes Henricus, Sergeant-Major 123rd Régiment de Ligny later Second-Lieutenant (1783 × 1813), 349.
John (1652), Table 8.
John *Iain McLachlan vc Allane alias McLeane* (1679), Table 3., 78, 81, 678.
John MA, Minister of Kilmorie in Arran and later in Antrim (1652–1729), Table 8, 95.
John MA, Minister of Billy (1699–1766), Table 8.
John (c.1750), Table 8.
John in Dantzig, (c.1750), Table 10.
John (1776), Table 11.
John, younger of Coll, (1542), Table 1.
John Abrach of Coll (1499 × 1519), Table 1, 6, 673.
John Cam of Coll (1528 × 1558), Table 1, 454, 672.
John Garbh of Coll (1443 × 1469), Table 1, 6, 431, 654.
John Garbh of Coll (1617 × 1675), Table 2, 21, 23, 24, 27, 28, 30, 31, 32, 33, 35, 41, 42, 43, 417, 651, 652.
John Garbh of Coll (1670–1688), Table 2, 91, 93, 97.
John Norman Hector of Coll Major-General (1829–1882), Table 2, 464, 466, 473, 530, 542, 552, 577, 648.
John Norman Hector Major-General (1839), 542, 552, 569.
John of Grishipol-Coll (1616 × 1621), Tables 1 & 7, 11, 24.
John of Grishipol-Coll (1652 × 1679), Table 8, 42, 263.
John of Mingary-Mull *Iain Gallda* (1627 × 1643), Table 2, 24, 30.
John in Mingary-Mull, officer in Jacobite Army (1711 × 1716), Table 2, 103.
John of Totronald-Coll (1640 × 1694), Tables 2 & 11, 2, 27, 37, 38, 39, 42, 49, 63, 65, 66, 67, 69, 77, 79, 116, 155, 430, 649, 651.
John MA, Minister of Kilmorie in Arran and later in Antrim (1652–1729), Table 8, 96, 99.
John MA, Minister of Billy (1699–1766), Table 8, 95.
John, Captain 2nd 1st Foot & Argyll Fencibles (1775 × 1809), Table 9, 168, 170, 180, 190, 191, 241, 323, 324, 342, 343, 344, 414, 417, 450, 544, 569.

John, Lieutenant Isle of Rum Company Inverness-shire Volunteers (1803), Table 5, 312, 318, 321, 353, 429.
John Francis Gray, Lieutenant 3rd Light Infantry HEICS (1790–1827), Table 9, 569.
John Leyburn, Captain 43rd Foot (1794–1873), Table 9, 342, 344, 352, 355, 385, 448, 452, 517, 518.
John, merchant at Virginia (1774 × 1781), Table 10, 117.
John *Bàrd Thigearna Collach* (1775), 169.
John, wine merchant at London (1808–1886), Table 4, 292, 430, 456, 457, 459, 462, 660.
John, wine merchant at Glasgow (1838), Table 8.
John, merchant at Danzig (1799), 355.
Julian, daughter of Mr Donald Minister of the Small Isles (1788–1858), 186.
Juliet Alexa, daughter of Hugh of Coll (1826–1909), 408, 411, 419, 427, 435, 440, 463, 464, 467, 468, 471, 473, 475, 480, 481, 494, 502, 503, 504, 505, 509, 520, 545–552, 555, 557, 559, 560, 561, 562, 563, 564, 565, 566, 568, 571, 677.
Katherine, daughter of Lachlan of Coll (1627), 24.
Katherine, daughter of John Garbh (1640), 28, 47.
Lachlan in Achacha, poet & officer in Jacobite Army (1717 × 1761), Table 2, 103, 114, 116, 120, 124, 126, 140, 305.
Lachlan of Auchnasaul-Mull (1659 × 1661), Table 7.
Lachlan of Coll (1403), Table 1, 5, 6.
Lachlan of Coll (1583 × 1631), Tables 1 & 2, 9, 10, 18, 19, 21, 22, 23, 24, 25, 27, 28, 34, 43, 53, 85, 102, 138, 158, 249.
Lachlan of Coll (1642 × 1687), Table 2, 42, 47, 52, 55, 56, 57, 58, 64, 65, 69, 70, 79, 81, 85, 89, 91, 93, 94, 96, 97, 201, 298, 305, 334, 349.
Lachlan of Craigendmuir of Provan, Glasgow and in Gallanach-Coll. formerly Captain HEICS (1729–1790), Table 8, 95, 143, 144, 146, 147, 148, 149, 155, 156, 161, 190, 292, 320, 334, 421.
Lachlan, shipwright at Kingston-Jamaica (1784 × 1814), Table 8, 292, 334, 419, 427.
Lachlan of Grishipol-Coll, Baillie of Tiree (1661 × 1681), Table 8, 42, 48, 49, 55, 56, 57, 58, 60, 63, 69, 70, 73, 83, 95, 96, 143.
Lachlan (1671), Table 9.
Lachlan in Grishipol-Coll, officer in Jacobite Army & merchant at Glasgow (1693–1772), Table 10, 103, 116, 125, 126, 130, 349.
Lachlan of Hynish-Tiree, Captain Royalist Army (1651), Table 3, 37, 39, 43, 78, 159, 454.
Lachlan of Isle of Muck, Captain Jacobite Army (1714 × 1726), Table 9, 103, 111.
Lachlan of Isle of Muck & Tower of London, Lieutenant-Colonel 1st BF (1771 × 1816), Table 9, 165, 171, 172, 178, 179, 180, 183, 190, 199, 202, 203, 204, 216, 225, 226, 227, 228, 230, 231, 232, 236, 237, 239, 241, 243, 245, 265, 287, 324, 325, 326, 327, 329, 331, 338, 341, 343, 344, 350, 361, 370, 386, 390, 533, 534, 569.
Lachlan of Torestan-Coll, soldier Dutch service (1689 × 1735), Table 10, 116, 392, 506.
Lachlan in Kilmore-Mull Lieutenant AV (1776 × 1798), Table 8, 163, 164, 259.
Lachlan, Assistant-surgeon EIMS (1776 × 1799), Table 11, 292.
Lachlan, merchant at Dantzig (1812 × 1816) Table 10, 349.
Lachlan Alexander, Lieutenant 67th Native Infantry (1837 × 1846), 534, 543.
Lachlan Hector Gilbert, Captain 49th Foot (1834 × 1847), 534, 535, 544.
Lachlin, MP for Arundel, Colonel (1728–1778), Table 8, 95, 96, 144.
Lillias [Lylyas], daughter of Mr Neil Minister of Tiree & Coll (1836), 453, 458, 460.

Louis, United States Ambassador at Court of St James (1829–1831), 117.
Louisa Maud, daughter of Colonel Alexander 94th Foot and wife of Dr Francis-Hawkins of Wimpole Street, London & Reading-Berkshire (1866–1935), 662.
Malcolm, (c.1540), Table 1.
Marjory, daughter of Lachlan of Torestan (1736), 112, 393.
Margaret, daughter of John Garbh (1640), 28.
Margaret, daughter of Hector Ruadh, younger of Coll (1673), 42.
Margaret, daughter of Hector of Coll (1689–1754), 128, 129.
Margaret, daughter of Mr Donald Minister of the Small Isles (1780–1845), 175, 186, 454, 458, 460, 463.
Margaret, daughter of Hugh of Coll (1815–1882), 464, 465, 468, 503, 563.
Maria, daughter of Alexander of Coll (1789–1862), 409, 503.
Marion, daughter of Hugh of Coll (1755), 358.
Marion, daughter of Roderick Neil (1790), 178.
Marion-Christina, daughter of Alexander Maclean of Coll (1792–1821), 405, 412.
Mary, daughter of Hector in Guirdal-Rum (1826), 425[?], 427.
Mary, daughter of Allan in Kinloch Scrisort-Rum (c.1800), 415, 423.
Mary-Gavine, daughter of Lachlan of the Isle of Muck (1816 × 1817), 386, 390, 391.
Mona Louisa, daughter of Hector Arthur Coulson and wife of Iain Pattullo, Langlogie-Perthshire (1909–1989), 662.
Mordaunt (1844), 517, 571.
Neil, Surgeon at Connecticut (1702 × 1784), Table 10, 116.
Neil of Drimnacross (1640 × 1698), Tables 2 & 10, 37, 42, 48, 49, 60, 63, 65, 66, 67, 69, 77, 79, 94, 97, 116, 158, 233, 234, 287, 336, 506.
Neil Mor of Quinish (1573), Tables 1 & 3, 8, 9, 11, 17, 78, 159, 160, 200, 431, 454, 626, 634, 650, 664.
Neil Buidh mac gille challum ic Eachan, (c.1570), Table 1, 10, 11, 200, 289, 310, 405, 437, 476, 494.
Neil Og (c.1600), Table 3, 11, 12, 15, 17, 106, 159, 454, 650.
Neil at Williamsburg, Virginia (1755), Table 2.
Neil MA DL, Minister of Tiree & Coll (1784–1858), Table 4, 151, 186, 311, 314, 315, 324, 326, 330, 344, 351, 355, 364, 375, 376, 379, 387, 388, 389, 390, 392, 396, 401, 430, 431, 432, 434, 436, 438, 441, 443, 444, 446, 453, 454, 457, 459, 472, 478, 483, 486, 492, 507, 514, 529, 530, 649.
Normand, Major 68th Foot (1759–1795), Table 2, 166, 167, 170, 199, 265, 273, 360.
Ronald mac Allan mhic John (1661 × 16710, Table 7, 48.
Roderick of Penmoloch, Mull (1674 × 1710), Table 8, 95, 143, 148, 334.
Roderick Neil, Lieutenant 81st Foot (1761–1794), Table 2, 167, 170, 178, 200, 265, 268, 360, 373, 402, 494.
Sibella, daughter of Hector of Coll (1689–1754), 140.
Sibbella, daughter of Alexander of Coll (1784–1830), 229, 408, 409, 410, 431, 675, 676, 677.
Una, daughter of John Garbh of Coll (1640), 28.
Una, daughter of Hector of Coll (1689–1754), 122, 140, 142.
Wellwood George Mowbray (1839), 542, 551.
William Hector [Moses] (1830–1867), Table 2, 502, 508, 509–513, 529, 531, 547–549, 558, 559, 560, 563.
William Swinton at Edinburgh (1818 × 1825), Table 11.

Tacksmen, Non-commissioned officers and their children.
Alexander MacAllan mhic Neil Og (1757), Table 3.
Alexander, Fiosgaradh-Coll Corporal 1st BF Sergeant Coll Company
AV (1776–1804), Table 6, 243, 244, 259, 310, 340.
Alexander, ship's captain at Connecticut (1747–1806), Table 10.
Alexander (c.1750), Table 9.
Alexander (c.1770), Table 9.
Allan (1661), Table 7.
Allan shopkeeper in Cliad-Coll (1776), Table 3, 159, 494.
Allan Mac Neil Og in Crossapol-Coll (1709 × 1725), Table 3, 103, 106, 140, 159, 160, 234, 454.
Allan in Fiosgaradh-Coll, Sergeant 1st BF (1776 × 1836), Table 6, 200, 225, 259, 289, 310, 340, 354, 414, 418, 451.
Allan in Grishipol-Coll (1710 × 1716), Table 10, 94, 116, 306.
Allan in Guirdal-Rum (1727 × 1764), Table 8, 141, 305.
Allan in Guirdal-Rum (1815 × 1826), Table 5, 304, 429.
Allan in Breacachadh, gardener (1776), 161.
Allan, 5 Glenview Terrace, Greenock (1921 × 1934), 355, 662.
Ann, daughter of Allan mhic Neil Og (c.1750), Table 4, 234
Ann, daughter of Neil in Crossapol-Coll (1776 × 1828), 291, 416, 430, 452.
Catherine, daughter of Sergeant Allan in Fiosgaradh-Coll (1808 × 1850), Table 6.
Charles Mac Neil Og (1716 × 1735), Table 3 & 5, 234.
Charles (c.1750), Table 8.
Charles in Guirdal-Rum (1737 × 1796), Table 5, 227, 300, 304, 305, 306.
Charles *alias McLachlin vic hearlich*, Merchant (1730), Table 8, 140.
Donald in Arileod-Coll (1826 × 1896), Table, 7, 467, 469, 471.
Donald in Caolis-Coll & Kilbride-Coll later in Crossapol-Coll & Knock-Coll alias *Donald McLachlane Vc A llane alias McLeane* (1679 × 1716), Table 3, 78, 678, 679.
Donald in Gallanach-Coll (1709), 118.
Donald in Gunna-Coll (c.1620), Table 7.
Donald in Totamore-Coll (1726), 110.
Donald in Uig-Coll (1726), 109.
Donald (c.1750), Table 9.
Donald Mac Allan mhic Neil Og (c.1770), Table 3.
Donald, Drill Sergeant AV (1799), 259.
Donald, student of divinity (1812–1834), Table 4.
Flora, daughter of John in Harris-Rum (1745 × 1764), Table 5, 234, 304, 306.
Hector in Auchnasaul-Mull (1722), Table 7.
Hector (c.1740), Table 8.
Hector (c.1750), Table 9.
Hector in Kilbeg-Mull (1688 × 1702), Table 8.
Hector in Knock-Coll alias *M cEan vic Ewin* 'Shopman' (1733 × 1771), Table 9, 135, 140, 154.
Hugh in Grimsary-Coll (1693 × 1715), Table 11.
Hugh in Knock-Coll (1776 × 1790), Table 11, 154, 155, 156, 191, 234, 245, 265, 292.
Hugh in Muck (1737 × 1764), Table 5 & 9, 234.
Hugh (1778 × 1824), Table 9.
Hugh, Fiosgaradh-Coll. Sergeant 1st BF (1776 × 1819), 243, 259, Table 6, 200, 246, 259, 289, 451.
James in Gallanach-Muck (1826 × 1838) Table 5, 427.
Janet in Triallan, daughter of Hector in Knock-Coll (1776), 161.
Janet, daughter of Neil Crossapol-Coll (1776 × 1790), Table 4.
Janet, daughter of Sgt Hugh in Fiosgaradh-Coll (1802–1885), Table 6.
John Mak neill vcGilliechallome, (1632), 24.
John in Arnabost-Coll (1776 × 1836), 398.
John in Arinagour-Coll (1776), Table 8.
John Og in Auchnasaul-Mull (1661 × 1692), Table 7.
John in Cove-Rum (1695 × 1771), Table 9, 141, 234, 321.
John (c.1715), Table 9.

Index

John in Gallanach-Coll (1796 × 1797), Table 8, 190, 263, 292, 320.
John in Grishipol-Coll (1716 × 1739), Table 10, 116, 117, 140, 349.
John in Guirdal-Rum (c.1740), Table 8, 304, 306.
John at Glasgow (1733 × 1780), Table 3.
John in Harris-Rum and later in Kinloch Scrisort-Rum (1724 × 1764), Table 5, 141, 234, 304.
John, Kinloch Scrisort-Rum (1803), 429.
John (c.1770), Table 9.
John in Leacruadh-Coll (1776 × 1860), Table 6, 289.
John in Sandeneisher-Rum (1803), Table 9, 321, 427.
John at Jamaica, 'Captain' (1805), Table 8, 334, 337.
Lachlan mac Lachain (c.1630), 11, 290.
Lauchlan mc Harlich vic Lauchlan alias McLean in Trialan (1710), 113, 114.
Lachlan (c.1715), Table 9.
Lachlan (c.1740), Table 8.
Lachlan (c.1750), Table 9.
Lachlan (c.1750), Table 11.
Lachlan Mac Neil mhic Allan (c.1760), Table 4.
Lachlan Mac Neil ic lachain at Ballyhough-Coll (1776), 290.
Lachlan in Fiosgaradh-Coll (1776 × 1795), Table 3 & 6, 161, 191, 243, 244, 246, 259, 274, 288, 340.
Margaret, daughter of Neil Crossapol-Coll (1776 × 1847), 386, 430, 496, 652.
Margaret, daughter of Lachlan in Fiosgaradh-Coll (1776), Table 6, 274, 352,
Marion, daughter Neil Crossapol-Coll (1774 × 1789), Table 4.
Mary, daughter of Allan in Grishipol-Coll (1688 × 1764), wife of John in Guirdal-Rum (c.1740), Table 10, 304, 306.
Mary, daughter of Neil in Crossapol-Coll (1776 × 1798), 366, 374, 430.
Murdoch, tailor, Arnabost later Torestan-Coll, 1st BF & Sergeant AV (1776 × 1848-9) Table 6, 200, 289, 310, 437, 494, 495, 506.
Neil (c.1750), Table 8, 334.
Neil (c.1755), Table 8.
Neil Mac Neil mhic Allan (1766–1787), Table 4.
Neil Og *Neillviz McLachlane Vc Allane* in Caolis-Coll & Kilbride-Coll & in Crossapol-Coll (1679 × 1716), Table 3, 42, 234, 259, 304, 454, 678, 679.
Neil in Crossapol-Coll (1712–1787), Table 3 & 4, 159, 160, 161, 174, 189, 235, 244, 292, 429, 433, 452, 454, 650.
Neil in Crossapol-Coll (1806–1855), Table 4, 431, 434, 438, 483, 485, 496, 497, 499, 500, 501, 506, 525, 529.
Neil of the Fiosgaradh family (1870), 662.
Nigello oig mak ean dowie in Gallanach-Muck.
Rorie, 'in Creisapoll' (Grishipol-Coll?) Merchant at Glasgow (1630), 28, 49.
Roderick (1710), Table 11.
Una, daughter of Neil Crossapol (1776 × 1809), 430, 433, 440, 450.
William, Kilmory-Rum, Sergeant 1st BF (1793 × 1810), Table 7, 201.

Tenants and their children.
Alexander, Acha-Coll (1822), 403.
Alexander (1849), 522.
Alexander, Cornaig-Coll Treasurer HLLRA-Coll (1885), 638.
Allan Roy, Feall-Coll (1776), 11, 294, 437, 450, 451.
Allan, Kilmory-Rum (c.1680), Table 7.
Allan, Kilmory-Rum (1764), Table 7.
Allan at Philadelpia (c.1750), 117
Allan, Totronald-Coll in charge of Coll's galley (1776), Table 7, 467.
Allan, Kilmory-Rum (1770), Table 7.

Allan, Kilmory-Rum (c.1800), Table 7.
Allan (1805), Table 11, 653.
Allan at Gorten-Coll (1822), 403.
Allan, Acha-Coll miller & boat builder (1837), 444, 445, 476[?].
Angus, Kilmory-Rum (c.1750), Table 7.
Angus author of *God & the Devil at Seal Cove* (1976), 450.
Ann, Ballyhough-Coll (1776 × 1800), 290, 402.
Ann, daughter of Hector, Cliad-Coll (1776), Table 5.
Ann, Grimsary-Coll (1801–1818), 373.
Archibald, Kilmory-Rum (c.1650), Table 7.
Archibald, Kilmory-Rum (1770), Table 7.
Barbara, Arnabost later Mibost & Cliad (1809 × 1841), 437.
Catherine, Feall & Totronald-Coll (1809), 373.
Catherine, Triallan-Coll, widow (1846), 477, 479.
Charles, soldier in Sir Allan Maclean of Brolas's Company in America (c.1756), Table 7, 134, 140, 201.
Donald, Kilmory-Rum (c.1710), Table 7.
Donald, Kilmory-Rum (1764), Table 7.
Donald, Totronald-Coll (1776 × 1800), Table 7, 472.
Donald Ban, Arnabost-Coll (1776), 452.
Donald (1776), Table 11.
Donald, Hyne-Coll (1822 × 1838), 403, 445, 452.
Donald, Hyne-Coll (1838), 445.
Donald, Kilbride-Coll (1766 × 1841), 402, 445, 450.
Donald (1806), Table 11, 653.
Donald, Kilbride-Coll (1830 × 1841), 402, 443.
Donald, cooper in Bute (1837), 446.
Donald junior, cottar at Acha-Coll (1837), 446,
Effy, daughter of John, Acha-Coll (1837), 446.
Ewen Mac Neil Og (1735), Table 3.
Flora, Acha-Coll (1839), 443.
Hector, Ballyhough later at Grimsary-Coll, (1782 × 1837), 290, 295, 437, 443.
Hector, Hyne-Coll (1776 × 1841), 294, 401, 402, 403, 443, 450.
Hector (1809), Table 11, 653.
Hector, Hyne-Coll (1822), 403.
Hector, Kilmory-Rum (1826) Table 7, 427.
Hector, Torestan later in Elean Ornsay-Coll (1848–9 × 1851), 494, 495.
Hugh, Caolis & later Torestan-Coll (1793 × 1841), 494, 495, 506.
Hugh, Hyne-later crofter Lagmore and then tenant in Kilbride-Coll (1822 × 1840), 401, 402, 403, 445, 450.
James, Totronald-Coll, later plumber in Greenock (1841 × 1896), Table 7, 450, 468, 469, 471, 482, 489, 494, 652, 655.
James, Torestan-Coll (1847), 495.
Jean, daughter of Hector, Cliad-Coll (1776 × 1819), Table 6.
John (1715), Table 11.
John, Arnabost-Coll (1776 × 1836), Table 6, 396, 437, 476.
John, Arnabost-Coll (1776 × 1810), 452.
John, boat builder (1837), 445.
John, Balard-Coll, joiner known as 'Iain Saor' (1794 × 1842), Table 7, 493.
John, Ballyhough-Coll (1782 × 1795), 290, 437.
John, Ballyhough-Coll (1837), 451.
John, Cliad-Coll, miller (1827 × 1834), 437, 442, 444, 450.
John, Acha-Coll (1839), 443, 446, 450.
John, Kilbride-Coll (1839), 443.
John, Grimsary-Coll soldier 93rd Foot 'Am Pensioner Mor' from Kilninian-Mull later at Grimsary-Coll (1841 × 1861), 644, 645, 646.
John, Kilmory-Rum, known as *Iain Gobha*. Soldier in Dutch service (c.1710), Table 7, 201.
John, Kilmory-Rum (c.1740), Table 7.

John, Kilmory-Rum (1764), Table 7.
John, Kilmory-Rum (1810), Table 7.
John, Kilbride-Coll (1814 × 1841), 443.
John, Freslan-Coll (1836), 442, 450.
John, Torestan and later Grishipol-Coll (1841 × 1851), 495, 497, 506.
John, Sorisdale-Coll formerly at Totronald-Coll (1857), 630.
Lachlan, Kilmory-Rum (c.1710), Table 7.
Lachlan, Kilmory-Rum (1764), Table 7.
Lachlan MacNeil ic Lachain at Ballyhough-Coll (1776), 290, 437.
Lachlan, Ballyhough-Coll later at Kilbride-Coll (1784 × 1836), 290, 400, 402, 405, 437, 443.
Lachlan, Arinagour, Arnabost and later in Freslan-Coll (1776 × 1841), Table 11, 2, 159, 400, 430, 437, 442, 651.
Lachlan, Harris-Rum (1803), 321.
Lachlan in Mibost-Coll (1777 × 1831), 289.
Lachlan, Arnabost-Coll later Mibost-Coll (1776 × 1784), Table 6.
Lachlan, Arnabost and later Mibost-Coll (1809), 437.
Lachlan, Feall & Freslan-Coll AV (1789 × 1807), 373.
Lachlan, Arnabost-Coll, author of *Adhamh agus Eubh* (1837), (1798–1848), Table 6, 431, 438.
Lachlan, Totronald-Coll, later merchant Tobermory (1823 × 1858), Table 7, 467, 468, 469, 489.
Lachlan, Fiosgaradh, later a cottar at Freslan-Coll (1828 × 1851), 451.
Lachlan, Fiosgaradh-Coll (1814 × 1835), 451.
Lachlan, Dervaig-Mull (1849), 522.
Malcolm, Arnabost Grimsary & Freslan-Coll (1783 × 1803), 373.
Margaret, Feall-Coll (1794 × 1810), 373.
Margaret, Muck (1820), 427.
Margaret [Peggy], Arnabost-Coll (1819), Table 6, 396, 397.
Mary, Kilbride-Coll (1830), 402.
Mary, Kilbride later in Grimsary-Coll (1834 × 1840), 443.
Mary, Acha-Coll (1839 × 1841), 445.
Mary, Fiosgaradh-Coll (1839), 451.
Murdoch, Arnabost-Coll Free Church Elder (1793–1867), 476.
Murdoch, Feall, Freslan &Gorten-Coll (1776 × 1811), 665, 373.
Murdoch, Kilmory-Rum (1704 × 1764), Table 7.
Murdoch, Kilmory-Rum (c.1800), Table 7.
Neil, Totronald-Coll (1841 × 1856), Table 7, 467, 468, 489.
Neil Bane, Ballyhough-Coll (1716), 290.
Neil, Ballyhough-Coll (1776 × 1797), 290.
Neil, Kilbride-Coll (1818 × 1841), 437, 443.
Neil, Feall-Coll (1776), 373.
Neil, Kilmory-Rum, soldier 85th Foot (c.1756), Table 7, 201, 427.
Neil, Gorten-Coll (1822), 401, 403.
Neil, Totronald-Coll (1846), 469.
Neil, Kilmore-Mull (1847), 493.
Roderick, Kilmory-Rum (c.1680), Table 7.
Roderick, Kilmory-Rum (1748 × 1810), Table 7.
Roderick, Kilmory-Rum (1764), Table 7.
Roderick, Gorten-Coll (1822), 401, 403.
Rory Mor, Ground officer Muck (c.1820), 467.
Sliochd Lachlin, 138.
Una, daughter of Lachlan, Freslan-Coll (1836), 442.
William, Arnabost-Coll (1776), 405.

No known landholding.
Allen (1746 × 1778), 117.
'Cailleach Eustin' at Dervaig (1846), 486.
Catriona nighean Eoghainn (c.1695), 100.
Charles, Corporal in Murray's Regiment in Dutch service (1685), 79, 81.
Charles, soldier 1st BF (1776 × 1799), 239.
Charles, Imperial Guard French Army (1793 × 1813), 349.
Christie, cottar at Kilbride-Coll (1760 × 1840), 437.443.
Donald soldier 1st BF (1795), 225.
Donald, cottar at Arnabost-Coll (1845 × 1847), 496.
Donald soldier 79th Foot (1812), 352.
Hector, cottar at Totronald later grasskeeper at Torrindeich-Arileod (1831 × 1834), 470.
James Coll's piper (1733), 114.
John, Roman Catholic servant in Muck (1765), 138.
John soldier 1st BF (1795), 225.
Neil, cottar at Torestan-Coll (1849), 524.

Other people living on the Maclean of Coll Estate & Two Ends of Coll, their descendants and those who were related to them by marriage.
An Gille Riabhach (c.1440), 7, 15, 433.
Beaton/Bethune
   Abraham 81st Foot, servant in Cliad later in Torestan-Coll (1776), 172, 201, 494.
   Christian, Mibost-Coll (1820), 421.
   Donald, Gallanach-Coll (1776), 201.
   Donald 1st BF (1793), 201, 204, 210, 213, 522.
   Donald, workman at Cliad-Coll (1819), 399, 400.
   Donald, Torestan later in Grishipol-Coll (1848–9), 494, 506.
   Donald, Arinagour-Coll (1849), 524.
   Flora (1793), 363.
   John 1st BF (1793), 201, 204, 363.
   John [?], Penmore-Mull (1849), 509.
   John, 11 High Street, Arinagour-Coll (1849), 524.
   Neil 81st Foot, servant in Cliad-Coll (1776), 201.
   Family, 201.
Bristol
   Paul, Lieutenant 1 KOSB (1957), 670.
   Timothy, Captain 1 KOSB (1962), Muscat Regiment (1967) 670.
Buchanan Alexander, Tiree (1886), 639.
Buckley
   George Alexander Maclean (1888), 650.
   Helen Maclean author of *From Little Towns in a Far Land we came* (1950), 661.
Caldwell drainage contractor (1848), 499, 523.
Cameron
   Alexander Wentworth (1850), 462.
   Catherina, Lady Coll, daughter of Captain Allan of Glendessary (1780 × 1802), 178, 225, 226, 228, 231, 233, 244, 298, 301, 305, 634.
   Christian (1706), 118.
   Dougald, 79th Foot (1814), 339, 347, 352.
   Isobel, daughter of Alexander Wentworth (1885), 626.
   Jean, daughter of Captain Allan of Glendessary (1795 × 1800), 226, 268, 550.
   John, Sergeant 42nd Foot (1801), Table 5, 274, 289, 352.
   Marion (1810 × 1831), Table 5.
   Miss, Calgary Castle-Mull (1841), 461.
Campbell
   family formerly of Barbreck-Mid Argyll, 3, 17, 260, 261, 262, 263, 295, 356, 365.
   family Ballyhough-Coll, 295.
   at Arinagour (1847), 493.
   Alexander, 'Captain' at Port Fairy (1805–1890), Table 4, 416, 418, 444, 445, 449, 454, 516, 517.
   Alexander of Caolis JP (1832 × 1848), 435, 483, 487, 498, 499, 500, 507.
   Alison McArthur, Melbourne, Australia (1973), 263.

Index

Angus, Coll, overseer at Talisker-Tasmania (1825 × 1828), 418, 420.
Ann, Totronald-Coll (1776), 295.
Catherine, Muck (1822), 427.
Catherine, Grishipol-Coll (c.1770), 356.
Catherine in Cliad-Coll (1861), 631.
Charles in Caolis-Coll (1832), 438.
Charles in Ballyhough-Coll (1845), 475, 477.
Cirsty, Ballyhough-Coll (1776 × 1782), 290.
Colin of Cornaig, Caolis & Auchnacloich (1796–1867), Table 4, 414, 416, 417, 418, 444, 515, 516, 517, 520, 631.
Colina, daughter of Colin of Cornag, Caolis & Auchnacloich (1886), 639.
Donald, Factor of Coll Estate, Captain (1815 × 1850), 3, 373, 374, 403, 429, 434, 436, 437, 467, 475, 478, 480, 481, 482, 483, 484, 485, 486, 487, 488, 489, 490, 491, 493, 494, 495, 496, 497, 498, 499, 500, 501, 502, 503, 504, 505, 508, 509, 512, 520, 521, 522, 523, 524, 525, 526, 527, 529, 531, 532, 629, 630.
Donald in Torestan-Coll (1776), 260, 506.
Donald, Grishipol-Coll (1800), 404.
Donald, Caolis-Coll (1820), 414, 418, 440, 513.
Duncan, Cornaig-Coll Chairman HLLRA-Coll (1885), 638.
Edward, Muck soldier 1st BF (1793 × 1813), 427.
Effie, Ballyhough-Coll (1776), 403.
Fionnvola, daughter of Sir Dugall of Auchinbreck (1620 × 1642), 23, 27, 30, 32, 33.
Hugh, Isle of Muck (1820), 399.
Hugh, Arnabost-Coll (1849), 524.
Hugh, Glencairn-Victoria (1851), 513.
John, apprentice (1776), 294.
John of Cornaig-Coll, in Gallanach-Coll (1828 × 1847), 434, 435, 437, 475, 483, 500, 507, 631.
John, Dervaig-Mull, soldier in 79th & 92nd Foot (1841 × 1892), 643, 644.
Malcolm, Ballyhough-Coll (1776), 290.
Malcolm, Mibost-Coll (1819), 396.
Malcolm in Breacachadh-Coll (1716), 104.
Malcolm in Cornaig-Coll (1776 × 1821), 241, 260, 261, 263, 356, 416, 518.
Malcolm 81st Foot in Feall-Coll (1778), 373, 402.
Malcolm, Trelvaig-Coll (1847), 493, 506.
Mary, daughter of Sir Duncan of Lochnell (1715), 103, 115.
Murdo tollick allias Campbell/Murchie Collich (1679), 79, 260, 675.
Murdoch in Cornaig-Coll (1776 × 1818), 260, 356, 414, 415, 416, 518.
Neil in Sunipol-Mull (1766 × 1854), Table 4.414, 420, 452.
Neil, Sunipol-Mull and later in Tasmania (1828), Table 4, 416, 418.
Neil, Feall-Coll (1778 × 1800), 402.
Neil, Feall-Coll (1790), 402.
Neil, Mibost-Coll (1819 × 1820), 396, 397, 419.
Neil, workman at Acha-Coll (1826), 401.
Mrs Neil (1826), 401.
William, MA (1633), 27.
Cotnam Hannah Barbara (1775), 171.
Davidson
  Ebenezer (1794–1815), 281, 282, 283, 284, 287, 295, 375, 377, 378, 379, 381, 384, 395, 475.
  John (1794 × 1806), 280, 281, 282, 283.
Day Olivia, daughter of the Rev. Samuel Day (1857 × 1908), 541, 608, 617.
Dennistoun Janet Baird (1814 × 1819), 363, 372, 405, 411.
De Roum Anna (1685), 79.

Douglas Mrs at Drumfin (1838), 468.
Fenwick Rose Eaden Abinger, daughter of Admiral William Fenwick (1889), 594, 595, 649, 650, 651, 652, 662.
Ferguson Jane (1849), 512.
Foster Mrs (1829), 411, 413.
Francis-Hawkins
  Alexander Symes Maclean, Second-Lieutenant KOSB (1897–1960), 662.
  Elspeth Maud Olivia Maclean, daughter of Dr Francis-Hawkins (1901–1961), 662.
Fraser
  Mr Alexander, Assistant Minister of Coll (1780 × 1791), 403.
  Rev. Donald Allan (1817), 398, 402, 403.
  Farquhar MA, Dean of the Isles (1640), 33.
Gillows
  John, servant Strathaven (1839), 451.
  Catherine (1839), 451.
Grant Jane Eliza (1835), 448.
Gray Hugh, ferryman at Port na Luing & land-steward in Ardnish-Coll (1798), 291, 295.
Gregorson Jane (1822), 429.
Hawke The Hon. Lavinia Mary (1964 × 2006), 664, 665, 669, 670.
Hamilton James of Barnes & Cochna-Dumbartonshire (1835), 467, 470.
Hamilton-Dundas, George youngest son of GHD of Duddingston, Linlithgow.
Hobart
  The Hon. George (1802), 326, 332.
  Lady Vere (1802 × 1820), 332, 408, 409, 410, 550.
Holmes Mathew, merchant Geelong-Victoria (1851 × 1864), 513, 514, 550.
Hunter
  Alexander WS (1820), 245, 409, 423, 424, 465, 476, 478, 480, 481, 482, 484, 485, 486, 487, 489, 490, 491, 494, 495, 496, 499, 503, 505, 507, 509, 512, 520, 521, 522, 524, 525, 526, 527, 529, 532, 563, 631, 651, 677.
  Frank (1897), 651.
Johnston
  family, 20, 94, 399, 403, 636.
  Alexander Maclean, Glasgow (1896), 650, 651, 662.
  AL (1906), 295.
  Allan, Feall-Coll (1792), 295.
  Alexander, Ballyhough-Coll (1776), 290, 295, 403.
  Alexander, Arnabost-Coll (1847), 493.
  Angus, Ballyhough later in Cliad-Coll (1819), 400, 403, 423, 488.
  Catherine, widow of James Johnston, Arnabost (1824 × 1876), 629.
  Donald, Feall-Coll (1801), 295.
  Donald, Arinagour-Coll (1819), 399.
  Donald, shoemaker Cliad-Coll (1840), 403.
  Duncan in Arnabost & Grishipol-Coll (1802–1890), Table 5, 287, 289, 396, 399.
  Hector, Arinagour-Coll (1819 × 1845), 399, 403.
  Hugh, Cliad later Arnabost-Coll & Inspector of Poor in Coll (1830 × 1855), 403.
  Iain dubh na Kille (c.1600), 94.
  James, Arnabost-Coll (1823), 629.
  John, Arnabost-Coll (1776), Table 5, 295.
  John, schoolmaster Torestan-Coll (1815), 380.
  John in Cliad-Coll (1832 × 1842), 403.
  John, Arnabost-Coll later in Totamore-Coll (1805–1896), Table 6, 636, 637, 651.

713

John in Totamore-Coll, sometime sanitary inspector &
    seanachaidh (1836–1921), Table 6, 116, 159, 295, 383, 385,
    386, 439, 494, 636, 637, 638, 639, 640, 642, 648, 651, 652.
Lachlan, Feall-Coll (1793), 295.
Lachlan, Grishipol-Coll (1819), 396, 399.
Lachlan, ground officer at Coll (1840 × 1848), 403, 488, 498, 502,
    508, 522, 525, 531, 532.
Malcolm in Penmolloch-Mull (1726), 110.
Murdoch, Arnabost-Coll (1847), 491, 493.
Mary (1819), 399.
Mary, Cliad-Coll widow (1847), 493.
Neil, Feall-Coll 1st BF (1791 × 1801), 295.
Neil 'on the Laird's wherry' (1847), 493.
Roderick, shoemaker (1819), 396, 397, 399.
RC, 158 Crecent Road, Toronto 5, Ontario, Canada, 355.
William, Captain 2nd Madras Infantry (1799–1861), Table 5, 329,
    491.
Kennedy
    family, 113, 118, 399, 402, 506.
    Angus, Knock-Coll (1716), 114.
    Donald, a cottar at Totronald-Coll (1837), 470.
    Donald, Trelvaig-Coll (1841), 506.
    Ferquhar Kinity alias Macoile eire in Sodistill (c.1700), 118.
    John in Torestan-Coll and later in Gallanach (1706), 118.
    John in Caolis-Coll (1716), 118.
    John in Caolis-Coll (1832), 438.
    John, Grimsary-Coll (1847), 493.
    John, Trelvaig-Coll (1841), 506.
    Lachlan, Dervaig-Coll (1892), 643.
    Malcolm in Gallanach-Coll (1710), 113.
    Malcolm in Knock-Coll (1716), 114.
    Malcolm, Torestan-Coll (1848–9), 495, 506.
    Marion, Mibost-Coll (1820), 419.
    Murdoch, in Cornaigbeg-Coll (1709), 118, in Knock-Coll (1716),
        114.
    Kirk Session Collector (1733), 118.
    Murdoch, Trelvaig-Coll (1841), 506.
Lamont Cirsty Arnabost & Freslan-Coll (1783 × 1803), 373.
Lang Major-General DB CB,DSO,MC, Director of Army Training
    (1967), 667.
Lloyd George of Clifton near York (1819), 405, 412, 411.
Lovat 'His daughter' (c.1520), 7.
MacCaill
    Donald at Gallanach-Coll (1846), 487.
    Martin ploughman at Gallanach-Coll (1846), 487, 494.
Macarthur
    family at Totamore-Coll (1841), 431.
    Isabella, Totamore-Coll (1839), 431.
MacCrimmon Janet, daughter of Macleod's piper (1785), 179.
Macdonald
    Alexander 1st BF (1793 × 1798), 205.
    Allan 'Darracha', Captain (1790), Table 4.
    Allan, *Ailein Muilleir*, Cliad-Coll (1776), 294.
    Allan, Ardnish-Coll (1776), 373.
    Allan, soldier 79th Foot & 92nd Foot (1880), 577.
    Angus roy, the piper at Arnabost-Coll (1716), 114.
    Ann, Ballyhough-Coll (1785 × 1847), 404, 493.
    Archibald, Mibost-Coll (1819), 396, 397.
    Catherine, servant Ballyhough-Coll (1818), 295.
    Charles, Totronald-Coll 1st BF (1793 × 1835), 201, 243, 245, 289,
        295, 467, 468, 470.
    Charles, Grishipol-Coll and Quinish-Mull (1847), 493.
    Charles, cottar at Trelvaig-Coll (1847), 495, 522.

Donald, Totronald-Coll (1793), 201.
Donald, Smith Ballyhough-Coll (1776), 290.
Donald, Achabhorolam-Coll (1776), 294.
Donald in Caolis-Coll (1832), 438.
Effy, (1815), 402.
Euphemia, widow MacEachren Torestan later in Grishipol-Coll
    (1848–9 × 1851), 495, 508.
Finlay the Smith in Uig-Coll alias *Finley McIllmickall smith in Uig*
    (1679), 79, 201, 675.
Finlay, Smith Ballyhough-Coll (1793), 200, 201, 290.
Flora, daughter of Macdonald of Morar (c.1670), 94.
Flora, daughter of Lachlan in Kilchoan-Ardnamurchan (c.1820),
    467, 468.
Hugh, Young Coll's servant (1773), 151, 161, 201.
Isabella, daughter of Major Alexander Macdonald of Vallay-
    North Uist (1814 × 1836), 392, 453, 454, 460.
John, *Am Buaile Bheag* Coll (c.1793), 373.
Lachlan, Arivarich then Torestan-Coll & later in Arnabost-Coll
    (1848–9 × 1851), 495, 506, 523.
Malcolm, Ballyhough-Coll (1776), 201, 290.
Malcolm, Crossapol-Coll (1790), Table 4.
Malcolm, Totronald-Coll (1844), 508.
Marion, daughter John of Moidart (1665), 42, 69, 334.
Marion/Meve, daughter John of Moidart's sister by *Alister
    MacRuary Ruarich* a son of Clan Glengarry (1665), 42, 44.
Marion, Triallain-Coll (1793), 205.
Mary, Gallanach-Coll (1787), 205.
Mary, Arnabost-Coll (1799), 213.
Mary, Freslan-Coll (1815), 366.
Mary, Cliad-Coll (1819), 399, 400.
Murdoch McMurchie, harper (1716), 103.
Neil, Mibost-Coll (1819), 398.
Neil, Totronald-Coll (1793), 201.
Neil, *Am Buaile Bheag* Coll (c.1860), 374.
Roderick, Ardnish & Lagmore-Coll 1st BF & Argyll Volunteers
    (1777 × 1818), 365, 373, 414.
Susanna, wife of Hector Rankin (1815), 399.
Widow, Arinagour (1815), 402.
Macdonelour
    Angus (1568), 7.
    Donald (1568), 7.
    Farchar (1568), 7.
    Jone baine (1568), 7.
    Neil (1568), 7.
    Ronald McMeldeny McIllacholm (c.1568), 7.
MacDougall Hector (1935), 628, 637.
Maceachren Mrs M (1848), 506.
MacFadyen
    family, 13, 291, 295.
    Allan in Totronald-Coll (1760–1847), 490, 493.
    Allan at Totamore-Coll (1841), 499.
    Angus, Ardnish-Coll (1716), 104.
    Angus, Sergeant AV (1797), 259.
    Aonghus Mac Ailein Mhic Aonghus, Ballyhough-Coll (1800–1886),
        629, 630.
    Archibald McNeill Vc Innes in Ardnish-Coll (1679), 79, 679.
    Catherine, widow of James Johnston, Arnabost-Coll
        (1823 × 1876), 629.
    Charles Roy, Ardnish-Coll (1716), 104.
    Charles, shoemaker in Totronald-Coll (1837), 470.
    Charles, Arinagour-Coll (1873 × 1892), 643.
    Donald, Trelvaig-Coll (1847), 493, 506.
    Donald Baine Mc Neill in Ardnish-Coll (1679), 79, 679.

Index

Donald alias *Mac Euin Roy in Breakachie* (1720), 140.
Duncan McDonald Vc Iain in Ardnish-Coll (1679), 78, 678, 679.
Dugall McDonald Vc Iain in Ardnish-Coll (1679), 78, 678, 679
Gwn Mc Neill Vc Innes in Ardnish-Coll (1679), 79, 679.
Flora from Salum-Tiree, wife of Archibald Mackenzie/Matheson pensioner at Cliad-Coll, widow of Lachlan Lamont (1841 × 1855), 648.
Hector, tailor Grimsary, Ardnish,Gorten, Freslan, Lagmore & Grimsary-Coll 1st BF (1776 × 1815), 365, 372.
Hector, Cliad-Coll (1819), 400.
Hector, Meibost-Coll (1784–c.1833), 629.
Iain Mc Neill Vc Innes in Ardnish-Coll (1679), 79, 678, 679.
John, Grimsary-Coll (1776), 372.
John, Clabach-Coll (1837), 451.
John, (1849), 513.
John, fiddler at Meibost and later tenant,Grishipol-Coll then to Canada post 1851 (1816 × 1851), 629.
John, *Iain Hyne* (1880–1974), 295, 374, 629, 630, 645.
Lachlan, Lonban-Coll (1847), 488.
Mary, Meibost-Coll (c.1820), 629.
Mòr nic Phàidein (c.1600), 11, 12.
Roderick (1840), 437, 443.
Macgregor
  Neil, ground officer at Quinish-Mull (1846), 486, 509, 510, 511, 514.
McIllphadrick Donald in Nealis [Caolis ?] (1679), 675.
Macinnes
  Angus, Arnabost-Coll (1847), 493.
  Archibald in Cornaig-Coll (1832), 435, 440.
  Donald, Grimsary-Coll Labourer& Pensioner (1861), 645, 646.
  Donald, mason Uig-Coll (1892), 642.
  Flora, maid at Acha-Coll (1822), 401, 405.
  John, Trelvaig-Coll (1847), 493, 495, 506, 522.
  Lachlan, Arnabost-Coll (1847), 493.
  Lachlan, cottar at Torestan-Coll (1849), 522.
  Margaret (1799), 263.
Mackay
  family, 645.
  Donald, Cornaig-Coll (1787 × 1804), 79th Foot, 338, 347.
  George, Cornaig-Coll 1790 × 1804), 79th Foot, 338, 347.
  Hugh, Cornaig-Coll (1785 × c.1840), 79th Foot, 338, 347, 645.
  Lachlan, Cornaig-Coll 79th Foot, (1794 × 1814), later of Green Swamp, Australia, 339, 347, 445.
  Neil in Keill-Muck (1803), 321.
  Patrick in Kiel-Muck (1726), 111.
  William soldier 79th Foot (1774 × 1804), 339, 347.
  William soldier 79th Foot [Cornaig-Coll] later Pensioner, Arileod-Coll 79th Foot (1784–1860), 338, 347, 644, 645.
Mackenzie
  Alexander, schoolmaster at Torestan & later Arinagour-Coll (1814), 379, 380, 381.
  Roderick, schoolmaster in Rum (1799), 284.
  see also Matheson.
Mackinnon
  Alister Mor (c.1520), 7.
  Allan, Rum later of Dalness-Tasmania (1822) Table 5, 415, 416, 421, 429, 666.
  Allan, Cornaig-Coll Secretary HLLRA (1885), 638.
  Ann, servant at Gallanach-Coll (1776), 155.
  Archibald, North Carolina (1792), 382.
  Catherine, Feall-Coll (1787), 373.
  Catherine, Gorten-Coll (1837), 451.
  Chrissie, wife of *Hughie Broadhill* (1974), 668.

Donald Ban (c.1520), 7, 9.
Donald Mugach (1583), 9.
Donald Freslan-Coll (1799), 373.
Donald of Dalness-Tasmania (1973), 666.
Duncan, Grimsary-Coll (1847), 488.
Flora, Glenalbyn-Natal (1858), 548, 561.
Hector, Feall-Coll (1776), 373.
Hector, Grimsary-Coll (1837), 446.
Hugh, Feall, Freslan,Gorten & Triallan-Coll 81st Foot & AV (1776 × 1808), 373.
Hugh, Totronald-Coll (1776), 295.
Hugh, Totronald later to Gorten-Coll (1831 × 1847), 470.
Hugh, Triallan-Coll (1792), 295.
Hugh, Torestan-Coll (1841), 506.
Hugh, Cnocleathan-Coll *Hughie Broadhill* (1959), 663.
Hugh, Grimsary joiner & house carpenter (1837), 446.
Janet, Totamore-Coll (1798), 205.
John, Caolis-Coll (1776), 356.
John in Grimsary-Coll later in Lagmore, soldier 1st BF (1776 × 1841), 225, 289, 295, 445, 446.
John, Keanouchcrach family (c.1800), 415, 421.
John in Gorten-Coll (1837), 453.
John, the Beadle in Clabbach-Coll (1781–1870), 401, 477.
John, Gorten-Coll (1836), 442.
John, Torestan later cottar at Arnabost-Coll (1848–9 × 1851), 495, 498, 506.
John, Torestan later at Knocleathan-Coll (1855), 506.
John, shepherd at Torestan [Cannada] later cottar at Grishipol-Coll (1841 × 1854), 522.
Julia, Grimsary-Coll (1837), 446.
Kenneth, Cornaigmore-Coll (1889), 632.
Lachlan, Grishipol-Coll (1819), 396, 397.
Lachlan, Glenalbyn-Natal (1858), 548, 549.
Mary, Arnabost-Coll (1776), 452.
Mary, Feall-Coll (1791), 295.
Mary, Feall-Coll (1789 × 1807), 373.
Mary, Gorten-Coll (1837), 451.
Mary, Hyne later cottar at Lagmore-Coll (1835 × 1841), 443.
Neil, in Caolis-Coll (1832), 438.
Neil, sailor 'on the Laird of Coll's wherry' (1848), 491.
Neil, Torestan (1848–9), 495, 496, 506.
Maclean
  Alastair, Royal Military College, Sandhurst (1900), 654.
  Alexander in Gott-Tiree & Mingary-Mull (1727 × 1797), Table 12, 163, 175, 181, 203, 224, 228, 242, 245, 328, 331.
  Alexander, Baillie of Coll in Arileod-Coll & Feall-Coll later in Freslan-Coll (1791 × 1836), Table 4, 191, 200, 228, 229, 235, 259, 293, 301, 310, 365, 366, 367, 373, 382, 385, 402, 430, 437, 450.
  Alexander, Freslan-Coll (1831), 437,
  Alexander in Acha later Lagmore-Coll 'The Cooper' (1776 × 1822), 401, 402, 442, 445, 446, 450, 522, 648.
  Alexander, Freslan-Coll (1822), 405.
  Alexandrina, daughter of Alexander, Lagmore-Coll 'The Cooper' (1837), 661.
  Allan in Acha later in Arileod-Coll eventually of Strathallan-Victoria (1776 × 1833) Table 4, 291, 381, 397, 414, 416, 433, 436, 445, 513.
  Allan in Bellachroy-Mull (1766) 163.
  Allan, Surgeon & Ensign 42nd Foot (1770 × 1781) 166, 171, 172.
  Allan, Lagmore-Coll & Lagmore-New Zealand (1837 × 1852), 446, 514, 517, 519, 522, 650.
  Ann 'from Lochaber' (1801 × 1841), 439.

Anne, daughter of Allan of Strathallan, Victoria formerly in Arileod-Coll (1851), 513, 550.
Anne, daughter of Alexander in Kinnegharair-Mull (1831), 430.
Catherine, wife of Neil Rankin (1776), 245.
Catherine, daughter of Charles at Arinagour-Coll (1791 × 1815), 437.
Charles, Baillie of Coll, at Arinagour and later in Gallanach-Coll (1776 × 1829), Table 4.191, 259, 292, 310, 320, 365, 382, 383, 384, 386, 423, 429, 437, 475, 496.
Charles S, Major-General CB, CIE Her Majesty's Consul General for the Province of Khorassan & Seistan-Persia (1836 × 1921), Table 4, 430, 437, 442, 452, 481, 542, 551, 552, 553, 555, 577, 578, 581, 582, 583, 584, 585, 586, 587, 588, 589, 590, 591, 593, 596, 652, 654, 662.
Christina Mackenzie, daughter of Dr Hector (1749 × 1773), 120, 129, 361.
Colin, Lietenant RN (1900), 654.
Donald, drill sergeant (1804), 315.
Donald, teacher at Arivichvarich-Coll (1836), 442.
Donald, Arileod-Coll later in New Zealand (1836 × 1859), 449, 550.
Donald, Isle of Rum (1842), 514, 517.
Donald, Captain the Royal Scots DSO (1900 × 1909), 654.
Dugald Lathanach (c.1450), 7.
Flora, daughter of John of Treshnish-Mull (1776 × 1807), 241, 260.
Flora, daughter of Hector, Cliad-Coll (1792), 439.
Flora, daughter of Allan in Arileod-Coll (1820), 414, 433, 440, 513.
Flora, Cornaig-Coll daughter of Norman in Freslan (1896), 651, 662.
Florence, daughter of Mr Hector (1747–1773), 155.
Hector, younger of Gruline (1704–1783), 1, 2, 14, 16, 31, 67, 94, 101, 120, 126, 136, 146, 160, 163, 324, 361.
Hector, Cliad-Coll (1776), Table 5, 289, 439.
Hector MA, Assistant Minister in Coll (1732 × 1773), 113, 139, 152, 155.
Hector, Mingary-Mull Lieutenant 14th Foot (1792–1812), Table 12, 328, 344, 351.
Hector, Hyne-Coll (1793 × 1841), 294.
Hector Lachlan Stewart VC (1889 × 1897), 593, 594, 597, 598, 599, 606.
Hector Charles Donald KBE, CB, DSC, Vice-Admiral RN (1908–2003), 654.
Hugh, Captain *John Dunscombe* (1801–1839), Table 4, 416, 433, 449, 450, 519.
Hugh in Achacharra-Mull (1766), 163.
Isobel, daughter of John Factor of Ardgour (1791), 190.
Isobel, daughter of Alexander of Sollas-Uist (1790), 190.
Isobel, daughter of Hector, Cliad-Coll (1776), Table 5.
Isabella, daughter of Charles at Arinagour-Coll (1822), 437.
Jan, Netherlands (1685), 79.
Janet [Jessie], daughter of Allan in Arileod-Coll (1836), 436, 666.
John, soldier 79th & 93rd Foot, later Pensioner Grimsary-Coll (1798 × 1871), 339, 648.
John in Mingary-Mull (1766 × 1775), 163.
John, Assistant Minister in Coll (1812), 379, 384, 396, 397, 437.
John, in Arileod formerly in Grishipol-Coll (1832 × 1849), 435, 440, 497, 498, 521, 522.
John, Lagmore-Coll & Lagmore & Morvern Hills-New Zealand (1837 × 1871), 446, 514, 517, 518, 522, 650.
John, Penmore-Mull (1849), 509, 510, 512.
Katherine, daughter of Allan of Strathallan-Victoria formerly in Arileod-Coll (1851), 515.

Lachlan in Rum, 'Dr' (1789 × 1881), Table 4. 292, 385, 423, 424, 427, 430, 441, 442, 475, 480, 481, 496, 514, 515, 529, 542, 544, 652.
Lachlan, Ardnish-Coll (1776), 292, 385.
Lillias, daughter of Alexander of Gott-Tiree & Mingary-Mull (1777 × 1780), 175, 303, 333, 334, 345, 346.
Malcolm, Ardnish-Coll (1776), 291.
Malcolm, Arileod-Coll (1836), 449.
Margaret, 1st wife of Alexander of Gott-Tiree & Mingary-Mull (1709–1783), 175, 185, 245, 331.
Margaret, 2nd wife of Alexander of Mingary-Mull later in Glasgow (1776 × 1805), 245, 328, 331.
Margaret (1794 × 1830), 288, 294.
Margaret, 2nd wife of Coun Rankin (1805), 329.
Marion, daughter of Donald of Arihualan-Ardgour (c.1720), 143.
Mary, daughter of Alexander the Bailie wife of the 'Cooper' (1788 × 1836), 401, 648.
Mary, daughter of John in Langamull-Mull (1812), 228.
Mary, Grishipol Coll (1798), 357.
Neil (c.1750), 356.
Neil, Captain *Lord Sausmarez* (1809 × 1899), Table 4, 433, 449, 458.
Norman in Freslan-Coll (1797 × 1871), Table 4., 293, 401, 403, 631, 651.
Robertson, Lagmore-Coll (1837), 446, 650.
Sibella, daughter of Charles at Arinagour-Coll and estranged wife of John Campbell of Cornaig(1798 × 1828), 437, 637, 651.
Maclean Buckley
  George Alexander (1888), 648.
  Helen (1950), 518, 659.
Maclean-Bristol
  Major Charles younger of Breacachadh Castle, late KOSB (1967), 667, 670, 671.
  Alexander, Captain A&SH (1970), 667, 671.
Macleod
  Anna, daughter of William of Harris (1403 × 1426), 5.
  Donald see Macleod of Talisker.
  Donald in Kilmory-Rum (1726), 111.
  Janet 'Lady Coll', daughter of Macleod of Talisker-Skye (1748 × 1780), 135, 154.
  Margaret (1826), 403, 404.
  Marion 'Lady Coll Elder', daughter of Sir Norman Macleod of Bernerah (1720), 140.
Maclonich family, 7, 135.
Macmaster Duncan, Coll's piper (1805 × 1819), 403, 405, 410.
Macmillan family
  Isle of Muck (1822), 419, 429.
  Lachlan, Muck (1822), 427.
  Margaret, Coll (1825), 401.
  Neil in Keill-Muck (1803), 321.
Macneil
  John weaver at Acha & later Totamore-Coll (1826), 401.
  Mrs (1826), 401, 402 see Margaret Macleod.
Macniven Christian, Ballyhough-Coll and later Kilbride-Coll (1809 × 1841), 400, 439.
  Dugal, Knocklean-Coll (1849 × 1851), 522.
Macphail Margaret (c.1800), 439.
Macpherson
  Lachlan in Cuin-Mull (1726), 110.
  Peter (1847), 487.
Macquarrie John in Harris-Rum (1726), 110.
Macqueen
  Donald MA, Minister of the Small Isles (1736), 112, 321, 393.
  Marion (1706 × 1764), 321.

Index

MacSween
    Sween (1776), 128, 154, 155, 156, 158, 162, 179.
    Hugh (1773), 154.
Matheson/Mackenzie
    family (1841), 644.
    Ann, North Carolina (1792), 382.
    Archibald, (1798 × 1872), 96, 277, 283, 294, 339, 356, 357, 363, 371, 381, 382, 385, 395, 396, 397, 398, 399, 423, 648.
    Archibald soldier later shopkeeper at Cliad-Coll in (1776 × 1851), 339, 648.
    Donald (1776), 339.
    Donald, Grishipol-Coll (1776), 646.
    Duncan (1872), 96, 277, 287, 294, 339, 356, 363, 382, 385.
    Hector (1776), 339.
    John soldier later Pensioner, Arinagour-Coll (1808 × 1857), 339, 648.
    Ludovic alias *Maoldòmhnich Mac Mhathain* (1698–1807), 287, 298, 356.
    Murdoch Allan (c.1690), 287, 339.
    Murdoch, Grishipol Murdoch *Murchie Ailean* (c.1690), 94.
    Neil (1794 × 1819), 287, 357, 371, 382, 395, 398, 399, 423.
    William Pensioner, Freslan-Coll (1851), 644.
Morison
    Charles Ensign AV (1774 × 1798), 163, 164, 260, 263.
    Coundullie Rankin (1856–1943), 263, 437.
    Donald Drill Sergeant AV (1793 × 1832), 163, 201, 259, 263, 310, 508.
    Flora (1805), 328, 440.
    Hector in Auchnasaul-Mull (1774), 163, 201.
    Hector, drummer (1804), 315.
    John, Torestan-Coll (1849), 526.
    Lachlan, Bellachroy-Mull (1848), 504.
    Niel, Cuin-Mull (1848), 504.
    Roderick, Drimnacross-Mull (1821), 400.
    Roderick in Bellachroy Hotel & Kilbeg-Mull (1847), 490, 493, 512.
    Roderick in Tobermory (1774 × 1789), Table 4, 182.
    Mr, from Mull in Tasmania (1835), 449.
Murphy Major Edmund KOSB (1999), 672.
Patronymics
    Rorie McDonald Vc wurchie in Uig, 678, 679.
    Donald McGreeht in Uig, 679.
    Charles McIllespick Vc Rorie in Arnabost, 679.
    Hector Og 'his good sonn', 679.
    Rorie Mor 'a papist', 678, 679.
    Donald McNeill Vc Illchallum, 679.
    Donald McInnes Baine, 678, 679.
Nicol Archibald Assistant Minister in Coll (1837 × 1848), 446, 472, 473, 475, 477, 478, 498.
Norris Robert strolling tin smith (1819), 396, 397.
Rankin
    Alexander Corporal 1st BF (1793), 200.
    Catherine, daughter of Neil in Cliad (1841), 494, 495, 506.
    Condullie (1793 × 1851), 200, 201, 242, 245, 293, 328, 329, 331, 332, 399, 400, 403, 434, 440, 506.
    Duncan, piper Isle of Muck (1765), 138, 179, 200.
    Duncan, Cliad-Coll (1815), 402.
    George (1806), 331, 434.
    Hector (1776 × 1819), 293, 399, 400, 434.
    Hugh, 47th Foot (1791 × 1803), 245, 265, 273, 293.
    Janet, daughter of Neil Rankin (1809), 163, 263.
    Neil in Arileod and later Cliad-Coll, piper (1776 × 1798), 161, 163, 191, 200, 245, 293, 399, 494.

Robertson Jane second wife of Hugh of Coll (1825), 406, 407, 408, 420, 435, 463, 465, 466, 468, 469, 473, 475, 477, 482, 505, 676, 677.
Smeaton Miller at Acha-Coll (1836), 442.
Smith-Windham Ashe, Resident MagistrateUmvoti-Natal (1830 × 1860), 550, 557, 558, 560, 561, 563.
Stewart
    Alexander, teacher (1848), 498.
    Ann of Green Swamp NSW (1837), 44.
    or Snodgrass, Alexander wright in Greenock (1679 × 1704), 94, 96, 234.
    Catherine, daughter of Alexander Stewart or Snodgrass (1776), 223, 234.
Sutherland
    Henry, Sergeant (1796), Table 4, 291.
    Henry (1796), 291.
    Betty, wife of John Mackenzie/Matheson at Arinagour-Coll (1841 × 1857), 648.
Thorburn in Isle of Muck (1848), 507.
Travers Elizabeth, daughter of Henry of Fairfield, Devon & Bengal Civil Service (1825), 417.
Van der Wiel Maria daughter of Peter (1685), 79.
Williams Anna Maria (1816), 389, 392, 393, 433, 440, 454, 455, 456, 457, 459, 461, 464, 529, 541.

* * *

The second part of the index consists of other people who play a part but are not members of the Family of Coll. The dates shown in brackets are when they became involved in the story.

Part 2 Other People.
Abercromby Lieutenant-General Sir Ralph (1798 × 1801), 237, 239, 267, 273, 289, 339.
Aberdeen Earl of
    (1775), 166, 167.
    (1835) Secretary of State for the Colonies, 451.
Abdur Rahman Amir of Afganistan (1881), 576, 581, 582, 583, 584, 586, 591.
Acheson Mr Thomas (1615), 19.
Adams Lieutenant-Colonel RB, VC Commanding the Queen's Own Corps of Guides (1897), 598, 599.
Alexander I Tsar of Russia (1801), 273, 338, 349, 386, 391, 575.
Alexander III Tsar of Russia (1887), 582.
Alfred HRH Prince, Duke of Edinburgh KG &c (1844–1900), 558.
Ali al-Rida 8th Ali al-Rida Imam of Shi-ite Islam (823), 583.
Allen Mr, Natal Carbineers (1860), 563.
Almsley Mr, Government Border agent, Natal (1860), 558.
Alikhanov Governor of Merv-Turcomanistan (1886), 582.
Amherst Lord, (1793 × 1796), 209, 211, 212, 213, 226.
Anderson
    James LL.D, author (1785), 156, 181, 192, 242.
    Lieutenant Fane's Horse (1860), 556, 555.
Anstruther
    Major PR (later Lieutenant-Colonel) 94th Foot (1879 × 1880), 572, 573, 579.
    Mrs (1880), 574.
Argyll
    Archibald 4th Earl (1529–1558), 9.
    Archibald 7th Earl (1584–1638), 20, 22, 26.
    Archibald 8th Earl & 1st Marquess (1607–1661), 21, 22, 23, 30, 31, 36, 37, 40, 41, 47, 55, 59, 531.

Archibald 9th Earl (1629–1685), 40, 43, 47, 48, 49, 51, 52, 53, 54, 55, 56, 57, 58,, 60, 61, 62, 63, 64, 65, 66, 67, 69, 70, 71, 72, 73, 75, 76, 77, 79, 80, 82, 83, 84, 85, 86, 89, 90, 91, 92, 96, 199, 421.
Archibald 10th Earl & 1st Duke (–1703), 85, 97, 98.
Archibald 3rd Duke (1682–1761), 122, 134, 145, 374.
Elizabeth Gunning, wife of 5th Duke (1773), 143, 148.
Elizabeth Talmash Countess, daughter of Elizabeth, Duchess of Lauderdale (1678 × 1735), 98.
John 2nd Duke (1680–1743), 113, 152, 157, 388.
John 5th Duke formerly Colonel Jack Campbell (1723–806), 122, 126, 142, 143, 148, 154, 156, 167, 168, 175, 181, 182, 188, 189, 190, 196, 199, 200, 258, 260, 262, 263, 291, 293, 309, 312, 326, 336, 356, 365, 367, 368, 369, 452, 673.
George 6th Duke (1768–1839), 356, 372, 421, 438, 457, 506, 520.
George 8th Duke (1823–1900), 483, 504, 625, 628.
Arkins Mathew, soldier 94th Foot (1846), 538.
Arthur Governor (1830), 445, 516.
Ashton Lieutenant 94th Foot (1846), 540.
Atholl
 Marquess (1678 × 1685), 61, 89, 90, 91, 92.
 Duchess (1908), 224.
 Duke of (1793), 196.
Auckland Lord, Viceroy of India (1840), 535.
Aust
 George, Under-Secretary of State for Foreign Affairs (1802 × 1811), 306, 334, 335.
 see Murray.
Avery Richard, architect (1970), 669.
Ayub Khan (1880), 576, 577, 583, 584, 585, 592.
Bahadur Shah, Delhi (1857), 551, 55.
Baillie
 Sir William Bart of Polkemmet (1838), 468, 470.
 Lady (1838), 466, 470.
 Family (1838), 464, 465.
Baird
 Charles, Secretary of the Glasgow Section of the Central Board of Management for Highland Relief (1836 × 1847), 523, 524, 525, 532.
 Sir David (1799 × 1805), 269, 327.
Bairnfather Margaret, wife of Major-General CS Maclean (1897), 598, 599.
Bathurst Henry KG, PC, FSA 3rd Earl of, Colonial Secretary (1820), 412, 413, 415, 419, 427.
Beaton
 James (1679), 77.
 John MA Minister of Kilninian & Kilmore (1683 × 1695), 89, 100.
 Robert son of James, apprentice (1682), 96.
Bedell Bishop (1686), 160.
Beresford Brigadier-General Marcus (1802), 332, 336.
Berry
 Agnes (1828), 409, 410.
 Mary (1828), 409, 410.
Bevins R, 8 Princes Square, Glasgow (1850), 520.
Beynon Lieutenant DSO, 3rd Gurkhas (1897), 601.
Binning Lord, Chairman of the Select Committee on Emigration (1829), 424, 428.
Blood Sir Bindon, Commander-in-Chief of the Malakand Field Force (1897), 599.
Blücher Field-Marshall (1815), 353, 354.
Boswell James younger of Auchinleck (1773 × 1778), 33, 113, 127, 128, 142, 143, 147, 150, 151, 152, 154, 155, 156, 158, 159, 160, 161, 162, 165, 166, 168, 300, 632, 635, 672, 674.
Botha Louis (1899), 609, 616.

Böttiger KA at Weimar (1798), 251.
Bowlby
 Thomas, correspondent for *The Times* (1860), 553, 555.
 Captain GRS 94th Foot (1879), 572.
Boyd Adam Archdeacon of Argyll (1630), 34, 85.
Boyter Dr Charles RN (1837), 445, 451, 498, 499, 500, 501.
Breadalbane see Campbell, John
Brewster Minister of Paisley (1805), 314, 315.
Brown of Fordell, Major-General (1651), 37, 38.
Brownrigg Colonel (1799 × 1813), 268, 351.
Bryce Drummer 1st BF (1793), 202.
Brydon Dr (1842), 536.
Buchan Lieutenant-Colonel Thomas in Dutch service (1684), 85, 89, 91.
Buchanan
 of Buchanan, George (1651), 37, 38.
 of Drumkill & Ross Priory, Dumbartonshire (1793), 358.
Buchanan
 Dugald (1716–1768), 277.
 John Lane MA (1782–1791), 157.
Buckinghamshire 5th Earl (1816), 413.
Bullen Captain (1746), 126.
Buller General Sir Redvers VC (1899), 609.
Burgers President of the Transvaal (1861), 565.
Burke Edmund (1793), 197.
Burn William architect (1825), 408.
Burns Robert poet, (1759–1796), 334, 629.
Burrard Major-General Sir Harry (1797), 238, 341.
Burrows Brigadier-General George (1880), 576, 583.
Cambridge HRH The Duke of, Commander-in-Chief (1879), 569, 594.
Cameron
 Clan (1746), 674.
 of Calgary Castle-Mull, Alexander (1838), 457, 462.
 of Callart, Allan (1746), 462.
 of Erracht, Major Alan 79th Foot later Sir Alan KCB (1793), 207, 208, 209, 210, 211, 214, 347, 670.
Cameron of Glendessary
 John (1675 × 1682), 53, 88, 91, 97, 98.
 Captain Allan (1750), 140.
Cameron of Lochiel
 Donald (1769–1832), 199, 207.
 Captain Donald (1796–1858), 410.
 Ewen Allansoun (1492), 6, 8, 672.
 Ewen (1629–1719), 40, 40, 50, 53, 54, 57, 58, 61, 66, 75, 76, 91.
 John (1663–1747), 102, 103, 106.
Cameron of Mount Cameron
 Mrs Jean (1745), 234, 305.
 Donald (1797), 225, 231.
Cameron
 Dr Archibald (1744), 673, 677.
 David, Leader of the Conservative Party (2006), 670.
 Donald formerly 'in the Guards' later at Morvern (1744), 119.
 Donald, tailor at Mannal-Tiree (1822), 403.
 Donald, MD, RN, of Fordon-Tasmania (1798 × 1820), 415, 418.
 John, Captain 1st BF (1797), 259.
 John, merchant at Greyfriars, Edinburgh (1798), 420.
 'a brave gentleman of the Locheil family' (c.1690), 78.
 Ferryman in Australia (c.1840), 515.
Campbell of Barcaldine
 Alexander (1678 × 1693), 65, 66, 68, 71, 98, 196.
 Duncan (1835), 470.
 Family (1838), 464.

Index

Campbell
- Alexander of Dunstafnage (1587 × 1619), 21.
- Alexander of Lochnell (1618 × 1635), 21.
- Alexander of Lochnell (1671 × 1714), 48, 52, 56, 65, 66, 67, 88, 102.
- Alexander, Governor of Heylipol Castle Tiree (1680), 83.
- Alexander of Srondour (1685), 92.
- Alexander, Major 77th Foot (1759), 134, 199.
- Alexander in Killundine (1754 × 1773), 436.
- Alexander of Glenfalloch (1793), 195, 204.
- Alexander, late Carolina Rangers (1793), 203.
- Alexander in Achlian (1793 × 1799), 196, 204.
- Alexander, Edinburgh organist (1815), 361.
- Angus of Kilberry (1679 × 1685), 71.
- Ann, wife of Captain Hector Maclean, Adjutant 1st BF (1793 × 1831), 231, 233, 235, 243.
- Archibald of Achnatene (1716), 106.
- Archibald of Inverawe *MacConachie* (1679), 80, 81, 88.
- Archibald of Jura, younger (1791), 242.
- Archibald of Stonefield, Chamberlain of Argyll (1729 × 1748), 119, 120, 125, 126, 147.
- Archibald of Strachur (1679 × 1685), 72.
- Archibald, Lieutenant AV (1803), 310.
- Charles, younger son of the 9th Earl of Argyll (1685), 89, 90, 92.
- Christian, Killundine (c.1800), 436.
- Colin of Atichuan (c.1685), 94.
- Colin of Ardkinglass, Baronet (1679 × 1709), 72.
- Colin of Achnaba (?), 204.
- Colin of Balimore (1746), 128.
- ? of Ballinaby-Islay (1756), 139.
- Colin of Blairintibbert (1685), 92.
- Colin of Glendaruel (1710), 102.
- Colin of Glenorchy, Knight (1594 × 1640), 53.
- Colin in Ballimartin brother of Donald of Ballinaby-Islay, Bailie of Tiree (1709), 101, 102.
- Colin of Ach at Inverawe (1793), 195, 203.
- Colin of Glenfalloch Lieutenant late 71st Foot (1793 × 1806), 202, 205, 216, 218, 228.
- Colin, late Lieutenant 74th Foot (1793), 203.
- Colin, Lieutenant 1st BF (1793), 203.
- Colin, General, later Lord Clyde (1857), 552, 625.
- D. Colonel, Chamberlain of Tiree (1833), 440.
- Dioysus, Dean of Limerick (1573 × 1603), 9, 10, 14.
- Donald of Airds (1704–1775), 143, 436, 663.
- Donald of Ardnamurchan, Baronet (1592 × 1651), 20, 21, 22, 24, 28, 33, 62, 78.
- Donald of Barbreck (1658 × 1690), 65.
- Donald, brother to Cawdor (1678), 64.
- Donald in Craig-Dalmally (1823), 414, 419.
- Donald in Gott-Tiree (1709), 102.
- Donald in Reef-Tiree (1832), 436.
- Donald in the 'Rock of Carnbulg' (1682), 88.
- Dugald, servant to Argyll (1678), 63, 70, 71, 77.
- Dugald in Achlian's son (1759 × 1799), 196, 204.
- Dugald MA, Minister in Mull (1802), 302.
- Dugall of Auchinbreck, Baronet (1622 × 1641), 21, 23.
- Duncan of Ardgadden, Baillie of Kintyre (c.1650), 96.
- Duncan of Auchinbreck, Baronet (1628 × 1645), 29, 31, 94.
- Duncan of Auchinbreck, Baronet (1679 × 1700), 62, 90, 92.
- Duncan, Baillie of Jura (1596 × 1695), 68.
- Duncan of Lochnell (1699 × 1765), 103.
- Duncan in Reef-Tiree (1832), 434.
- Flora, Countess of Loudoun (1804), 327, 390.
- Frederick, Colonel the Lord (1775), 167, 169, 200.
- George of Airds, Tutor of Cawdor (1661 × 1685), 62.
- George of Kinnochtrie, Sheriff Clerk of Argyll (1642 × 1659), 30, 41, 43, 58.
- Governor of Duart Castle (1679), 80.
- Hugh of Cawdor, Knight (1660 × 1716), 51, 52, 54, 64, 71.
- Hugh of Loudoun formerly Cessnock (1639 × 1686), 88.
- Hugh, Captain 72nd Foot (1787–1788), 274.
- Hugh in Killundine-Morvern (1775 × 1796), 436.
- James of Ardkinglas, Baronet (1666 × 1752), 101, 105.
- James of Ardkinglas, Baronet (1775), 167.
- James of Auchinbreck, Baronet (1702 × 1756), 102.
- James of Lawers, later Earl of Loudoun (1777), 327.
- James of Stonefield, Chamberlain of Argyll (1706 × 1729), 157, 223.
- James, late 40th (1784 × 1850), 203, 206.
- James, ensign 1st BF (1793), 203.
- James, Captain in Calve Island-Mull (1817), 372.
- John of Ardnamurchan DSO Baronet, Commandig Officer 11 Royal Scots (1917), 661, 671.
- John of Glenorchy later Earl of Caithness and later still 1st Earl of Breadalbane (1674 × 1690), 49, 50, 52, 55, 57, 58, 59, 61, 62, 65, 66, 67, 68, 71, 72, 73, 84, 88, 90, 133.
- John of Breadalbane, 4th Earl & 1st Marquess (1762–1834), 189, 195, 196, 199, 200, 201, 202, 203, 207, 208, 209, 210, 211, 212, 213, 214, 217, 219, 220, 221, 230, 231, 232, 236, 240, 243, 247, 249, 259.
- John son of Duncan the Baillie of Jura (1679), 65.
- John, 4th Lord Loudoun (1705 × 1782), 122, 127.
- John of Barcaldine (1759), 134, 139.
- John, junior (1788), 148, 149.
- John WS (1793), 195, 199.
- John of Airds (1793), 195, 199.
- John ensign 1st BF (1793), 203.
- John, Sergeant 1st BF (1793), 200.
- John, Captain in Calve Island-Mull (1817), 373.
- Katherine, widow of 'old Torloisk' (1684), 89.
- Lorne, Ensign 3rd Foot Guards (1801), 326.
- Lord Neil of Ardmadie (1630 × 1685), 102, 51, 52, 64, 67, 72, 73, 77, 199.
- Patrick, son of Balevolin (1793), 195, 204.
- Pedro, deserter in Argentina (1814), 406.
- Robert of Benmore (1793), 195.
- Robert, son of Balevolin (1793), 196, 204.
- Robert, Major Argyll Militia (1797), 263.
- Thomas, poet (c.1800), 518.
- William, captain of Argyll's frigate (1679), 72.
- William, ensign 1st BF (1793), 203.
- of Jura, his son 'ensign & surgeon's mate' (1793), 196.
- of Lockdochart (1793), 196.
- of Lockdochart's son (1793), 196.
- son of Lieutenant Ronald Campbell, Achrioch (1793), 196.
- Dugald in Achlian's son (1793), 196, 203.
- in Sunipol family, (c.1800), 515.
- of Sonachan (1793), 199.
- Lieutenant (1794), 219.
- Lieutenant, Tiree (1841), 460.
- Lieutenant-Colonel (1795), 230, 236.

Campsie Lieutenant 64th Foot (1816), 387.
Cardwell Edward Secretary of State for War (1873), 596, 597.
Carnarvon Lord, Colonial Secretary (1861 × 1875), 564, 565, 569.
Candlish Dr. Free Church Minister (1843), 472, 476, 477.
Cathcart Lord (1805), 326.

Cavagnari Sir Louis (1879), 576, 594.
Cetewayo see Ketchwyo.
Chaka of Zululand, the 'South African Attila' (1820), 508, 559.
Chambers Major Courtenay 25th Foot (1829), 596, 599.
Chalmers The Rev. Thomas (1843), 471, 478.
Chamberlain Joseph (1897), 608.
Chanda Sahib (1751), 144.
Charles I (1642 × 1649) 27, 36, 40, 86.
Charles II (1651 × 1685) 36, 37, 40, 41, 42, 47, 50, 51, 54, 60, 70, 73, 80, 84, 86, 88, 90, 405.
Charles X of France (1830), 434.
Chatham Countess of (1805), 326.
Chelmsford Lieutenant-General Lord, Commander-in-Chief South Africa (1879), 566, 572.
Chermiside Major-General Commanding 14th Brigade (1900), 610, 614, 615, 617.
Chitral Amir of (1891), 593
Churchill
    Randolph MP (1888), 586.
    Winston MP (1916), 659.
Clark of Ulva, William (1846), 483, 486, 488, 494.
Clarke of Comrie, Mrs (1793), 196.
Clarke Edward (1797), 277, 297, 298, 299, 304, 309, 382.
Clerk John estate officer at Netherlorn (1695), 98.
Clephane of Carslogie
    Major-General William (1803), 360.
    Margaret Maclean (1809 × 1815), 360, 363.
Clerk or Clarke
    Captain Colin The Rifle Brigade (1817), 391, 392.
    John estate officer at Netherlorn (1695), 98.
Clifford the Hon RE, Dillon's Regiment (1788–1817), 257.
Clinton
    Colonel the Commander-in-Chief's Military Secretary (1804), 329, 331.
    General Sir Henry (17780), 330.
Clive Robert (1751 × 1773), 144, 145, 146, 543.
Coats Elizabeth widow of AndrewMaclean MA (1695), 105.
Cochrane Hon. Andrew (1793), 207, 208.
Cobbett Colonel Robert (1653), 40, 41.
Coffin
    General (1815), 329.
    Sir Edward Pine (1846), 483, 484, 488.
Colenso
    Bishop of Natal, Pietermaritzburg-Natal (1858 × 1875), 549, 550, 559, 560, 563, 564, 566.
    Mrs, Pietermaritzburg-Natal (1858 × 1863), 549.
Colley Major-General Sir George Commander-in-Chief in South Africa (1881), 574, 616.
Colman George the younger (1781), 153.
Colville Major-General HE (1900), 611, 613.
Compton Lord (1815), 363.
Corbett Royal Glasgow Volunteers (1794), 219.
Cornwallis Lord (1792), 269.
Cowan Mason in Ballyhough-Coll (1856), 630.
Craig John in Crossapol-Coll, formerly in Ayrshire (1856 × 1871), 631.
Crawford
    Charles, Ballimartin-Tiree (1779), 333.
    Donald at Kingston, Jamaica (1805), 333, 334.
Cromartie Earl of (1745), 677.
Cromwell Oliver (1650), 36, 40, 41, 47, 54.
Cronje Piet (1899), 609, 610, 611, 612, 613, 614, 615, 616.
Cross Lord, Secretary of State for India (1887), 582, 584, 585.

Cunningham
    of Aikenbar, Provost of Dumbarton (1678), 63, 67, 69, 71.
    William late 17th Foot (1793), 203.
    Captain 1st BF (1794), 216.
Curzon George Nathaniel MP (1889), 591, 594.
Cyrus the Great (559–580), 579.
Darlington Lord (1796), 227.
Darroch Alexander, Factor of Coll (1887 × 1892), 640, 641, 642, 643.
Darwin Charles author of *Origin of the Species* (1859), 563.
Davenport W Davenport late 94th Foot, of Bramall Hall, Cheshire (1841), 464.
Davidson Andrew Notary Public (1793), 210.
Day
    Rev. Samuel Emory Vicar of St Philips & Jacobs, Bristol (1845), 536, 541.
    William Deane Hoare Guinness, Ensign 94th Foot (1845), 536, 541.
Deccan Nizam of the (1748), 144.
Deedes WF, journalist, (2006), 670.
De Ile Donald Lord of the Isles (1387–c.1423).5, 559.
De La Rey Boer Commando (1901), 619.
Dempster of Dunnichen, George MP (1786), 187.
Dennistoun
    of Colgrain, James (1796), 363, 372, 406.
    Elizabeth Dreghorn (1835), 470, 565.
    Dame Mary Lyon (1835), 467, 468, 470, 565.
Derriman Paul (1970), 515.
Desbrough Captain Laurence 94th Foot (1849), 540, 541.
Desta Prince Alexander of Ethiopia (1963), 663, 664, 667, 668.
Devine TM (1988), 480.
Devonshire Duke of (1892), 651.
Dewar
    Rev. Daniel (1812), 375, 376.
    Lieutenant KDG (1879), 572.
De Wet Christian (1900), 611, 612, 614, 615, 616, 618, 619.
Dickson
    Alec, Founder of VSO (1967), 665.
    Mora author of *A World Elsewhere: Voluntary Service Overseas* (1964), 665.
Dillon
    Edward (1801), 273.
    Hon Henry (1801), 273.
Dingaan of Zululand (1835 × 1838), 508, 546, 559
Disraeli Benjamin, Prime Minister (1876), 575.
Dixon
    James Captain of the *Skelton* (1820), 415.
    Lieutenant-Colonel Commanding Officer 2KOSB later Brigadier-General in South Africa (1897 × 1901), 602, 606, 620.
Donhill Lieutenant George 94th Foot (1849), 540.
Donkin Major 44th Foot (1797), 238, 239, 241.
Douglas Mrs (1838), 466.
Doyle Conan (1900), 617.
Dreghorn
    Margaret (c.1820), 470
    Robert of Blochairn (c.1800), 470.
Drummond
    of Balhaldie (1685), 91.
    of Kelty, Gavin his brother late 42nd Foot (1793), 195, 198, 201, 202, 203, 216, 218.
Drummond Wolff, Sir Henry MP (1830–1908), 586, 587, 589, 594.
Duncan Captain of the *Herald* (1858), 548.
Dundas Sir David (1810), 343, 347.

Index

Dundas
- Henry 1st Viscount Melville (1742–1811), 187, 196, 197, 204, 207, 208, 209, 211, 212, 215, 219, 220, 247, 249, 251, 256, 265, 266, 267, 411.
- Robert, the Lord Advocate (1794), 215, 251.
- Family (1838), 464, 465.

Dundonald Earl of (1748–1778), 207.
Dunlop John Provost of Glasgow (1794), 215, 217, 218, 219, 224.
Dunn Border representative, Natal (1860), 559.
Duff Captain Robert of *HMS Terror* (1746), 124, 126.
Dumbarton Earl of (1685), 89.
Durand HM, Secretary to the Government of India (1885), 581, 582, 583.
Eastwood Mr, Umvoti-Natal (1858), 550.
Edinger George author of *The Twain Shall Meet* (1960), 665, 669.
Eglinton Lord (1756), 142, 673.
Egerton Lieutenant, Transport Officer 94th Foot (1880), 573, 594, 606.

Elliot
- Colonial Office, (1849), 510, 511.
- Admiral (1840), 535, 543.
- Captain Charles RN (1840), 543.

Erskine
- Archibald of Cardross Captain 42nd Foot (1775), 171.
- Mary sister of Viscount Fentoun later Earl of Kellie (c.1600), 23.
- Major (1860), 561.
- Colonel, Colonial Secretary (1860), 562.

Exmouth Admiral Lord (1816), 389.
Eyre Coote Major-General (1797), 238, 675.
Fair Thomas financier in South America (1816), 407.
Fane Captain Walter (1860), 553, 555.
Fan So servant of John & Allan Maclean, Lagmore-Coll in Australia (1852), 517.
Farell Captain 43rd Foot (1812), 350.
Farewell Dr, explorer of Natal (1823), 508.
Fawcett Colonel Scots Guards (1774), 224.
Feilding General the Hon. WHA, Inspector-General of Recruiting for the Army (1894), 594.
Fenwick Admiral William RN (1889), 594.

Ferguson
- Sir Adam MP (1786), 187.
- Captain 81st Foot (1775), 167.

Ferrier James Chamberlain of Argyll (1790), 190.
Fessey William, soldier 1 KOSB (1900), 610, 613, 614, 615, 616, 617.
Fincastle Lord VC, ADC to Sir Bindon Blood (1897), 599.
Findlater Piper VC, Gordon Highlanders (1897), 601.
Fisher Captain Edward RA (1850), 543.
Flett William, builder on Coll (1968), 667.
Forbes of Culloden, Duncan Lord President (1737 × 1746), 126, 223.
Forsyth of Quinish-Mull (1857), 643.

Foster
- Mrs (1828), 411.
- Sir Augustus John, Bart (1828), 411.

Francia Dr José Dictator of Paraguay (1814), 406.

Fraser
- Alexander in Gualachaolish-Mull (c.1760), 176, 177.
- Alexander MA Assistant Minister of Coll (1780), 176, 190, 191.
- Rev. Alexander, Free Church Minister at Coll (1885), 631, 637.
- Andrew, Master Mariner (c.1700), 402.
- Brigadier David, Commander 19Brigade (1964), 664.
- Donald, soldier 1st BF (1794), 216.
- Hector in Ruaig-Tiree (1671 × 1679), 48, 79.
- John, Captain 82nd Foot (1760), 402.
- John MA Dean of the Isles & Minister of Tiree & Coll (1671 × 1695), 48, 97, 99, 100, 105, 176, 402.
- John, Assistant-Director Project Trust (1982), 669.
- Simon, see Lovat.
- Simon in Kingharair-Mull, Colonel 80th Foot & Emigration agent (1818), 398.
- William MA (1779), 174, 175.

Fraser-Macintosh, Charles MP (1892), 643.
French Major-General John commander of the cavalry at Paardeberg (1900), 611, 612, 613, 614, 615, 616.
Frere Sir Bartle, Governor of Cape Colony (1876), 565, 566.
Frome Captain 94th Foot (1879), 571.
Galbraith John, Ayrshire miner later in Cliad-Coll (1856), 635.
Gatacre General Sir William (1899), 609.
George I (1716), 102.
George III (1793 × 1801)198, 208, 209, 210, 211, 212, 220, 247, 250, 251, 252, 253, 273, 461, 596, 599.
George IV, formerly Prince Regent (1815 × 1822), 385, 390, 405, 406.
Gillespie Major-General RR (1811), 351.

Gilchrist
- Mr, architect (1831), 432.
- John in Totronald-Coll formerly at Islay (1856), 630.

Gladstone William, Prime Minister (1881), 574, 576, 580, 581, 583, 690, 611, 639.
Glencairn Earl of (1653), 40, 41, 47. (1787), 363.
Glenelg Lord (c.1815 × 1837), 430, 446, 447, 448, 451, 452, 542, 544.
Godfray Colonel (1901), 619.
Going Captain 1 KOSB (1901), 617.

Gordon
- Duke of (1793), 207, 233.
- Duchess of (1793), 207, 211, 625.
- Lord Adam (1775), 169, 207, 208, 209, 210, 212, 213, 214, 217, 218, 219, 220, 229, 231, 232, 239, 240, 362.
- Colonel the Hon. William (1775), 166.

Grafton Duke of (1816), 391.

Graham
- of Claverhouse, John Viscount Dundee (1648–1689), 72, 596.
- of Glenny, Walter his brother (1793), 195.
- Grahame, Professor of Botany at Glasgow University (1837), 444, 452.
- Humphrey, Chamberlain of Argyll (1797), 259, 309.
- Colonel John (1812), 508.
- Bishop of the Isles (1680), 84, 90.

Granger Drummer 1st BF (1793), 202.

Grant
- of Grant Sir James (1795), 127, 247, 248, 249, 250, 251, 252, 253, 254, 255, 256, 310, 311, 313, 315, 317, 319, 328, 352, 353.
- of Redcastle, Patrick (1830), 448, 452.
- General Clerk of Lieutenancy for Inverness-shire (1804), 316, 317.
- General Sir Hope (1860), 553, 554, 555.
- Francis J, Lyon Clerk (1898), 653.

Gray
- the Hon. Francis (1765–1842), 203, 205, 216, 236, 243, 259.
- Malcolm, author of *The Highland Economy 1750–1850* (1956), 397.

Greaves Lieutenant (1897), 598, 599.
Gregorson of Ardtornish, John Sheriff-Substitute at Tobermory-Mull (1822), 429.
Gregory Donald author of *History of the Highlands and Islands of Scotland* (1836), 626, 662.
Grenville Lord (1798), 267.

721

Grey
  Sir George, 2nd Bart (1837 × 1858), 447, 448, 452, 547, 548.
  Henry George 3rd Earl (1849), 509, 510, 511.
  Colonel 85th Foot (1860), 563.
Grimes
  Private David 94th Foot (1849), 540, 541.
  Private James 94th Foot (1849), 540, 541.
Guinness
  family, 649.
  Olivia, daughter of Arthur of Beaumont, County Dublin, (1781–1809), 541.
  Sir Benjamin Lee 1st Baronet (1798–1868), 541.
Guthrie Mr (1786), 187.
Haig Captain AE 2 KOSB later Major 1 KOSB (1897 × 1901), 602, 603, 606, 619.
Haile Selassie Emperor of Ethiopia (1963), 663, 668.
Haines Commander (1839), 536.
Hamilton
  Duke (1685), 50, 93, 96.
  Ann Duchess of (1685), 93, 96.
  George, Tasmania (1834), 434.
  Lieutenant RN (1846), 537.
  Lieutenant-Colonel 2nd Lancers Hyderabad Contingent (1888), 579.
  Major-General Ian (1901), 619.
  Family (1838), 465.
Hannay Colonel OC Commander of the mounted infantry at Paardeberg (1900), 613, 618.
Hanning Hugh, journalist (1967), 667.
Hardinge Viscount, Viceroy of India (1844), 537.
Harris Lord (1799), 269.
Hassan Ali Khan Nawab (1889), 587, 588, 590.
Hastings Francis Rawdon, Earl of Moira (1804 × 1811), 327, 331, 390, 392.
Hay Captain John (1746), 124.
Hearsay General, Commander Calcutta garrison (1857), 551.
Hill Field-Marshal Lord, Commander-in-Chief (1838), 455.
Hoare Rev. William, Vicar General of Limerick (1823), 541.
Hobart
  George see Buckinghamshire (1816), 411.
  [Robert] The Rt.Hon. Lord, Secretary of State for War (1801–1804), 326, 413, 430, 437.
Hodson Major WSR (1857), 552.
Holburne Lieutenant-General (1651), 37, 38.
Home Popham Captain RN (1797), 238, 327, 336, 408.
Home Captain Roddam of *HMS Caesar* (1798), 263.
Hope
  Lady Georgina (1793), 207.
  Lady Margaret (1822), 411.
  Admiral (1859), 553.
Hore Colonel (1901), 619.
Hunter
  Professor (1805), 315.
  James author of *The Making of the Crofting Community* (1976), 476, 627, 636.
Huntly Marquess of
  (1679), 82, 85.
  (1803), 315, 391.
Huruhuru Maori chief (1858), 518.
Hyder Ali (1766), 674, 675.
Hyderabad Nizam of (1766), 674.
Irving Edward (1792–1834), 470.
James VI & I (1609 × 1616), 9, 19, 82, 153.

James VII & II (1679 × 1702), 73, 82, 83, 84, 86, 88, 97, 99.
James VIII & III (1715), 103.
Jamieson Mr at Sandy Island-Canna (1803), 321.
Jardine Guy & Jean, Isle of Coll Hotel (1959), 663.
Jhansi Rani of (1858), 552.
Johnson Dr Samuel, (1773 × 1778) author of *A Journey to the Western Islands of Scotland* (1817), 16, 108, 112, 142, 143, 146, 150, 151, 154, 155, 157, 158, 160, 161, 162, 164, 165, 168, 260, 287, 294, 298, 300, 361, 672.
Joseph
  Johnson's servant (1773), 161.
  King of Spain (1812), 352.
Junot Marshall (1808), 341.
Kay Captain (1746), 124.
Keate Surgeon-General (1805), 334, 335.
Kekewich Colonel RG (1901), 620.
Kelly Colonel James (1895), 593, 596.
Kelly-Kenny Major-General Commander of 6th Division (1900), 611, 612, 613.
Kemp
  Dr J, Secretary of SSPCK (1794), 280, 281, 282.
  General (1901), 622.
Kennedy John President of the United States of America (1917–1963), 665.
Kenneth MacAlpine (841 × 858), 311.
Ketchwyo of Zululand (1860 × 1879), 559, 560, 561, 562, 563, 564, 565, 566, 572, 574, 576.
Kimberley Lord, Viceroy of India (1885), 580. .
Kitchener Lord, Chief of Staff to Lord Roberts (1899 × 1914), 609, 610, 611, 612, 613, 615, 618, 620.
Knowles Clerk-Sergeant Alexander 1st BF (1795), 224.
Knox
  Andrew MA Bishop of the Isles (1609), 19, 20.
  John, Bookseller (1786), 187, 369, 421.
  Thomas MA Bishop of the Isles (c.1609), 19, 20.
Koch Mr, merchant in Natal trading with Zululand (1858), 547, 548, 549.
Kruger Paul, President of the Transvaal (1881), 574, 608, 618.
Lalor James Fintan, Irish political writer (1807–1847), 627.
Lambert Major-General (1651), 37, 38, 39.
Lamont
  of Lamont, Sir James (1670 × 1700), 88.
  Neil at Balevulin-Tiree (1755), 115, 359.
Lang Major-General DB, CB, DSO, MC (1967), 665.
Langalialele Chief of the Hlubi of Natal (1873), 564.
Langlands George & Son (1794), 242, 286.
Lauder of Fountainhall, Sir John (1679), 82, 86, 87.
Lauderdale John Maitland 2nd Earl & 1st Duke (1665), 48, 61, 73, 82, 83, 84, 85.
Lawrence
  Sir Henry, Governor of Oudh-India (1857), 551.
  Sir John (later Lord), Lieutenant-Governor of Punjab (1857), 551.
Lees Gamekeeper on Coll (1898), 633.
Lennox Lord, Colonel of the 25th Foot (1782), 596.
Lesley John Bishop of the Isles (1632), 24.
Leslie
  David Major-General (1647), 33, 36.
  Lieutenant-General (1793), 203.
  Major & ADC (1794), 218, 220.
Leven Earl of (1689), 596.
Lewis Major the Hon. Peter 15/19th Hussars (1972–1973), 666, 667.
Lilburne Colonel Robert (1653), 40.

Index

Lindsay Ian G (1961), 669, 671
Linlithgow Earl (1678), 61, 75.
Lister Ann (1820), 405, 409, 410, 413.
Lloyd Archdeacon (1875), 564.
Lockhart Lieutenant-General Sir William (1897), 599, 603, 605.
Long Mr at Harley Street, London (1828), 409.
Lord Simeon of Sydney NSW (1825), 416.
Lord Provost of Edinburgh (1829), 597.
Lord Lyon King of Arms (1896), 650, 653.
Louis
    XVI King of France (1793), 198.
    XVIII King of France (1815), 353.
Lovat
    Lord, Simon (1675 × 1746), 166.
    Simon, General (1745 × 1775), 165, 166, 294, 673.
Low Major-General Sir Robert (1895), 593, 596.
Lumsden General Sir Peter (1884), 580, 591.
Lynn Major (1796), 227.
Lytton Lord, Viceroy of India (1876), 575, 576, 579.
MacAlasdair of Loup
    Alexander (1573 × 1580), 11.
    John (1685), 90.
Macallum Donald soldier 1st BF (1794), 219.
MacAlpine family (1803), 311.
Macarthur
    Archibald MA, Minister of Kilnian & Kilmore-Mull (1776 × 1810), 152, 160, 175, 279, 280, 283, 435.
    Dr Donald MA, Minister of Kilninian & Kilmore-Mull (1810 × 1848), 435, 504.
Macaskill
    family (c.1600), 24.
    Captain Allan of Calgary Castle-Mull (1823), 457.
    Captain Donald in Keildonan-Eigg MD (1797), 251, 252, 254, 255, 256, 311, 312, 345, 346.
    Lieutenant Hugh 1st BF (1796), 226, 234.
    Malcolm MA, Minister of the Small Isles (c.1785), 234, 346.
Macaulay
    family (c.1400), 5.
    Aulay MA, Minister of Tiree & Coll (1704), 100, 105.
MacCulloch John (1824), 422.
MacCrimmon
    Donald Roy (c.1780), 405.
    Pàdraig (c.1716), 115.
Macdonald
    of Dalilea, Alexander (1812), 382, 383, 397.
    of Knockrinsay, Sir James (1596 × 1626), 12, 14.
    of Keppoch, Archibald (1672 × 1682), 53, 71, 76.
    of Lindill (1797), 242.
Macdonald of Vallay-North Uist
    Major Alexander (1814), 390, 414, 419.
    Alexander (1820), 414.
    William (c.1800), 391.
Macdonald Captain Alexander (1775), 171, 173.
    Alasdair MacColla (1644 × 1645), 31, 37, 71.
    Alasdair mac Mhaigstir Alasdair (1745), 116, 303.
    Angus, younger in Laig-Eigg (1797), 251, 252, 253, 257, 311, 414.
    Angus, Canna (1804), 319.
    Anthony, priest at Eigg (194), 257.
    Iain Lom (1678), 38, 62, 63.
    Colin in Galmisdale-Eigg (1794), 250, 251, 252, 253, 254, 255, 257.
    Donald, Laig-Eigg (1820), 416.
    Donald in Balure-Appin, Lieutenant Donald (1820), 414.
    Donald, Ardnamurchan (1843), 468.
    Hugh, Hough-Tiree (1775), 169, 170, 216.
    Hugh changekeeper in Sandavore-Eigg (1794 × 1803), 257, 321.
    James MA (1807), author of *A General View of the Agriculture of the Hebrides* (1811), 251, 286, 287, 288, 291, 292, 293, 294, 303, 366, 367, 368, 369, 370, 421, 422.
    James, writer at Inveraray-Argyll (1841), 467, 468, 469, 472, 491, 494.
    John, late 76th Foot (1793), 203.
    John in Cliadale-Eigg (1797), 251, 255, 256, 257.
    John, Kilchoan-Ardnamurchan (1847), 489.
    JFM, Major-General Commanding 52 (Lowland) Infantry Division (TA) & Lowland District (1958 × 1960), 662.
Macdonald Lachlan
    Bailie of Eigg (1709 × 1710), 101, 102.
    Bailie of Canna (1709), 101.
Macdonald
    Lachlan in Kilchoan-Ardnamurchan (1841), 467.
    Neil in Kenovay-Tiree (1812), 383.
    'Old Macdonald' (1773), ship's captain, 151.
    Ranald in Five Pennies-Eigg (1794), 257.
    Ranald in Laig-Eigg (1776 × 1802), 257, 303, 311.
    Ranald, Howlin-Eigg (1794), 257.
    Lieutenant-Colonel Robert, of Inchkenneth & Gribun-Mull CB, JP, DL, Late RHA (1841), 457, 460, 462.
    Rory, cousin of Lord MacDonnell (1678), 62, 72, 73, 76.
    William, fisher (1786), 188.
Macdonald of Boisdale
    Alexander (1745 × 1747), 128, 134, 358.
    Alexander (1793), 195, 390.
    Colin (c.1750), 358.
Macdonald
    of Clanranald see MacRuari
    of Dalilea, Alexander (1797 × 1812), 252, 253, 382, 383, 397, 399.
    of Knockrinsay, Sir James (1596 × 1626), 12, 14.
    of Keppoch, Archibald (1672 × 1682), 53, 71, 76.
    of Lindill (1797), 242.
    of Morar, Captain John (1794 × 1797), 250, 252, 253, 254.
    of Staffa, Sir Ranald later Seton-Stewart (1814), 390.
MacDonald of Slate, 4th Baron (1809–1863), 504.
MacDonald of Sleat
    Alexander, Baronet (1720–1746), 119, 122.
    Donald, Baronet (1679 × 1718), 66, 76, 99.
    James, Baronet (1651 × 1678), 51.
MacDonald of Vallay-North Uist
    Major Alexander (1814), 390, 414, 417.
    Alexander (1820), 414.
    William (c.1800), 391.
Macdonnell of Barisdale Coll (1744), 673, 677.
Macdonnell of Glengarry
    Aeneas 1st Lord Macdonnell & Aros (1678 × 1680), 40, 53, 55, 58, 61, 62, 63, 71, 72, 73, 75, 76, 82, 83.
    Alasdair Ranaldson (1773–1828), 362, 405, 406.
    Alexander 'Pickle the Spy' (1753), 133.
Macdonnell
    of Lochgarry, Charles (1753), 133.
    Coll Lieutenant-Colonel (1804), 319.
    Captain (1858), 547.
Macdonald Buchanan, Hector WS (1820), 245, 358, 390.
Macdougall
    Duncan brother to Dunach (1676), 58.
    Rev. Neil Minister of Coll (1877 × 1895), 632, 637, 638.

MacDougall of MacDougall
    Alexander younger (1796), 228.
    Iain Ciar (1715), 106.
MacDougall
    of Ardincaple, John (1793), 195.
    of Gallanach, ? (1793), 196.
Maceachern Rev. Dougall Minister of Coll (1898), 634.
MacFadyen, family, 30.
Macfarlane
    Malcolm 1st BF (1794), 216, 220, 240.
    A black servant (1820), 419.
    Captain 2 KOSB (1897), 603.
    DH, Liberal MP for Argyllshire (1885 × 1886), 639.
Macgregor
    Lieutenant Fane's Horse (1860), 554.
    Major-General Sir Charles, Quartermaster-General of the Indian Army (1884), 581.
Macians
    of Ardnamurchan family (1620), 20, 21, 26.
    John (1611), 20.
MacIlendrish Duncan, in Beach-Morvern (1664), 48.
MacIlvernock of Oib Angus (1665 × 1685), 65.
MacIllivoill John (1746), 124.
Macinnes
    Allan I, author of *Clanship, Commerce and the House of Stuart, 1603-1788* (1996), 1, 2, 12, 13, 29, 47.
    John, author of *The Evangelical Movement in the Highlands of Scotland 1688-1800* (1951), 283.
Mackay
    of Scourie, Colonel Hugh in Dutch service (1640–1692), 85, 89.
    Aeneas, second son of Lord Reay (1684), 85, 89.
    Charles (1793), 200.
    Captain Charles, Campbeltown (1850), 628, 629.
    Captain, Loudoun's Highlanders (1746 × 1747), 127.
    John, Messenger at Fort William (1781), 129.
    Lieutenant-Colonel (1793), 209.
    Dr Macintosh Free Church Minister at Dunoon (1845), 475, 476, 479, 489.
    Piper at Dunvegan (1780), 403.
Mackenzie
    of Applecross (c.1800), 430.
    of Gairloch family, 663.
    of Hartfield, Captain Donald (c.1800), 430.
    of Suddie (1685), 92.
    Christina, Dervaig-Mull (1790), 361.
    Colin son to the Laird of Redcastle (1733), 129.
    Isabella, daughter of Captain Donald of Hartfield (c.1820), 430.
Mackillop
    Mr at North Sannox-Arran (1812), 383.
    Andrew author of '*More Fruitful than the Soil*' (2000), 180, 185, 200, 202, 205.
Mackinnon
    Angus, Talisker-Tasmania (1825–1828), 416.
    Donald MA, Minister of Strath (1731–1831), 415.
    Hector, Ensign Eigg Company Inverness-shire Volunteers (1803), 311.
    Hector in Derrichuag-Mull (1815 × 1837), 437.
    John in Gallanach-Muck (1803), 321.
    John in Keill-Canna (1803), 321.
    Lachlan in Howlin/Holoun-Eigg (1795 × 1803), 230, 236, 251, 257, 311, 320, 321, 415.
    Margaret, daughter of Hector Derrichuaig-Mull (1830), 437.
Mackinnon of Mishnish, Ewen (1519), 7.

Mackinnon of Strathordill
    John *balbhan* (1627), 24.
    John Dubh (1715 × 1746), 119, 126.
    Lachlan Dubh (c.1557 × 1580), 320.
    Sir Lachlan (1616), 19, 24.
Macintosh of Borlum, Brigadier (1715), 104.
Maclachlan of Maclachlan, Lachlan (1746), 121.
Maclachlan
    Alexander Bailie of Tiree & Two Ends of Coll (1693 × 1709), 97, 98, 103, 113.
    Eoin of Killiemre at Laudle-Morvern (1821), 438.
    John in Ardnamurchan (1679), 66.
    Lachlan vc ewen in Hynish-Tiree (1663), 81.
Maclane
    Archibald of *Maclane & Son* London (1764), 146.
    Duncan (1764), 146, 147.
    Rebecca (1775), 148.
    Thomas Ashurst (1764), 146.
Maclaine of Lochbuie
    Archibald (1774), 163, 179.
    Hector (1669 × 1716), 357.
    Murdoch (1814–1850), 504.
Maclaine
    Lieutenant-General Sir Archibald, 94th Foot (1777–1861), 459, 462.
    Rev. A Minister of Ardnamurchan (1835), 449.
    Gillean of Scallastle (1760), 363.
    John (1751 × 1773), 147, 149.
    John in Gruline, Lochbuie's factor (1788), 182.
    Murdoch (1775 × 1804), 165, 172, 178, 179, 182, 185, 357, 358, 363.
Maclaurin Lieutenant (1794), 216.
Maclean
    of Ardgour family [Clan Ewen], 48, 49, 53, 57, 67, 70, 75, 77, 98, 99, 359, 406.
    of Boreray family, 223.
    of Duart family, 48, 372, 421, 431.
    of Hynish family, 359.
    of Kingerloch family, 48.
    of Kinlochaline family, 129.
    of Lehir, 136, 229.
    of Lochbuie family, 48.
    of Pennycross family, 626.
    of Ross family, 38, 39, 264.
    of Torloisk family, 48, 129, 372.
    Alexander of Ardgour (1780 × 1855), 411.
    Alexander of Otter, Knight (1655–1707), 85.
    Alexander of Pennycross-Mull, surgeon in Mull (1760 × 1786), Table 12, 118, 129, 139, 142, 626, 634.
    Alexander MA, Minister of Kingarth (1689), 99.
    Alexander MA, Minister of Kilninian & Kilmore (1760), 274, 336.
    Alexander, Lieutenant Western Fencibles (1775), 167.
    Alexander, Sergeant-Major 72nd Foot (1795), Table 12, 224, 268, 274.
    Alexander, Surgeon HEICS (1810 × 1821), Table 12.
    Alexander, soldier 1st BF (1794), 216.
    Alexander in Hosta-North Uist, Captain 79th Foot (1815), 341, 385, 391.
    Alexander, Dr Langamull-Mull (1810), 346, 383.
    Alexander, in Kengharair-Mull (1831), 430.
    Allan of Ardgour (1668–1756), 96.
    Allan of Ardtornish-Mull (1594 × 1630), 23.

Index

Allan of Brolas-Mull, later of Duart Baronet (1725–1783), Table 12, 119, 122, 127, 129, 134, 139, 140, 142, 143, 147, 148, 149, 163, 178, 181, 182, 186, 199, 626, 673.
Allan of Drimnin-Morvern (1654 × 1680). 64.
Allan of Drimnin-Morvern (1745 × 1788), 121, 123, 124, 147, 149.
Allan of Duart, Baronet (1661 × 1674), 42, 47, 48, 49, 84, 89, 223.
Allan of Gruline-Mull (1671 × 1702), Table 12.
Allan of Inverscadell (1674 × 1686), 55.
Allan, Captain Dalziel's Regiment (1710 × 1722), Table 12.172.
Allan, Marjoribanks Regiment in Dutch service (1744), 120.
Allan, General late Scots Dutch, 60th, 114th & 84th Foot (1748), 134, 178, 199, 274, 337, 626, 673.
Allan MD, Lieutenant 2/1st Foot, 1st BF & Captain AV (1759–1837), Table 12, 168, 172, 228, 229, 243, 259, 309, 310, 366.
Allan, Sergeant Western Fencibles (1775), 171.
Allan, of the 'Black Swan' Hobart-Tasmania (1820 × 1824), 414, 417, 420.
Angus of Knock, Minister of Morvern (1620), 34.
Ann, daughter of John Langamull-Mull (1812), 386.
Anna, daughter of Sir Allan (1773), 148.
Anna Isabella, daughter of Baron David (c.1750), 402.
Anne, daughter Charles of Kilunaig-Mull (c.1740), Table 12.
Archibald MA, Archdeacon of Argyll (1689), 99.
Archibald 'of the family of Lochbuy' (c.1700), 160.
Archibald in Scour-Mull, Lieutenant-Colonel 79th Foot (1793), 340, 357.
Archibald in Kilmaluag-Tiree (1785), 190, 191.
Archibald of Pennycross-Mull (1893), 649.
Charles of Ardnacross, formerly in Fuinary, Bailie of Aros (1660 × 1694), 51, 64.
Charles of Drimnin (1716 × 1746), 123, 130.
Charles of Inverscadell (1686 × 1705), 95.
Charles of Kilunaig-Mull (1674 × 1743), Table 12, 120.
Charles of Kinlochaline-Morvern (1783 × 1787), 147.
Charles Fitzroy of Duart, Baronet 3rd Foot Guards & 81st Foot (1816 × 1883), 626.
Christian, daughter of Captain Allan Dalzell's Regiment (1718 × 1808), Table 12, 172, 234.
Christian, daughter of Donald Maclean of Torloisk-Mull (1750), 274.
Daniel, Secretary of the Clan Maclean Association (1896), 650.
David, Baron Maclean of Gasevadholm, Sweden (1646–1708), 402.
Donald of Boreray-Uist (1615), 233.
Donald of Arihualan-Ardgour (c.1700), 143, 148.
Donald in Kilunaig-Mull (1746 × 1762), Table 12, 120, 123, 129, 130, 229.
Donald of Brolas-Mull, Lieutenant-Colonel Royalist Army (1645 × 1658), 37, 39, 40, 41, 289, 626, 652.
Donald of Brolas-Mull, Lieutenant-Colonel Jacobite Army (1695 × 1725), Table 12, 122.
Donald of Kingerloch (1674 × 1719), 58.
Donald of Tarbert-Jura later of Torloisk-Mull (1715 × 1748), 106, 119.
Donald, merchant at Glasgow sometime Collector of Customs at Montego Bay-Jamaica (1751 × 1769), 626.
Donald, 74th Foot (1778–1783), 264.
Donald, Major 1st Foot (1795 × 1820), Table 12.
Donald, Excise Stirling (1762), 129.
Donald in Sorn (c.1780), Table 4, 234.
Donald in Kengharair-Mull (1848), 504.
Dugald, Second-Lieutenant Western Fencibles (1775), 168, 172, 264.
Eachann Bacach (1651), 38, 39.
Ewen of Treshnish-Mull, Captain Argyll's Regiment (1644 × 1651), 31, 37.
Farqhar, Oscamull-Mull (1760), 358, 363.
Fitzroy Jeffreys Grafton of Duart, Baronet (1789 × 1839), 626.
Fitzroy Donald of Duart, Baronet (1835–1936), 626, 629, 649, 650, 663.
Florence, daughter of Donald of Arihualan-Ardgour, 148.
Florence, daughter of Hugh in Balliphetrish-Tiree (1695), 234.
Francis, Major-General, Colonel 82nd Foot (c.1720–1781), 171, 173.
Francis, volunteer Western Fencibles (1775), 171, 173.
Hector in Ballimartin-Tiree (1693 × 1698), Table 12, 101, 120, 121, 223.
Hector in Balliphetrish-Tiree (1695 × 1776), Table 12, 223, 224, 233, 234.
Hector in Cornaigmore-Tiree (1709), 101.
Hector Allansoun, *Eachann mac Ailean na Sop* (1547 × 1579), 8, 9.
Maclean, Hector
  of Duart-Mull (1390 × 1411), 6.
  Og of Duart-Mull (1587 × 1632), 14, 18, 19, 22.
  Younger of Duart-Mull (1632), 24, 25.
Maclean
  Hector of Duart-Mull, Baronet (1651), 36, 37, 38, 39, 47.
  Hector of Duart-Mull, Baronet (1704–1750), 104, 134.
  Hector of Duart-Mull, Baronet, Ensign 84th Foot (1778 × 1818), 626.
  Hector, merchant at Jamaica (1771), 626.
  Hector Reaganach of Lochbuie-Mull (c.1360), 8.
  Hector of Lochbuie-Mull (1602 × 1628), 20.
  Hector of Lochbuie-Mull (1669 × 1717), 85, 91.
  Hector, Sergeant-Major 3rd Foot Guards & Captain 1st BF (1751–1830), Table 12, 196, 198, 203, 216, 217, 218, 221, 223, 224, 225, 226, 227, 228, 229, 230, 231, 232, 235, 236, 237, 241, 242, 246, 328, 345, 367, 389.
  Hector of Killene, later of Torloisk-Mull (1630 × 1685), 28, 34, 40, 41, 51, 55.
  Hector of Killean, in Ardfinaig-Mull Lieutenant in Argyll Fencibles (1756–1763), 261, 264.
  Hector of Kinlochaline-Morvern (1630 × 1642), 28, 34.
  Hector of Knock-Morvern MA, Bishop of Argyll (1605–1787), 84, 85.
  Hector Mor, illegitimate son of Donald of Brolas and *not* of Donald of Coll (1680), 652.
  Hector Og in Cornaigbeg-Tiree, brother of Brolas (1675 × 1679), 56, 60, 79, 83, 626, 652.
  Hector, cousin to Torloisk-Mull (1678), 64.
  Hector, brother of Torloisk-Mull (1679), 77.
  Hector of Torloisk, writer in Edinburgh (1744 × 1765), 119, 126, 374.
  Hector in Torren-Mull (1744), 120.
  Hugh, younger of Ardgour (1671 × 1690), 70, 91, 93, 96.
  Hugh, in Balliphetrish-Tiree, Baillie of Tiree (1663 × 1698), Table 12, 48, 53, 56, 79, 83, 101, 158, 223, 233.
  Hugh in Barchindroman-Mull (1760), 358.
  Hugh of Carna-Morvern's grandson (1679), 80.
  Hugh of Kingerloch (1745 × 1784), 122, 123, 126, 127, 129, 140.
  Hugh, brother to Kilmory-Scarba (1744), 120.
  Hugh, writer at Glasgow (1779), 117, 118.
  Hugh (1718), Table 12.
  Hugh alias *mac Eachan vic Ewen vic Ewen vic Ilchalum* (1734), 136.

Hugh in Langamull-Mull, Lieutenant Scots Dutch & 114th Foot (1748–1771), 139, 140.
Hugh, Tigh-a loin-Mull (1789), 182.
Hugh (c.1800), Table 12.
James at the Cecil Street Coffee House formerly soldier 77th Foot (1756 × 1775), 166, 172.
Janet, daughter of Donald, sometime Collector at Montego Bay-Jamaica (1782), 628.
John in Cornaigmore-Tiree (1679), 79.
John Dubh of Morvern (1561 × 1585), 626.
John Crubach of Ardgour (1637 × 1690), 51, 53, 55, 57, 64, 66, 88, 96.
John, 1st Adlad Macklier of Sweden (1649) & 1st Baronet of Dowart (1650), 402.
John of Duart-Mull, Baronet (1674 × 1715), 49, 52, 53, 54, 55, 58, 61, 82, 84, 86, 89, 97, 98, 102, 103, 104, 106, 143, 423.
John, in Kilfinichen-Mull (1727), 626.
John, Kingerloch's brother (1743 × 1746), 120.
John of Kinlochaline-Morvern (1649 × 1687), 56, 64, 66, 233.
John of Knock-Morvern (1642), 34.
John of Tarbert-Jura, brother to Torloisk (1685), 91.
John Diùrach in Ballimartin-Tiree (1651 × 1663), Table 12, 39, 101, 121.
John MA, WS at Edinburgh (1670 × 1695), Table 12, 155, 158.
John 42nd Foot (1739), 129.
John MA in Treshnish, Minister of Kilninian & Kilmore-Mull *Maighstir Seathan* (1737), 120, 129.
John of Killean-Mull, in Ardfinaig-Mull (1748), 129.
John in Icolmkill-Mull (1737 × 1746), 120, 124, 125, 126, 129.
John in Hosta-North Uist (c.1770), 392.
John, Captain Jacobite Army (1709 × 1746), Table 12, 105, 120, 121, 122, 123, 229.
John the poet *Iain Mac Ailein* (1716), 114.
John MD at Brolas-Mull (1729 × 1779), Table 12.172.
John, Surgeon at Glasgow (1770), 166, 172.
John in Langamull-Mull (1783 × 1787), Table 12, 228, 229, 386, 402.
John in Lagganulva-Mull (1782), 181, 186.
John, late Lieutenant 74th Foot (1793), 203.
John, Ensign 6 WIR (1798), 264.
John, Regimental Sergeant-Major 1st BF (1758 × 1798), Table 4, 200, 224, 235, 239.
John, Ensign 43rd Foot (1811), 343, 355.
John the Laird of Coll's bard *Iain Mac Ailein mhic Thearlaich mhic Lachain mhic Eoghain mhicLachainn Fhin* (1807), 359, 360, 363, 364, 370, 371, 372, 398, 662.
John in Tiroran-Mull (1812), 383, 386.
John of Ardow-Mull MD 84th Foot (1821), 421, 436.
Julia, at Ballimartin-Tiree (1779), 333, 334.
Lachlan Odhar of Ardchraoishnish-Mull (c.1600), 38.
Lachlan of Ardnacross-Mull [*Lachlann Barrach*] (1618), 21, 26, 28.
Lachlan of Brolas-Mull (1650 × 1686), Table 12, 49, 51, 52, 53, 54, 55, 57, 61, 64, 66, 71, 80, 83, 84, 88, 91, 93, 97, 626.
Lachlan Lùbanach of Duart-Mull (1367 × 1390), 8.
Lachlan Cattanach of Duart-Mull (1465–1523), 32.
Lachlan of Duart-Mull, Knight (1558–1598), 8, 9, 10, 11, 12, 14, 20, 21, 36, 96, 626.
Lachlan, 3rd son of Donald of Boreray-North Uist (c.1651), 233.
Lachlan of Kingerloch (1716 × 1758), 127.
Lachlan of Knockroy-Mull (c.1720), 358.
Lachlan of Lochbuie-Mull (1669 × 1685), 47, 50, 51, 55, 64, 66, 70, 85, 91.

Lachlan, Sir Lachlan of Morvern, Baronet later of Duart (1632 × 1649), 24, 25, 31, 32, 33, 34, 35, 41.
Lachlan of Torloisk-Mull (1674 × 1687), 64, 66, 70, 83, 91, 92, 97.
Lachlan of Torloisk-Mull (1793), 199.
Lachlan of Craigbete-Renfrewshire, Captain Madras Army 'Tiree Lachlan' (1751), 145, 146, 147, 148.
Lachlan, guardsman in 3rd Foot Guards & Captain Jacobite Army (1710 × 1739), Table 12, 104, 105, 107, 120, 121.
Lachlan, Colonel 60th Foot (1754–1829), 224, 268, 273, 274, 332, 336.
Margaret, daughter of Lachlan of Knockroy-Mull, in Oscamull-Mull (c.1760), 358.
Margaret, daughter of John in Langamull-Mull (c.1800), 402.
Maria, eldest daughter of Sir Allan (1773), 142, 147, 163.
Marianne, heiress of Lachlan of Torloisk-Mull (1803), 360.
Mary of the family of Ardgour (1695), 98, 99.
Mary, daughter of John in Killean-Mull (1748), 129.
Mary, daughter of Hugh Bailie of Tiree (c.1700), Table 12, 223.
Mary, daughter of Donald in Kilunaig-Mull (c.1780), Table 12.
Murdoch of Lochbuie-Mull (1635 × 1661), 25, 36.
Murdoch younger of Kilmory-Scarba (1746), 123.
Murdoch, Lieutenant Western Fencibles (1775 × 1799), 167, 173, 199[?].
Murdoch of Kingerloch (1793), 196.
Neil in Fanmore-Mull (1744), 120.
Neil, Lieutenant RN (1793 × 1800), 261, 262, 323, 324.
Peter, the Rev. Free Church Minister at Tobermory-Mull (1843), 472, 473, 474, 475, 476, 478.
Sibbella, daughter of Sir Allan (1773), 142.
Maclean Sinclair Alexander author of *Clan Gillean* (1896 × 1899), 108, 398, 403, 429, 442, 450, 651, 652, 652, 654, 662.
Maclennan Major Stewart REME (1971), 667.
MacLeod of MacLeod
  John Breac (1664–1693), 76.
  Malcolm (1390), 24.
  Norman (1706–1772), 119.
  Norman (1793), 197, 248, 256.
  Sir Rory Mor (1595–1626), 19, 20, 21, 23, 24.
Macleod
  Lord (1781), 677.
  Family, 57,
Macleod of Bernerah
  Donald (c.1745), 675.
  Norman, Knight (1614 × 1675), 24, 42, 47, 58.
Macleod of Greshornish Donald (c.1640), 24.
Macleod of Hamer
  William (c.1640), 24.
  Donald (c.1760). 135, 140.
Macleod of Muiravonside
  John (1745), 127, 672.
  Alexander *McCruslick* (1745), 127.
Macleod of Raasay Lieutenant-Colonel James (1805), 327, 390.
Macleod of Talisker
  Major Donald (1794 × 1828), 396, 397, 412, 414, 415, 416, 417, 418, 433, 436, 440, 445, 517.
  Colonel John (1718 × 1795), 122, 126, 127, 136, 159, 247, 417.
  Colonel Magnus (1798), 417.
  Roderick, Knight (1650 × 1660), 24, 654.
Macleod
  Colonel Alexander, EICS (1820), 415.
  Captain Alexander (1760), 675.
  Alexander (1825), 416, 675.
  Anne, sister of Lieutenant-Colonel James of Raasay (c.1780), 430.

Index

Hector Allan (c.1850), 555.
Magnus (1825), 416, 433, 675.
Marion Christina Lloyd, daughter of Major Donald Macleod of Talisker (1844), 517.
Norman *Caraid nan Gaidheal* (1783–1862), 314, 431, 441, 486, 494
Roderick, Professor of King's College, Aberdeen (1773), 135, 186, 248, 372.
Roderick merchant at Glasgow (1724–1740), 140.
Roderick Maclean (c.1890), 555
Macmahon Lieutenant Maurice, Ultonia Regiment in Spanish service (1746), 124.
Macmartin John soldier 1st BF (1794), 219.
MacMhuirich Neil Mor (c.1620), 23.
MacNachton Alexander Roy (1660), 42.
Macnab of Degnish (1820), 414, 419.
Macnaughton Ludovick soldier 1st BF (1794), 220.
Macneil of Barra
   Roderick (1409), 6, 7.
   (c.1650), 626.
   Robert Lister (1889–1970), 663.
Macneill
   in Canna, Donald (1804), 319, 321.
   of Colonsay (c.1810), 432.
MacNeill
   of Gualacholie, Donald (1684 × 1689), 88, 92.
   John, Colonsay's brother (1746), 124.
   John, GCB, FRSE, PC (c.1810), 430, 439, 523, 527, 528, 529.
   Neil, catechist in Eigg (1765), 137.
Macniven
   James 'from Oban' (1847), 489.
   John in Ledmore & Lettermore, Letterbeg & Strone-Mull (1817), 372.
Macpherson
   Captain Duncan 42nd Foot (1775), 171.
   Ewan MA, schoolmaster in Badenoch (c.1755), 136.
   James 'Ossian' (1760), 136.
   John, MP (1781), 675.
   John, Minister, Skye (1773), 675.
Macrae Rev. Finlay (1829), 391.
MacRuari of Clanranald
   Allan (c.1429), 6.
   Donald MacAllane (1616), 19, 20.
   Donald (1644 × 1686), 51, 57, 58, 66, 71, 76.
   John *Iain Muirdeartach* (1618), 21, 23, 70.
   John (1787), 182, 183.
   Ranald (1692 × 1746), 119.
   Ranald George (1799), 241, 250, 370, 372.
Macquarrie family, 55.
Macquarrie of Ulva
   Allan (1651), 37.
   Lachlan (1679), 64.
   Lachlan (1726–1818), 139, 141, 358.
   Lachlan, Major-General & Governor of New South Wales (1804 × 1822), 412, 413, 414, 417, 419.
Macqueen Rev.
   Donald Minister of North Uist (1770), 392.
   James Minister of North Uist (c.1800), 391.
Mac Uilleim (c.1716), 115.
'Mad Fakir' (1897), 597.
Mahdi (1884), 581, 609.
Mahratta Confederacy (1800), 270, 271.
Maitland Lieutenant 1st BF (1794), 216.
Malcolm John W, younger of Poltalloch MP (1886), 639.

Malloch John soldier 1st BF (1794), 220.
Mangal Pandy sepoy 34th Native Infantry (1857), 551.
Mar
   Earl (1710), 102, 103.
   John Thomas younger of (1793), 195.
Markham Edward Surveyor of Van Diemeen's Land (1833), 433.
Martin
   Captain 11th Foot (1799), 239.
   Frañois (1693), 143.
   Martin (1703), 278.
Maser Mrs, Governess (1825), 676.
Masserene Viscount (1690), 95.
Matheson
   Alexander (1848), 543.
   Donald (1848), 543.
   Reverend William (1920–1980), 163.
Maurice Major-General Sir J Frederick KCB author of *History of the War in South Africa 1899–1902* Vol. II (1907), 612, 614, 615.
Maxwell James in Aros (1817), 372.
Mayne Major KOSB (1897 × 1901), 601, 606, 615, 620.
McColl Archibald MA Minister of Tiree & Coll (1780), 175, 176, 191, 192, 242, 281, 380.
McCorquodale of that Ilk, Duncan [McKorkindale] (1672), 60.
McCorkindale Duncan, estate clerk (1885), 637.
McGilchrist in Balliphetrish-Tiree (1709), 101.
McNab Dr attached to the Guides (1897), 599.
McNiven John in Ledmore & Ledbeg-Mull (1817), 373.
McVean
   Lieutenant John 1st BF (1797), 237.
   Minister of Kenmore's son (1793), 196.
Meik Lieutenant 94th Foot (1849), 542.
Mercer Captain 94th Foot (1849), 540.
Melbourne Lord (1838), 465.
Melfort John Earl of (1688), 97.
Menzies of Culdares, Colonel James (1665 × 1679), 42, 66, 71, 77, 79, 84, 89.
Methuen Lieutenant-General Lord Commander of 1st Division (1899), 609, 610, 612, 619.
Middleton
   Earl (1663), 50.
   Ensign later Captain, 3rd Foot Guards (1674), 50, 52, 55.
Milne Miss, headmistress in Edinburgh (1841), 458.
Milner
   Lieutenant-Colonel HR 94th Foot (1842), 543.
   Alfred, High Commissioner for South Africa (1897), 608, 609.
   Mr Harry, Natal (1858), 548.
Milton Lord (1745), 119, 126.
Mitchell Andrew Ensign 1st BF (1793), 203.
Mohammed Ali Nawab of Arcot (1751), 144, 675.
Monck General (1657), 41.
Monboddo Lord (1775), 168.
Monmouth James Duke of (1685), 90.
Montague
   Captain WE 94th Foot (1879), 568, 569, 571.
   Mrs [Nelly] (1879), 570.
Montgomery
   of Coilsfield, Major Hugh (1775), 167, 169, 170.
   Colonel (1794), 219.
Montrose James
   Marquess of (1646), 31, 32, 33, 35, 36, 37, 54, 71, 80, 127, 672.
   3rd Duke of (1822), 406.
Moore Major-General Sir John (1799), 267, 339, 341.
Moray Earl of (1675 × 1679), 50, 62, 72, 73, 76, 77.

Morison of Penmore
  family, 372.
  Magnus (1679), 77.
  Magnus (c.1750), 163.
Morison
  Brothers, Nova Scotia (1826), 427.
  John (1746), 124.
  William MA Minister of Tiree & Coll (1732), 112, 113.
Morrison
  Lieutenant-Colonel William Maxwell (1793), 195, 202, 207, 209, 210, 218, 221.
  Alexander (1793), 200.
Mordaunt Colonel of Dragoons (1775), 169.
Munro
  Angus Glasgow Regiment (1794), 216, 240.
  Sir Hector (1797), 231.
Murdoch John, Inland Revenue officer & founder of *The Highlander* (1818–1903), 627, 628, 648.
Murray of Octertyre, William (1793), 196, 204.
Murray
  Lord George (1715 × 1746), 123.
  The Hon. Mrs of Kensington, author of *A Companion and Useful Guide to the Beauties of Scotland and the Hebrides* (1810), 293, 295, 300, 301, 302, 304, 305, 306, 320, 334, 335, 336, 369, 374.
  Lieutenant-Colonel 94th Foot (1879), 572, 574.
Myrtle Brigadier AD, CB,CBE late KOSB (2006), 671.
Nairne
  Alexander Ensign Scots Brigade & later commanded 3rd BF (1793 × 1799), 202, 205, 216, 219, 478.
  of Drumkilbo, David, (1844), 205, 473, 475, 478.
  Miss (1844), 473.
  Mrs (1844), 473.
Nana Sahib Peshwa, Cawnpore-India (1857), 551, 552.
Napier Lord (1883), 628.
Napoleon (1799 × 1815), 269, 272, 273, 323, 338, 339, 341, 349, 350, 353, 365, 373, 385, 458, 575.
Nash Beau (1674–1762), 404.
Nasser Gamal Abdul President of Egypt (1964), 666.
Necker de Saussure LA author of *A Voyage to the Hebrides* (1822), 301, 304, 306, 421.
Nelson Admiral Sir Horatio (1773 × 1800), 261, 272.
Newcastle Duke of (1830), 434.
Newdigate Major-General (1879), 571.
Nicholl Captain 94th Foot (1849), 540.
Nicolson
  Arthur Chargé d'Affaires at the Legation in Tehran (1887), 583, 585, 586, 592.
  Sheriff (1892), 643, 646.
Nisbet Henry banker in Tobermory, trustee on the Caolis & Cornaig estates (1847 × 1848), 497, 504, 522.
Nielson Sergeant 1st BF (1794), 216.
Norman Lieutenant 11th Bengal Lancers (1897), 598, 599.
Northbrook Thomas George 1st Earl (1884), 579.
Nugent
  General Governor of Jamaica (1801 × 1805), 265, 266, 332.
  Mrs (1801 × 1805), 265, 266, 332, 333, 334.
Ó Baoill Colm author of *Eachann Bacach & other Maclean Poets* (Scottish Gaelic Texts, 1979), 305.
O Donnell Father (1679), 73.
O' Ham son of King Panda of Zululand (1860), 559, 560.
O'Keefe John (1770), 150.
Ò Muirgeasáin see Morison.
Oughton Lieutenant-General Sir Adolphus (1775), 168, 169, 172.

Paget Hon. Berkeley (1797), 297, 305.
Paine Thomas (1793), 197.
Palmerston Foreign Secretary (1840), 535.
Panda of Zululand (1840 × 1872), 508, 509, 513, 558, 559, 560, 561, 563, 566.
Paradis Monsieur (1746), 143.
Parish John, retired Scots Hamburg merchant at Bath (1816), 409.
Park Sir James Allan (1828), 274.
Paton Mr, merchant in Zululand (1858), 550.
Patterson
  John Hunter, Riverina-Tasmania (1829), 444.
  John in Arnabost-Coll formerly in Ayrshire (c.1862), 636.
  Mr, overseer Greytown-Natal (1860), 561.
Pattle Brigadier-General, Commander of the Cavalry Brigade (1860), 555.
Peatt Lieutenant 94th Foot (1849), 540.
Peblis Hew (1615), 19.
Peter the Great Tsar (1700), 575.
Peel Sir Robert (1832), 435, 484.
Pelham Henry (1753), 133.
Peshwa of Poona (1800), 270.
Peters Mr, settler Greytown-Natal (1860), 561.
Picton General (1815), 354.
Pine Sir Benjamin Lieutenant-Governor of Natal (1860 × 1875), 561, 562, 564, 568.
Pitt
  William the Elder (1766), 133, 140.
  William the Younger (1793 × 1798), 207, 208, 211, 253, 265, 266, 324, 326, 330.
Pöe Captain 94th Foot (1879), 571.
Prebble John, author of *Mutiny* (1975) 168, 172, 215, 216, 221, 224.
Pretorious Mr Duval, settler near Greytown-Natal (1860), 561, 562.
Primrose Sir Archibald (1660), 42.
Probyn Major (1860), 554, 555.
Proudfoot W, Carbineers (1860), 563.
Portland Duke of (1794 × 1808), 217, 218, 219, 221, 249, 253, 256, 338.
Queen
  Anne (1710), 102.
  Victoria (1838), 465, 566, 570, 595, 643.
Rae Lieutenant George (1797), 237.
Raleigh Sir Walter, 23.
Ramsay
  Major David Commissary of the Isles (1675), 55.
  John, 55.
Rankin Conduiligh at Kilbrennan-Mull (1716), 115.
Retief Piet (1838), 508.
Reitz
  FW, State Secretary of the Transvaal (1899), 609, 618.
  Denys, author of *Commando* (1930), 618.
Reynolds
  Gerry MP, Parliamentary Under-Secretary for the Army (1967), 665.
  Lewis, Oatlands-Natal (1858), 548, 550.
  Mr (1857), 547, 548.
  Tom, Oatlands-Natal (1858), 549.
Rhodes Cecil (1867), 563
Rider Haggard H author of *A Farmer's Year* (1909), 302, 306, 632, 633, 663.
Richmond Duke of (1782), 596.
Ripon Lord (1848), 502, 542.

Index

Roberts Lord, Commander-in-Chief in India and later in South Africa (1885 × 1899), 575, 576, 577, 581, 609, 610, 611, 612, 613, 615, 616, 618.
Robertson
   of Lude, Major (1793), 198.
   Hugh, soldier 1st BF (1794), 216, 217.
   James Robertson, Sheriff-Substitute for North Argyll (1842), 435, 439, 472, 473, 475, 476, 478, 481, 517.
   John Parish, merchant in South America (1806 × 1847), 406, 407, 408, 464, 468, 481, 503, 504, 505, 507, 520.
   William, Assistant Secretary of the Bank of Scotland, Edinburgh & merchant in South America (1792 × 1825), 406, 676.
   William Parish (1814), 406, 407, 408, 464.
   Miss (1838), 463.
   Mrs, Hotelier in Glasgow (1896), 650.
Robinson Provost of Aberdeen (1797), 233.
Rose
   General Sir Hugh (1858), 552.
   General Sir John, Inverness, (1841), 457.
Ross Baillie Lady (1794), 280.
Ross
   Rev. David Minister at Tobermory-Mull (1844), 473, 474, 475, 478, 485.
   Rev. Roderick Free Church Minister at Coll (1882 × 1892), 637, 638, 639, 640, 641, 642.
Rothes John Earl of (1679), 70.
Rousseau Jean Jaques (1770), 150.
Roxburgh Duke of (1725), 145.
Rowse Professor EAA, Technical Agency, Ethiopia (1963), 663.
Russell Miss later Mrs Barrie PA to GOC 52 (Lowland) Infantry Division (TA) & Lowland District (1958 × 1960), 662, 663.
Salibury Marquis of
   (1845), 475.
   (1877 × 1884), 565, 567, 581, 585, 586, 587, 594, 608, 609, 649.
Saunders
   Governor of Madras (1751), 144.
   Major David, Gordon Highlanders (1971), 666.
Scott Sir Walter (1793 × 1805), 358, 359, 360, 361, 362, 364, 405, 406.
Scott Moncrieff Mr Rob. (1794), 281.
Scrimgeour John 1st BF (1794), 219.
Seaforth Earl of (1676), 58.
Selkirk Earl of (1800), 180, 340, 347, 382, 383, 397, 400.
Sekukuni Chief of the Bapedi in the Transvaal (1861), 565, 572, 574, 576.
Seton-Stewart Sir Ranald, formerly Macdonald of Staffa (1814), 392.
Shadwell Captain (1897), 599, 600, 601, 602, 604, 605, 608.
Sharp
   James Archbishop of St Andrew's (1618–1679), 79.
   Corporal 51 Highland (1970), 666.
Shah of Persia
   (1830), 531.
   (1885), 577, 586, 587, 590, 591.
Shaw William 1st BF (1794), 216, 240.
Shepstone
   John (1870), 564.
   Theophilus Secretary for Native Affairs to the Governor of South
   Africa & later Governor of the Transvaal (1860 × 1877), 559, 560, 561, 563, 564, 565, 566, 569, 573, 632
Sher Ali Amir of Afganistan (1876), 576, 592.
Simson ship owner (1773), 151.

Sinclair
   George 6th Earl of Caithness (1681), 50.
   Dugald, Baptist preacher (1814), 388.
   George or Patrick late 42nd (1793), 203.
Skobelev General Mikhail (1880), 580.
Sladen Captain DSO 2 KOSB (1898), 606.
Small Major John (1775), 165, 171, 173.
Smith
   Sir Harry, Governor of Cape Colony (1849), 511.
   John Director of Studies Madras Academy, St Andrews (1830), 542.
   C Webb (1850), 542, 544.
Smijth-Windham Joseph of Wawne Hall, Yorkshire DL, JP (1830), 557.
Smuts Jan (1899), 608.
Snodgrass
   of Cunninghamhead-Renfrewshire (1818), 373.
   John merchant in Paisley-Renfrewshire (1681), 94, 96.
   Major JJ author of *Narrative of the Burmese War* (1827), 543.
   Neil of Cunninghamhead (1823), 543.
Somers Robert (1840), 520, 625.
Somerset Major-General Lord Fitzroy (1834), 455, 540.
Speirs Graham Sheriff of Mid-Lothian (1845), 476, 477, 478.
Spens Colonel (1901), 621.
Spooner Inspector of Drainage (1849), 524.
Stalker Alexander schoolmaster (1790), 279.
Stevenson Colonel (1800), 270, 271.
Stephenson Major-General Commander of 18 Brigade (1900), 613.
Stewart
   of Appin (1675), 57, 88.
   of Ardshiel (1745), 628.
Stewart of Coll
   John Lorne (1856 × 1878), 373, 374, 563, 628, 629, 630, 631, 632, 637, 638, 639.
   Colonel John Lorne (1886), 632, 635, 636, 638, 640, 642, 643, 644, 648, 652.
   Kenneth (1959), 663.
Stewart
   of Garth, Major-General David (1768–1829), 406.
   Allan brother to Duncan younger of Appin (1673), 42.
   Allan, Innerhaden (1795), 196.
   Charles MA, Preacher of the Gospel in Appin (1773), 152, 174.
   Duncan soldier 1st BF (1794), 220.
   James, brother to the Minister of Killin (1793), 195.
   Robert Viscount Castlereagh (1801), 326, 330, 406.
   Selkirk, late Scots Brigade (1793), 203.
   William Lieutenant 42nd Foot (1775), 171.
   of Ballechin (1685), 89, 90, 93.
   in Cornaigbeg-Tiree (1779), 94.
Stirling
   of Keir (1665), 48.
   Sir James Bart, Lord-Provost of Edinburgh (1805), 374.
   Sir Gilbert Bart, late Coldstream Guards (1781–1830), 374.
Straker Lieutenant 73rd Foot (1813), 350.
Streaphan later Strachan
   Lieutenant JWH 73rd Foot (1812–1815), 355, 389, 392.
   Mary (1812 × 1815), 355, 389, 454, 457.
Strachan Colonel Henry 39th Foot (1841), 458, 459, 461.
Stuart
   HRH Prince Charles Edward (1745 × 1788), 121, 126, 127, 133, 252.
   A (1789 × 1791), 242.
   Charles, Baron Stuart de Rothesay (1828), 408, 409, 410, 411, 464.

James, Colonel 72nd Foot (1795), 268.
Louisa, widow of Lieutenant-General Sir Charles (1820), 408, 409, 410.
Stubbs Lieutenant 43rd Foot (1812), 350.
Sturgeon Robert, postmaster (1892), 643.
Sutherland
soldier Alexander 1st BF (1794), 218, 220.
George [*Fear Cuairt*], Highland Ladies Association's schoolmaster at Bousd-Coll (1883 × 1888), 628, 630, 631, 636, 637, 638, 639, 640, 648.
Syed Ishmael (1846), 537.
Sykes Lieutenant 94th Foot (1849), 540
Taylor Mr. 85th Foot (1860), 561.
Tait Captain RN (1807), 336
Tantia Topi (1858), 552
Teignmouth Lord (1827) author of *The Coasts & Islands of Scotland* 2 vols (1836), 400, 423, 429.
Templer Field-Marshal Sir Gerald (1968), 666.
Thomson ERC, Vice-Consul for Khorassan & Seistan-Persia (1889), 587, 589.
Tippoo Sahib (1792), 269, 675.
Todd Lieutenant-Colonel Kenneth RHF (1972), 667.
Torrens Colonel Military Secretary to the Commander-in-Chief (1810), 343, 350.
Toussaint (1798), 266.
Travers Henry of Fairfield,Devon (c.1800), 417, 542.
Trevelyan Charles Assistant Secretary at the Treasury (1845), 483, 484, 485, 523, 527, 529.
Tucker Lieutenant-General Charles Commander of 7th Division (1900 × 1901), 610, 612, 617, 618
Turner Sir James (1645), 22.
Tytler Alexander Fraser Judge Advocate (1794), 219, 221.
Tullibardine Marchioness of see Atholl.
Tweedale Marchioness of (1895), 595
Umbulazi son of King Panda of Zululand (1860), 559.
Umkungo son of King Panda of Zululand (1860), 561, 563.
Umra Khan of Swat (1895), 593, 594.
Villeneuve Admiral (1805), 327.
Wade General (1725) , 133.
Waheer Khan Sowar Fane's Horse (1856), 555
Walker Dr John (1766 × 1771), 136, 137, 139, 152, 162, 242.
Walmsley Mr, Border Magistrate, Natal (1860), 559, 562.
Walpole
Horace (1800), 410.
Robert (1725), 145.
Ward Colonel EJS, MVO, MC, Commander od The Life Guards (1950) & Household Cavalry (1953–1956), 666.
Warren Colonel (1746), 126.
Watt James Schoolmaster Eigg (1794), 257.
Wavell Major-General AG Commander of 15th Infantry Brigade (1901), 617.
Wayeer Khan sowar Fane's Horse (1860), 557.
Weir
Lieutenant William (1775), 167.
Mr in Gallanach-Coll formerly in Ayrshire (1885), 637, 638.
Wellesley Sir Arthur later Duke of Wellington (1799), 240, 270, 271, 272, 341, 342, 344, 350, 352, 353, 354, 385, 410, 538, 576.
Wellesley Marquess Governor-General of India (1799), 270.
West Lieutenant, Adjutant 1st Battalion 3rd Gurkhas (1897), 605.
Westmacott Brigadier-General Commanding 4 Brigade Tirah Field Force (1897), 600, 601, 605.
Wheeler Mr of Player & Wheeler, general merchants Maritzburg-Natal (1860), 561.

Wilberforce William (1799), 239, 240
Will Sir John, Director General of Ordnance Hospitals (1841), 458.
William
III (1688), 97.
IV (1832), 596.
Williams
family, 390.
Lieutenant John Poulton RN (1809), 389.
Lieutenant Thomas RN (1805 × 1812), 389, 392.
Lieutenant Poulton RN (1816 × 1836), 389, 453.
Williamson Patrick maltman at Dumbarton (1679), 69, 73.
Wills
family, 651.
WH, MP later Lord Winterstoke (1892), 649, 662
Wilson
Miss, headmistress in Edinburgh (1838), 457.
WS late 94th Foot (1880), 573, 576, 579.
Witter Captain Joseph (1657 × 1659), 27, 41.
WolmariansCommandant (1901), 622.
Wolseley General Sir Garnet Commander-in-Chief South Africa(1879), 572, 574.
Woodcock Frank [Dingaan], Natal (1858), 548.
Yakub Khan Regent of Afganistan (1878), 576, 583, 592.
Young Lieutenant 1 KOSB (1901), 617.
York Field-Marshal HRH the Duke of (1795 × 1799) 228, 231, 267, 270, 324, 329, 343, 455.
Yorke Charles Secretary at War (1803), 319, 321.

Battles.
Aboukir Bay, Egypt (1798), 272.
Alexandria, Egypt (1801), 273, 339.
Alford, Aberdeenshire (1644), 32.
Algiers, Algeria (1816), 391.
Alma, Crimea (1854), 541.
Argaum, India (1803), 271, 272, 456, 463.
Arni, India (1751), 145.
Assaye, India (1803), 270.
Austerlitz, Austria (1805), 326.
Batwa, India (1857), 554.
Blarnicara, Corpach, Lochaber (c.1520), 6, 7, 12, 18, 135.
Blood River, South Africa (1840), 508.
Bronkhorst Spruit, South Africa (1880), 573, 574.
Busaco, Portugal (1810), 645.
Cape Town, South Africa (1805), 327.
Chinhat, India (1857), 551.
Coire na Creiche, Skye (c.1600), 17.
Corunna, Spain (1809), 339, 340, 645.
Crater, Aden (1846), 537.
Culloden, Inverness-shire (1746), 123, 124, 127, 128, 229, 464, 674.
Dargai, Pakistan (1897), 603.
Dunbar, East Lothian (1650), 36–40.
Dunkeld, Perthshire (1689), 97, 116.
Eilean Gheirig, Cowal, Argyllshire (1685), 90.
El Alamein, Egypt (1943), 662.
Falkirk, Stirlingshire (1745), 122.
Fontenoy, Belgium (1744), 133.
Fuentes de Oòoro, Spain (1811), 645
Grimsary Hill, Coll (c.1400), 5.
Gruinart, Islay (1598), 12.
Grishipol, Coll (c.1425), 6, 7, 431.
Harlaw, Aberdeenshire (1411), 6, 559.
Ingogo, South Africa (18810), 576.
Inverlochy, Lochaber (1645), 31, 32.

Index

Inverkeithing, Fife (1651), 36, 78, 121, 233, 360, 659.
Isandhlwana, South Africa (1879), 566, 568, 571, 572.
Kambula, South Africa (1879), 572.
Kandahar, Afganistan (1880), 577.
Karee Siding, South Africa (1901), 616, 617, 618.
Kilsyth, Stirlingshire (1645), 32.
Laing's Nek, South Africa (1881), 574.
Landakai, Pakistan (1897), 598.
Ligny, Belgium (1815), 353.
Loos, Belgium (1916), 659.
Maiwand, Afganistan (1880), 576, 583, 584.
Majuba Hill, South Africa (1881), 574, 616.
Malakand Pass, Pakistan (1895), 597.
Marengo, Italy (1800), 272.
Minden, Germany (1759), 596.
Nanking, China (1841), 535.
Nitrals Nek, South Africa (1901), 621.
Nivelle, France (1813), 645.
Omdurman, Sudan (1898), 609.
Orthez, France (1814), 596.
Paardeberg, South Africa (1900), 613, 614,.
Patna, India (1764), 146.
Pei-ho River, China (1859 × 1860), 553, 554.
Peninsula, Spain & Portugal (1805–1814), 458.
Preston, Lancashire (1715), 104.
Prestonpans, East Lothian (1745), 122.
Philiphaugh, Selkirkshire (1645), 32.
Piscattang, North America (1777), 171.
Pyrenees, France & Spain (1814), 645
Plassey, India (1757), 146.
Quatre Bras, Belgium (1815), 354, 389.
Radfan, South Arabia (1964), 664.
Saif-un-din, Afghanistan (1880), 577.
Salamanca, Spain (1812), 350.
Saratoga, North America (1777), 166.
Sekukuni's Kraal, South Africa (1879), 574.
Sheriffmuir, Perthshire (1716), 103, 104, 115, 121, 223.
Sruthan nan Ceann, Coll (c.1583), 9, 431.
St Malo, France (1805), 391.
Swat Valley, Pakistan (1897), 600, 601.
Talavera, Spain (1809), 341, 361.
Third Battle of Ypres (1917), 661.
Tirah, Pakistan (1897), 599–606, 620, 664.
Toulon, France (1809), 391.
Toulouse, France (1814), 645.
Trichinopoly, India (1772–1773), 545.
Trafalgar, Spain (1805), 327, 332, 337, 338, 352, 391, 429.
Ulundi, South Africa (1879), 572.
Vimeiro, Portugal (1808), 341.
Vitoria, Spain (1813), 352, 596.
Vlakfontein, South Africa (1901), 622.
Waterloo, Belgium (1815), 353, 354, 384, 385, 391, 456, 501, 541, 643, 645.
Wurdah River, India (1858), 552.

Regiments.
Regiments originally took the name of their Colonel but from 1751, to avoid confusion, regular army units were numbered, with the oldest having the lowest number. In 1782 for the first time some regiments added the name of a particular county to their title. The names of regiments listed here are taken from the *Army List* from Young, Peter & Lawford, JP *History of the British Army* (1970) or WWW. Regiments.org.

When, at the end of a war, a regiment was disbanded it ceased to exist. Its number was then allocated at the start of the next war to a completely new unit. Dates in brackets should help identify which regiment is being referred to.

In 1873 regular and reserve forces were welded together. Two battalion regiments were formed from the old numerical units. One battalion was intended to serve overseas whilst the other stayed at home. In 1881 territorial titles and regimental districts were introduced. The innumerable amalgamations that have taken place since the Second World War have complicated the situation.

Argyle or Western Fencible Regiment (1778–1783), 167, 168, 169, 170, 171, 172, 202, 215, 259, 264.
Argyllshire Regiment of Fencible Men in North Britain (1793), 200, 219, 239.
Argyllshire Militia (1745–1746), 122, 123, 127, 674.
Argyllshire Volunteers, (1795–1802), 230, 258, 259, 260, 273, 313, 669.
Argyllshire Volunteers (1803–), 309, 310, 372, 373, 496.
Breadalbane or 4th Fencibles (1793–1797), 1, 195, 198, 200, 201, 205, 207, 208, 209, 210, 211, 212, 213, 214, 215, 216, 217, 218, 219, 220, 221, 223, 224, 225, 226, 228, 229, 231, 232, 233, 234, 235, 236, 237, 239, 240, 242, 243, 244, 245, 246, 249, 259, 320, 372, 368, 389, 429, 467, 478, 496.
Bengal Infantry (1839), 542.
Bombay Infantry (1844), 542.
Brown's Horse (1650–1651), 38.
Buchanan's Foot (1650–1651), 37.
Cambrian Rangers (c.1778), 206.
Canadian Fencibles (1803), 338.
Carolina Rangers (c.1778), 203.
Cape Corps (1860), 561.
Derbyshire Yeomanry (1901), 618.
Dillon's Regiment in the Irish Brigade (1798), 257, 265, 273.
Dragoons, 217, 218.
Dumbartonshire Militia (1796), 363.
Edward Dillon's Regiment of Émigrés (1800), 273.
Fane's Horse (1860), 553, 554.
Fencible Cavalry, 217, 218.
Fencible Men of Argyllshire (1756–1763), 264.
First (or Argyll) Regiment of North British Militia (1797), 263.
Fraser's Highlanders. 63rd or Second Highland Battalion (1756–1758). Later (1758–1763) 78th Highland Regiment of Foot, 165.
Fraser's Highlanders (1775–1783) see 71st Foot, 166.
Glasgow Volunteers (1778), 168, 216, 219.
Guides Infantry (1857), 552, 593, 597.
Guides Cavalry (1895), 594, 596, 597, 598.
HEIC's Eoropean Regiments (1748), 144.
HEIC's Indian Regiments (1748), 144.
Holburn's Foot (1648–1651).
Household Cavalry (1953–1956), 668.
Indian Staff Corps (1891), 593.
Inverness Fencibles (1797), 254, 362.
Inverness-shire Volunteers, Isle of Eigg Company (1794 × 1802). 249, 250, 251, 252, 253, 254, 255, 256, 257, 310, 311, 312.
Inverness-shire Volunteers (1803 × 1810), 311, 312, 313, 314, 315, 346, 352, 412, 419.
Inverness-shire Militia (1808), 419.
King's Dragoon Guards (1859), 553, 554, 555, 572.
King's German Legion (1815), 353.
Kitchener's Horse (1900), 613.
Lochaber Fencibles (c.1795), 234.

731

Loudoun's (Highland) Foot (1745–1746), 122, 127, 128, 129.
Sir Lachlan Maclean's Foot (1645–1646), 32, 33.
Sir Hector Maclean's Foot (1650–1651), 37–40.
Sir John Maclean's Foot (1715–1716), 103, 104, 223.
Mackenzie's Foot (1715–1716), 121.
Maclachlan's Foot (1745–1746), 121.
Madras European Battalion (1751), 145, 146, 329.
Marquis of Argyll's Foot (1642–1649), 29, 30, 31, 32.
Marjoribank's Regiment of Foot in the Service of the States General (1755).
Montgomery's Highland Battalion of Foot see 77th Foot.
Mr Barter's Karkloof Troop Natal Carbineers (1860), 561.
Mr Proudfoot's Troop Natal Carbineers (1860), 561.
New Brunswick Fencibles (1804), 328, 329, 332.
New South Wales Corps, 415.
King's Regiment of Guards (1675–), 50, 65, 71, 83.
Probyn's Horse see 1st Sikh Irregular Cavalry.
Punjaub Cavalry (1853).
Queen's Own Corps of Guides (1897), 591, 593, 597, 598, 599.
REME (1971), 669.
Royal African Corps (1807), 335.
Royal Artillery (1798 & 1900), 238, 545, 555, 611.
Royal Glasgow Volunteers later 83rd Regiment of Foot (1779), 219.
Royal Highland Emigrants see 84th Foot.
Royal Horse Artillery (1841), 459, 464, 618.
Royal Marines (1805), 431.
Royal North British Veterans Battalion see 6th .
Royal Regiment of Scotland (2006), 673, 677.
Scots Brigade in Dutch service, 78, 79, 95, 116, 122, 134, 148, 201, 202, 203, 247, 458, 463.
Scotch Brigade 1st Regiment
   [Hugh Mackay's 1677–1692], 79, 81.
   [Alexander Marjoribank's 1745–1773].
Scots Brigade Earl of Drumlanrig's (1747–1752), 127.
Scots Greys (1901), 619.
Scottish Horse (1901), 618.
The Life Guards (1950), 668.
Yorkshire Militia (1873), 597.
1st Regiment of Guards or Grenadier Guards (1798), 238.
2nd Regiment of Guards or Coldstream Guards (1798), 238, 374.
3rd Regiment of Guards or Scots Guards (1700), 104, 121, 195, 203, 223, 224, 238, 326, 336, 361, 627.
1st Foot The Royal Scots (or Royal Regiment of Foot) (1780), 168, 170, 190, 554, 597, 654, 661.
1st Sikh Irregular Cavalry or Probyn's Horse (1857 × 1860), 552, 553, 554.
1st Punjab Cavalry (1880), 577.
2nd Foot or Queen's Royal Regiment (1834), 534.
2nd Lancers. Hyderabad Contingent (1882), 577.
2nd West India Regiment (1838), 456.
2nd Native Infantry Battalion (1764), 146.
2nd Madras Infantry Battalion (c.1840), 329.
2nd Lancers Hyderabad Contingent (1870), 579.
2nd (Prince of Wales's Own Gurkha (Rifle) Regiment (1897), 601, 605.
3rd Battalion Connaught Rangers (1894), 594, 653.
3rd European Regiment (1854), 542.
3rd South Mayo Militia (1881), 594.
3rd Gurkha (Rifle) Regiment (1897), 601, 602, 604, 605, 607.
4th Foot or King's Own (1879), 573.
5th Foot or Northumberland Fusiliers (1889), 593.
5th Native Infantry Battalion (1775), 166, 674.
6th West India Regiment (1798), 264.

6th (Royal North British) Veterand Battalion (1810), 324, 342.
6th North Mayo Militia (1881), 594.
7th Madras Light Cavalry (1845), 542, 552.
7th Mounted Infantry (1900), 613.
8th Native Infantry Battalion (1762), 146.
8th West India Regiment (1801), 234, 265.
8th Foot (1816), 329.
9th Foot or Norfolk Regiment (1901), 617.
9th Madras Native Infantry Battalion (1800), 270, 271.
10th Regiment of Dragoons (1778), 169.
10th Foot or Lincolnshire Regiment (1900), 615, 617, 619.
11th Foot North Devon (1795), 227, 231, 234, 237, 238, 239, 245, 265, 328.
11th Bengal Lancers (1897), 598.
12th Foot or the East Suffolk Regiment of Foot (1799), 269.
14th Foot or Buckinghamshire Regiment (1811), later Pince of Wale's Own (West Yorkshire Regiment) (1901), 328, 351, 620.
15/19th Hussars (1970), 666.
16th Foot or the Bedfordshire Regiment (1809), 342.
17th Regiment of (Light) Dragoons (1798), 238.
17th Foot or the Leicestershire Regiment of Foot (1795), 203.
18th Foot or the Royal Irish Regiment (1805), 332, 334, 337, 543.
18th Field Battery Royal Artillery (1900), 613.
19th Lancers see Fane's Horse.
19th (Light) Dragoons (1803), 271.
21st Foot or the Royal North British Fuzileers (1807 × 1897), 204, 572, later Royal Scots Fusileers [RSF], 605, and later still Royal Highland Fusiliers (1972), 669, 677.
23rd Foot or the Royal Welsh Fuzileers (1798), 238.
25th Foot or King's Own Borderers formerly Leven's Regiment (1840), 509, from 1887 King's Own Scottish Borderers, 595, 596, 597, 599–611, 614, 615, 616, 617, 618, 619, 620, 654–660, 663, 664, 665, 666, 670, 673.
27th Foot or Inniskilling Regiment (1840), 509.
31st Bombay Native Infantry (1844), 544.
32nd Madras Native Infantry (1839 × 1857), 542, 552.
34th Native Infantry (1857), 551.
36th Foot or Herefordshire Regiment of Foot (1795), 234, 268.
36th Sikhs (1897), 602, 603, 604, 605.
37th Foot or the North Hampshire Regiment of Foot (1758), 172.
39th Foot or the Dorsetshire Regiment (1841), 460.
40th Foot (c.1778), 203, 206.
42nd Foot The Black Watch (Royal Highland Regiment), originally 43rd Foot (1739), 133, 166, 171, 172, 185, 203, 220, 222, 267, 274, 320, 352, 358, 668.
43rd Foot or Monmouthshire Regiment (1809), 342, 344, 352, 385, 450.
44th Native Infantry (1854), 542.
46th Foot or South Devonshire Regiment of Foot (1801), 327, 341.
47th Foot or Lancashire Regiment (1792 × 1799), 245, 273.
48th Foot or Northamptonshire Regiment (1897), 601, 602, 607, 619.
49th Foot or the Hertfordshire Regiment of Foot (1798), 238, 265, 268, 320, 534, 542.
50th Foot or The West Kent Regiment (1830), 450.
51st (Highland) Volunteers (T&AVR) (1970), 666.
60th or Royal American Regiment (1794 × 1803), 220, 221, 268, 274, 309, 337, 344, 350, 351.
61st Foot or the South Gloucestershire Regiment (1809), 341, 342, 350.
64th Foot or 2nd Staffordshire Regiment (1815), 355, 385, 386, 388, 393.
67th Foot or Hampshire Regiment (1860), 554, 617.
67th Native Infantry (1839), 533, 534.

Index

68th Foot or the Durham Regiment of Foot (1790), 199, 265, 273.
71st Foot or 71st Highland Regiment of Foot (1775–1782), 202, 268, 327, 674, 677.
71st Native Infantry (1857), 551.
72nd Foot or Seaforth's Highlanders (1793 × 1807), 204, 224, 268, 274, 327, 350, 412, 419, 461.
73rd Foot originally 71st Highland Regiment of Foot (1782 × 1813), 170, 259, 268, 269, 350, 351, 415.
73rd Highland Regiment of Foot originally 2nd 42nd Highland Regiment of Foot (1815), 389, 413, 461, 543.
74th Foot or Argyle Regiment of (Highland) Foot (1778), 203, 264, 269, 271, 272, 274.
74th (Highland) Foot (1807), 461, 677.
75th (Highland) Foot (1807), 461.
76th Foot or Macdonald Regiment of (Highland) Foot (1778), 203, 419.
77th Foot Montgomery's Highlanders (1758–1763), originally 62nd or First Highland Battalion (1757–1758), 134, 142, 166, 201, 202.
78th Foot (1778–1763) see Fraser's Highlanders.
78th Foot or the Ross-shire Highlanders (1803), 271, 272, 339, 340.
79th Foot (1793 × 1815), or Cameronian Volunteers later Cameron Highlanders (1793 × 1815), 207, 209, 210, 213, 214, 221, 265, 338, 339, 340, 341, 351, 352, 354, 357, 385, 393, 447, 542, 552, 579, 643, 644, 645, 646 later still Queen's Own Cameron Highlanders, 668, 670.
80th Foot or Staffordshire Volunteers (1800), 400.
81st Foot or Aberdeenshire Highland Regiment (1777–1783), 167, 170, 172, 373, 404, 496.
81st Foot or (Loyal Lincoln Volunteers) Regiment of Foot (1793–1881), 627.
82nd Foot (1760), 404.
82nd Foot (1778–1784), 173, 181.
84th Foot formerly Royal Highland Emigrants (1775–1784), 165. 172, 173, 178, 199, 202, 273, 336.
84th Foot or York & Lancaster Regiment (1815), 438.
85th Foot (1779–1783), 201, 429.
85th Foot or The King's Regiment of Light Infantry (Buck's Volunteers) (1860), 561.
86th Foot (1808), 173.
87th Foot (1779–1783), 170.
87th Foot or Prince of Wales's Own Irish Regiment
88th Foot or Connaught Rangers (1881), 596, 598, 653.
91st Foot or Argyllshire Regiment (1807), 461.
92nd Foot or Gordon Highlanders (1857), 552, 577, 601, 611, 643, 668.
93rd Foot or Princess Louise's (Argyll & Sutherland Highlanders), 644, 646, 668, 669,
94th Foot, formerly the Scots Brigade (1803), 271, 272, 456, 458, 459, 461, 462, 464, 533, 536–541, 566, 568, 569, 570, 571, 572, 573, 574, 594, 628, 651, 672 after 1881 2nd Battalion The Connaught Rangers, 594, 596, 597, 655, 670.
95th Foot later The Rifle Brigade (1817), 393.
99th Foot (1805 × 1807), or Duke of Edinburgh's (Lanarkshire) Regiment, 335, 336, 337, 344, 363.
104th Foot see New Brunswick Fenciles (1815), 329.
114th Foot or Royal Highland Volunteers (1761–1763), 134, 139, 185, 358.

Ships.
Airly Castle (1790 × 1791), 245.
Augustine Caesar (1805), 332.
Australian (1854), 552.
Belvidere (1845), 487.
Braemar Castle (1900), 609.
Brilliant (1837), 445, 446, 451.
Britannia (1840), 450.
Castle Forbes (1822), 415, 421.
Chesterfield (1761), 146, 148.
China (1879), 569, 570.
City of Edinburgh (1825), 416, 433.
Commerce (1822), 419.
Devondale (1857), 545
Diamond (1840), 456, 457.
Dunnotar Castle (1900), 610.
Earl of Durham (1837), 450.
Economy (1818), 398, 399.
Edward Johnston (1854), 528.
Fingal (1898), 632.
Flora Macdonald (1852), 451.
Furnace (1746), 128.
Good Hope (1798), 415.
Harriet (1811), 344, 352.
Harmony (1828), 428.
Happie (1746), 125, 126.
Herald (1858), 547, 548.
Highlander (1822), 405.
Highland Laddie (1828), 428.
HMS *Agamemnon* (1805), 429.
HMS *Argo* (1793), 261.
HMS *Bellerophon* (1798), 262, 385.
HMS *Caesar* (1798), 261, 263.
HMS *Ceylon* (1815), 385.
HMS *Chichester* (1807), 336, 337.
HMS *Crescent* (1809), 338, 346.
HMS *Euryalius* (1804), 323, 391
HMS *Flora* (1806), 338.
HMS *Ganges* (1807), 338.
HMS *Kent* (1800), 324.
HMS *Leda* (1804), 323.
HMS *Lyra* (1858), 548.
HMS *Majestic* (1805), 324.
HMS *Minerva* (1810), 350.
HMS *Opussum* (1812), 391.
HMS *Prince George* (1900), 654.
HMS *Pygmy* (1812), 391.
HMS *Terror* (1746), 124, 126.
HMS *Theseus* (1805), 332, 333.
HMS *Ville de Paris* (1797), 262.
HMS *Zealand* (1800), 325
Hornet (1854), 530.
Hornet (1851), 528.
John Dunscombe (1819–1832), 433, 435, 449, 458, 666.
Loch Seaforth (1970), 667.
Lord Sausmarez (1841), 458, 459, 460.
Marmion (1852), 528.
Mars (1835), 517.
May of Glasgow (1746), 125, 126.
Middlesex (1796), 245.
New Zealand (1853), 528.
Persian (1857), 637.
Princess Amelia (1792 × 1793).
Princess de Conti (1746), 125.
Saint Lawrence (1828), 424.
Scotia (1845), 539.

733

Sir William Wallace (1835), 517.
Skelton (1805), 416, 415, 433.
Symmetry (1825), 409.
Torch (1847), 502.
Toward Castle (1844), 472.
Triton (1825), 416.
Waldenstein (1857), 545.

Sieges.
Amboor, India (1781), 674.
Arcot, India (1751), 144, 145.
Asseeghur, India (1803), 270.
Badajoz (1812), 352, 596.
Batavia, Indonesia (1811), 351.
Bergen-op-Zoom, Netherlands (1748), 134.
Breacachadh Castle, Coll (1679), 77, 79.
Burhanpore, India (1803), 270.
Carnaburg Catle, Treshnish Islands (1679), 41, 79.
Carnassary Castle, Mid Argyll (1685), 92.
Cawnpore, India (1857), 551.
Chitral, Pakistan (1895), 595.
Chuenpi, China (1840), 537.
Cuidad Rodrigo, Spain (1811–1812), 342.
Delhi, India (1857), 553, 593.

Djokjakarta, Indonesia (1812), 351.
Etshowe, South Africa (1879), 572.
Eureka Stockade, Victoria (1854), 516.
Fort Matagorda, Spain (1810), 464.
Gibraltar (1779 × 1783), 170.
Gawilghur, India (1803), 271, 272.
Heylipol Castle, Tiree (1679), 79.
Jhansi, India (1858), 552.
Kimberley (1900), 614.
Kinlochaline Castle, Morvern (1679), 80.
Lucknow, India (1857), 551, 552.
Musilipatam, India (1759), 146.
Policat, India (1778), 170.
Pondicherry, India
  (1693), 143.
  (1778), 170.
  (1793), 224, 268.
Port Louis, Mauritius (1810), 350.
Port Natal, South Africa (1840), 511.
Seringapatam, India (1799), 269, 456, 463, 596.
Taikoktow, China (1840), 537.
Taku Forts, China (1860), 553, 555.
Trinchinopoly, India (1751), 144.
Trincomalee, Ceylon [Sri Lanka] (1795), 268.